THE CAMBRIDGE
ANCIENT HISTORY

VOLUME VII
PART 2

THE CAMBRIDGE
ANCIENT HISTORY

SECOND EDITION

VOLUME VII

PART 2

The Rise of Rome to 220 B.C.

Edited by

F. W. WALBANK F.B.A.

*Emeritus Professor, formerly Professor of Ancient
History and Classical Archaeology, University of Liverpool*

A. E. ASTIN

*Professor of Ancient History,
The Queen's University, Belfast*

M. W. FREDERIKSEN
R. M. OGILVIE

Assistant Editor

A. DRUMMOND

*Lecturer in Classics,
University of Nottingham*

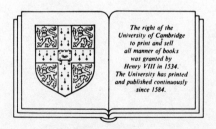

The right of the
University of Cambridge
to print and sell
all manner of books
was granted by
Henry VIII in 1534.
The University has printed
and published continuously
since 1584.

CAMBRIDGE UNIVERSITY PRESS

CAMBRIDGE

NEW YORK   PORT CHESTER

MELBOURNE   SYDNEY

Published by the Press Syndicate of the University of Cambridge
The Pitt Building, Trumpington Street, Cambridge CB2 1RP
40 West 20th Street, New York, NY 10011, USA
10 Stamford Road, Oakleigh, Melbourne 3166, Australia

First published 1989

Printed in Great Britain at the University Press, Cambridge

British Library cataloguing in publication data

The Cambridge ancient history. – 2nd ed.
Vol. 7
Pt. 2: The rise of Rome to 220 B.C.
1. Ancient world
I. Walbank, F. W. (Frank William)
930

Library of Congress card number 75-85719

ISBN 0 521 23446 8

CONTENTS

v

BIBLIOGRAPHY

NOTE ON THE BIBLIOGRAPHY

The bibliography is arranged in sections dealing with specific topics, which sometimes correspond to individual chapters but more often combine the contents of several chapters. References in the footnotes are to these sections (which are distinguished by capital letters) and within these sections each book or article has assigned to it a number which is quoted in the footnotes. In these, so as to provide a quick indication of the nature of the work referred to, the author's name and the date of publication are also included in each reference. Thus 'Ogilvie 1965 [B129], 232' signifies 'R. M. Ogilvie, *A Commentary on Livy Books 1–5*. Oxford, 1965, p. 232, to be found in Section B of the bibliography as item 129'.

TABLES

MAPS

TEXT-FIGURES

xiii

PREFACE

The subject-matter of this volume is the history of Rome from the earliest times until shortly before the Second Punic War. In the planning of a new edition of Volume VII it was recognized from the start that major changes were required in both the scale and the disposition of the material to be presented. The undivided volume of the first edition embraced both this period of Roman history and Hellenistic history from 301 to 217 B.C.: two fields in which the scholars of the last half century have made exceptional advances, both of discovery and of interpretation. Accordingly, in this second edition Volume VII has been divided. Part 1, published in 1984, is given over entirely to the Hellenistic history, while the present volume contains a much expanded treatment of the Roman history.

The reconstruction of the early history of Rome presents special problems of its own. One of these is the rapid and continuing increase in the archaeological evidence for Rome and its immediate environs, and indeed for Central Italy as a whole. More fundamental, however, is the peculiar mix of archaeological evidence with literary evidence which was written centuries later. This gives rise not only to disputes about particular conclusions but to much diversity in methodology and principles of interpretation. Consequently no single account may be taken as definitive, and the editors of this volume, far from seeking a uniform approach to the problems, have consciously embraced a variety of responses.

The volume begins, therefore, with an examination of the sources, undertaken by R. M. Ogilvie and A. Drummond. The earlier history of Rome is then discussed at length by four scholars who each bring distinctive insights to bear upon an aspect of ancient history which has generated more deep-rooted controversy than most. A. D. Momigliano and M. Torelli, adopting contrasting approaches, discuss the origins and early development of Rome, after which A. Drummond and T. J. Cornell explore the history of the Republic to the eve of the Pyrrhic War. Pyrrhus himself and his war with Rome are the subject of a chapter by P. R. Franke. E. S. Staveley writes on Rome and Italy in the third

century, while H. H. Scullard in his chapter on Rome and Carthage
discusses the institutions of Carthage and the development of Rome's
extra-Italian interests, culminating in the First Punic War and its aftermath. To the latter chapter A. E. Astin appends a short section on the
emergence of the Roman provincial system. J. A. North examines early
republican history with a different emphasis and from a different point of
view in his chapter on society and religion. Broadly speaking the volume
follows Roman history to the eve of the Second Punic War, but it was
decided to reserve for Volume VIII the Illyrian wars and the involvement of the Carthaginians in Spain, both of which are advantageously
considered in conjunction with later events. A full discussion of Roman
provincial administration will appear in Volume IX. Another consideration which invites attention is the wider context within which Rome
developed, embracing other peoples of Italy and the Western Mediterranean; and much of this material also is to be found in other volumes.
Especially relevant are chapters 12–15 of Volume IV, but Volumes III.3,
V and VI all contain pertinent sections.

This volume has been in the course of preparation for a considerable
time, most of the contributions having been first submitted by 1985 and
some as early as 1980. In many cases it has not been possible to take
account of the most recent work in the field. The bibliography, however,
has been updated (as far as possible) to 1986. The editors regret to have to
record several deaths which occurred during that period. M. W.
Frederiksen, who died in consequence of a road accident in 1980, was a
member of the original editorial team which planned the second editions
of Volumes VII and VIII. A. D. Momigliano and H. H. Scullard were
contributors to this volume. R. M. Ogilvie, who died in 1981, was both
contributor and the member of the team who initially took special
responsibility for the volume. It is a cause for deep regret that he did not
see the completion of a volume which already owed much to his work
and his remarkable scholarship.

Following R. M. Ogilvie's death the outstanding chapters were edited
by F. W. Walbank and A. E. Astin, while A. Drummond undertook the
considerable task of editorial co-ordination. The editors acknowledge
with gratitude his invaluable assistance with such matters as bibliography, maps, illustrations and proofs, and generally with the format of
the volume and its preparation for the Press.

The editors wish to thank also several other persons for their assistance, as well as the contributors for their patience. Judith Landry
translated M. Torelli's contribution from the Italian, and Lyndall von
Dewitz translated P. R. Franke's from the German. A. Drummond
acknowledges generous assistance received from the British Academy
and the Sheffield University Research Fund towards the cost of research

for Chapters 4 and 5; and also the painstaking and constructive comments made on those same chapters by Professor P. A. Brunt. David Cox
of Cox Cartographic Ltd drew the maps. The index was compiled by
Barbara Hird. Finally warm thanks are due to the staff of the Cambridge
University Press for their constant encouragement, care and help.

A.E.A.

F.W.W.

CHAPTER 1

THE SOURCES FOR EARLY ROMAN HISTORY

R. M. OGILVIE AND A. DRUMMOND

The first section of this chapter deals with the main literary and archaeological sources for early Roman history. The second considers the type of material which was at the disposal of the historians of Rome for the regal period and the fifth century and how they used it.[1]

I. THE SURVIVING EVIDENCE

(a) *Literary sources*

There were three, possibly four, main historical strands – Greek, Roman, Etruscan and Carthaginian. The Carthaginian can be discounted, because, although probably used at second-hand by the Greek historian Polybius, nothing survives or can be recovered independently. The Emperor Claudius in a famous speech preserved at Lyons (*ILS* 212) refers to 'Tuscan authors' ('auctores . . Tuscos') in connexion with the legend of Mastarna and the Vibennae (see p. 94f). There are a few other references to Etruscan historians and Claudius' account is strikingly corroborated by frescoes from the François tomb at the Etruscan city of Vulci. Nevertheless, there is no evidence for Etruscan writers who were active in the fifth or fourth century. Claudius' 'Tuscan authors' were learned scholars with an Etruscan background, like A. Caecina, writing in the first century B.C. We cannot reconstruct their work or judge how reliable it was.

The Greeks, on the other hand, knew about Rome from an early date. Aristotle was aware of the capture of Rome by the Gauls in 390 B.C., and a series of minor historians interested themselves in the foundation legends of the city. One or two early Greek writers are of considerable importance even though their works do not survive. Imbedded in the history of Dionysius of Halicarnassus (*Ant. Rom.* VII.3ff) is an extensive excursus about Aristodemus, the tyrant of Cumae, and his defeat of the

---

[1] Professor Ogilvie was primarily responsible for Section I, Dr Drummond for Section II. The draft of Section I was edited by Dr Drummond after Professor Ogilvie's death but its substance remains as originally written.

Etruscan Porsenna near Aricia *c.* 504 B.C. The source is clearly Greek and probably originates from not long after the event. If he is not a local historian, he is likely to be Timaeus of Tauromenium (Taormina in Sicily) who wrote on the Western Greeks and on Pyrrhus. Timaeus was born in the mid-fourth century and, although he spent much of his working life, fifty years he said, in exile in Athens (Polyb. XII.25d.1: perhaps *c.* 315–264 B.C.), he always retained his interests and contacts in Magna Graecia. He knew much about the growing power of Rome.

Four other Greek historians are of fundamental importance for our knowledge of early Rome, although they were writing after Roman historiography had established itself. The first is Polybius (born in Megalopolis *c.* 210–200 B.C.), who was detained by the Romans in 167 B.C. as politically unreliable (XXVIII.13.9–13). Later he made many friends among the Roman nobility, particularly Scipio Aemilianus, and wrote a detailed history from the antecedents of the First Punic War to 146 B.C. For early Roman history and the Punic wars Polybius seems to have used as a main source the Roman Fabius Pictor and also (for Romano-Carthaginian affairs) the Greek Philinus (p. 486 n.1). It is probable, despite his sharp criticisms (XII.3–16), that he also consulted Timaeus regularly and in detail. Whether he used other Roman historians, such as L. Cincius Alimentus, C. Acilius, L. Cassius Hemina or Cato, is quite unknown, but he was familiar with and critical of the *pragmatike historia* 'political (and military) history' written in Greek by A. Postumius Albinus (*cos.* 151 B.C.). Only Thucydides rivals Polybius as a scientific and critical investigator. Unfortunately, of the forty books which he wrote, only six survive in substance and Book VI, in which he dealt with the affairs of early Rome, is itself fragmentary. We do not, therefore, have a full or continuous account of what Polybius thought of the first few centuries of Rome and even what we do have is clearly coloured by a philosophical view of history, ultimately derived from Plato, which thought of epochs as cyclically determined, but which is further complicated by an intricate and perhaps inconsistent attitude to the role which Fortune (Tyche) played in those events.

Nonetheless, Polybius' ideas exercised some influence on later accounts of Rome's development, most notably that in Cicero's *De Republica* (II.1–63), written in 54–1 B.C. and itself preserved in a fragmentary condition. Here the discussion operates formally in terms of a constitution comprising elements of monarchy, aristocracy and democracy which are all already present in the regal period but are only brought into a true balance in the early Republic. The overall theme owes much to the argument of Polybius' sixth book, although Cicero is more positive in his evaluation of the contribution of the component elements in the constitution (which for Polybius functioned principally as checks on each other) and stresses above all the moral qualities needed to maintain the proper constitutional balance. Unfortunately, however, for the details of his historical sketch Cicero may depend on later annalists alongside Polybius and he cannot, therefore, be used to fill the lacunae in Polybius' text or be taken as a sure guide to the historical traditions already current in the mid-second century or beyond.[2]

Like Polybius, Diodorus Siculus (so named because he was born at Agyrium in Sicily) also was the author of a history in forty books (of which fifteen are extant) written in Greek, although he obviously spent much of the thirty or more years which he devoted to its composition in Rome (probably from c. 70 to at least 36 B.C.). It was a 'universal history' covering the affairs of all the known countries of the civilized world. As one would expect, it is derivative and for the sections on early Roman affairs (where the narrative is preserved in full only for the Varronian years 486–302 B.C.) Diodorus used an unidentified historian as his main or only source.[3] Whether the brevity and character of his account indicate dependence on an early annalist[4] is uncertain: they may reflect his own comparative neglect of Roman history before the late fourth century (cf. p. 310).

Dionysius of Halicarnassus was born about 60 B.C. He made his name as a rhetorician and came to Rome in 30 B.C. after the decisive battle of Actium. He seems to have won an entrée to distinguished critical circles at Rome but he also had a deep interest in Roman history and devoted twenty-two years of research to the writing of his twenty books of *Roman Antiquities*. Eleven books, taking the story down to 444 B.C., remain and there are excerpts from the other nine (concluding with the start of the First Punic War). Dionysius relied largely on the same sources as his contemporary Livy – namely the annalistic historians of the early part of the century (see below) – but he has some valuable and recondite versions of regal history and for pre-regal Rome even uses authors like the Greek historians Pherecydes and Antiochus of Syracuse. For that period especially he was a serious researcher (cf. *Ant. Rom.* 1.32.2; 32.4; 37.2; 55.2; 68.1–2, et al.) and quotes over fifty authorities.

He remains, however, the moralizing rhetorician as historian. His work is formally structured, with sharp divisions into 'Domestic' and 'Foreign' affairs, and is distinguished by the prolific elaboration of the speeches and the similarly detailed (and fictitious) reconstruction of events as both a guide to statesmen and a source of literary diversion. Episodic treatment rather than a coherent philosophy characterizes much of Dionysius' approach to political developments but he remains

---

[2] Cf. Rambaud 1953[B147], 75ff.
[3] See Perl 1957[D25], 162ff for suggested identifications.
[4] As Stuart Jones in the first edition of *CAH* VII (Cambridge, 1928) 318f.

heavily indebted to the traditions of Greek political theory and historiography. These are reflected, for example, in the occasional employment of the notion (again influenced by Polybius) that Rome's political structures developed into a combination of monarchy, aristocracy and democracy, in his detailed discussion of constitutional innovations and their significance, in the attention paid to legal formalities. He is no less interested in the forms of economic and social dependence by which the aristocracy reinforced its position. Above all, he owes to Greek traditions the strongly political character of his history and his robust, often cynical attitude to political conflict, which on occasions even transcends his fundamental aristocratic sympathies but seldom rises above the stereotyped and superficial.

Finally, Plutarch. Born at Chaeronea in central Greece c. A.D. 46, Plutarch studied at Athens and travelled widely as a young man – especially to Egypt and Italy. His most important contribution to history was the *Parallel Lives* which range from the mythical (e.g. Romulus) to the historical (e.g. Julius Caesar): their value can only be as good as that of his sources (and even so Plutarch recast his material to suit his own artistic and moral objectives), but although he relied on authors still extant, such as Dionysius of Halicarnassus, he also had access to many works which no longer survive, and it is the unexpected details which crop up from time to time in his writings that make Plutarch such a vital authority. He also wrote a series of books on religious, philosophical and moral matters and his *Roman Questions* contains much previous information and speculation on early Roman religion.[5]

Roman historiography began at the end of the third century B.C. but the earliest historical work was almost certainly the epic poem on the First Punic War written in the later third century by one of the combatants, Cn. Naevius from Campania. This was as factual as it was dramatic and was followed by another epic, the *Chronicle* (*Annales*) of Q. Ennius (239–?169 B.C.) from Rudiae in Calabria. Ennius recounted Roman history to his own day in eighteen books, the first three covering the Aeneas legend and the monarchy, the next two the fifth and fourth centuries. The fragments from the regal period demonstrate the already detailed development of several major episodes. The early Republic is less well represented but Ennius' primary interest here (as perhaps that of the older prose historians) was evidently military. How far his work was later used as a historical source is controversial, but the *Annales* was widely read in the last two centuries B.C. and with its apparent emphasis on ancient traditions of conduct, on Rome's religious institutions, on her

[5] The much later account of Cassius Dio (early third century A.D.) is preserved for this period only in fragments and in the twelfth-century epitomizing universal history of Zonaras (who also used Plutarch). It is derivative (not least from Livy) but occasionally preserves variants otherwise lost.

military achievement and on individual heroism and renown it must have exercised an important influence on Roman attitudes to their past.

The *Annales* was probably begun *c.* 187 B.C.[6] If so, Ennius almost certainly had available the first prose history, that of Q. Fabius Pictor. Fabius had served as an official delegate to Delphi in 216 B.C. (App. *Hann.* 27). His history has perished but an inscription from a library at Taormina[7] gives a summary of the contents, and citations by Dionysius, Livy and other historians enable us to gain some insight into its scope, sources and purpose. Fabius wrote in Greek, the only available literary language at the time, with a view to establishing Rome in the eyes of the world, especially the Greek world, as a civilized and great nation. Whether he wrote in the dying days of the Second Punic War or, more probably, in the immediately succeeding years, his aim was chauvinistic. Attention was concentrated on the foundation legends of Rome and on events of Fabius' own day, while there seems to have been little detailed account of events of the fifth and fourth centuries, presumably for lack of evidence. Fabius has been condemned for wide-spread falsification of early Roman history[8] but extant fragments only admit of a verdict of non-proven.

Fabius was followed by L. Cincius Alimentus, but of his work we know nothing, except that he also wrote in Greek, had been captured by Hannibal and was a senator. Only five fragments survive but again they reveal an interest in very early legend (fr. 3–6P) and contemporary Punic affairs (fr. 7P). The great hiatus of early republican history remains. Of C. Acilius, another senator who wrote *res Romanas* in Greek early in the first half of the second century, and A. Postumius Albinus (*cos.* 151 B.C.) who was devoted to Greek language and studies (Polyb. XXXIX.1) and also wrote a history of Rome (p. 2), nothing of significance is left.

The new start came with M. Porcius Cato, the elder (234–149 B.C., consul in 195 B.C., censor in 184 B.C.), who was the first historian to write in Latin. At least for history before his own day Cato abandoned the annalistic method, employed by historians before and after him, who recorded events year by year, in favour of a much broader outlook. The first three books dealt with the foundation of Rome and other Italian cities. Cato took advantage not only of the *fable convenue* but also made a serious effort to seek out original documents (cf. e.g. fr. 58P, which gives a list of Latin communities who made a dedication at Aricia (p. 272)). Books 4 and 5 dealt with the Carthaginian Wars and brought the story down to 167 B.C. The date of publication is not certain but the shape

---

[6] See, e.g., Jocelyn 1972[B81], 997–9; cf. also Skutsch 1985[B169], 2ff (*c.* 184 B.C.).

[7] Manganaro 1974[B101], 389–409; 1976[B102], 83–96.

[8] Most notably by Alföldi 1965[I3]; see pp. 248ff.

of the work raises an unanswerable question: how did Cato deal with the fifth and fourth centuries?

For a generation Roman historians do not seem to have added much. Acilius and Postumius are shadowy figures; a descendant of Q. Fabius Pictor (?N. Fabius Pictor) may have translated some or all of his predecessor's work into Latin; L. Cassius Hemina (*fl.* 146 B.C.: see fr. 39P) was quoted as an authority by the elder Pliny (e.g., *HN* XVIII.7) and later scholars, but we do not know the scale or originality of his work. Book 2 was still dealing with immediately post-regal figures such as Porsenna (fr. 16P); Book 4 is entitled 'Bellum Punicum posterior', 'The later Punic War' (fr. 31P). It can, therefore, be assumed that Cassius also gave very little attention to the early years of the Republic.

It is this gap which raises such intriguing questions as the second century draws to an end. In or after 130 B.C. the chief *pontifex* (*pontifex maximus*), P. Mucius Scaevola, ended the practice by which every year a whitened board was put up outside his residence which probably recorded calendaric events (e.g. the dates of festivals) and also, as they occurred, other events of a semi-religious significance (e.g. elections, triumphs, portents and prodigies). The evidence for Scaevola's action is clearly given by Cicero (*De Or.* II.52: 'usque ad P. Mucium pontificem maximum res omnes singulorum annorum mandabat litteris pontifex maximus'[9]). Quite separately the Vergilian scholar Servius records that the contents of these records were published in eighty books (*ad* Verg. *Aen.* 1.373), but Servius gives no date and does not mention Scaevola. Until recently it has been taken for granted that the material from these pontifical *Annales Maximi* was published by Scaevola and first used by L. Calpurnius Piso Frugi (*cos.* 133 B.C.) in his historical *Annales*, scathingly described by Cicero (*Brut.* 106) as 'very meagrely written' ('sane exiliter scriptos') but often quoted, for instance by Livy. There are, however, difficulties. Dionysius of Halicarnassus (*Ant. Rom.* 1.74.3) claims that Polybius used the pontifical *tabula*,[10] and that must have been many years before P. Mucius Scaevola. Secondly, we would expect a huge expansion of fifth- and fourth-century material in Piso's history but, once again, he was already dealing with the affairs of 305 and 304 B.C. in his Book 3 (Livy IX.44.2; Gell. *NA* VII.9). Therefore, the archival material which fills the first Decade of Livy cannot have been available to Piso or, if it was, was not exploited by him. Thirdly, ancient references to the *Annales*, while containing a few curiosities (such as the eclipse of 400 B.C.: Cic. *Rep.* 1.25 (cf. p. 21)), also contain much fiction (especially in the quotations from the fourth-century A.D. *Origo gentis Romanae*). So it may be that

---

[9] 'Down to the time when P. Mucius was *pontifex maximus*, the *pontifex maximus* used to commit to writing every event of each year.'

[10] For a different interpretation see Walbank 1957–79[B182], 1.665 (on Polyb. VI.11a.2).

the annual notices were transferred by the *pontifex maximus* every year (perhaps from about 500 B.C. or as a result of the activities of Cn. Flavius *c.* 300 B.C. (p. 396)) into continuous commentaries which could be used for practical purposes, such as providing precedents for dealing with religious emergencies. Historians like Q. Fabius Pictor or Polybius, because of their social position, could always have consulted such commentaries, if they had been interested. But the publication in eighty books looks much more like an antiquarian venture, typical of the first century B.C.[11] and it is hard to see Piso's history as the turning point which it has so often been assumed to be.

There are other historians known from this period[12] but we cannot appreciate their contribution. It is in the first half of the first century B.C. that a new impetus was given to Roman historiography and it was inspired by two important factors – a growing awareness of documents, inscriptions and other archival materials, on the one hand, and, on the other, a desire to understand history politically (and if necessary to rewrite it politically). In this period the names of four authors stand out although their works survive only in miserly fragments: Q. Claudius Quadrigarius, C. Licinius Macer, Valerius Antias and Q. Aelius Tubero. One thing is immediately apparent. Their works were much longer – Quadrigarius at least twenty-three books, Macer sixteen,[13] Antias no less than seventy-five. The sudden wealth of detail has arrived, although interestingly Quadrigarius seems to have begun his history in 390 B.C., presumably because he regarded fifth-century and earlier history as largely legendary.[14]

C. Licinius Macer is the best known. Tribune of the plebs in 73 B.C. and father of the poet C. Licinius Calvus, Macer was a *popularis* in politics, a supporter of Marius in the troubles of the eighties. It cannot be doubted that this coloured his interpretation of history, especially in the desire to see antecedents of more recent political measures (e.g. the Gracchan proposals) in the remote past. This must have helped to swell the size of his account of early Roman history and can be traced in Livy. But Macer, as the fragments show, was also an antiquarian. He found in the temple of Iuno Moneta some Linen Books (*libri lintei*) which gave a list of magis-

[11] Frier 1979[B57] makes out a case for the Augustan antiquarian Verrius Flaccus as the author.

[12] Notably Cn. Gellius, who has sometimes been credited with at least ninety-seven books. In fact, however, in the relevant passage Charisius cites from Book 27 (*Gramm.* p. 68B).

[13] Or even twenty-one. Priscian's allusion (*Inst.* XIII.12, *GL* III p. 8K) to Book Two as dealing with Pyrrhus must be a textual corruption.

[14] Cf. p. 21. Quadrigarius' first book probably covered most or all of the fourth century from 390; extensive consecutive treatment began only with the Samnite, Pyrrhic and Punic wars. For an assessment of his history and the question of his relationship to C. Acilius, whose Greek history he supposedly partly or wholly translated into Latin (Livy XXV.39.12; cf. XXXV.14.5), see Zimmerer 1937[B194]; Klotz 1942[B89], 268–85; Badian 1966[B6], 18–20 (emphasizing his patriotic distortion and devotion to entertaining narrative).

trates[15] and he also unearthed a treaty between Rome and Ardea which he dated to 444 B.C. (fr. 13P). Cicero had a poor opinion of him (*Brut.* 238) and criticized his loquacity (*Leg.* 1.7), just as Livy criticized him for inventing stories for the greater glory of his own family (VII. 9.5: his son's name Calvus is itself romantic).

Valerius Antias is more problematical. We do not know his *praenomen* or his family background. There was a L. Valerius Antias who commanded some ships in 215 B.C. (Livy XXIII.34.9), which indicates that his family played a cadet role in the Roman political life of the Valerii. Nor can we be sure about his date. Velleius Paterculus (II.9.6) makes him a contemporary of Sisenna (praetor in 78 B.C.), P. Rutilius Rufus (praetor before 118 B.C.; exiled in 92) and Claudius Quadrigarius, which should place him in the eighties and seventies B.C., but he is not mentioned by Cicero in his judgement of historians before his day and this has led scholars, without adequate justification, to argue that he was writing as late as the time of Caesar. There are no certain allusions to mid-first-century events in the fragments. On the other hand, like Macer, he clearly publicized his own *gens* and many Valerian laws and actions from the early centuries have to be disregarded. He was censured even in antiquity for his reckless assertion of numbers (e.g. military casualties) which must have come from his fertile imagination rather than from newly discovered documents, although he does seem to have had a real interest in Roman institutions such as the triumph or the secular games. His political affiliations are not known: if he was writing in the early part of the century, perhaps an admiration for the Sullan restoration. But Antias was certainly prolific and provided much of the raw material for Livy's own history.

Q. Aelius Tubero came from a literary family (L. Tubero, a legate of Q. Cicero in 60 B.C., was something of an historian (*Q Fr.* 1.1.10)) and Dionysius of Halicarnassus addressed a long essay *On Thucydides* to a Q. Aelius Tubero. There was also a notable jurist of the same name (Gell. *NA* 1.22.7). Livy quotes Q. Tubero as an annalistic source from time to time. It is probable that the jurist, the annalist and Dionysius' patron were one and the same person, the father of the consul of 11 B.C.[16] Tubero's history was at least fourteen books long (fr. 10P) and so designed on the same larger scale as his immediate predecessors, but the fragments give little or no idea of its character, except that he too had consulted documents (Livy IV.23.1) and conducted independent research (fr. 9P). He would have been writing in the forties and thirties B.C.

[15] The Linen Books are cited four times in Livy for issues concerning the identity of magistrates between 444 and 428 B.C. (cf. p. 18). How far they went outside these chronological limits and whether they contained more than a list of magistrates is not known, although Livy IV.13.7 suggests that at most they included only brief notices.

[16] See Ogilvie 1965[B129], 16–17; 570–1 (on Livy IV.23.1).

It is ironic but perhaps not accidental that the only work which does survive is Books I–X (753–293 B.C.) and XXI–XLV (219–167 B.C.) of the massive 142-book history of T. Livius (Livy) from Padua (*c.* 59 B.C.–A.D. 17). Unlike all his predecessors Livy did not belong to the Establishment. He held no public office; he did not even have the family background of a Valerius Antias; he was criticized by Asinius Pollio for his 'provincialness' ('Patavinitas'); although he was acquainted with Augustus (Tac. *Ann.* IV.34) and acted as literary tutor to the young Claudius (Suet. *Claud.* 41.1), he never figured in the literary world of Augustan Rome and died at Padua, not Rome. His knowledge of Greek was competent but not more than competent; his interest in research minimal. Yet he in part survived and Quadrigarius, Macer, Antias and Tubero did not. Why? Obviously sheer literary genius accounted for much; obviously too the combination of freedom, moral earnestness and patriotic fervour, which is also the hall-mark of the *Aeneid*.

Livy's *History* deals only briefly with the mythical events preceding the foundation of Rome and the regal period is also covered in a reduced compass by comparison with the early Republic. These appear to be innovations on Livy's part and they signify his predominant concern with Rome's historical achievement, above all in the military sphere, and its moral and political background. Livy lays less emphasis than Dionysius on constitutional developments for their own sake (the establishment of both the quaestorship and plebeian aedileship, for example, is omitted) and conveys little sense of inherent institutional imbalance in the early Republic. What matters to him (even more than to Dionysius) are the moral qualities, of both leaders and led, which are essential to the preservation of internal harmony and thereby to external success. In this general preoccupation and its detailed elaboration Livy is, of course, reacting to the experiences of the late Republic and his approach to his material is strongly conditioned by his view of Rome's contemporary failings. Nonetheless, he is basically retailing at second, third or fourth hand the evidence of earlier historians and doing so with prejudice and without a critical or scholarly intent. Since the works of these earlier historians do not survive, it is a nice judgement how far Livy has reproduced them accurately and how far they, for their part, were in any position to give an authoritative account of early Roman history. Every scrap has to be scrutinized.

(b) *Antiquarian writers*

Livy was an annalist, recording history year by year, however improbable. So was Dionysius of Halicarnassus. But in the first century B.C. there was also a new development. Pure antiquarianism became fashionable, again largely as a result of Hellenistic influences, especially the

Museum at Alexandria, and there emerged a group of learned writers who devoted their energies simply to antiquarian scholarship for its own sake, who looked at records, however uncritically, because they saw them as the raw material of history, and who, above all, studied the enduring history of Roman religion and institutions.

Two scholars of major importance merit special consideration but from the late second century B.C. onwards there were many more – Iunius Gracchanus and Sempronius Tuditanus (both writing works on the Roman magistracies), Cincius, Q. Cornificius, Nigidius Figulus ('On Thunderclaps'), Cornelius Nepos (*c.* 99 B.C. to *c.* 27 B.C.) and then Atticus (110 B.C. to 32 B.C.), who made the first serious attempts to utilize the principles set by Eratosthenes to establish Roman chronology, Tarquitius Priscus, A. Caecina and Fenestella (d. A.D. 19), to name only a few who investigated the byways of history. Of the greatest of them, M. Terentius Varro (116–27 B.C.), only two works survive (partially) and neither of them is of fundamental relevance to Roman history (*De Lingua Latina* ('On the Latin Language') and *De Re Rustica* ('On farming')), but his output was phenomenal (620 volumes, so it is said). Much of this abstruse scholarship was passed on through various channels to the Middle Ages and Renaissance (the most important intermediaries were the Latin Fathers of the Church). Varro, following on the work of Nepos and Atticus, may have established the dating system for early Roman history which has become standard (*ab urbe condita*, 'from the foundation of the city': he probably placed the foundation of Rome in the year which by our practice is known as 753 B.C.).[17] It is presumed that this was set out in his work entitled *Annales*, the date of which is unknown. Varro also published forty-two volumes on *Human and Divine Antiquities*, probably in 42 B.C. (although the date is disputed and the publication may have been spread over a number of years). This work included the explanation of many religious cults and many legendary tales. From the *De Lingua Latina* we know that one of his main tools of research was the use of etymology, often erratic, if not eccentric (e.g. the role of one Cornelius (cf. *cornu* 'horn') in the sacrifice of a miraculous cow by King Servius Tullius: Plut. *Quaest. Rom.* 4; cf. Livy 1.45.3ff). But Varro was thorough and systematic and if, as is probable, the digression in Livy VII.2.3ff on the origins of Roman comedy is derived from him, then it reveals painstaking investigation of Etruscan and Roman institutions; and although he was concerned not with the philosophical panorama of history but with the idle tit-bits, any citation from his works must be treated as very serious evidence, even if only to be discarded.

In contrast to Varro, a man of position who had written a constitu-

---

[17] On the 'Varronian' chronology (used throughout this volume) and other chronological systems for early Roman history see pp. 347ff; 625ff.

tional hand-book for the young Pompey, Verrius Flaccus was a freed-man. We do not know his antecedents but he was recognized by Augustus, who gave him a house, a pension and the over-sight of his grandsons' education. Verrius was obviously inspired by Varro, to whom he often refers, and he wrote a wide miscellany of books on a variety of antiquarian topics. His longest work was a dictionary, *On the Significance of Words* (*De Verborum Significatu*), which reflected Varro's linguistic interests but which adopted, perhaps for the first time in Latin, the principle of listing words alphabetically rather than by subject-matter. It was so huge a work (the letter A took four books alone) that, as was increasingly the custom in the Empire, it was abridged by Pompeius Festus at the end of the second century and further abridged in the Carolingian age. It is these abridgements which survive, and they contain a rare collection of antiquarian oddities, which are invaluable to a modern historian. Verrius is also quoted by the Fathers and other later writers whose works survive, such as Servius and Macrobius.

There are other names to conjure with. The geographers contribute much and of them Strabo (Aelius Strabo, born *c.* 64 B.C.) has left a *Geography* of great erudition. Like Dionysius he had come to Rome after the Battle of Actium in 31 B.C. He was widely travelled and had also composed a *History* which has perished, but the *Geography* reveals an interest in early Etruria and Latium and contains some precious facts.

(c) *Inscriptions*

Although the alphabet was introduced into Central Italy from the Greek world *c.* 700 B.C. (Fig. 1) and inscriptions appear at Rome at the end of the seventh century,[18] it is surprising how little actual epigraphic material survives from the period 600–250 B.C. This may be a fact of chance; or it may be that writing was at first an aristocratic and hieratical phenomenon and not until Rome's increasing contact with other powers such as Greece and Carthage was it employed on a major scale as an instrument of government and communication. At all events the surviving inscriptions earlier than the tombs of the Scipios in the third century are meagre and often highly controversial,[19] adding little to our knowledge of early Roman history.

Yet there was an alternative history of Rome. Probably not all that different, but it would be interesting to have it. There is a fresco from a

---

[18] P. 81. On the introduction of writing to Central Italy cf. Cristofani 1972[G43], 466–89; 1978[G45], 5–33; and in Ridgway and Ridgway 1979[A111], 373–412.

[19] So, for example, the early sixth-century inscription on a stele from the Lapis Niger shrine in the Comitium which apparently prescribes penalties for sacral violations but has defied complete elucidation.

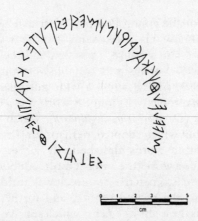

Fig. 1. Perhaps the earliest known Etruscan inscription on the foot of a proto-Corinthian kotyle from Tarquinii (*c.* 700 B.C.). The inscription (from right to left) reads:
   mi velelθus kacriqu numesiesi putes kraitilesθis putes
The full sense is uncertain but the text apparently records the making or giving of the vase by a Velthu for or to a Numerius. See M. Cristofani, *ASNP* ser. III.1 (1971) 295–9 (drawing after ib. 296).

tomb of the Fabii on the Esquiline hill at Rome (Fig. 2), probably recording some unknown events of the Samnite wars; there are the much more famous frescoes from the François tomb at Vulci which confirm a tradition, known otherwise only from an odd reference in Claudius' speech (*ILS* 212) and a mutilated fragment in Festus (486L), that a *condottiere* called Mastarna (? = Lat. *Magister*) with other warriors from Vulci, notably the brothers Vibennae (also known independently: cf. Varro, *Ling.* v.46), was in fact the king known to history as Servius Tullius.[20] Perhaps the most dramatic instance of this alternative history is the recently discovered inscription from the second temple at Satricum which dates from *c.* 500 and records a dedication by the *suodales* (comrades) of Publius Valerius to Mars (p.97). One Publius Valerius, surely this one, is well-known to history (see p. 174). But who are these *suodales*? Why to Mars?

Other inscriptions fill out or reinforce the information derived from our literary sources. A Greek inscription of the late sixth century from Tarquinii ('I belong to Apollo of Aegina, Sostratus made me'[21]) adds a new dimension to our understanding of the intercourse between Etruscans and Greeks (p. 49). From Tarquinii also come some commemorative inscriptions (*elogia*) recounting stirring deeds which have left no other trace in the annalistic record (p. 300). No doubt other discoveries will be made.

[20] For further discussion see p. 94f (with a different view).   [21] Torelli 1971[G499], 44ff.

But what is tantalizing is the epigraphic evidence which is lost. Greek and Roman scholars often (although uncritically) cite inscriptions, but many of these must either be bogus or be renewals as the result either of the decay of the original or of the need to update them so that a modern generation could actually understand what was written. One clear case of such modernization is an inscription preserved in Festus (180L) and, therefore, certainly derived from Varro or Verrius Flaccus, commemo-

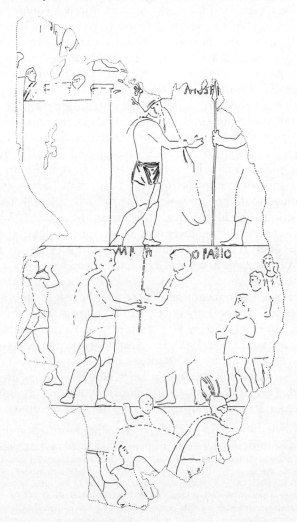

Fig. 2. Fresco from Esquiline tomb (third century?). The interpretation of the scenes is uncertain; they may depict actions involving Q. Fabius Maximus Rullianus (*cos.* 322; 310; 308; 296; 295) during the Samnite wars (p. 412). After *Roma medio-repubblicana 1973* [B401], fig. 15.

rating nine ex-consuls killed in the Volscian Wars of the early fifth
century. Festus' version must be false (it contains *cognomina*),[22] and yet
Varro or Verrius cannot have invented it. Another is a censors' document of 392 B.C. (Dion. Hal. *Ant. Rom.* 1.74.5): it also anachronistically
employs *cognomina* and uses a literary rather than a documentary form of
dating ('in the 119th year after the overthrow of the kings'); indeed, there
may have been no census in that year (cf. Festus 500L).

There is, in fact, a large quantity of inscriptions (genuine or spurious)
which were known to ancient scholars but which no longer survive.
Obviously the most important of these for early republican history is a
fifth-century law-code (the Twelve Tables), many of whose provisions
can be recovered from later references. But also of international consequence are the treaties with Carthage reported by Polybius (III.22–5) and
Livy (VII.27.2; Diod. XVI.69) which the Pyrgi inscriptions (p. 256) have
to some extent corroborated. More disputable but not really in doubt is
the dedication which Dionysius of Halicarnassus (*Ant. Rom.* IV.26)
describes as 'written in archaic Greek letters' and which set out the rules
for the cult of Diana on the Aventine (p. 267). It also must bear some
relation to the cult inscription from Aricia (p. 272). There was the corslet
of the Roman military hero Cossus (Livy IV.20.7: p. 298) and the Linen
Books consulted by Macer, quite apart from the *Annales Maximi* themselves. There were 'Commentaries of Servius Tullius' (Livy 1.60.3)
which alleged to give instructions on the election of consuls: in fact, they
are probably the same document as that compiled between *c.* 213 and 179
B.C. which gives the orthodox Servian 'Constitution' (p. 164) with its five
classes and consequent centuries. There was the law of the annual nail in
the temple of Iuppiter (Livy VII.3.5 (p.187)). From the fifth century also
there are mentions of surviving texts of Sp. Cassius' treaty with the
Latins (*c.* 493 B.C.: Dion. Hal. *Ant. Rom.* VI.95 (p. 274)); a law inscribed
on a bronze column by L. Pinarius and Furius (*coss.* 472; Varro *ap.*
Macrob. *Sat.* 1.13.21); the Ardea treaty (see p. 174 n.8). In the fourth
century this list of inscriptions and documents increases, but the questions surrounding ·their authenticity are not greatly altered.

[22] Roman nomenclature became progressively more elaborate: the original single name (the later
'forename' (*praenomen*)) was gradually supplemented by a lineage or clan name (*nomen gentile*:
originally a patronymic (p. 98)). The date of the use of inherited additional names (*cognomina*), never
obligatory or universal in the republican period, is uncertain: in Etruscan occasional additional
names may appear as early as the sixth century (M. Pallottino, *Gnomon* 36 (1964), 804) but are not
common on inscriptions before the third century. Their adoption as inherited names at Rome was
probably largely conditioned by the desire to distinguish different branches of the same 'clan' (*gens*)
and presumably therefore varied from one *gens* to another (some never employed them). It therefore
seems unlikely that all fifth- and fourth-century magistrates had *cognomina* as our surviving lists
pretend (p. 628), and as they are otherwise not cited on inscriptions of official documents until the
second century, their alleged appearance in such a context three centuries earlier is highly suspect.

(d) *Archaeological and other evidence*

The tombs, the buildings, the artefacts of a nation tell a great deal about their character and about their development (or decline) and about their relationships with their neighbours. This is particularly true of early Rome. Recent discoveries in Latium and Campania, as well as in Etruria, have shown that Rome was not peculiar or distinct in her development – except in the sense that eventually she, because of her geographical position and her tenacity, triumphed. In the sixth and fifth centuries there was almost a common culture throughout Central Italy. Etruscan towns like Veii or Vulci had similar lifestyles to those that can be recognized at Rome, Lavinium (Pratica di Mare), Ficana, Gabii, Decima and elsewhere. This phenomenon extends right down to Campania, because the entire network of communities, however ethnically different, was bound together by commercial ties which were of far greater significance. This characteristic is seen in the very strong Etruscan and Greek influence on Rome and, more vitally, on other neighbourhood towns; it is to be seen in the Valerius inscription (however we should interpret it; p. 97); it is to be seen in the Latin influences on Campanian artefacts; it may be seen in the way in which Roman constitutional organs and social patterns evolved.[23] It is wrong to think that the Etruscans, Latins and Greeks in the sixth century were fundamentally different in their way of life.

Rome itself is an impossible place to excavate: too many layers of priceless heritage have covered it. Only a few holes at occasional places can be dug (in the Forum, or in the Forum Boarium at the present-day church of Sant' Omobono) but even from these trifling excavations enough has emerged to confirm, at least in general, the traditional account of the growth of the city (e.g. traces of a primitive Palatine settlement have been found; the draining of the Forum area can be approximately dated; various structural phases of the Regia (in the republican period the seat of the 'priest-king' (*rex sacrorum*) and perhaps used by his regal predecessors) have been identified; unearthed antefixes suggest a date *c*. 500 B.C. for the temple of Iuppiter Optimus Maximus on the Capitoline hill[24]). Conversely the excavations disclose no evidence for a Gallic conflagration in *c*. 390 B.C. (p. 308). They do, however, bear testimony to the cultural affinity of early Rome with its Etruscan and Latin neighbours. Any idea of a uniquely different style of 'Latial pottery', for example, must be abandoned and we should not think of an 'Etruscan conquest' of Rome but of a synoecism which resulted in

[23] The exact extent to which similarity of material culture and 'commercial' ties implies uniformity of social and political structure is, however, variously evaluated (cf., e.g., p. 187).
[24] But see p. 22 n. 41.

Etruscan families settling permanently in Rome (as at Ardea or Satricum), in Etruscan political and religious institutions being adopted and in Etruscan art being welcomed for all its aesthetic beauty.

By contrast, so far the fourth and early third centuries have produced little significant archaeological material, either inside Rome or outside. It might be expected, for instance, that some of the Roman campaigns in Samnium could be traced by forts and marching camps, but the discoveries so far are negligible (although evidence has accumulated of the Samnites' own hill-forts). Some evidence has emerged about the fate of Etruscan cities captured by Rome (e.g. Falerii or Bolsena) but less than might be expected. Various public buildings at Rome have been uncovered, such as the great double temple of Fortuna and Mater Matuta at Sant' Omobono. However, in this phase, as indeed in the earlier period, detailed, historical information comes mainly from the annalists (particularly Livy), who viewed history from a different standpoint, and it is only from the time of Pyrrhus that more abundant archaeological material, together with more reliable historical accounts, provide a solid foundation for a full history of Rome.

II. THE CREATION OF EARLY ROMAN HISTORY

(a) *The available data*

To the Greek historian Timaeus in the third century early Rome already represented a remote past and for most of the period covered by this volume an interval of centuries separated even the first Roman historians from the events they described. Historical reconstruction of events before the later fourth century[25] relied on a slender repertoire of documentary and oral sources and even Livy (VI.I.Iff) concedes the deficiency of authentic records, assigning as a principal cause the Gallic Sack in 390 B.C. That is probably erroneous,[26] but a survey of the sources potentially available to Fabius Pictor and his successors confirms the essential fact: the surviving early documentation, at least before the mid-fourth century, was sparse and inadequate.

The existence of early Etruscan historical accounts is speculative and the use of Etruscan material by Roman sources seems in general to have been late and occasional (p. 89). Even the Etruscan legends associated with Mastarna and the Vibennae (p. 94f) found no place in the main-stream Roman historical tradition, to which Mastarna as such remained

[25] From that period on, more extensive and reliable archival and oral material, coupled with the increasing interest of contemporary Greek historians, provided a more substantial basis for the historians' accounts (p. 311).

[26] Castagnoli 1974[E85], 425–7; below, p. 308.

largely or wholly unknown and the Vibennae merely the focus of aetiological legend.

Greek authors from the late fifth century B.C. gave various accounts of Rome's foundation and a few events in the early history of the Western Greeks were also relevant to Rome, but it will have been from the late fourth century, as Roman history became increasingly entwined with that of Campania, Samnium, South Italy and Sicily, that Greek material will have become more plentiful; Pliny (HN III.57) states firmly that Theophrastus (c. 370–288/5 B.C.) was the first Greek to treat Rome in any detail. Although we do not know what topics he covered, Greek interest is likely to have focused particularly on contemporary external affairs,[27] but that in turn presumably prompted some interest in Rome's earlier internal and external history. According to Dionysius (Ant. Rom. 1.6.1) the first to 'run over' the early period of Rome was Hieronymus of Cardia in the late fourth–early third century B.C.,[28] but the major contributor here was undoubtedly Timaeus. He treated early Rome twice, in the introduction to his history of the Western Greeks and in that to his supplementary books covering the emergent rivalry of Rome and Carthage. The scope of these accounts, however, is problematic. Timaeus certainly included the foundation of the city, explained (in the supplement) at least one of its rituals thereby and, in a highly controversial fragment,[29] referred to a 'monetary' reform of Servius Tullius. His own focus of interest may have led him to trace briefly Rome's external development, at least in the late fourth and early third centuries, and he may well have outlined the growth of Roman political institutions in the common Greek manner.[30] For most such material, however, he would have been reliant ultimately on local traditions, presumably those subsequently available to Roman historians, and although Fabius Pictor and others probably knew and used his work, its ultimate basis would largely coincide with theirs.

Few documentary sources can have survived from the regal period (cf. p. 87) and even for the early Republic their significance was probably limited. One possible major exception, however, is a consecutive list of republican chief magistrates. These were the eponymous officials by which each year was distinguished and lists of them were apparently kept for chronological purposes since the term *fasti*, by which such records are later known, refers in origin to the calendar proper. Such lists of

27 Frederiksen 1968[J47], 226–7. Duris of Samos (c. 340–c. 260 B.C.) apparently recorded Rome's victory over Etruscans, Gauls and Samnites at Sentinum in 295 (Jac. FGrH 76 F56); p. 379.

28 Cf. Hornblower 1981[B78], 140ff.

29 Jac. FGrH 566 F61; cf. De Martino 1977[H23], 51–3; below, p. 417.

30 The allusion in Eratosthenes (Geog. IIC 24 Berger (= Strabo 1.4.9, p. 66c)) to the admirable government of Carthage and Rome confirms early Greek interest in the form of the Roman state and may well reflect some previous treatment of the topic.

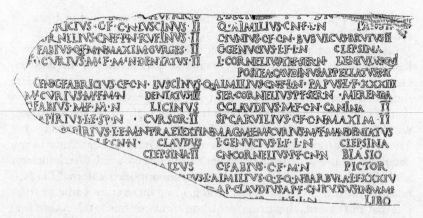

Fig. 3. Fragment of the Capitoline Fasti recording the principal magistrates of the years 279–267. After Degrassi 1947 [D7], 40.

eponymous magistrates were frequently published alongside the calendar from the first century, and their function as a chronological key would clearly have made such a record desirable from the inception of the Republic. If a list was kept from that date, however, it has not survived; the sequence of magistrates has now to be reconstructed from the surviving historians (above all Diodorus, Livy and Dionysius), from inscribed lists of the late Republic and early Empire (particularly the so-called Capitoline Fasti, a learned reconstruction published on the Arch of Augustus in c. 30 or c. 17 B.C. (Fig. 3)), and from closely related late imperial compilations. These lists, however, show a high level of uniformity, and this, together with indications of an original common order of names even within colleges of up to six officials, suggests that all derive ultimately from a single exemplar or at least a common tradition.[31]

Moreover, the surviving authorities do not indicate major discrepancies or omissions in their sources on a scale to suggest that they contained radically different consular lists or consequent major differences in their overall republican chronology.[32] This is true even of the Linen Books discovered by Licinius Macer (p. 7f). Within the period from which our citations of the Books come (444–428 B.C.) only two significant variants are attributed to them.[33] Under 444 B.C. the Books apparently gave as an additional consular college the alleged censors of

---

[31] Beloch 1926[A12], 4ff. Uncertainties surrounding the *praenomina* and *cognomina* of many individual magistrates in the early part of the list do not weaken this conclusion, since it is the family names which are significant here; indeed, the *cognomina* probably represent later reconstruction. See further pp. 627ff.   [32] See pp. 173ff.

[33] Livy IV.7.12 (cf. Dion. Hal. *Ant. Rom.* XI.62.1ff) = Licinius Macer fr. 13P; Livy IV.23.1ff = Licinius Macer fr. 14P; Aelius Tubero fr. 6P. On the problem of the magistrates of 444 B.C. see further p. 174 n. 8.

443, under 434 B.C. two consuls rather than three consular tribunes. In neither instance can the truth be established definitively, but even if the Linen Books were correct here, that need mean only that in these cases they contained elements deriving from a comparatively early stage in the transmission of the consular list, which was perhaps subsequently manipulated to enhance reconstruction of the consular tribunate and censorship. Moreover, although presumably Macer considered the Books of some independent value in relation to his principal sources, the ancient references do not prove that they were of great antiquity, and their inclusion of L. Minucius Augurinus in an unknown capacity under the years 440–439 B.C. (cf. p. 183) does not encourage confidence in their reliability.

The hypothesis, therefore, of a common source to the surviving consular lists remains unimpaired. Any estimate of that source's antiquity must depend on a systematic analysis of its intrinsic reliability but if a case for its accuracy can be sustained (p. 173f), it is difficult to resist the conclusion that it must derive from an early documentary record. Even so, however, the evidence which it provided to the early historian was limited. At most it offered some guidance on republican chronology, the fortunes of aristocratic families, the form of the principal magistracy and the admission of plebeians to office, but of itself it could not yield even a skeleton outline of early republican history.

Some more specific evidence for external history might have been derived from lists of triumphs. In the late Republic an inventory of triumphal dedications appears to have been kept in the Capitoline temple of Iuppiter[34] but the antiquity of this practice is unknown. Equally uncertain are the basis and reliability of the principal surviving list, the so-called Acta Capitolina Triumphalia or Fasti (Capitolini) Triumphales, set up in parallel to the Fasti Capitolini on the Arch of Augustus (Fig. 4). The general accuracy of its data can be determined only in the context of a detailed consideration of the traditions for Rome's territorial and military expansion, but a record which commences with the fiction of Romulus' triumph over the Caeninenses has clearly undergone at least some re-working, as other manifest inventions and the genealogical details also show. There can, therefore, be no *a priori* confidence in most of its notices, at least before the third century,[35] and there is much uncertainty as to the sources on which it ultimately depends for those which are authentic. If, as is commonly assumed, it drew directly or indirectly on the annual pontifical records (rather than a temple inventory) for such material, the question becomes one further aspect of a much wider and more fundamental issue of early republican history: the

---

[34] *CIL* I², 78 (Henzen).
[35] For a defence of their reliability from the fifth century cf. p. 289f.

Fig. 4. Fragment of the Acta Capitolina Triumphalia recording triumphs ascribed to Ancus Marcius, Tarquinius Priscus and Servius Tullius. After Degrassi 1947 [D7], 64.

scope of the pontifical records and the date from which they were authentically preserved.

That the *pontifex maximus* should have sought to keep a historical record of the Roman state centuries before the development of literary history at Rome is clearly implausible: presumably his primary interest lay in recording events of immediate concern to the pontifical college itself, perhaps on what was, in origin, principally a calendar, although that need not have restricted his purview to events which would now be classed as 'religious' (cf. p. 587). A slighting reference in the elder Cato (*Orig.* fr. 77P (= Gell. *NA* 11.28.6)) indicates that the annual whiteboard recorded eclipses and high corn prices, in contrast apparently to the material of 'true history'. This obviously cannot be taken to exhaust the tablet's contents (at least in Cato's day) and other, admittedly vague references suggest that a wide range of public events was covered.[36] However, that may be the result of a progressive increase in the tablet's scope, and the character and range of the material originally recorded remain purely conjectural. All that can be said with confidence is that the tablet can have given no details of episodes noted.

If in origin the whiteboard served principally the pontifical college itself, preservation of its data may have been important from an early date but such material certainly did not survive from (or at least was not used for) the monarchy (p. 88) nor even necessarily the early Republic. In their accounts of the fifth and early fourth centuries the extant historians seldom include certain categories of occurrence (above all prodigies and portents) which might reasonably be expected to have been noted by the

---

[36] See especially Cic. *De Or.* 11.52 (above, p. 6); Serv. *Aen.* 1.373.

priests, there are still in Livy's account occasional years where nothing memorable was recorded (e.g. IV.30.4 (429 B.C.)), and even in antiquity doubts were entertained about the reliability of material which allegedly derived from records kept before the Gallic Sack. Although Cicero (*Rep.* 1.25) cites the pontifical record for an early eclipse, probably that of 21 June 400 B.C.,[37] a certain 'Clodius' (possibly Claudius Quadrigarius) denounced as forgeries the available genealogical records which purported to date from before the Sack. They were, he declared, the work of individuals anxious to flatter those who claimed a spurious descent from distinguished figures of the past[38] and while he does not specify the pontifical tablets, he might not have written so confidently if in his view they had survived intact from that period. Livy (VI.1.2) too presumably has them in mind when he more cautiously ascribes the unreliability of early Roman history to the loss of most of the pontifical records (*commentarii*) in 390. Even if the Sack was not in fact responsible for the scantiness of genuine earlier documentation, the existence and scope of such documentation from the fifth century were evidently controversial. Whilst, therefore, the survival of a pontifical record from that period cannot be excluded, it is too insecurely attested to justify confident acceptance of the relevant annalistic traditions. Since in any case it could have provided only rudimentary information, the scale of the later elaboration by the historians themselves would make it difficult to assign any individual item to this source with confidence, even presuming (what is controversial) that the early historians used these records to their fullest extent.[39]

Equally problematic (as Livy's evidence indicates) is the availability of other priestly documents (alongside ritual hymns). Perhaps lists of priests and accounts of priestly actions were kept from an early date, not least as a source of procedural examples (cf. p. 577), but whether, as Dionysius (*Ant. Rom.* VIII.56.1) might suggest, they or other documents (e.g., dedicatory inscriptions or, again, the pontifical tablets) were regularly available to provide details even of such fundamental events as temple dedications must be uncertain in view of the character of many surviving traditions. Some early temple inscriptions survived but it is not certain that dedicants were recorded on the building at Rome in this period[40] and if they were, many were presumably erased in the course of later reconstruction. A number of temple foundations were spuriously attributed to the early monarchy and at a more general level the extant

[37] Skutsch 1974[B167], 78–9; 1985[B169], 311–13.　[38] Plut. *Num.* 1.
[39] For a less sceptical account see above, p. 6f.
[40] Dionysius' statement (*Ant. Rom.* v.35.3) that M. Horatius Pulvillus 'τὴν ἐπιγραφὴν ἔλαβε' in the case of the Capitoline temple may mean only that he received the credit for the dedication (K. Hanell in *Les origines de la république romaine* 1967[A98], 41).

historical sources show little or no serious grasp of the introduction of temple building (or of the major transformation in the public appearance of Rome (p. 75f)) in the late seventh and early sixth centuries. Moreover, they apparently omit shrines now revealed by archaeology, whereas none of the temples they ascribe to the late sixth or early fifth centuries has been conclusively located in this period by archaeological evidence, except for that of Castor.[41] Even the detailed literary evidence for the date or circumstances of individual dedications is often contradictory, anachronistic or otherwise unsatisfactory; the temple of Saturn, for example, was apparently dated to the late fifth or early fourth century by Cn. Gellius, to 501 or 498 B.C. by Varro and to 497 B.C. by Dionysius and Livy.[42] Nonetheless, the archaeological data do suggest that the historians are correct in implying a major phase of temple construction in the sixth and early fifth centuries, followed by a comparative lull until the late fourth century, and their assignation of particular shrines to this period is not implausible. Conceivably the names of dedicants or the dates of dedication alone were preserved in some form[43] and the variant traditions in the case of some shrines are due to rebuilding (frequent in this period) or subsequent reworking of an authentic tradition. But in other cases the apparent (or inferred) antiquity of these shrines may have prompted their attribution to the monarchy or very early Republic. Even in late republican Rome the physical heritage of the early period remained a potent reminder of her past.

Other epigraphic evidence was sporadic (p. 13f) and appears not to have been employed systematically by the historians. It is frequently adduced almost as an extraneous element, suggesting that it has often been incorporated into a narrative whose basic outline was already established. The manner in which Livy draws on the antiquarian Cincius for the regulations governing the nail set every year in the wall of the Capitoline temple in order to develop a schematic history of the ritual (Livy VII.3.5ff) is typical. So is the incorporation of the alleged Latin treaty of 493 B.C. in Dionysius (*Ant. Rom.* VI.95.1ff). Some such documents were in fact largely ignored, most notably the Twelve Tables; for ancient writers war and politics were the spheres in which the individual

[41] That one phase of the sanctuary of Mater Matuta or Fortuna in the Forum Boarium may fall within the traditional but purely conventional chronology of its reputed founder, Servius Tullius (p. 76), offers no realistic basis for faith in the literary tradition. Similarly, although some sixth-century antefixes have been plausibly assigned to the Capitoline temple (509 B.C.), there is no clear proof. For the temple of Castor see I. Nielsen and J. Zahle, *Acta Archaeologica* 59 (1985) 1–29. The earliest phase of the temple of Saturn is currently being investigated.

[42] Cn. Gellius fr. 24P (= Macrob. *Sat.* 1.8.1); Varro *ap.* Macrob. *Sat.* 1.8.1 (cf. Dion. Hal. *Ant. Rom.* VI.1.4); Livy II.21.2; Dion. Hal. *Ant. Rom.* VI.1.4; Macrob. *Sat.* 1.8.1.

[43] Cf. also the signatures of two Greek artists on the early fifth-century temple of Ceres (Pliny *HN* XXXV.154 (from Varro); Le Bonniec 1958[G360], 257ff).

demonstrated his qualities and won renown and those in which the historical development and achievements of the state were to be observed; legal or social history in themselves were of little account.

The possible contribution of oral traditions (chiefly Roman but also Latin and even perhaps Etruscan) to the formation of historical accounts of Rome's past has yet to be evaluated thoroughly, particularly on a comparative basis. At Rome itself the existence of such traditions is most readily traced in the early development of the foundation myth (cf. p. 56f). It is also reflected in the information which percolated, albeit sometimes in garbled form, to late fourth- and early third-century Greek sources. Aristotle knew of a Lucius who had saved Rome after the Gallic Sack, while Callimachus applied a Greek motif to the story of a Gaius wounded in killing the enemy leader during an assault of the 'Peucetii' on Rome.[44] So also Timaeus' accounts of the historical Rome, whatever their scope, must have relied substantially on oral data (p. 89).

How reliable or extensive such data were is another matter. Much of what relates to the earlier period and may derive from popular belief is merely aetiological fiction (an abiding source of inspiration also in the later historical and antiquarian authors). Certain epochal events, such as the overthrow of the monarchy and the Gallic Sack, were presumably recalled and progressively elaborated, and the continuing need to defend the prerogatives of the plebeian officers may have fostered a lively oral tradition on their origins, although one continuously reworked to suit the contemporary situation. Some memory (also subject to constant recasting) may also have been retained of personalities, historical or legendary, and of episodes which were politically or morally edifying, although the famous heroic 'lays' to which the elder Cato referred contributed little to the historians, at least directly (p. 88). At a more general level it is an attractive conjecture that in a traditional, predominantly oral society a broad consensus on the major phases or landmarks of Rome's internal and external development had become established among the aristocracy[45] but if so, this can have operated only in very general terms; it will have been highly (and unpredictably) selective and much will have been vague and malleable, subject to progressive reinterpretation and modification as the perspectives and needs of society changed. Moreover, there is no reason to suppose that the earliest historians would have refrained from altering or (especially) supplementing such pre-existing traditions if (for whatever reason) that appeared justified; and such revisions might well have imposed themselves on subsequent writers if they were sufficiently plausible, possessed a convenient patriotic or moral character or proved otherwise attractive;

[44] Aristotle ap. Plut. Cam. 22.4; Callim. Aet. IV fr. 107 Pfeiffer; cf. Fraser 1972[A52], 1.763–9.
[45] Cornell 1986[B35], 82ff.

there can, after all, seldom have been specific evidence to refute such versions, even if they contained a generous quantity of invented material.

What is certain is the prevalence of family pretensions in early republican history, including probably such famous episodes as the migration to Rome of Att(i)us Clausus in 504 B.C. or the defeat of the Fabii by Veii at the Cremera in 477 B.C. (apart from a few legendary clan founders with regal connexions, such material is scarce under the monarchy (p. 89f)). Authentic information of this type must be oral in origin. Portrait masks of distinguished ancestors, perhaps with inscriptions recording their deeds, adorned the halls of late republican aristocratic houses, but there is no reliable evidence that any such had survived from the early Republic and comparable funerary inscriptions are found only for men of the late fourth century onwards (even then the most famous early example, the funerary inscription of L. Cornelius Scipio Barbatus (*cos.* 298), is notoriously at variance with Livy's account (p. 377)). The preservation of funerary orations is not reliably attested before the third century and other documents attributed to family records, such as the census records of 393/2 B.C. cited by Dionysius (p. 14), are likely to be fiction. Roman aristocratic families, as perhaps their Tarquinian counterparts,[46] will proudly have retailed their distinguished past, particularly in the military sphere, and such memories or claims may lie behind the early republican legends of Brutus, Coriolanus, Cincinnatus or Servilius Ahala (cf. Fig. 5); but many apparently notable figures of the fourth century and earlier remain shadowy in the surviving narratives, suggesting that detailed family information was not available, or if it was, it was not used. Moreover, such material as was known to be available was notoriously suspect (Cic. *Brut.* 62; Livy VIII.40.2ff), particularly that deriving from later funeral eulogies (where the family past was lavishly paraded); and whilst some authentic achievements may have been recalled, the discernible family material in the historians more usually merits a healthy scepticism, at least in its detail.

(b) *Techniques of reconstruction*

Even on the most optimistic assumptions the first historians of early Rome faced a chronic shortage of reliable information: a few random epigraphic texts and (perhaps) other documents, a quantity of popular and family traditions (of highly uncertain reliability), perhaps some Greek (and even Etruscan) literary material, a consular list and, from some uncertain date, the notes of the *pontifex maximus*. They, as conceivably Timaeus before them, may have filled out the regal period with the

---

[46] Torelli 1975[B266], 96–7; Cornell 1978[B209], 173.

Fig. 5. Coin of M. Iunius Brutus (54 B.C.) depicting his reputed ancestors L. Iunius Brutus and C. Servilius Ahala, perhaps as a gesture of opposition to Pompey's supposed autocratic ambitions (*RRC* n. 433.2).

creation of several fundamental Roman institutions and they probably established or reiterated much of the broad pattern of Rome's development, both internal and external, which thereafter became accepted in the historical tradition. Nonetheless, their narrative of Roman history before the third century was inevitably restricted; according to Dionysius (*Ant. Rom.* 1.6.2) they dealt with events between the foundation of Rome and their own day 'in summary fashion'.

It was from the late second or early first century that a more extensive narrative was created. This will reflect the desire to produce a readable and suitably informative history on the approved Hellenistic model and to make history serve more adequately the ends of ethical instruction in particular. History, it was felt, should not be a mere chronicle (a demand already voiced by Sempronius Asellio (fr. 1P (= Gell. *NA* v.18.7ff)) in the late second century); it should both improve and instruct the reader and engage his emotions. The historian must explain the events recounted, especially in terms of human motivation; he must develop and emphasise the moral aspect and provide a wealth of detail that would not merely enhance the credibility of his narrative but also make it come alive for the listener or reader.[47] To achieve that, however, it was necessary to invent. However deplorable in theory, the absence of detailed sources made historical reconstruction on a large scale both unavoidable and possible.

The means employed for this purpose by the later annalists are most evident in the surviving accounts of early republican political history

---

[47] Although many of these objectives are first clearly articulated in extant Latin literature by Cicero, they were common coin in the Hellenistic period and the surviving fragments of early first-century historians, together with the character of the surviving narratives, suggest that some or all of them were already pursued in that period (cf. Badian 1966[B6], 18–23; also 11–12 (Cn. Gellius)); indeed, individual episodes in the earliest historians may have been elaborated along lines popular among Hellenistic historians (Walbank 1945[B181], 12f; but cf. also J. Poucet, *Historia* 25 (1976) 200ff; G. P. Verbrugghe, *Historia* 30 (1981) 236ff).

(where the major expansion may have occurred[48]). Theories about the nature of political conflict and its causes, moral preconceptions or implicit assumptions about human character and behaviour provided general guidelines, but for the reconstruction of individual events particular models might be sought, consciously or not. Greek parallels were sometimes invoked for both historical and literary effect, as already in the earliest historians (cf. p. 214), but the historian looked above all to later Roman experience for colour, amplification and even entire episodes. Thus the numerous early tribunician prosecutions before the centuriate assembly appear to be a fictitious reconstruction from mid-republican practice (p. 222) and the whole treatment of the agrarian agitation of the early Republic, focusing on patrician occupation of public land, may be modelled largely on the tensions that developed progressively over the second century and the political conflicts to which they led (cf. p. 238).

Inevitably accounts of the distant past came to reflect the political views of their authors. Dionysius, for example, embraces a tradition (or traditions) openly hostile to Sulla, favourable or indulgent to Caesar and bitterly antagonistic towards his murderer Brutus, whose alleged plebeian forebears are constantly pilloried. The treatment of particularly contentious episodes may also have been conditioned by their use as precedents in contemporary political argument (cf. e.g. p. 183 n. 35). Since early Roman history was apparently comparatively little regarded,[49] however, it cannot be assumed that it was chronicled purely for propagandist purposes. Where historians drew on contemporary or recent experience, that may merely reflect the search for plausible explanatory detail, the provision of which Dionysius (with others) regarded as central to the historian's task: it was recent history which offered the best guide to the probable course of events.

Literary effect also became of increasing importance,[50] conditioning not only the organization, treatment and focus of the individual episode but also the structural unity of the overall narrative. In particular, the employment of certain recurrent themes offered one convenient approach by which a pattern of events might be created or at least satisfactorily explained and both literary and historical coherence achieved. The notion that internal disunity results from the absence of external threat becomes in Livy especially a major thematic thread which enables him to weld his disparate raw material into an integrated whole

---

[48] Even then the political background to certain major events (e.g. the sudden and temporary influx of plebeians into the consular tribunate in the years 400–396 (p. 239)) remains inadequately explored or developed.

[49] Cic. *Leg.* 1.5ff; Livy *Praef.* 4.

[50] An explicit concern with literary style is already attested in the late second-century historian of the Second Punic War, L. Coelius Antipater (fr. 1P).

(above all in Book II). So too the spurious interpretation of the consular tribunate as an office open to plebeians from the outset (cf. p. 193) became the basis for a series of invented conflicts between patricians and plebeians over the appointment of consular tribunes or (exclusively patrician) consuls, intended to explain the irregular alternation of the two offices.

Although events may indeed on occasion have taken a broadly similar course, such fictitious repetition of entire episodes is not infrequent in the early narrative, albeit often with the individual variation of detail which literary considerations demanded. The reasons for the duplication may be various: genuine uncertainty, rival chronologies (p. 349), the conflation of variants or simply the stereotyped repetition of a well-worn theme. Livy's battle narratives, for example, are a familiar instance of carefully graduated variations on a restricted repertoire of stock situations and, as their frequent anachronisms confirm, can only be the product of his or his predecessors' imagination.

One particularly significant source of inspiration was again the claims of noble families, such as the Fabii, Postumii and Licinii, to a distinguished role in the early Republic. Most notorious in this respect were the Valerii. Even before Valerius Antias further adorned their past, they seem to have secured recognition of their alleged services in the establishment of liberty, the promotion of political concord and the provision of constitutional safeguards, especially through the actions of P. Valerius Poplicola (*cos.* 509; 508; 507; 504 B.C.) and L. Valerius Potitus (*cos.* 449 B.C.). In the case of Poplicola this was further aided by a general tendency to attribute fundamental institutions and popular rights to the first years of the Republic and his career was extensively elaborated with a series of popular innovations, above all a law of appeal against extreme magisterial penalties (duplicating that of 300 B.C.) and a measure inflicting outlawry on those who sought monarchic power.

In notable contrast the Claudii are repeatedly disparaged. In the surviving accounts of Ap. Claudius the Decemvir (p. 227) and of Ap. Claudius Caecus (*cos.* 307; 296 B.C.: p. 395f) there are traces of a version which saw them as demagogues in the pursuit of personal power. These, however, have been largely overlaid by a portrait of the clan as arrogant, self-assertive patricians, brutally unremitting in their hostility to the plebs. The authorship of this tradition is unknown. The stereotyped arguments and attitudes involved, together with Cicero's apparent ignorance of it before 46 B.C., have suggested that it is largely the work of a single, comparatively late annalist but neither consideration is conclusive. What is more important is the light it sheds on annalistic procedures and its implication that the overall character of the surviving accounts is often a more significant consideration than the intrinsic credibility of individual details.

(c) *Conclusion*

The deficiencies of the sources available in antiquity for the reconstruction of early Roman history, together with the historians' own lack of a systematic critical approach, their freedom in recreating the past and their accelerating attention to literary effect, render stringent criticism of the extant narratives a prerequisite of any historical enquiry. Not only does any assessment of their value depend on a scrutiny of their internal consistency and inherent plausibility, their wider preoccupations, assumptions and methods, their compatibility with other data, their possible anachronisms and (to the limited extent usually attainable) the development of the individual traditions they embrace, but the severely limited quantity and scope of the authentic material which could have survived from early Rome make it imperative at least to demonstrate how a particular datum might have been preserved before it can be considered as potentially reliable. There can, for example, be no justification for accepting details for which no means of preservation can be plausibly conjectured whilst jettisoning other, more substantial elements in the extant accounts.

As the fictitious early census figures (p. 136) and other data show, Roman historians were aware that in the early days Rome was much smaller and weaker (although even so they grossly overestimated her population). It was not, after all, until the early third century that Rome achieved firm control over Central Italy and her experiences in that period and in the first two Punic wars hardly encouraged the belief that her history had been one of remorselessly successful advance. Indeed, the effects of one major calamity (the Gallic Sack) have been grossly exaggerated in surviving accounts even if patriotic sentiment (half-) suppressed the actual capture of the city (cf. p. 307). Moreover, even if the annalists' recreation of Rome's early history often reflects a moralizing idealization, it may on occasions come near to the truth simply through the retrojection of factors which remained broadly unchanged, through the attribution of characteristics typical of comparatively modest agrarian communities or through plausible inference from surviving institutions or from general probability. Even unexceptional material, therefore, may be the historians' own work; there is no known means by which the detail could have been reliably transmitted and the frequent discrepancies between individual versions themselves suggest (although they do not prove) that it merely reflects the annalists' attempts to produce credible as well as readable history.

Inevitably even the proper and consistent employment of critical principles leaves considerable scope for diverse evaluation both of the literary tradition in general and of its individual data (as is exemplified by the different approaches adopted in this volume). Of especial importance in this respect are the doubts surrounding the availability and use of records from the early Republic, above all the pontifical tablets. Given that uncertainty, however, the possible existence of such records cannot alone justify faith even in the general outline of early republican history in Livy and Dionysius. Rather, the availability of such records must itself depend to a considerable extent on the credibility of that outline as determined by other criteria.

The primary focus of the modern historian must, therefore, be the critical dissection of the literary tradition and, still more, those non-literary sources of evidence which both serve as a touchstone of the annalistic data and, in a number of areas, offer a more secure basis for reconstruction. The most important of these sources are constitutional, legal and religious institutions and practices which survived into a much later period as self-evident fossils from the distant past; the consular list (with some reservations); laws, formulae and other documents which are preserved in classical writers and whose date and authenticity can be credibly supported; modern philological investigation; the results of archaeological excavation and survey; and (yet to be exploited fully) comparative data from other societies. For many aspects of early Roman history all such material is sparse and inadequate. The picture drawn from it must inevitably be restricted, defective and, to varying degrees, conjectural. In consequence, a detailed narrative of political or military history can seldom be essayed at least before the later fourth century. The principal concern must be those general trends and developments which are of greater significance for an understanding of early Rome, even where the absolute chronology of the relevant phases is uncertain.

The scope of such an enquiry is not, however, to be determined, and therefore limited, by the preoccupations of the Roman annalists. Such issues as the development of settlement at Rome and throughout Central Italy, of demographic changes, of the emergence of the city-state, of its economic and social structures, of its religious and legal institutions and of its cultural life and influences were, to the ancient historian, at best of subsidiary interest. Modern research may regard them as both more central and more fruitful, for, though often deficient, the information available on such topics from non-annalistic sources frequently makes possible the framing of relevant questions and even the formulation of reasonable hypotheses. Above all, the history of Rome has to be under-stood in the context of the development of Central Italy as a whole, a subject no less important in its own right and one increasingly illumi-nated by archaeological discovery. The history of the period covered by this volume is as much the history of the peoples of Italy whom Rome brought under her hegemony as it is that of Rome herself.

CHAPTER 2

ARCHAIC ROME BETWEEN LATIUM AND ETRURIA

M. TORELLI

I. INTRODUCTION

Rome's geographical position makes her earliest history a very special and exemplary instance of 'frontier history': situated on the first ford and easiest landing-place on a large river, the Tiber, which itself formed the natural boundary between ethnic groups differing from one another in language and in their level of social and economic development (the Etruscans, Faliscans, Latins, Sabines and Umbrians), the settlement of Rome was able to benefit from exceptionally easy communications, both with the hinterland and in the direction of the sea, to an extent virtually unequalled in the whole peninsula. The historical traditions concerning the asylum of Romulus, the Latin-Sabine union and the emergence of the Etruscan monarchy (pp. 57f; 91f), whose first representative was said to have had Greek ancestry, are themselves excellent evidence for the effects of this open situation, which influenced the economy, society and culture of the emerging city.

All this has been stressed repeatedly in modern historical research but it is worth noting again here in the specific context of an assessment of the evidence contributed by the archaeological data. As has already been noted (p. 15), this is in fact as scarce for Rome, with her history of successive building over a period of nearly three thousand years, as it is relatively abundant in the neighbouring cities and areas of Etruria and Latium, where it constitutes a valuable tool for reconstructing the phases of social and cultural development between the end of the Bronze Age and the beginning of the Republic. However, such a procedure[1] requires that particular caution which is integral to the very process of historical reconstruction from archaeological evidence; for, as A. Momigliano has pointed out in connexion with E. Gjerstad's monumental work,[2] such evidence does not always automatically reflect social structures, ethico-political forms or their various modifications. Moreover, still greater caution is needed in the specific approach which it is

---

[1] Torelli 1974–5[G148], 3–78; 1981[J122].
[2] Momigliano 1963[A83], 101–8 (= id. *Terzo Contributo* 558–71).

30

intended to adopt here because, at least in theory, the archaeological sequences of one area are not necessarily identical with those of another, even of one very close at hand, in terms either of the actual material or of its implications. Nonetheless, the contacts between southern Etruria (particularly Veii) on the one hand and the settlements of Latium Vetus (particularly Rome) on the other do in practice justify such a comparison, although here this will be strictly limited to major sequences and data and will ignore casual points of similarity and isolated phenomena. Furthermore, as we shall see, an independent analysis of the archaeological data tends to confirm the picture which emerges from a non-reductive interpretation of the literary tradition, of the kind to be found in Chapter 3.

II. ARCHAEOLOGY, URBAN DEVELOPMENT AND SOCIAL HISTORY

The first and most important results of a parallel study of the archaeological data from southern Etruria and Latium concern not only the typology but the continuity or discontinuity of human settlement over the very long period which separates the Bronze Age from the sixth century B.C.[3] The Final Bronze Age in its Sub-Appennine form, which can be assigned in general terms to the eleventh century B.C., is only sporadically attested in Latium and, with the single exception of Ardea, makes no appearance in any of the later Iron Age centres. In contrast, Etruscan territory frequently yields evidence of this same Sub-Appennine culture in conjunction with the later Proto-Villanovan culture, which also belongs to the Final Bronze Age; this is the case, for example, with the settlements of the Tolfa hills. Conversely, while in Latin territory the First Latial Period, parallel in chronology and cultural character to the Proto-Villanovan,[4] appears frequently in a continuous sequence with materials belonging to all or some of the later periods in Etruria, with the odd rare exception (for instance a Proto-Villanovan tomb in the very centre of the large Villanovan necropolis of Casale del Fosso at Veii),[5] there is a widely accepted sharp discontinuity between Proto-Villanovan and Villanovan: Proto-Villanovan settlements, often situated not far from Villanovan, vanish with the appearance of the latter at the start of the Iron Age.[6] It is quite clear that in this context the difference between the Etruscan and Latin environments is not without relevance to the mythical–historical traditions which record the origins and remoter history of the two peoples.

---

[3] The principal cultural phases of this period, with approximate dates, are tabulated on p. 64.
[4] R. Peroni in *Civiltà del Lazio primitivo* 1976[B306], 19–25.
[5] Vianello Cordova 1967[B418], 295–306.   [6] Colonna 1977[B313], 189–96.

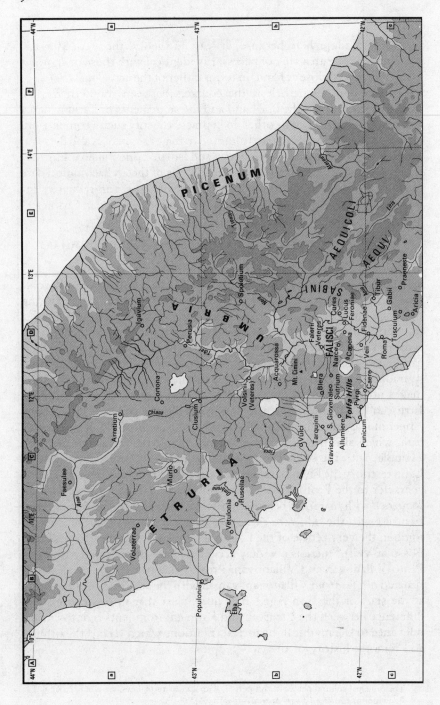

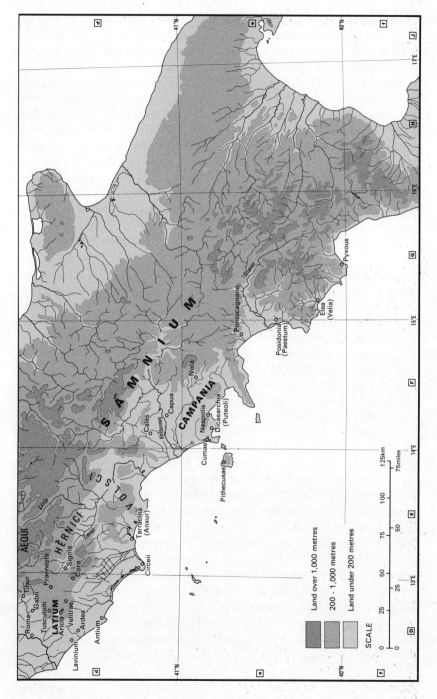

Map 1 Central Italy in the archaic period.

The burials and settlements of the First and Second Latial Periods, between the tenth and the middle of the ninth centuries B.C., do not differ from those of the same period in Etruria, particularly southern Etruria, being smallish in size and not at all close-packed. Admittedly, the communities which they reveal sometimes turn out to have been fairly close together, as in the Alban Hills or at Rome (where traces of settlements occur near the Arch of Augustus and on the Palatine), and, lying only a few hundred metres apart, indicate economic and social formations based on kinship structures. If the production of utilitarian and ritual pottery undoubtedly took place within the domestic sphere, metallurgy seems to have been organized on a regional scale and thus not to have been centred on the family nucleus.[7] Though this did not affect social structure directly, it nonetheless suggests a rapid economic growth, with the mass production of work tools and weapons.

On the ideological level, synchronic and diachronic differences in funerary ritual offer additional material for profitable speculation on possible social structures.[8] Throughout the ninth century B.C. such ritual appears coherent and consistent in southern Etruria and Latium, with the universal custom of cremation in biconical funerary urns in southern Etruria and in simple urns, sometimes hut urns, in Latium, accompanied by a funerary deposit comprising a small number of miniaturized objects (including panoplies of armour and weapons in Latium). In the second half of the ninth century B.C., however, the miniaturization of the funerary material was apparently superseded by the practice of placing objects of normal size in the tomb, while the ritual of cremation was gradually replaced by that of inhumation. The latter was virtually general by the middle of the eighth century B.C. and the only exceptions are some male burials in hut urns in Latium and in biconical funerary urns in southern Etruria (more rarely hut urns): in both regions the custom seems to have persisted for a long time, even if sporadically, throughout the orientalizing period[9] as is demonstrated by the very recent discovery of the princely tomb of Monte Michele at Veii[10] or the well-known case of the Regolini-Galassi tomb at Caere, which is again a princely burial.[11] The retention for particular members of society of the archaic crematory ritual with a tomb which had heroic overtones served to stress the eminence and prestige of the head of a specific lineage. The similarity of such tombs to the heroic tombs of Eretria has been noted by several scholars, and is an indication not only of the Hellenization – though in a very individual sense – of Etruscan and Latin funerary customs, but also of the importance which particular family groups had gradually assumed within society from the middle of the eighth century onwards, thus

---

[7] *La formazione della città nel Lazio* 1980[I27].   [8] Colonna 1974[B311], 286–92.
[9] Bietti Sestieri 1979[B295], 24–9.   [10] Boitani 1982[B299], 95–103.   [11] Pareti 1947[B374].

destroying the original economic and social homogeneity which is reflected by the cemeteries of the previous phase.

The emergence of the Etruscan and Latin aristocracies between the eighth and seventh centuries B.C. finds its exact counterpart in the growth in size of some of the settlements in both areas. Lesser settlements were absorbed by larger neighbours, others disappeared to the obvious benefit of stronger and more powerful communities, while sites which had clearly been relatively more extensive from the early Iron Age onwards now grew out of all proportion. Modern interpretations of this phenomenon in terms either of synoecism or of nuclear expansion appear, in this rigidly polarized form, not to comprehend the true import of what was undoubtedly an extremely complex process. Recent research on various sites in Etruria and Latium, from Veii to Falerii, Tarquinii and Lavinium, has shown that the phenomenon was frequently the result of both tendencies, active over a period of time which is often of very long duration, running from the ninth to the sixth century B.C.:[12] some towns grew by the concentration within a single settlement of several villages scattered over quite a wide area, others developed by leaving outside their perimeter whole sections of the built-up area as 'dead zones'. Synoecism and nuclear expansion are not therefore contradictory phenomena, but form part of a single drive towards concentrating the population, and this was no doubt set in motion by the economic and social developments which were dominated by the emergence of the aristocracies of southern Etruria and Latium.

Along with this expansion in settlements came the definitive establishment of the hoplite phalanx in the last years of the seventh century B.C. (reliably confirmed from archaeological material found in tombs, but above all from painted or relief representations of the phalanx itself (Fig. 6)) and the monumental organization of the sacred and public areas of the city during the same period. The first phenomenon, the diffusion over the whole area of Etruria and Latium of the technique of hoplite warfare, has implications both on the social level and in the sphere of urban organization. The need for closer co-operation (for increasingly pressing military reasons) appears both to foster and to hinder the gradual consolidation of the power of the aristocracies: in both Etruscan and Latin representations the hoplite phalanx appears consistently to be led and guided by heroic figures on chariots, who are quite clearly the dominant heads of the aristocratic clans.[13] These aristocratic groups had therefore to adapt their own social and economic system of clients and dependants to the new techniques of hoplite combat, broadening their own social base with some difficulty and supplying its members with the

12 Torelli 1982[B413], 117–28.   13 Torelli 1981[J122], 128–30.

Fig. 6. Hoplite column depicted with cavalryman and war-chariot on ostrich egg from Vulci (late seventh century). From P. Ducati, *Storia dell'arte etrusca* (Rome–Milan, 1927), pl. 74.222.

means of acquiring heavy bronze armour. Furthermore, the joint requirements for defence, which often went far beyond the invariably limited force fielded by the aristocratic groups, offered increasingly greater opportunities to social classes not restricted by the links of dependence imposed by the aristocracies. In archaeological terms a particularly telling example of this entry into the citizen hoplite phalanx of individuals who did not form part of the dominant aristocratic structure, is furnished by the Tomb of the Warrior at Vulci, a 'chamber' tomb *a cassone* (a typical individual tomb, that is, not a family one) of 530 B.C., with its complete hoplite armour and a rich set of Attic pottery.[14] The final confirmation of this process must undoubtedly be seen in the centuriate organization of Servius Tullius' *classis*, traditionally assigned to the middle years of the sixth century B.C. (p. 92; 103).

This new military reality, with its economic and social implications, which we see under way from the last thirty years of the seventh century B.C., naturally finds expression in an increasingly complex and effective system of urban defence. Though there are insufficient examples of urban excavation in Etruria, except at Rusellae in the north, we now have numerous cases of settlements in Latium – such as those at Lavinium, Castel di Decima and Ficana (Map 2: p. 244) – where the presence of primitive defence structures[15] from the eighth and seventh centuries has been revealed. These structures comprise banks (*aggeres*) of earth and tufo chips and their memory may possibly have survived at Rome in the 'earth wall of the Carinae' (*murus terreus Carinarum*: Varro, *Ling.* v.48; 143). They normally rest against, or are replaced by, a real wall consisting of

---

[14] Dohrn 1964[B320], 491–2.

[15] C.F. Giuliani in *Enea nel Lazio* 1981[E25], 162–6 (Lavinium); Guaitoli 1981[B339], 117–50 (Castel di Decima); T. Fischer-Hansen in *Ficana. Catalogo della Mostra* 1981[B325], 59–65 (Ficana).

blocks of stone, usually built during the first half of the sixth century B.C. (this is the date traditionally given to the building of the walls of Servius Tullius) and equipped with gates and defensive devices consonant with the siege techniques generally employed in this period throughout the area of Greece and Magna Graecia.

If *aggeres* and walls represent the response, as far as urban organization was concerned, to the changed conditions of warfare and its techniques, it is significant that during the same period, between the penultimate and last quarter of the seventh century B.C., we see the first signs of religious ideology emerging. Up to this point archaeological traces of cult, other than specifically funerary cult, have been practically non-existent: hitherto the sacral dimension, whether in a family or collective context, has not in fact appeared in forms distinct from those of everyday life. Now, between 630 and 600 B.C., the framework of political and religious life is created at Rome around the Forum (p. 75): the second and more complex paving of the area (625 B.C.), the construction, on the site of former huts, of the royal shrine-dwelling of the Regia (630 B.C.), the building of the Comitium (assembly area) and the Curia Hostilia (senate-house) (600 B.C.), the first tangible evidence, in the shape of material taken from a well, of the cult of Vesta (600 B.C.).[16] The phenomenon is echoed closely elsewhere in Latium, at Satricum[17] and at Gabii,[18] but above all in Etruria,[19] at Veii in the so-called 'sanctuary of Apollo' (in fact dedicated to Minerva) and at Rusellae with its unusual building of sun-dried brick discovered under the forum area of the Roman period.

The production and circulation of luxury goods, Hellenic in form and origin, which from the middle of the eighth century had been the exclusive prerogative of the emerging aristocracy, in whose tombs they were offered in remarkable quantities, now find a new focus of accumulation in the votive deposits of sanctuaries. And it is no coincidence that gradually, from this moment onwards, tombs prove increasingly bare of prestige objects both at Rome and also at nearby Veii. Status tends rather to find expression, not in the accumulation and exhibition of luxury objects, but in the particular attention paid to burial rites or in the deliberately austere grave apparatus, as with the marble urn from the Esquiline or the tomb of the horseman-athlete of Lanuvium.[20] At the same time this phenomenon reveals the diffusion, particularly in the Latin area (though not in Etruria), of customs which tended to restrict funerary luxury, unless one chooses rather to interpret it as the result of a different pattern of wealth circulation in which shrines and collective buildings occupy a central position.

[16] M. Torelli in *Roma arcaica e le recenti scoperte archeologiche* 1980[A113], 13–15.
[17] *Satricum – una città latina* 1982[B405], esp. 53–4.   [18] Zaccagni 1978[B423], 42–6.
[19] Torelli 1981[J122], 164–74.   [20] Colonna 1977[B312], 131–65; below, Figs. 35 and 39.

In this way, through archaeology, we can trace a long process of economic and social development which, in Latium and Etruria, moves from village-based structures in the final phase of the Bronze Age to the definite establishment of urban forms in the crucial last years of the seventh century B.C., with the parallel establishment of a dominant aristocratic class. Furthermore, the hard core of certain facts which can be recovered from a critical perusal of the data recorded in the literary tradition is considerably reinforced by the organic sequence of archaeological data on the two banks of the lower reaches of the Tiber. In Latium between the tenth and the middle of the ninth centuries B.C. the Alban Hills occupy a position of great importance, thanks to the quality and quantity of the evidence which they offer; the society is defined as a village society, characterized by an extremely small number of settlements, probably linked among themselves by ties of kinship, with a social division of labour shared out according to sex and age groups, and a strictly subsistence economy, in which the production of poor quality cereals and some vegetables seems to have predominated. But the most valuable evidence is afforded by the stability of the settlements, compared with the relative impermanence and fluctuations of the Bronze Age; this stability is inseparable from the family ownership of what was, in the ancient world, the means of production *par excellence*, land. This form of ownership, which probably existed side by side with collective possessions of tribal origin, seems to have been the lynch-pin of later developments and a main source of that element of contradiction of which signs may already be visible in the 'crisis' in funerary ideology that can be observed in the course of the ninth century B.C.

Beginning in the second half of the ninth century B.C. and lasting until halfway through the following century, these signs of 'crisis' become increasingly pronounced, with a visible impoverishment of the hill centres of the Alban Hills, where the tombs diminish in quantity and richness, and a parallel blossoming of settlements on the plains, such as Rome, Lavinium, Ficana, Gabii. There are similar developments in the Etruscan area, where again the abandonment of the Proto-Villanovan hill centres and the sudden appearance of Villanovan settlements on modest heights surrounded by wide fertile plains implies the importance of the ownership and working of the land. For the Villanovan culture one may conjecture a genuine and positive colonizing movement, starting in the course of the ninth century B.C.; and in Latium likewise the appearance of new centres with similar characteristics, from the Quirinal in Rome to Castel di Decima, Laurentina and perhaps Tivoli, makes it possible to speak of parallel impulses towards colonization, an indication that the search for better land and more profitable agricultural production played a vital role in the development of the forces of production.

And that a process of this kind could not occur peacefully is demonstrated by the progressive changes in military techniques, defensive structures and the size of settlements.

The most obvious social change is that which occurs in the middle of the eighth century B.C. and becomes fully established in the course of the seventh century. A rudimentary social stratification emerges and takes root, the outcome of the developments of the previous periods which had witnessed a complex interaction of such factors as the appropriation of the means of production (whose implicit and profound inequality of output should be stressed), the strong tendency to conflict between separate communities, and within the individual communities the need to integrate groups of varying origins. Without doubt it is at this point that we should see the emergence of relations of production based on client dependence, the pivot of aristocratic economic power: the enormous growth of some settlements (this is the time at which, in Rome, the necropolis is moved to the Esquiline) and the 'disappearance' of many others in this and the following century prove that the very conquest of further territory and the subjection of all or part of the settlements there (an event symbolized by the royal conquests of Tullus Hostilius and Ancus Marcius) brought into play a mechanism for the accumulation of riches in the hands of an aristocratic class, an accumulation encouraged by improvements in cultivated crops and in technology, both agricultural and non-agricultural, and by the increasingly marked division of labour, factors once again revealed to us by archaeology. Nor should it be forgotten that the entrenchment of the aristocracies found basic support in the acquisition not only of objects imported from the East and from Greece, but also of cultural models, originating in the same areas, such as the symposium and the ceremonial ritual governing the display of wealth; and the acquisition of these in its turn generated greater local demand and for that very reason brought about the consolidation of specialized craft activities, which served as a further basis for more complex social stratification.

The conclusion of this economic and social process is therefore the 'birth' of the city as an organism with tangible monumental evidence, walls, sacred and communal buildings, and permanent and enduring dwellings which, from the last decades of the seventh century B.C., come to constitute the first real urban landscape in the history of Latium and Etruria.

III. SANCTUARIES AND PALACES

One of the most obvious and important signs of the economic and social development of the seventh century B.C. is the creation of dwelling structures in material which is not entirely perishable.[21] At the beginning of the seventh century, as the well-known case of hut VI at Satricum shows, the dwelling unit is still a hut of the type which had developed in the early Iron Age. About half-way through the century, however, both the great Caeretan aristocratic tombs of the Painted Lion type, and the appearance of clay tiles and of dwelling structures with stone foundations, articulated on complex bipartite or tripartite plans, attest a fundamental change in the lifestyle of the ruling classes.

The discoveries at the settlement of Acquarossa near Viterbo, with houses on a rectangular plan embracing several rooms and a courtyard[22] and decorated with painted architectural terracottas of the mid-seventh century B.C., and the excavation of the great palace building of Murlo near Siena,[23] which was originally built at the same time and then rebuilt at the beginning of the next century, have completely redefined our perspectives for the interpretation of monumental archaeological data of the seventh to sixth centuries B.C. While earlier evidence seemed to indicate that architectural terracottas were a feature of temples alone, the new data reveal that until the end of the sixth century B.C. these decorated clay revetments could be applied both to sacred edifices and to public and private structures. It should, however, be emphasized that for this phase the distinction between private, public and sacred is anything but precise or workable, as the evidence from Murlo makes all too clear.

In its definitive version the palace of Murlo is an almost square structure, its sides some 60 m. long (Fig. 7). It is arranged around a huge central courtyard with wooden columns on three sides and with four identical corner rooms, and bears close comparison to eastern palace buildings such as the Cypriot palace of Vouni or the palace of the *tyrannos* of Larissa on the Hermos. The four wings of the building around the courtyard were planned with varying internal divisions; on the north-east and south-east sides long rooms may have functioned as service areas, ranging from storerooms to stables and servants' quarters, while the banquet hall and women's quarters were probably situated on the south-west side. The north-west side, divided exactly into three parts, open at the centre (in obvious relationship to the *tablinum* of Roman tradition) and without a colonnade, frames a small *oikos* which is displaced towards the centre of the courtyard and is to be identified as the building used for the family cult. The terracotta decoration is a true synthesis of aristocratic ideology: images of ancestors are proudly displayed on the roof beams, amid a mythical bestiary of gryphons and gorgons; on the side porticoes, friezes on terracotta plaques with scenes of games, a wedding celebration, a banquet and a group of chthonic and

---

[21] Torelli 1983[J125], 471ff.   [22] Östenberg 1975[B368].
[23] Nielsen and Phillips 1976[B367], 113–47.

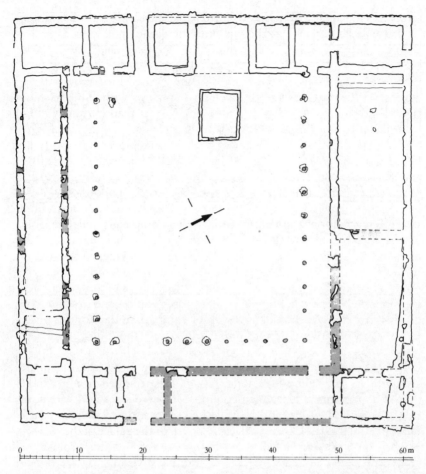

Fig. 7. Plan of early sixth-century 'palace' building at Murlo (Poggio Civitate). From Nielsen and Phillips 1976 [B367], fig. 1.

heavenly divinities (Fig. 8a–c) hint at the ceremonial use of the courtyard and the rooms opening off it, and give perfect expression to the aristocratic owners' desire to make the building the political and ideological centre of the world.

In the palace of Acquarossa (Fig. 9), dating from the third quarter of the sixth century B.C. but likewise preceded by a building of the mid-seventh century, we can make out a central courtyard with only two colonnaded sides (Fig. 10);[24] the east side houses the banquet hall and possibly the women's quarters, while the north side is a tripartite space

[24] Östenberg 1975[B368], 15–26.

Fig. 8a. Reconstruction of (wedding) procession frieze from Murlo 'palace' (early sixth century). From T. N. Gantz, *MDAI(R)* 81 (1974), fig. 1.

Fig. 8b. Reconstruction of banquet frieze from Murlo 'palace' (early sixth century). From J. P. Small, *Stud. Etr.* 39 (1971), 28 Fig. 1.

Fig. 8c. Reconstruction of seated divinities frieze from Murlo 'palace' (early sixth century). From T. N. Gantz, *Stud. Etr.* 39 (1971), 5 fig. 1.

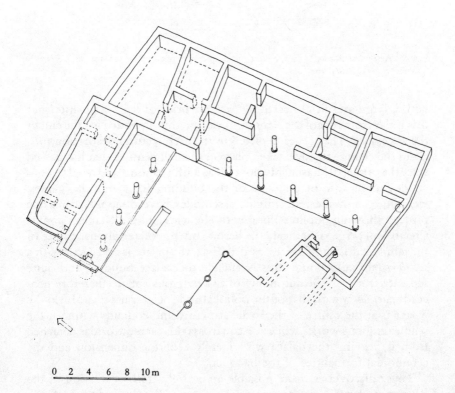

0   2   4   6   8   10m

Fig. 9. Plan of 'palace' building at Acquarossa: phase III (*c.* 550–525 B.C.). From Östenberg 1975 [B368], 140.

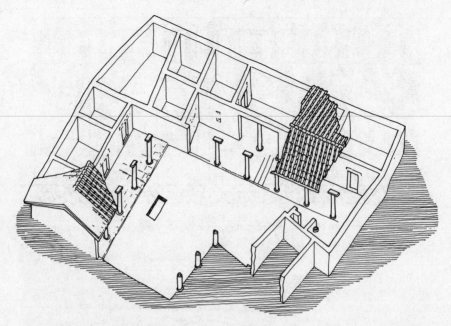

Fig. 10. Reconstruction of 'palace' building at Acquarossa: phase III (*c.* 550–525 B.C.). From Östenberg 1975 [B368], 164.

with a large sacrificial hearth (*eschara*) in front of it, in a position not dissimilar from that of the *oikos* at Murlo and thus intended for the cult of the ancestors. The scenes depicted in the architectural decoration proclaim the change that has taken place in the half century that has passed since the principal phase at Murlo: a frieze with a banquet and revel (*komos*) alludes to the use of one side of the building for symposia (games, wedding ceremonies, and divine assemblies have disappeared), while plaques showing hoplites along with Heracles and the Nemean lion or Cretan bull (Fig. 11) indicate the heroic, but no longer divine, nature of the family cult. Significantly, as at Larissa, the palace is on an axis with a *sacellum* (shrine), though this is outside the palace building and quite separate from it. The autonomy of the religious sphere therefore proceeds *pari passu* with that of the political and social sphere: at Murlo the palace is at the centre of the social structure and contains within it the whole religious world, while at Acquarossa this sacred world is detached from it, leaving the palace with merely a heroic dimension and the ceremonial formalities of the banquet.

These discoveries make possible an entirely fresh evaluation of the Roman evidence – not only the decoration of the Regia and the Curia Hostilia, both adorned with architectural terracottas which are taken from the same mould and represent the Minotaur (Fig. 12), possibly an

Fig. 11. Reconstruction of architectural terracotta frieze from Acquarossa 'palace' depicting hoplites, Heracles and the Cretan bull, and chariot (c. 550–525 B.C.). From Östenberg 1975 [B368], 182.

Fig. 12. 'Minotaur' architectural terracotta frieze plaque from the temple of Caesar in the Roman Forum (ultimately probably from the Regia). First quarter of the sixth century.

archetypal image of the 'city', but even the actual plan of the Regia (Fig. 13a–d) which repeats the basic lines of the type of palace exemplified at Acquarossa and Murlo. No less significant for the identification of the form of social organization dominant in Latin society is the presence of a structure of the palace type, though of smaller proportions, at Ficana, while some very recent discoveries at Satricum[25] seem to point to the

[25] Pavolini and Rathje 1981[B376], 75–87; G. I. W. Dragt in *Satricum – una città latina* 1982 [B405], 41–2.

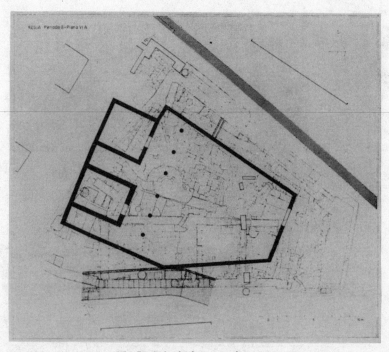

a. The Regia in the late seventh century

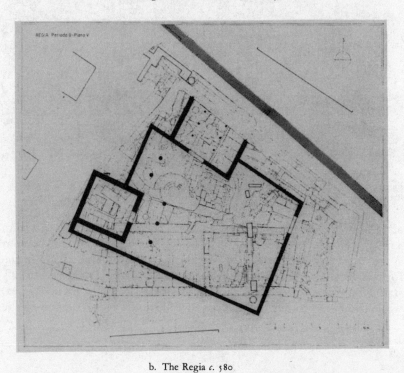

b. The Regia *c.* 580

Fig. 13a–d. Phases of the Regia in the archaic period: after Brown 1974–5 [E79], figs. 10. 12. 14 and 4.

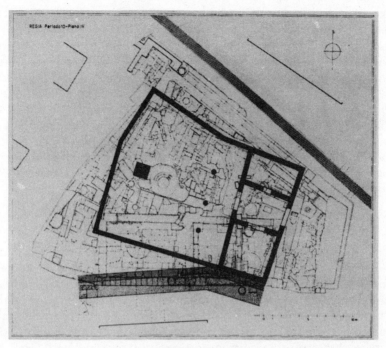

c. The Regia c. 530

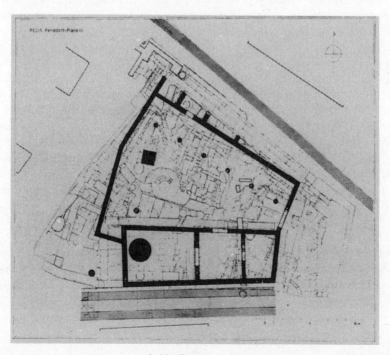

d. The Regia c. 510–500

existence of a similar building in this other great Latin city. At the end of the sixth century, however, with the political movement towards institutions of a republican type, the Regia, now the seat of a *rex* reduced to a purely religious function, was to present – in a kind of frozen state – the typical form of the palace-shrine of the previous period, just as at Caere the shrine of Montetosto – in all probability a sacred place dedicated to the rite of *enagismos*, that is, the rendering of offerings to the shades of Phocaean prisoners impiously put to death after the battle of Alalia in *c*. 540 (Hdt. 1.167) – was to repeat yet again the plan of the palace building, perhaps to emphasize the expiation of a 'religious crime' perpetrated by some local ruler in accordance with the Homeric (and aristocratic Etruscan) model for the sacrifice of such prisoners.[26]

IV. EMPORIA AND SHRINES AT EMPORIA

The emergence of urban structures which take on monumental forms also marks an important change in the processes of trade. Since very ancient times the Etruscan and Latin world had been in contact with the eastern Mediterranean and with the protagonists of maritime trade, the Phoenicians and the Greeks.[27] Materials from the East appear in tombs and archaeological contexts of the Etrusco-Latin coastal area from the early eighth century B.C.: from this period onwards Phoenicians and Greeks brought luxury goods with ever increasing frequency to the shores of Etruria, where they were destined to satisfy the similarly increasing needs of the emergent aristocracies. The Tiber, with its landing-places on both the Veientan and the Roman banks, was perhaps one of the earliest settings for the development of these contacts, attested by Euboean-Cycladic pottery found in tombs at Veii and in urban contexts at Rome. Until the late seventh century B.C. trade seems to have been controlled by the emergent classes, to judge by the presence of oriental objects, or imitations of them, in aristocratic tombs. But from that date onwards we find emporium shrines appearing near the landing-places, where exchanges between Greek, Etruscan and Latin merchants took place under the apparent control of deities brought in from Greece or the East, even though these were soon assimilated to local divinities.

The fullest and clearest picture is that furnished by Gravisca,[28] the port of Tarquinii, where an emporium shrine was established around 590–580 B.C. to Aphrodite-Turan: to this the cults of Hera-Uni and Demeter-Vei were soon added, under the growing influence of the trade with Samos and also to some extent as a result of the social pressure produced by the massive influx into the port of agents of the great emporia of Ionia and,

[26] Torelli 1981[J124], 1–7.   [27] Torelli 1981[J123], 67–82.   [28] Torelli 1977[G500], 398–458.

Fig. 14. Reconstruction of terracotta frieze plaque from the second phase of the Sant'
Omobono temple (c. 530 B.C.?). From Sommella Mura 1977 [E135], fig. 7.

from the late sixth century B.C. onwards, of Aegina; at Gravisca we have
evidence of the votive gift of an anchor given by the man whom
Herodotus (IV.152) considered 'the most fortunate of the merchants
known to him', Sostratus son of Laodamas of Aegina (see *CAH* IV, Fig.
39).

Cults like those of Gravisca are known or can be surmised throughout
the whole coastal area of western central Italy. A grandiose temple of the
late sixth century at Pyrgi, the port of Caere, has revealed the name of a
local *tyrannos*, Thefarie Velianas, the author of an inscribed bilingual
dedication in Etruscan and Phoenician, set up to commemorate the help
received in his ascent to power from the goddess Ishtar, assimilated to
the Etruscan Uni. This dedication and the grandiose character of the
temple buildings at Pyrgi, colossal in comparison with the far more
modest fabric of the emporium at Gravisca, reveal clearly the importance
which the emporia and the classes directly connected to them assumed in
this Etruscan metropolis.[29]

At Rome, the oriental Aphrodite brought by the merchants was
installed at the gates of the city at the edge of the Portus Tiberinus and
took on the name of Fortuna, modelled on that of the Greek Moirai, of
whom Aphrodite Urania was the *presbytate*, the eldest (Paus. 1.19.2). Her
temple has been identified with that of the sacred area of Sant' Omobono

[29] *Die Göttin von Pyrgi* 1981[G338]; Verzar 1980[G507], 35–86. For a different dating of Thefarie
Velianas see below, p. 256.

and, like the numerous other sanctuaries of Fortuna once scattered throughout the surburban area of the archaic city, it was closely linked by tradition with the 'tyrannical' figure of Servius Tullius. Its Etruscan and Latin inscriptions, rich votive offerings from the beginning of the sixth century B.C. and sumptuous decoration are evidence of the splendours of the regal period and confirm the importance which the cult – and those who brought it to Rome – had for the royal power during the years of the Etruscan monarchy. Even more significant perhaps is the fact that the popularity of the shrine and its prosperity seem to follow the fortunes of the Etruscan kings of Rome. The last votive offerings belong to the late sixth century B.C., and it may be no coincidence that, in the very years which saw the birth of the republican state, the temple was abandoned, not to be rebuilt until over a century later.[30]

Nonetheless, the Aphrodite of the emporia appears not only in the great cities of southern Etruria, but also in others along the Latin coastline. From the mouth of the Liris, where the goddess Marica was explicitly identified with Aphrodite of the Sea (Pontia), to the beaches of Antium, which venerated the Fortunae in the two guises of the goddess, as virgin and as matron, to Satricum, where the aspect of Mater Matuta predominated (at Rome, in the shrine of Sant' Omobono, she was associated with Fortuna the Maid (Virgo)), to Ardea with its Aphrodisium, and indeed to the great pan-Latin Aphrodisium of Lavinium, the guardian goddess of the emporia secured trade and navigation by her presence. The evidence from Lavinium (p. 59f; Fig. 21) illustrates the importance the goddess had assumed: the shrine 'of the thirteen altars', almost certainly identifiable with the pan-Latin Aphrodisium, which was inaugurated in its monumental form around 570 B.C. with an altar and with the 'consecration' of a princely tomb of a century earlier for the divine cult of Pater Indiges-Aeneas,[31] is the most eloquent demonstration of the impact on local religious traditions of those who thronged the emporia. It is therefore logical that around this Aphrodisium there should have grown up the complex ritual of the Vinalia Rustica, the sacred celebration of the grape harvest and the 'mystery' of the fermentation of the wine, of a cultural inheritance, that is, which the Etruscan–Latin world had taken over during the eighth century from ancient Greek and oriental technology. No less part of the same picture is the appearance in this same context of the cult of the Dioscuri, a Greek borrowing openly acknowledged as such epigraphically by the well-known inscribed bronze plaque from Lavinium (Fig. 63: p. 579), which may be dated to the first phase of the monumental shrine.[32]

[30] For another discussion of the history of this temple see below, pp. 76ff.
[31] For an alternative, later, dating of this shrine see below, p. 69.   [32] Torelli 1984[I70].

It was through the agency of those who frequented the emporia that Etruscan and Latin culture acquired the whole of its vast ideological and technological Greek heritage and adapted it to its own needs, reshaping rites and remoulding divine images to serve the whole complex social stratification which had gradually been created over the three centuries that saw the slow formation of urban structures.

V. CONCLUSION

The 'archaeological' history which has been briefly outlined above does not claim to be in any way exhaustive. Rather, our aim has been to draw attention to the considerable potential of this evidence, which should not be understood either as supporting a particular interpretation of the literary tradition, itself shrouded with ancient and modern uncertainties and misunderstandings, or as a self-sufficient reality, devoid of links with the real dynamics of historical events. Limitations on the space available for this exposition have made it necessary to stress only certain aspects of the whole range of evidence. Nevertheless, it may confidently be hoped that the historian's attention has been drawn at least to the main lines of an economic, social and cultural complex which can at once be integrated with the broad picture that emerges from a critical and non-reductive interpretation of the literary tradition.

The reader will be able to co-ordinate for himself this sequence of major archaeological events with the historical data which emerge from the following chapter by A. Momigliano, and it is therefore unnecessary to attempt that task here. A single uniform approach to the world of southern Etruria and Latium (while making proper allowance for differences due to diversity in the social and cultural rather than in the ethnic background) is undoubtedly fruitful; it helps to restore to the long-term historical process the basic unity which existed between these two worlds, and also enhances our understanding of the diverse destinies which the passage of time allotted to Etruria, Latium and Rome. But the relatively provisional character of an 'archaeological history' should always be borne in mind, since by its very nature it is destined to undergo progressive modification in the course of time. Hence in integrating the one type of history with the other an even greater degree of caution must be exercised than that indicated in the opening paragraphs of this chapter – yet without abandoning completely such an attempt in the manner which has unfortunately become an increasingly dangerous and regrettable habit amongst both historians and archaeologists.

CHAPTER 3

THE ORIGINS OF ROME

A. MOMIGLIANO

I. THE PROBLEMS OF CONTEXT

The question whether Rome was a Greek polis was asked in Greece in the fourth century B.C. by scholars like Heraclides Ponticus who at least in theoretical terms were well qualified to answer (Plut. *Cam.* 22). An alternative question was suggested by other Greek scholars whom Dionysius of Halicarnassus leaves unidentified (*Ant. Rom.* 1.29.2): whether Rome was or had been an Etruscan polis. The definition of Rome as a Greek polis evidently still appealed to philhellenic historians such as the senator C. Acilius (?) in the second century B.C., when Rome was turning into an empire of unprecedented structure (Jac. *FGrH* 813 F1). On the other hand the question of Etruscan influence on Roman institutions and customs was still very much in the mind of historians like Strabo (v.2.2, pp. 219–20C). These alternative interpretations – of Rome as a Greek city or as an Etruscan city – remain significant for us too. But we are now more aware of one of the difficulties inherent in the opposition: the Etruscans themselves developed their cities with an eye to Greek models.

As we know, between approximately 850 B.C. and 700 B.C. a profound social transformation started in Greece and spread to Italy, the outcome of which was the creation of the classical city-state. Initially this transformation involved the displacement of groups which either went to remote places, often overseas, in what we call colonization or simply created a new town in the neighbourhood where they used to live. Forcible removal of inhabitants from one place to another was not excluded. The technological conditions of these developments are not always evident. However, improvements in the control of waters – either through irrigation or by navigation; better metallurgy with increased and more skilful use of iron and with wider exchange of tin and copper; availability of surpluses of wheat, oil and wine in certain places and in certain years with consequently a wider range of trade; and finally, most elusive of all, the military superiority of certain groups seem to be the main factors. The creation of colonial establishments such as Al-Mina in

Syria and Pithecusae on the island of Ischia during the eighth century gives some measure of the range of Greek trade and of the countries involved. By importing iron and copper from Etruria Pithecusae established direct contact between Greeks and Etruscans and initiated a migration of Greek artisans, traders and aristocrats into Etruscan towns which led to widespread assimilation of Greek cultural patterns by the Etruscans and their neighbours, among whom were the Latins and more specifically the recent settlers of the new town of Rome.

The formation of city-states in Italy under the influence of Greek models is therefore indisputable. But several factors complicate our understanding of it. First of all we are not yet in a position to account for the authority, skill and rapidity with which the Etruscans turned the Villanovan culture of Central Italy (whether it was native or alien ground to them) into one of the most enduring networks of cities history has ever known. It is only too obvious that the Etruscans remained different from the Greeks, however much they learned from them; and it will become apparent from what follows that what the Romans learned from the Greeks does not coincide with what the Etruscans learned from them. In particular we are still in the dark about what the near-Etruscan population of Lemnos contributed both to the contacts between the Etruscans and the East and to their peculiar interpretation of Greek social and cultural models: the presence of Greeks at Lemnos prior to the conquest by Miltiades seems now to have been established.[1]

Furthermore we cannot forget the parallel phenomenon of urbanization, trade and colonization among the Phoenicians who competed with the Greeks in the western Mediterranean and shared with them many basic attitudes to social life. The co-operation between the Etruscans and the Phoenicians of Carthage became close, and was extended to Rome only in the sixth century B.C., but it had developed from old contacts with the Phoenicians in general since at least the eighth century (cf. Fig. 15). Though it now seems probable that both the Etruscans and the Latins got their alphabetic writing from the Greeks rather than from the Phoenicians, Phoenician imports appear in tombs, and one in Praeneste has a Phoenician inscription.[2] There is no conclusive evidence for the existence of a Phoenician (Tyrian) quarter in Rome in the seventh century, as suggested by R. Rebuffat, but D. van Berchem has made out a strong case for the Phoenician origin of the cult of Hercules (= Melqart) in Rome.[3] Phoenician contributions to the development of urban life in Central Italy must at least be treated as a serious possibility.

Going beyond the events – or the traditions – of the eighth to the sixth

---

[1] Heurgon 1980[J65], 578–600.   [2] Amadasi 1967[K1], 157.
[3] Rebuffat 1966[K162], 7–48; van Berchem 1967[G504], 73–109, 307–38.

Fig. 15. Figured friezes from a faience vase depicting the Egyptian pharaoh Bocchoris. In the upper frieze he stands by a table between the deities Neith and Horus and is then seen conducted by the gods Horus (l.) and Thot (r.). The lower frieze shows negro prisoners sitting among palms. The vase is either Phoenician or Egyptian work and was made before Bocchoris' death in 715. It was found in a female grave at Tarquinii, probably of the first quarter of the seventh century. After A. Rathje in Ridgway and Ridgway 1979 [A111], 151, fig. 11.

centuries B.C., recent research has been considering Mycenaean influences and Indo-European survivals in Latium. They undeniably exist, but their extent is still very controversial. Evidence is increasing for Mycenaean imports into Italy. Greek-speaking people traded and probably even settled in Sicily and southern Italy at given moments between 1500 and 1100 B.C. No Mycenaean sherd has, however, been securely identified on the site of Rome; and altogether Latium remains poorly represented on the 1981 map of Mycenaean finds in Italy. Believers in a strong Mycenaean influence on early Rome, among whom the most authoritative is E. Peruzzi,[4] therefore have to rely on linguistic data and Greek myths for the hypothesis that there was a Mycenaean settlement on the Palatine. The evidence so far adduced fails to persuade, being made up of doubtful etymologies and of an unorthodox use of the legend of Euander (p. 58f).

In comparison, the case for the Indo-European heritage in Rome is far stronger. In a general sense it is in fact indisputable. The Latins, and therefore the Romans, spoke an Indo-European language and worshipped some unmistakably Indo-European gods (though not many). The point in dispute is more specific. It has been the life-work of an exceptionally able and influential scholar, Georges Dumézil, to try to demonstrate that the institutional and intellectual patrimony of the

[4] Peruzzi 1980[150].

Romans was organized according to a coherent Indo-European pattern.[5] In his earliest works Dumézil identified this pattern in a division of archaic Roman society into three 'functional' tribes, one of rulers and priests (Ramnes), one of producers (Tities) and one of warriors (Luceres). A tripartite religion, culminating in the triad Iuppiter, Mars and Quirinus (where Mars is the god of war and Quirinus of peace and production), would have corresponded to the three 'functional' tribes or castes. Later, however, Dumézil changed his mind. He admitted that the three Romulean tribes were no castes and explicitly stated that no Indo-European institution was recognizable in Rome except at the level of terminological continuity (e.g. *rex* ('king') compared with Indian *raj(an)* and Celtic *rīg*). Consequently, in this second phase Dumézil confined himself to seeking the tripartite ideology in religion and myth. He has suggested that the stories about the origins of Rome from Romulus to Ancus Marcius are Indo-European myths turned into history by a peculiar twist of the Roman mind. It is generally admitted that Dumézil has succeeded in showing various degrees of similarity between Roman myths (or legends) and myths (or legends) circulating among other Indo-European groups. The story of the contest between three Latin and three Alban brothers, the Horatii and Curiatii (Livy 1.24.1ff; Dion. Hal. *Ant. Rom.* III.13–22; etc.), is an example. But it is less certain that Dumézil and his followers have been able to re-interpret the history of the Roman monarchy persuasively as the projection of a collective mentality obsessed by tripartition. There is of course an element of truth both in the earlier and in the later Dumézil. Any society has to operate with priests, warriors and producers, and has to place its leaders somewhere between priests, warriors and producers. It is not surprising that Dumézil's tripartition could easily be applied in the study of the western Middle Ages. What Dumézil cannot do, because it is contradictory in terms, is to postulate an invariable Indo-European pattern as the explanation of the continuously changing relations between the social groups of Rome. Nothing is gained, however, by replacing Dumézil's Indo-European model with A. Alföldi's 'nomadic' model.[6] Taking his cue from descriptions of Iranian and Turkish nomads, Alföldi postulated two stages in archaic Roman society, one matriarchal based on tripartite institutions (such as three tribes and 30 *curiae*) and the other patriarchal with binary institutions (such as double monarchy). This is no more demonstrable than the existence of a rule of exogamy in the patriarchal society of the second stage. But Alföldi's researches have raised problems which cannot be disregarded, such as the importance of the cavalry and of youth-groups in archaic Roman society.

[5] See Dumézil 1941–5[G395]; 1944[A41]; 1958[A43]; 1968–73[G396]; 1969[G397]; 1974 [G398].
[6] See Alföldi 1974[A1].

At present the traditional alternative, of interpreting archaic Rome as a society similar either to a Greek or to an Etruscan city-state, is complicated by the emergence of other, often more remote, factors, which have not yet been defined with sufficient clarity. It must be added that even some fundamental features of Roman society of the seventh to the sixth centuries B.C. are in themselves obscure. It is enough to remind ourselves that the regime of land-ownership is an unsolved problem, because of the uncertainties surrounding the key-term *heredium* (p. 100), and that the structure of Roman monarchy is obfuscated by our ignorance of the original meaning and function of the *lex curiata de imperio* which may (or may not) have given legitimacy to a new king (p. 105). In these circumstances it has seemed prudent to give separate accounts of the archaeological and of the literary evidence and to refrain from more tentative hypotheses which would be justified and welcome in a personal monograph. In the past centuries, even down to the time of B. G. Niebuhr and Th. Mommsen, any study of archaic Rome was an examination of the traditional account transmitted to us by the surviving ancient texts, the most important of which belong to the late first century B.C. (Diodorus, Dionysius of Halicarnassus and Livy): the Dutchman J. Perizonius (1685) and the Frenchman L. De Beaufort (1738) are usually considered the pioneers of this critical examination of the literary sources, but names could easily be multiplied. What is new in our century is the accumulation of new archaeological (including epigraphic) evidence. It is now ample enough to provide a story of its own which can be used to check the literary evidence and *vice versa* can be checked against the literary evidence. As archaeological research can, to a certain extent, be planned with specific problems in mind, it has increasingly been directed towards obtaining answers to questions (especially about material conditions of life and social stratification) for which the literary evidence is insufficient or unreliable, being much later than the events themselves.

II. THE MYTHS OF FOUNDATION

Before we turn to archaeology, it is, however, wise to give some attention to the foundation legend of Rome as it appears in our literary sources. The peculiar Roman synthesis of the legend of Romulus with the legend of Aeneas no doubt developed slowly through the centuries with materials which are partly indigenous, partly Greek and perhaps partly Etruscan. It is important as an indication of what the Romans thought about themselves at least from the end of the fourth century B.C. onwards. When the Romans decided that they were ultimately Trojans, they were in effect saying that they were neither Greeks nor Etruscans – an answer in anticipation to the question put by the Greeks whether Rome was a Greek or an Etruscan polis.

The notion that Aeneas founded Rome either with Odysseus or after Odysseus (the text is uncertain) is attributed by Dionysius of Halicarnassus (*Ant. Rom.* 1.72.2) to Hellanicus. When Hellanicus wrote in the late fifth century B.C., the text of Hesiod's *Theogony* had been circulating for a long time with lines, perhaps interpolated, announcing that Circe bore Odysseus two sons, Agrius and Latinus 'who was faultless and strong . . . they ruled over the famous Tyrrhenians in a distant recess of the holy islands' (1010–1016). These passages, of course, belong to Greek speculations about the peregrinations of the heroes of the Trojan War. We owe also to a Greek writer – the Sicilian Alkimos – the earliest reference which associates Romulus with Aeneas, if it is true that Alkimos lived about 350 B.C. (Jac. *FGrH* 560 F4). He stated that Romulus was the only son of Aeneas by Tyrrhenia and the father of Alba whose son Rhomos (an obvious emendation of the 'Rhodios' of the MSS) became the founder of Rome. Though Romulus makes his first appearance in this Greek text, it can hardly be doubted that his connexion with Aeneas was artificial and imposed by the existence of a native, Roman legend which the Greeks had to take into account.

As it appears in our main sources of the Caesarean and Augustan age, the Roman version of the foundation legend preserves the connexion of Romulus with Aeneas through a series of kings of Alba Longa who were the descendants of Aeneas. A daughter of one of these kings was raped by the god Mars (though there were other versions of the story) and gave birth to the twins Romulus and Remus. The subsequent events can be divided into four sections. In the first the twins, who had miraculously survived by being fed by a wolf, start a career as youth leaders, decide to found a new city and quarrel between themselves at the moment of the ritual foundation, so that the foundation of the city was also an act of fratricide. In the second sequence Romulus, by now alone, pursues the policy of a robber chief, collects male citizens for Rome indiscriminately and gives them wives by a collective act of rape of Sabine women. In the third scene Romans and Sabines become united under the joint leadership of Romulus and Titus Tatius (the only dual kingship in the Roman tradition) and are organized into three tribes and thirty *curiae*. In the fourth section the episodes, mainly of military conquest, are less neatly characterized, except for the final disappearance of Romulus which · represents the model for the Roman divinization of sovereigns. Though it is easy to produce parallels to individual episodes or even to individual sections of this foundation story (and of course Cain and Abel, Moses, Cyrus, the twin Indian Nāsatya and the wars between Asi and Vani in the Icelandic saga have all been invoked in turn) there is no obvious general model for the story. The substance of the legend must already have been elaborated long before 296 B.C. when a statue of the wolf with the twins was solemnly set up (Livy x.23.1). The conventional account was to be found in the first of the Roman historians Fabius Pictor (writing in Greek) about the end of the third century B.C. Plutarch (*Rom.* 3.1; 8.7) says that Fabius Pictor's account corresponded to that given previously by the Greek Diocles of Peparethus. This basically confirms that the compromise between a Greek and a Latin version of the origins of Rome had already become canonical in the second half of the third century. The compromise was increasingly easy because it became evident that if the foundation of Rome had to be put about 250 years before the beginning of the Republic, it could not be attributed either to Aeneas or to his immediate descendants. Hence the creation of a series of intermediate Alban kings, which the poet Naevius had not yet considered necessary, but which his contemporary Fabius Pictor admitted. Thus Aeneas and Romulus became perfectly compatible.

The sum total of the legend represented in itself an ideological orientation. The first characteristic of the myth about the foundation of Rome is precisely that it is a myth about a city, not about a tribe or a nation. The citizens of Rome were always conscious of belonging to the comparatively small nation of the Latins which in its turn was identifiable by its specific language, its specific sanctuaries and (at least for a long time) federal institutions. The Roman story recognizes the existence of the Latins and of their centres Lavinium and Alba Longa, but does not explain the origins of the Latins as a whole. Secondly, the Roman legend emphasized in its most authoritative versions that both Aeneas and Romulus had one divine parent (but on the opposite side, Aeneas having a divine mother and Romulus a divine father: Venus and Mars were not unknown to each other in Greek myths). Both were leaders of migrant bands which in turn absorbed alien elements. The ultimate impression the Romans wanted to give of themselves was of a society with divine, but by no means pure, origins in which political order was created by the fusion of heterogeneous and often raffish elements, after a fratricide had marked the city's foundation. No doubt, as we shall see, the legend transmitted some awareness of the part played by juvenile bands of adventurers under aristocratic leaders in the archaic societies of Central Italy. In the ritual of the *ver sacrum* (the 'sacred spring'), as a consequence of a previous vow, a band of young people was sent away to seek new land under a leader who in his turn was supposed to follow a sacred animal (p. 284). But the *ver sacrum* was only the most sacralized version of these juvenile migrations. Significantly, Romulus did not lead a *ver sacrum*. The Romans, while giving notice that they did not consider themselves either Greek or Etruscan, also displayed considerable sophistication in defining the mixed origins of their citizen body.

Having made their point in the main story, they acknowledged an early relationship with the Greeks in its later developments, by allowing the Palatine hill to be occupied by the Arcadian Euander before Aeneas reached Latium. We do not know who first invented this story. The Romans also came to recognize an Etruscan contribution to the original population of the city by various devices, including the artificial connexion of one of the three Romulean tribes, the Luceres, with the Etruscans. There is more than a premonition of the future attitudes of the Romans to empire in their stubborn defence of their own identity against the Greeks and Etruscans, while declaring themselves a nation ready to assimilate foreigners without racial prejudices or even moral pretensions.

Strikingly enough in this context, the Romans at an early period gave signs that they were ready to identify themselves with the Sabines. Showing another element of guilt about their origins which superimposed itself on that of fratricide, they believed that Romulus had achieved fusion with the Sabines by raping their women. His successor Numa Pompilius, a model religious leader, was a Sabine. It is no less puzzling that the Sabine Titus Tatius should appear as a joint king with Romulus. Why should Rome have had first a potential joint king, Remus, and then a temporary joint king, Titus Tatius? The possible connexion with the double consulate of the Roman Republic adds to the obscurity rather than detracting from it. We should have to know more about the early contacts between the Latins and the neighbouring Sabines, who, with their forays into the plains and hills of Latium (such as Rome still experienced in the middle of the fifth century B.C. when Appius Herdonius occupied the Capitol (p. 286)) and, probably, with attempts to secure land for themselves among the Latins, must have created anxiety among the Romans.

What we have said is not, however, intended to explain the myth of the Roman foundation – only to indicate the direction which the Romans gave to their future by the political ideology implicit in this myth. We would understand it better if we knew whether the Etruscans had used similar ingredients for their myths. A wolf feeding a human child appears on an Etruscan stele from the Certosa of Bologna attributable to the fifth or fourth century B.C. (Fig. 16). An Etruscan scarab of about 500 B.C. (Luyne Collection in Paris) represents Aeneas carrying his father. Statuettes of Aeneas in the same posture were found at Veii. But we are far from knowing what the Etruscans made of children fed by wolves or of Aeneas carrying his father, the more so because the Veii figurines may well belong to the time when Veii was Roman. We cannot be certain that the Attic vases with representations of Aeneas found in Etruria express the taste of Etruscan customers, rather than that of the Athenian painters. Another factor about which we should like to know more is the role of the Latin city of Lavinium in shaping the legend of Aeneas. Dionysius of Halicarnassus saw a *heroon* of Aeneas in the town (*Ant. Rom.* 1.64.5).

Fig. 16. Stele from Bologna depicting wolf suckling child (first half of the fourth century).

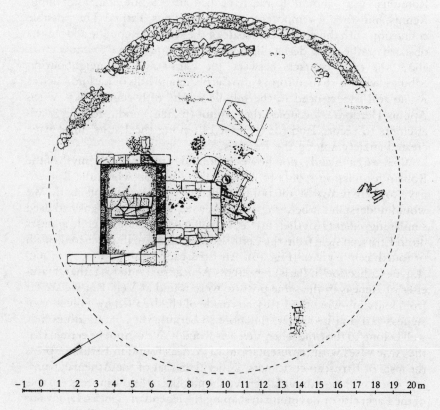

−1 0 1 2 3 4 5 6 7 8 9 10 11 12 13 14 15 16 17 18 19 20m

Fig. 17a. Lavinium 'heroon': plan. From *Roma medio-repubblicana* 1973 [B401], 314 fig. 24.

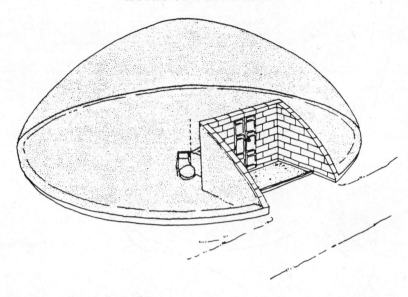

Fig. 17b. Lavinium 'heroon': reconstruction. From C. F. Giuliani and P. Sommella, *PP* 32 (1977), 368 fig. 8.

Italian archaeologists believe that they have identified it in a sacred building of the fourth century B.C. which includes a tomb of the seventh century (Fig. 17; cf. p. 50). In the early third century B.C. Timaeus learned from natives of Latium that Aeneas brought sacred objects of his own to Lavinium (Jac. *FGrH* 566 F59). These objects must be identified with the Penates Populi Romani which the Roman consuls and praetors were required to visit in Lavinium each year (Varro, *Ling.* v.144; Macrob. *Sat.* III.4.11). Furthermore, the Greek poet Lycophron in the *Alexandra* (third or second century B.C.) seems to be the first to state that Aeneas founded Lavinium (implied in l. 1259). Livy and other writers knew that Aeneas had died by drowning in the river Numicus not far from Lavinium and was worshipped under the name of Iuppiter Indiges. An inscription from Tor Tignosa, near Lavinium, with its mention of 'Lar Aeneas'[7] has been taken by many as a reference to this cult of Aeneas. Cumulatively the evidence suggests an old concern in Lavinium with Aeneas which may have preceded and inspired Rome's interest in him. In any case when the Romans decided to be Trojans they knew they could count on the sympathy of other Latin towns.

[7] *ILLRP* 1271. On the problems of the reading cf. Kolbe 1970[E37], 1–9; Guarducci 1971[E34], 74–89.

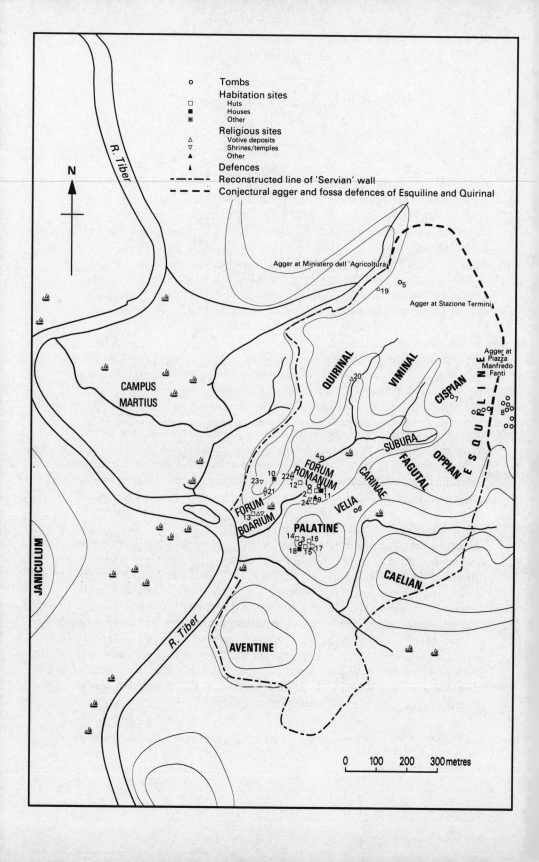

Tombs ○

Habitation sites
  □ Huts
  ■ Houses
  ▣ Other

Religious sites
  △ Votive deposits
  ▽ Shrines/temples
  ▲ Other

Defences ▲

— · — Reconstructed line of 'Servian' wall

- - - Conjectural agger and fossa defences of Esquiline and Quirinal

N

R. Tiber

Agger at Ministero dell 'Agricoltura

△19   ○5

Agger at Stazione Termini

Agger at Piazza Manfredo Fanti

CAMPUS MARTIUS

QUIRINAL   VIMINAL   CISPIAN

△20   ○7   ○8

SUBURA   OPPIAN   ESQUILINE

FAGUTAL

FORUM ROMANUM

CARINAE

4○
10■   22△
23▽   12□
21△
2□ ▲9 □11
24△

VELIA
○6

FORUM BOARIUM
13□ △▽

PALATINE
14□   ■16
18■   ○   □17
15

JANICULUM

CAELIAN

R. Tiber

AVENTINE

0   100   200   300 metres

III. SETTLEMENT, SOCIETY AND CULTURE IN LATIUM AND AT ROME

We can now turn to the archaeological evidence (Maps 1 and 2; Fig. 18). Rome has been a city for the living for about three thousand years. The living inevitably destroy the past in order to live. What is left for archaeologists in the best of cases raises the problem of how typical and representative the finds are of the period to which they belong. In recent years modern technology has increased the danger of total destruction of the traces of the past. Any new building in Rome or any new road – especially any new motorway – in Latium is likely to erase ancient remains. Many of the recent archaeological discoveries (for instance at Castel di Decima) are the result of emergency rescue work. What has been achieved remains exceptional both in quality and in quantity. We shall try here to summarize the main historical results, and we shall obviously give special attention to the more recent, and only partly published, excavations.

At the beginning of the first millennium B.C. there were many more forests in Latium than we might imagine. Even the Roman hills looked considerably different, with the Oppian still united with the Palatine and the Quirinal with the Capitoline. A little lake stood on the site of the present Colosseum, and the Campus Martius included a lake of its own, Lacus Caprae. Wheat (*triticum turgidum*, L., as distinct from emmer, spelt, barley and oats), wine, olive oil and even apples were apparently relative novelties in the early eighth century B.C. With the harbour of Ostia still in the future – tradition puts it in the late seventh century B.C., archaeology seems to scale it down to the fourth century – only the place we call Antium was a safe coastal harbour. The seasonal movement of livestock – transhumance – being then as now an essential feature of Italian pastoral life, the internal roads of Latium along the rivers Tiber and Anio

---

Fig. 18. The archaeology of early Rome: location map. After Gjerstad 1953–73 [A56], figs. 1–2.

1. Sacra Via necropolis	13. Sant' Omobono
2. Temple of Caesar	14. 'Scalae Caci'
3. House of Livia	15. Atrium of Domus Augustana
4. Forum Augusti	16. Aula Regia of Domus Augustana
5. Quirinal	17. Lararium of Domus Augustana
6. Velia	18. Palatine (near House of Livia)
7. Cispian	19. S. Maria della Vittoria
8. Esquiline necropolis	20. Villino Hüffer
9. Regia	21. Capitol (SE)
10. Capitoline habitation strata?	22. Lapis Niger
11. Sacra Via	23. Capitoline temple
12. Equus Domitiani	24. Temple of Vesta

maintained contacts with the outside world of Etruria, Campania and Umbria, each with its peculiar mixture of languages, religious rituals and political institutions. Groups of huts formed the villages which in the seventh century were slowly replaced by wider settlements both of unbaked and baked bricks. The earlier fortifications of the villages were earthworks. Varro still saw some of them inside Rome (p. 36). The place where Rome ultimately developed was attractive to those who wanted to cross the Tiber on their way from Etruria to Campania or, more urgently, needed the salt to be found abundantly in the salt beds at the mouth of the Tiber.

The thin population, which to present-day archaeologists seems to be indistinguishable from other groups of the Appenninic bronze culture, begins to thicken and to acquire characteristics of its own in the tenth century. Though there are competitive systems of classification, the following scheme which basically goes back to H. Müller-Karpe[8] has become a sort of internationally recognized code:

Latial Culture

Phase I	(Final Bronze Age)	1000–900 B.C.
IIA	(Early Iron Age)	900–830 B.C.
IIB		830–770 B.C.
III		770–730 B.C.
IVA	(Early and Middle Orientalizing Style)	730–630 B.C.
IVB	Late Orientalizing	630–580 B.C.

Continuity with preceding sites can (as far as present data tell us) seldom be proved. Traces of preceding occupation have, however, been found – among others – on the site of the later Rome not far from the Forum Boarium (going back to the fifteenth century B.C.), in Pratica di Mare (that is, Lavinium) and towards the coast at Ardea. One must add immediately that our knowledge of cemeteries is far better than that of residential settlements. The fact that in Phases I and IIA cremation prevailed, almost exclusively, on certain sites does not further reduce our chances of understanding how people lived, because the ashes were often put into urns representing the huts of the dead, while miniature (and even normal-size) reproductions of the dead person's belongings were strewn about. The urn was in its turn inserted into a large jar with a wide mouth, the *dolium*. Negatively, Phase I is characterized by the absence of the typical bi-conical Proto-Villanovan urns which are present at Allumiere, La Tolfa, etc. Allumiere and Phase I of Latium, however, share the custom of the double container for the ashes. Valley bottom

[8] Müller-Karpe 1959[E114].

settlements may be replaced by sites on the west slopes of the Alban hills. The Alban hills – where Alba Longa was situated (more or less modern Castelgandolfo) – have been described as the cradle of Iron Age culture in Latium, but so far the evidence about Alba Longa itself has been most disappointing (p. 265), to the extent that some scholars have asked whether it ever existed. In Phase IIA inhumation begins to compete with cremation. It is unnecessary to say that the theories which explained the co-existence of inhumation and incineration as the sign of co-existence of two different ethnic groups are now discredited. But it is as well to remember that fifty years ago it was the right thing to believe that cremators spoke an Oscan–Umbrian dialect, when they did not speak Etruscan, whereas inhumation was a sign of competent Latinity. F. von Duhn's archaeology and G. Devoto's linguistics were both, alas, marred by this mythology.[9] It is true that Lavinium seems to lead in inhumation practices (though incineration has been located there too), and Lavinium was supposed to have been founded by Aeneas and to preserve the gods (Penates) brought by him from Troy. But what can we deduce from that?

In the ninth and early eighth centuries the villages were often in clusters. No central power seems apparent, at least in archaeological terms. One would like to see the state of Latium in those centuries reflected in the list of the thirty peoples of Latium which Pliny gives in his *Natural History* (III.69). Pliny certainly preserves the memory of an old ritual: the title of his list is 'triginta carnem in monte Albano soliti accipere populi Albenses'.[10] But the names of the thirty peoples given by Pliny are dubious for various reasons (p. 267f), and even their number creates difficulties.[11] We have no way of deciding whether the list is due to conjectures by antiquarians or reflects authentic data and, if authentic, to which century it belongs. What we learn from excavations is that in Phases IIA and IIB, that is, from roughly 900 to 770 B.C., there was an enlargement and reorganization both of the several cemeteries and of the very few villages we happen to know. In the place which was to be known in classical times as Tibur (present-day Tivoli), on the hill where the Rocca of Pius II now stands, the reshaping of the burial area is evident: individual tombs are surrounded by circular enclosures. At the same time a tendency to enlarge the occupation of the plains became manifest: we ultimately owe to it the rise of Rome. A most impressive necropolis began to be excavated in 1971 on the modern Via Prenestina

---

[9] von Duhn 1924–39[B323]; G. Devoto, *Gli antichi Italici* (Ed.1, Florence, 1931); cf. id. *Stud. Etr.* 6 (1932) 243–60; *Athenaeum* N.S. 31 (1953) 335–43; *Stud. Etr.* 26 (1958) 17–25.

[10] 'The thirty Alban peoples who regularly received (sacrificial) meat on the Alban Mount.'

[11] Lycoph. *Alex.* 1253ff; Dion. Hal. *Ant. Rom.* III.31.4; cf. Diod. VII.5.9; Dion. Hal. *Ant. Rom.* v.61. Dion. Hal. *Ant. Rom.* IV.49 gives the members as forty-seven.

on the western edge of the now dried-up Lake of Castiglione. It has become known as the necropolis of the Osteria dell'Osa. It was perhaps one of the cemeteries of the city of Gabii, a mysterious little place where Romulus and Remus were supposed to have been educated (Dion. Hal. *Ant. Rom.* 1.84.5). Gabii was absorbed into the Roman state during the sixth century B.C. The treaty between Gabii and Rome inscribed on a leather shield was preserved in the sanctuary of Semo Sancus on the Quirinal and was one of the antiquarian oddities dear to the writers of the Augustan age.[12] About two hundred tombs were found in the cemetery of the Osteria dell'Osa where the teachers of Romulus, if any, must be supposed to have found their final rest. Cremation tombs *a pozzo* (in the form of a pit) and inhumation tombs *a fossa* (trench) were mixed, the latter being in the majority. From the tomb furniture it would appear that cremation was reserved to adult males, though some of the deceased were inhumed like the women and children. The other peculiarity is that only cremation graves contain weapons. Here cremation clearly implies status, and the ashes are placed in urns representing dwellings – presumably emphasizing that the man was a *pater familias* (household head). In the process of time (IIB) inhumation seems to become the absolute rule. We may add here that Gabii itself seems to have been identified, and a seventh-century sanctuary and a sixth-century building have been explored. The seventh-century sanctuary yielded Italo-Geometric and Corinthian pottery and votive statuettes.

Phase III (about 770–730) presents throughout more precise signs of social differentiation. Iron is by now in general use, and bronze has a prestige value. In Phase III of the Osteria dell'Osa (which is still largely unpublished) wheel-made pottery makes its appearance, and some tombs stand out as particularly wealthy ones. Weapons abound everywhere in men's tombs; chariots appear both for men and for women, and are therefore signs of status. Some of the painted pottery appears to be inspired by Greek Geometric models. We are reminded that the island of Ischia was colonized by Euboean Greeks about 775 B.C. and that Greek imports surround Latium, at Veii in Etruria and Pontecagnano, Capua, and Cumae in Campania. Taking the area as a whole, artisan production seems to go beyond local needs and to be due, at least partly, to itinerant or immigrant smiths and potters. A rich deposit of bronze objects belonging to this Phase III was discovered by chance at Ardea in 1952.

This is in chronological terms the age of Romulus according to the conventional date. But so far archaeology has not yet revealed any inscription or any other sign pertaining to the foundation act, if there was one (as tradition states), a point of some relevance. There are on the

---

[12] Dion. Hal. *Ant. Rom.* IV.58; Hor. *Epist.* II.1.5; cf. Paul. Fest. 48L.

contrary signs that the Palatine and the Forum had been occupied earlier, at least since the tenth century, to which some tombs discovered in the Forum belong (Fig. 24). As already mentioned, on other neighbouring sites the occupation may be even more ancient. The excavations of the area of Sant' Omobono have revealed materials going back to the fifteenth century B.C., though mixed with later strata. There is no archaeological confirmation of, and some evidence against, the traditional date of the foundation of Rome in the eighth century. True enough, three hut floors belonging to the eighth century were discovered on the Palatine, more precisely on the Germalus side of it, in 1948. They include holes for the wooden posts which must have formed the solid framework for the walls (Fig. 19a). With the help of the dwellings represented by funerary urns it is possible to reconstruct one of these huts (Fig. 19b) and to give oneself the pleasure of imagining that it is the *casa* or *tugurium Romuli*, Romulus' hut, which was preserved on that spot to the end of antiquity. But there would be no substance behind these fancies. The Forum, which has yielded numerous tombs (both inhumation and cremation) for the ninth and possibly early eighth century B.C., ceased to be used for burials in the early eighth century. The Esquiline cemetery seems to have acted as the main substitute. Only children were still buried in the Forum, under huts, in the eighth and

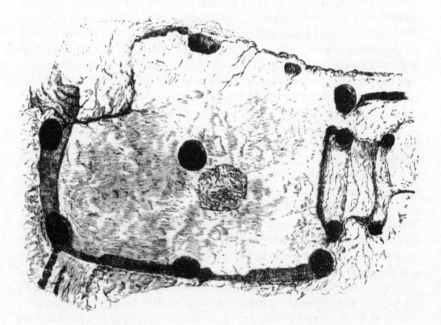

Fig. 19a. Palatine hut: plan. From Gjerstad 1953–73 [A56], IV.46 fig. 4.

Fig. 19b. Palatine hut: reconstruction. From Gjerstad 1953–73 [A56], IV.46 fig. 5.

seventh centuries. The Forum was certainly a residential area in the seventh century, and there are signs of occupation on the Capitoline hill. The archaeological data we have do not allow us to decide whether Rome resulted from the association of pre-existing villages or from the creation of a central organization, say, on the Palatine – apart from the possibility that the two phenomena were concurrent (cf. p. 35). Marks of wealth appear in some of the tombs on the Esquiline, at least one of which had a chariot among its furniture. The Esquiline cemetery must have lasted, to judge from some Greek vases found there, until at least 630 B.C.: in fact, it was probably used much later. Outside Rome, the discovery at La Rustica on the Via Collatina in 1975 of a previously unknown proto-historic site has added to our knowledge of Phase III and of its wealth in bronze objects.

We are approaching a stage (Phase IV) which we can appreciate better because it reminds us immediately of things we have seen elsewhere in civilizations which have long been familiar. The orientalizing style in Italy is in fact a mixture of techniques and objects coming from Greece and the East. No doubt Greek and eastern artisans could have been on the spot to work for the new wealthy aristocrats and tyrants; but after all the Greeks were appearing in strength on the Tyrrhenian coast (Cumae) and in Sicily, and the Phoenicians were both in Sardinia and in Sicily. As for the Etruscans, they may or may not have come from the East in the ninth and eighth centuries. To the sites which we have so far mentioned one at least must be added, with due emphasis on its importance. On the ancient road to Lavinium, 18 km. south of Rome, the place of Castel di Decima has been famous since 1971 when it became obvious that an archaic necropolis was in danger of destruction because of the work for the new Via Pontina. Though there are tombs of earlier periods, Castel di Decima is essentially a document of the orientalizing phase of Latium with its new display of wealth, sometimes of exotic origin. One interesting feature of this necropolis is that some of the tombs (all inhumation) have swords only among their furniture, others spears only, while there are some with both spears and swords. The known tombs of the new necropolis are said to be more than 350. The element of chance in the finds of tombs containing swords and spears makes it hard to explain the distribution pattern. It may have something to do with rank and age. In the Roman archaic army the 'hastati hasta pugnabant', as Varro says (*Ling.* v.89), 'principes gladiis'. That is, the younger soldiers (*hastati*) had spears, the senior ones swords. The tombs offer intimation of family groups, and of continuity through a few generations. Chariots are again found both for men and women. Two tombs deserve special mention: tomb xv, which must have belonged to a very powerful man to whom hunting and fighting were both familiar. He had accumulated much bronze wealth (Fig. 20), some Greek vases (such as a Proto-Corinthian aryballos of the end of the eighth century) and at least one Phoenician amphora. The other tomb, ci, was occupied by a woman who could afford not only a chariot, but refined silver and gold jewellery. A gold and amber pectoral, a silver robe sewn with carved amber and glass beads and gold spiral hair-rings suggested the title of 'Tomb of the Princess' for this burial. One would like to be able to name the place where the princess lived. Politorium, a place said to have been conquered by Ancus Marcius on his way to Ostia (Dion. Hal. *Ant. Rom.* iii.38; Livy 1.33.3), has been proposed. The town corresponding to the necropolis of Ponte Decima has been probably identified not far from it on Monte Cicoriaro. If its defence work in *cappellaccio* belongs to the sixth century the identification with Politorium would not be affected, but the destruction of Politorium by Ancus Marcius before 600 B.C. would become hard to believe.

Nothing so spectacular has been found from this phase either in Rome or at Lavinium. As we have already mentioned, a remarkable multi-period monument has been discovered at Lavinium (Fig. 21). The monument has in its earliest stratum a tomb with seventh-century orientalizing material to which a sixth-century bucchero oinochoe was later added. The tomb was renewed and turned into a shrine in the fourth century, for which identification with the *heroon* of Aeneas has been suggested (p. 59f;

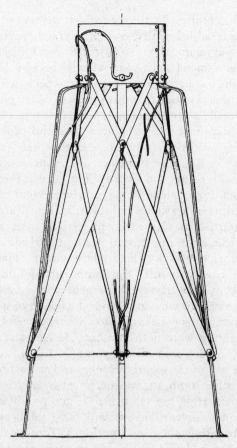

Fig. 20. Reconstruction of bronze tripod from Castel di Decima tomb xv (c. 720–700 B.C.).
From *Civiltà del Lazio primitivo* 1976 [B306], tav. LXII.

Fig. 17 a–b). Another sanctuary (ib.) goes back to the late sixth century
and may have been connected with both the cult of Aeneas and the Latin
League: in its final stage in the fourth century it had thirteen altars, one of
which was no longer in use. These sanctuaries are extra-urban, like
another where about sixty large statues were found dating from the sixth
to the fourth centuries. Four statues represent Minerva. The largest, of
the sixth century, shows Minerva accompanied by a Triton (Fig. 22), the
Tritonia virgo ('Tritonian maiden') of Virgil (*Aen.*II.171; V.615). A sanctuary of Minerva in Lavinium was known to Lycophron (*Alex.* 1281).

   Let us add some details for the orientalizing period from other recent
explorations. At the so-called 'Laurentina' site, at a place called Acqua
Acetosa on the Via Laurentina, a necropolis was discovered in 1976
which may well rival Castel di Decima in importance; it is so far

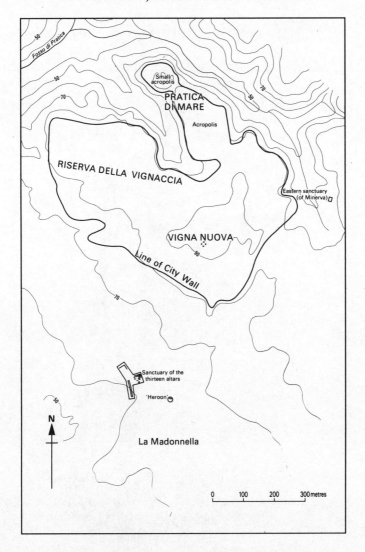

Fig. 21. Lavinium and environs (after Castagnoli et al. 1972 [I16]).

represented by about 50 tombs. They are rich, with gold and silver ornaments for women. The later tombs are organized in distinct groups forming a circle, with one or two more important tombs at the centre. These central tombs contain chariots (also for women) and prestige goods with large amounts of pottery, some of Greek and Phoenician origin. The interest of the place is increased by the identification of the residential area. Attic black figure pottery of the last quarter of the sixth

Fig. 22. Fifth-century statue of Minerva accompanied by Triton from the eastern sanctuary at Lavinium. From F. Castagnoli, Accademia Nazionale dei Lincei, anno 376. Problemi attuali di scienza e cultura, *Quad.* 246 (1979).

century was found nearby. Two sherds incribed 'Manias' and 'Karkafaios' are apparently among the oldest personal names found in Latium. Finally, another settlement of the orientalizing period has been identified as the ancient Ficana on the hill of Monte Cugno overlooking the plain of the Tiber (between Rome and Acilia). The fortification (*agger*) seems to belong to the late eighth century. From the middle of the seventh century B.C. huts give place in some cases to two-roomed buildings. One sanctuary or public building was decorated with terra-cotta revetments representing a procession of chariots and warriors (late sixth century). A necropolis of about sixty tombs shows a steady decline in funeral furniture. Towards the end of the seventh century all display of wealth ends, though the cemetery goes on. From this point of view Ficana raises with particular clarity the general problem of what caused the change from prestige tombs to austerity tombs which is observable throughout Latium at the end of the orientalizing period between 600 and 580 B.C. (cf. p. 37). The same problem is posed by the chamber tombs of Torrino near the Via Laurentina.[13] People ceased displaying or rather concealing prestige, and therefore fruitless, wealth in their tombs.

Earlier archaeological discoveries, in the last century, first revealed what the wealth of the upper class in the seventh century could be at its peak. Praeneste (modern Palestrina), in a splendid (but not yet exactly identified) fortified position on Mount Ginestro, began to attract the interest of archaeologists and looters in 1738 when one of the master-pieces of archaic art – the Ficoroni Cista (p. 412) – was discovered. It was a reminder that Praeneste had been famous in antiquity for its fine bronzes. The first great tomb in the orientalizing style to be properly recognized was the Tomba Barberini of Praeneste. Discovered in 1855, it is now in the Museo di Villa Giulia in Rome. The Tomba Castellani was discovered in 1861–2; the Tomba Bernardini appeared in 1876. These tombs are characterized by the almost unbelievable wealth and beauty of their metal and ivory objects. The most obvious comparison is with the Tomba Regolini-Galassi of Caere (now Cerveteri) which is preserved in the Vatican Museum. Some of the objects are certainly of Eastern origin (Assyria, Urartu, Phoenicia, Cyprus), but some oriental artists may have been at work in Latium or at Ischia. Not all the objects were kept together by the discoverers. One, the gold fibula (Fig. 23) inscribed 'Manios me vhevhaked Numasioi' ('Manios (Manius) made me (or 'had me made'?) for Numasios (Numerius)') – perhaps the most famous inscribed object from the whole of Latium – raises two doubts, one about its origin and the other about its authenticity. It was published in 1887 by an eminent archaeologist, W. Helbig,[14] without indication of its origin.

---

[13] Bedini 1981[B288], 57ff.   [14] Helbig 1887[B232], 37–9.

Fig. 23. Manios fibula with retrograde inscription. From *Civiltà del Lazio primitivo* 1976 [B306], tav. c.

Later Georg Karo declared that he had been told by Helbig that the fibula, being of gold and obviously valuable, had been stolen from the Tomba Bernardini.[15] However, doubts have repeatedly been expressed about the authenticity of the fibula and therefore of its inscription, which if genuine would be the oldest known Latin text, perhaps of the late eighth century B.C. While Professor A. E. Gordon of Berkeley,[16] after careful examination of all the elements involved, inclined to take the fibula as authentic, M. Guarducci has not only concluded that it is a forgery but has identified the forger as the first editor, Helbig; she is supported on linguistic grounds by E. P. Hamp.[17]

With or without the Manios fibula Praeneste offered such a wealth of archaic objects as to overshadow any other place in Latium. But Tibur provided something less precious yet in a different way remarkable, in a tomb with several ivory objects of the orientalizing style; and Satricum (between Anzio and Cisterna) brought to light an extremely remarkable collection of artistic objects in the *stips* (offerings) of the temple of Mater Matuta in its orientalizing phase. The *stips* also contained a vase, a bucchero kylix of about 620–600 B.C., with an Etruscan inscription by a man of Caere:[18]

> mi mulu larisale velχainasi
> I given by Laris Velchaina

It remains an open question whether Rome had anything to offer of comparable wealth, especially in the matter of tombs, in the eighth and seventh centuries B.C. The Esquiline tombs, as far as our knowledge goes, do not provide anything so opulent. It is possible, of course, that this is misleading. The richest tombs may have been looted long ago, or may still await discovery. But we must also consider the other two possibilities, that Rome never had an aristocracy possessing wealth comparable with that of Praeneste or that in Rome law or custom

[15] See Zevi 1976[B274], 50–2; cf. Karo 1904[B351], 24.   [16] Gordon 1975[B224].
[17] Guarducci 1980[B226], 413–574; 1984[B228], 127–77; Hamp 1981[B229], 151–4.
[18] M. Cristofani Martelli, *Stud. Etr.* 44 (1974) 263f (n. 217).

intervened earlier than in surrounding places to discourage the accumulation (or elimination) of wealth in tombs. In the sixth and fifth centuries B.C. Rome clearly shared the ideals of aristocratic austerity of her Latin (but not Etruscan) neighbours.

The finds from Rome are disappointing in the sense that they tell us very little about what was happening outside the zone of the Forum and Palatine. It would be very interesting to know something about the Quirinal, which our historical tradition connects with a Sabine population. But the few tombs of the eighth century found there do not give us any exact information about the date, extent and ethnic features of the site. A deposit in a pit near the church of S. Maria della Vittoria with pottery, bronzes and other objects discovered in 1875 may come from a sanctuary of the Quirinal belonging to the eighth to the seventh century, but is no more revealing. Even less is known about the other hills, such as Mons Caelius and the Aventine. These are quarters of modern Rome where one cannot choose to dig *ad lib*. It is, however, symptomatic that the Palatine–Forum zone (Fig. 24) remains central for modern archaeologists, as it was for the Roman historians of the Augustan age. The centre of power does indeed seem to have been there – and to have been expressed, not in terms of rich tombs, but rather of progressive urban organization. There are clear signs that in about 635–575 B.C. the Forum was paved and transformed from a residential to a public place with ceremonial buildings. The area of the Comitium seems to have been ready to receive assemblies from 600 B.C.: a building in it has been

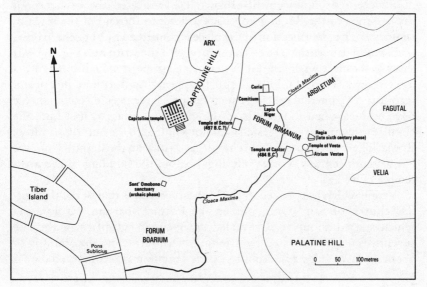

Fig. 24. Central Rome: Location map.

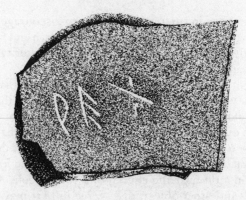

Fig. 25. Fragment of bucchero bowl from the Regia with inscription 'rex' ('king'). *c.* 530–510 B.C.?

hypothetically identified with the first Curia Hostilia, a place for the senate. At a slightly later stage (575–550 B.C.) the place included the Lapis Niger ('Black Stone') – the so-called tomb of Romulus discovered in 1899. Whether a fragment of an Attic black figure vase with a representation of Hephaestus helps to prove that the place was the Volcanal (p. 579) remains to be confirmed. Frank Brown, the excavator of the Regia, had at first thought that, notwithstanding the name, it had been built for the priest called *rex sacrorum*, that is the priest who took over some of the sacred functions of the kings after the end of the monarchy. But in his more recent pronouncements Brown has indicated the existence of earlier strata of the Regia going back at least to the end of the seventh century.[19] The identification of the place is confirmed by a bucchero bowl of disputed date within the sixth century with the word *rex* (Fig. 25).[20] If this was the place where the kings performed some of their duties, it was a modest one. Temple buildings begin to appear in and around the Forum: terracotta ornamental reliefs of such temples have been discovered. We have no idea when the temple of the goddess Vesta was first built; its circular structure has suggested a dubious link with the huts of primitive Rome. There are also signs of religious activities on the Capitol from the late seventh century (votive offerings) before the building of the great temple (Fig. 42).

A zone which has proved of the highest interest is that of the present-day church of Sant' Omobono in the Forum Boarium. Exploration which started about 1938 revealed an open-air cult-place of the late seventh century, followed by a temple with terracotta decorations of about 575 B.C. (Fig. 27). About 525 the temple was reconstructed on a

[19] Brown 1974–5[E79], 15–36; cf. above, p. 45f with Fig. 13a–d.
[20] Guarducci 1972[B225], 381–4.

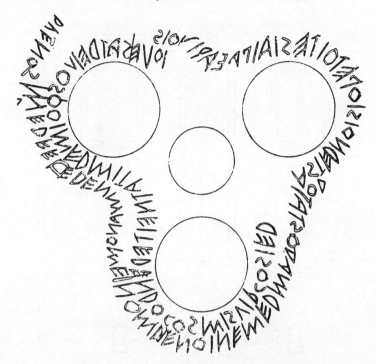

Fig. 26. The 'Duenos vase' (first half of the sixth century) from the Villino Hüffer votive deposit on the Quirinal. The inscription seems to begin (in the extreme upper left) 'Duenos med feced' ('Duenos made me (or had me made)') but has not been fully elucidated. From Gjerstad 1953–73 [A56], III.163, figs. 102 and 104.

VICVS   IVGARIVS   N

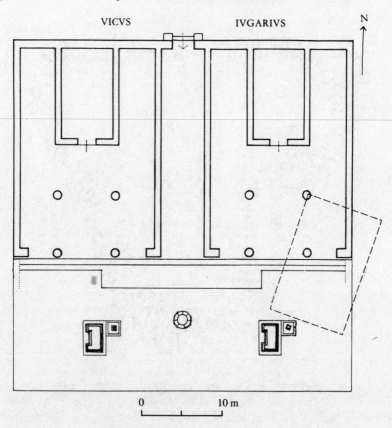

0   10 m

Fig. 27a. Plan of the republican temples of Fortuna and Mater Matuta at Sant'Omobono in the Forum Boarium, with outline of the archaic temple. After G. Ioppolo, *RPAA* 44 (1971), 6, fig. 2.

larger scale and on a new podium. After destruction at the end of the fifth century a new higher podium supported *two* temples which are certainly to be identified with those of Fortuna and Mater Matuta, attributed by tradition to Servius Tullius. The cult of these two goddesses may, of course, be earlier[21] and therefore due to Servius' initiative; but the archaeological evidence offers no support. Greek and Etruscan influences – indeed Greek myths – are evident in the decoration of these temples and also in the offerings of the *stips votiva* (votive donation) with their varieties of imported and local pottery (including Attic ware). One significant item is an ivory lion bearing an Etruscan inscription with a personal name (Fig. 28). By turning to such public buildings we get a flavour of the organized social life and of the cultural contacts of sixth-century Rome.

[21] For the view that the original temple was dedicated to Fortuna see p. 49f.

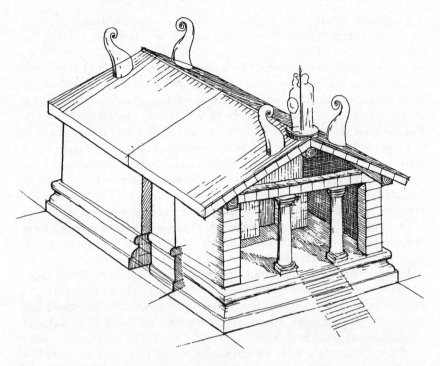

Fig. 27b. Reconstruction of the archaic temple at Sant'Omobono (second half of the sixth century). From *Enea nel Lazio* 1981 [E25], 117.

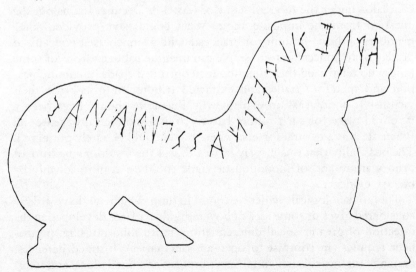

Fig. 28. Inscription on ivory lion from Sant'Omobono (first half of sixth century). From M. Pallottino, *Stud. Etr.* 47 (1979), 320.

Curiously enough, we are not yet quite certain how this city was protected against attack. The prevailing opinion seems to be that the oldest defences of Rome are represented by an earth wall (*agger*), five to six metres high, accompanied by a ditch which one can follow for a stretch round the Quirinal, Viminal and Esquiline. The earth wall would have preceded the stone one, the *murus lapideus*, dated after the Gallic invasion of 390 B.C., which is in the typical Grotta Oscura tufa (p. 332). But there are three questions about the earth wall – one of date, another of extent and the third of its relation to strange pieces of a different stone wall (in the stone locally called *cappellaccio*). In the foundations of the earth wall, the *agger*, one piece of an Attic vase has been found which can be dated about 490–470 B.C. Some scholars – including E. Gjerstad[22] – are convinced that one piece of Greek pottery is enough to date the whole of the earthwork. This would mean that the *agger* should be dated slightly later than 470 B.C. But can we really date an earth wall on the basis of one piece of Greek pottery? Secondly, even if we accept the earth wall as the oldest type of fortification we are not yet certain that it crossed the valleys and embraced the Caelius, the Palatine and the Capitol. In its turn the suggestion that the sections of *cappellaccio* wall might also be archaic and meant to supplement the earth ramparts is based on dubious chronological premises.

With or without a wall, the citizens of Rome seem to have been less able or ready to display wealth in their tombs than some of the citizens of Praeneste and even of Satricum, Tibur and the unknown little place concealed under the modern name of Castel di Decima. Let us put the question from the opposite angle. What could have provided some members of the community of Praeneste with so much useless wealth to display or to conceal in tombs? We can imagine robber barons of some kind who terrorized their neighbours, controlled roads of communication and therefore trade, and extracted tributes or gifts from their victims. It is not easy to explain why Praeneste should have been a favoured place for such robber barons to live and die in, but after all Praeneste was a natural fortress where booty could be safely preserved. The possibility that this display of wealth was the result of a mixture of band warfare and of monopolistic trade could be confirmed only by literary evidence.

The archaeological evidence about Latium which we have briefly considered gives us some idea of how individual places developed in the direction of greater social differentiation, more solid housing, permanent temples (in contrast to open-air sanctuaries), fortified defences, drainage for agricultural and urban purposes and finally local and long-range exchange of goods. The formation of military and economic élites

[22] Gjerstad 1951[E104], 413–22; 1954[E105], 50–65; 1953–73[A56], III.37ff; IV.352ff.

goes together with the acquisition of goods either by gift exchange or by straight commercial transactions. Foreign influences are at work in the style of objects – principally from Etruria and from Greek centres and less commonly from Phoenicia and, perhaps through Phoenicia, from other Near-Eastern countries (including Urartu). The presence of foreign traders and artisans is *a priori* probable and in a few cases epigraphically confirmed. Latin, Greek and Etruscan appear in Rome and no doubt were spoken there. But the only official text (the Lapis Niger (p. 11 n. 19)) is in Latin. So far there is no evidence that Etruscan was ever the language of government in Rome. Writing appears in Rome about 600 B.C. The existence of inscriptions is in itself an index of the rise of self-conscious individuals and groups who are concerned to advertise themselves in sanctuaries. Some of them are certainly foreigners like Laris Velchaina of Caere who makes an offering to Mater Matuta of Satricum and, probably, the companions of Publius Valerius in the same place, to whom we shall return later. Mobility from place to place is, indeed, generally suggested by the inscriptions: thus there is a Tite Latine at Veii[23] and a Kalaturus Phapenas at Caere (*TLE* 65), the Latin origins of whom seem evident. A Rutile Hipukrates at Tarquinii (*TLE* 155) has a name which is half Latin and half Greek (see below, p. 91). A member of the *gens Veturia*, later to be found in Rome, is mentioned in a tomb of Praeneste.[24]

Even the epigraphical evidence is sufficient to reveal the existence of a revolutionary development in the onomastic system of Central Italy which happened between the eighth and the sixth centuries B.C. Latin, Etruscan, Faliscan and Osco-Umbrian dialects slowly replaced the combination of the personal name with the patronymic by a combination of a personal name (later often abbreviated and called *praenomen* in Latin) with a name indicating membership of a clan, that is descent from a common ancestor (the *nomen gentile* of the Romans). The implications of this change for social life can of course be worked out only with reference to the literary evidence. Once again the archaeological evidence, whether accompanied or not by epigraphic evidence, refers us back to the literary tradition. The same applies to the other big question raised by the archaeological evidence. Weapons and armour found in tombs or exhibited on reliefs indicate that Greek tactics in cavalry and infantry fighting penetrated into Latium (and Etruria) in the seventh century B.C. (p. 35), though double axes and chariots survived for ceremonial purposes if not for actual fighting (Fig. 29). But archaeology alone cannot clarify the modes, the limits and the social consequences of the hellenization of warfare in Central Italy.

---

[23] Palm 1952[B373], 57.   [24] Torelli 1967[B265], 38–45; below, p. 285.

Fig. 29. Reconstruction of architectural frieze plaque (late sixth century?) from the Comitium depicting pairs of riders; the left hand rider of the first two pairs each wear a helmet, carry a round shield and brandish a double-axe or sword respectively. After Gjerstad 1953–73 [A56], IV.2, 483 fig. 147.1.

IV. THE DEVELOPMENT AND GROWTH OF ROME

On three points the literary tradition can be immediately compared with the archaeological evidence. The first is the date of the foundation of Rome. Those who took Aeneas either as the founder or one of the near ancestors of the founders of Rome were bound to date Rome not much after the Trojan war. Such was apparently the choice of Ennius who considered Ilia, Romulus' mother, to be the daughter of Aeneas. He said somewhere in the *Annals* (154 Skutsch) 'septingenti sunt paulo plus aut minus anni, augusto augurio postquam incluta condita Roma est'.[25] The question, of course, is from where he started to count his 700 years. If, as seems probable, he attributed these words to Camillus, he placed the origins of Rome in the early eleventh century B.C. If so, it becomes still more remarkable that Roman historians and antiquarians gave dates for the foundation of Rome in the eighth century B.C.: Fabius Pictor in 748 B.C., Polybius apparently in 751, Atticus (Cicero's friend), followed by Varro, in 753, while the antiquarians who put together the Fasti Capitolini chose 752. The most aberrant date among historians of Rome is 728 B.C., preferred by Fabius' contemporary Cincius Alimentus. The date given by Timaeus, 814 B.C., was apparently dictated by the desire to date the foundations of Carthage and Rome in the same year, that is, it was determined by the date attributed to the foundation of Carthage: it is, however, in broad agreement with Roman dates. The Roman historians were obviously starting from the date of the foundation of the Republic, which was fixed by the list of the consuls (*fasti*) about 509–506 B.C. But why did they attribute a period of 250 years to the monarchy? The length

[25] 'Seven hundred – a little fewer or a little more – are the years since far-famed Rome was founded with august augury.'

of the individual reigns of the seven canonical kings of Rome is not plausible (an average of 35 years for each king) and seems rather artificially concocted. But we simply do not know why Roman tradition chose to fix the date of the birth of Rome in the eighth century. It is easier to explain why Rome was supposed to have a precise foundation date. Though undoubtedly many cities were never founded and simply evolved from one or more previous villages, ritual foundations of cities were known to Etruscans, Greeks and Latins. The Romans, being themselves founders of cities, considered themselves to have been ritually founded. They may even not have been entirely wrong in their surmise. The character of some of the basic Roman institutions (three tribes, thirty *curiae*) presupposes the intervention of some organizing mind at a very early stage. The man who organized Rome into three tribes and thirty *curiae* may be called the founder of Rome. The trouble is that we do not know who he was or when he lived.

Secondly, the literary tradition helps to determine at least certain stages of the gradual extension of the Roman territory in its various aspects. The Romans always made a distinction between the sacred boundary of the city (*urbs*) and the boundary of the *ager Romanus* (territory of Rome). There is no reason to doubt that the distinction goes back to the origins of the city. The oldest sacred boundary (*pomerium*) of the *urbs* seems to have defined a settlement on the Palatine. Tacitus (*Ann.* XII.24) gives some details about it, we do not know on what authority. The Palatine *pomerium* may have coincided with the itinerary of the Luperci who ran round the foot of the hill at their festival in February – or it may have been deduced from it by some speculative antiquarian of the late Republic. Tacitus also states that Forum and Capitol were incorporated in the *pomerium* by Titus Tatius, in Romulus' time, while Livy 1.44.3 states that Quirinal, Viminal and perhaps Esquiline were added by Servius Tullius. The tradition on the Mons Caelius is particularly confusing: the first six kings are involved. There is no further mention in our sources of later extensions of the *pomerium* until Sulla. The *pomerium* came (gradually, one would think) to signify the zone within which the head or heads of the state had civil, not military, power. The centuriate assembly (*comitia centuriata*), which was a military assembly, had to be summoned outside the *pomerium* in the Campus Martius.

It is very difficult to grasp the nature of the relation between the *pomerium* and the Septimontium. In itself the Septimontium was a festival, almost certainly including a procession, which involved sections of the Palatine (Germalus, Palatium) and the Velia, the three sections of the Esquiline (Oppius, Cispius and Fagutal), the Caelian and apparently also the Subura valley betwen Cispius, Oppius and Velia (Festus 458; 476 L). The Septem Montes ('Seven Hills' – plus a valley!) are evidently not the seven traditional hills of Rome (Palatine, Quirinal, Viminal, Esquiline, Caelius, Aventine, Capitol). The Septimontium implies a special bond between three of the seven hills. The bond may have developed before Rome extended to the seven traditional hills, but there is no certainty that it did not develop at a later date inside the larger city. Another ceremony which may or may not point to an otherwise unattested stage in the development of Rome is that mysterious festival of the Argei, the topography of which is accurately described by Varro (*Ling.* v.45). Puppets called Argei were collected from 27 chapels scattered throughout Rome with the exclusion of the Aventine and the Capitol: they were thrown into the Tiber by the Vestal Virgins.

The dimensions of Rome inside the *pomerium* at the end of the Republic have been calculated as 285 ha. Outside the *pomerium* there was the *ager Romanus* which in its turn required yearly purifications. Some information about these allows us to define what is for us the oldest territory of the Roman state. The ceremony of the Ambarvalia ('Around the fields') was carried out between the fifth and the sixth mile from the Forum (Strabo v.3.2, p. 230C) and that of the Terminalia ('Boundary rites') at the sixth mile on the Via Laurentina (Ovid, *Fast.* II.679). The Fossae Cluiliae, which appear in various traditions as the border of Rome on the Via Latina, were at five miles from the Forum (cf. Livy 1.23). An approximate calculation gives about 150 km.^{2} to the oldest known *ager Romanus*. Naturally there were gains and losses: we know that the so-called 'septem pagi' ('seven cantons') were a bone of contention with the Etruscans. But at the end of the monarchy, when Rome had absorbed more or less finally many neighbouring communities, such as Alba Longa, Crustumerium, Nomentum, Collatia, Corniculum, Ficulea, Cameria, etc., the Roman territory amounted to something like 800 km.^{2} It was either then or later distributed among sixteen 'rustic' tribes (as opposed to four 'urban' tribes) which received their individual names mainly from the leading clan (*gens*) owning land in the territory of each (p. 179).

Thirdly, and finally, the literary evidence allows us to say something more (but not much) about the ties which connected Rome with the other Latin-speaking communities.[26] From time immemorial Rome had belonged to a Latin League. When this League was entirely under Roman control, say in the late fourth century B.C., its centre was in the temple of Iuppiter Latiaris on the Mons Albanus. The priests for the annual festival of the League were called Cabenses Sacerdotes, Cabum being reputed to be a village in the neighbourhood of Alba Longa, the city of the ancestors of Romulus allegedly destroyed by the Romans

[26] For a further discussion (with some differences of view) see Chap. 6.

Fig. 30. *Denarius* of P. Accoleius Lariscolus (43 B.C.) with bust of Diana Nemorensis on the obverse, triple cult statue of Diana Nemorensis on the reverse (*RRC* 486.1).

under Tullus Hostilius (Pliny, *HN* III.64). As we mentioned (p. 65), the membership of the League consisted traditionally of 30 *populi* or communities that were entitled to share the meat of the sacrifices and refrained from fighting each other during the festival (Dion. Hal. *Ant. Rom.* IV.49; Macrob. *Sat.* 1.16.16). In addition to the temple of Iuppiter Latiaris, the city of Lavinium played a special role in this League. 'Sacra principia' (the 'sacred origins') of the Romans, the gods Penates, were kept there (*ILS* 5004; Varro, *Ling.* V.144). It is obvious that this later situation preserved elements of earlier times when Rome was not yet the ruling power in Latium. But we do not know whether in those earlier times the League centred on the Mons Albanus pursued definite political aims; nor do we know what was the exact relation between the sanctuary of the Mons Albanus and other Latin sanctuaries, such as the one 'ad caput aquae Ferentinae' ('at the source of the Ferentine water'), apparently not far away (Festus 276 L), or the other of Diana in a wood near Aricia (Fig. 30). The latter may have become an anti-Roman centre at the beginning of the fifth century B.C. (this is at least what one can infer from an inscription quoted by Cato *Orig.* fr. 58 P (p. 272f)). We have, however, definite indications that under the two Tarquinii and Servius Tullius the Romans succeeded for a time in controlling a large portion of Latium. Servius Tullius was legitimately credited on the basis of a surviving document with having established a Latin sanctuary of Diana just outside the *pomerium* of Rome on the Aventine (Dion. Hal. *Ant. Rom.* IV.26; Varro, *Ling.* V.43; *ILS* 4907), which was meant to attract the Latins to Rome and perhaps represented a 'zona franca' where they could trade under divine protection. Even at the time of the beginning of the Republic, in their first treaty with Carthage (if Polybius III.22 is correct in his dating of it), the Romans claimed a hegemonic position in Latium (p. 253f). More precisely, the Romans divided the peoples of Latium into three groups: those directly incorporated in the Roman state (not mentioned as such); those who were 'subject' (Ardea, Antium, Circeii, Tarracina and perhaps Lavinium are singled out); and those who were not subject, but from whom the Carthaginians had to keep away all the same (no names given). The young Republic was evidently not capable of maintaining such claims for long. Not much later it had to make a treaty of alliance with the Latins, the 'Cassian treaty' (*foedus Cassianum*), on a different basis (p. 274). The text reported by Cato on the league centred in the sanctuary of Diana near Aricia may well represent a stage between the Roman claims in the treaty with Carthage and the more modest settlement of the *foedus Cassianum*. In relation to individual Latin cities a variety of settlements (with a corresponding variety of legal formulae) must have developed during the expansion of Rome in Latium. Only a few traces remain. The special position maintained by the small city of Gabii in sacred law may go back to the monarchic period: the *ager Gabinus* ('Gabine territory') held a middle position between the *ager Romanus* and the *ager peregrinus* ('alien territory') (Varro, *Ling.* v.33). The Twelve Tables imply pre-existing privileges for the mysterious communities of Forctes and Sanates (about whom the later Romans remembered almost nothing; cf. Festus 474 L).

We may end this section by saying that so far no archaeological support has been found for the self-assured Roman tradition that the Latins of Romulus soon combined with the Sabines of Titus Tatius. Tradition also suggests, though not very consistently, that the Sabine settlement was on the Quirinal, that Quirinus was a Sabine god (Varro, *Ling.* v.74; but cf. Livy 1.33) and that 'Quirites' was a second name of the Romans because of their Sabine component. The notion that Quirinus was Sabine was so deep-rooted that in the third century B.C. the Roman magistrates decided to call Quirina the tribe which was created to incorporate the Sabine inhabitants of Reate, Amiternum and Nursia (p. 431). A few details of Roman religious institutions may support the notion of a Sabine Quirinal hill. Those archaic priests, the Salii (p. 109), were divided into two groups, one called Salii Palatini, the other Salii Collini (where *collis* ('hill') seems to stand for *Quirinalis*). There are traces of an 'Old Capitol' (Capitolium Vetus) on the Quirinal as opposed to the true Capitolium (Varro, *Ling.* v.158; Mart. v.22 and VII.73). One can go further. The Luperci were divided into two groups, Fabiani and Quinctiales. The division, unlike that of the Salii, is according to clans (*gentes*), not places. But the *gens Fabia* is known to have had cultic connexions with the Quirinal (Livy v.46.2; 52.3) and may therefore be assumed to have represented the Sabines in the Lupercalia. The case, however, for a Sabine settlement on the Quirinal is not very strong. It cannot be reinforced by linguistic arguments. The Sabines spoke a dialect of the Umbro-Oscan group which was clearly distinguished from Latin. They came, no doubt, to influence Latin (as they themselves were influenced in their speech by Latin). It is probable that such common words in Latin as *lupus* ('wolf'), *bos* ('bull/cow'), *scrofa* ('sow'), *rufus* ('red') (instead of the undocumented *lucus, vos, scroba* and of the existing alternative *ruber*) are a sign of Sabine infiltration. But Titus Tatius is not needed to explain all this. In fact, if Quirinus and Quirinal had been authentic Sabine words we would have them in the form Pirinus, Pirinal. It is also very uncertain whether the terminological distinction between *montes* and *colles* for the hills of Rome (Mons Palatinus but Collis Quirinalis) should be treated as evidence for the co-existence of Latins and Sabines on the hills of Rome. At the moment the primeval fusion of Sabines and Latins must be considered a respectable traditional datum for which there is no strong support (if it is a fact) nor obvious explanation (if it is a legend).

V. THE ROMAN KINGS

Beyond this point we are left more or less alone with the literary tradition, the only one which gives us a story of the Roman kings. This tradition, which is for us chiefly represented by writers of the Caesarean and Augustan period, Diodorus, Dionysius of Halicarnassus and Livy, is remarkably consistent. It seems to go back in its essentials to the first historians of Rome who wrote in Greek at the end of the third century B.C., Q. Fabius Pictor and L. Cincius Alimentus (p. 5). The vital question is from *where* these early annalists (as they were called) derived their information about the monarchic period of Rome. Roman historians consulted, or at least knew of, some documents for early Rome (p. 13). We can add the treaty with the neighbouring Gabii written on a shield (Dion. Hal. *Ant. Rom.* iv.58.4; Festus 48 L) to the *lex sacra* concerning the temple of Diana on the Aventine (Dion. Hal. *Ant. Rom.* iv.26.5) and the treaty between Rome and Carthage (Polyb. iii.22) already mentioned. But such texts were not numerous enough to represent an essential element of the tradition. Some may in fact have been rediscovered (like the text of the first treaty with Carthage) when the tradition had already been established in its essential features. In addition, certain existing sacred objects were deemed to be connected with certain legends and therefore helped to keep them alive. Such were the Pila Horatia (interpreted as the 'Horatian Column' or the 'Horatian Spears') and the Tigillum Sororium (interpreted as the 'Sister's Beam') in the saga of the Horatii and Curiatii. But such objects seldom constituted the origin of the legend: more often they presupposed it and therefore they do not serve to explain it. All in all, documentary evidence seems to have played a minor part in the formation of the tradition about Roman origins. The Roman annalists of the late Republic were rather more conscious of being the continuators of the annals of the pontiffs. We are told that the *pontifex maximus* published a list of events every year. This pontifical registration was finally discontinued under the *pontifex maximus* P. Mucius Scaevola *c.* 130 B.C. and was edited in eighty books at an uncertain date which can hardly be later than Augustus (p. 6f). We are also told that the Pontifical Chronicle in its edited form contained stories about the origins of Rome (which are quoted by the anonymous *Origo gentis Romanae* and by the *SHA Tac.* 1.1). If we accept this information as authentic, we must also accept the consequence that the Pontifical Chronicle devoted at least four of its eighty books to the Alban prehistory of Rome. As no one can believe that the Alban pontiffs transferred their historical registrations to Rome when Alba disappeared, we have to assume that somebody (perhaps even the editor of the Pontifical Chronicle in eighty books himself) added the prehistory of Rome to the later events in order to make the Chronicle more interesting. This is only the most conspicuous element of uncertainty in a Chronicle about which almost everything else is uncertain (p. 20f). We do not know when it was started, we have very little information about what it contained, but above all we do not know how much it was really used by the historical annalists of the late Republic, some of whom, if not all, wrote before the pontifical registrations were collected in eighty books. In any case the annalistic form which the pontiffs used for their registrations is based on the list of the Roman consuls: the monarchic section looks like a later addition. The Pontifical Chronicle is hardly an answer to the question as to where the historians of the late Republic found their stories about early Rome. Nor are we made much wiser by our scanty information about the songs (*carmina*) the ancient Romans sang, while banqueting, in praise of their ancestors. These songs were no longer sung at the time of Cato the Censor.[27] It is therefore not surprising that our sources are divided on the point whether the *carmina* had been sung by adults or children. Dionysius (*Ant. Rom.* 1.79.10; VIII.62) seems to indicate Romulus and Coriolanus as specific subjects for such *carmina*. Acquaintance with other cultures which have preserved their 'historical' ballads better does not encourage us to take them as scrupulous records of events. Besides, we are struck by the fact that not much in the tradition about early Rome looks 'poetic'. The exception is represented by some of the stories about Romulus, the fight between Horatii and Curiatii and the rape of Lucretia (a counterpart to the rape of the Sabine women) at the end of the monarchy. But even for these 'poetic' episodes a poetic source is not the most obvious origin. Livy (1.24.1) was uncertain whether the Horatii or the Curiatii represented the Romans in the famous fight. A ballad would not have left this in doubt. The importance of the *carmina*

---

[27] Cic. *Brut.* 75; *Tusc.* IV.3; Varro, *De Vita p.R.* II *ap.* Non. p. 107L.

(which have played a conspicuous role in modern discussions on early Rome from B. G. Niebuhr to G. De Sanctis) is as questionable as the importance of the Pontifical Chronicle.

Greek historians, as we have already implied, began to look at Rome in the late fifth century B.C., if not earlier. The Roman historians of later centuries could and did read them. But the first Greek historian to give an organized account of early Rome was the Sicilian Timaeus, writing in Athens in the first part of the third century B.C. He was in no better position to know about the eighth to sixth centuries B.C. than the Romans were two generations later. It would be surprising if Timaeus revealed to the Romans something they did not know, though no doubt he taught them how to write history in Greek. It is therefore not surprising to hear from Plutarch (*Rom.*3) that Fabius Pictor followed the Greek Diocles of Peparethus in his account of the foundation of Rome. Assuming that Plutarch is correct about the priority of Diocles, this simply means that Diocles registered the tradition prevailing in Rome itself in a way Fabius found acceptable. Accounts of Roman history by Greek historians must not, however, be confused with occasional allusions to Rome in the chronicles of neighbouring cities. Roman historians became aware that some of the chronicles of neighbours of Rome (both Greek and Etruscan) contained references to Roman events which had affected them. Some writers of Cumae in Campania told stories about the intervention in Latium by a tyrant of Cumae at the end of the sixth century (Dion. Hal. *Ant. Rom.* VII.3ff; cf. Ath. XII.528d). Etruscan annals or histories are mentioned by Pliny, *HN* II.140 and by Censorinus, *DN* 17.6. Etruscan evidence was tapped by the Emperor Claudius (*ILS* 212) and his near contemporary Verrius Flaccus (Festus 38 L), perhaps through translations into Latin. It contained some information about the kings of Rome. This acquaintance, to judge from Dionysius and Claudius, started late and was very limited. The neighbours of Rome did not supply much material to the Roman tradition.

We have finally to consider the contribution which clan traditions may have made to the history of early Rome. The Roman aristocratic *gentes* certainly preserved memories and records of their eminent ancestors. The discovery of the epigraphic *elogia Tarquiniensia* (p. 300) proved that in the Augustan age Etruscan aristocratic families also preserved recollections of their own ancestors. Some of these Etruscan aristocrats had by then been mingling with Roman aristocrats for centuries. Once again, however, we are disappointed in our expectations about the monarchic period. With the exception of some information about Mastarna (see below) there is nothing in what the Romans knew or thought they knew about their kings which bears the mark of an Etruscan aristocratic source. More unexpectedly, the Roman *gentes* which played a leading part in the Republic had little to say about the monarchic period and claimed almost no role in it for themselves. The Fabii who believed themselves to be as old as Romulus and had some right to think so, as the existence of the Luperci Fabiani shows, had nothing to say about their ancestors under the kings. The Valerii thought that they had come to Rome from the Sabine countryside with Titus Tatius, but did not make their own first big public appearance until the foundation of the Republic, that is, with the consulate of P. Valerius Poplicola. The other great clan, the Claudii, firmly maintained, with the probability of being correct, that they had migrated to Rome after the fall of the monarchy about 504 B.C. These great clans either did not have or chose not to have any responsibility for the events of the monarchy. The only exception are the Marcii who were proud of their namesake King Ancus Marcius and put him and his uncle Numa Pompilius on the coins they minted for the Roman state in the first century B.C. Yet even in the case of the Marcii there is no sign that they helped substantially to shape the vulgate about Numa and Ancus Marcius. On the whole the events and individuals of the monarchic period are outside the main stream of the Roman aristocratic tradition. A Iulius was said to have announced Romulus' ascent to heaven (apotheosis), a Valerius was credited with the position of the first *fetialis* or priest in charge of war and peace. This is not much. We may aptly add at this point that in the late Republic a list was made of the noble families which claimed to be of Trojan origin and to have moved from Alba to Rome under the first three kings. Altogether we must admit that we do not yet know how the Roman tradition about the monarchic period took shape.

This is why we cannot be sure about anything the tradition tells us of the first three successors of Romulus (Numa Pompilius, Tullus Hostilius, Ancus Marcius). We also have great difficulty in making up our minds about the events of the last (?) three kings (the two Tarquinii and, between them, Servius Tullius) who, being nearer to the foundation of the Republic, had a better chance of being remembered correctly. The end of the monarchy in Rome, like the beginning of the monarchy among the ancient Hebrews, may in itself have been transformed beyond recognition by unreliable details, yet it marks a new era in historiographical terms: better chronology and constitutional continuity make tradition more reliable. In any case the monarchy did end.

However, the tradition about the Sabine Numa Pompilius, the Latin Tullus Hostilius and the partly Sabine Ancus Marcius cannot have been entirely invented. Only the first is a coherent figure. He is represented as the creator of the religious institutions of Rome (including at least part of the *flamines*, the Salii, the Vestals, the *pontifices* and the calendar). The second is a warrior who, however improbably, allowed a war between Rome and Alba Longa to be turned into a contest between three Roman and three Alban brothers (the Horatii and Curiatii). The third is a peaceful man who conquered and destroyed the neighbouring towns of Politorium, Tellenae and Ficana, annexed the Janiculum hill to the city, planted a colony at Ostia and established the first prison (*carcer*) in the city. The coherence of Numa and the incoherence of his successors are not explained by taking them as gods or heroes. It is not altogether impossible that the reform of the calendar goes back to a king Numa and that the elimination (if not the total destruction) of Alba as a Latin power happened under a Tullus. An expansion towards Ostia under Ancus Marcius is credible even if the permanent settlement at Ostia is not earlier than the fourth century B.C. and Politorium, if properly identified with the settlement near Castel di Decima, cannot have been destroyed so early.

L. Tarquinius nicknamed Priscus, Servius Tullius and L. Tarquinius nicknamed Superbus are placed in a more recognizable historical context, which is Greco-Etruscan. Tradition has it that Tarquinius Priscus was the son of the Corinthian Demaratus who had emigrated to Etruria and married in Tarquinii. The arrival and fortunes of Demaratus' son in Rome look likely enough in relation to what we know from elsewhere about aristocrats trying their luck in neighbouring cities. Emigration of Greeks to Etruria is equally plausible. An archaic inscription of Tarquinii (*TLE* 155) referring to 'Rutile Hipukrates' (Rutilus Hippocrates, a combination of a Latin and of a Greek name in Etruscan dress) opens up speculations about a man of Greek origin who may have reached Tarquinii after having passed through Rome, whereas Tarquinius, the son of a Greek, reached Rome through Tarquinii. The colourful wife of Tarquinius, Tanaquil, whom tradition presents as an expert in Etruscan lore, seems plausible in that society of adventurers. It is another matter when it comes to believing that Tarquinius doubled the Roman cavalry or that he was murdered by a faction of the sons of Ancus Marcius and succeeded by his protégé Servius Tullius. In some cases tradition wavered between the two Tarquins, for instance about the foundation of the tripartite temple which established the supremacy of the new (?) triad Iuppiter-Iuno-Minerva on the Capitol. There seems to be some support for the tradition that under both Tarquinii Rome controlled most of the Latins and at least some of the Etruscans. Admittedly Livy is far more reticent on this matter than Dionysius of Halicarnassus. But the first treaty with Carthage seems to confirm what Dionysius claims. Furthermore, an appendix to Hesiod's *Theogony* states that Latins ruled over the Etruscans (l. 1015). It is not easy to find another situation to which this strange statement would apply.[28]

Servius Tullius, a Latin king and reformer thrown in between two

[28] See further p. 253f.

Etruscans, is too improbable a figure to have been invented. His name suggested (we do not know how early) a tale of servile origins and of special luck (*fortuna*). Some of his real achievements increased his qualifications for being treated as a second Romulus. Hence his twofold aspect – of an Italic mythical figure and of a Greek political reformer. One of the best-documented facts of his reign seems to be the foundation of a sanctuary of Diana on the Aventine as a meeting place with the other Latins. The sanctuary (originally around an altar (*ara*)) preserved the text of a pact between Servius and the Latins (Dion. Hal. *Ant. Rom.* IV.26). Furthermore, the *lex arae Dianae in Aventino* ('statute of the altar of Diana on the Aventine') became the model for the regulations of later sanctuaries. The cult statue of this sanctuary has been shown to go back to a sixth-century type, exactly as stated by Strabo IV.1.5, p. 180C, who derives it from Massalia (Fig. 31; cf. p. 267).

Above all, tradition makes Servius Tullius the great reformer who superimposed on the three tribes and thirty *curiae* of the Romulean order a new division of the citizens into five *classes* and 193 or 194 centuries according to wealth. Military obligations were fixed on the new basis. The rather simple army of Romulus, divided into a uniform cavalry and a uniform infantry, tradition tells us, was supposedly replaced by an army of the hoplitic type in which there were various kinds of infantry soldiers and possibly two types of cavalrymen, one with two horses and the other with one (Granius Licinianus, p. 2 Flemisch). This is clearly what existed in Rome from the fourth century onwards. The general assembly of the Romans by *curiae*, though not by then abolished, was considered less important than the new assembly according to *classes*: juniors and seniors of each 'class' were summoned to approve laws and to act as an appeal tribunal in the so-called centuriate assembly (*comitia centuriata*). As the first class included 40 centuries of juniors and 40 centuries of seniors out of 193 or 194 centuries of the whole organization, and each *centuria* had one vote, Servius Tullius reputedly put the state in the hands of the wealthy. Tradition also recounts that Servius Tullius introduced coinage

Fig. 31. *Denarius* of L. Hostilius Saserna (48 B.C.) depicting the archaic cult statue of Artemis at Massalia (*RRC* 448.3).

(a piece of information already available to Timaeus) and took a census of the population; he extended the urban territory of Rome and divided it into four quarters; he completed its fortification – the Servian walls – and divided the territory of the Roman state outside the urban zone into local departments or tribes.

Simple reflection shows that what was in fact the centuriate organization of the middle Republic cannot be retrojected wholesale into the sixth century B.C. Coinage of the type attributed to Servius was perhaps known at Gela in Sicily more or less at the time in which Servius is supposed to have lived,[29] but Rome – not alone in this – seems to have done without coins until the third century B.C. In the same way most of the archaeological evidence we can safely date takes us down to the fourth century B.C. for the oldest circuit of the Roman walls. However, we shall see that there are indications that a simpler form of the centuriate organization existed in the sixth century. Traces of a more primitive system of fortifications have also been identified.

The great reforming king Servius Tullius may indeed have been murdered, as tradition has it, by his daughter Tullia and her husband L. Tarquinius Superbus, either a son or a grandson of Tarquinius Priscus. However embellished by successive layers of popular and literary elaboration, the career of Tarquinius Superbus makes sense in the context of sixth-century tyranny. The transition from Servius Tullius to Tarquinius Superbus reminds us of the transition at Athens from Solon to Pisistratus. There may even be some truth in the story of how Tarquinius managed to become master of Gabii with the co-operation of one of his sons who posed as an enemy of his father and was accepted, according to custom, by the men of Gabii as their military leader. The text of the treaty between Gabii and Rome was dated to the reign of Tarquinius by ancient scholars who were still able to read it (Dion. Hal. *Ant. Rom.* IV.58).

The prevailing account of the end of the monarchy had difficulty in defining the attitude of the neighbouring powers to the overthrow of the Tarquinii. These powers included Aristodemus, the Greek tyrant of Cumae; the Latin League, which saw its chance of recovering its freedom from Rome; and finally those Etruscan cities which took no pleasure in the expansion of Rome, albeit under Etruscan kings. The annalistic tradition presented Porsenna, the sovereign of Clusium, as the champion of those Etruscans who would have liked Tarquinius back in Rome (p. 257f). According to this tradition the bravery of Horatius Cocles, Mucius Scaevola and Cloelia persuaded Porsenna to abandon the enterprise. He then turned against the Latins and was finally defeated at the battle of Aricia by the joint forces of the Latin League and of Aristodemus. But

---

[29] Ampolo 1974[B196], 382–8. On the Timaeus passage see further p. 417.

historians of the first century A.D. discovered somewhere, perhaps in Etruscan sources, that Porsenna had actually taken Rome and imposed humiliating conditions (Tac. *Hist.* III.72; Pliny, *HN* XXXIV.139). Porsenna, however, did not bring back the Tarquinii and obviously did not last long as master of Rome. His final defeat, resulting from the intervention of Aristodemus, seems to have been registered in the chronicles of Cumae. The probability that Porsenna was ultimately eliminated by the alliance of the Latins with Aristodemus throws an entirely different light on the end of the monarchy in Rome. It may still be true (as Roman tradition says) that a conspiracy of the Roman aristocrats (of which L. Iunius Brutus and L. Tarquinius Collatinus, two relatives of the king, are said to have been the leaders) threw Tarquinius out. But Porsenna's army must have imposed a new Etruscan ruler on Rome. Whether the Romans had time to elect their first consuls before the arrival of Porsenna becomes of course doubtful. The Romans simplified the process of the installation of the Republic in order to obliterate the shame of having been liberated from Porsenna by the joint forces of the other Latins and of Aristodemus of Cumae.

The dedication of the temple of Iuppiter on the Capitol by the consul M. Horatius Pulvillus is the first act of the new republican government we can consider certain. It was already a pillar of Roman chronology at the end of the fourth century B.C., as an inscription by Cn. Flavius quoted by Pliny (*HN* XXXIII.19; p. 627 n. 13) shows. With the fluctuation of a few years, due to the uncertainty of the consular list in its very beginning, it tells us that there were yearly ruling magistrates in Rome (later generally known as consuls) about 509–507 B.C. This is, approximately, the date of the end of the monarchy. Porsenna (or his nominee) is very probably only the last of a series of kings of Rome which the annalistic tradition did not register, while it includes a King Romulus who is probably an entirely mythical figure. Titus Tatius may well have been an authentic monarch who was later inserted into the mythical period of Romulus as co-regent. But the most interesting name we must now consider as a possibly forgotten monarch of Rome is that of Mastarna.

In the Roman tradition he appears first in a speech of the Emperor Claudius (*ILS* 212), where he is considered identical with Servius Tullius. In the Etruscan tradition Mastarna (or Macstrna) appears much earlier in a series of scenes painted and inscribed in the François tomb of Vulci which are most usually dated in the fourth or third century B.C. (Fig. 32). Mastarna liberates Caeles Vibenna, while Aulus Vibenna kills a man apparently from Falerii, and Marcus Camillus (or Camitilius; 'Camitlnas' in the inscription) kills a Gnaeus Tarquinius Romanus (?) ('Rumach'). Caeles and Aulus Vibenna reappear elsewhere as 'condottieri': they are sometimes associated with Romulus (Varro, *Ling.* v.46;

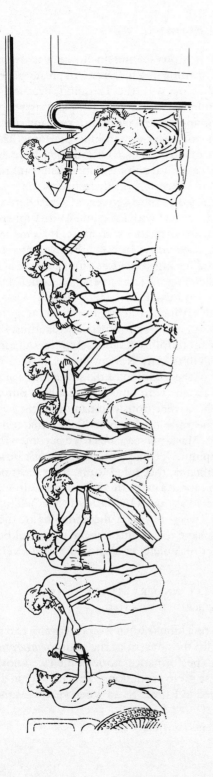

Fig. 32. Wall paintings from the Tomba François at Vulci (*c.* 300 B.C.?). From the left: Macstrna frees Caile Vipinas, Larth Ulthes stabs Laris Papathnas Velznach, Rasce strikes Pesna Arcmsnas Sveamach(?) and Avle Vipinas kills Venthi Cal [· ·] plsachs(?). In a separate scene Marce Camitlnas moves to kill Cneve Tarchunies Rumach. After F. Coarelli, *D·Arch.* ser. 3.2 (1983), 54 fig. 7 and 47 fig. 4.

Festus 38 L); and the name of Mons Caelius in Rome was deemed to
honour Caeles Vibenna. The painting of Vulci seems to presuppose some
connexion of the brothers Vibenna with the Tarquinii, because one of
the men in the scene is a Tarquinius from Rome. The painting represents
some historical episode involving several cities, but perhaps centred in
Vulci. Gnaeus Tarquinius is not necessarily a king of Rome (the two
traditional kings were both called Lucius): he too may have been a
'condottiere', as one of the sons of Tarquinius Superbus is said to have
been. The historicity of Aulus Vibenna, and therefore of the group to
which he belonged, was confirmed by the discovery of a bucchero vase in
Veii of the sixth century B.C. inscribed with the name Avile Vipiiennas.[30]
Mastarna (Macstrna) is not an ordinary Etruscan name. It seems to be an
Etruscan form of the Latin *magister*. Just as the Romans turned
'Lucumon', the Etruscan word for king (*lauχume*), into a personal name,
so the Etruscans may have taken *magister* to be a personal name. Mastarna
would therefore be another band chief (= *magister populi*?) who, after
having operated under Caelius Vibenna in various cities, migrated to
Rome, according to the Etruscan tradition followed by Claudius. It is left
to us to decide whether we want to follow Claudius' sources in identifying Mastarna with Servius Tullius. Any Roman historian or Etruscan
historian under the influence of the tradition of the seven kings of Rome
was compelled to identify Mastarna with one of these kings. But we are
under no such obligation. The adventurous companion of the brothers
Vibenna is so different from the traditional Servius Tullius that it appears
prudent to keep the two apart. Mastarna may well have become a ruler in
Rome in the age of the Tarquinii. We may consequently ask ourselves
whether Aulus and Caeles Vibenna, too, ruled Rome for a short period.
There was an obscure tradition about a man Olus who supposedly gave his
name to the Capitol, interpreted as *caput Oli* ('head of Olus'). This Olus
was a king according to the *Chronogr.a.* 354. Aulus and Olus are the same
name, and the tradition may have had Aulus Vibenna in mind because
Olus is called 'Vulcentanus' ('of Vulci') by Arnobius, *Adv. Nat.* VI.7.

VI. THE SOCIAL, POLITICAL AND RELIGIOUS STRUCTURES OF THE REGAL PERIOD

Not everyone could claim to be a king (*rex*) in Rome. Royalty had sacred
aspects, it was proclaimed with the consent of the gods (*inauguratio*) and
was accompanied by religious performances about which we know very
little. The importance of these sacred functions explains why in a sense
monarchy was never abolished in Rome. Even when yearly magistrates

---

[30] Pallottino 1939[B245], 455–7.

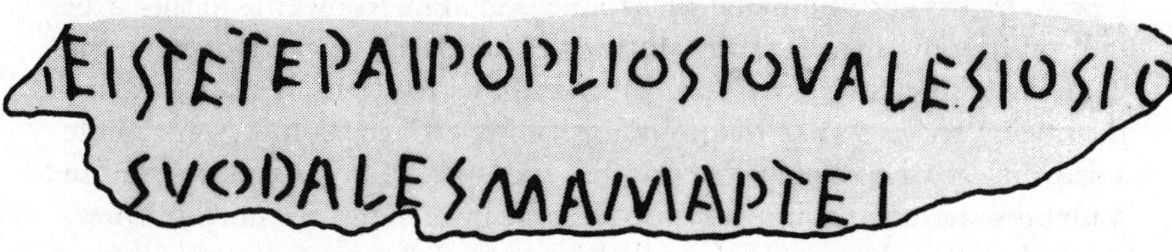

Fig. 33. 'Publius Valerius' inscription from Satricum (*c.* 500 B.C.?).

had replaced the *rex*, a life *rex* bearing the title of *rex sacrorum* or *sacrificulus* remained in the old royal house (Regia) to perform religious acts while being debarred from the ordinary political career (p. 610f). He was later displaced from the Regia, but not deprived of all his functions, by the *pontifex maximus*. Kingship was not hereditary, and its priestly functions were subordinated to its military aspect. As far as we can judge, the majority of the kings of Rome were band chiefs, not necessarily of Roman, or even of Latin, extraction, who persuaded or coerced the local aristocracy to accept their rule. There was probably only a thin dividing line between the band chief called in to help an existing *rex* and a band chief called in to replace him and therefore to rule in his stead. Tradition seems to imply that Tarquinius Superbus had not been properly inducted. Others – such as Mastarna (if he is not identical with Servius Tullius), Aulus Vibenna and Porsenna – may never have obtained full religious confirmation. Such band chiefs might try their luck in more than one city. We saw a Gnaeus Tarquinius (explicitly called Roman) active in Etruria, perhaps at Vulci, while Mastarna and the two Vibennas are on record both in Vulci and in Rome: Aulus Vibenna also reappears in Veii. An epigraphical confirmation of this situation has now been provided for the period around 500 B.C. by the so-called Lapis Satricanus,[31] a dedication in Satricum by the followers of a Publius Valerius (Fig. 33). The text says:

> . . . iei steterai Popliosio Valesiosio
> suodales Mamartei

It is tempting to recognize in this Publius Valerius the P. Valerius Poplicola who, according to Roman tradition, played a part in the foundation of the Roman Republic and even replaced the original leaders Brutus and Collatinus in consolidating it. This inscription is not complete, and we have the choice between referring the word 'sodales' either to Publius Valerius (in the genitive) or to the god Mamers (in the dative). In the former interpretation we have a dedication by the 'sodales'

[31] Stibbe et al. 1980[B263].

(companions) of Publius Valerius to the god Mamers (Mars). In the latter interpretation (which assumes a word like 'socii' in the lacuna at the beginning) the followers ('socii') of Publius Valerius, who were also members ('sodales') of a religious corporation for the cult of Mars, made a dedication to another god or goddess (possibly Mater Matuta, in whose precincts the inscription was found). We prefer the former interpretation, but the ultimate meaning is not very different in either version: followers of Publius Valerius appear in a prominent position, and possibly with military connotations, at Satricum. If the identification of Publius Valerius happens to be correct we must face the paradox that a band chief in Satricum contributed to the introduction of the new republican regime at Rome. This early republican regime was neither able nor perhaps anxious to avoid interference from band chiefs. The best Roman tradition has it that the band chief Attus Clausus, the founder of the fortunes of the clan of the Claudii, migrated with his retinue to Rome from the Sabine country just in time to reinforce the still shaky new Republic. (Later tradition made the Claudii come to Rome under Romulus: what else could one expect from the ancestors of the future Claudian emperors?) The Fabii still acted as band chiefs in a famous private war with the Etruscans a few decades after the foundation of the Republic (p. 297). Their defeat may have saved Rome from a Fabian monarchy. Later, in about 460 B.C., the Sabine chieftain Appius Herdonius managed to occupy the Capitol by a surprise attack (p. 286). By ousting him, with the help of the Latins, the Romans spared themselves another Sabine king.

The phenomenon of the band chiefs which tradition, reasonably enough, had some difficulty in reconciling with the rigid and schematic structure of the 'Romulean' state must be connected with one of the most striking features of Central Italian society of the eighth to sixth centuries B.C., the rise of the *gentes*. As we have mentioned, epigraphical evidence allows us to perceive the growth of a peculiar onomastic system whereby a person (most often a man) is designated by two names, the personal name (in Rome, *praenomen*) and the name of the clan to which he belonged (in Rome, *nomen gentile*). Even if formally the *nomen gentile* might appear as an ordinary patronymic (Servius Tullius = Servius son of Tullus), it was taken to indicate membership of a wider group than the nuclear family. The *nomen gentile* was displayed in identical form not only by all the theoretical descendants of a common ancestor, but also by certain clients who had joined the group in a subordinate position and apparently without blood relationship. The emigration of the Claudii is paradigmatic of what a *gens* could do: the clients of the *gens Claudia* obtained land in Rome through the agency of their band chief Attus Clausus. If our evidence is not misleading, there was a close relationship between bands (*sodales*), clients and *gentes*. The prestige and attraction of a band chief would make the fortunes of a *gens*: the band chief would both establish the reputation of his kin and reward his clients with land, booty and employment. It is not impossible that the *gens* as an institution acquired consistency before the urban development of the archaic age, as P. Bonfante[32] and others have assumed. But we see the dual onomastic system characteristic of the *gens* gaining strength concurrently with the urbanization of Central Italy. In Rome it is interesting to observe that only Romulus, among the kings, is without the *nomen gentile*. The other point worth noticing is that as soon as the system of organization by *gentes* gathered momentum (we do not know from what centre), it spread through all social classes. There is no firm evidence to show that in Rome only the aristocracy was organized by *gentes*. Even less do we know of a time in which the *gentes* could be identified with that special type of hereditary aristocracy which was known as the patriciate. The isolated polemical utterance attributed in Livy to his patrician opponents by a plebeian of the fourth century B.C., 'vos (patricios) solos gentem habere' ('that you (patricians) alone have a clan') (Livy x.8. 9), cannot be turned into a statement of fact, 'plebeii gentes non habent' ('plebeians do not have clans'), as modern students are apt to do. At best the sentence represents Livy's notion of archaic Roman society. In societies where the powerful become more powerful by asserting kinship ties and annexing volunteers, the weaker groups may well try to react by asserting in their turn kinship solidarity in the form of gentilicial ties. Later on the reaction of the weaker took the form of the organization of the plebs.

Correspondingly, there is no evidence that land or other ordinary property was owned by the *gens*, though the *gens* obtained some second-ary rights of inheritance in the absence of closer relatives. We hear (which is a different matter) of gentilician cemeteries and cults – also of delibera-tions by a *gens* with a view to consolidating a common style of life. But we do not know who summoned the *gentiles* (members of a *gens*) to an assembly. The leader of a clan (*princeps gentis*), unless one means a band chief like Publius Valerius or Attus Clausus, is a modern fiction. Together with the notion of clan ownership any illusion of catching Roman private property *in statu nascendi* must be abandoned. Existence of private landownership and instability of the upper class must have been connected. The band chiefs and their followers gained or lost land held as private property. Other people found an incentive to move from city to city in trade and professional activities. We know of Etruscan (and perhaps Greek) artists in archaic Rome. The onomastic evidence seems to confirm this social mobility. We have already noted Demaratus from

---

[32] Bonfante 1925–33[G177], I.5ff; VI.37ff; 1926[G178], 18ff; 1958[G179], 67ff.

Corinth, Rutile Hipukrates of Tarquinii, Tite Latine in Etruscan Veii and a Kalaturus Phapenas (Calator Fabius?) at Caere (p. 81). We also have evidence of long-standing connexions of the Claudii with Etruria, and even with Etruscan elements in Corsica.[33] The growth of powerful *gentes* must therefore have resulted in inequality in land holdings. This seems to be confirmed by the names of the sixteen oldest tribes (or divisions) of the Roman territory which almost all bear gentilician names (Pollia, Fabia, Claudia, etc.). The families of a specific *gens*, together with their *clientes*, evidently owned a great deal of land in the tribal district bearing its name. Nothing, however, suggests that the territory of the tribe had been the collective property of a *gens*.

There was in Rome the notion that two *iugera* of land (= 5047 m.[2]) represented the *heredium* (Varro, *Rust.* 1.10.2; Pliny, *HN* XVIII.7); Romulus was supposed to have given two *iugera* to each citizen, and later two *iugera* were the smallest portion of land given to each settler at the foundation of a Roman colony (Livy VIII.21.11 for Anxur (Tarracina)). Two *iugera* may have been enough to feed one man in the rather primitive conditions of archaic Italian agriculture; they would not keep a family. The notion that the standard land holding was two *iugera* (and therefore represented the *heredium*, the land one leaves to one's children) may be a survival from the period in which stock-raising on communal land (*ager publicus*) was the main activity; alternatively, it may indicate the minimum of agricultural land which one had the moral obligation to transmit to one's children. Some ancient lawyers who were puzzled by the word *heredium* suggested that *heredium* was the *hortus*, the kitchen-garden, as opposed to agricultural land (Pliny, *HN* XIX.50), but this does not solve the problem. There is no firm evidence that in Rome private land-property was ever limited to two *iugera* or that it was inalienable. When the two *iugera* appear as the basis of colonial distribution of land, we have no evidence to prove that the colonist was prevented from purchasing and owning more land; in any case he must have had the use of extra land if he had a family.

Archaic Rome clearly had its aristocrats, like any other city of Latium or Etruria, though perhaps not so flamboyant. These aristocrats inscribed their names (personal or *gentile*) on their valuables and exchanged gifts, though the most ancient and famous of the gift inscriptions, the Fibula Praenestina with its inscription 'Manius made me for Numerius', is now under suspicion of being a nineteenth-century forgery (p. 73). On one jar we read of toasts men proposed to women (Fig. 34), probably their wives, who, like Etruscan wives, but unlike Greek wives, took part in symposia.[34] Their lives were made pleasant and interesting by foreign-

---

[33] J. Heurgon in Jehasse and Jehasse 1973[B347], 551.   [34] Colonna 1980[B208], 51ff.

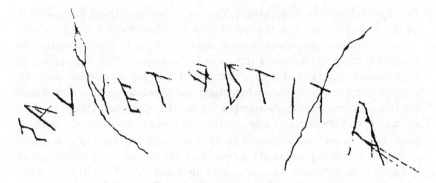

Fig. 34. Inscription on impasto jar from Osteria dell' Osa tomb 115 (c. 630 B.C.?). The inscription wishes good health to Tita ('salvetod Tita'). From Colonna 1980 [B208], 51 fig. 1.

ers who visited Rome and other cities and perhaps settled there as traders, artisans and artists. Slowly it must have become evident that the newcomers, especially Greeks, brought with them new social and religious notions. It would be interesting to know how the idea of associations of artisans (*collegia opificum*) developed in Rome. The creation of the most ancient *collegia* was attributed to Numa (Plut. *Num.* 17.1–4; cf. Pliny, *HN* xxxiv.1; xxxv.46). *Collegia* are presupposed by the Twelve Tables. They must have been one of the elements which prepared the way for the emergence of a unified *plebs*.

The question is when and how inequality in Rome hardened into the distinction between patricians and plebeians: a subordinate question is the relation between plebeians and clients. If an answer to both questions were possible it would help us to make up our minds on Servius Tullius' reforms and on the limits of the 'Hellenization' of Roman institutions under the last kings. It was a well-established opinion in the first century B.C. that Romulus himself had introduced the distinction between patricians and plebeians (Cic. *Rep.* 11.23; Dion. Hal. *Ant. Rom.* 11.8). There is furthermore some basis in ancient texts (prominently in Dion. Hal. *Ant. Rom.* 11.9) for the theory most clearly formulated by Th. Mommsen[35] that the plebeians were originally the clients of the patricians. Our tradition is more uncertain about the distinction within the patriciate between 'greater' and 'lesser' clans (*maiores gentes* and *minores gentes*) which was remembered, but had lost significance, during the late Republic. Only the *gens Papiria* is mentioned as having belonged to the *minores gentes*, and even that was debatable (Cic. *Fam.* ix.21; cf. Suet. *Aug.* 1.2). The creation of the *minores gentes* was attributed either to Tarquinius Priscus (Cic. *Rep.* 11.35; Livy 1.35.6) or – in one of the dissenting opinions about archaic

---

[35] Mommsen 1859[G115], 322–79.

Rome which are characteristic of Tacitus (*Ann.* XI.25) – to the founders of the Republic. Now it is evident that the basic structures of Roman society – such as the tribes, the *curiae* and the army (cavalry included) – do not imply the separation of patricians and plebeians. Nor is it implied in the reforms of Servius Tullius. The notion that the cavalry was filled by the patricians is a modern one for which there is no unambiguous ancient evidence either in the monarchic or in the republican period. The existence of (apparently) one century of *procum patricium* (? 'leading patricians') in the *comitia centuriata* of the late Republic tells us something about the vestigial powers of the patricians at the time when the centuries of the *comitia centuriata* were no longer identical with the centuries of the real army, but not about the army itself. The Roman kings do not bear names of *gentes* which were considered patrician in later times; and the same applies to the names of Roman hills (e.g. Caelius) connected with the names of *gentes*. Even in the first years of the Republic some of the consuls bear *gentile* names which are not patrician, including Iunius Brutus.

For centuries the separation between patricians and plebeians was clear-cut in the priesthoods and in the senate (originally the council of the kings). The three *maiores flamines* (of Iuppiter, Mars and Quirinus), the Salii, the *pontifices*, but apparently not the Vestals, were all uniformly and exclusively patrician until the reforms of the fourth century B.C. As for the senate, even in the late Republic the patrician senators were the only ones entitled to elect the *interrex* – or rather the successive *interreges* necessary to fill the gap between two kings – and to give their consent (*auctoritas patrum*) to the laws passed by the *comitia*. The formula *auctoritas patrum* implies that the patrician senators alone were called *patres*. Another formula, 'qui patres quique conscripti' ('those who are *patres* and those who are enrolled'), used to define the whole of the senate (Livy II.1.11 and, most significant, Festus 304 L), seems to indicate that the non-patrician senators were called *conscripti*.

This state of affairs may indicate that the formation of a privileged group of *gentes* (later known as patricians) began when they secured for themselves exclusive access to certain priesthoods and to special powers in the council of the kings (senate). It is easy to envisage how certain family groups would monopolize certain priesthoods. It is less easy to imagine how they would dominate in the senate if the selection of the individual members of the senate remained a prerogative of the king and there were always senators (later known as *conscripti*) belonging to unprivileged *gentes*. But Roman monarchy, as we have seen, was not hereditary, and the kings were often foreigners. They needed support from the local aristocracy, and they would have had to recognize the power of the strongest *gentes* even if they retained the right to choose their own councillors. Though we know deplorably little about the senate of the monarchy we can at least perceive that it was a powerful corporation. Greek models may have had some influence on it. Its members were chosen *de facto* for life. The number of senators was high: apparently 300 at the end of the monarchy (with confused traditions asserting that it was originally made up of 100 members and gradually raised to 300). The number 300 suggests some connexion, obscure to us, with the three tribes and the thirty *curiae*. The rights to approve laws and to choose the interim head of state (*interrex*) are in themselves indications of the prestige gained by the senate or rather by its most powerful members.

If this view is accepted, the distinction between patricians and plebeians developed in the senate during the monarchy and established itself as a principle of organization of the Roman state in the initial stages of the Republic. It affected the priesthoods and the principal magistracies of the Republic, but not, at least directly, the Roman assemblies and the army. Those excluded from the privileged patrician *gentes* might be their clients: in this case they would presumably derive advantage from their connexions and perhaps even be called to the senate as *conscripti*. But there is no *a priori* reason for denying that some *gentes* had clients, yet were excluded from the privileges of the patriciate. Though large groups of clients would necessarily reinforce the success of certain *gentes* in establishing themselves as patricians, clientship is not to be considered a preserve of the patricians.

The real difficulty is the position of the plebeians in the Roman army. As we have already emphasized, there is no sign that the Roman army ever made major distinctions between patricians and plebeians. In the Servian reform as traditionally described, the criterion for being assigned to the hoplite infantry (and perhaps to the cavalry) was wealth, not hereditary nobility. If we accept that the traditional description is unlikely to correspond to the sixth-century situation, the question arises whether there are traces of an earlier stage of the Servian organization and whether these traces, if any, have a bearing on the condition of the plebs. Now we know that even in the late Republic the first of the five traditional Servian 'classes' was called *classis*, that is 'army' *par excellence*, and all the other 'classes' were labelled together as *infra classem* ('below the army': Gell. *NA* vi.13 from Cato; Festus 100 L). This suggests the possibility that an earlier, perhaps the earliest, version of the Servian order was a simple distinction between *classis* and *infra classem*. The *classis* would have been the infantry legion, and the *infra classem* would have provided the auxiliary, light-armed troops. In line with Greek principles, though not yet with the sophistication of a Solonian reform, the *classis* would have been chosen according to qualifications of wealth. Servius perhaps meant to codify the introduction of hoplitic tactics into Rome and to reduce the tension between a budding hereditary aristocracy and the non-aristocratic well-to-do. He may also have found a way of giving citizenship to foreigners by admitting them to the army at an appropriate level. But property qualifications would in themselves make the *classis* a place for the patricians, as only a minority of plebeians could gain access to it. The prevalence of the patricians would be reinforced by the co-operation of their clients, to whom admission to the *classis* could hardly be refused if the backing of the patricians was strong enough. Though there might be a clear distinction between city-army (divided into *classis* and *infra classem*) and private bands of noblemen with their clients, the structure of the private bands was likely to influence the city-army. One wonders, therefore, whether the rise of the patriciate to the position of ruling class in the early Republic was accompanied by patrician assumption of control over the *classis*, with a corresponding tendency to push those who were not patricians or clients of patricians into the *infra classem*. There is a traditional formula ('populus plebesque': Livy xxv.12.10; Cic. *Mur.* 1) which seems to separate the notion of 'populus' (= army: cf. the verb *populor* to indicate the activity of the army) from that of 'plebs'. This formula may go back to a time at which few, if any, plebeians managed to enter the *classis*. P. Fraccaro's hypothesis[36] that during the monarchy the *classis* came to be divided into sixty centuries, that is, to have a nominal strength of 6000 soldiers, remains attractive. The creation of the two consuls at the end of the monarchy was probably the occasion for splitting the *classis* into two legions, in each of which there were sixty centuries, but in which each 'century' had a strength of about sixty men. It became a peculiarity of the centuries of the Roman legion that they consisted, not of a hundred, but of sixty men.

The fact that the Roman legion was still based on sixty centuries during the late Republic is a reminder of the part the original three tribes and thirty *curiae* played for a long time in shaping the Roman state, either directly or by duplication of the original structures. The 6000 infantry-men who were accommodated in two legions in the early Republic corresponded to the 600 knights (*equites*) who in their turn were the duplication of the original strength of the Roman cavalry. The knights maintained their direct connexion with the Romulean tribes longer because they went on being called Tities, Ramnes and Luceres (the official order). The qualification of *priores* ('first') and *posteriores* ('secondary') to distinguish the two centuries of each tribe indicated the rise from 100 to 200 knights per tribe. It is likely that the *celeres* mentioned by the tradition were identical with the 300 'Romulean' knights. The name was preserved by the tribunes of the *celeres* (*tribuni celerum*) who still existed in

---

[36] Fraccaro 1931[G579], 91–7; 1934[G581], 57–71.

the early Empire, no longer as military commanders but as minor priests. The Romulean tribes thus continued for a long time to influence the organization of the army. Similarly, their subdivisions, the *curiae*, remained, even after the creation of the centuriate organization by Servius Tullius, one of the operative principles of political and social grouping. There are some doubtful indications that the *curiae* owned land (Dion. Hal. *Ant. Rom.* 11.7). But, as such, the *curia* was an association of given *gentes* which met in rooms of their own (each called *curia*) for communal meals and religious ceremonies. The rooms of all the *curiae* were originally in one building, but at an uncertain date twenty-three *curiae* moved elsewhere and left the other seven (of four of which we know the names: Foriensis, Rapta, Veliensis, Velita) in the old house; the seven became known as *curiae veteres* ('old curiae': Festus 174 L). Each *curia* had a head, *curio*, and a priest, *flamen*. A *curio maximus* presided over all the *curiae* – a patrician in early republican times. Each *curia* acted as a voting unit in the oldest assembly of Rome (*comitia curiata*). This principle of voting, not individually but by group, was transmitted by the *comitia curiata* to the later assemblies of the Roman people (*comitia centuriata* and *tributa*). It is an uncommon one in the history of political assemblies and resulted in diminishing personal initiative and responsibility in Roman assemblies (with a consequent increase in aristocratic patronage within the voting units). What the *curiae* had to vote for or to bear witness to in the monarchic period is a difficult matter to establish. It seems probable that the *lex curiata de imperio*, which in the late Republic was a formal confirmation of the appointment of Roman magistrates elected by the centuriate assembly, was originally the act which conferred power on the elected king – and consequently, at a later date, on the consuls. As the kings were not hereditary and often imposed themselves from outside, recognition by an assembly must have been necessary to legitimize their authority. It is also probable that as early as the monarchic period two meetings of these assemblies (*comitia*) were set aside each year to give an opportunity to the Roman heads of household (*patres familias*) to make a public testament. Transition from one *gens* to another and adoption by another family within the same *gens* were acts that had to be performed before the *comitia curiata*. It is more doubtful whether the *comitia curiata* were asked to take part in legislation and treaties with other states. It is equally doubtful whether the *comitia* had the right to act as a court of appeal (*provocatio*) in criminal cases dealt with by the king or other magistrates. With the creation of the *comitia centuriata* by Servius Tullius, in whatever form that creation happened, a military assembly founded upon wealth and meeting outside the *pomerium* with military symbols began to compete with the curiate assembly. We are simply unable to define the terms of this competition which proved to be of momentous

importance for the future development of Rome. The *curiae* were originally, and remained even in their decline, an organization suitable for
moderate social differentiation where face-to-face contacts prevailed.
They remind us of the Greek phratries and are certainly one of those
features of archaic Rome which explain why Rome was capable of
appreciating Greek political ideas and of evolving on lines parallel to
those of Greece.

We are left still wondering whether Servius Tullius knew of Solon,
who may have been his contemporary. Servius Tullius is the one king to
whom we can at least attribute a political programme. He had to confront
the steady increase in power (and therefore in clients) of a restricted
number of *gentes*, the future patricians, who aimed at securing hereditary
privileges. As far as we can see, Servius recognized social and economic
differentiation, but no hereditary privileges, in his centuriate and tribal
reform. He was partially unsuccessful: two or three generations later the
aristocrats managed to get rid of the kings and to assume power. The
comitia centuriata in their original form did not stop the rise of the
patriciate; they may even have favoured it, if the patricians were the main
holders of wealth. On the other hand, in its more developed form the
centuriate order proved to be helpful in providing a meeting place, and
therefore a basis for compromise, between the patricians and the wealthiest plebeians.

What the other kings tried to do in coping with the situation inside
Rome is more difficult to guess. Themselves products of this unstable
society, they were more like Greek tyrants than traditional Greek *basileis*.
They were heavily dependent on their own military bands – that is, their
own clients. But at the same time they had to be acknowledged by the
local senate and by the *curiae*. In the intervals between kings an *interrex*
was chosen in turn from the senators according to regulations that
remained in force (though perhaps somewhat modified) during the
Republic, on the occasions when both consuls died in office (p. 184). On
the other hand, the king had to appear in the *comitia curiata* on stated
occasions; he could not dispense with it. In the circumstances we must
assume that military command was the most important function of the
king. It is therefore unlikely that the dictator, or *magister populi* ('commander of the army'), who makes his appearance as the supreme military
commander in emergencies during the Republic, should have been
originally an auxiliary of the king. Victory in war, justice and public
works in peace time were obviously what the Romans expected of their
kings. But, as we have seen, the king was also a priest. To judge from the
priest-king of Diana Nemorensis made famous by J. G. Frazer (Strabo v.
3.12, p. 239C; Suet. *Calig.* 35 etc.), Latium had some strange combinations of priest and king in the archaic age, but the Roman combination

was simple enough. Even during the Republic the successor to the king, the *rex sacrificulus*, still had the highest position in the formal hierarchy of the public priests (*ordo sacerdotum*), especially at banquets (Gell. *NA* x.15.21; Serv. *Aen.* 11.2). The king organized games (*ludi*) in honour of gods. He performed purificatory rites on behalf of the community, such as the mysterious flight from the Comitium (Regifugium) on 24 February, perhaps at that time the last day of the year. This flight had its counterpart in the equally mysterious flight of the people (Poplifugia) from the Comitium on 15 July. Romans dated events by the years or at least by the names of kings. The king's wife, too, was a priestess. The king had an official residence and a sacred place, the Regia, and he had close relations with the virgin priestesses who preserved the sacred fire for Rome, the Vestals. Stories about kings generated by divine fire were told: about Romulus (as an alternative to the story about Mars as his father) and about Servius Tullius. The connexion between king and fire is found elsewhere, for instance in Iran. In Rome it seems to have remained an element of secondary importance, like the other story of Numa Pompilius being the pupil or even the lover of the nymph Egeria (he was also considered a pupil of Pythagoras, against all chronological probabilities). Where the intervention of kings in the religion of Rome can be more clearly perceived, at the time of the Tarquinii, we find an admixture of Greek elements. The consecration of the temple to Iuppiter, Iuno and Minerva has at least one Greek feature, the elevation of Minerva to protectress of Rome as Athena was of Athens. According to a good tradition (Dion. Hal. *Ant. Rom.* IV. 62) the Tarquinii imported the Greek Sibylline books into Rome from Cumae to be consulted under state control.

We must assume *a priori* that the Roman kings made laws and regulations, though the mechanism of such early legislative activity (whether or not in collaboration with the senate, the *comitia* and the pontiffs) is unknown to us. Nor is there any difficulty in admitting that some royal enactments (*leges regiae*) may have been remembered and even obeyed in later centuries. We know in fact that collections of *leges regiae* existed (cf. Livy VI.1.10) and that some of these laws were attributed to specific kings (most frequently to Romulus, Numa and Servius Tullius). According to Dionysius of Halicarnassus (*Ant. Rom.* III.36.4) the *pontifex maximus* Gaius Papirius who lived after the expulsion of the kings collected those laws of Numa which had been transmitted to Ancus Marcius. According to a different version of the same story reported by Sextus Pomponius, the lawyer of the Antonine age, a Sextus (or Publius) Papirius living under Tarquinius Superbus made a collection of laws enacted by all the kings (*Dig.* 1.2.2. 36). In any case a collection of *leges regiae* was known as Ius Papirianum ('Papirian law') and was commented upon by antiquarians such as Granius Flaccus who apparently lived under Caesar (*Dig.* L.16.144 compared with Censorinus, *DN* 3.2). It remains strange that Cicero, who shows a special interest in the *gens Papiria* (*Fam.* IX.21), should seem to be unaware of the Ius Papirianum, though he is familiar with individual *leges regiae*. It can in general be said that, where we have the full text, the *leges regiae* attributed to Numa seem more archaic than those attributed to other kings.[37] More particularly, there is an evident difference in style and content between Numa's laws and the laws attributed to Romulus by Dionysius (*Ant. Rom.* II.7–29) which must derive from a tendentious political pamphlet of the first century B.C. But even for Numa's laws there is no guarantee that they are authentic legislation of the monarchic period. They may easily be the product of pontifical lore of later centuries which ascribed them to the authority of King Numa. We shall not therefore use these laws as evidence for the monarchic period, though in doing so we may well miss some interesting facts.

Archaic Roman religion[38] has a well-deserved reputation for punctilious respect of formulae, for an almost inextricable identification of legal and sacral acts, and finally for perceiving the intervention of the gods as essentially discontinuous. Without indulging in social interpretations of religion which our insufficient knowledge of archaic Roman society would make particularly fragile, one can admit a certain connexion between these attitudes and the predicament of people who were used to quick and violent changes in their leadership and who were unsure of the foundations of their own models, part of which came from Etruria and Greece. One of the characteristics of Roman piety was to keep separate the spheres of gods and men, but to take equal precautions in both. This resulted in the use of very precise formal language for anything which affected either divine law (*fas*) or human law (*ius*). The earliest stratum of the Roman calendar goes back (as has been generally recognized since Mommsen) to the time when the triad Iuppiter-Iuno-Minerva had not yet been established on the Capitol at the centre of the Roman official cult: this means, in all probability (though attempts have been made to modify this conclusion), to before the beginning of the Republic. The names of the month Aprilis and of the day Idus seem to be Etruscan. One third of the days in the calendar are *dies nefasti*, that is, days reserved to the gods (almost all odd days of the month), and two thirds are *dies fasti*, that is, suitable for ordinary political transactions. Ceremonies directly referring to the opening, conduct and conclusion of military campaigns are scheduled on days reserved to the gods. Connexions between the military and diplomatic activities of the state and the sacred sphere were further-

---

[37] Gabba 1960[B60], 202.   [38] See further Chap. 12.

more maintained by special priestly corporations, such as the Salii who propitiated war (whatever that meant), the *fetiales* who were responsible for the ritual correctness of the diplomacy leading to war or concluding it, or the Arval Brethren (*fratres arvales*) who seem to have been responsible for the purification of the borders of the *ager Romanus*. One interesting implication of the institution of the *fetiales* is the careful elaboration of a doctrine of just war, according to which a war is justified when the opponent refuses to make amends for past offence (p. 384). It was normal practice, no doubt going back to the monarchic period, that the heads of the Roman state were advised by technicians (*augures*) in the interpretation of signs indicating approval or disapproval by the gods before a specified course of action. There were offences within the city which made a man *sacer*, that is, deprived of his civil rights and open to divine punishment. By *devotio* a general could magically bind himself to the enemy in such a way that he and they were vowed to destruction together. By *evocatio* the gods of the enemy were invited (or compelled) to migrate to Rome where cult was promised and help against the previous worshippers expected. When in danger, the state could dedicate the produce of one spring (*ver sacrum*) to Mars. And the king would celebrate a 'triumph' (the Greek word ϑρίαμβος, which apparently reached Rome through Etruscan) when victorious according to recognized criteria. He may have enjoyed divine status for the duration of the ceremony, but this is not evident.

It would be easy to multiply the examples of the intense sacralization to which the public life of the Romans was submitted. One would, of course, have to add all the rites, the prayers, the precautions and the straight magical practices with which a head of a household surrounded his family and his earthly goods in daily practice. This formalism has also something to do with the Roman inclination to turn abstract concepts (such as *fides* ('faith')) or momentary events (such as the voice which warned the Romans before the arrival of the Gauls in 390 and originated the cult of Aius Locutius) into divine forces. Gods were about everywhere: in gates (Janus), on specific hills (Quirinus on the Quirinal; Diva Palatia on the Palatine). The river Tiber was a god, and possibly Diva Rumina was a specific goddess of the whole of Rome connected with the Ficus Ruminalis, a fig-tree near the Lupercal associated by legend with the suckling of Romulus and Remus (Dea Roma is a later, basically non-Roman, creation). The multiplication of gods and rituals went together with discontinuity of religious life and technical specialization in rituals. Specific gods were left to the care of specific priests. Various sources (of which the most important are Cic. *Leg.* II.20 and Varro, *Ling.* v.84; VII.45) allow us to compile a list of fifteen priests (*flamines*) for as many gods. Some of the gods (Falacer, Pomona and Flora) do not appear in the calendar, and the whole order of the *flamines* seems hardly ever to have enjoyed a collective activity. The first three *flamines* (*Dialis, Martialis, Quirinalis*) seem to have had special prestige, but there was no triad of Iuppiter, Mars and Quirinus comparable with the triad of Iuppiter-Iuno-Minerva to which the Tarquinii gave sanctuary on the Capitol. The ritual of the *spolia opima* ('spoils of honour': p. 168) – which was probably more ancient than the triumph and celebrated victory in individual combat of a pre-hoplitic type – may have involved the three gods Iuppiter, Mars and Quirinus (Festus 202 L; Serv. *Aen.* VI.859). It was left to the *flamen Dialis* to preserve to the end of the Republic, and beyond, the remnants of old and by then inexplicable taboos. The *flamen Dialis* and his wife were hardly allowed to leave their house, and even less the city. Ordinary people obviously relied on the purity of the *flamen Dialis*, as they relied on the chastity of the Vestals (who were cruelly punished for their weaknesses). But nobody found a model in, or stopped to think about, these priestly performances. It is significant that, with all this multiplication of gods, family gods (Manes, Lares, Penates, Lemures) remained very impersonal and that there is little trace of specific gods of *gentes*. A *gens* could have a favourite hereditary common cult (such as the *gens* of the Pinarii had for Hercules, and the Nautii for Minerva), but there was no exclusive god, say, of the Claudii. Nor is there any clear evidence that the Genius was the god of the *gens* rather than the god of each individual male.

Just because there were specific places of cult for a specific family or *gens*, and specific sanctuaries for the federal activities of the Latins, it should not cause surprise that when the plebs began to organize its resistance against the patricians during the early Republic, it managed to connect itself with certain cults and temples, most conspicuously with that of Ceres, Liber and Libera. But very little guidance came to political life from temples and priests. The priestly group which ultimately proved to be most influential in the Roman Republic and undoubtedly had its roots in the monarchic period was that of the *pontifices*, who belonged to the upper class (in the early Republican period to the patriciate), were eligible for ordinary magistracies and altogether brought the layman's experience to bear on sacral business rather than *vice versa*. Originally five life members, one of whom acted as *pontifex maximus*, they perpetuated their own college by co-optation. Whether they were originally the 'bridge-makers', as their name seems to imply, is irrelevant to what they turned out to be: authorities on the law, in both its sacred and its profane aspects. In Rome the priestly machinery produced technicians of the law rather than spiritual and political leaders.

We are back where we started. At the end of the monarchy, the Romans were giving themselves a basically Greek structure of government notwithstanding the rapid changes in the ruling class and the constant interference of military bands seeking their fortune in whatever part of Central Italy they could penetrate. The main annalistic tradition, by playing down these bands, perhaps unwittingly exaggerates the Greek elements in Roman constitutional developments; but these elements are real enough. They are more important than the trappings (such as the *fasces*) which the Romans borrowed from the Etruscans (Sil. *Pun.* VIII.483ff). Hellenization included the dualism of senate–popular assemblies, the hoplitic organization, the introduction of the census and of the local tribes, and the progressive secularization of priesthoods. It finally inspired the ways of life of the patriciate and the democratic opposition of the plebeians. It prepared the way for future absorption of Greek gods and of Greek theological thinking. Political and cultural hellenization, partly derived from direct Greek contacts, partly mediated by the Etruscans, went together with a self-conscious dissociation both from the Greeks and from the Etruscans. Though some Greeks were ready to look upon Rome as a Greek city, the Romans opted for Troy. If the style of social, political and religious life in Rome became different from that of the Etruscan cities, it could not be confused with that of any Greek city we happen to know. The Roman plebs, for instance, does not seem to have an exact counterpart either in Etruria or in Greece (Magna Graecia included). Conversely, there seems to be little evidence in Rome for that identification between aristocracy and cavalry of which there are good examples in Greece.

What part literature played at such an early stage of Rome is more obscure. We cannot be certain that the most famous Latin verse form, the Saturnian, was a Greek import, as has been suggested. Some Greek influence seems undeniable in the formulae of archaic hymns, such as the *carmen* of the Salii which has come down to us. By 450 B.C. the Romans were able to formulate laws in a way which leaves no doubt about their acquaintance with Greek legislators, though it does not necessarily imply the borrowing of individual laws. The word *poena* ('indemnity', 'penalty') in the Twelve Tables is a manifest Graecism. Contacts with the Greeks of Italy are enough to account for most of this cultural movement, but tradition insisted that the friendship between Rome and Massalia (mod. Marseilles) went back to the age of the Tarquinii (Justin. XLIII.3; Strabo IV.1.5, p. 180C): the friendship was old and firm enough by 390 B.C. for the Romans to use the official house or 'treasure' of the Massaliotes in Delphi to make an offering there. Through Massalia and the Etruscans Rome was also put in touch with Carthage, and there, too, the Romans encountered assimilation of Greek institutions and legal patterns. The first treaty between Rome and Carthage – for the early date of which the discovery of the bilingual (Etruscan–Phoenician) tablets of

Pyrgi in the territory of Caere (p. 256) have provided an additional argument – is another example of the adoption of Greek formulae. The spontaneous, unprompted character of this orientation explains why we can never exactly correlate Greek and Roman developments. If Servius Tullius instituted in Rome some of the reforms which Solon and Cleisthenes introduced in Athens, this did not lead, as in Athens, to a democratic republic, but to a very aristocratic one.

CHAPTER 4

ROME IN THE FIFTH CENTURY I: THE SOCIAL AND ECONOMIC FRAMEWORK

A. DRUMMOND

I. THE TWELVE TABLES

The documentation for early Roman social and economic structures is sparse and inadequate. The literary narratives, preoccupied with war and politics, commonly ignore such topics except where they are relevant to their central themes, and even then their lack of detailed information often confines them to speculation or inference from more recent conditions. Archaeology throws some light on contemporary material culture, but its evidence is severely restricted. We lack tombs securely datable to the fifth century, apparently because it was then customary to bury the dead without grave goods,[1] and fifth-century material is also absent from certain major sacral sites, notably the Lapis Niger votive deposit and the Sant' Omobono sanctuary. Linguistic, religious and other institutional survivals from the early period provide significant clues to particular aspects of both economic and social behaviour but seldom yield a precise context into which these individual items can be placed in terms either of chronology or of overall development. Evidence from other societies presumed to be of a broadly similar character may offer possible models for the reconstruction or interpretation of the Roman evidence and, in the case of the early economy, the known geographical features of the region, together with the limitations on economic development common to ancient societies, supply at least a rudimentary framework for reconstruction. None of this, however, suffices for more than tentative hypothesis, and even then we must often rely partly on inference from later Roman conditions, with the inevitable risk that the distinctive features of sub-archaic society may become blurred or escape detection altogether.

There is, however, one reputedly fifth-century document of which numerous fragments survive and which purports to offer important contemporary evidence for Roman social and economic structures in this

---

[1] Colonna 1977[B312], 131ff; above, p. 37.

period. This is the Twelve Tables, the law-code assigned to *c.* 450 B.C.[2]
Although the law is restricted in its scope, has its own preoccupations
and may not always accurately reflect current patterns of social or
economic behaviour, the preserved provisions of the Twelve Tables
remain the most significant potential indicator of the character of early
republican society.

The compilation of the Tables is attributed to two ten-man commis-
sions (*decemviri legibus scribundis*) which replaced the consulship as the
chief magistracy in 451 and 450 B.C. and which should, therefore, have
been recorded in the list of eponymous magistrates (the *fasti*). Are these
Decemvirates authentic? The composition of the first board shows two
suspect features: although it purportedly (Dion. Hal. *Ant. Rom.* x.56.2)
comprises ex-consuls,[3] no two members had held the consulship
together and none had held it more than once, despite the fact that
repeated tenure of the office was not unusual in this period (p. 206, n. 84).
However, the exclusion of consular colleagues may be mere accident,
deliberate policy or largely a further consequence of the omission of the
most distinguished ex-consuls. That in turn may have a political motivation. The years 455–452 B.C. had seen a sudden influx into the consulship
of new families (Table 3; p. 207); according to the literary tradition these
still belonged to the exclusive ruling class of Rome, the patriciate (p.
179), but had not hitherto held the principal magistracy. Three of these
newcomers appear in the First Decemvirate, along with a further new
name (Genucius). The remaining Decemvirs belong to more distinguished patrician families but not the pre-eminent half-dozen. Hence the
particular composition of this board may reflect the temporary success of
patrician families which did not normally enjoy political distinction and
which were, perhaps in consequence, more amenable to demands for the
publication of the law, whilst no less anxious to reinforce the internal
cohesion of the patriciate itself (p. 233).

The Second Decemvirate is more difficult to defend. Half of its
members have names which are elsewhere held only by men of plebeian
(i.e. non-patrician) status and they can scarcely belong to obsolete
patrician families since, with one exception (Antonius (p. 193)), none
appears elsewhere in the early *fasti*; a major commission of this kind
could hardly include so many non-consular patricians. Evidently then
the second board is divided equally between patricians and plebeians.[4]

---

[2] Text: Bruns n. 15; *FIRA* 1.21ff. English translation: A. C. Johnson, P. R. Coleman-Norton and
F. C. Bourne, *Ancient Roman Statutes* (Austin, Texas, 1961) n.8.

[3] Apart from Genucius ('Minucius' in Diod. xii.23.1) and, for Livy and Dionysius, Ap. Claudius
(whom the Capitoline Fasti apparently identified with the consul of 471). On the problems of the
consular status of the Decemvirs cf. Fraccaro 1947[D10], 247 n. 1; Ogilvie 1965[B129], 456f.

[4] Dion. Hal. *Ant. Rom.* x.59.4 supposes that three were plebeian, Livy iv.3.17 that all were
patrician. Diodorus' variant Sp. Veturius (xii.24.1) has probably been erroneously carried over from
the First Decemvirate (cf. Perl 1957[D25], 47, 57, 83f).

Yet such a composition is difficult to reconcile with the patrician dominance in this period or with the political measures in the Tables designed to strengthen the patriciate's reputed monopoly of power, most notoriously the ban on marriage between patricians and plebeians (which curiously is often ascribed specifically to the Second Decemvirate). Conceivably plebeian discontent with the work of the first commission led to its replacement by a mixed board, while the patriciate reacted by ensuring that plebeian members were elected who would be reluctant to adopt an independent stance, but so speculative a scenario is hardly satisfactory as a demonstration of authenticity.

Whilst, therefore, the First Decemvirate at least may well be historical, neither it nor its successor is so unequivocally trustworthy as to demonstrate the traditional date of the Twelve Tables beyond cavil. Of course, even if both Decemvirates were spurious, the very fact that the Tables were the work of the early Republic may have been preserved, along with the Tables, in oral tradition, but the vital consideration is whether the Tables themselves, so far as they survive, can reasonably be assigned to a fifth-century context.

The preservation of such a document presents no difficulty. Even Livy (VI.1.10; cf. IX.34.6f) seems to imply that the Tables survived the Gallic Sack of Rome (390 B.C.) in some form (cf. p. 308), and since they were intended to make public the law and remained a principal basis for much private law into the second century B.C., their continued display in the Forum (presumably in front of the Rostra where our sources unanimously locate them) is to be expected. Whether the Tables were still visible in the first century (when their importance had declined sharply) is more doubtful,[5] but in any case knowledge of their contents in the extant sources does not rest on direct acquaintance with a publicly displayed text but on oral and, increasingly, literary traditions. The spelling and phonetics of the extant citations betray a long and continuous process of modernization, certain provisions are the subject of well-established variants, and others again are clearly transmitted inaccurately. Indeed, down to the early first century children might still learn the Tables by heart[6] and they formed the basis of the earliest attempt at a general treatment of Roman private law, the *Tripertita* of Sex. Aelius Paetus (*cos.* 198 B.C.), as well as being the subject of a number of later commentaries by the imperial jurist Gaius and others.

The Tables are known only from individual references and citations in juristic, antiquarian and other literary authors, with the inevitable dangers of loose quotation from memory, misinterpretation in the light of

---

5 Dion Hal. *Ant. Rom.* II.27.3 may imply so but cannot be pressed.
6 Cic. *Leg.* II.59; cf. Plaut. *Mostell.* 118ff; Plut. *Cat. Mai.* 20.6.

later law and even the false ascription of provisions believed to be of early date; hence, for example, doubts surround Tacitus' attribution of a maximum interest rate to the Tables (*Ann.* VI.16; cf. Cato, *Agr. praef.*) since it duplicates a law recorded in Livy (VII.16.1) under 357 B.C. Nonetheless, where provisions are cited in more than one author, the discrepancies are insufficient to suggest the existence of radically different versions of the whole code, and certain broad consistencies of style (e.g. in expressing contingent regulations) indicate a comparatively homogeneous tradition. Moreover, a number of archaic linguistic features suggest that the archetype which must lie behind this tradition was of relatively early date. Thus the cumbersome expression of complex provisions[7] or the frequent failure to specify the subject of a verb and the unmarked changes of subject (e.g. Table 1.2) reflect a very early stage in the development of legal drafting; and the citations contain a wealth of archaic words and usages, one at least already unintelligible to their earliest commentator (Cic. *Leg.* II.59).

Other considerations date particular regulations before the third century. The provisions on personal injury (Table VIII.2–4) must antedate considerably the Aquillian law (usually dated to *c.* 286 B.C.) which established new and more sophisticated penalties for damage to persons and property, required explicitly that the damage be inflicted 'wrongfully', re-categorized injuries to slaves and probably employed a far more advanced legal style. The crude expression of accidental homicide[8] must also belong to a very early stage of legal development. The penalty of talion for a particular form of serious injury, the selling into slavery or execution of the judgement debtor, the archaic house search 'with dish and band' ('quaestio cum lance et licio') were all almost certainly a dead letter by the mid-Republic, whilst the procedures of adoption, freeing from paternal power and the will 'by bronze and balance' (p. 147f) had already then been developed through a creative application of Decemviral provisions. Moreover, certain clauses most properly belong specifically to a fifth-century context: the sale of the judgement debtor 'across the Tiber' (presumably before the capture of Veii in 396 B.C.); the exclusion of full marriages between patricians and plebeians; the special arrangements with two forgotten peoples, the Forctes and Sanates (p. 86); and the restrictions on aristocratic funerals (p. 233). It has been supposed[9] that the Tables represent a mid-republican compilation, principally on the basis of a few provisions regarded as anachronistic in a

---

[7] E.g. X.8: 'at cui auro dentes iuncti escunt, ast im cum illo sepeliet uretve, se fraude esto' ('but a man whose teeth are fastened with gold, if further (anyone) shall bury or cremate him with that (gold), let it be without risk of punishment').

[8] VIII.24: 'si telum manu fugit magis quam iecit' ('if the weapon escaped from his hand rather than he threw it . . . ').

[9] Lambert 1902[G249], 149ff; 1903[G250], Section VI; 1903[G251], 501ff.

fifth-century context.[10] Such anachronisms, however, are few in number and may rather reflect spurious attribution by authors anxious to accord a prestigious origin to measures believed to be of some antiquity, and it is difficult to see why a published document of this kind should, on this hypothesis, have included so many obsolete provisions. Overall the style and stage of legal development represented by the vast majority of the code's provisions make an early republican date highly plausible; it should be accepted.

Modern reconstructions of the Tables' internal organization are based principally on a few ancient attributions of specific rules to individual Tables and what little is recorded of the distribution of material in Gaius' six-book commentary. These data confirm that the code did not represent a systematic treatment of the law (in the modern legal sense) but are insufficient to determine the disposition even of some major topics. Nor do the fragments provide a complete picture of the Tables' contents. This is adequately demonstrated by allusions to expressions which evidently appeared in provisions no longer extant. As most topics, and many specific rules, appear in both juristic and non-juristic sources, the preserved citations probably reflect the main areas of law included, but some significant provisions may well have failed to survive, particularly those of little later relevance. As even the Decemviral recognition of oral contract (*stipulatio*) rests on a single passage in a papyrus fragment of Gaius, arguments from silence cannot be pressed.

The Tables need not have restricted themselves to what would now be regarded as private law (cf. Livy III.34.6) and certain norms (e.g. the ban on nocturnal meetings (VIII.26)) clearly have a political or semi-political character. However, unless the scope of the extant fragments is grossly misleading, the public law in the Tables was confined to a few matters, perhaps those of particular contemporary importance. Private law formed the core of the code, so far as it is known, and here the purpose of publicity which lies behind its publication (p. 232) made comprehensive treatment a desideratum. The Tables fulfilled that requirement sufficiently to be regarded later as the fundamental basis of civil law but even so, despite the fragmentary character of our evidence, it is probable that a variety of topics were passed over. The most serious omissions concerned the details of the individual modes of legal action (*legis actiones*), not formally published until the late fourth century (p. 396f). Certain other matters were probably taken for granted (e.g. the rights and duties of guardians or supervisors), others still regarded as the province of social obligation (p. 155). Other deficiencies, such as the notorious

---

[10] E.g. Table XII.5 (p. 203).

failure to define offences, betray the undeveloped state of the law, and even where a particular topic was included, the code probably concentrated on those aspects where clarification, reform or publicity was desirable; the comparatively rare testate inheritance was treated before intestate (Ulpian, *Dig.* xxxviii.6.1pr.), and at intestate succession itself the rights of the immediate heirs are simply assumed; the law stresses principally the respective rights of other kinsmen where no immediate (or 'automatic') heir is forthcoming (p. 149). Similarly in delicts the emphasis is on the remedies available to the injured party; that the action itself entitled the victim to redress required no overt statement but rested on tacit social recognition.

In summary, the haphazard means by which the fragments of the Tables have survived and the probability that they were in any case an incomplete statement of the law imply defects in our knowledge of the Tables and of the law in the fifth century. In addition, even some of the extant provisions may have been mis-attributed to the Tables, reinterpreted or modified in the light of later law. Nonetheless, the ancient tradition that the Tables represent a fifth-century law-code remains credible. It is supported by both the form and content of a number of extant citations, and the authors of the code may even have been known from the *fasti*. With due allowance, therefore, both for the lacunae in the Tables as preserved and for the limited and specialized perception of contemporary society which they provide, their evidence for fifth-century conditions is solidly based and material.

II. ECONOMY

(a) *Agriculture*

To the limited extent that later writers concerned themselves with economic matters they saw early republican Rome as essentially a farming community. Although they were aware of the natural advantages of the site of Rome for commerce (e.g. Cic. *Rep.* ii.7ff) and casually refer, for instance, to imports of wheat, they make little of craftsmen, industry or trade. In thus emphasizing the central role of agriculture they merely rehearse an obvious truth. As in most ancient city-states, comparatively low agricultural production, the prevalence of subsistence or near subsistence farming, difficulties of transport, lack of incentives for the production of a surplus and other factors will have combined to restrict the development of the market and of non-agricultural production. Hence possession of land was apparently regarded as the characteristic qualification for military service[11] and Roman military colonies were explicitly communities of farmers (*coloni*); agricultural metaphor permeates later Latin vocabulary; and agriculture occupies a central position in early law and in religious ritual. Thus one of the functions of the archaic sale 'by bronze and balance' (*mancipium*), in which certain objects were purchased against a payment of bronze weighed out before five witnesses and a 'balance-holder' (*libripens*), seems to have been to protect farmers concluding purchases vital to their livelihood. This procedure gave the purchaser the right to call on the seller to help uphold his title to ownership if that was challenged by a third party before the period needed to establish ownership by continuous possession elapsed; and should the third party be successful, the purchaser could then sue the seller for twice the purchase price. Only certain objects, however, could be so purchased, and for the most part these *res mancipi* were items of central importance to agricultural operations. In this period they probably comprised land subject to full citizen ownership, yoked and draught animals, persons (including slaves) under the authority of a family-head and certain so-called rustic praedial servitudes (in particular the rights to walk, to drive animals or carts and to take water through another's property).

As the elaborate cycle of public religious festivals concerned with the sowing, growth, health, harvesting, and storage of crops demonstrates, cereals (with viticulture) had long been dominant in the rural economy. These probably included barley[12] but above all *far*, almost certainly emmer (*triticum dicoccum*), a hulled wheat which is unsuitable for bread-making but was particularly well adapted to Roman conditions (p. 135) and probably consumed mainly as porridge (*puls*) (cf. Pliny, *HN* XVIII.83f). Still in the Twelve Tables the chained debtor is to receive one pound of *far* a day, the death penalty is exacted for stealing, spiriting away or setting fire to crops, remedies are provided for damage to property by drainage operations or animals, special procedures are prescribed for reclaiming material being used as vine-props (to protect the current user), the leasing of draught animals is regulated in certain circumstances and there is extensive provision for the precise fixing and preservation of property boundaries.

Cereals and viticulture will not, however, have enjoyed a monopoly in the agricultural regime. The seasonal character of the labour requirements of cereal crops and the need to safeguard against their failure may

---

[11] The term *assiduus* ('occupier') seems to have been used in a contrast with *proletarius* to denote those qualified for regular military service (cf. Twelve Tables 1.4: below, p. 166 n. 127).

[12] Used in part for animal fodder; cf. the 'barley money' (*aes hordearium*) later granted to the cavalry for maintenance of their mounts.

already have been significant factors in encouraging diversification. So may crop rotation, although here the wide variety and unscientific character of rotation practices even in nineteenth-century Italy[13] warn against the assumption of a uniform or wholly rational pattern. Many holdings were probably insufficient to permit an annual fallow, desirable though that might be,[14] and hints in Varro (*Rust.* 1.44.2) and Pliny (*HN* XVIII.187; cf. also Columella, *Rust.* 11.10.7) suggest a later tendency of peasants to alternate cereals with other crops: beans, lupines and perhaps root crops such as turnips. Such staples are likely to have been popular from an early date. However, given the probable lack of manure or other fertilizer for the main area under cultivation, such successive cropping must have reduced yields. That would also be true if interculture was practised, as in later periods.

How far, in addition, production for the market encouraged specialization or a wider range of crops is difficult to estimate. The need to purchase certain essential commodities presumably necessitated some surplus production, either on the peasant's own farm or through hiring his labour to a larger landowner. There may also have been some growing of cash or barter crops, particularly those low in labour requirements. Yet the evidence is scanty even for olives (the most obvious candidate) whose cultivation appears to have been introduced into Central Italy from the Greek world *c.* 600 B.C. and rapidly established itself in Etruria.[15] Although olive stones occasionally appear in archaeological contexts (notably at Sant' Omobono[16]) and oil containers are not unknown, olives are accorded no specific treatment in state ritual (p. 601), and in the Twelve Tables the destruction of trees entails only a comparatively modest pecuniary recompense. While some specialized production must be assumed (particularly by the more affluent), for the majority the danger of individual crop failure and the consequent unreliability of the market in essentials will doubtless have encouraged the tendency to satisfy all possible needs from the peasant's own resources. In this context especial importance will have been attached to the kitchen-garden, as the elder Pliny[17] plausibly assumes, perhaps on the basis of later practice. In contrast to more extensive areas of cultivation, such a specialized plot could be given intensive watering and fertilization and thus be made to yield, in relatively high quantities, a variety of vegetables

13 Porisini 1971[G123], 6–16; 42–59.
14 E.g. Columella, *Rust.* 11.9.4. That occupancy (*usucapio*) for two years rather than one was required to establish title in the case of land (Twelve Tables VI.3) may reflect its importance rather than a normal annual fallow (as Watson 1975[G317], 153).
15 Vallet 1962[G154], 1554ff.   16 P. Virgili in Colini *et al.* 1978[E96], 428.
17 *HN* XIX.49ff (interpreting thus the *heredium* of the Twelve Tables (Table VII.3): see p. 100).

and fruit to supplement the basic cereal diet, which of itself would be deficient, particularly in vitamins A and C.

Even so, given the probable small size of many early holdings, numbers of citizens must have derived no more than bare subsistence from their land. Admittedly, Varro's notion (*Rust.* 1.10.2) that all citizens had originally been allocated two *iugera* (= 0.5 hect.) should be rejected as a myth based on later surveying practice for land allocation in Roman colonies[18] and (probably) on a spurious parallel with archaic Sparta. More persistent and credible is the figure of seven (or, less commonly, four) *iugera*, found, for example, in accounts of the viritane allotments of Veientan territory[19] or of the impoverished circumstances of leading political figures.[20] Although these accounts are often suspect, the figure may indicate the size of holding later considered to be the minimum for subsistence.[21]

The difficulty is to estimate the productive capacity of a plot of this size. In particular, we have no evidence for average yields in this period, with the result that modern estimates are based essentially on analogy with later conditions, which themselves vary considerably and whose applicability is open to challenge.[22] The fluctuations in annual yields, the disparities in soil fertility even within a given area in Central Italy and the uncertainties surrounding the combinations of crops grown, crop rotation and the extent and return of the kitchen garden further complicate the problems of a realistic estimate of yield and indeed warn against broad generalization. However, it seems likely that to support a family on such a holding it must often have been necessary either to supplement one's income through wage labour (presumably paid in kind) or more probably through use of common land for further cultivation or pasture. Although the treatment of public land (*ager publicus*) in the literary

---

[18] Gabba 1978[G74], 250ff; id. in Gabba and Pasquinucci 1980[G76], 55–63. Livy even purports to record early land assignations of this size (IV.47.7; VIII.11.14; 21.11; cf. V.24.4; VI.16.6). For other possible explanations of the figure see above, p. 100.

[19] Livy V.30.8; Diod. XIV.102. Cf. early second-century allocations in citizen colonies (Brunt 1971[A21], 193).   [20] Heitland 1921[G88], 131ff.

[21] Cf. also Varro, *Rust.* 1.2.9; Columella, *Rust.* 1.3.10; Pliny, *HN* XVIII.18.

[22] For some discussion of the relevant problems see Ampolo 1980[C2], 20–4; De Martino 1979[G50], 241–55; 1984[G53], 241–63 (neither entirely satisfactory). There is further difficulty in estimating the weight yield of kernels from emmer; on this cf. Jasny 1944[G91], 154ff.

Ampolo estimates net yields of milled emmer (with future seed excluded) at *c.* 85–90 kg. per *iugerum*; De Martino gives 125–45 kg. per *iugerum*, apparently as the total yield in usable wheat (the net yield would then be *c.* 100–25 kg.). Neither calculation allows for loss during storage (probably at least 5 per cent, even for a husked wheat). The subsistence food requirements of an individual (average for adults and children) are reckoned at *c.* 210 kg. of unmilled grain (= *c.* 190 kg. of milled grain) if little else is consumed (C. Clark and M. Haswell, *The Economics of Subsistence Agriculture* (ed.4, London, 1970), 57ff); this rises to the equivalent (in cost) of at least *c.* 250 kg. of unmilled wheat if allowance is made for some diversity of diet and the provision of clothing (ib. 83).

sources for the most part merely retrojects later controversies, there are possible traces of a tradition that an individual might exploit as much such land as he could immediately work[23] and this may represent an early convention, allowing a limited quantity of public land to be used for cultivation. Since access to common land was also vital for timber, fuel, wild fruits, fungi and other edible plants, game, pannage and pasture, some convention on the individual's right to its use is to be expected. Nonetheless, the availability of such an additional resource must often have been crucial. The small size of land allocations attested from the later fourth century presupposes similar additional opportunities for occupation and may well reflect a pattern of peasant economy already familiar in the environs of Rome itself.[24]

The pig was probably the animal normally kept on small-holdings. The Twelve Tables (VII.10; cf. also VII.9; VIII.11) assert the right of landowners to collect mast (*glans*) which has fallen onto a neighbouring property (although this might also be used for draught animals) and pigs occupy a pre-eminent position in the blood-sacrifices of the family cult, including funerals. Sheep were a valuable source of milk, cheese, wool and, to a much lesser extent, meat, but both they and the almost equally versatile but destructive goat might prove difficult to maintain in the summer drought through lack of water and adequate pasture. Pigs presented less of a problem since they could probably find pannage throughout the year in the still abundant woodland and the flitch, no less than the kitchen garden, could assume a significant function in the rural diet (cf. Cic. *Sen.* 56).

Even so, animal husbandry probably played a restricted role in the peasant economy, as this stratum was least able to generate the capital required for the purchase of livestock. Sheep and cattle may, however, have occupied a more central place in the holdings of the wealthy, although reliable direct evidence for the fifth century is scanty. Even if *pecunia* ('wealth', 'money') derives from *pecus* ('flock', 'herd') and implies that pasture animals were an archetypal form of wealth-holding at an early date,[25] by the fifth century the term may have denoted any kind of wealth (especially perhaps movable wealth) in whatever form it was held[26] and need not imply continued substantial holdings of livestock.

---

[23] Tibiletti 1948[G147], esp. 219ff, citing Siculus Flaccus, *Condic. Agr.* p. 136.10–13 Lachmann; cf. p. 138.8–10 Lachmann; Columella, *Rust.* 1.3.11. This may in practice have already included the right to use dependent labour to work such land but that perhaps became a major phenomenon later (certainly for agriculture) with the rapid increase in such labour resources. Cf. further p. 326.

[24] For further discussion cf. p. 325f.

[25] E.g. Cic. *Rep.* II.16; cf. Gnoli 1978[G79], 204–18.

[26] So already in the Cassian treaty (493 B.C.) if the quotation in Fest. 166L derives from there (p. 275). Cf. also the (controversial) usage attributed to the Twelve Tables (v.3; v.7; x.7), with Diósdi 1964[G202], 87–105; 1970[G203], 23ff.

Certainly there was a tradition, supported by or based on apparently archaic formulae,[27] that until the mid-fifth century fines imposed by magistrates were assessed and paid in sheep or cattle, but the two innovations reputedly introduced at that time are inconsistently recorded: the introduction of a maximum fine is variously ascribed to a Lex Aternia Tarpeia of 454 B.C. or a Lex Menenia Sestia of 452 B.C., and the fixing of 'money' equivalences (i.e. specified amounts of weighed bronze) to a Lex Aternia of ?454 B.C., a Lex Tarpeia apparently after 452 B.C. or a Lex Iulia Papiria of 430 B.C.[28] Such confusion inspires no confidence in the authenticity of any of these specific enactments and the dating of these innovations to the mid-fifth century may be based merely on the fact that the Twelve Tables uniformly express penalties in 'monetary' terms. Even if, however, the practice of assessing fines in terms of livestock persisted into the early Republic, it presumably originated in the regal period when pasturage may have been more prevalent and the confiscated animals went to form part of the royal or priestly estates.[29] They were, therefore, even then a form of wealth-holding rather than a unit of exchange, and agreed equivalents of weighed bronze may have been accepted in practice long before fixed valuations were established by law. There is, therefore, no reliable clue here to the economic significance of livestock in the early republican period.

Pasturage on some scale must, of course, have been practised in Roman territory. Some of its products were indispensable and some areas, especially towards the coast, will scarcely have tolerated any other productive use. The lower, though permanent, labour requirements involved should have made it a more attractive, as well perhaps as a more prestigious, form of large-scale wealth-holding than intensive cultivation, provided sufficient land and labour were available, and wealth may well have been often so maintained and transmitted, particularly where cattle could be grazed throughout the year on permanent riverside meadows (cf. Dion. Hal. *Ant. Rom.* 11.2.1). Elsewhere, however, transhumance was probably necessary. This presented problems of access to upland pastures, supervision and security which may well have increased in the disturbed conditions of the fifth century. Moreover, it is impossible to gauge how far the flocks which wintered in Roman territory were the property of Roman citizens rather than of outsiders

[27] Varro *ap.* Gell. *NA* xi.1.4; Non. p. 319f; cf. Varro, *Rust.* ii.1.9.

[28] Cf. Cic. *Rep.* ii.60; Dion. Hal. *Ant. Rom.* x.50.1f; Festus 268/270L; Gell. *NA* xi.1.2.

[29] If the wager required of both parties for most early civil law procedures was originally in livestock (cf. Cic. *Rep.* ii.60), that of the loser was probably forfeited to the *pontifices* (Varro, *Ling.* v.180), perhaps to be used for an expiatory sacrifice (either directly or as a means of defraying the cost) or (as the later money wager) for normal state ritual (Festus p. 468L).

domiciled in the hills. Pasturage was not necessarily, therefore, a universal (still less the sole) activity even of those whose wealth took them comfortably above subsistence level.[30] If the Licinio-Sextian proposal of 376–367 B.C. sought to regulate large-scale use of public land for pasture (p. 328f), that may reflect a development which had been strongly fostered by the seizure of the territory of Veii.

(b) *Market development and trade*

The apparent scarcity of other early communities in her close vicinity suggests that Rome had long acted as the market centre for her immediate territory, a function illustrated by the early importance of the market held every ninth day (by inclusive reckoning). That role was extended with the progressive absorption of small independent communities in the wake of Roman expansion in the later regal period. Although these may have retained some defensive and religious functions, political and legal activities, together with the major popular religious celebrations, were concentrated in Rome, which may itself have experienced an increase in population (p. 139). Roman institutions, epitomized in the sacral and political distinction between intra- and extra-urban space (p. 585), show the city occupying the same central role that the evidence of settlement and roads has suggested for Veii;[31] and this must have enlarged the market's potential clientèle despite the distances involved (probably up to 15 km. or more in most directions south of the Tiber) and the activities of travelling pedlars and craftsmen. By contrast, the already small-scale role of the absorbed communities as market centres will gradually have been eroded, contributing to their progressive decay.

Rome's strategic position at a major Tiber crossing and on the route up the Tiber valley will also have acted as a stimulant to market development. So too presumably did the important salt deposits at the river mouth and the need for metals and perhaps luxury goods. The requirement that those liable for military service should provide their own armour and weapons will certainly have stimulated some surplus production; so too the competition in lifestyle, display and liberality among the aristocracy, along with the irregular and often unpredictable demands of social and family obligations. Moreover, market exchange in general may have been facilitated by an increasing use of metal as a unit of exchange, initially in the form of irregular lumps of bronze (*aes rude*). Although the use of cumbersome blocks of imported metal must have severely restricted the volume of such transactions, the sale 'by bronze

---

[30] As, for instance, Ménager 1972[H56], 367ff. Pasturage appears to make little impact on early law or ritual, although special factors (including our imperfect knowledge of the law) may be partly responsible.   [31] Kahane, Threipland and Ward-Perkins 1968[B350], 71.

and balance' certainly originated as a purchase against an agreed weight of bronze; and while the exclusive use of the bronze pound for reckoning penalties in the Twelve Tables may reflect primarily the need for clarity and ostensible equity, it was evidently an established medium of value and exchange.

Nonetheless, certain important potential stimuli to market development were absent. Rome had no significant and distinctive natural resources to form the basis of extensive manufacture for external trade. Surplus capital in the form of booty may have been available in some quantity in the sixth century when Rome was militarily more successful, but how far this created any large-scale domestic production of luxury items is not clear (even the local decorated pottery is of comparatively modest quality) and the difficult external position of Rome and the Latins for much of the fifth century must have sharply diminished this source of stimulus. Although the growing of some cash crops is likely, peasant agriculture will have tended towards self-sufficiency so far as possible and taxes or other financial obligations played little role in stimulating the creation of a surplus: army-pay (*stipendium*) and its corollary, the property tax (*tributum*), will have become necessary on a regular basis only in the Samnite wars of the fourth century when armies first commonly operated away from Rome for long periods. Neither, therefore, can go back to the regal period as the historians assume and if the accounts of their alleged re-introduction in 406 B.C.[32] have any basis, they may refer to temporary measures associated with the siege of Veii.[33]

So far as larger-scale agriculture or pastoralism is concerned, this may have been seen in part at least as a reservoir of wealth and status rather than as a productive enterprise, but even where surplus production for the market was involved, the returns may have been curtailed by the comparative expense and restricted pool of permanently exploitable labour. Slavery in particular will have been small-scale, since the sources of supply were limited. No doubt, as the historians presume, capture in war was the principal source but for much of the fifth century such captives were necessarily few. Domestic breeding may have been practised where feasible but in view of the expense involved it is unlikely to have occurred on a large scale. There may also have been some trade in slaves, perhaps fostered by Etruscan piracy, but it can hardly have been extensive, not least in view of the similar needs for such labour within each community. The inclusion of slaves among the items bought 'by bronze and balance' is a token of their value and also perhaps of the restricted volume of such purchases; and provisions to regulate the sale

---

[32] Livy IV.59.11; 60.5ff; Diod. XIV.16.5 (*stipendium* only).
[33] For a different view cf. Gabba 1977[G587], 13–33; below, p. 301.

of allied captives are noticeably absent from the first Carthaginian treaty[34] in contrast to the second, although this may merely reflect a development of sensibilities by the contracting parties, not least for political reasons.

As a corollary of the shortage of slaves other forms of dependent labour were apparently exploited on some scale. Those subject to paternal authority who committed certain offences could be surrendered to their victims, who presumably might use them as labour. So also the controversial rule (Table IV.2b) that a son sold by his father three times should be free of his control is probably best interpreted as imposing a *de facto* restriction on the father's right to sell his children, perhaps as a debt-pledge or in effect as a form of hire; in either case the need for labour is probably implied and the quasi-servitude here and in other instances may have threatened to become permanent. Above all, the principal consequence of debt-bondage (p. 215), and probably its primary advantage to the 'creditor', was to leave the 'debtor' working as his bondsman and it is significant that it was precisely in the late fourth century, when Rome's growing military success brought an increased reservoir of slave-labour, that such debt-bondage was formally abolished (p. 333). Even so, debt-bondage was a comparatively unpredictable and inflexible form of labour and may even have involved maintenance of the debtor's family as well as himself, thus further restricting its profitability. The ease and rapidity of its supersession by slavery, as a cause or consequence of its prohibition in the fourth century, may indicate that its contribution to the creation of an economic surplus had been relatively limited.

Nor, so far as we can tell, did the state take a strong interest in promoting or protecting trade, with the possible exception of a few vital commodities. Rome's discernible military objectives were security, booty, land and self-aggrandisement (particularly by her aristocratic leaders), not commercial protection or expansion,[35] and she developed no major naval forces to match those of her Etruscan neighbours. Whereas the first Carthaginian treaty carefully specifies the conditions under which Romans may trade in Carthage's claimed spheres of influence, Carthaginian traders at Rome are neither regulated nor protected (in contrast to the second treaty); and if, as is probable, Rome exacted no harbour or market dues,[36] that denotes the undeveloped condition and requirements of the Roman treasury, not a desire to stimulate trade. Our sources allege that the state took a hand in the occasional import of corn supplies to meet a local shortage and in control of the production and sale of salt,[37] but if true, this demonstrates only concern with the supply of

[34] Polyb. III.22.1ff; cf. p. 520f.   [35] For a different view see p. 297.
[36] Even the supposed abolition of harbour dues in 508 must be fictitious (Ogilvie 1965[B129], 258).   [37] Cf. Clerici 1943[G32], 461–6 (sceptical).

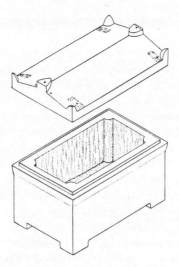

Fig. 35. Marble cinerary chest from the Esquiline (found inside a large peperino chest). Perhaps made on Paros. Late sixth century- early fifth century. From Colonna 1977 [B312], 143 fig. 5.

essentials (and in time with the enrichment of the treasury), not a general interest in the market. The same is probably true of the cult of Mercury, whose temple was allegedly dedicated in 495 and whose introduction may also reflect anxieties about the corn supply.[38] In contrast, the preserved fragments of the Twelve Tables give only limited attention to market transactions: no specific provisions are preserved, for example, on surety or pledge, little on lease or hire. Our defective knowledge of the Tables' contents may be partly responsible but not wholly so in view (for instance) of the later ill-developed character of the law of credit.[39] The severe procedures for debt execution hardly encouraged the borrowing of capital and if the Tables did restrict interest rates to $8\frac{1}{3}$ per cent (p. 116), this must be a monthly rate, designed for short-term loans to meet an immediate crisis, particularly among the peasantry.[40] A flexible form of oral contract (*stipulatio*) was recognized but could not be concluded by agents. The law of sale formally protected only purchase by *mancipium* against defective title (p. 119); to secure comparable protection other purchasers had to conclude a separate oral contract to that effect, a clear admission of the defective character of the law in this area. That is not a reliable index of Rome's actual status as a commercial centre but it does

[38] Wissowa 1912[G519], 304.
[39] The Twelve Tables may, however, have offered rudimentary protection for informal credit sales: cf. Iust. *Inst.* II.1.41 (=Table VII.11); Watson 1975[G317], 145–7.
[40] Zehnacker 1980[G168], 353–62.

suggest that her legal institutions were not designed with such a role in view.

Assessment of the actual scale and nature of market transactions is severely hampered by the inadequacies of our evidence, in particular the paucity of relevant archaeological data. Thus the only significant material evidence for foreign trade in this period concerns Attic pottery (chiefly cups) which continued to be imported until the mid-fifth century. Even this trade is impossible to quantify in absolute terms and although these vases indicate some private purchasing capacity, even as luxury items they will hardly have been of major economic significance. Moreover, there is no certain indication that Attic vases were accompanied by other significant imports from Greece itself or the Greek colonies of South Italy and Sicily. A few pieces, such as the Greek cinerary chest of Parian marble from the Esquiline necropolis (Fig. 35),[41] were almost certainly imported in this period rather than in the wake of later expansion but they reveal only a limited acquisition by a few individuals with the means to indulge their tastes. And of trade with Etruria and Latium, which should have been far more significant, there is little concrete trace.

The literary sources supplement this meagre record with the temple of Mercury, allegedly dedicated in 495 B.C. and accompanied by the institution of a 'guild of traders', accounts of wheat imports in times of shortage (p. 133f) and two treaty provisions. The first Carthaginian treaty (p. 521f) regulates trade by Romans and their allies in North Africa, Sardinia and Sicily but the extent of the trade which it reflects is impossible to assess. No relevant archaeological material has been discovered and although the trade might have been entirely in perishable commodities, the treaty may simply incorporate conditions required by Carthage in her dealings with the Etruscan coastal states.[42] According to Dionysius (*Ant. Rom.* VI.95.2) the Cassian treaty of 493 B.C. between Rome and the Latins (p. 274) ordered the hearing of lawsuits relating to private contracts between a Roman and a Latin within ten days in the courts of the state where the contract was made.[43] The mutual trading rights which certainly existed later (and included the right of Latins to acquire property by *mancipium*) may well reflect a formalization of an earlier freedom of exchange and acquisition (p. 270), but all this again provides scant indication of the character, extent or economic effects of the transactions involved.

[41] The quantity of such imports would be much increased if a series of early fifth-century Greek marble sculptures from Rome (Paribeni 1969[G121], 83–9) was imported in this period, but they may, of course, have arrived much later.

[42] The treaty itself may be framed on the Carthaginian model; cf. Täubler 1913[J235], 254–64.

[43] The Twelve Tables (II.2) also provided for cases involving foreigners, although not necessarily only Latins.

The problems are no less acute when we turn to artisan production at Rome itself. There is a similar shortage of relevant archaeological material and because of the lack of datable tomb groups no firm chronology has yet been established for much of the domestic pottery (an issue further complicated by the likely survival of earlier shapes and forms). The most that can be said is that such pottery shows a continuing general decline in quality from the sixth century, that comparison with Veientan material suggests it was largely of local fabrication, and that Rome seems neither to have produced herself nor imported from Etruria any truly high quality work.

In metals local production of mirrors, other ornaments or major bronze sculpture is not clearly attested and Pliny (*HN* xxxiv.34) notes that bronze cult statues were rare; terracotta and wood were apparently still the norm. Several votive and honorary statues are attributed to the fifth century,[44] but although some were no doubt ancient, their literary identifications and dates are probably pure conjecture: in some instances, for example, they presuppose that Rome anticipated Greece by up to a century in erecting honorary statues to the living. Two possible major fifth-century bronzes discovered in Rome's territory (a head from the Janiculum (the 'Sciarra youth') and the Capitoline wolf) highlight further difficulties in our evidence. For both may derive from Etruscan workshops and their appearance in Rome may be the result (for example) of the plundering of captured Etruscan cities at a much later date; the Capitoline wolf (even if a fifth-century work) is first securely attested at Rome in the tenth century A.D.

Whether or not as a consequence of the deficiencies of the archaeological record, there is little clear evidence that specialization in artefact production was far advanced. The material remains do show that pottery, tiles and metalwork had long been specialist products and the large-scale construction of public buildings at Rome from the sixth century, together with a more advanced house architecture, clearly created a demand for a variety of building skills, even if some of the principal artists and craftsmen may have come from elsewhere. The Twelve Tables refer directly to flute-players and goldwork, and carpenters and smiths appear separately organized in the developed centuriate organization, along with trumpeters and horn-players. Whether the alleged early guilds (flute-players, goldsmiths, carpenters, dyers, leather-cutters, curriers, smiths and potters)[45] were already established we do not know.[46] All were probably specialist occupations by this stage but apart

[44] Richardson 1953[G129], 77–8.

[45] Plut. *Numa* 17.1f; cf. Pliny, *HN* xxxiv.1; xxxv.159; Flor. 1.6.3.

[46] The identity of the earliest guilds became politically important with the restrictions imposed on such *collegia* in the first century B.C. and the list may be an invention of that period.

from flute-players (needed *inter alia* for cult purposes) and goldsmiths, represent only the trades required to service the basic needs of a largely peasant community.

This does not mean, however, that the aggregate volume of transactions involved even at this level was insignificant but the scale both of this and of the acquisition of 'luxury' items is impossible to assess. In view of the Decemviral restrictions on grave goods and the flourishing trade in Attic painted pottery in the late sixth century and in black-glaze and black painted ware in the early fifth we should not discount the possibility that Rome had generated notable levels of consumption (and competition) among her most affluent citizens, but the direct evidence at our disposal for trade and local production is insufficient to demonstrate such a hypothesis. Apart from Attic pottery and a few other high quality goods, the only known imports are metals and possibly on occasion wheat. What Rome exported, apart from salt, can only be conjectured; animal products (especially skins and leatherwork) and timber are perhaps the two most obvious possibilities. Domestically there is evidence at most only for a modest luxury output for consumption and no sign that Rome was a major centre of artistic innovation. On the other hand, in the sixth and early fifth centuries she did erect a remarkable series of well-decorated public temples and sometimes employed outside specialists for the purpose: at least two surviving terracottas seem to be of Greek workmanship and were probably made in Rome,[47] while literary sources cite epigraphical evidence for two Greek artists, Damophilus and Gorgasus (evidently of non-Ionian extraction), engaged on the temple of Ceres,[48] and claim, on unknown authority, Etruscan workmanship for the statuary of the Capitoline temple. How far this apparent contrast (also observable at Veii) between the modesty of artistic production for private purchasers and the relative scale and splendour of public building at least into the early fifth century is merely a consequence of the peculiar character of the archaeological record it is obviously impossible to determine, although the city as a whole evidently still offered worthwhile prospects of plunder to the Gauls in 390.

(c) *Economic changes in the fifth century*

A number of factors are commonly taken to indicate a general recession throughout Central Italy in the fifth century, particularly in the later decades:[49] a sharp decline in temple construction, in imports of Attic pottery, in local quality work and in the scale and splendour of funerary

[47] Andrèn 1940[B279], Rome: Forum II.11; Gjerstad 1953–73[A56], IV.456f.
[48] Le Bonniec 1958[G360], 256–62.
[49] E.g. Torelli 1974[J120], 828–9; 830–1; Ogilvie 1976[A96], 104–7.

deposits. Yet even in central and southern Etruria, where these changes are most apparent, their extent and momentum vary. Indeed, the fifth century seems to see a new prosperity at Falerii and, further north, at Orvieto and Clusium. The decline in temple building, for example, is much less strongly marked here and whereas imports of Attic painted pottery appear to decline in the coastal cities from *c.* 500 B.C., they increase further inland, although all areas show a marked decline after the mid-fifth century.

Even the contemporary deterioration in the quality and quantity of south Etruscan artistic production is not uniform.[50] It is to be seen primarily in the pottery, continuing, in Black Figure and bucchero, a trend already established in the later sixth century. Red Figure proper is restricted to a discontinuous and small-scale production from the late fifth century, although even so Etruscans were among the first to imitate this difficult technique. Other forms of Etruscan art, however, are more resilient. Mirrors and bronzes were probably produced in South Etruria and at Praeneste throughout the century, if for a restricted clientèle; and although there is little sculpture from the coastal states, there are some notable mid- or late fifth-century pieces from Veii and Falerii.

Thus the picture in Etruria is complex, varying according to the locality or factor involved. Moreover, one of the most uniform developments, the general decline in Attic pottery imports from *c.* 450 B.C., may be due to special causes. New markets probably became available to the Greeks, notably the Adriatic port of Spina whose imports increase in precisely this period. For external reasons now beyond detection the carriers in the pottery trade may have changed or at least become more diverse *c.* 480 B.C. and a more scattered pattern of distribution have reduced concentration on Central Italy.[51] At the same time new outlets seem to have opened up for Etruscan metals and metalwork (probably a principal item of exchange for Attic imports) in North Italy and beyond the Alps. In any event, since this was a luxury trade in a specialized commodity, its decline does not necessarily imply any general diminution of external commerce, the bulk of which was presumably limited to Central Italy.

If we turn specifically to Rome, there may be some individual local peculiarities, particularly in imports of Attic pottery where the available evidence has revealed an extraordinary surge in imports of figured pottery in the period 525–510, followed by an equally sharp decline.[52] However, these statistics are vulnerable and their evidence to be treated with caution, particularly perhaps in their implication that the decline at

---

[50] E.g. Sprenger 1972[J115], esp. 83–94.   [51] Cf. Johnston 1979[B348], 51–2.
[52] Meyer 1980[G112], 47ff.

Rome both preceded and outstripped the general decline in the Etruscan coastal states from c. 500.[53] Their explanation is also uncertain[54] but so far as the economic implications are concerned, the deficiency in the early fifth century was largely remedied by imports of Attic black-glaze and black painted ware, which indicates at most only a relative decline in purchasing capacity. The further decline of Attic imports after the mid-fifth century is no more marked at Rome than elsewhere in Central Italy and so may be largely a localized consequence of this wider phenomenon, without specific implications for the city's own economic fortunes. Admittedly domestic production does not seem to have expanded to fill the gap and local pottery even deteriorates in quality, but this continues a trend already established in the later sixth century; Rome seems to have had no strong tradition of local quality work from which to build up her own production subsequently. Moreover, our general knowledge of artisan production in this period is small, and sweeping conclusions about this or the general level of prosperity it implies unwise (p. 129). The major find of votive statues at Lavinium[55] shows that elsewhere in Latium some large-scale sculpture was still being produced, albeit in a cult context.

The only firm indicator of a reduction in prosperity at Rome is the decline in temple construction, which seems as true of her as of the Latin and south Etruscan cities. Here, however, much turns on the source of finance involved. If there was an element of private contribution by aristocrats anxious both to validate their monopoly of political power and to outdo each other by public benefactions, the decline may indeed imply a general decrease in wealth at the higher social levels, which might be the result of some wider economic decline. Later analogy suggests, however, that the principal contribution will have come from booty.[56] If so, the virtual cessation of temple construction after the early fifth century simply reflects Rome's more difficult military position in the subsequent decades. Moreover, so far as a decline in prosperity is evident

[53] In contrast to the Etruscan material, that from Rome derives from non-funerary contexts, especially votive deposits of varying lifespan; thus Meyer's statistics (loc. cit.) include the Sant' Omobono deposit (20% of the total) which appears to end c. 500 (and the Vesta deposit (10%) which ends c. 475). There is in any case an inherent danger in relying on statistics based on the vagaries of archaeological discovery and potentially subject to the effects of local variations in cultural practices.

[54] The hypothesis of a sudden decline in prosperity in the last decade of the sixth century and associated with Rome's loss of hegemony in Latium (Meyer loc. cit. 63ff) does not accord with the record of temple-building into the first two decades of the fifth century (below).

[55] *Enea nel Lazio* 1981 [E25], 221–70.

[56] P. 287. There may also have been some use of public labour; the legends associating this with the regal period (so already Cassius Hemina fr. 15P) are unreliable but the obligation itself may be authentic (it reappears later in the Caesarean colony at Urso (*lex. col. Gen. Iuliae* (*FIRA* 1 n. 21) 98)). Also to be noted here is the responsibility of landowners to mark the course of roads passing between their properties (Wiseman 1970[J244], 140f; 147, so rightly interpreting Table VII.7).

Fig. 36. *Denarius* of C. Minucius Augurinus (135 B.C.) depicting a column statue anachronistically alleged to honour L. Minucius for relieving a corn shortage in 440–439 B.C. The figure on the left may be P. Minucius Augurinus (*cos.* 492) or M. Minucius Augurinus (*cos.* 491), that to the right is probably M. Minucius Faesus, among the first plebeian augurs in 300 (*RRC* 242.1).

in some south Etruscan coastal cities, a number of specific developments can be cited which might have precipitated a relative impoverishment there but which would have had for the most part little significant effect on Rome: the growing isolation of Campania, the new impetus to metalwork in northern Etruria, the probable limitations on Etruscan piratical activities, the defeat inflicted by Cumae and Syracuse in 474 B.C., increasing Syracusan intervention (including a direct raid in 454) and perhaps growing Carthaginian pressure. Of these only the decline in trade with Campania, together with a reduced market in these south Etruscan states themselves, will have impinged directly on Rome and even their effects are impossible to assess.[57] For Rome her own comparative lack of military success until late in the century is likely to have been at least as important a factor in reduced public and private demand as a decline in her external market, but again the overall economic impact is impossible to gauge. Lack of booty may obviously have had some effect in reducing opportunities for acquiring (*inter alia*) luxury goods among the comparatively affluent, and even among those of the smaller peasantry who might serve on campaign it removed one potential, if limited, resource against impoverishment. For them, however, as for those usually excluded from military participation, the underlying problems probably lay elsewhere, in the recurrent difficulties of agriculture in the Roman Campagna, perhaps exacerbated by land shortage.

The Roman historians record at various stages in the fifth century famines alleviated by imports from Etruria, the Pomptine plain and occasionally Campania, Cumae and Sicily; indeed, as early as the 130s

---

[57] Any interruptions to the salt trade (vital to those in the hinterland) through warfare must have been temporary.

coins commemorate L. Minucius' supposed alleviation of a corn shortage in 440/439 B.C. (Fig. 36).[58] The reliability of such records, however, is
another matter. High corn prices, with eclipses, were entered on the
pontifical whiteboard (Cato *Orig.* fr. 77P; cf. also Dion. Hal. *Ant. Rom.*
VII.1.6) but the survival and use of such pontifical records from the fifth
century is highly contentious (p. 20). The extant historians seldom
record eclipses and the absence of corn shortages in Livy's account of the
fourth century after 383 B.C. renders suspect those assigned to the fifth;
even if allowance is made for increased prosperity and the establishment
of a regular import trade in grain as a result of Rome's expansion, it seems
difficult to believe that no such crises occurred in that period, particularly in view of the growth of the city itself and the apparent occurrence
of such difficulties in the early third century.[59] Where the reports of fifth-
century imports can be tested they prove suspect, most obviously in the
anachronistic details of Greek tyrants who aided Rome in 492/1 and
411,[60] and there is no solid evidence that these transactions were recorded
in Greek sources. Moreover, the issue of consular initiatives to deal with
shortages was already of topical interest in the mid-second century B.C.[61]
and may have influenced annalistic writing on the subject.

Nonetheless, the possibility cannot be excluded that some general
memory of early famines and attempts at their alleviation survived in oral
if not in documentary form. If the alternative was starvation for numbers
of its citizens, some initiative by the state, provided sufficient public or
private resources were available, is not unlikely.[62] Certainly the occurrence of such crises is beyond dispute; even the most fertile regions of the
Mediterranean world in antiquity did not escape poor harvests and
consequent shortage. The same will have held good of Roman territory,
even though generalization on conditions there is misleading since the
differing qualities of local soils, particularly in their reaction to variable
climatic conditions, were probably as significant a feature of agriculture
in ancient as in modern times. As later, the arid coastal sand dunes and
often ill-drained quaternary dunes immediately inland will have been
given over to marshland, woodland and pasture. Agriculture will have
been restricted to the fertile alluvial soils of the river valleys and the
primary volcanic soils of the broad ridges which comprise most of the
Campagna. Here winter drainage was probably a recurrent difficulty;
evidence from Veientan territory suggests that in antiquity these areas
may often have had a heavy clayey soil which tended to retain moisture

[58] Ogilvie 1965[B129], 256; *RRC* nos. 242–3.   [59] For a different view see p. 409.
[60] Dion. Hal. *Ant. Rom.* VII.1.1ff (= Cn. Gellius fr. 20P; Licinius Macer fr. 12P); cf. Livy II.34.2ff
(492 B.C.); IV.52.5ff (411 B.C.).   [61] Cf. Val. Max. III.7.3 (138 B.C.).
[62] If public cults of Mercury and Ceres, Liber and Libera were established in the early Republic,
they may attest state concern over grain supplies.

in winter and present a stiff resistant crust during a spring or summer drought.[63] How soon these soils also began to suffer from lack of depth (the major deficiency in modern times as a result of progressive erosion) it is impossible to say. By the late Republic the *ager Pupinius* north-east of Rome was a by-word for its thin and arid soil (Cic. *Leg. Agr.* II.96; Varro, *Rust.* 1.9.5; etc.) and Livy (VII.38.7; cf. Dion. Hal. *Ant. Rom.* XV.3.5) has mutinous Roman troops in 343 B.C. generalize its pestilential and dry qualities to the entire area around Rome. This, however, is clearly rhetorical exaggeration even for Livy's own day; Strabo (V.3.7, p 234C) under Augustus attests the fertility of the wider environs of Rome[64] and his reference (V.3.12, p. 239C) to their extensive occupation is amply confirmed by the surviving remains. Nonetheless, in the early period the poor drainage of these soils may have made proper cultivation difficult, particularly given the likely prevalence of wooden implements, with resultant low yields. The preference for emmer was presumably due precisely to its capacity to withstand moist as well as arid conditions.

The other principal factor affecting cereal yields is the variability of climate which characterizes Rome and its environs. Lack of autumn rain or an unusually cold winter may hinder germination. An excessively wet winter may slow root development, particularly where the soil is retentive of moisture or poorly drained. The most serious problem, however, is lack of spring rainfall in precisely the period of maximum absorption by wheat (April–May). The piecemeal information available on ancient climatic conditions indicates that these followed broadly the same pattern as in the modern period, but the greater forestation of the whole region and notices of the timing of Tiber floods[65] suggest a heavier and more evenly distributed rainfall and also perhaps some mitigation of the extremes of winter and summer temperatures, although other, fragmentary evidence of uncertain reliability points to an occasional severity of winter conditions in the early Republic which is unparalleled in modern experience.[66] Whatever modest variations were in evidence, however, the same fluctuations of temperature and rainfall which are characteristic of the modern climate seem to be attested by later literary references to unusually severe or dry winters and excessive summer drought, and the effects of adverse climatic conditions on grain crops were sufficiently

---

[63] Judson and Kahane 1963[G93], 77, 91.

[64] Cf. also Dion. Hal. *Ant. Rom.* II.25.2; VIII.8.2.

[65] Le Gall 1953[C8], 27–31. Cf. also the probable greater area of standing water (Quilici and Quilici Gigli 1975[C13], 8–23).

[66] Dion. Hal. *Ant. Rom.* XII.8; cf. Livy V.13.4 (400 B.C.); Zonar. VIII.6; August. *De civ. D.* III.17 (270 B.C.). Cf. Saserna *ap.* Columella, *Rust.* 1.1.5 (alleging generally colder conditions at an unspecified date before the first century B.C. on the dubious basis of the spread of vine and olive-growing); Heuberger 1968[C7], 270ff (Alpine evidence). For climatic variation in general in antiquity cf. Vita-Finzi 1969[C19].

familiar to be retrojected as the cause of failure in the fifth century (e.g. Livy IV.12.7). A more even rainfall may have reduced summer deficiencies a little, but a periodic shortfall was clearly a familiar problem since specific religious remedies were early instituted to meet it. Hence barley may have been attractive as an alternative to emmer precisely because of its early maturation (which also reduced attack by mildew).

Climatic variability, coupled with soil conditions, poor seed quality, inadequate rotation practices, lack of fertilizer, periodic flooding in low-lying areas and the incidence of locusts, mildew and other crop diseases are likely to have resulted in wide fluctuations of return (as in early nineteenth-century Italy[67]). Further problems were caused by the dangers of sudden rain during threshing and the need for protection against vermin and damp during storage. Given the lack of incentive to produce a substantial surplus beyond the normal market requirements (since there was no discernible external outlet), periodic shortages are certain in early republican Rome. The sanctuary to Ceres, Liber and Libera (traditionally dated to 493 B.C.) will belong in this context, as does the general concern of public ritual with agricultural prosperity.

In the fifth century such difficulties will have been aggravated by Rome's external position. Enemy raids threatened the outlying areas and some territory may even have been temporarily lost to Veii (cf. p. 297). Deteriorating relations with the hill peoples may have hindered access to summer pastures (with consequent increased competition for access to public land), whilst one cause of friction may itself have been pressure on lowland resources which led to attempts to exclude the hillmen from the winter pastures of the coastal plain. In turn, the advances of the Aequi and Volsci (p. 282f) may have prompted some influx of fugitive Latins. Above all, Rome's agreement with the Latins in the early fifth century (p. 274) will have precluded further territorial expansion at their expense. As a result, there was little scope for new settlement until the capture of Fidenae and Veii.[68]

How far Rome in fact experienced population pressure in the fifth century is difficult to assess. The recorded census figures (Table 1) imply a sharp decline in military manpower (or total population) early in the century but their evidence is spurious. As enumerations of adult males they allow insufficient growth in the fourth and third centuries, whilst as figures of total population (cf. Pliny, *HN* XXXIII.16) they still yield an impossibly high density of population (at least 120 per km.^{2} in 493 B.C.), the decline from 150,700 (498 B.C.) to 110,000 (493 B.C.) is impossible to

67 Porisini 1971[G123], 1–6.
68 The fifth-century colonies are probably all Latin foundations (Salmon 1953[I62], 93–104). Roman citizens may have participated in some numbers (p. 278) but were not necessarily predominant. Only two such colonies are in any case recorded between 492 and 418 B.C.

Table 1. *Roman Census Figures to 234/3* B.C.

Servius Tullius	80,000	Fabius Pictor fr. 10P (Livy 1.44.2) (83,000: Eutr. 1.7; 84,700: Dion. Hal. *Ant. Rom.* IV.22.2)
508	c. 130,000	Dion. Hal. *Ant. Rom.* v.20
503	120,000	Hieronymus Ol. 69.1
498	150,700	Dion. Hal. *Ant. Rom.* v.75.3
493	over 110,000	Dion. Hal. *Ant. Rom.* vi.96.4
474	a little over 103,000 (or 133,000)	Dion. Hal. *Ant. Rom.* ix.36.3
465	104,714	Livy III.3.9
459	117,319	Livy III.24.10, etc.
393/2	152,573	Pliny, *HN* xxxiii.16
340/339	165,000	Euseb. Armen. Ol.110.1 (160,000: Hieronymus Ol.110.1 and Prosper Aquitanus 1.539 Ronc.)
c. 323	150,000	Oros. v.22.2; Eutr. v.9 (250,000: Livy ix.19.2; 130,000: Plut. *Fort. Rom.* 13)
294/3	262,321	Livy x.47.2 (*alii alia*)
290/89–288/7	272,000	Livy, *Epit.* xi
280/79	287,222	Livy, *Epit.* xiii
276/5	271,224	Livy, *Epit.* xiv
265/4	292,234	Eutr. ii.18 (382,234: Livy, *Epit.* xvi)
252/1	297,797	Livy, *Epit.* xviii
247/6	241,212	Livy, *Epit.* xix
241/0	260,000	Hieronymus Ol.134.1 (250,000: Euseb. Armen. Ol.134.3)
234/3	270,212	Livy, *Epit.* xx

Source: after Beloch 1886[G10], 339ff; Brunt 1971[A21], 13.

justify and the transition to a later enumeration of adult males alone is difficult to explain: the census procedures were from the outset concerned predominantly with those qualified for some form of military service.[69]

Even though the census figures are spurious, they perhaps imply a belief on the part of those who fabricated them that Rome's manpower declined in the early fifth century. If so, however, the basis of that view remains unknown. Little in the extant narratives suggests any ancient belief that Rome suffered a major long-term loss of territory in the early fifth century[70] and although five (Latin) colonial foundations are assigned to the period 503–492 B.C., emigration elsewhere (Dion. Hal. *Ant. Rom.* VII.18.3) hardly offered a viable escape on any scale from

[69] Beloch 1926[A12], 216; cf. Frank 1930[G70], 313–24 (defending authenticity).
[70] Thomsen 1980[F62], 118–21.

whatever pressures were experienced at Rome. The annalists do record a series of pestilences but their basis is subject to the usual uncertainties; some at least may be a convenient explanation for a series of uneventful years (cf. Livy IV.20.9) and the details of all will certainly be later reconstruction. Plague, of course, will have been a recurrent factor (often linked to malnutrition) and religious remedies, such as the nail set annually in the wall of the Capitoline temple,[71] the shrine of Apollo (431 B.C.) and the *lectisternium* (399 B.C.), testify to its dangers if the relevant traditions are reliable. Whether, however, this represented anything abnormal by ancient standards or had significant demographic effects we do not know. All that can be said is that there is no clear evidence of any major impact on Rome's military capacity or policy. If malaria was already established in Central Italy, it did not prevent Latin or Volscian occupation of the southern part of the Latin coastal plain or fourth-century Roman viritane allocations in the area (which was notoriously infested later); certainly nothing in the historical record demonstrates that it was introduced into Central Italy in this period with a resultant heavy initial mortality.

Some assistance in determining population trends might be sought from the results of archaeological survey but the evidence available is limited and of uncertain significance. The only attempt to investigate a substantial block of relevant territory concerns an area (designated for convenience 'Collatia') between Rome and Gabii.[72] In the sixth century this reveals several significant settlements on the Anio, together with a progressive concentration of occupation in the sector towards Gabii. By the mid-Republic important sites on the Anio remain but elsewhere settlement is much more evenly distributed, perhaps in larger units, and tending to gravitate towards the major highways. Less systematic evidence from elsewhere in Latium suggests that this transformation is a general phenomenon, as archaic concentrations of population gave way to a more dispersed pattern of occupation. The apparent decline of some of the major archaic centres and the development of road-side sanctuaries from the fourth century will reflect the same process. Several factors are presumably involved here: the political and economic decay of the older foci, the increasing importance of the major roads, the re-settlement of population elsewhere, the premium on estates near Rome, but above all progressively more secure conditions.

Most of these factors, however, apply only from the fourth century and the position in the fifth century is unclear. In the Collatia survey the evidence for this period largely comprises fragments of tile and impasto pottery which easily escape detection, are often difficult to classify

---

[71] Magdelain 1969[G654], 257–86; cf. p. 187.   [72] Quilici 1974[B388].

precisely and whose chronology and relationship to archaic wares are inadequately known. Moreover, the quantities involved are often insufficient for a realistic assessment of the size of the site concerned or the duration of its occupation. The material at present assigned to the fifth century would suggest a *depopulation* of the countryside here, perhaps in favour of concentration around the larger centres,[73] but until the pottery is more securely classified and other surveys conducted, no firm general conclusions can be drawn.

At the Iron Age and archaic settlements absorbed by Rome funerary practice virtually excludes specifically fifth-century evidence from the cemeteries and the hitherto limited investigation of habitation sites is again severely hampered by the uncertainties of pottery chronology and classification. So far as it goes, survey and excavation material suggests no decline at some sites (e.g. Antemnae and Marcigliana Vecchia)[74] but at others (e.g. Monte Cugno (Ficana?) and Castel di Decima) few traces of an early republican presence have hitherto appeared. Even if, however, these centres were already in decline, that need not be true of the surrounding territory, whose pattern of occupation remains to be explored. The rural population of Veii apparently continued at virtually the same level in the fifth century (Fig. 37);[75] despite the immediate impression of some of the archaeological evidence, the same might still be true of Rome.

The survey evidence does, however, seem to reveal a rapid growth in settlement in the seventh and sixth centuries, which will have created increasing competition for land, particularly in the vicinity of the major centres. The analogy with Veii (cf. Fig. 37a–b) suggests that little territory will now have been available near Rome for occupation, and if a tribunician bill of 456 B.C. to open up the Aventine for settlement is genuine and correctly dated,[76] it presumably reflects increased pressure of population in and around the city. The detailed provisions concerning the delimitation of, and title to, private land in the Twelve Tables, the sacral character attached to boundary stones and alleged capital sanction against their removal also indicate considerable intensity of occupation in certain areas. In the more outlying districts a much lower density of settlement might be expected and is suggested by the survey evidence. Land across the Anio was allegedly available for distribution to the Claudii in 504 (although that may be aetiological fiction to explain the

[73] Cf. possible contemporary changes in settlement in Faliscan territory: Potter 1979[B385], 89.
[74] Varro (*Ling.* vi.18) believed that some absorbed communities retained sufficient sense of identity to revolt after the Gallic Sack.   [75] Potter 1979[B385], 89.
[76] Dionysius (*Ant. Rom.* x.32.4) claims that a bronze copy of the law was set up in Diana's Aventine temple but his own account of the measure's contents (ib. 2) seems to be another retrojection (with varied application) of later controversies over the occupation of *ager publicus*.

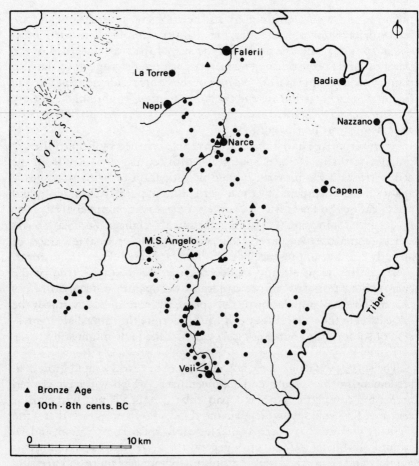

a. *c.* 1500–700 B.C.

Fig. 37a–d. The South Etruria survey: evidence of settlement density and patterns.

particular configuration and location of the Claudian tribe), and in lowland Latium as a whole there were evidently still large quantities of uncleared woodland in the fourth century (Theophr. *Hist. Pl.* v.8.3). Nonetheless, whether in public or private ownership, much of this territory may already have been reserved for extensive forms of exploitation (notably pasturage), particularly by the major families. They will assuredly have profited from the expansion of the sixth century, as the use of clan names to designate the newly created rural tribes (p. 179) perhaps indicates, and they may well have sought to extend their holdings where possible on existing territory to compensate for the reduced availability of pasture elsewhere and for the lack of fresh

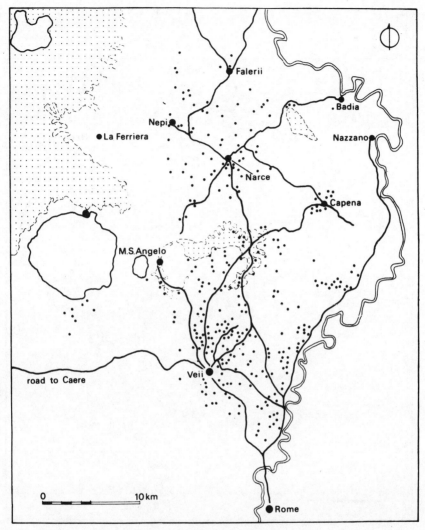

b. seventh to sixth centuries B.C.

territorial gains. The sharp reduction in booty through much of the fifth century may also have encouraged the aristocracy (whose competition in status and therefore in display and liberality will not have diminished in the new republican order) to focus more purposefully on the exploitation of land and the labour of impoverished citizens to generate the income required to sustain their position.

Thus, while an overall demographic increase in the fifth century cannot be demonstrated (and may even be deemed unlikely), there may at

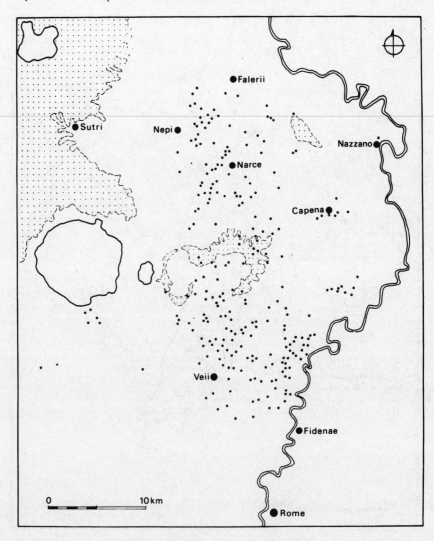

c. fifth and fourth centuries B.C.

least have been population pressure around the major political, defensive
and market centre and increasingly little land available for occupation
elsewhere: the determination with which Rome prosecuted the conquest
of Veii and the subsequent viritane distributions within her territory
certainly imply some potential demand for land. That is in any case
readily intelligible since peasant impoverishment must have been a
recurrent phenomenon throughout the early Republic. The fluctuating
expenses of family life, the probable small size of many holdings, the

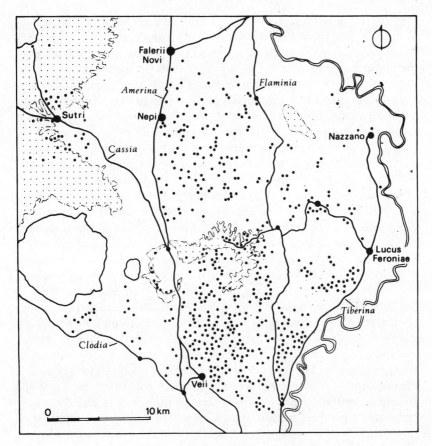

d. third, second and first centuries B.C.

From Potter 1979 [B385], figs. 12, 21, 25 and 27.

considerable hazards and inherent defects of small-scale peasant agriculture, coupled with a system of intestate succession whereby all children
under their father's authority inherited equally, ensured that debt and
destitution were endemic in Roman society. Hence the need to resort to
debt-bondage or the sale of children to avoid starvation.

III. SOCIAL STRUCTURES

(a) *Introduction*

The social structures encountered in the fifth century must in large
measure reflect the developments of the regal period and even beyond.
Unfortunately, it is seldom possible to discern with any certainty their

origins, the causative factors behind their emergence or the changes to which they had been subject over the intervening period. Our ignorance of so central an issue as the development of private land-ownership (p. 100) is an apposite instance. So also is the related controversy over the origins and functions of the *gens* or 'clan' (ib.). Was it, for example, once a (or the) primary social unit, linked perhaps to a regime of common clan ownership or occupation of land?[77] Or was it a progressive development, particularly among the aristocracy, of the regal period, reflecting the emergence of an elite which created these putative kin-groups as a means of reinforcing its solidarity?[78] Any answer to such questions is necessarily hypothetical, for it is only in the fifth century, in particular through the evidence of the Twelve Tables and early republican political institutions, that we can begin even to glimpse these social structures in operation. Nonetheless, it does remain possible to isolate certain factors which are closely associated with the patterns of social organization found in this period, which may have exercised an important influence on their origin and growth and which certainly contributed either to their maintenance or to their modification in response to new conditions.

Early Rome practised settled agriculture based on a prevalence of comparatively small-scale, privately owned farms which provided the fundamental resource of the great majority of the citizen body. Hence not only does the primacy of the family unit reflect this pattern of economic activity but the entire structure of kin-group classification and the regulation of kin prerogatives show a pre-eminent concern with the transmission of property. As will be seen, rights of inheritance are closely correlated with membership of a kin-group (in particular subjection to the authority of a head of household), the power of an individual to dispose of his property as he wished at death was limited by custom if not by law, and the rules governing both guardianship and marriage are decisively conditioned by issues of property transmission. The apparent lack of opportunities for personal enrichment and new settlement through much of the fifth century can only have further reinforced these concerns as well as confirming the basically static character of wealth distribution; few could anticipate any substantial improvement in their fortunes.

It is a further consequence of her comparatively restricted economic development that, even had she wished to do so, early republican Rome was in no position to create an elaborate state apparatus which could have provided positive intervention to protect the individual citizen against abuse and injury. The entire structure of the law in the Twelve

[77] Cf., e.g., Mommsen 1887–8[A91], III.3–53; Guarino 1975[H40], 56ff; 272ff.
[78] E.g. Botsford 1907[G20], 663–92.

Tables implies that already under the monarchy a regime of individual self-help to maintain personal rights and avenge injuries was deep-rooted, even probably in cases where the penalty was death;[79] and there was no increase in resources in the fifth century that would have facilitated greater public initiative in this sphere. Indeed, whereas individual monarchs might sometimes have found it politically expedient to attempt to check flagrant oppression,[80] the advent of an aristocratic political regime offered little prospect of a willingness to develop active state intervention on behalf of the populace at large, at least on a regular basis. Moreover, the population of Rome in this period, whatever its exact numbers (p. 163f), was clearly of modest dimensions. It had certainly not reached a size where the scale and anonymity of crime were such as to threaten public safety and make the private pursuit of wrongs impossible in principle in the majority of cases.

The resultant responsibility on the individual to assert and uphold his own rights, coupled with his reliance on his own private production for his livelihood and the absence (again in part through restricted economic development) of corporate financial institutions or any public or private organizations of social or economic assistance, inevitably meant that patterns of co-operative behaviour were a central feature of Roman social relations, a fact mirrored in the slow development of the law in significant areas of economic and social life. Moreover, the long-established and substantial inequalities of wealth and status within the community as a whole meant that, alongside the horizontal relationships between men of broadly similar status, there was a strong impetus to the development of vertical bonds whereby men of inferior status sought protection and assistance from their more powerful fellow-citizens. These patronal relationships were of major significance. Not merely did they provide the individual with a resource against abuse and thus help to mitigate social tensions, but in their turn they served to buttress the power of the aristocracy by making its exercise of patronal responsibility central to social organization and assistance, by increasing its prestige, and by incorporating into a position of personal dependence men of lower status who might otherwise have sought to remedy their plight by collective action amongst themselves.

Rome was also, however, a citizen community in which, notionally, its members enjoyed certain common rights, were members of certain common institutions (e.g. the *curiae*) and contributed, so far as they were able, to its military needs. This sense of communal identity had probably

---

[79] Kunkel 1962[G245], 97–130.

[80] Similarly, if the restrictions on funerary extravagance incorporated in the Twelve Tables go back to the monarchy (cf. Colonna 1977[B312], 160–1), they may reflect efforts by one or more of the kings to curb aristocratic excess and resultant social tensions.

been strengthened by the development of the city itself as the major centre of population and the focus of legal, political and religious life.[81] The relatively exposed position of the city and its territory made united action in its defence essential, and both the adoption of a military structure centred on a massed heavy-armed infantry and the resultant institutional changes in the sixth century (p. 103) can only have sharpened the sense of collective responsibility for the community's interests on the part of a substantial element in its population. At the same time the institution of a more systematic assessment of military responsibility introduced wealth as a possible formal determinant of status and privilege, although in the face of inherited patterns of social differentiation and organization this seems to have been unable to effect major changes of status definition in Roman society as a whole.

The social structures of the early Republic which were influenced by, or correlated with, these factors must now be treated in detail. The discussion will first examine those at the individual level before considering the wider divisions and status groups. It will begin with the bonds which linked men of broadly equal status (kinship, friendship and other ties of obligation) and then pass on to those patronal relationships where the differences of status between the participants were of central significance. The development of these vertical bonds in turn contributed to the essential complexity of the patterns of social differentiation within the citizen body as a whole, which cannot be reduced to a single common formula; only the patriciate stands out as enjoying an institutionalized but increasingly contentious position of privilege.

(b) *Family, agnates and clan*

Three principal forms of kin-group classification are attested for early Roman society: (i) the family unit, comprising a male head (*paterfamilias*) and those under his authority, in particular his descendants in the male line and wife (if she passed into his power (*in manum*) at marriage); (ii) the agnates, probably defined as the individual's relatives in the male line up to the sixth grade (i.e. second cousin); (iii) the 'clan' (*gens*),[82] composed of

---

[81] In the countryside the territorial units known as *pagi* are regarded by Dionysius (see esp. *Ant. Rom*: IV.15) as providing a focus of local defence, religious celebrations and administrative functions. Much of this is clearly anachronistic, implausible fantasy or based on false premises (Brunt 1969[G540],265; Frederiksen 1976[G583], 344–5), but the apparently early festival of the Paganalia attests their religious identity and their use for other local purposes (e.g. defensive emergencies) is not to be excluded.

[82] In conformity with common usage 'clan' is here used to translate the Latin term *gens*. It is arguable, however, that such a translation prejudges the size, coherence and collective activity of the *gens* and that a term such as 'lineage' is preferable (although even that is misleading for the late Republic when proof of kinship was not in practice a necessary qualification for membership of a *gens*: Brunt 1982[H102], 3).

several families all bearing the same name and allegedly related in the male line.

The Twelve Tables establish that the patriarchal family was by the fifth century the fundamental social unit. Roman civil law essentially regulated the relations between the heads of such families and private cult (as it is known from later evidence) also centred around the individual household (p. 605), reflecting its function as the immediate focus of communal life and activity. As has been noted, that centrality corresponds closely to an economy based on small-scale, largely self-sufficient peasant agriculture; the Latin term *familia* was probably already used, at least in part, to denote all the persons and property under the control of the family head (cf. Twelve Tables v.8), thus making explicit its proprietorial aspect.

The same factor, together with the gerarchic character of Roman social and political life, is also reflected in the family's internal structure. As a legal entity the *familia* was implicitly defined by reference not to blood relationship but to the powers exercised for life by the family head over both the persons and property subject to him, and the patrimonial rights of children and wives were determined on the basis of their membership of it. Thus, under the rules for intestate succession, children and wives subject to a *paterfamilias* shared equally in his estate as 'automatic heirs' (*sui heredes*), whereas those not subject to him (e.g. illegitimate children) were entirely excluded; if he had no 'automatic heirs', his property passed to his nearest agnate, or failing that, to all his clansmen.

Thus an essential connexion was created in Roman law between the total and perpetual power of the family-head and the intestate inheritance rights of those free persons subject to him, both reflecting in turn their continuing economic dependence on the family property. In the fifth century the probable scarcity of new land for settlement, coupled with the system of equal division of the inheritance among the 'automatic heirs', could only increase that dependence. It was only later, for example, presumably in the fourth and third centuries when new territory periodically became available at some distance from Rome, that procedures were developed for freeing sons from their father's power (which otherwise continued until his death). These gave the son legal independence (including the right to own land) but also, as an automatic concomitant, removed his intestate inheritance rights.

The power of the family-head is notorious, extending even to the right to kill those subject to him. This presumably reflects a strong collective emphasis on the need for rigorous discipline in the component elements of the community, not least to regulate the relations between *familiae*, since the heads of households were responsible to each other for the private actions of those subject to them. Moreover, in later periods at least their powers could be used to vindicate the family honour where an individual member had committed a heinous public offence. Nonetheless, in the normal course of events paternal power was subject to important restrictions. Public rights and obligations were not affected and, given low average life-expectancy, paternal power (*patria potestas*) probably ended for many during or soon after childhood. Moreover, communal attitudes will normally have ensured its reasonable exercise. The right to kill a descendant, for example, was obviously implemented only in exceptional circumstances and probably, as later evidence indicates, after the consultation of a family council; although the Twelve Tables allegedly confirmed the right, they may also have prohibited its exercise without proper cause.[83]

Social attitudes and their legal reflection also controlled the exercise of property rights. Although the *paterfamilias* had full powers of disposal of his property during his lifetime, he could not waste his substance, whether through lunacy or prodigality. In such a case his nearest agnate (or, failing that, his clansmen) acted as his supervisor, clearly in their own interests (as his prospective heirs) or in that of his 'automatic heirs'. Moreover, the individual's discretion in bequeathing his property was probably strictly limited, although the evidence regarding testamentary disposition in this period is inadequate and controversial. Twelve Tables v.3 ('As he has bequeathed in relation to [his property and the guardianship of] his possessions, so let the law be') was later interpreted as sanctioning the will 'by bronze and balance', by which the whole property was bequeathed, a specific heir instituted and guardians might be named; but in fact the original provision probably referred only to bequests of individual items and perhaps the appointment of guardians.[84] The wills made before the curiate assembly and on the battlefield were probably well established but their normal scope is purely conjectural. That before the assembly can only have been available to a minority, and it is a reasonable assumption that the battlefield will was originally its military equivalent[85] and therefore similarly restricted in application. Overall, therefore, the evidence does not suggest a widespread use of testamentary disposition for the entire estate and there are certainly positive indications that, as we might expect, intestacy was common, if

---

[83] Table IV.2a; cf. Gai. *Inst. fr. Augustod.* 85–6; Kunkel 1966[G246], 242ff.

[84] Watson 1975 [G317], 56–60. For other interpretations see e.g. Gaudemet 1983[G217], 109ff (comitial or libral will); Magdelain 1983[G272], 159ff (comitial will). It was believed later that the Twelve Tables permitted manumission by will (cf. Table VII.12), though the form of will involved is not specified.

[85] Kaser 1971[G240], I.106; for another possibility cf. Wieacker *ap.* Watson 1975[G317], 66 n. 38.

not the norm. The rules governing wastrels (later at least) applied only to property which the wastrel had acquired by intestate succession and were evidently instituted to protect those who would similarly inherit from him. So also the intestate guardianship of minors and women (who could not make a will) was exercised by their prospective intestate heirs in their own interest. Moreover, the 'automatic heirs' of intestate succession were clearly privileged; they were expected to succeed to the property and therefore did so without any formal act of acceptance. Hence also Table v.4 ('if a man who has no automatic heir (*suus heres*) dies intestate, the nearest agnate shall take the property'[86]) concentrates on the rules for intestate succession where there are no 'automatic heirs'.

Clearly, therefore, the provision for legacies in Table v.3 cannot have been intended to undermine the position of the heirs. Presumably such legacies were not as yet on a scale which would seriously jeopardize their inheritance; whether they served principally to bequeath particular items (e.g. personal effects) to individual heirs or were left to third parties as a token of social esteem we cannot say. However, by confirming (or establishing) the validity of such bequests the Tables did recognize some rights of the family head over the posthumous disposition of his property without external sanction; and this in a sense paved the way for the subsequent creation of the will 'by bronze and balance' and for the later form of adoption before a magistrate. Both of these procedures would procure an heir, thus enhancing the control of the *paterfamilias* over the destiny of his property and undermining the prospects of his agnates and clansmen. No less significantly, neither procedure required the participation of the assembly. The older comitial witnessing or approval of wills and adoptions (p. 105) implies a strong communal interest in, or control of, the devolution of property and family cult and this may be reflected also in the 'court of one hundred' (*centumviri*) which comprised judges drawn equally from the tribes and dealt with inheritance cases, perhaps from an early date.[87] Practical considerations obviously contributed to the decay of comitial involvement in such matters but the earlier communal participation must also reflect the positive interest of the early city-state and its pre-occupation with upholding the normal succession of property, not least in the interests of its own manpower (and perhaps social harmony). In contrast, as Rome expanded and opportunities for personal enrichment grew, the aristocracy in particular may have found such restrictions irksome, although it was still expected that descendants or near relatives would be instituted as heirs.

[86] For this interpretation of the provision cf. Daube 1964–5[G192], 256–7.
[87] Kelly 1976[G244], 1–39.

The near kin (agnates) will have occupied a position of particular importance within the individual's range of social relationships. It was they, apparently, who were responsible for avenging a man's murder since at unintentional homicide the offender had to surrender a ram to them to avert their revenge.[88] In contrast to the *familia*, however, the agnates never enjoyed any corporate existence, each individual being enmeshed in a variety of such relationships. Agnates had no common religious rituals and there is no abstract collective noun in Latin to describe them. Agnatic relationship as such was principally a wider kinship definition for the purposes of inheritance (and hence guardianship and supervision) and marriage. Agnatic rights are individual, not collective, and those in the nearest degree exclude the rest. Thus the agnates' rights are secondary to the patriarchal family and tend to reinforce its primacy since the family property was thereby retained as close as possible to the original line of male descent.

There was one particular circumstance in which a restricted group of agnates might act together on a more formal and long-term basis, but here too it was prior membership of a family group rather than agnatic relationship as such which was the crucial factor. At intestate inheritance the 'automatic heirs' might leave the estate undivided and exploit it jointly. Such arrangements were later sometimes associated with poverty, and although that is not a necessary conjunction, progressive impoverishment may have contributed to their frequency in the early Republic. They might also, however, allow a more effective exploitation of larger agricultural units (e.g. through maintenance of a plough team) or a more diversified pattern of farming; and they may have been popular where the elder son(s) acted as guardian to his sisters or younger siblings and worked the whole estate. In all such cases, however, the partnership is again a secondary phenomenon, contingent on the prior existence of a single family unit which forms the common inheritance. It was also ill-adapted to serve as a permanent institution[89] since it had no formal head and each inheriting son could dissolve the partnership at any time by unilateral application to the courts.[90]

It is sometimes supposed that the inheritance rights of agnates were an innovation, perhaps of the Twelve Tables themselves; previously the clan had inherited immediately in default of 'automatic heirs'; now the rights of the near kin were being decisively strengthened.[91] Such views

---

[88] Serv. *Ecl.* IV.43; *Georg.* III.387; Cic. *Top.* 64 (= Twelve Tables VIII.24a); Fest. 470L, 476L.
[89] Cf. Crook 1967[G47], 113–22.
[90] Gaius' statement (*Dig.* x.2.1pr.) that the Twelve Tables first introduced the procedure for the dissolution of such partnerships cannot be based on reliable knowledge of earlier law and therefore deserves little credence.   [91] For this view see, e.g., Michon 1921[G275], 119–64.

are often linked to theories of an early clan ownership of property that subsequently declined, but they cannot be proven. For although the law specifies that all clansmen without distinction shall inherit whereas amongst the agnates it is the nearest alone who qualified, this may merely reflect the practical difficulty of determining degrees of relationship beyond the sixth grade, not a primordial regime of collective clan property. Moreover, a system under which agnates had no specific inheritance rights would prevent siblings from retaining the whole property of a brother or sister who died without 'automatic heirs'; it would also automatically dissolve a common partnership in such cases. In view of these obvious deficiencies we need better evidence before we can assert an earlier absence of specifically agnate inheritance rights which was then remedied in the early Republic.[92]

In one respect, however, the position of agnates had significantly improved in or by the time of the Twelve Tables. Where a woman passed at marriage under her husband's control, he acquired full ownership of any property she possessed. At his death under intestate succession the wife in turn inherited from him, equally with each child, and came under the tutelage of his kin. Clearly where the woman already owned property in her own right such a marriage was highly disadvantageous to her nearest agnate(s), who would otherwise inherit from her at her death. They did, of course, act (up to her marriage) as her guardian(s) and had to authorize any disposal of her property, including probably her conclusion of an *in manum* marriage, but they could not marry her themselves; marriages within the seventh degree of relationship were not permitted.[93] Marriage to other clansmen was allowed but there is no clear evidence that it was mandatory even for widows or heiresses; the apparent later requirement that a freedwoman could not marry outside her patron's *gens* without express permission (Livy XXXIX.19.5) cannot be generalized to free-born clan members at a much earlier date without supporting evidence. Much here depends on our view of the relative rights of clansmen and agnates in the archaic period, particularly with respect to inheritance, but little else suggests that the claims of agnates would be deliberately denied in order to favour other clansmen, and the ban on patrician–plebeian intermarriage in the Twelve Tables, together with the probable right of intermarriage with Latins (p. 270), may indicate

[92] On the later restrictive interpretation of the rule regarding the nearest agnate (cited by De Zulueta 1953[G200], II.122–3; Watson 1975[G317], 68f) cf. Yaron 1957[G333], 385–9.

[93] Cf. Livy, fr. 12W; Tac. *Ann.* XII.6; Plut. *Quaest. Rom.* 6; Ulpian, *Tit.* 5.6; August. *De Civ. D.* XV.16. While we have no reason to suppose that female intestate inheritance was a later innovation and it provides the most satisfactory explanation of 'free' marriage (below), its combination with a bar on marriage to the near kin is remarkable. It may in part reflect an earlier abundance of land for settlement and occupation.

that marriage outside the clan was common.[94] In practice families may
have regularly contracted *in manum* marriages within a restricted group[95]
but if, for example, a system of preferential cross-cousin marriage was
ever practised at Rome,[96] there is no clear evidence for it in this period,
and both later practice and the wording of Livy, fr. 12W suggest that in
the mid-Republic at least marriage to near cognates[97] and not merely
agnates was barred. If such a strongly 'open' marriage-regime did obtain
in the early Republic, it presumably functioned as a means by which the
individual family enlarged the range of social relationships on whose
assistance and support it might call. From the community's viewpoint it
may also have checked any separatist tendencies of kin-groups and
reinforced a wider social cohesion, particularly among the aristocracy.
The disadvantage remained, however, that in this form of marriage, if
the woman owned property in her own right, the claims of her agnates
were definitively extinguished, whether or not she (re)married inside the
clan.

The secondary, 'free' form of marriage, already found in the Twelve
Tables (VI.5) and perhaps in some measure a reaction to growing
pressure on land resources, avoided this inconvenience. Here the husband acquired ownership only of the dowry and had no legal control
over his wife, who remained under the authority of her *paterfamilias* or (if
he was dead) her guardian. In consequence, she retained her inheritance
rights in her original kin-group and did not succeed to her husband's
estate. Her kinsmen's claim to her property was preserved and they could
now control her remarriage if her husband died. For her husband's
family there was the compensation that she had no claim to a share in his
estate, which might have passed out of their control if she remarried.[98]

For the role of the clan (*gens*) even in the fifth century evidence is scant.
Individual clans in the mid- and late Republic might have a common cult
(p. 621), burial place or customs, but even these are often limited to a
particular branch or to the patrician clan members, and the prevalence of
such foci then or earlier is impossible to determine. There may have been
a variety of practice and, as a corollary, considerable variation in the
degree of internal cohesion within each clan. Hence even if these

---

[94] August. *De civ. D.* xv.16 is too vague, in terms of chronology, reference and authority, to
demonstrate the contrary.

[95] Cf. perhaps the use of *adfinis* ('neighbour') as the generic term for relations by marriage.

[96] Benveniste 1973[A14], 1.223ff; Moreau 1978[G116], 41–54.

[97] I.e. relatives traced through the mother's line as well as the father's.

[98] The particular respect accorded to those who remained widowed and apparent emphasis on the
permanence of marriage in the early period (Williams 1958[G164], 16–29), reflected in the limited
availability of divorce (Watson 1965[G313], 38–50), may partly reflect the desire to avoid this
eventuality in marriages where the wife came into the husband's *manus*.

practices reflect an erstwhile solidarity within a few clans, it certainly cannot be assumed that all acted as close-knit units in the early Republic; there is, for example, no good evidence that the *gens* functioned as an economic unit in this period, beyond presumably the social obligation of mutual assistance when necessary. The known clan cults do not mark it out as fulfilling a central economic or social purpose comparable to that of the household; their function is rather to enhance its prestige and perhaps strengthen its sense of identity. Whether clans as such co-operated in private military ventures at this date is also doubtful. The Roman procedure for the declaration of war, which centres on demands for the restoration of property seized by an enemy, may reflect an original situation in which conflict often originated in the appropriation of booty by private individuals or groups but if so, the danger that such enter-prises might implicate the whole community in a major confrontation must early have prompted attempts to curtail or at least disown them. Rome's early fifth-century treaty with the Latins (p. 274), for example, would certainly preclude such activities against her immediate neigh-bours south of the Tiber, although such ventures might be permitted in the raiding warfare with the encroaching hill peoples (p. 291). Moreover, while legend portrays a number of sixth- and fifth-century individuals in Central Italy sufficiently powerful to engage in ventures of this type (p. 96f) and no doubt clansmen figured prominently in their following, the only evidence for common clan action as such is the expedition of the Fabii against Veientan territory in 478 B.C. (Livy II.48.8ff; Dion. Hal. *Ant. Rom.* IX.15.2ff; etc.). Another version (Diod. XI.53.6), however, turned that episode into an operation by the Roman army, with Fabii at most merely prominent in it. That may simply reflect efforts to regularize the event, but the alternative possibility, that members of the clan subsequently exaggerated their own role, perhaps to explain the ending of their successive run of consulships (485–479 B.C.) and under the influence of the Spartan stand at Thermopylae, cannot be entirely ruled out. In any case, this is the only possible evidence for clan military action and does not necessarily reflect a common pattern;[99] as their extraordi-nary domination of office at this date perhaps suggests, the Fabii may have enjoyed an unusual degree of clan solidarity, and their calamitous defeat would have acted as a powerful warning to would-be imitators.

Probably the principal function of the clan, at least in the fifth century, was the mutual aid (social, political and economic) of its individual members, together perhaps with a certain social and political éclat among the aristocracy. Individual clans, for example, seem once to have had

[99] Even if it does, this was clearly not the only form which private military ventures took (p. 292): here, as in other spheres, (putative) kinship bonds co-exist with, and fulfil similar functions to, other forms of individual association.

charge of particular public cults or rituals (e.g. the Luperci) and membership of the patriciate itself was apparently determined by clan.[100] While
the clan was not restricted to the patriciate (p. 99), an aristocracy whose
stress on ancestry inevitably brought a keener awareness of clan links
(real or alleged) may well have found it a particularly useful institution in
social and political contexts. The apparent bar on two clansmen holding
office together throughout much of the fifth century (p. 206) perhaps
indicates its potential value in this regard, but our evidence does not
permit us either to assess directly the practical significance of clan units in
the early Republic or to discern whether its importance increased or
diminished in this period. Those who regard the clan as a (or even the)
primordial form of social grouping will naturally see the fragmentary
evidence for its fifth-century role as a sign of its progressive decline. If,
on the other hand, it is viewed as a more recent, largely aristocratic
epiphenomenon, that role may be accorded greater prominence than our
evidence strictly warrants. Whatever its earlier history, however, it
would be rash to assume that its development and functions followed a
rigidly schematic course in any given period or that its role conformed to
a uniform pattern in all cases. In an age where the deficiencies of state
control and protection reinforced the individual's reliance on his social
associates, the clan might naturally play a significant role but not
necessarily or solely as an entity in its own right. Rather than the clan *per
se* acting as a unit in social or political life, greater importance may often
have attached to the individual links which it created, enabling each
member to call on a wide circle of putative kinsmen as and when
required. At the least it is clear that Roman social organization even
among the aristocracy cannot be reduced to the relationships obtaining
between a series of wider kin-groupings of which each individual
household was merely a component.

(c) *Kinsmen, friends and neighbours*

It is a corollary of the secondary character of agnatic and clan bonds in the
early Republic that it would be misleading to regard kinship as the
determining basis of Roman social organization in the sense that such
bonds necessarily formed the overwhelmingly pre-eminent form of
social categorization. Rather, alongside kinship there will have been
other modes of social grouping often fulfilling many of the same
functions; and patterns of mutual co-operation in particular are likely to
have developed outside as well as within the kin-group. Such practices as
work-exchange, minor loans or assistance in times of difficulty will have

---

[100] Cf. the distinction between 'greater' and 'lesser' clans (p. 101).

been regarded as part of the normal social arrangements and duties, and, initially at least, as entirely outside the law. Hence, for example, both the custom of making informal loans without interest and the apparent slowness of the law in the provision of actions for their return.[101] Similarly, the importance of personal sureties and guarantors in contractual dealings presupposes the existence of individuals willing to assume a potentially ruinous personal liability, and the grounding in 'good faith' of many legal actions introduced from the third century (however that is exactly interpreted) must imply a centrality of social norms and obligations which was presumably long established.

What must, therefore, be assumed is that already in the early period Roman social relations were dominated by a nexus of informal and personal bonds of mutual obligation broadly comparable to those familiar from the mid- and late Republic. The obligation imposed by the receipt of a service to repay it as and when the benefactor needed assistance, the potentially permanent bond of mutual expectation of assistance thereby created and the multiplicity of such connexions which any one individual might contract and inherit were fundamental to social life. Their rationale was the need of the individual for protection and aid, but they also reinforced the cohesion of the community and their basis was a strong collective sense of the rights and duties involved.

The importance of such ties is perhaps most evident in the pursuit of wrongs. Whether or not the origins of Roman legal procedure are to be sought in an initially unregulated regime of 'self-help', early Roman law clearly presupposes the private pursuit of wrongs and condones the use of force to assert one's rights where this was deemed necessary or justified. Indeed, for the most part the individual *paterfamilias* alone could initiate legal action for any wrong he or those subject to him had suffered. He was responsible for bringing the defendant to court, for producing witnesses (whom the magistrate would not compel to attend) and if successful, for executing the judgement. The defendant was no less responsible for the conduct of his own case.

Underlying this personal responsibility for seeking legal redress lay a strong element of the desire for vengeance. Indeed, the Twelve Tables attest clearly the desire of the law to moderate and control the exaction of revenge (cf. Lucr. v.1136ff); whatever the extent of their own innovations to this effect,[102] they expressly prescribe a pecuniary penalty in many instances, regulate in detail the circumstances under which physical vengeance is permitted and make special provision for unintentional

---

[101] Daube 1973[G194], 129–30.

[102] In particular *talio* (below) need not once have had a general application which the Tables then curtailed (cf. Diamond 1971[G201], 98–101; 398–9; whether Cato, *Orig.* fr. 81P (from Book IV) refers to Rome is uncertain).

homicide. Nonetheless, revenge continued to be an accepted motive for legal and extra-legal action, most evidently perhaps in the provision that the perpetrator of one type of personal injury (*membrum ruptum*) was liable to suffer the same injury himself (*talio*) unless he could persuade his victim to come to some alternative arrangement (Table VIII.2). There were even circumstances in which the exaction of revenge was tolerated without formal authorization: the Decemviral permission to kill the thief who comes by night or the manifest thief who resists arrest (Table VIII.12–13) reveals a readiness to countenance direct action where the victim's person is potentially at risk.

Moreover, in both asserting and contesting a disputed right, both parties may be permitted to employ force. Where, for example, an individual claimed authority over a slave or free person he was entitled to seize that person and those who contested his claim were no less entitled to resist. The action for claiming ownership of any object was itself framed on the model of a physical struggle for possession. Similarly, in an action against a person, if the defendant resists the plaintiff's summons to court the plaintiff is entitled to haul him off physically (later a ritual but probably real enough in origin); he can be prevented, however, by the intervention of a *vindex* ('champion') who himself 'gives notice of force' (*vim dicere*) and repels the plaintiff's physical hold on the defendant. So also at execution of judgement the plaintiff leads a defaulting defendant off into confinement unless again a *vindex* intervenes.

These procedures betray the readiness with which legal action was conceived in terms of the metaphor of force and the law itself in terms of regulating the conditions under which such force might be employed. In this context the assistance of neighbours, friends and kinsmen becomes paramount. At the lowest level witnesses were needed at summons (if the defendant resisted), in the legal suit itself, at the immediate killing of the manifest thief who resisted arrest,[103] at informal house search, etc. Defendants might require champions, guarantors or sureties, all willing to assume some form of personal liability. A man seized as a slave had to have his claim to free status asserted by a third party, whilst the regulations governing the public production of the judgement debtor on three successive market days seem similarly to presuppose a strong social obligation on his immediate circle to extract him from his desperate plight.

Moreover, the more support an individual could muster, the greater his chance of avoiding litigation by direct assertion or defence (by force if necessary) of the right claimed. An individual faced with oppressive

---

[103] Table VIII.13. Originally neighbours may have been summoned to provide assistance but here their presence is a safeguard against a charge of wanton killing.

action by a magistrate or private citizen might appeal to the protection of his fellow-citizens in general (cf. p. 220). In the pursuit of a private wrong the offended party might organize a ritualized cry at his opponent's door or against him personally in public to shame him into meeting his obligations; the Twelve Tables (II.3) expressly permit such a shout outside the door of the defaulting witness. More generally, popular fury might spontaneously erupt against those deemed to have flouted the social order.[104] Later evidence suggests that such demonstrations commonly took the form of public abuse outside the miscreant's door but in extreme cases might involve the burning of his house or even lynching.

It is a mark of the public humiliation which such demonstrations could inflict and the force of public opinion to which they appealed that the Twelve Tables may even have prohibited the singing or composition of public chants directed at an individual on pain of death.[105] That in turn would imply the high value attached to personal reputation, particularly among the aristocracy to whom personal honour was no doubt of great importance and against whom this may have been the only weapon available to the poorer would-be litigant unless he enjoyed the support of a powerful patron. It is no less significant that here the assistance of the citizen community as such may be invoked on behalf either of the individual or the social order and that 'private' conduct is not exempt from public scrutiny and disapprobation. Although for the most part the citizen is reliant on his immediate circle for aid and protection, he may on occasion be able, or be forced, to transcend this narrower range; beyond kinsmen and clan, beyond friends and neighbours there may lie the common interest of his fellow-citizens in his defence.

(d) *Comrades and dependants*

The forms of mutual assistance already described must have characterized the aristocracy no less than the rest of the citizenry. Dionysius speaks of *hetaireiai* (brotherhoods or factions) among the Roman patriciate, Livy of their kinsmen, friends and comrades. These motifs may reflect Greek or later Roman experience, but both historians have rightly sensed the importance which such ties will have had both for the individual and for the nexus of bonds thus created within the aristocracy as a whole.

Occasionally such relationships may have emerged from a collective context, particularly in the religious sphere. Cult brotherhoods such as the Arval Brethren (p. 109) may have implied mutual bonds extending

---

[104] Cf. Usener 1901[G152], 1–28. Even within the law the culpability of specific types of action rested principally on tacit general recognition of their delictal character (p. 118).

[105] Table VIII.16; Fraenkel 1925[G211], 185–200 (= 1964, II.400–15). *Contra*, e.g. Wieacker 1956[G326], 462ff.

beyond their immediate cult function as may the aristocratic fraternities (*sodalitates*) which met for ritual performances and common feasts. According to Gaius (*Dig.* XLVII.22.4 = Twelve Tables VIII.27), the Twelve Tables sanctioned the existence of *sodalitates* provided they did not conflict with public legislation. Gaius interprets the provision as embracing all clubs but the term *sodalitas* may originally have characterized specifically cult fraternities,[106] perhaps largely of an aristocratic character. If so, the concern of the Tables with their possible violation of public law (whatever originally that meant) suggests that their activities might in practice extend beyond their immediate cult context.

For the most part, however, ties of comradeship and obligation will have been individual both in origin and nature. The potential importance of marriage customs in fostering a web of such relationships within the aristocracy has already been noted (p. 152) and we must assume that at this level also the individual contracted or inherited a network of personal alliances based on mutual obligation which, by their sheer number and complexity, reinforced the cohesion of the elite. It may be in this context that we should locate the *socii* ('associates') or *sodales* ('comrades') of a P. Valerius attested on the recently discovered inscription from Satricum (p. 97) but regrettably we cannot further define the nature of the bond involved here. Was it a temporary or long-term association (of the type envisaged by the Twelve Tables)? Was it exclusive in character? How great a degree of cohesion was involved? What was the relative status of those concerned? Whether or not he was Roman, had Valerius exercised leadership over his fellows and if so, of what type? It is tempting but speculative to connect this inscription with the literary evidence which suggests that on occasion leading figures in Central Italy in the sixth or early fifth centuries B.C. might acquire bands of comrades, sometimes of comparatively high social status,[107] and that these bands might be used for private ventures without reference to a particular community or even in open opposition to its interests (p. 94f). If such bands were an authentic feature of this period and were to be found also at Rome,[108] this would explain the patriciate's evident concern with individual usurpation at the start of the Republic and the comparatively early legends alleging individual attempts at tyranny. Whereas marriage practices and other social ties might help to cement the bonds within the aristocracy as a whole, here the individual association, temporarily at least, assumes so particular and close a character that it may even threaten the internal stability of that aristocracy.

---

[106] Cf. Marquardt-Wissowa 1881–5[A77], III.134–7. For the Satricum inscription as revealing a possible instance cf. Guarducci 1981[B227], 479–89.

[107] Cf. *ILS* 212 (Mastarna and Caeles Vibenna).

[108] The attested cases all involve men who were at that stage outsiders.

It is also in this context of personal obligation that the ties which bound together men of different status in a relationship of patron and client must be set, although the evidence for early clientship is insufficient to elucidate its character fully since the two principal ancient texts are intrinsically unreliable.[109]

(i) Dionysius attributes to Romulus regulations in which the obligations of the patron comprised primarily support in lawsuits while in return the client afforded his benefactor financial assistance (*Ant. Rom.* II.9–11). This account merits little credence. It appears in an artificial, idealizing context which seeks to turn Romulus into a legislating founder of the Greek type; the references to monetary contributions, to public fines and to the pursuit and expenses of office are clearly anachronistic for the early regal period; and Dionysius proceeds to record individual patronage of communities and peoples in terms which are specifically relevant to late republican conditions. Such relationships can in any case hardly have been the subject of formal state definition from the outset as Dionysius pretends, particularly given the restricted use of legislative enactment in the early period. Only the law penalizing breach of faith by patron or client merits consideration as a possible early provision and that, in part at least, duplicates a regulation elsewhere attributed (not necessarily correctly) to the Twelve Tables (VIII.21).

Dionysius' account must, therefore, be a reconstruction. It is presumably founded in part on mid-republican conditions since he evidently believed that this form of clientship lasted down to the late second century, but it also incorporates etymological speculation and misstatement. Thus Dionysius' belief that patrons could take legal action on behalf of clients can hardly be credited given the strictness of the rules governing the appointment of personal representatives under the older *legis actio* procedures; it is probably a misleading formulation of the patron's later right to act as his client's advocate (e.g., Plaut. *Men.* 571ff), perhaps prompted by the assimilation of the patron's position to that of a father. That comparison in turn clearly depends on the etymological derivation of *patronus* ('patron') from *pater* ('father'), just as the belief, shared by Cicero (*Rep.* II.16), that plebeians were initially all in clientage to individual patricians will derive from a tradition which equated the *patroni* with the *patres/patricii* (cf. Fest. 262L).

(ii) Festus (288L; 289L) derives the name *patres* ('fathers'), applied to the Roman senate, from the fact that Romulus' senators had granted parcels (*partes*) of land to the poor as if to their own sons. This passage,

[109] The following discussion has been much strengthened through access to an unpublished treatment of republican clientage by Professor P. A. Brunt (see now id. *The Fall of the Roman Republic* (Oxford, 1988) 382–442).

which clearly has in mind the identification of senators (*patres*) and patrons (*patroni*), rests on a complex of etymological speculations: the play on *patres–partes*, the equation of *patronus* and *pater* (with again the consequent assimilation of the client's position to that of a son), even perhaps the ancient derivation of *cliens* ('client') from *colere* ('to farm' as well as 'to show respect').[110] Festus cannot, therefore, be used to create an elaborate juristic model in which the client, like a son, received land as a revocable gift (*precarium*) from his patron[111] since the basic comparison of client and son itself rests on spurious conjecture.

The annalists record clients as an important factor in patrician supremacy in the early Republic and purport to show something of their role in political and military affairs, but they provide few clues to the character of the bond itself. We are therefore compelled to rely largely on inference from apparently old established features of the patron–client bond as it existed later between individual free-born citizens.[112] Even this allows tentative inference only at a general level since its precise form(s) may have changed to meet new conditions. In particular it was held in antiquity that clients had been much more closely tied to their patrons in the early and mid-Republic than was true later (so apparently Dionysius). Traditionalists in the second century B.C. might put obligations to a client above those to blood relatives (Cato, *Orat.* fr. 200 Malc.) and a rigid taboo on legal action between patron and client is still attested then. The hereditary character which the relationship still sometimes assumed in the mid-Republic may also indicate the early closeness of the bond.

Nonetheless, the later form assumed by clientship indicates that it was (in theory at least) a voluntary relationship which conferred on the patron no formal rights against the client's person or property.[113] The term *patronus* itself, although again perhaps suggesting a familial character to the association, need imply only a protective or gubernatorial function, not anything comparable to paternal power. Similarly, the fact that the client is said later to be *in fide* to his patron may convey no more than that the latter's position is one of protection deriving from a position of socio-economic superiority and based on social obligation (it can denote no more in the late republican contexts in which it appears). The client bond was not, therefore, akin to serfdom;[114] patronage did not, so far as is known, affect the client's citizen status, personal or

110 Serv. *Aen.* VI.609; *Comm. Eins. gramm. suppl.* 216.24; Lydus, *Mag.* 1.20; Isid. *Orig.* X.53; cf. Sen. *Ep.* XLVII.18; Pliny, *HN* XXXIV.17.   111 Mommsen 1864[G115], 366.

112 Other forms of 'patron–client' relationships (notably that of freedman and ex-master) may have varied to suit their particular context and function and should not be used in this connexion.

113 The circumstances of the case cited in Cic. *De Or.* 1.177 are too obscure (cf. Badian 1958[A8], 7–9) to attest patronal rights of inheritance even in the (much later) period to which it refers.

114 Dionysius' comparison with the *penestai* of Thessaly and *thetes* of early Athens (*Ant. Rom.* II.9.2) is principally concerned to point up the difference.

property rights nor did he become a member of (or the client of) his patron's *gens*. He may even, as later, have been able to enjoy more than one patron. Had clients regularly received land grants (as Festus suggests), one might expect some recompense in the form of share-cropping or periodic labour on the patron's estate but there is no evidence for such a system. If grants were made to clients, therefore, they were probably gifts for which no fixed return was required; but in any case the frequency and even existence of such benefactions entirely escapes us.

In general it may be said that any formalized position of power (patrimonial or personal) enjoyed by the patron or a relationship in which economic exchange was overtly and as such the definitive factor, would so conflict with the later putative character of the patron–client bond that we should hesitate to attribute either to its early republican counterpart, particularly in the absence both of concrete evidence and of a satisfactory explanation for the subsequent transformation of the institution into its later form.[115] There the obligations involved are founded on social expectation, not legalized power, and the services exchanged between patron and client take the form of gifts and mutual aid as required. The traditional ranking of obligations among those to relatives and guest-friends perhaps suggests that the relationship had had that character from an early date; although *cliens* always implied dependence,[116] it denoted a relationship which should, in this application, be based on mutual respect and obligation between fellow-citizens. It is, of course, possible that early clientage was a much more formalized and overtly exploitative relationship than the later ideal, but our evidence provides no firm basis for assuming that this was so, at least in principle,[117] and a number of factors can be cited which would tend to influence the character of the bond to the client's advantage, at least in a fifth-century context. The existence of a substantial, apparently independent stratum in Roman society which formed the backbone of the plebs, developed its own sense of identity and gradually created its own mechanisms for seeking individual and collective redress (p. 212f) implies that clientship (at least to a patrician patron) was not universal. Together with aristocratic rivalry, this may have encouraged competition for the adhesion of clients, who, if they were men of some substance, might also have alternative or supplementary sources of assistance in the continuing obligations of kinsmen, neighbours and friends. And more generally, the

[115] For other views cf., e.g., Mommsen 1859[G115], 322–79; Meier 1966[A78], 24–9; Magdelain 1971[G109], 103–27; Torelli 1974–5[G148], esp. 33–6; Rouland 1979[G134], 23–110.

[116] The etymology of the word and its implications are, however, disputed: Richard 1978[H76], 159–60.

[117] That the Twelve Tables supposedly sought to reinforce the bond by providing a sanction at least against patrons who violated it (Table VIII.21) does not imply a radically different character to the bond itself.

corporate traditions of the community, especially in the context of the city-state, may have helped to restrict abuse and exploitation. Indeed, a putative basis of social obligation between patron and client may be precisely the means whereby the fact of dependence, which the need for protection and assistance created, was integrated into the structure of the citizen community without at the same time undermining it. In contrast, debt-bondage, which did involve formal subjection and manifest exploitation, created sufficient social tensions to prompt its abolition at the end of the fourth century.

As later, legal assistance must have been a major benefit to the client in the early Republic when the difficulties in pursuing a lawsuit were considerable, particularly for the ordinary citizen (p. 233f); but at a wider level also, the protection of the powerful was the best guarantee that the individual's rights would not be infringed, as well as a potential resource when other forms of assistance were required. In return, the patron might anticipate political or other support but above all prestige and approbation as a benefactor able to attract and maintain a following. As such clientship may have operated at relatively high social levels, particularly if (as the annalists suppose) clients were a major source of political support. That belief may be mere conjecture, an attempt to explain the patrician ability to counteract and frustrate the plebs, but if so, it is plausible; the patrician retention of power until the early fourth century is far more readily explicable if collectively they were able to muster substantial numbers of dependants.[118] Dionysius even supposes that they took the field when the plebs refused to serve in the army. That again may be conjecture but it is hardly a retrojection based on the exceptional later instances of politicians raising regular military forces from their clients (essentially Scipio in 134 and Pompey in 83 B.C.) and may represent a dim echo of the use of personal followings in a military context in the early period.[119] This does not, of course, exclude the possibility of much humbler dependants (for whom the protection and other aid afforded would be still more crucial) but they would bring less obvious benefit to the patron and if the relationship functioned at these levels, it apparently did little to prevent impoverishment and subsequent exploitation through debt-bondage.

Similarly, we cannot tell whether the patron–client relationship over-

[118] However, the notion, found occasionally in the sources, that the clients of an individual patron (or of patrons belonging to a single *gens*) might run into several thousands is pure fantasy. Given the likely population levels and patterns of client distribution they can have numbered no more than one or two hundred even in the most exceptional cases, and probably in practice clientship was on a very much smaller scale still.

[119] Cf. also e.g. Fest. 450L. Conceivably such practices had been more common in the less urbanized areas of Italy in historical times: cf. Latte 1936[G639], 68f = id. *Kleine Schriften* 349f; Salmon 1967[J106], 83f; below, p. 292.

lapped with, or ran parallel to, other ties, how large the category of patrons was or from which social groups they were drawn. It should not, however, be assumed that patronage was necessarily the prerogative of a very few or even limited to the patriciate. That the patriciate as a whole did succeed in holding individual ambition and power reasonably in check may indicate a wide distribution of dependants within its ranks and although its political control gave it a particular advantage, the gradual emergence of a powerful plebeian leadership may in part rest on, or have encouraged, the adhesion of clients of their own, particularly if patrician followings were largely recruited at the higher social levels.

(e) *Social stratification*

Within the free-born Roman citizen body the patterns of social differentiation can be sketched only in the crudest outline, not least because the literary sources offer little except vague and unreliable data. As a preliminary, however, we should consider the likely pattern of wealth distribution and here comparatively solid evidence is provided by the so-called 'Servian organization' in which the entire adult male citizenry was assigned to one of five *classes* (with some additional units, particularly for the cavalry and for the poorest citizens (*proletarii*)) according to wealth. Each *classis* contained a given number of units ('centuries'), half for the older men (*seniores*: those over forty-five), half for the younger (*iuniores*) (Table 2). The literary sources ascribe this classification to Servius Tullius, but whilst membership of a *classis* continued to determine liability for military service, what they describe is clearly a later, essentially political structure which developed out of an earlier, much simpler 'hoplite' force (*classis*) with accompanying cavalry and light-armed troops (p. 92f; 103f).

In the fifth century Rome probably needed to have available all possible manpower and therefore kept the qualifications for service to a minimum; leather, for example, may have been widely used for some defensive equipment. Nonetheless, the ability to purchase the necessary armour presumes ownership of property some way above subsistence level and the employment of such a 'hoplite' force therefore implies the existence of a substantial peasantry. The size of this class and its strength in proportion to the total population are, however, impossible to estimate. Whether even the single legion of 6000 infantry had been achieved by the fifth century cannot be determined. At the start of the republican period the maximum extent of Roman territory was *c.* 822 km.[2] (and did not significantly increase until the late fifth century) but too little is known of its agricultural resources, pattern of exploitation and degree of market development to assess even the total population; and even

Table 2. *The centuriate organization according to Livy*

Class	Number of centuries		Wealth qualification (in asses)	Arms
	junior	senior		
I	40	40	100,000	helmet, round shield, greaves, breastplate, spear and sword
	+ 2 centuries of engineers (*fabri*)			
II	10	10	75,000–100,000	oblong shield; no breast-plate. Otherwise as Class I
III	10	10	50,000–75,000	no greaves. Otherwise as Class II
IV	10	10	25,000–50,000	spear and javelin
V	15	15	11,00–25,000	slings and stones
	+ 3 centuries of supernumeraries (primarily or entirely musicians) 1 century of *proletarii* (below 11,000 asses) 18 centuries of cavalry with public horse			

Source: Livy 1.43.1ff; cf. Dion. Hal. *Ant. Rom.* IV.16–18.

attempts to assess the likely *maximum* population are bedevilled by uncertainties, particularly over cereal yields and the extent of land in cultivation.[120] However, retrospective application of the highest population density figures for Central Italy in 225 B.C.[121] suggests that even with a territory of 822 km.[2] Rome would have found considerable difficulty in mustering a 'hoplite' force of 6000[122] and could have fielded a significantly lower total. It has been argued[123] that the progressive increase in

[120] Thus the calculation of Ampolo 1980[C2], 27–30, who suggests 35,000 as the maximum total population, assumes that only *c.* ⅔ of the land was under cultivation, that the net surplus of cereal production was of the order of 315–67 kg. per hectare (problematic: p. 121), that the entire population lived at subsistence level and (implausibly: p. 120) that there was a universal annual fallow. Most seriously, it underestimates subsistence needs (which should for this purpose be based on modern calculations of the level required for long-term viability rather than the starvation rations of the Twelve Tables or the Syracusan stone quarries). The cumulative effect of these uncertainties cannot be estimated, but if modern subsistence needs are taken as the basis (p. 121 n. 22), it seems unlikely that the *free* population can have exceeded Ampolo's figure even if somewhat higher cereal yields and a somewhat greater area under cultivation are assumed. The actual free population may well have been markedly lower.

[121] That of the Latins (Brunt 1971[A21], 54) which would yield a total free population of *c.* 33,000 on an area of 822 km.[2], although the greater incidence of slavery in the third century, the disparity in the areas compared and possible changes in the density and patterns of settlement may all affect the comparison.

[122] A maximum free population of 33,000 correlates with an adult male population of *c.* 10,000 (Brunt, loc. cit.). This, however, not only includes *seniores* (not necessarily exempt from regular field service at this stage) but the large proportion (possibly a majority) who did not qualify for service in the heavy infantry or cavalry.   [123] E.g. Sumner 1970[G728], 67–78.

the numbers of the consular tribunate from three (444 B.C.) to six (406 B.C.) reflects an increase in army strength from an original complement of 3000 to one of 6000 in the later fifth century but this is both unproven and unlikely. Rome enjoyed only a modest increase in territory in this period and it is difficult to believe that she had previously set the qualifications for 'hoplite' service so high that she could now double her effective manpower by their reduction. Clearly the figure of six thousand was reached before the creation of a second legion (for which it also provided the notional complement) but that may be no earlier than the mid-fourth century; if this division of military forces is connected with the dual consulship, it may reflect the re-institution of that office in 366 rather than its (controversial) initial creation in the late sixth century.[124]

The 'Servian organization' also suggests the existence of large numbers of citizens well below the 'hoplite' level. Its structure was designed to leave the decisive political voice with the cavalry and the more prosperous heavy infantry by allocating a much smaller number of centuries to each of the four lowest classes. Yet the thirty centuries of the lowest class (V) exceed those assigned to each of classes II–IV. Presumably, therefore, those qualified only for the most basic light-armed service were far too numerous to be confined to the twenty notional centuries allocated to the preceding three classes. The actual ratios involved cannot be determined but the implication that there were substantial numbers of very small property-holders can scarcely be avoided; and even if the 'Servian organization' in its developed form may be no older than the fourth century, the position clearly cannot have been radically different in the fifth, when the general economic pressures were probably more severe. Moreover, Class V did not include the poorest citizens, the *proletarii*, used for military service only in an emergency. Their numbers are unknown,[125] but they were at least sufficiently numerous to be the subject of a special provision in the Twelve Tables (I.4). The overall impression is that a distinguishable proportion of the population lived at or not far above subsistence level and this accords with the prevalence of debt, the practice of selling children and the possible growing pressure for the acquisition or at least use of new territory for settlement.

Equally important, however, to the political conflicts of the early Republic are the possible differentiations among the comparatively wealthy. An aristocratic lifestyle and the exercise of political responsibilities implied a substantial level of wealth and the leisure which accompanied it. The naming of rural tribes after patrician clans (p. 179) may

[124] Cf. above, p. 104; see further below, p. 248.
[125] Dionysius' belief (*Ant. Rom.* IV.18.2; VII.59.6; but cf. V.67.5) that they accounted for half the population (cf. also Cic. *Rep.* II.40) must be based, at best, on later conditions.

reflect important land-holdings by their members in the area concerned. Certainly the regulations of the Twelve Tables restricting funerary extravagance attest families able to afford such flamboyant and prestigious demonstrations as well as other aristocratic activities (notably the racing of chariots). Yet not all patricians may have been able to match the affluence of their peers. In particular, the rapid eclipse of many families, apparent from the consular *fasti*, may in part reflect economic weakness, exacerbated by the system of partible inheritance, *in manum* marriage and dowry provision. Moreover, the Decemviral prohibition on full marriages between patricians and plebeians (p. 180) and the subsequent success of certain plebeian families in establishing political dynasties suggest that some of these could already match the economic status of many patricians.

As the preceding paragraph implies, distinctions of wealth cannot necessarily be correlated with differentiation of status in early republican Rome. Indeed, it is possible to assemble from the Twelve Tables and other evidence a variety of antitheses which express differing modes of status classification or particular social relationships within the citizen body in the early Republic: patrician and plebeian, patron and client, *classis* and *infra classem* (p. 103), cavalry and infantry, *assidui* and *proletarii*, seniors and juniors. Most of these contrasts are specific to one particular context (political, social or military) and cannot be correlated with each other or, usually, extended beyond their original reference. That patrons and clients were originally identified with patricians and plebeians, for example, is merely spurious ancient conjecture (p. 159). Similarly, there is no direct evidence that the pairing 'people and plebs' (*populus plebesque*) in certain later formulae goes back to the early Republic and shows that the plebs were then the *infra classem*, i.e. those outside the army (the *populus*); the pairing would prove only that the two terms were not coextensive, not that they referred to two entirely distinct groups, and may in any case be a later pleonasm deriving from the use of 'populus' and 'plebs' for the centuriate and plebeian assemblies respectively.[126]

Where these individual contrasts are, on occasion, employed outside their original context, it is usually for a particular purpose. So the *assiduus–proletarius* contrast, which was ultimately wealth-based, is introduced into Twelve Tables 1.4,[127] either as a measure of relief to *proletarii* or to protect the legal adversaries of *assidui* by ensuring that anyone who intervened on their behalf (probably after judgement) was able to meet the potential liabilities involved.[128] In either case the contrast has here

---

[126] Cf. Stuart Jones 1928[A128], 450–2. For a different view see p. 104.
[127] 'For an *assiduus* let an *assiduus* act as champion (*vindex* (p. 156)), for a *proletarius* let anyone who wishes act as champion.'   [128] Cf. *lex col. Gen. Iuliae* (*FIRA* I, n. 21) *c.* 61.

been employed for a highly specific purpose and hence does not appear elsewhere in the preserved fragments of the Twelve Tables. In general these antitheses seem to be confined to their original application and their multiplicity and probable lack of correlation appear to imply the absence of a formalized social hierarchy which acted as the determinant of status throughout public and social life.

The partial exception is the patrician–plebeian contrast. Fundamentally in the early Republic this was political in character, marking off the patriciate as a hereditary privileged group which reputedly monopolized office. So far, therefore, as the 'plebs' are simply the non-patricians, the term does not necessarily denote any homogeneous body within Roman society (p. 235). It is the patriciate which here forms a distinct and self-contained group and their exclusiveness impinged on other spheres also, notably control of public religion and the prohibition of patrician–plebeian intermarriage.[129] These, however, are themselves linked to their political predominance (and efforts to preserve it) and although that in turn implies (and, in the final analysis, rests on) the exercise of considerable social and economic leverage, there is no good evidence that the patriciate itself represents the totality of a particular social or economic class (however defined), that it was marked out by a peculiar source of wealth (e.g. pasturage as opposed to agriculture or land as opposed to 'commerce') or that its roots lay in some other distinction (for example, ethnic differences or priority of presence at the site of Rome). Nor are there solid grounds for believing that the patriciate enjoyed a specifically military origin, as the regal cavalry.[130] Admittedly, while the military tactics and functions of the cavalry in the era of 'hoplite' warfare are highly controversial,[131] they do seem to have enjoyed a special prestige and status, conceivably greater than their purely military role warranted and perhaps indicative of their aristocratic character. They were, for example, recruited and organized separately from the infantry, in divisions which were apparently based on the pre-Servian tribes, and on the nomination of a dictator they were assigned their own subordinate commander, the 'master of horse' (*magister equitum*). Both horse and fodder were, of course, provided at public expense but this in itself, if not a later innovation,[132] may be as much a mark of honour as a form of financial relief. Moreover, the right to a public horse was conferred by

---

[129] The distinctive marriage form known as *confarreatio*, required for certain priests and their parents, may have been reserved to patricians but this is not directly attested.

[130] As Alföldi 1952[H1]; id. 1965[H2], 21–34; 1967[H3], 13–47; 1968[H4], 444–60. For further discussion see above, p. 102.   [131] Cf. Stary 1981[G719], 95–9, 124–5, 157–8, 165–8.

[132] The system of using the contributions of widows and orphans to finance the equestrian subventions can hardly precede the regular imposition of *tributum*: cf. Gabba 1977[G587], 24–6 (citing Plut. *Cam.* 2.4; *Publ.* 12.4 against Cic. *Rep.* II.36; Livy 1.43.9). Cf. also the changes in the supply of horses for chariot-racing (Rawson 1981[G126], 1ff, esp. 4f).

the magistrate conducting the census who would presumably give preference to those of his own class with the leisure to acquire and practise the skills involved. The popularity of equestrian scenes in archaic Etruscan art, the tendency to represent persons of rank in a chariot or on horseback and the probable participation of aristocrats in equestrian sports serve to confirm this elitist character, as does the fact that at Rome the cavalry centuries originally voted first in the centuriate assembly.[133] In both the military and political spheres, therefore, cavalry service may well have provided a distinctive and prestigious role for the aristocratic young, but this does not prove a formal identity between cavalry and patriciate. The alleged coincidences of equestrian and patrician dress and ornament have largely proved illusory[134] and there is no evidence that service in a corps which probably required particular attributes of skill and physique (cf. Gell. *NA* vi.22.1) was formally restricted to a specific social or political group.[135]

Of the lifestyle and values of this aristocracy little is known, although the importance of revenge for injuries suffered, of personal honour and of social obligation have already been noted. The hereditary character of the patriciate will certainly have reinforced the emphasis on ancestry and it is a reasonable assumption that the traditions of private generosity were paralleled by an expectation of public liberality also. Aristocratic display is obviously implied in the Twelve Tables' restrictions on funerary extravagance and other evidence also suggests a milieu similar to the exuberant world of games, banquets, hunts and war so vividly illustrated in archaic and sub-archaic Etruscan art (cf. also Fig. 38). The elder Cato recalled the distant practice of celebrating heroic deeds at aristocratic feasts (Cic. *Brut.* 75; *Tusc.* iv.3) and such banquets formed an integral part of some religious celebrations. The taste for the heroic may explain the popularity of such figures as Hercules, and the old traditions of aristocratic combat still survived, notably in the 'spoils of honour' (*spolia opima*) gained (according to the usual version) by a commander who killed an enemy commander. Those traditions, reputedly exemplified by A. Cornelius Cossus' slaughter of a Veientan king in 437 B.C. in a cavalry duel, conflicted sharply with the disciplines of 'hoplite' warfare, as the legends narrating the executions of a Postumius (432 or 431 B.C.) and a T. Manlius (347 B.C.) for defying orders may originally have demonstrated. The adoption of 'hoplite' tactics will have reduced the

[133] Livy 1.43.11, not necessarily contradicted by Dion. Hal. *Ant. Rom.* iv.18.3; vii.59.3; x.17.3. For a different view cf. Momigliano 1966[H59], 21ff (= id. *Quarto Contributo* 387ff).

[134] See Momigliano 1966[H59], 16–24 (= id. *Quarto Contributo* 377–94); 1969[H62], 385–8 (= id. *Quinto Contributo* 635–9).

[135] That assumption would be justified if the century or centuries termed 'procum patricium' were exclusively patrician and identical with the six earliest equestrian centuries (so, for the early Republic, Thomsen 1980[F62], 193–8) but neither contention is more than conjecture.

Fig. 38a. Terracotta frieze plaque depicting chariot race (late sixth century?). Reconstructed from fragments found on the Palatine and corresponding examples from Velletri. From Gjerstad 1953–74 [A56], iv.480 fig. 145.

Fig. 38b. Terracotta frieze plaque depicting banqueting scene (late sixth century?). Reconstructed from one fragment found at Rome and corresponding examples from Velletri. From Gjerstad 1953–73 [A56], iv.481 fig. 146.

Fig. 39. Incised discus from warrior tomb at Lanuvium (second quarter of the fifth century?).
From Colonna 1977 [B312], 156f fig. 10/A and B.

scope for this form of aristocratic prowess but will not have undermined the values which it represented,[136] and the rewards of military valour were probably specifically exempted from the Decemviral restrictions on grave goods. So also were the victory wreaths won by the aristocrat, suggesting that he might himself participate in equestrian or other contests on the Greek model[137]. The tomb of a warrior at Lanuvium,[138] buried with discus (Fig. 39), strigils and containers for sand, oil and perfumes, still more obviously reflects the influence of Greek athletic traditions, although in this case not necessarily in a competitive context.

The emergence of the patriciate, its establishment of its political pre-eminence and attempts to reinforce its dominance by (*inter alia*) social exclusivity epitomize the potential tensions inherent in the social and political organization of the Roman city-state. On the one hand substantial material inequalities had helped to foster the emergence of an elite which was able to capitalize on its position of privilege to reduce numbers of fellow citizens to a position of dependence, whether in the form of debt-bondage or clientship. At the same time, the progressive transformation of this elite (or a part of it) into a closed hereditary caste created an artificial distinction which was almost inevitably open to challenge, since its position increasingly failed to reflect the realities of social and economic status; it enjoyed, it seems, a monopoly neither of wealth nor, increasingly, of that military prestige which was a major determinant of reputation and status. Moreover, the pre-eminence of the patriciate stood in potential conflict with the needs and aspirations of the citizen community as a whole. If the vertical bonds of patron and client encouraged (to an extent that is unknown) the fragmentation of the ordinary populace, the established patterns of mutual co-operation, common membership of the citizen body and, above all, the regular participation of a large proportion of the community in its major military force necessarily fostered a sense of common commitments and therefore of common rights; and it was to be the translation of this awareness onto the political level which was to provoke the major internal confrontations of the fifth century B.C.

---

[136] For its later survival and function cf. Oakley 1985[G686], 392ff.
[137] Rawson 1981[G126], 1ff.   [138] Galieti 1938[B332], 282–9; Colonna 1977[B312], 150–5.

CHAPTER 5

ROME IN THE FIFTH CENTURY II:
THE CITIZEN COMMUNITY

A. DRUMMOND

I. POLITICAL AND CONSTITUTIONAL DEVELOPMENTS

(a) *The ancient account*

The literary sources present a broadly uniform picture of the constitutional developments of the early Republic.[1] In *c.* 509 B.C. the forcible seduction of Lucretia (wife of L. Tarquinius Collatinus) by Tarquinius Superbus' son Sextus and her subsequent suicide prompted a revolution, led by L. Iunius Brutus. Superbus was driven from Rome and an already well-established hereditary aristocracy, the patriciate, assumed control of the state, monopolizing political office. From the first the secular powers of the kings were vested in two magistrates, later known as consuls but at first as praetors, who were elected by the people and held office for one year. They did not, however, inherit the king's sacral powers, although they had the right and duty on prescribed occasions to ascertain the will of the gods by 'taking the auspices'. Some of the king's sacrificial duties were committed to a newly established *rex sacrorum*, a priest holding office for life, but control of religious practices is, later at least, found in the hands of the *pontifex maximus*.

The consuls commanded Rome's armies and exercised civil (and potentially at least criminal) jurisdiction. They also presided over the senate and assemblies and in general acted as the chief executives of the state. Originally they took the census but this function was transferred in 443 B.C. to two censors elected at intervals, who also at some stage acquired from the consuls the duty of compiling the list of senators. If both consuls were absent from Rome they would appoint a prefect of the city to see to its protection and any necessary domestic administration. They were also assisted by two junior magistrates called quaestors (raised to four in 421 B.C.) who were charged chiefly with financial duties.

Romans saw the establishment of the consulship as the beginning of

---

[1] The principal accounts are those of Livy (Books II–V), Dionysius of Halicarnassus (*Ant. Rom.* Books V–XIII (only fragments after 443 B.C.)), Cicero (*Rep.* II.53–63), Plutarch (*Publicola, Coriolanus* and *Camillus*) and Dio-Zonaras (Dio Books III–VI (vol. I, pp. 35–77 Boiss.); Zonar. VII.12–22).

freedom, but acknowledged an early predominance of the aristocracy and unhindered exercise of power by the consuls who, it was supposed, jointly possessed the plenitude of regal authority. However, it was also believed that the collegiate character of the office itself acted as a limitation; each consul had equal power and could thus take action to nullify abuses by his colleague. Moreover, the consuls normally sought and complied with the advice of the senate on any issue of substance; for the annalists the senate is already the central instrument of government.

In emergencies, often because their powers were insufficient to deal effectively with plebeian recalcitrance, one of the consuls, in conformity with a decree of the senate, would nominate a single man as dictator; assisted by a 'master of horse' (*magister equitum*) of his own choice, he was exempt from the limitations gradually imposed on the power of the consuls but he was expected to resign his office not later than six months after nomination. In 451/450 B.C. the consulship was replaced by the Decemvirates (p. 114) and was also in abeyance in most years between 444 and 366 when consular power was vested in three, four or six military tribunes.

Some at least believed that this 'consular tribunate' was open to plebeians from the start, although none were in fact elected until 400, and that plebeians were granted access to the quaestorship in 421. With these exceptions, however, both magistracies and priesthoods were a patrician preserve. Only when the consulship was reinstituted in 366 was it made a rule that one consul should be plebeian. The admission of plebeians to other political offices followed fairly rapidly but entry to the two most politically important priesthoods, the pontificate and augurate, came only in 300 B.C.

Much of this account has been challenged by modern scholars. For instance, it has often been held that the kings were not immediately replaced by a dual magistracy; some think that the fall of the monarchy must be placed much later than was believed in antiquity, others that the patriciate itself or its monopoly of office was only gradually established. Crucial to any consideration of these theories is the reliability of the consular list, which purports to record the names of the chief magistrates of the Roman state from the last decade of the sixth century and provides the basis for key elements of the traditional narrative. Hence a consideration of the accuracy of the *fasti* must precede a more detailed discussion of early republican constitutional history.

(b) *The consular fasti and the date of the Republic*

The consular lists current in the late Republic betray a number of possible spurious additions. The register for the first year of the Republic suffered progressive interpolation.[2] P. Valerius Poplicola's subsequent series of consulships, two with a Lucretius (in 508 and 504) and one (in 507) with Horatius[3] (suspiciously parallel to the famous Valerio-Horatian consulship of 449), is also disturbing, even if perhaps reflecting an initial political dominance of a peculiarly powerful figure. Later in the fifth century Diodorus has (or had) two or three additional years whose authenticity is dubious[4] and the Second Decemvirate, if not the First, is open to suspicion (p. 114). In the era of the consular tribunate (444–367) the evidence of the Linen Books may reveal one or two added names (p. 18), two apparently plebeian names (in 444 and 422 respectively) are highly dubious (p. 193), and there are some puzzling irregularities in the lists for 389, 387, 380 and 379.[5] At the end of this period the 'five year period without magistrates' or 'anarchy' (375–371 B.C.)[6] is historically implausible (cf. p. 348) and was probably intended to correlate the (pre-Varronian) Roman date for the Gallic Sack with an independent synchronism of that event in Greek sources (perhaps originally Philistus or Timaeus): the surviving consular list(s) had preserved five years too few to meet that Greek date (ol. 98.2 (387/6 B.C.)) and the anarchy made up the deficit. Finally, four 'dictator years' (333, 324, 309 and 301), in which dictators with their *magistri equitum* supposedly held office alone, were added to the *fasti* in a few sources, probably in the first century B.C. (ib.).

Alongside these interpolations we must also reckon with the possibility of omissions in the surviving lists. Indeed, given the hazards of transmission, loss of names or colleges may be as significant a factor as interpolation. If, for example, the Greek synchronism for the Gallic Sack is accurate, it seems to imply the loss of entire colleges from the fourth-century list[7] and the same would presumably then also be true of the fifth-century *fasti*,[8] although not necessarily on a large scale.

---

[2] Cf. Ogilvie 1965[B129], 232; Richard 1978[H76], 474ff.

[3] 'Lucretius' in Livy II.15.1.

[4] Between 458 and 457; 457 and 456; 428 and 427. Cf. Drummond 1980[D9], 69–71.

[5] Below, p. 193 n. 58. The uneven occurrence and variations in size of the early colleges of consular tribunes also present an intractable problem (p. 195) but allegations of widespread interpolation in Livy and the Capitoline Fasti cannot be substantiated on the basis of Diodorus' abbreviated lists (cf. Drummond loc.cit.).

[6] In Diod. xv.75.1 this has been reduced to one year, perhaps through negligence (Perl 1957[D25], 113). In compensation for this and for his omission of the college of 367 B.C. Diodorus repeats the colleges of 394–390 B.C.

[7] There seems to have been no fixed date for the start of the consular year in the early Republic and if both consuls left office early or the appointment of successors was delayed, the new consuls probably counted their year of office from their own entry date. This alone, however, cannot explain the apparent defects in the fourth-century list.

[8] A possible instance may lie behind the variants under 444 B.C., where according to Licinius Macer the Linen Books gave a consulship of L. Papirius Mugillanus and L. Sempronius Atratinus, also allegedly recorded in a treaty with Ardea (presumably in an accompanying protocol): Livy

None of these defects, however, casts serious doubt on the core of the preserved list; they may merely represent the inevitable corruption that results from repeated transmission over the centuries or (in some cases) deliberate manipulation for specific and limited purposes. More significant reservations concern a number of early fifth-century consuls. Their family names are known later only as plebeian but they hold office in a period in which, according to the literary sources, the patriciate monopolized the chief magistracy. The following list of such consuls[9] is typical:

L. Iunius Brutus (509)
Sp. Cassius Vicellinus (502; 493; 486)
Post. Cominius Auruncus (501; 493)
M'. Tullius Longus (500)
M. Minucius Augurinus (497; 491)
P. Minucius Augurinus (492)
T. Sicinius (or Siccius) Sabinus (487)
C. Aquillius Tuscus (487)
T. Numicius Priscus (469)
P. Volumnius Amintinus Gallus (461)
L. Minucius Esquilinus Augurinus (458)
Q. Minucius Esquilinus (457)
Sp. Tarpeius Montanus Capitolinus (454)
A. Aternius Varus Fontinalis (454)
T. Genucius (*cos. des.* 451; Decemvir 451)
M. Genucius Augurinus (445)

These names are sometimes accepted as both authentic and plebeian with, in consequence, no patrician monopoly of office in this period.[10] Alternatively, that monopoly is accepted and these consuls repudiated as fiction.[11] Both solutions, however, assume that these names are not patrician. Yet two of these families (the Tarpeii and Aternii) are never reliably recorded as plebeian and six of the remaining ten (the Aquillii, Cassii, Cominii, Numicii, Tullii and Volumnii) show a considerable interval between their last appearance in an ostensibly 'patrician' office and their first in a clearly plebeian post. There may, therefore, be no direct descent involved, particularly since the Italic practice of using patronymics as family names (p. 98) readily leads to the adoption of the same name by unrelated individuals and clans. Even where consular names were held also by plebeians in the early Republic (as, allegedly,

---

IV.7.10–12; cf. Cic. *Fam.* IX.21.2; Dion. Hal. *Ant. Rom.* XI.62.3f. The accuracy of this account is contentious (despite Livy the evidence of the Linen Books and the Ardeate treaty need not be mutually independent and therefore confirmatory) but if it is reliable, this cannot be a college of suffect consuls, replacing the consular tribunes of the year as Livy and Dionysius pretend (Mommsen 1859[D22], 93f); it would be an additional consular year already lost in the early annalists (Livy IV.7.10).   [9] Based on Beloch 1926[A12], 9–22.
[10] So first Schaefer 1876[H84], 569ff.   [11] Beloch loc. cit.

with the Iunii, Siccii/Sicinii, Genucii and Minucii), the plebeian status of these consuls would remain unproven, for the co-existence of patrician and plebeian homonyms is familiar from the late Republic, above all among the Claudii, Servilii and Veturii.

Moreover, the criteria of plebeian status applied to these *gentes* (that they hold no clearly patrician post after 367 but have homonyms in plebeian offices in the republican period) imply that other early consular families are also plebeian: the Menenii, Curiatii, Sestii/Sextii, Aebutii, Curtii, Lucretii and perhaps Verginii and Sempronii. Since these clans appear in office until the early fourth century, their acceptance as plebeian entails either that there has been large-scale interpolation throughout the fifth century *fasti* or that there was no period at which the patriciate alone held office.[12] Such radical conclusions are difficult to accept. It is easier to believe that, as with the Papirii in the late Republic, these are all patrician houses which progressively died out or at least declined into obscurity, especially as the sharp decrease in the number of posts available to, or reserved to, patricians after 367 meant reduced opportunities for the lesser families to hold offices that would reveal their patrician status.

There are, therefore, no solid grounds for disputing the general credibility of the core of the preserved consular list,[13] and certain of its features taken together indicate that it is substantially reliable even for the fifth century. A notable number of rare or obsolete family names appear. The forenames (*praenomina*) employed by the consuls are progressively restricted to the later canonical range. The most overtly Etruscan names also gradually disappear and no room seems to have been found initially for such famous legendary figures as Coriolanus and Cincinnatus. Moreover, the list presents a coherent picture of changing fortunes within the aristocracy itself and of the decline of individual families at least from the mid-fifth century.[14] It also tacitly implies important and plausible principles governing the aristocratic sharing of office (p. 206). Whilst, therefore, the list may suffer both from omissions and from some later interpolations, its evidence for the early chief magistrates is probably broadly accurate.

The general reliability of the *fasti* implies acceptance also of the traditional chronology of the Republic which is based on them. Although strictly consuls were recorded as the eponymous officials of the year rather than as the chief magistrates of the Roman state, their use for this purpose is *prima facie* evidence that they were already the

---

[12] So Palmer 1970[A102]; cf. Cornell 1983[H18], 101ff.
[13] For reservations based on doubts about the initial form of the chief magistracy cf. p. 186f.
[14] Beloch 1926[A12], 22–6; cf. also Tables 3 and 4 (p. 207–8).

principal magistrates and the ancient assumption that the inception of the consular list implies the overthrow of the monarchy seems unexceptionable.[15] Hence, if the surviving *fasti* are substantially reliable, the Republic was instituted in or by the late sixth century and modern attempts to redate it to *c.* 475 or 450 B.C.[16] must fail, especially since the further arguments adduced to support such a redating are inadequate.[17] Moreover, the ancient chronology for the establishment of the Republic provides the most satisfactory context for the political developments of the early fifth century, above all the emergence of the plebeian movement which sought to assert and defend the rights of some or all non-patricians. That chronology may also be supported by archaeological evidence from the 'king's house' (Regia), which appears only at the end of the sixth century to have assumed the form which became invariable thereafter;[18] a link with the creation of the priest-king (*rex sacrorum*) at the establishment of the Republic is plausible, though not provable.

Other data which are sometimes cited in support of the traditional chronology are less certain. Thus Dionysius dates to 505/4 the Latins' appeal to Aristodemus of Cumae for aid against Porsenna soon after the Romans' expulsion of their last king (*Ant. Rom.* VII.5.1) and it is possible that he derived this date from the independent Greek source on which he evidently drew for his account of Aristodemus (p. 1f). We cannot be sure, however, that this is the case or that his Greek source was not itself available to the earliest Roman historians and used by them to date the Porsenna episode. Similar uncertainty surrounds Cn. Flavius' alleged dating of the dedication of the Capitoline temple to 507 B.C. (p. 627 n. 13). It is again possible that this date was established independently of the consular *fasti* and on that basis might confirm the date of the first year of the Republic in which (according to later tradition) the temple was dedicated. However, both hypotheses are fragile: we do not know how Flavius calculated his date, and the date of the dedication of the Capitoline temple is a notorious crux. There is no reason to doubt a sixth-century date for the temple as such,[19] but unless this was a reconsecration occasioned by the expulsion of an earlier dedicator (i.e. Tarquinius Superbus), the traditional location of the dedication in the first year of

---

[15] The inference would be reinforced if (i) the Capitoline temple was dedicated by a consul (M. Horatius) in the late sixth century and (ii) the rule that the 'greatest praetor' should insert a nail in the temple wall each year (p. 187) was established at the time of the dedication. Neither, however, is certain: Horatius' dedication may be an inference (below) and analogous later documents suggest that temple regulations in this period would not be explicitly dated.

[16] Hanell 1946[G611]; Gjerstad 1962[A57]; id. 1953–73[A56]; Bloch 1959[F9], 118ff; Werner 1963[A134].

[17] See e.g. Momigliano 1963[A83], 101–6 (= id. *Terzo Contributo* 558–67); Ogilvie 1964[A95], 85–7.   [18] Brown 1974–5[E79], 15ff; cf. above, Fig. 13a–d (p. 46–7).

[19] See Drerup 1974[G394], 1–12.

the Republic is too obviously symbolic to be accepted.[20] All this, however, is of secondary significance. The essential fact is that the Republic was established in or very close to the last decade of the sixth century, a date which rests ultimately on the consular list.

(c) *The patriciate and the senate*

In explaining the origins of the Republic the Roman tradition concentrated on proximate causes linked to their depiction of the last king in terms of the stereotyped features of Greek tyrants, where the sexual abuse of subjects is a recurrent theme. Even so, the surviving narratives are unsatisfactory, for they seem to reflect a combination of two distinct motifs. Lucretia and Brutus have no integral connexion and presumably represent independent narratives subsequently combined or the interpolation of Brutus into a pre-existing legend. Both motifs betray a characteristic aristocratic tendency to assign an individualist explanation to political change but whether either has any basis in fact we do not know. The narrative itself is generally reminiscent of the overthrow of several Greek tyrannies essentially for reasons of individual vengeance (cf. Arist. *Pol.* v.1311a32ff) but has no exact Greek parallel and neither the patrician Lucretii (who disappear after 381 B.C.) nor their plebeian namesakes were of sufficient prominence to be able to impose the legend of Lucretia on Roman tradition themselves. Brutus' role was no less widely accepted and his statue allegedly appeared alongside those of the kings on the Capitol, but his involvement may reflect merely the spurious claims of the later (plebeian) Iunii Bruti or a deduction from his appearance at the head of the consular list.

However, even if it were authentic, in part or in whole, the revolution narrative would identify only the immediate background to the expulsion of an individual king, ascribing it to motives of personal honour and revenge among his own circle. It does not illuminate the more fundamental factors which determined the transition from monarchy to aristocracy. Nor does the attractive modern conjecture that it was in fact Porsenna's seizure and subsequent abandonment of Rome which opened the way to aristocratic government (cf. p. 258f). Nonetheless, it does appear that, in one way or another, the monarchy was ended by force. That some of the king's religious functions passed to a *rex sacrorum* is no evidence that the transition to the Republic was achieved only by a gradual reduction in the king's powers.[21] The *rex sacrorum* was almost

---

[20] The name of the alleged dedicator Horatius may not have been recorded epigraphically (p. 21 n. 40) and may simply be derived from the consular *fasti* for the first year of the Republic. The dedication is dated to Horatius' *second* consulship by Dion. Hal. *Ant. Rom.* v.35.3; Tac. *Hist.* III.72.

[21] De Sanctis 1907–64[A37], I.401; cf. Guarino 1948[F31], 95ff; 1963[F32], 346ff; 1971[G533], 312ff; 1975[H40], 135ff; 305ff.

certainly not an independent Roman creation but derived directly or indirectly from Greek models.[22] Since in historical times he was selected by the *pontifex maximus* in the manner of other major priests and was barred from political office, there is no reason to doubt that his institution was a deliberate act after the last king was expelled. That seems to be indicated by subsequent Roman hostility to monarchy, which is evident both in individual legends detailing the fate of those accused of aiming at autocratic power in the early Republic (p. 183) and in the whole structure of republican government (cf. esp. p. 205f). The (re)construction of the Regia in the late sixth century may also offer further confirmation.

For Roman sources the revolution represented a seizure of power by a clearly defined patriciate, which already in the regal period had monopolized the priesthoods, the senate and the *interregnum* procedure (p. 184) by which a new king was appointed.[23] Much of this account cannot be controlled, but if the sixteen earliest rural tribes were instituted under the later monarchy,[24] they indicate already a powerful presence of families included in the historical patriciate since ten are named after known patrician *gentes* (the remaining six names are similarly formed and may derive from clans which subsequently disappeared). Still more, the later patrician monopoly of positions (such as that of the chief *curio* (*curio maximus*)) which were of increasingly little significance under the Republic and of other archaic priesthoods like the Salii can be plausibly attributed to the regal period. Such religious prerogatives in turn may imply a major role in the formulation and preservation of the law, which rested with the *pontifices* as far back as we can trace. Indeed, the aristocracy's position may owe much to the development of religious and legal traditions not publicly accessible and demanding both expertise and the leisure and opportunity to acquire it. Though the king himself had significant ritual functions and may have assumed overall charge of religious matters, by the end of the monarchy there was a wide variety of specialized priesthoods immediately responsible for most public religious ordinances and observances (pp. 582ff) and patricians may already have monopolized most of these. In addition, the patriciate may have acquired political prerogatives under the kings, notably the right to a predominant or even exclusive position in the senate (and thereby perhaps control of the *interregnum* procedure). The term *patricius* itself clearly derives from the appellation *patres*, whose later use both for the patrician

---

[22] E.g. Momigliano 1971[F50], 357–64 (= id. *Quarto Contributo* 395–402).

[23] On the patriciate in the regal period and the *interregnum* procedure see also above, p. 101f.

[24] Taylor 1960[G733], 3–7; cf. Sherwin-White 1973[A123], 195–7; below, p. 245f. For other views cf. Humbert 1978[J184], 49–84; Thomsen 1980[F62], 115–43 (both dating the establishment of many or all of the early rural tribes to *c.* 495 B.C. on the basis of Livy II.21.7).

senators and for the senate as a whole[25] may indicate that the patriciate
had once monopolized that body, presumably again at an early date. A
nascent patriciate may, therefore, have acquired an identity, status and
privileges under the later monarchy, which, reinforced by its wealth and
nexus of social ties and dependants, would have enabled it to seize and
monopolize power after the expulsion of the kings.

This belief is, however, frequently challenged, principally on the basis
that the consular list shows plebeians in office as late as 445 B.C. and thus
demonstrates that the patriciate was established only at that date or, at the
least, that it was only then that its composition and prerogatives received
final and formal definition.[26] There is, of course, no intrinsic difficulty in
believing that whilst a privileged hereditary elite developed in the later
regal period, its composition was only finally determined in the early
Republic, when it became crucial to control the right both to hold office
in the new Republic and to sit in its chief decision-making body, the
senate. Indeed, if the legend of Att(i)us Clausus' emigration to Rome and
admission to the patriciate c. 504 B.C. is to be believed, it offers a concrete
instance of an initial continuing readiness to admit new blood and there
may have been a corresponding fluctuation in the status of some marginal gentes. Whether, however, the early fifth-century 'plebeian' consuls
in fact represent families subsequently excluded from an emerging
patriciate or non-patricians admitted to office in the early Republic as a
means of securing support for the new political regime must be much
more dubious, since the alleged 'plebeian' names in the early fasti may as
easily be patrician (p. 175f) and the principal supporting arguments
adduced to prove a republican origin for the patriciate are inadequate.

Thus, it is argued that some of the kings (Numa Pompilius, Ancus
Marcius, Tullus Hostilius and Servius Tullius), curiae and hills of the
Septimontium bear family names held later only by plebeians. This,
however, demonstrates nothing for the emergence of the historical
patriciate in the early Republic rather than the later monarchy, particularly since in every case the link between the early clans concerned and
their much later plebeian namesakes is highly speculative (most obviously in the case of Servius Tullius). Similarly, the ban on full marriage
between patricians and plebeians in the Twelve Tables (Table XI.1) does
not prove a development of patrician exclusivity in the mid-fifth century;
even if the prohibition was here expressly formulated for the first time,
that is as likely to indicate that an ailing or threatened custom now needed
legal expression.[27] No less inconclusive are the traditions of senatorial

[25] Stuart Jones 1928[A127], 413f.
[26] See, e.g., Bernardi 1945–6[H9], 3–14; cf. Momigliano 1969[A87], 1–34 (= id. Quinto Contributo
293–332); Richard 1978[H76], esp. 519ff.
[27] According to legend as late as 295 B.C. patrician marital exclusivity was enshrined in the
exclusion from the (supposed) sanctuary of Pudicitia Patricia in the Forum Boarium of patrician
women who married plebeian husbands (Livy x.23.4ff).

address, also invoked in this context.[28] Livy (II.1.11) and Festus (304 L)
quote the phrase 'those who are fathers (*patres*) (and) those who are
enrolled (*conscripti*)' as the formula for summoning the senate, and
interpret both this and the formal mode of address to the senate, *patres
conscripti* (literally 'fathers enrolled'), as originally referring to two
distinct groups: the patrician senators and those non-patricians admitted
at the start of the Republic. This, it is argued, reveals the participation of
non-patricians in government in the early fifth century, an inheritance
from a position of influence already attained in the regal period. Again
the deduction is insecure: the summons formula may be a mere pleonasm
and other sources[29] regard *patres conscripti* as a unit ('enrolled fathers')
with the participle 'conscripti' dependent on 'patres'. Even if *conscripti*
does refer to non-patricians as a separate group, the formula does not
indicate when they were first admitted: indeed, it may imply that they
were a subsequent addition to a senate monopolized by *patres*, but in that
case the diversity of ancient accounts of the date and identity of the
conscripti suggests that there was no firm tradition on either topic; and
that the *patres* in historical times monopolized the *interregnum* procedure,
for example, does not imply the existence also of *conscripti* in the regal
senate.

If these arguments to prove a republican origin for the patriciate are
indecisive, there is still less reason to suppose that patrician status itself
was based, in whole or in part, on a family's tenure of the chief republican
offices.[30] It is an unwarranted assumption that in describing the procedure at the *interregnum* as 'the reversion (*redire*) of (the) auspices to the
patres' Cicero (*ad Brut.* 1.5.4) reflects a deep-seated tradition that the *patres*
were here ex-magistrates reviving the auspices they had previously
held while in office. It may rather, for example, express the fact that
interregna were a recurrent, if irregular, feature of political experience and
that, just as the commonwealth itself may be said to revert to an
interregnum (Livy IV.43.7), so also at such an *interregnum* the auspices may
be conceived as reverting from the regular magistrates to the patrician
senators. It is equally arbitrary to suppose that when Livy 1.8.7 attributes
the appellation *patres* to the respect (*honos*) enjoyed by the patrician
senators, he in fact misrepresents a source which intended the term
'honos' in its concrete sense of political office; and when he and other
sources refer to the first of a clan to hold the chief magistracy as 'the
originator of his clan' (*princeps gentis*) or 'the originator of (its) nobility'
(*princeps nobilitatis*) they do not thereby necessarily indicate the basis of
its patrician status.

There is, therefore, no compelling reason to discount an origin of the

[28] Momigliano 1969[A87], 23–4 (= id. *Quinto Contributo* 319–20).
[29] Notably Dion. Hal. *Ant. Rom.* II.12.3; *Schol. Dan. Aen.* 1.426; cf. Cic. *Phil.* XIII.28.
[30] Magdelain 1964[H50], 427–73. Cf. also Palmer 1970[A102]; Ranouil 1975[H74].

patriciate in the pre-republican period or a patrician monopoly of the consulship in the fifth century. Indeed, the alternative view fails to explain satisfactorily why and how the patriciate excluded certain families which on this hypothesis had already held office. There is also little evidence that those non-patricians allegedly excluded from office after the early fifth century subsequently went to form the core of the plebeian leadership in their struggle to check and modify the patrician hegemony, as might be expected; only the Genucii are self-evidently prominent among the plebeians seeking office in the early and mid-fourth century.[31] Yet the plebeian movement, which was already electing its own officers (the plebeian tribunes and aediles) in the early fifth century, must have enjoyed vigorous leadership by men of some standing from the outset. That too is more easily explained if the consulship was already a patrician preserve. Moreover, if the ancient account is in error on so central an issue as the right to hold office, little else in it would have any claim to credence: so fundamental a misconception would leave us with little grounds for faith in the rest of its narrative. In itself, of course, that is hardly a solid counter-argument, but fortunately scepticism of this magnitude is not necessary. What the 'plebeian' names in the *fasti* reflect is the abiding process of change within the aristocracy,[32] but the foundations of that aristocracy's power were already becoming established under the later monarchy and it is their growing self-assertion and distaste for regal rule which must ultimately lie behind the establishment of the republican system.

Although the patriciate was by definition a political entity, its power clearly rested on an interconnecting complex of factors: wealth, a strong kin-group structure, the nexus of associations within its own ranks, the patronage of dependants perhaps of varying social and economic status, ties of guest-friendship and probably marriage with aristocrats in other neighbouring communities, Etruscan and Latin. Patrician families probably had strong traditions of military prowess and it can be assumed that the later kings drew their subordinate commanders from aristocratic partisans, who thus acquired experience of military leadership. Finally, it has been seen that patricians were probably already the repositories of legal and religious expertise. It was in fact a particular feature of the Roman state that it had no separate priestly caste. The tenure of certain priesthoods precluded political activity but even these were reserved to the patriciate and later at least those which passed judgement on major

---

[31] In the present writer's view the fifth-century tribunates of the Iunii, Minucii and Siccii are almost certainly fictitious.

[32] The increasingly dominant position of a few patrician clans from the mid-fifth century on (p. 207) is especially relevant here.

religious issues, in particular the pontificate and augurate, were normally held by active politicians (p. 588). Moreover, the principal priestly colleges were kept clearly distinct in their spheres of competence, the initiative in taking cognisance of, and the final decision on, the most important religious issues rested with the senate, and many of the most important religious acts were performed by the magistrates (p. 589). There could, therefore, be no permanent separate religious focus of power and interests and the patriciate was probably able to use its religious predominance not merely to enhance its standing but to reinforce its hold on political power.

The patriciate may well, however, have experienced difficulty in maintaining its own internal cohesion, particularly if it included some individuals who were able on occasion to assemble sufficiently powerful followings to act as quasi-autonomous agents (pp. 96ff). If the narratives of Att(i)us Clausus' defection from the Sabines, Coriolanus' alleged desertion of Rome for the Volsci, or the campaign of the Fabii against Veii contain even a kernel of truth, they would be relevant here. So very probably would be the narratives of early republican figures who sought monarchic power.[33] One such account speaks of a Sp. Maelius who courted popular support by organizing relief in a corn shortage and was assassinated by C. Servilius Ahala in 439 B.C. This, however, may be fiction, based on an aetiological explanation of a site in Rome known as the Aequimaelium, which was interpreted as the 'level of Maelius'. Here, it was supposed, a Maelius' house had been destroyed, reputedly a normal procedure after the execution of traitors in the early Republic. This core was then expanded, probably as early as Cincius Alimentus or even Ennius,[34] by a similar attempt to explain the Servilian *cognomen* Ahala as the 'armpit' (*ala*) where Servilius hid his sword or lopped off Maelius' arm, and by the incorporation of an independent family legend (cf. Fig. 36: p. 133) of an early Minucius who had relieved a corn shortage and who was later paraded by the historians as an anachronistic 'prefect of the corn supply' and/or supernumerary plebeian tribune; in the early historians the whole narrative may have served as an illustration of the obligation on any citizen to remove a potential tyrant, itself indicative of the continuing danger of individual ambition.[35] Whilst, however, the legend of Sp. Maelius may illuminate later aristocratic concerns rather than historical reality, those of Sp. Cassius, executed in 485, and of M.

[33] For these narratives see Lintott 1970[F39], 12–29 (defending the historicity of Maelius' execution).

[34] Cf. Dion. Hal. *Ant. Rom.* XII.4.2 (Cincius Alimentus); Skutsch 1971[B166], 26ff; 1985[B169], 306f(Ennius).

[35] At a later stage the story was 'normalized' for political purposes by transforming Ahala into the *magister equitum* of a dictator (L. Quinctius Cincinnatus): Lintott 1970[F39], 16–17.

Manlius Capitolinus, executed in 385 or 384, are less obviously invented. In their developed form both men are presented as demagogic agitators but this reflects subsequent elaboration under the influence of Greek theories of tyranny and late republican political propaganda; the agitation of Cassius in particular is largely modelled on events of the Gracchan period.[36] The most that can have been recalled or recorded of either man was the execution for seeking autocratic power. That is not implausible in the context of sub-archaic society but though popular support might well be sought for such an enterprise, the proper context for such ambitions is the individual power which could be exercised in that period. To judge by his three consulships (502; 493; 486 B.C.) Sp. Cassius was amongst the most prominent political figures of his day and his fall coincides with the onset of an unparalleled series of seven Fabian consulships (485–479 B.C.), suggesting rivalry within the aristocracy itself as a pre-eminent factor in his demise. It is notable that, as Table 3 (p. 207) shows, some of the most politically successful patrician families enter office for the first time in these years (the Cornelii, Aemilii and Manlii as well as the Fabii themselves).

It is readily intelligible, therefore, that at the outset the major preoccupations of the patriciate were the maintenance and stability of the new political regime against the threat of a reversion to monarchy and that to this end the patriciate made strenuous efforts to reinforce its own internal cohesion both politically and socially. The ban on marriage with plebeians, probably already customary before its inclusion in the Twelve Tables, was obviously intended to prevent the dilution of its traditions of exclusivity, whilst the forms in which patrician political power was institutionalized from the start of the Republic sought both to forestall abuse and usurpation by individual magistrates and to ensure a major role for the collective voice of the patriciate as a whole.

The principle of collective aristocratic responsibility is, indeed, already implicit in the *interregnum* procedure. Under this, individual patrician senators were successively nominated to hold elections if the chief magistrates died or left office without electing successors; indeed, the first such *interrex* was appointed by the patrician senators as a whole after the necessary auspicial observances (Livy VI.41.6; cf. Cic. *ad Brut*. 1.5.4; p. 181). Furthermore, the patrician senators are here entitled to take the auspices for a public act and perform that act without authorization by any other organ of state. This suggests that the patrician monopoly of political office was reinforced by claims to special competence in the religious acts necessary to such office.[37] Even if we do not trust Livy's

---

[36] Gabba 1964[B62], 29–41.

[37] Even if in origin the right to take public auspices depended on public position rather than individual 'charisma' (Heuss 1982[G618], 391), that does not exclude the subsequent development of claims to a peculiar patrician competence, especially in the face of plebeian demands.

rhetoric on the subject (VI.41.5ff), it may be significant that plebeians secured access to the pontificate and augurate some time after their admission to secular office (p. 343), and it is presumably similar considerations which explain why a plebeian censor first performed the closing purification ceremony of the census (the *lustrum*) only in 279 B.C., sixty years after plebeians entered the office (Livy, *Per.* XIII).

The *interregnum* procedure also helps to bring into focus the character of the patrician senate, for in the last resort the patrician senators themselves are responsible for the continuity of government. Thus the senate is not restricted to a purely advisory function; *in extremis* it can and does take action on its own initiative. This collective sense of patrician responsibility is further illustrated by the institution of the *patrum auctoritas* (p. 343). The sources regard this as a formal sanction given by the patrician senators to legislative and electoral acts of the curiate and centuriate assemblies but its precise function is obscure; it may have been a declaration that the formalities of the legislative procedures (particularly in their religious aspect) had been correctly observed or a more general act of approval, but there are difficulties in either view. Livy believed that the *patrum auctoritas* had originated in the regal period for the confirmation of the election of the early kings[38] but whether that has any basis it is again impossible to determine. What is known is that the procedure was modified in the late fourth century or early third. Originally the *patrum auctoritas* had been given after the election or comitial approval of legislation,[39] but by an alleged Publilian law of 339 it had to be given in advance for centuriate legislation and by a Maenian law (?early third century) in advance also for elections. That does not necessarily imply, however, an early origin for the prerogative itself: it could still, for example, be a safeguard introduced after the admission of plebeians to the consulship in 366 B.C. However, whilst it was required for acts of the curiate as well as the centuriate assembly, it was not perhaps required for the decisions of the tribal assembly meeting under the presidency of a state magistrate[40] and this may indicate an origin earlier than the development of such tribal assemblies (perhaps in the mid-fourth century). In that case it should probably be seen as a general check on the magistrates instituted or inherited in the early fifth century.

Whatever its date and exact purpose, however, the *patrum auctoritas*, along with the *interregnum* procedure, indicates clearly that the patriciate was concerned to give the senate (or at least its patrician members) a role

---

[38] E.g. Livy 1.17.9; cf. also Dion. Hal. *Ant. Rom.* 11.60.3.

[39] Dionysius seems in his account of the fifth century (contrast *Ant. Rom.* 11.14.3) to misinterpret it as a preliminary senatorial decree, perhaps misled by Sullan propaganda (App. *BCiv.* 1.59.266) or later non-technical usages such as 'ex auctoritate patrum' ('with the senate's sanction').

[40] Cf. the references solely to the centuriate and curiate assemblies in Cic. *Dom.* 38; Livy VI.41.10. But note Livy VI.42.14; VII.16.7.

and powers which exceeded those of a body of advisers.[41] Indeed, from the outset it probably envisaged the senate as exercising a central function in the decisions of the state. It was a public body which had to meet on sacred or public ground formally constituted as a *templum*, its deliberations being preceded by the taking of public auspices and other rituals. Admittedly, it was dependent on the magistrate for its summons and, largely, for the subject and conduct of its debates, and senatorial resolutions were presumably, as later, formulated in the language of advice. That, however, in no way weakened their force in a society where custom and the collective will of the aristocracy were at least as important as statute in determining the effective character of political institutions. Moreover, the individual magistrate would ignore or flout senatorial advice at the expense of his own future interests. The ex-consul would hope to spend most of his remaining years as a member of the senate in which he had probably often sat before election. He was thus inevitably more sensitive to the views of his peers than a life-long king to those of his councillors. Indeed, his permanent importance depended far more on the long-term influence he could wield in the senate than on the legal power he enjoyed often for only a single year. If the weapons available to the senate as a means of curbing magisterial independence increased in the mid-Republic (p. 346), they may also have become more necessary as Rome's commanders operated for longer periods and at increasing distances away from the city. In any case, the actual relations of consul to council were always subject to variation according to the personalities involved, the issues at stake and the general constellation of political forces. In this respect the experience of the fifth century will have been no different from that of the mid- and late Republic. Neither that nor the later extension of the senate's concerns with the growth of empire, however, constitutes a valid ground for discounting the strong probability that the senate had already acquired a central role in the decisions of state.

(d) *The consulship*

For the Roman upper class in the late Republic the institution of the annual dual consulship, in which two colleagues with equal powers

[41] The fact that consuls controlled enrolment in the senate in the early Republic does not justify Festus' attempt (290 L) to explain the purpose of the Lex Ovinia by the hypothesis that previously kings, consuls or consular tribunes had enlisted only their own associates. This supposition is based on an over-literal interpretation of the senate as the consuls' council (Mommsen 1887–8[A91], III.856 n. 4), presumably on the analogy of the *ad hoc* domestic council of the Roman *paterfamilias*. In practice personal prudence, aristocratic expectations and public policy would combine to maintain considerable continuity in the senate's composition, with consuls more often supplementing than replacing the existing membership (there was no formal ceiling); and such stability, if not inherited from the regal period, will rapidly have been established as the norm. For a different view see p. 393f.

formed the chief executive of the state, was almost synonymous with the republican system of government. Since it ensured the sharing of power, it was a bulwark against domination by an individual and for the elite at least a fundamental guarantee of their collective and personal political liberty. Yet the uniform ancient view that such a dual magistracy was established immediately after the overthrow of the monarchy has often been challenged, usually in the belief that a single chief magistrate (with or without subordinates) was essential for effective government. The arguments adduced to support such a position[42] are for the most part, however, *a priori*. Other central Italian communities, for example, do appear later to have had constitutions with a single magistrate at their head but we cannot assume that this pattern was or had been uniform throughout the region or that the Roman aristocracy would have felt obliged to follow it.[43] So too there is no reason to suppose that the aristocracy regarded unified direction of the Roman state as of such importance that it would not countenance the sharing of supreme power. On the contrary, both political and administrative needs may have recommended such an arrangement; indeed, collegiality (in the sense of two or more colleagues with equal powers) seems rapidly to have established itself as the hallmark of both the state and plebeian offices. Nor was the consul's power of effective action hampered by a general right of veto exercised by his colleague, as is often assumed. Such a general prerogative is not attested for the Roman state magistracies;[44] the veto powers they did possess (which concerned predominantly judicial rulings, summary punishments and senatorial decrees) were probably the result of subsequent development, perhaps originating in the magistrate's ability to issue contrary orders and in some cases parallel to, or a consequence of, the recognition of tribunician veto against the magistrates. The only possible solid evidence for an original single chief magistracy is an inscription discovered in the Capitoline temple, which provided that 'he who is the greatest praetor ('qui praetor maximus sit') shall fix a nail on the Ides of September' (Cincius *ap.* Livy VII.3.5). Even here, however, the term 'greatest praetor' does not necessarily refer to a single chief magistrate.[45] *Praetor maximus*, for example, may itself have been an archaic term for the consul and, as occasionally in later documents,[46] the singular may have been used without further distinction even though the act is normally performed by either or both of two equal

---

[42] For a convenient summary cf. Heurgon 1967[G616], 97ff.

[43] Cf. also the uncertainty surrounding the progress and timetable of the eclipse of monarchies in Central Italy: p. 262f.

[44] App. *BCiv.* 1.12.48; III.50.206 refers to the tribunate alone, Cic. *Leg.* III.11 to the veto of legislation (cf. III.42), *lex mun. Salp.* (*FIRA* 1 n. 23) 27 apparently only to veto on appeal by a private citizen (and not at Rome).

[45] Momigliano 1968[G676], 159–75 (= id. *Quarto Contributo* 403–17).

[46] *Tabula Heracleensis* (*FIRA* 1 n. 13) 142ff.

colleagues. Since it would then be possible to retain the consular list and accept an early creation of the dictatorship (otiose if there were a regular sole chief magistracy) an explanation along these lines is probably to be accepted and with it an early institution of the consulship. This would accord in particular with the manifest prevalence of collegiality in the other republican offices, a principle to be extended still further in the consular tribunate.

Ancient writers, influenced by Greek political theory and anxious to emphasize the continuity of Roman political development, see the republican chief magistracy as heir to the power of the kings. In contrast, an influential modern view[47] draws a fundamental qualitative distinction between the absolute power of the kings and the more restricted, essentially conferred power exercised by the consuls. Both perspectives are false, since they erroneously presuppose that the powers of the king or magistrate were already conceived as an abstract unity distinct from the office to which they pertained and as potentially or in fact conferred by an act separate from appointment to the office itself. For such conferment there is no certain evidence (the curiate law may originally have served a different purpose (p. 198f)); the powers of an office may have been implicitly regarded as a necessary concomitant of election or appointment.

Even if, however, such powers were separately conferred, they were not necessarily conceived as a single all-embracing unity. The term *imperium* was used quasi-technically in a much later period to denote the sum total of the magistrate's powers; but as such it is apparently reserved to those who might independently command Roman armies and is employed principally in relation to military command, which may, therefore, represent its original sphere of application. Whether *imperium* already had even this restricted sense in the early Republic is not known but the slow crystallization and differentiation of abstract general notions of power and ownership in private law suggest that no precocious growth of precisely defined concepts is to be expected here in the public sphere.[48] It may have been when the powers of a magistrate were prolonged beyond his term of office or conferred on individuals not holding the magistracy concerned that they were first clearly conceived as a distinct entity, although even then it is doubtful whether they were felt to form a unity except by reference to their concentration in the office in which they originated. If Roman tradition could be trusted, such a process was already under way in 444 B.C. with the appointment of

---

[47] Coli 1951[F14], 1–168.

[48] There is no evidence for, or basis to, the view that 'auspicium' was originally used as a general term for magisterial power (as Bleicken 1981[G532]; Heuss 1982[G618]).

'military tribunes with consular power', but the title at least is probably a later reconstruction (p. 193); at most these were military tribunes who in practice exercised consular functions and therefore enjoyed comparable powers.

What, therefore, was created in 509 was a magistracy with certain functions and, as a necessary consequence, the powers deemed appropriate to those functions. So at the institution of the censorship certain specific functions were taken from the regular chief magistrates and the appropriate privileges and powers were accorded to the new office: the censor may summon the people only for the purpose of the census itself; he neither proposes legislation (despite Zonar. VII.19) nor supervises elections; he normally enjoys no right of military command (and therefore no *imperium* in the later quasi-technical sense); he has neither capital powers of punishment nor lictors. He does, however, possess (in later terminology) the greatest right to auspices, required for the conduct of the census ceremonies, and is entitled to the curule chair and purple-bordered toga (*toga praetexta*) worn by the higher magistrates .

Similarly, in relation to the consulship itself, there is no evidence that military command and civil jurisdiction were conceived as the exercise of a single common authority except by reference to their concentration in the same hands. Jurisdiction as such was not later limited to those with *imperium* nor even is it represented in its entirety as a function of *imperium*; although later theory treats some legal actions as attached to *imperium*, *imperium* and *iudicium* ('(power of) judgement') can still appear as alternatives (e.g. *lex rep.* 72; *lex agr.* 87). Earlier the diversity of the consuls' functions was even reflected in their titulature: alongside the initial *praetor* ('(military) leader') or later consul,[49] *iudex* ('judge') was also at some stage used in formal contexts (Varro, *Ling.* VI.88).

In terms of concrete powers and functions the early consuls probably differed little from their regal predecessors. They will have enjoyed full military command, exercised jurisdiction, controlled public finance, maintained public order, conducted the census, selected the senate, perhaps appointed criminal judges and been responsible for vows, games and other religious acts no less than the kings. The powers associated with these various functions (probably largely determined by custom) may also initially have been little different: in the military sphere the republican magistrate enjoyed or acquired an unfettered authority which can scarcely represent any dilution of the corresponding powers of the monarchy, whilst in civil administration he possessed a discretionary power only gradually subjected to certain formal limitations. Similarly, certain magisterial insignia were attributed, probably correctly, a regal

---

[49] For the initial use of 'praetor' cf. Stuart Jones 1928[A128], 437f.

origin: the curule chair, and above all, the lictors and *fasces* denoting the right to scourge and execute.[50] A parallel continuity is observable also in much of the religious activity of the magistrates (cf. e.g. p. 612).

What the aristocracy clearly found distasteful in the monarchy was not its functions, powers and traditions as such but its permanent concentration of authority, power and status in the hands of a single individual; and it is here that the fundamental differences between the kingship and the republican magistracies are to be found. These lay principally in the limitation of office to a year, the probable provision of a colleague with equal powers and growing comitial participation in the appointment of magistrates (and, later, legislation). In addition, the general context and perception of the magistrate's role seems to have differed from that which obtained under the monarchy. Some of the ritual functions of the king were separated from the political and invested in a specially created priest-king (*rex sacrorum*) with his own 'house' (Regia) on the Sacred Way, close to the temple of Vesta. The ostensible status of the Regia as both house and public shrine, and its proximity to the Vestals, their public hearth and its sacred fire reflect a coherent religious structure in which the monarch had been identified with, and acted as the symbol of, the community itself. No comparable structure was created for the new political and military executive, even though it too performed major religious acts on behalf of the state: the consuls were not priests.[51] Moreover, the freedom of action enjoyed in practice by the republican magistrates was probably far more restricted by their integration into an aristocratic system in which the senate was to play a central role and by the collective will of the aristocracy itself. In the military sphere the disciplines of 'hoplite' warfare and the potential for autonomous action or displays of personal virtuosity by individual aristocrats made a strong command essential and may even have accentuated its severity, but outside that the aristocracy will hardly have regarded its magistrates as possessing universal and unlimited authority; their extensive discretionary powers may not have been formally defined and may have been progressively modified, but that does not imply that they either were or were conceived to be absolute.

(e) *The dictatorship*

Alongside the consuls the historians chronicle the occasional naming of a dictator who would assume supreme command of the state for a limited period. The dictator was appointed after the appropriate religious obser-

---

[50] And the magistrates celebrating a triumph may have resurrected for that day the trappings of monarchy; cf. for discussion Versnel 1970[G742], esp. 56ff; Weinstock 1971[G517], 64–6; below, p. 614.   [51] And hence were not inaugurated as the king may have been (p. 96).

vances at night by one of the consuls (or consular tribunes) and his assumption of office was recognized by a curiate law (p. 198). Livy (II.18.5) cites an alleged law that only men of consular rank were eligible but our admittedly suspect records indicate that that was true only from the early third century. The dictator was originally termed 'master of the army'[52] (*magister populi*), while his subordinate (and appointee) was still known as the 'master of cavalry' (*magister equitum*) in the late Republic. In antiquity the institution of the office was sometimes attributed partly to a desire to remedy internal discord or frustrate plebeian agitation (e.g. Dion. Hal. *Ant. Rom.* v.70.1ff; Zonar. vII.13; *ILS* 212), a conception which may owe much to Licinius Macer and the example of Sulla (cf. Dion. Hal. *Ant. Rom.* v.77.4ff); but the titles of the dictator and his assistant, the restriction of the office to a maximum of six months and the accomplishments of those early dictators with the strongest claims to credence demonstrate that, as other ancient authorities supposed (Pomp. *Dig.* 1.2.2.18; *Suda* s.v. δικτάτωρ; cf. Livy II.18.2ff), the office was specifically military in purpose.

The ancient conception that the new office was required to circumvent restrictions placed on the consulship by the Valerian law of appeal of 509 B.C. cannot be accepted, not least because that law is fiction (p. 220). Nor was it perhaps intended purely as a crisis office; unless the requirement of a law passed by the curiate assembly to confirm or acknowledge the appointment is a later innovation, it implies no necessarily immediate urgency in the appointment (there was no memory of a dictator named to meet the initial Gallic assault of 390). The magistracy may have been as much intended to provide unified leadership for a sustained major campaign. Indeed, four of the most significant military successes of this period are attributed to dictators: the defeat of the Latins at Lake Regillus (499 or 496), victories against the Fidenates and Veientans by Mam. Aemilius (probably duplicated under 437, 434 and 426), a major defeat of the Aequi by A. Postumius Tubertus (432 or 431) and Camillus' capture of Veii (396). The reliability of these dictatorships, as of others in the fifth century, is difficult to assess. Since the dictatorship was not eponymous, its tenure may not have been recorded in the consular list and the preservation of the names of many dictators was probably largely due to family traditions (which were notoriously suspect). However, if triumphal records survived from the fifth century (p. 289) they will have registered the more successful incumbents. Certainly Camillus' capture of Veii appears beyond cavil and the other successes involved are at least credible (p. 289; 298f). If historical, they too indicate that the dictatorship was not restricted to sudden emergencies.

---

[52] So still in the augural books (Cic. *Rep.* 1.63). For this sense of 'populus' cf. p. 104.

The haphazard survival of early dictatorships excludes any assessment of their frequency. Even the date of the office's institution is uncertain. Very early sources named T. Larcius as its first incumbent[53] but the date of his tenure was evidently unknown since it was implausibly located in his first (501) or second (498) consulship. Larcius, however, belongs to an obsolete *gens* for whom a claim to the first dictatorship might hardly be invented, although the means by which the memory of his colourless tenure was preserved remain problematic.[54] The provisions that the dictator should be appointed at dead of night and might not mount a horse suggest that it was an archaic office. It is not unlikely that it was created soon after the establishment of the Republic, when external pressures may well have illustrated the need for a unified military command and the cavalry may still have enjoyed a distinct, if subordinate, military role, but more than that we cannot say.[55]

Whether the office had earlier precedents is unknown. Given its initial purely military character (dictators, for example, never supervised civil jurisdiction), it is unlikely to be a temporary reversal to an earlier system of a sole chief magistrate[56] or to be borrowed from similar systems elsewhere (as Licinius Macer fr. 10P). If the *dictator* (or *dicator*) of the Latin League was appointed to take charge of a specific campaign, his office may have exercised some influence on the Roman institution, despite the initial difference of nomenclature: at least some dictators may have served as league commanders (so presumably Postumius in 432 or 431, if authentic)[57] and the Latin title have been transferred to the Roman magistracy. Alternatively, there may have been some regal provision for the appointment of a commander when the king himself could not take the field and this precedent was subsequently reshaped to meet republican needs, but such possibilities lie beyond the limits imposed by our evidence.

(f) *The consular tribunate*

In the preserved *fasti* between 444 and 427 B.C. colleges of two consuls alternate irregularly with colleges of three 'military tribunes with con-

---

[53] Livy II.18.5. A later Valerian tradition claimed the distinction for M.' Valerius (Festus 216 L; Livy II.18.6).

[54] Unless he was initially credited with the defeat of the Latins at L. Regillus (cf. Livy II.18.3; Dion. Hal. *Ant. Rom.* V.76.1–4; Zonar. VII.13), the variant datings of which (499 and 496) run parallel to those of his dictatorship.

[55] An obvious alternative is to date its introduction to the period of the consular tribunate, when there would, on occasion, be still greater need for a single supreme commander.

[56] Staveley 1956[G724], 90ff.

[57] It is possible, however, that some individuals in fact appointed as league commanders were later erroneously interpreted as dictators (Pinsent 1959[B139], 85).

sular power'; between 426 and 406 there is a similar fluctuation between two consuls and three or four consular tribunes. From 405 to 367, however, there is an almost uniform series of six-member colleges (albeit often abbreviated in Diodorus)[58] interrupted only by a temporary reversion to the consulship in 393/2.

The ancient characterizations of the consular tribune as 'military tribune', 'military tribune with consular power' or the equivalent imply that he was later regarded essentially as a military tribune acting as a substitute for the consuls.[59] Yet there is no evidence or probability that the 'consular tribunes' differed in function or in powers from the 'consuls'; that no consular tribune triumphed (Zonar. VII. 19) may merely reflect the defective character of the triumphal records or the custom of appointing a dictator for the most important campaigns. In consequence, it is difficult to see why the larger colleges should have been separately named, at least if the late fifth-century fluctuations are accepted. Conceivably in years where they were elected, they fulfilled the functions of both consuls and military tribunes but the reason for the adoption of the subordinate title remains obscure. In character, therefore, and perhaps even in nomenclature the consulship and consular tribunate may have been identical (both offices are often held interchangeably by the same individuals, even though ancient sources carefully distinguish between repeated tenure of each). The distinction drawn by Roman historians would then be a false deduction from the subsequent constant association of the consulship with a dual magistracy and from the later practice of electing six military tribunes for each of the first four legions.[60]

If this is correct, the dominant ancient explanation of the office, that it was designed to facilitate admission of plebeians to office without compromising the patrician monopoly of the consulship, can hardly be sustained. It is in any case implausible since on Livy's own showing plebeians only secured election in 400 and admission to the more junior quaestorship in 421. Two consular tribunes with names known otherwise only as plebeian do appear before 400 (L. Atilius Luscus (444) and Q. Antonius Merenda (422)) but that is hardly sufficient to justify the ancient interpretation of the office, especially as both are suspect. The

[58] Hence only four consular tribunes are recorded in 376, for which Diodorus alone gives a regular list. The five-member college of 385 is also probably due to abbreviation. The eight- or nine-member colleges of 389, 387, 380 and 379 probably result from the incorporation either of names from colleges now lost or of names interpolated in one or more earlier sources to compensate for a defective transmission of the original list: cf. Drummond 1980[D9], 57ff; below, p. 239f.

[59] So also, e.g., Sealey 1959[G709], 521–30; Sumner 1970[G728], 70–3; Pinsent 1975[D26], 51–61.

[60] This is also presumably the basis for the strange notion (e.g. Livy IV.16.6) that there were six places as consular tribune available each year from the outset, three for patricians and three for plebeians according to Dionysius (*Ant. Rom.* XI.60; cf. Zonar. VII.19), here evidently influenced by the later partitioning of the consulship.

Antonii are absent from office until the second century, with the exception of T. Antonius Merenda of the problematic Second Decemvirate and a dubious *magister equitum* of 333. The Atilii may be a Campanian family, which would certainly exclude an appearance in the *fasti* at this date,[61] but in any case the magistrates of 444 B.C. are a notorious crux (p. 174 n. 8) and the election of a single plebeian followed by a patrician monopoly until 400 cannot be accepted. More probably the alleged later admission of plebeians to the consular tribunate created the notion that the office was introduced for that reason. Antonius or Atilius may, of course, be the scions of obsolete patrician clans; otherwise they represent spurious additions or an early corruption of the authentic names.

An alternative ancient conjecture, attributing the consular tribunate to increasing military needs (Livy IV.17.2), is probably nearer the truth. The later fifth century in general may have seen a more aggressive (or progressively more successful) external policy, the establishment of the six-member colleges in 405 was swiftly followed by a major offensive against Veii and the reversion to the dual consulship in 393/2, if authentic, may mark an interlude in Roman military activities. Yet it is difficult to see why it should be necessary to increase the numbers of the principal military commanders to this extent; in 367 B.C. when the consular tribunate was abolished, three at most were deemed sufficient. Their progressive enlargement and variation in numbers has sometimes been interpreted as reflecting changes in army strength, each consular tribune taking charge of 1000 men, but a doubling of army manpower in the late fifth century is difficult to credit (p. 165), as is the assumption that the field forces required could be calculated in advance each year. Moreover, there is no evidence that the consular tribunes commanded individual contingents rather than (as the consuls) the entire force nor is it likely that they all took the field for a particular campaign. More probably increasing military needs were accompanied by a general growth in domestic administration, of which the institution of the censorship and alleged increase in the quaestorship in 421 may also be symptomatic; when the six-member college was abolished in 367, it was replaced by two consuls, one praetor (primarily in charge of civil jurisdiction) and two curule aediles (with various subordinate domestic responsibilities).

Political factors may also have contributed to the office's later development. There may have been a desire to extend further the collegiate character of the chief magistracy. The establishment of six-member colleges from 405 B.C. may be partly attributable to the fact that two members of the same clan held office together for the first time in 406

---

[61] Heurgon 1942[J59], 288–94; but cf. Schulze 1904[G138], 151 n. 3; Beloch 1926[A12], 338f; Frederiksen 1984[J48], 231.

B.C.; from 405 this becomes a frequent practice. The consular tribunate also gave greater opportunities for the repeated tenure of office (even on occasions in successive years) without thereby denying access to the magistracies to others. It thus allowed a regular blending of experienced men with new blood and in the developed period of the office (from c. 426) few colleges include no previous holder of the chief magistracy.

One major puzzle remains: how are the variations between the dual consulship and three or four member consular tribunates in the later fifth century to be explained? It has been argued that they are unlikely to reflect prospective army strength. A more promising solution is that they are due to corruption in transmission, concealing what was in fact a regular pattern of increase.[62] However, while a few interpolations may be suspected (p. 174), there is no evidence for widespread invention. On the other hand, if loss of names was the major factor, such losses would have had to be large-scale and early if the enlargement of the office was more orderly than the surviving lists indicate, and it would then be difficult to explain why the larger colleges from c. 405 B.C. are far more faithfully preserved. If, however, the variation in the size of the late fifth-century colleges is authentic, perhaps the most plausible approach is to suppose that until 405 the presiding magistrate at elections exercised discretion in the number elected, depending on anticipated military and other needs and perhaps also on the number of well-qualified candidates who secured the necessary quota of votes.

(g) *The quaestors, quaestores parricidii and duoviri (perduellionis)*

Specialized offices to relieve the consuls of individual responsibilities were slow to develop. The earliest were probably in the spheres of criminal law and finance. Later sources regard the chief magistrates as possessing a reserve right to conduct criminal trials but in practice regular criminal jurisdiction in the early Republic is attributed to other, subordinate officials. The financial officers (quaestors) are very occasionally described as conducting capital criminal prosecutions on a variety of charges (treason, false witness and peculation), but these trials are uniformly fictitious[63] and though quaestors in the mid-Republic certainly conducted some criminal prosecutions (Varro, *Ling.* VI.91–2), the charges are unknown; they may have concerned only the misappropriation of public funds, an offence closely connected with the quaestors' financial functions.[64] In the early period cases of treason at least seem to have been handled by a specially appointed two-man

[62] Beloch 1926[A12], 260–2; cf. Pinsent 1975[D26].   [63] Kunkel 1962[G245], 34–5.

[64] On Oros. v.16.8 (Jones 1972[G228], 5f) cf. Kunkel 1962[G245], 47 n. 179 with Badian 1984[G169], 306–9.

commission (*duoviri*). For (kin-?)murder the Twelve Tables (IX.4) recorded other specific officials (the *quaestores parricidii*), although whether these presided over private suits or themselves conducted a publicly initiated enquiry is disputed. In either event they, like the *duoviri*, were presumably appointed on an *ad hoc* basis.

If this is so, there is unlikely to be any continuity between the *quaestores parricidii* and the financial quaestors since the transformation of an *ad hoc* judicial office into a regular magistracy of much wider purpose is not readily explained. Moreover, the *quaestores parricidii* were evidently still a distinct office at the time of the Twelve Tables and the financial quaestors can also hardly be dated later than the fifth century.[65] Their institution is variously ascribed by our sources to the regal period or the first year of the Republic, and certainly in the fifth century the financial activities of the state, together with the increased workload of the chief magistrates, may well have made specialist surveillance desirable. Tacitus' view (*Ann.* XI.22) that the quaestors were originally nominated by the king or consuls seems more probable than the supposition[66] that the office was elective from the start, although its basis is problematic.[67] Tacitus also ascribes the introduction of election to 447 B.C. and if plebeians held the office in 409 (but cf. p. 239), it was presumably elective then. The quaestors were later, however, elected by the tribal assembly whose official use is not otherwise attested until the mid-fourth century,[68] and Tacitus' record of a Valerius, probably the consul of 449, among the first elected quaestors inspires no confidence in his accuracy.

Originally two in number, the quaestors were reputedly raised to four in 421. That tradition cannot be controlled. Livy (IV.43.4) and Tacitus (loc. cit.) describe the earliest quaestors as urban or military respectively but such precision (and the resulting disagreement between them) may be misplaced; the original pair may have fulfilled both functions, which were distinguished only when the office was enlarged. In the military sphere later practice suggests that the quaestors acted as general assistants to their commander and were not limited to the supervision of the war chest and supplies. Comparable unambiguous evidence is lacking for the exercise of domestic functions beyond those associated with their

[65] The use of 'quaestor' (from Latin *quaerere* ('to investigate' or 'to exact')) for both types of consular assistant is unlikely to have arisen independently. The term may have been first created for the regular quaestors as financial officers (cf. Ed. Meyer 1907–37[A79], III.481) and then reapplied to the *ad hoc* judicial commissioners (*quaestores parricidii*) on the basis of the inquisitorial connotations of its verbal root. Alternatively, the financial officers may also have exercised some 'judicial' responsibilities in the financial sphere or initially have conducted the preliminary capital enquiries subsequently entrusted to the *tresviri capitales* (cf. Varro, *Ling.* v.81).

[66] Iunius Gracchanus *ap.* Ulp. *Dig.* 1.13.1pr.; Plut. *Publ.* 12.3.

[67] The curiate law for L. Iunius Brutus (*cos.* 509) to which Tacitus has just referred can hardly have been authentic.

[68] Apart from a fictitious narrative under 446 B.C.: Livy III.72.6; Dion. Hal. *Ant. Rom.* XI.52.3; Ogilvie 1965[B129], 523.

responsibility for the treasury, but here too they may initially have had a potentially much broader role than was to be true later.

(h) *The censorship*

The attribution of the censorship to the mid-fifth century rests on a slender basis, since most of the six preserved colleges before the Gallic Sack are suspect. In particular, the first censors (L. Papirius Mugillanus and L. Sempronius Atratinus in 443) appeared as consuls the previous year in the Linen Books and Ardeate treaty. If that evidence is reliable (p. 174 n. 8), their immediate joint tenure of the censorship may represent a transformation of their consulship when it was lost from the annalistic tradition.[69] The first censors would then be those of 435 (C. Furius Pacilus Fusus and M. Geganius Macerinus); a tradition to that effect may be reflected in the supposition that they first used the censors' building (*villa publica*) in the Campus Martius (Livy IV.22.7) and that their tenure of office was now limited to eighteen months by a Lex Aemilia, although this narrative itself (Livy IV.24.2ff) is replete with suspect detail and probably fictitious.

The new office was self-evidently established to relieve the consuls of the burden of the census. There may have been other duties early attributed to the censors (e.g. the leasing of a few minor state contracts) but most of their other functions and powers were probably subsequent accretions (so too Livy IV.8.2). Thus they seem only in the fourth century to have taken over from the consuls responsibility for the composition of the senate (p. 393) and their role as arbiters of conduct will have developed progressively out of their supervision of the census.

Whether their institution (whatever its date) signals a widening of the basis or function of the census itself is unknown. The census may originally have taken the form of a full military review;[70] it always retained that character for the equestrian centuries and the traditional summons of the citizen infantry to the census, under arms and with no restriction to heads of households (Varro, *Ling.* VI.86f), suggests that it had once performed the same function in their case also. Nonetheless, its periodic character indicates that it was more than a military inspection, which would more appropriately be conducted annually, not least to permit the incorporation of those newly qualified by age for service. The census must already have comprised an individual assessment of liability for military service on a wealth basis,[71] if not tribal registration of the entire citizen body. With the development of the centuriate assembly as a

---

[69] For a defence of the censors of 443 B.C. cf., e.g., Leuze 1912[G645], 95–133; Klotz 1939[G629], 27ff.   [70] Pieri 1968[G689], 47–75.

[71] The Twelve Tables may have included the term 'duicensus' (*fr. incert.* 12) to denote a man assessed with his son.

political forum, these functions may have been extended in some way and
if (as is possible) obligation for military service had hitherto been based
purely on the capacity to provide the relevant weapons, the introduction
of the censorship may also be linked to the introduction of a formal
assessment in 'monetary' terms.[72] What is certain is that the dual character of the census, as determining not only military responsibilities but
also political rights, must have become increasingly evident as the
powers of the centuriate assembly grew and a gulf gradually developed
between the military and political organization of the citizen body.

(i) *The assemblies*

The oldest Roman assembly, the curiate (*comitia curiata*), still witnessed
or sanctioned comitial wills and the adoption of men not subject to
paternal power in the early Republic, although already comitial involvement in acts affecting the *familia* was declining and was not required for
at least some of the procedures whereby slaves received both freedom
and citizenship. Quasi-political decisions are also still attributed to the
curiate assembly: it allegedly voted Camillus' restoration from exile and,
according to one tradition, was used initially for the election of plebeian
tribunes. That, however, is probably mere conjecture, based on the belief
that the tribal plebeian assembly was introduced only in 471 B.C.; if that
belief is correct (cf. p. 217), voting may earlier have been by general
acclamation, not specific units.
    The only significant regular act of the curiate assembly was the curiate
law which allegedly confirmed at least the principal magistrates in office.
If this was not an inheritance from the regal period (p. 105), it will belong
to the very early Republic since the comparable law for the censors was
already entrusted to the centuriate assembly (*comitia centuriata*). The
function of the law is controversial. In the late Republic it was regarded
as necessary to the full validity of the magistrate's position and sometimes to the exercise of his office, particularly in the military sphere. Yet
lack of the law seems, on occasion at least, to have imposed no concrete
restriction on magisterial action. In part this may be due to the decay of
the curiate assembly into a mere form. It may also, however, reflect an
ambiguity which had arisen through changed perceptions of the law's
function. Assertions that it confirmed the grant of the magistracy are
evidence only for its later interpretation, which may be influenced by
contemporary notions of statute as an order of the people and of the
people itself as the source of magisterial authority. Originally the *lex
curiata* may have served a different purpose, as a formal acknowledge-

[72] Pieri 1968[G689], 125–50.

ment by the community of the magistrate's assumption of office. Such a hypothesis would explain the apparent duplication between election to office and the passage of the curiate law. It would also explain how in the late Republic the law could sometimes be dispensed with in practice, yet also on occasions be conceived as essential to the proper tenure of magisterial powers: a declaration that A. Sempronius and Q. Fabius should be consuls, originally a formal act of recognition (perhaps carried over from the monarchy and executed by acclamation (*suffragium*)), could be readily reinterpreted later as a constitutive act confirming their appointment, particularly if some general description of the powers of the office was gradually added. It is a further attractive conjecture[73] that in origin such a curiate law was an act of the army meeting in curiate divisions, which thereby acknowledged the assumption of military command and the obedience owed to the new commander. This would also provide an illuminating backcloth for the later development of the centuriate organization as a political assembly. However, such a particular character to the curiate law would have disappeared once the *curiae* ceased to be the basis of the army, probably in the sixth century, and no trace is evident in the vestigial assembly responsible for the law in the late Republic.

Whilst the curiate assembly probably suffered no diminution of its role (accounts of it exercising wider functions under the monarchy are not to be credited (cf. p. 105)), such new functions as were acquired by popular assemblies in the fifth century accrued to the centuriate assembly. However, the stages by which this body evolved from a single military *classis* of heavy-armed infantry with accompanying cavalry and light-armed troops into the later complex political structure of five wealth-based *classes*, each organized into units ('centuries') for voting purposes, are controversial. Behind the later political organization seems to lie a structure based on a hoplite force of 6000 (the later notional complement of a Roman legion) since in the historians' account it was the sixty centuries of young men from the first three *classes* who had the heavy infantry armour (cf. Table 2: p. 164). The division of that force into three *classes* (the first including forty centuries of younger men, the second and third ten each) has been thought to reflect a situation in which a single *classis* of 4000 was supplemented by the progressive enlistment in the later fifth century of 1000 younger men not previously employed for 'hoplite' service into each of two new *classes*,[74] perhaps as a result of a new readiness to admit to the infantry men who could not afford the full 'hoplite' panoply. Yet in our sources the differences in armament be-

---

[73] Cf. Latte 1936[G639], 59–73 = id. *Kleine Schriften* 341–54.
[74] E.g., Sumner 1970[G728], 67–78.

tween classes II and III at least were minimal, concerning merely the presence or absence of greaves.[75] This provides no convincing basis for a separate military classification. Moreover, if the later ratio of property valuations between the classes obtained from their inception, those qualified for the first class would, on this hypothesis, enjoy twice the numerical strength of those with property valued at 50 per cent or more of the minimum required for admission to class I. That is improbable *per se* and such substantial differences of wealth cannot be realistically correlated with the comparatively small distinctions in armament involved, particularly again between classes II and III.

More probably, therefore, these distinctions, at least in their historical form, were established later for political reasons, when military manpower exceeded considerably the sixty notional centuries allotted to those who qualified for the heavy infantry. The reason for the innovation can only be conjectured but the probable regular exaction of *tributum* in the later fourth century may have sharpened claims for enhanced political status by the relatively affluent. The newly established ratio of values and allocation of centuries among the first three *classes* were designed explicitly to favour those who now qualified for the first class and it was they who retained (or appropriated) the appellation of the 'classis' in traditional parlance. The cavalry even more effectively preserved their privileged position since increases in the number of those granted a public horse (the eventual total of 1800 can hardly antedate the late fourth century) were accompanied by a corresponding increase in the number of equestrian centuries, each maintained at 100 strong.

The differentiation of *classes* within the 'hoplite' force as it is known later may not, therefore, belong to the fifth century,[76] but the growing political role of the centuriate organization was probably already responsible for some innovations. The later system of allocating the older men (*seniores*) the same number of centuries as the *iuniores* has no military justification since each would have perhaps no more than a third of the complement of the corresponding junior century. It must, therefore, be viewed in political terms. That it should give their vote disproportionate weight, both in numerical terms and in terms of their military contribution, is indicative of the influence and authority generally accorded to the older members of the community. It also broke decisively with any concept of the century as a unit of a hundred men, thus accelerating the

---

[75] Both classes II and III are also given the oblong shield called the *scutum* rather than the round hoplite *clipeus* but for the sixth and fifth centuries that may be anachronistic (Kienast 1975[H45], 94), perhaps betraying the late origin of the differentiation of equipment. See, however, Saulnier 1980[G706], 71ff for a possible example of the combination of the two types of armament from Bologna.

[76] In defence of earlier dates cf., e.g., Fraccaro 1931[G579], 91–7 (= id. *Opuscula* II.287–92); 1934[G581], 57–71 (= id. *Opuscula* II.293–306); Last 1945[G638], 42–4.

divorce between the organization of the political assembly and the army. In the former the century was now a unit of variable size and the total number of centuries (junior and senior) could remain unchanged despite their lack of correlation with actual manpower; the fixing at sixty of the political centuries assigned to those 'younger men' who qualified for the heavy infantry is presumably a consequence of this.

The light-armed may similarly have claimed some place in the assembly. Presumably they too already had their own military organization but whenever they were incorporated into the centuriate political assembly, their units must have been adjusted to reduce the significance of their votes drastically. When the single century of *proletarii* (those levied only in emergencies) was similarly established is impossible to determine, but two of the major sources of political discontent in the fifth century may precisely have been claims to an enhanced political role for the centuriate assembly and, as a consequence, demands that it include the entire adult male citizen body.[77]

The use of the centuriate organization as a political assembly was certainly well under way in the early Republic; the red flag raised on the Janiculum during its meetings to warn of enemy attack belongs most appropriately before the destruction of Veii (396 B.C.) and the use of a centuriate rather than a curiate law for the censors presumably dates from the establishment of that office. In seeking to demonstrate the illegality of his exile in 58 B.C. Cicero (*Sest.* 65; *Rep.* II.61; *Leg.* III.11; cf. Twelve Tables IX.1–2) alleged that the Twelve Tables prohibited the passage of bills concerning an individual's status except through the 'greatest assembly' (*comitiatus maximus*) and identified the 'greatest assembly' as the *comitia centuriata*. If that is correct, it implies that the centuriate assembly had already eclipsed the curiate.

Cicero interpreted this provision as confining all capital jurisdiction to the centuriate assembly and elsewhere attributed both this and a ban on *privilegia* (interpreted as bills directed at specific individuals) to otherwise unknown 'hallowed laws' (*leges sacratae*).[78] By *leges sacratae* Cicero may understand measures sponsored by the plebeian tribunes (p. 223) but the rules of the Twelve Tables, if authentic, seem designed to curb tribunician attempts to force through plebiscites inflicting penalties on those who defied their intervention. Thus the restriction of measures imposing a capital penalty to the centuriate assembly (to which the tribunes can have had no access in the fifth century) clearly refers only to the passage of comitial proposals, not to the infliction of legally sanctioned penalties, and is evidently intended to prevent their presentation

---

[77] The centuries of 'engineers' (*fabri*) and musicians are also artificial but could have been created for the purposes of military review.   [78] Cic. *Dom.* 43; *Sest.* 65.

to the plebeian assembly.[79] Hence the Decemviral measures provide no basis for fathering a wide-ranging capital jurisdiction on the *comitia centuriata*. Indeed, since the alleged quaestorial comitial prosecutions of this period are fiction and the *duoviri* at least seem to have passed judgement in cases of treason without reference to the people, the centuriate assembly may not at this stage have been involved in first instance criminal jurisdiction at all.[80]

Its most important role in the Roman tradition is the election of chief magistrates. That has sometimes been regarded as an error: the consul initially either merely named his successors or brought for the assembly's approval the number of names required to fill the available places.[81] The two principal arguments for such views are the wide discretionary powers later enjoyed by the presiding magistrate and the fact that he is said to 'create' (*creare*) the new magistrate when announcing his election. These arguments are inconclusive. The announcement of the result of an election was the constitutive act by which the successful candidate formally secured office and the term *creare* is therefore appropriate to it. It is notable in fact that *creare* is seldom used of the consul's nomination of a dictator (for which *dicere* ('name') is normal) and it is commonly employed in contexts where a popular vote is involved. As to the later rights of the presiding magistrate to bar candidates, these served principally as a check on the assembly if it sought to elect individuals whom he deemed unacceptable on grounds of their qualifications or the interests of the state or aristocracy (not his own personal preference). There was no formal requirement, at least in the mid-Republic, that only those whose candidacy had been notified to, and accepted by, the presiding magistrate could present themselves for election (though that may have become usual) and the assembly itself might even elect from outside the number of declared candidates.

The control exercised by the presiding magistrate is therefore negative in character and, if anything, an argument against an original naming of his successors. Admittedly, the nomination of the dictator, city prefect and (probably) quaestors shows that a popular vote was not regarded as fundamental to the magistracies in the early Republic, but we have no clear evidence of such a practice for the early consulship and the aristocratic requirement of the successive rotation of office (p. 206) may have demanded some more broadly based system of selection.

---

[79] The Decemviral ban on *privilegia*, if Cicero's interpretation is correct, may also have specifically applied to the tribunes (it is otherwise difficult to reconcile with the passage of bills inflicting a capital penalty).

[80] On 'appeal to the people' against magisterial penalties cf. p. 219f.

[81] Cf. Mommsen 1887–8[A91], 1.470–1; Tibiletti 1950[G738], 3–21. Against the view (Staveley 1954/5[G722], 193–211) that throughout the republican period the *interrex* also nominated the new consuls for approval by the assembly cf. Jahn 1970[G623], 25–7.

Conceivably that could have been secured by making consular nomination subject to senatorial and even popular approval but it is no less possible that from the outset it was found politically expedient to allow any patrician who wished to stand and to give the military forces of the new Republic an active role in the appointment of their regular commanders (which might reinforce their allegiance in the field). If not, such episodes as the Fabian domination of office between 485 and 479 may rapidly have led to the introduction of election. Certainly whenever the right was conceded, it will have acted as a significant factor in moderating antagonism towards aristocratic rule, although patrician interests were safeguarded by the right of the presiding officer to debar unacceptable candidates and by making the election subject to the *patrum auctoritas*. Hence even if plebeians formed a majority of the assembly there were formal mechanisms to reinforce the patrician monopoly of office should it be challenged.

Given the original military character of the centuriate organization, the declaration of war was presumably also amongst its earliest functions, if not a major starting point for its whole development as a political assembly. It may also have sanctioned treaties but the evidence here is inconclusive. In these cases, as in all its legislative dealings, the assembly was, of course, entirely dependent on magisterial summons and magisterial proposals which it could only accept or reject; and the measures which it accepted had then to receive the sanction of the *patrum auctoritas*. Even so, the extent of its legislative role at this date is doubtful. The measure cited by Livy (vii.17.12; cf. ix.34.6f; Twelve Tables xii.5) from the Twelve Tables ('let what the people has ordered last be the law and valid') would suggest considerable legislative activity but its authenticity is dubious. Although it is manifestly designed to resolve conflicts between laws or other acts of the people and need not imply any active belief in popular sovereignty,[82] the wording of the law has certainly been modernized, a reference to the need for patrician sanction (*patrum auctoritas*) of the legislation concerned might be expected and there is little other evidence for extensive use of comitial enactment. The law of 472 B.C. recorded on an inscription still available to Varro (Macrob. *Sat.* 1.13.21) indicates that some legislative activity occurred but its content is unknown. The Twelve Tables may have envisaged the possibility of capital proposals directed against individuals but if so, this was largely to outlaw tribunician proposals to the plebs. Statute made only a restricted contribution to the development of private law in the later republic and, with the possible exception of the Twelve Tables themselves, can hardly have been more widely employed in the fifth century. The political order

---

[82] Contrast Appian's interpretation of a similar bogus regal enactment (*Pun.* 531).

itself was largely moulded by custom and practice and even the most fundamental constitutional innovations may have no statutory basis, despite the procedural anxieties of some later writers to supply one. There is no firm evidence for general laws defining an individual magistracy, its functions and prerogatives, and even the creation of new offices may have had no legislative foundation. Livy's alleged law creating the dictatorship is clearly a later fiction (p. 191), as is that of Dionysius (*Ant. Rom.* v.70.5) leaving the senate to make the first appointment. A measure creating the consular tribunate as an office open to both plebeians and patricians (Livy iv.35.11) is equally spurious and little faith can be placed in essentially casual references to other laws establishing the consulship (Pomp. *Dig.* 1.2.2.16) or censorship (Livy ix.34.7). Such innovations are in general not attributed a legislative basis and the same is true even of the creation of the praetorship and curule aedileship in 367 b.c. The other alleged political legislation of this period is largely fabrication, none entirely free from doubt. So far as our evidence goes, therefore, whilst the centuriate assembly was the principal, indeed probably sole source of comitial legislation, the scope and quantity of such legislation are likely to have been limited. That may reflect only our ignorance but more probably these functions developed gradually, one major consequence of the emergence and success of popular demands for political reform.

(j) *Conclusion*

The piecemeal development of the republican organs of government reflects their origin as a response to immediate political or administrative needs rather than as the implementation of a preconceived overall design or the application of a general constitutional theory. Indeed, early innovations such as the dictatorship betray the potential inadequacy of the original arrangements. Such theoretical treatment as the constitution was accorded was essentially a development of the late Republic and therefore *post eventum*; in the fifth century even the powers of the magistrate were probably not treated as a unitary concept. Although certain recurrent principles can be seen in the form and structure of the magistracies, these must be viewed in the context of contemporary political requirements, predominantly those of the ruling patriciate.

This hereditary aristocracy had probably largely crystallized under the later monarchy as a result of increasing economic power (fostered by Roman expansion), the growing need for legal and religious expertise, which the kings could not meet alone, their own military prowess and the comparative weakness of the central authority which encouraged the acquisition of personal followings. The importance of the aristocracy already in the regal period is emphasized in the *interregnum* procedure, which implies at some stage a non-hereditary concept of monarchy with the aristocracy playing a central role in the appointment of a new incumbent; and even where rulers seized power by force, they had to come to terms with at least a substantial element of the elite if they were to survive. Indeed, it was presumably the anxiety of the more powerful clans to buttress their own position with respect to the monarchy which led to the assertion of collective rights, particularly in relation to senatorial membership, and this was further reinforced by demands that important offices (notably the major priesthoods) should be filled from the ranks of those so privileged.

The evolution of such an aristocracy into a closed caste is difficult to trace. Although a number of families may have achieved a *de facto* position of hereditary privilege comparatively early, the notion of this as an exclusive group may have been slow to take root and its composition may therefore have remained elastic. Names of Etruscan origin in the historical patriciate, for example, may largely reflect sixth-century immigrants, some taking advantage of the 'open' character of contemporary aristocratic society (p. 261), others perhaps partisans whom individual monarchs had sought to promote. Equally, the fall of a particular ruler may have resulted in the removal of some of his adherents; it is not necessary to accept the legend of Tarquinius Collatinus' exile in 509[83] in order to suppose that such expulsions followed the departure of Tarquinius Superbus. Conceivably, it was only at the overthrow of the monarchy, when the right to hold supreme office in the new Republic became a critical issue and created a powerful motive for fixing irrevocably the circle of those qualified to exercise political power, that the concept of a closed patriciate was finally established and even then there may have been some fluidity in its composition (now untraceable in detail) with individual families unable to retain their status while others (like the Claudii) secured later recognition. Nonetheless, it is the growth in power of this aristocracy in the sixth century and its progressive development of a sense of common collective interests and privilege which must lie behind the revolution of 509, and the political system then established served principally its interests.

Arguably the most urgent domestic problem was the stability of the patriciate itself, threatened from within by powerful individuals attended by clansmen, comrades and clients. Certainly the patriciate sought to express in constitutional terms its collective role in the government of the state. Hence the maintenance of the *interregnum* procedure, the institution (at whatever date) of the *patrum auctoritas*, and also probably

---

[83] Piso fr. 19P; Cic. *Rep.* II.53; Livy II.2.1ff; Dion. Hal. *Ant. Rom.* v.9ff; etc.

the ascription to the senate of a major role in decision-making. Though each chief magistrate possessed in his own right the wide powers deemed necessary, particularly for military command (his likely principal function), tenure of office was limited to a year and probably from the outset collegiality was an invariable feature of the regular Roman magistracies, offering the possibility of a check on personal misuse of power, but still more encouraging co-operation in the execution of their responsibilities. Moreover, the pattern of entry into office (Table 3) shows a rapid introduction of numerous families in the first three decades of the Republic. Although office might be held more than once, for most of the fifth century it apparently could not be held in successive years[84] nor could two members of the same clan hold the chief magistracy together, a rule or practice which sought to prevent individual monopolization of power and thus ensure its distribution among the aristocracy. Admittedly the enlargement of the consular tribunate was accompanied by some relaxation of these rules, but this rapid expansion of the chief magistracy itself serves to emphasize its collective and co-operative character. Only in one circumstance was an exception made; characteristically that was in the military sphere where it was expected that on occasion a consul would voluntarily forego his own position as the state's chief executive and in particular as its military leader by appointing a dictator who exercised supreme command alone. Even here, however, the dictator's tenure of office was restricted to a maximum of six months and the aristocratic distaste for such unfettered power insisted that in practice he resign once he had accomplished the purpose for which he was appointed.

These political arrangements could not entirely forestall individual aristocratic ambition, at least if the legends of Sp. Cassius and Manlius Capitolinus have a core of truth, and individual followings may have continued to be a potent factor. In the last resort, however, the patriciate's cohesion withstood these challenges. A number of factors no doubt contributed: the social bonds within the aristocracy itself may have become more wide-ranging and complex; private free-booting was probably progressively restricted, at least on land;[85] above all, whereas

---

[84] Apart from the dubious examples of P. Valerius Poplicola (*cos.* 509; 508; 507), C. Iulius (*cos.* 435; 434) and C. Servilius Axilla (*cons. trib.* 419; 418; 417), the first instance agreed in our sources appears to be C. Servilius Ahala (*cons. trib.* 408 and 407).

The incidence of iteration of office in the first half century of the Republic is not abnormally high, except that a few individuals succeed in holding three consulships. In the period 509–452 sixty-six men hold the consulship once, thirteen twice and six three times. This compares with (for example) the period 277–220 when twenty-five individuals hold the consulship twice, although the value of such comparisons is limited since the third-century iterations are often prompted by military needs and whilst the same may have been true in the fifth century, we have insufficient reliable evidence to explain repeated tenure in that period.

[85] At sea men of Latin extraction could still act, apparently autonomously, in piratical ventures in the fourth century: cf. Diod. XVI.82.3.

Table 3. *The entry of gentes into office: 509–401*

509 Horatius (8)	498 Cloelius (3)	471 Quinctius (27)
Iunius (1)	497 Minucius (5)	469 Numicius (1)
Lucretius (12)	Sempronius (8)	461 Volumnius (1)
Tarquinius (1)	495 Claudius (6)	455 Romilius (1)
Valerius (37)	Servilius (23)	454 Aternius (1)
506 Herminius (2)	492 Geganius (7)	Tarpeius (1)
Larcius (4)	489 Iulius (16)	453 Curiatius (1)
505 Postumius (13)	Pinarius (3)	Quinctilius (2)
503 Menenius (11)	488 Furius (35)	452 Sestius (1)
502 Cassius (3)	Nautius (8)	451 Genucius (5)
Verginius (13)	487 Aquillius (2)	445 Curtius (1)
501 Cominius (2)	Sicinius(?)(1)	444 (or 441) Papirius (19)
500 Sulpicius (18)	485 Cornelius (36)	444 Atilius (3)
Tullius (1)	Fabius (28)	437 Sergius (11)
499 Aebutius (3)	484 Aemilius (19)	433 Folius (1)
Veturius (10)	480 Manlius (19)	422 Antonius (1)

Note: the table gives the year in which each *gens* first appears in the chief magistracy with (in brackets) the total number of such posts (excluding the Decemvirates) held in the period 509–367. The data are based on the uncorrected consular *fasti* since any attempt to remove dubious elements would be highly contentious.

under the monarchy aristocrats were faced at best with a choice between rival claimants to the throne, now they had a vested interest in the maintenance of their own collective power and would naturally close ranks against any who threatened to destroy it. The rise of the plebs can only have furthered this sense of common self-interest. Tensions and imbalance within the aristocracy remained, however. Clans such as the Cornelii, Fabii, Furii, Quinctii, Servilii and Valerii enjoyed a disproportionate hold on political office (Table 4). The most striking instance is the run of seven consecutive Fabian consulships between 485 and 479, which is perhaps linked to the fall of Sp. Cassius in 486/5 and signals the potential dangers which such internal rivalry and aristocratic ambition repeatedly posed. More insidiously, despite the enhanced opportunities for office-holding which it brought, the era of the consular tribunate seems to have seen an advance in the hold over the magistracies enjoyed by the major clans. In contrast, many other families appear rarely in office and some were probably already threatened with extinction. Their anxieties may find indirect reflection in the Twelve Tables (p. 233).

Nor could the patriciate ignore the new forces emerging in Roman society. The creation of the 'hoplite' army in or by the sixth century had established an organization which, whatever its initial size, can hardly have been manned exclusively by some fifty patrician clans and their

Table 4. *The distribution of office: 509–445 and 444–367* B.C.

Office-holding *gentes*: 509–445 B.C.

Valerius	11	Cassius*	3	Cloelius	1
Fabius	10	Menenius	3	Curiatius*	1
Verginius	10	Nautius	3	Curtius*	1
Furius	7	Sulpicius	3	Iunius*	1
Servilius	6	Aebutius	2	Numicius*	1
Aemilius	5	Cornelius	2	Quinctilius	1
Horatius	5	Cominius*	2	Sestius*	1
Minucius*	5	Geganius	2	Sicinius(?)*	1
Postumius	5	Genucius	2	Romilius*	1
Quinctius	5	Herminius*	2	Tarpeius*	1
Claudius	4	Manlius	2	Tarquinius*	1
Iulius	4	Pinarius	2	Tullius*	1
Larcius*	4	Sempronius	2	Volumnius*	1
Lucretius	4	Aquillius	1		
Veturius	4	Aternius*	1	Total:	134

Office-holding *gentes*: 444–367 B.C.

Cornelius	34	Postumius	8	Titinius (pl.)	2
Furius	28	Sempronius	6	Trebonius (pl.)	2
Valerius	26	Veturius	6	Aebutius	1
Quinctius	22	Geganius	5	Albinius (pl.)	1
Papirius	19	Nautius	5	Antistius (pl.)	1
Fabius	18	Atilius	3	Antonius	1
Manlius	17	Horatius	3	Duillius (pl.)	1
Servilius	17	Genucius	3	Aquillius	1
Sulpicius	15	Verginius	3	Folius	1
Aemilius	14	Claudius	2	Pinarius	1
Iulius	12	Cloelius	2	Pomponius (pl.)	1
Sergius	11	Licinius (pl.)	2	Quinctilius	1
Lucretius	8	Maelius (pl.)	2	Sextilius (pl.)	1
Menenius	8	Publilius (pl.)	2		
				Total	316

Note: each table gives the number of consulships or consular tribunates held by each *gens* in the period concerned, based on the uncorrected consular *fasti* (cf. Table 3). *Gentes* whose names first appear in or after 401 and which are generally regarded as non-patrician are marked 'pl.'; some other *gentes* may also be non-patrician, at least in part (cf. p. 175; 336). Names asterisked in the first list do not appear in the second.

adherents.[86] The possibility that the demographic increases of the seventh and sixth centuries and, in particular, Roman territorial expansion in the sixth century had fostered the enlargement of the independent peasantry and that common 'hoplite' service will gradually have stimu-

---

[86] For a different view see above, p. 104. For the probable small size of many patrician *gentes* cf. Botsford 1907[G20], 681–3.

lated an awareness of their own common interests and identity cannot be excluded. In the fifth century the members of the 'hoplite' *classis* had probably little active role in political decision-making, but the right of the army (meeting as a political assembly in rudimentary form) to elect magistrates and declare war may have been granted early, thus establishing for the future a new timocratic basis to the distribution of political rights at Rome. Initially that aspect probably played only a very secondary role; the military associations of these functions made the army a natural forum and what was immediately significant was the concession of these rights to some form of popular assembly. Nonetheless, it must soon have become apparent that these new-won rights were sharply gradated according to wealth and then age.

Even so, it would be hasty to assume that those more substantial peasantry who were not patrician clients necessarily regarded themselves, or always acted, as a distinct category within the Roman political and social order. For alongside the emergence of a hereditary aristocracy formally monopolizing office and the incipient development of a timocratic structure no less formally determining effective rights of political suffrage, there persisted another tradition, that of the citizen community. Indeed the distinction between citizen and non-citizen was fundamental to the whole legal and political order. That is evident, for example, in the continuing gulf in status between citizen and slave even where in practice they might be subject to similar physical constraints. Although the restricted scale of slavery may have given it a more familial character than it often possessed in the later days of mass slavery,[87] the slave was legally the disposable property of his owner and, so far as we know, without rights, whereas the Roman citizen who had entered debt-bondage or been sold to another seems to have retained his public and other personal rights intact (at least in theory). Similarly, the rule that the insolvent judgement debtor be sold into slavery 'across the Tiber' (Twelve Tables III.5) must reflect a desire to prevent one Roman citizen falling into legal servitude to another.[88]

The basis of citizenship was presumably no different from that in force later when it went to the legitimate offspring of a Roman male citizen or (notably) the illegitimate children of a female citizen irrespective of other qualifications. One version of Twelve Tables 1.4 ('proletario iam civi' 'a *proletarius* who is now a citizen') might imply that the citizen status of the virtually landless *proletarii* was a contemporary innovation, but the simple 'proletario civi' ('a *proletarius* citizen') has better manuscript

---

[87] Their participation in the family cult, for example, is presumably an inheritance from this period.

[88] Some held later, however, that manifest thieves surrendered to their victim became the latter's slave (Gai. *Inst.* III.189).

authority and is to be preferred.[89] There is, therefore, no good evidence
that citizenship was ever linked to property ownership; birth was the
normal criterion.

Citizenship was not, however, exclusive (cf. p. 261). Whether or not it
was already a formally recognized right, Latins and Romans could
probably change citizenship by a change of cities and certain cities
(including Rome) may have acknowledged the right of their exiles to find
refuge in each other's community. As in an earlier period, when central
Italian communities appear to have had a corresponding 'open' character, Rome may also have been receptive to some immigrants from
outside Latium and her repeated absorption of conquered peoples into
her citizen body was rightly seen by Dionysius (*Ant. Rom.* 11.16.1f;
XIV.6.1ff) as a major factor in her later success. Above all, this receptivity
was evident in the grant of citizen status to freedmen, which seems
already by this date to have accompanied the concession of liberty to
these former slaves.[90] The provisions in the Twelve Tables concerning
the guardianship of, and inheritance from, freedmen betray no sign that
they were of non-citizen status[91] and Table v.8 even allegedly envisaged
that a freedman might make a will (presumably a comitial will). If so, they
had certainly achieved citizenship and that principle is in any event best
dated to a period when freedmen were few and usually presumably of
central Italian origin.[92]

Roman practice here was notoriously different from that of many
Greek states where ex-slaves remained in a position analogous to that of a
resident foreigner (metic). The reason probably lies in differing implications of citizen status. In the ancient Greek city-states at least this was
commonly regarded in terms of political participation and rights.[93] To
the Roman freedman, still probably regarded as of inferior social status
and as the dependant of his former owner,[94] citizenship meant above all
certain rights at civil law, most of which Greek states could accord

[89] Even here 'civi' ('citizen') is superfluous and probably a later addition.

[90] In a confused statement Plutarch (*Publ.* 7.7; cf. also Livy 11.5.10) seems to assert that
manumission conferred citizen status only from 509 or 312 B.C. but little trust can be placed in this (or
in Dionysius' deduction from Ser. Tullius' alleged creation of the census (and own servile origins?)
that he first granted freedmen citizen status (*Ant. Rom.* IV.22.4)).

[91] Ulpian, *Tit.* 29.1 explicitly understands these rules as applying to freedmen who are citizens (in
contrast presumably to the Augustan categories of non-citizen freedmen).

[92] One or both of the procedures used to give slaves their liberty during their patron's lifetime
implies also the grant of citizen status (Cosentini 1948 & 1950[G187], 1.9–17). For other views on the
date of the concession of citizenship cf. Chantraine 1972[G182], 59–67.

[93] Note, however, Frederiksen 1984[J48], 196–8 on the more fluid situation which obtained
among the Western Greeks in particular.

[94] There is no clear evidence, however, for patrons exercising automatic formal powers over their
freedmen: cf. Cosentini 1948 & 1950[G187], 1.69–103; Treggiari 1969[G150], 68–75.

through quasi-metic status. The principal exception, apart from the right to beget free citizens, was land ownership but this was not so integrally linked to full rights of political participation at Rome, at least in origin, as it was in much of the Greek world.[95] Indeed, for the citizen body at large, political rights can have had at most a very restricted scope under the monarchy and only developed gradually in the early Republic. Nonetheless, the concept of the citizen community was central and found expression in a variety of forms: in the particular character assumed by social relationships between men of different status (p. 162), in the absence of a formalized social hierarchy, in the common citizen dress (the *toga*), in participation in the religious life of the community (p. 606), in its defence and perhaps in public works,[96] in common membership (apparently without status distinction) of the *curiae* and participation in their common meals and assemblies, in curiate comitial involvement in acts affecting individual status and property, in the custom of appealing for aid to the citizen body (p. 220), and above all in common (and, in theory, almost certainly equal) enjoyment of the rights given by the civil law; indeed, the *ius* ('right') asserted as the basis of the individual's claim to ownership was the 'right of the citizens' (*ius Quiritium*).

Yet even apart from the demands for a greater role in political decision-making, the patrician seizure of power and its social exclusivity might seem both anomalous and a threat to that citizen order. Public supervision of the production and sale of salt or of corn imports in time of famine may, if authentic, testify to a rudimentary conception of state concern with the welfare of the whole citizen body, but the forms in which political power was in practice exercised might readily impinge on individual citizen rights: the definition, knowledge and administration of the law lay entirely in the hands of the ruling elite and even for those of 'hoplite' status there was little protection against the wide coercive and other discretionary powers of the magistrate. Indeed, it was the lack of defined limits to magisterial power that was to make the relationship of magistrate and private citizen fundamental to the Roman view of the development of the magistracies and of popular liberty. Later evidence of such concern is to be seen in the likely development of magisterial veto powers against a colleague's judicial or coercive acts as a response to appeals for assistance by individual citizens. If the fifth-century establishment of a maximum fine (imposed as a coercive penalty) is authentic (cf. p. 123), it also belongs in this context. Above all, it is principally here that

---

[95] The later restriction of freedmen to the four urban tribes (erroneously retrojected into the early Republic when it can have served no useful function) will have been motivated by the growth in freedmen numbers and their acquisition of some small political role through the development of the tribal assemblies.   [96] P. 132 n. 56.

we must seek the origins of the most remarkable development in Roman internal history: the political self-assertion of the plebs.

II. THE PLEBEIAN MOVEMENT

(a) *Introduction*

Since the prerogatives and functions of the plebeian tribunes remained a focus of political controversy and juristic comment to the close of the Republic, the origin and development of plebeian rights may have been the subject of a comparatively strong oral tradition, but one continuously modified and elaborated to suit later political or historiographical preoccupations. The surviving literary narratives must therefore be rigorously scrutinized in an attempt to distinguish the authentic features of the emergence of the plebs as a political force. In those narratives two fifth-century episodes occupy a key role in the assertion of plebeian prerogatives: the First Secession (494/3) saw the emergence of the plebs as a political force and the creation of the specifically plebeian officers, while agitation for the publication of the law culminated in the appointment of the First and Second Decemvirates, to be followed immediately by the Second Secession (449), which secured the restoration of the tribunate with enhanced powers. These two episodes and the reforms associated with them are here analysed in detail, as a prologue to a general assessment of the composition and aims of the plebeian movement.

(b) *The First Secession and the plebeian officers*

In the existing narratives[97] problems of debt, caused by enemy raids, the burdens of military service and taxation, and, in Sallust and Livy, wanton patrician severity provoked a military strike by the plebs (494 B.C.), who withdrew to the Aventine or the Sacred Mount or both successively. This First Secession was ended by the mediation of Menenius Agrippa (*cos.* 503) whose fable comparing the mutual dependence of patriciate and plebs with that of the parts of the body convinced the people of the need for reconciliation. Nonetheless, the plebs secured a major concession: the creation of their own officers (the tribunes) to act as a check on the consuls by providing assistance (*auxilium*), in the form of personal intervention, to individual plebeians threatened with oppressive magisterial action. Their appointment and recognition was the subject of a

---

[97] See especially Piso frs. 22–23P; Valerius Antias fr. 17P; Ascon. *Corn.* p. 76–7Cl; Cic. *Rep.* II.57; *Brut.* 54; Sall. *Iug.* 31.17; *H.* I fr. 11; Livy II.23–33; Dion. Hal. *Ant. Rom.* VI.23–90; *Inscr. Ital.* XIII.3 nos. 60, 78; Festus 422/4 L; Dio fr. 17 vol. I, pp. 43–9 Boissevain; Zonar. VII.14f.

patrician–plebeian agreement (Livy II.33.1) or even a formal treaty (Dion. Hal. *Ant. Rom.* VI.89.1; cf. VI.66.3f).

The number of tribunes initially appointed was disputed. Piso, Cicero, Atticus and perhaps Diodorus (p. 217) gave two, a total raised to four (Diodorus) or five (Piso) in 471 B.C. That is probably the original version but already in the late second century Sempronius Tuditanus (fr. 4P) alleged that the first two tribunes had co-opted three colleagues, yielding a total of five, a figure also found in the sources used by Livy and Dionysius. This left no scope for an increase in 471 but one significant change was still (or now) attributed to that year: voting in the plebeian assembly was henceforth by tribal units.

The tribunician prerogative of providing assistance, guaranteed in some accounts by the agreement of 493, was reinforced by tribunician 'sacrosanctity'. One tradition traced this to an oath sworn by the plebs to protect their officers as inviolate, with a prescription of outlawry against anyone who assaulted their person. The same conception may lie behind the ascription of tribunician sacrosanctity to a 'hallowed law' (*lex sacrata*) passed at the First Secession. One ancient version derived the term 'hallowed law' from the penalty of outlawry (*sacer esto*) which it contained, while others again referred it specifically to laws sworn by the plebs at the Secession (Fest. 422L).

Armed with this popular backing, the tribunes rapidly (in the historians' view) acquired all the prerogatives associated with the office in the late Republic. Thus Dionysius carefully charts the usurpation of the right to hold meetings of the plebs (492), to prosecute patricians before the people (491), to summon the senate and lay proposals before it (456), to impose fines on their own authority (455) and to propose plebiscites binding on the whole populace (449).[98] If the same sense of development is not explicit in Livy, that is merely a token of his comparative indifference to constitutional issues.

Much of the narrative of the First Secession can be swiftly eliminated. The depiction of Ap. Claudius (*cos.* 495) as an unremitting opponent of plebeian demands or of M'. Valerius as the leading advocate of reconciliation merely reflects established literary postures (the Valerii even claimed that M'. Valerius as dictator in 494 was responsible for ending the Secession). Dionysius' formal treaty can also be disregarded as a misplaced legalism characteristic of his history; it was evidently repeated in the context of the Second Secession (cf. XI.49.3; also Livy IV.6.7).

The disagreement over the location of the First Secession or the

[98] Dion. Hal. *Ant. Rom.* VII.16ff; 35ff (esp. 65.1ff); X.31.1ff; 50.1ff; XI.45.1ff.

number of tribunes originally appointed similarly betrays the process of reworking to which the episode was subject, as does the controversy concerning the identity of the first tribunes.[99] Even a demonstrably early element in the narrative of the tribunate's creation, the fable of Menenius, is an accretion from Greek literary or philosophical sources.[100] It appeared in 'all the old histories' (Dion. Hal. *Ant. Rom.* VI.83.2), but though the early political decline of the Menenii may indicate that Menenius Agrippa's role as a conciliator was established early and though the fable itself implicitly upholds and justifies patrician hegemony, it must be doubtful whether it could have become known at Rome before the third century.

The date of the Secession is no less precarious. Although the surviving accounts give it no prominence, the coincidence that the tribunate was established in the year of the dedication of the temple of Ceres, the principal religious focus of the plebeian movement, is rendered doubly suspicious by the parallel with the dedication of the Capitoline temple in the first year of the Republic (p. 177). The tribunate must belong to the very early Republic, probably before the Twelve Tables, which presumably resulted from concerted plebeian pressure and may even have sought to curb tribunician activities. Nonetheless, unless the temple of Ceres itself has been redated, the precise year of the First Secession may be the result of later reconstruction.[101]

Superficially at least the surviving accounts of the causes and results of the Secession also contain a serious incoherence: the Secession originates in economic distress (debt) but culminates in an essentially political solution (the tribunate). Later authors[102] alleged that the release of debtors featured among the terms by which the Secession ended, but that must represent a subsequent attempt to resolve the puzzle. Livy (II.33.1; cf. also Cic. *Rep.* II.59) ignores such a solution and may see the tribunate itself as a remedy for the oppressive treatment of debtors. Is that plausible?

In their discussions of debt execution in the fifth and fourth centuries Livy and Dionysius speak mainly of debtors who have been formally surrendered (*addicti*) by the magistrate to their creditor and have entered quasi-servitude as a direct consequence. Aulus Gellius (*NA* xx.1.19; 39–52; cf. Twelve Tables III.1ff) cites the Twelve Tables for the addic-

[99] Cf. *MRR* 1.15f. The records of fifth-century tribunes as a whole are highly suspect, as the apparent duplication of names in the lists for 470 and 449 illustrates (e.g. Momigliano 1931[G674], 164–6 (= id. *Quarto Contributo* 301–2)). The plebs may have kept some records of their activities but the tribunes were not eponymous and there was, therefore, no reason to keep a register after the manner of the consular *fasti*.

[100] Nestle 1927[H66], 350–60.

[101] For a possible ancient tradition which dated the establishment of the tribunate in the mid-fifth century see p. 228.

[102] Dion. Hal. *Ant. Rom.* VI.83.4f, 88.3; Dio fr. 17 vol. 1, p. 47 Boiss.; *Inscr. Ital.* XIII.3 nos. 60, 78.

tion of judgement debtors, who would include those in default of debts incurred by oral contract (*stipulatio*),[103] but he mentions no entitlement of the creditor to retain the addicted debtor as a quasi-slave; rather, at the end of a prescribed period of enchainment to allow for repayment of the debt, the insolvent debtor was either to be killed or sold into slavery 'across the Tiber'. The retention of the debtor as a tied bondsman may have been gradually permitted and might well often have resulted from an agreement (*pactum*) between the parties by which the debtor avoided the prescribed modes of vengeance, but even so there must be a strong chance that in their treatment of addiction the annalists' picture is based on later procedure, where quasi-servitude could certainly in practice result from a debt-judgement,[104] and on an assimilation of addiction to debt-bondage proper.

The history of debt-bondage (*nexum*) is obscure because it was reputedly abolished by a Lex Poetelia of 326 or 313 B.C. and little knowledge of it therefore survived into later periods. In Livy II.27.1 it appears to require a formal magisterial addiction and *nexi* enter bondage under compulsion. This may, however, be again merely a consequence of the assimilation of the two different procedures, occasioned here by the desire to involve the consul Ap. Claudius in the oppression of debtors. Elsewhere Livy (VIII.28.2; cf. VII.19.5; Val. Max. VI.1.9) and Varro (*Ling.* VII.105) tend to suggest (though they do not prove) that men entered bondage voluntarily. The form of the transaction, however, is singularly ill-attested. It is even uncertain whether it was an original loan on the person or a self-sale resulting in immediate servitude by those unable to meet a pre-existing debt.[105] The latter might suggest that the institution arose mainly as a means of avoiding the severe consequences of addiction but in that case it is difficult to see why its abolition should be regarded as a major popular advance. It seems more likely that, whatever its legal form, it was a loan directly on the person of the debtor who was subject to bondage either immediately or on default after a prescribed period.[106] Whether the bondsman could work off such a debt is doubtful, for in talking of his redeeming his debt Varro (loc. cit.) may refer to repayment. For many the servitude must in practice have been permanent.[107]

If debt-bondage was a purely private transaction with no magisterial involvement, the tribunate is unlikely to have been created specifically and principally to regulate it since in the mid- and late Republic tribunes

[103] For which cf. Gai. *Inst.* IV.17a.

[104] E.g. Peppe 1981[G283], 100–1; 188–208. Livy's apparent belief (VIII.28.8) that the Lex Poetelia (below) prohibited any enchainment for debt probably rests on a confusion between debt-bondage and *addictio*.   [105] For modern theories cf. Behrends 1974[G172], 141–50.

[106] Naturally it might also then be applied where a pre-existing debt remained unpaid, as the ancient sources often seem to assume.

[107] For further discussion of debt-bondage and its political significance see below, p. 329f.

rarely intervened in the relations between individual citizens. It may have been different in the early Republic (p. 218), especially in the case of bondsmen, who were in no position to assert their own rights in court (cf. Dion. Hal. *Ant. Rom.* xvi.5), but given that such intervention was not later part of the tribunate's function, it would be bold to assume that this was its sole initial purpose, for it would then be necessary (and difficult) to explain why the tribunate abandoned a tradition of intervention that was so central to its original creation. It would probably be consistent with the office's later character for the tribunes to intervene in the addiction of the judgement debtor so far as this was being conducted oppressively (so Livy vi.27.8ff), but in such cases the law made provision for the intervention of a champion (*vindex*) and it again seems improbable that a permanent office should be established purely to deal with cases where condemnation appeared unjustified and no *vindex* was forthcoming.

This is not to deny that economic discontent may well have been a significant factor in mobilizing support against the ruling patriciate[108] or that the tribunate may have been intended from the outset to act as a vehicle for reform. Indeed, the importance of economic grievances in the First Secession was probably an early element in the historical tradition since it seems implicit in Menenius' fable: the patriciate is Rome's stomach, enjoying (by implication) the profits of others' labours. However, the failure of Livy and Dionysius to cite debt as a source of major discontent again until the fourth century suggests that the exclusive centrality of its role in the agitation of 494/3 may be an artificial construction, perhaps based on the Secession of 287/6 (p. 400) where debt does seem to have been a determinant factor and where the political outcome (recognition of the universal validity of plebeian decrees) did have a direct potential relevance to its remedy. Certainly their allegations that military service and taxation were among its principal causes cannot be sustained. In this period personal taxation did not exist and although campaigns might sometimes have interfered with the harvest, they were in general short and close to home.

What remains of the literary tradition for the First Secession is therefore meagre: a military strike in the early fifth century which resulted in the creation of the tribunate, with economic distress as a significant but not necessarily decisive factor. Even this minimum has been questioned[109] on the supposition that both the First and Second Secession are entirely modelled on that of 287/6 B.C. The similarities are not, however, sufficient to prove duplication on that scale and there was

---

[108] For possible evidence of difficulties over grain supplies in the early fifth century cf. above, p. 133f with n. 62.   [109] E.g. Beloch 1926[A12], 283.

every reason for the plebs in the third century to employ again a tactic which had previously proved effective. What is crucial here is the character of the tribunate itself. As an office designed to represent plebeian interests against the state magistrates in particular it must result from a major act of self-assertion by a substantial element outside the ruling aristocracy. In that context the First Secession is entirely credible; it provides a plausible mechanism by which the plebs sought to secure acceptance of its right to organize in this way and its particular form (a military strike) coheres with the probable original purpose of the tribunate itself.

The initial functions and development of the tribunate must be largely conjectured from its later character and history. The derivation of the name 'tribunus' from 'tribus' ('tribe') has been taken to indicate that the tribunes were initially linked to the four urban tribes.[110] There is, however, no good evidence that the tribunes originally numbered four: Diodorus' account of the election of four plebeian tribunes in 471 (XI.68.8) probably refers not to the office's foundation but to its later enlargement, as his own language and the parallel with Piso (p. 213) suggest.[111] So far as is known, the tribunes never acted as representatives of individual areas of the city and the early breaking of the association at the increase in the tribunate to ten would require detailed explanation. The title of the office may be explained by the plebeian use of the tribes as the basis of their assembly. Admittedly, this form of assembly is supposed to have been introduced only later, by the tribune Publilius in 471 B.C., but the ancient belief that a different electoral forum (a curiate assembly) was originally used is itself irreconcilable with an association between the early tribunes and the urban tribes and may, in any case, be a fiction suggested by the alleged Publilian law of 339 giving general validity to the decisions of the plebeian tribal assembly. The uncertainties surrounding the date of the tribes themselves (p. 245f) further complicate the issue, but the possibility that they were used as the basis of the plebeian assembly from the outset cannot be excluded. Alternatively, the title *tribunus* may have been modelled on the military tribunes, who had probably long ceased to act as the commanders of tribal infantry contingents. That again would accord with the character of the Secession as a military strike.

The tribunate's later character indicates that the provision of assistance to the individual citizen against action by the magistrates was amongst its most fundamental and probably therefore earliest features.

[110] Ed. Meyer 1895[H57], 1–18 = 1924, 1.333–55.
[111] Urban 1973[H97], 761–4. If so, Diodorus presumably recorded the tribunate's foundation in his now lost account of the period before 486 B.C.

Tribunician inviolability must have served precisely to protect the tribune's person when he intervened in this way and the requirements that he could not spend a night or an entire day away from the city and that his door must always be open clearly reflect the importance of this aspect of his duties. The later technical term for vetoing a magisterial act (*intercessio*) derives from the physical act of 'stepping between' (*intercedere*) the two parties concerned and the tribunes' later wider veto powers (e.g. of legislation), for which a term such as 'prevent' or 'prohibit' (*prohibere* or *interdicere*) would be more appropriate, are therefore secondary to, and probably developed from, this original intervention on behalf of the individual. Indeed, the extension of tribunician prerogatives will often have been secured through the tribunes' powers of obstruction, particularly at the levy, a tactic prominent in the annalistic accounts of the early Republic. This lever was not so employed from the mid-third century and may, therefore, derive from authentic memory, at least for the fourth century and very early third.

Such tribunician assistance was probably, as later, used particularly in relation to the magistrate's role in civil jurisdiction and the levy since it was here that the magistrate most commonly confronted the individual citizen. In its early days, however, the tribunate presumably intervened wherever plebeian sentiment demanded protection. Thus the tribunes will certainly have attempted to intervene in other instances of summary coercion by the magistrate, particularly where this was directed against plebeian agitation, and even their normal confinement to the city and exclusion from the military sphere may be later developments. They may also on occasion have sought to check oppression by private individuals (cf. Zonar. vii.15), although throughout its history the tribunate never actively broke with the principle that the private individual was primarily responsible for the pursuit of personal wrongs. Throughout the Republic the tribunes seem neither to have claimed nor exercised any positive powers of civil or criminal jurisdiction against individuals acting in a private capacity (cf. Gell. *NA* xiii.12.9) and the later development of the office is confined almost exclusively to the public sphere.

Since the office was clearly intended as a check on the consuls, it may well have initially numbered two, but we have no means of controlling either this or the varying traditions of subsequent increases to a total of ten in 457 (Livy iii.30.7; Dion. Hal. *Ant. Rom.* x.30.6), perhaps 449 (Diod. xii.25.2) or even 493 (cf. Livy ii.44.6; Val. Max. vi.3.2).[112] The physical nature of early tribunician intervention clearly made a rapid increase in numbers desirable and reflects its usurpative nature. Hence

[112] Cf. also Zonar. vii.15; 17; Stuart Jones 1928[A128], 453f.

provision for the continuity of the office must also have been a high priority. Some echo of this may be found in the requirement (Diod. XII.25.3 (449 B.C.); Val. Max. VI.3.2 (486 B.C.)) that tribunes ensure the election of successors or be burned to death,[113] but in Valerius Maximus this appears to be an aetiological explanation of the monument commemorating the 'nine cremated' (p. 13f) and so may be later speculation. The possibility that a full complement of tribunes could not be found appears in an alleged ban on co-option, dubiously attributed to a Trebonian plebiscite of 448 (or 401 B.C.) but without parallel in the state offices. Clearly the tribunate in its early days was precarious and, despite the historians, recognition of its rights must have been slow and bitterly contested. Hence popular support was essential and the tradition that the inviolate status of the tribunes was secured by a general plebeian oath is highly plausible;[114] ultimately the tribunate rested on a general principle of plebeian self-help.

It is a credible corollary of this development that the individual who was subject to magisterial abuse should often couple an appeal to the people with that to the tribunes. Given their importance in social life (cf. p. 157), such appeals probably already had a long history and might, through sheer pressure of public disapprobation, if not the latent threat of violence, force the magistrate into concessions. In Livy (e.g. II.55.5–7) this appeal for popular protection is sometimes used as a reinforcement of the right of 'appeal to the people' (*provocatio ad populum*), which is often associated with tribunician assistance as one of the twin pillars of popular liberty. 'Appeal to the people' appears later to have been conceived as an appeal not for aid[115] but to a judgement of the people, meeting on occasion at least in formal assembly, to uphold, modify or reject the penalty inflicted by an official on an individual citizen. According to our sources such a right of appeal had been formally guaranteed against execution or scourging by a Lex Valeria of 509 B.C.[116] This was reinforced by a Lex Valeria Horatia (or Duillian plebiscite) of 449 prohibiting the appointment of magistrates not subject to appeal and its

---

[113] Cf. also Dio fr. 22 vol. I, p. 61 Boiss.; Zonar VII.17.

[114] The oath of obedience to their commanders and of willingness to fight to the death which was sworn by the Samnite 'linen-clad corps' (Livy x.38.5ff; cf. p. 292) is sometimes adduced as a parallel (Altheim 1940[H5]), but the circumstances, purposes and consequences of such military oaths (as of the 'hallowed laws' by which Italic military forces were sometimes assembled) were entirely different.

[115] *Contra*, Lintott 1972[H48], 229f. But in Livy II.55.5–7 the appeal for popular assistance follows the consuls' refusal to heed an 'appeal to the people' and may, therefore, be separate. The episode, which contains clear anachronisms (Ogilvie 1965[B129], 375), is comparable to, and may be based on, later incidents (Lintott loc.cit. 231) where individuals seek implementation of their citizen rights by rallying popular support. Livy III.56.5ff may be explained similarly.

[116] According to Dion. Hal. *Ant. Rom.* v.19.4 and Plut. *Publ.* 11 magisterial fines were also covered.

provisions were repeated by a Lex Valeria of 300. Only the last of these can be authentic. Valerius' consulship in 509 is itself almost certainly spurious[117] and having established the new republican magistracy with implicitly extensive coercive powers the aristocracy is not likely to have imposed a major restriction on their exercise forthwith. Moreover, the existence of such a law makes the early concern of the tribunes with oppressive magisterial action less easy to explain. The law is a clear duplication of that of 300; it reflects both later Valerian populist ambitions and a general tendency to attribute key elements of popular freedom to the first year of the Republic. If it is fiction, so also must be the statute(s) of 449, and in any case our sources suppose that magistrates not subject to *provocatio* continued to be appointed in the person of dictators.

These two fictitious measures and the Lex Valeria of 300 probably concern primarily appeals against the coercive actions and penalties of the magistrates, but when Cicero claims (*Rep.* 11.54) that the Twelve Tables contained several provisions making appeal permissible from every penalty and judgement, he may envisage its application also to regular judicial decisions. Even if, however, he refers only to the coercive penalties imposed by a magistrate and magistrates were not obliged to heed the appeal (an issue Cicero does not elucidate), the potential range of appeal involved here is much more extensive than that covered by later legislation. Unless we are here to recognize a major potential encroachment of popular sanction into the sphere of magisterial enactment which is otherwise unattested and remained largely unfulfilled, Cicero's information must be rejected as at best a misunderstanding (perhaps under the influence of Solon's example) of the restriction of capital penalties to the centuriate assembly and/or other provisions now lost. Whether, as was assumed in the first century, the decisions of the *duoviri* (*perduellionis*) were appellable in this way must also remain dubious, although some involvement of the assembly in cases of treason at least would not be surprising.

Even if, however, our sources have grossly exaggerated the formal rights of appeal in the early Republic, it remains entirely plausible that informal appeals were made for protection against oppressive magisterial action, as part of the traditions of citizen assistance. To judge by later evidence it was explicitly to one's fellow-citizens (*Quirites*) that the appeal was made, often perhaps with the implication that citizen rights were under threat, and it may have been precisely the need to give these appeals some more formal and effective means of expression that prompted the creation of the tribunate itself, perhaps on the basis of the emergence of individual spokesmen for the popular mood on such

[117] E.g. Ranouil 1975[H74], 71–2; cf. above, p. 173f.

occasions. Faced with such popular hostility the magistrate might press on with his action, if he could enforce his will, or give way entirely. Alternatively, he might seek to determine the true strength of popular feeling by summoning an assembly and proposing a formal motion for the punishment of the accused. Hence what had originated as an appeal for popular assistance becomes transformed into an appeal to the popular judgement and the conjecture that *provocatio ad populum* in its later conception developed from, and initially depended on, such informal requests for aid[118] is entirely plausible. In practice, however, even after the right of appeal was sanctioned by law, it seems seldom, if ever, to have been implemented. The explanation is probably that where the magistrate refused to yield entirely but yet felt obliged to heed popular opinion, he 'saved face' by simply modifying the penalty involved. That may well in fact have been the permanent consequence of the Lex Valeria of 300 B.C. According to the received text of Livy, *Per.* xiv M'. Curius in 275 was the first to order the sale of the property of a defaulter at the levy (and perhaps of the man himself: cf. Varro *ap.* Non. p. 28L; Val. Max. vi.3.4);[119] execution or scourging were now in effect prohibited penalties but an almost equally severe substitute was provided.

As has been seen, popular support was not only a vehicle of redress in its own right but also essential to the effectiveness of tribunician intervention. The tribunes may, as was later believed (cf. e.g. Dion. Hal. *Ant. Rom.* x.31.3), have claimed that where that intervention was disregarded or the tribune's person otherwise violated, the individual concerned was liable to be executed without trial, although it is characteristic of the concern of the Gracchan age with tribunician prerogatives that the first known historical attempt to enforce such a right is that of the tribune C. Atinius in 131 B.C. (Livy, *Per.* LIX; Pliny, *HN* vii.143). More commonly in the later period the tribune might of his own initiative 'consecrate the property' of (usually) a magistrate. That also presumably reflects an ancient practice (cf. Cic. *Dom.* 123)[120] but no examples of this or of lynch justice are recorded from the early Republic. That may merely reflect the inadequacy of our sources and forcible action of this kind may well have been attempted, but it must often have been difficult to implement. In that event the tribunes' only recourse was to turn to the plebeian assembly to secure a formal declaration that their sacrosanctity had been violated and that the offending magistrate was in their eyes an outlaw and

[118] Lintott 1972[H48], 226–67; cf. Staveley 1954–5[H90], 412–28.
[119] Dion. Hal. *Ant. Rom.* viii.81.3 (cf. x.33.3) attributes sale of the defaulter's property and seizure of his person to the early fifth century, but this may be in part or whole an anachronistic anticipation of later practice.
[120] So perhaps may the imprecations of C. Ateius Capito on the departing Crassus in 55 B.C.; cf. p. 621.

his property should be confiscated. It was perhaps such capital proposals which the Twelve Tables sought to prohibit (p. 201).

Such decrees of the plebeian assembly may lie at the root of the later tribunician right to prosecute former public officials before the people for misconduct in office. The annalists suppose that such a prerogative was already widely exercised in the fifth century in a series of comitial trials, principally against ex-magistrates for military failure. These cannot be historical. They are suspiciously concentrated in the fifth century in contrast to the fourth. Some (such as that of Coriolanus) are manifestly spurious. The fines in which they often result are anachronistic in scale, and for capital trials patrician magistrates would not have allowed any tribune the access to the centuriate assembly which, according to Cicero, the Twelve Tables had made necessary. Nor can the tribunate have acquired such extensive powers or so general a function in this period.

The tribunes' dependence on popular support implies also that the plebs must have been essentially self-regulating. The right to organize in this way may have been secured by the Secession but so far as the plebeians were able to determine their own affairs, they presumably did so without reference to any external approval. Dionysius' assumption that senatorial sanction was required for such decisions before 471 B.C. is merely a consequence of his erroneous belief that hitherto the plebs had met in the full patricio-plebeian curiate assembly (see *Ant. Rom.* IX.41.3f) and that a preliminary senatorial decree was necessary for any measure passed by that body to become binding (p. 185 n. 39).

It is another matter whether many of the recorded fifth-century plebiscites which sought to regulate and protect the plebeian movement are in fact historical. Dionysius (*Ant. Rom.* VII.17.5) can cite a plebiscite of 492 protecting a tribune from interruption at a public meeting, Livy (III.64.10) a clearly fictitious formula for the tribunician elections before 448 B.C., Festus (424 L) a 'first law concerning the tribunate', but the authenticity of all such documents is at best unproven. Similarly, though the plebs probably made comparatively free use of formal decisions, much need not have been the subject of specific enactment. That, for example, the exclusion of patricians from the tribunate required a 'hallowed law' (Cic. *Prov. Cons.* 46; *Sest.* 16) or a patricio-plebeian agreement (Livy II.33.1) must be extremely doubtful. Although the annalists have sensed correctly the precarious character of the early plebeian movement, no doubt on the basis of later experience and political argument,[121] they have again fallen prey to the recurrent temptation to regularize constitutional innovation, and in particular the plebeian movement, by attributing to it a formally unexceptionable basis.[122]

---

[121] Clodius' attempt to have the tribunate opened to patricians (Dio XXXVII.51.1 (60 B.C.)) no doubt revived interest in the issue.

[122] For further instances cf. Stuart Jones 1928[A128], 454, 460.

It was not only on matters internal to the plebs that tribunes will have sought expression of their sentiments. The office must early have acted as a focus of agitation for reform and plebiscites were an obvious and necessary means both of ensuring support and impressing the ruling elite with the strength of popular feeling. First-century writers, particularly Cicero, apparently assume that all early plebiscites were 'hallowed laws' (*leges sacratae*), involving probably a penalty of outlawry and perhaps a plebeian oath, and it is possible that this procedure was adopted as a means of exerting pressure where the plebeian demand could be implemented unilaterally. It might, for example, have been so used in the attempt to open up the Aventine for settlement in 456 B.C. (cf. Livy III.32.7), although Dionysius claims (*Ant. Rom.* X.32.4) that the relevant measure, subsequently set up on a bronze tablet in the temple of Diana, had been formally passed by the centuriate assembly. Certainly where active patrician co-operation was required, a unilateral 'hallowed law' alone is hardly likely to have been sufficient.

Initially plebiscites can only have been expressions of plebeian opinion. According to the annalists their general validity was recognized by a Lex Valeria Horatia of 449 B.C. but this clearly duplicates a similar Publilian law of 339 and Hortensian law of *c.* 286 B.C. The fiction was no doubt designed to explain the validity of certain later plebiscites, especially the Canuleian law (445), the Licinio-Sextian laws (367) and the Genucian laws (342). So far as these are authentic, however, their implementation may have been a matter of *de facto* acceptance, consular action or subsequent approval by the centuriate assembly: the history of the plebeian struggles and of the difficulty in implementing their demands, even in the annalists, is hardly intelligible on the assumption of an early general recognition of plebeian enactments. It has been supposed[123] that the Lex Valeria Horatia made such plebiscites binding if they received the approval of the patrician senators (*patrum auctoritas*) or some other form of senatorial sanction. There is, however, no clear evidence for such a provision or for its removal by the Lex Publilia or Lex Hortensia. It would in any case be a meaningless concession (since with or without it the plebs would still be dependent on patrician acceptance of their demands if these were to be formally enacted). The securely attested legislative successes of the tribunes in the fifth century are in any event negligible: at most they comprise the bill of Icilius on the Aventine traditionally dated to 456 B.C. (and therefore before the Lex Valeria Horatia) and that of Canuleius on patrician–plebeian intermarriage (445 B.C.).

That the tribunes, holding a usurpative office with restricted and contested functions, were admitted to the senate in the fifth century is

---

clearly not to be credited, despite the historians' implication that they were regularly present at senatorial debates; indeed, Valerius Maximus (II.2.7) and Zonaras (VII.15) report that they originally took up their station outside the senate. Similarly, their right to summon the senate or refer matters to it can have developed only when plebiscites achieved automatic general validity, probably by the Lex Hortensia: then it would have become essential if the senate were to discuss tribunician proposals before their presentation to the assembly.

Zonaras and Valerius Maximus indicate that the tribunes' original interest in the senate was purely negative, to prevent the implementation of any decree of which they disapproved. This must be set in the wider context of tribunician rights to veto magisterial legislative proposals, elections and other acts. These powers probably grew out of, or were considered analogous to, the older right of assistance (p. 218), but although there may have been early attempts to disrupt public business or declare particular actions or decisions unacceptable, these cannot yet have rested on a formally recognized right of veto. Indeed, some of the veto rights directed specifically at magisterial initiative may have achieved ultimate acceptance less in the popular interest than in that of the senatorial majority which could thus check recalcitrant magistrates. Their recognition was probably a gradual process but cannot have become definitive before the mid-Republic as the tribunate came to achieve a more generally recognized role in the Roman pattern of government.

The right of a tribune to veto the proposals or positive actions of a colleague is also not likely to have been original to the office (cf. Diod. XII.25.3) since it would have frustrated its basic purposes. Tribunician veto of a colleague's plebiscite will have arisen only when these became automatically binding on the whole community, that of their senatorial decrees only when they had secured the privilege of proposing them. Veto of popular trials is also improbable when these merely represent tribunician attempts to seek backing for intended retribution on those who had violated their persons. Still less can it be believed that tribunes would intervene to prevent their colleagues from taking action against magistrates seen to be acting oppressively.

The tribunate originated, therefore, in a determined act of self-assertion by the plebs. Its initial function was probably that of intervening on behalf of the individual citizen against oppressive or irregular magisterial action, particularly at the levy and in civil jurisdiction. For this purpose the office had to be permanent and provision made for annual elections and for the necessary organization of the plebs itself (soon, if not from the first, on a tribal basis). The success of the tribunes relied essentially, however, on mass popular support, which found expression in tribunician inviolability, perhaps in attempts to reinforce that inviolability by penalties voted against those who infringed it, and in the parallel development of appeal to the people. The tribunate must have early become a mouthpiece for plebeian demands but its other prerogatives, those of capital prosecution before the centuriate assembly, of proposing plebiscites of general validity, of summoning the senate and seeking its advice, of vetoing the acts of state magistrates or a colleague were established only at a much later date. In this period it was a usurpative and precarious office restricted in scope.

Two further plebeian officers, the plebeian aediles, were also reputedly created at the First Secession. That is perhaps an anticipation, but the office was evidently well established by 366 B.C. when two additional curule aediles (initially patrician) were instituted as state officials in imitation. It is possible that the office was borrowed from elsewhere in Central Italy, where it occasionally appears later;[124] but there is no certainty that in most of these instances the title at least does not derive ultimately from Rome, and since the functions of the municipal aediles may themselves have undergone progressive modification (at Tusculum, for example, the dual aedileship became at some stage the local chief magistracy), they offer little guidance to the original scope of the Roman office. The various ancient suggestions concerning its initial functions[125] are also of little assistance since they largely reflect either particular later aspects of its responsibilities or deductions from its title; in themselves they are of little independent value. The historians' treatment of the aediles in the early Republic is no less unreliable, particularly in their implicit assumption that they acted as an organ of the Roman state, a role they can have acquired only from 366 B.C. at the earliest. It is difficult to accept, for example, that already in 449 the aediles were officially charged with preserving senatorial decrees or that the state commissioned them to remove foreign cults in 428. The supervision of public games clearly belongs after 366 and their role in the corn-supply is also probably a later development from their control of markets. The aediles' general policing and supervision of the roads, temples and other public buildings must also be a subsequent accretion; the plebs would hardly appoint their own officials for that specific purpose.

The title *aedilis* (from *aedes* 'house' or 'temple') is the best evidence for their original function. It suggests that the aediles acted as guardians of plebeian interests in the precinct of the (public) temple of Ceres, Liber

[124] E.g. Momigliano 1932[G674], 217–28 (= id. *Quarto Contributo* 313–23); Mazzarino 1945[F47], 127–52.
[125] Varro, *Ling.* v.81; Dion. Hal. *Ant. Rom.* VI.90.1f; Fest. 12 L; Pomp. *Dig.* 1.2.2.21; Theophil. *Inst.* 1.2; Lydus, *Mag.* 1.35; Zonar. VII.15.

and Libera which had intimate associations with the plebeian movement. The existence of an early plebeian archive there seems unlikely since it presupposes a highly developed sense of the plebs as a permanent organized institution, but dedications were made in the shrine to Ceres, not least from the property of those who violated tribunician rights; and there may also have been a market, associated perhaps with plebeian meetings. The supervision of such a market is the most plausible starting-point for the development of the aediles' subsequent functions and can be illustrated by Greek parallels.[126] Whether, as Dionysius (*Ant. Rom.* VI.90.2) supposes, the aediles also acted as general tribunician assistants (a role which they did not usually assume later) must remain an open question, although their subordination to the tribunate is evident in tribunician supervision of their election.

Dionysius (loc. cit.) further states that the tribunes referred certain judicial cases to the aediles who were also known as 'judges', and under 454 an aedile is credited with a comitial prosecution of an ex-consul for military misconduct (Livy III.31.5f) or offences against the plebs (Dion. Hal. *Ant. Rom.* X.48.3f). Both suppositions are to be rejected: the tribunes never exercised jurisdiction in the historical period of the Republic and the recorded fifth-century comitial trials are fictitious. Dionysius or his source may have been misled by the later comitial prosecutions by the aediles for a variety of offences against the common interest and by the tribunician practice of hearing appeals for their assistance in quasi-judicial form. The same practice has probably also influenced the claim in Zonaras (VII.15) that the tribunes either heard cases of violation of their sacrosanctity themselves or referred them to 'certain judges' or to the people.

Zonaras (and perhaps Dionysius) may also be reflecting interpretations of the term 'judges' or 'board of ten judges' (*iudices decemviri*) recorded ambiguously alongside the aediles and tribunes in an alleged law of 449 B.C. ('whoever harms the plebeian tribunes, aediles, judges board of ten, his person shall be consecrate to Iuppiter' (Livy III.55.7)). The identity of these 'judges' was and is disputed. Modern interpretation has centred around their possible identification with the later 'board of ten for the judging of lawsuits' (*decemviri stlitibus iudicandis*) who were responsible for hearing claims to free status and perhaps other matters, but Pomponius (*Dig.* 1.2.2.29) implies that these were established after 242 B.C. and although the pairing of *iudices decemviri* in this order is possible,[127] the terms could equally well refer not to a unit ('board of ten judges') but to two separate offices ('judges' and 'board of ten'). If so,

---

[126] Latte 1936[G639], 74f = id. *Kleine Schriften* 356.
[127] Thus in a few cases of municipal titulature the more general title precedes the qualifying numerical term (e.g., *praetores duoviri* 'praetors board of two'); the earliest preserved examples derive from Sullan colonies (*ILLRP* 606, 675).

however, their further identification remains mysterious. Dionysius or his source may have thought that 'judges' here qualified 'aediles', Zonaras' source that they were distinct officials appointed to hear cases of the violation of tribunician sacrosanctity. Others apparently identified the 'iudices' as the consuls (Livy III.55.11f); but if that was the original reference, the law must be spurious since it would thus confer inviolate status on the state magistracies as well as the officers of the plebs. For that we have no supporting evidence and consuls already had extensive powers to deal severely with citizens who infringed their authority and persons.

(c) The Decemvirate, Second Secession and Twelve Tables

For both Livy (III.9–64) and Dionysius (*Ant. Rom.* x.1–xi.50) the history of the Decemvirate commences with the proposal of the tribune C. Terentilius Harsa in 462 B.C. that a commission be created either to publish the laws and legal principles (Dionysius) or to draw up legislation restricting the power of the consuls (Livy). After years of fruitless wrangling a compromise was reached in 454: a three-man legation was despatched to Athens and other Greek cities to bring back the laws of Solon and others, in preparation for the appointment (in 452) of a ten-man legislative board. That board, exclusively patrician and not subject to popular appeal (*provocatio*), replaced both consuls and tribunes in 451 B.C. Its conduct of affairs was exemplary. Ten Tables of laws were drafted, subjected to popular scrutiny, approved by the centuriate assembly and eventually set up publicly in the Forum.

A second Decemviral board was elected for the following year (450 B.C.), entirely patrician (Livy) or including three plebeians (Dionysius). Led by the ambitious Ap. Claudius, this Second Decemvirate added two further Tables (including the notorious ban on patricio-plebeian intermarriage) but also abused its unrestricted powers to assume arbitrary control of the state and prolong its term of office indefinitely, without reference to senate or people. Attacks by the Sabines and Aequi eventually forced consultation of the senate, where M. Horatius and L. Valerius vigorously opposed the decemviral regime; but it was the armies levied to meet the emergency that brought about their overthrow. That encamped near Crustumerium was early alienated by the murder of a legendary military hero L. Siccius Dentatus, and both forces revolted when Appius Claudius attempted to get control of a plebeian girl Verginia through a client (M. Claudius) who claimed her as his slave. L. Verginius killed his daughter to protect her chastity and appealed successfully to both armies and to the urban populace to rise against their oppressors.

The resulting Second Secession drove the senate to an agreement, negotiated by Valerius and Horatius, whereby the Decemvirs resigned. Major legislation followed, more fully reported in Livy than in Dionysius (whose account is in any case partly lost). One of the newly elected tribunes, M. Duillius, passed plebiscites re-establishing the consulship, ensuring the continuity of the tribunate and prohibiting the future appointment of magistrates not subject to appeal. The new consuls, Valerius and Horatius, passed measures guaranteeing the inviolability of the plebeian officers, prohibiting the appointment of magistrates exempt from appeal and making plebiscites binding on the whole community; in addition, senatorial decrees were now to be preserved by the plebeian aediles in the temple of Ceres. Finally, in 448 L. Trebonius carried a plebiscite ensuring the election of a full complement of tribunes.

Although the conception of the Decemvirate as a major political turning-point was established as early as Polybius,[128] the version of the reforms found in Livy and Dionysius was not universally accepted. In Diodorus (XII.24–6) they comprise the appointment of ten tribunes with the highest powers as guardians of freedom, the reservation of one consulship and the opening of the other to plebeians, the obligation on the tribunes to arrange the election of successors on pain of being burned alive and (probably) the institution of the tribunes' right of mutual veto. Moreover, all this is the result of a patrician–plebeian agreement, not legislation; in Diodorus Valerius and Horatius merely compile the two additional Tables and place all twelve on display. Zonaras (VII.18f) also ignores the Valerio-Horatian laws (perhaps through over-compression of his source (Dio)), attributing instead to their consulship the change of title from praetor to consul and the grant to the tribunes of auspicial rights (probably that of hindering a magistrate or colleague by declaring an unfavourable omen (*obnuntiatio*)).

Finally, and most radically, some may have ascribed the creation of the tribunate itself to 449. Varro (*Ling.* v.81) attributes the origin of the title 'tribunes of the plebs' to their initial appointment from among the military tribunes 'in the secession of Crustumerium'. Crustumerium appears in the surviving accounts only in the Second Secession and it is notable that in the description of that episode in Livy and Dionysius both mutinous armies appoint ten military *tribuni* as their leaders, clearly as a prelude to the re-election of plebeian *tribuni* (cf. Livy III.51.8). Unless, therefore, Varro or his source knew of a similar but now lost version of the First Secession (or was merely confused), the tradition on which he drew evidently associated the establishment of the tribunate with the revolt of 449.

---

[128] Polyb. VI.11.1 with Walbank 1957–79[B182] ad loc.

The relative antiquity of these different versions is difficult to determine. Even their deep-seated belief in the constitutional importance of the Decemviral period may merely reflect a tendency to attach undated developments to a known major event, especially since there is a substantial lack of agreement about the measures involved and those measures themselves are often suspect in their individual content. Thus the admission of plebeians to the consulship (Diodorus) occurred only in 366 B.C. The provision for the perpetual election of tribunes (Diodorus and Livy) seems elsewhere presupposed already for the time of Sp. Cassius (Val. Max. VI.3.2). Even if that merits no greater trust (p. 219), the date was apparently not firmly established. Its location here is intimately linked with the suspension of the tribunate during the Decemvirate but it is difficult to see why the institution of such a legislative commission should have placed the tribunate in abeyance. That notion may be related to an early view of the Decemvirate as a mixed commission replacing both patrician and plebeian offices (cf. Livy III. 31.7f; Dion. Hal. *Ant. Rom.* x.58.4), to an attempt to explain why its tyrannical behaviour went initially uncontested or even to efforts to accommodate a tradition that the tribunate itself was created after the Decemvirate's overthrow.

Similarly, the election of ten tribunes (Diodorus) is dated by other sources to 457 or even 493 B.C. (p. 218), while mutual veto (Diodorus) or *obnuntiatio* (Zonaras) can scarcely have been established so early. The Trebonian plebiscite of 448 prohibiting the co-option of tribunes (Livy) seems in another version to have been dated to 401 (cf. Livy v.10.1ff). The Duillian plebiscite and Valerio-Horatian law on appeal (Livy) are duplicates and neither is authentic (p. 219f). The Lex Valeria Horatia on plebiscites (Livy and Dionysius) is equally fictitious (p. 223). The Valerio-Horatian bill recognizing the inviolate status of plebeian officers in part duplicates the annalists' patrician–plebeian agreement of 493 B.C., as Livy (III.55.6) realizes; and his account implies that even ancient critics found some difficulty in reconciling the law with the accepted basis of tribunician sacrosanctity in the plebeian oath of 493.[129] Conceivably the plebs, angered by restrictions placed on their representatives by the Twelve Tables (p. 201f), sought to secure formal recognition of their status, and the law's inclusion of the otherwise unknown *iudices decemviri* (p. 226) among the plebeian officers may also support its authenticity, but its appearance among a series of fictitious measures reinforcing the tribunate makes its historicity or at least its date highly suspect.[130]

---

[129] If one version attributed the actual creation of the tribunate to 449 B.C., the law may well derive from there.

[130] For a more favourable assessment of the alleged measures of 449 B.C. cf., e.g., Ogilvie 1965[B129], 497–501.

Analysis of the Second Secession also reveals much that merits rejection. The Second Decemvirate itself may be fictitious (p. 114f). The two armies seem to belong to duplicate accounts and there were also varying versions of the negotiations which ended the Secession. Verginia, originally anonymous (her name was inspired by the Latin *virgo* 'maid'), probably belongs to the oldest stratum of the legend but as the late annalists half-realized, she is merely a pale imitation of that Lucretia whose rape provoked the overthrow of the monarchy, and her potential violator was conjured from the established literary portraits of the Claudii.

This entire narrative, therefore, yields little worthy of serious consideration: at most perhaps a Secession intended to reassert the role of the tribunate in the face of attempts in the Twelve Tables to restrict its activity, and recognition or reaffirmation of its right to fulfil its basic function. Even this may have begun life merely as a variant version of the creation of the tribunate itself or as a superfluous attempt to explain the abolition of the Decemvirate but it is not *per se* implausible.

The ancient sources offer varying interpretations of the plebeian agitation for the publication of the law and the creation of the Decemvirate. Thus for Cicero (*Rep.* II.61ff) the Decemvirate represents primarily a peaceful transition to absolute aristocratic rule; its legislative activity is largely secondary. For Dionysius its establishment reflects plebeian agitation not merely to ensure the equitable administration of justice but to establish *isegoria* ('equal rights of free speech' or 'political equality') and *isonomia* ('equality before the law' or 'equality of rights'), the cornerstones of democracy (cf. also Zonar. VII.18). For Livy the plebeian objective was to limit the power of the consuls. None of these extravagant interpretations can be sustained, at least in this form. Even the view (common to Livy and Dionysius) that equality of rights or law was the Tables' specific intention lacks any foundation, unless it refers merely to the previous inaccessibility of the law and the potential arbitrariness of its administration; there is no evidence that in its formulation the law had hitherto discriminated between different categories of citizen in matters where they were now put on an equal footing.[131]

A true assessment of the purpose and achievement of the Twelve Tables (and therefore the Decemvirate) must depend on analysis of their

---

[131] Significantly in Livy Canuleius (IV.5.5) and Licinius and Sextius (VI.37.4) by implication regard the Tables as having failed to establish true or full *aequa libertas* or *aequum ius*, which can only be achieved by granting plebeians access to the magistrates (perhaps suggesting that for Livy at least these phrases were predominantly political in their connotations (cf. also Tac. *Ann.* III.27)). Cf. the discussion in C. Wirszubski, *Libertas as a Political Idea at Rome during the Late Republic and Early Principate* (Cambridge 1950) 9ff.

extant provisions, although here too there is much uncertainty. For example, with the exception of one or two regulations of obvious immediate political impact, it is impossible to gauge how far the Tables introduced major innovations in the law, since neither we nor the ancient sources possess any reliable knowledge of earlier law on which to base an opinion. It was, of course, believed in antiquity that the Tables included new measures derived from Greek sources and two competing legends sought to explain this influence: the embassy to Athens and elsewhere (first in Livy and Dionysius) and the presence at Rome of the Ephesian legislator Hermodorus (Pliny, *HN* XXXIV.21; Pomp. *Dig.* 1.2.2.4; cf. Strabo XIV.1.25, p. 642C).[132] Ultimately both fictions probably spring from the observation of similarities between the Tables and Greek legislation. In his *Laws* (*Leg.* II.59ff; cf. Table x.1ff) Cicero derives certain Decemviral restrictions on mourning from Solon.[133] Gaius' commentary on the Tables added Solonian models for the laws governing brotherhoods (*sodalitates*) (Table VIII.27) and the adjudication of property boundaries (Table VII.2), but here at least the parallels are insufficiently close to show direct dependence. In any case, these specific instances do not touch the main corpus of private law which had clearly developed independently of Greek influence (cf. also Dion. Hal. *Ant. Rom.* XI.44.6) and despite some possible immediate debts to Greek models for the formulation of certain provisions,[134] it might be expected that detailed acquaintance with contemporary Greek legislation would have resulted in a significantly higher level of juristic and stylistic sophistication than that encountered in the extant fragments.

Nonetheless, the notion of making public the law and the appointment of a special commission for this purpose do probably derive directly or indirectly from contemporary external sources, presumably again the Greek colonies of the West. Even so, the scope and purpose of the Tables, so far as we know them, remain fundamentally distinct. There is little concern with the avoidance of material inequalities; few signs that the laws were seen as a general education in socially desirable conduct (only in specific areas do the legislators seek to control the individual or group); and in no sense is the code itself or the law it enshrines regarded as of divine origin or inspiration. Whether or not the Tables were the subject of formal comitial approval, their acceptance rested on general public recognition of the law they enshrined.

Although the mere act of recording and publishing the law may

---

[132] Cf. Münzer 1913[G278], col. 859–61.

[133] For discussion cf. Wieacker 1971[G328], 772–81. If they are of Greek origin, one or more of the western colonies is more probably the source (cf. also Dion. Hal. *Ant. Rom.* x.51.5; 54.3) and the borrowing, like some others (Norden 1939[G454], 254–8), may go back to an earlier period (Colonna 1977[B312], 160–1). [134] E.g. Wieacker 1967[G327], 351f.

initially have imposed a brake on its development, the Tables did not deprive the *pontifices* and magistrates of their role in determining or advising on the law. The limited use of writing ensured that legal knowledge, beyond the contents of the Tables, remained largely a priestly preserve, and the omission from the code of the forms of action and of technical legal definitions left a wide discretion in their hands. This was also frequently employed to extend or modify the scope of existing provisions or to use them as the basis for new legal procedures and institutions; adoption, the freeing of a son from paternal power and the will 'by bronze and balance' were all created by a re-application of Decemviral rules and institutions. Indeed, whereas initially alterations to substantive law, the establishment of new actionable claims and the extension of the right to execute a claim without judgement seem to have been reserved to statute, increasingly the priests and, later, the magistrates were not restricted to principles, claims and procedures which could be claimed to enjoy a legislative basis, however slight. As the will 'by bronze and balance' was developed, the *pontifices* surrounded it with a series of regulations designed in particular to ensure maintenance of the family rites. Magistrates were evidently prepared to countenance the seizure of pledges in certain cases not covered by statute (cf. Gaius, *Inst.* IV.26f) and by the third century to institute new actions for claims based on 'good faith' where no statutory remedy was available. As the Twelve Tables became progressively inadequate, requiring supplementation and, increasingly, revision, no objection seems to have been raised to the use of magisterial initiative for these purposes.

What continued to be voiced was the demand that the law, whatever its source, should be publicly known, openly administered (at least at the *in iure* stage before the magistrate) and not subject to arbitrary variation. These must be the primary motives also behind the compilation and publication of the Tables (whence perhaps Livy's distorted notion (III.9.1ff) that the plebeian objective was to limit consular power). In the private sphere the fixing of the law, where conflicting practice made it uncertain and recent developments needed formal recognition, may have been as important as specific innovation. There was also the need to clarify legal rights and liabilities and to publicize the severe consequences of particularly heinous acts: hence presumably the detailed treatment of the conduct of cases and execution of judgements, of penalties for delictal offences, of family law and relations between neighbours. The procedures and in particular penalties of the law were now clearly fixed and freely accessible (cf. Dion. Hal. *Ant. Rom.* II.27.3f; X.1.1ff), and the Tables specify that hearings, at least before the magistrate, are to take place in the Comitium or Forum.[135]

---

[135] Table 1.7 (with Kelly 1976[G244], 103–4).

All this not only informed the individual of his legal position (thus opening a small breach in the patrician monopoly of legal knowledge); it also imposed clear restrictions on magisterial discretion and abuse. Nonetheless, the Tables in no way affected the political structure of the state in the way Dionysius and others imply. Indeed, the few known measures of political import seem largely intended to reinforce both the patriciate's internal cohesion and its political dominance. If the restrictions on bills directed at individuals or inflicting a capital penalty are authentic, they were probably designed to curb such proposals on the part of plebeian tribunes (p. 201f), and the formal enunciation of the ban on patrician–plebeian marriages clearly sought to maintain patrician exclusiveness. The restrictions on funerary extravagance, mourning and grave goods may also be relevant. Originally these were perhaps designed to avoid more general social tensions, but their detailed reaffirmation may also relate to the strains which such displays by the more powerful families might create within the aristocracy itself, a matter of particular concern to those less distinguished families which supplied members of the first Decemviral board (p. 114).

All this points to the Tables as the work of patrician legislators. That is in any case to be expected since they alone were familiar with private law. It was this, however, which occupied the bulk of the code and whose publication was presumably the chief objective of plebeian pressure. The precise rules protecting defendants, the careful regulation of the position of the judgement debtor, the measures against judicial corruption and defaulting witnesses, the emphasis on the public character of judicial proceedings suggest a background of uncertainty and at least potential abuse similar to that which provoked unrest and opposition to aristocratic rule in archaic Greek states.

Even so, the publication of the code can have had little direct relevance to the poorer citizenry. So far as it is preserved, it contains few provisions which might specifically protect them. The right of *proletarii* to have anyone intervene on their behalf (Table 1.4) may have been designed in their interest, but if so, its practical importance is doubtful since the *proletarius* is in any case the least likely to find such a champion. In the relations between patron and client the Tables as known imposed at most a largely unenforceable sanction in cases of (undefined) gross misconduct against the client (Table VIII.21). If regulations governing debt-bondage were included,[136] they were evidently insufficient to make its nature clear to late republican authors. Above all, the Tables did little if anything to remove the vast barriers which virtually excluded the poor from legal action. The deterrent wager (*sacramentum*), for example, was

---

[136] None are certainly preserved since Table VI.1 may not refer specifically to debt-bondage: cf. Behrends 1974[G173], 137–84.

still required for the pursuance or defence of most claims: fifty pounds of bronze for cases involving items or penalties below 1000 lb. in value, five hundred for those above that figure, to be deposited before the case began and forfeited if it was lost.[137]

Some concessions were incorporated. Where a man's freedom was at stake the wager was only fifty pounds (Table II.1a) and the individual remained free until the case was decided. Although it is doubtful whether the Tables fixed a maximum interest rate (p. 116), debts arising from oral contract were pursued by a procedure where no wager was involved (Table II.1b) and the rights of defendants and treatment of the adjudged debtor were also carefully defined (Table III.1–6). It would be attractive to conjecture that these provisions are new, but even so the creditor's position remained largely protected: he too benefited by the exemption from a wager and after judgement he could use chains above the prescribed weight, was obliged to provide only starvation rations and ultimately, if the debt remained unpaid, could sell the debtor into slavery or kill him. It must in any case be doubtful whether this form of actionable loan was commonly available to the poor (who could offer little as security) rather than the more substantial peasantry.

Even for this more affluent stratum the pursuance of claims against their peers or superiors was hindered by the failure to publish the forms of legal action, although the belief that precise verbal adherence to particular formulae was required for any legal action is probably errone-ous. Gaius (*Inst.* IV. 11; 30) seems to imply that the later strictness was the progressive result of fastidious juristic attitudes, perhaps attempting to limit use of the old forms of action in favour of the later formulary procedure; even then what was demanded was not verbal accuracy for its own sake so much as adherence to the established statutory basis of the claim.[138] Nonetheless, the failure to include the relevant formulae in the Tables meant that much must often have depended on the willingness of priest or magistrate to prompt or assist if such a claim were to be pursued correctly and successfully, and of course, even for the more securely placed peasantry legal action against an aristocratic opponent was always likely to prove problematic in practice unless he enjoyed the vigorous support of a powerful patron.

However, it must have been this more substantial element within the populace who principally benefited from the publication of the code. They probably represent the minimum social and economic level which could seriously contemplate independent legal action and some individ-ual regulations seem to apply solely or principally at or above this level:

---

[137] For this and other difficulties in litigation cf. von Ihering 1909[G226], 175–232; Kelly 1966[G242].   [138] Daube 1961[G191], 4–5.

the furnishing of transport to the sick defendant; the precise rules governing the driving of a cart (or plough team) through another's land; the careful protection of those who purchase 'by bronze and balance' (*mancipium*); the reference to the lease of draught animals; the plethora of regulations protecting peasant proprietors and defining their obligations; the provisions regarding slaves and freedmen. The law embodied in the Tables was not, of course, intended purely to satisfy a particular social or political group. Its primary purpose is often to establish social peace through the definition of mutual rights and responsibilities, the restriction of the extra-legal exaction of vengeance, the encouragement of mutual agreement between the parties (itself perhaps reflecting a substantial use of private arbitration) or the imposition of an equitable accommodation. Moreover, many of the regulations cited above (and others, such as the recognition of clan inheritance and guardianship rights) were also relevant to the highest levels within Roman society, some of whom may have seen some concrete advantage in the publication of the code. Nonetheless, the Tables were clearly the result of popular pressure and this must be assumed to derive principally from those who stood to benefit most: the more prosperous and independent peasantry and those families of yet higher status which were excluded from the patriciate.

(d) *The character and objectives of the plebeian movement*

The term 'plebs' is notoriously vague, denoting little more than the mass excluded from a particular limited group or groups, and it can be used in a variety of contrasts. In accounts of the early Republic 'plebeian' is usually contrasted with 'patrician', but the implied assumption that all non-patricians (except perhaps clients) were involved in the fifth-century plebeian movement may be schematic, and the historians offer no more than a superficial development of the contrast. Uncertainties over the prevalence and character of clientship, the social strata which it primarily concerned and the political behaviour of clients further obfuscate the issue.

It is sometimes held[139] that the plebeian agitation was predominantly an urban phenomenon, the work of artisans, craftsmen and traders seriously affected by economic recession and reacting against a patriciate whose power depended on substantial followings of rural clients. Such views are based primarily on the rapid growth of Rome as an urban centre in the sixth century, the later restriction of the activities of the

---

[139] See especially Ed. Meyer 1895[H57], 1–18 = 1924, 1.333–55; Beloch 1926[A12], 273–83; 336–8; Ogilvie 1965[B129], 294.

plebeian tribunes to the city and a derivation of the title *tribunus* from an original association with the four urban tribes. These arguments are, however, insufficient. There is no evidence for any link between the tribunate and the urban tribes (p. 217). The restriction of the tribunes to the city is directly related to their function as a check on activities of the magistrates conducted within or in proximity to the city boundary (notably at the levy and in jurisdiction), and is designed above all to exclude direct intrusion by tribunes in military campaigns. That cannot have been formally prohibited in this period when all tribunician activity against the magistrates was probably usurpative and conceivably the tribunes initially intervened here also. If not, that may indicate merely recognition by themselves and their following of the peculiar requirements of military command.

That urban based trades had developed over the sixth century is not to be denied nor that they may have been peculiarly vulnerable to unfavourable economic circumstances in the early Republic. Apart from the sudden decrease in temple construction, however, the rate, scale and effects of any decline are impossible to determine (p. 130f). So far as it went, its principal impact may only have been felt when the plebeian movement had already emerged and, in any case, given the routine quality of Rome's domestic production even in the sixth century and the relatively modest development of her market, the proportion of the population engaged primarily in urban occupations must have been small. And unless the apparent neglect of trade and artisan activity in the Twelve Tables is entirely due to the accidents of transmission, it does not suggest that the agitation of their practitioners was the primary motive force behind that reform.

Moreover, a sharp distinction between city and country is likely to be gravely misleading. The analogy of Veii[140] and the strongly centralized character of Roman political and economic life make it overwhelmingly probable that many of those peasants who owned property close to Rome lived in the city itself; indeed, only thus can the vast area covered by the city be satisfactorily explained. Nor can a clear line be drawn between peasant and artisan; some trades (e.g. tile manufacture) may have been semi-seasonal and combined with small-scale farming; other craftsmen may well have owned at least a kitchen garden. More fundamentally, craftsmen and peasants were bound together in a pattern of recognizable mutual dependence, which revolved around the supply of raw materials, finished products and agricultural surplus. The supposition that they saw themselves and acted as distinct groups with distinct interests is not proven.

[140] Kahane, Threipland and Ward-Perkins 1968[B350], 70–1.

If the Icilian plebiscite of 456 opening up the Aventine for settlement is authentic (p. 139), it may imply a demand for land in or near the city as one significant element in the plebeian agitation. Even so, however, the principal factor here is likely to have been immigration from the rural areas, as a result of poverty or external threat, and other considerations suggest that the major role in the plebeian movement was in fact played by the more substantial peasantry. In particular, the early adoption of the tribal form of assembly gave a dominant voice to those registered in the rural tribes and they were also the principal beneficiaries of the most notable early plebeian successes. They above all profited by the publication of the Twelve Tables and they also had a particular (though not exclusive) interest in the tribunician right of assistance if, as seems likely, that was employed primarily against magisterial judicial decisions and the operation of the levy.

Common military service also offers some explanation for the immediate and long-term success of the plebs. This presupposes a greater political muscle than a movement composed largely of urban artisans or the poor could have commanded. It also helps to account for the ability and readiness of the plebs not only to organize itself initially but to maintain its determination to assert its collective will where necessary. Service in the 'hoplite' army, transcending individual social groupings and reinforcing the sense of citizen rights and duties, probably stimulated an awareness of common identity and grievance amongst the independent peasantry who served in it, particularly in the context of the increasingly heavy and unrewarding military demands of the fifth century, and it created the most potent weapon which they could use to seek a remedy.

Not that those of the 'hoplite' infantry who participated in the plebeian agitation necessarily saw themselves as a distinct group rather than as part of a wider popular movement. The adoption of the tribal rather than the centuriate mode for the plebeian assembly presumably reflects a very broad basis to the plebeian movement in its initial stages. Those, for example, who qualified for the light-armed forces also had an interest in checking magisterial abuse; and the impoverished and indebted within and below their ranks may also have been active early with their own demands, although, with the possible exception of the Lex Icilia of 456 B.C., we cannot determine how far there was specific championing of their interests. Periodic corn shortages are certainly to be assumed and it is presumably significant that the temple of Ceres became a focus of plebeian activity, but to what extent the plebeian officers were active in seeking remedies to such crises we do not know. Debt was a persistent problem, but although the Twelve Tables deal with judgement debtors, there is a curious dearth of evidence for popular or tribunician agitation about debt-bondage after the First Secession. That probably reflects only the inadequacy of our sources since so potent a source of tension can hardly have lain dormant for so long, but in any case little concrete alleviation of the problem seems to have been achieved.[141] The historians do record proposals concerning the allocation of public land, beginning with the agitation of Sp. Cassius, but the details of his demagogy are based on events of the Gracchan period (p. 184) and it is difficult to see how any record of the subsequent tribunician activity could have survived since it yielded no solid results. There is no evidence that plebeians were legally excluded from public land and the accounts of their expulsion by rapacious patricians (so already Cassius Hemina fr. 17P) are clearly retrojected from later abuses which probably gained in momentum (or at least in public awareness) over the course of the second century and came then to form part of the background to the Gracchan reforms. Nonetheless, local conflicts over public land set aside for common use are almost inevitable and may even have been generalized into agitation over the rules governing its use and availability for settlement, particularly if competition for access to such land intensified as a result of an increasing need for summer pasture.

All this, however, is conjecture and any remedies secured by the plebs were presumably short-term responses to immediate crises or the exploitation for public benefit of the new opportunities for settlement which arose late in the century (itself sometimes the subject of tribunician agitation according to Livy): on the evidence available to us it was not until 367 that institutional economic reform (even on the most modest scale) was attempted, to mobilize support for the realization of the political ambitions of the plebeian elite. And in the fifth century the known institutional and more enduring successes of the plebs were largely political not economic: the creation and development of the tribunate, the Twelve Tables, perhaps the rescindment of the ban on patrician–plebeian intermarriage and the first admission of plebeians to office (conceivably also increasing popular participation in the appointment of the state magistrates and in some decision-making). These are ultimately a response to the patrician seizure and exercise of power after the overthrow of the monarchy and the work, above all, of those who could use their military service as a lever to preserve and advance their interests. In contrast, significant progress on land reform or the amelioration of debt bondage was achieved only in the fourth century and was largely a consequence of renewed expansion.

The political achievements of the plebs, in particular the maintenance

---

[141] Public pressure may, however, have modified the severe penalties prescribed for judgement debtors in the Twelve Tables since no instance of their implementation is recorded.

of the tribunate, also presuppose a reservoir of able leaders of an economic and social status which provided the leisure, determination, independence and standing to carry out the functions of the office, and it is clear from the ban on legal marriages between patricians and plebeians, from its later abandonment (allegedly by formal rescindment in 445 by a plebiscite of the tribune Canuleius) and from the eventual admission of plebeians to high office that such a core of plebeian families early existed. When first such families ventured to press for admission to the magistracies is impossible to determine. Some sources suppose that plebeians were admitted to the senate as early as the regal period or the first year of the Republic[142] but this is merely conjecture based on explanations of the traditional designation of the senate as *patres conscripti* (p. 181). Presumably once plebeians held the highest offices of state they could no longer be barred from senatorial membership, but whether Livy is right (v.12.11; cf. also Cic. *Sest.* 137) in his belief that some achieved admission before this we cannot say. Livy and Dionysius do suppose erroneously that the consular tribunate was accessible to plebeians from the outset (p. 193), but otherwise in Livy's narrative they achieve office only in the last decades of the fifth century. The quaestorship was opened to them in 421 and three plebeians were first elected for 409, an account which again cannot be controlled but is notable for its suspect names and detail. Finally, in 400 one plebeian, P. Licinius Calvus, held the consular tribunate. In fact the surviving lists (including Livy's) show four plebeians in office that year, five more in 399 and five again in 396. Whether L. Aquillius Corvus in 388 is plebeian is questionable, but Livy's M. Trebonius under 383 must be, and Diodorus gives four or five further plebeians under 379, of whom three also appear in Livy.[143]

The accuracy of these records is hard to judge. None of the names involved is demonstrably spurious, unless the Campanian origin of the Atilii is accepted (p. 194), but it is perhaps disquieting that whereas the consular tribunes of 400, 399 and 396 belong largely to clans which achieved considerable prominence in the fourth or third centuries, all or nearly all those of 383 and 373 come from families of no subsequent importance at least until the second century. Of course, the sheer obscurity of these names argues for their authenticity, but it is remarkable that only one at most[144] should hold the consulship when that was opened to plebeians in 366. The issue is further complicated by the fact that for 379 Diodorus has an implausible total of eight consular tribunes,

142 Ogilvie 1965[B129], 236.

143 C. Licinius under 378 (Diod. xv.57.1; cf. Livy vi.39.3) is, however, probably a corruption of Licinus Menenius (Livy vi.31.1).

144 Emending 'Erenucius' (Diod. xv.51.1 (379 B.C.)) to 'Genucius'.

suggesting that his list for this year includes some spurious accretions (perhaps to supplement an originally defective record). Whether or not these later plebeian consular tribunes are authentic, however, they only marginally modify the temporary character of the success of 400, 399 and 396. It makes sense that the plebs should have forced acceptance of their candidates during the war with Veii, perhaps out of military impatience (though the patrician consular tribunes of the previous years were certainly not disgraced), and the Roman voting system would encourage the election of several plebeian candidates as the assembly sought to ensure that at least some plebeians were successful.[145] After the capture of Veii by the patrician dictator Camillus, however, the patriciate was evidently able to reassert its position. In this reaction the old networks of personal ties, cutting across status distinctions, and the traditional criteria of individual prestige and standing may have reaffirmed their role in maintaining patrician pre-eminence. The Gallic Sack too may have contributed to a temporary cessation of internal argument. Hence the plebeian insistence later on the reservation of one consulship to them alone.

Political will provides only the immediate explanation of the progressive breaking of the patrician monopoly: other underlying factors must have played a significant role. The advent of 'hoplite' warfare may have begun to undermine any aristocratic monopoly of military expertise, as well perhaps as fostering a sense of plebeian unity. Earlier plebeian advances may have weakened the patrician hold over some of their more securely placed dependants or associates and whilst the emergence of the plebs as a political force may initially have encouraged the aristocracy to close ranks, in time leading plebeians may have developed ties with individual aristocratic families which made their absorption into the ruling elite both easier and more palatable. The plebeian Licinii even claimed that they had contracted a series of marriage ties with major patrician houses in the late fifth and early fourth centuries (Livy v.12.12; vi.34.5f; 39.4) and whilst such claims must be treated with reserve, the implication that patrician–plebeian intermarriage was already developing and even that the lead was taken by those patrician families whose political position was most secure is entirely credible; the Decemviral ban may have been prompted specifically by the incipient disintegration of earlier custom (p.180).

Despite all the uncertainties, the plebeian movement of the fifth century emerges as complex in its composition[146] but limited in its

---

[145] The very fact that plebeians enter the consular tribunate so suddenly and in such numbers indicates that this is the result of popular pressure to break the patrician stranglehold rather than simply a continuation of an alleged earlier occasional toleration of non-patricians in the chief magistracy.   [146] For a different view see below, p. 325f.

aspirations. It owed much to the vigorous leadership of prominent plebeian families, and although the core of its support probably came from the more substantial peasantry, it was clearly intended to be open to the entire non-patrician citizen body without distinction. Nonetheless, as a permanent political entity the plebs existed primarily in its more negative aspects, as a check on the magistrates through the activity of its tribunes and the support which it accorded them. As a movement for reform its existence was probably fitful, often more potential than actual. Although the deficiencies of our evidence do not permit us to gauge the frequency of such agitation, positive successes were sporadic and continuous pressure difficult to maintain; even the election of plebeians to the consular tribunate could only occasionally be secured. Demands for change were also probably contingent on immediate circumstances and those active in their support will have varied, depending on the group(s) whose interests were directly involved. To treat the plebs as a permanent and coherent political force for change is to underestimate its essentially discontinuous character and fluctuating composition.

It follows that the (rudimentary) plebeian organization was not a coherent focus of permanent opposition to the organs of the Roman state as such,[147] and still less did the plebeian movement constitute itself as a 'state within a state'[148] in any meaningful sense. Although its offices were to some extent modelled on the magistracies and it employed the tribes as the basis of its assembly, the movement as it is known in the historical period had no priests or (probably) prescribed rituals, it imposed no taxes and probably had no treasury, it raised no armies, it had no council, and it almost certainly exercised no distinctive civil or criminal jurisdiction, except against those who violated the sacrosanctity of its officers.[149] Indeed, as with appeal to the people (p. 220), the creation of the tribunate, its early functions and demands may have rested partly on appeals to the traditions of the common interests of the citizen community and of the personal rights of the citizen. In practice at least tribunician actions consistently reflect a broader conception of those rights and interests than the patrician monopoly of political power and the forms in which it was exercised might allow. Conceivably, although the early tribunate consistently expressed popular distrust of magisterial power, it claimed to act as a check on its misuse in the interests of the community as a whole. Such a stance would explain in particular its non-intervention in the conduct of military campaigns and would have facilitated its later development into an instrument of government.

If this conjecture is correct, it may also assist in explaining why

[147] For a different view see below, p. 340.   [148] Mommsen 1887–8[A91], III.145.
[149] Mommsen 1887–8[A91], III.146f.

plebeian objectives are never known to have included a fundamental transformation of the social, economic or political order, although other factors were no doubt primarily responsible. In a traditional society the nature of the patrician claim to privilege, in particular its strong religious character (p. 184), may have determined some to leave that claim unchallenged, and Rome's military difficulties throughout most of this period created a paramount need for experienced commanders which the patriciate may have been able to capitalize upon, at least until the end of the century. The institution of clientship would fragment some potential opposition; indeed, the patriciate could probably mobilize substantial numbers of followers (of varying rank) to counter plebeian opposition. The essentially transitory tenure of the tribunate itself, even with the possibility of re-election, made the sustained pursuit of long-term aims extremely difficult and in the short term too it was a weak instrument of reform except on those few issues where vigorous mass support could be mobilized. Moreover, those plebeians with the most effective leverage (through 'hoplite' service) to press their demands may not themselves have suffered major and persistent economic difficulties which might have provoked a challenge to the existing order. Their concern was primarily with the abuse of magisterial power and a more clearly defined civil jurisdiction, and the developing role of the centuriate organization provided a mechanism by which they (and to a lesser extent other plebeians) could begin to be integrated into the process of political decision-making. The primary interest of the plebeian leaders lay in the removal of barriers to their personal advancement within the existing framework rather than a major shift in the balance of power between the various organs of government. Neither they nor many of their followers sought to modify fundamentally the relative spheres of concern of the state and the private individual nor did they, in contrast to some Greeks, develop any concept of the territory of the state as the collective property of the citizen body in which each individual was entitled to share. A general redistribution of property was never actively proposed in any period, so far as is known. If a remedy for land shortage was the subject of conscious political decisions, it was conceived to lie in the allocation of public land, essentially of territory acquired by military conquest, and that became possible again on any scale only late in the fifth century.

CHAPTER 6

ROME AND LATIUM TO 390 B.C.

T. J. CORNELL

I. THE GROWTH OF ROMAN POWER UNDER THE KINGS

When King Tarquinius Superbus was overthrown in 509 B.C., Rome was by all accounts a powerful city-state with a relatively extensive territory (see below, Figs. 40–1), a developed urban centre, an advanced institutional structure and a strong army. We are told moreover that the Romans exercised a kind of formal hegemony over the other Latin peoples, and dealt on equal terms with the great cities of Etruria and Campania. Their horizon extended as far as Sicily and Magna Graecia; they had diplomatic and commercial links with Carthage, and perhaps also with Massalia, the Greek colony at the mouth of the Rhone.[1]

This situation did not come into being overnight, however, but was the result of a process of expansion and conquest undertaken by the kings. Our knowledge of the process is naturally uncertain. One is bound to be sceptical of narrative accounts which purport to describe campaigns led by mythical or semi-mythical figures such as Romulus or Tullus Hostilius. Although some of the stories may have a factual basis, the circumstantial details given in the surviving sources are completely unhistorical. Generally speaking they are the product of secondary elaboration by annalists writing in the late Republic who had no clear idea of the social and economic conditions of the archaic period and did not appreciate how far they differed from those of their own age. The annalists had no understanding of the character of primitive warfare, and the imaginary details with which they enlivened their accounts are largely anachronistic.

Even so, we need not doubt that under the kings armed conflicts with neighbouring communities did take place, and it is possible that some memory of them survived into the historical period. A notable fact about the traditional narratives is that the wars are set within a topographical framework that is both logical and historically plausible. The earliest campaigns took place within a radius of a few kilometres of the city. Even

---

[1] Dion. Hal. *Ant. Rom.* VII.1.4–5 (Sicily); Polyb. III.22 (Carthage); Justin. XLIII.5 (Massalia: cf. above, p. 111).

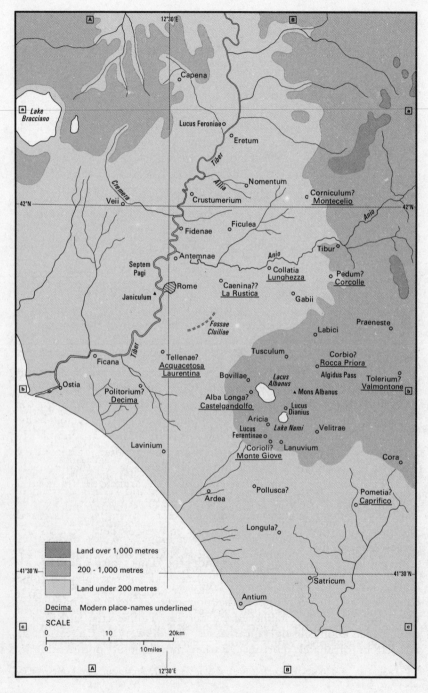

Map 2 Archaic Latium.

in cases where the Romans allegedly fought against entire nations such as the Sabines or Etruscans, the scene of the action does not move beyond the territory of Veii and Caere in the one case, or of Eretum and Lucus Feroniae in the other. In Latium we hear of campaigns against the Prisci Latini, the 'Ancient Latins',[2] whose centres included Antemnae, Caenina, Corniculum, Ficulea, Cameria, Crustumerium, Ameriola, Medullia, Nomentum, Tellenae, Politorium and Ficana. The sources themselves provide a general idea of the location of these places, some of which have been identified with relative certainty (see Map 2), and suggest that Rome's earliest military operations were confined to a narrow area extending a few kilometres to the north east of the city in the district between the Tiber and the Anio, and in a south-westerly direction along the Tiber towards the coast.

The extent of Rome's territory at this period is indicated by certain ancient festivals concerned with boundaries (p. 84). Such ceremonies as the Terminalia, the Robigalia, and particularly the Ambarvalia, in which a procession of priests traced a boundary around the city (Strabo v.3.2, p. 230C), appear to date from a time when Rome's territory extended for about five Roman miles (a little over 7 km.) in each direction, and thus embraced an area of between 150 and 200 square kilometres. Physical traces of this ancient boundary also survived, for example the Fossae Cluiliae, a primitive earthwork which lay five miles to the south of the city and supposedly marked the boundary between Roman territory and that of Alba Longa.

Expansion beyond these earliest known limits of the *ager Romanus* began with the war against Alba Longa, which tradition ascribes to the reign of Tullus Hostilius. As a result of Tullus' victory the Romans destroyed Alba, absorbed its population and annexed its territory. Further gains were made by Ancus Marcius, Tullus' successor, who is said to have conducted a series of campaigns down the Tiber valley. Ancus destroyed the towns of Ficana, Politorium and Tellenae, extended the boundaries of the Roman state as far as the coast, and founded Ostia at the mouth of the Tiber. The territory thus acquired was further increased and consolidated under the last kings, and was divided by Servius Tullius into a number of administrative districts which, together with the four regions of the city, formed new local 'tribes'.

The surviving sources are very confused on the subject of the local tribes, and give no idea either of the function or of the actual number of the tribes originally established by Servius Tullius (the situation is discussed in Dionysius of Halicarnassus, *Ant. Rom.* IV.15.1, a text which is itself unfortunately corrupt). Rather more definite information is

---

[2] Livy 1.38.4; cf. Ennius, *Ann.* 22 Skutsch, who calls them *casci Latini.*

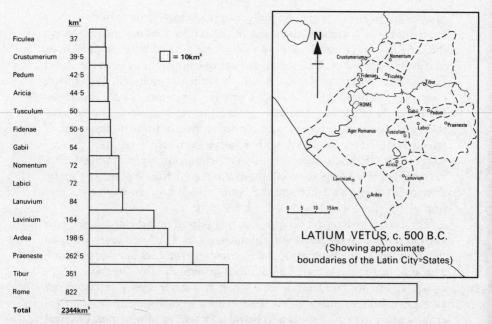

	km²
Ficulea	37
Crustumerium	39·5
Pedum	42·5
Aricia	44·5
Tusculum	50
Fidenae	50·5
Gabii	54
Nomentum	72
Labici	72
Lanuvium	84
Lavinium	164
Ardea	198·5
Praeneste	262·5
Tibur	351
Rome	822
Total	**2344km²**

☐ = 10km²

LATIUM VETUS, c. 500 B.C.
(Showing approximate
boundaries of the Latin City-States)

Fig. 40. Territories of the Latin city-states at the end of the sixth century B.C. After Beloch
1926 [A12], 178.

given by Livy (II.21.7), who tell us that in 495 B.C. the number of local
tribes was fixed at twenty-one: *tribus una et viginti factae* (cf. Dion. Hal.
Ant. Rom. VII.64.6). Livy's statement probably means that in that year
some new tribes were added to the existing ones, to bring the total up to
twenty-one. In any case the figure of twenty-one remained unchanged
until 387 B.C., when four new tribes were created after the annexation of
the territory of Veii (Livy VI.5.8). The clear implication of these reports is
that Rome's territory at the time of the conquest of Veii (396 B.C.) had
been in her possession since the beginning of the Republic, and that most
of it was the result of expansion under the kings.

The territory which our sources attribute to Rome at the end of the
monarchy, and which was incorporated in the local tribes, measured
some 822 square kilometres, according to K. J. Beloch's estimate.[3] This
amounts to 35 per cent of the total land area of Latium Vetus. The other
Latin cities were tiny by comparison. According to Beloch's calculations,
which are based on a conjectural reconstruction of the territorial boundaries of the Latin cities, Rome's two biggest rivals, Tibur and Praeneste,
possessed territories of 351 and 262.5 km.² respectively, and among the
rest only Ardea and Lavinium had more than 100 km.² each (see Fig. 40).
These figures are admittedly only conjectural; adjusting the boundaries
would produce marginally different figures and alter the relative propor-

[3] Beloch 1926[A12], 169–79.

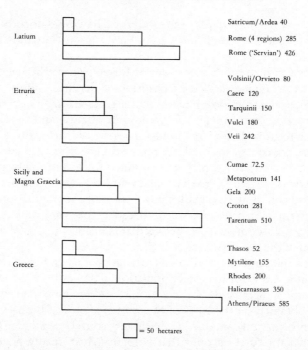

Latium — Satricum/Ardea 40 / Rome (4 regions) 285 / Rome ('Servian') 426

Etruria — Volsinii/Orvieto 80 / Caere 120 / Tarquinii 150 / Vulci 180 / Veii 242

Sicily and Magna Graecia — Cumae 72.5 / Metapontum 141 / Gela 200 / Croton 281 / Tarentum 510

Greece — Thasos 52 / Mytilene 155 / Rhodes 200 / Halicarnassus 350 / Athens/Piraeus 585

☐ = 50 hectares

Fig. 41. The size of cities in the archaic and classical periods. Some comparisons. After Ampolo in *La formazione della città nel Lazio* 1980 [I27], 175.

tions, but would not affect the general picture to any significant extent.

A recent study has calculated that if 15 per cent of the total land surface was under cultivation in each year, Rome's territory of 822 km.[2] would have been able to support a maximum population of around 35,000 persons.[4] No doubt the actual figure was lower than this theoretical maximum, and on balance Beloch's conjecture of between 20,000 and 25,000 seems not unreasonable. Such a figure would make Rome a large and important state by the standards of the archaic period.

This hypothetical conclusion is compatible with other quantifiable data that can be obtained from the traditional account. For instance, we are told that the urban centre of Rome had expanded beyond the original nucleus of the Palatine and Forum, and that under Servius Tullius, who established the sacred boundary (the *pomerium*), it included the Quirinal, Viminal, Esquiline and Caelian hills (e.g. Livy 1.44). This area, the so-called 'city of the four regions', was reckoned by Beloch to comprise some 285 hectares. Comparable figures can be cited for major settlements in Etruria and Magna Graecia, but those Latin cities whose urban areas can be measured were much smaller; the largest of them, Satricum and Ardea, occupied only about 40 hectares apiece (see Fig. 41). The standard

[4] Ampolo 1980[C2], 15–31; cf. above, p. 164 n. 120.

of comparison is admittedly crude, but the data would nonetheless seem to indicate that 'Servian' Rome was by far the largest and most powerful of the Latin city-states.

Another indication of the power of Rome is given by the centuriate organization, again ascribed by tradition to Servius Tullius. The most probable reconstruction of the centuriate system in its original form presupposes an army (*classis*) of 6000 hoplite infantry and 600 cavalry.[5] It has been reckoned that free adult males would normally amount to around 29 per cent of the total free population of an ancient community.[6] But the Servian *classis*, which was confined to men of military age who could afford to equip themselves and excluded old men and proletarians, must have constituted a smaller proportion of the population of sixth-century Rome. If it was between 20 and 25 per cent of the total, the population would have been between 26,400 and 33,000. A rival interpretation of the Servian *classis*, which argues for a body of 4000 infantry,[7] would by the same method of calculation produce a figure of between 18,400 and 23,000 for the total population. The figures in either case are of the same general order of magnitude, and are consistent with those already obtained on the basis of the estimated size of the *ager Romanus*.

The information contained in the literary sources can therefore help us to construct a basic account that is logical, historically plausible and internally consistent. Briefly stated, it tells us that by the end of the sixth century B.C. successful wars of conquest had made Rome a large and populous city which dominated its nearest neighbours. It is a matter of considerable dispute, however, whether this conventional picture is historically authentic. We do not know how the earliest Roman historians, writing in the third century B.C., conducted their research, or where they obtained their information about the archaic period, and it is therefore not surprising that the extant narratives should have been treated with considerable scepticism by modern scholars. This is particularly true of the remote age of the kings, about which even Livy was doubtful.

Recent scholarship has nevertheless inclined towards the view that Roman historians and antiquarians, wherever they obtained their information, somehow succeeded in establishing a basically reliable outline of the development of early Rome, even if they are not to be trusted in matters of detail. This view is not, however, universally accepted; indeed the most original and influential recent book on the subject (A. Alföldi 1965[I3]) was written with the explicit aim of challenging the whole basis of the traditional account. Alföldi argued that Rome under the kings was

[5] Fraccaro 1931[G579], 92–5 (= id. *Opuscula* II.288–90); 1975[G582], 29–40.
[6] R. P. Duncan Jones, *The Economy of the Roman Empire* (edn 2. Cambridge 1982), 264 n. 4.
[7] Richard 1978[H76], 364.

an insignificant place with a restricted territory, and that the alleged Roman hegemony in Latium is a fiction; indeed, during the sixth century B.C. Rome was itself conquered and ruled by the Etruscans. This unpalatable fact, according to Alföldi, was suppressed by the Roman historians, who constructed in its place a completely false picture of Roman power under the Tarquins. On this view the Roman conquest of Alba Longa and of the lower Tiber valley took place in the middle of the fifth century B.C.; the area embraced by the twenty-one local tribes did not come under Roman control in 495 B.C., as Livy maintains, but only towards the end of the fifth century, when the city emerged for the first time as the dominant power in Latium.

The question of whether the tradition is acceptable in its main out-lines, or whether it is to be rejected in favour of some alternative reconstruction such as that of Alföldi, cannot be answered with any certainty in the present state of our knowledge. The balance of the argument, however, seems to favour the view, adopted in this chapter, that the traditional picture of Rome's development is at least as credible as any of the modern hypotheses that have been designed to replace it, and that radical theories such as Alföldi's create more problems than they solve.

The traditional picture can be supported by three main arguments. First, the conquests that are traditionally ascribed to the kings cannot easily be fitted into the existing record of events in the fifth century B.C., which is presented in the sources as a period of weakness and difficulty for the Roman state and its allies. To date an event like the conquest of Alba Longa in the middle of the fifth century creates all sorts of particular difficulties. For example, in historical times there were six noble clans that were supposed to have come to Rome from Alba Longa: the Iulii, Servilii, Quinctii, Cloelii, Geganii and Curiatii (Livy 1.30.2; Dion. Hal. *Ant. Rom.* III.29.7). But the fact that these 'Alban' *gentes* were patrician, and are all represented in the consular *fasti* in the early decades of the Republic (e.g. in 498, 495, 492, 482, 471 and 453 B.C.), must imply that they migrated to Rome under the monarchy, and is in any case incom-patible with the view that Alba was not conquered by Rome until the mid-fifth century.

Secondly, the internal consistency and general plausibility of the traditional account, which have already been remarked on, are in them-selves an argument in favour of its basic authenticity. One would not expect such a result if the Roman historians and antiquarians had grossly misunderstood the evidence in front of them; one would rather imagine that wholesale errors and misunderstandings would have led to confu-sion, disagreement and inconsistencies in the literary tradition. It is partly because of the general coherence of the traditional account that sceptical historians such as Alföldi have suggested that it was the product of deliberate and systematic falsification; they believe that the annalists, finding the evidence either inadequate or unsatisfactory, created a totally false picture of the early history of the city, wilfully distorting such evidence as was available, and freely inventing facts when evidence was lacking. On this view the internal consistency and general plausibility of the tradition come ultimately from the minds of the men who created and organized the material of the story. For Alföldi the organizing genius was Fabius Pictor, the first Roman historian, who, in an attempt to make a favourable impression on his Greek readers, constructed an exaggerated and overblown picture of Rome as a powerful independent state in the sixth century B.C.

The chief objections to this theory are, first, that there is no good reason to doubt the honesty of Fabius Pictor, and secondly that as far as we can see Fabius was not in a position to impose a fraudulent version of Rome's past on successive generations of Roman historians. Quite apart from the fact that earlier Greek historians such as Timaeus had already written something about Rome in the regal period, it is hard to believe that an intelligent and independent-minded historian like Cato the Censor would have meekly accepted Fabius' view of early Rome if the primary evidence, which he knew well, had said something radically different. Again, if the Roman historians had been in the habit of perpetrating wholesale lies and distortions, it is surprising that the general structure of the narrative is so uniform in all the sources.

The third general argument is that the archaeological evidence, such as it is, is consistent with the traditional picture of Rome as a flourishing urban centre in the sixth century B.C. It is important, however, not to exaggerate the force of this argument, and to be clear about precisely what archaeological evidence can prove, and what it cannot prove. The material that has been unearthed in recent excavations has greatly increased our knowledge of the cultural development of early Rome and the conditions of its material life; but it can hardly be expected to provide much direct information about the external relations of the city. Attempts to verify the conquests of Tullus Hostilius or Ancus Marcius by means of archaeological evidence have not surprisingly met with little success. It is indeed hard to imagine what kind of archaeological evidence, short of an explicit inscription, would be adequate to prove or disprove the claim of our sources that the Romans conquered as far as the coast and the Alban hills in the sixth century B.C.

Archaeology has not yet been able to confirm that the urban area of Rome extended as far as the line of the 'Servian' *pomerium* in the sixth century; nor is there any archaeological proof that the city was surrounded by defensive fortifications in the late regal period (p. 80), although the sources attribute the construction of city walls to both

Tarquinius Priscus and Servius Tullius (Livy 1.36.1; 38.6; 44; Dion. Hal. *Ant. Rom.* III.67.4; IV.13). The earth rampart (*agger*) which encloses part of the Esquiline, Quirinal and Viminal is of uncertain date, and may not have embraced the whole of the city. A further limitation on the value of archaeological evidence in the present context is the fact that we still know very little about the other settlements of Latium Vetus during the archaic age. The main reason for this deficiency is that most recent archaeological work has concentrated on sites which by definition lay outside the main areas of habitation – cemeteries and extra-mural sanctuaries. Archaeology has shown that Rome underwent dramatic changes and developed into an urbanized community in the years around 600 B.C.; but it has not so far made it clear whether the same process was simultaneously taking place elsewhere in Latium. Our sources imply that Rome outstripped its Latin neighbours during the last century of the monarchy, but this alleged fact cannot yet be demonstrated archaeologically.

This is not to say, however, that archaeology has no contribution to make in the present context. Excavations have given us a glimpse of the monumental developments that occurred during the sixth century B.C. in the area around the Forum Romanum (p. 75f), itself formally laid out as a public meeting place in the later seventh century. Temples and other public buildings have been located, some of them showing several successive phases of construction. These finds provide a general confirmation of the tradition that the last kings engaged in extensive and grandiose building projects in the city. The most important of these constructions was the great temple of Iuppiter on the Capitol, which was built by the Tarquins and dedicated in the first year of the Republic. Archaeological evidence, in the form of fragmentary architectural terracottas, confirms the dating of the temple, and traces of the foundations and substructure serve to corroborate what tradition tells us about the immense scale of the building (Fig. 42). The platform on which it stood measured some 61 metres long by 55 metres wide (cf. Dion. Hal. *Ant. Rom.* IV. 61.3–4), making it one of the largest temples in the Mediterranean world at the time. This fact in itself must lend support to the tradition that Rome under the Tarquins was the leading state in Central Italy. Artefacts from votive deposits and other contexts point in the same direction, indicating as they do a highly developed material culture and widespread external contacts.

In the light of this evidence there seems no good reason to reject the tradition concerning the ambitious and successful foreign policy of the last kings. We are told that they not only reduced the Latins to subjection, but also won victories against the Etruscans and Sabines, from whom they made territorial gains (e.g. Dion. Hal. *Ant. Rom.* IV.27:

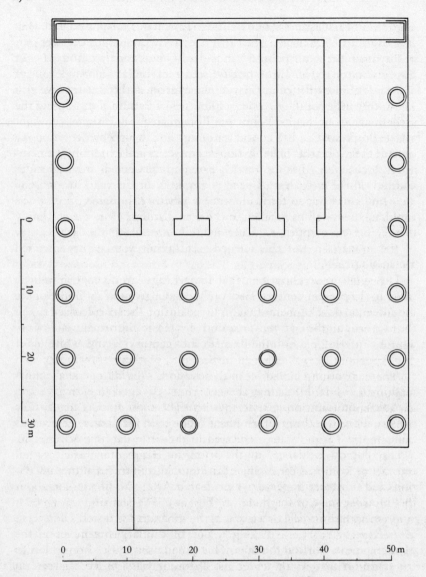

Fig. 42. Plan of the Capitoline temple of Iuppiter Optimus Maximus, Iuno and Minerva. From Gjerstad 1953–73 [A56], III.181 fig. 116.

Servius Tullius). It is likely enough that the scale of operations in these conflicts has been exaggerated in the sources. For example Dionysius of Halicarnassus would have us believe that the whole Etruscan nation, the 'Twelve Peoples', had united in opposition to Rome, and that all of them submitted to her on more than one occasion. But this idea, though unacceptable as it stands, may well be the result of a misunderstanding of a genuine historical fact, namely that successful campaigns were conducted against Etruscan peoples whose lands bordered on Rome's. The fantastic notion that Tarquinius Priscus received the surrender of the Twelve Peoples of Etruria derived in part from antiquarian speculation about the origin of the *fasces* (e.g. Dion. Hal. *Ant. Rom.* iii.61); but this does not rule out the possibility that Roman armies occasionally ravaged the territories of Caere, Veii and Tarquinii, and that the *ager Romanus* was extended beyond the Tiber under the kings. At least three of the earliest rural tribes, the Romilia, the Galeria and the Fabia, were probably located on the right bank (see Fig. 43), and the district known as the Septem Pagi, which was the object of continual disputes between Rome and Veii, seems to have fallen into Roman hands before the end of the monarchy (Livy ii.13.4; 15.6; Dion. Hal. *Ant. Rom.* v.36.4; 65.3).

In Latium itself the Romans had established an extensive hegemony by the time of Tarquinius Superbus. The basis of this king's success is said to have been his reorganization of the Latin League into a regular military alliance (Livy i.52). In the course of his reign Tarquin captured Pometia by storm, gained control of Gabii by means of a ruse, colonized Signia and Circeii, and won over Tusculum by marrying his daughter to its leading citizen Octavus Mamilius;[8] at the time of the coup which led to his expulsion, he was engaged in besieging Ardea.

There is nothing incredible in these reports. The story that the spoils of Pometia paid for the construction of the Capitoline temple may well be an authentic tradition connected with the building (cf. Tacitus, *Hist.* iii.72), while the treaty which Rome made with Gabii was preserved in the temple of Semo Sancus and was still there in the time of Augustus (Dion. Hal. *Ant. Rom.* iv.58.4). Two further pieces of evidence confirm the fact of Rome's ascendancy in Latium at this time. First the author of lines 1011–1016 of the *Theogony* wrote that Agrios and Latinos, the sons of Odysseus and Circe, 'ruled over the famous Tyrsenians, very far off in a recess of the holy islands' (p. 57). If the appendix to Hesiod's *Theogony* is correctly dated to the sixth century B.C., these lines probably represent a contemporary allusion to the power of the Latins under Roman leadership during the age of the Tarquins. The second and most crucial piece of evidence is the treaty between Rome and Carthage transcribed by Polybius (iii.22), and dated by him to the first year of the Republic.[9] In this remarkable document the Romans and Carthaginians agree to be friends and not to act contrary to each other's interests. In particular, the Carthaginians pledge themselves 'not to injure the people of Ardea,

---

[8] The sources call him Octavius (*sic*) Mamilius. But it is probably better to presume a *praenomen* Octavus (cf. Quintus, Sextus, Septimus, Decimus) than a name composed of two *gentilicia* (cf. Beloch 1926[A12], 189 n. 1).　　[9] Cf. below, pp. 520ff (with further discussion).

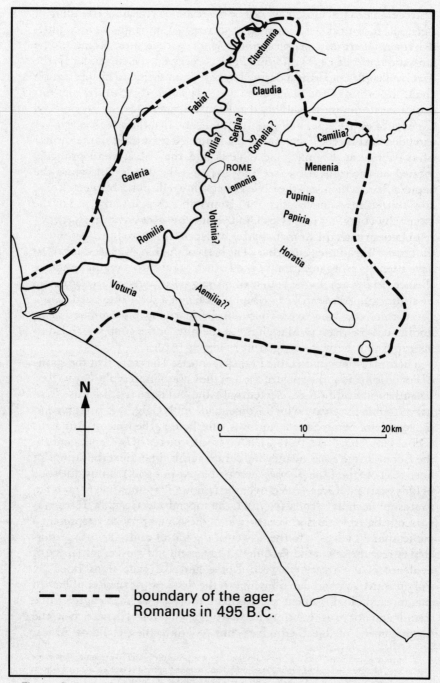

Fig. 43. Conjectural location of the earliest rural tribes (495 B.C.) (after Taylor 1960 [G733]).

Antium, Lavinium, Circeii, Tarracina or any other city of the Latins who are subjects of Rome. As for the Latins who are not subjects, they shall keep their hands off their cities, and if they take any such city they shall hand it over to the Romans unharmed. They shall build no fort in Latin territory. If they enter the territory in arms, they shall not spend a night there.'

Obviously, if this evidence is genuine, there can be no doubt about the extent of Roman power in Latium. But is it genuine? The document quoted by Polybius has long been the subject of dispute. The idea that it was a deliberate forgery need not be entertained; but it is a serious question whether Polybius (or his informant) was correct to date it to the first year of the Republic. Livy makes no mention of any treaty between Rome and Carthage before the one he records under the year 348 B.C. (VII.27.2); while Diodorus explicitly says that the treaty of 348 was the first between the two states (XVI.69.1). On the other hand Livy implies that there had been earlier treaties, because in his next reference to a treaty he speaks of it being renewed 'for the third time' (IX.43.13: 306 B.C.; cf. IX.19.13: *foedera vetusta* ('old treaties')). In fact there is much confusion in the sources on this whole question. But Polybius is a reliable authority whose statements cannot be lightly cast aside. The arguments for accepting his date for the Carthaginian treaty were clearly set out in the first edition of this work by H. M. Last,[10] whose discussion remains fundamental and whose conclusions have not been seriously weakened by subsequent efforts to discredit Polybius' testimony.

The principal argument in favour of Polybius' date is precisely the fact that the contents of the treaty accord with the historical circumstances of the late sixth century B.C. The treaty makes Rome the overlord of a miniature 'empire' in Latium extending down the coast as far as the Pomptine plain. This conforms precisely to the situation described in the sources as obtaining under Tarquinius Superbus, whose control of the region is implied by his capture of Pometia and his foundation of a colony (whatever that precisely means) at Circeii. We may note that a later date is ruled out by the fact that the Pomptine district and much of southern Latium were overrun by the Volscians at the beginning of the fifth century and were not regained by Rome until a hundred years later. In short, unless we choose to believe that the treaty is itself an integral part of some mischievously contrived scheme of falsification, we may reasonably conclude that its close agreement with the surviving accounts of Tarquin's military and diplomatic achievements is a guarantee both of the correctness of Polybius' date and of the general authenticity of the rest of the tradition.

[10] Last 1928[K152], 859–62.

That a treaty should have been concluded between Rome and Carthage at the end of the sixth century B.C. is not in itself particularly surprising. Carthaginian interest in the area of the Tyrrhenian Sea during this period is well documented, and it is probable that the treaty with Rome was one of a number of such agreements which the Carthaginians made with friendly states in the area. Aristotle refers to treaties between Carthage and the Etruscans as classic examples of a particular type of trading agreement (*symbolon*) which provided for a mutual exchange of rights and privileges; according to Aristotle, the contracting parties became 'like citizens of one city' (*Pol.* III.1280 a 36). The purpose of these *symbola* seems to have been to ensure rights of access to foreign trading ports and to protect the interests of traders resident in them.

The presence of communities of Phoenician traders in Etruscan ports is indicated by the existence of a coastal settlement called Punicum (S. Marinella) in the territory of Caere, and by the bilingual (Etruscan and Phoenician) inscriptions that were discovered in the early 1960s at Pyrgi (S. Severa), another Caeretan port. The Pyrgi inscriptions, which date probably from the early fifth century B.C., record a dedication to the Phoenician goddess Astarte (Etruscan Uni) by Thefarie Velianas, the ruler of Caere (Fig. 44). The fact that he claimed to be ruling by favour of the goddess suggests that the resident Phoenician merchants had consid-

Fig. 44. Gold tablet from Pyrgi: the longer Etruscan text (early fifth century?). From M. Cristofani in Ridgway and Ridgway 1979 [A111], 406 fig. 6.

erable political influence. Close ties between Caere and Carthage were of
long standing. A generation or so before the time of Thefarie Velianas (in
c. 540 B.C.), their combined fleets had fought a naval battle against the
Phocaean Greeks in the Sardinian Sea (Herodotus 1.166–7).

It is possible, though not yet demonstrable, that there was a colony of
Phoenician traders resident in Rome during the archaic period (cf. above,
p. 53). In any case it is likely that the Carthaginians would have wanted to
establish good relations with the city on the Tiber that controlled a
long stretch of the central Italian coastline, and it would obviously have
made sense for them to keep on good terms with the new republican
regime that established itself in Rome after the fall of Tarquin, when all
existing agreements would have been automatically terminated. For
their part, the new Republic's leaders might have hoped to obtain
recognition for themselves by a formal agreement with Carthage, and at
the same time would have wanted to assert their claim to the position of
hegemony in Latium which the kings had formerly possessed. The first
year of the Republic is therefore a plausible context for a treaty between
Rome and Carthage.

II. THE FALL OF THE MONARCHY AND ITS CONSEQUENCES

If the Republic's founding fathers had been hoping to carry on where
Tarquin had left off, they would have been disappointed. In the event the
downfall of the monarchy was attended by an upheaval which threatened
to undermine Rome's dominant position and profoundly affected the
political relationships of all the peoples of Central Italy. But it is
uncertain whether this upheaval was a cause or a consequence of
Tarquin's expulsion. The events themselves are difficult to reconstruct,
and a proper understanding of them is beyond our grasp. The reason for
this difficulty is that the aristocratic tradition of the Republic, with its
proverbial hatred of kingship, transformed the memory of the events
into a heroic struggle by the Roman people to preserve their newly won
liberty in the face of repeated attempts by Tarquin to regain his throne.

Tarquin is said to have applied first to Veii and Tarquinii, and
persuaded them to mount an armed invasion of Roman territory; this
initiative was thwarted at the battle of Silva Arsia in which the Romans
were victorious, in spite of the loss of their consul, L. Brutus. Tarquin
then turned to Lars Porsenna, the king of Clusium, who marched on
Rome and besieged it from his camp on the Janiculum; but the heroism
of Horatius Cocles, Mucius Scaevola and Cloelia persuaded Porsenna to
relent, and to send his forces instead against the Latin town of Aricia. The
expedition ended in failure, however, when the Etruscans were defeated
by the Latins and their allies from Cumae. Tarquin then enlisted the aid of

his son-in-law, Octavus Mamilius of Tusculum, who mobilized the Latin League in his support and led a general revolt against Rome. Finally, after the defeat of Mamilius and the Latins at the battle of Lake Regillus (499 or 496 B.C.), Tarquin took refuge with Aristodemus the Effeminate, the tyrant of Greek Cumae and the leader of the Cumaean army that had helped the Latins against Lars Porsenna. It was as an exile at the court of Aristodemus that the hated Tarquin finally ended his days, in the consulship of Appius Claudius and Publius Servilius (495 B.C.: Livy II.21.5).

This romantic story is exciting but does not carry much conviction as a historical account. That is not to say, however, that the events themselves are unhistorical. The expedition of Lars Porsenna, for instance, is almost certainly authentic, in spite of recent efforts to prove the contrary.[11] The destruction and abandonment of a number of archaeological sites in southern Etruria at the end of the sixth century would seem to indicate some kind of violent unrest at this period; more explicit evidence is provided by the account in Dionysius of Halicarnassus of the life and deeds of Aristodemus of Cumae, which recent studies have shown to be based on an independent Greek source (Dion. Hal. *Ant. Rom.* VII.3–6).[12] This remarkable account, which probably derives ultimately from local traditions of Cumae, describes Aristodemus' victory over the Etruscans at Aricia and gives a precise date (504 B.C.).

The biography of Aristodemus confirms what one might otherwise have suspected, namely that the Roman tradition has distorted the truth by placing the exiled Tarquin at the centre of the stage. In fact the change of regime in Rome was only one element in a more complex and far-reaching set of events. The received tradition gives a particularly misleading account of the role of Lars Porsenna. This conclusion is based on the fact that some writers knew of a variant tradition, according to which the Romans surrendered to Porsenna and were obliged to submit to humiliating terms (Tac. *Hist.* III.72; Pliny *HN* XXXIV.139). If that is true, and it is hard to see why anyone should invent anything so perverse, then it helps to explain the strange story that survivors of Porsenna's army were given refuge in Rome after their defeat at Aricia (Livy II.14.8–9); on the other hand the conventional version of the beginning of the Republic is placed under severe strain, and it becomes impossible to believe that Porsenna's principal aim was to reinstate Tarquin. It has indeed been suggested that, so far from attempting to install Tarquin, Porsenna actually removed him, and either ruled in his place or set up a puppet

[11] Werner 1963[A134], 381.
[12] Alföldi 1965[I3], 55f; Momigliano 1966[A84], 664f; Gabba 1967[B63], 144f; Cornell 1974[B32], 206f.

regime (the 'consuls') to govern the city on his behalf.[13] However that may be, and the precise details are obviously not now recoverable, Porsenna's sojourn in Rome cannot have lasted for long, and we may safely assume that after the battle of Aricia Rome's monarchic age was definitely at an end.

The complex narrative of the overthrow of King Tarquin and the related story of Lars Porsenna's attack on Rome raise in an acute form the general problem of Rome's relations with the Etruscans in the archaic period. The standard interpretation, which can be found in the majority of modern works, is that the expulsion of the kings marked the end of a period of Etruscan rule in Rome, and the reassertion by the Romans of their national independence. The most radical version of this theory maintains that Lars Porsenna's adventure was merely the last in a series of Etruscan conquests, by which Rome was subjected to the rule of one Etruscan city after another.[14] These conquests were part of a wider pattern of expansion in Italy which led to the formation of an Etruscan 'empire' extending from the Po valley to the gulf of Salerno. By occupying Rome the Etruscans gained control of a vital crossing of the River Tiber; once this strategic point was secure they were able to continue their advance towards Campania, where they took over existing settlements at Capua and Nola, probably in the second half of the sixth century B.C.

The corollary of this thesis is that the fall of the Roman monarchy at the end of the sixth century severed the link between Etruria and the Etruscan settlements in Campania, and was a major cause of their ultimate decline; the process was aggravated by the defeat of Porsenna's army at Aricia, and later by the destruction of an Etruscan fleet by Hiero of Syracuse off Cumae in 474 B.C. (Diod. XI.51; Pind. *Pyth.* 1.72). The final blow came when Campania was overrun by Oscan-speaking highlanders in the 420s (see below, p. 284f).

That Rome under the Tarquins was in some sense an Etruscan city cannot seriously be denied. The process of urbanization that began in the second half of the seventh century B.C. was at least in part the result of Etruscan influence, and the effect of Etruscan ideas on the development of Roman religious cults, political institutions, and social customs was far-reaching. We may note that the Roman tradition makes no attempt to conceal this fact; on the contrary, the written sources provide most of the evidence. Archaeology too has shown that in terms of its material culture regal Rome belonged to the world of the Etruscan cities.

But it does not necessarily follow from the fact of Etruscan cultural

---

[13] Ed. Meyer 1907–37[A79], III.752 n.1; cf. Alföldi 1965[I3], 77; above, p. 178.
[14] E.g. Homo 1927[A66], 115; Alföldi 1965[I3], 206ff; Heurgon 1973[A64], 140–1.

influence that Rome was politically dominated by the Etruscans. The literary sources do not, and the archaeological evidence cannot, provide support for the proposition that Rome was subjected to alien rule in the archaic period. The Elder Cato may have written that 'almost all of Italy was once in the power of the Etruscans' (*Origines* fr. 62P; cf. Livy 1.2.5; v.33.7–11). But Cato certainly did not mean to imply that *Rome* was once in the power of the Etruscans; rather, the context makes it clear that his reported statement referred to the time of the legendary Metabus, a contemporary of Aeneas, and consequently has no relevance to the question of Rome's position in the archaic age.[15]

The widely canvassed notion that the Etruscans needed to control Rome and other Latin places in order to secure a direct overland route to their colonial settlements in Campania is a modern myth. Nothing compels us to believe that the Etruscan settlements in Campania required the support of a direct umbilical link with the mother country. A much more reasonable hypothesis is that under the Tarquins Rome was an independent power, but that the Etruscan element in its population was politically dominant and ruled the city in the Etruscan interest. Thus it has been argued that 'the presence of an Etruscan ruling family may well have facilitated Etruscan control of the land route to Campania'.[16] Such a statement would be unexceptionable if its leading assumption could be shown to be true. But there is no evidence that the foreign policy of the Tarquins was in any way 'pro-Etruscan'. In fact, as we have seen, tradition maintains that they ruled as independent kings of Rome and fought wars *against* the Etruscan cities. Again it is not necessary to suppose that the coup which drove out the Tarquins entailed a change in Roman policy towards the Etruscans, nor is there any evidence for such a change.

As far as internal politics are concerned, it is important to stress that the Tarquins do not appear to have favoured the Etruscan element in the population at the expense of other groups. There is no trace of racial discrimination in any of the institutions attributed to the Tarquins (or Servius Tullius). Attempts to prove that archaic social distinctions, such as that between patricians and plebeians, were founded on racial differences have been discredited by modern scholarship.[17] In short, the fact that the Tarquinii were an Etruscan family does not necessarily imply that the ruling class of Rome was wholly or predominantly Etruscan.

Recent research has shown that the ethnic composition of the popula-

[15] Colonna 1981[F15], 159. The same considerations apply to Cato, *Origines* fr. 12P, on which see Momigliano 1967[I44], 213 (= id. *Quarto Contributo* 492–3).

[16] Ridgway 1981[J103], 31. For the view given in the text see Colonna 1981[F15], 165.

[17] On the history of this question see Richard 1978[H76], 27ff; Momigliano 1977[H63], 10ff (= id. *Sesto Contributo* 480ff).

tion of archaic Rome was very diverse, and that there was a complex interaction of different ethnic elements at all social levels. This situation, which has been analysed in detail in a series of papers by C. Ampolo,[18] was made possible by a high degree of horizontal social mobility which characterized all the communities of Tyrrhenian Central Italy in the archaic age. The most important evidence for this proposition comes, once again, from the literary tradition. The Romans of later times were well aware of their mixed origins, and made a positive virtue of the fact that their ancestors had been willing to admit foreigners into their midst. The tradition records many examples of individuals and groups who migrated to Rome and were accepted into the ruling elite. They include the kings Titus Tatius and Numa Pompilius, the adventurer Mastarna of Vulci, and Attius Clausus, the ancestor of the Claudian house. But for the Romans the most striking example of their ancestors' willingness to admit foreign immigrants was precisely the story of the family of the Tarquins.

According to tradition Tarquinius Priscus migrated to Rome with his wife and family because he knew that it was a place where he would be accepted and where he would be able to make his fortune. Conversely the exile of Tarquinius Superbus did not involve the expulsion of all Etruscans from the city, but merely that of the Tarquinii. Thus, Livy tells us, 'in accordance with a decree of the senate, Brutus brought before the people the proposal that every member of the Tarquin family should be banished from Rome' (Livy II.2.11). These accounts are consistent with the model of an 'open' society in which individuals and groups could move freely from one place to another without loss of rights or social position. The phenomenon is attested at other places besides Rome. The tradition of the Corinthian Demaratus, supposedly the father of Tarquinius Priscus, who migrated from Corinth to Tarquinii, is exactly parallel to the story of Tarquin's own move to Rome. Another example is Coriolanus, the Roman who went to live among the Volscians and became their leader. Considered in the light of these examples, even the tale of Sextus Tarquinius, the tyrant's younger son, who persuaded the people of Gabii to accept him under false pretences, is perhaps not as improbable as it might otherwise seem (Livy 1.53–4).

Whether or not these stories are literally true does not really matter. What is important is that they reflect a genuine feature of the archaic society of Central Italy. In the Etruscan cities inscriptions have revealed the presence of families of Greek, Latin and Italic origin occupying positions of high social rank.[19] In Rome the same phenomenon is attested

---

[18] Ampolo 1970–1[G2], 37–68; 1976–7[G3], 333–45; 1981[G4], 45–70.
[19] Ampolo 1976–7[G3], 333ff.

by the consular *fasti*, which show that many immigrant families held the supreme magistracy during the early years of the Republic. The presence of Etruscan names among the consuls of the early Republic proves incidentally that the end of the monarchy did not entail the wholesale expulsion of Etruscans from the city; and the archaeological record shows that Etruscan cultural influence continued without a break well into the fifth century.

These facts accord with the literary tradition, which contains no hint of any anti-Etruscan reaction at the time of the fall of the monarchy. The story that after his expulsion Tarquin received help from Octavus Mamilius and the Latins (a much more credible version than that which makes him a protégé of Lars Porsenna) is a further indication that these events should not be seen as symptoms of a wider racial conflict between Etruscans and Latins. In fact there is no good reason to distrust the clear message of the sources, that the Romans overthrew Tarquinius Superbus, not because he was an Etruscan, but because he was a tyrant. Forever after the Romans hated the very idea of a king; but there is no trace in the Roman historical tradition of any residual prejudice against Etruscans as such.[20]

If the fall of the monarchy was not a symptom of a general collapse of Etruscan power in central Italy, it nevertheless had far-reaching effects on the city's external relations. The most important of these repercussions were the disintegration of Roman power in Latium and the subsequent restructuring of the Latin League in the early years of the fifth century. But it is not immediately obvious why such developments should have been occasioned by a change of regime in Rome, which might at first sight appear to have been an entirely domestic affair.

How Rome's neighbours might have reacted to the foundation of the Republic is not a question that can be answered with any certainty because we are poorly informed about their internal political and constitutional systems. It has been argued, however, that this was a period in which the institution of monarchy was everywhere under threat, and that republican regimes were being established throughout Central Italy, in Etruria as well as in Latium, in the late sixth and early fifth centuries B.C.[21] Unfortunately this attractive theory cannot be substantiated by detailed evidence. While it is certain that republican governments were eventually set up in all the cities of Central Italy about which we know anything, and that there is no trace of monarchy anywhere after the beginning of the fourth century B.C., nevertheless the details of the process are unclear.

---

[20] In fairness it must be said that some scholars view the matter differently. For example D. Musti 1970[B119] argues that the surviving tradition is a complex tapestry of pro-Etruscan and anti-Etruscan threads; but these threads are not visible to me.

[21] E.g. Mazzarino 1945[F47].

As far as the Latin cities are concerned, there is little trace of the institution of kingship in the surviving tradition, which makes no reference to kings in the period after the destruction of Alba Longa, and if anything implies that the Latin communities were governed by aristocratic regimes in the sixth century. In Etruria, on the other hand, we know that some monarchies survived well into the fifth century, for example at Caere and Veii; indeed Veii was still ruled by a king at the time of its capture by the Romans in 396 B.C. We may also note that the institution of tyranny lasted longer in the Greek cities of Sicily and Magna Graecia than on the Greek mainland, and was not generally superseded until around the middle of the fifth century.

It is most probable that the political upheaval in Rome provoked a variety of different reactions in neighbouring states. Some might well have taken the opportunity to follow suit by expelling their own rulers, and indeed we read in Livy that Sextus Tarquinius was assassinated by the people of Gabii as soon as they heard the news of the revolution in Rome (Livy 1.60.2). On the other hand, a hostile reaction was to be expected in places where the Tarquins had established good relations with the local ruling families, for example at Tusculum, where Superbus' son-in-law Octavus Mamilius began to organize a revolt against Rome (it is worth noting that none of the sources describe Mamilius as king of Tusculum). In general, however, it is likely that most of the Latins would have welcomed the opportunity provided by the fall of the Tarquins to free themselves from Roman domination.

The Latin revolt, according to the most probable reconstruction, was a continuation of the organized resistance of the Latins to the forces of Lars Porsenna, whose brief occupation of Rome had temporarily isolated the city from the rest of Latium and was partly responsible for the fall of the Tarquins. The link between Tarquinius Superbus, Octavus Mamilius and Aristodemus of Cumae makes political sense not because of a shared attachment to the idea of kingship but because of their common opposition to Lars Porsenna. After the battle of Aricia, and the withdrawal of both Porsenna and Aristodemus, the stage was set for a conflict between Rome and the rest of the Latins, with the Romans attempting to regain their former ascendancy, and the Latins determined to resist. There is no reason to doubt that Tarquinius Superbus was closely involved in these events, although it is probable that his role was secondary.

The issue was settled, so we are told, at the battle of Lake Regillus in either 499 or 496 B.C. (Livy II.21.3-4), where the Romans under the dictator A. Postumius Albus won a memorable victory. The battle was followed, after an interval of a few years, by a treaty between Rome and the Latins (traditionally 493 B.C.). The treaty, known to posterity as the *foedus Cassianum* from the fact that it was signed on Rome's behalf by the

consul Sp. Cassius, defined the formal relations between Rome and the
Latins which were to persist for the next 150 years. But before we
consider the terms of the treaty, it will be necessary to attend briefly to the
previous history of the Latin League.

III. THE LATIN LEAGUE

In the fifth and fourth centuries B.C. the communities of the 'Latin name'
(*nomen Latinum*) were joined together in a political and military federation that we traditionally call the Latin League. Political relations
between the Latin states during this period were regulated by the
provisions of the treaty of Spurius Cassius. It is certain, however, that the
treaty did not itself create the Latin League, but merely introduced
modifications to a pre-existing structure, and in particular redefined the
position of Rome in relation to the other Latins. But we have only a very
sketchy and unreliable picture of the league in the period before the
Cassian treaty, and since our knowledge of the treaty itself is poor, there
is also much uncertainty and controversy about the organization and
character of the league even in the fifth and fourth centuries.

This uncertainty arises from the fact that our sources have all, to a
greater or lesser extent, been influenced by later developments. In the
third and second centuries B.C. the Latin name had ceased to have an
exclusive ethnic or territorial significance, and the phrase was used
instead to describe a particular juridical category of non-Roman communities in Italy. The important point about these later 'Latin' communities
is that they possessed a special status vis-à-vis the Roman state. As
individuals the Latins could exercise certain rights and privileges in their
dealings with Roman citizens. In other words, Latinity was defined in
terms of a bilateral relationship (or, rather, a series of bilateral relationships) between unequal partners, rather than by membership of a wider
community or federation of states.

The sources have allowed this state of affairs to colour their picture of
the Latin League in the archaic period. From the very earliest times the
Latins are presented as a mere appendage of the Roman state, a group of
subject allies who were under a formal obligation to furnish troops for
Rome's armies, and who were condescendingly granted a privileged
status in comparison with other subject communities.

The traditional account maintains that the league had military and
political functions from the beginning. The basis of this conception was
the belief that all the peoples of Latium Vetus were the colonies of a
single city, Alba Longa, which consequently exercised a position of
hegemony in the period before its destruction by Tullus Hostilius:
'Albanos rerum potitos usque ad Tullum regem' (Cincius *ap.* Festus 276

L). This seems to be an anachronistic and artificial construction modelled on the relationship that existed in historical times between Rome and its colonies, many of which possessed Latin rights and by the middle of the third century formed the majority of the *socii nominis Latini* ('allies of the Latin name'). According to the traditional account, the victory of Tullus Hostilius gave Rome the hegemony that had formerly belonged to Alba (e.g. Dion. Hal. *Ant. Rom.* III.34.1). The new dispensation was solemnly enshrined in a treaty (Livy I.32.5; 52.2) which was subsequently renewed on several occasions following Latin 'revolts'. The *foedus Cassianum* was merely one such renewal. Thus it became possible to present relations between Rome and the Latins as persisting unchanged from the time of Tullus Hostilius to the end of the Latin War in 338 B.C. This reconstruction, as Mommsen said, is not history, but rather a way of representing a constitutional doctrine.[22]

The theoretical possibility that there really was some kind of 'Alban hegemony' in very early times cannot be entirely discounted, although it is not supported by any reliable evidence. The archaeological record, which shows that a number of small settlements existed in the region of the Alban Hills during the earliest phases (I and IIA) of the 'cultura laziale' (p. 34f), cannot really help to clarify the political role of the city of Alba Longa, of which no archaeological trace has yet been found, and presumably never will be, since 'Alba' was traditionally destroyed in the pre-urban period.

It is in any case much more likely that the prominence of Alba Longa in the traditional story derives not from any supposed political hegemony but from the historical fact that the national festival of the Latin peoples was celebrated each year within its former territory, on the Mons Albanus. There can be no doubt about the antiquity of this cult, or of its importance in the national consciousness of the Latin peoples. In the historical period it was the Latin cult par excellence. The annual festival, known as the Latiar or Feriae Latinae, was in honour of Iuppiter Latiaris, who was identified in legend with Latinus, the eponymous ancestor of the tribe (Festus 212 L). The site of the cult, the summit of the Alban Mount (Monte Cavo), is the highest point in the region (949 m.) and dominates the plain of Latium.

The Feriae Latinae, which were celebrated in the spring of each year, continued to take place long after the dissolution of the Latin League in 338 B.C., and were still being performed in the time of the emperors. The central element of the ritual was a banquet to which each of the communi-

---

[22] Mommsen 1887–8[A91], III.611: 'Es ist das nicht Geschichte, wohl aber die staatsrechtliche Darlegung des Verhältnisses welches der Auflösung des latinischen Bundes unmittelbar vorherging, der Hegemonie Roms über die übrige in föderativer Geschlossenheit neben ihm stehende Nation.'

ties taking part contributed lambs, cheese, milk, or something similar
(Dion. Hal. *Ant. Rom.* IV.49.3; the pastoral character of the ceremony is
evidence of its extreme antiquity). A white bull was sacrificed, and each
community received its share of the meat.[23] A curious list of thirty '*populi
Albenses*, who . . . used to receive meat on the Alban Mount' is given by
Pliny the Elder (*HN* III.69) and perhaps represents an early stage in the
development of the cult (see below, p. 267). It is probable that the
division of the meat into thirty portions had a special significance and
was artificially maintained for ritual purposes throughout the history of
the Feriae Latinae. This would explain the repeated references in our
sources to the 'thirty peoples of the Latin name' (e.g. Livy II.18.3; Dion.
Hal. *Ant. Rom.* VI.63.4, etc.). The ceremony was evidently an expression
of tribal solidarity, and constituted an annual renewal of the ties of
kinship that united the Latin peoples. Participation in the cult was a
badge of membership; the Latin name could be said to consist exclusively
of those peoples who received meat at the annual banquet on the Alban
Mount. If one of the Latin peoples failed to obtain its proper share of the
meat, the whole ceremony had to be repeated (see e.g. Livy XXXII.1.9;
XXXVII.3.4).

What is uncertain, however, is the relationship between the cult of
Iuppiter Latiaris and the political league of Latin states that existed at the
end of the sixth century B.C. Although it might seem simple enough to
argue that the latter evolved naturally out of the former, or that the
annual reunions on the Alban Mount were merely a religious function of
the Latin League, most scholars are careful to distinguish between the
two institutions. This caution is justified for a number of reasons. We
may note for instance that the Latiar was not the only cult that the Latin
peoples shared in common. Festivals of the same kind were also celebrated at Lavinium, an important religious centre and the home of the
Penates (*ILS* 5004). There was a major common shrine in the grove of
Diana at Aricia (see below, p. 272), and from casual references in the
literary sources we hear of others near Tusculum and at Ardea (Pliny,
HN XVI.242; Strabo V.3.5, p. 242C). It is perfectly possible moreover that
there were other common shrines of which we now know nothing.

Archaeological evidence has yielded some further information about
these cult places. For example at Gabii an archaic sanctuary has been
discovered outside the walls of the city, suggesting a cult open to
outsiders.[24] It seems that the common sanctuaries were generally situated
outside the walls of the cities to which they belonged. At Lavinium
(Pratica di Mare) excavations during the last twenty-five years have

[23] Dion. Hal. *Ant. Rom.* IV.49.3; Cic. *Planc.* 23; Schol. Bob. ad loc., p. 128 Hild.; Varro, *Ling.*
VI.25; Serv. *Aen.* 1.211; cf. Alföldi 1965[I3], 19–25.   [24] Cornell 1980[B315], 85.

revealed traces of a complex of extra-mural sanctuaries which are probably to be connected with the federal cults referred to in the written
sources.[25] It is in this context that we can best understand the tradition
that Servius Tullius founded a temple of Diana on the Aventine as a
common shrine for all the Latins (p. 85; 92). Since the Aventine was outside the *pomerium*, the sacred boundary of the city, the Dianium was clearly
an extra-urban sanctuary of the kind that already existed at other places in
Latium. There is no reason to doubt that the cult of Diana was, in fact,
founded by Servius Tullius, although the original sixth-century shrine
was probably not a temple, but an open air sanctuary with an altar (cf.
ILS 4907). The inscription which recorded the founding of the cult still
survived in the time of Augustus.[26] The Aventine cult of Diana was
influenced by Greek ideas; the cult image of the goddess was modelled
on that of Ephesian Artemis – or, rather, on the copy of the Ephesian
Artemis that had been set up shortly before in the Ephesion at Massalia.
Representations on coins of the later Republic confirm the sixth-century
date of the statue of Artemis at Massalia and, by implication, of the
Roman copy.[27]

The proliferation of common cults at different sites in Latium does not
at first sight seem compatible with the idea of a united Latin League.
Various attempts have been made to explain this difficulty. One suggestion is that the multiplicity of cult centres was the result of ancient
political conflicts within the league. They would indicate that the leadership of the federation passed in the course of time from one centre to
another, and that each was in turn reduced to a ritual function ('ad sacra')
when a new leader emerged to take its place. Thus the hegemony passed
from Alba to Lavinium, then to Aricia, and finally to Rome.[28]

The majority view, however, is that the several common shrines were
originally the centres of separate religious federations, each comprising a
number of small local communities within a relatively restricted area.
This notion of small local leagues is thought by some to be corroborated
by Pliny's list of *populi Albenses* (see above), which may describe a
federation of small village communities in the immediate vicinity of the
Alban hills.[29] Other local leagues would have existed elsewhere in
Latium, with their centres at Lavinium, Ardea and so on. On this
hypothesis it was only at a later stage, and then perhaps only as a

[25] Castagnoli et al. 1972[I16]; Castagnoli 1977[G373], 460ff; Poucet 1978[B386], 583–601;
1979[B386], 177–90; Dury-Moyaers 1981[E24], 95–162; above, p. 50; 69f.
[26] Dion. Hal. *Ant. Rom.* IV.26.5. The inscription should probably be identified with the *lex arae
Dianae in Aventino* ('statute of the altar of Diana on the Aventine'), which served as the model for all
later sanctuaries of the same kind: *CIL* XII.4333 etc.; Mommsen 1887–8[A91], III.614ff.
[27] The cult statue: Strabo IV.1.5, p. 180c. The coins: *RRC* n. 448.3; cf. Ampolo 1970[G343],
200–10; above, Fig. 30.   [28] Alföldi 1965[I3], 236ff.   [29] E.g. Bernardi 1964[I11], 230ff.

consequence of the development of a politically conscious federation, that some of these sacred associations came to embrace all the Latins.[30]

One difficulty with this reconstruction is that identifying the peoples in Pliny's list is a largely arbitrary exercise. Alternative identifications have been proposed which would spread the names over a much wider area.[31] But the main objection to these attempts to explain the proliferation of common cults in Latium is that they are unnecessary. The difficulty seems in fact to be the result of a misconception – or, rather, of two distinct but related misconceptions. These are, first, that a league or federation could only have a single cult centre (membership being defined by participation in the cult); and secondly that control of a common cult centre implied political hegemony.

These misconceptions are rooted in the sources. For example, the tradition assumes that the location of the Latiar on the Alban Mount was a reflection of the political hegemony once exercised by Alba Longa. A natural consequence of this assumption is that when the Romans under Tullus Hostilius destroyed Alba and overran its territory, they not only took over the supervision of the Latiar but also gained control of a political federation of Latin states. Similarly our sources take it for granted that in instituting a common cult of Diana on the Aventine Servius Tullius was making a bid for political supremacy; when the Latins agreed to take part in the cult, their acquiescence signified that they accepted the hegemony of Rome: 'ea erat confessio caput rerum Romam esse' (Livy 1.45.3). But if the Romans had already obtained the leadership after the defeat of Alba, Servius' initiative would appear to have been superfluous. The two accounts are mutually contradictory, and probably both wrong. Another tradition asserts that Rome's hegemony was established by Tarquinius Superbus. There may well be some truth in this, but the additional statement that it was Superbus who founded the cult of Iuppiter Latiaris (Dion. Hal. *Ant. Rom.* IV.49) cannot be accepted; it must also be a consequence of the procrustean notion that the political and religious associations of the Latins are inseparable.

In fact the evidence seems to point to a variety of different forms of association among the Latins rather than a single 'league' (for which there is no precise equivalent in Latin). The confusion that surrounds this subject arises from the fact that both ancient and modern accounts fail to distinguish properly between different forms of association and communal activity which functioned independently of one another and originated in different ways. In the discussion that follows, sacral, juridical and political aspects of the Latin community will be discussed separately and in turn.

[30] Thus, e.g., Sherwin-White 1973[A123], 15; Catalano 1965[J151], 151ff.
[31] E.g. Werner 1963[A134], 440.

We have already described the religious festivals, celebrated at different sites in Latium, in which some or all of the Latin communities took part. These shared cults should be seen as a relic of the pre-urban period. The common shrines, which were mostly very ancient, were originally the sacred places of a tribally organized Latin nation which later, in the archaic age, came to be divided into politically separate units. The persistence of the common cult celebrations is the clearest sign of the fact that, throughout their history, the Latins were conscious of belonging to an integrated community that transcended the boundaries of the individual city states. They shared a common name (the *nomen Latinum*), a common sentiment, and a common language. They worshipped the same gods and had similar political and social institutions. A shared sense of kinship was expressed in a common myth of origin. The archaeological record shows moreover that a distinctive form of material culture (the so-called 'cultura laziale') was diffused throughout the region of Latium Vetus from the period of the Final Bronze Age onwards.

This sense of cultural unity was never completely submerged by the growth of the city-state, with its exclusive institutions and its distinctive concept of restricted local citizenship. The reason is that the model of the city-state was itself only partially adopted by the Latins during the archaic age. The phenomenon of urbanization occurred in Latium during the 'late orientalizing' period (*c.* 630–580 B.C.), certainly at Rome (p. 36f) and probably at other centres as well, although the process is not so well attested at sites other than Rome. It was accompanied by a radical transformation of political and social institutions, a process that is reflected in the traditional account of the reigns of the last three Roman kings. The emergence of city-states in Latium was not however the result of a spontaneous evolution, but rather the revolutionary transformation of a peripheral native culture brought about by contact with socially more advanced communities in Etruria and Magna Graecia. The result was a unique amalgam in which city-state structures were superimposed upon a substantial residue of pre-urban or 'pre-political' institutions.

This simplified model of the development of the city-state in Latium can help to explain the survival of other communal institutions which appear to be a legacy of the pre-urban period. In particular it can account for the body of social and legal privileges that were shared in common by the Latins and were in historical times defined as specific rights (*iura*). These included *conubium*, the right to contract a legal marriage with a partner from another Latin community; *commercium*, the right to deal with persons from other Latin communities and to make legally binding contracts (especially important was the right to own real property within the territory of another Latin state); and the so-called *ius migrationis*, the capacity to acquire the citizenship of another Latin state simply by taking up permanent residence there.

The origin of these 'Latin rights' is much disputed. It is unlikely that they were the product of formal diplomatic agreements, although this view has recently been restated.[32] It is more probable that such institutions as intermarriage and free exchange were characteristic of a society 'where the concept of the state, with its attendant concept of the fixed domicile, is not strongly developed'.[33] This is not to say that Latium was not yet urbanized in the sixth and fifth centuries B.C., but rather that only a very imperfect model of the city-state had been adopted there. In its classical Greek form the polis was a closed society which admitted outsiders to citizen rights only in the most exceptional circumstances. In particular the right to contract a legal marriage and the right to own land within the territory of the polis were rigidly confined to persons of citizen birth. The contrast with Rome could not be more striking; but it is precisely its divergences from the ideal type of the polis that make Rome such a distinctive political community.

On the other hand it is probably wrong to seek the origin of the 'Latin rights' in the tribal inheritance of the *nomen Latinum*. Rather the rights of *conubium*, *commercium* and *migratio* seem to recall the phenomenon of horizontal social mobility that characterized Central Italy in the archaic period (cf. above pp. 81; 261). Two features of this horizontal mobility need to be stressed here. First it was not confined to any particular ethnic group, but seems rather to have led to the integration of Etruscans, Latins, Sabines and others within individual communities. Secondly it was principally an aristocratic phenomenon. In the orientalizing period (*c.* 730–580 B.C.) Central Italy was dominated by aristocratic clans, whose members led a luxurious way of life and maintained close contacts with one another through intermarriage and the exchange of gifts.[34]

The horizontal mobility that prevailed at this time was however matched by a contrasting vertical immobility. That is to say, the aristocracies maintained close links with one another, but held themselves aloof from the lower classes in their own communities. This state of affairs still persisted in the fifth century; in Rome we find that the patricians were willing to admit to their own ranks an aristocratic clan leader, the Sabine Attius Clausus, and to provide land for him and his dependants (Livy 11.16.4–5), but rigidly excluded fellow citizens who did not belong to the patriciate. The most extreme example of this policy was their attempt to introduce a ban on intermarriage between the orders (*c.* 450 B.C.), even though they were at the same time willing to practise intermarriage with aristocracies of other communities.[35]

It can be said, therefore, that the 'Latin rights' were an institution-

---

[32] Humbert 1978[J184], 81–4.   [33] Sherwin-White 1973[A123], 14–15.
[34] Cf. Cristofani 1975[J32], 132–52.
[35] Cf. De Visscher 1952[G569], 411–22 (= 1966, 157–67).

alized version of the horizontal mobility that characterized the society of
Central Italy in the pre-urban period. Formal interstate agreements such
as the *foedus Cassianum*, so far from conceding these rights for the first
time, probably curtailed them, by restricting their exercise to the communities that signed the treaty. Thus it came about that the mutual rights
and privileges which Dionysius of Halicarnassus describes as 'isopolity'
(see below p. 275) were confined to Latium, which became a kind of
closed jural community. This reconstruction would explain the provision of the Twelve Tables, that a Roman citizen enslaved for debt could
only be sold 'trans Tiberim peregre' ('in foreign territory across the
Tiber');[36] in other words, the rule that no Roman could become a slave at
Rome in fact applied throughout the territory of the Latin community;
enslavements therefore had to take place 'across the Tiber', where the
ager Romanus bordered on Etruscan territory.

We may now turn to the political and military league of Latin states
which we know existed at the end of the sixth century. There are several
reasons for thinking that this Latin League was an artificial phenomenon
that came into being at a relatively late stage and is to be firmly
distinguished from the religious associations and the community of
private rights that we have just been discussing. The principal reason is
the consistent and unequivocal view of our sources that Rome was never
a member of the Latin League. In fact the traditional account maintains
that the League was a political coalition of Latin states formed in
opposition to Rome. Its meetings took place outside Roman territory at
the Grove of Ferentina (Lucus Ferentinae or, more properly, *lucus ad
caput aquae Ferentinae*; it was probably in the territory of Aricia), and its
purpose was to organize resistance to the growth of Roman power.

Our sources refer to this league as a going concern early in the regal
period. For example, Dionysius of Halicarnassus describes a war between the Rome of Tullus Hostilius and an organized coalition of Latin
states meeting at Ferentinum (*sic*) (Dion. Hal. *Ant. Rom.* III.34.3).
Dionysius' report is probably unhistorical, but it may be an anachronistic
reflection of a situation that actually existed in the later part of the sixth
century. In the time of Tarquinius Superbus we hear of another meeting
at Ferentina, at which a certain Turnus Herdonius of Aricia attempted to
stir up the Latins against Rome (Livy 1.50; Dion. Hal. *Ant. Rom.* IV.45).
Turnus was however outwitted by Tarquin, who had him killed and then
persuaded the Latins to accept an agreement in which they formally
acknowledged the supremacy of Rome. The treaty entailed joint military
co-operation, with Rome and the Latin League each contributing an

---

[36] Twelve Tables III.5 *ap*. Gell. *NA* 20.1.46–7: 'tertiis autem nundinis capite poenas dabant aut
trans Tiberim peregre venum ibant' ('but on the third market day they suffered a capital penalty or
were sold in alien territory across the Tiber').

equal number of troops to the allied army, but with the Romans taking command (Livy 1.52.6).

The details of this traditional account are certainly dubious, and some scholars have suggested that all of it should be rejected as fiction. But there is some reason to think that it may have a historical basis. In particular we may note that it is entirely consistent with the situation presupposed in the Carthage treaty (above pp. 85; 253f). It is a reasonable hypothesis that the Latin states which met at Ferentina and which made the agreement with Tarquin are to be identified with the 'subjects' (ὑπήκοοι) of Rome mentioned in the treaty. The Greek term would be a perfectly acceptable way of referring to 'subject allies'. The treaty admittedly distinguishes between the 'subjects' and 'those Latins who are not subjects', but that does not rule out the interpretation being offered here, since there is no reason to assume that all Latin cities other than Rome belonged to the organization centred at Ferentina. In any case the treaty does not appear to provide evidence of a well-defined category of 'non-subjects', but rather to be covering all possible contingencies by referring to 'non-subjects, if any'.[37]

The fact that the Carthage treaty specifies by name only five of the subject cities (all of them on the coast) need not rule out the identification of the subjects with the members of the league of Ferentina. It would after all have been reasonable to expect that any possible Carthaginian attack would come from the sea; the draftsmen of the treaty were therefore content to mention only the coastal cities by name, and to subsume the inland cities under the general heading of 'others who are subject to the Romans'.

When the Latins broke away from Rome after the overthrow of the Tarquins and the occupation of the city by Porsenna, their resistance was once again organized from Ferentina, this time under the leadership of Tusculum and Aricia. This phase of Latin history is documented for us by two important texts that have a better claim than most to preserve authentic information about the period. The first is Dionysius' account of the life and deeds of Aristodemus, which has already been referred to (above, p. 258); the second is a fragment of the Elder Cato's *Origines*, which records a joint dedication of a grove of Diana at Aricia by a group of Latin peoples. The text, which was probably transcribed by Cato from the original dedicatory inscription, reads as follows:

---

[37] ἐὰν δέ τινες μὴ ὦσιν ὑπήκοοι: Polybius III.22.12. A less satisfactory alternative is that the subjects mentioned in the treaty are to be identified with those Latin communities with which Rome had concluded individual treaties, on the model of the *foedus Gabinum*, whether or not they were members of the league. On this view the non-subjects would be the members of the league of Ferentina which did not have separate agreements with Rome (p. 524; cf. e.g. Sherwin-White 1973[A123], 17ff). On balance this reconstruction seems unnecessary and contrived; moreover all the indications are that the status of Gabii was unique (see e.g. Varro, *Ling.* v.33).

Egerius Baebius of Tusculum, the Latin dictator, dedicated the grove of Diana in the wood at Aricia. The following peoples took part jointly: Tusculum, Aricia, Lanuvium, Laurentum (i.e. Lavinium), Cora, Tibur, Pometia, Rutulian Ardea . . .

(Cato, *Origines*, fr. 58 P)

The quotation as we have it tells us nothing about the date or significance of the event in question, nor is it clear how the passage fitted into Cato's narrative. But the majority of scholars are now agreed that the most suitable context for it would be the period around 500 B.C., when the Latins were co-ordinating their efforts against Rome.

The grove of Diana mentioned by Cato is not to be identified with the Lucus Ferentinae, although both were situated in the territory of Aricia. The Dianium has been located below the north-east edge of the crater of Lake Nemi; parts of the historic sanctuary were excavated in 1888 and in the 1920s.[38] The grove of Ferentina, on the other hand, was situated near the course of the later Via Appia, and is probably to be identified with the Laghetto di Turno (Lacus Turni) near Castel Savelli, about two km. west of Albano.[39] It follows that the fragment of Cato does not itself record the formation of the anti-Roman alliance, but rather a parallel religious event.

It is probable that the cult foundation recorded by Cato represents an attempt by the Latins to isolate Rome and to set up a new 'federal' cult of Diana which would rival – and perhaps supplant – the shrine on the Aventine at Rome. It is not really a serious objection to this view that some sources seem to regard the Arician cult of Diana as older than the 'Servian' cult at Rome (e.g. Stat. *Silv.* III.1.59ff). The Diana cult at Aricia was indeed very ancient, and displays a number of primitive features, most notably the institution of the *rex nemorensis*, the runaway slave who obtained his priesthood by killing the former incumbent, and held on to it for as long as he could defend himself against aspiring successors. Such features must go back a long way before the sixth century. But the difficulty can easily be overcome by assuming that the document quoted by Cato did not record the initial foundation of the cult of Diana at Nemi, but rather an attempt to give it a new role as a religious centre for the Latin League.

The list of peoples given in the fragment is probably not complete, since the grammarian who preserves it for us, Priscian, was only interested in the form of the name 'Ardeatis'; it seems that, in conformity with his usual practice, Priscian cited only enough of the text to convey its sense, and did not bother to list any names after 'Ardeatis Rutulus'. It

38 Morpurgo 1903[B364], 297–368; 1931[B365], 237–305.
39 See Ampolo 1981[I5], 219–33.

follows that we cannot use the Cato fragment to reconstruct in full the membership of the Latin League at the end of the sixth century B.C. An alternative list given by Dionysius of Halicarnassus (*Ant. Rom.* v.61.3) is suspect for a number of reasons – it is probably based on erudite conjecture rather than on genuine records – and cannot safely be used to supplement Cato.

Cato's evidence does however confirm the leading part taken by Tusculum, the city which heads the list and whose representative, Egerius Baebius, performed the dedication as 'dictator Latinus'. This apparently official title is another important element of the text. It can be argued that the Latin dictator was the chief official of the Latin League, and that it was as dictator that Octavus Mamilius commanded the confederate Latin forces at Lake Regillus. It has been suggested however that Cato may have written 'dicator' rather than 'dictator';[40] but it is not clear how much of a difference this would make, since 'dicator' does not necessarily signify a purely religious official, any more than 'dictator' necessarily indicates a secular magistrate. It seems that Egerius Baebius could have been either the chief magistrate of the Latin League or a functionary appointed for the specific purpose of dedicating the grove. Both interpretations are equally possible, but the rest of the evidence, such as it is, seems to favour the view that the Latin League was commanded by a dictator.

IV. ROME AND HER ALLIES IN THE FIFTH CENTURY

Such, then, was the federation which was defeated at Lake Regillus and with which the Romans concluded the Cassian treaty in 493 B.C. The historicity of the treaty is not in doubt. Sp. Cassius, whose name was mentioned in the text, was a historical figure who appears three times in the consular *fasti* of the period. The terms of the treaty were inscribed on a bronze pillar which was set up in the Forum and was still there in the time of Cicero (*Balb.* 53; cf. Livy II.33.9). In Dionysius of Halicarnassus we find what purports to be an account of the contents of the treaty (*Ant. Rom.* VI.95). Dionysius' version is not inherently improbable, and has every right to be regarded as authentic. Why should Dionysius, or his source, have fabricated the contents of a treaty if the actual text was publicly available?

The treaty summarized by Dionysius was a bilateral agreement between the Romans on the one side and the Latins on the other. This fact is the strongest single argument for saying that Rome was not at that time,

[40] Rudolph 1935[J211], 12. Cf. Sherwin-White 1973[A123], 13.

and perhaps never had been, a member of the Latin League. The treaty lays down perpetual peace between the two parties, and a defensive military alliance by which each will go to the aid of the other if it is attacked. Each agrees not to assist or give free passage to enemies of the other. The spoils of any successful campaign are to be shared equally. Finally, provision is made for the settlement of commercial disputes between the citizens of different states.

It should be emphasized that Dionysius of Halicarnassus gives only a brief summary of what must have been a longer document. Elsewhere he states that the treaty established a relationship of 'isopolity' between Rome and the Latins (*Ant. Rom.* vi.63.4; vii.53.5 etc.), no doubt a reference to the 'Latin rights' that were discussed in the previous section, although Dionysius gives no further details. Two brief quotations in Festus (166 L) may have been taken from the *foedus Cassianum*, but if so they belong to a clause not mentioned by Dionysius.

One matter which Dionysius does not refer to, but which was obviously of great importance, is the question of the organization and command of the allied army. Some information on this point is, however, given in a fragment of the antiquarian L. Cincius, quoted by Festus (s.v. *praetor*, 276 L). Cincius tells us that, down to the consulship of P. Decius Mus (340 B.C.), the Latins used to meet at the Grove of Ferentina to discuss arrangements concerning the command. He goes on to describe a curious procedure that was put in hand 'in a year when it was the responsibility of the Romans to supply a commander for the army by order of the Latin name'.[41]

The meaning of this passage is unfortunately ambiguous. The phrase 'quo anno' ('in a year when') appears to imply that there were years when the allied supreme commander was *not* summoned from Rome, and consequently that the command was exercised in turn by the Romans and the Latins in alternate years.[42] But this interpretation is open to the objection that there is no hint in the sources of any such system ever having been put into practice. In the surviving accounts of the fifth and fourth centuries B.C. there is no reference to a joint army of Romans and Latins being commanded by anyone other than a Roman. The passage should therefore be taken to mean that there was a regular annual meeting of the Latins at Ferentina, but not necessarily a regular annual

---

[41] 'Itaque quo anno Romanos imperatores ad exercitum mittere oporteret iussu nominis Latini, conplures nostros in Capitolio a sole oriente auspicis operam dare solitos . . . etc.'

[42] Thus e.g. Schwegler 1853–8[A117], II.346f, and many others after him. The view of Rosenberg (1919[I59], 147ff; cf. Alföldi 1965[I3], 119f, et al.), that there was a system of rotation by which all Latin cities, *including Rome*, took turns to hold the supreme command, must be ruled out as incompatible with the text of the *foedus Cassianum*, and on grounds of general improbability.

campaign; so that it was only in years when military action was contemplated that a commander would be needed – a commander who was invariably summoned from Rome.[43]

In the years after the *foedus Cassianum* we can observe the alliance at work. In the first half of the fifth century Rome and the Latins faced enemies on all sides, and were seemingly engaged in continuous warfare. The wars themselves will be examined in more detail in the next section: here we need only note that the alliance made effective resistance possible and saved Latium from being overrun. It has indeed been suggested that it was the pressure of hostile forces on the borders of Latium that brought Rome and the Latin League together in the first place, and gave rise to the *foedus Cassianum*.[44]

An important development occurred in 486 B.C., when the Hernici were brought into the alliance. The Hernici were an Italic people, related (it seems) to the Sabines,[45] who inhabited the strategically vital region of the Trerus (Sacco) valley. In the absence of any archaeological or epigraphic material the Hernici are now little more than a name to us. The only relics are some impressive remains of polygonal walls, dating from the pre-Roman period, which can still be seen at the chief Hernican centres: Anagnia, Verulae, Ferentinum and (especially) Aletrium. But we do not know whether these places were fully developed urban settlements in the fifth century. More probably they were fortified places of refuge. An isolated reference in Livy (IX.42) suggests that the Hernici were organized in a league centred at Anagnia.

The alliance with the Hernici was attributed, once again, to Spurius Cassius, who was consul for a third time in 486 B.C. The Hernici are said to have been admitted on terms identical to those of the earlier Cassian treaty (Dion. Hal. *Ant. Rom.* VIII.69.2). It is not clear, however, whether the result was a tripartite alliance involving the Latins, or whether it was a separate pact between the Romans and the Hernici. The sources contain no hint of an agreement between the Hernici and the Latins, who in later times operated independently of one another in their dealings with Rome. It is certainly tempting to argue that Rome's characteristic policy of making separate bilateral alliances originated at this time. In any event it seems likely that, as the alliance widened, Rome increasingly became the focus of its activities; by co-ordinating the efforts of two disparate sets of allies she inevitably came to control them both. The addition of

[43] Mommsen 1887–8[A91], III.619 n. 2. Mommsen proposed to emend the text to read *quando* in place of *quo anno*.   [44] De Sanctis 1907–64[A37], II.97.
[45] Ancient scholars believed that their name derived from the Sabine or Marsic word 'herna' = 'rock' (Schol. Veron. & Serv. *Aen.* VII.684; Festus 89 L). Cf. Devoto 1968[J39], III.

the Hernici to the alliance therefore had the paradoxical effect of weakening the position of the allies and strengthening that of Rome.

We have no reliable information on how the military alliance was organized in practice. All we can say is that the Latins and Hernici fought in separate contingents under a unified (Roman) command. But we have no idea what proportion of the total allied force was contributed by each of the three partners. Our sources are undecided on this question, sometimes asserting that each contributed an equal number of troops (thus e.g. Livy III.22.4), and sometimes that the allies (Latins and Hernici together) contributed half the army, the Romans the other half (e.g. Dion. Hal. *Ant. Rom.* IX.13.1; 16.3–4; XI.23.2). In fact it is doubtful if either view was based on any genuine record of what really happened.

The same uncertainty naturally surrounds the question of the division of the spoils. Here again the sources sometimes state that the spoils were divided into three equal portions, but on other occasions they imply only that the Romans generously 'conceded' some of the loot to the allies. An equitable division of the spoils as laid down in the treaties would presumably have entailed a distribution to the various contingents in proportion to their size. In any event we can be certain that the division of the spoils was a matter of great importance. It is not only mentioned explicitly in the *foedus Cassianum*; it is also frequently referred to in the course of the traditional narrative (on this point see further below, p. 293).

Booty consisted of movable goods, livestock, slaves and land. In the nature of things, the distribution of land acquired by conquest presented a special problem, particularly where the Latins were concerned, since the Latin League did not constitute a unitary state, but rather a coalition of states. Probably the same was true of the Hernici. To divide a single tract of land into separate allotments belonging to different sovereign states would have been unthinkable from an administrative point of view as well as legally absurd. The problem was overcome by the institution of the colony. By this simple device conquered land was allotted to colonists who were organized into a new political community. The new community became an independent sovereign state with its own citizenship and its own territory.

The sources record the foundation of many such colonies during the fifth and fourth centuries (see Table 5, below). The majority of them were on the borders of Latium, or indeed at sites that had formerly been Latin and were now reconquered from the Volsci and Aequi. In most cases the territories of the colonies did not border on *ager Romanus*. It was therefore logical for the new settlements to become members of the Latin League. As such they were obliged to send contingents to the allied army along with the other Latins, but they also possessed full Latin rights. Consequently they were known as 'Latin colonies' (*coloniae Latinae*). An exception to this pattern was Ferentinum (not to be confused with the Grove of Ferentina, above p. 271), which was conquered (or reconquered) from the Volsci in 413 B.C. (Livy IV.51.7–8). Since Ferentinum was in Hernican territory, it was attached to the Hernican federation, rather than to the Latin League. The same principle probably applies to Veii and other places such as Labici which were directly incorporated into the Roman state (see below p. 281).

It is true that Livy often refers to the new foundations as 'Roman' colonies rather than 'Latin' ones; he takes it for granted that they were founded by the Roman state, and he seems to imply that in normal circumstances the colonists all came from Rome. But since Livy speaks in exactly the same way about the Latin colonies that were founded in the third and second centuries B.C., there is no reason to doubt that these early colonies were *coloniae Latinae* of the normal kind.

It is important however to point out that the appellation 'Latin colony' refers solely to the legal status of the newly founded community, and has nothing to do with either the ethnic origin of the settlers or the manner in which it was founded. In any Roman colonial enterprise the largest single group of settlers would normally have been drawn from Rome. Beloch cannot have been far wrong in asserting that normally at least 50 per cent of the colonists would be Romans.[46] The rest would be taken from the allies, either Latins or Hernicans or both. The Romans continued to allow their Italian allies to share in colonial schemes right down to the time of the Social War (91 B.C.). In this way they fulfilled their treaty obligations in the matter of sharing the spoils of conquest. But it is typical of the Rome-centred outlook of the sources that they rarely record the fact of allied participation, and tend to refer to these shared enterprises as if they were exclusively Roman. In fact, although the Roman colonists would invariably be the largest single group of settlers, they might still constitute a minority of the total population, since many of the early colonies were established at existing towns, whose surviving inhabitants were then enrolled in the colony. This is actually recorded as happening at Antium in 467 B.C., where native Volscians were included together with Romans, Latins and Hernici (Livy III.1.7; Dion. Hal. *Ant. Rom.* IX.59.2). It is noteworthy that the sources misunderstand this story, and attempt to explain the presence of allies and native Antiates by suggesting that an insufficient number of Romans volunteered to join the colony

---

[46] Beloch 1880[J137], 152.

(incidentally this misunderstanding is a strong argument in favour of the authenticity of the event).

The inclusion of the existing inhabitants is not in fact particularly surprising. The alternative would have been to expel, massacre or enslave them en masse, and it is doubtful whether the Romans and their allies could have afforded the wastage of manpower that such a course would entail, whatever they might have felt like doing. The fact that some colonies are said to have rebelled against Rome can be the more easily accounted for if we assume that Roman colonists formed only a minority of the resulting population. Antium is a case in point: within three years of the founding of the colony it had become disaffected (Livy III.4), and openly rebelled in 459 (Dion. Hal. *Ant. Rom.* x.21.4–8).

On the question of how a colony came to be founded, the sources tell us that the Roman state was responsible for the entire exercise. In recent years, however, it has become fashionable for scholars to reject this tradition and to argue instead that the colonies were founded by the Latin League.[47] This line of argument seems to the present writer to be at best unhelpful and at worst simply mistaken. The strict constitutional position must have been that all matters regarding the distribution of conquered land had to be decided jointly by Rome and the allies in consultation. But to say that a colony was founded by Rome is probably only a technical error. It is most likely that in practice the decisions were taken by the Romans, and that the consultation of the allies was a formality. Roman officials were probably always responsible for the practical tasks of founding the colonies and distributing land. This conclusion proceeds both from the analogy of the military command and from the fact that in every case the largest single group of colonists were Romans. In any event the extreme idea that the Romans took little or no part in decisions regarding the early colonies is surely inadmissible. As it happens, on more than one occasion Livy gives us the names of the commissioners who supervised colonial enterprises – and they are always Romans. For example the 'triumvirs' who led the colony to Ardea in 442 B.C. were Agrippa Menenius Lanatus, T. Cloelius Siculus, and M. Aebutius Helva, all prominent members of the senate (Livy IV.11.5–7). As R. M. Ogilvie sardonically remarked, 'we are not compelled to disbelieve either the notice or the names'.[48]

The record of colonization during the fifth and early fourth centuries can be tabulated as follows:

[47] Following Rosenberg 1919[I59], 161ff, and Salmon 1953[I62], 93ff; 123ff. *Contra* Gelzer 1924[I30], 958–9.   [48] Ogilvie 1965[B129], 549 ad loc.

Table 5. *Early Roman/*
Latin colonies with
attributed or probable dates

Fidenae	Romulus
Signia	Tarquinius Superbus
Circeii	Tarquinius Superbus
Cora	Tarquinius Superbus
Pometia	Tarquinius Superbus
Fidenae*	498 B.C.
Signia*	495
Velitrae	494 (reinforced 492)
Norba	492
Antium	467
Ardea	442
Labici	418
Velitrae*	401
Vitellia	395
Circeii*	393
Satricum	385
Setia	383
Sutrium	383
Nepet	383

(* = second recorded foundation)

One point arising from this list calls for brief comment. Under the year 209 B.C. Livy gives a list of all the colonies that had been founded by the Romans until that date (Livy XXVII.9). As usual Livy calls them Roman colonies, although they should strictly speaking be termed Latin colonies (see above). The problem is that Livy's list, which contains thirty colonies in all, includes only seven of the early colonies enumerated above in Table 5, viz. Signia, Norba, Setia, Circeii, Ardea, Sutrium and Nepet. The rest are ignored.

Livy's omission of colonies whose foundation he himself had recorded in his earlier narrative is indeed a difficulty, and has led some scholars to argue that many of the earlier notices are false. But the omissions can be more satisfactorily explained on the assumption that the communities in question no longer had the status of colonies in 209 B.C. Some had perhaps ceased to exist altogether (e.g. Fidenae, destroyed in 426 B.C.), while others were incorporated in the Roman state as communities of Roman citizens after the Latin War of 340–338 B.C. (e.g. Velitrae and Antium).

It is possible however that some of the earlier colonial settlements never became Latin colonies. For example, if the conquered land bordered on the *ager Romanus*, it may have been simply annexed and assigned *viritim* (i.e. in individual allotments) to Roman citizens who were not formed into a new community but remained citizens and were directly administered from Rome. This procedure was adopted when Veii was conquered in 396 B.C., and it may have happened earlier, for example at Labici in 418, when Livy simply tells us that 1500 colonists were sent out 'from the city' (Livy IV.47.6–7). It is possible, indeed likely, that in these cases some of the land was assigned to allies in accordance with the treaties. If so, they will automatically have become Roman citizens on taking up residence within Roman territory. In the same way it is probable that Romans and Latins were able to take part in the settlement of Ferentinum when it was recaptured in 413 and handed over to the Hernici. It seems that the treaties gave the Latins and Hernici the right to take part in any programme of colonization that the Romans might undertake, and that this right continued to be exercised. Strangely enough we know about this because of an incident involving Ferentinum; Livy records that some Ferentinates had enrolled as settlers in a Roman citizen colony in 195 B.C., and had thereby obtained Roman citizenship (Livy XXXIV.42.5).

V. THE INCURSIONS OF THE SABINES, AEQUI AND VOLSCI

It has already been explained in an earlier section how the fall of the Roman monarchy was followed by a brief period of confusion and turmoil. But in the years that followed the situation gradually stabilized, and in the 490s a new structure of political relationships seemed to be emerging in Latium. The Romans were able to regain at least a measure of the power they had held under the kings. A number of successful campaigns against the Sabines are recorded in the period 505–500 B.C. (see below, Table 6); they were followed by a Roman advance into the region between the Tiber and the Anio. Fidenae and Crustumerium were taken (and perhaps also Ficulea – although we have no explicit information regarding the history of Ficulea in the fifth century).

These gains are reflected in the creation of new local tribes in 495 B.C. (see above, p. 246). The new tribes must have included the Claudia, in the district where the Claudian *gens* was settled after its arrival in 504 B.C. (above, p. 98), and the Clustumina, the former territory of Crustumerium. At this point Rome's territory to the north-east of the city extended as far as the borders of Nomentum; she also controlled the Via Salaria, which runs along the left bank of the Tiber, almost as far as the Sabine stronghold of Eretum. As a result the area embraced within the *ager Romanus* will have increased to *c.* 949 km.² (cf. above, Fig. 40, p. 246). Further expansion at the expense of the Latins was checked by the *foedus Cassianum* of 493. But that agreement itself represented a consolidation of Rome's position in Latium.

As has been mentioned, the formation of the military alliance between Rome and the Latin League was a response to an external military threat which became apparent during the 490s. The colonies at Velitrae, Signia and Norba probably represent an attempt by the alliance to strengthen the borders of Latium against the threat of hostile invasion.[49] But in spite of these precautions the newly established stability of Latium was violently disrupted at the end of the 490s by incursions of the Volsci and Aequi, who first begin to feature prominently in the traditional narrative at this time.

We have no way of knowing how or when the Volscians succeeded in occupying the southern half of Latium. It is certain, however, that for most of the fifth century they were in control of the Monti Lepini (the hill country to the west of the Sacco valley), most of the Pomptine plain, and the whole of the coastal district from Antium to Tarracina which in the sixth century had been part of the 'empire' of Tarquinius Superbus (cf. above, p. 253). A brief remark in Livy shows that the strongholds of Cora and Pometia were in their hands by 495 B.C. (II.22.2); Antium was occupied before 493 (Livy II.33.4), and was shortly followed by Velitrae, on the southern edge of the Alban massif.

The ethno-linguistic affiliations of the Volscians are problematic. Onomastic evidence and general probability suggest that they were an Osco-Sabellian people who had moved down from the central Appennines before the end of the sixth century. This is to some extent confirmed by the fact that another branch of the Volscians was established at an early date in the region of the middle Liris valley, around Sora, Arpinum and Atina (see e.g. Livy x.1). Linguistic evidence is furnished by the so-called Tabula Veliterna, a four-line bronze inscription from Velitrae, dating from the third century B.C. and written in a language that is usually taken to be Volscian.[50] The language of the inscription has close affinities with Umbrian, and for this reason scholars generally postulate a 'northern' origin for the Volscians, and suppose that they migrated down the Liris valley from beyond the Fucine Lake during the course of the sixth century.[51]

It is in any case most probable that the appearance of the Volscians in

[49] According to the traditional chronology the colonies at Signia (495) and Velitrae (494) were founded before the *foedus Cassianum* (493). But the precise dating of events at this period is so uncertain (cf. above, p. 265 n. 22) that it would be unwise to press the point. On general grounds the most probable reconstruction is that Signia, Velitrae and Norba were Latin colonies founded jointly by Rome and the league in the immediate aftermath of the *foedus Cassianum*.

[50] Vetter 1953[J129], no. 222. It is possible that the Tabula Veliterna was not in fact inscribed at Velitrae in the local dialect, but was brought there as booty from somewhere else at a later period (thus Crawford 1981[J31], 542). In that case all bets are off.   [51] Devoto 1968[J39], 113–14.

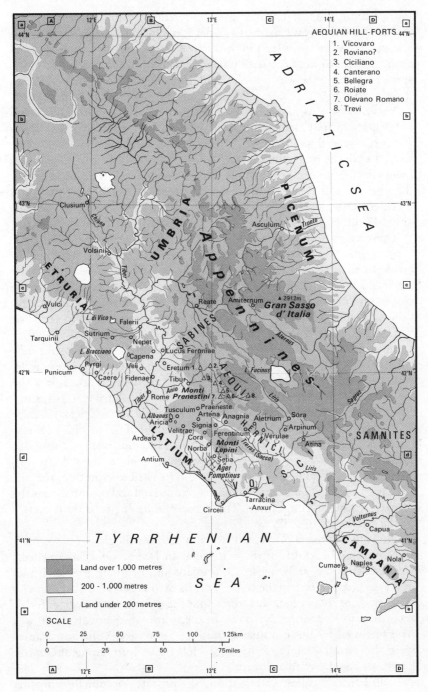

AEQUIAN HILL-FORTS

1. Vicovaro
2. Roviano?
3. Ciciliano
4. Canterano
5. Bellegra
6. Roiate
7. Olevano Romano
8. Trevi

ADRIATIC SEA

PICENUM

UMBRIA

Appennines

ETRURIA

Clusium

Chiana

Volsinii

Asculum

Tronto

Reate
Amiternum
▲ 2912m
Gran Sasso
d' Italia

Tiber

SABINES

Vulci

L. di Vico
Falerii
Sutrium
Nepet
Tarquinii
L. Bracciano
Capena
Lucus Feroniae
Pyrgi
Veii
Eretum 1. △ 2.
Caere
Fidenae
Tibur
Anio
Monti
Prenestini 7. △ 6.
Punicum

AEQUI
△3.
△4.
△5. △8.

L. Fucinus

Liris

Sagrus

Rome
Tusculum
L. Albanus
Aricia
Velitrae
Ardea
Cora
Norba
Antium

Praeneste
Artena
Anagnia
Signia
Ferentinum
Monti
Lepini
Setia
Ager
Pomptinus

Aletrium
Sora
Arpinum

HERNICI
Verulae
Atina

Trerus (Sacco)

Liris

SAMNITES

Circeii
Tarracina
-Anxur

VOLSCI

LATIUM

Volturnus
Capua

CAMPANIA

TYRRHENIAN

SEA

Cumae
Naples
Nola

Land over 1,000 metres

200 - 1,000 metres

Land under 200 metres

SCALE

| 0 | 25 | 50 | 75 | 100 | 125km |

| 0 | 25 | 50 | 75miles |

Map 3 Central Italy in the fifth century B.C.

the southern part of Latium was the result of a migration from the interior, and that it was part of a wider movement of peoples which, we know, affected most of Italy in the fifth century B.C. Our literary sources report a succession of tribal migrations at this time which resulted in the spread of the Sabellian peoples and the diffusion of Osco-Umbrian dialects throughout the central and southern regions of the peninsula.

This process was described in detail by the Elder Cato in his work on the origins of Italy, which unfortunately does not survive in full. But a fragment quoted by Dionysius of Halicarnassus tells us that the process started with the migration of the Sabines from a place near Amiternum (beneath the western slopes of the Gran Sasso) to their later homeland in the hills around Reate; from there they sent out further colonies and founded settlements in the form of 'unwalled cities' (Cato, *Origines*, fr. 50P = Dion. Hal. *Ant. Rom.* 11.49).

These migrations resulted from a series of 'sacred springs'. The sacred spring (*ver sacrum*) was a drastic ceremonial remedy for a famine or similar crisis. In such circumstances all the produce of a given year would be sacrificed to Mars. The animals were slaughtered, but the children were spared and designated *sacrati*. When they reached maturity this genera-tion of young people would be sent out into the world to fend for themselves, under a leader who was obliged to follow a wild animal; they would then settle wherever the animal stopped to rest, and form a new tribe. This myth accounted for the origin of the Picentes, for example, who had followed a woodpecker (*picus*) in their migration down the Tronto valley to Asculum (Ascoli Piceno) and the Adriatic coast; simi-larly the Samnite tribe of the Hirpini had followed a wolf (*hirpus*) in their southward trek from the Sabine hills. The legend of the origins of Rome contains similar elements, since Romulus and Remus were envisaged as leaders of a band of young shepherd warriors living in the wild (p. 58). The myth corresponds to reality at least in its basic assumption, that the pressure of overpopulation in a region of poor natural resources was the primary cause of emigration. The *ver sacrum* itself probably reflects a primitive rite of initiation.

The migrations set off a chain reaction, and the shock waves were felt the length and breadth of the peninsula. In Magna Graecia the effects were catastrophic, as Iapygians, Lucanians and Bruttians pressed down upon the Greek cities on the coast. The disastrous defeat of Tarentum by the Iapygians in 473 B.C. was 'the worst the Greeks have ever suffered' according to Herodotus (VII.170). In the south-west, city after city was overwhelmed by the Lucanians, until by about 400 Velia and Naples were the only remaining centres of Hellenic culture along the entire length of the Tyrrhenian coast.

Inland from Naples, Oscan-speaking Samnites occupied Campania and formed themselves into a new Italic nation (the 'Campani') after taking over the principal cities. This movement seems to have begun as a gradual infiltration of Samnite immigrants rather than as an organized invasion. At Capua the Etruscan inhabitants admitted the newcomers into the citizen community after an initial period of resistance; but this gesture did not prevent the Samnites from overthrowing the Etruscan ruling class in a violent coup one night in 423 B.C. (Livy IV.37.1).

Returning to Latium, we can see that the incursions of the Sabines, Aequi and Volsci in the fifth century were local manifestations of this wider phenomenon, and that they had similar effects on the settlements in the coastal plain. As we have seen, the Volscians occupied the cities of southern Latium probably shortly after 500; in the east the cities of Tibur, Pedum and Praeneste were threatened by the Aequi, a mountain people who inhabited the upper Anio valley and the surrounding hills.

We know nothing about the language and culture of the Aequi, although it is a fair presumption that they too were a Sabellian people speaking an Oscan-type dialect. Once again the archaeological evidence consists solely of remains of polygonal fortifications that can be seen at a number of hilltop sites in the Monti Prenestini (see Map 3). The forts should presumably be equated with the defensive positions (*oppida*) which are referred to in the literary sources (e.g. Livy II.48.4; x.45; Diod. xx.101). It was from these mountain fastnesses that the Aequi made their frequent raids into the Latin plain.

There are good grounds for thinking that Tibur, Pedum and Praeneste were overrun by the Aequi at the start of the fifth century. Tibur had taken part in the foundation of the grove of Diana at Aricia (see above, p. 273), but then vanishes from the record until the fourth century. Praeneste is said to have defected from the Latin League to Rome in 499 B.C. (Livy II.19.2) – not an impossible occurrence, given that one of the consuls of 499, C. Veturius, belonged to a clan that had long-standing connexions with Praeneste[52] – but that is the last we hear of Praeneste for the rest of the century. Pedum is likewise missing from the traditional account of the fifth century, apart from a brief appearance in the saga of Coriolanus (see below).

The best explanation of these silences is that Tibur, Praeneste and Pedum had been taken over by the Aequi. This possibility becomes a virtual certainty when we take account of the fact that in the wars against the Aequi the principal scene of action was the Algidus pass and the

---

[52] The connexion is established by the inscription 'vetusia' (i.e. Veturia) on a silver cup found in the Tomba Bernardini (early seventh century B.C.; see *Civiltà del Lazio Primitivo* 1976[B306], 374). Veturia could have been a Roman lady who married a prince of Praeneste; alternatively one could suppose that the Veturii had migrated to Rome from Praeneste. Thus Torelli 1967[B265], 38ff and 1981[J122], 135–6.

region around Tusculum, which is presented as the most vulnerable of the Latin cities. This state of affairs would not make sense if the Latins still controlled Praeneste.

The chief victims of the Volscian and Aequian attacks were therefore the outlying Latin cities, which protected Roman territory from the worst effects of enemy action. But in the case of the Sabine incursions it was Rome that was directly affected. Wars between the Romans and the Sabines had been going on for centuries. After all, the first event of Roman history, after the death of Remus, was the rape of the Sabine women and the consequent war between the husbands and their fathers-in-law. This legend expresses in the most dramatic form the deeply rooted belief of the Romans that they were a mixture of Latins and Sabines. The fact that two later kings, Numa Pompilius and Ancus Marcius, were Sabines was a further reminder to the Romans that relations with the Sabines had been characterized by peaceful infiltration as well as by armed hostility. Many of the noblest Roman families, including the Valerii and the Postumii, claimed a Sabine origin, and the undoubtedly historical story of the migration of the Claudii in 504 B.C. is evidence that the process of integration was still going on in the republican period. Sporadic warfare between the Romans and the Sabines also continued down to the middle of the fifth century.

How the story of Appius Herdonius fits into the general pattern is not clear. In 460 B.C. Herdonius, a Sabine nobleman, attempted to take over Rome by seizing the Capitol with a band of 4000 companions. After a few days the Romans, with the aid of a force from Tusculum, managed to dislodge Herdonius, who was killed along with most of his Sabine followers. The episode, which is certainly genuine, has no parallel in the tradition. It could perhaps represent a putsch by a group of under-privileged immigrants (they are presented as clients in Dionysius of Halicarnassus *Ant. Rom.* x.14–17, and as slaves and exiles in Livy III. 15–18); it may be that Herdonius and his band of conspirators failed where the Samnites at Capua later succeeded. But there can be no certainty about the incident, which remains a mystery.[53]

The wars against the mountain tribes in the early part of the fifth century had a disastrous effect on the economic and cultural life of Rome and the Latins. This point is not simply an *a priori* inference from the fact that half of Latium fell into enemy hands; it is also confirmed by clear evidence of an economic recession in Rome in the fifth century. As we have seen (above, pp. 75f; 250f), the archaeological evidence shows that Rome was a prosperous and rapidly expanding community in the sixth century. The fifth century, by contrast, is a dark age. At the time of

[53] See Capozza 1966[G28], 37ff.

writing (1983), it is still true to say that the period after *c.* 475 has yielded virtually no distinctive archaeological material from Rome, with the exception of a few stone sarcophagi and some modest quantities of imported fine pottery.[54] In fact the import of Attic pottery fell off dramatically in the fifth century as compared with the sixth; a recent study has demonstrated that although a general reduction in the level of Attic imports can be observed in the Etruscan cities too, the decline was much more drastic in Rome than in Etruria.[55]

This archaeological argument, which is admittedly an argument from silence, can be supported by other evidence. For example, our sources record the dedication of several major temples in the first years of the Republic. Apart from the great temple of Capitoline Iuppiter (509 B.C.), they include those of Saturn (497), Mercury (495), Ceres (493), and Castor (484). But after 484 the tradition, which is normally meticulous in registering details of this kind, has no further record of any temple dedications until that of Apollo in 433. We are given no explanation of this pattern in the sources, but it is a reasonable conjecture that temple construction was normally financed by booty (as the tradition makes clear in the case of the Capitoline temple), and that no temple constructions took place after the 490s because the Romans were no longer engaged in successful and lucrative warfare.

Taken together with the archaeological evidence (or lack of it), the record of temple foundations appears to support the idea of an economic decline. On that assumption it would be reasonable to regard the political and social upheavals, famines and epidemics, which are such a marked feature of the Roman Republic's domestic history in the fifth century, as direct or indirect consequences of this recession.

Historians traditionally, and rightly, attribute Rome's difficulties in this period to the military reverses she suffered at the hands of the invading highlanders. The most serious of these setbacks occurred in the years 490–488 B.C., when the Volscians, led by the Roman renegade Cn. Marcius Coriolanus, invaded Latin territory in two devastating annual campaigns. Capturing one city after another, Coriolanus' forces advanced as far as the Fossae Cluiliae on the outskirts of Rome (see above p. 84). In the traditional story, of which Livy gives the most moving – and the least accurate – version (II.36–41), the city was saved only by the entreaties of Coriolanus' wife and mother, who persuaded him to turn back.

The Coriolanus episode was a popular legend, celebrated in poetry and song for centuries afterwards (cf. Dion. Hal. *Ant. Rom.* VIII.62.3). Its historical credentials are naturally suspect, and it has been criticized from

[54] Ryberg 1940[B402], 51ff; cf. Colonna 1977[B312], 131ff.   [55] Meyer 1980[G112], 47ff.

almost every point of view.[56] But in spite of many unmistakable signs of
late literary embellishment (for example the attempt to assimilate Coriolanus to Themistocles), there is no doubt – at least in the mind of the
present writer – that the basic elements belong to a long-established oral
tradition. A notable feature, characteristic of epic tales, is the emphasis
on topographical details, and especially the catalogues of obscure place
names that occur in the narrative of Coriolanus' victorious campaigns. In
his first march he took Tolerium, Bola, Labici, Pedum, Corbio and
Bovillae, and in his second Longula, Satricum, Setia, Pollusca, Corioli
and Mugilla (Dion. Hal. *Ant. Rom.* VIII. 14–36; Livy II.39 conflates the
two campaigns into one). It has been rightly remarked that the narrative
of the famous march reveals vestiges of a 'village system' that had long
since disappeared in the historical period.[57]

Leaving aside the romantic details, we can reasonably accept that the
story reflects a genuine popular memory of a time when the Volscians
overran most of Latium and threatened the very existence of Rome. The
chronology is however very insecure, since none of the leading persons
in the story appears in the consular *fasti*; but the Romans' belief that the
events took place in the early years of the fifth century is probably correct
in general terms.

The Volscian wars continued intermittently throughout the fifth
century. Their raids into Latin territory either alternated, or coincided,
with those of the Aequi. During the period from *c*. 494 to *c*. 455 a Roman
campaign against one or other, or both, of these peoples is recorded
virtually every year; after the middle of the fifth century, the record
becomes more sporadic (see below, p. 293). The spectacular successes of
the Volscians under Coriolanus were never repeated, as far as we know,
although occasionally we hear of armies of Aequi and Volsci advancing
right up to the gates of Rome (e.g. Livy III.66.5 – 446 B.C.).

The most memorable episode of the Aequian wars is the story of L.
Quinctius Cincinnatus, who, during an emergency in 458 B.C., was
summoned from the plough to assume the dictatorship. Within fifteen
days Cincinnatus had assembled an army, marched against the Aequi
(who were besieging a consular army encamped at the Algidus), defeated
them, triumphed, laid down his office, and returned to his ploughing. It
must be admitted, however, that this exemplary story tells us more about
the moralizing ideology of the later Roman elite than it does about the
military history of the fifth century B.C. Even if Cincinnatus was a
historical character (as he probably was), the supposedly crushing victory of 458 B.C. is more than a little suspect, especially as the Aequi came
back the following year, and again in 455.

[56] Most notably by Mommsen 1870[I45], 1–26. But see De Sanctis 1907–64[A37], II.103ff.
[57] Sherwin-White 1973[A123], 8–9.

On the other hand, the story of a major Roman victory over the Aequi and Volsci at the Algidus in 431 B.C. (Livy IV.28–9) has more right to be regarded as historically authentic. This account shares certain features in common with the saga of Coriolanus and the surviving descriptions of the battle of Lake Regillus. These narratives are exceptional in that they are embroidered with a wealth of incidental detail that is qualitatively different from the transparent rhetoric that we find elsewhere. A particular feature of the story of the battle of the Algidus (and of that of Lake Regillus) is the record of the names and exploits of individual combatants on *both* sides. This feature, which gives the battle descriptions an 'epic' character, is not due in the first instance to Livy (although he exploits it to the full), but is rather a sign that the events had been celebrated in popular memory for centuries, and had perhaps formed the subjects of those historical ballads that were wistfully recalled by the Elder Cato.[58]

But such episodes are exceptional. For the most part the literary tradition consists of a vacuous and insipid narrative of annual campaigns of which the most we can say is that they probably took place. The accompanying details that we find in Livy and Dionysius of Halicarnassus are transparently rhetorical exercises and are not taken seriously by anyone. But it is obviously an important question whether the basic structure – the bare record of events, stripped of all rhetorical embellishment – is soundly based and derived from an authentic tradition.

Alleged Roman successes form the most dubious category of material. It seems likely enough that the annalists sometimes took the opportunity to exaggerate minor successes, and to turn indecisive engagements into victories. Under the year 446 B.C. Livy reports a major victory over the Aequi and Volsci, but adds that, as far as he could discover, the victorious consuls did not go on to celebrate a triumph, a fact which he then attempts – unconvincingly – to explain (Livy III.70.14–15). But it is worth noting that as a general rule major Roman victories are comparatively rare in the tradition as we have it. This point can be illustrated by the record of Roman triumphs between the overthrow of the kings and the Gallic Sack (which are listed in Table 6).[59] The list reveals the comparative infrequency of triumphs during this period. In the middle Republic triumphs were held, on average, in two out of every three years,[60] and they were especially common at the time when the first Roman histories were being written – that is, in the late third and early

---

[58] Cato, *Orig.* fr.118P; cf. Cic. *Tusc.* 1.2.3; *Brut.* 75. See Momigliano 1957[B111], 104–14 (= id. *Secondo Contributo* 69–88); above, p. 88f.

[59] Information taken from Degrassi 1947[D7], 535ff.

[60] Harris 1979[A61], 26: 'through most of the middle Republic about one consul in three celebrated a triumph . . .'.

Table 6. *Roman triumphs 509–368 B.C.*

B.C.	Triumphator	Defeated enemy
509	P. Valerius Poplicola	Veii and Tarquinii
505	M. Valerius Volusus	Sabines
505	P. Postumius Tubertus	Sabines
504	P. Valerius Poplicola II	Sabines and Veii
503	P. Postumius Tubertus (*ovatio*)	Sabines
503	Agrippa Menenius Lanatus	Sabines
502	Sp. Cassius Vicellinus	Sabines
499 (or 496)	A. Postumius Albus	Latins
494	M'. Valerius Maximus	Sabines and Medullini
487	T. Siccius Sabinus	Volsci
487	C. Aquillius Tuscus (*ovatio*)	Hernici
486	Sp. Cassius Vicellinus II	Volsci and Hernici
475	P. Valerius Poplicola	Sabines and Veii
474	A. Manlius Vulso (*ovatio*)	Veii
468	T. Quinctius Capitolinus	Volsci Antiates
462	L. Lucretius Tricipitinus	Aequi and Volsci
462	T. Veturius Geminus Cicurinus (*ovatio*)	Aequi and Volsci
459	Q. Fabius Vibulanus	Aequi and Volsci
459	L. Cornelius Maluginensis	Volsci Antiates
458	L. Quinctius Cincinnatus	Aequi
449	L. Valerius Potitus	Aequi
449	M. Horatius Barbatus	Sabines
443	M. Geganius Macerinus	Volsci
437	M. Valerius Maximus	Veii, Falerii and Fidenae
431	A. Postumius Tubertus	Volsci and Aequi
428	A. Cornelius Cossus	Veii
426	Mam. Aemilius Mamercinus	Veii and Fidenae
421	N. Fabius Vibulanus (*ovatio*)	Aequi
410	C. Valerius Potitus Volusus (*ovatio*)	Aequi
396	M. Furius Camillus	Veii
392	L. Valerius Potitus	Aequi
392	M. Manlius Capitolinus (*ovatio*)	Aequi
390	M. Furius Camillus II	Gauls
389	M. Furius Camillus III	Volsci, Aequi and Etruscans
385	A. Cornelius Cossus	Volsci
380	T. Quinctius Cincinnatus Capitolinus	Praenestini

second centuries B.C. By contrast, only twenty-two triumphs (and ovations) are registered for the whole of the fifth century; this must suggest that the record is relatively free from contamination, and that it was not simply a fraudulent projection into the remote past of the conditions of the middle Republic.

Whatever later generations of Romans might have wanted to believe about the heroic achievements of their ancestors, the fact is that they did not succeed in effacing the dismal memory of the fifth century as a period of hardship and adversity. Indeed the sources frequently record Roman defeats (e.g. against the Volsci in 484: Dionysius of Halicarnassus, *Ant. Rom.* VIII.84–6; and 478: Livy II.58–60). It is clear that Livy for one found these defeats embarrassing, and did his best to minimize them. He tried to find mitigating circumstances, and he used diversionary tactics, for example by highlighting individual acts of Roman heroism. An obvious instance of the use of this technique is the story of Sex. Tampanius, a cavalry commander who distinguished himself at the disastrous battle of Verrugo in 423 B.C. (Livy IV.38). The clear inference to be drawn from such passages is that Roman historians, so far from scribbling whatever they pleased, accepted the traditional facts for what they were and tried to make the best of them.

But the most striking feature of the surviving narratives is that most of the annual campaigns are presented neither as victories nor as defeats, but as indecisive and often uneventful raiding expeditions. This seems an unlikely pattern for an annalist to invent; it is much more likely that it represents the true character of actual events.

We should note that the warfare of the fifth century was a very different kind of phenomenon from the organized military activity of the Roman state in the later Republic. The annalists clearly failed to understand the difference, and in describing the wars of the early Republic in terms of later concepts and practices they inevitably distorted the facts. If the wars of the fifth century are conceived as full-scale military operations, then it does indeed become difficult to explain their frequency and regularity over such a long period of time.

Livy, an honest and intelligent man, was himself puzzled by the apparent capacity of the Aequi and Volsci to field armies year after year in spite of continual defeats (VI.12.2). He offered a variety of possible explanations: several different branches of the Aequi and Volsci may have been involved at various times; Central Italy could have been more densely populated in the fifth century; and so on. But the true explanation is surely that what was happening was not warfare as Livy understood it, but rather a much less intensive pattern of raiding and skirmishing. The scale of operations was probably small, pitched battles few and far between, with casualties relatively light.

It is obvious that a political or Clausewitzian model of war cannot easily be imposed on the archaic world of Central Italy in the fifth century. Instead we find an indistinct pattern of annual razzias. Warfare is recorded regularly, but there is no continuity from year to year. One year the Volsci might attack, the next year the Aequi, the next both together – in a seemingly random pattern. On the Roman side, each year's campaign was treated as an entirely self-contained affair. New

consuls would take office, and a new army would be enrolled. Every
spring and autumn special rituals were performed to mark the beginning
and end of the campaigning season. This rhythmic pattern of annual
warmongering was certainly not confined to Rome, but was characteristic of Italic society in general during the archaic age.

The legalistic conception of war as a political phenomenon presupposes the full development of the state. But in the warfare of the fifth
century there was often no clear distinction between the actions of states
and those of private individuals and groups. Much of the recorded
warlike activity of this period involved mysterious bands of warriors
who accompanied individual leaders as clients or 'companions', and
functioned as private armies.[61] Not surprisingly the literary sources do
not properly explain the role of these bands or 'conspiracies', but they
provide ample evidence of their activities, for example the incident of
Appius Herdonius (above, p. 286), the migration of the Claudii (above
p. 281), and the private war of the Fabii against Veii (below p. 297). The
phenomenon is now attested by a contemporary document, the recently
discovered inscription from Satricum, which records a dedication to
Mars by the 'companions' (sodales) of Publius Valerius.[62] These private
'conspiracies' are analogous to the armies of Volscians and Samnites that
were levied by means of leges sacratae. A lex sacrata was an ancient Italic
rite which bound the soldiers to follow their leaders to the death (Livy
IV.26.2; VII.41.4; IX.39.5; X.38.2–12). The milites sacrati recall the bands of
young men sent out in consequence of a ver sacrum. The myth of the ver
sacrum may well reflect a primitive pattern of initiation by which young
men who had reached a certain age were segregated from the rest of the
tribe and sent away to fend for themselves by raiding and pillaging. It is
certainly possible that some of the raiding parties which entered Latium
during the fifth century were in fact semi-autonomous marginal groups
of this kind.

It follows that in Central Italy in the fifth century there was little
difference in practice between warfare and brigandage – a fact acknowledged by Livy, who frequently speaks of periods in which there was
'neither peace nor war' (e.g. Livy II.21.1; 26.1; etc.). At all events the
rationale behind these wars was always the same. They were predatory
raids by highland peoples upon the relatively prosperous and advanced
settlements on the plain. The notion of the 'just war' (p. 384), and the
traditional claim that Rome's wars were fought in retaliation against
external aggressors, probably derived from the experiences of the fifth
century. This interpretation is borne out by the fact that the fetial

---

[61] For this phenomenon in the sixth century cf. p. 97f.
[62] Versnel 1982[B268], 199; above, p. 97.

procedure, the ritual performance by which wars were formally declared, was centred around the *rerum repetitio*, a demand for the return of stolen property; the expression *res repetundae* should certainly be taken in this literal sense, which it still retained in the *leges repetundarum* of the later Republic.[63] The *rerum repetitio* also underlines the crude economic character of fifth-century warfare. The principal objective was always the acquisition of booty. The capture of large quantities of spoils is referred to again and again in the traditional accounts of the campaigns, and the importance of this feature is confirmed by the explicit provisions in the *foedus Cassianum*. The expectation that in the normal course of events booty would be obtained from any successful military effort is a striking feature of ancient treaties,[64] and is a revealing indication of contemporary mental attitudes to warfare.

We may conclude this discussion with two brief quotations from Livy and Dionysius of Halicarnassus. They describe a campaign that supposedly took place in 479 B.C., which is chosen as a typical example. Comment is unnecessary: between them these two passages provide a model of the kind of warfare that was endemic in Central Italy in the fifth century, and which left many traces in later Roman practice. Although later Roman warmongering was far more organized and sophisticated, the idea of war as an annual performance with a crude economic function was never effaced from the Roman mind. It was a crucial element in the development of Roman imperialism. The two passages are as follows:

Caeso was commissioned to deal with the situation in Latium, where raids by the Aequi were causing trouble. He marched thither with a body of troops, and then crossed into Aequian territory to carry out reprisals. The Aequians withdrew inside the defences of their various strongholds (*oppida*), and no action of any note was fought.

(Livy II.48.4)

The consuls, having drawn lots for the armies, took the field, Fabius against the Aequi, who were plundering the fields of the Latins, and Verginius against the Veientines. The Aequi, when they learned that an army was going to come against them, hastily evacuated the enemy's country and returned to their own cities; and after that they permitted their own territory to be ravaged, so that the consul possessed himself at the first blow of large amounts of money, many slaves, and much booty of all sorts.

(Dion. Hal. *Ant. Rom.* IX.14.1–2)

This pattern of raiding and counter-raiding seems to have diminished considerably after the middle of the fifth century. The Sabines disappear from the record after 449 B.C., and attacks by the Aequi and Volsci are reported far less frequently. In the period of thirty-two years between

---

[63] Sherwin-White, *JRS* 72 (1982), 28.   [64] Garlan 1972[G591], 50f = 1975, 76f.

442 and 411 B.C., campaigns against the Volsci are recorded in only three years (431, 423 and 413), and against the Aequi in only four (431, 421, 418 and 414). The most likely explanation is that the Aequi and Volsci gradually developed a more settled mode of existence, rather than that the record is defective in some way. This deduction is based on the fact that the sources continue to report other 'routine' events, such as plagues and grain shortages, during the period in question. They also give full accounts of wars against the Etruscan city of Veii, and it is to these wars that we must now turn.

VI. VEII AND ROME'S OFFENSIVE

Situated on a rocky plateau some 15 km. to the north of Rome, Veii was the nearest of the Etruscan cities to the borders of Latium. Rome and Veii shared a common border along the right bank of the Tiber, and it is hardly surprising that the sources should trace their rivalry back to the very beginning of Roman history. The first war is said to have occurred under Romulus, who captured and colonized Fidenae and gained control of the district known as the Septem Pagi on the right bank, as well as the salt beds to the north of the river mouth. The legend may be based on nothing more than the fact that the Septem Pagi were part of the tribe Romilia; but in any event it is likely that during the regal period Rome gained possession of a strip of territory on the right bank stretching from what is now the Vatican to the coast.

Intermittent wars between Rome and Veii must have occurred under the monarchy, even though we cannot reconstruct them in detail from the unreliable narratives of Livy and Dionysius of Halicarnassus. The evidence for the three major conflicts that occurred during the republican period is however much more secure. The three encounters were well-defined events which we may legitimately call the First, Second and Third Veientine wars. This fact in itself clearly differentiates the struggle between Rome and Veii from the more primitive pattern of organized brigandage that characterized the Aequian and Volscian wars. The difference arises simply from the fact that Veii, like Rome but in contrast to the Aequi and Volsci, was a well developed and centralized city-state.

During the last fifty years our knowledge of the city of Veii and its territory has been greatly increased by archaeological finds, which have resulted partly from excavations and partly from the extensive field survey of South Etruria (including much of the *ager Veientanus*) that was carried out by the British School at Rome in the years between 1950 and 1974.[65] In the present context it will be sufficient merely to give a brief

---

[65] Potter 1979[B385], 1–18.

summary of the main historical conclusions that have emerged from this work.

During the sixth century Veii was a flourishing urban centre. Not much is known about the actual layout of the town, although the evidence of surface finds suggests a fairly open pattern of loosely scattered buildings running the whole length of the plateau from the north-west gate to the sanctuary at Piazza d'Armi (see Fig. 45). There was probably some concentration around the point where the major roads converged, which formed the centre of the later Roman town, but this has yet to be confirmed by excavation. The sanctuary sites at Portonaccio, Campetti and Piazza d'Armi have been more systematically explored, and it is clear that at each of them substantial buildings were erected during the sixth century. The famous acroterial statues from the Portonaccio temple are an indication of the wealth of the city and of its high level of artistic achievement. It is not fanciful to attribute the Portonaccio terracottas to the school of Vulca, the Veientine sculptor who was summoned to Rome by Tarquinius Priscus to make the statues for the Capitoline temple.

Veii controlled an extensive and fertile territory, measuring some 562 km.^{2}.[66] Field surveys have revealed an even and relatively dense pattern of rural settlement in the sixth and fifth centuries, indicating that most of the land was under cultivation or grazing (Fig. 37). Its productive capacity was greatly improved by the elaborate system of drainage tunnels (*cuniculi*) which are common in the *ager Veientanus*, the majority of them probably dating from the fifth century. The territory of Veii was also served by a network of carefully engineered roads which were probably constructed during the seventh and sixth centuries and are in any case of pre-Roman date. The roads facilitated the movement not only of rural produce into the city, but also of objects of long-distance trade on which Veii's prosperity must have been largely based. An important recent study, which has provided much of the information for the above summary, has concluded that 'both roads and drainage schemes quite clearly reflect the control and organization of a major city, setting its *territorium* in order'.[67]

The wars between Rome and Veii in the fifth century were organized conflicts between developed states, confined to three well-defined and relatively brief bouts of fighting, separated by periods of peace guaranteed by treaty (*indutiae*). As befits their character, the wars arose from a complex variety of economic and political causes, and the two sides had long-term objectives that went beyond the mere acquisition of booty – although raiding naturally went on during the course of the fighting (e.g. Livy 11.48.5–6).

[66] Beloch 1926[A12], 620.   [67] Potter 1979[B385], 87.

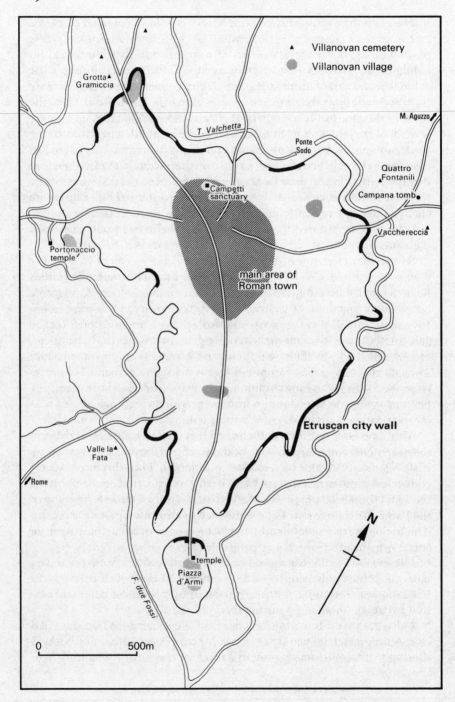

Fig. 45. The Etruscan and Roman town of Veii (Source: Ward Perkins 1961 [B421]).

The economic prosperity of both Rome and Veii depended to a large extent on their control of major natural lines of communication. Traffic passing along the western side of Italy from north to south could go either through Rome or through the territory of Veii, crossing the Tiber at Fidenae or Lucus Feroniae. But the rivalry between the two cities arose from their attempts to control the routes along the Tiber valley from the coast to the interior. It seems that the Veientines could threaten Rome's control of the left bank by holding a bridgehead at Fidenae; while Rome, by occupying the right bank, could cut off the Veientines' access to the coast and the salt beds at the mouth of the river. It is not therefore surprising that in the wars between them the principal objective of the Romans should have been to gain permanent control of Fidenae, which changed hands frequently in the course of the fifth century, while the Veientines concentrated their efforts against the Roman possessions on the right bank.

Of the First Veientine War (483–474 B.C.) the most we can say for certain is that the Veientines had the best of it. The sources record a Roman victory at a pitched battle in 480, the details of which are plausible but possibly imaginary.[68] In any event it did not stop the Veientines from advancing into Roman territory and occupying a fortified post on the Janiculum. It was in an attempt to counter this move that the Fabian clan, accompanied only by their own clients and 'companions', marched out in 479 B.C. to occupy a small frontier post on the river Cremera. Two years later they suffered a catastrophic defeat in which the entire clan, 306 persons in all, was wiped out, with the exception of a single youth who escaped to keep alive the name of the Fabii.

Although later tradition embellished this tale with details taken from the nearly contemporary episode of the 300 Spartans at Thermopylae, its basic historicity cannot be seriously questioned. The story is obviously connected with the fact that the Fabian tribe was situated on the border of the *ager Veientanus*, which was marked by the river Cremera. The war of the Fabii was therefore fought in defence of their own private interests. The incident represents one of the last vestiges of an archaic form of social organization which was probably already in an advanced state of obsolescence. Finally we should note that in the years from 485 to 479 B.C. one of the annual consuls was invariably a Fabius; but after 479 the Fabii disappear from the *fasti* until 467, when the supreme office was held by Q. Fabius Vibulanus, the survivor of the Cremera.

The truce that was made in 474 left the Veientines firmly in possession of Fidenae, which they must already have controlled before the Cremera disaster.[69] Thus Fidenae became the focus of the Second Veientine War

[68] A matter of opinion. I prefer to trust the intuition of De Sanctis 1907–64[A37], II.120.
[69] Cf. De Sanctis 1907–64[A37], II.122.

which broke out in 437 B.C. when four Roman ambassadors were murdered on the orders of Lars Tolumnius, the tyrant of Veii. Another memorable and certainly authentic event of this conflict was the battle in which Aulus Cornelius Cossus killed the Veientine leader Lars Tolumnius in single combat. For this he was awarded the *spolia opima* (p. 168), a distinction which had previously been achieved only by Romulus. The inscribed linen corslet which Cossus dedicated in the temple of Iuppiter Feretrius was – notoriously – still there in the time of Augustus, when it became the object of a political controversy (Livy IV.20.5–11). Shortly afterwards (435) Fidenae was besieged, and captured when Roman soldiers entered the citadel by means of a tunnel.

According to Livy, Fidenae later rebelled again, only to be recaptured and destroyed in 426 (Livy IV.31–5). It is not impossible that Fidenae should have changed sides yet again after 435, and that there really were two wars; but in this instance a strong case can be made for saying that the tradition has mistakenly recorded the same events twice. This is a highly complex and technical problem, which largely turns on the question of whether or not Cornelius Cossus won the *spolia opima* during his consulship (as the Emperor Augustus maintained), in which case the event will have to be dated to 428 B.C., rather than to 437, when Cossus was military tribune. However this matter is resolved, the final outcome was that Rome had established a permanent hold on Fidenae by 426 and was poised to take the offensive.

In the Third Veientine War (traditionally 405–396 B.C.) the Romans took the initiative and launched a full-scale attack on the city of Veii itself. The siege that ensued is said to have lasted for ten years; it ended with the capture of the city by the dictator M. Furius Camillus. The bare facts – the fall of Veii in 396 B.C. and the subsequent incorporation of its territory in the *ager Romanus* – are historically certain and mark the end of an epoch in Italian history. But the traditional details of the war, as recorded by Livy and others, are mostly legendary.

The story of the fall of Veii was elaborated in two distinct ways. First, the idea of a ten-year siege was obviously modelled on the Greek legend of the Trojan War, and traces of a superficial attempt to assimilate the two events are clearly visible in the surviving narratives. Secondly, the whole account is pervaded by an atmosphere of mysticism and religiosity. The story consists of a succession of supernatural happenings. The end of Veii, predicted in its 'Books of Fate' (Livy v.14.4; v.15.11), was the consequence of a religious offence committed by its king (Livy v.1.4–5). The fall of the city was portended by a rise in the level of the Alban lake, a prodigy which the Romans expiated by constructing a drainage tunnel on the orders of the Delphic oracle. This bizarre story must be connected in some way with the tradition that the Romans entered Veii by means of a tunnel, a motif which itself has a bewildering variety of associations (the earlier siege of Fidenae, the *cuniculi* in the countryside around Veii, etc.). Another legend connected with the tunnel is best told by Livy:

There is an old story that, while the king of Veii was offering sacrifice, a priest declared that whoever should remove the victim's entrails would be victorious in the war. The priest's words were overheard by some of the Roman soldiers in the tunnel, who thereupon opened it, snatched the entrails, and carried them to Camillus.

(Livy v.21.8–9; the sober historian goes on to absolve himself of any responsibility for the story.)

Camillus, the Roman commander, is portrayed as an instrument of Fate (*dux fatalis*) carrying out a religious mission. The story ends with the 'evocation' of Iuno Regina, the goddess of Veii, who was persuaded to abandon the city and go over to Rome. Her cult statue was transported – with miraculous ease – to Rome, where it was installed in a temple on the Aventine dedicated by Camillus (Livy v.22.3–6).

The mystical quality of the events is reflected in the language of Livy, whose fifth book is an artfully constructed sermon on the theme of religious obligation.[70] The sanctimoniousness did not however originate with Livy (as the above quotation about the entrails makes clear), but was obviously part of the received tradition. It has been suggested that the whole account was ultimately derived from Etruscan sources, and that its peculiar mysticism was a characteristic of Etruscan historiography.[71] This is theoretically possible but cannot be certain. Etruscan historiography is a subject about which we do not, in fact, know anything.

Some elements of the story turn out on examination to be more soundly based than might have been expected. For example, the consultation of the Delphic oracle is an elaboration of the historical fact that the Romans sent a thank-offering to Delphi after their victory. The offering, a golden bowl, was placed in the treasury of the Massaliots. It was later stolen and melted down by Onomarchus in the Sacred War, but its base remained at Delphi for everyone to see (App. *Ital.* fr. 8.3). The tradition is further confirmed by the story of the Liparan pirate Timasitheus, who escorted the Roman ships to Delphi and was rewarded by the senate with a grant of *hospitium publicum* (p. 313). The memory of this event was preserved by the descendants of Timasitheus, who were honoured by the Romans when the Lipara islands were annexed in 252 B.C. (Livy v.28.3; Diod. XIV.93.3; Plut. *Cam.* 8.8).

The wars between Rome and Veii illustrate an important fact about

---

[70] Ogilvie 1965[B129], 626.
[71] Sordi 1960[J230], 10–16; 177–82; Ogilvie 1965[B129], 628.

Etruscan political history, namely the particularism of the individual
cities. The fact that Veii received no significant support from the other
Etruscan cities evidently ran counter to the expectations of the Roman
annalists. In Livy's account there is an underlying assumption that the
other cities ought to have assisted Veii and would have done so had it not
been for special circumstances, such as the impious behaviour of the
Veientine king at the national games (Livy v.1.3–5). We hear repeatedly
of meetings of the Etruscan 'League' at the Fanum Voltumnae (near
Volsinii) at which the assembled delegates of the 'Twelve Peoples'
refused, for one reason or another, to give aid to Veii (e.g. Livy IV.24.2;
61.2; V.1.7; 17.6–7).

In fact it is highly questionable whether the federation of twelve
peoples that met at the shrine of Voltumna ever functioned as a political
or military league. There is no historically verified instance in the sources
of an action involving an Etruscan federal army, and many scholars have
supposed that the league of Voltumna was a purely religious association.
On the other hand there is abundant evidence of antagonism and warfare
between the Etruscan cities. This state of affairs is now documented by
the *elogia Tarquiniensia*, Latin inscriptions of the first century A.D. which
refer to events of the history of Tarquinii in the fifth (and perhaps also the
fourth) century B.C.[72] The inscriptions refer to hostile interventions by
magistrates of Tarquinii in the affairs of Caere and Arretium, as well as a
war against the Latins (Fig. 46).

During the wars between Rome and Veii Tarquinii seems, if anything,
to have supported Veii (Livy v.16.4). Clusium on the other hand
remained neutral (Livy v.35.4), while Caere favoured the Romans. Any
suggestion that the wars were part of a continuing racial conflict between
Latins and Etruscans (cf. above pp. 259ff) can therefore be ruled out.

This conclusion is definitively confirmed by the fact that the most
consistent and loyal supporters of Veii were the Capenates and Faliscans.
These peoples, who lived in the region to the north of Veii between the
Tiber and the Lakes of Vico and Bracciano, spoke a dialect of Latin and
were ethnically distinct from the Etruscans. But both politically and
geographically Capena and Falerii belonged to the catchment area of
Veii, and they never failed to give her active support in the struggle
against Rome. After the fall of Veii, the Romans quickly reduced them to
submission (in 395 and 394 respectively).

These events all form part of a new phase in the history of Rome's
external relations. In the last years of the fifth century there are clear signs
of a more aggressive policy, not only against Veii and its satellites, but
also in southern Latium. In a series of sparse notices, Livy records the

---

[72] Torelli 1975[B266]. For the date see Cornell 1978[B209], 171–2.

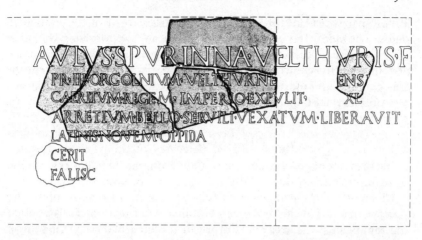

Fig. 46. Fragments of commemorative inscription ('elogium') of Aulus Spurinna of Tarquinii set up in the early imperial period. It records events relating to the expulsion of a king from Caere, a slave war at Arretium and nine strongholds of (?) the Latins (?). Reconstruction (in part conjectural) and supplements after Torelli 1975 [B266], tav. IV.

capture of Bola (415 B.C.), Ferentinum (413), Carventum (410) and Artena (404). These successes were matched by occasional setbacks, but there can be little doubt about the overall success of the thrust, which had the effect of driving the Aequi out of the Algidus region and extending Roman control in the direction of the Sacco valley. In the coastal region Rome defeated the Volscians at Antium in 408, captured Anxur (Tarracina) in 406 and colonized Circeii in 393. The details are confused, but the basic trend is unmistakable.

This change of stance coincides with a reform of the Roman army (the precise details of which remain obscure) and the introduction of pay (*stipendium*) for the troops (Livy IV.59–60; Diod. XIV.16.5). At the same time the sources first begin to refer to the *tributum*, a property tax that was levied in order to meet the cost of military expenditure, and to the imposition of indemnities on defeated communities, starting with Falerii in 394 (Livy V.27.15). These innovations are probably connected with a reform of the centuriate system, and the introduction of graded property classes in place of the old 'Servian' *classis* (above, p. 199f).[73]

Our knowledge of this period is still pitifully inadequate. But through the gloom we can dimly discern the outlines of a decaying archaic society in a state of radical and dynamic transition. The sack of the city by a

[73] Crawford 1976[G42], 204ff. A curious reference in Livy to the 'classis' operating at Fidenae in 426 B.C. (IV.34.6, completely misunderstood by Livy, who thought the fleet was meant!) seems to indicate that the Servian system was still in being at that time. *Contra* Ogilvie 1965[B129], 588–9, ad loc.

raiding party of Gauls in 390 B.C. was an unexpected and momentarily shattering blow, but its long-term effects were negligible. Within a generation or so Rome emerged even stronger than before. The peoples of Central Italy would shortly find that the newly refounded city of Camillus was a far more aggressive and dangerous force than the old city of Romulus.

VII. THE GALLIC DISASTER

In the summer of 390 B.C. a horde of Celts from the Po valley crossed the Appennines into northern Etruria. Advancing southwards down the Val di Chiana they stopped briefly at Clusium, and then pressed on to the Tiber valley and made for Rome. A Roman army was hastily assembled and sent against the invaders, but it was routed at the river Allia on 18 July, which for ever after was marked as an unlucky day. The survivors fled to Veii, leaving Rome at the mercy of the Celts, who entered the defenceless city a few days later and sacked it. Everything is said to have been destroyed, with the exception of the Capitol, where a small garrison held out. The Gauls then departed, either because the Romans paid them to go away, or because they were driven out by a Roman army formed by Camillus from the survivors of the Allia.

These basic elements make up one of the most dramatic episodes in Roman history. That it happened is certain. The Sack was referred to by Greek writers of the fourth century B.C., including the philosopher Aristotle (fr. 568 Rose = Plut. *Cam.* 22.3–4) and the historian Theopompus (Jac. *FGrH* 115 F317 = Pliny, *HN* III.57); it was the first event of Roman history to impress itself on the consciousness of the Greeks. There is almost certainly a sound historical basis for the statement of Polybius (1.6.1) that the Sack occurred in the same year as the Peace of Antalcidas and the siege of Rhegium by Dionysius I of Syracuse – that is, in 387 or 386 B.C. It follows that the traditional 'Varronian' chronology (which is retained here for convenience) was three or four years adrift at this point (see below, Chapter 7, p. 347f).

A historical analysis of the catastrophe entails a consideration of three problems. First, we must look for some explanation of the sudden appearance of the Gauls. What were they doing in the vicinity of Rome in 390 B.C.? Secondly, we must try to identify and account for some of the legends that became attached to the event. Thirdly, we must assess the extent of the disaster, and ask how seriously it damaged the city and disrupted the lives of its inhabitants. Let us deal with these three questions in turn.

First, then, why did the Gauls attack Rome? The Gallic invasion of Italy in 390 B.C. can only be understood against the general background of the movement of Celtic peoples into Northern Italy during the previous centuries. This point was clearly appreciated by Livy, himself a native of Cisalpina, who devoted two important chapters to a discussion of the subject (v.34–5). Livy describes a succession of migrations by different tribes, beginning with the Insubres, who moved into the region around Milan under the leadership of the legendary Bellovesus in around 600 B.C. They were followed, in the course of the next two centuries, by the Cenomani, Libui, Salui, Boii and Lingones. The last group to arrive were the Senones, who by the start of the fourth century B.C. had occupied the strip of land along the Adriatic later known as the *ager Gallicus* (see Map 4).

It was these same Senones, according to Livy, who crossed the Appennines and invaded the peninsula in 390. Their aim, he says, was to find land for settlement. This view is corroborated by other sources which, although less informative, tell much the same story (e.g. Polyb. II.17; Dion. Hal. *Ant. Rom.* XIII.10–11; Plut. *Cam.* 15). All of them are agreed that it was the produce of its land, and especially of its vineyards, that tempted the Gauls to invade Italy. In the traditional story they were enticed by a certain Arruns of Clusium, who was hoping that with their assistance he would be able to take revenge on his wife's lover. In any event Clusium was the Gauls' first destination.[74] Rome became involved when three Roman ambassadors, all sons of M. Fabius Ambustus, fought alongside the men of Clusium in a battle against the Gauls and thus provoked their anger.

There are many difficulties in this account. Livy's description of the Celtic occupation of the Po valley has been much criticized, particularly for its 'long' chronology. But it is in fact compatible with the versions of other sources (which are much less precise on the question of dating). Although there is no definite archaeological evidence of Celtic migrations into Northern Italy before the fifth century and the beginning of the La Tène culture, there is equally nothing that tells against Livy's scheme. The principal difficulty is that it is not clear exactly how Celts are to be recognized archaeologically. For example there are close resemblances between some burials of the so-called Golasecca culture in Lombardy and those of the Hallstatt culture beyond the Alps. These same Golasecca sites during the fifth and fourth centuries contain increasing amounts of La Tène material, but at no stage is there any recognizable break in continuity. The most reasonable assumption is that there was a gradual infiltration of Celtic elements over a period of several centuries. In the Romagna supposedly Celtic cemeteries have been found

---

[74] Some scholars argue that the role played by Clusium in the events of 390 B.C. is unhistorical: Wolski 1956[B193], 37–9; Ogilvie 1965[B129], 699–700.

304

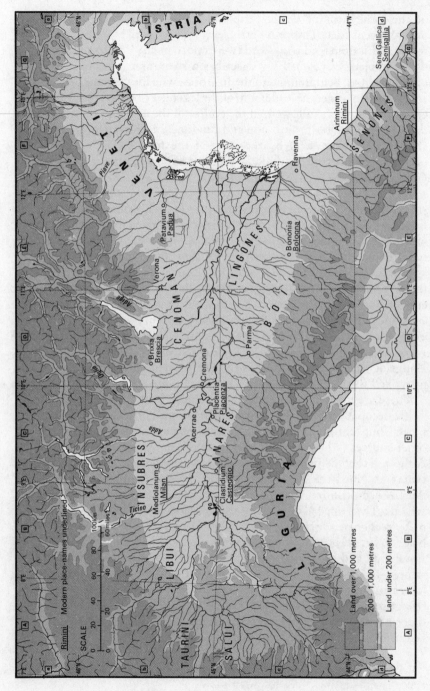

Map 4 The Celts of Northern Italy: fourth and third centuries B.C.

with material dating from the sixth and fifth centuries, for example at Casola Valsenio and S. Martino in Gattara (both near Ravenna). But the 'Celtic' identification of these finds remains uncertain. Generally speaking it is still true that the arrival of the Celts in Northern Italy cannot yet be documented by archaeological means.[75] More explicit evidence is provided by the famous grave stelae of Bologna, showing combats between Etruscan horsemen and naked Celtic warriors, which confirm Livy's account of the insecure position of the Etruscan cities of the Po valley in the years after 400.

Livy's general picture of the Celtic occupation of Northern Italy may therefore be more reliable than has sometimes been supposed. Less certain however is the notion that the Gauls were tempted to move from the Po plain into peninsular Italy in the hope of finding more productive land. The tale of Arruns of Clusium was certainly an old tradition (it was known both to Polybius and to Cato),[76] but its connexion with the Gallic invasion of 390 B.C. is nonsensical. So too is the traditional explanation of the attack on Rome. The idea that the Romans were punished for a breach of the *ius gentium* by their ambassadors at Clusium is a legalistic fiction with strong anti-Fabian overtones.

A major inconsistency in the tradition is that the invading force is clearly envisaged as a war-band – the followers of Brennus (cf. Polyb. II.17.11; Caes. *BGall.* VI.15.2 on the importance of these 'Gefolg-schaften') – rather than a mass folk migration in search of land for settlement. A migrating tribe would not have advanced as far as Rome, at least not in the first instance: on the other hand, the story makes more sense if Brennus and his men were a band of warriors who moved into the Italian peninsula in search of plunder and adventure. Stripped of its romantic details, the story of Arruns of Clusium would imply that the Gauls intervened in an internal political struggle in Clusium at the bidding of one of the warring factions; in other words, they were a mercenary band, not a migrating tribe. Their route, via Clusium and Rome, becomes comprehensible if we assume that their ultimate destination was the Mezzogiorno, since the natural route to Campania and Magna Graecia was across the Appennines and down the valleys of the Chiana and Tiber.

We are specifically told that, a few months after the sack of Rome, the Gauls enlisted as mercenaries in the service of Dionysius of Syracuse, and helped him in his wars against the Italiot Greeks (Justin. xx.5.1–6). This information seems to be confirmed by the report that *on their way back*

---

[75] For a succinct account of the problems see Chevallier 1962[J24], 366ff; Barfield 1971[J7], 127ff. On Livy's account see Mansuelli in *I Galli e l'Italia* 1978[J49], 71–5.
[76] Polyb. II.17.3; and see Walbank 1957–79[B182] ad loc.; Cato, *Orig.* fr.36P with Peter's note ad loc.

from the South the Gauls were caught and defeated in the 'Trausian Plain' (wherever that was) by an Etruscan army from Caere (Diod. xɪv.117.7). Strabo confirms this story, and adds that it was the Caeretans who recovered the gold which the Romans had paid over to the Gauls (Strabo v.2.3, p. 220C). This Caeretan victory, not mentioned in the surviving Roman tradition, almost certainly provided the factual raw materials for the fabricated story of Camillus' face-saving victory.

It has been suggested that subsequent Gallic attacks were orchestrated by Dionysius of Syracuse, whose principal aim was to undermine the power of Rome's ally Caere.[77] In 384 the Caeretan port of Pyrgi was sacked by a Syracusan fleet (Diod. xv.14.3); if Dionysius had organized a simultaneous attack on Caere from the interior by his Gallic mercenaries, we should have a plausible context for the battle of the Trausian Plain. This hypothetical reconstruction cannot be proved, but it certainly provides a plausible explanation of events that would otherwise be very hard to understand.

The close friendship between Rome and Caere is presupposed in the traditional story, which records that the Vestal Virgins and the sacred objects they looked after were given refuge in Caere. They were escorted there by a plebeian named Lucius Albinius, who is probably a historical figure and in any case belongs to the very earliest level of the tradition. Aristotle apparently wrote that the city was saved by 'a certain Lucius', who is presumably to be identified with Albinius. Aristotle's statement is one of the reasons why scholars tend to reject Camillus' part in the story. We might add that Camillus is not mentioned by Polybius either.

In the developed legend Camillus was in exile at Ardea when the Gauls descended (he had been wrongfully accused of mishandling the spoils of Veii), and was appointed dictator only after the fall of the city. He then proceeded to form a new army out of the remnants of the old, marched on Rome and defeated the Gauls in the Forum at the very moment when the gold was being paid out. It is obvious that this legend was fashioned in an attempt to compensate for the most humiliating fact of all: the payment of the ransom. It is said that when the gold was being weighed out the Romans complained about the weights; whereupon Brennus threw his sword into the scales with the words 'vae victis' ('woe to the vanquished') – an incident which has immortalized the Gallic chief in contrast to the lifeless figure of Camillus, the most effete of all Rome's heroes.

The part played by Camillus in the Gallic saga is demonstrably a late and artificial accretion. Even the story of his exile may be no more than a device to dissociate him from the disaster of the Allia. It is not simply that

[77] Sordi 1960[J230], 62–72.

his alleged contribution is implicitly denied by Aristotle and Polybius. It is equally significant that other traditions existed concerning the departure of the Gauls and the recovery of the gold. Polybius for instance maintained that the Gauls voluntarily left the city because they had received news of an attack on their homeland by the Veneti. The family of the Livii Drusi claimed on the other hand that the gold was paid, but then recovered at a later date by their ancestor, who defeated a Gallic chief in single combat during a campaign in Northern Italy (Suet. *Tib.* 3.2). Another version, as we have seen, gave the credit to Caere. These alternative traditions could not have had any currency if the Camillus story had been either true or an element of the earliest tradition.

In general, it can be said that the Camillus legend serves to replace the historical role of Caere, and that he himself is a substitute for the person of L. Albinius, who is an integral part of an original tradition in which Caere held the centre of the stage. A second function of Camillus in the developed narrative is to lead the opposition to a popular proposal to rebuild the city on the site of Veii. If anything, this story is a reflection of the tensions that arose concerning the distribution of the conquered territory of Veii, and of plebeian agitation for a share in its allocation. This is one of a number of anti-plebeian elements in the story of Camillus.[78]

Suspicion attaches also to the figure of M. Manlius Capitolinus, who supposedly saved the Capitol from capture; it was he who was aroused by the cackling of the sacred geese just as the Gauls were about to scale the citadel. This story would certainly have to be rejected if we were to accept an alternative tradition, of which traces have been detected in the literature,[79] that the Gauls succeeded in taking the Capitol. Other legendary elements that remain entirely uncertain include the story of the aged senators who 'devoted' themselves and the enemy to the infernal gods, and then calmly sat around the Forum awaiting death. These and other stories present a general picture of a catastrophe that was nevertheless redeemed by individual acts of heroism and piety.

The sources certainly do not attempt to minimize the extent of the disaster. They report widespread loss of life, total moral collapse and the physical destruction of the city. There are however good grounds for thinking that these reports are exaggerated. The Allia was certainly a rout, but casualties may have been light since we are given to understand that the Romans ran away at the first encounter. It has been reasonably suggested that the flight of the soldiers to Veii was not a spontaneous act arising in the panic of the moment, but part of a pre-arranged plan;[80] in

[78] M. Torelli in *I Galli e l'Italia* 1978[J49], 226–8.
[79] Ennius, *Ann.* 227–8 Skutsch; Tacitus, *Ann.* XI.23; Sil. *Pun.* 1.525ff; IV.150ff; VI.555ff. See Skutsch 1953[J226], 77f; 1978[J227], 93f; 1985[B169], 405–8.   [80] Alföldi 1965[I3], 356–7.

other words the Romans, realizing that their cause was hopeless and that
they would be unable to save the city, evacuated it in advance. This
would be consistent with the story of Albinius and the Vestals.

Most suspicion attaches to the accounts of the destruction of the city.
The traditional idea that everything was destroyed serves as an aetiology
for two things. First, it was advanced as an explanation for the uncertainty of early Roman history; information about the sixth and fifth
centuries was scarce because all the records had been destroyed by the
Gauls (Livy VI.1.2; Plut. *Num.* 2). Secondly, it was believed that the
haphazard and unplanned character of the later city resulted from the
haste with which it was rebuilt after the Sack (Livy V.55).

In fact both explanations are fallacious. It is obvious that the haphazard plan of the city resulted from its gradual development, rather than
from hasty rebuilding. If it had been entirely rebuilt from nothing, one
might rather have expected evidence of deliberate planning. As for the
destruction of the records, what is striking is not that so many ancient
documents, buildings, monuments and relics were destroyed, but rather
that so many of them survived. Some of these ancient documents and
relics have been discussed in this chapter. The best explanation of all the
evidence is that the Gauls were interested in movable booty, and that
they left most of the monuments and buildings alone. They ransacked the
place, and made off with whatever they could carry. The story that they
had to be bought off with gold is consistent with this interpretation – and
is most probably true.

This conclusion is in line with common sense and is moreover
consistent with the fact that no archaeological trace of the Gallic disaster
has yet been positively identified. The 'burnt layer' beneath the second
paving of the Comitium is clear evidence of a destructive fire which was
once thought to have been the work of Brennus; but it has recently been
established that the destruction of the Comitium took place in the sixth
century B.C. and was perhaps part of the same fire that burned down the
Regia and the first temple in the Forum Boarium – evidence of a
widespread upheaval that is perhaps to be connected with the accession
of Servius Tullius.[81] In any event the absence of any archaeological
evidence of destruction at the beginning of the fourth century B.C. must
surely support the general conclusion that the physical effects of the Sack
were superficial. But the strongest argument for a 'minimalist' interpretation of the Gallic disaster is the speed and vigour of the Roman recovery
in the following years. The story of this recovery forms the subject of the
next chapter.

[81] F. Coarelli in *I Galli e l'Italia* 1978[J49], 229–30; id. 1977[E92], 181f; 1982[B309].

CHAPTER 7

THE RECOVERY OF ROME

T. J. CORNELL

I. ROME'S WIDENING HORIZONS

The ancient tradition maintained that Rome had suffered terribly at the hands of the Gauls, but that the calamity was followed by a miraculous recovery. We are asked to believe that, with their city in ruins, their manpower drastically reduced, and their allies in tacit or open revolt, the Romans were able to restore their former position almost immediately. Within a year of the Gauls' departure the city had been completely rebuilt, and spectacular victories had been won against enemies on all sides. These extraordinary achievements allegedly owed much to the inspired leadership of Camillus, who was regarded as a second founder of Rome.

Modern historians have not allowed this edifying story to pass un-challenged, however, and are apt to modify it in one of two ways. Either they accept that the Sack was indeed calamitous, but dismiss the story of the rapid recovery as fiction; or they accept the basic outline of events in the years after 390, but minimize the effects of the Sack. Both opinions have points in their favour. In support of the former it has been argued that the invention of compensating victories in the aftermath of defeats was a regular habit of the later Roman annalists; that the received version is at variance with that of Polybius, our oldest surviving authority; and that there is no mention of Camillus' victories in Diodorus, who is generally supposed to have followed an early source.[1] On the other hand, we saw in the previous chapter that there is good reason to doubt the picture of extensive destruction and loss of life which is presented in the annalistic accounts. It was suggested there that the physical damage to the city was superficial, that the civilian population had been evacuated and that the manpower losses at the Allia were not great.

A reasonable compromise would seem to be that the patriotic annalistic tradition exaggerated both the extent of the disaster and the magnitude of the subsequent victories. But if the actions of Camillus in

---

[1] The idea that Diodorus followed an early source goes back to Mommsen 1864–79[A90], 221ff. For a critical review of the question see Perl 1957[D25], 162ff.

the aftermath of the Gallic raid have been exaggerated, it does not necessarily follow that they are the product of pure invention. Camillus himself is certainly historical, and there is no good reason to doubt that he dominated affairs in the years after the Sack. He figures prominently in the *fasti*, which credit him with three consular tribunates and three dictatorships in the years from 389 to 367 B.C. Such a career, although remarkable, is not without parallel in the surviving record of the period. In fact Camillus can be regarded as the first of a series of such leaders who held a multiplicity of offices and dominated the political life of the state in the fourth century (see further below, pp. 344ff).

It is true, however, that the successes of Camillus are not mentioned by Polybius or Diodorus. This point raises the more general issue of the relative merits of our sources, and the question of how they are to be approached. Some modern historians, including contributors to the first edition of this work, have taken it as axiomatic that the versions of Polybius and Diodorus should be preferred to the late annalistic tradition followed by Livy, Dionysius of Halicarnassus, Plutarch and Dio Cassius.[2] This approach appears to the present writer to be unsound, if only because the two groups of sources do not, in fact, represent two parallel but conflicting traditions. Polybius does not give a systematic account of the events of the period, but merely alludes to them in passing in the course of an interesting digression on Rome's Gallic wars (Polyb. II.18–35). As for Diodorus, the identity of the source he followed for his Roman history remains a mystery (cf. above, p. 3). That it was the work of an early annalist is possible, but by no means certain. In any event Diodorus' notices of early Roman history are so scarce, and his choice of events is so idiosyncratic, that nothing can legitimately be inferred from his silence on any particular topic. The fact remains that Livy is the only source to give a full-length narrative history of the fourth century, and it is not good method to regard as automatically suspect anything in Livy that is not corroborated by other sources.

In particular, there is no warrant for the view that there are two traditions about the decades following the Gallic disaster. Polybius tells us that, after the destruction of Rome by Brennus, thirty years elapsed before the Gauls returned to Latium. He also states that during the interval the Romans regained their supremacy over the Latins (II.18. 5–6). This appears to be a specific allusion to the fact, acknowledged by Livy, that the Latin and Hernican federations withdrew their support from Rome after the Sack, and that the Cassian treaty remained in abeyance until it was renewed in 358 B.C. (Livy VI.2.3–4; 9.6; VII.12.7; and see further below). This need not mean, however, that the Romans were

2 Homo 1928[J178], 554–5.

reduced to impotence for thirty years; nor does it necessarily indicate that it took them thirty years to restore the *status quo ante*. In fact, the position of the Roman state was far stronger in the 350s than it had been a generation earlier. By the middle of the fourth century the scope of Rome's military and diplomatic activity had expanded greatly, and for the first time its power and influence were felt beyond the borders of Latium.

It is worth noting that at this period the main outline of events as reported in the literary tradition can be accepted with a much greater degree of confidence. The information in our sources improves notice-ably in both quantity and quality from the 360s onwards. It is true that Livy himself has a rather different view of the matter. He argues that the record is both fuller and more reliable for the period after the Sack (VI.1.1–3), and he marks a second break in 343 B.C. when the scale of his narrative changes (VII.29.1–2). But Livy's arguments are based not on a first-hand acquaintance with the primary evidence, but on purely subjec-tive impressions.[3] To a modern reader of Livy's text it is clear that the evidential basis for the narrative of the decades after 390 B.C. is not better (though not necessarily worse) than for the period before the Sack; whereas there *is* a marked change in the character of the tradition from *c.* 366 B.C. onwards, when Livy's account becomes much more detailed.

There seem to be two reasons for this improvement. First, we are now beginning to approach the period that was within the living memory of the first Roman historians and their informants. The earliest Roman historian, Fabius Pictor, was born probably in the second quarter of the third century B.C., and would have met and spoken to men who remem-bered the Great Samnite War (327–304 B.C.) and the censorship of Appius Claudius (312), and who had themselves known men of the generation of M. Valerius Corvus (*cos.* 348; 343, etc.). Secondly, we should note that from the 360s Livy begins to include many more routine notices of annual events, for example the deaths of officials, the appoint-ment of dictators for religious or electoral purposes, and, at the outbreak of a war, the dispatch of the *fetiales* and the formal vote of the centuriate assembly (e.g. Livy VII.6.7, 362 B.C.). Such notices must indicate the increasing use of documentary evidence from official archives. It is tempting to connect the greater availability of official records with the constitutional changes of 367 B.C. In any event, the improved quality of the record is not in doubt.

The evident growth of Roman power between the 390s and the 350s B.C. must serve to authenticate the Roman military successes that are recorded in the aftermath of the Sack – indeed it requires us to presup-

3 Cornell 1980[B34], 24–5.

pose them. There is nothing particularly surprising in the fact that, even without the support of the Latins and Hernici, the Romans were able to embark on an aggressive military policy. As we have seen, their physical resources were probably not seriously diminished by the Gallic raid, and circumstances generally favoured them. The point can be illustrated by a brief survey of how things stood at the time of the raid.

I. The most important single factor contributing to the strength of Rome at this time was the annexation of the territory of Veii (*ager Veientanus*) in 396 B.C., which had increased the size of Rome's territory by some 562 km.[2] If account is taken of other territorial gains made during the fifth century (Crustumerium, Ficulea, Fidenae, Labici), it is possible to calculate that the *ager Romanus* had doubled in size since the fall of the monarchy, from *c.* 822 km.[2] in 509 B.C. to *c.* 1582 km.[2] in 396.[4] It is reasonable to assume a corresponding increase in manpower resources.

In the aftermath of the Gallic Sack the Romans consolidated their hold on the new territories. Hostile attacks by the Etruscan cities to the north were repulsed by Camillus in 389 and 386 B.C.,[5] after which we hear of no further threats to Rome's northern borders for nearly thirty years. The principal adversary was presumably the city of Tarquinii, with which Rome now shared a common border on the north-west of the *ager Veientanus*, although the tradition speaks (probably wrongly) of a joint enterprise by the entire Etruscan nation (Livy VI.2.2). In 388 the Romans themselves invaded the territory of Tarquinii and captured two other-wise unknown towns, Cortuosa and Contenebra (Livy VI.4.8–10). The general aim of Rome's policy was to establish a firm frontier along the Monti Cimini, which form a natural barrier; an important stage in the process was the foundation of Latin colonies at Sutrium (Sutri) and Nepet (Nepi), probably in 383, although there is some confusion in our sources about the exact date.[6] The strategic importance of these two outposts was recognized by Livy, who likens them to 'barriers and gateways of Etruria' ('Etruriae . . . claustra . . . portaeque': Livy VI.9.4).

Meanwhile, the Roman state was organizing the settlement of the *ager Veientanus*. Some years previously allotments of Veientine land had been distributed to Roman citizens (Livy V.30.8; Diod. XIV.102.4). Then in 389 Roman citizenship was conferred on the surviving native popula-tion, as well as on the inhabitants of the territory that had been seized from the Capenates and Faliscans in 395 and 394. Livy regards this grant

[4] Beloch 1926[A12], 620.

[5] If these are not, in fact, 'doublets' of one another, as Beloch supposed (Beloch 1926[A12], 305). See chronological note, p. 349.

[6] Livy does not record the foundation of Sutrium, but dates Nepet to 383 (VI.21.4). Velleius Paterculus (1.14) says that Sutrium was founded seven years after the Sack, and Nepet ten years later. On this problem see Harris 1971[J175], 43–4.

of citizenship as a reward for a handful of pro-Roman quislings (VI.4.4), and suggests that the bulk of the population was sold into slavery (V.22.1). Although some historians accept Livy's version,[7] it seems in fact to reflect the attitudes and practices of a later age, when Roman citizenship was highly prized, and mass enslavements were a regular feature of Roman policy. It is much more likely, given the absence at this period of a market for such a vast number of slaves, that only a minority of the defeated Veientines were sold.

The resettlement of the *ager Veientanus* was probably complete by 387 B.C., when four new local tribes were created: the Stellatina, Tromentina, Sabatina and Arniensis (Livy VI.5.8). The Romans' control of the region was symbolized by the fact that shortly after the Sack they began to construct a new city wall, made of squared stones from the Grotta Oscura quarries near Veii. It is also relevant to note that the wall, which was over eleven kilometres long, enclosed an area of *c.* 426 hectares. By the start of the fourth century B.C. the city of Rome was the largest urban settlement in Central Italy.

II. Another circumstance that worked to the Romans' advantage was their alliance with Caere. Caere had supported Rome against Veii and had provided a refuge for the Vestal Virgins at the time of the Gallic Sack (p. 306). This was the product of a long-standing entente that continued after the Sack. But the precise juridical terms of the relationship are uncertain and have given rise to much debate. The question has important implications, and it will be necessary to outline the main points of the controversy in a brief digression.

At some stage in its history Caere was incorporated into the Roman state with the restricted form of citizenship known as *civitas sine suffragio* ('citizenship without suffrage'). Some sources maintained that this act of union came about after the departure of the Gauls from Rome in 390 B.C., and that Caere was the first community to receive the *civitas sine suffragio*. It was noted that a grant of citizenship without full political rights was a rather poor reward for the help which the people of Caere had given the Romans in their hour of need (Strabo V.2.3, p. 220C). Livy's version is rather different. He defines the relationship between Rome and Caere as 'public guest-friendship' ('hospitium publicum': Livy V.50.3), which probably means that when in Rome a citizen of Caere could enjoy all the private rights and privileges of Roman citizenship but would be free from its burdens and obligations. The same would apply to Romans at Caere.[8] Somewhat later, in the 350s, Livy records a war between Caere and Rome which ended in 353 with a truce (*indutiae*) of 100 years (VII.20). This report must imply that Caere was still an independent sovereign

---

[7] Harris 1971[J175], 41 and n. 6.   [8] Sordi 1960[J230], 110ff.

state, and would appear to rule out any possibility that the Caeretans had been made Roman citizens *sine suffragio* in either 390 or 353 B.C., although both dates have been widely canvassed.[9]

As a compromise it has been suggested that the institution of *civitas sine suffragio* did not originally entail incorporation in the Roman state, but was a form of potential or honorary citizenship similar to the Latin right (see above, p. 269); and that what Livy referred to as *hospitium publicum* was, in fact, nothing other than this original *civitas sine suffragio*.[10] Some support for this contention is provided by a passage of Aulus Gellius (*NA* XVI.13.7), who writes that the Caeretans became the first *municipes sine suffragio*, and received the honour of citizenship without any of its commitments or burdens (on *municipes* see below, p. 319).

But an equally plausible solution is that Roman antiquarians were simply mistaken when they dated the *civitas sine suffragio* of the Caeretans to the time of the Gallic invasion. Their mistake would have resulted from a facile interpretation of a document or group of documents known as the Tabulae Caeritum (the 'Register of the Caeretans'). The Tabulae Caeritum were apparently lists on which the censors used to enter the names of Roman citizens who did not possess full rights of suffrage. The fact that the lists were called Tabulae Caeritum was taken to imply that there was a time when the only names they contained were those of Caeretans, and consequently that the Caeretans were the first to possess the *civitas sine suffragio*. This inference may or may not be correct – as a matter of fact there are other perfectly possible explanations;[11] but in any event the point is of no great consequence. What is important is that the relationship between Rome and Caere in the years after 390 B.C. involved a reciprocal grant of honorary citizenship, and it does not much matter whether we choose to regard it as *hospitium publicum* or as an early form of *civitas sine suffragio*.

The problem that remains is the question of when Caere was finally absorbed into the Roman state with *civitas sine suffragio* in its later form – which entailed all the burdens and obligations of Roman citizenship but none of the political rights. Here the most attractive theory is still that of Beloch, who dated the incorporation of Caere to 273 B.C., when the city was deprived of half its territory following a revolt.[12]

The origin of the *civitas sine suffragio* is fundamental to our understanding of the development of the juridical framework of Rome's foreign

[9] 390 B.C.: Sordi 1960[J230], 36–49; Harris 1971[J175], 45–6. 353 B.C.: Mommsen 1887–8[A91], III.572; De Sanctis 1907–64[A37], II.243; Sherwin-White 1973[A123], 51; Humbert 1978[J184], 410ff.   [10] Sordi 1960[J230], esp. 107ff.

[11] For one suggestion see Brunt 1971[A21], 515–18.

[12] Dio fr. 33, vol. I, p. 138 Boiss.; Beloch 1926[A12], 363; see below, p. 423.

relations, and it is this abstract question that has been the focus of modern discussion. Less attention has been paid to the more specific problem of how the link between Rome and Caere affected the political and military affairs of Central Italy in the fourth century B.C.[13] On this the sources are not helpful. For example, we have no idea to what extent, if any, the understanding between the two cities entailed military co-operation. But on any view it is clear that together they were a formidable coalition. That they were a threat to the ambitions of Dionysius of Syracuse has been plausibly argued (cf. above, p. 306).

One consequence of the entente was that the Romans began to pay more attention to the wider world of the western Mediterranean. A set of disconnected and seemingly improbable reports can be formed into a coherent story which makes sense in the general context of the alliance with Caere. Justin tells us that in 389 B.C. Rome made a formal alliance with Massalia, and adds the specific information that Massaliot visitors to Rome were to enjoy certain privileges (Justin XLIII.5.10). This clause appears to recall the institution of *hospitium publicum*, which was probably a common feature of international treaties at this period, and not a native Roman institution at all.[14] Shortly afterwards Diodorus records that the Romans sent a colony of 500 citizens to Sardinia (Diod. XV.27.4); and an anecdote in Theophrastus (*Hist. Pl.* V.8.2) refers to a Roman attempt to colonize Corsica, but with no indication of the date. We should note, moreover, that the most recent study of the archaeological evidence dates the foundation of a fortified settlement at Ostia to the period 380–350 B.C.[15] We know no more than this, so it is impossible to tell whether this Roman spirit of adventurism had commercial or piratical aims, or whether there was some broader strategic purpose.[16]

This evidence of Roman maritime activity is surprising, and uncharacteristic of the Romans, who were later renowned for having a healthy dislike of the sea. Some scholars have indeed rejected the reports on that account. But the fact that they do not appear in the annalistic sources is not necessarily an argument for rejecting them. That they derive from an independent Greek tradition (directly in the case of Theophrastus) could well be in their favour. And it is surely unwise to reject evidence simply on the grounds that it does not conform to expectations.

III. A third circumstance that favoured the Romans at this time was the relative weakness of their southern neighbours. In the course of the

[13] This aspect is considered at length, however, by Sordi 1960[J230], esp. 91ff.
[14] Sordi 1960[J230], 111ff. [15] F. Zevi in *Roma medio-repubblicana* 1973[B401], 343ff.
[16] Sordi 1960[J230], 91ff has suggested that the object was to avert the threat of Dionysius of Syracuse. For a different assessment see Momigliano 1936[F48], 393–8 (= id. *Quarto Contributo* 355–61).

fifth century Rome had come to dominate her Latin and Hernican allies, and by about 400 B.C. she had reduced the Volsci and Aequi to virtual impotence. Successful actions against these peoples at the end of the fifth century had given the Romans a position of supremacy in the upper Trerus valley and the Pomptine region, although they were not as yet able to maintain a permanent presence there, apart from the isolated strongpoints where Latin colonies were established, such as Velitrae, Vitellia and Circeii. In the half century after the Gallic Sack we find the Roman state engaged in almost continuous warfare in the Pomptine region, the district that for over a century had been in Volscian hands. It is sometimes suggested that the Volscians were able to take advantage of Rome's weakness after the Gallic raid, and that in the following years the Romans had to struggle against a renewed Volscian offensive. But this view has no support in the sources. In fact, the record shows that Rome's campaigns were not defensive operations aimed at warding off hostile attacks, but were rather a concerted attempt to extend her control in the region. The results confirm the general reliability of the record. Bearing these points in mind, then, we may now turn to an examination of the events themselves.

In the year after the departure of the Gauls Camillus defeated the Volscians of Antium at a place south of Lanuvium called 'ad Maecium'. This campaign was perhaps a response to a Volscian attack, but it is not inconceivable, given the location of the battle, that the Romans had decided on a show of strength. At any rate the sources are all agreed that the result was decisive. The victory was followed by what in current jargon would be called a 'pre-emptive strike' against the Aequi; the Aequi were taken by surprise as Camillus and his army descended on them near Bolae, which was then captured at the first attack (Livy VI.2.14). The next year (388) the military tribunes 'led an army against the Aequi, not to make war (for the Aequi admitted they were defeated), but out of hatred, intending to destroy their lands and leave them no strength for future designs' (Livy VI.4.8). After this the sources make no further mention of the Aequi until their ill-fated rebellion in 304 B.C.

An indication of the Romans' aggressive posture at this time is given by the report of their intention to annex the Pomptine plain. In 388 and 387 the tribunes of the plebs are said to have agitated for the 'viritane' distribution of the ager Pomptinus or 'Pomptine territory' (Livy VI.5.1; 6.1 – i.e. its distribution in individual allotments). A victorious campaign by Camillus in 386 (if it is not a 'doublet' of the one in 389 – see chronological note, p. 349) was followed by the foundation of colonies at Satricum (Le Ferriere) in 385 and Setia (Sezze) in 382, fortress sites which overlooked the Pomptine plain from the north and east respectively. In 383 a five-man commission was appointed to distribute the ager

Pomptinus (*quinqueviri agro dividendo* – Livy VI.21.4). The task was not fully accomplished until 358 B.C., and we cannot say how much progress was made in the intervening period. The delay was almost certainly due in part to the desperate resistance put up by the Volscians of the Pomptine district, whose very existence as a separate people was directly threatened; the Romans had clearly decided to pursue the same policy in this region as they had against Veii.

It is against this background that we can begin to understand the puzzle of the relations between the Romans and their Latin and Hernican allies. Livy speaks of a revolt (*defectio*) immediately after the Sack, but the record of events shows that Rome was not faced with a full-scale armed uprising of the kind that had occurred after the fall of the monarchy and that was to occur again in 340 B.C. Rather it seems that the arrangements of the *foedus Cassianum* simply lapsed, and that the military partnership ceased to function. Livy writes, under the year 386 B.C., 'in the same year satisfaction was demanded from the Latins and Hernici, who were asked why in recent years they had provided no military contingents as they had agreed to do' (Livy VI.9.6). What clearly puzzled Livy and his sources was the fact that the Romans took no active steps to rectify this state of affairs. The suggestion that they were prevented from doing so on various occasions because of greater dangers on other fronts is a transparent rationalization (Livy VI.6.2; 10.9; 14.1 etc.).

The answer is probably that it no longer suited the Romans to enforce the terms of the *foedus Cassianum*. The treaty had after all come into being at a time when Rome and the Latins were threatened by external forces, and it had served the interests of both parties; but now that the external threats had receded it was no longer in the Romans' interest to subscribe to a treaty that inhibited their chances of further territorial expansion.

Many of the Latin communities seem to have remained loyal to Rome. This is attested in the case of Tusculum and Lanuvium, and is probably true of other cities as well, such as Aricia, Lavinium and Ardea.[17] These communities probably continued to send troops and to take part in the Latin colonies that were founded by Rome. The difference was that the Romans were now dealing with each of them individually rather than with all of them collectively.

Some Latin peoples, however, were overtly hostile, and joined the Volscians in armed resistance to Rome. The result was a reversal of what had happened in the fifth century, when the Latins had joined forces with Rome in response to Volscian attacks; now they were uniting with the Volscians against the threat of Roman encroachment. The secessionists included the Latin colonists of Velitrae and Circeii. Their action can be

17 De Sanctis 1907–64[A37], II.232–3.

explained partly on the assumption that most of their population actually consisted of the original Volscian inhabitants, and partly by the fact that they were especially threatened by the Romans' plan to overrun the Pomptine Plain. It is not at all surprising that the nearest of the old Latin communities, Lanuvium, is also recorded as joining the Volscians in 383 B.C., although it had hitherto been loyal (Livy VI.21.2).

Of the Latin states that opposed the Romans during this period the largest and most powerful were Tibur and Praeneste. It is probable that these cities had not belonged to the Latin League in the fifth century (see above p. 285), and only began to play a part in the affairs of the region after the withdrawal of the Aequi. At all events they became formidable adversaries of the Romans in the fourth century. As far as we know, hostilities between Rome and Tibur did not begin until 361 B.C., but already in 382 the Praenestines are recorded as attacking Rome's allies and joining the Volscians. Livy's account of Roman successes against Praeneste in 380 B.C. has an authentic ring: 'Titus Quinctius (Cincinnatus) then returned in triumph to Rome. He had won one victory in pitched battle, taken nine towns by assault and accepted the surrender of Praeneste, and brought with him a statue of Iuppiter Imperator which he had carried off from Praeneste. This he dedicated on the Capitol between the shrines of Iuppiter and Minerva, with a plaque fixed below it to commemorate his exploits bearing an inscription to this effect: "Iuppiter and all the gods granted that the dictator Titus Quinctius should capture nine towns"'.[18]

To the south there was fierce fighting in the Pomptine district, with Satricum and Velitrae at the centre of the action. Satricum was repeatedly taken and retaken in the period between 386 and 346 B.C. (Livy VI.8; 16.5; 22; 32; VII.27); Velitrae was the object of continual attack by the Romans, and its capture is reported in 380 (Livy VI.29.6) and again in 367 after a long siege (Livy VI.36.1–6; 42.4; Plut. Cam. 42.1).

There can be no question about the generally aggressive and expansionist nature of Roman policy at this time. The clearest demonstration of the Romans' intentions occurred in 381 B.C., when they annexed Tusculum. In a sense this was a logical step, since Tusculum was by now completely, or almost completely, surrounded by Roman territory. The sources suggest that the Tusculans had become disaffected, and had actually joined the Volscians (Livy VI.25.1); given the menacing character of Rome's recent actions, that would not be altogether surprising. Camillus was dispatched with an army against Tusculum, which surrendered without a blow. The free inhabitants were forthwith admitted to Roman citizenship.

[18] Livy VI.29.9; cf. Diod. XV.47. Festus 498 L gives a different version of the text. Cicero, II Verr. 4.129 wrongly connects the dedication with T. Quinctius Flamininus, cos. 198. On this see De Sanctis 1907–64[A37], II.237 n. 31.

The later Roman tradition was pleased to regard this act as one of great generosity, a sign of the humanity of the Romans in general and of Camillus in particular (Livy v.25.6; Dion. Hal. *Ant. Rom.* xiv.6). But this anachronistic presentation conceals the fact that the incorporation of Tusculum marked the political annihilation of an independent community. We need not be surprised that Tusculum joined the insurgents at the time of the great Latin revolt (340 B.C.), nor should we cast doubt on reported attempts by the other Latins to detach Tusculum from Rome (e.g. Livy vi.36.1–6: 370 B.C.).

It seems certain that the Tusculans received full Roman citizenship (*civitas optimo iure*) rather than *civitas sine suffragio*. They nevertheless retained their corporate identity and were internally self-governing, but were subject to all the duties and obligations of Roman citizens (above all the payment of *tributum* and service in the legions). Tusculum thus became a Roman *municipium*, a word whose original significance is uncertain, but which in later times was the standard term for any community incorporated into the Roman state as a self-governing body of Roman citizens. The view that the term originally applied only to *cives sine suffragio*, and not to *cives optimo iure*, is probably mistaken.[19] We may conclude therefore that Tusculum became the first *municipium*, a conclusion that receives some support from the sources (Cic. *Planc.* 19).

According to the traditional narrative the period from 376 to 363 B.C. was one of comparative peace, interrupted only by the siege of Velitrae (370–367) and a Gallic raid in 367 which may be apocryphal (see below). It is true that the period in question has been artificially lengthened in the Varronian tradition for chronological reasons (see below p. 348), but even after allowance has been made for this, one is left with an interval of some ten years without any serious campaigns. The explanation offered by our sources is that the Romans were preoccupied by domestic problems – first a political crisis and then a plague – which prevented them from engaging in warfare. This explanation would be absurd if the Romans had been defending themselves against hostile attacks; but it does make sense in terms of the aggressive policy which has been postulated in the foregoing pages, and is indeed an indirect confirmation of it.

The resumption of warfare in 362 B.C. opened a new phase in the history of Rome's external relations. A decade of vigorous and successful campaigning brought an unprecedented series of victories (eight triumphs and one ovation are recorded in the period from 361 to 354; see below p. 363, Table 7) and placed Roman power on a new footing. This general point can be asserted with some confidence, even if the exact pattern of events is difficult to reconstruct in detail. The sources record

---

[19] Humbert 1978[J184], 283–4. *Contra*, e.g. Sherwin-White 1973[A123], 40ff.

simultaneous Roman campaigns against a bewildering variety of different adversaries, but they do not properly explain the relationship between them. Moreover, the annalistic tradition probably contains errors
and doublets. In these circumstances it seems best to offer a brief and
tentative summary of what the tradition records, and to comment in
passing on the salient points.

Rome's new offensive apparently began with a war against the
Hernici. After an initial reverse in 362 the Romans captured Ferentinum
in 361 and won further victories in 360 and 358. The outcome was
probably the renewal, in 358, of the alliance which had been in abeyance
since the Gallic Sack. We know at any rate that the treaty with the Latins
was revived in 358 (Livy VII.12.7). It may be that the new agreements
were made on terms that were much more favourable to the Romans than
in the original treaties, but the sources do not help us on this issue. At all
events the Latins were now obliged to assent to the Roman occupation of
the *ager Pomptinus*, and at the same time the Hernici were forced to cede
part of their territory in the Trerus valley for occupation by Roman
settlers. These annexations were formally carried out in 358 B.C., when
the two districts were formed into new Roman tribes, respectively the
Pomptina and the Publilia (Livy VII.5.11).

The Romans renewed their alliance with the Latin and Hernican
Leagues at a time when Latium was once again being menaced by attacks
from outside – a fact that is unlikely to be a coincidence. Indeed this very
point is made explicitly by Livy (VII.12.7–8) and implicitly by Polybius
(II.18.5), both of whom refer to the renewal of the Latin treaty in the
context of an attack by the Gauls. Livy records several Gallic incursions
at this period – in 367, 361, 360, 358 and 357 B.C. – whereas Polybius
refers to just one, which he dates thirty years after the original Sack.
Again, Livy's account includes a number of Roman victories, whereas
Polybius says that the Romans avoided meeting the Gauls in the field
(Polyb. II.18.6).

It is possible that some of Livy's reports are doublets or errors.
Particular suspicion attaches to the alleged victory in 367 B.C., which
enabled the aged Camillus to crown his career with one final Gallic
victory. Livy himself appears to be aware of some confusion here,
because he notes that a single combat between T. Manlius Torquatus and
a gigantic Gaul, which he narrates under 361 B.C. (Livy VII.10), was dated
to 367 by some of his sources (Livy VI.42.5; cf. Claudius Quadrigarius fr.
10–11 P). But we should not necessarily conclude that all Livy's notices
are fictitious. In fact there is much to be said for the view that the attacks
recorded by Livy were carried out by Gallic war-bands operating from
southern Italy,[20] whereas Polybius only took note of invasions from the
north.

[20] Sordi 1960[J230], 164–5. Note esp. Livy VII.1.3 (Apulia); 11.1 (Campania), etc.

An integral part of the Livian tradition, and one that is unlikely to have been invented, is the war with Tibur, which lasted from 361 to 354 and in which the Tiburtines joined the Gauls in their attacks on Rome. Evidently Tibur was excluded from the new agreement Rome had made with the Latin League in 358 B.C. There is nothing particularly surprising about this, since as far as we can see Tibur had never been a member of the Latin League (see above p. 285). The same probably goes for Praeneste, which was also hostile to Rome in the 350s. In 354 both Tibur and Praeneste were compelled to surrender and to make separate agreements with Rome (Livy VII.19.1; Diodorus XVI.45.8).

In 358 B.C. the Romans also found themselves at war with the Etruscans of Tarquinii, who were joined in 357 by Falerii and by Caere in 353. In 356 Livy records a victory by the dictator C. Marcius Rutilus over the entire Etruscan nation (VII.17.6–9), but this is probably an annalist's misunderstanding of a notice in which the Tarquinienses and their allies were referred to by the general name of Etruscans. The origin of this war is totally obscure, and its character is difficult to assess from the brief notices we are given in Livy. One notable – and probably authentic – episode was the killing of 307 Roman prisoners of war in the forum of Tarquinii following an Etruscan victory in 358 (Livy VII.15.10). There is some reason to believe that this act was an expiatory ritual for the dead of Tarquinii, and is to be seen as a form of gladiatorial performance.[21] The gesture was repaid in kind in 354 B.C. when 358 noble Tarquinienses were put to death in the Roman Forum (Livy VII.19.2–3; cf. Diod. XVI.45.8). The outcome of the war was a truce of 100 years with Caere (353 B.C.) and truces of forty years each with Tarquinii and Falerii (351).

In 350 and 349 the Gauls once again attacked Latium. In 349 the Latin League refused to send troops to the army, and a Greek fleet ravaged the coast. But in spite of these difficulties the Romans managed to defeat the Gauls (in a battle in which M. Valerius Corvus fought a celebrated duel with a Gallic champion – Livy VII.26), and the Greek fleet eventually withdrew. Livy's speculation (VII.26.15) that the ships were Syracusan was probably well founded.[22] The incident was not repeated, as far as we know, a fact which may have something to do with the overthrow of Dionysius II and the upheaval that followed in Sicily. Equally we hear of no further Gallic attacks for several decades. In 331, according to Polybius (II.18.9), the Romans made peace with the Gauls, who did not return for another thirty years.

The significance of the Gallic wars of the fourth century B.C. is difficult to assess. It is not clear whether we should visualize the periodic attacks as large-scale invasions by terrifying and irresistible barbaric

---

[21] Torelli 1981[J124], 3ff; cf. id. 1975[B266], 82ff.
[22] Sordi 1960[J230], 68; her view is that the Syracusans had organized a simultaneous attack by their fleet and by a land-based force of Gallic mercenaries.

hordes, sweeping aside everything in their path in orgies of destruction (which is how the first great invasion of 390 was seen by all the sources, and how Polybius envisaged the subsequent incursions down to the third century), or whether they were petty raids by relatively small marauding bands operating from within the peninsula (which is the model that some historians have drawn from Livy). On this view they represented little more than a minor irritation to Rome, once she had learned how to deal with them. The view adopted in the present chapter has tended towards the latter alternative, but in the knowledge that the available evidence does not permit any certainty. The main reason for this approach is that the Gallic raids – even the great invasion of 390 B.C. – had little long-term effect on wider developments and did not upset the general pattern of interstate relationships in Central Italy. The Gauls thus represent an extraneous and largely irrelevant factor in Italian history at this time.

That is not to say, however, that the inhabitants of peninsular Italy were able to view the Gauls with equanimity. The raids were terrifying and unpredictable, and aroused deep and irrational fears. Their effect on the collective mentality of the Roman people was remarkable. In later times the threat – even the merest possibility – of a 'Gallic outbreak' (*tumultus Gallicus*) called for emergency troop levies and induced a state of extreme panic. The clearest example is the series of bizarre happenings in 114–13 B.C. that were provoked by news of the approach of the Cimbri (who were assumed to be Celts). On this occasion human sacrifices were performed and Vestal Virgins were put to death (because the danger to the state seemed to prove that they had been unchaste). The same procedures are known to have been carried out on earlier occasions – specifically in 228 and 216 B.C., both times in connexion with Gallic invasions of Italy. The human sacrifice involved the burial in the Forum Boarium of a pair of Gauls and a pair of Greeks. It has been suggested that this curious rite had its origins in the mid-fourth century B.C., and represented a magical performance designed to neutralize the threat of the two great external foes, the Gauls and the Sicilian Greeks.[23] But this may be too rational an interpretation of a ritual which we cannot really hope to understand.

There can be no doubt, however, about the main trend to emerge from the bewildering array of brief and obscure campaign reports of the mid-fourth century. These are the inexorable growth of the Romans' military power, the increasingly ambitious nature of their foreign entanglements and the ever widening scope and scale of their warlike operations. There is no good reason to deny the historicity of the Roman raid against Privernum in 357 (Livy VII.16.3–6), the attack on the Aurunci in 345

[23] A. Fraschetti 1981[G404], 51–115, esp. 90ff.

(Livy VII.28.1–3) or the capture of Sora in the same year (Livy VII.28.6). These ventures make sense in relation to the events that were to follow; and the widening horizons of Rome are confirmed by two cardinal pieces of evidence: the treaty between Rome and the Samnites in 354 B.C. and that between Rome and Carthage in 348.

Of the former we know only what we are told by Livy, who simply reports that a treaty of alliance (*foedus*) was granted to the Samnites, who had requested it because they were so impressed by a recent Roman victory over the Etruscans (Livy VII.19.4). Of the background to the treaty, of its purpose and of its terms we know absolutely nothing, but presumably the two parties pledged themselves to respect one another's interests, however defined. Whether any kind of military alliance was entered into at this stage cannot be known.[24] The Carthage treaty, on the other hand, is almost certainly to be identified with the second of the three treaties which are quoted and discussed by Polybius (III.24; see pp. 526ff). The text given by Polybius is unfortunately vague about the precise extent of Roman power, and merely recognizes Roman overlordship of Latium and the fact that there were other peoples outside Latium with whom Rome had formal relations. These 'non-subject' peoples, who are described as having written peace treaties with Rome, are normally identified with Tibur, Praeneste, Caere, Tarquinii and Falerii. The existence of places in Latium not subject to the Romans is also implied; presumably the reference is to towns such as Antium, which was still under Volscian control. As far as these places are concerned, the treaty does not forbid all hostile actions by the Carthaginians (as the treaty of 509 B.C. had done); on the contrary, it permits them to keep the spoils from any such place that might fall into their hands, but insists that they hand over the town itself to the Romans. Probably what is implied is the possibility of Carthaginian piratical raids, rather than joint warlike operations by the Romans and Carthaginians acting together, although the latter view cannot be entirely ruled out.

II. ECONOMIC AND SOCIAL PROBLEMS IN THE FOURTH CENTURY: POVERTY, LAND HUNGER AND DEBT

The years of recovery and gradual expansion after the Gallic Sack also witnessed dramatic changes in Roman social structure and political organization. The archaic society that is revealed to us in the Twelve Tables and other early sources was in a state of radical transition by the end of the fifth century. As we have seen, the Gallic raid was only a temporary setback in the growth of Roman power in Latium; on the

---

[24] Salmon 1967[J106], 192–3 gives a speculative reconstruction of its terms.

other hand it must have exacerbated the difficulties of the poorest class and can only have increased social tensions and hastened the process of internal change.

The period is represented as one of profound crisis and continual strife, leading to an attempted coup d'état in 384 and culminating in the 'anarchy' of the Licinio-Sextian Rogations at the end of the 370s. These years are not well documented, however, and the details of the events are uncertain. The sources are agreed that there were three main underlying issues: land, debt and the political rights of the plebeians. But although they have much to say on these matters, it is clear that they did not properly understand them. This is not really surprising, since the main institutional features of the archaic period had either been abolished or become obsolete by the beginning of the third century B.C., and its true character had long been forgotten by the time Fabius Pictor began to write. Nevertheless some record of the major events and issues of the struggle were preserved: for instance, the attempted coup of M. Manlius Capitolinus, the basic content of legislative enactments, changes in the rules governing eligibility for the chief magistracies, measures to alleviate debt and to alter the condition of debtors. The historians and annalists of the late Republic did their best to make sense of these traditional facts, and to construct around them a coherent narrative that would explain the behaviour, attitudes and aspirations of the groups and individuals who took part in the story. In doing so they inevitably distorted the historical reality, because their understanding of the institutional background was very limited and their interpretations were often naive and mistaken. Above all they were not fully aware of how different the archaic age of Rome was from that in which they themselves lived; the result was that they unconsciously modernized the story. They made false and anachronistic assumptions about the economic and social organization of Rome in the fifth and fourth centuries B.C.; and they modelled their accounts of political struggles on the experience of more recent times, adopting the political vocabulary of the late Republic and assimilating the early leaders of the plebs to the Gracchi, Saturninus and Catiline.

In a sense the procedure of the annalists was understandable enough. The issues that dominated the crisis of the early fourth century were in some respects similar to those of the second and first centuries B.C. This point deserves emphasis. It has been suggested that the traditional stories of agitation about *ager publicus* and debt-bondage were fabrications modelled on the events of the age of the Gracchi and later. But such scepticism is unjustified. Land and debt were constant issues in political struggles in the Greco-Roman world. Moreover, the conflicts of the fourth century B.C. as recorded in our sources have certain distinctive features which clearly puzzled later historians; and whatever the shortcomings of the late-republican annalists, it would be difficult to believe that they invented things that were beyond their own powers of comprehension.

In this chapter it will be assumed that the sources were right to stress the issues of land and debt in their accounts of the social conflicts of the fourth century. However obscure the details, it seems certain that the conflict between the patricians and the plebeians in early Rome was principally a struggle against oppression by a large class of poor peasants who were in subjection to the rich.[25] The domination of the rich rested on their control of large landed estates; while the small size of the majority of peasant holdings was the cause of the indebtedness of the poor and of the state of bondage to which they were reduced.[26]

In the present state of the record, however, it is impossible to proceed with any confidence from this level of generality to more specific details. As long as it is accepted that no credence can be given to the social and economic framework that is presupposed in the literary narratives, the historian has no alternative but to fall back on conjecture and intuition in an attempt to construct an alternative and necessarily hypothetical model of the early Roman economy. Much of what follows is therefore admittedly hypothetical, and combines what appear to the present writer to be the most convincing elements of several modern reconstructions. The criteria of selection have been, first, the capacity of any given model to explain puzzling and contradictory data in the literary sources, and secondly its general plausibility, particularly in the light of comparative evidence from other archaic societies.

A fact of prime importance for our understanding of the early Roman economy is the land hunger of the peasantry.[27] References in the sources to the small size of peasant holdings are frequent and pervasive, and cannot reasonably be rejected out of hand. Whatever view is taken of the tradition concerning the heritable property (*heredium*) of two *iugera* (= 0.5 hectares) that Romulus gave to each of the original Roman citizens (p. 100), there is plenty of evidence that smallholdings of seven *iugera* or less were common in early Rome. It is remarkable, for instance, that when the Romans redistributed part of the extensive territory of Veii to plebeian settlers in 393 B.C., the individual allotments were no bigger than seven *iugera* apiece (Livy v.30.8; Diod. xiv.102.5 gives four *iugera*).

These figures are interesting because a plot of seven *iugera* (let alone one of two or four) would not be sufficient to support a family at a

---

[25] A different view is adopted in Chap. 5 (pp. 235ff).

[26] With this statement I do not mean to rule out the possibility that the plebs included landless artisans and traders, but I doubt if such persons were more than a small minority of the population.

[27] For discussion of these issues in a fifth-century context cf. pp. 133ff.

minimum level of subsistence. Modern estimates vary, but most experts reckon that, in ancient conditions of agricultural technology, more than ten *iugera* would be needed to feed a family of four. Roman historians and antiquarians offer no explanation of this peculiarity in the tradition, and leave us to guess how peasants in early Rome made their living. The only realistic assumption is that they were able to supplement their incomes by working some additional land other than their own, and in particular the so-called 'public land' (*ager publicus*). But here we step into a minefield. The nature and function of the *ager publicus*, and the rights of Roman citizens in relation to it, are among the most fundamental but at the same time the most intractable problems in all of Roman history.

It seems reasonably certain that public or domain land had comprised a substantial proportion of the *ager Romanus* from the earliest times, and that it was continually supplemented by conquest. Its theoretical function seems to have been to provide a reserve supply of land for Roman citizens whose own properties were not sufficient for their needs. As such it was made available for communal grazing or for occupation by cultivators (the tradition implies that originally the *ager publicus* was uncultivated land). The small size of traditional land-holdings would seem to indicate that the peasants were dependent on access to the *ager publicus* for their livelihood. According to a traditional custom a man was permitted to occupy as much public land as he was able to cultivate on his own (Sic. Flacc. *De condic. agr.* p. 136 Lachmann). A more sophisticated 'timocratic' version of this customary limitation was that a Roman citizen could occupy as much of the public land as his patrimonial resources would permit (Columella, *Rust.* 1.3.11). But this is in fact a very different matter, since the wealthy patricians and their clients could dispose of relatively large resources of capital and labour, and would have been able to extend their control over a much wider area than is implied by the simple notion of what one man could work on his own.

Apparently that is precisely what happened. The original customary limitations were ignored, and the public land came to be occupied exclusively by the rich. We are told that permitted holdings of *ager publicus* began to include areas which the occupier 'hoped' to cultivate ('quod . . . in spem colendi occupavit': Sic. Flacc. *De condic. agr.* p. 137L). This cynical formulation, if it is in any sense historical, was probably invented as a way of justifying the growth of extensive holdings. At all events the literary sources make it plain that the wealthy patricians encroached on the public land to the point of excluding plebeians altogether. The earliest reference to this process occurs in a fragment of the annalist Cassius Hemina, who wrote in the period before the Gracchi (fr. 17P). The rich simply annexed the *ager publicus* to their estates and treated it as their own heritable property; the poor were reduced to indigence and total dependence on the wealthy landowners.

It is important to stress that the power of the patricians and the oppression of the plebs derived from the particular regime of land tenure that obtained on the *ager publicus*. It is this that gives Roman agrarian history its distinctive character. The epoch-making work of Berthold Niebuhr at the beginning of the nineteenth century established once for all that the movements for agrarian reform that occurred during the Republic were not aimed at redistribution of land in private ownership, but were solely concerned with the manner of disposal and use of the *ager publicus*. This fundamental thesis, which is now universally accepted even by the most literal-minded interpreters of the ancient sources, is as valid for the period of the early Republic as it is for the age of the Gracchi.[28] The discontent of the plebeians was caused by the fact that the public land, on which they depended for survival, was controlled and permanently occupied by the patricians and their clients.

The remarkable story of how the plebeians formed their own independent organization and fought for their rights during the fifth century has already been dealt with in Chapter 5. The details of the struggle are obscure, but its principal results are clear: by the beginning of the fourth century we find an active and fully developed plebeian organization which was pressing, through its elected leaders the tribunes, for specific concessions on a range of issues, including the use of public land.

On this question the plebs adopted a two-pronged approach. First, they continually demanded that newly conquered land should be distributed in allotments which would become the private property of the individual recipients (*assignatio viritana*), rather than remaining the property of the state and thus a target for encroachment by wealthy possessors. In the period from 486 to 367 B.C. our sources record no fewer than twenty-two separate agrarian proposals of this kind. Some of the reports may be unhistorical, but it is arbitrary to reject the entire tradition as an invention, as some modern scholars have done.[29] It is noteworthy that very few instances of agitation for land assignation are recorded during the middle years of the fifth century, whereas they are frequent in the period after 424 B.C.;[30] it is not a coincidence that at precisely this time a series of successful military operations opened a new phase in the history of Roman conquest (see above, p. 300f).

Naturally the plebeian demands for viritane assignations were resisted by the patricians, who stood to benefit from the occupation of new additions to the existing stock of *ager publicus*. It is extremely probable that a dim memory of this struggle over the disposal of newly conquered territory is concealed within the story of the attempt by the plebeians to

---

[28] Niebuhr 1838[A94], II.129ff. On this whole question see Momigliano 1982[A89], 3–15.

[29] E.g. Niese 1888[H68], 410ff; Beloch 1926[A12], 344; Ogilvie 1965[B129], 340. The tradition is defended by De Martino 1980[G51], 14–15.

[30] See Rotondi 1912[A114], 197–212, and cf. 212–15.

abandon the city of Rome after the Gallic Sack and move to the site of Veii, an attempt that was foiled by an emotional appeal from Camillus (Livy v.51ff). The result of this particular conflict was a compromise, since although some of the *ager Veientanus* was distributed to the poor, the individual allotments were relatively small (see above).

The second line of attack that the plebs adopted was the introduction of a statutory limit on the amount of *ager publicus* that any one *paterfamilias* could occupy, and on the numbers of animals he could graze on it. This was one of the principal ingredients of the Licinio-Sextian legislation, which, in spite of fierce opposition, became law in 367 B.C. The aim of the law was to allow poor plebeians some access to the *ager publicus*. There is no evidence that before 367 plebeians had been legally denied the right to occupy *ager publicus*, as is sometimes asserted, but it is likely enough that that is what happened in practice. It is important to note that the Lex Licinia merely imposed fines on those who held public land in excess of the prescribed limit. It did not set up any machinery for the reclaiming of such excess in the name of the state, nor did it contain any provision for the assignation of public land to the plebs. It was concerned solely with rights of occupation (*possessio*), and in this respect it differed from the agrarian law of Tiberius Gracchus, for which it provided only a partial model. This crucial distinction is a strong argument in favour of the authenticity of the Lex Licinia, and clearly undermines the view that it was a fictitious anticipation of the legislation of the Gracchi.

It is generally accepted that the Lex Licinia was a genuine early example, if not in fact the earliest example, of a law to limit holdings of public land (*lex de modo agrorum*). The details of the prescribed limits are, however, a matter of controversy. Livy and other sources maintain that a maximum of 500 *iugera* was laid down for individual holdings; but in the course of a precise digression on the subject Appian adds two further clauses: that the number of animals that could be put to pasture on public land should not exceed 100 cattle or 500 smaller animals (i.e. sheep or pigs),[31] and secondly that a certain number of the workers should be free men (App. *BCiv.* 1.8.33). These details are said by some historians to be anachronistic, more appropriate to the age of the great slave-run estates (*latifundia*) of the second century B.C. than to the simple peasant society of the fourth century. That may be so; in any event it is probable that the two additional clauses mentioned by Appian were later modifications of the original Lex Licinia. That does not mean, however, that we should reject the statement of other sources, including authoritative writers like Varro (*Rust.* 1.2.9), that the Lex Licinia imposed a limit of 500 *iugera*.

---

[31] Tibiletti 1950[G147a], 248f and Gabba 1958[B59], ad loc. have argued that these figures are not alternatives, but should be taken as cumulative. This is possible, but the precise wording of Appian should not be pressed too far.

The *ager Romanus* is likely to have embraced large areas of *ager publicus* already at the beginning of the fourth century. We cannot know how much of the territory of Veii was assigned to freeholders, how much was left in the possession of the original inhabitants (who were given full rights of ownership in accordance with the law of Roman citizens – *ex iure Quiritium*), and how much was left as *ager publicus*, but on any reasonable estimate the latter category must have been a substantial proportion of the total; modern scholars have suggested as much as half or two thirds – that is, *c.* 112,000 or *c.* 150,000 *iugera*.[32] If we remember that this amount would have been an addition to the *ager publicus* that already existed in the old *ager Romanus*, then it becomes evident that some individual holdings might well have exceeded 500 *iugera*, or at least threatened to do so. It is probable that the 500 *iugera* limit, so far from being a second-century figure applied anachronistically to the early fourth century, was on the contrary a fourth-century figure that had become little more than an archaic survival by the second, when some landowners possessed estates embracing thousands of *iugera* of *ager publicus*. That would explain the hysterical reaction of the Roman ruling class when Ti. Gracchus proposed to enforce the ancient limit. A moment's reflection is sufficient to show that, unless some holdings of *ager publicus* in 133 B.C. were vastly in excess of the ancient limit, Gracchus' land commission would not have been able to obtain much land for distribution to the poor.

We may now turn to the problem of debt, which was one of the main issues in the conflict over the Licinio-Sextian Rogations and had always been a major grievance of the plebs. Once again it will be necessary to digress briefly on the background, and to discuss the general nature and causes of indebtedness in archaic Rome.

Debt[33] was a direct consequence of poverty and land hunger, and itself gave rise to the condition of servitude to which many of the plebeians were reduced. The institution of debt-bondage is well attested in early Rome and has parallels in many other archaic societies. Indeed it can be regarded as a defining characteristic of such societies, and a dominant feature of their relations of production. In Rome the situation of debt-bondage was known as *nexum*. Our sources, however, knew little more about it than that, and were unable to define it in precise juridical terms. It has been endlessly discussed in modern times, especially by students of Roman law. It must be said, however, that most of the modern literature is more concerned with abstract legal questions than with the problem of setting the institution of *nexum* in its social and economic context.

---

[32] De Martino 1980[G51], 26. The general point made in the text was already clearly set out by H. M. Last in the first edition of *CAH* VII: see (Stuart Jones and) Last 1928[H92], 539–40.

[33] For this issue in a fifth-century context cf. pp. 214ff.

A particular problem is the relationship between the institution of *nexum* and the procedures outlined in the Twelve Tables for executing judgement on defaulting debtors. Such persons were called *addicti* or *iudicati*, and following judgement they could be seized by their creditors and either killed or sold into slavery across the Tiber.[34] Since these penalties clearly did not befall the *nexi*, it seems reasonable to accept the conclusion reached by many historians and romanists that seizure (*manus iniectio*) and bondage (*nexum*) were distinct institutions.[35] The most probable interpretation is that *nexum* was the result of an agreement voluntarily entered into by the debtor, who placed himself in the power of the creditor in order to avoid the extreme consequences of a judgement for default. This distinction seems to be reflected in the language of Livy, who implies that it was normal practice for a poor man to 'enter into bondage' (*inire nexum*).[36]

This interpretation can provide a solution to the puzzle of why a rich man should have been prepared to issue a loan to an impoverished peasant who had no prospect of repaying it. Since the loan was secured upon the person of the debtor, the original transaction was made precisely in order to create a state of bondage. The 'loan' was therefore a payment for the labour services of a bondsman, who effectively sold himself (or one of his children) to the 'creditor'. From the lender's point of view the object of the exercise was to obtain the labour services of the debtor rather than profit through interest. The difference between such an arrangement and a wage contract is that the debt-bondsman is placed under constraint, and his person is completely at the disposal of the employer. In fact the most striking aspect of the tradition about *nexum* in early Rome is the prevalence of stories of maltreatment of debtors, who were apparently beaten and sexually abused as a matter of course.

The precise legal details of the *nexum* contract are unknown, and there is a wide range of possibilities. It is for example uncertain whether the *nexus* had to give his services until his debt was repaid, whether he gave his labour in lieu of interest, or indeed whether he gave it in lieu of payment – i.e. 'worked off' his debt. In such a case the payment can hardly be viewed as a loan at all, but rather as part of a service arrangement. Equally we do not know whether the bondage was permanent or restricted to an agreed term. In the latter case the bondage could have become permanent in practice because of the necessity (for the debtor) of renewal. It is probable that some or all of these possible variations actually existed, and that *nexum* was a flexible institution. At all events we may reasonably assume that its most important function was to provide

[34] See e.g. Watson 1975[G317], 121ff.
[35] E.g. Mitteis 1901[G276], 96ff; Watson 1975[G317], 111ff; Finley 1965[G65], 172 (= 1981, 158).   [36] Livy VII.19.5; cf. VIII.28.2; on these texts see MacCormack 1967[G260], 350ff.

dependent labour for exploitation by large landowners. This conclusion becomes inescapable if we accept the standard view that there was no alternative source of available labour.

Although chattel slavery existed in early Rome,[37] and probably some form of hired wage labour as well, these categories cannot have accounted for more than a small part of the total labour force. For the most part wealthy landowners must have relied upon the labour of their dependants. Some of these may have been clients who were granted privileged tenancies on lands controlled by their patrons; but many of them will have been debt-bondsmen. If we accept this, together with the tradition that much of the power of the patricians came from their occupation of the *ager publicus*, we can see that the issues of *ager publicus* and *nexum* are directly related. As the control of the public land became concentrated in the hands of a small class of wealthy aristocrats, more and more peasants were reduced to servitude. They were denied the possibility of working the *ager publicus* for their own benefit, and instead worked it for the patricians under constraint. In this way the majority of the peasants were prevented from rising above the level of subsistence, and from obtaining a share of the surplus, which was entirely expropriated by the patricians and their clients.

This state of affairs forms the background to the crisis of the early fourth century. Livy refers frequently to the problem of debt at this period, and argues that it was greatly exacerbated by the Gallic Sack. There may be some justification for this opinion. Although the physical damage caused by the invaders was superficial, and the long-term effects on the economy slight or indeed negligible, nevertheless the presence of a hostile barbarian army living off the land for several months must have been catastrophic in the short term; many poor peasants must have lost everything and been faced with starvation. In such circumstances a growing incidence of debt and debt-bondage was inevitable.

The sources affirm that the problem was widespread and that large numbers of citizens were affected. According to Livy the tribunes of 380 B.C. complained that one class of citizens had been ruined by the other ('demersam partem a parte civitatis': Livy VI.27.6). The first major upheaval that occurred in connexion with the debt crisis of the 380s B.C. was the celebrated affair of M. Manlius Capitolinus, who was condemned and executed in 384 for allegedly aiming at tyranny. The surviving accounts of this obscure event are unreliable and highly elaborated rhetorical narratives. Much is made of the fact that Manlius, who had saved the Republic when he prevented the Gauls from storming the

---

[37] Slavery was certainly important at the time of the Twelve Tables, when, according to Watson (1975[G317], 82), 'the slave presence at Rome was considerable'.

Capitol, was later condemned for attempting to subvert it. There was further irony in the manner of his death: he was hurled from the Tarpeian rock (an outcrop of the Capitol), the very precipice from which he had once thrown the Gallic intruders. In Livy Manlius is presented as a tragic figure, consumed by pride and jealousy, and unable to tolerate the superior reputation of Camillus (who plays a prominent but scarcely comprehensible role in the affair). This romance was spun out of a very few authentic facts. But we can be sure that some kind of upheaval did take place, and that Manlius was a historical person.[38] This is borne out by certain incidental details, for example the story that after his death the Manlii decreed that in future no member of the clan should ever again bear the given name Marcus (a rule that was rigidly observed, so far as we know). But the important fact about the event, as far as this discussion is concerned, is that it arose directly out of the debt crisis. Manlius obtained the mass support of the plebs by taking up their cause (he was the first patrician to do so, according to Livy vi.11.7) and paying their debts out of his personal fortune.

Manlius was suppressed, but the crisis continued, in spite of attempts to alleviate it by the foundation of colonies (this point is made explicitly by Livy in connexion with Satricum – vi.16.6–7). Unrest over debt is recorded in 380 and again in 378. In the latter year Livy mentions the construction of the new city wall, and states that taxes levied to pay for it led to increased indebtedness among the plebs. It is difficult to know how much truth, if any, there is in this observation. It is certain that the wall itself was an immense undertaking, and must have imposed heavy demands on the available workforce. It was eleven kilometres long, over ten metres high and four metres thick at the base. The huge blocks of tuff with which it was built (measuring on average *c.* 1.5 m. × 0.5 m. × 0.6 m.) came from the Grotta Oscura quarries near Veii, which was fifteen kilometres from Rome. As far as I know the economics of the wall's construction have never been seriously studied.[39] But even on the roughest estimate it can be conjectured that the labour expended on the tasks of quarrying, transporting and laying the hundreds of thousands of blocks must have amounted to several million man-hours.

The problem is that we do not know who supplied the labour or how it was organized. Livy speaks of taxes and censorial contracts, but in this he may have been guilty of anachronism. It is perhaps more probable that the government distrained directly on the labour services of Roman citizens as a form of tax or an extension of military service, and only contracted with specialized craftsmen and engineers, some of whom

---

[38] He appears in the *fasti* as consul in 392 B.C., and is listed as *interrex* in 388 (Livy vi.5.6).

[39] The construction of the wall is treated in detail by Säflund 1932[E130]. Säflund's approach is largely antiquarian, however, and is not much concerned with social and economic questions.

perhaps came from abroad. On the other hand if Livy is correct and the whole of the work was farmed out to contractors (the fact that the wall was built in distinct and clearly identifiable sections may give some support to this idea), we still do not know how the contractors obtained the necessary labour. It is not impossible that wealthy contractors used the labour of slaves and debt-bondsmen, and were thus themselves the sole beneficiaries of a major investment of funds raised from taxes, booty and indemnities. The plebeians cannot have gained anything from the work unless there was a considerable redistribution of resources through the payment of wages. If this did not happen, Livy must be right that the building of the wall increased the burdens of the poor.

The debt issue featured prominently in the struggle over the Licinio-Sextian Rogations. The legislation apparently laid down that on all outstanding debts the interest paid should be deducted from the capital sum and the remainder paid off in three annual instalments (Livy VI.35.4). The following decades saw further enactments restricting interest rates and easing the terms of repayment (e.g. in 357 and 347). In 344 Livy records that severe penalties were inflicted on usurers (VII.28.9); two years later a Lex Genucia prohibited interest charges altogether, a law that remained in being for centuries, but was only rarely enforced (cf. App. *BCiv.* 1.54.232ff). Under 352 Livy records a law which apparently introduced a system of state mortgages and bankruptcy proceedings under the supervision of a commission of five men, two patricians and three plebeians.

Some of the details of these various reports may seem anachronistic or improbable, but there is no reason in general to doubt that debt relief was the object of much legislation in this period. It is true that our sources only rarely refer to *nexum*; but that is almost certainly the result of bias. Ancient writers naturally concentrated on the monetary aspects of the debt problem, and refer constantly to monetary loans, usury and default, because these were aspects that were familiar to them. In fact we are dealing with a society that did not yet use coinage; and although that does not rule out monetary transactions, it probably does mean that they were not the most common forms of debt contract, especially where the peasants were concerned. Rather, we should imagine loans of items such as seed corn, with repayment and interest in kind. The silence of the sources does not mean that the legislation of the mid-fourth century did not also contain measures to alleviate the conditions and terms of debt-bondage. The *nexum* certainly continued to exist (see e.g. Livy VII. 19.5 – 354 B.C.) until in 326 B.C. it was formally abolished by a Lex Poetelia (Livy VIII.28; Dion. Hal. *Ant. Rom.* XVI.5; Cic. *Rep.* II.34 (Varro, *Ling.* VII.105 places the law in 313 B.C., when a C. Poetelius was dictator)).

The Lex Poetelia marks the end of a long process of transformation.

By that time the land hunger of the plebs had been largely satisfied by the conquest and settlement of new territories. The improved economic conditions that resulted from successful warfare and extensive schemes of land assignation and colonization would have meant that the plebeians were gradually freed from the necessity of entering into bondage. It is probable that by the start of the Second Samnite War (327–304 B.C.) the institution of *nexum* had already become a relic of a bygone age. Its disappearance did not, however, put an end to indebtedness, which persisted as a major social evil to the end of the Republic. The Lex Poetelia merely abolished the *nexum* as a form of labour contract; from now on only defaulting debtors were placed in bondage, following a judgement in court.[40]

The decline and eventual abolition of debt-bondage at the end of the fourth century must have created a demand for an alternative supply of labour to work the large estates of the rich. The demand was met by the importation of slaves. The growing importance of slavery in fourth-century Rome is indicated by the tax on manumissions which was introduced in 357 B.C. (Livy VII.16.7). The tax implies that manumissions were frequent, which in turn presupposes a large number of slaves. By the end of the century freedmen were so numerous and so influential that their status had become a major political issue. From the beginning of the Samnite wars our sources regularly record mass enslavements of prisoners of war, a phenomenon which must imply that the Roman economy was by that time largely dependent on slave labour.

The idea that Rome did not become a slave society until after the Hannibalic War is unacceptable;[41] the process was in fact already well advanced by the end of the fourth century, together with the closely related phenomenon of imperialism. War and conquest both created and satisfied the demand for slaves. Finally we should note that the emancipation of the citizen peasantry and the increasing use of slave labour on the land made it possible for the Roman state to commit a large proportion of the adult male population to prolonged military service, and thus to pursue a course of imperialism and conquest.

III. CONSTITUTIONAL REFORMS AND THE RISE OF THE NOBILITY

In the space of barely two generations the social and economic structures of the Roman Republic had been radically transformed. This process coincided with a reform of the constitution and a profound alteration in the composition and character of the governing class. The change

[40] Brunt 1958[G22], 168; 1971[H17], 56–7.
[41] Cf. Finley 1980[G66], 83. See further below, pp. 413ff.

resulted from the power struggle that preceded the legislation of 367 B.C., and it is to this political conflict that we must now turn.

In general we are better informed about the development of Roman political institutions than about other matters, for two reasons: first because they were a matter of direct concern to the ruling class, to which the Roman historians and antiquarians themselves belonged, and upon which they concentrated their attention; and secondly because the results of the changes can be monitored through the evidence of the *fasti* and other relatively reliable indicators. Even so, the background remains obscure and controversial, and although we can document the changes we are often a long way from being able to explain them. Once again the literary sources do not seem to have been able to account adequately for the facts at their disposal, and we cannot trust their interpretations of them. In particular, the narrative of the Licinio-Sextian Rogations in Livy (our main source) is a tissue of confusion and misunderstanding.

Livy's version is roughly as follows: in 376 B.C. the plebeian tribunes C. Licinius Stolo and L. Sextius Lateranus brought forward three proposals (rogations). Two of these concerned land and debt (see above); the third dealt with the admission of plebeians to the consulship (Livy VI.35.4–5). Faced with patrician opposition and the veto of their own colleagues, Licinius and Sextius nevertheless persisted with their demands. The conflict lasted for ten years (376–367), during which the two reformers were continually re-elected. They countered the veto of their colleagues by themselves blocking the election of consular tribunes; for a period of five years (375–371) the state was without magistrates and no public business could be conducted (Diodorus XV.75 shortens the anarchy to one year). The crisis continued until 367, when the rogations were finally enacted by the plebs and accepted by the patricians in a compromise deal worked out by the aged Camillus, who emerged once again as the hero of the hour (Livy VI.35–42).

Very little of this narrative can be accepted as it stands. But of the following facts we can be reasonably certain. In 367 B.C. the consulship was restored as the chief annual magistracy and made accessible to plebeians. A new magistracy, the praetorship, was created; although the praetor held *imperium* and could be appointed to military commands if necessary, his principal tasks were judicial. At first the praetorship was held only by patricians, but in 337 B.C. a plebeian was elected. Another innovation was the appointment of two 'curule' aediles on the model of the existing plebeian aediles. Though confined to patricians at first, the curule aedileship was soon made accessible to plebeians, who held it in alternate years. Finally the Board of Two in charge of sacred performances (*duumviri sacris faciundis*) was enlarged to a Board of Ten (*decemviri*), comprising five patricians and five plebeians.

The most important of these measures was undoubtedly that concerning the consulship. The background to the reform is puzzling. In 444 B.C. it had apparently been decided that in certain years the consulship should be suspended and that three or more 'military tribunes with consular power' (*tribuni militum consulari potestate*) should hold office instead. We do not know why this change was instituted, nor what determined the decision to have tribunes rather than consuls in any given year (p. 192f). Two possible explanations are offered by the sources, but both are unsatisfactory. The idea that consular tribunes could provide more army commanders in times of serious military crisis is open to the objection that consular tribunes were often appointed when there was no obvious need for several commanders; what usually happened was that one or two of the consular tribunes commanded the army while the rest stayed at home. In times of extreme emergency the Romans continued to appoint dictators. An interesting fact noted by our sources is that no tribune ever celebrated a triumph. On the other hand, the explanation preferred by Livy, that the new magistracy was accessible to plebeians and was devised in order to allow them to take some part in the government, seems hard to accept in view of the fact that in the first few decades of the experiment the military tribunes with consular power were all patricians. Moreover it may not even be true that the patricians had a complete monopoly of the consulship in the period down to 444; some of the names in the *fasti* of the early fifth century appear to be plebeian.[42]

The only certain facts are that in the course of time consular tribunes came to be elected more frequently than consuls, and replaced them altogether after 392; that the number of consular tribunes in each annual college gradually increased, until by the end of the fifth century six had become the regular number; and finally that from 400 onwards the consular tribunes began to include men who were not patricians. The last point inevitably raises the question of why there should have been such resistance to the measure proposed by Licinius and Sextius, and why, if plebeians were already eligible for the chief magistracy, the enactment of the Licinio-Sextian Laws in 367 B.C. should have been regarded as such a landmark in the struggle for plebeian rights.

The answer provided by the tradition is that the law was a breakthrough, not because it allowed plebeians to hold the consulship, but because it required that one of the two annual consulships be *reserved* for a plebeian. The difficulty with this interpretation is that the alleged rule was not adhered to, and in several years between 355 and 343 both consuls were patricians. This is described by some scholars as a 'patrician

---

[42] Cf. above, pp. 175ff (with a different conclusion).

reaction'.[43] From 342 onwards, however, the two orders shared the consulship every year without exception for nearly two centuries. The introduction of this regular system is surely to be connected with a mysterious set of plebiscites which some of Livy's sources recorded under the year 342 B.C. and attributed to the tribune L. Genucius (Livy VII.42; and cf. below p. 345).

Strangely enough, however, Livy maintains that the reported Lex Genucia allowed plebeians to hold *both* consulships, a possibility that was not in fact realized until 172 B.C. Thus we find an apparent discrepancy between the literary tradition and the evidence of the *fasti* concerning the laws of 367 and 342. According to the annalists the first law stated that one of the consuls *must* be plebeian, the second that both *might* be. The *fasti* on the other hand suggest that the law of 367 made it possible for a plebeian to hold one of the annual consulships, and that the law of 342 made it obligatory.

The second of these two alternatives is clearly preferable. If a law of 342 B.C. had given the voters freedom to elect two plebeian consuls they would certainly have done so long before 172 B.C. The confusion in the sources concerning the Lex Genucia is easily explained, however, if we assume that it gave plebeians a guaranteed right to one of the consulships but did not specify any similar guarantee for patricians. At the time it was not necessary; the patricians' right to hold one of the consulships would have been taken for granted, and was in practice guaranteed by traditional custom.

In this connexion it is relevant to note that the Roman *comitia* made their decisions not by a show of hands but by a complex system of group voting. At the consular elections each of the constituent voting units (in this case the centuries) returned two names, and the two candidates who achieved a majority of the centuries were declared the winners. A curious feature of the system was that the centuries voted, and declared their results, in succession, and that as soon as a candidate achieved the votes of 97 of the 193 centuries he was declared elected. When a second candidate had gained 97 votes the election was considered complete and the voters went home. But since each century had two votes it would have been perfectly possible, if the people had had a free choice among all the candidates, for more than two men to obtain the required number of 97 votes.

Historians usually offer a cynical interpretation of this strange feature, and argue that its purpose was to give the power of decision to the wealthier centuries which voted first.[44] In the late Republic that was indeed what happened. But it is much more probable – indeed virtually

[43] Münzer 1920[H120], 21.   [44] Staveley 1972[G726], 180ff.

certain – that in earlier times (beginning in 342 B.C.) the presiding officer at the consular elections asked each of the centuries to return the name of a patrician and the name of a plebeian. It follows that a consular election was not a competition for two places between an undifferentiated group of candidates; rather, patrician candidates competed for one of the annual places, and plebeian candidates competed for the other. As we shall see, this fact has important implications for our understanding of the Roman political system in the fourth and third centuries B.C.

When the power-sharing system was ended at the consular elections of 173 B.C. it was no doubt argued that the change did not contravene the provisions of the Lex Genucia, since that law had only specified that plebeians should have a reserved right to one of the consulships. In 342 B.C. it had not been necessary to go further than that in order to ensure power-sharing. But once it was accepted that an all-plebeian college was in accordance with the Lex Genucia, historians could easily have made the mistake of supposing that it was what Genucius had originally intended.

If it was the Lex Genucia that introduced the system of power-sharing, it would seem to follow that the law of 367 B.C. had done no more than restore the consulship in place of the military tribunes with consular power. It has in fact been argued that the purpose of the Licinio-Sextian Laws was administrative reform;[45] the undifferentiated college of six consular tribunes was replaced by a more sophisticated system of five magistrates with specialized functions: two consuls, one praetor and two curule aediles. In this respect the reform continued a trend that had been initiated in 443 B.C. when the censorship was created. The difficulty with this interpretation is that it does not explain why the law should have been regarded as a victory for the plebs.

One possible answer is that the consular tribunate had not given the plebeians a chance to exercise 'real' power, since they were only being admitted to membership of a committee. It could be that whenever an important task presented itself the patricians arranged for it to be given to consular tribunes from their own class; thus in 379 B.C., according to Livy, a military command was given to two patrician tribunes 'because of their superior birth' ('quod genere plebeios . . . anteibant'), and their plebeian colleagues were left behind to guard the city (Livy VI.30.2–3). Alternatively recourse could be had to a dictator, who would always be a patrician. In these ways the patricians may have found the consular tribunate easier to control and manipulate than a dual magistracy.

There may be some truth in an explanation such as this. But it does not seem to tell the whole story. The tradition clearly implies that before 367

---

[45] E.g. von Fritz 1950[H32], esp. 39ff.

plebeians had been systematically excluded from the magistracies. The celebrated achievement of L. Sextius Lateranus, the first plebeian consul in 366 B.C., becomes rather less of a breakthrough if in fact he simply happened to be the first to hold an office after an administrative adjustment. The point is surely that he was the first plebeian to hold any kind of supreme office, just as L. Genucius (*cos.* 362) was the first plebeian to conduct a military campaign under his own auspices (Livy VII.6.8). Unless we dismiss the whole of the Roman tradition as worthless, we must accept that the Licinio-Sextian Laws radically changed the plebeians' rights in relation to the magistracies.

In one significant way L. Sextius did set a precedent. As far as we know he was the first Roman to hold both plebeian and curule offices in the course of his career. Admittedly our knowledge of the tribunician *fasti* at this early period is extremely limited; but the tribunes of the plebs we do hear about were the leaders of the plebeian movement, and it is surprising not to find any of them among the plebeian consular tribunes. Is it possible that before 367 B.C. former tribunes (and aediles) of the plebs were excluded from the curule magistracies?

The suggestion is admittedly hypothetical, but it has several points in its favour.[46] In the first place it is compatible with Momigliano's attractive theory that the so-called plebeian consuls of the early fifth century were clients of the patricians, and were drawn from the ranks of the *conscripti* (i.e. non-patrician senators). The *conscripti* were plebeian only in the negative sense that they did not belong to the patriciate. They certainly had nothing in common with the plebeians who took part in secessions, and who formed the alternative plebeian 'state' that emerged in the fifth century. Obviously the story of the Struggle of the Orders would not make historical sense if the organized plebs had included all Roman citizens who were not patricians. It is very much an open question whether groups such as clients or *conscripti* should be classed as plebeians at all.[47]

According to the model suggested by Momigliano, patricians and plebeians were not antithetical categories; rather they were two components of a wider and more complex structure which comprised a range of variously differentiated groups (e.g. clients and *conscripti*). Once it is accepted that there were Roman citizens who were neither patricians nor plebeians, the problem of eligibility for the magistracies is easily resolved. We can simply assume that the consular tribunate (and before that the consulship) were not exclusively reserved for patricians, but

---

[46] The case is argued more fully in Cornell 1983[H18], 101–20.

[47] For the general theory see Momigliano 1967[H60], 199–221 and 1967[H61], 297–312 (= id. *Quarto Contributo* 419–36 and 437–54); also 1975[A88], 293–332.

were nevertheless closed to plebeians, and *a fortiori* to men who had held plebeian office.

The assumption is not unreasonable, given the nature and aims of the plebeian movement. The movement was not a 'state within a state' (which is how it is often described) so much as a separate organization that was set up in opposition to the state and existed independently of it. The patricians at first refused to recognize the plebeian organization; then they attempted to isolate it by imposing disabilities on its leaders. The Lex Canuleia (445 B.C.) revoked a ban on intermarriage between patricians and plebeians; in the same way, perhaps, the Lex Licinia Sextia of 367 removed a prohibition which excluded the leaders of the plebs from the senate and the magistracies.

The most compelling argument in support of this reconstruction is that it makes sense of the story of the Licinio-Sextian Rogations. The aim of Licinius and Sextius was to abolish all forms of discrimination against plebeians as such. The enactment of the law was a victory for the leading plebeians, many of whom were wealthy, talented and politically ambitious. Such men had been attracted into the vigorous and well-organized plebeian movement in preference to the alternative of attaching themselves to a patrician patron. The latter course offered prestige and the hope of honours, but no opportunity to exercise real power. On this view the non-patricians who held the consular tribunate in the years before 367 were mere ciphers; not surprisingly they played no part in the leadership of the reformed state.

However that may be, it is generally agreed that only a small group of rich and aspiring plebeians derived any advantage from the constitutional reforms of 367 B.C. In the struggle against patrician exclusiveness this group had made common cause with the poor and had used the institutions of the plebeian movement to gain entry into the ranks of the ruling class. Whether the mass of the plebs benefited from their success is more doubtful. The poor gained some temporary economic relief, but lost control of their own organization. Once the plebeian leaders were admitted into the ruling class on an equal footing with the patricians they immediately acquired all the characteristics of the incumbent group and ceased to represent the interests of the plebs. The plebeian leaders were themselves wealthy landowners, and shared the same economic interests as the patricians. The point is well illustrated by the story that C. Licinius Stolo, one of the legislators of 367, was later fined for occupying more *ager publicus* than had been permitted by his own law (Livy VII.16.9). There is no way of knowing whether this story is historical. But if it is not true, it is *ben trovato*.

It seems clear that the plebeian leaders, having scaled the patrician citadel, pulled the ladder up after them. The process is a familiar one in all societies. That the outcome of the Licinio-Sextian Laws should have been the emergence of a joint patrician–plebeian aristocracy (the so-called *nobilitas*) is not in the least surprising, and could perhaps have been foreseen at the time. In Livy's account of the struggle over the Rogations the opposition to Licinius and Sextius is said to have come not only from the patricians, but also from within the plebeian movement itself. The two reformers were resisted both by their fellow tribunes and by a strong radical element of the membership, who favoured the proposed laws on land and debt but opposed the admission of plebeians to the consulship. We are told that at one stage the plebeian assembly was on the point of enacting the first two proposals and rejecting the third, but that Licinius and Sextius were somehow able to insist that all three measures were voted on together (Livy VI.39.2). Livy's account naturally raises procedural questions that we are not equipped to answer. Our ignorance in this matter does not, however, give us the right to reject the whole narrative out of hand, as some historians tend to do.[48] The basic point of Livy's story, that the Licinio-Sextian Rogations contained two very different kinds of reform, is clearly true, and his suggestion that the plebeian movement was sharply divided as a result is perfectly credible. The radical opposition had good reason to be suspicious of the proposed admission of plebeians to the consulship. Such a measure, they knew, would destroy the plebeian movement.

The Licinio-Sextian Laws radically transformed the political structure of the Roman state. By ending all forms of discrimination against plebeians the reform brought about the complete assimilation of all non-patrician Roman citizens, who were henceforth subsumed under the general designation of *plebs*. The consequence was that the plebeian movement lost its identity and ceased to exist as a separate organization. Its institutions were incorporated into the structures of the state. The tribunate and aedileship virtually became junior magistracies, open to all except patricians, and were increasingly occupied by young nobles who treated them as stepping stones to the consulship. Since these plebeian offices no longer entailed disqualification from curule magistracies, the men who held them did not consider themselves in any way bound to promote the interests of the mass of the plebs (cf. Livy X.37.11, where some tribunes are described as 'slaves of the nobility' – *mancipia nobilium*). The plebeian assembly (*concilium plebis*) was assimilated to an assembly of the people (*comitia populi*) and its resolutions (*plebiscita*) eventually became equivalent to laws (*leges*). The two terms are used interchangeably, not only in the ancient literary sources, but also in official documents from the late Republic.[49]

[48] E.g. von Fritz 1950[H32], 11 and n. 17.
[49] E.g. *lex agraria* of 111 B.C. (*FIRA* I n. 8) ll.77–82.

The precise legal status of plebiscites in the fourth century is, however, a matter of controversy. There are two basic problems. First we are told that on three separate occasions, in 449, 339 and 287 B.C., the people enacted that plebiscites should have the force of law and be binding on the whole community. Some scholars have suggested that only the law of 287 (the Lex Hortensia) is historical and that the other two are inventions. But this view runs foul of the second problem, namely that a number of plebiscites are recorded in the period before 287 B.C. which obviously did have legal force. For example the laws of Canuleius (445 B.C.), of Licinius and Sextius (367), and of Genucius (342) were in fact plebiscites. The probable answer to the puzzle is that the law of 449 conceded the general principle that the plebeian assembly could enact legislation, but in some way restricted its freedom to do so, for example by making plebiscites subject to senatorial assent or to a subsequent vote of the *comitia populi*. On this view the supposed restrictions would have been partly removed by the law of 339, and completely abolished by that of 287. It is not possible to say more than this on the evidence that is presently available.[50]

It has been argued in this chapter that the aim of the constitutional reform of 367 B.C. was to remove the civil disabilities suffered by plebeians, rather than to abolish the privileges enjoyed by patricians. In fact, the patricians retained their prestige and many of their political prerogatives; although these were gradually eroded in the course of the next two centuries they were never entirely eliminated. The fact that a very small number of patrician clans were able to claim the right to one of the consulships each year until the second century B.C. should not be overlooked. But their monopoly of important magistracies was rapidly ended in the years after 367. The first plebeian dictator was appointed in 356, and a plebeian censor soon followed (in 351). An important stage in the process is represented by the Leges Publiliae of 339, proposed by the dictator Q. Publilius Philo (who was subsequently to become the first plebeian praetor in 336). Three Publilian Laws are recorded. The first, modelled on the Genucian plebiscite of three years earlier, extended the system of power-sharing to the censorship. It too gave no specific guarantee to the patricians, who nevertheless continued to provide one of the censors as of right; no legislation was needed when two plebeian censors were elected for the first time in 131 B.C. (Livy, *Per.* LIX). The second Lex Publilia, 'that a decision of the plebs should be binding on the people' (Livy VIII. 12.14), has already been discussed. The third was a closely related measure which laid down that the 'authorization of the

Fathers' (*auctoritas patrum*) should be given before a law was voted on by the *comitia populi* rather than afterwards. The 'Fathers' (*patres*) were the patrician senators, and their right to sanction the people's decisions before they could become law was apparently a powerful weapon in their arsenal.

It is very uncertain precisely what the *auctoritas patrum* amounted to (p. 185), and what effect the Lex Publilia had on the people's freedom to make laws. It does not seem likely that the *auctoritas patrum* gave the patrician senators a general right of veto over measures of which they did not approve. If it had been a general power of assent the Lex Publilia would have increased rather than diminished the power of the patricians; obviously the capacity to kill off a proposal before it could be put to the vote would have been more effective than the right to sanction a decision that had already received the support of a majority of the people. But Publilius's law was certainly a liberal measure which enhanced popular sovereignty. It follows that the *auctoritas patrum* must have been some kind of confirmation that the law in question was technically acceptable, and in particular that it did not contain any religious flaws (the word *auctoritas* is etymologically related to augury, and implies religious 'authority'). The Lex Publilia therefore reduced the *auctoritas patrum* to a formality by laying down that any proposed measure had to be checked for religious defects in advance of the people's vote. It took away the patricians' power to overturn a popular enactment on a technicality.

The *auctoritas patrum* was one aspect of a more general religious aura that surrounded the patriciate. It was believed that the gods were especially intimate with the patricians, who consequently had exclusive control of many religious institutions and monopolized the chief priesthoods. The change in the composition of the committee in charge of sacred performances (*decemviri sacris faciundis*, see above) in 367 was the first attempt to break the patricians' hold on the priesthoods. The second and decisive stage occurred in 300 B.C. when a plebiscite (the Lex Ogulnia) admitted plebeians to the two major colleges of priests on a power-sharing basis (Livy x.6–9). Four plebeians were added to the four existing pontifices, and five plebeians were added to the four existing augurs. These priests held office for life; but whenever death created a vacancy in one of the colleges a successor was chosen from the same order as the deceased (see e.g. Livy XXIII.21.7). Thus the ratio of plebeians to patricians in the colleges of pontiffs and augurs remained constant (at 4:4 and 5:4 respectively) until the end of the Republic. In the late Republic only minor archaic priesthoods, such as the corporation of the Salii, were exclusively filled by patricians.

The character of the new regime that took power in 366 B.C. can be illustrated by an analysis of the consular *fasti*, which tell an interesting story. They make it clear that the beneficiaries of the reform were the aspiring plebeian leaders together with a relatively small group of patrician associates who supported them. The principal figures of this liberal or progressive wing of the patriciate were C. Sulpicius Peticus, L. Aemilius Mamercinus and Q. Servilius Ahala (who between them shared all the patrician consulships in the years 366–361), and M. Fabius Ambustus (censor in 363 and father-in-law of Licinius Stolo), who is said by Livy to have given active support to the reformers.

The victory of this 'centre party' (as it has been called) was won at the expense of the rest of the patricians, who found themselves excluded from office in the years after 367. It is striking, for instance, that not one of the eighteen patricians who held office as consular tribunes in the years 370–367 survived to hold a consulship after the reform;[51] moreover several old established patrician clans faded away altogether and do not reappear in the *fasti* after 367 B.C. 'Disappearing' patrician *gentes* include the Horatii, Lucretii, Menenii, Verginii, Cloelii and Geganii – to mention only some of those that are well represented among the consular tribunes in the early fourth century. One could add the Sergii and the Iulii, who came in from the cold only at the end of the Republic.[52]

Another conspicuous change is that in the decades after the Licinio–Sextian Laws office-holding was restricted to a small and exclusive group. The number of available opportunities was drastically curtailed, not only by the reduction of the size of the supreme annual college from six to two (or three, if the praetorship is included), but also by the frequency of the practice of 'iteration' – that is, the repeated tenure of the same office by the same man.

Iteration was extremely common in the reformed state. In the 25 years from 366 to 342 B.C. the 50 annual consulships were shared by only 27 men. The pattern is remarkable. Not only were 35 of the consulships (70 per cent) held by men who were consul more than once; even more striking is the fact that a majority of the individual consuls ($15/27 = 55.5$ per cent) held the office more than once. It follows that iteration was the norm at this period, and that any man who reached the consulship had a better than average chance of being consul again. This situation has no parallel in the entire 900-year history of the consulship.

The pattern also contrasts sharply with the record of consular tribunates in the period before 367. Although iteration had been frequent under the old regime, it had not unduly restricted the number of opportunities available to aspiring office holders. In the 25 years from 396 to 367 B.C. (excluding the 'anarchy') some 75 individuals were

---

[51] Data in *MRR* I.110ff. The point was made already by Münzer 1920[H120], 10–11.
[52] Data in Ranouil 1975[H74], 205ff.

consuls or consular tribunes, a sharp contrast with the 27 who held the consulship in the corresponding period after the reform.

No doubt it was the exclusiveness of the newly formed nobility, as well as the patrician reaction after 355, that prompted a shake-up in 342 B.C. In that year Livy reports a mutiny among the soldiers who were serving in Campania (VII.38–42). This mysterious affair, which is linked to a debt crisis and a secession in other sources, is one of several indications that the Roman state underwent a major upheaval at this time. The others include a complete volte-face in Roman foreign policy in 341 (see below, p. 360), and the appearance of several 'new men' in the consular *fasti* in the following years.

All these phenomena must be in some way connected with the Leges Genuciae of 342. Two of the Genucian laws, those concerning usury and the sharing of the consulship between patricians and plebeians, have already been referred to (above, pp. 333 and 337). The third law apparently provided that no one could hold more than one magistracy at a time, or hold the same office twice within ten years. The latter clause seems to be reflected in the *fasti*. In the next twenty years no one held two consulships within ten years of each other, with one doubtful exception. The contrast with the preceding period is so striking that we must conclude that the Lex Genucia was not only enacted but enforced.[53] The election in 321 of two able and experienced men (L. Papirius Cursor II, Q. Publilius Philo III), in both cases in breach of the ten-year rule, was clearly a response to exceptional circumstances; 321 B.C. was after all the year of the Caudine Forks (p. 370). The general crisis of the Second Samnite War caused a revival of frequent iterations. Not for the last time the Romans sacrificed constitutional principle on the altar of military expediency. In the space of just thirteen years (326–313) L. Papirius Cursor managed to hold five consulships, two of them in succession (in 320 and 319).

But Cursor's remarkable record was an exception and stands out against a more general trend away from multiple iterations and towards a wider distribution of consular honours among the elite. In 295 B.C., significantly a year of extreme crisis, the two consuls were men who between them could boast nine consulships (Q. Fabius Maximus Rullianus V, P. Decius Mus IV), but nothing like this was to occur again until the Second Punic War, when military exigencies caused another temporary reversion to multiple iterations. In the period from 295 to 215

[53] This has frequently been denied, even by Mommsen (1887–8[A91], 1.519 with n. 5). It is true that one of the consuls of 341 and one of those of 340 had held the consulship a few years previously; but we need not suppose that the law was made retrospective. The possible exception is L. Papirius Crassus, *cos.* 336 and 330; but there may have been two men of this name at this period. See F. Münzer 1949[H121], 1035–6; 1949[H122], 1036.

only three men held three consulships, of whom M'. Curius Dentatus (*cos*. III, 274) was the last. The most telling statistic is that in the thirty-five years from 289 to 255 the seventy consulships were shared among sixty-five different individuals; in other words there was virtually no iteration at all.

We may conclude by observing that from the end of the Third Samnite War (290 B.C.) until the dictatorship of Julius Caesar Roman nobles could normally expect, at best, to be consul just once in their careers. Second consulships were rare, and indeed were prohibited by law in 151 B.C. Exceptions to this general rule occurred only at times of extreme military emergency or civil strife (the Hannibalic War, the invasion of the Cimbri, the domination of Cinna). The pattern of office-holding in the period 366–290 B.C. is therefore significantly different from that which prevailed in the last two and a half centuries of the Republic. This fact surely has important implications for our understanding of the structure of Roman politics in the fourth century.

In the 'classical' Republic, say from 287 to 133 B.C., the state was in the hands of a senatorial oligarchy. By the end of the third century the senate controlled all aspects of government activity, and had subordinated the executive magistrates (who were themselves senators) to its authority. This is not surprising in view of the fact that individual senators held high office only occasionally and for short periods. The senate's opinions, and especially those of its leading members who had themselves been consuls, effectively controlled those individual senators who happened to be exercising magisterial *imperium* at any particular time. It is generally agreed that the most important mode of control was the restriction of the possibility of iteration. In this way the senatorial oligarchy was able to curb the ambition of individuals and to prevent them from exercising independent power (see further below, pp. 392ff).

In the fourth century, evidently, matters were very different. It should be emphasized that we know little about either the organization or the function of the senate at this time. But there are good grounds for supposing that in the fourth century the senate did not possess the wide-ranging supervisory powers that it had in the classical period. In later practice there are many residual traces of a system in which major initiatives, such as the founding of colonies, the declaration of war and the conclusion of treaties, were decided on by popular assemblies summoned by the magistrates.

There is no reason to suppose that in the fourth century popular enactments were merely formal ratifications of decisions that had already been taken in advance (and in secret) by the senate. That is not to say that the advisory role of the senate was unimportant; but when the Roman

state was a relatively compact territorial unit with only simple administrative needs, the popular assemblies probably took a more central part
in determining policy than they did later. Again, the senate's control of
finance would have been less important and perhaps less absolute in the
pre-coinage economy of the fourth century than in the relatively complex
world of the second. In the third and second centuries the senate's right
to terminate or extend the *imperium* of a serving commander (*prorogatio*)
was a crucial weapon of control. But in the fourth century the practice of
prorogatio hardly existed. Moreover the earliest known instance, the
appointment of Q. Publilius Philo *pro consule* against Naples in 326 B.C.,
was the result of a *popular* vote (Livy VIII.23.11–12).

We must surely reckon with the possibility that in the fourth century
political power rested not with a collective oligarchy but with a handful
of talented and charismatic individuals who shared the senior
magistracies among themselves and largely directed the policy of the
state. In the seventy-two years between 366 and 291 B.C. fifty-four
consulships were held by only fourteen individuals, thirty-eight of them
by just eight, each of whom was consul four or more times. They include
the patricians C. Sulpicius Peticus, L. Papirius Cursor, M. Valerius
Corvus and Q. Fabius Maximus Rullianus, and the plebeians M.
Popillius Laenas, C. Marcius Rutilus, Q. Publilius Philo and P. Decius
Mus. These men and their associates ruled by virtue of the offices which
they held, and their tenure of office was dependent on popular appeal and
electoral success. This point highlights the fact that the system involved a
substantial democratic element that was largely absent in the later period
when the senate controlled the government and the outcome of the
annual elections had little effect on the general direction of policy.

APPENDIX

The chronology of the fourth century B.C.

The Romans dated events by the names of the annual consuls. For us to
give a 'Christian' date (B.C. or A.D.) to any given consular year is a
relatively straightforward matter for the period after 300 B.C., for which
we possess a full and accurate list of consuls (the *fasti*). Before 300 B.C.
matters are more complicated because the *fasti* are reconstructed differently by different sources, and because there are discrepancies between
the several versions of the *fasti* and chronological data provided by
independent evidence.

The present chapter has followed standard procedure in using the so-
called 'Varronian' chronology. This canonical system, established by
scholars (including Varro) at the end of the Republic, placed the founda-

tion of the city in 753 B.C., the first consuls in 509, the Gallic Sack in 390 and the first plebeian consul in 366. This is the system followed by the Fasti Capitolini, the inscribed lists of consuls and triumphs which were set up in the Forum in the time of Augustus.[54]

The problem is that the Varronian chronology is a secondary reconstruction based on an artificially revised version of the *fasti*. In particular there are clear signs of an attempt to lengthen the chronology by means of bogus insertions into the list. The most notorious are the four so-called 'dictator-years' – i.e. (Varronian) 333, 324, 309 and 301 B.C. In each of these years, according to the Fasti Capitolini, a dictator and *magister equitum* held office instead of consuls, and gave their names to the year. It is obvious, however, that the dictator-years were a relatively late fabrication. They do not appear in any sources other than the Fasti Capitolini, and it is impossible to believe that such an extraordinary constitutional anomaly as a dictator-year should have gone unnoticed by historians if it had had any foundation either in fact or in tradition. The point can be further confirmed by other means (see for an example, p. 374 n. 29).

The Fasti Capitolini also include five years of 'anarchy' (Varronian 375–371 B.C.) during the turmoil of the Licinio-Sextian Rogations, in which no curule magistrates were elected. Livy's version is similar (VI.35.10, and cf. above, p. 335), but Diodorus, more plausibly, has only one year without magistrates. The five-year anarchy is obviously unlikely to be historical, and is best seen as a device, similar to the dictator-years, for extending the chronology of the fourth century. The need for such lengthening was already implicit in the Roman historical tradition at an early stage. For example Fabius Pictor wrote that the election of the first plebeian consul (Varronian 367 B.C.) occurred in the twenty-second year after the Gallic Sack (Gell. *NA* v.4.3), although the *fasti* record only nineteen colleges of consular tribunes for the period in question. Again, Polybius maintains (II.18.6) that the Gauls returned to Latium (Varronian 361 B.C.) in the thirtieth year after the Sack, a period covered in the *fasti* by only twenty-five colleges of consular tribunes.

The most important piece of independent evidence was the synchronism of the Gallic Sack with the Peace of Antalcidas and the siege of Rhegium by Dionysius of Syracuse. The synchronism, which was recorded by Polybius (1.6.2), but was probably worked out by an earlier historian such as Philistus or Timaeus, would place the Sack in the spring

[54] But note that the years of the Varronian era, which are reckoned in numerical sequence from 21 April 753 B.C. (the traditional foundation day), are equated in the Fasti Capitolini with the years in which the consuls entered office. Thus for example the consuls who took office in the early months of 362 B.C. (Q. Servilius Ahala II, L. Genucius Aventinensis) are placed in *a(b) u(rbe) c(ondita)* 391 (i.e. 21 April 363–20 April 362).

of the Julian year 386 B.C. The Romans knew that the Sack had occurred under the consular tribunes Q., K. and N. Fabius Ambustus, Q. Sulpicius Longus, Q. Servilius Fidenas and P. Cornelius Maluginensis; but in the *fasti* only eighty-one colleges of consular tribunes and consuls were listed between that year and the consulship of M. Valerius Corvus V and Q. Appuleius Pansa (= Varronian 300 B.C.).

Those who attempted to establish a general chronology in the late Republic would have been able to infer from such evidence that the available versions of the *fasti* were deficient in the period after the Sack. In particular, the synchronism of the Sack with the Peace of Antalcidas would have indicated that the list of magistrates was four years short. It is probable that the four dictator-years and the extension of the 'anarchy' from one to five years were alternative ways of lengthening the *fasti* by the appropriate amount. But by adopting *both* devices, the Varronian chronology placed the Sack in 390, four years *earlier* than the Polybian date.

The precise mechanics of the Varronian chronology need not concern us. The important point for the present purpose is that the later-republican annalists had access to several rival chronologies, which differed from one another by only a few years at most. But the discrepancies, though trivial in themselves, may have created confusion in the historical tradition by causing annalists to duplicate events which their sources placed in different years.

The frequency of such 'doublets' is debatable, but in the view of the present writer should not be exaggerated. We should note that what really mattered as far as the Romans were concerned was the consular year in which an event took place, rather than the location of that year in any general scheme of absolute chronology. For instance, one historian has recently written that the capture of Veii occurred 'in (Varronian) 396 according to Livy, in 388 according to Diodorus'.[55] This implies that Livy and Diodorus reported the fall of Veii under different years; but in fact they place the event in the same 'Roman' year – the consular tribunate of L. Titinius, P. Licinius, P. Maelius, Q. Manlius, Cn. Genucius and L. Atilius; it is only their general schemes of chronology that are different. In fact Livy, who omits the dictator-years and therefore does not follow the Varronian chronology, places the fall of Veii in 391 B.C.,[56] whereas Diodorus synchronizes the year in question with Olympiad 96.4, the archonship of Demostratus (i.e. 393/2 B.C.).

[55] Harris 1971[J175], 41.

[56] Livy's chronology is five years adrift from the Varronian at this point, because he omitted not only the four dictator-years, but also the consular tribune year Varronian 376 B.C. (see MRR I.108–9).

Many readers of Livy are quite unaware that his chronological scheme is different from the Varronian one. The reader is not affected by this because Livy records events under the heading of the annual magistrates, who by a simple process of conversion can be given their appropriate Varronian dates (which are inserted in the margins of many modern editions). No doubt ancient readers were equally unconcerned about the absolute chronology of the annalistic histories they consulted. A historian using a variety of annalistic sources would be unlikely to duplicate events which were 'dated' differently by his sources, provided that they were recorded in the same consular year.[57]

[57] On the rival chronologies of the republican period see further, pp. 625ff.

CHAPTER 8

THE CONQUEST OF ITALY

T. J. CORNELL

I. ROME'S FIRST STRUGGLE WITH THE SAMNITES, THE DEFEAT OF THE LATINS AND THE FORMATION OF THE ROMAN COMMONWEALTH

The emergence of the nobility and the competition for honours among its individual members, described in the previous chapter, were directly related to the development of Roman imperialism. The great political figures who dominated public life in the second half of the fourth century B.C. initiated and directed a policy of military conquest which in the space of little more than half a century brought all of peninsular Italy under Rome's control. This process was dominated by the struggle between Rome and the Samnites, which began in 343 B.C.

The Samnites were a powerful federation of tribes who occupied a large area of the southern central Appennines. Samnium was a land-locked region, roughly rectangular in shape, which stretched diagonally from the river Sagrus (Sangro) in the north-west to a point beyond the Aufidus (Ofanto) in the south-east. On its north-eastern side it was separated from the coast by the lands of the Frentani and Apuli, and on the south-western side by those of the Volsci, Sidicini, Aurunci, Campani and Alfaterni. The precise line of the frontier in 343 B.C. cannot be drawn with any certainty; its probable course is most easily indicated on a map (see Map 5).[1]

The area defined by these conjectural limits measures some 12,500 km.[2] Both in antiquity and in more recent times Samnium seems to have been densely populated by comparison with other rural areas of

---

[1] I have followed E. T. Salmon's reconstruction of the borders of Samnium (Salmon 1967[J106], 23–7). It has been argued on the basis of the fourth-century *Periplus* of the Ps. Scylax (XI.15) that the Samnite territory stretched from coast to coast (e.g. De Sanctis 1907–64[A37], II.266); but the reference is probably to the territories of the Frentani (on the Adriatic side) and the Alfaterni (on the Tyrrhenian), who were not members of the Samnite League. Cf. Salmon 1967[J106], 40–1.

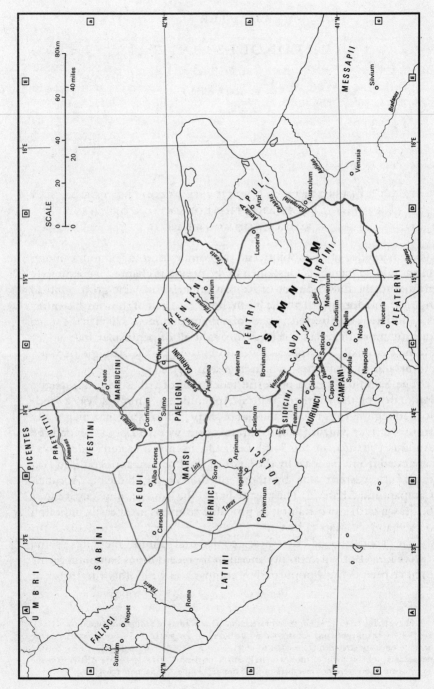

Map 5 The peoples of Central-Southern Italy *c.* 350 B.C. (after Salmon 1967 [J 106]).

peninsular Italy. On the basis of modern calculations the total population of Samnium in 343 B.C. can be estimated at around 450,000 persons.[2]

The region consists of a mountainous plateau intersected by steep re-entrant valleys, especially those formed by the upper reaches of the rivers Sangro, Trigno and Biferno, which give access to central Samnium from the north-east. On the southwestern side the land rises steeply from the Volturnus valley to the great massif of the Mons Tifernus (Montagna del Matese), which is the backbone of the region. Even so, Samnium is relatively easily traversed, at least in peacetime; and although more than 65 per cent of it rises above 300 m., a surprisingly large proportion of its land surface is capable of arable cultivation.

The upland valleys contain many pockets of fertile agricultural land, which were densely settled even in the pre-Roman period. Archaeology has confirmed this pattern of dense rural settlement, and has led to a modification of the traditional picture of the Samnite economy as essentially pastoral.[3] Stockraising, especially of sheep and pigs, was nevertheless an important element in the economy. It is probable that Samnite shepherds practised transhumance – that is, the seasonal move-ment of flocks from the plains to the mountains in the summer months – a system that has persisted in the central Appennines since time immemorial.[4]

But if archaeological research has shown that the Samnite economy was more complex and diversified than was once assumed, it still remains true in general that before the Roman conquest the region was poor and relatively backward, with few, if any, urban centres, no coinage and little trade. The inhabitants supplemented their livelihood by warfare and raiding, and in times of extreme hardship their only remedy was forced emigration in the form of a *ver sacrum* (see above, p. 292).

The political organization of the Samnites was correspondingly sim-ple and unsophisticated. The basic local unit was the *pagus*, a canton comprising one or more villages (*vici*), which was economically self-

[2] The estimate is based on the calculations of Afzelius 1942[J134]. Afzelius concluded (from Polybius) that the population density of Samnium could be reckoned at 37.8 persons per km.[2] (p. 106). He argued further that the pattern of relative density among the various regions as given by Polybius was confirmed by the figures for the rural population recorded in the 1936 census (p. 123). Afzelius himself reckoned that the area controlled by the Samnite League in *c*. 350 B.C. measured 21,595 km.[2], and gave the total free population as over 650,000 persons (p. 138); but he included the territory of the Frentani, Larinates and Alfaterni, and large parts of Apulia and Lucania in his total. If these are excluded, we arrive at a total of 12,665 km.[2] for Samnium proper, a more accurate estimate than the 14,000–15,000 given by Beloch (1926[A12], 368–9) or the 15,000 of Salmon (1967[J106], 27 and n. 4).

[3] Note especially the field survey, by a British team, of the Biferno (Tifernus) valley: Barker 1977[J9], 20ff and Barker *et al.* 1978[J11], 135ff. Some good general comments in La Regina 1975[B352], 273. For a concise statement of the traditional view see Tibiletti 1978[J119], 33.

[4] See e.g. Varro, *Rust.* II.2.10; III.17.9; *CIL* IX.2438 ('the Saepinum inscription'). On transhumance in general see Skydsgaard 1974[G140], 7ff; (Gabba and) Pasquinucci 1979[G76].

354

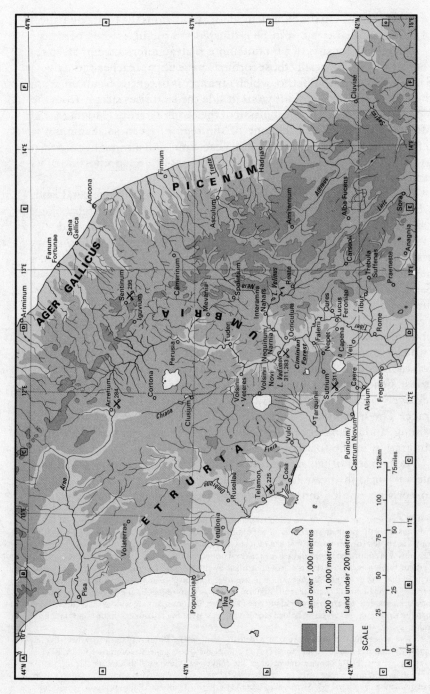

Map 6 The Roman conquest of peninsular Italy (North).

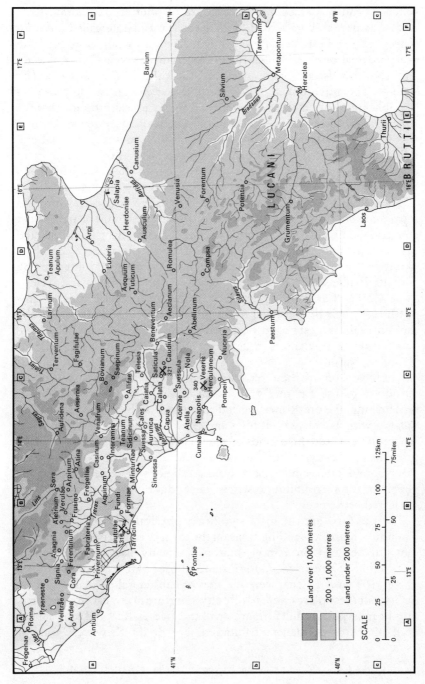

Map 7 The Roman conquest of peninsular Italy (South) (after Salmon 1967 [J106]).

sufficient and possessed a large measure of political autonomy. Each *pagus* was probably governed by an elected magistrate called a *meddiss* (Latin *meddix* – Festus 110 L). A group of such *pagi* would together form a larger tribal unit, for which the Oscan term was *touto* (Latin *populus*). The chief magistrate of the *touto* had the title *meddiss tovtiks* (*meddix tuticus*). The governmental system of the *touto* can be described as 'republican' rather than monarchical on the technical grounds that the *meddix tuticus* was an annually elected official; but in more general terms it was a very simple political structure in which military, judicial and religious functions were performed by the same man. Some sort of electoral machinery must be presupposed, but of the composition and functions of tribal councils or assemblies we know nothing at all.[5]

The Samnite League consisted of four tribal groups, each forming a separate *touto*. Of these the Hirpini inhabited the southern part of the country; their main centres were Aequum Tuticum (Sant'Eleuterio) and Malventum (Benevento). The Caudini occupied the western edge bordering on Campania, their chief places being Caudium (Montesarchio), Trebula Balliensis (Treglia), Saticula (S. Agata dei Goti) and Telesia (Telese). The Carricini, the smallest of the four, lived in the extreme north-east; their political centre was probably Cluviae (Casoli). Finally the Pentri, the largest group, occupied central and eastern Samnium, and had centres at Bovianum (Boiano), Saepinum (Sepino) and Aufidena (Castel di Sangro?).

The character of these 'centres', which are referred to in literary narratives of the Samnite wars, is uncertain. The general pattern of settlement in the pre-Roman period seems to have been one of scattered villages with associated hill forts and rural sanctuaries. The functional separation of these three kinds of site is characteristic of a non-urban or pre-urban society.[6] For instance, the elaborate sanctuary at Pietrabbondante seems to have been a religious meeting place for the people of the surrounding districts, but it did not form part of a large nucleated settlement.

The hill forts are the most significant physical relics of pre-Roman Samnium (Map 8). Standing ruins, in the form of rough polygonal walls, can still be seen on remote hilltops in many parts of the central Appennines. Some of them, for instance those at Monte Vairano, Castel di Sangro and Alfedena, were the sites of substantial permanent settlements; but these places were hardly cities, and are in any case exceptional. For the most part the hill forts are small and inaccessible, and cannot have been places of permanent habitation. No doubt they were used as

[5] A full account of the meagre evidence in Salmon 1967[J106], 77–101.
[6] La Regina 1975[B352], 273.

temporary refuges, although some of them may have had a more positive strategic purpose as military strongholds.[7]

Of the organization of the league we know only what we are told by Livy, who refers to some kind of central council and a single commander-in-chief who led the Samnites in war (e.g. IX.1.2; 3.9; X.12.2 etc.). Otherwise the sources tell us nothing, apart from implying that the Samnites maintained a remarkable unity in the face of common enemies. The individual tribes are hardly ever mentioned by name in the surviving accounts of the Samnite wars, which almost always refer simply to the Samnites.

This sense of national solidarity distinguishes the four tribes of the Samnite League from their neighbours. But we should not forget that in cultural terms the Samnites belonged to a much wider community of Oscan-speaking peoples who as a result of migrations in the fifth century (see above p. 284) had spread throughout the Mezzogiorno. The only exceptions were southern Apulia and the Sallentine peninsula in the extreme south-east (the 'Heel'), where a native culture and language persisted in isolation from the rest of Italy, and the coastal regions occupied by the surviving Greek colonies. Otherwise Bruttium, Lucania, northern Apulia, Samnium and Campania were all inhabited by peoples who spoke the same language and shared common religious beliefs, social customs and political institutions. This Oscan koine also included the peoples of the Abruzzi region which, then as now, belonged economically, socially and culturally to the South, although it is geographically on a parallel with Rome. The region was a patchwork of fragmented tribal groups: the Marsi, Paeligni, Vestini, Marrucini and Frentani.

It only remains to discuss the situation in Campania. Here the Oscan-speaking invaders had occupied a wealthy and highly developed region which had been colonized by both Greeks and Etruscans and in which urbanized city-states were well established. Although the immediate effects of the Oscan invasion at the end of the fifth century were dramatic, the city-states soon began to flourish once again under their new overlords. A remarkable mixture of influences led to the formation, in the fourth century, of a distinctive Campanian culture. Many of the old Greek and Etruscan cultural traditions and institutional structures survived, and were adapted to the social needs and values of the Oscan

[7] The matter is much disputed. The whole subject of central Italian hill forts still awaits a comprehensive and systematic study. For the present see the brief general survey of La Regina 1975[B352], 271ff. The excellent account of Conta Haller 1978[B314] unfortunately restricts its attention to the region of the lower Volturnus valley. Cf. the review by E. Gabba 1979[B331], 171–2. On this and other matters I have received invaluable assistance from S. P. Oakley, who has treated the subject extensively in his unpublished PhD thesis, *A Commentary on Livy Book IX, 1–28* (Cambridge, 1984).

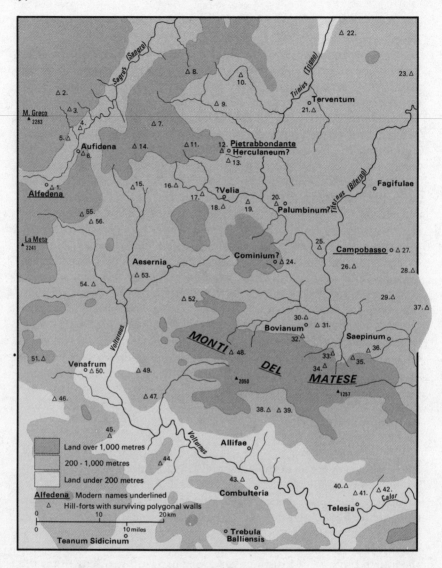

Map 8 Central Samnium.

Key to hill-forts

1. Alfedena
2. Rivisondoli
3. Roccaraso
4. Rocca Cinquemila
5. Castel di Sangro (Aufidena)
6. Castel di Sangro (Aufidena)
7. Monte Cavellerizo

8. Monte San Nicola
9. Agnone
10. Monte Rocca Labate (Belmonte del Sannio)
11. Staffoli
12. Pietrabbondante (Herculaneum?)
13. Monte Saraceno
14. Monte Miglio (S. Pietro Arellana)

conquerors. A case in point is their addiction to horse-breeding and cavalry prowess. As M. W. Frederiksen noted, this horsiness can hardly have been brought with them from Samnium; in fact it is virtually certain that the Campanian cavalry, which played such an important part in the political history of Capua in the fourth and third centuries, was originally a Greek institution.[8]

An intense rivalry existed between these city-states. In the fourth century the cities of northern Campania formed a league, centred on Capua and led by a *meddix tuticus*. Among the member states of this confederation were Casilinum, Atella and Calatia. Other Campanian towns such as Nola and Abella remained separate, while the Alfaterni in the south formed their own league under the hegemony of Nuceria. Naples, the only surviving Greek city in Campania, was strongly affected by Oscan influences, but retained its political independence. An equally strong antagonism existed between them and their Samnite kinsmen in the interior. This tangled web of internecine rivalry and conflict was further complicated, in 343 B.C., by the intervention of Rome.

The events of the so-called First Samnite War are described only by Livy, whose account (VII.32–38.1) can be briefly summarized. In 343 the Samnites attacked the Sidicini (an Oscan-speaking people about whose history and culture we have no specific information), and subsequently the Campanians, who had gone to their assistance. When the Samnites

15. Bosco Pennataro (Rionero Sannitico)	36. Terravecchia
16. Carovilli	37. Monte Saraceno (Cercemaggiore)
17. S. Maria dei Vignali (Pescolanciano)	38. Monte Cila
18. Chiauci	39. Castello d'Alife
19. Civitanova	40. Faiccio
20. Duronia	41. Monte Acero
21. Trivento (Terventum)	42. Monte Pugliano (Telesia)
22. Montefalcone	43. Dragoni
23. Serra Guardiola (Guardalfiera)	44. Monte Auro
24. Frosolone (Cominium?)	45. Presenzano
25. Castropignano	46. S. Pietro in Fine
26. Monte Vairano	47. Monte Castellone (Torcino)
27. Campobasso	48. Letino
28. Ferrazzano	49. Capriati
29. Vinchiaturo	50. Monte S. Croce (Venafrum)
30. Boiano (Bovianum)	51. Monte Sambucaro
31. Boiano (Bovianum)	52. Longano
32. Monte Crocella (Boiano)	53. La Romana (Castel Romano)
33. Campochiaro	54. Monte S. Paolo (Colli al Volturno)
34. Le Tre Torrette	55. Monte Castellone (Montenero Valcocchiara)
35. Guardiaregia	56. Monte S. Croce (Cerro al Volturno)

NOTE: This map is based on information supplied by Dr S. P. Oakley.

[8] Frederiksen 1968[J46], 3–31.

began to besiege Capua the Campanians appealed to Rome. In spite of their alliance with the Samnites (above p. 323), the Romans responded positively to the appeal and intervened on the Campanian side. Livy says that they took this step because the Campanians had surrendered themselves completely into the power of the Roman people (Livy vii.31.3–4) – a questionable excuse and perhaps also a doubtful piece of history.

A more convincing explanation of the Romans' action can be deduced from the speech which Livy attributes to the Campanian envoys (Livy vii.30). Here the suggestion is made that the Romans could not afford to ignore the opportunity that was being offered to them, nor to risk letting the Samnites gain control of Campania. The speech is unhistorical and full of rhetorical commonplaces – in particular its main argument is borrowed from Thucydides (1.32–36) – but it nevertheless contains an important historical truth. Campania is the most fertile and productive region in peninsular Italy, and by gaining control of most of it the Romans vastly increased their available economic and military resources and became more than a match for the Samnites. It is not an exaggeration to say that 'in the contest between Rome and Samnium the control over Campania was the key to ultimate victory'.[9]

Hostilities began when the Romans sent two consular armies to Campania in the summer of 343 B.C. After a number of victorious engagements they succeeded in driving out the Samnites and occupying Capua. Livy gives an improbably detailed account of these events, of which the basic outline at least can be accepted. We need not doubt that the Roman armies did enough to earn triumphs for both consuls (Fasti Capitolini) and the congratulations of a Carthaginian embassy (Livy vii.38.2). The theory that the whole First Samnite War was invented by the annalists[10] has not been widely accepted.

In 342 the Romans were preoccupied by an army revolt and a political crisis (see above, p. 345); when hostilities resumed in 341 the Samnites apparently sued for peace at the first appearance of a Roman army. The Romano-Samnite alliance was then renewed, with the consequence that the Sidicini and the Campanians at once allied themselves with the Latins and Volscians, who were already in revolt against Rome. There was, therefore, a complete reversal of the situation of two years earlier, when the Romans had aided the Campanians and Sidicini *against* the Samnites. This volte-face is indeed strange, but not by any means incredible. A possible explanation is that after an internal struggle in Rome a 'pro-Samnite' faction came to power (see above, p. 345).

Be that as it may, the Romano-Latin War, which began in 341, was a major turning point in Italian history. There is no reason to doubt Livy's

---

[9] Toynbee 1965[A131], I.91.   [10] Adcock 1928[J133], 588.

view that the war arose out of the Latins' resentment at being treated as subjects rather than allies. However, the specific demands that he attributes to the rebel leaders – that the Latins should be admitted to the Roman citizenship and should supply one of the consuls and half the senate (Livy VIII.4.11) – are clearly anachronistic. In part they reflect the aspirations of the Italian insurgents at the time of the Social War (91 B.C.).

The actual events of the war cannot be reconstructed in any detail. This point raises the general question of the reliability of the traditional narrative of the wars of conquest. Livy's account, which covers the period down to 293 B.C., is full of rhetorical battle-pieces and similar devices in which much of the detail is likely to be imaginary; such items as the numbers of enemy casualties are largely the product of enthusiastic guesswork. But the general outline of the campaigns need not be fictitious; there is no reason to think that any of the principal events were deliberately fabricated out of nothing by Livy or his sources. It is clear, however, that Livy's understanding of geographical and strategic realities was weak – and sometimes non-existent. Livy did not carry a map of Italy in his head, and certainly made no attempt to reconstruct campaigns on the ground. We do not know if he had ever visited Samnium, for instance, but it seems unlikely. Mostly Livy was content to reproduce the place names and other topographical indications that he found in his sources, without necessarily having any idea of their precise location or character. The fact that the sources he was following may themselves have done the same thing naturally increases the chances of misunderstanding and distortion.

In interpreting Livy's account, the method adopted by many modern commentators is that of the armchair strategist. That is to say, the historian rejects whatever seems implausible to him, and substitutes a reconstruction based on his own assessment of what the military situation required. The results are largely arbitrary, for obvious reasons. For instance, Livy's statement that the consuls of 340 B.C. marched through the country of the Marsi and Paeligni on their way to Campania (Livy VIII.6.8) is sometimes rejected as implausible – surely an 'anticipation' of the Romans' campaigns in Central Italy in the Second Samnite War. Other scholars, however, see the consuls' detour as a deliberate manoeuvre to surprise the Latins, who would have been expecting a direct attack.[11] In fact our knowledge of the general military situation is nowhere near good enough to allow us to decide on a matter of this kind. How can we know what the Latins were expecting? All that we can say is that seemingly implausible events should not be rejected automatically.

---

[11] For the former interpretation see e.g. De Sanctis 1907–64[A37], II.262; for the latter A. Alföldi 1965[I3], 412.

Indeed it is arguable, on the principle of the *lectio difficilior*, that statements in our sources are 'the more credible the more odd they look'.[12]

The revolt that began in *c.* 341 was crushed after four years of hard campaigning. The Volscians of Privernum were defeated in 341; in the following year the Latins and Campanians suffered at least two major defeats, one of them at the celebrated battle of Veseris (perhaps at Fenseris (Sarno); at any rate it was somewhere near Mount Vesuvius: Livy VIII.8.19). The battle was remembered in the Roman tradition for two incidents. First, T. Manlius Torquatus, the son of one of the consuls, slew an enemy champion in single combat, but was executed by his father for disobeying a command not to engage the enemy. The second incident involved the other consul, P. Decius Mus, who 'devoted' himself and the enemy to the gods of the underworld, and by riding headlong into the opposing ranks brought about their destruction along with his own. Whether these episodes are in any sense historical naturally cannot be known, but neither should be ruled out *a priori*. The first possibly, and the second probably, has some basis in fact.

The campaign of 340 brought a temporary end to the fighting. Rome punished her enemies by confiscating some of the territory of the Campani and Privernates (the future tribes Falerna and Oufentina) and of the Volscians and Latins to the south of Velitrae and Lanuvium (later incorporated in the tribes Maecia and Scaptia). Those who had remained loyal were rewarded. They included Lavinium, which was given a privileged status that is now obscure to us, and 1600 of the *equites Campani*, the aristocracy of Capua, who received economic privileges and honorary Roman citizenship.[13] Some of the Latin peoples took up arms again in 339, but were defeated after two more years of warfare. In 338 the Romans captured the stronghold of Pedum, and then proceeded to reduce the other rebel communities one by one (Livy VIII.13.8). In the following years mopping-up operations were carried out in Campania, and against the Sidicini, Aurunci and Volsci.

A skeletal version of these events can be found in the list of triumphs recorded in the Fasti Capitolini, which are well preserved for the second half of the fourth century; they represent a tradition, independent of Livy, that seems to be generally reliable. The triumphs of the period are listed in Table 7.

During the years 343–329 B.C. the Romans completely reorganized their relations with their conquered subjects. The result was the formation of a Roman 'commonwealth' (to borrow Arnold Toynbee's convenient phrase) which embraced all of the lowland district along the

[12] Alföldi 1965[I3], 410 n. 2.
[13] Livy VIII.11.16. This tradition, often rejected by scholars, is defended by Humbert 1978[J184], 172–6, who is followed in the text.

Table 7. *Roman Triumphs 367–264 B.C.*

B.C	Triumphator	Defeated enemy
367	M. Furius Camillus IV	Gauls
361	T. Quinctius Capitolinus	Gauls
361	C. Sulpicius Peticus	Hernici
360	C. Poetelius Libo	Gauls and Tiburtes
360	M. Fabius Ambustus	Hernici
358	C. Sulpicius Peticus II	Gauls
358	C. Plautius Proculus	Hernici
357	C. Marcius Rutilus	Privernates
356	C. Marcius Rutilus II	Etruscans
354	M. Fabius Ambustus II	Tiburtes
350	M. Popillius Laenas	Gauls
346	M. Valerius Corvus	Antiates, Volsci, Satricani
343	M. Valerius Corvus II	Samnites
343	A. Cornelius Cossus	Samnites
340	T. Manlius Torquatus	Latins, Campanians, Sidicini, Aurunci
339	Q. Publilius Philo	Latins
338	L. Furius Camillus	Pedani, Tiburtes
338	C. Maenius	Antiates, Lanuvini, Veliterni
335	M. Valerius Corvus III	Caleni
329	L. Aemilius Mamercinus	Privernates
329	C. Plautius Decianus	Privernates
326	Q. Publilius Philo II	Samnites, Palaeopolitani
324	L. Papirius Cursor	Samnites
322	L. Fulvius Curvus	Samnites
322	Q. Fabius Rullianus	Samnites, Apuli
319	L. Papirius Cursor II	Samnites
314	C. Sulpicius Longus	Samnites
312	M. Valerius Maximus	Samnites, Sorani
311	C. Iunius Bubulcus Brutus	Samnites
311	Q. Aemilius Barbula	Etruscans
309	L. Papirius Cursor III	Samnites
309	Q. Fabius Rullianus II	Etruscans
306	Q. Marcius Tremulus	Anagnini, Hernici
305	M. Fulvius Curvus	Samnites
304	P. Sempronius Sophus	Aequi
304	P. Sulpicius Saverrio	Samnites
302	C. Iunius Bubulcus Brutus II	Aequi
301	M. Valerius Corvus IV	Etruscans, Marsi
299	M. Fulvius Paetinus	Samnites, Nequinates
298	Cn. Fulvius Maximus	Samnites, Etruscans
295	Q. Fabius Rullianus III	Samnites, Etruscans, Gauls
294	L. Postumius Megellus	Samnites, Etruscans
294	M. Atilius Regulus	Volsones (=Volsinienses?), Samnites
293	Sp. Carvilius Maximus	Samnites
293	L. Papirius Cursor	Samnites
291	Q. Fabius Maximus Gurges	Samnites

Table 7 (*cont.*)

Lacuna of *c.* 21 lines, room for about nine triumphs

282	C. Fabricius Luscinus	Samnites, Lucani, Bruttii
281	Q. Marcius Philippus	Etruscans
280	T. Coruncanius	Volsinienses, Vulcientes
280	L. Aemilius Barbula	Tarentini, Samnites, Sallentini
278	C. Fabricius Luscinus II	Lucani, Bruttii, Tarentini, Samnites
277	C. Iunius Brutus Bubulcus	Lucani, Bruttii
276	Q. Fabius Maximus Gurges II	Samnites, Lucani, Bruttii
275	M'. Curius Dentatus IV	Samnites and King Pyrrhus
275	L. Cornelius Lentulus	Samnites, Lucani
273	C. Claudius Canina	Lucani, Samnites, Bruttii
272	Sp. Carvilius Maximus II	Samnites, Lucani, Bruttii, Tarentini
272	L. Papirius Cursor II	Tarentini, Lucani, Samnites, Bruttii
270	Cn. Cornelius Blasio	Regini
268	P. Sempronius Sophus	Picentes
268	Ap. Claudius Russus	Picentes
267	M. Atilius Regulus	Sallentini
267	L. Iulius Libo	Sallentini
266	D. Iunius Pera	Sarsinates
266	N. Fabius Pictor	Sarsinates
266	D. Iunius Pera II	Sallentini, Messapii
264	M. Fulvius Flaccus	Volsinienses

Source: Fasti Capitolini, ed. Degrassi 1947[D7].

Tyrrhenian coast from north of the Tiber to the bay of Naples. The settlement which the Romans imposed after 338[14] was of crucial importance in that it established a pattern for the future development of Roman expansion in Italy. It combined a number of constitutional innovations that gave the Roman commonwealth an unprecedented – indeed unique – structure. We do not know who devised the scheme,[15] but whoever it was made a vital contribution to the development of the Roman empire. In the opinion of G. De Sanctis this was the turning-point of Roman history.[16]

The settlement seems to have been drawn up on the basis of two broad principles. First, the Romans dealt with the various defeated communi-

[14] Livy (VIII.14) dates the settlement to 338, but Velleius Paterculus (1.14.2–4) is probably correct to imply that it was worked out over a period of several years.

[15] Inevitably the name of Q. Publilius Philo has been linked with the formation of the commonwealth: Toynbee 1965[A131], 1.139 n. 9. I agree with Toynbee that this seems 'a safe guess'. Livy gives a prominent role to the consuls of 338, especially L. Furius Camillus, the grandson of the conqueror of Veii (Livy VIII.13.10–18). Statues of the younger Camillus were set up in the Forum: Pliny, *HN* XXXIV.23; Asconius p. 14C.

[16] De Sanctis 1907–64[A37], II.267: 'Fu questo il momento critico della storia di Roma'.

ties individually rather than in groups. Leagues and confederations were dissolved. The consequence was that the constituent units of the Roman commonwealth were bound together not by mutual ties but by the fact that each had a fixed relationship with Rome. Secondly, a set of distinct types of relationship was established, so that Rome's subjects were divided into formal juridical categories defined by the specific rights and obligations of each community in relation to the Roman state. Thus a hierarchy of statuses was created among the member states of the Roman commonwealth.

The details of the settlement are systematically outlined in a careful chapter of Livy (VIII.14) which is the main source for what follows. Livy deals with the matter under three headings:

(a) *Latium: incorporated communities*

Some of the defeated Latin cities were incorporated in the Roman state and their inhabitants made Roman citizens. Livy specifies Lanuvium, Aricia, Nomentum and Pedum. Each of these places became a self-governing *municipium* on the model of Tusculum (see above, p. 319). Tusculum itself had taken part in the revolt (its cavalry commander, Geminus Maecius, had been killed by T. Manlius in the duel before the battle of Veseris) but its citizenship was restored in 338 after the ringleaders had been executed.

Specially harsh treatment was reserved for Velitrae and Antium. Velitrae's walls were razed and its ruling class was banished. The land of the dispossessed aristocrats was distributed to Roman settlers, and the remaining Veliterni were given Roman citizenship.[17] The inhabitants of Antium also became Roman citizens, but were forced to surrender their fleet. Some of the ships were immediately destroyed; their prows or beaks were displayed as trophies in the Roman Forum on the front of the speakers' platform, which was afterwards known as the Rostra (i.e. 'the Beaks'). A Roman garrison was then established at Antium in order to guard the coast. This so-called 'Roman-citizen colony' (*colonia civium Romanorum*) was modelled on the garrison that had been founded at Ostia a generation earlier (see above p. 315 and n. 15). Further coastal garrisons of the same type were later established at Tarracina (329 B.C.), Minturnae and Sinuessa (both 296 B.C.), and other places. They were manned by a small number of Roman citizens (usually 300) who were exempt from service in the legions but forbidden to leave their colonies.

There has been considerable discussion of whether or not the enfran-

---

[17] Livy obscurely states that they were already Roman citizens (VIII.14.5), which must be a mistake; he is presumably referring to the colonial status of Velitrae.

chised communities referred to above acquired full Roman citizenship. The most probable answer is that they did, since they are clearly distinguished by Livy from the states that received half citizenship (*civitas sine suffragio*). There is no warrant for the widely held view that the *civitas optimo iure* was reserved exclusively for Latins, and that the Volscians of Antium and Velitrae could therefore only have received *civitas sine suffragio*.[18] We have no reason to suppose that the Romans discriminated between newly enfranchised communities on the grounds of race or language.

The practical business of registering the new citizens was carried out by the censors of 332 B.C. (one of whom was the omnipresent Q. Publilius Philo). Most of the communities in question were registered in existing tribes, but Lanuvium and Velitrae were incorporated in two new tribes, respectively the Maecia and the Scaptia (Livy VIII.17.11). The new tribes also included Roman citizens who had been settled on land confiscated from the two cities. The inclusion of both old and new citizens in newly created tribes had occurred earlier in the settlement of the *ager Veientanus* in 387 B.C., and had become the normal practice.

(b) *Latium: communities not incorporated*

Of the Latin cities that were not enfranchised, Tibur and Praeneste retained their status as independent allies, but were forced to cede some of their territory. The Latin League was broken up, but those of its members which were not incorporated in the Roman state continued to exist as sovereign communities and to possess the rights of *conubium* and *commercium* with Roman citizens (see above, p. 269). But they were no longer permitted to exercise such rights among themselves and were forbidden to have political relations with one another. It is tempting in this context to invoke the cliché 'Divide and rule'; but it should be remembered that the (apparently short-lived) ban on mutual *conubium* and *commercium* did not isolate these communities entirely, since the majority of the old Latin peoples, whose territory bordered on theirs, were now Roman citizens.

From this time on Latin status no longer depended on membership of a distinct ethnic, jural and sacral community, but rather on possession of legally defined rights and privileges that could be exercised in dealings with Roman citizens. A Latin state could therefore be created simply by an enactment of the Roman people conferring Latin rights on it. Thus it

---

[18] Most clearly Salmon 1982[J219], 46–7 and *passim*. This view is now apparently shared by Sherwin-White 1973[A123], 205, 212. The old idea of Mommsen, that all incorporated communities, including the Latins, received the *civitas sine suffragio*, is no longer widely accepted. It seems to be contradicted by Dio VII.35.10. In general cf. Humbert 1978[J184], 177 n. 78.

came about that the peoples of the Latin name (*nomen Latinum*) were continually augmented by the foundation of new Latin communities in a revived programme of colonization that began in 334 B.C.

(c) *Communities outside Latium*

In the part of the Roman commonwealth that lay outside the boundaries of Latium Vetus – the region later known as Latium Adiectum (Pliny, *HN* III.56–9) – the Romans imposed partial citizenship (*civitas sine suffragio*) on the peoples whom they had defeated. Livy specifies the Campanian cities of Capua, Suessula and Cumae, to which Acerrae was added in 332 (VIII.17.12), and the Volscian towns of Fundi and Formiae, with the addition of Privernum in 329 (VIII.21.10). This partial citizenship was the most striking innovation of the whole postwar settlement. The *cives sine suffragio* were liable to all the burdens and obligations of full citizens – especially military service – but possessed no political rights. They could not vote in Roman assemblies nor hold office at Rome. As communities they retained their native institutions, and became self-governing *municipia*. Since they possessed the rights of *conubium* and *commercium* their status was in practice similar to that of the Latins, although the two categories were juridically quite distinct, since the Latins were technically foreigners (*peregrini*), whereas the Oscan-speaking Campanians and Volscians were technically citizens (*cives*).

The size and population of the Roman commonwealth after the Latin War have been analysed in detail by A. Afzelius, who estimated the size of the *ager Romanus* (i.e. the territory occupied by Roman citizens of all kinds) at 5525 km.^{2}, and of the commonwealth as a whole at 8505 km.^{2} This was considerably smaller than the territory of the Samnite League, but it included the best agricultural land in peninsular Italy, and in terms of manpower Rome commanded resources that were at least equal to, and perhaps greater than, those of the Samnites: Afzelius estimated the total population of the *ager Romanus* at 347,300 free persons, and that of the commonwealth at 484,000.[19]

The Roman commonwealth was a dynamic structure with an almost infinite capacity for growth. The institution of the self-governing *municipium* enabled the Roman state to go on extending its territory and incorporating new communities without having to make any radical changes to its rudimentary system of centralized administration; and by the invention of the *civitas sine suffragio* the Romans could increase their citizen manpower but still maintain the essential character of Rome as a city-state and the integrity of its traditional political institutions.

[19] Afzelius 1942[J134], 153.

On the other hand, colonization gave Roman citizens the chance to acquire conquered land even in distant regions, and thus to benefit directly from the commonwealth's territorial expansion; while the state was able to consolidate its conquests by planting strategic garrisons in troublesome areas. Since the colonies were self-sufficient autonomous communities with Latin status, their distance from Rome did not place any strain on its traditional city-state structure. These points were clearly outlined by Arnold Toynbee, who noted that the main constitutional innovations of the settlement 'gave the Roman commonwealth the maximum capacity for expansion, combined with the maximum solidity of structure, that could be obtained by "political engineering" with no institutional materials except city-states manned by citizen soldiers, governed by unpaid nobles, and maintained by subsistence farming'.[20]

II. THE SECOND SAMNITE WAR

In 334 B.C. the Romans established a colony at Cales, which they had captured from the Aurunci a year before. Cales (Calvi) was a crucial strategic site on the main route from Rome to Capua; it protected the vulnerable stretch of this route at a point where it swerved inland in order to cross the river Volturnus, and shielded Capua from the Sidicini.[21] The 2500 men and their families who colonized the site were drawn largely from the Roman proletariat, but also included Latins and other allies. They received allotments of land and were constituted as an autonomous community with Latin rights. The government of the colony was placed in the hands of a small group of well-to-do colonists (*equites*) who received large allotments of land and formed the ruling class of the new community.[22] Cales became a model for later colonies which were established at strategic points throughout the Italian peninsula during the course of the next two generations. As well as being military strongholds, these colonies were romanized enclaves in which Latin was spoken and the Roman way of life was practised; as such they contributed more than any other single factor to the consolidation of the conquest and the eventual unification of Italy under Rome.

Six years later a second colony was founded at Fregellae (Ceprano) on the eastern bank of the Liris, at the junction with the Trerus (Sacco). The colonization of Fregellae provoked the hostility of the Samnites, who had overrun the region a few years previously and regarded the Romans'

[20] Toynbee 1965[A131], 1.140.

[21] On the strategic importance of Cales see Toynbee 1965[A131], 1.136–7.

[22] This is not specifically attested for the early colonies, but can safely be assumed. Strangely enough the text that refers explicitly to the practice (Plutarch, *C. Gracch.* 9.1) is usually misinterpreted, e.g. by Salmon 1969[J218], 120.

action as an occupation of their territory (Livy VIII.23.6). Relations between Rome and the Samnites then deteriorated rapidly, and within two years they were formally at war. The sources, which naturally describe events from a Roman point of view, accuse the Samnites of aggression on three different fronts. It is alleged, first, that they were preparing to attack the Roman colonists at Fregellae; secondly, that they had incited the Greek city of Neapolis (Naples) to attack Rome's possessions in Campania; and thirdly, that they were encouraging Privernum, Fundi and Formiae to revolt.

The Naples affair, of which our sources give conflicting reports, was evidently crucial. When the Romans declared war on Naples (or 'Palaeopolis', as Livy calls it, apparently under the impression that they were two different places – e.g. VIII.23.3), the Samnites immediately came to its assistance and installed a garrison (327 B.C.). It appears, however, that the city was internally divided, with the mass of the people (the *demos*) favouring the Samnites and receiving support from other Greek cities (especially Tarentum), while a section of the propertied class supported Rome (Dion. Hal. *Ant. Rom.* xv.6.5 etc.). In 326 the pro-Roman group succeeded in getting rid of the Samnites and handing over the city to the Roman commander Q. Publilius Philo. The subsequent alliance with Naples was Rome's first success of the Second Samnite War, which had formally begun a few months previously, in late 327 or early 326.

Our sources give a very imprecise account of the early years of the war. Little can be said about the character of the campaigns except that the Romans seem to have adopted a broadly offensive strategy. At no point in the period down to 320 B.C. did the Samnites attack the territory of Rome or its allies;[23] on the contrary, the Romans invaded western Samnium in 326 (Livy VIII.25.4) and attacked the Vestini, who were allies of the Samnites, in the following year (VIII.29.1;6; 11–14). Large-scale victories over the Samnites are recorded in 325 and 322, the former apparently somewhere 'in Samnium', although the exact site of the battle (Imbrinium) is not identifiable. This campaign was the scene of a celebrated quarrel between the dictator L. Papirius Cursor and his *magister equitum* Q. Fabius Maximus Rullianus, of which Livy gives a detailed account; it probably derives from Fabius Pictor (who is quoted at VIII.30.9).

The campaign of 322 is not located at all and is problematic from other points of view. Livy (VIII.38–9) ascribes the victory to the dictator A. Cornelius Arvina; but in a later chapter (VIII.40) he records an alternative tradition (followed by the Fasti Capitolini) which gave the credit to the

[23] Harris 1979[A61], 177.

consuls. In an exasperated aside he remarks that the record had been falsified by aristocratic families who claimed the credit for great victories by falsely attributing them to their ancestors (cf. Cicero, *Brutus* 62). Our sources contain many similar cases of uncertainty about which of the magistrates should be credited with a particular action or exploit. The obvious inference would seem to be that the original records – the pontifical chronicle, or whatever – did not make the matter clear. It is important to note, however, that these instances cast doubt on the identity of the magistrates who took part in the events, but do not necessarily imply that the events themselves are fictitious. Indeed, if anything they rather imply the contrary.

In 321 B.C. the Romans suffered a disaster at the Caudine Forks. Our sources give a highly coloured but largely unreliable account of this event. All we can be sure of is that it was one of the most humiliating and discreditable episodes in Roman history. Apparently the consuls had led the Roman army into a remote mountain glen where it was surrounded and forced to surrender. The Romans were set free under an agreement, after being forced to march, unarmed and half-naked, under a 'yoke' of spears.

Livy's account attempts to attenuate the disgrace by suggesting that the Samnites had tricked the Romans and enticed them into a rocky defile from which there was no escape (Livy IX.2). But other sources clearly imply that the Roman army surrendered after a defeat (e.g. Cic. *Off.* III.109). Moreover Livy's description of the Caudine Forks does not match the topography of any of the valleys in the region between Calatia and Caudium, where the débâcle is said to have taken place (Livy IX. 2.1–2; the Forks are traditionally identified with the valley between Arienzo and Arpaia).

But whatever the precise circumstances, the fact of a Roman surrender is undeniable. The doubtful part of the story is the sequel. We are told that when the army returned to Rome the senate and people rejected the truce which the consuls had made and voted to continue the war. In the next two years the Romans avenged the disaster with a series of victories. In particular they captured Luceria in northern Apulia, recovered the lost standards and freed the 600 knights whom the Samnites had taken hostage. The 7000 Samnite prisoners who surrendered at Luceria were then sent under the yoke.

This end result seems too good to be true, and is usually dismissed as fantasy. Another doubtful element is the claim that the truce was not a treaty (*foedus*), but a *sponsio*, a provisional agreement made by the consuls who offered themselves as guarantors ('sponsores'). When the Roman people refused to ratify the truce, the consuls were handed over to the Samnites, naked and bound. This looks like a piece of legalistic special pleading and does not carry conviction.[24] The standard modern view is that a regular *foedus* was made, that the Romans were forced to comply with its terms (which included the surrender of Fregellae and Cales – Livy IX.4.4; App. *Sam*. 4.5), and that all hostilities between Rome and the Samnites ceased until 316 B.C. On this interpretation the repudiation of the agreement and the subsequent Roman victories are nothing more than dishonest fabrications.

But in spite of its wide currency this critical view is not necessarily compelling. For one thing it requires us to believe that the annalists invented the most shameful part of the story, namely the abrogation of the treaty. It is perhaps more reasonable to assume that the Romans really *did* break a treaty, and that the annalists attempted to whitewash this fact by introducing the notion of a *sponsio*. Although the details of the victory at Luceria are obviously imaginary, it is nevertheless possible that some fighting did take place in 320 and 319 and that the Romans achieved some successes (the Fasti Capitolini record a triumph *de Samnitibus* in 319). There is moreover some positive reason to think that the record of these campaigns may belong to an early layer of the tradition.[25]

In general it must be admitted that the facts surrounding these events are not now recoverable. It seems likely enough, however, that by 318 open hostilities between Rome and the Samnites had ceased, either as a result of the original *foedus* or a subsequent truce at the beginning of 318 (Livy IX.20.1–3). This left the Romans free to strengthen their position in Campania (Livy IX.20.5 and 10), and to create two new tribes, the Oufentina and the Falerna, on territory that had been settled twenty years previously (see above p. 362). At the same time they campaigned in Apulia and Lucania, and forced a number of communities there to make treaties of alliance (including Arpi, Teanum Apulum, Canusium, Forentum and Nerulum – Livy IX.20). These regions had for some time been the object of Roman attention, and earlier alliances are recorded by Livy in 326 B.C. (VIII.25.3). Rome's efforts on this front form part of a broad strategic policy aimed at isolating and encircling the Samnites. The pattern is one of consistent aggression, a conclusion that is not necessarily incompatible with the modern view that the Romans' principal intention was to preserve their own security.

On the other hand, there is no sign of any corresponding aggression or urge to expand on the part of the Samnites, although both ancient and modern writers frequently assert the contrary.[26] Samnite 'inactivity' in the years before 316 B.C. does not need to be either explained or explained away; as a tribal confederation the Samnite League could organize united

[24] Crawford 1973[J156], 1–7.   [25] See Frederiksen 1968[J47], 226.
[26] See e.g. the references cited by Harris 1979[A61], 176 nn. 1–2.

resistance against external attack, but would hardly have been able to implement any kind of long-term offensive strategy. Rome, by contrast, was a developed unitary state with strong aggressive tendencies.

The only occasion when the Samnites invaded the territory of the Romans or their allies in force was in 315 B.C. This attack was a response to Roman aggression, as Livy himself admits. Hostilities had resumed in the previous year when the Romans attacked Saticula (Livy IX.21.2), which fell in 315 after a long siege. But in the same year the Samnites seized the (unknown) stronghold of Plistica and advanced across the Liris. At Lautulae near Tarracina they defeated the Romans in a pitched battle; it must have been on this occasion that they entered Latium and devastated the coastal region as far as Ardea (Strabo v.3.5, p. 232C; v.4.11, p. 249C). But in the following year they were themselves defeated by the Romans, possibly again at Tarracina.[27] The Romans then proceeded to reassert their control of Campania, where some cities had become disaffected, and dealt severely with a revolt of the Aurunci. If Livy is to be believed, the Aurunci were massacred (IX.25.9). The Romans also recovered Sora, which had gone over to the Samnites in the previous year.

These events mark the turning-point of the war. In 315 the Romans captured (or recaptured) Luceria and founded a colony there a year later. In 313 they recovered Fregellae, which had been either ceded to the Samnites by the Caudine treaty or taken by them in a night attack in 320 (Livy IX.12.5–8); further Latin colonies were established at Suessa Aurunca, Saticula and on the island of Pontia (in 313) and at Interamna on the Liris (in 312). A Roman attack on the Pentrian capital of Bovianum is also recorded in 313, and further successes occurred at Nola and Calatia in Campania, and at Atina in Samnium (Livy IX.28.3–6). The result of this activity was that by 312 Samnium was encircled by military allies of Rome, and confronted in the sensitive Liris–Volturnus region by a string of Latin colonies on strategic sites stretching from Fregellae to Saticula. At the same time the Romans strengthened their grip on the whole of the lowland region along the Tyrrhenian coast. A potent symbol of their permanent control of this area was the construction of the Appian Way, the great highway from Rome to Capua, which was started in 312 B.C.

III. THE ROMAN CONQUEST OF CENTRAL ITALY

After the consolidation of 313–312 B.C. the outcome of the Second Samnite War was no longer in doubt. In the years that followed the

---

[27] Diod. XIX.76.2. The MSS have περὶ κίνναν πόλιν; the emendation περὶ Ταρακίναν πόλιν was Burger's conjecture.

Romans were able to extend the scope of their military activities to other parts of Central Italy, and to embark on a series of vigorous offensives which in little more than a decade transformed the political map of Italy. By 299 the Roman state had surpassed all its rivals and controlled most of the Italian peninsula.

The increased scale of Roman operations during this period is revealed by a notice of Livy (IX.30.3), which states that in 311 B.C. the military tribunes of the four legions were elected by the people rather than appointed by their commanders. This innovation presupposes an increase in the normal size of the army from two to four legions, and probably coincides with it. Whether it was also at this time that the Romans introduced the manipular formation that characterized the later army is uncertain, but probable. Livy assumes the existence of a manipular army much earlier, and includes an interesting digression on the subject before his account of the battle of Veseris in 340 B.C. (VIII.18.3–14), while other sources trace its origin back to the time of Camillus (Plut. Cam. 40); but it is more likely that both the manipular formation and the use of oblong shields and javelins were borrowed by the Romans from the Samnites at the end of the fourth century (thus Sall. Cat. 51.37–8; Ined. Vat. (Jac. FGrH 839 F 1.3)).

Our sources do not give a very clear picture of the last years of the Second Samnite War; instead they provide a shapeless catalogue of annual campaigns, the details of which are often uncertain. Similar problems attend the narrative of the Etruscan wars of 311–308 B.C. In 311 the Etruscans attacked Sutrium (we are not told why) and prompted Roman intervention in a region that had been quiet since the 350s. It is not clear precisely who these 'Etruscans' were, but they probably included the 'inland' cities of Volsinii, Perusia, Cortona, Arretium, and Clusium. The coastal cities, such as Caere, Tarquinii and Vulci, do not seem to have taken part.

The surviving accounts of this war are confused and contradictory in detail, but are broadly in agreement on the main points, which can be briefly summarized (Livy IX.32; 35–7; 39–41; Diod. XX.35 and 44.8–9). The Romans drove back the army that had laid siege to Sutrium and followed up their success in 310 with a bold advance into central Etruria under the consul Q. Fabius Maximus Rullianus. We hear of pitched battles at Lake Vadimon in the Tiber valley and near Perusia. Perusia, Cortona and Arretium were forced to make thirty-year truces with Rome. A celebrated episode of this campaign was the reconnaissance mission by the consul's brother, who crossed the trackless Ciminian forest and continued as far as Camerinum in Umbria, which he persuaded to become an ally of Rome (Livy IX.36.1–8).[28] In the next year (i.e. 308;

[28] Camerinum seems rather out of the way; but it may be a mistaken reference to Clusium, which Livy says was originally called 'Camars' (X.25.11). This would make better sense of the story,

309 was a 'dictator year') the consul P. Decius Mus campaigned successfully in Umbria and made an alliance with Ocriculum. He also arranged
for the renewal of the forty-year truce between Rome and Tarquinii,
which implies that Tarquinii had not been involved in the fighting in
311–310.[29]

The historical reliability of this narrative has been the subject of
controversy among modern historians, some of whom have rejected
almost all of it as fiction. The tradition as it stands is certainly not above
criticism. The surviving narratives contain much exaggeration and
rhetoric and are confused about the location of events. For instance Livy
is uncertain whether Fabius Rullianus' second major victory in 310
occurred at Sutrium or near Perusia (IX.37.11–12). He maintains that
Fabius made two expeditions to the interior in 310, defeated the
Etruscans at Sutrium on two separate occasions, and twice received the
submission of Perusia. These look like classic examples of 'doublets' –
that is, duplications that arose when an annalist, faced with two different
versions of the same event, mistakenly inferred that they were different
events and recorded them both.

But these acknowledged faults do not necessarily impugn the basic
structure of the narrative, which is regarded by many historians as
broadly historical. This 'conservative' position concedes that much of
the narrative detail is the product of rhetorical elaboration, and that the
annalists introduced much confusion, but nevertheless holds that the
main outline of the traditional account is probably reliable and based on
authentic records. This view of the matter explains the nature of the
sources much better than the 'hypercritical' alternative, and has been
adopted throughout the present chapter.[30]

In any event both the quantity and the quality of available information
noticeably improves in the last years of the Second Samnite War. Livy's
account in the later part of Book Nine and in Book Ten includes far more
substantive data than previously, and begins to resemble the narrative
format of the later decades. From 318 B.C. onwards Livy can be
supplemented by the regular annual notices of Roman events in
Diodorus (down to 302 B.C.), and by the entries in the triumphal *fasti*.
Discrepancies between these sources occur frequently; but we should not
necessarily infer that when two different sets of events are reported one
or both sources must be wrong. Sometimes both could be right; in other

---

especially as Livy implies that the town gave military aid to Fabius in the subsequent campaign
(IX.36.8).

[29] The interval from 351 to 308 works out at exactly forty years if the 'dictator-years' (333, 324,
309) are excluded. The renewal of the *indutiae* with Tarquinii in 308 B.C. thus reinforces the
presumption that the dictator-years are a fiction.

[30] For a clear statement of the conservative case see Harris 1971[J175], esp. 49–84.

words, they complement, rather than contradict, one another. It is also worth noticing that in this section of his work Livy refers frequently to discrepancies between *his* sources (e.g. x.17.11–12). These instances bear witness to his conscientiousness, and increase the value of his account.[31]

Roman campaigns in Samnium are recorded every year down to 304 B.C. A major victory is attributed to L. Papirius Cursor in 310, but after that only minor Roman successes are registered until 307; in that year the Samnites took the initiative and seized Sora and Caiatia (Livy ix.43.1; Diod. xx.80.1). Although apparently defeated in a battle (Livy ix.43. 8–21), they returned to the attack the next year and invaded Roman territory in northern Campania (Livy ix.44.5; Diod. xx.90.3). The Romans retaliated with a full-scale invasion of Samnium which led to the capture of Bovianum; the Samnites were then destroyed in a pitched battle in which their leader Statius Gellius was killed. The Romans proceeded to recapture Sora and to take Arpinum and Cesennia (Livy ix.44.16). In 304 the Samnites sued for peace; the 'old treaty' (presumably that of 354 and 341) was renewed, and the twenty-years war was at an end.

The conclusion of the Samnite War did not, however, result in an immediate or drastic reduction in the level of Rome's military commitments. The reason is that, from around 312 B.C. onwards, the Samnite War as such had ceased to be the Romans' principal concern. Other theatres of war now predominated, as the Romans concentrated their efforts in other directions, first in Etruria and Umbria, and then in the mountainous region of Central Italy. A crucial stage in the conquest of Central Italy was marked, in 307, by the decision to begin construction of the Via Valeria, the military road which extended beyond Tibur into the central Appennines and eventually reached the Adriatic (Livy ix.43.25).

In 306 B.C. some communities of the Hernican confederation, which had remained faithful to Rome since 358 B.C., were accused of rebellion. After a brief resistance they were rapidly forced to surrender to a consular army. The dissident communities, the most important of which was Anagnia, were incorporated with *civitas sine suffragio*. At the same time they were deprived of the right of *conubium* (*sc.* with other Roman citizens and with non-Romans who did possess *conubium*) and of the rights of assembly and self-government (Livy ix.43.26). It has been suggested that because the people of Anagnia were deprived of *conubium* they cannot have been Roman citizens, and consequently that *civitas sine suffragio* did not mean citizenship.[32] This paradoxical view is mistaken; in Roman thinking *conubium* was not an inseparable and automatic ingredi-

[31] Cf. Harris 1971[J175], 52–3.   [32] E.g. Sherwin-White 1973[A123], 49.

ent of Roman citizenship, but a positive right which could be granted or taken away according to circumstances independently of other citizen rights. The classic case is the law of Augustus which forbade intermarriage between freed slaves and members of the senatorial order. It would not be legitimate to infer from this that under Augustus senators were not Roman citizens.

The Hernican states that had remained loyal to Rome (Livy names them as Aletrium, Ferentinum and Verulae) retained their independence and all their privileges under the existing treaty. Livy states that they preferred this condition to Roman citizenship. This is an important reference because it indicates that at the time *civitas sine suffragio* was regarded as a punishment, and not in any sense a privilege (Livy ix.43.23; cf. ix.45.7–8).

In 304 the Romans turned on the Aequi, and overwhelmed them in a campaign that lasted a mere fifty days. Their hill towns were systematically destroyed, and the population massacred almost to a man (thus Livy ix.45.17: 'nomen Aequorum prope ad internecionem deletum'). Immediately the other peoples of the Abruzzi region hastened to conclude permanent treaties of alliance with Rome: the Marsi, Paeligni, Marrucini and Frentani in 304 (Livy ix.45.18; Diod. xx.101.5), the Vestini in 302 (Livy x.3.1). The peoples of the central Appennines had been associated in a loose federation which moderns call the 'Sabellian League'. This league seems generally to have favoured the Romans in the Second Samnite War, at least to judge from the ease with which Roman armies were able to cross the peninsula in order to operate in Apulia. As far as we know relations with Rome became strained only at the end of the war, and actual clashes were infrequent (Diod. xix.105.5 – 312 b.c.; Livy ix.41.4; Diod. xx.44.8 – 308; Diod. xx.90.3 – 305). There is no justification for the view that the Abruzzi peoples were continuously at war with the Romans from 308 onwards, still less than they consistently supported the Samnites throughout the Second Samnite War.[33] Apart from some minor insurrections in 302 and 300 (Livy x.1.7–9; 3.2–5; 9.7) the Romans' control of the region of the central Appennines remained unshaken until the time of the Social War.

These conquests were consolidated by the foundation of colonies at Sora (303 b.c.), Alba Fucens (303) and Carseoli (298). In 299 the Umbrian stronghold of Nequinum was captured, and the colony of Narnia founded on its site (mod. Narni). In 303 the towns of Trebula Suffenas (Cicilliano) and Arpinum (Arpino) were annexed with *civitas sine suffragio* (Livy ix.1.3); Frusino (Frosinone) suffered the same fate, but not before many of its leading citizens had been executed and one-third of its land

[33] For the view criticized in the text see Letta 1972[J81], 67–79.

confiscated (Livy ib.; Diod. xx.80.4 dates the subjection of Frusino to 306). In 299 the tribes Aniensis and Teretina were created; the former was situated on land taken from the Aequi in the upper Anio valley, and the latter in the Liris valley on land that had been annexed from the Aurunci in 314 B.C. (see above p. 372).

These acts of enfranchisement and annexation mark the end of a further stage in Rome's conquest of Italy. The process of expansion had by now developed its own momentum; the logical result was Roman domination of the entire Italian peninsula. This outcome could only have been averted by positive and concerted action by the peoples who still retained their independence. It was perhaps around the turn of the century that the free peoples of Italy first perceived what might be in store for them; at any rate it was then for the first time that they began to make serious efforts to organize a united front against Rome.

IV. THE THIRD SAMNITE WAR AND THE COMPLETION OF THE CONQUEST OF PENINSULAR ITALY

By 298 the Romans were once again fighting on several fronts. Annual Roman campaigns in Etruria and Umbria are recorded from 302 B.C. onwards, but until the great clash of 295 these seem to have been minor and desultory affairs, with the exception of the siege and capture of Nequinum in 300–299. A Gallic invasion of Etruria in 299, though ominous, did not involve the Romans in any large-scale military action, if we are to believe Polybius (II.19.1–2); on the other hand, by making an alliance with the Lucanians, who had been attacked by the Samnites, they provoked the so-called Third Samnite War (298–290).

The first campaign of this war is referred to in the epitaph of L. Cornelius Scipio Barbatus (*cos.* 298), an inscription which probably dates from the early second century B.C. and is therefore by some way the oldest surviving document concerning the history of the Samnite wars (*ILLRP* 309). Its account of Scipio's achievements in Samnium is at variance with Livy, who makes him campaign in Etruria. This well-known puzzle is further evidence of the confusion in the tradition about the distribution of consular commands in the Samnite wars, and of the fact that many different versions proliferated in the late Republic.

As consuls for 297 the Romans chose two of their most experienced military leaders, Q. Fabius Maximus Rullianus and P. Decius Mus. Both men had their commands extended in 296 and were again elected consuls for 295. In 295 at least five men held *imperium* as 'pro-magistrates'. They included one of the consuls of the previous year, L. Volumnius Flamma, who was retained *pro consule* (his colleague in the consulship of 296, Ap. Claudius Caecus, was praetor in 295). The other four, who held commands *pro praetore*, were the two consuls of 298, L. Cornelius Scipio Barbatus and Cn. Fulvius Maximus Centumalus, and two other ex-consuls, M. Livius Denter (*cos.* 302) and L. Postumius Megellus (*cos.* 305).

The pattern is extraordinary and unprecedented. If we ignore some doubtful fifth-century cases, there had only been two previous instances of prorogation – those of Q. Publilius Philo in 326 (above, p. 347) and of Q. Fabius Maximus Rullianus in 307 (Livy IX.42.2). Now in 296–295 several simultaneous prorogations are recorded. Even more remarkable is the fact that four of the pro-magistrates of 295 did not have regular commands prorogued, but had *imperium* conferred upon them at a time when their legal status was that of private citizens (*privati*). Appointments of this kind were always regarded as anomalous; in Roman constitutional language they were *extra ordinem*, and were juridically quite distinct from the more regular 'prorogations'.

How are we to account for the multiple prorogations and extraordinary commands in 296/5 B.C.? There can be no doubt that at this time the pattern of distribution of offices and commands among the Roman elite was in a state of transition. Two aspects of the change deserve attention. First, as we have seen, the practice of iteration of senior magistracies became much less frequent after the 290s (above, p. 345f). Secondly, this period witnessed the demise of the dictatorship as a regular military office. Dictators had frequently been appointed to undertake military tasks in the period down to 310 B.C.; but after that year military dictatorships are attested only in 302 (301) B.C., in 249 at a critical moment of the First Punic War, and finally in the emergency that followed the battle of Trasimene (217).

Our sources give no explanation of these changes. But it would be reasonable to see the unprecedented number of pro-magistracies in 296/5 B.C. as a response in a period of constitutional experiment to a grave military threat. Our sources give no hint of an impending military crisis until the end of 296. In 297 the consuls Fabius and Decius had both commanded in Samnium, and ravaged it continuously for four months (Livy x.15.3–6). These operations continued in the following year, when the towns of Murgantia, Romulea and Ferentinum fell to the proconsuls. At the same time the consul L. Volumnius Flamma put down a revolt in Lucania and defeated the Samnites at the river Volturnus. But in spite of these successes the Romans were not able (or did not choose) to prevent the Samnite general Gellius Egnatius from leading an army northwards into Etruria and joining forces with the leaders of the Etruscan states.

The Roman commander in Etruria, the consul Ap. Claudius, defeated a joint force of Etruscans and Samnites in a pitched battle (in which he vowed a temple to Bellona), but the result was far from decisive. At the end of the year Appius reported to the senate that a grand coalition had been formed in northern Italy, involving Samnites, Etruscans, Umbrians and Gauls (Livy x.21.11–15). This alliance of convenience must have been several years in the making, as Livy himself implies (x.16.3). The extraordinary pattern of military appointments in 296 and 295 shows that the Romans had been conscious of a growing threat since the end of 297 at the latest.

Matters came to a head in 295 when a combined army of Samnites and Gauls met the Romans at Sentinum in Umbria. At this celebrated battle the Romans fielded four legions together with contingents of allied soldiers who, according to Livy, outnumbered the citizen troops. If we estimate the size of a legion at around 4500 men, the total number of troops on the Roman side will have been over 36,000, a huge army by the standards of the time, and probably the largest that the Roman state had ever put into the field. The size of the opposing force is completely unknown. The sources naturally maintain that the Romans were heavily outnumbered, and fantastic figures such as 650,000 were given in some accounts known to Livy (x.30.5). The Greek historian Duris of Samos, who was a contemporary of the event, apparently reported that 100,000 men were killed (Jac. *FGrH* 76 F 56). Livy's more modest account gives a figure of 8700 killed on the Roman side, and 25,000 of the enemy (x.29.17–18). Such figures are more realistic, and may be based on more than guesswork.

However that may be, there can be little doubt that, in terms of the size of the forces engaged, the ferocity of the fighting and the decisiveness of the result, Sentinum was the greatest military engagement that had ever taken place in Italy. Livy's detailed account of the battle may well contain authentic elements, probably for the first time. The reference to it in the work of a contemporary Greek historian has already been noted; moreover Romans of the generation of Fabius Pictor would have been able to speak to survivors of the battle, and it would be extraordinary if Pictor himself had not in fact done so.

The Roman victory was total, but apparently far from easy. In Livy's opinion, the result might have been different if the Etruscan and Umbrian contingents had been present (Livy x.27.11); as it was they were drawn away from Sentinum when the Roman reserve armies moved up from Rome and attacked Clusium. The battle itself was closely fought, but at the critical moment the consul P. Decius Mus followed the example of his father and devoted himself (cf. above p. 362). This undoubtedly historical incident turned the tide of the battle in favour of the Romans. After the victory Fabius returned to Rome in triumph, with an assured place in the Roman tradition as the hero of the Samnite wars.

Sentinum sealed the fate of Italy. After the battle the Romans lost no time in settling accounts with the Etruscans and Umbrians; in 294 they captured Rusellae and imposed terms on Volsinii, Perusia and Arretium. At the same time Roman armies continued to operate in Samnium, where fierce fighting is reported in 295 and 294 (details in Livy x.31–6; once again his sources disagreed about the identity of the commanders serving in the various theatres – x.37.13–16). In the following year the Samnites made a final effort by calling up every available man in a mass levy under a *lex sacrata* (p. 292); of the 36,000 who were assembled, 16,000 were chosen to form a specially equipped elite force, the so-called 'linen legion' (Livy x.38). But this great army came to grief at the battle of Aquilonia in 293.

The Roman victory at Aquilonia was the most notable event in a year in which innumerable Roman successes are recorded, including the capture of Duronia, Cominium, Aquilonia, Saepinum, Velia, Palumbinum and Herculaneum. With the exception of Saepinum (Sepino) the identification of these towns is uncertain, and the geography of the campaign of 293 is a long-standing puzzle; but according to the most probable modern reconstruction the events should be located in the area to the north of the Monti del Matese stretching between the upper reaches of the rivers Trigno and Biferno (see Map 8).[34]

Livy's tenth book ends with the events of 293. The succeeding books do not survive, and we are compelled to rely on later epitomes and secondary accounts that preserve only the barest outline of Livy's narrative. The complete text of Diodorus ceases with the events of 302, and to complete the dismal picture of our sources for this period the section of the Fasti Capitolini containing triumphs from 290 to 283 is missing. A proper narrative of the final stages of the Roman conquest of peninsular Italy is not really possible from the few scraps of evidence we have. The following facts seem, however, to be reasonably certain. In the years from 292 to 290 Samnium was overrun by the Romans, who annexed a large area of territory on the south-eastern borders of Samnium where the colony of Venusia was founded in 291. A year later the Samnites surrendered and were forced to become allies of Rome, no doubt on unequal terms.

The Roman advance continued. In 290 the consul M'. Curius Dentatus conquered the Sabines and Praetuttii, who were incorporated into the Roman state as citizens *sine suffragio*; some of their land was seized and distributed to Roman settlers. As a result of this poorly documented episode Roman territory was extended right across the peninsula to the Adriatic coast, where a colony was founded at Hadria (Atri) probably between 290 and 286 (Livy, *Per.* XI). Some years later the territory of

---

[34] La Regina 1975[B352], 271–82.

Picenum was added, following a revolt in 269 B.C.[35] The Picentes were made *cives sine suffragio* (with the exception of Asculum), and a colony was established at Firmum in 264.

After their defeat at the battle of Sentinum the Gauls seem to have remained quiet for a time; but after an interval of ten years they once again penetrated into Etruria. The events of the Gallic war of 284/3 B.C. are difficult to reconstruct in detail;[36] the most probable sequence is that in 284 a Roman army under L. Caecilius Metellus was destroyed in a battle at Arretium, but that the Romans retaliated in the following year and won a decisive victory at Lake Vadimon. Shortly afterwards they annexed the territory along the northern Adriatic that was occupied by the Senones (the *ager Gallicus*). It is probable that the Gauls continued to inhabit the region on sufferance, until they were expelled in consequence of an agrarian law in 232 B.C. (p. 432f). The Romans' control of this district was secured by the foundation of a Latin colony at Ariminum (Rimini) in 268 B.C.

Warfare in Etruria and Umbria continued, although very few details are preserved. Vulci and Volsinii were defeated in 280, and Caere in 273. The process of conquest was certainly complete by 264, when Volsinii was destroyed in the aftermath of a revolution in the city. The Etruscan and Umbrian communities remained nominally independent but were bound to Rome by treaties of alliance. The exception was Caere, which was incorporated with citizenship *sine suffragio* following its defeat in 273; in the same year a colony was founded on the Tuscan coast at Cosa.

In the south the Romans faced renewed problems with the intervention, in 280 B.C., of King Pyrrhus of Epirus, whose adventures are dealt with in Chapter 10. As a result of Pyrrhus' defeat (275 B.C.) the Romans overran Magna Graecia, and captured the leading Greek city, Tarentum, in 272. But the arrival of Pyrrhus coincided with a revolt of the Samnites, Lucanians and Bruttians which lasted for over a decade. Although our meagre sources provide very few details about this war, it was evidently a serious affair, as is proved by the fact that no fewer than ten triumphs over these peoples (in varying combinations) are listed in the *fasti* between 282 and 272 B.C. The final defeat of Samnium and Lucania was marked by the foundation of colonies at Paestum (273 B.C.), Beneventum (268) and Aesernia (263). By 264 B.C. the Roman conquest of peninsular Italy was complete.[37]

It is as well to remind ourselves that this definitive result had been achieved in a remarkably short space of time; only seventy-five years previously Rome's power had not extended beyond the relatively minute

35 For discussion of the episode cf. below, p. 425.
36 Texts, bibliography and discussion in Torelli 1978[B177], 80–4.
37 For events of the period 275–264 B.C. see Chapter 9.

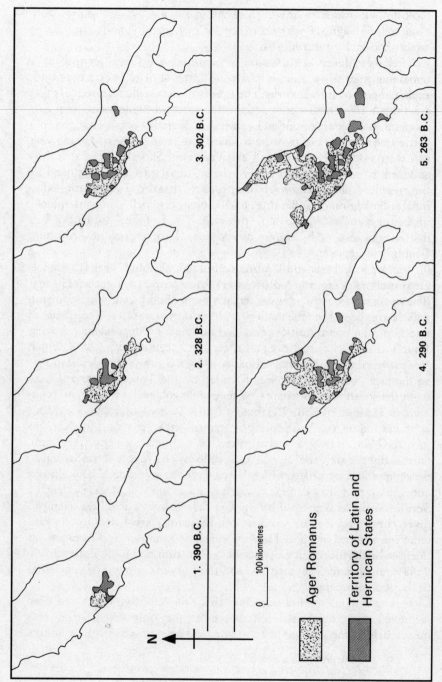

Fig. 47. The growth of Roman power, 390–263 B.C.

1. 390 B.C.

2. 328 B.C.

3. 302 B.C.

4. 290 B.C.

5. 263 B.C.

N

0   100 kilometres

Ager Romanus

Territory of Latin and Hernican States

region of Latium Vetus (cf. Fig. 47). On the other hand, the Romans established their control so thoroughly that, if we exclude the special circumstances of the Hannibalic War, they faced no serious revolts in Italy for nearly 200 years. The only exceptions to this consistent pattern were the isolated and short-lived rebellions of Falerii (241 B.C.) – if rebellion this was, and not an act of Roman aggression (see below p. 431) – and Fregellae (125 B.C.), which attracted no support from the other allies and were both easily crushed. The speed and thoroughness of the Roman conquest are astounding, and demand some kind of explanation.

The first point that calls for comment is the Romans' extraordinary belligerence. The conquest of Italy was the result of warfare that was both intensive and continuous. The record speaks for itself. In the historical period of the Republic the Roman state engaged in warfare as a matter of course. This pattern of constant military activity was firmly established by the time of the Samnite wars, when campaigns took place literally every year, with the doubtful exceptions of the period after the Caudine Forks (when some scholars have argued against Livy that the Romans were at peace – see above, p. 370f), and the years 289–285 B.C., when our sources simply fail us.[38] The peace that was marked, in 241 B.C., by the closing of the temple of Janus was genuinely exceptional (Varro, *Ling.* v.165; Livy 1.19.3 etc.).

The Roman state's bellicosity is indicated not only by the frequency with which it went to war, but also by the high proportion of its citizen manpower that was regularly committed to military service. The size of the citizen population before the mid-third century can only be guessed at, but estimates such as those of A. Afzelius must be of the correct order of magnitude. Afzelius' figures imply a total of *c.* 100,000 adult male citizens in 338 B.C., rising to *c.* 115,000 in 304, and to *c.* 160,000 after 290.[39] The regular annual levy in the fourth century was two legions (*c.* 9000 men), and was raised to four legions (*c.* 18,000 men) during the Second Samnite War (see above p. 373). It follows that, throughout the period of the Italian wars of conquest, between 9 and 16 per cent of all adult male citizens were regularly serving in the army. In times of crisis the proportion was even higher, for example in 295 B.C. when six legions were under arms, representing around 25 per cent of the probable adult male population. These figures, which are consistent with those of later and better documented periods, represent a very high level of military involvement of Roman citizens, which as far as we know cannot be matched by the record of any other pre-industrial state.[40]

[38] Harris 1979[A61], 256–7.
[39] Afzelius 1942[J134], 153, 171, 181. I have calculated the numbers of male *iuniores* as *c.* 29 per cent of Afzelius's totals for the free population of the *ager Romanus*.
[40] De Sanctis 1907–64[A37], II.191; Hopkins 1978[A67], 31–5; Harris 1979[A61], 44–5.

The social and economic implications of this degree of commitment to warfare have already been touched upon (above, p. 333f); but it also reveals much about Roman culture and Roman values. In the middle Republic Rome was a warrior society pervaded at all levels by what has justly been called a 'militaristic ethos'. This characteristic feature was most clearly expressed in ceremonies like the triumph (p. 600f), and in the cult of warlike deities such as Bellona and Victoria. These divinities feature prominently in the record of temple foundations in the age of the Samnite wars (see below, Table 10: p. 408), and among the types on the earliest Roman coins, which also date from this period.

Not surprisingly, in its relations with other states Rome was consistently aggressive. No value judgment is intended in this use of the term 'aggressive'; it is simply meant as a descriptive comment on Roman military activity, which *was* intensive and continuous, and *as a matter of fact* resulted in territorial expansion, increased wealth and the political domination of other peoples. That the Romans were imperialists is a truism. We may also observe that the campaigns in which they were engaged took place for the most part in enemy territory rather than in their own or in that of their allies.[41]

Whether the Roman state's actions were either legally or morally justified is another matter, and one that need not concern the historian. Equally, questions of motive and intention are only of marginal relevance. We cannot know for certain whether the Romans were consciously or cynically aggressive, but it seems unlikely. In fact the tradition maintains that the Romans only fought 'just wars' in defence of their own or their allies' legitimate interests. When war was declared, special rituals were performed by the fetials to confirm the justice of the Roman cause and to ensure the support of the gods. The idea of the 'just war' has sometimes been dismissed as a cynical pretence or as the naive fabrication of patriotic annalists;[42] but it is far more likely that the Romans were able to persuade themselves that their case really was just (whatever its 'objective' merits) and that the gods were on their side.

Evidently the Romans were prepared to use war as an instrument of policy in support of what they considered to be their rightful claims. This willingness to engage in warfare was perfectly rational, as W. V. Harris has shown.[43] Successful warfare brought tangible gains in the form of movable booty, slaves and land, as well as the intangible benefits of increased security, power and glory. The Romans, who were not imbeciles, were obviously aware of these advantages of successful warfare, and no doubt saw them as desirable.

[41] Harris 1979[A61], 176–82.   [42] E.g. Harris 1979[A61], 165–75; Badian 1966[B6], 19.
[43] Harris 1979[A61].

The essential requirement, however, was victory. In any rational calculation, the potential advantages of military success would have to be weighed against the possible consequences of defeat. The remarkable fact is that the Romans do not seem to have been deterred by the risks; they evidently expected to win, and generally did so. What needs to be explained, therefore, is not only why the Romans fought so many wars, but why they were so successful. In the final analysis the answer to both questions is the same: they had at their disposal a very efficient military machine, and could call upon resources that their opponents could not hope to match.

The foundations of Rome's military power were firmly laid in the settlement that followed the Great Latin War in 338 B.C. As we have seen, the resulting Roman commonwealth comprised a single territorial unit whose inhabitants were divided into full citizens, citizens *sine suffragio*, Latin colonists and Latin allies. These various groups had one thing in common: the obligation to provide troops for the Roman army in time of war. In consequence the Roman commonwealth in 338 B.C. was able to dispose of unrivalled resources of manpower, and was already the most powerful military state in peninsular Italy. Its successes led to expansion and a further increase in its manpower resources. At the same time, the practice of continuous warfare inevitably led to improved organization and tactical skills, and greater military effectiveness.

A point that deserves attention is that the Roman state reinvested the profits of successful warfare in further military enterprises. The cost of mobilizing large armies every year was met by the imposition of a property tax called *tributum*, which was probably instituted at the end of the fifth century (see above, p. 301). Part of this tax was no doubt paid in kind, in the form of supplies for the army, and the remainder in uncoined bronze, a fact that is reflected in the Latin term for soldiers' pay, *stipendium*, which implies the weighing out of uncoined metal. The *tributum* was an irregular levy, imposed whenever the need arose.[44] But the income derived from booty and indemnities was also used to cover the cost of warfare. A major political issue, which is continually referred to by our sources on the history of the Republic, concerned the destination of booty acquired by the victorious armies. The commander, with whom the power of decision lay, could either distribute the booty at once among his troops (and thus supplement their existing pay) or hand it over to the state, in which case it could be used to pay a refund to the tribute-payers, or to pay for the *stipendium* of Roman soldiers in forthcoming campaigns and thus make the payment of future instalments of *tributum* unnecessary.

44 Nicolet 1976[G682]; cf. id. 1980[G685], 149ff.

Another way in which the Romans made their wars pay for themselves was to impose indemnities on defeated enemies, who were thereby compelled to provide supplies, equipment and pay for the Roman army for a stated period of time. For example in 306 B.C. the Hernici were granted a truce by the consul Q. Marcius Tremulus, who ordered them to supply two months' pay and provisions, and a tunic for every soldier (Livy IX.43.6; for other instances see Livy VIII.2.4; 36.11–12; IX.41.5–7; X.5.12–13; 37.5). According to the Elder Pliny an equestrian statue of Marcius was set up in front of the temple of Castor in recognition of his services, which included two victories over the Samnites, the capture of Anagnia and freeing the people from war-tax (*stipendium*: Pliny, *HN* XXXIV.23; the statue is also referred to by Livy IX.43.22 and Cic. *Phil.* VI.13).

But the most important feature of the Roman military machine was the system of alliances in Italy. By the mid-third century Rome had concluded permanent treaties with over 150 nominally independent Italian communities, which had either been defeated in war or had voluntarily agreed to become allies.[45] The treaties (*foedera*) probably differed from each other in detail, but the basic provision common to all of them was the allies' obligation to supply military aid to the Romans in time of war. In return they received Rome's protection and a share in the profits of successful military enterprises.

From 338 B.C. onwards, every Roman army that took the field comprised both citizen troops (in the legions) and contingents of allies. This fact is easily overlooked, since the contribution of the allies tends to be ignored by the Rome-centred sources. But the presence of the allies was a crucial factor in Rome's military success. Already at the battle of Sentinum the Latins and other allies outnumbered the Roman legionaries (according to Livy X.26.14 – a notice that would hardly have been invented). It can be estimated, on the basis of figures supplied by Polybius (II.24), that in 225 B.C. the allied population of Italy included some 360,000 men of military age whom the Romans could have mobilized if necessary; of the troops actually under arms in 225, the allies outnumbered the Romans by three to two. In subsequent years the ratio fluctuated between 1:1 and 2:1 down to the time of the Social War.[46]

These facts have an important bearing on the problem of Roman imperialism. The availability of Italian manpower gave the Roman state immense military potential and an almost infinite capacity for absorbing losses, as the events of the Pyrrhic and Hannibalic wars were to de-

[45] For a list of allies see Afzelius 1942[J134], 134–5.
[46] Brunt 1971[A21], 44–60 for a discussion of the population in 225 B.C.; N.B. p. 45, table IV for the figure cited in the text; pp. 677–86 for the ratio of allies to Romans in the army down to the Social War.

monstrate. But equally important was the fact that the system of alliances had an exclusively military function, and was only of use to the Romans in time of war. It was therefore logically necessary for the Romans to engage in warfare if they were to avail themselves of the services of the allies and to keep them under control. This functional interpretation of the Roman alliance was first outlined by A. Momigliano, whose description of its operation is worth repeating:

The machine worked for about two centuries, from about 280 to 100 B.C.; and the way it worked was that Rome passed from war to war without giving thought to the very metaphysical question of whether the wars were meant to gain power for Rome or to keep the allies busy. Wars were the very essence of the Roman organisation. The battle of Sentinum was the natural prelude to the battle of Pydna – or even the destruction of Corinth and the Social War.[47]

The system was exploitative in the sense that the allies carried a substantial part of the burden of the wars of conquest, and a corresponding share of the risks; and in particular they incurred a proportion of the cost, since they were obliged to pay for their contingents out of their own resources. In this way the Romans taxed the allies without imposing a direct tribute, and created the possibility of fighting wars at a relatively low cost to themselves. For their part the allies were evidently prepared to accept this state of things, and in fact remained consistently loyal to Rome. This attitude of compliance may at first sight seem surprising, but can probably be accounted for in two ways.

In the first place the Romans received the support of the propertied classes in the allied states, who turned naturally to Rome whenever their local interests were threatened. During the Italian wars of conquest the Romans frequently profited from the actions of pro-Roman elements within the Italian communities; the events at Naples in 326 B.C. (above p. 369) provide a good example. On a number of recorded occasions the Romans actually intervened with military force to put down popular insurrections on behalf of the local aristocracies of allied communities, for example at Arretium in 302 B.C. (Livy x.3 and 5), in Lucania in 296 (Livy x.18.8) and at Volsinii in 264 (Zonar. VIII.7.4–8). In return they received the active co-operation of the ruling classes of the allied states, an arrangement that ensured their continuing loyalty even in times of crisis. It was especially effective in regions where deep social divisions existed, as in northern Etruria, where archaic forms of dependence and clientage appear to have survived well into the Roman period.[48]

The second reason for the co-operation of the Italian allies is that as military partners of Rome they obtained a share of the profits of successful warfare. There is good evidence that when movable booty was

[47] Momigliano 1975[A88], 45–6.   [48] Harris 1971[J175], 114–44.

distributed to a victorious army the allied soldiers received an equal share along with the Roman legionaries. The only known exception to this, the occasion in 177 B.C. when the allies received only half of what was given to the Romans (Livy XLI.13.8), was probably an isolated act of meanness.

The quantities of booty taken and the numbers of captives enslaved during the Samnite wars were very considerable, to judge from the figures given by Livy, which may well be based on an authentic record (the data are listed in Table 8). The most important gain that was made from the conquests was land, which was confiscated from conquered enemies and used for colonization (Fig. 48) and distribution to individuals. Although the sources do not give us much help on this issue, it is virtually certain that the colonists included non-Roman Italians (Latins and allies) as well as Roman citizens.

This conclusion is based not only on what we know of colonization at later periods (e.g. Livy XXXIV.42.5–6; XLII.4.3–4; etc.), but also on the simple demographic argument that the Roman population on its own could not have sustained such a high rate of emigration as the record implies.[49] According to the sources Latin colonies comprised between 2500 and 6000 adult males. This means that in the period from 334 to 263 B.C., when nineteen such colonies were established (see Table 9), as many as 70,000 adult males and their dependants were resettled. It is unlikely that the Roman population on its own (on which see above p. 383) could have withstood such a drain on its citizen manpower. The only reasonable explanation of the facts is that a substantial proportion of these settlers were drawn from the allied communities.

The participation of the allies in the settlement of conquered territories should be set against the fact that as a general rule the Romans confiscated large areas of land from defeated peoples. The Roman system has been compared to a criminal operation which compensates its victims by enrolling them in the gang and inviting them to share the proceeds of future robberies.[50] This sinister but apt analogy brings us back to the point about the Roman state's need to make war. Any self-respecting criminal gang would soon break up if its boss decided to abandon crime and 'go legitimate'.

By joining a large and efficient operation and sacrificing their political independence, Rome's Italian allies obtained security, protection and profit at a relatively modest premium. Although the allied soldiers serving in the Roman army might often (if not always) outnumber their Roman counterparts, the burden placed on the manpower of Roman

---

[49] Hopkins 1978[A67], 21 and n. 27 questions the authenticity of the records; but his figures are in need of modification (see Badian 1982[A9], 165), and he takes insufficient account of the participation of the allies.

[50] This notion has been lifted from Bickerman and Smith 1976[A17], 149.

Table 8. *The mass enslavement of prisoners in the Third Samnite War*

Date (BC)	City or people	Number of captives enslaved	Livy ref.
297	Cimetra	2,900	x.15.6
296	Murgantia	2,100	17.4
296	Romulea	6,000	17.8
296	Samnites	c. 1,500	18.8
296	Etruscans	2,120	19.22
296	Samnites	2,500	20.15
295	Samnites and Gauls	8,000	29.17
295	Samnites	2,700	31.7
294	Milionia	4,700	34.3
294	Rusellae	more than 2,000	37.3
293	Amiternum	4,270	39.3
293	Duronia	fewer than 4,270	39.4
293	Aquilonia	3,870	42.5
293	Cominium	11,400	43.8
293	Velia, Palumbinum, Herculaneum	c. 5,000	45.11
293	Saepinum	fewer than 3,000	45.14
		66,330	

Source: Harris 1979[A61], 59 n. 4.

citizens was proportionally much heavier. In 225 B.C. the Roman citizen troops accounted for about 40 per cent of the combined Roman and Italian army, but at that time Roman citizens represented only about 27 per cent of the total population of peninsular Italy.[51] By drawing up this kind of balance sheet it becomes possible to understand the position of the allies in relation to Rome, and to explain both the efficiency and the cohesiveness of the system.

What we cannot do, in the present state of our knowledge, is to proceed from these schematic generalizations to an appreciation of how the wars of conquest affected the lives of the people who had the misfortune to live through them – what Toynbee calls 'the human balance sheet' of Rome expansion (Toynbee 1965[A131], 1.161). All we can say is that the unification of Italy under Roman leadership was achieved at an immense cost in terms of human suffering. Southern Central Italy was especially badly affected by the endless succession of Romano-Samnite wars. It is impossible to quantify the extent of devastation and loss of life that are referred to in a general way by our sources; and the consequential effects of war, such as mass starvation and disease, and the social and economic dislocation of the peasantry, can only be

[51] Afzelius 1942[J134], 133-5.

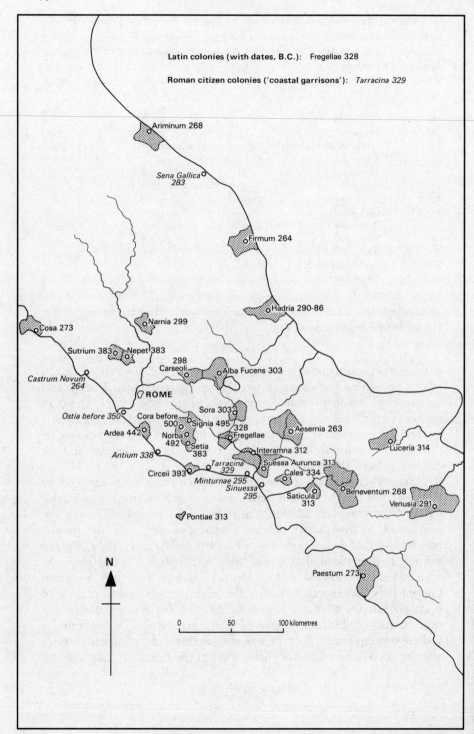

Latin colonies (with dates, B.C.):   Fregellae 328

Roman citizen colonies ('coastal garrisons'):   *Tarracina 329*

Ariminum 268

Sena Gallica 283

Firmum 264

Hadria 290-86

Narnia 299

Cosa 273

Sutrium 383   Nepet 383

Castrum Novum 264

298
Carseoli   Alba Fucens 303

ROME

Ostia before 350

Cora before 500   Sora 303

Signia 495

328
Fregellae

Aesernia 263

Ardea 442

Norba 492   Setia 383

Luceria 314

Antium 338

Interamna 312

Tarracina 329   Suessa Aurunca 313

Circeii 393   *Minturnae 295*   Cales 334

Sinuessa 295   Beneventum 268

Saticula 313

Venusia 291

Pontiae 313

N

Paestum 273

0   50   100 kilometres

imagined. Our evidence is confined to impressions and anecdotes, such as the following story about Pyrrhus, preserved by Cassius Dio: 'Pyrrhus became afraid of being cut off on all sides by the Romans while he was in unfamiliar territory. When his allies showed displeasure at this, he told them that he could see clearly from the country itself what a difference there was between them and the Romans. The subject territory of the latter had all kinds of trees, vineyards, tilled fields, and extensive farm fixtures; whereas the districts of his own friends had been ravaged to such an extent that it was impossible to tell whether they had ever been inhabited' (Dio ix, fr.40.27, vol. i, p. 126f Boiss.).

V. ROME IN THE AGE OF THE ITALIAN WARS

(a) *Politics and government*

During the period of the Italian wars between 338 and 264 B.C. the Roman commonwealth was internally transformed. It was at this time that the characteristic political, social and economic structures of the classical Republic began to take shape. As far as political institutions are concerned, the most striking development was the emergence of the senate as the dominant element in the state, and of the nobility as the controlling force within the senate. How this situation came about is difficult to assess, largely because of the extreme poverty of the sources for the third century. Matters are particularly bad for the period from 293 to 218 B.C., when virtually no information survives concerning Rome's domestic history. But when the record resumes in 218 B.C. with the full-scale narratives of Livy and Polybius, we find ourselves dealing with a

Fig. 48. Roman colonization in Italy, to 263 B.C.
Latin colonies
Before 500 Cora

495 Signia	298 Carseoli
492 Norba	291 Venusia
442 Ardea	290–286 Hadria
393 Circeii	273 Cosa
383 Setia	273 Paestum
383 Sutrium	268 Ariminum
383 Nepet	268 Beneventum
334 Cales	264 Firmum
328 Fregellae	263 Aesernia
314 Luceria	*Citizen colonies*
313 Saticula	Before 350 Ostia
313 Suessa Aurunca	338 Antium
313 Pontiae	329 Tarracina
312 Interamna	295 Minturnae
303 Sora	295 Sinuessa
303 Alba Fucens	283 Sena Gallica
299 Narnia	264 Castrum Novum

stable and efficient regime that had evidently been firmly established for several decades.

It was this established system that Polybius attempted to analyse in his account of the Roman constitution at the time of the battle of Cannae (VI.11–19). In spite of Polybius' celebrated theory that the government of the Roman state consisted of a balanced mixture of monarchic, aristocratic and democratic elements, to a modern observer the distinctive feature of the classical republican constitution is its strongly oligarchic character. Political power was concentrated in the hands of a wealthy landowning class which monopolized the magistracies and filled the senate. The nobility was a narrow political elite within the upper class, and consisted of patricians and leading plebeians who had held curule office. Former office-holders were a dominant group in the senate, and controlled the policy of the state. They passed their nobility on to their descendants, who thereby obtained a better chance of holding curule office in their turn.

There was considerable mobility within the upper class, however, and the nobles were far from being an exclusively hereditary group. At all times during the Republic there were many 'new men' (men without senatorial ancestors) in the senate, whose descendants could aspire to curule office and perhaps even the consulship. For a new man to reach the consulship himself was, naturally, a rare event; but that does not mean that the chief offices were monopolized by the descendants of former holders. Indeed it can be shown that under the Republic a considerable proportion of consuls, perhaps as many as 20 per cent, had no consular antecedents; on the other hand, many who were descended from consuls failed to achieve the office themselves.[52] The political elite was therefore a relatively open and competitive group, and was continually being invaded by newcomers.

The important point, however, is that the nobles exercised power because of their influence in the senate, rather than through office-holding *per se*. That is to say, tenure of the consulship, while it gave a man supreme executive authority for a year, was politically important in the long term because it admitted him to the elite group of *consulares* (ex-consuls), who were the most influential group in the senate and controlled its deliberations.

Roman nobles occupied executive offices not only for very short periods (usually for a year), but also infrequently; as we have seen, the practice of iteration was gradually brought to an end in the early decades of the third century (see above, p. 346). By then the most that a successful politician could hope for was to be consul once during his career. On the

---

[52] Brunt 1982[H102], 1–22; K. Hopkins and G. P. Burton in Hopkins 1983[A68], 31 ff.

other hand, all those who held curule magistracies were lifelong members of the senate, which consequently is where real power came to reside. In the developed Republic the magistrates were the servants of the senate. They consulted it as a matter of course before taking any action, and were in practice bound by its decrees. The senate meanwhile controlled the state's finances, the levying and disposal of military forces, the allocation of magisterial tasks ('provinces'), relations with foreign powers, and the maintenance of law and order in Rome and Italy. The senate also had complete charge of all matters relating to the state religion. It was not only the governing body of the Roman state; it was also a repository of political wisdom and experience, and the guardian of traditional moral values.

The emergence of the senate as the principal organ of government in Rome can be located in the period of the Samnite wars. In part it was an inevitable consequence of the growth of the Roman state and the increasing complexity of its affairs. But equally important was a change in the character of the senate and in the method by which it was recruited.

The senate of the early Republic is for us an ill-defined and elusive entity.[53] We know little about its composition and even less about its function. It seems reasonably certain, however, that in archaic times the main function of the senate was to act as an advisory body (*consilium*), first to the kings, and subsequently to the chief magistrates (consuls and consular tribunes), who apparently chose their own advisers and thus determined its membership. The senate was therefore not a permanent body, but was liable to change from year to year at the discretion of the magistrates in office.

This general conclusion emerges from an important passage of Festus (290 L) which states that originally no disgrace attached to men who were passed over (*praeteriti* – i.e. excluded from the senate), because the consuls (or consular tribunes), following the precedent of the kings, used to choose their closest friends from among the patricians, and then from among the plebeians. According to Festus, this informal system was changed by the Ovinian plebiscite, which transferred to the censors the task of drawing up the roll of the senate, and enjoined them to select 'the best man from every rank' (whatever that means).

The date of the Lex Ovinia is unknown, but it probably belongs to the fourth century, and is certainly earlier than 318 B.C., when we know the senate was selected by the censors.[54] Its most important consequence was

[53] Cf. above, p. 185f (with a different view).

[54] The standard view is that the first censorial *lectio* was that of 312 B.C., and that the Lex Ovinia was enacted in the years 318–312 (see e.g. Rotondi 1912 [A114], 233–4). But Diodorus xx.36.5 refers explicitly to Τὴν [sc. σύγκλητον τὴν] ὑπὸ τῶν προγεγενημένων τιμητῶν καταγραφεῖσαν – that is, the senate enrolled by the censors who preceded Appius Claudius (viz. those of 318 B.C.).

that those who were chosen became senators for life; their position was no longer dependent on the favour of the magistrates in office. By laying down the criteria of selection (which are unfortunately obscure to us) the law also restricted the discretionary powers of the censors; and while it gave the censors the power to omit names from the roll of the senate, it appears to have specified that only men who had shown themselves to be morally unfit for membership should be passed over. The Lex Ovinia therefore marks an important stage in what Mommsen called 'the emancipation of the senate from the power of the magistrates'.[55]

The growing ascendancy and increasing independence of the senate in the third century served the interests of the most conservative elements of the Roman political elite. The independent power of the executive magistrates was gradually diminished, and popular participation in the affairs of state was confined within increasingly narrow limits. These developments systematically undermined the rudimentary democracy that had occasionally been evident earlier in the fourth century. At that time, as we saw (p. 347), political leadership had been exercised by charismatic individuals who depended on popular favour, and the people's assemblies had been more prominent in the administration of affairs. The operation of this 'plebiscitary' system[56] is best exemplified by the career of Q. Publilius Philo, whose supremacy was based on the electoral support of the people. Philo's laws of 339 B.C. (above p. 342) advanced the principle of popular sovereignty, and aroused the hatred of the nobility, which persisted throughout his life.

This antagonism came to a head in 314 B.C., when Philo was accused of complicity in a plot to subvert the Republic. The affair is exceedingly obscure. Livy, the only source to refer to it, evidently had no clear notion of what he was supposed to be reporting. What began as an inquiry into disaffection among the aristocracy of Campania was apparently extended to Rome, where it became a full-scale witch hunt against those who had 'conspired against the state' by forming caucuses for the purpose of obtaining magistracies (Livy IX.26.8–9). Livy (or his source) seems to have regarded the event as a reaction by the nobility against the threat of competition from parvenus ('new men'). In this respect it recalls his earlier reference to the Lex Poetelia of 358 B.C. This was a law against electoral 'malpractice', designed to inhibit the ambition of new men 'who had been accustomed to frequent markets and meeting places', a practice that was now curtailed or forbidden (Livy VII.15.12). That is to say, the law restricted the freedom of candidates to canvass support from the voters.

---

55 Mommsen 1887–8[A91], III.2.880.
56 I use the term 'plebiscitary' in the modern sense, as in Weber 1976[A133], 156 etc.

In both cases the reference to 'new men' seems anachronistic, since in the generations after the Licinio-Sextian laws most plebeian office-holders were new men by definition; moreover, one of those impeached in 314 was a patrician (M. Folius). It is more probable that the law of 358 B.C. and the inquisition of 314 were directed against demagogic practices in general and form part of a wider attempt by the emerging oligarchy to limit eligibility for high office to 'acceptable' persons, and to prevent the rise of charismatic individuals.

The events of 314 B.C. can thus be understood in terms of a conflict between the oligarchic tendencies of the newly established 'patricio-plebeian' elite and the plebiscitary leadership of men such as Q. Publilius Philo. The existence of such a conflict can help to explain the extraordinary career of Appius Claudius Caecus, the dominant figure in Roman public life in the years on either side of 300 B.C. Appius Claudius is often described as the political heir of Philo.[57] Although there is no explicit evidence of a direct connexion between the two men, it is nevertheless extremely probable that they were associated in some way; and it is certainly reasonable to argue that Appius' programme was a continuation of Philo's. Philo disappears from the record after his trial in 314 B.C., at which he was acquitted; perhaps he died soon afterwards. Two years later, in 312, Appius took office as censor.

Although he was already an established political figure, aged perhaps about forty, Appius had not yet done anything that the later tradition considered worthy of remark. But his tenure of the censorship was truly sensational, and created a political upheaval.

The main events can be briefly summarized. Appius first ordered the construction of the great public works that bore his name: the highway from Rome to Capua, and Rome's first aqueduct, which brought fresh water into the city from the Sabine hills. Both projects entailed a vast expenditure of public funds; nevertheless, according to one source (Diodorus xx.36), Appius acted without authorization from the senate and emptied the treasury. In drawing up his list of the senate he outraged the Establishment by passing over men who were considered better than some of those chosen (Livy ix.30.1–2). His selection of new senators was regarded as wilful and partisan; and great offence was caused by the fact that many of them were the sons of freedmen.

Appius Claudius' most important measure as censor was a reorganization of the tribes, which had the effect of increasing the voting power of the city proletariat in the tribal assemblies. The precise nature of the change is unclear; Livy merely says that Appius corrupted the Forum and the Campus (that is, probably, the electoral and legislative assemblies) by distributing the lower classes (*humiles*) throughout all the tribes. The *humiles* were presumably the propertyless inhabitants of the city (artisans, traders and so forth), who had hitherto been confined to only four of the thirty-one tribes, and were therefore under-represented in the assemblies in proportion to their numbers. A large number of them, probably the great majority, appear to have been freedmen or the descendants of freedmen.[58] Appius' reform will have distributed them among all the tribes, including the so-called rustic tribes, which had formerly been the exclusive preserve of country dwellers and landowners. The measure had far-reaching implications; in Livy's words it transferred the control of the assembly from the 'honest citizens' (*integer populus*) to the faction of the Forum, the 'lowest of the low' (*forensis factio . . . humillimi*: Livy IX.46.13–14).

Appius also interfered with the organization of the state religion; our sources have some entertaining anecdotes about his activities in this sphere, but we are not in a position to understand their political significance (if any). What is clear is that Appius' radical reforms aroused a storm of protest from conservative nobles. It is said that even his own colleague in the censorship, C. Plautius, was so scandalized by the new senatorial roll that he resigned his office, leaving Appius to carry on alone (and with a free hand). It is further alleged that Appius failed to lay down his office when the full eighteen-month term had elapsed. Indeed, according to some sources he was still in office as censor in 308 B.C., when he stood (successfully) for the consulship (Livy IX.42.3).

However that may be, there can be no doubt about the intensity of the opposition that Appius' measures aroused. His new list of senators was not recognized by the consuls of 311 B.C., who continued to summon the senate using the old list that had been drawn up by the previous censors. Conceivably the consuls' justification was that by enrolling his own clients and passing over more 'worthy' choices Appius had contravened the Lex Ovinia.[59] In any event, Appius' designs in regard to the senate were thwarted. His reform of the tribes, however, remained in force for a time, and was directly responsible, according to Livy, for the election of Cn. Flavius as curule aedile for 304 B.C. (Livy IX.46.10).

Cn. Flavius, a secretary (*scriba*) of Appius Claudius, was the son of a freedman and the first of his class to hold a curule magistracy. The conservative establishment was appalled, and many of the nobles refused to treat Flavius with the customary respect due to a curule magistrate (Piso fr. 27P); Livy records moreover that some removed their gold rings and military decorations in protest. As aedile Cn. Flavius published

---

[58] As implied by Plut. *Publ.* 7. This is a highly controversial matter. I have followed the interpretation offered by Treggiari 1969[G150], 39–42.

[59] Thus Staveley 1959[H128], 413.

an account of the legal procedures known as *legis actiones*, which had not hitherto been accessible to the people, and posted in the Forum a calendar which indicated the *dies fasti* – the days on which legal business was permitted. There seems no reason to question the view of all the sources that the publication of the *ius Flavianum* (as it was later called) and the calendar was a politically motivated act, nor the clear implication of most of them that Flavius was acting as Appius Claudius' agent.[60]

A reaction soon followed. In the same year as Flavius was aedile, the censors Q. Fabius Rullianus and P. Decius Mus reversed Appius' tribal reorganization, and confined the *humiles* once again to the four 'urban' tribes. Then, when Cn. Flavius dedicated a shrine of Concord in the Comitium, much to the annoyance of the leading nobles, a law was immediately enacted that no one should dedicate a temple or an altar without the authorization of the senate or of a majority of the tribunes of the plebs.

The actions that are attributed to Appius and his agents clearly mark him out as a radical populist who aimed to build a personal following among the mass of the people. The sources lay stress on the size of his *clientela* (e.g. Cic. *Sen.* 37; Val. Max. VIII.13.5); one text even alleges that he attempted to take over all Italy by means of his clients.[61] This general assessment of Appius Claudius as a revolutionary democrat is clearly set out in the surviving sources, especially in Diodorus, who gives the most coherent account of his censorship (xx.36). It was accepted by Mommsen (who likened Appius to Cleisthenes and Pericles) and remains the standard view, in spite of hypercritical and revisionist challenges.[62]

It is true that the later annalistic tradition was hostile to the whole clan of the patrician Claudii,[63] and that Livy's stereotyped picture of Appius Claudius as a tyrannical and overbearing patrician cannot be accepted as it stands (the facts which Livy himself records are against it!); on the other hand, there is no reason whatever to doubt the basic outline of Appius' actions, as they are reported in the sources, nor to modify the record so as to reduce him to the level of a run-of-the-mill politician who did nothing out of the ordinary. Some of the traditional hostility to Appius may in any case reflect contemporary rhetoric; as we have seen, Fabius Pictor had access to traditions going back to the time of Fabius Rullianus, who was a personal enemy of Appius Claudius.

---

[60] Pomponius, *Dig.* 1.2.2.7, claims that Flavius stole the formulae from Appius, who had been planning to publish them himself.

[61] Suet. *Tib.* 2. Mommsen argued persuasively that the 'Claudius Drusus' of the MSS must be a reference to Appius Caecus (Mommsen 1864–79[A90], 1.308–9).

[62] The 'hypercritics' include Palmer 1970[A102], 269–70, and most recently Wiseman 1979[B190], 85–9. The chief revisionist is Garzetti 1947[H112], 175ff, who attempted to 'normalize' all of Appius' political acts.

[63] Mommsen 1864–79[A90], 1.287ff; cf. Wiseman 1979[B190], 85–9.

The chief difficulty in seeing Appius as a democrat is the fact that on a number of occasions he appears as the upholder of patrician privileges and an opponent of the plebs. In 300 B.C. he vigorously opposed the Ogulnian plebiscite, which admitted plebeians to the two senior priestly colleges, and on two separate occasions he attempted to exclude plebeians from the consulship and to bring about the election of an all-patrician college.

But aristocratic pride is perfectly compatible with demagogic methods, as Mommsen noted (citing the examples of Pericles and Caesar). Appius' opposition to the Lex Ogulnia is not really a major difficulty because that law was in no sense a democratic measure. Like other political reforms in the Conflict of the Orders, it benefited only a narrow group of well-to-do plebeians and did nothing for the rights of the lower classes. Under the Lex Ogulnia the major priestly colleges became self-perpetuating oligarchic cliques, divided equally between the patrician and plebeian members of the new nobility and recruiting new members by co-option. The choice of pontiffs and augurs was not in any way subjected to popular will (the colleges were not opened to election until much later), and anyone not acceptable to the conservative establishment could be excluded. Appius himself was not a member of either college.

As for his attempts to contrive the election of an all-patrician college of consuls, the most probable explanation is that Appius was challenging the system of power sharing between the two orders, rather than the right of plebeians as such to hold the consulship (which is how Livy and his sources interpreted it – x.15.8–9). The target was not the political rights of plebeians in general, but rather the privileged position of the plebeian nobility, which had acquired a guaranteed share of the senior magistracies, irrespective of the wishes of the electorate.

The point can be illustrated by the consular elections of 297 B.C., in which Appius himself was a candidate (Livy x.15.7–12). When it became clear that the people's first choice was Q. Fabius Rullianus, who was not even a candidate (as consul in office Fabius was presiding over the elections; his candidature would have been technically illegal), Appius proposed that the rules should be waived and that both he and Fabius should be consuls. This was evidently what the result of a free election would have been.

In the event Fabius withdrew, allowing Appius Claudius to take the patrician place in the consular college, and thus resolving the immediate issue. But the point of principle was whether or not the *comitia* should be entitled to elect whomsoever they wished, regardless of the rules. Appius evidently contended that they should, on the basis of the clause of the Twelve Tables which stated that 'the people's last decree is the effective law' (Livy VII.17.12; Cic. *Balb*. 33). The argument, in other words, was that an electoral vote constituted a decree of the *populus*, and as such automatically overruled any previous enactment that might conflict with it.

Livy explicitly attributes this line of reasoning to Appius at the time when his prolonged tenure of the censorship came under attack (IX.33.9); and the case is outlined in full in a speech ascribed to Appius Claudius Crassus, Caecus' grandfather, at the time of the Licinio-Sextian Rogations (Livy VI.40.15–20; cf. X.7.2). The argument which Livy or his source(s) thus foisted on the Claudian house is so distinctive, and so obviously accords with Appius Caecus' actual view of popular rights, that we might reasonably conjecture that the tradition has preserved a genuine example of the political thought of Appius Claudius Caecus.

This speculation is not necessarily improbable, given that much reliable information about the political debates of this period would have been available to Fabius Pictor; moreover, we happen to know that some of Appius' own words survived in written form. Appius Claudius has a place in the history of literature as the father of Latin prose. Works attributed to him include political speeches (Cicero refers to the one in which Appius opposed peace with Pyrrhus in 279 B.C. (p. 471) – *Sen*. 16; *Brut*. 61) and a work of jurisprudence (Pomponius in *Dig*. 1.2.2.36); and a collection of his sayings (*carmina*) circulated in the late Republic, and was already known to the Greek philosopher Panaetius in the second century B.C. The most famous of the sayings to survive is the adage *faber est suae quisque fortunae* ('each man is the architect of his own fortune'). The various works attributed to Appius Claudius are sometimes dismissed as late forgeries, but without any good reason.[64] The fact is that the traditional picture of Appius *does* have some authentic touches. That is what makes him so different from Furius Camillus, Manlius Torquatus, Valerius Corvus and the other lifeless heroes of the early Republic. As De Sanctis observed, he stands out as the first living personality in Roman history.[65]

It is clear, however, that in his political actions Appius was swimming against the tide. His efforts to democratize the assembly and to assert its sovereignty were ultimately abortive; popular government was never established in Rome. On the contrary, the outcome of the political struggles of the fourth century was the formation of a self-serving and self-perpetuating oligarchy which restricted the magistrates' scope for independent political action and at the same time emasculated the theoretical sovereignty of the people's assemblies.

---

[64] E.g. A.S. Gratwick in the *Cambridge History of Classical Literature II: Latin Literature* 1982[B24], 138–9.   [65] De Sanctis 1907–64[A37], II.216.

This may seem at first sight a somewhat paradoxical result, given that
the Roman tradition regarded the political history of this period as a long
but ultimately successful struggle for liberty and the assertion of the
rights of Roman citizens. Moreover, some modern scholars have argued
that at this time Rome was progressing towards democracy.[66] But we
must recognize that there is a great difference between what the Romans
regarded as liberty (*libertas*) and the modern (or for that matter the
ancient) concept of democracy. For the ordinary citizen *libertas* signified
equality before the law, and the right of appeal (*ius provocationis*) against
the arbitrary decisions of a magistrate. Both principles were enshrined in
the Twelve Tables, and reinforced by subsequent legislation; for
example a Lex Valeria of 300 B.C. confirmed the citizens' right of appeal
(Livy x.9.3–6). The history of the institution of appeal (*provocatio*) in the
Roman Republic is very obscure (pp. 219ff), and the circumstances in
which it operated in practice are the subject of much controversy. But,
however we interpret the significance of *provocatio*, the fact is that the
Roman ideal of juristic liberty and equality for all citizens was never
matched by true political liberty or equality of political rights. In political
terms *libertas* was an aristocratic concept, which signified the unhindered
operation of a system of hierarchical institutions, and the freedom of
members of a noble elite to compete equally and openly for political
honours.

The theory that in the fourth century Rome was gradually advancing
towards democracy is based on the fact that at this time the people's
assemblies gradually acquired the right to pass legally binding enactments. The final stage in the process was the Lex Hortensia, a measure
passed in circumstances that are entirely obscure to us. Even the date is
uncertain, but it was between 289 and 286 B.C. We are told that Q.
Hortensius, a plebeian who is otherwise unknown, was appointed
dictator to deal with a plebeian secession caused by debt. How the
emergency arose, and how it was resolved, we cannot say (but it is
interesting to observe that the Lex Poetelia of 326 B.C. had not, in fact,
abolished the problem of indebtedness). The memorable result of the
crisis of c. 287 B.C., however, was a law that appeared to endorse the
principle of popular sovereignty.

But this impression is largely illusory. To regard the Conflict of the
Orders as a struggle for democratic rights is to misunderstand the facts
(and perhaps also to submit to a whiggish fallacy). The problem,
naturally, is that the apparent success of the plebs did not in the event
result in democratic government. This has led historians to speak about
the 'frustration of democracy by the Roman establishment', and to argue

[66] Cf. the remarks of De Martino 1972–5[A35], 1.491ff.

that the embryonic growth was somehow aborted almost at the moment of its birth.[67] Alternatively it has been suggested that the Roman state became so prosperous as a result of war and imperialism that the masses were content to leave the conduct of affairs to the senate and did not bother to exercise the democratic rights which they had actually managed to acquire.[68]

There is certainly some truth in these propositions. The alleviation of economic discontent by successful conquest undoubtedly caused the people to acquiesce in the rule of the oligarchy, and created a consensus that was to last until the time of the Gracchi. But that is not to say that Rome was a latent democracy, or that the people possessed the constitutional means to withdraw their consent at any time. In fact the political reforms of the fourth century had the effect of reducing the powers of the plebeian assembly. As we have seen (above, pp. 334ff), the leading plebeians fulfilled their aspirations and obtained admittance to the nobility, but by doing so they ceased to represent the political interests of the rest of the plebs.

The Lex Hortensia was certainly an important concession (the legislation of the Gracchi would have been impossible without it), but it did not radically affect the basic structure of Roman political institutions. Democracy never materialized at Rome because the popular assemblies could not function as autonomous institutions. They did not meet as a matter of course, as the Athenian *ecclesia* did, but only when summoned by a magistrate – a consul or praetor in the case of the *comitia* (the full state assemblies), a tribune in that of the *concilium plebis* (the assembly of the plebs). Moreover they could not initiate anything; they merely answered 'yes' or 'no' to questions (*rogationes*) that were put to them by the magistrates, or chose between candidates who were presented to them. Their role in politics was therefore passive rather than active, and depended absolutely on the magistrates who had the right to 'deal with the people' (*agere cum populo*). In this sense every election, enactment or judicial verdict was a bilateral act, as Mommsen saw.[69] The problem was that the two parties to this form of contract were potentially, and often actually, antagonistic. The magistrate did not necessarily share the people's interest, and was under no obligation to represent them; although elected by the people, he was not in any way accountable to them either during or after his term of office.

Ordinary citizens had little freedom of speech, in the basic sense that they were denied access to all formal means of making their views known and of taking political initiatives. Only magistrates were entitled to

---

[67] Toynbee 1965[A131], 1.315ff.   [68] E.g. Scullard 1980[A119], 129-30.
[69] Mommsen 1887-8[A91], III.303-4.

address the people and to propose laws. The citizens had no right either to debate or to amend the proposals put to them. It follows that the Roman people could advance their own interests only in collusion with a magistrate; and for them to do so against the wishes of the ruling class required a kind of conspiracy between magistrate and people. Not surprisingly this did not occur very often, and when it did the oligarchy was still able to use a variety of devices to thwart a proposal, for instance by using the tribunician veto or by the announcement of unfavourable omens before or during an assembly. When in 133 B.C. a tribune of the plebs allied himself with the assembly in a systematic attempt to promote the interests of the poor against those of the possessing classes, the result, not surprisingly, was violence, bloodshed, and the start of the Roman revolution.

Two further points need to be made in connexion with the subject of democracy (or its absence) at Rome. First, the voting in the assemblies was organized by groups, rather than on the basis of a simple majority of all those present and voting. In the *comitia tributa* and the *concilium plebis* the voting units were the local tribes, which numbered thirty-three after 299 B.C. (the definitive figure of thirty-five was reached in 241 B.C., when the last two tribes were added). Four of them were the so-called 'urban' tribes, the rest were 'rustic' tribes. The significance of this distinction is that (after the failure of Appius Claudius' reform) only landowners and country dwellers were registered in the rustic tribes, while the landless inhabitants of the city were confined to the four urban tribes, and consequently had very limited voting power in proportion to their numbers. Since the assemblies were held only in Rome, the system artificially favoured the wealthy landowners who lived in the city but owned country estates, and discriminated both against the urban proletariat and the far-flung peasant small-holders who for practical reasons were unable to attend the *comitia* in person.

The voting units of the *comitia centuriata* were the 193 centuries, which were distributed among five economically defined 'classes' (p. 165). But the distribution of the centuries among the classes went in inverse proportion to the actual numbers of citizens, so that the wealthiest class, which was numerically relatively small, contained by far the largest number of centuries; together with eighteen centuries of aristocratic knights, the eighty centuries of the first class could command an absolute majority of the total. At the other extreme proletarians who fell below the minimum property qualification for membership of the fifth class were enrolled in a single century, and were often not called upon to vote at all.

The assemblies were thus organized to give the greatest influence to the propertied classes. Another factor that gave the *comitia centuriata* in particular an inherently conservative character was the division of the centuries between *iuniores* (men aged between 17 and 45) and *seniores* (men aged 46 and over). Since both had an equal number of centuries within each class, it followed that the seniors, who represented fewer than 30 per cent of the total electorate, carried more than twice as much political weight as the juniors.

The second point is that only members of the elite could stand for magisterial office. Whether or not there was a formal property qualification, it is obvious that only the wealthy could put themselves forward for positions that were unpaid and might entail considerable expense. Moreover, given the restrictions on canvassing and the absence of any means of making oneself known to the electorate, an outsider without powerful connexions and backing would have had no chance at all. It is significant that the term *nobilis* means literally 'well-known'.

(b) *Economic and cultural developments*

The period of the Samnite wars saw an unparalleled increase in the public and private wealth of the Romans. Their most obvious gain was in land. The *ager Romanus*, which after the conclusion of the Latin war in 338 B.C. had comprised *c.* 5525 km.^{2} and supported a population of around 347,300 persons (see above, p. 367), had expanded by 264 to 26,850 km.^{2} with a population in the region of 900,000 (Fig. 47: p. 382). On these figures the Romans possessed more than 20 per cent of the total land surface of peninsular Italy (reckoned at 125,445 km.^{2}) and nearly 30 per cent of its population (estimated in total at something over 3 millions).[70]

The process of expansion entailed a considerable redistribution of landed property within the annexed territories, where large numbers of impoverished Roman citizens were resettled on small allotments. The principal stages in this process were marked by the formation of new rustic tribes (Fig. 49), the Scaptia and Maecia in 332 B.C., the Oufentina and Falerna in 318, and the Aniensis and Teretina in 299. A further large-scale resettlement of Roman citizens took place on land annexed from the Sabines and Praetuttii after the campaigns of M'. Curius Dentatus in 290 B.C. The original proprietors were wholly or partly dispossessed. Many of them were killed, enslaved or deported *en masse* to other areas.

We have no means of knowing how many people were involved in these schemes, but a reasonable guess would be that between 20,000 and 30,000 adult male Romans were resettled, together with their dependants. In addition, Romans and their allies benefited from the foundation

[70] Afzelius 1942[J134], 192; cf. Brunt 1971[A21], 59.

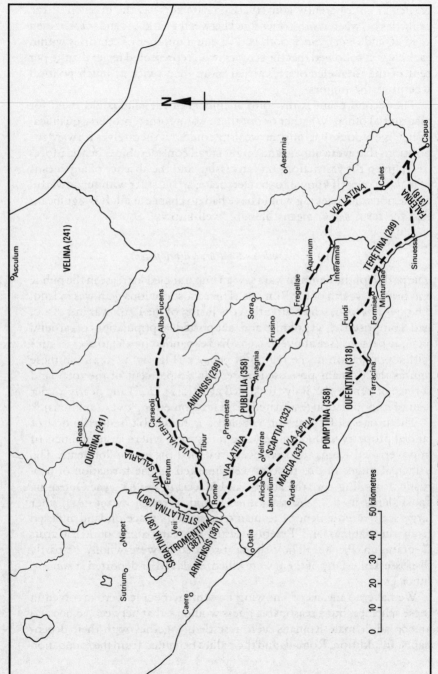

Fig. 49. Development of the Roman tribes, 387–241 B.C. (and principal Roman roads).

Table 9. *Latin colonies, 334–263 B.C.*

Date (B.C.)	Colony	Region	Adult male settlers	Cum. Total	Area (km²)	Cum. Total
334	Cales	Campania	2,500*	2,500	100	100
328	Fregellae	Latium	4,000	6,500	305	405
314	Luceria	Apulia	2,500*	9,000	790	1,195
313	Saticula	Samnium	2,500	11,500	195	1,390
313	Suessa Aurunca	Latium	2,500	14,000	180	1,570
313	Pontiae Islands	(Latium)	300	14,300	10	1,580
312	Interamna Lir.	Latium	4,000*	18,300	265	1,845
303	Sora	Latium	4,000*	22,300	230	2,075
303	Alba Fucens	Central Appennines	6,000*	28,300	420	2,495
299	Narnia	Umbria	2,500	30,800	185	2,680
298	Carseoli	Central Appennines	4,000*	34,800	285	2,965
291	Venusia	Apulia	6,000	40,800	800	3,765
289	Hadria	Central Appennines	4,000	44,800	380	4,145
273	Paestum	Lucania	4,000	48,800	540	4,685
273	Cosa	Etruria	2,500	51,300	340	5,025
268	Ariminum	Umbria	6,000	57,300	650	5,675
268	Beneventum	Samnium	6,000	63,300	575	6,250
264	Firmum	Picenum	4,000	67,300	400	6,650
263	Aesernia	Samnium	4,000	71,300	385	7,035

(All figures are rough estimates, except for those marked *, which are recorded by Livy.)
Source: A. Afzelius 1942[J134], with modifications.

of Latin colonies, which in the period 334–263 B.C. took up a further 7000 km.² of conquered land and involved the resettlement of over 70,000 men and their families (see Table 9).

Rome's increasing prosperity is reflected in the development of the city (Fig. 50) and the growth of its population. The profits of conquest, in the form of booty and indemnities, were used to finance a programme of public building on a scale that had not been seen since the great age of the Tarquins. The literary sources record the construction of fourteen temples in the years from 302 to 264 B.C. (see Table 10), but this is certainly not a complete list of those actually built; eight of the fourteen are known from Livy, and belong to the period before 293 B.C., for which his text is fully preserved. Moreover, archaeology provides evidence of other temple construction, either not mentioned in literary sources, or not securely identified with otherwise known buildings. These include the temples of Portunus and Hercules Invictus (see below), and two of the temples of the Largo Argentina (temple C and temple A) which

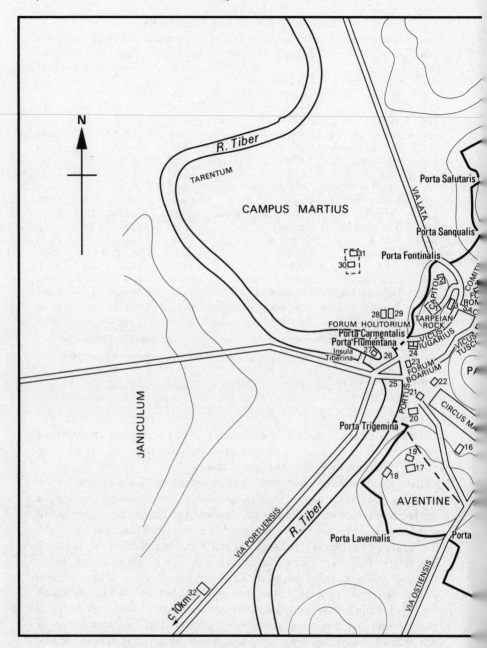

Fig. 50. The city of Rome in the early third century B.C.

1 Iuppiter Optimus Maximus (509); 2 Iuno Moneta (344); 3 Saturn (497); 4 Rostra (338); 5 Janus; 6 Semo Sancus (466); 7 Salus (302); 8 Quirinus (293); 9 Iuno Lucina; 10 Tellus (268); 11 Castor (484); 12 Regia; 13 Vesta; 14 Atrium Vestae; 15 Iuppiter Stator (294); 16 Mercury (495);

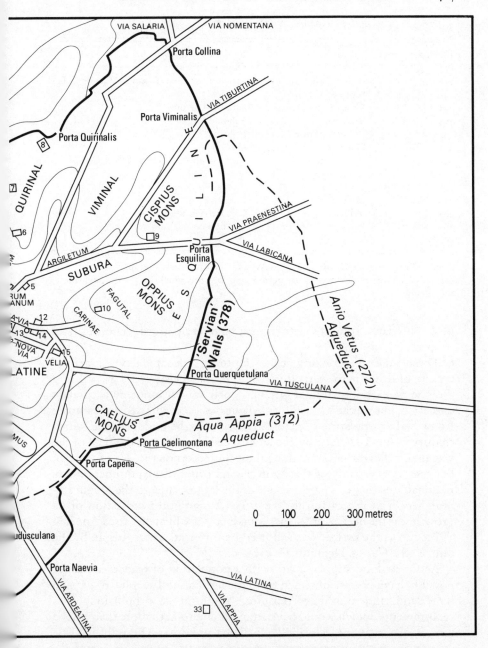

VIA SALARIA   VIA NOMENTANA

Porta Collina

VIA TIBURTINA

Porta Viminalis

Porta Quirinalis

QUIRINAL   VIMINAL   CISPIUS MONS

VIA PRAENESTINA

⬜9   VIA LABICANA

ARGILETUM   SUBURA   Porta Esquilina

RUM ANUM   FAGUTAL   OPPIUS MONS   Anio Vetus Aqueduct (272)

CARINAE   ⬜10   'Servian' Walls (378)

A-VIA   12

13   14

NOVA VIA   15

VELIA   Porta Querquetulana   VIA TUSCULANA

LATINE

CAELIUS MONS   Aqua Appia (312) Aqueduct

MUS   Porta Caelimontana

Porta Capena

0   100   200   300 metres

udusculana

Porta Naevia   VIA LATINA

VIA ARDEATINA   VIA APPIA   33⬜

17 Diana; 18 Iuno Regina (392); 19 Minerva; 20 Ceres (493); 21 Ara Maxima Herculis; 22 Hercules Invictus; 23 Portunus; 24 Fortuna and Mater Matuta (396); 25 Pons Sublicius; 26 Pons Aemilius; 27 Aesculapius (291); 28 Apollo (431); 29 Bellona (296); 30 Largo Argentina, Temple 'C'; 31 Largo Argentina, Temple 'A'; 32 Fors Fortuna (293); 33 Tomb of the Scipios.

Table 10. *Roman temple construction, 302–264 B.C.*

Date (B.C.)	Temple	Location
302	Salus	Quirinal
296	Bellona Victrix	Circus Flaminius (Campus Martius, S.E.)
295	Iuppiter Victor	Quirinal?
295	Venus Obsequens	Circus Maximus
294	Victoria	Palatine
294	Iuppiter Stator	Palatine
293	Quirinus	Quirinal
293	Fors Fortuna	Right bank of Tiber, at 6th milestone
291	Aesculapius	Tiber Island
278	Summanus	Circus Maximus
272	Consus	Aventine
268	Tellus	Carinae (Esquiline)
267	Pales	Unknown
264	Vertumnus	Aventine

Source: Wissowa 1912[G519], 594–5; Wissowa lists a further 18 temples which certainly or probably belong to the period 293–218, for which Livy's full text does not survive.

probably date from the late fourth and early third centuries B.C. (respectively).[71]

These public undertakings are a symptom of the rapid development of the city of Rome in the early third century. Its precise rate of growth and the size of its population at any particular stage cannot be accurately measured, but we can make informed guesses. According to one estimate Rome had a population of *c.* 30,000 persons in the middle of the fourth century, rising to 60,000 by 300 and exceeding 90,000 at the time of the war against Pyrrhus.[72] If anything these figures err on the side of caution, but they are certainly of the right general order of magnitude; on any reasonable estimate, Rome was one of the largest cities in the Mediterranean world in the early third century. A significant indication of its growth was the need to construct aqueducts, of which the Aqua Appia in 312 B.C. was the first; it was followed by the Anio Vetus, begun by the censor M'. Curius Dentatus in 272 B.C.

As for its food supply, a city with a population of 90,000 could not possibly have been maintained from the agricultural surplus of its own hinterland, and must have imported a substantial proportion of its requirements, which would have amounted in total to more than 18,000 tonnes of wheat (or calorific equivalent) per year. The only realistic assumption is that the necessary imports were transported by water. As

[71] F. Coarelli in *Roma medio-repubblicana* 1973[B401], 117–20.
[72] Starr 1981[A125], 15–26.

there was as yet no harbour in use at Ostia (the small Roman settlement founded early in the fourth century was no more than a fort to guard the estuary), we must suppose that a substantial traffic made its way along the Tiber to the Portus Tiberinus, the river landing situated opposite the eastern tip of the Tiber island.

As it happens the literary tradition confirms that the Tiber had been used for the importation of grain since the beginning of the Republic (if not earlier). Food shortages are recorded on a number of occasions in the fifth century, when the Romans sent to Etruria, Campania and Sicily for emergency supplies.[73] These places are all accessible from Rome either by river or by sea. Under the year 411 B.C. Livy explicitly reports that grain was brought down the Tiber from inland Etruria as well as by sea from coastal Etruria and Sicily (IV.52.5–8).

The authenticity of these fifth-century notices is naturally far from certain, but most scholars are now prepared to accept them.[74] The fact that there are far fewer records of similar shortages in the fourth century is, if anything, a point in their favour, for two reasons. First, in the fourth century one of the principal causes of food crisis – enemy action – had been largely eliminated; as we have seen, the Romans took care to fight their wars on other peoples' territories, rather than on their own. Secondly, the growth of the city made it necessary for the Romans to import grain on a regular basis, and not just in times of exceptional shortage; moreover their military power was such that they were no doubt always able to procure whatever they needed, by force if necessary, and thus to minimize the effects of a food crisis. Even so, occasional shortages still occurred fom time to time, as in 299 B.C. (Livy X.11.7).

The use of the Tiber for grain transport naturally raises the question of the scale and nature of Rome's maritime trade in general. Archaeological research has shown that the area of the Portus had been frequented from a very remote epoch;[75] more important for the purposes of the present discussion is the fact that a substantial redevelopment seems to have taken place there at the end of the fourth century B.C. The earliest phase of the temple of Portunus, the god of the harbour, belongs to this period, as does the temple of Hercules Invictus, which stood beside the Ara Maxima. The Ara Maxima was itself the site of a cult of Hercules and had long-standing associations with foreign trade. It is tempting to speculate that the late fourth-century buildings reflect the growing importance of Rome's maritime trade at that period; and the attractive suggestion has been made that the redevelopment of this part of the city should be dated to the censorship of Appius Claudius, since it was he who transformed

[73] References and discussion in Ogilvie 1965[B129], 256–7; cf. above, pp.133ff.
[74] The case was made by Momigliano 1936[F48], 374ff (= id. *Quarto Contributo* 331ff).
[75] La Rocca 1977[G99], 380ff.

the worship of Hercules at the Ara Maxima from a private concern of the Potitian clan into a publicly administered cult.[76]

At this point it may be noticed that the picture of Rome as a major importing centre conflicts with the conventional view of the Roman economy at the start of the third century. This view[77] maintains that Rome was a simple agrarian community with a near-subsistence economy and little trade. Local craft production was at a rudimentary level and of poor quality; such luxuries as were to be found at Rome must have been imported from more advanced centres of production in Etruria, Campania or Magna Graecia. The Roman ruling class was culturally unsophisticated and not particularly rich by comparison with other contemporary elites or in relation to the mass of the peasantry. Tradition itself told stories of horny-handed senators who worked their own fields, lived in unplastered hovels and cooked their own turnips (see especially the account of M'. Curius Dentatus in Plutarch, *Cat. Mai.* 2.1). Above all the Romans were indifferent to maritime activity. According to Seneca (*Brev. Vit.* 13.4) the man who first persuaded the Romans to take to the sea was Appius Claudius Caudex, consul in 264 B.C. Polybius tells us that in 260 the Romans possessed no naval resources at all, because 'they had never given a thought to the sea' (1.20.12).

This traditional view has been challenged, however, and in the extreme form outlined above it is certainly unacceptable. We cannot take Polybius literally, nor Seneca seriously. The foundation of coastal garrison colonies, the Latin settlement on the Pontine islands, and the Decian plebiscite of 311 B.C., which established a small fleet under two naval commanders (*duumviri navales*: Livy IX.30.4), show that the Romans had not been entirely unconcerned about naval defence in the late fourth century. Nevertheless, it remains true that the object of these measures was primarily to guard the coast of Latium against pirates or enemy attacks, and possibly to provide naval assistance for land forces where appropriate (as in 310 B.C. – Livy IX.38.2); they do not necessarily have any bearing on the question of Rome's status as a commercial centre. The negative point made by the traditionalists, that the Roman government cannot be shown to have had any 'commercial policy', remains valid. The second treaty between Rome and Carthage of 348 B.C. (it was renewed in 305 according to Livy IX.43.26) contains clauses dealing with trade; but while they envisage the possibility that Roman traders might visit Sicily or Africa, the primary object of these clauses was clearly to protect the commercial interests of Carthage, not those of Rome (text in Polybius III.24: cf. p. 527).

---

[76] Livy IX.29.9–11; cf. Coarelli 1975[B308], 279.

[77] E.g. Frank 1933[G71], 1.6; M. Rostovtzeff, *Social and Economic History of the Roman Empire*, Oxford 1957, 13. For a reasoned critique of the conventional view see Starr 1981[A125], who is closely followed in this section.

On the other hand, it cannot be seriously maintained that the Romans were not engaged in trade at all. Archaeological evidence shows beyond doubt that Rome was an important manufacturing and trading centre in the years before and after 300 B.C. As usual, pottery is the most plentiful category of material, and the evidence it provides is decisive in this case. It is virtually certain that several different kinds of pottery, including wares of high quality, were manufactured in Rome in the early third century. The material includes not only decorated plates of the so-called 'Genucilia' type, but also black-glaze ware – of which the *pocula* form a particularly interesting group.[78] The most characteristic body of material, however, is a group of black-glaze pots decorated with small embossed stamps which come from a Roman workshop known as the 'Atelier des petites estampilles'. The significant point about this high-quality fabric, which was produced in large quantities in the early years of the third century, is that it was widely exported; examples have been found not only in many parts of Central Italy, but also along the coasts of southern France and North-East Spain, in Corsica and the Punic part of Sicily, and in the Carthaginian territory in North Africa.[79]

It is important that we should be clear about the limitations of this evidence. We might reasonably argue that the distribution of finds of Roman fine pottery represents the tip of an iceberg, and implies a geographically extensive trade, not only in ceramics but in other items as well. But we have no means of reconstructing the content, volume or mechanism of this trade, nor of assessing its general economic importance. We cannot say, for instance, what percentage of Rome's gross product (itself unknowable) was represented by manufacture and trade.

But the evidence that is currently available nevertheless supports a position that is qualitatively different from the traditional idea of third-century Rome as a simple rustic community. It should be emphasized that the original proponents of the traditional view were not attempting to set up a 'primitivist' model of the early third-century economy in the manner of the Cambridge school.[80] On the contrary, they were (if anything) 'modernists', whose purpose in stressing the supposedly primitive character of Rome was precisely to isolate it from the more advanced economic and cultural conditions that prevailed elsewhere in the Mediterranean (and even in Italy) at the beginning of the third century B.C.[81]

But an unprejudiced assessment of the archaeological facts shows

[78] J.-P. Morel in *Roma medio-repubblicana* 1973[B401], 43–6.

[79] Morel 1969[B361], 94ff.

[80] For a lucid summary of the views of the 'Cambridge primitivists' (principally A. H. M. Jones and M. I. Finley) see K. Hopkins in Garnsey, Hopkins and Whittaker 1983[G77], x–xiv.

[81] This is clear at least as far as Frank is concerned; his explicit rejection of all theory (Frank 1933[G71], I.viii) makes him an unconscious modernist.

decisively that Rome was neither isolated nor culturally backward at this time. A high level of material culture is attested not only by the products of fine pottery workshops, but by a whole range of artefacts: terracotta sculptures and miniature funerary altars ('arule'), carved stone monuments (among which the sarcophagus of L. Cornelius Scipio Barbatus, *cos.* 298, holds pride of place), bronzes, and even a fragment of an extremely fine fresco painting (Fig. 2: p. 13). The latter item, from a tomb on the Esquiline, depicts a historical scene involving a certain Q. Fabius. According to the most probable interpretation, the tomb was that of Q. Fabius Rullianus, and the painting part of an illustrated account of episodes from the Samnite wars.[82] The finest example of Roman craftsmanship to survive from this period is the Ficoroni Cista, an engraved bronze casket that was found in a tomb at Palestrina (Praeneste); one leading authority has dated it to around 315 B.C.[83] An inscription on the handle tells us that the Cista was made in Rome by a craftsman named Novius Plautius. Although it is sometimes dismissed as a unique exception, there is in fact no reason to suspect that the Ficoroni Cista is not a representative example of the bronzework that was being produced in Roman workshops in the years around 300 B.C. It is exceptional only in the sense that no other surviving Cista is demonstrably of Roman origin.

Literary evidence moreover indicates that at this time bronze statues began to be erected in Rome. They include the equestrian statue of Q. Marcius Tremulus, consul in 306 B.C. (cf. above p. 386), and the bronze group of the twins Romulus and Remus with the she-wolf, which was set up by the curule aediles Cn. and Q. Ogulnius in 296 B.C. These two also placed a bronze statue of Iuppiter in a four-horse chariot on the roof of the Capitoline temple, in place of the terracotta one that had been there since the end of the sixth century (Livy x.23.11–12). Three years later colossal bronze statues of Iuppiter and Hercules were set up on the Capitol; and in the Comitium, according to a strange story in Pliny, the Romans put up statues of Pythagoras and Alcibiades, 'the wisest and bravest of the Greeks' (historians have not failed to point out the 'western' bias apparent in this strange choice). The only surviving remnant of republican bronze sculpture is the head of the so-called 'Capitoline Brutus'. Although it is usually ascribed to this period, the date – and even the authenticity – of the 'Brutus' remain controversial.[84]

The only testimony that conflicts with this picture of Rome as a prosperous and culturally sophisticated place is the fact that later tradition portrayed its aristocratic leaders as models of frugality and sim-

[82] F. Coarelli in *Affreschi romani dalle raccolte dell'Antiquarium comunale*, 1976[B277], 3–11.
[83] Dohrn 1972[B321].
[84] For the standard date (early third century B.C.), see Bianchi Bandinelli 1972[G14], 29.

plicity. But in reality the supposed poverty of men like M'. Curius Dentatus and C. Fabricius Luscinus is a myth. The stories that were told about them are more revealing of later Roman ideology than of the economic conditions of the early third century; in any case the later tradition was less concerned with the precise economic status of these men than with the moral example they set. It is relevant to note that these improving tales were almost certainly propagated by the Elder Cato, who fashioned Dentatus and his like in his own self-made image; and it would be unwise to base a historical account of the lifestyle of Roman aristocrats in the third century on the ideological constructs of the Elder Cato.

The nature of the economic and cultural changes we have been discussing can be further illustrated by an examination of three specific developments that occurred during the age of the conquest. The first is the growth of slavery. We have already seen that Rome was well on the way to becoming a slave society before the end of the fourth century B.C. (above, p. 334); the mass enslavements that are recorded in the early years of the third century must have advanced the process still further. We have little specific information about the social and economic effects of the process, but it is possible to construct a plausible account of the changes that occurred.

It is reasonable to suppose, first, that many slaves were employed in the houses of the rich and in trading and manufacturing enterprises in the city; they added to the size of the urban population and in the course of time changed its composition. Throughout the history of the Republic the most important single cause of the growth of the urban plebs was the importation, and subsequent manumission, of slaves. The social effects of the process were already beginning to be felt at the time of Appius Claudius' censorship, as we have seen.

It is also extremely probable that slave labour was being used on a large scale in agriculture. This contention is not seriously weakened even if we choose to accept the moralizing tales about third-century senators working their own land. It is sufficient merely to notice a revealing story about Cato, who took pride in the fact that as a young man he had worked with his own hands *together with his slaves* (Plut. *Cat. mai.* 3.2).

The development of large slave-run estates (*latifundia*) is normally dated to the period after the Hannibalic War, but there is no warrant for this assumption. On the contrary, there is good reason to believe that slaves were employed on the land from the late fourth century onwards. The case rests on three connected arguments. First, as we have seen, the ending of debt-bondage (formally abolished by the Lex Poetelia of 326 B.C.) must have created a demand for an alternative supply of agricultural labour to work the estates of the rich, a demand that can only have been met by slaves. Secondly, the impoverished peasants who were freed from dependence on the rich were left with no means of livelihood other than their own inadequate landholdings. Their plight was remedied by successful war and the colonization of conquered territories. Thirdly, the mass emigration of tens of thousands of poor peasant families must have led to a gradual depopulation of the old *ager Romanus* – a phenomenon that is in fact referred to in the sources of the classical period[85] – and implies a radical change in the organization of landholdings and the manner of their exploitation. What must have happened is that the land was concentrated into larger holdings, which were worked by slaves who were brought in to replace the former peasant small-holders.

The model therefore implies a continuous exchange of populations; poor Roman citizens were sent away to colonize lands whose original inhabitants were brought back to Rome as slaves. The process was complicated by a change in the relative distribution of the inhabitants in the old *ager Romanus*, with a greater proportion than before living in the city, and a corresponding reduction in the population of the countryside. The same land was worked by a smaller number of people; since they were slaves they could be worked harder and organized more effectively so as to produce a greater surplus. Increased productivity was stimulated by the development of an urban market in the growing and prosperous city of Rome.

In the absence of any specific testimony this reconstruction must remain hypothetical; but it has the virtue of being able to account for the mass enslavement of war captives (who must have been employed somehow), and the economic growth that is presupposed by the increase in the non-agricultural population of the city.

The second exemplary development is the appearance of Rome's first coinage. Precisely when, where and why the Roman state first issued coined money are much debated questions, each involving complex technical matters. The following is a brief summary of what seems to the present writer to be the most convincing modern reconstruction, presented in the knowledge that many areas of doubt still remain to be settled.[86]

The use of coined money was a Greek practice and was introduced into Italy by the cities of Magna Graecia at an early date. Coins produced

---

[85] Brunt 1971[A21], 345ff, with full references. Brunt notes that ancient writers who complained about depopulation had in mind only the free population, and ignored the slaves.

[86] I have followed the version of Crawford 1974[B210]; 1985[B212], 25ff and Burnett 1977[B202], 92ff; 1978[B203], 121ff. A different dating and interpretation of some issues is adopted in Chapter 10 (p. 476).

Fig. 51a. Silver didrachm with head of Mars on obverse, horse's head and legend ROMANO on reverse (*RRC* 13): *c.* 310 B.C.?

by the Italiot Greeks mostly had a local circulation, but by the end of the fourth century had begun to penetrate into some of the native regions of the Mezzogiorno. Indeed by this time some non-Greek communities (especially in Campania, but also in Apulia and Lucania) were producing their own coins on the Greek model. Moreover some formerly Greek communities such as Cumae, which had been overrun by Oscan-speaking natives at the end of the fifth century (see above, p. 284f), had continued to mint coins after the Oscan takeover without any noticeable break in the regularity of issues.

Early Roman coinage forms part of the monetary history of Campania, which is where the first coins to be issued in the name of the Republic were minted. Coinage was therefore a consequence of Rome's political involvement in Campania. The earliest 'Romano-Campanian' coins can be dated to the fourth century, and belong to isolated and sporadic issues. A small group of bronze coins, with a head of Apollo on the obverse, and the forepart of a manheaded bull with the Greek legend *ΡΩΜΑΙΩΝ* on the reverse (*RRC* 1), was probably the first. The types are purely Neapolitan, and it is reasonable to infer that they were minted at Naples shortly after the treaty with Rome in 326 B.C., and perhaps in commemoration of it. These coins probably circulated only in Campania, and belong more properly to the monetary history of Naples than to that of Rome.

Much more important is the first issue of Roman silver coins, the didrachms with Head of Mars/Horse's Head ROMANO (*RRC* 13; Fig. 51a). This appears to have been an isolated coinage datable to the years around 310 B.C. It was a substantial issue, to judge from the number of dies, and it circulated widely in the South (though not, apparently, in Rome). The mint is uncertain, but probably Campanian; the weight standard is that of Naples. An isolated issue of this kind was almost certainly minted for a specific purpose, presumably on the occasion of some project involving large state expenditure. The most likely candidate is the construction of the Via Appia in the years 312–308 B.C. Once again a major innovation appears to be associated with Appius Claudius Caecus.[87]

These sporadic isolated coinages did not give way to a regular sequence of Roman coins until the time of the Pyrrhic War, which seems to have been a crucial event for the monetary history of Italy. The demands of the war led many Greek cities to reduce the weight of their coins; some ceased to strike coins altogether. On the other hand coined money began to circulate much more widely in non-Greek Italy than it had done previously; and for the first time coins penetrated into Samnium and the region of the central Appennines. This development was a consequence of Roman activity, and almost certainly reflects the fact that men from these regions were now serving in the allied contingents of the Roman army.

The Pyrrhic War witnessed a second issue of Roman silver didrachms (Apollo/Galloping Horse ROMANO – RRC 15; Fig. 51b) and the beginning of a remarkable series of bronze issues. The bronze coins were cast rather than struck, in units weighing a pound (324 gr.) and fractions of a pound. The basic unit was the *as*, and the fractions the *semis*, *triens*, *quadrans*, etc. Associated with the cast bronze coins were large bronze ingots ('currency bars') weighing about five pounds each (RRC 3–12). The cast bronze coinage is a very characteristic form, unparalleled outside Italy. Within Central Italy, however, it was widespread, and was produced at a number of different centres, mostly, if not entirely, in imitation of Rome.

The date at which silver coins were first minted at Rome (as opposed to Campania) is uncertain, but the most probable answer is 269 B.C., which the literary sources regard as a crucial date in the history of Rome's silver coinage. The coinage that can be ascribed to this year is the very large issue of silver didrachms with Hercules/Wolf and Twins ROMANO (RRC 20; Fig. 51c). The types are interesting, and serve to remind us that coined money was a medium through which a state could advertise itself to the world at large. The Hercules/Wolf and Twins coinage was followed, on the eve of the First Punic War, by an issue of didrachms with a helmeted head of Roma/Victory ROMANO (RRC 22; Fig. 51d). Such types are an indication of Rome's growing self-confidence, and awareness of her immense power.

In economic terms the introduction of coinage is not of great significance in itself; the important stage in the early history of money is the official designation of a specific quantity of metal as a monetary unit, irrespective of whether the fixed unit is issued in the form of a coin. In

---

[87] Crawford 1982[B211], 99 and 1985[B212], 28ff, revising the opinion given in Crawford 1974[B210], I.37–8, 133.

Fig. 51b. Silver didrachm (*c.* 275–270 B.C.) with head of Apollo (legend: ROMANO) on obverse, prancing horse on reverse (*RRC* 15).

Fig. 51c. Silver didrachm (269–6 B.C.) depicting head of Hercules on obverse, wolf suckling twins (legend: ROMANO) on reverse (*RRC* 20).

Fig. 51d. Silver didrachm (265–42 B.C.) with helmeted head of Roma on obverse, Victory with legend ROMANO on reverse (*RRC* 22.1).

Rome the fixed metallic unit was the *as*, a pound of bronze, which had existed as an official measure of value long before the introduction of coins. The Greek historian Timaeus seems to have attributed the designation of the *as* to king Servius Tullius, according to the most likely interpretation of a highly problematic text.[88] However that may be, Rome's monetary history goes back a long way before the fourth century B.C.

[88] Crawford 1976[G42], 198ff.

It follows that we need not search for elaborate explanations of the introduction of coinage by Rome. In general ancient states issued coins for financial, rather than for economic reasons. That is to say, coinage was a convenient means of distributing the proceeds of booty, or of making payments to large numbers of people such as soldiers or work-men. It was not produced in order to facilitate exchange, or in further-ance of any kind of monetary policy. For the Romans of the fourth century B.C. the decision to issue money in the form of coin must have been taken principally for reasons of prestige. Its economic importance may have been minimal, but the appearance of Roman coins was an event of great cultural significance. Coinage was a Greek device, and the Romans' adoption of it marks a conscious effort on their part to enter the cultural milieu of the Hellenistic world. This brings us to the last of the three developments referred to earlier, namely the increasing influence of Hellenism on Roman life.

The influence of Greek culture on Rome can be traced back to the beginning of Roman history. The archaeological record shows that Greek artefacts and techniques were being imported as early as the eighth century B.C., and in the archaic age the influence of Greek ideas on Roman political, legal and religious institutions was pervasive. But during the course of the fifth century Rome's contacts with the Greek world diminished, as the city entered a long period of recession and isolation.

When Rome emerged in the second half of the fourth century as a powerful military state, relations with the Greek world were re-estab-lished on a new footing. The renewed influence of Greek culture manifested itself not only in monuments and artefacts, as Rome, along with the rest of Italy, adopted Hellenistic styles and techniques, but also in the field of politics and religion. That leaders such as Q. Publilius Philo and Appius Claudius Caecus were infected by democratic political ideas and practices seems certain. A point of particular interest is that the former was, as far as we know, the first Roman noble to adopt a Greek surname. He was followed by P. Sempronius Sophus (cos. 304 B.C.) and Q. Marcius Philippus (cos. 281).

A number of Greek cults were established in Rome at this time. The most spectacular example is that of the healing god Aesculapius, to whom a temple was dedicated on the Tiber island in 291 B.C. A series of appropriately militaristic cults were set up in the period of the Samnite wars; they include those of Victoria, Iuppiter Victor, Bellona Victrix and Hercules Invictus. These 'victory cults' were evidently based on contem-porary Hellenistic models.[89]

[89] Weinstock 1957[G515], 211ff.

In contrast to the one-sided relationship of the archaic age, the long and not always easy love affair that began in the fourth century was reciprocated. The Romans' enthusiasm for Greek culture was matched by the close attention which the Greeks began to pay to Rome. A list of the Greek intellectuals who were attracted to the subject of Rome and the Romans at this time reads like a *Who's Who?* of contemporary Greek learning: the philosophers Aristotle, Theophrastus and Heraclides Ponticus, the historians Duris, Hieronymus, Callias and Timaeus, the poets Callimachus and Lycophron, and the scientist Eratosthenes. The detailed evidence is well known and has been assembled many times; there is no need to reproduce it here.[90]

The Greeks were attempting to understand the little-known Italian Republic which had grown from nothing into a world power, and which in 275 B.C. had won a sensational victory in the war against Pyrrhus. But one senses that at the same time the Romans were also trying to come to terms with the position in which they found themselves. The enthusiastic adoption of Hellenism was itself a part of this search for an identity. This became apparent at the end of the third century when Fabius Pictor presented a definitive account of the Roman tradition to the public. His *History of Rome*, the first ever by a Roman, was written in Greek.

[90] A penetrating and witty account in Momigliano 1975[A88], 12–21.

CHAPTER 9

ROME AND ITALY IN THE EARLY THIRD CENTURY

E. S. STAVELEY

I. THE ROMAN COMMONWEALTH

By the year 280 B.C., when Pyrrhus of Epirus first set foot in Italy, Rome had already established control, direct or indirect, over a broad band of the Italian peninsula extending from coast to coast and lying along its length for a distance in excess of 240 km. (Maps 6–7). The *ager Romanus* alone, the territory which was in the *dominium* of the Roman state, had swollen eightfold in the space of just sixty years from a mere 2000 to approximately 16,000 km.[2] (cf. also Fig. 47 (p. 382)). From the central zone which incorporated the original urban tribes and those established on Veientan territory it radiated in three distinct spurs. One of these, by far the longest, embraced virtually the entire coastal belt from the Tiber to the township of Cumae in the south-east corner of the Campanian plain. Much of it was occupied by citizens with full voting rights – the inhabitants of the enfranchised Latin states of Lanuvium, Aricia, and Lavinium, and Roman settlers who were incorporated into the six new tribes which had been formed both along the line of the Via Appia north-west of Tarracina and in the fertile lower reaches of the Liris and Volturnus rivers. With the exception of the old Latin settlements at Ardea and Circeii and the very small maritime colonies at Antium, Tarracina, Minturnae, and Sinuessa, the remainder of this strip, comprising principally Velitrae, Privernum, Fundi, Formiae, and the Campanian townships, was occupied by *cives sine suffragio*.[1] A second spur of *ager Romanus* extended from Rome in a more easterly direction and was separated from the coastal strip for most of its length by a succession of Latin colonies and allied townships. This incorporated the fully enfranchised *municipia* of Nomentum, Pedum, Tusculum, and (perhaps) Labici, and also the lands which had been used for viritane settlement in the *tribus Aniensis*, east of Tibur, and the *tribus Publilia*, north of Anagnia.[2] Though broken up by those friendly Latin and Hernican townships that

---

[1] For a different view of the status of Lavinium and Velitrae see above, pp. 362, 365f.

[2] This is the location of the *tribus Publilia* favoured by Taylor 1960[G733], 52f. Beloch (1926[A12], 357f) placed it further south on the coastal strip.

had retained their independence, it extended through the territories of the Aequi and of the townships of Frusino and Anagnia as far as Arpinum on the middle Liris. The third spur incorporated the territories that Rome had acquired most recently in her determination to drive a solid wedge across the peninsula. It stretched in a north-easterly direction from the middle reaches of the Tiber to hit the Adriatic coast just south of Asculum, and it took in the country of the Aequicoli and the Sabines, very probably the Umbrian townships of Spoletium and Fulginiae, and at least part of the lands of the Vestini. Further, after the victory at Lake Vadimon and the routing of the Senones in 283 B.C. Rome had appropriated a separate strip of Adriatic coastland, the so-called *ager Gallicus*, where was founded in the same year the small Roman citizen colony of Sena Gallica. Although M'. Curius Dentatus had already initiated a programme of extensive land settlement, none of the territory in this eastern spur was as yet included in the Roman tribes.

Hand in hand with the annexation of new lands had proceeded the planting of Latin colonies, settlements designed originally as fortress communities, and so positioned as to serve as defensive bulwarks between the territory of a potential enemy and that of Rome and her friends (Table 9; Fig. 48). Thus the five colonies of Fregellae, Interamna Succusana, Suessa, Cales and Saticula, occupied much of the area dividing the coastal strip of *ager Romanus* from the Samnite tribes to the north: Luceria was more isolated, and safeguarded Rome's position in northern Apulia: while a later series of colonies planted around the turn of the century, comprising Sora, Carseoli, Alba Fucens and Narnia, played a vital part in Rome's move to cut off the Samnites from Etruria. The two most recent settlements lay at a considerably greater distance from Rome but served a similar purpose in the changed circumstances which prevailed following the Samnite collapse: one, Venusia, founded in 291, was strategically placed on the common borders of the southernmost Samnites, the friendly states of northern Apulia, and the potentially hostile Lucanian tribes: the other, Hadria, founded in 289, lay on the Adriatic seaboard where it dominated the coastal road between north and south and helped to control the tribes of Picenum.

The identity and number of the communities already allied to Rome by treaty in 281 is less certain; but, although no permanent decision had yet been taken with regard to the Samnites, there is little doubt that the system of individual treaties which was to form the lasting basis of Rome's relations with her Italian neighbours had already begun to take shape. Several independent townships situated along the line of the Via Latina to Capua, among them Fabrateria, Aquinum, and Teanum, had for some time been numbered among her allies, and the victory at Sentinum helped Rome to cement her existing relationship with the tribal peoples of the Marsi, Paeligni, Vestini, Marrucini, and Frentani, and with townships in northern Apulia extending along Samnium's eastern flank at least as far south as Canusium. In Etruria Rome probably based her relations on a series of truces (*indutiae*) of varying duration rather than on treaties (*foedera*),[3] and it is probable that the four communities of Arretium, Cortona, Perusia, and Clusium, which had made peace with Rome for a period of forty years in 294, lay on the northern boundary of Rome's present sphere of interest. To the east of the Tiber, on the other hand, in Umbria, we know of only two states which were bound to her by treaty, Ocriculum in the far south-west, and Camerinum in the north.

Such was the extent of Rome's commonwealth in 281 B.C. Yet in the mere sixteen years between Pyrrhus' invasion and the outbreak of the First Punic War the advance of her authority in Italy was even more spectacular than it had been in the preceding sixty. A detailed account of her intervention in the affairs of the Greek townships of the south and of her consequent confrontation with Pyrrhus is given elsewhere.[4] The outcome was the absorption of the entire southern half of the peninsula. The Greek cities, which, like Rome, enjoyed a city-state form of government and which had long contained pro-Roman elements, received the most favourable treatment, and, irrespective of whether they had played a largely friendly or hostile role, were allied to Rome without loss of territory. The tribal peoples of Lucania and of Bruttium in the toe of Italy, who had for many years been a source of harassment to the Greeks, were deprived of part of their land, Bruttium of forest terrain, which was requisitioned to provide timber for shipbuilding, Lucania of the fertile coastal plain on the Salernian Gulf on which in 273 the large Latin colony of Paestum was founded, and also of a strip of territory to the north where, according to Strabo,[5] some of the Picentes were transplanted some years later. The thickly populated region of southern Apulia and Messapia was disregarded until 267–266, when a Roman army advanced into the area to dictate treaties of alliance and perhaps to use token resistance as a pretext for confiscating lands around the natural harbour of Brundisium – the township which became the site of a Latin colony in 244 and later a thriving commercial port at the terminus of an extended Via Appia. After Pyrrhus' departure a final solution was also found for Samnium. The tribal confederation was broken up into three parts, an area retaining the name of Samnium in the north, Hirpinum in the south, and Caudium – later to be subdivided into a series of townships – in the west. Further, a broad belt of land covering the area later controlled by

---

[3] See Scullard, 1967[A118], 274; Harris 1965[J174], 282–92 and 1971[J175], 94–6 argues that regular *foedera* were employed.

[4] See Chap. 10.   [5] Strabo v.4.13, p. 251C; cf. Pliny, *HN* III.70.

municipia at Allifae, Venafrum, Casinum, Atina, and probably Aufidena, was annexed to produce a wedge of territory between the Samnite tribes and the Marsi and Paeligni further north; and in accordance with well-established practice two Latin 'watchdog' colonies were planted at strategic points – the first in 268 at Beneventum on the common border of the three new Samnite regions, the second five years later at Aesernia in the angle of the arc of the Samnite territory newly annexed.

Despite her protracted involvement in the south of the peninsula in this period, however, Rome found the time and the energy to consolidate her position to the north and east of the city both through the further annexation and settlement of land and through an extension of her network of alliances. In her relations with her Etruscan neighbours in particular she appears to have adopted a singularly aggressive stance. When the Boii had advanced south in 283, certain of the Etruscan cities had renounced their treaties with Rome and joined in the attack, with the result that Roman armies had been occupied in Etruria for two full years after the battle of Lake Vadimon.[6] Unfortunately, the Fasti Triumphales name only the people of Volsinii and Vulci as those defeated in 280 and record a triumph simply *de Etrusceis* ('over the Etruscans') in the previous year, so making it difficult for us to assess the extent of the defection. Moreover, there is no record of any punitive action taken at the time or of any consequent revision of treaties. What is certain, however, is that the Romans gave the area their serious attention as soon as Pyrrhus set sail from Italy. According to Dio,[7] it was in 274 or 273 that their nearest Etruscan neighbour, Caere, with whom they had enjoyed a special relationship of *hospitium* for over a hundred years (p. 313f), was called upon to surrender half its land and was incorporated as a *municipium sine suffragio*. The occasion for this action is not known, but, as Caeretan aggression is most unlikely at this juncture, it can only be supposed that it was an act of opportunism, which the Romans may have sought to justify on the basis of the treachery, true or alleged, of some elements at Caere during the war of 282–280. For Rome there was clearly sound sense in annexing territory so close to the city which provided the natural maritime outlet for the expanding Roman hinterland; and her further interest in the area is illustrated by the planting of three coastal citizen colonies there during the First Punic War.[8] This same year may well have seen the reshaping of Rome's relations with Caere's northern neighbours. Vulci and Volsinii, which are known to have broken faith in 283–280, were mulcted of a sizeable block of territory, on part of which was founded in 273 the Latin colony of Cosa. Tarquinii, which lay between

---

6 On the problem of dating these events see above, p. 381.
7 Dio fr.33, vol. I, p. 138 Boiss.
8 These were at Castrum Novum (264 B.C.), Alsium (247 B.C.), and Fregenae (245 B.C.).

these townships and Caere, is not mentioned by name in the tradition, but, as the settlement of the second-century colony of Graviscae suggests, she too was at some stage deprived of part of her land. A favoured date for this act of confiscation and for the rewriting of the Romano-Tarquinian alliance is 268 B.C. at the expiry of the existing forty-year treaty, but the mere lapse of a truce could not in itself have justified the confiscation of land, and if, as is more probable, the pretext for this action lay in the role the Tarquinians had played at the time of the Boian invasion, it is not unreasonable to suppose that Rome waited to dictate her terms only until her hands were free and her demands irresistible. Significantly perhaps, it was also in 273 that diplomatic contacts were first established with Ptolemy, reportedly at the Egyptian monarch's request.[9] In view of Egypt's long-standing interest in the Etruscan iron trade it is not improbable that her approach to the senate was prompted by news of Rome's new thrust northwards and by recognition of the undisputed mastery of the Etruscan coastline which it afforded her. This is still more likely to have been the case if, as Beloch believed,[10] Rome used this opportunity to bring the more distant northerly states of Populonia, Volaterrae, Rusellae, and Pisa into her net as allies and so effectively to extend her sphere of influence to the line of the Arnus.

There was one further intervention in Etruria at the end of this period, which is worthy of note. In 265 a request was received from the Volsinian aristocracy for help in suppressing their freedmen, who, as Zonaras has it,[11] had succeeded in seizing all the magistracies, making themselves senators, and setting up a democratic constitution. An army was sent from Rome, which began a siege that lasted over twelve months before the city was finally stormed, razed to the ground, and rebuilt at a nearby site for occupation by the aristocrats and by those who had remained loyal to them (Fig. 52). The incident is of interest not only because it is a rare, if not unique, example of major Roman interference in an ally's internal affairs, but also because it throws some light upon the consideration that Rome may have extended to the governing class in many of the communities on which she imposed her terms (p. 387). The favoured treatment of pro-Roman aristocracies in Campania is well attested, but it is not unlikely that in Etruria also the Romans ensured that friendly aristocrats suffered less than most from land confiscation, perhaps permitting and even encouraging them to farm on the annexed *ager publicus*. The statement of Orosius that the Volsinian rebels criminally seized the land of their rulers[12] suggests that the revolt may have been provoked by just such a private arrangement; and, if this was so, Rome could obviously not afford to ignore it.

---

    [9] Eutropius II.15. Cf. Livy, *Per.* XIV; Val. Max. IV.3.9; Dion. Hal. *Ant. Rom.* XX.14; Dio fr.41, vol. I, p. 139 Boiss.   [10] Beloch 1926[A12], 457–8.   [11] Zonar. VIII.7.   [12] Oros. IV.5.5.

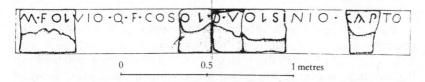

Fig. 52. Inscription on *donarium* (found at the Sant'Omobono sanctuary) recording its erection by M. Fulvius (Flaccus) after the capture of Volsinii in 264. From M. Torelli, *Quaderni dell'Instituto di Topografia Antica dell'Università di Roma* 5 (1968), 71ff.

It is a common assumption that Rome's further advance into the Umbrian highlands in this period was occasioned by the revolt of her allies, the Picentes, which broke out in 269 and was quelled by the combined consular armies in the following year. Certainly, steps designed to consolidate her hold in the north-east followed this incident in quick succession: the foundation in 268 of the Latin colony of Ariminum, which was carved out of the northern section of the *ager Gallicus* annexed some thirteen years earlier; the annexation of the whole Picentine land save for the Greek coastal township of Ancona and an arc of territory around Asculum; the transportation of large numbers of Picentes to the *ager Picentinus* on the west coast; and finally in 264 the planting of a second large Latin colony on the coast at Firmum. Yet it is difficult to believe that the Picentes acted without direct provocation or that they freely selected this date to invite a trial of strength rather than one some ten years earlier, when Rome was fully engaged with Pyrrhus. Rome's interest in the region is illustrated by her decision, surely taken before the Picentine revolt, to colonize Ariminum with a view to protecting the as yet largely unoccupied *ager Gallicus*; while her determination to entrench herself further south is illustrated both by the grant of the full franchise to the lowland Sabines in the same year and by the progress which must by then have been made in the settlement of the highland Sabine region and of the coastal strip north of Hadria to warrant the creation of two further tribes in these areas in 241. It is not, therefore, improbable that she also actively sought a pretext for linking the two areas of *ager Romanus* by further annexation. Significantly, within two years of the events of 268 a Roman consul was engaged in a campaign against the Sarsinates in the highlands of northern Umbria. This suggests that in the east, as in the west, the policy of Rome was to distance the Gallic threat by establishing a line of defence across the peninsula some 130 miles north of the city. Evidence about Rome's treaty arrangements with the Umbrians is scant, but it is a fair assumption that by 264 Rome had extended her commonwealth to a line which lay roughly along the river Arnus to Arretium and then through the upper Tiber valley to Ariminum.

What can be said about the nature of this commonwealth, which had assumed what must have appeared to the senate of that time to be its optimum size? As Toynbee rightly emphasized, the much-used term 'federation' as applied to the association of communities which made up Roman Italy is a misleading one. Federalism implies some form of participation by member states in the policy-making process, however indirect. Yet in Italy there existed not even the machinery for effective consultation: the determination of the all-important issues of foreign policy remained firmly with the senate, magistrates, and assemblies of Rome, which together reflected the views only of the full citizens who were registered in the tribes. Moreover, any meaningful co-operation among the unenfranchised communities themselves was effectively precluded both by the general considerations of distance and poor communications and by the deliberate policy which Rome had adopted of breaking up existing leagues and tribal associations into their basic parts and of contracting separate alliances with the smallest units (p. 364f). But, though the member states of Rome's commonwealth fell far short of federal states, they nevertheless enjoyed an appreciable measure of autonomy in the management of their domestic affairs. Italian allies, Latin colonies, even the *municipia sine suffragio* ('municipalities without voting rights (at Rome)'), may more appropriately be described as having been Rome's satellites rather than her subjects.

The Italian allies for their part enjoyed near-total sovereignty in the domestic sphere. Each maintained its own form of government and laws; each retained its own language and the right to manage its own economy by levying its own taxes and minting its own coinage; and none, with the exception of Tarentum, Rhegium and Metapontum, where special circumstances obtained, was ever called upon to accept a Roman garrison. The sole obligation of the allies to Rome was to contribute to her military or naval needs. A select few, indeed – those who had contracted treaties with Rome at an early date or who had voluntarily entered into an alliance without being directly or indirectly subjected to the constraint of Roman arms – enjoyed an association based upon a *foedus aequum* ('equal treaty'), under which the contractual arrangement was simply that each party should render assistance to the other in the event of its being the victim of aggression: in these cases a decision as to whether to send assistance to Rome, and, if so, how much, lay at least in theory with the ally. The vast majority, on the other hand, were bound by treaties which required them to contribute armed contingents on request up to a stipulated maximum. Even this military commitment, however, did not represent a serious encroachment upon sovereignty. The units were raised and financed by the allied states and served under their own commanders; and, even if Rome had requisitioned the maxima permitted, she would still herself in proportion to the total population have shouldered a military burden at least twice as heavy as that of her Italian allies.[13]

The Latins enjoyed the same freedom as the Italians in the management of their own affairs and were subject to the obligation to provide Rome with military contingents on a similar basis. What particularly distinguished them from the Italians was that they had an acknowledged affinity with Rome which, had circumstances been different, would have sufficed to qualify them for the Roman franchise. Many of the members of the more recently founded Latin colonies were actually themselves Romans or of Roman descent, while the people of the older Latin townships, which had been either original members or colonies of the Latin League, even though they may have cherished their independence, were of the same culture as the Romans. It was this affinity which was recognized by the *iura Latina* ('Latin rights') which they enjoyed (cf. p. 269), and in particular by the *ius migrationis* ('right of transfer') and the *ius suffragii ferendi* ('right to cast a vote'), the former guaranteeing to any Latin the right to move to the *ager Romanus* and by the very act of so doing to become eligible for enrolment as a *civis*, the latter providing that any Latin present in Rome should be able to cast a vote in a single voting-unit to be determined by lot. It is improbable that the right of *migratio* was invoked to any great extent before the second century, when it began to be abused and was consequently restricted, and it is certain that the limited suffrage was viewed as symbolic rather than politically meaningful; but it was the possession of this body of rights, together perhaps with the fact that the Latins were called on to bear less onerous burdens of taxation and military service than citizens, which reconciled them to their non-citizen status even when the obstacles of distance and poor communications that had originally dictated it had been removed.

Unfortunately, we have little information about Rome's administration of those areas which had been incorporated into the territory of Rome *sine suffragio* ('without voting rights (at Rome)'), nor are we told very much either about the attitude of the half-citizens towards their status or about Rome's long-term intentions as to their future. All that can be said with assurance is that in the period between 338 and 268 the concept of *civitas sine suffragio* ('citizenship without voting rights (at Rome)') had been adapted to suit very different situations and needs. The original recipients, the Campanian states (p. 367), may well have regarded it as in some measure a privilege; for the establishment of a close tie with Rome not only served to lend support to the authority of a ruling class part of which had already established links with the Roman nobility:

---

[13] For a slightly different calculation see above, p. 388f.

it also facilitated the promotion of a profitable commercial partnership, which, though perhaps sought by the Romans, was not without its benefits for the Campanians themselves. The special nature of this relationship is exemplified by the right which the Campanians perhaps retained of serving in their own separate *legio*,[14] and by the close co-operation on the economic front which underlay the production of a joint Romano-Campanian coinage (cf. p. 415); and it is reflected also in the tendency of the ancient writers to refer to the Campanians as *socii* ('allies'), whether or not the use of that term had a juridical basis.[15] Nevertheless, it is probably a mistake to overstress this aspect of the association or to liken it in any way to the Greek concept of isopolity (ἰσοπολιτεία). The Campanians, it is true, retained their own form of government and code of law, and it is possible that with their tradition of independence they would have spurned the Roman franchise in 338, had it been offered, as being inconsistent with municipal autonomy; but nonetheless it should not be forgotten that the Campanians had been defeated in war and that they had subsequently been incorporated in the Roman state and subjected to the *munera* ('obligations') of Roman taxation and military service.

In many respects the circumstances and the nature of the grants of *civitas sine suffragio* which were made to the Campanians and to the neighbouring city-states to the north were markedly similar. The annexation of these latter townships was normally consequent upon some hostile act, and, except in the isolated cases of Satricum and Anagnia,[16] where treachery had been blatant, the new citizen municipalities continued to enjoy a considerable measure of local autonomy. Moreover, although land was often mulcted in the first instance for settlement by Romans, there is little evidence of extensive redistribution within the area left under municipal control. Indeed, the decision of Rome to introduce a constitutional anomaly into her commonwealth by despatching small groups of colonists to key points on the Tyrrhenian seaboard who, on account of the very small allotments made available to them, needed to be enticed to volunteer by promises of a *vacatio militae* ('exemption from military service') and the retention of the franchise, is at least partly to be explained by her desire to minimize any offence to the local population. But in terms of Roman motivation there was an important difference between the grants of citizenship made to

[14] Livy, *Per.* xv; Oros. iv.3.4. There is considerable disagreement among scholars on this issue. Compare Beloch 1926[A12], 576; Heurgon 1942[J59], 201ff; Bernardi 1942[J141], 91ff; Toynbee 1965[A131], 1.397ff.   [15] Diod. xix.76.4; Livy ix.6.4; 7.1.

[16] Following its revolt and reconquest in 306 Anagnia was incorporated as a *civitas sine suffragio* with certain restrictions on its magistrates (Livy ix.43.24); Satricum, which revolted after the battle of Lautulae and was recovered in 313 (Livy ix.16.9–18), was probably deprived of self-government.

Campania and those made to her northern neighbours. In the case of the Campanian states Rome's object had been to devise a form of association which would be lasting and mutually beneficial. In the case of the other *municipia* she had viewed the *civitas sine suffragio* as no more than a convenient instrument of annexation which, on account of the extent of devolution involved, had the supreme advantage of relieving her of any significant increase in her administrative responsibilities.

Into yet another category fall the tribal lands such as the *ager Gallicus* and the extensive areas of *ager publicus* which were seized from states which retained their independence. The feature of these areas was that they were not dominated by existing townships and had therefore to be administered centrally by prefects responsible to the *praetor urbanus* at Rome. Unfortunately, the distribution of citizens and non-citizens in these parts of the Roman territory is an unknown quantity. In many cases full citizens will have moved on to the territory to farm *ager publicus*, while, to judge by the allied complaints made at the time of the Gracchan land act,[17] substantial tracts of the border lands continued to be occupied and farmed on sufferance by members of neighbouring Italian communities; but of the size and economic standing of the native population there is no record. It was perhaps only in the well-populated Samnite uplands that Rome succeeded in encouraging the development of new municipal centres, to which eventually she could delegate the tiresome administrative duties which she was herself so ill-equipped to discharge. Elsewhere, even the bringing of roads will have led only to the formation of modest communal centres, *fora* or *conciliabula* so named, which were too small to be self-administered and which primarily served the needs of the fully enfranchised settler.

The question of when these very different types of half-citizen area received the franchise is one on which there is little ancient evidence and no modern consensus. The sources record the upgrading of *civitas sine suffragio* on only three occasions – in 268 for the lowland Sabines, in 211 for the Campanian *equites*, and in 188 for the municipalities of Fundi, Formiae, and Arpinum.[18] Were these exceptional grants, or did many others go unrecorded? There is one school of thought which maintains that the *civitas sine suffragio* came at some stage to be viewed by the Romans themselves as probationary, and that it must consequently have been transmuted into the full franchise as soon as the barriers of distance had been broken down by the building of roads, and those of language and culture by a process of planned exposure to Roman law and manners. Toynbee has further argued for early enfranchisement, particularly in the non-municipalized areas, on the ground that Rome could not have

---

[17] Cic. *Rep.* 1.31; III.41; App. *BCiv.* 1.21.   [18] Vell. 1.14.5; Livy XXIII.5.9; XXXVIII.36.7–9.

afforded to harbour such a disproportionate number of potential mal-
contents in the form of underprivileged citizens when she engaged upon
her life-and-death struggle with Hannibal.[19] But there is little warrant for
either of these assumptions. The first – that the *cives sine suffragio* were
regarded as novitiates – is belied by the fact that, in marked contradistinc-
tion to the Latins, they did not enjoy token voting rights and, on the most
natural interpretation of an admittedly garbled entry in Festus,[20] they did
not as a class possess the *ius migrationis* or the right of holding office. The
second – that they were fundamentally dissatisfied with their lot –
presupposes that they attached less value to the more tangible privileges
of citizenship than to a right of suffrage which very few would have had
either the inclination or the opportunity to exercise. It is true, of course,
that a sense of grievance was perhaps betrayed by the Campanians when
they defected at the time of Hannibal's invasion. But, as we have seen,
theirs was a special case: they may have long ceased to harbour constitutional objections to accepting the Roman franchise, and it is possible
that, seeing the currency of the *civitas sine suffragio* so markedly debased,
they came peculiarly to regard their non-voting status as a stigma.

Perhaps, therefore, the grants of full franchise recorded by our sources
were indeed exceptional. Each grant at least can readily be explained as a
response to a special circumstance. The Sabines of Cures not only
enjoyed ties with Rome that reached back to the age of legend, but were
situated immediately between the old tribal area of *ager Romanus* and the
region north of Reate which, from 290 B.C. on, was extensively settled by
Roman citizens. The grant to the Campanian *equites* simply recognized
their loyalty at the time of the defection in 216 as well as the special nature
of the Romano-Campanian relationship. Fundi and Formiae, apart from
having the most natural claim after Campania, lay directly between the
territory of the *tribus Falerna* and *Teretina* and that of the chain of Roman
tribes to the north. That Arpinum was also enfranchised in 188 may
possibly indicate that by the second century the development of closer
ties and the attractiveness of a potentially influential *clientela* was beginning to dictate a more liberal attitude on the part of the nobility towards
the *municipia* south of the city, but it is likely that elsewhere at least the
status of *civitas sine suffragio* survived until the universal enfranchisement
of Italy which followed the Social War.

[19] Toynbee 1965[A131], 1.403f.
[20] Paul. Fest. 127 M 155 L: 'Municipes. Id genus hominum qui cum Romam venissent neque cives
Romani essent participes tamen fuerunt omnium rerum ad munus fungendum cum Romanis civibus
praeterquam de suffragio ferendo aut magistratu capiendo' ('*Municipes*: The category of men who,
although they came to Rome but were not Roman citizens, nonetheless shared with Roman citizens
in everything pertaining to the fulfilment of their obligation (*munus*) except in the casting of a vote or
the holding of office.')

II. THE NORTHERN FRONTIER: ROME AND THE GAULS

If further evidence be needed that Rome's wars in the north of the Italian peninsula were largely of her own devising, we need point only to the almost total lack of activity in that quarter during the entire twenty-four years of the First Punic War and to the launching of a full-scale assault upon the Etruscan township of Falerii in the very year in which peace with Carthage was signed. The Romans marched out in 241 with two consular armies, destroyed the fortified city of the Faliscans, transplanted the inhabitants to a new town some three miles distant from the old site, and confiscated half their territory. The pretext for the attack was some unspecified act of non-compliance with the instructions of Roman officials which could well have been wholly justified by the expiry of the fifty-year treaty that had been contracted between the two states in 293, but it is evident that Rome's true motive for her action was to strengthen her hold upon Etruria by meting out to Falerii similar treatment to that which had been meted out before the war to her western neighbours, and to bring the community into the commonwealth on the basis of a permanent *foedus*.

While the consuls of 241 were so engaged, the censors were also busy taking steps to consolidate Rome's hold upon the area north of the city. The Latin colony of Spoletium was founded in southern Umbria on land which lay along the direct route to Ariminum and just north of the recently settled Sabine uplands, and a start was probably made on the building of the Via Aurelia up the western seaboard towards Pisa. Two new tribes, the *Quirina* and the *Velina*, were also created in this year, and were the last to be formed. They accommodated respectively the settlers in the highlands around Reate and those who had established themselves on the Adriatic coast north of Hadria, but the circumstances which dictated their creation in this particular year are obscure. The names of the new tribes strangely did not fit the locations which they covered, and there is much to be said for the suggestion of Lily Ross Taylor that the plan to form new tribes with these names had all but been implemented about thirty years earlier with a view to incorporating in them the new citizens in the lowland Sabine region near Cures (Quirina) and in the highland area round the Lacus Velinus (Velina).[21] Political differences or personal rivalry could well have accounted for the dropping of this scheme in 268, when the original Sabine population was in fact enrolled in the existing *tribus Sergia*. One possible explanation for the revision and revival of the proposal in 241 may be that the settlement of citizens in the

[21] Taylor 1960[G733], 59ff. Compare Toynbee 1965[A131], 1.377ff.

more distant areas covered by the new tribes had been progressive and had only recently reached such proportions as were thought to warrant the creation of new tribes.[22]

The events of 241 demonstrate Rome's concern both to extend and strengthen her communications with her northern frontier, and to consolidate her position in the rear. Just three years later she initiated offensive operations at both the western and eastern ends of her line (Map 4: p. 304). The war in the west was directed against the mountain tribesmen of Liguria, who dominated the territory north of the Arnus. The campaign, which continued intermittently for eight years from 238 to 230, was no doubt originally associated with the rape of Corsica and had as its limited objective the clearance of the coastal strip north of Pisa, from which in conjunction with Corsican pirates the Ligurians may well have threatened shipping in the Tyrrhenian Sea. On the course of events at the eastern end of the frontier there is some dispute. In a condensed summary Polybius refers only to a combined assault upon the Roman colony of Ariminum launched by the Boii and tribes from Transalpine Gaul. This, he informs us, proved abortive on account of dissension born of distrust within the Gallic ranks which led the Boii to murder their own kings; and a Roman army that had been despatched to meet the threat was speedily withdrawn.[23] The annalistic version preserved by Zonaras presents a fuller and more acceptable picture, which accords with Polybius' own statement that the peace with Gaul had lasted just forty-five years. According to this, the Romans waged an offensive war against the Gauls in 238, and again with combined consular armies in 237. The raid on Ariminum was thus a counter-offensive. Furthermore, so far from treating the Boian act of self-destruction as an excuse for disengagement, the Romans capitalized on it by temporarily abandoning the Ligurian campaign, carrying the war into the territory of the Boii, and confiscating a large portion of their land.[24]

After this incident an uneasy peace with the Gauls reigned for eleven years. The Romans, however, remained very conscious of the Gallic threat, and when in 232 the tribune, C. Flaminius, introduced a controversial bill providing for the distribution to individuals (*viritim*) of the *ager Gallicus*, which had been seized in 283 and which lay to the immediate south of Ariminum, both he and his political opponents were doubtless very much aware of the relevance of the proposal to the whole question of frontier security. Indeed, the bill is represented by Polybius as the cause of the next Gallic war. There has been much debate about the true

---

[22] Another possibility is that an increase in the number of tribes to a total of thirty-five was deemed constitutionally desirable in order to facilitate the remodelling of the centuriate organization. The precise date of this reform is, however, uncertain. See below, p. 440f and p. 454.

[23] Polyb. II.21.   [24] Zonar. VIII.18.

purpose of the Flaminian plebiscite and about the reasons for the spirited resistance which it met with at the hands of the senatorial majority. Influenced by the hostile tradition which represents Flaminius as a demagogue and a forerunner of the Gracchi, many scholars have interpreted the measure in a domestic context, as an attempt to secure generous allotments of fertile land for the Roman poor at the expense of wealthy *occupatores* ('appropriators').[25] But this is to presuppose without warrant that there was still widespread land-hunger among Roman citizens in the second half of the third century, and to underestimate the impact which had been made upon Roman society by the very extensive programme of colonization and land allotment that had been implemented since the fall of Veii.[26] More credible is the view that the Flaminian bill had a military purpose, and that it aimed to establish a strong block of loyal citizens behind the existing frontier line, thus turning the *ager Gallicus* into a zone which could serve both as an effective bulwark against enemy raids and as a possible launching-pad from which a full-scale attack could be mounted against the Gauls of the Po valley. From the resistance which Flaminius met in carrying his bill we might be tempted to conclude that there were few who shared these general objectives; but this would be a mistake. Although there doubtless were influential men within the senate who favoured the adoption of a more pacific and less provocative stance, the vehemence of the opposition to the measure is to be explained less by widespread disapproval of his broad strategic aims than by unease over the method by which he sought to achieve them. Like M'. Curius Dentatus a generation earlier, Flaminius chose to flout the accepted constitutional proprieties of the day by proposing that citizenship should be retained by settlers who would be debarred by distance from exercising their basic rights. In opting for *viritim* distribution he no doubt alienated many who might otherwise have been his sympathisers; but it is a measure of the importance which he attached to attracting a sufficient number of settlers for his purpose that he was prepared to offer the retention of citizen status and so to put himself in the position of having in the last resort to legislate in the *concilium plebis* against senatorial advice.

The war which according to Polybius was presaged by the Flaminian plebiscite eventually broke out in 225 with the invasion of Roman Italy

---

[25] For this interpretation see De Sanctis 1907–64[A37], III.332f; Jacobs 1937[H115], 33ff, 71ff; Càssola 1962[H103], 211ff.

[26] See Fraccaro 1919[H110], 81ff; Tibiletti 1949[G147], 3ff; cf. above, p. 388. It may be estimated that some 50,000 to 60,000 Romans had secured plots as colonists over the preceding century, not to mention an unspecified number who had benefited by viritane assignation. That there was not a pressing demand for land in 232 B.C. is indicated by a Gracchan boundary-stone found near Pisaurum (*CIL* I².719; *ILLRP* 474), which reveals that part of the *ager Gallicus* was still in the hands of *occupatores* a hundred years later.

by a combined Gallic force of some 150,000 foot and 20,000 horse. This massive army, drawn in the main from the four tribes of the Boii, Insubres, Taurini, and Lingones, who between them occupied the plains of the middle and upper Po, and buttressed by a contingent of the Gaesati from the Rhone valley, struck swiftly south through the mountains of central Etruria as far as Clusium, and after plundering the countryside inflicted severe losses upon the praetorian army which had been stationed in the centre to bar its progress. The Roman response was speedy and unusually effective. One consul, L. Aemilius Papus, who had been awaiting the expected onslaught at Ariminum, marched south, so inducing the Gauls to seek an escape route up the west coast of the peninsula, while the other, C. Atilius Regulus, who had been serving in Sardinia, crossed with his legions to Pisa to cut off their retreat. The Gauls found themselves surrounded by the two consular armies at Telamon, and the resulting battle was one of the bloodiest to be fought on Italian soil. The defeated Gauls alone lost 40,000 dead and 10,000 captured, and both the consul, Atilius, and one of the Gallic kings were among those killed in action.

That the Gauls on this occasion were the aggressors cannot be disputed: it was they who made the first move, and then with an army which had been carefully assembled for the purpose over many months. This is not to say, however, that the Roman stance had been wholly defensive in advance of the invasion or that the Gallic tribes had not viewed their attack as a pre-emptive strike: Polybius himself confesses that 'many of the Gauls entered upon the war in the conviction that the object of Rome in her wars with them was no longer just supremacy and dominion over them, but their total expulsion and destruction.'[27] It is, of course, fair to allow that the Romans may themselves have harboured a similar fear, but one cannot but be struck by the unparalleled state of readiness in which Rome entered upon this war. As has been noted, her preparatory moves may be traced back to the settlement of the *ager Gallicus* in 232. Soon afterwards she had attempted to deprive the Gauls of the wherewithal to buy mercenary assistance by banning the purchase of Gallic merchandise for gold or silver; she had cultivated the friendship of the Veneti and of the Cenomani, who occupied the land to the northwest of the Po delta, and had sent in troops to help man their borders with the Insubres; and finally in 226, perhaps at some cost to her commercial interests, she had contracted the Ebro treaty with Hasdrubal in Spain in what proved to be a successful attempt to buy Carthaginian neutrality. Polybius, further, supplies revealing details of the sheer size of the military forces which Rome had amassed for a Gallic campaign. In

[27] Polyb. 11.21.5.

addition to the two consular armies, each of which consisted of two legions, supported by allied contingents of 30,000 foot and 2000 horse, she had at her immediate disposal the praetorian army of 50,000 foot and 4000 horse which was stationed in Etruria, the 20,000 Umbrians who had been sent north to join with the Cenomani, and in Rome itself a mighty reserve of 23,000 citizens and 32,000 Italians. Furthermore, in 225 she took the unusual step of conducting a census of all her allies to determine the full potential of armed soldiery on which she might call if the need arose. In the circumstances it is difficult to believe that these vast forces would have remained undeployed if the Gauls had not themselves struck an early blow.

Whatever might have been their earlier intentions, the victory at Telamon undoubtedly gave the Romans encouragement, and, in the words of Polybius, 'inspired them with hope that they might be able to expel the Gauls totally from the Po valley'.[28] In 225 the surviving consul pursued the Boii into their own territory before returning to triumph, and in the following year both consuls, though hampered by illness and bad weather, succeeded in forcing this tribe into submission. In 223 the consuls, C. Flaminius and P. Furius Philus, carried the war still further into enemy territory by attacking the warlike Insubres, who dominated the central northern plains of Italy which lie between the Po and the Italian lakes. After crossing the river near Clastidium they made a detour into the lands of the friendly Cenomani, whence they attacked the Insubres from the east at a point on the river Oglio west of Brescia. The ensuing battle, in which the enemy force of some 50,000 men was totally routed, was a notable triumph for Flaminius, who had staked all on victory by destroying the river bridges in the rear of his army and so cutting off his line of retreat. It is one, however, for which he was given little credit either by his political opponents or by the tradition which they helped to mould, and it was left to the popular assembly, rather than to the senate, to vote him the triumph which he had so richly deserved.

The final blow to the Insubres was delivered in the following year by the consuls, Cn. Cornelius Scipio and M. Claudius Marcellus, but not before they had overcome spirited resistance. When they crossed the Po to lay siege to Acerrae, the Gauls, recently reinforced by 30,000 of the transalpine Gaesati, created a diversion by launching an assault upon the Roman supply base of Clastidium, south of the river. Marcellus was consequently forced to detach himself from his colleague and to march west to counter this threat, but, having surrounded and defeated the enemy, he was able to rejoin Scipio, fresh from the capture of Acerrae, and to stage a successful frontal attack upon the chief township of the

[28] Polyb. 11.31.4.

Insubres, Mediolanum (Milan). Thereafter resistance crumbled, and the tribesmen surrendered unconditionally, ceding territory to Rome and withdrawing into the Alpine foothills.

Thus in the space of four years' campaigning the whole of Cisalpine Gaul was brought under Rome's sway, and the frontiers of Roman Italy were extended to the Alps. In 221, in order to tidy up the operation, the senate despatched the two consuls north of Venice into Istria to make war upon, and to receive the submission of, all the tribes occupying the area between the coast and the Julian Alps. This meant that all the low-lying areas of present-day Italy were now secured and that only the Ligurians in the mountain fastnesses of the north-west remained unsubdued. Appropriately in 220 the supreme office of censor was conferred upon C. Flaminius, who both as tribune and as consul had been one of the principal architects of the Roman advance, and who now set the seal upon his work both by commissioning the building of the Via Flaminia, which was to link Rome initially with Ariminum and the *ager Gallicus*, and by founding two Latin colonies in the central Po valley, at the key points of Cremona and Placentia.

III. THE CONSTITUTION: MAGISTRACY AND ASSEMBLIES

The dramatic widening of Rome's horizons in the late fourth and third centuries naturally imposed severe strains upon institutions which had been designed for the government of a city-state. In the period before the Samnite wars her modest establishment of magistrates had supposedly not been overstretched, and the two consuls in particular, though frequently called upon to command armies in the field, had normally been able to find time out of the campaigning season to devote attention to the more important aspects of domestic government. Thereafter the pressures built up rapidly. Wars became progressively more prolonged and were fought at ever-increasing distances from Rome, with the result that they not only demanded the undivided attention of the consuls but also often called for the services of additional military commanders. The rapid growth of the Roman commonwealth in Italy and the eventual acquisition of overseas territories also placed heavy additional burdens of a governmental and administrative character upon the ancillary magistrates. Furthermore, the extension of the Roman frontier affected the very character of the city-based voting assemblies. At one time easily accessible to, if not always well attended by, the majority of citizens, they became increasingly beyond the reach of vast numbers, who will have lacked not only the inclination, but also the time and finance, to under-take journeys of up to 240 km. simply to record their vote. With the benefit of hindsight it can, perhaps, be convincingly argued that in the circumstances it would have best served the long-term interests both of

Rome and her leaders if the senate had at this stage undertaken a thorough and innovatory review of the organs of government. But the full significance of change is rarely obvious to those who live through it, and to a nobility jealous of its privileged role as a governing class the prospect of such a radical reform held out few attractions. In the event, therefore, the senate chose to meet each new crisis by sanctioning restrained, and often ingenious, modifications to the existing constitution, which had the merit of providing effective medium-term solutions without seriously undermining the balance of political power.

As far as the consuls were concerned, two developments in particular served to ease their burden. One was the invention of the concept of promagistracy – a device whereby with the approval of senate and assembly the *imperium* of a senior magistrate could be prorogued beyond the date at which he was obliged to lay down his office. This expedient, first used in 326 B.C. (p. 347) and thereafter only sparingly until the time of the Punic wars, had originally been designed to ensure continuity of command in a vital area of war, but it was soon recognized to provide Rome with the means of augmenting its supply of legionary commanders without unduly increasing the number of annual magistrates or breaking the traditional link between political leadership and military command. The other development which lightened the consular load was the mobilization of the plebeian officers, and of the tribunes in particular, in the service of government.[29] By the close of the fourth century the economic burdens which had weighed upon the Roman poor had been substantially eased by means of a programme of land settlement and colonization. This had deprived the *tribuni plebis* of their raison d'être as a quasi-revolutionary pressure-group. Furthermore, the measure of official recognition which the tribunes and the assembly through which they operated had received, first in 449, and then more recently by the Lex Hortensia of 287 (p. 400), had rendered them a highly convenient potential instrument of domestic government. The tribunes of the middle republican period were in fact for the most part prominent plebeian members of the governing class who viewed the office as a stepping-stone to a higher magistracy. As a class they came to behave and to be viewed, in the words of Livy, as *mancipia nobilium* ('slaves of the nobles');[30] and, if our sources tend to highlight occasions when tribunes ran foul of the senatorial majority, this merely reflects the fact that these officers had a unique opportunity to give expression to a minority view and in no way belies the essential truth that some of them could always be found to relieve the major magistrates of much of their responsibility in the field both of jurisdiction and of routine legislation.

Inevitably, of course, some addition to the number of her annual

---

[29] Cf. pp. 340ff (with some differences of view).   [30] Livy x.37.11.

magistrates was necessary to enable Rome to meet her growing commitments. In 267 the college of quaestors was raised from four to eight. These officers, whose duties had originally been investigative and inquisitorial,[31] were used during the Republic to perform a variety of seemingly unrelated tasks, but prominent among their functions was a broad responsibility for financial administration, which they appear to have discharged in such varying capacities as those of city treasurer or of senior quartermaster attached to a military or provincial command. There can be little doubt that the doubling of their number in 267 was closely associated both with the increase in revenue resulting from the recent extension of the *civitas sine suffragio* and with Rome's decision made two years earlier to face up to her Italian responsibilities by minting her own silver coinage.

After the First Punic War additions were also made to the college of praetors. In 242 Rome's sole praetor was given a colleague – the *praetor peregrinus* – who was to have responsibility for the administration of the law among non-citizens. Fifteen years later, in 227, two more praetors were added specifically to provide Rome with annual governors for the newly acquired overseas provinces of Sicily and Sardinia (p. 571). It is clear that during the third century the Romans still laid considerable stress upon the status of the praetor as a holder of *imperium* and as an unequal colleague of the consuls. The first praetor, or *praetor urbanus* as he came to be known, was frequently called upon to assume legionary command in the early years and was still being occasionally so employed as late as 232, while praetors were obviously considered to be best equipped for the new provincial governorships on account of their capacity for military command. Yet the very need to create the *praetor peregrinus*, and the eventual carrying of a Lex Plaetoria of uncertain date, which, among its other provisions, may well have restricted the term during which the *praetor urbanus* might be away from Rome to ten days,[32] serve to illustrate the increasingly heavy responsibilities which they were called upon to shoulder as administrators of the law. By the early second century it came to be seen that the pro-magistracy was a far more flexible instrument than the praetorship for dealing with the growing demand for army commanders in that its use both obviated a proliferation of senior annual magistrates and greatly facilitated a more appropriate use of available talent.

The effect which Rome's expansion had upon attendances at her

[31] For discussion (and a different view) see above, p. 195f. For other views on the innovation of 267 B.C. cf. p. 549 with n. 62.

[32] The restriction is implied by Cicero, *Phil.* II.31. The Lex Plaetoria is known to have defined the attendants of the *praetor urbanus* (Censorinus, *DN* 24.3), and is likely to have specified his rights and duties upon the creation of the new office of *praetor peregrinus*.

assemblies was of course profound. In all assemblies the vote which had once been freely exercised by every citizen became for all practical purposes the preserve of the few; but in the *comitia tributa* and *concilium plebis*, where the unit of vote was the tribe, the very process of creating new tribes in which to enrol ever more distant pockets of citizens had three additional consequences of no small significance. First, it gave to these bodies a representative aspect by assuring as much weight in the vote to the few who attended from a remote tribal area as to the many who, living on the doorstep of the Forum, were registered in one of the urban tribes; second, it provided the rural community with an inbuilt majority and so denied any effective voice to those who were domiciled in Rome and were engaged in urban occupations; and third, it guaranteed that for the foreseeable future neither candidates nor legislators would have the opportunity to promote their cause by making a direct appeal to voters *en masse*. These were developments in which Rome's rulers for the most part appear readily to have acquiesced. It is true that in 312 B.C. the censor, Appius Claudius, had sought to change the rules governing tribal registration (p. 395f), perhaps with the intention of affording greater voting strength to the commercially orientated citizens of Rome, but he had been very much a political maverick; and, when his rival, Q. Fabius Rullianus, had undone his work and once more relegated the city dwellers to the four urban tribes, he had set the seal of official approval upon the tribal group-vote principle and upon all that it implied.[33] We cannot know what considerations had most influenced Rullianus to take this stand in 304. We can, however, be sure that the *nobiles* came quickly to recognize as the supreme merit of the tribal group-vote that it removed the opportunity for demagogy and provided them with an effective means of subjecting the assemblies to their corporate control. Because the nature and size of the attendance from the more remote areas of the *ager Romanus* was so crucial to the outcome of votes, it became possible to lay the emphasis in pre-comitial activity not upon the wooing of the voters, but almost exclusively upon the delivery of a committed vote. The reduction of the assemblies to such an instrumental role may ill accord with present-day concepts of democracy: yet it had the undeniable advantage of reserving serious political debate for a responsible and informed forum while at the same time affording the people a form of participation in the decision-making process which was meaningful in the very real sense that it guaranteed substantial benefits to individuals and to the communities they represented from the hands of the patrons who called upon their votes. That in the absence of more radical constitutional reform the *nobiles* were right to cast the assembly in

[33] See Staveley 1959[H128], 414ff, 433.

this role is indicated both by the long period of political stability which Rome enjoyed during the middle Republic and by the chaos into which she speedily plunged when in the post-Gracchan years the rigid application of the group-vote principle was successfully undermined by power-seeking opportunists and would-be demagogues.

The impact of rapid enfranchisement upon Rome's senior electoral assembly was less dramatic. One reason for this is that the outcome of votes in the *comitia centuriata* had even from earliest times been determined more by the mobilization of clients than by efforts at direct persuasion. Another is that the wealthier citizens, who alone had an effective voice in these assemblies, were somewhat more immune than others to the cost and time of travel. But until the second half of the third century the most fundamental distinction between centuriate and tribal assemblies lay in the fact that the composition of the centuries bore no necessary relation either to tribe or to place of domicile. The censors were required to classify citizens according to age and wealth, but to the best of our knowledge the principle according to which they assigned citizens from a common age and property group to individual centuries was arbitrary and discretionary. For this reason the progressive increase in the number of tribes did not in itself affect the distribution of interest within the *comitia centuriata* as it did in the tribal assemblies. It is therefore of particular interest and significance that in, or soon after, 241 the Roman government deliberately set out to change this situation by carrying out a reform of the centuriate assembly of which the principal constituent was at least the partial co-ordination of the voting centuries with the tribal system. There is much uncertainty about the precise structure of the revised assembly, since any reconstruction must be based largely upon oblique references in Livy and Cicero,[34] but there is at least a wide measure of agreement on three of its essentials: first, that the right of prerogative voting (the right, that is, both to register a vote and to have a result declared in advance of the voting of the rest of the assembly) was transferred from the eighteen cavalry centuries (*centuriae equitum*) to one of the first-class centuries selected on each occasion by lot; second that the total number of voting units remained unchanged at 193; and third, that the complement of centuries in the first property-class was reduced from eighty to seventy to produce an exact multiple of the number of tribes, which had been brought up to a final total of thirty-five by the censors of 241. There are other questions which remain unsolved, as for example whether the co-ordination of centuries with tribes was extended to any or all of the other four classes, and in what proportion the remaining centuries were distributed among them; but fortunately

[34] Livy 1.43.12; Cic. *Rep.* II.39.

these have little direct bearing on what for the historian are the most interesting aspects of the reform – its purpose and its effect.

The traditional view that the change was democratically inspired is now largely discredited. One need point only to the minimal reduction in the number of centuries assigned to Class I, to the complete absence of any indication from the *fasti* that the reform weakened oligarchic control of elections, to the failure of any source to report controversy, and to the obvious difficulties involved in reconciling democratic change with censorial authorship. Not even the loss by the *equites* of their prerogative voting rights implies an attack upon the Establishment; for the enjoyment of a privileged vote by a predetermined aristocratic group, which suited a situation such as existed in the early Republic when the assembly was to be used as an instrument of a class, was less suited to an age when the assembly's loyalty was no longer a serious consideration and when the nobles were more free to indulge their personal and factional rivalries.

It is evident that the principal motive of the reform was closely related to what is so obviously the essence of the change – the co-ordination of the more important centuries with the tribes. One well-established view, expounded first by Rosenberg and developed since with variations by others,[35] is that the reform mirrored the action of Rullianus relating to the tribal assemblies and sought by restricting the urban voters to eight out of seventy centuries in the first class to stifle the influence of an emergent commercial interest and to assert the dominance of the yeoman farmer. This interpretation has its attractions; but it implies the existence of what for so late a date is perhaps too rigid a demarcation between the interests of the wealthy town and country dwellers, and it fails to account for the successful promotion of expansionist policies in the years which followed the reform.

More convincing is the theory that the reform was dictated by a need on the part of the nobility to exercise more effective control over the very considerable number of new citizens whose names had been added to the list. This vital connexion between the reform and enfranchisement was first recognized by Fraccaro, although his argument was bedevilled by a preoccupation with the comparative voting influence of old and new tribes.[36] His suggestion that the object of the reform was to reserve power for the citizens of the old tribes by ensuring that their voice prevailed in a majority of centuries obscures the fact that under the original Servian arrangement the predominant influence of the older citizens would have been guaranteed, not only by the censor's tactical use

---

[35] Rosenberg 1911[G703], 8off. Compare, more recently, Staveley 1953[G720], 28ff; Càssola 1962[H103], 99ff.   [36] Fraccaro 1929[G578], 119ff, followed by Taylor 1957[G732], 337ff.

of their discretionary powers in constituting the individual centuries, but also, more particularly, by the much larger attendance at the electoral vote of those who lived in or near Rome. The possibility that larger numbers of new citizens living at a distance actually made a habit of attending the assemblies unsolicited seems remote. Nevertheless, there is a rather different sense in which under the old order the extensive enrolment of new citizens on the register could have proved a serious embarrassment. In essence, the Roman election was a trial of personal strength: success depended in the last resort upon the ability of an individual candidate to marshal and deliver the maximum vote. So long as the electoral roll remained comparatively small, this task of canvassing support can have presented few problems. After the large-scale extension of the franchise, however, candidates must have found themselves confronted with a sizeable, unpredictable element among the potential voters – an element which, owing to the random composition of the century lists, could not be systematically or conveniently canvassed. There is no suggestion that at any time these voters constituted a threat to the nobility as a whole, or that they even wished to challenge the nobility's claim to rule. As with the new citizens after the Social War in 89 B.C., they constituted not a threat, but an imponderable, the very existence of which struck at the root of what the nobility believed the electoral contest should truly be. To this problem the reform of the *comitia centuriata* provided a convenient solution. By effecting the co-ordination of the first-class centuries with the tribes it ensured that in future the *nobilis* would have at his disposal in the map of the *ager Romanus tributim discriptus* ('the Roman territory divided by tribe') an all-important key to the composition of the individual voting units. With this as an aid he would be able to concentrate effort where it was needed and to contend with his rivals on equal terms by conferring *beneficia* and cultivating *clientelae* with predictable effect.

It is very possible that this fundamental change in the structure of the *comitia centuriata* was closely associated with another measure of the period, which had the effect of concentrating the freedman vote for the first time in the urban tribes.[37] The question of the electoral loyalties of freedmen has been much debated. It has in the past been commonly held that they were bound by ties of *clientela* to their former masters, but this carries with it the obvious and improbable corollary that any restriction of the freedman franchise represented an attack upon the control of the nobility. A more likely case is that many of those who themselves acquired such wealth as to afford them an effective voice in the centuriate

---

[37] Livy, *Per.* xx. The measure, like the centuriate reform, was the work of one of the colleges of censors who held office between 241 and 220.

assembly broke free from their bonds of dependence, and that, while retaining their original tribal registration, they moved their place of domicile, often to Rome itself. If this was so, then with the co-ordination of centuries and tribes in the main electoral assembly such men would have constituted a threat to the efficacy of the group-vote principle, and it would therefore have been only reasonable for the reformer to legislate at the same time to restrict their influence.

IV. *NOBILITAS* AND SENATE

The interpretation of the reform of the centuriate assembly which has just been given carries with it the implication that the average member of the Roman electorate regarded his vote as essentially something to be traded for benefits received, and that in casting it he consequently paid little heed to the merits either of the candidates or of the policies which they advocated. There is little reason to dispute this view. There were no doubt occasions, most probably at times of national crisis, when the outstanding qualifications of a candidate inspired the voters to an excess of zeal and resulted in the attendance at the *comitia* of many upon whom no call was made, but in the absence of any easy means of mass communication these occasions must have been few. In effect, therefore, the outcome of most consular elections, and consequently the course of Roman foreign and domestic policy, which whether by executive or legislative initiative the consuls were in a strong position to mould, was determined not by the electorate itself, but by those in the *nobilitas* and the senate who largely controlled both the size of the attendances at the assemblies and the sense in which the votes were cast. It is the nature and structure of this governing class, and not that of the electorate, which thus provides the key to any meaningful examination of Roman politics in the middle Republic.

There are notable respects in which the new *nobilitas* that emerged in the late fourth and third centuries differed from the patriciate which it succeeded. The patriciate, for one thing, had been a closed caste, perhaps of artificial creation, a group of influential families whose principal object had been to arrogate to themselves certain constitutional and religious privileges and to work for the exclusion from office of all but their own members. With the oligarchy of the later period the case was very different. The *nobilitas* was no closed circle (p. 392), and there is no evidence that the deliberate introduction of new blood into the ruling class either by an individual or by a group was regarded as a breach of faith by the remainder. Again, the unity of the patriciate had been based to a considerable degree upon class prejudice. Together with the few non-patrician families which they had been forced at a very early date to accept into the governing circle they had formed a distinct social group: they had constituted the landed aristocracy of Rome, while their plebeian opponents had for the most part been drawn from an entirely different stratum of society – wealthy no doubt, but in riches derived from meaner trades.[38] The *nobilitas*, by contrast, formed no such social or economic elite. Admittedly all, as their ability to pursue a political career implies, possessed a substantial capital, and all, although the wealth of some may originally have been derived from other sources, were landowners. But they were not the only large-scale landowners on the *ager Romanus*, and, as time passed, they came to represent an ever-diminishing minority. Despite these differences between the two groups, however, there are clear signs that this new and enlarged ruling class, composed as it was of diverse elements from both Rome and Latium, very quickly came to be regarded by its members as a corporate entity which could command of them a modicum of loyalty and impose upon them a code of political conduct. The new families introduced to the consulship throughout the entire third century numbered only sixteen, and the concerted attitude of exclusiveness which is suggested by this statistic is attested by a revealing story which the elder Pliny tells of the aedilician elections of as early as 304 B.C.[39] In that year, we are told, the entire nobility staged an ostentatious display of mourning on learning that two newcomers had defeated the official candidates – and this even though the families of the Poetelii and Domitii, to which these official candidates belonged, had themselves attained consular rank only a generation earlier.

This sense of unity and cohesion which pervaded the new *nobilitas* was, of course, dictated in part by a narrow self-interest and by instincts of self-preservation. Yet it undoubtedly also reflected the bond of a common responsibility. The succession of long and extensive wars in which Rome engaged as she advanced from city-state to, first, an Italian, and then a Mediterranean, power called not only for skill and experience in her executive magistrates, but also for a certain consistency and stability in policy-making, for which the Roman system of government by annually elected magistrates made little provision; and it was for this reason that a considerable burden of responsibility fell upon the one body which, although having no legal authority, could claim to enjoy a certain degree of permanence – the senate. It was membership of this august council, composed as it was for the most part of ex-curule magistrates, which was largely instrumental in welding men of different origin and background into a coherent whole and in causing them to abide by unwritten rules of conduct. It is true that after the Hannibalic War the combination of a fast-growing empire and an ill-adapted consti-

---

[38] For discussion cf. above, p. 167f (with a different view).   [39] Pliny, *HN* XXXIII.17f.

tution conspired to present individual *nobiles* with opportunities for personal self-aggrandizement which they found it hard to resist, but during the third century at least the authority of the senate was by and large respected by its members, with the result that Rome then enjoyed a golden age of stable and ordered government.

It has sometimes been suggested that the cohesion of the *nobilitas* was threatened throughout the third century, and even beyond, by a continuing conflict between its patrician and plebeian members. This view is almost certainly misconceived. We read of protests which were raised in 209 B.C. against the appointment of a plebeian, C. Mamilius, to the religious office of *curio maximus*;[40] but this is an isolated incident, and we cannot be sure that such protests, unsuccessful as they were, were inspired by class prejudice rather than by personal animosity or even by religious scruple. To infer the existence of a continuing rift from the fact that a patrician held one consulship annually until as late as 172 B.C. is even less reasonable. The most likely explanation of the continued regular appointment of patricians to this office is that it was universally approved by the entire *nobilitas* as a matter of policy. In this instance, as in others, patrician and plebeian senators no doubt agreed to utilize the prestige and prerogatives of the patriciate in order to facilitate the attainment of their common ends, for by establishing the principle that one of the two consuls in every year should be a patrician they notably diminished the chances of new men who may have aspired to the highest office. The patrician claim to one consulship was dropped in 172 – notably without any political conflict – no doubt simply because the numbers of eligible patricians had by then so declined as to make it difficult for rival groups to offer a fully qualified and suitable candidate in every year. It was upheld in 215, when a plebeian suffect was forced to stand down 'in order that there should not be two plebeian consuls', not on account of patrician intransigence, but simply because the senate opposed the establishment of a dangerous precedent at a critical period.[41]

To lay stress upon the community of interest and responsibility which characterized the nobility of the third century, however, is not to deny the existence of real conflict within its ranks. The annual electoral contest was itself the most obvious manifestation of such conflict, and in recent times it has become fashionable for scholars to represent at least the inner circle of the senate as divided into two or more identifiable groups or factions, whose principal object was to promote the electoral chances of their members. The nature and raison d'être of these so-called factions, even their very existence, are subjects of a continuing debate, and, since

[40] Livy XXVII.8.1.
[41] Livy XXIII.31.13. Scullard (1973[H127], 58) also accepts collusion, but chooses to interpret this incident in the context of factional politics.

the evidence provided by the annalistic tradition is slight and indecisive, it must suffice here simply to state where the probabilities may lie.

Münzer,[42] who pioneered the application of prosopographical study to republican Rome, maintained that the association of families in factions was for the most part based both upon long-standing and inherited ties of friendship, and upon links which were deliberately forged either through intermarriage or through the extension of political patronage. He consequently tended to endow the faction with a greater degree of stability and permanence than many have been prepared to accept. His most severe critics have challenged his use of evidence, and in particular his attempts to establish family associations by attaching what they regard as unwarranted significance to patterns of collegiality, and even succession, in office as they appear in the magisterial lists.[43] But, justified as some of their strictures may be, the most damaging criticism that may be levelled against Münzer and his school is that they failed to make any allowance for the part played by political outlook in determining the composition of noble factions. Great as may have been the respect which Romans held for the obligations imposed by *amicitia* ('friendship') and *gratia* ('favour'), it is scarcely credible that in the context of a consular election these took precedence over political attitudes, whether dictated by self-interest or principle, in influencing the level and direction of effort that was expended in the canvass. And since it is far from being an invariable rule that statesmen either inherit their political stand from their fathers or share the outlook of their kinsmen, there must be some considerable doubt as to whether factions at Rome commonly embraced entire families or even retained their identity for more than a limited period. Of course, the long-standing family ties peculiar to Roman society provided a firm basis for potential co-operation on the political front, and they may frequently have led to an active co-ordination of effort in cases where this was not precluded by either political or personal differences. Yet conversely it must be conceded that a strong community of interest or conviction must also on occasions have sufficed to induce a working association among *nobiles* who were linked by no such ties. Many of the partnerships into which nobles entered are, therefore, likely to have been ephemeral. There was little question of a binding commitment or even of a moral obligation to work in harness, and enthusiasm for pooling electoral effort and resources is likely to have waxed and waned both with the level of acceptability of the individual candidates and with the adjudged importance of the issues upon which the outcome of the election might have bearing. Provided, however, that this is clearly

---

[42] Münzer 1920[H120].

[43] For a well-balanced critical appraisal of the methods adopted by Münzer and to some extent by Scullard 1973[H127], see Càssola 1962[H103], 8ff.

understood, it may still be meaningful and useful to classify potential allies as members of a group or faction and even to speculate as to their identity.

Although the principal raison d'être of the faction as here defined was to control policy by influencing the outcome of the major elections, we should not make the mistake of supposing that in these elections the comparative strength of rival groups was in itself always a deciding factor. The faction did not extend beyond the inner circle of the governing class; yet outside that circle there were many members of the senate who together must surely have been in a position to deliver a sizeable vote at the *comitia*. It was these 'backbenchers' in their capacity as potential harvesters of votes who were the equivalent of the 'floating voters' on the Roman electoral scene. It was their changing political attitudes, and their electoral zeal or indifference, which perhaps more than any other factor decided the changing fortunes of the noble factions. In this sense, therefore, the often changing course of Roman policy was largely dictated not by individual magistrates, or even by factions, but by the senatorial majority of the day.

V. POLICIES AND PERSONALITIES

In the absence of any continuous annalistic narrative covering the period 291 to 219 B.C. it is difficult, if not impossible, to identify with any assurance the particular issues which may have divided Rome's politicians in any given year. Nevertheless, it may with reason be assumed that throughout this time the senate continued to engage in the wide-ranging debate over the future political and economic role of Rome which had characterized its deliberations in the latter part of the fourth century. From as early as 340 there had been conflict within the nobility over the advisability of cultivating the Campanian connexion (cf. p. 360); and it is likely that towards the turn of the century this had come to a head with the attempt of the censor, Appius Claudius, to effect radical changes in Rome's social structure and constitution designed to enable her to play a more prominent part in the Italian world of commerce.[44] This move, it is true, had been successfully countered by Q. Fabius Rullianus, who, in turn, together with his political associates, appears to have pursued a policy of northward advance which positively discouraged urban expansion and which led to the settlement of large numbers in colonies and on the Sabine land.[45] But the debate concerning the extent to which Rome should involve herself in the affairs of the Greek South nevertheless

[44] On Appius' censorship see above, pp. 395ff (with a different interpretation).
[45] See Càssola 1962[H103], 154ff.

continued. This is revealed by the only two concrete references which we have to serious senatorial discussion before the Punic wars – the first relating to the year 279 B.C., when the aged Appius Claudius delivered a masterly oration to divert the senate from contracting a dishonourable peace with Pyrrhus (p. 471), the second relating to the year 264 itself, when the senate allegedly referred a decision on offering assistance to the Mamertines of Messana to the assembly (p. 542). On both occasions the senate was evenly divided and clearly open to persuasion, and, whatever the moral or military considerations which may have had a bearing on its decisions in each case, it is certain that the chief underlying doubts among the uncommitted related to the long-term consequences for Rome of her assumption of a Mediterranean role.

It is important that we should not misunderstand the nature of this debate or the attitudes which gave rise to it. In recent years there has been a tendency to treat it as a manifestation of class war, the nobles who favoured a policy geared to commercial expansion being represented as a narrow capitalist elite, their opponents as champions of the *populus*, or, slightly more plausibly, of the yeoman farmer whose interests were tied to the maintenance of an essentially agrarian economy.[46] There are reasons for questioning this assessment. For one thing, the so-called imperialists among the senators could presumably call for voting purposes upon as broad a base of clients and adherents as their opponents, and, if we are able to judge by their relative success, the support of such clients was clearly not undermined significantly by political hostility. For another, the very assumption that yeomen farmers of the first property class were opposed to a policy of maritime and commercial expansion has no basis. The high incidence of what was in all probability speculative debt in the late fourth century[47] indicates that there was no lack of enthusiasm even among the generality of Rome's wealthier citizens to invest in new enterprises for a profitable return; and the introduction of a more sophisticated coinage can only have hastened on the day when, according to Polybius, the majority took some interest, direct or indirect, in the lucrative contracts of Empire.[48] Warfare in the richer Mediterranean sphere also had its appeal, holding out the prospect of personal booty – a deciding factor, we are told, in the assembly's endorsement of intervention in Sicily in 264 – and of a gradual easing of taxation, made possible by the inflow of funds into state coffers. Those in the senate, therefore, who opposed southward expansion should not be viewed as the champions of a particular social or economic group. Their motives

[46] Compare, for example, Càssola 1962[H103], *passim*; De Martino 1972–5[A35], III.2.76ff.
[47] Cf. pp. 329ff (with a different interpretation).
[48] VI.17.2: Polybius refers in this passage to the situation as it was in the middle of the second century.

were more complex. Some may have been influenced by a respect for the traditional ethos of Roman society, some by an idealistic scorn for excessive wealth such as is exemplified in anecdotes told of men like Curius and Fabricius (p. 410); but the majority undoubtedly took the stand which they did because they deeply feared the long-term effects which Rome's projected Mediterranean involvement would have not only upon the fabric of society but upon the political system of which they and their fellow nobles formed so integral a part.

A recognition that political divisions within the senate were not based essentially upon diverse loyalties or economic interests should warn us against undue schematization in an interpretation of Roman policy-decisions in the third century. It may indeed be that in the opening decade the conflict within the nobility had been manifested by an enthusiasm for either northward or southward expansion; but, if so, the object of those who advocated a northward thrust in these years had been to counter the policies of their opponents and not to satisfy the needs either of land-hungry citizens, if indeed these existed in any numbers, or of the agrarian community at large. It should not, therefore, be assumed that the question of Rome's engagement on her northern borders continued to be a serious political issue once the absorption of southern Italy into her sphere of interest became accepted as a *fait accompli*. Although the resistance encountered by M'. Curius Dentatus in 290, and perhaps again later when he advocated the creation of new tribes, may indicate that there were differences over the method to be employed in extending Roman influence and control in the region, there is little reason to doubt that the aggressive stance which was adopted towards Etruria, Umbria, and Picenum in the immediate aftermath of the Pyrrhic War had the backing of an all-but-united senate. Indeed, the establishment of diplo-matic contacts with Egypt in 273 and the introduction of a silver coinage at Rome in 269[49] suggest that those who held sway in these years had in some measure come to terms with the economic reality of Rome's new role.

There is little information on the political leanings of individual nobles in the period immediately prior to the First Punic War. Even the knowledge that particular magistrates were involved in specific courses of action yields few sure clues, since consuls were frequently bound to pursue policies set in motion by their predecessors and to campaign vigorously in wars of which they may not have approved. Little purpose can therefore be served by an attempt to reconstruct the composition of senatorial groups on the strength of inadequate evidence. The only explicit reference to a form of political alliance in these years comes from

[49] See above, pp. 414ff, for the beginnings of Roman coinage.

Cicero, who singles out a group of five *amici*, M'. Curius, C. Fabricius, Ti. Coruncanius, P. Decius Mus, and Q. Aemilius Papus.[50] The first three of these were *novi homines* ('new men': p. 392), two of them from Tusculum, which may indicate that there were those in the established governing class – among them Aemilius Papus – who had been spurred to support their advancement by a desire to broaden the group of families who shared their political outlook. The indications are that this group favoured the conservative approach. The association of P. Decius Mus with Rullianus, for example, extended over several terms of office: Curius came into conflict with Appius Claudius Caecus[51] and was largely responsible for the annexation of the *ager Sabinus*: and Fabricius, for all his vigorous campaigning, came to be regarded by Pyrrhus as the man most likely to influence the senate in favour of a compromise settlement.[52] Another name could reasonably be added to this list, that of M. Fulvius Flaccus, who collaborated with Curius on the Anio aqueduct project, who was appointed *magister equitum* by one of Cicero's five, Ti. Coruncanius, when he held the dictatorship to hold the elections in 258, and who as tribune in 270 opposed the move to woo the favour of Rome's new Greek allies by sacrificing the Campanian mercenaries of Rhegium (p. 539f).[53] He too was of Tusculan stock – which prompts the speculation that the Latin elements in the nobility may have brought with them a deep distrust of Rome's South-Italian connexion, which had so soured Romano-Latin relations at the time of the Latin War. In the opposing camp also we can identify only the odd individual with any degree of confidence. The aged Appius Caecus, of course, holds pride of place; and with him should no doubt be coupled his two kinsmen, Appius and Gaius Claudius, who as consul and military tribune in 264 exerted what influence they could to draw Rome into conflict with Carthage. Other possible associates are the C. Aelius who as tribune in ?285 was responsible for Rome's first intervention in Thurii,[54] and P. Cornelius Rufinus, who is reported to have been assisted by friends within in capturing the Greek city of Croton in 277[55] and who was later expelled from the senate by Fabricius and Aemilius Papus for possessing an excess of silver vessels.

It must be assumed that during the twenty-four years of the First Punic War there was some abatement of political controversy at Rome. Certainly a recent suggestion that the composition of rival factions can be

---

[50] Cic. *Sen.* 43; *Amic.* 39.   [51] Cic. *Brut.* 55; [Aur. Vict.] *De Vir. Ill.* 34.3.
[52] Zonar. VIII.4.
[53] Val. Max. II.7.15. Càssola (1962[H103], 171ff) argues with some force that the Campanian mercenaries had earlier been encouraged to massacre the anti-Roman elements at Rhegium by C. Fabricius.   [54] Pliny, *HN* XXXIV.22.
[55] Zonar. VIII.6: καὶ ἐπὶ Κρότωνα ὥρμησεν ἀποστάντα Ῥωμαίων μεταπεμψαμένων αὐτὸν τῶν ἐπιτηδείων. Below, p. 480.

reconstructed by examining the role which successive generals played in the conduct of the war is totally unconvincing.[56] With the coming of peace, however, the old divisions reasserted themselves. The emphasis in political debate was naturally somewhat modified, for the defeat of Carthage, bringing in its train the permanent annexation of Sicily, had established Rome as a Mediterranean power. But the basis of dissent remained largely unchanged. There were those who looked to capitalize on the humiliation of her enemy by maintaining Rome's naval power, strengthening contacts with trading centres such as Massalia, and totally usurping Carthage's one-time maritime ascendancy in the west. There was also a powerful group who viewed the pursuit of such a course with grave misgivings and for whom a policy of aggressive expansionism threatened to put at stake much that they deemed of greater value – the prosperity of Italian agriculture; the survival of traditional Roman values; even the oligarchy itself, which depended in the last resort upon the ability of the senate to exercise effective control not only over the electorate but also over its own members. In the early second century, when Rome was already being swept along irresistibly by the tide of imperialism, it fell to the elder Cato and to a comparatively small band of sympathizers to voice these conservative sentiments. But before the war with Hannibal the advocates of containment had a more powerful voice. They may have lost the argument, but there are indications of a continuing and lively debate within the senate. There was a clear difference of view about the terms of the peace treaty in 241, which were eventually amended to the detriment of Carthage (p. 565). There was vacillation as to the appropriate action to be taken in Sardinia, where an original policy of strict neutrality at the time of the Mercenary War gave way in 238 to one of opportunist aggression. And in 219 on the eve of the Second Punic War there took place, according to Dio,[57] a notable senatorial debate on what should be the proper response to Hannibal's attack upon Saguntum. For the rest, much of the evidence for political controversy during the interwar years centres around the personality and activities of the *novus homo*, C. Flaminius; and we should, therefore, consider how, if at all, this related to the basic argument of the day on the appropriate course of foreign policy.

Flaminius has been commonly represented either as a man of the people or as the champion of the small proprietors. The former view, which rests essentially upon Polybius' description of the man as a thorough mob-orator and demagogue,[58] is effectively belied by the fact

[56] Compare Lippold 1963[H117], 104ff.

[57] Dio XIII fr. 55, vol. I, pp. 194–7 Boiss. Cf. Zonar. VIII.22.

[58] Polyb. III.80.3 (ὀχλοκόπον μὲν καὶ δημαγωγὸν τέλειον). Compare also Livy XXI.63.3–4; XXII.1.5.

that his stormy tribunate was followed by election to the highest offices of state. The latter is based upon a fundamental misinterpretation of two of his public acts. One of these – his promulgation of a bill in 232 B.C. providing for the *viritim* distribution of the *ager Gallicus* – has already been discussed (p. 432). It bears sufficient resemblance to the provisions of M'. Curius for the division of the Sabine territory two generations earlier to invite the suggestion that it was inspired by a similar motive; but, except for the detail that both men offended the proprieties of their age by calling for the settlement of citizens on lands unduly distant from the political centre, the analogy is far from apt. As we have seen, a preoccupation with the north of the peninsula had long since ceased to be the monopoly of those who were opposed to commercial interests; and the motives of Flaminius on this occasion were almost certainly military. His other act said to be indicative of an anti-commercialist stance was his alleged solitary support for the Claudian plebiscite of 218 B.C., a measure which provided that no senator or father of a senator should possess a ship with a capacity of more than 300 *amphorae*. But any suggestion that such a restriction could stay the development of Rome's maritime activities or effectively deprive the more imperialistic of senators of an incentive to further their policies is facile. Introduced as it was on the eve of the Hannibalic War, this measure is best understood as designed to ensure that the senators upon whose counsels in war the fate of the Republic rested would devote their time to public affairs. That a majority of the senate should have opposed it can be explained simply by their natural resentment at a legalized interference with their freedom, but that Flaminius gave it his support need mean no more than that he was intent on forestalling the more serious constitutional consequences of economic policies to which he gave his full approval.

A surer clue to Flaminius' political stance is provided by the several indications that he was a bitter opponent of Q. Fabius Maximus, the great-grandson of Rullianus, who voiced the arguments of appeasement in the debate of 219. Fabius is mentioned by Cicero as the consul who strongly opposed the Flaminian bill for the distribution of the *ager Gallicus*;[59] it was very probably Fabius who as the dominating voice in the augural college was primarily responsible for the efforts which were exerted to secure Flaminius' abdication during his first consulship and subsequently to deny him a triumph; and it is almost certainly Fabius' kinsman and probable associate, the historian Q. Fabius Pictor, who should be held responsible for the hostility shown to Flaminius in the surviving tradition. Furthermore, Flaminius' own known associations

---

[59] Cic. *Sen.* 11; *Acad. Pr.* II.13. The clash almost certainly belongs to Fabius' first consulship (233 B.C.), with which the tribunate of Flaminius overlapped.

within the governing class tend to confirm that the two men belonged to opposing political camps. Among other allies we should mention Fabius' arch-opponent of 217 B.C., M. Minucius, who appointed Flaminius his *magister equitum* in 220,[60] and L. Cornelius Lentulus, the protagonist of war in the debate of 219, who can only have owed his appointment as *princeps senatus* ('leader of the senate') in preferment to the oldest living ex-censor, M. Fabius Buteo, to the good offices of the censors of 220, of whom Flaminius was one. In the light of these indications the northern policy of Flaminius should be seen as one which accorded with the designs of the expansionist group within the senate. The plan to consolidate further the frontiers of Italy by driving the Gauls back into the Alpine foothills and taking possession of the Po valley was viewed as a necessary preliminary to a major confrontation with Hannibal, which it was no doubt hoped and expected would take place not on Italian soil but in Spain.[61]

Perhaps because political controversy in these years centred on one overriding issue – that of war or peace, aggression or retrenchment – it becomes possible not only to detect the periodic swings of senatorial opinion, but even at times to relate these swings to the electoral fortunes of identifiable groups. After the peace a hardening of attitudes is first evident in 238. In that year Rome went on to the offensive with the occupation of Sardinia and the commencement of operations against the Ligurians and Gauls, and but two years later she turned her attention to Corsica and, as we are told, even contemplated a renewed assault on Carthage in defence of her merchant shipping. Significantly, the two patrician consuls of 237 and 236 were the later *princeps senatus*, Lucius Cornelius Lentulus, and his brother, Publius.

The year 235 by contrast saw a reversion to a more pacific stance. There was notably no follow-up to the rout of the Gauls after the raid on Ariminum, and, as if to make a political point, the consuls took the unusual course of ceremoniously closing the doors of Janus.[62] For three years, in the last of which Q. Fabius Maximus held his first consulship, Rome engaged in no warfare save that which was forced upon her by the actions of insurgents. It was perhaps because Carthage was widely believed to have been responsible for instigating revolt in the offshore islands and in Liguria at this time that the 'hawks', as it appears, regained

---

[60] The tradition found in Plutarch (*Marc.* 5.5) which has M. Minucius as dictator in 220 B.C. is convincingly defended by Dorey (1955[H108], 92ff). Valerius Maximus, who represents Flaminius as the *magister equitum* of Fabius (1.1.5), was almost certainly confused by the fact that Fabius was appointed dictator in the same year and was immediately declared *vitio creatus* ('faultily appointed').

[61] For an exposition of a similar view see Kramer 1948[J188], 1ff.

[62] In the consulship of T. Manlius Torquatus (Livy 1.19.3; Varro, *Ling.* v.165); but Livy adds 'after the end of the First Punic War' and many scholars assume a confusion with A. Manlius Torquatus (*cos.* 241) and put the closing of the temple in that year (see above, p. 383).

the initiative in the years 232–230. In 232 was carried the Flaminian bill, which in principle, if not in detail, can only have been inspired by senior members of the nobility. Then in the following year came the investigatory embassy to Hamilcar in Spain, which may well have led to the contraction of an agreement between Rome and the township of Saguntum.[63] Whether those responsible for this treaty actually intended that it should at some future date provide the pretext for renewed hostilities with Carthage is unclear: but the move was undoubtedly provocative. Finally in 230 the long-overdue protest was sent to Teuta of Illyria, warning her to desist from piratical attacks on Italian shipping. There can be little question that all three steps were inspired by a similar political outlook. They reflect a determination to incur, even to provoke, war rather than sacrifice any one of Rome's rapidly expanding interests. Furthermore, they were all taken in a period of years when the consulship was dominated by what scholars have tended to identify as an emerging group which centred at this time around leading families of the Aemilian and Cornelian *gentes* and was to centre in the next generation around the Scipios. Certainly, two of the six consuls were Aemilii, and two others, C. Papirius Maso and the new man M. Pomponius Matho, belonged to families which were soon to forge marriage alliances with both the Scipios and the Aemilii Pauli.[64]

The first half of the next decade saw little activity except for the Illyrian campaign, to which the senate was already committed and on which again there was no attempt to capitalize. Q. Fabius Maximus held his second consulship in this period (228 B.C.) and may have exercised a weighty influence, particularly if, as is very possible, he had enhanced his reputation by carrying through the centuriate reform as censor in 230.[65] It is even possible that the Ebro treaty, which was contracted with Hasdrubal in 226 and which appeared superficially to conflict with Rome's obligations under the Saguntine alliance, reflects the viewpoint of those like Fabius who were genuinely prepared to compromise. From the time of the Gallic attack in 225, however, senatorial attitudes discernibly hardened once more, and Rome was carried forward on an offensive tide which brought successively in its wake the subjection of

---

[63] Dio fr. 48, vol. i, p. 178–9 Boiss.

[64] The daughter of C. Papirius Maso married the son of L. Aemilius Paulus (Plut. *Aem.* 5.1). Scipio's mother was a Pomponia (Sil. *Pun.* XIII.615f), and his wife an Aemilia Paula (Livy XXXVIII.57.6).

[65] So Vitucci 1953[B270], 54ff, who sought to identify Q. Fabius Maximus with the Fabius honoured in a fragment of an *elogium* found at Brundisium. The incomplete sentence 'primus senatum legit et comiti . . .' ('he was the first to revise the membership of the senate and . . . assembly(?)') certainly refers to censorial activity, but some doubts exist over the identification of the Fabius concerned, over Vitucci's restoration of the words *comiti[a ordinavit]* ('he regulated the assembly'), and over his claim that they refer to the reorganization of the centuriate system at Rome (cf. Taylor 1957[G732], 352f).

Transpadane Gaul, the Istrian War, the second intervention in Illyria, and eventually the fateful declaration of war against Carthage. It has been claimed that the so-called Aemilio–Cornelian group largely dominated the elections in these seven years. This may indeed be so; but, if such an alliance existed, a glance at the lists of magistrates is enough to establish that the dominant political figure of the group was Flaminius, twice consul and once censor in the short space of six years. Like Cato in the next generation, Flaminius was clearly a *novus homo* whose exceptional talents and strength of personality enabled him to establish himself as a leader even among those members of the older nobility who had been instrumental in promoting his political advancement. Unlike Cato, however, it was his misfortune to be killed in his prime and so to have his name and reputation fall defenceless victims to the vilification of his opponents. It is indeed ironical that it was not he, but Q. Fabius Maximus, his chief rival and the apostle of appeasement, who survived to win enduring fame as an architect of the victory over Carthage which was to set Rome beyond recall upon the road to empire.

CHAPTER 10

PYRRHUS[1]

P. R. FRANKE

I. THE CONFLICT BETWEEN ROME AND TARENTUM

There was a treaty between Rome and the South Italian Greek city of
Tarentum, certainly from 303–302 B.C., perhaps even as early as 332/1,
which prohibited the Romans from sailing northwards beyond the
Lacinian Promontory (south of Croton) and penetrating the Gulf of
Tarentum (Map 10).[2] But a squadron of ten Roman ships nevertheless
did make a surprise appearance in the harbour of Tarentum, probably in
the autumn of 282 – the first time, incidentally, that mention is made of
Roman warships in ancient times. Only shortly before the consul C.
Fabricius Luscinus had liberated the city of Thurii from a Lucanian siege.
The Lucanians, along with the Bruttii, were increasingly terrorizing the
Greek settlements in southern Italy. The consul left a garrison behind to
protect the city and its oligarchic government which was loyal to Rome.
The Tarentines therefore had good reason to fear that this would
severely weaken their own position in relation to Thurii, their constant
rival in reputation and power. No one in the city believed for one
moment that the Roman ships were only making a sightseeing tour of
Magna Graecia on their way to visit Thurii or, perhaps, the three Roman
colonies of Sena Gallica, Hadria and Castrum Novum which had been
founded on the upper Adriatic coast after the Third Samnite War. On the
contrary, they feared a political purpose behind the visit on the part of the
new rising power in Latium whom they had been watching with suspicion for some time and who, they imagined, had come to overthrow the
demos (the mass of the people) in Tarentum in order to reinstate the

[1] Sources: the *Hypomnemata* ('Memoirs') of the king and his treatise on *Tactics* have been lost, as
has also the work by Cineas mentioned by Cic. *Fam.* IX.25.1. Only fragments of the *Epeirotika* by the
historian Proxenus, who was a member of Pyrrhus' court, survive, as also of Timaeus' history of the
Western Greek world and of the work of Duris of Samos, who was hostile to Macedonian rule. But
these works, and also the history of the Diadochi by Hieronymus of Cardia, were all used to some
extent by Plutarch for his *Life of Pyrrhus* – our main source alongside scattered notes in Diodorus
(Books XXI–XXII), Pompeius Trogus-Justinus (Books XVI–XVIII, XXIII–XXV), Pausanias, Livy,
Dionysius of Halicarnassus, Appian and others. In addition, there are a few inscriptions and the
extensive coinage of Pyrrhus himself and of the South Italian Greek cities and Rome.

[2] Schmitt 1969[J224], 60 n. 444.

aristocrats who were sympathetic towards Rome, just as they had done in Thurii. The friendly relations Rome enjoyed with Naples (which had signed a *foedus aequo iure* – a contract making the two cities equal partners with equal rights[3] – with Rome as early as 326, the first of the Greek communities to do so), as well as with other Greek cities including Massalia, also gave grounds to fear the decline of Tarentum's traditional predominance in South Italy. This fear grew all the stronger when, in about 306/5 B.C., the first signs of an economic, and soon also a political, relationship between Rome and the island of Rhodes[4] made it clear that Rome was beginning to think beyond the narrow confines of Central Italy and show an interest in the Greek world to the east as well. In addition to this, the city on the Tiber had succeeded in 306 in reaching a new, third agreement with Carthage, marking out the boundaries of each other's spheres of influence and reflecting the new conditions of power in Italy. Though this barred Rome from Graeco-Punic Sicily, it also closed the whole of the Italian peninsula to the Carthaginians.[5] The Greek settlements on the other hand must have felt this to be at least an indirect threat to themselves.

Spurred on by the demagogue Philocharis, an incensed mob therefore fell on the Roman ships, which had clearly contravened the existing treaty. They sank four and seized a fifth, whilst the rest managed to escape by the skin of their teeth. The Tarentine army then marched to Thurii and forced the ruling aristocracy, who sympathized with Rome, as well as the Roman garrison, to withdraw from the city. For Rome, this brusque action meant not only a severe loss of prestige; it was also a serious blow to her efforts to establish greater influence in South Italy. A Roman embassy therefore arrived in Tarentum at the end of 282 or early the following year demanding satisfaction. But it left again empty-handed and, if the pro-Roman annalistic tradition is not exaggerating here as in so many other places,[6] the victim of heavy insults. As a result a Roman army under the command of the consul L. Aemilius Barbula invaded Tarentine territory and soon reduced the city to an extremely precarious position. The people's assembly, no longer trusting in their own strength and leadership, and in defiance of the vehement opposition of the aristocrats, decided, as so often in the past, to ask the help of a foreign commander. In 343–338 it had been Archidamus of Sparta. In 334 the Molossian King Alexander I of Epirus came in the hope of

[3] Schmitt 1969[J224], 22 n. 410; above, p. 369.
[4] Cf. Polyb. xxx.5.6: in 167 the Rhodians had 'shared in the most glorious and finest achievements of the Romans for nearly 140 years'. This assertion has given rise to much controversy. For discussion see Schmitt 1957[J223], 1–49 and, briefly, Walbank 1957–79[B182], III.423–6.
[5] Schmitt 1969[J224], 53 n. 438; cf. below, p. 532f.
[6] App. *Sam.* 7.1–6; Zonar. VIII.2.1–2.

carving out an empire for himself in battle with the Lucanians and Bruttians, and paid with his life in 331. In 303 the Spartans responded to a further appeal from Tarentum by sending Acrotatus' brother Cleonymus to South Italy, where he took and briefly held Metapontum; but while he was absent in Corcyra, the Tarentines turned against him and his attempt to recover their city in a night attack failed dismally. Eventually the Romans drove him from the area and he was reduced to pursuing an unsuccessful career of brigandage in the northern Adriatic. King Agathocles of Syracuse too had repeatedly intervened in South Italy between 298 and 295 at the instigation of Tarentum, and fought against the Bruttians and the Iapygians, who had been threatening the Greeks. His death robbed the Greeks of a strong protector and left behind a power-vacuum which Rome thought to fill.

It was not mere chance that the choice this time fell on King Pyrrhus of Epirus, on the other side of the Adriatic. Not long before, in 282/1, Tarentum had placed a number of ships at the Molossian king's disposal for the purpose of winning back the island of Corcyra, which he had received in 295 as dowry from his second wife Lanassa, daughter of Agathocles, but had lost again in 290 to Demetrius Poliorcetes when Lanassa left him and married Demetrius. Pyrrhus was therefore under an obligation towards Tarentum. There were also various trade connexions between Epirus, South Italy and Sicily, reflecting the fact that groups of Thesprotian and Chaonian peoples from Epirus had earlier settled there. Records that Tarentines had consulted the oracle at Dodona around the turn of the fourth to the third century[7] and inscriptions on a number of votive offerings in this chief sanctuary of the Epirotes show that the links must in fact have been fairly intensive.[8] Furthermore, Pyrrhus was considered an outstanding commander and tactician, who never shrank from personal danger and who inspired enthusiastic obedience in his soldiers. The memory of the powerful personality of Alexander the Molossian, brother-in-law to Alexander the Great and Pyrrhus' uncle and predecessor on the Molossian throne, was also undoubtedly still vivid at Tarentum.

II. PYRRHUS AS KING OF THE MOLOSSIANS; HIS POLICY IN GREECE TO 281 B.C.[9]

There were of course other reasons for Pyrrhus' willingness to answer the Tarentine plea for help. Pyrrhus was born in 319, the son of the

[7] *SGDI* 1567; cf. also the προξενία granted by the Molossians to the people of Acragas around 300 (*SIG* 942).   [8] Franke 1961[B220], 276f.

[9] For the wider Hellenistic background and personalities concerned here see also E. Will in *CAH* VII.1 (Cambridge,[2] 1984), Chaps. 2 and 4.

Molossian king Aiacides who, in 317, was deposed and banished by popular decree. Pyrrhus therefore spent his youth as a refugee at the court of the Illyrian king Glaucias. In 306 the latter restored Pyrrhus by force to the Molossian throne under the kind of regency government which was customary in Epirus and Macedonia. But only a few years later, in 302, Pyrrhus was once again ousted, this time by Cassander of Macedonia. He was forced to leave the country and went to serve as an officer in the army of his brother-in-law Demetrius Poliorcetes (son of Antigonus the One-eyed), who had married Pyrrhus' sister Deidameia. In 298, as a sequel to a short-lived peace between Demetrius and Seleucus, the latter as go-between arranged a peace settlement between Demetrius and Ptolemy I and in connexion with this Pyrrhus went to the Alexandrian court as a hostage. Here he won the favour of Berenice, Ptolemy's mistress and later his queen, and he married Antigone, her daughter by her first marriage to an otherwise unknown Macedonian noble. Only a year later, in 297, following the death of Cassander, Pyrrhus returned to his homeland with considerable military and financial support from Ptolemy I. At first he ruled together with Neoptolemus II, his relative and a protégé of Cassander, but very soon had him murdered.

As king of the Molossians – he never styled himself king of the Epirotes and certainly never king of Epirus, a title found especially in the Roman tradition – Pyrrhus was at the same time the *hegemon* of the Epirote League which was founded around 325/20 and describes itself as the *ΣYMMAXOI TΩN AΠEIPΩTAN* ('the Epirote allies') on inscriptions.[10] The League united the three main peoples of Epirus (Map 9) – the Molossians, the Thesprotians and the Chaonians, who were evidently the last to join; each of these in turn consisted of numerous sub-groups. The constitution set the powers of the Molossian king within relatively narrow confines, both as far as his own people were concerned and also as regards the Epirote League. The minting of coinage, the conferment of προξενία (public guest-friendship), of citizenship and of freedom from taxation, the granting of the right to asylum and other privileges lay exclusively in the hands of the κοινόν (commonalty) of the Molossians, at the head of which was the προστάτης, roughly comparable in function and standing to the ephors of Sparta. Likewise it was the συμμαχία (alliance) of the Epirotes and not the king, its nominal head and general, which possessed both the right to mint coinage and also the right to grant freedom from customs duties, as is apparent from inscriptions. First and foremost the Molossian king was through long tradition head of the army in time of war, but to declare war he needed the consent of the

[10] *SGDI* 1336.

460

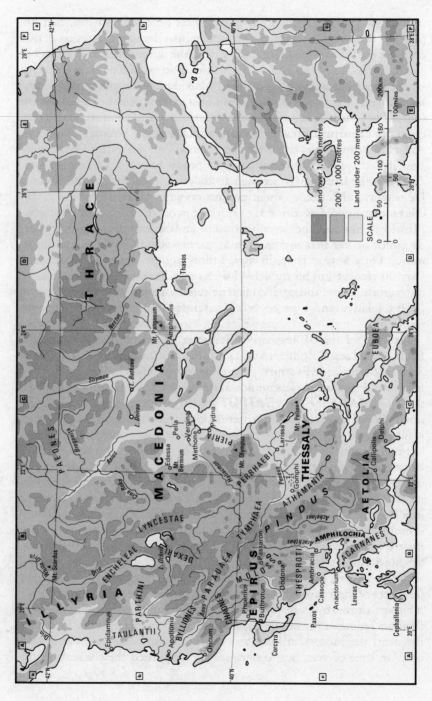

Map 9 Northern Greece in the time of Pyrrhus.

military assembly. He also acted as high priest and supreme judge, except in cases of capital offences, which were judged by the military assembly. But the king was entitled to conclude foreign treaties and to recruit mercenaries in his own name. In his *Life of Pyrrhus* (5.5), Plutarch records that it was the custom for the Molossian king to swear an annual oath at the temple of Zeus at Passaron – not far from modern Jannina – that he would govern according to the constitution. The Molossian people then swore in their turn to support and protect his kingship as laid down by the constitution. There is evidence that on several occasions rulers who violated these laws were expelled or deposed.

For a man like Pyrrhus, who yielded nothing to the other Diadochi or Alexander the Great in his ambitions, energy and desire for glory, this was a very limited and limiting field in which to develop his personality. Thus Pyrrhus soon began to thrust his way beyond the narrow borders of Epirus. After occupying Corcyra (and possibly Leucas?), which he had acquired in 295 through his marriage to Lanassa, daughter of Agathocles, he then in the following year gave support and help to Alexander V, the son of his former enemy Cassander, in his attempt to gain the Macedonian throne. In 294, as the price of his help, Pyrrhus was given the region of Ambracia in southern Epirus, Acarnania, Amphilochia and the regions of Tymphaea and Parauaea in the border country between Epirus and Macedonia. In this connexion a special agreement embodied in a treaty appears to have been made between him and the Acarnanian League.[11] With these extensive land acquisitions Pyrrhus had begun to build up the foundations of a personal power-base in the form of a Hellenistic personal monarchy, and this found an appropriate focal point when he built himself a residence in Ambracia – outside his own native territory. Polygamy being the typical marriage form for the Diadochi, Pyrrhus married, in 292, for the third and fourth time, in quick succession and for purely political ends, first the daughter of the Illyrian prince Bardylis and then a daughter of King Audoleon of the Paeonians. In this way he could safely turn his back on the northern boundaries of Epirus whilst also gaining important allies for his further plans, which were now directed towards winning for himself the throne of Macedonia. Not unnaturally, Lanassa felt herself slighted and left Pyrrhus to marry his keenest rival Demetrius Poliorcetes, to whom she also gave Corcyra as her dowry. After years of strife, Pyrrhus won a victory, through his own personal courage, over Demetrius' general Pantauchus in 289. Disregarding the peace treaty which was subsequently signed, and cleverly emphasizing his relationship with Alexander the Great, whose mother Olympias did indeed come from the

11 Schmitt 1969[J224], 94 n. 459.

ruling house of the Molossians, Pyrrhus succeeded in 287 in persuading
the Macedonian army to proclaim him king of Macedonia. In this
capacity he shortly afterwards paid a visit to Athens and offered a
sacrifice to Athena.

But he could not hold out for long against Lysimachus, a former
bodyguard of Alexander the Great now based in Thrace, whose army
was far superior and who was equally interested in the throne of
Macedonia and the role of successor to Alexander. By the year 284
Pyrrhus had already had to retreat again to Epirus, and he now tried to
extend his kingdom northwards towards Illyria. By 282/1 he had won
Corcyra back again, subjugated some of the neighbouring tribes on the
borders of northern Epirus and Illyria and probably also gained control
of Apollonia, the colony founded by Corcyra on the Adriatic coast in 588
B.C.[12] After the death of Lysimachus in the spring of 281 and that of
Seleucus I in the late summer of the same year, Pyrrhus saw another good
opportunity to assert his claims to Macedonia and took up arms against
the new king Ptolemy Ceraunus, who was as yet by no means firmly
established on the throne. But before any serious fighting began the
Tarentine embassy (p. 457f) reached Pyrrhus. The prospect of gaining
new power and glory in the Western Greek world and – if we can believe
the account in Plutarch (*Pyrrh.* 14.8ff) which was presumably derived
from Pyrrhus' court historian Proxenus – the further possibility of being
able to conquer Sicily and perhaps even to invade North Africa and
Carthage, like his father-in-law Agathocles, all seemed so enticing to the
Molossian king that he speedily concluded a treaty with Ptolemy
Ceraunus. This placed Ceraunus under an obligation to put troops at
Pyrrhus' disposal in support of the planned campaign in Italy, whilst
Pyrrhus in his turn renounced his claims to the Macedonian throne. Now
there was nothing to prevent him going westwards, and for the first time
in her history Rome saw herself face to face with one of the Hellenistic
powers.

III. PYRRHUS IN TARENTUM. THE BATTLE OF
HERACLEA 280 B.C.

The consul Aemilius Barbula's rigorous action against Tarentum resulted first of all in the choice of a new general, by the name of Agis,
whose good connexions with Rome, it was hoped, would bring about a
peaceful end to the conflict. But shortly afterwards two of Pyrrhus'
advance divisions anchored in the city's harbour in quick succession.
The first 3,000-strong division was commanded by Pyrrhus' closest

---

[12] App. *Ill.* 7.

confidant and adviser, Cineas the Thessalian, whilst the second was led by the general Milo. Any further attempt to reach an amicable settlement with Rome was immediately halted and Agis was replaced by a man acceptable to the king. But Pyrrhus' negotiations in Macedonia and the military preparations for his expedition across the Adriatic dragged on and the new magistrate in Tarentum renewed the appeal to the king for help, supported by the Samnites, Lucanians and Messapians, who likewise felt threatened by Rome. Their doubtless wildly exaggerated promise to provide Pyrrhus with over 350,000 soldiers and at least 20,000 horsemen resulted in official endorsement of the Italian campaign by the authorities in the Epirote League and the levying of a federal army. This was only possible once the king had laid his plans and objectives before the assembly of the League. As already mentioned, Pyrrhus was certainly as outstanding a strategist as he was a tactician in the military field. He was impetuous and daring in battle, but he was equally an immensely prudent, skilful and – if it should prove necessary – also unscrupulous politician. By proclaiming his undertaking to be a kind of panhellenic campaign to free all Greeks in southern Italy once and for all from the perpetual threat of the barbarian world, he succeeded first and foremost in securing the essential participation of the troops of the Epirote League, which were to form the core and backbone of what was otherwise a pretty motley army. Over and above this he succeeded in winning the support of the other Hellenistic states, whose rulers were no doubt only too glad to see this restless and dangerous man seek an arena for his activities elsewhere. Thus he received Macedonian auxiliary troops and twenty Indian war elephants from Ptolemy Ceraunus. Antigonus Gonatas put at his disposal the ships which were indispensable for the sea crossing and the securing of reinforcements. Antiochus I of Syria sent money; and a series of gold coins later minted in Syracuse and bearing the portrait of Berenice as Artemis suggests that in all probability he also received money from Ptolemy I of Egypt. In his cleverly thought-out propaganda campaigns in Greece, southern Italy and later in Sicily, Pyrrhus deftly referred to his descent from Achilles and from Alexander the Great. He took the stage as their heir and equally as avenger of the death of his uncle Alexander the Molossian who had been murdered in southern Italy. The coins minted under Pyrrhus in Tarentum, Locri and Syracuse at the time of his campaigns make this particularly clear. On all the tetradrachms, which, on the evidence of die-links, were all issued from a single mint, probably at Locri, we find the picture of Zeus of Dodona and his consort Dione (Fig. 53b), the two main Epirote gods, who were also worshipped on the other side of the Adriatic. On other denominations appear the figure of Athena Promachos as champion against the barbarians, the head of Athena and a Nike bearing a trophy,

464

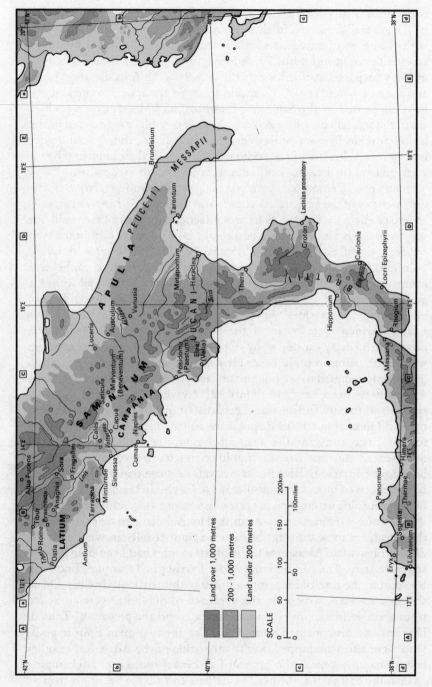

Map 10 South Italy in the time of Pyrrhus.

SCALE

Land over 1,000 metres

200 - 1,000 metres

Land under 200 metres

0   50   100   150   200km

0   50   100miles

LATIUM

Rome
Tibur
Praeneste
Ostia
Antium
Tarracina
Anagnia
Sora
Fregellae
Alba Fucens
Minturnae
Sinuessa
Cales
Volturnus
Capua
Cumae
Naples

CAMPANIA

SAMNIUM
Saticula
Malventum
(Beneventum)
Caudium
Luceria

APULIA
PEUCETII
Ausculum
Aufidus
Venusia
Metapontum
Heraclea
Siris
Posidonia
(Paestum)
Elea
(Velia)
LUCANI

Tarentum

Brundisium

MESSAPII

Thurii
Siris

BRUTTII
Hipponium
Croton
Laginian promontory
Caulonia
Locri Epizephyrii
Rhegium
Messana

Himera
Panormus
Thermae
Segesta
Eryx
Lilybaeum

Fig 53a . Didrachm with head of Achilles on obverse, Thetis with legend *ΒΑΣΙΛΕΩΣ ΠΥΡΡΟΥ* ('of King Pyrrhus') on reverse.

Fig. 53b. Tetradrachm with head of Zeus of Dodona on obverse, Dione with same legend on reverse.

clearly in imitation of the gold staters of Alexander the Great, which were in circulation everywhere at this time. The head of Heracles in the lion's skin is similarly a deliberate link with both the great Macedonian king and also the most famous of the Greek heroes – both likewise symbols of the fight against the barbarians. Later Pyrrhus was to hold a great display of festive games in honour of his ancestor Heracles on Mount Eryx in Sicily. On the obverse of the didrachms there is a representation of his ancestor Achilles (Fig. 53a), possibly bearing the features of Pyrrhus himself – like silver coins of Alexander the Great which portray him as Heracles. Because of the constitutional restrictions on his rule in Epirus there were no coins with an official head of Pyrrhus, as was customary among all the other Hellenistic rulers of the time. On the reverse of these didrachms there is a figure of Thetis who, as in the *Iliad*, is depicted taking a costly shield and other new weapons across the sea to her son Achilles, fighting outside Troy. For his contemporaries this meant that just as the great Achilles conquered the Trojans, so likewise, with the aid of the gods, the Aeacid Pyrrhus, his descendant, would fight and conquer the barbarian Romans, who were the descendants of the Trojans. Other coins show figures such as Artemis, Demeter and Persephone, others again Phthia, who could signify either the king's mother or a personification of the Thessalian countryside, the homeland of Achilles. Taken as a whole these coins conjure up an impression of

South Italy or Sicily, without surrendering their general Greek character.

The army with which Pyrrhus left Epirus in the spring of 280 – after consulting the oracle of Zeus at Dodona and receiving a favourable response – consisted of 22,500 foot soldiers, including 2000 archers and 500 armed with slings, 3000 cavalry and 20 war elephants. At its core was the combined Molossian, Thesprotian and Chaonian levy, reinforced with mercenaries from Aetolia, Thessaly, Athamania, Acarnania and the rest of Hellas. The so-called φίλοι – the friends of the king – commanded the individual divisions and together formed the royal council of war, being in this respect entirely comparable to the leading Hetairoi, the Companions of Alexander the Great.

The crossing to Italy, made with the help of Tarentine and Macedonian ships, proved difficult. A severe storm scattered the armada so that to begin with Pyrrhus arrived in Tarentum with only part of his army. But even so he was immediately chosen as στρατηγὸς αὐτοκράτωρ – that is, as supreme commander, with unlimited authority. He adopted vigorous measures to strengthen the city's defensive capabilities, not only occupying the fortress immediately with his own Epirote troops so that he had a better hold on the city, but also forbidding all theatrical performances, closing the gymnasia and prohibiting the συσσίτια, or communal messes, which met there according to Laconian custom: Tarentum was the one colony founded by Sparta. He conscripted all able-bodied young men for military service and demanded heavy financial sacrifices from the rest of the citizens. Any dissipation or desertion was harshly punished. He aimed to increase the effectiveness of his army to the optimum through continual training. When some of the aristocrats tried to exploit the unrest and discontent which soon arose in Tarentum, by stirring up the people against the Molossian king, they were immediately deported to Epirus or put to death without further ado. Pyrrhus even brought his influence to bear on the city's mint, whose autonomy he always formally recognized, for alongside the picture of the dolphin-rider there appeared subsidiary symbols referring to the king on the Tarentine staters: the lightning and eagle of Zeus of Dodona, a spearhead as a symbol of 'the house of Aeacus powerful with spears' – as Leonidas of Tarentum calls Pyrrhus' line in an epigram[13] –, an elephant and the helmet of the Macedonian kings with the two goat's horns, worn both by Pyrrhus and by Alexander the Great before him.[14]

The news of the king's arrival in Tarentum caused consternation in

---

[13] *Anth. Pal.* VI.130.

[14] In the Alexander Mosaic in Naples the horned helmet lies on the ground beneath the king, who is fighting bare-headed. For Pyrrhus cf. Plut. *Pyrrh.* 11.11; for Philip V, Livy XXVII.33.3.

Rome. The Romans had only recently succeeded in defeating the united army of the Boii and Etruscans at Lake Vadimon and had at long last managed to bind the most important Etruscan communities by treaty to Rome. Nor had it proved easy for Rome to defend herself against the Senones who had descended upon her from northern Italy in the same year, although everything had ended extremely satisfactorily with the annexation of the *ager Gallicus* and the founding of the colony of Sena Gallica on the Adriatic. The heavy losses incurred during the Third Samnite War (298–290), which had finally brought Rome and her allies to supremacy in Central Italy, were still a painful memory. The fact was that Rome urgently needed a long period of peace in which to consolidate what she had achieved so far. Since the city on the Tiber was also involved time and again in battles with the Etruscans, and since the Samnites and Lucanians still remained bitter enemies, Rome had to strain every muscle if she was to succeed against Pyrrhus. Additional troops were therefore levied, allegedly even from the *proletarii* – that class of citizen without means which was normally exempt from taxation or military service and which could only be called up in time of *tumultus maximus*, in cases, that is, of extreme emergency. Roman troops were quartered in allied Greek cities such as Rhegium, Thurii and Locri (Map 10). Rome itself was placed under the protection of a strong garrison.

In 281/0, contrary to normal practice, L. Aemilius Barbula had not led his army from Tarentum back to their winter quarters, but had withdrawn to the area around Venusia so as to be able to keep the Samnites and Lucanians in check. P. Valerius Laevinus, one of the two new consuls for the year 280, marched with another contingent towards the king and tried to cut him off from the Lucanians, who had promised him reinforcements. It would seem that both Roman commanders achieved their aim at first, for Pyrrhus set up camp in the plain between Pandosia and Heraclea, north of the river Siris, and bided his time. His army was outnumbered by the Romans, who were about 30,000 strong, for he had left some of his troops behind for the protection of Tarentum. As the hoped-for reinforcements from the local tribes and the other Greek cities had not yet materialized, the king had to try to gain time. So he sent an envoy to Valerius Laevinus with the suggestion that the dispute with Tarentum should be settled by a neutral court of arbitration. This was a perfectly customary procedure among the Hellenistic states at that time and even earlier. It was also a procedure which Pyrrhus himself recommended in his treatise on tactics – a document which has unfortunately since disappeared – where he argued that before any battle priority should be given to exploring all possible diplomatic means of reaching a settlement in order to avoid unnecessary bloodshed. Pyrrhus held to this principle of negotiation both now and later, after his victory at Heraclea, even though he was in fact in a favourable position; as a result he appears not at all a man who thrived on the adventure of war, who sought decisions by battle alone – as some ancient sources and modern research alike would have him.[15]

But the Roman consul, who was on the opposite side of the river, declined the suggestion, although acceptance would have meant friendship and alliance with the Epirote. Perhaps the Roman feared that the setting up of a court of arbitration of this kind would inevitably be to Rome's disadvantage, or perhaps he hoped to bring about a military decision before Pyrrhus' army outnumbered his own. It was the Roman consul too who opened the attack and ordered his cavalry, which was stationed on the wings, to cross the Siris. This manoeuvre meant that the Epirotes, who were drawn up beside the river, were in danger of being trapped in a pincer movement, and they withdrew hurriedly, leaving the way open for both legions to cross unhindered. When the Greek phalanx clashed with the Romans it was in great danger for a while, though Pyrrhus appeared everywhere among his men, inspiring courage wherever he went. Pyrrhus usually had his elephants in the centre acting as a wedge, but on this occasion he had divided them between the two wings on either side and when he brought them into action against the Roman cavalry the legions were terrified at the unaccustomed sight of the wild, loudly trumpeting beasts and began to flee in panic. The great Hannibal himself – who in conversation with Scipio Africanus is said to have called Pyrrhus the best commander after Alexander the Great – repeated this tactical concept with great success at the battle on the Trebia in 218. Pyrrhus took the enemy camp and only nightfall put an end to the pursuit of the enemy. The remnant of the Roman army escaped to Venusia but over 7000 men had fallen and 1800 had been taken prisoner. Yet the Molossian king is said to have exclaimed, 'Another such victory and we are lost!', for he too had lost 4000 soldiers, among them some of his trusted friends and best officers, and replacing them would prove extremely difficult. (The expression 'Pyrrhic victory' is derived from this statement, though it is in fact modern.) Pyrrhus was impressed by the courage of the enemy soldiers and gave orders that the dead – allegedly all wounded in the breast only – be given an honourable burial. He celebrated his victory with votive offerings of captured enemy weapons at his native temple at Dodona. A modest bronze tablet still survives with the votive inscription: 'King Pyrrhus and the Epirotes and the Tarentines to Zeus Naius from the Romans and their allies' (Fig. 54).[16] He sent his own armour and βουκέφαλα – the heads of sacrificial beasts – to the temple of Athena at Lindus on the island of Rhodes. Zeus of

---

[15] Cf. Carcopino 1961[J253], 11ff.   [16] SIG 392.

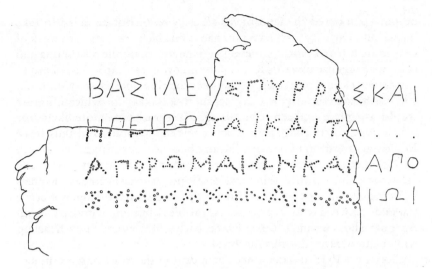

Fig. 54. Dedicatory inscription (with supplements) from Dodona recording Pyrrhus' defeat of the Romans and their allies at Heraclea (*SIG* 392). From Franke 1955 [J257], fig. 2.

Tarentum also received rich votive offerings and the Tarentines likewise sent offerings to Athens to demonstrate the significance of this victory over the barbarians. On Tarentine coins a small elephant and a flying Nike proclaimed the victory they had gained together.

IV. NEW NEGOTIATIONS WITH ROME. THE BATTLE AT AUSCULUM 279 B.C.

Pyrrhus' first great military success had far-reaching consequences, for now not only the Lucanians, Samnites and Bruttii but also the Greek cities, which had so far sat on the fence, openly declared their support for the victor – led by the city of Croton. When Pyrrhus appeared outside Locri the citizens hastily delivered up the Roman garrison, but Pyrrhus immediately let 200 men go free without demanding a ransom. Rhegium, whose inhabitants also wanted to join Pyrrhus, could only be kept loyal to Rome by the exercise of brute force on the part of the Campanian troops stationed there and by the murder of the most influential of her citizens.

But Pyrrhus, like Hannibal after him, did not know how to exploit his victory to the full. His opponent, King Antigonus Gonatas of Macedonia, is said to have remarked mockingly that, as a player, Pyrrhus made many good throws but he did not know how to use them. He now marched the reinforcements he had been awaiting from his allies northwestwards through Lucania and Campania whilst his troops periodically plundered the land of his allies *en route*. But he failed to take Naples and Capua, which Laevinus had been able to occupy in the nick of time as he hurried past. So the king advanced along the Via Latina and through Fregellae towards Rome. His intention can hardly have been to beleaguer the city, protected as it was even at that time by a city wall, and still less to take the city by surprise, an undertaking for which his army would scarcely have been large enough. It seems much more likely that his aim was to try to make contact with the Etruscans and thus force Rome into a war on two fronts. Meanwhile, however, the other consul, Ti. Coruncanius, had defeated and concluded a peace treaty – or at any rate a cease-fire – with Volsinii and Vulci and was free to come to Rome's assistance. It was now Pyrrhus' turn to be faced with the danger of being trapped between the two consular armies and he withdrew from Anagnia, about 60 km. south of Rome, back to Tarentum where he set up winter quarters in the autumn of 280.

From here Pyrrhus tried once again during the following months to reach an amicable agreement with Rome. Ancient records of these negotiations are contradictory and in addition the Roman annalistic tradition is padded out with innumerable anecdotes and imaginative tales which were intended to cast a particularly favourable light on Rome. However, a tradition which goes back to Livy (the most reliable source here), reveals that first of all a legation of three former consuls (*viri consulares*) came to Pyrrhus in Tarentum to negotiate the release of the prisoners of war in return for a ransom or in mutual exchange. They were C. Fabricius Luscinus and Q. Aemilius Papus, the consuls of the year 282, and P. Cornelius Dolabella, who had held that office in 283. Pyrrhus, who was impressed by the personality of Fabricius, took Cineas' advice and, in the hope of achieving acceptable peace terms, released all the prisoners without demanding a ransom, and sent them, probably in the late autumn of 280, back to Rome with Cineas. The Thessalian, whose eloquence was compared by contemporaries to that of Demosthenes, set before the senate the terms under which enmity could be ended: (1) The recognition of freedom (ἐλευθερία) and self-determination (αὐτονομία) for Tarentum and all the other Greek cities in southern Italy – a demand which was raised time and again (and never properly realized) during the struggles for power among the individual Diadochi and which at the same time represented the programme with which Pyrrhus had answered Tarentum's cry for help. (2) The return of all lands taken from the Samnites, Lucanians and Bruttii to their original owners. This probably also included the Roman colonies of Luceria (founded in 314) and Venusia (founded in 291). It implied withdrawal from the whole of Apulia, Bruttium, Lucania and Samnium, possibly of Campania too, and would in effect have reduced Rome's sphere of influence to Latium alone. (3) The conclusion of an alliance, which the sources do not further elaborate, with King Pyrrhus – not, that is, with the Epirotes, nor with Tarentum, which casts a telling light on Pyrrhus' position.

In accordance with Hellenistic and oriental custom, Cineas took costly gifts with him to Rome which he offered to the most influential personalities and their wives and children. But in ignorance of Greek tradition the Romans took this to be an attempt at bribery and refused the gifts. Nevertheless, a majority in the senate appears to have been inclined to accept the Molossian king's undoubtedly harsh conditions because their own strength seemed at an end. Since Pyrrhus had made it clear that he sought peace, they doubtless hoped that further negotiations might achieve some concessions. It was only when Appius Claudius Caecus, now almost blind, spoke out resolutely against the peace proposals that the senate rejected them. Ever since the construction of the Appian Way, which had been named after him, he had taken a particular interest in Campania and southern Italy (cf. p. 447f). His speech must have been quite remarkably vivid and persuasive. It was still frequently read in Cicero's day[17] and was regarded as the oldest document of its kind to be preserved in the Roman archives. Despite this decision, however, Fabricius was sent once more to Pyrrhus to negotiate about the fate of the prisoners-of-war, who now faced the prospect of being returned to Pyrrhus and sold as slaves. With a generous and characteristic gesture, Pyrrhus released them and declared that he did not wish to haggle over the price of their freedom but would prefer to pit his strength against Rome once more on the battlefield. Cineas is said to have considered the Roman senate to be like an assembly of kings[18] but Pyrrhus was quite their equal in dignity and self-assurance.

After the breakdown of negotiations with Rome, the king reinforced his military capability and also recruited new mercenaries, mostly from southern Italy. Not unnaturally the Greek cities, for the sake of whose liberty and independence, after all, the whole campaign was being undertaken, were now called upon to finance operations. Tarentum had to reduce the average weight of her silver staters from 7.9 g. to 6.5 g. so that she could mint more money. The so-called Temple Archives of Locri show what immense sums of money Pyrrhus also managed to obtain elsewhere, and reveal too how rich and flourishing these cities were. The archives consist of thirty-eight bronze tablets with inscriptions from the temple of Zeus Olympios which once stood in Locri, and were found in a stone box in the winter of 1958–9.[19] Seven of the inscriptions can be dated to the time of Pyrrhus, between September 281

---

[17] Cic. *Brut.* 61; *Sen.* 16; cf. Sen. *Ep.* 114.13.   [18] Plut. *Pyrrh.* 15.6.

[19] De Franciscis 1972[J44]; cf. Panuccio 1974[J98], 105–20. The dating of these archives is still controversial. Musti in Musti 1979[J118], 211ff envisages three possibilities: (1) that the king referred to is indeed Pyrrhus, (2) that he is Agathocles, or even (3) – though this is unlikely – that he is a city magistrate with the title of βασιλεύς.

and September 275. They reveal that during these six years no fewer than
11,240 silver talents were paid out of temple funds 'to the king' in the
form of loans or taxes. The Greek word συντέλεια is used, which could
perhaps best be translated here as 'contribution towards the common
cause'. This sum represents approximately 295 metric tons of silver, an
amount corresponding to 45.3 million of the Tarentine silver coins of the
time, weighing 6.5 g. each, or 53.6 million of Pyrrhus' drachmai weighing 5.5 g. each. With this huge sum about 20–24,000 mercenaries could
be paid their customary daily drachma each for six years. At Ausculum
Pyrrhus' army numbered some 40,000 but it was considerably smaller the
rest of the time. Temple income was derived from taxes, collections,
various special dues, and gifts to the gods, from the sale of wheat, barley,
wine and olive oil grown on temple lands, from the sale of tiles and bricks
of the temple's own production and lastly but by no means least from the
considerable revenue from temple prostitution which was customary at
Locri in times of crisis. Locri had to raise the highest sums of 2685 talents
after the battle of Heraclea and of 2452 talents in September 276 after the
king's return from Sicily. These annual accounts also reveal that, contrary to the statements of some ancient authors, Locri never fell into
Roman hands during the wars with Pyrrhus and certainly never joined
Rome voluntarily. It can, of course, be assumed that Pyrrhus received
similar sums of money, given more or less voluntarily, from other cities
allied to him, and especially from Tarentum which was most immediately
concerned.

In the spring of 279 Pyrrhus marched slowly northwards through
Apulia with an army reinforced by his allies to about 40,000 men, taking a
series of small towns on the way. The two new consuls, P. Sulpicius
Saverrio and P. Decius Mus, marched towards him to protect the
colonies of Venusia and Luceria and to prevent the king from penetrating as far as Samnium and from thence threatening Rome herself. The
two armies, about equal in strength, met near Ausculum, by a bridge
over the River Aufidus, swollen with flood-water. It was wooded
country, very unsuitable for the deployment of the cavalry, the Greek
phalanx and the elephants. Cicero's account of the battle,[20] as well as
those of other authors, shows the significance Rome attached to this
conflict, for the consul P. Decius Mus was alleged to have followed the
example of his famous father in 295 (p. 379) (and of his grandfather in
340? (p. 362)) and to have 'devoted' himself to the gods of the Underworld, prepared to die to ensure a Roman victory. But this cannot be
true, for he is still mentioned in other sources as alive in 265 and the Fasti
Capitolini do not record his death in office in 279 as they would normally
have done.

[20] Cic. *Fin.* 11.61; *Tusc.* 1.39.

The battle raged for two days, but we only have relatively detailed, if sometimes contradictory, accounts of the second day, when Pyrrhus moved his army before daybreak to the open plain which suited his tactics better. He then placed his cavalry on the wings beside the Samnites and Macedonians, with the elephants behind them, whilst in the centre, from left to right, were the formations of Greek mercenaries, the Epirotes, the Bruttii and Lucanians, the Tarentines and the Ambracian and Italiote mercenaries. They faced four Roman legions and their auxiliary units. For some time the battle raged back and forth without decision. When the elephants were first sent into the fray, they are said to have failed because of a counter-offensive by the waggons which the Romans had equipped with scythes mounted on movable poles. The Greek left wing retreated and when Pyrrhus extended the centre to cover his left the Romans pushed forward here too. The king's camp was already being plundered and set on fire by Roman allied troops. But eventually Pyrrhus himself, with his cavalry and elephants, penetrated the front of the third and fourth legions who were fighting in the centre and decided the outcome of the battle in his own favour, although he was himself seriously wounded during this personal inter-vention. Though over 6000 Romans fell, the rest managed to retreat to a mountain fort and there hold out against further attacks. The king had lost about 3500 men. He withdrew to Tarentum, all pleasure in his victory overshadowed by the heavy losses. In addition he there received bad news from home. The death of Ptolemy Ceraunus, who had been killed along with most of his army early in 279 in a battle against the Celtic tribes which had once again descended upon Macedonia, had plunged the country into serious internecine struggles.[21] None of the various claimants to the throne were at first able to assert themselves. The Molossians also felt increasingly threatened by these hordes of barbarians who had thrust their way as far as Aetolia, plundering and murdering as they went, for there was no longer the protection which Ptolemy Ceraunus had previously given to Epirus. At all events there were risings and unrest and Pyrrhus had to decide whether or not he ought to return to Greece. The temptation to do so was all the greater since he was forced to admit that there was scarcely any chance of quick successes in Italy in view of the intensified Roman opposition on the one hand and a growing aversion to himself in Tarentum on the other.

V. SYRACUSE CALLS FOR HELP. THE ROMANO-PUNIC TREATY AGAINST PYRRHUS 279–8 B.C.

While Pyrrhus was still hesitating, messengers arrived in Tarentum from Syracuse, offering the king the supreme command in the war against

---

[21] On the Celtic invasion and Ceraunus' death see E. Will in *CAH* VII.1 (Cambridge², 1984), 115.

Carthage. This offer was an open admission of the city's own incompetence and weakness. In fact, not only Syracuse but Greek Sicily generally had been in a state of anarchy since the death of Agathocles in 289. Syracuse itself, torn apart between the army and the civil leader Hicetas, had been obliged to make a treaty with Carthage, by which she lost the towns formerly under her control. Hicetas was soon faced with a series of tyrants – Heracleidas in Leontini, Tyndarion in Tauromenium and Phintias in Acragas – and was himself led to seize supreme power in Syracuse. Phintias was defeated by Hicetas and several cities combined to overthrow him. But soon afterwards, in 279, after being defeated by the Carthaginians, Hicetas was replaced by Thoenon. However, he was unable to assert himself for long. At the time of the offer to Pyrrhus the Syracusans, embittered by Thoenon's despotic rule, and aided by Sosistratus, the new tyrant of Acragas, had driven him out of the city to the off-shore island of Ortygia. From this island with its strong fortress, and with the help of the fleet that was left to him, Thoenon caused much harm to the citizens of Syracuse and disrupted the entire economic and political life of the city. At the same time the Mamertines, the 'sons of Mars', Campanian mercenaries who had formerly fought for the tyrant Agathocles and had settled in Messana on the north-east coast of Sicily in 289,[22] exploited time and again the weakness of the Syracusan state by invading Syracusan territory, plundering, ravaging and taking as slaves any inhabitants who fell into their hands. As the main power in Sicily, Carthage too took the opportunity to do all she could by means of continual raids and skirmishes to reduce the power of what had hitherto always been her most dangerous opponent on the island. Thanks to a situation which resembled civil war in Syracuse and the resultant weakening of Syracusan defences, Carthage could now hope at long last to achieve the goal she had persistently followed for centuries – to bring all Sicily under her sway.

The Syracusan offer seemed extremely tempting to Pyrrhus. As erstwhile son-in-law to Agathocles he could put forward an entirely legitimate claim to his realm, especially since Lanassa, the tyrant's daughter, had borne him the son Alexander whom he, for this reason, designated later as heir to the kingdom of Sicily. Possession of this immensely rich and fertile island, whose wealth was symbolized by the Greek goddess Demeter, would doubtless put him in a far better position than before to play a decisive role in the political life of the Hellenistic states. At the same time it opened up the possibility of pursuing the war against Rome on quite a different basis. It no doubt also appealed to his broad vision and wide-ranging notions to liberate the Greeks on Sicily

<hr/>

[22] For a different and slightly later date for the Mamertine seizure of Messana see below, p. 539.

from the perpetual fear of the Carthaginians whom they despised as barbarians, and possibly even, like Agathocles, to carry the battle over the sea to Africa. Even if there really were renewed peace talks between Pyrrhus and Rome after the battle at Ausculum, as is implied by some, admittedly unreliable, sources, all negotiations were doomed to failure from the moment the king learnt that Rome and Carthage were on the point of forming an alliance against him.

Both Rome and Carthage were pursuing extremely selfish ends. Carthage saw the Syracusan plea for help as a threat to her endeavour to bring all Sicily, Syracuse at long last included, under her own control – an ambition which seemed to be so near fulfilment. However, she feared still more the lust for action and the military genius of the Molossian king who, once landed in Syracuse, would have the support not only of the Syracusans, but doubtless, thanks to his name, of the other Greek cities on the island as well, as he marched against the Carthaginians whom they all feared and hated. Rome on the other hand hoped at last to be rid of the pressure which the king, with his great military experience and his outstanding strategic and tactical skills, had now for some time been exerting on the city and which also meant the continual additional danger of renewed battle with the Etruscans and Samnites, whose sympathies were unequivocally on Pyrrhus' side. But it was Carthage who took the initiative. As early as the autumn of 279 a fleet of 120 Carthaginian warships arrived in Ostia, Rome's harbour at the mouth of the Tiber, and its commander, Mago, offered the senate military aid. The offer was politely refused, but then a new treaty was signed after all, retaining the earlier mutually agreed clauses of the so-called Philinus treaty of 306 – which Polybius incorrectly represents as an anti-Roman fabrication of the Greek historian Philinus, who lived in Acragas in the second half of the third century B.C.[23] This new treaty was the fourth in the long history of Romano-Punic relations, which began in 508/7. The text, which must be understood, it is true, more as a preliminary contract, is preserved in Polybius, but an interpretation of the first part and an exact translation both present difficulties, for the historian, writing in Greek, has obviously tried to give as literal a rendering as possible of the text, which was originally written in antiquated Latin and in the Punic language. Both parties pledged themselves to give mutual military assistance, whereby Carthage was to provide transport ships in both directions for the troops of both powers whenever necessary. Each state was, however, responsible for the payment of its own soldiers. Since the Romans at this time did not yet possess a large, effective war-fleet, the Carthaginians pro-

---

[23] Polyb. III.25.1–6; cf. Schmitt 1969[J224], 101 n. 466. For further discussion both of the treaty of 279/8 and of the problems surrounding the Philinus treaty see below, pp. 532ff.

mised Rome active support at sea, with the express proviso, however, that Carthaginian sailors were not to be forced to fight on land against their will. The individual specifications make it clear that it must have been an alliance against Pyrrhus and not a general treaty. The historical situation also virtually rules out the interpretation held by some that the introductory words refer to a possible agreement or even to a separate peace treaty between either Rome or Carthage and Pyrrhus.[24] Further, there is no mention in the text which has come down to us of a monetary payment to Rome by the Carthaginians: earlier assumptions that the first minting of a silver coinage by the Romans was linked with this treaty and with financial support for Rome, stipulated in a section of the treaty which has not been preserved, have been proved wrong. For only the first two series of what are today known as the Romano-Campanian didrachms can be dated back to the time of the war with Pyrrhus: (1) the coins with the head of Mars on the obverse and a horse's head, possibly in imitation of a Punic model, on the reverse, which can be dated to the years 280–270; (2) those with a laureate head of Apollo on the obverse and a galloping horse and star on the reverse, which were probably minted in 275–270.[25] But the limited number of proven mint-marks and preserved coins reveals that this must have been a very small issue, which would hardly have sufficed to finance a war. The coins were mainly used, along with the heavy cast bronze money, the *aes grave*, for trade with South Italy.[26] There were however two series of *aes grave* whose design demonstrates a clear connexion with the war with Pyrrhus and which must have been made during its final phase or soon after its conclusion. Firstly, there were those currency bars weighing approximately a Roman pound, or 334 g., one *as* in value, with the picture of an Indian elephant on the obverse and a sow on the reverse (Fig. 55).[27] The elephant certainly appears here because Pyrrhus was the first to bring this animal to Italy and employ it in battle, though the discipline and courage of the Roman troops overcame the terror it first aroused. And it is certainly for the same reason that we meet the elephant shortly afterwards as a motif in Latin-Etruscan vase-painting (p. 411). Ancient tradition has it that, in the decisive battle of the war at Beneventum in 275, the king's elephants were put to flight by the sow and its pungent smell, hence the sow on the reverse of the currency. Secondly, there were similar pieces of the same value with the eagle of Iuppiter Capitolinus on the obverse and a Pegasus on the reverse.[28] The latter is frequently found on coins as a symbol of

---

[24] On this issue cf. below, p. 536 with n. 46.   [25] *RRC* nos. 13 and 15.
[26] Cf. p. 415 (with an alternative dating of the Mars/horse's head didrachm and variant interpretation of the purpose of these issues).
[27] *RRC* n. 9.   [28] *RRC* n. 4.

Fig. 55. Cast bronze bar (so-called 'aes signatum') depicting Indian elephant and sow (*RRC* 9; 275–242 B.C.).

Carthage and is here perhaps a definite allusion to the Romano-Punic treaty of 279/8.

The agreement was especially advantageous for Rome, for with the help of the Carthaginian fleet she was in a far better position to attack and blockade Tarentum from the sea – by land the king was stronger. It also seemed possible that in this way reinforcements could be prevented from arriving from Greece, or at any rate their journey could be made extremely hazardous. On the other hand Rome had by no means undertaken to give Carthage massive support against the Greeks in Sicily, no doubt partly out of consideration for the Greek cities in southern Italy, some of which were friendly towards Rome. Carthage believed that the treaty would prevent Rome from making peace with Pyrrhus, thereby rendering it unsafe for the king to leave Italy and so keeping him well away from Sicily and Syracuse. For the Molossian king the treaty meant a strong shift in the relative strengths of the combatants in Italy to his own disadvantage, for from now on he had to reckon not only with Italian troops under Rome's command but also with the Carthaginian fleet and possibly even with Carthaginian land troops as well. But on the other hand, the conquest of Syracuse by the Carthaginians would virtually mean the collapse of his whole policy so far, which had advertised the liberation of the Greeks from the barbarian threat as its foremost objective, and this would be sure to have an extremely negative effect on his reputation both in Italy and in Greece itself. So Pyrrhus, not unwillingly, now turned his attention towards Sicily, the possession of which seemed to open up far greater future possibilities for his ambitions than did Italy.

VI.   PYRRHUS IN SICILY

So, in the spring of 278, after further indecisive fighting in Apulia – it was at this time that Pyrrhus is alleged to have narrowly escaped being

murdered by his personal physician, thanks to a magnanimous warning
from the consul C. Fabricius – the king began to make the necessary
preparations for the crossing to Sicily. It would seem that Rome expected
a decision of this nature, for at this time, and evidently very soon after the
ratification of the treaty for mutual assistance, the Carthaginians transported 500 Roman soldiers on their ships to Rhegium. But the attempt to
take the city in a surprise coup and thereby to gain control of the
strategically important straits between Sicily and the southern tip of Italy
failed, though it did prove possible to win over the Mamertines in
Messana to an alliance with Carthage.[29] Not long afterwards the Punic
fleet of about 130 ships, under the command of the admiral Mago,
appeared off Syracuse and blockaded the great harbour. The Syracusans'
cry for help became more insistent than ever and the king was forced to
take action. Once again he sent first his trusted friend Cineas to negotiate
in advance with the Greek cities on the island and thus by diplomatic
means to prepare the ground thoroughly before his own arrival. Then, in
the summer of 278, he himself set out for Sicily with a relatively modest
army of only 8000 foot soldiers and a small number of horsemen and
elephants, leaving a large garrison behind in Tarentum under the command of the reliable general Milo. Other Epirote troops remained
stationed in various places allied to him, as protection against the
Romans and against the danger of betrayal, though they could not
prevent the two new consuls, C. Fabricius Luscinus and Q. Aemilius
Papus, from winning back, in the course of the year, some of the peoples
and cities which had previously gone over to Pyrrhus. In Rome in the
winter of the same year, they celebrated a triumph over the Lucanians,
Samnites, Tarentines and Bruttii, which shows that their successes must
have been considerable.

On his voyage with the expeditionary corps southwards from
Tarentum along the coast, Pyrrhus landed first at Locri, which still
had to provide strong financial backing. Then he crossed over to
Tauromenium in Sicily. Tyndarion, the tyrant there, was willing to join
him and placed his army under the king's command. When he landed at
Catana Pyrrhus was greeted jubilantly as the long-awaited liberator and
honoured with wreaths of gold. Not only this, but he also received
reinforcements in the form of a citizen levy. The army then proceeded
overland towards Syracuse, the fleet of about 60, mostly Tarentine, ships
sailing ready for action along the coast and covering the advance of the
land troops. As the king approached Syracuse the Punic admiral hastily
lifted the blockade, for although he had about 100–130 ships at his
disposal, he was in danger of being caught between the 140 Syracusan

[29] Diod. XXII.7.4.

ships that lay in the harbour and Pyrrhus' fleet at sea. The Carthaginian army also lifted the siege and beat a hurried retreat. Pyrrhus was thus able to enter Syracuse in triumph amid the cheers of the Greeks, and the city was formally handed over to him by Sosistratus. Thoenon then likewise handed over Ortygia and the fleet, a welcome reinforcement. Thus Pyrrhus' skilful negotiations even succeeded – perhaps under threat – in reconciling the two antagonistic former rulers of the city. The other Greek cities on Sicily, hopeful of a near and final end to the ever-present Punic threat, all sent envoys to Syracuse announcing their desire to support Pyrrhus and to subordinate themselves to him. Among them, for example, was Heracleidas, the tyrant of Leontini, who sent Pyrrhus an army of 4000 foot soldiers and 500 horsemen. Very soon the Molossian king had at his disposal an army of over 30,000 men and 2500 horse and the Carthaginians withdrew to their original dominions, their *epikratia*, in the west of the island.

In spring 277 Pyrrhus marched via Enna, which of its own accord had forced its Punic garrison to withdraw towards Acragas. Here the tyrant Sosistratus, who had shared in the invitation to Pyrrhus to come to Syracuse, joined the king, allegedly with thirty other towns within his territory, and strengthened the king's army by a further 8000 foot soldiers and 800 horsemen. In a triumphal march Heraclea Minoa, Azonae, Selinus, Halicyae, Segesta and the other towns of the interior, both large and small, fell into Pyrrhus' hands one after another in rapid succession. Even the inaccessible, strongly fortified hill fortress on Mount Eryx (Map 15: p. 561) on the north-west coast was besieged and taken. Splendid victory celebrations and contests were held there in honour of Heracles, who had been revered here since ancient times and who was, of course, held to be an ancestor of the Aeacid line. After his first successes, if not earlier, Pyrrhus – who at first appears to have had only a hegemonial position in Sicily – seems to have been proclaimed king – βασιλεύς – according to Greek custom by the Siceliot troops and was thus confirmed as legitimate successor to Agathocles. Other accounts, however, imply that it was on his arrival in Syracuse that he was greeted with this honorary title, which was tied to the person and not to a particular territory. Be that as it may, he designated Alexander, his son by Lanassa, as heir to the Sicilian kingdom, whilst Helenus was to succeed to his dominions in Italy – whatever one is to understand by that – and Ptolemy to those in Epirus.[30]

When Panormus also fell and the Mamertines had suffered several serious defeats in the north-east of the island, the Carthaginians were left with only the important harbour of Lilybaeum on the west coast under

---

[30] Justin. XXIII.3.

their control. Since they had reason to fear losing even this last bastion and with it every vestige of influence they had on the island, they offered Pyrrhus peace talks. They declared themselves willing to pay a large war-indemnity and – despite the treaty with Rome – to put ships at the king's disposal for further operations. This implies that they hoped – indeed even expected – that the king would return to Italy. At first Pyrrhus was indeed willing to accept what appeared to be a favourable offer, for the situation in Italy had certainly not developed in his favour during 277. The consul C. Cornelius Rufinus had conquered Croton, now therefore lost to Pyrrhus' cause, though contrary to later literary tradition the newly found inscriptions from the temple archives (p. 471f) show that Locri had been able to hold out. But Caulonia had fallen into the hands of the enemy and the Samnites, Lucanians and Bruttii had suffered repeated defeats as is evident from the records of triumphal processions held in Rome in 277 and 276. The enthusiasm for Pyrrhus' cause and willingness to support a king fighting in Sicily – that is, relatively far away – were decreasing steadily. But the royal council summoned by Pyrrhus, which included not only his trusted confidants but also repre-sentatives of the individual Sicilian cities, decided after lengthy debate to turn down the Punic peace offer. The whole of Sicily must be liberated; otherwise all effort and sacrifice would have been in vain. Every single Carthaginian base on the island was a potential starting-point for future new conflicts.

But the determined siege of Lilybaeum which was now begun had to be broken off after two months without result. It was virtually imposs-ible to take the city from the landward side, and there was scant hope of carrying out a successful sea blockade – Pyrrhus' fleet was just not large enough. For this reason he now set his hopes upon a campaign in Africa. Like Agathocles, he wanted to transport the war in a newly built fleet across the sea to the homeland of the enemy and force a conclusive decision there. But he tried to put his plans into practice with characteris-tic impatience and this very soon led to serious conflict with his allies. For not only did he begin – like Agathocles and like other Hellenistic rulers of his time – to exact taxes from them as though they were his subjects, but he also demanded the provision of oarsmen and sailors for his new fleet and the money with which to pay them. Not surprisingly, the cities were even more angered at his encroachment on their own autonomy, especially when he interfered with their jurisdiction and took upon himself the direction of individual cases in which he had a particular interest. He also confiscated as royal lands property which had once belonged to Agathocles, dispossessed the present owners and made gifts of vast stretches of land to his friends and followers. Thus the latter in turn acquired substantial influence in the cities and these Epirotes, who had so suddenly risen to rank and wealth, tended frequently to despise the local population which was in fact culturally far their superior. In this way a body of strong opposition developed, especially in Syracuse, similar to that which had grown up in Tarentum – an opposition which did not shrink from renewing broken links with Carthage and betraying the Greek cause, as so often, for its own selfish ends. This led Pyrrhus to take vigorous action. Thoenon and other Syracusans suspected of conspiring with the enemy were put to death. Sosistratus managed to escape in time but by his actions the king lost one of his most valuable allies, who ruled not only over Acragas but also over a large area of the rest of the island. Pyrrhus' measures did not, however, prevent some of the cities from openly joining the Mamertines and others the Carthaginians, and the latter, unhindered by Pyrrhus, proceeded to bring a powerful new army over to Sicily, because they could now hope to reverse the setbacks they had suffered so far. The situation worsened when envoys arrived in Syracuse from the Samnites, Lucanians and Bruttii urgently begging Pyrrhus to return as soon as possible to Italy, for Rome had increased the pressure on these tribes still further and they saw in Pyrrhus their only hope of changing the situation. Pyrrhus also had reason to fear that his overland link with Tarentum, which led through Bruttium, might be cut off and that all his plans would collapse like a house of cards if Samnium and Lucania should fall to the Romans. His decision to abandon the Sicilian expedition and to return to Tarentum was made the easier since he was forced to admit that the Sicilian cause was already all but lost – an outcome for which he himself was certainly not free from blame.

VII.   PYRRHUS RETURNS TO ITALY. THE BATTLE OF
BENEVENTUM 275 B.C.

Plutarch[31] records Pyrrhus as saying that he left the island behind him as a wrestling ground for the Romans and Carthaginians, as he set sail from Syracuse in the late summer of 276, with 110 warships and numerous cargo ships. But as he sailed northwards along the Sicilian coast he was surprised by a Punic fleet not far from Rhegium and suffered heavy losses. Over seventy of his warships were sunk and many others badly damaged. Only a dozen escaped unharmed. Yet the Carthaginians had not achieved their real objective – the destruction of Pyrrhus' entire army, for the fleet of transport ships was able to get away and land unhindered at Locri. From Locri, Pyrrhus went to Rhegium, but he was unable to take the city because of the strong resistance put up by the Campanian garrison there, which was under Roman command and

---

[31] Plut. *Pyrrh.* 23.8.

reinforced by Mamertines from Messana. As he was retreating from the city he was ambushed by the Mamertines and suffered further heavy losses. His army only escaped from this precarious situation with the help of the personal intervention of the king himself who, in single combat, allegedly cut an opponent in two with a single blow of his sword. He finally arrived back in Locri with 20,000 men and 3000 horsemen – even now a considerable army – and once again exacted a particularly high sum in taxation from the city (p. 472) in order to cover his losses and recruit new mercenaries. Not content with this, he also confiscated the treasures of the temple of Persephone in Locri, to the great indignation of the Greeks. He gave most of them back again, however, when the ships carrying the booty to Tarentum ran into a severe storm, which he took to be a bad omen. We do not know for certain whether Pyrrhus now also turned once more to Greece, and in particular to Antigonus Gonatas of Macedonia and Antiochus I of Syria, with a plea or even a demand for further support. The Samnites and Lucanians, weary after three years of heavy losses in their war with Rome, showed little inclination to continue to support the king without reservation. But on the other hand, the consuls of the year 275 found it equally difficult to mobilize a new army, the more so as Rome had been visited in 276 by an outbreak of plague which had taken a heavy toll of lives. Livy reports a drop in the number of citizens from 287,222 in the year 280 to only 271,224 in 275. The consul M'. Curius Dentatus threatened any citizen who sought to evade military service with the sale of his person into slavery and the disposal of all his property,[32] the first time such a threat had ever been issued and a sure indication of just how war-weary the Romans also were.

In the spring of 275 both consuls moved their armies into strategic positions to prevent Pyrrhus from advancing towards Rome once again. L. Cornelius Lentulus stationed himself in Lucania in order either to intercept Pyrrhus at this early stage if possible or to cut him off from his lines of communication in the event of an attack on Rome. M'. Curius meanwhile occupied the passes near the town of Malventum, which later, in 268, became a Roman colony with Latin rights and was renamed Beneventum. His aim was to hinder Pyrrhus from advancing towards Capua and Rome. Pyrrhus ordered one division to protect his south flank against Lentulus and himself marched against M'. Curius. For the first time his army was seriously outnumbered by the Romans, so he tried to gain a tactical advantage by finding a favourable height from which he could make a surprise attack on the enemy camp. But his Epirote troops, unacquainted with the terrain, got lost during a night-time advance to the planned position for attack and were beaten back with relative ease

---

[32] Livy, *Per.* xiv; Val. Max. vi.3.4.

next morning by the Romans, who had been observing their approach. In the ensuing battle on the plain the exhausted Greeks broke down in face of the onslaught of the legions and the Romans succeeded in so frightening the king's elephants with burning arrows that they stampeded and charged towards their own ranks. Eight of the animals were captured and shown in Rome for the first time in 272, in Curius' triumphal procession. The Romans also took Pyrrhus' camp, thus giving their officers their first opportunity to see for themselves how the Greeks managed undertakings of this kind. Later, when he was censor, M'. Curius had Rome's second great aqueduct, the Anio Vetus, built from some of the booty which was taken here and allotted to him as commander (p. 408).

VIII. RETURN TO EPIRUS. DEATH OF PYRRHUS, 272 B.C.

Pyrrhus was now in danger of being trapped between the armies of the two consuls and he withdrew with all speed to Tarentum after his defeat. There are no reliable figures for his losses – later Roman sources exaggerated shamelessly – but they were at any rate high enough for him to decide to return to Epirus, and in the autumn of 275 he set sail for Greece with only 8000 soldiers and 500 horsemen. He left his son Helenus and his general Milo behind in Tarentum with a relatively strong contingent of troops to demonstrate that he had by no means abandoned his Italian plans and would continue to intervene on behalf of the freedom of the Greek cities and especially of Tarentum. But in reality he had been defeated by a stronger opponent, and he knew it.

It is true that Pyrrhus did win back the title of king of Macedonia in 274, within a mere few months of his return, in a battle against Antigonus Gonatas. Already decked out in the insignia of this office, he was able, through the continuing magnetism of his personality, to bring the Macedonian phalanx over to his side during a battle in the gorges of the Aous, near present-day Tepelene in Albania. But even this success did not put him in a position to return to Italy, and in addition, his reputation in Macedonia, at first immensely high, shrank very rapidly when he left his own occupying troops in Macedonian towns and allowed his Celtic mercenaries to plunder the tombs of the Macedonian kings at Aegae. These tombs were rediscovered in 1976 near the Hellenistic palace of Vergina, not far to the south of Beroea in the foothills of Olympus. In the winter of 274/3 he summoned his son Helenus back from Tarentum, though Milo still remained for the time being. Restlessly pursuing one new scheme after another, he appeared with an army in the Peloponnese in the following spring of 272, on the excuse that his general Cleonymus, son of the Spartan king Cleomenes II, wished to be reinstated in his

ancestral rights in Laconia. At the same time he announced his desire to
free all Greece from the domination of Antigonus Gonatas – a slogan
which was, of course, far too transparent to take anybody in, though the
Aetolians did make an alliance with him. But an attack on Sparta failed,
with considerable losses, and his own son Ptolemy was among the dead.
In the late autumn of 272, after a few skirmishes in Laconia, Pyrrhus
marched to Argos, where Antigonus had appeared with an army. Thanks
to the secret help of a friend, a citizen of Argos, and ignoring the city's
neutrality, Pyrrhus forced his way into the town – despite unfavourable
sacrificial omens. But in the ensuing street fighting he was mortally
wounded by a tile, hurled down by a woman from the roof of her house,
when she saw him threaten her son – an ignominious end for so famous a
man. His body was burnt by the victors and later a memorial was erected
to him on the site, with the king's weapons and pictures of his elephants.
The records are contradictory as to whether his mortal remains were
taken to the temple of Demeter in Argos or laid to rest in the Pyrrheum in
Ambracia where he had built his residence.

IX. EPILOGUE

Doubtless influenced by the news of the Molossian king's death,
Tarentum soon afterwards (in 272) surrendered to the Romans and was
included among the naval allies (*socii navales*).[33] Milo and the Epirotes
were granted safe conduct. The long years of war with Pyrrhus and their
heavy losses nevertheless continued to determine Roman policy towards
the other Hellenistic powers and especially towards Philip V of Macedonia[34] for a long time to come. The king's personality, to which statues at
Athens, Olympia and Callipolis in Aetolia bear witness, also continued to
fascinate Roman authors from Ennius[35] until long after Plutarch, in a
way quite different from that of Hannibal. For Pyrrhus, like Alexander
the Great, whom he took for his example and whose heir he felt himself
to be, united military genius with personal courage, diplomatic skill with
winning charm, charisma even, and was totally devoid of the 'Punic'
slyness and cruelty which were later to become proverbial in Rome.
Under Pyrrhus, remote Epirus played a brief but significant role within
the sphere of Graeco-Roman politics – indeed, if the king had been
successful, its role would have had significance on the stage of world
politics. Despite his wars, Pyrrhus pressed ahead with the construction
of his residence in Ambracia, and with new buildings for the sanctuary at
Dodona and other places in Epirus. He found time to encourage the arts

[33] Schmitt 1969[J224], 128 n. 475.   [34] Livy XXXI.7.8–12.   [35] Cic. *Div.* 11.116–17.

and foster trade with southern Italy and Sicily which continued to flourish from then on.[36]

It comes as no surprise that the rediscovery of Plutarch in England, which was to influence so greatly the works of Shakespeare, led also to works inspired by Pyrrhus. In 1695 Charles Hopkins dedicated an – admittedly mediocre – drama called *Pyrrhus* to the Duke of Gloucester[37] as a kind of *Fürstenspiegel*. Nicolas Poussin painted *The young Pyrrhus on his Flight to Illyria* in Paris as early as 1665. Still earlier, the Albanian national hero George Kastrioti Skanderbeg called up memories of both Pyrrhus and Alexander the Great in his struggle against the Turks in 1443–68, and for this reason also wore like them a helmet with goat's horns in battle. His contemporaries called him *princeps Epirotarum* and the Albanians call themselves to this day 'Skipetars' – Sons of the Eagle – the name Pyrrhus, the 'eagle', used to flatter his Epirote soldiers.[38]

---

[36] Breglia 1941[J252], 193ff.

[37] C. Hopkins, *Pyrrhus, King of Epirus*. A Tragedy, acted at the New Theatre in Little Lincolns-Inn-Fields, by his Majesty's Servants, printed for Samuel Briscoe in Covent-Garden: Peter Buck, at the Sign of the Temple, and Daniel Dring, at the Harrow and Crown, in Fleet-street, 1695.

[38] Plut. *Pyrrh.* 10.1; cf. Nederlof 1940[B122], 48.

CHAPTER 11

CARTHAGE AND ROME[1]

H. H. SCULLARD

I. CARTHAGINIAN PUBLIC AND PRIVATE LIFE

(a) *The Carthaginian state*

The Carthaginian state impressed the ancient world not only for its
wealth, but also for its stability and endurance. Its riches may have
provoked envy, and its increasing corruption contempt, but its tenacity
evoked respect even from Greeks and Romans, its age-long enemies.
Thus Cicero wrote (*Rep.* fr. 3) 'Carthage would never have held an
empire for six hundred years had it not been governed with wisdom and
statesmanship', and Aristotle classed its constitution with those of Sparta
and Crete as one of the three actual states which through their stability
most nearly approached the ideal 'mixed' polity (*Pol.* 11.127 b ff): it was in
fact the only non-Hellenic constitution that he included in his long series
of constitutional studies. Isocrates (*Nicocles* 24) echoes the same theme:
'the Carthaginians and Lacedaemonians, who are the best-governed
peoples in the world' (τοὺς ἄριστα τῶν ἄλλων πολιτευομένους). Wealth
and constitutional stability were closely linked. The wealth of Carthage
derived from her territorial empire in North Africa and the western
Mediterranean; it was safeguarded by naval protection of her overseas

---

[1] If Carthaginian historians ever recorded the story of their city and civilization, their works
have perished, together with any other literature that Punic writers may have produced. Thus the
surviving literary sources for Carthaginian history are Greek and Roman authors, men who
belonged to peoples to whom the Punic way of life was alien and whose own states were for long
periods politically hostile to Carthage. But enmity, prejudice and lack of sympathy have not totally
obscured the Carthaginian achievement: thus, for example, Eratosthenes believed that many of the
'barbarians' were civilized, peoples such as Indians, Persians, together with Romans and
Carthaginians 'who are so admirably governed' (*ap.* Strabo 1.4.9, p. 16 c). But for an understanding
of Carthaginian civilization we have largely to depend on the ever increasing body of archaeological
evidence from the countries of the western Mediterranean.

For the First Punic War we have Polybius Book I, which is based on the pro-Roman Fabius Pictor
and the pro-Carthaginian Philinus, though it is not always easy to attribute specific passages to either
the one or the other (further difficulties arise from the possibility that Fabius himself may have used
Philinus). Diodorus' account of the First Punic War is based on Philinus, but he follows Polybius for
the War of the Mercenaries (which Philinus probably did not record). For detailed discussion and
other possible views see Walbank 1945[B181], 1–18; 1957–79[B182], 1.65; 1968–9[B184], 493ff;
1972[B185], 77–8.

trade which in turn provided her with financial means to maintain a strong navy. Further, her commercial success gave political power to a timocratic oligarchy which, by providing the state with the means of hiring a mercenary army instead of depending upon a large citizen militia, decreased the risk of military *coups* and enhanced political stability.

The early history of Carthage has already been described in earlier volumes,[2] including the gradual way she dominated the other Phoenician settlements in the West and added her own quota to the number of Semitic colonies; her extending influence in North Africa, Spain, Sardinia and Sicily; her establishment of a commercial monopoly in western waters and the consequential struggles (at times in concert with the Etruscans) with the Greek cities which challenged her ascendancy; her continuing success in the extreme west and her fluctuating fortunes in Sicily. At times she acted aggressively, but her driving motive was to protect and extend her commerce rather than to seize land for its own sake. It was in response to these needs that her constitution and institutions developed, and her successes came and went. By the sixth century she had emerged as a powerful state, and though in the fifth century her trade with the Greek world declined, she began to exploit further the resources of her rich hinterland and her Libyan subjects. By the mid-fourth century her commerce was flourishing again and she became increasingly open to hellenizing influences; after the death of Alexander the Great she was one of the five great Mediterranean powers, balancing with Roman Italy in the West the three Successor States of the East. It is at this point in her history, in the century or so before her clash with Rome in 264 B.C., that we may glance briefly at her public and private life.

Although the Carthaginian constitution was relatively stable, it naturally underwent considerable change during the centuries, and our knowledge of it is very limited and patchy. Despite the loss of Aristotle's separate treatment, his comparative account of it in his *Politics* provides much useful information for its institutions during his life-time, but its early development is not clear; somewhat more is known about its final stages during the struggles with Rome. As a 'mixed' constitution it allegedly combined the best elements of monarchy, aristocracy and democracy, but in practice it was an oligarchy in which wealth predominated (p. 492). The nature and history of the head of state, representing the monarchical element, is obscure: king or magistrate? Tyre, the mother city of Carthage, had been ruled by hereditary kings, and Greek authors referred to βασιλεῖς at Carthage, while in later times the executive officers

2 See G. Charles-Picard, *CAH* vi, Chap. 11e.

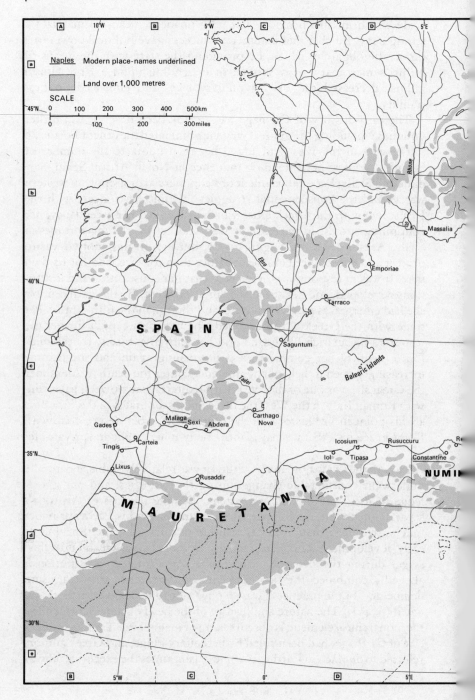

Map 11 The western Mediterranean in the third century.

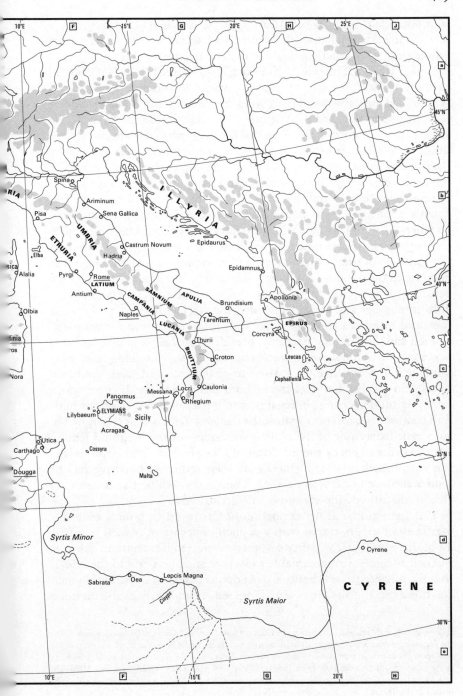

were not called kings (*melekim*) but judges (*shophetim* or in Latin *sufetes*). It remains uncertain whether the word βασιλεύς necessarily implies regal power (and, if so, whether single or dual monarchy) or was loosely used for 'magistrates'. If monarchy did exist, it was based not on birth but on election at least as early as 480 B.C. when according to Herodotus (VII.166) Hamilcar was chosen king because of his courage, and it remained so in the time of Aristotle who records that the βασιλεῖς (he always uses the word in the plural) at Carthage were drawn, not from a single family but from any outstanding family, and were chosen by election and not by seniority. Whatever the nomenclature, these men at this time were not *ipso facto* generals: twice Aristotle (*Pol.* 11.1273 a 30, 37) distinguishes 'kings' and 'generals'. Since the word βασιλεύς was frequently applied to some predominant military leaders, particularly to members of the Magonid family, military power could be, and apparently often was on specific occasions, vested in these magistrates though not inherent in their office – unless it be supposed that originally the βασιλεῖς enjoyed military authority which they lost as a right some time before Aristotle. Roman writers called these executive officers *sufetes*. Two in number and elected annually, they lacked military power, but exercised more than judicial functions: thus they could summon the council and the popular assembly, preside over them and present business to them. Some scholars who believe in an early life-long monarchy think that the *sufetes* even existed at that time, and later gradually overshadowed the kings as the archons did at Athens. If there was a relatively sudden change in regal power, it may well date from the mid-fifth century, as a reaction against the dangers to the state created by the autocratic behaviour of the army commanders of the Magonid family, since in order to check them a Court of One Hundred and Four Judges was established to which generals on their return to Carthage had to render account (Justin. XIX.2.5–6). This might well be the occasion to change the title of the executive officers to *sufetes*.[3]

The discussion and determination of Carthaginian policy, both domestic and foreign, rested with a council or senate of several hundred (300?) life-members, whether co-opted or elected is uncertain. When it reached an agreement acceptable to its own members and to the *sufetes*, this did not need to be submitted to a popular assembly of citizens, which was however consulted in case of disagreement and perhaps also on some

---

[3] Maurin 1962[K82], 16ff argues that the Court of One Hundred and Four Judges was created at the beginning of the fourth century, not in the mid-fifth as is usually believed. For the view that the two eponymous magistrates named *sufetes* in various Punic inscriptions were the annual presidents of the Court of One Hundred and Four Judges see Pareo 1978[K95], 61–87. Inscriptions: Mahjoubi and Fantar 1966[K79], 201–10; Dupont Sommer 1968[K33], 116–33; Garbini 1968[K49], 11ff; Teixidor 1969[K129], 340–4; Garbini 1974[K50], 20ff.

matters which had already been carefully prepared by the senate. In the assembly however there was great freedom of speech, at least in later times, and it was the assembly which, with certain restrictions, elected the *sufetes* and the generals and possibly also the members of the senate. But in practice the choice of candidates was presumably restricted by prior arrangement. Beside the (300?) senators acting as a body, thirty or so of them formed an inner council, which doubtless helped to prepare and facilitate business as a committee of the larger body, but also probably gained great power as a smaller cabinet. It was functioning in the third century, but its earlier history is obscure, partly because of the confusing titles used by ancient writers. Polybius (x.18.1), referring to 209 B.C., implies that the thirty were called γερουσία and the senate σύγκλητος (though occasionally he names one or other συνέδριον), but it is less certain that such a clear distinction is to be found in Diodorus' use of the words in his account (xiv.47.1–2) of a letter sent by Dionysius to Carthage in 397 B.C., while the γερουσία which Aristotle compares with that of Sparta may not be the γερουσία of Polybius (or the *consilium* which Livy xxx.16.3 indicates was a committee of the *senatus*) since this would involve the consequence that he had overlooked the existence of the larger senate.

Two other bodies gained increasing power in the state: the Court of One Hundred and Four Judges and the Pentarchies. The former has already been mentioned. Designed to keep ambitious generals in check, after Aristotle's time its competence was extended to include all public officials who had to render to it an account of their year of office; this function was similar to, but more extensive than, that of *euthyne* at Athens and was compared by Aristotle to the watch-dog activities of the ephors at Sparta. Its members were chosen from the senate, and (at least in the second century) held office for life. Its powers gradually expanded until it was universally feared and hated and Livy could write (xxxiii.46.1) that in the second century it dominated (*dominabatur*) the whole city, magistrates and people alike. At some point the election of its members was entrusted to a number of mysterious Boards of Five (Pentarchies) which are mentioned only by Aristotle, who says that they held office longer than other magistrates and exercised authority both before and after office. These bodies elected themselves and supervised various parts of the administration, including probably finance but not military or imperial affairs. Since they elected the Judges, the Pentarchs could themselves pass into this Court, and the two bodies together could virtually control the state.

Membership of the popular assembly must have been confined to the male citizens of Carthage of a certain age, and just possibly of a certain financial standing. Nothing is really known about qualifications for citizenship, especially whether artisans may have been excluded. Although Aristotle, in discussing the principle of this class sharing in citizenship (*Pol.* III.1277 b 33 ff), concluded that the best form of state will not make a *banausus* ('artisan') a citizen, unfortunately he does not specifically refer to Carthage, while it is somewhat hazardous to generalize from the fact that after his capture of New Carthage in 209 B.C. Scipio treated the artisans (χειροτέχναι) among his prisoners differently from the citizens (Polyb. x.16.1): a recently founded colony may well not have reflected all the features of its centuries-old mother-city. Carthage, however, is perhaps unlikely to have been liberal in granting her franchise: since she employed few citizen soldiers, there was little military inducement to generosity, while she was far from liberal in her dealings with her allies. Whatever its composition, the assembly was theoretically strongest in the electoral field, but it probably had no judicial authority and met but seldom except for elections: the senate is likely to have remitted to it only referenda on very serious matters. Aristotle also records (*Pol.* II.1272 b 33–4) that the citizens were divided into groups which met for common meals (τὰ συσσίτια τῶν ἑταιριῶν) like the 'messes' (φιδίτια) at Sparta. These may have had some political as well as social or religious importance, but any comparison with Greek *phratriai* or Roman *curiae* – or indeed, in any detail, with Spartan *phiditia* – is purely hypothetical.

Polybius and Cato might see in Carthage, as in Sparta and Rome, a mixed constitution of royal, aristocratic and popular power, but the three elements were not equally balanced, and effective power rested with an oligarchy, as both Aristotle and Isocrates recognized.[4] The original Phoenician settlers may have formed an aristocracy of birth but commercial and industrial activities probably transformed them into an aristocracy of wealth. This in turn may have become somewhat exclusive: the leaders of the state known to history belong to a remarkably small number of families, and their names, which recur in many generations, comprise only a very small proportion of the names revealed by Punic inscriptions. How far this oligarchy tried to exclude 'outsiders' and how far it was weakened by a division of interest between commercial and agricultural interests must remain uncertain. As to its exclusiveness, it is likely that successful wealthy businessmen could win an entry, and in fact the great Barca family, which emerged in the third century B.C., seems to have been a new family. The needs of a growing population and the attractiveness of the hinterland may have led many Carthaginians to turn to agriculture, and a class of large landowners who cultivated their

---

[4] Polyb. VI.51.2; Cato *ap.* Serv. *Aen.* IV.682; Aristotle, *Pol.* II.1272 b 24ff, esp. 1273 a 13ff; Isocrates, *Nicocles* 24: Καρχηδονίους . . . οἴκοι ὀλιγαρχουμένους.

estates with slave labour emerged. Such men, it has been suggested, became so involved in their estates that from the fourth century they tended to leave the pursuit of commerce to others, and indeed that this division of interest was reflected in the political field, with the *sufetes* and senate representing them, while the commercial interests were championed in the One Hundred and Four and the Pentarchies.[5] But such a dichotomy is probably over-schematic: clashes of interest there may have been, but many men may have had a foot in both camps.

Behind the façade of the constitution lurked an all-pervading influence: money. Aristotle (*Pol.* II.1273 a 35ff) criticized the Carthaginians for making the highest offices, those of king and general, open to simple purchase (ώνητάς), while Polybius in contrasting Roman and Carthaginian attitudes to wealth writes (VI.56.1–4) that 'at Carthage nothing that results in gain is disgraceful . . . candidates for office obtain it by open bribery (φανερῶς)'. Punic greed was traditional: indeed Polybius (IX.25) tells how Massinissa personally discussed with him 'the love of money shown by the Carthaginians in general'. Candidates for office may well have been required to possess a fixed minimum of wealth: at any rate votes had to be bought and success paid for. Corruption appears to have increased in the later days of Carthage until Hannibal (who himself was taunted by his enemies with the national weakness) with popular support struck at the power of the oligarchs and cleansed the administration by constitutional and financial reforms. But this was over six hundred years after the traditional date of the founding of the city. The constitution had certainly shown the stability which attracted Greek and Roman attention: despite some attacks from within, in general it had withstood the tensions that had produced temporary tyrannies and *stasis* in so many Greek states. This it owed not least to the fact that the primary interest of so many of its citizens was money-making rather than politics: they were quite prepared in the main to leave the direction of affairs to the few, provided peace and prosperity were secured.

At the height of her power Carthage needed a strong army and navy to safeguard her far-flung interests. The original founders of the city, which was built on a defensible peninsula, required a relatively small citizen militia which was no doubt trained and equipped like the forces of Phoenician Tyre. But as the Carthaginians gradually acquired an ever-widening control in North Africa and in the lands of the western Mediterranean, the strain of maintaining an army as well as a fleet created an unacceptable drain on her limited manpower, and in any case the

[5] (Meltzer and) Kahrstedt 1879–1913[K83], III.138ff, 582ff; rejected by Groag 1929[K53], 18f.

average citizen preferred trading to fighting, and only accepted war as a means of protecting the city and its commerce. Thus from the time of Mago in the mid-sixth century, the Carthaginians decided to use part of the wealth derived from their lands and trade to employ others to fight for them; in this way their economic prosperity would not be disrupted by periods of military service. The phasing out of the citizens was gradual: some are still found serving on expeditions to Sicily in the fifth and fourth centuries, and in 339 an elite corps of some 3000 Carthaginian citizens, called by the Greeks 'The Sacred Band', makes its appearance, but after 311 citizens did not serve in the ranks in war outside Africa. When the homeland of Carthage itself was threatened, either by invasion (as by Agathocles, Regulus or Scipio) or by disturbances in Africa (as in the Mercenary War), levies of Carthaginians were naturally raised. Further, armies serving overseas continued to be commanded by Carthaginian officers. When occasion demanded, the Carthaginians could fight with great tenacity and the city produced many fine commanders. But military service was obviously not popular and for the most part armies were raised only for specific needs or expeditions, though garrisons were kept where required.

Thus the armies of Carthage came to consist primarily of three groups: native peoples in territory dominated by Carthage, in Africa, Spain and Sardinia, who were compelled to offer military service; secondly, mercenaries who were enrolled under contract to serve for a given campaign; thirdly, and of lesser importance, were contingents of auxiliaries furnished by friends or allies of the Carthaginian state. The subjects received pay, as naturally did the mercenaries; possibly the allies also. The amount will have varied, since a light-armed Ligurian or a conscripted African will not have received as much as a Greek serving as a hoplite. A corn ration was also granted: this is mentioned at the end of the fifth century (Diod. XIII.88.2), while the mercenaries who revolted after the First Punic War claimed arrears of rations ($\sigma\iota\tau o\mu\epsilon\tau\rho\iota\alpha$: Polyb. 1.68.9) as well as of pay. Mercenaries are first mentioned in the army which Hamilcar commanded at Himera in Sicily in 480; it consisted of Phoenicians, Libyans, Iberians, Ligurians, Sardinians and Corsicans. At this time the Libyans may have been mercenaries, but soon afterwards as Carthaginian power spread in North Africa they became conscripts and formed one of the most important elements in the army: thus of the troops in Sicily in 311 B.C., said to be 40,000 strong, Libyans formed a quarter (Diod. XIX.106.2). They served both as light infantry, especially useful for quick raids, and also, suitably armed, as infantry of the line where they distinguished themselves not least in later battles such as Cannae. In preparation for a campaign against the Sicilian Greeks at the end of the fifth century the Carthaginian generals summoned contingents from allied African peoples: Moors, Numidians and Cyrenaeans; the Numidian cavalry was particularly useful in the campaigns of Hannibal. Large numbers of Iberians served in the wars in Sicily against Greeks and, later, Romans; before the conquests of Hamilcar Barca in Spain, they will have been mainly mercenaries rather than subjects; the Celtiberians, who remained independent of Carthage, also provided some mercenaries in later times (e.g. 4000 at the battle of Campi Magni in 203). These Spanish troops, like the Libyans, were valuable for quick-moving guerrilla tactics and as light-armed cavalry. Corsicans and the Balearic Islanders, who were trained from childhood as slingers and were said to be paid in women rather than in cash, served as mercenaries, not as subjects, e.g. in 406 and 311 (Diod. XIII.80.2; XIX.106.2). The status of Sardinians must have depended on whether or not they came from those parts of the island controlled by Carthage. Ligurians, Celts (first mentioned about 340, they were often courageous, impetuous and fickle fighters), Campanians, who were also regarded as unreliable but extremely effective (e.g. in 410: Diod. XIII.55.7), and Etruscans (mentioned only once, in 311: Diod. XIX.106.2) are also among the mercenaries, while even Greeks in Sicily sometimes deserted their national cause to fight for the Carthaginians (e.g. in 409, 398, 343, while the help given by the Spartan Xanthippus in 255 is famous). But Greeks, Celts and Italians were probably employed only on a relatively small scale: the bulk of the Carthaginian army was formed by the native peoples of the western Mediterranean lands.

Such diverse units could not be welded into a completely uniform structure; they served as national or tribal groups, each commanded by its own leaders under the overall command of Carthage whose own citizens continued to supply the senior officers. To a large extent they retained their national arms and armour and manner of fighting, though when they were employed as heavy-infantry of the line, Carthage may well have supplied their weapons. Methods of fighting depended on the opponents: lighter troops would be employed against the native peoples of Africa and Spain during the years of expansion, but against Greek and Roman armies the Carthaginians fought hoplite battles on normal lines, with variations devised by the skill of the generals, culminating in the resourceful genius of Hannibal. Two special armaments were used at different times: chariots and elephants. War-chariots were used in the wars of the fourth century in considerable numbers (according to Diod. XVI.67, in 345 B.C. three hundred four-horse chariots and two thousand two-horse chariots were deployed, though these figures may be doubted). Their use however was discontinued before the Carthaginians crossed swords with the Romans, when greater importance was given to cavalry, and elephants were brought into service. These were African elephants, who were captured in the hinterland of the coast of North Africa; they were smaller than both the great Bush elephant of equatorial Africa and Indian elephants. In battle they did not carry 'towers' and they often proved two-edged weapons, running amock and doing damage to their own side as well as to the enemy, but extremely formidable on occasion.

The use of native subjects and of mercenaries enabled Carthage to extend her colonial empire, and it also minimized the disastrous results of any defeats, since these involved the shedding of little Carthaginian blood. Though the native Africans might become discontented and a potential danger, the mercenaries on the whole fought well and bravely as professionals, even when they were faced by other mercenaries such as those employed by Dionysius or Agathocles. But pay and booty could not always produce the same results as ardent patriotism, while any delay in payment or better offers from others might lead to unrest or desertion. Further, diversity of race, language and customs made co-operation difficult. Many soldiers had little contact with Carthage itself, except perhaps when they were enrolled or discharged, but served mainly overseas. Hence their attachment might centre on their Carthaginian commander, who could on occasion be tempted to use their loyalty to help him challenge the Carthaginian state, as for instance Bomilcar did in 308 B.C. But for the most part Carthage managed to restrain ambitious generals, who were sometimes hampered by mutual rivalry and jealousy, while they were subjected to control by the One Hundred and Four and might face crucifixion as the penalty even for military failure, let alone for revolt. The potential weakness of the use of mercenaries can be exaggerated. When well-led they served Carthage efficiently and when a general of genius welded them together into a cohesive fighting force they provided Hannibal with one of the great armies of antiquity. Nor should the valour of the Carthaginian citizens, when forced to fight, be forgotten: with their lives at stake in the three years of siege which ended in the final destruction of 146 B.C., they displayed unsurpassed tenacity and courage. Virgil sums up the national character of Carthage (*Aen.* 1.14): *dives opum studiisque asperrima belli* ('rich in resources and ferocious in the pursuits of war').

The Carthaginians had arrived at the site of their city in ships, and throughout their history they needed ships, both merchantmen for their commerce and warships to help establish and safeguard their colonial ventures and to maintain the widening monopoly which they asserted in western waters. Derived from the naval traditions of their Phoenician ancestors, their skill at sea, exemplified not least by their daring voyages of exploration in the stormy waters of the Atlantic, was widely recognized by Greeks and Romans. The size of their navy was determined by the numbers of enemy ships that faced them at different times: in 398 B.C., for instance, Dionysius of Syracuse, who had a fleet of more than 310 vessels, sent some 200 of them against Punic Motya. Carthaginian fleets varying between 200 and 270 ships are mentioned during the fourth century, and some 200 may well be the kind of effective force that Carthage liked to keep in being, though not necessarily afloat: when not needed, some would be laid up. Appian (*Pun.* 96), following Polybius, says that the inner naval harbour at Carthage (Fig. 56) contained ship-sheds for 220 vessels and this figure is borne out in general terms by recent excavations in the circular harbour area: the admiral's island in the centre was equipped with 30 sheds, while the outer circuit, apparently over 1100 metres in length, was sufficient for about another 160 sheds.[6] The type of ships used probably followed roughly the same pattern as in Greek construction: pentecontors, then triremes, and later quinque-remes (the quadrireme was invented by the Carthaginians, according to Aristotle (*apud* Plin. *HN* VII.207) and Clement of Alexandria (*Strom.* 1.16.75), while the Punic admiral at Mylae used as his flagship a *hepteres* which had been captured from Pyrrhus in 276). By the time of the wars with Rome, the quinquereme was the favoured vessel: thus the fleet left by Hannibal in Spain consisted of 50 quinqueremes, 2 quadriremes and 5 triremes. The discovery of a wrecked Punic ship off Lilybaeum, perhaps a Liburnian, has thrown much light on constructional methods: it was carvel built, the ribs being inserted into the already assembled planks; the keel was of maple, the ribs of oak and the planking of pine; the ram was encased in bronze, and the hull covered with lead sheeting. It was some 35 m. long and 5 m. wide (the ship-sheds at Carthage, for quinqueremes, were 5.9 m.).[7]

The complement of a quinquereme, according to the numbers attri-buted to the Roman vessels at Ecnomus in 256 B.C., consisted of 300 rowers and 120 soldiers: thus a fleet of 200 ships required no less than 60,000 rowers. They were presumably normally raised at Carthage itself and perhaps the Libyphoenician cities, but could be supplemented from subject peoples (thus the Barcid Mago in 206 received some from the Balearic Islands), while Hasdrubal, awaiting the subsequent Roman invasion of Africa of 204, bought 5000 slaves for use as rowers. In a sea-faring people there would be no shortage of pilots and captains, while no doubt the higher commands were reserved for the Carthaginian aristo-cracy: in general there was no sharp distinction between admirals and generals, since land and sea forces are found under the same commander. Thanks to this fleet Carthage was enabled to withstand constant pressure

---

[6] Hurst 1976[K62], 177–97; 1977[K62], 232–61.
[7] Frost 1972[K46], 113ff; 1973[K47], 229ff.

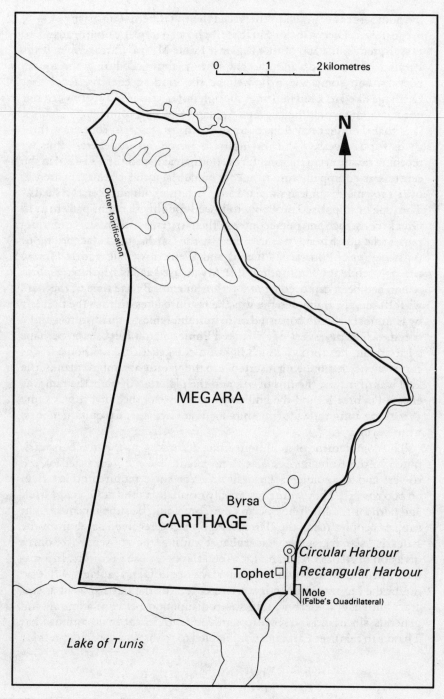

Fig. 56. Carthage (after Huss 1985 [K65], 45).

from the Greeks by sea and land and to repel or sink any intruders in
western waters, where she had no other rival competitors: she was allied
both to the Etruscans, whose power was gradually declining, and to the
Romans, who were so indifferent to her expansion that in the fourth
century they readily recognized by a treaty a wider extension of the Punic
mare clausum (pp. 526ff).

(b) *City and empire*

The site of the city (Fig. 56) resembled that of many other Phoenician
settlements. It lay on a triangular peninsula which projected eastwards
into the Mediterranean; the narrow isthmus, which linked it to the
mainland in the west, was bounded on the north by the sea (now Lake
Sebka Er Riana) and on the south by the Lake of Tunis. This strong
position was backed by a fertile hinterland. The citadel, named Byrsa, lay
on a hill (St Louis) some 200 feet high and less than a mile from the sea. In
the first centuries of its history the town's general appearance presumably resembled that of Tyre and other Phoenician cities, as represented
on the reliefs of Sennacherib: above turreted walls rose up the top storeys
of the houses, some having balustrades supported by small palm-shaped
columns. The houses at Tyre had even more storeys than those at Rome
according to Strabo (XVI.2.23, p. 757 C), while the houses between the
forum and Byrsa at Carthage in 146 B.C. had no less than six storeys (App.
Pun. 28). Gradually Carthage will have approximated more closely to the
cities of the Hellenistic world. But so thorough was the Roman destruction of the city in 146 that very little of Punic Carthage survives, though
its general lay-out is known from literary references and archaeological
investigation, not least that conducted under the auspices of the
UNESCO 'Save Carthage Project'.

The city walls were so strong that they deterred Agathocles from
attacking them and held at bay the Roman assault for three years. They
were said to have been 37 km. in length, including presumably the
stretches along the coast. The strongest part was the length across the
isthmus, with four-storeyed towers at intervals of 55–65 m.: within the
walls were said to be stables for 300 elephants, and store-houses and
barracks for 20,000 infantry and 4000 cavalry. In front of the wall was an
intermediate rampart and a ditch backed by a palisade; this was identified
from the air in 1949 and proved to consist of an outer ditch 20 m. wide
and an inner ditch 5.3 m., with post-holes for a palisade in between. The
Byrsa hill and its neighbourhood were surrounded by a separate wall,
some two miles in circumference. In the absence of any surviving
stretches of these Punic walls, their date and development remain
uncertain, but the system was probably strengthened perhaps from the

time of the First Punic War. The skill of the Carthaginians in fortification and the appearance of some of the walls of the city itself are doubtless reflected in parts of the walls of Selinus which were constructed in the last years of the fourth century when the city was becoming more Punic than Greek, while the fortifications at Lilybaeum, though known only fragmentarily, are certainly Punic.[8] At Carthage after about the fifth century the whole of the peninsula within the walls may have been inhabited, but not in equal density: the quarter in the north-west named Megara contained orchards, gardens and scattered houses.

The harbours of Carthage formed the centre of her economic life. The outer rectangular commercial harbour and the inner circular naval harbour, described by Appian, have long been identified with the surviving 'lagoons', and after decades of debate their character is now being revealed by excavation. The word 'Cothon', which strictly applied to the naval harbour, was loosely used for the whole complex. As we have seen (p. 497), Appian's description of the splendid naval harbour has recently been confirmed in general terms (though perhaps not applicable before the late fourth century), with its thirty ship-sheds radiating from the central admiral's islet and the rest built around the outer circuit: 'two Ionic columns stood in front of each shed, giving the appearance of a continuous portico to both the harbour and the island'. From his central tower the admiral could get a clear view to sea and issue orders, while a double wall surrounded the harbour so that activities within could not be seen from outside, even from the commercial harbour. The early history of the circular harbour is still uncertain, but radical changes were made in the fourth century, after which first timber and then stone ship-sheds and other installations were provided.[9] The entrance to the harbours was in the south, and east of the entrance a large stone structure (*choma*), called by archaeologists 'Falbe's quadrilateral', sheltered the entrance and provided a massive quay for merchant shipping: over 300 yards of it survive underwater.

Between the harbours and the Byrsa lay the main public square: its early lay-out may not have closely resembled a Greek agora or a Roman forum, but it was probably regularized in the fifth or later centuries. Here was the senate-house, outside which the judges (*sufetes*) administered justice in the open air; three very narrow streets, lined by six-storeyed houses, led up to the Byrsa. Temples and shrines were numerous and varied greatly in appearance. Many shrines followed the traditional

---

[8] Isthmus wall: Duval 1950 [K35], 53–9. Selinus: Winter 1971[K207], 120f; 230f; Martin 1977[K80], 61f; de la Genière 1977[K52], 251ff. Lilybaeum: Frederiksen 1977[B328], 74f.

[9] See Hurst 1975[K62], 11–40; 1976[K62], 177–97; 1977[K62], 232–61.

Phoenician and Canaanite form: small sacred enclosures (*tophets*), marked by stones or *stelae*; these in some way represented the deity, which could not be embodied in graven images. The most ancient and revered *tophet*, dating from the eighth century, was that of Tanit in the area of Salambo near the rectangular harbour: it consisted of a chamber only about a metre square, in front of which was an almost equally small courtyard with an altar; this shrine was reached through three concentric curved walls. In its precinct offerings and funerary monuments, as altars, urns and *stelae*, continued to be provided throughout the Punic period. The idea of giving the gods more elaborate dwelling-places gradually increased under Egyptian and then Greek influences. Thus a *stele* of the end of the fourth century from Hadrumetum (Sousse) depicts Baal Hammon enthroned in an Egyptian-like temple, while Carthaginians serving in Sicily became more familiar with Greek temple architecture. The temple of Demeter and Kore, built in 396, must surely have been Greek in form. The Salambo chapel, discovered in 1916, retained an older design, but the decoration was Greek. The richest temple in the city in 146 B.C. was that of Eshmun which crowned the Byrsa and was approached by a flight of sixty steps; here the last defenders rallied. When the Romans plundered the temple of Apollo, they found the god's statue, covered with gold, in a shrine of beaten gold, weighing 1000 talents.

Several cemeteries lay within the city, their locations marking its expansion. The predominant rite was inhumation, but cremation appeared alongside it in the eighth–seventh centuries, and then after a long lapse reappeared in the third. Richer burials were made in coffins laid in underground chambers (sometimes superimposed) which were reached by vertical shafts with footholds cut in the sides; these might reach a depth of 7.6 or 9 m. Alternatively, built chambers might be set in shallow cuttings, with access by a dromos or by a staircase as at Cap Bon. Thus, unlike many Greek and Roman cemeteries, those at Carthage were comparatively inconspicuous, although in later times a funerary monument might be built above the burials. Four anthropomorphic coffins survive at Carthage, two showing bearded priests, and one a priestess, in which Egyptian and Hellenistic influences combine.

The district around the forum and harbours, which contained living-quarters as well as public buildings, was the heart of the bustling commercial and industrial life of the city. On the southern slope of the Byrsa hill part of a residential quarter of the Hellenistic period has been uncovered: the straight but narrow streets separated rectangular *insulae* of dwellings (at least in the third and second centuries) and were provided with sewers; flights of steps gave access to the higher ground. The houses were simple, with square or rectangular rooms and stuccoed walls.[10] They resemble the houses discovered in the 1950s in the Carthaginian town at Dar Essafi near Kerkouane on Cap Bon, which flourished from the fifth century until its destruction, either by Regulus in 256 or by the Romans in 146.[11] Here the walls were made of unbaked brick, resting on local stone foundations, but strong enough to carry several storeys; outside they were white-washed, broken only by a door to the street, while inside was a central courtyard. In one such courtyard nine columns of a peristyle survive. The rooms had pink cement floors, inlaid with fragments of white marble or broken glass, and some houses had bath-rooms. Two-storey houses are represented on a fourth-century painting in a tomb at Cap Bon which shows a town surrounded by a turreted wall; the strongly-built houses depicted within vary in size and each is crowned by a columned loggia, above which are rows of rounded arches, or perhaps cupolas. These houses, with flat or vaulted roofs, probably looked much like those of modern Tunisia and they indicate in the Hellenistic period a considerable degree of comfort in a town which owed its prosperity to purple-dye workers and fishermen. There is little evidence for street-planning, and the public buildings have not yet been found, but there were good sewers and drains. At Carthage the water-supply derived from a spring in the north at the 'Fountain of the 1000 amphorae', and from many cisterns which though surviving in Roman form had a Punic origin.

Any estimate of the population of Carthage must be extremely hazardous, since we do not know what reliance to put on Strabo's figure of 700,000 for the population in 149 B.C. (XVII.3.15, p. 833 c) nor to what area of the city it should apply. On the basis of a suggested 114 hectares U. Kahrstedt estimated 125–130,000 souls, whereas K. J. Beloch reckoned nearly double that figure.[12] Whether 700,000 has any validity if the population of Cap Bon and the rest of the *chora* is included, is quite uncertain. Army figures, themselves not always above suspicion, refer to 45,000 men hurriedly raised to meet Agathocles' unexpected invasion at the end of the fourth century (Diod. xx.10.8); during the Truceless War Carthage raised two armies of 10,000 each; during the last siege

[10] Byrsa houses: C. Picard 1951–2[K99], 117–26; Ferron and Pinard 1955[K40], 31–81; 1960–1[K42], 77–170; G. C. Picard 1958[K104], 21ff; Harden 1962[K58], 135–6. The recent French excavations have confirmed the late-Punic dating of these houses (Lancel 1977[K76], 19ff) and revealed an extension of this built-up area on the southern slope of the Byrsa hill (Carrié and Sanviti 1977[K18], 67ff). See also S. Lancel, G. Robine and J.-P. Thuillier in *New Light on Ancient Carthage* 1980[K93], 13ff: the area appears to have been a cemetery until *c*. 500 and then remained unused until occupied by iron-workers (*c*. 250–200); then came peace, prosperity and urban development. The houses appear to have risen at least two or three stories, but evidence is lacking for Appian's six stories (*Pun*. 128).

[11] Cap Bon: Cintas 1953[K26], 256–60; G. C. and C. Picard 1961[K113], 46f, pl. 1; Warmington 1969[K135], 132f; Morel 1969[K84], 473–518; Fantar 1972–3[K39], 264–77.

[12] (Meltzer and) Kahrstedt 1879–1913[K83], III.23f; Beloch 1886[G10], 467.

Hasdrubal commanded 30,000 combatants (App. *Pun.* 120), while another force was in the surrounding country; at the end of the siege 50,000 men and women survivors surrendered on the Byrsa (App. *Pun.* 130). Guesswork might suggest a total population, including slaves, of some 200,000 at this time, and perhaps nearly double this at the time of Carthage's greatest prosperity. In fact we really know little more than that Carthage became one of the great cities of the Hellenistic world, both in population and public building.

A large population had been made possible only by the acquisition of considerable territory in North Africa which helped to feed the capital city (Maps 11 and 12). This expansion, which occurred especially from the fifth century onwards, cannot be traced in detail but by the time of Agathocles' invasion it appears to have included the coastal plain behind Hadrumetum and reached south-westwards as far as Dougga. The land nearest the city, including the Cap Bon peninsula where many rich Carthaginians had estates, probably was considered city land, while the inhabitants of the Mejerda (= anc. Bagradas) valley were subjected to taxation and conscription and came to be called Libyans, by a restricted application of this word. At times Carthage exercised some control over the tribes of Numidia and further west and by the beginning of the fourth century she dominated the coast of North Africa from the Atlantic to Cyrenaica where she established numerous settlements or took over earlier Phoenician colonies. Lepcis, Oea, Sabrata, Hadrumetum, Utica (traditionally founded before Carthage itself, and enjoying a privileged relationship of alliance), Hippo Diarrhytus, Hippo Regius, Rusuccuru, Rusaddir, Tingi, and on the Atlantic coast, Lixus and Mogador – all came under Punic control, and beyond there the hand of Carthage stretched to southern Spain, Sardinia and western Sicily. The inhabitants of these African towns (called Libyphoenicians by the Greeks who later extended the term to those natives who had absorbed some Phoenician culture) were probably bound to Carthage by separate treaties and enjoyed a privileged status; Polybius (VII.9.5) says that they had the same laws as the Carthaginians, meaning probably the same civil rights, with local officials and constitutions, thus perhaps approximating to the status of Latins *vis-à-vis* Rome (at any rate they had the right of intermarriage, ἐπιγαμία: Diod. XX.55.4). On these Libyphoenicians Carthage imposed some direct taxes and dues on imports and exports, as well as the requirement of military service, including probably rowers for the fleet (Lepcis is said by Livy XXXIV.62.3 to have paid no less than a talent a day in the second century, but perhaps this vast sum represents the tax of a large area which was gathered together at Lepcis). Her increasing control was shown when in her second treaty with Rome Carthage disallowed the somewhat wider trade in Africa recognized under her first treaty:

now all such commerce had to be channelled through Carthage itself (see p. 527f). The Libyphoenicians seem to have accepted their subordinate position, helped no doubt by their ties of common race, language and religion – if the absence of revolt indicates lack of will rather than of means.

The Libyans on the other hand were treated more harshly. Their tribute may have amounted to a quarter of their crops (in the First Punic War they had to pay half: Polyb. 1.72) and they provided many soldiers who at least in later times may have received some payment as well as booty. Visiting Carthaginian officials no doubt ensured prompt fulfilment of their obligations, acting possibly under orders from regular governors (στρατηγοί). In other respects as long as they remained peaceful they were probably left to live their own lives under their own chiefs in their little settlements and they were doubtless reasonably prosperous (some may even have employed slaves), but they hated their masters and revolted several times from the fourth century onwards. According to Polybius the Carthaginians admired and honoured the governors who exacted the greatest amount of supplies and treated the inhabitants ruthlessly, rather than those that treated the subjects with moderation and humanity. True, the Libyans for the most part were culturally very inferior to their masters (though some gained sufficient acquaintance with Punic civilization to be classed loosely as Libyphoenicians), but Carthage seems to have made little effort to win their loyalty. By a more generous policy to the defeated peoples of Italy the Romans built up a strong confederacy: Carthage had to pay the price for her lack of understanding. Her hand rested perforce somewhat more lightly on the Numidians further west: some of their chiefs might be regarded as allies, but they were in fact 'client princes' and had to offer troops, especially cavalry, and other services when required.

The grip of Carthage on her overseas dependencies is harder to assess. By the third century B.C. Carthage had turned to the aggressive acquisition of a land empire and the creation of the administrative means of governing the territories that she had conquered, but in her early days her moves overseas were clearly directed to establishing and protecting her commerce rather than to acquiring land for its own sake. Her policy in the centuries between has been variously assessed. In western Sicily for example the Phoenician and Elymian cities at first retained their own institutions and during the fifth century were allowed the right to issue coins, but when at the end of that century Carthage conquered some of the Greek cities we hear of a Carthaginian ἐπικράτεια in the island. But does this imply a province with the imposition of tribute (perhaps a tithe on produce) and Carthaginian garrisons in some cities, or merely a 'sphere of influence'? It is not feasible to discuss the question in any detail here, beyond noting a recent reaction against the more 'imperialist' interpretation of Carthaginian policy in this period. It has been argued that in the early Classical period Carthage did not annex cities in the western Phoenician orbit but considered the securing of trading rights in emporia more important than the acquisition of territory. These were ports where either Carthaginian traders settled and operated under licence of a foreign power (e.g. Carthaginians in Syracuse or Acragas) or which were under Carthaginian control (including Carthage itself) with trade conducted under the eyes of state officials (e.g. in Libya and Sardinia, as under the first treaty with Rome: below, p. 521f). Clearly it was in the interest of Carthage to extend the latter class of emporia by negotiating new treaties. Further, Carthage sought control, not in order to limit but rather to increase the number of traders who came to her ports, where she offered protection and fair trading, with the exclusion of undesirable foreigners. However, the balance of such agreements of reciprocity, which started as treaties between equals, often began to swing in favour of the greater power.[13]

Trading conditions may gradually have stiffened. Thus the trade allowed to the Romans in Libya and Sardinia in the first treaty (509) was denied to them in the second (348), although they were still allowed in the Punic area in Sicily as well as at Carthage itself where the trader received the same rights as a Carthaginian citizen. In the second treaty Carthage extended her commercial monopoly to south-west Spain, where some of the natives had probably been reduced to subjection and the rest commercially exploited for many years. But even after the conquests of the Barcids in the third century the Carthaginians avoided direct administration there as far as possible: a show of force and the exaction of hostages secured the obedience of tribal chiefs and the prompt supply of money and troops. But before this more aggressive imperialism of the third century Carthage sought to secure peace, the necessary background for a flourishing commerce, and one way of promoting this was by the establishment of good personal relationships. Thus powerful Carthaginian families might intermarry with Greeks (e.g. Mago c. 500 B.C. married a Syracusan), while others established formal ties of hospitality (*xenia*) by the exchange of *tesserae* (tokens). (So in 357 the Punic governor at Heraclea Minoa was a guest-friend of the Syracusan Dion, and a private token of guest-friendship (*tessera hospitalis*) between a Carthaginian and a Greek has been found at Lilybaeum.[14]) Indeed this policy was continued even in the later days of more aggressive empire-building: both Hasdrubal and Hannibal married Spanish wives, but by

[13] Whittaker 1978[K137], 59–90.
[14] See Plut. *Dion* 25. Tessera: *IG* xiv.279, on which see Masson 1976[K81], 93f.

that time a fully-fledged provincial system of government was being developed to control the 'empire', at least in Africa.[15]

(c) *Economic and social life*

The wealth of Carthage was proverbial. A Syracusan speaker, according to Thucydides (VI.34.2), stated that she possessed 'an abundance of gold and silver', and nearly three hundred years later Polybius said (XVIII.35.9) that at the time of her fall Carthage, even after the loss of Spain, was reckoned the wealthiest city in the world (πολυχρημονεστάτη). Over the years her fortunes fluctuated wildly but her phenomenal powers of economic recovery were attested by her offer in 191 B.C. to pay off the remaining forty years' balance of her war-debt to Rome only ten years after incurring this burden and after the loss of the Spanish mines. The sources of her prosperity are obvious: the agricultural and mineral wealth of homeland and empire (including gold from western or central Africa and silver from Spain), the energy displayed by her citizens in developing her overseas trade, whether as carrier of foreign-made goods or exporter of the products of her own industry and agriculture, and the exploitation of the manpower of her empire. But we are ill-informed about the management of the state finances. Expenditure on the civil administration was probably not very large (magistracies were apparently honorary), but included public building and religious responsibilities (she sent an annual tribute to the mother-city of Tyre, at first allegedly a tenth of her revenue: Diod. xx.14.2); she paid large sums to her mercenaries and other troops and maintained a large navy; and after frequent defeats she often had to pay heavy war-indemnities (e.g. 2000 talents after Himera in 480 B.C. and 2200 after the First Punic War). To meet these expenses Carthage levied taxes on her subjects and probably on the Libyphoenicians but apparently did not normally lay any direct tax on her own citizens, who in later days seem to have been free from this burden as well as that of military service except in times of emergency: thus in 196 B.C. when Hannibal reformed the administration, the poor state of the public finances *threatened* to impose a *tributum*.[16] Details of indirect taxation, which must have been pervasive and complex, escape us: references, such as 'vectigalia quanta terrestria maritimaque' ('the amount raised by the land and sea revenues') in relation to 196 B.C. (Livy XXXIII.47.1), are very vague (they will scarcely have been less than the one million drachmas which Rhodes derived from customs-duties *c.* 170

[15] Administration in Africa: G. C. Picard 1966[K109], 1257–65.

[16] 'tributum grave privatis imminere videbatur' (Livy XXXIII.46.9; cf. 47.2), but to meet the shock of the first payment of the Roman indemnity *c.* 201 B.C. 'tributum ex privato conferendum est' ('tax had to be paid from private resources': Livy XXX.44.11).

B.C.: Polyb. xxx.31.12). Nor can we assess the extent of corruption in earlier years, though Hannibal's reforms reveal an ugly state of affairs in the early second century. Fines and confiscations provided a minor source of revenue: thus in the First Punic War Hanno had to pay 6000 pieces of gold as the price of military incompetence (Diod. xxiii.9.2: he was lucky to have escaped crucifixion), while the estates of Hamilcar were confiscated in 200 B.C. (Livy xxxi.19.1).

The late adoption of the Greek practice of coining money by the Carthaginians has often caused surprise. Since they were such keen businessmen, they must be presumed to have assessed their own interests and concluded that the nature of their trade would not have benefited by following the Greek example until a fairly late date. Apart from the coins that she allowed Punic settlements in western Sicily to issue, Carthage did not issue her own coins until *c.* 410 B.C. and then not for commercial reasons but for payment of her troops in Sicily. The occasion was probably when she decided to intervene to help Segesta against Selinus. The coins, which were probably minted at Carthage itself, carry as legends the city-name (QRTHDST) and MHNT, i.e. the camp or military head-quarters; the types (Fig. 57a) are horse and (reverse) palm-tree (it is uncertain whether the palm (*phoenix*) is a pun on 'Phoenician' (or 'Punic') or else an emblem of fertility only). This series ceased *c.* 390 B.C. and Carthage only resumed her minting *c.* 350 B.C. when she started to produce a prolific gold coinage; for the Siculo-Punic silver, the mint was probably transferred to Sicily, and the type changed to head of Tanit and (reverse) horse and palm-tree (Fig. 57b). At this time (350–340)

Fig. 57a. Carthaginian coin with forepart of horse, corn grain and legend QRTHDST on obverse, palm tree with legend MHNT on reverse (*c.* 410–390 B.C.).

Fig. 57b. Carthaginian silver coin with female head (of Tanit?) and legend QRTHDST on obverse, horse walking in front of palm tree on reverse (*c.* 350–340 B.C.).

Carthage was facing the challenge of a Greek revival in Sicily under Timoleon, and also negotiated her second treaty with Rome: she was 'mobilizing herself to a more active policy concerning her whole strategic position' (G. K. Jenkins).[17] Coinage provided the sinews of war even more than of commerce. In line with this slow emphasis on the economic importance of coins and despite the volume of her trading Carthage does not seem to have developed banking and trading systems to match those of Hellenistic Alexandria or Rhodes.

As Carthaginian power extended in North Africa agriculture joined commerce as one of the main sources of her economic life, but these need not necessarily have been mutually exclusive pursuits and interests. Men who had become rich through investing in commerce and industry may well have regarded the acquisition of land chiefly as a further source of wealth, the more so since they exploited the land by the use of slave labour. True, Mago, who wrote twenty-eight books on agriculture, seems to suggest a certain dichotomy when he urged that any one who bought land should sell his town house, while 'the man who takes greater pleasure in his city residence will have no need of a country estate' (Columella, Rust. 1.1.18). But while many Carthaginians may have enjoyed country life and have appreciated their country houses in the heat of the summer, perhaps few are likely to have devoted exclusive attention to them, unsupported by some commercial interests. Despite the use of slave labour, the country estates do not appear to have been very large, but their prosperity impressed Agathocles' invading troops: well-irrigated gardens, luxurious country houses, covered with stucco, well-stocked farm buildings, vines, olives, orchards, cattle, sheep and horses (Diod. xx.8.3f), while later Regulus' invading force captured more than 20,000 slaves in the area of Aspis, just south of Cap Bon. Beyond the area fairly close to Carthage itself, the cultivation of the interior was left to the Libyans, whose main produce was grain, much of which went to the capital as tribute. Whether or not the vine, olive, fig and almond were first introduced into North Africa by the Phoenicians, they were cultivated with skill, while the pomegranate (*mala Punica*) became popular and the date-palm was advertised on the coinage, as was the horse. In fact Polybius (xii.3.3f) doubted whether so large a number of horses, oxen, sheep and goats could be found in the rest of the world. These animals, together with fowls and pigeons, are sometimes depicted on votive *stelae*, while the local bees were noted for their honey and wax, a *cera Punica* being used for medicinal purposes. The *stelae* also show the type of simple wooden plough used in cultivation, and Varro (*Rust.*

[17] On this coinage see Jenkins 1971[K71], 25ff; 1974[K72], 23ff; 1977[K73], 5ff (quotation from 1977, 6).

1.52.1) records a special harvesting machine (*plostellum Punicum*). The general success of Carthage in scientific agriculture is best attested by the decision of the Roman senate that Mago's work should be translated into Latin and its subsequent popularity among a nation of farmers who already possessed their own Cato's work on agriculture.

Industry had to supply the basic needs of a large city and also to provide a means of exchange in those areas overseas where money was not used. While the state employed men, both free and slave, in the docks and arsenals, most industry was in the hands of private citizens and was on a small scale: evidence for large factories owned by the aristocracy is lacking. A great variety of trades was followed. The carpenters and wood-carvers of Carthage kept up the traditions of their Phoenician ancestors who had worked the cedars of Lebanon and supplied Solomon with craftsmen for building his temple. Punic skill is displayed especially in ship-building and furniture; the Romans made mention of *lectuli Puniciani* (Punic couches) and *fenestrae Punicianae* (Punic windows), while a head of Demeter, carved in cedar, was found on the Ste Monique hill at Carthage. Their stone-masons, beside the main tasks of building walls and houses, provided stone coffins and could draw on local quarries: a large underground quarry at Cap Bon had exits on the seashore to enable stone to be shipped direct across the bay to Carthage. While much spinning and weaving was done at home, some was organized on a commercial scale, with a dozen or so slaves, to produce carpets, cushions and embroideries, and also the eastern form of dress which the Carthaginians inherited from the Phoenicians: the women seem to have followed Greek fashions more readily than the men, who retained the long coloured embroidered robes of their ancestors. The dyeing industry, inherited from Tyre and Sidon, flourished at Carthage; at Dar Essafi heaps of myrex shells and rock-cut vats show that it, together with fishing, was the main industry of the town. Although good clay existed in parts of the Carthaginian peninsula, Punic pottery remained plain and utilitarian: the better pottery found in the tombs is all imported – from Greece, Etruria and southern Italy. A potters' quarter has been found in the Dermech district of Carthage, containing an oven, still stacked with its pots; it is 6 m. high, 4 m. being below ground level. The industry aimed at mass production and cheapness, not at artistic merit. It provided everyday objects, such as vases, amphorae and terracottas. These last include the masks, both smiling and grimacing, of the seventh and sixth centuries; the later Greek-style statuettes were often made by immigrant Greek workmen. Although the Phoenicians were famed for their metal-work, especially in bronze and copper, most of the bronze works of art found at Carthage are of foreign manufacture. However, the copper razors, often engraved with figures of deities or sacred symbols (p. 512), were a typical product of the Carthaginian metal-workers, who also mass-produced copies of Greek original bronze vases. Some of their tools have been found in graves, others are depicted on *stelae*. Phoenician gold and silver jewellery is found at Carthage, but probably not much of real artistic merit was manufactured there. Carved ivory from the tusks of African elephants decorated furniture or provided small objects such as boxes, combs and hairpins, as also did bone on a humbler scale. At first some of these objects were imported from the East, but by the fourth century at least Carthage was manufacturing her own. Another luxury trade was in painted cups made from ostrich eggs. The discovery of a glass-maker's furnace at Dermech (of the fourth century or later) shows that Carthage maintained something of the old Phoenician tradition of making glass vessels and trinkets such as beads, scarabs and amulets. Thus in general, although the Carthaginians had access to plentiful supplies of raw material, especially metals, their lack of artistic talent, of originality and of a creative interest in such work prevented the production of many objects that would sell in overseas markets: their industry mainly supplied the home market with the objects of daily life: more artistic goods, for those who could afford and appreciate them, had to be imported.

In the early centuries of her history, the overseas trade of Carthage had fluctuated with the rise and fall of her political fortunes and had been determined largely by her relations with Etruscans and Greeks. The development of her commercial monopoly in the western Mediterranean is described below in connexion with her treaties with Rome (pp. 520ff) since these provide much of our detailed evidence for this expansion. In the fifth century her overseas interests had contracted, but they extended again in the fourth, especially after the break-up of Alexander's empire. Despite the extent of her trade, the surviving evidence is woefully small, partly because some of the main goods handled, such as slaves, textiles, crude metals and food-stuffs, were perishable and have left no archaeological record. About the typical Carthaginian trader, however, we can form some idea: he showed the same energy in establishing new trading colonies and exploring the remoter parts of the earth as his Phoenician ancestors, 'whose merchants are princes, whose traffickers are the honourable of the earth' in the words of Isaiah (23.8), though Homer (*Od.* XIV.288f) stressed less attractive aspects of the Phoenician merchant, 'a man well versed in guile, a greedy knave' (ἀνὴρ ἀπατήλια εἰδώς, τρώκτης). In a later age Hanno, the Punic trader in Plautus' *Poenulus*, is portrayed in a more kindly light, at worst a figure of fun; presumably this also reflects the attitude of the lost Greek New Comedy play used by Plautus. These plays show that Punic merchants were visiting Greece again with the improvement of relations after

Alexander's day and that a Roman audience, probably just after the Hannibalic War, could laugh, perhaps unmaliciously, at an ex-enemy, a loosely robed pious foreigner with rings in his ears. Further, Plautus counterbalances Homer's picture of Phoenicians as kidnappers of children (*Od.* xv.415ff) by telling of the seizure of Carthaginian children by Greek slave-dealers, while he indicates that Hanno had one of the prerequisites of the good international trader, the ability to speak the language of his customers: 'he knows all languages' ('is omnis linguas scit': *Poen.* 112); he also made use of individual reciprocal contracts of hospitality (*tesserae hospitales*) to build up his trade relationships. More official were the ties established by proxeny: thus we hear of Nobas, a Carthaginian *proxenos* who was honoured at Thebes *c.* 364 B.C. (*SIG* 1.179).

A large proportion of Carthaginian commerce comprised a carrier trade: Carthage acted as middleman and helped to distribute the products of more industrial peoples and the raw materials of less civilized peoples to appropriate markets. Her control of the western Mediterranean and her own key position enabled her to build up, sustain and indeed enforce on others this transit trade. Thus foreign traders could visit Carthage, but not sail further west, so that most of the products of Greece, Egypt and Italy found in North Africa, Spain and Sardinia must have been conveyed in Punic ships which re-exported the goods that arrived at Carthage: she was a great Mediterranean clearing-house. But it is not easy to define her imports and exports in any detail. In Hellenistic times she presumably exported some corn, oil, food-stuffs, textiles, horses and slaves, and she acquired precious metals from the backward natives of the West in return for trinkets and the cheaper products of her own industry which can have found markets only in areas less civilized than herself and could not compete with the more artistic wares of the East. These metals, which enabled Carthage to produce her own spectacular gold and silver coinage, were required by other states such as Ptolemaic Egypt with whom Carthage had good relations, as witnessed by her request to Ptolemy for a loan during the First Punic War and by the possibility that she even allowed a Ptolemaic officer to sail to Carteia in southern Spain.[18] But here as elsewhere detailed knowledge is lacking: 'though there may have been considerable trade between the two cities [Alexandria and Carthage] in the earlier Ptolemaic period, there is little surviving trace of it . . . it is not possible to form any clear idea of the goods exchanged in either direction'. Such is the cautious conclusion of P. M. Fraser[19] and it reinforces the view that we must simply trust to a

---

[18] On this officer, Timosthenes of Rhodes, see Fraser 1972[A52], 1.52 and relevant note.
[19] Fraser 1972[A52], 1.153.

large extent the unanimous impression of the ancient writers about the
wealth of Carthage and the extent of her trade.

Little need be said here about Carthaginian art, since amid Egyptian
and Greek influences it is extremely difficult to isolate a distinctively
Punic contribution of any high aesthetic value or inspiration. These
influences weakened in the fifth and earlier fourth centuries, but they
revived in full force thereafter. We have already glanced at some of the
products of the workshops of Carthage. Two of the most attractive and
interesting of these, although the work of Greek or Greek-trained Punic
artists, are the large number of sculptured limestone *stelae* and the copper
razors which probably had a ritualistic rather than a purely practical
function. While the early *stelae* of the seventh to fifth centuries, which
hark back to Phoenician models, are shaped like thrones and altars, later
stones generally had a triangular top; from the fourth century they
sometimes portray the dead, priests and worshippers, while later their
repertoire was extended to include a great variety of animals, as well as
chariots, ships, vases, knives and jewel-cases, though the human figure is
rare. Many *stelae* were found in other towns, such as Sousse (from the
fifth century) and Constantine (third century); indeed this very typical
Punic product survived the fall of Carthage and continued to flourish in
the Neo-Punic period, for instance at Dougga (second–first centuries).
Most of the engraved razors, which come from fourth-century or later
tombs in Carthage, Sardinia and Ibiza (but not Spain), concentrate on
religious themes, such as deities and sacred symbols, of which the
majority are Egyptian and Punic rather than Greek: thus Baal had to
compete with Isis and Horus. Egyptian gods, animals and divine symbols are also depicted on amulets; their use was frequent in the seventh
and sixth centuries, less so in the fifth, and revived in the fourth and third
but not to the same extent. Though many were imported from Egypt,
some are thought to have been manufactured in Carthage: at any rate
they indicate the interest of the Carthaginians in superstition and magic.
Some Egyptianizing and Graecizing motifs are seen in the scarabs and
jewellery; when *c.* 400 B.C. the scarab was no longer made in Egypt, the
Carthaginians either imported them from Sardinia or made them themselves. Some of the early jewellery was very good, such as circular gold
pendants and ear-rings from Carthage and Tharros in Sardinia, but in
later pieces Greek influences have largely replaced the earlier Phoenician
inspiration. In general the Carthaginians' lack of artistic impulse accords
with Plutarch's picture (*Mor.* 799D): 'they are a hard and gloomy people,
submissive to their rulers and harsh to their subjects . . . they keep
obstinately to their decisions, are austere, and care little for amusement
or the graces of life'.

The Punic language came of a sturdy stock, the North Semitic family, and survived in North Africa for many centuries after the fall of Carthage itself. Evidence exists for Carthaginian books and libraries, but little is known about their authors or contents, though St Augustine could say (*Ep.* XVII.2) that 'in Carthaginian books there were many things wisely handed down to memory' ('multa sapienter esse mandata memoriae'). There were Carthaginian histories, written by a certain Hiempsal and by King Juba, which may have provided information for the Emperor Claudius' history of Carthage in Greek. The main work known to history is Mago's treatise on agriculture, but we have no references to poetry or philosophy, though it was a certain Hasdrubal, born at Carthage, who settled in Greece, changed his name to Clitomachus and became head of the New Academy (but he wrote in Greek). The official account of Hanno's voyage of exploration down the west coast of Africa was commemorated in a long inscription set up in the temple of Melkart, but whether such tales of adventure circulated also in book form we do not know. Numerous inscriptions survive, but most are brief epitaphs or dedications. The great literature of many Old Testament authors showed that a Phoenician people had a precedent for developing literary gifts, but the Carthaginians seem to have neglected all fields of artistic pursuit, concentrating rather on more material objectives. Unlike the early Roman authors who began by translating Greek epic and tragedy, the Carthaginians seem not to have felt the need for any imaginative litera-ture – and yet we cannot be quite certain: were all the books in the Punic libraries technical manuals? At any rate some Hellenized Carthaginians must have read some Greek literature, and the historical work of the Sicilian Philinus and the accounts of Hannibal's exploits written in Greek by Sosylus and Silenus seem to have been aimed at Carthaginian as well as Greek readers.

The religious beliefs and practices which the Carthaginians inherited from their Phoenician ancestors played a significant part in their life. Many Carthaginian citizens had theophoric personal names, and the evidence of tombs and votive *stelae* suggests a considerable personal involvement in religion. However, it is not easy to distinguish the nature and functions of some of the gods, who were seldom depicted in anthropomorphic shape, and little mythology survives to attest beliefs about their mutual relationships. Further, difficulties arise from uncer-tainty whether a name is being used in a general or in a more individual-ized sense for the deity. The chief god of Tyre, Baal Melkart, was worshipped in Carthage, as also in the Phoenician settlement at Gades, and was later equated with Heracles. Equally important was Eshmun, originally from Sidon and assimilated to Aesculapius. Other Phoenician gods who also received temples in Carthage included Resheph, god of lightning (Apollo) and many minor Baals. The two deities most fre-

quently named in the numerous votive inscriptions, either together or
separately, are Baal Hammon and Tanit Pene Baal (Tanit, Face of Baal).
Their early history is obscure. Baal Hammon is already found in the East,
and was later perhaps connected with another deity, the Egyptian
Ammon whose cult had spread in Libya; he was identified by the Greeks
with Kronos (and probably also with Zeus), by the Romans with Saturn.
On a *stele* from Sousse he is shown bearded, wearing a tall crown and a
long robe, and seated on a throne flanked by winged sphinxes. Tanit
hardly appears in Phoenicia and is found in Carthage only after the fifth
century; she corresponds to the eastern Astarte (Ashtoreth), a mother-
goddess; her symbols, dove, pomegranate, fish and palm-tree, indicate
fertility (the precise significance of the ubiquitous 'sign of Tanit', a
triangle on which rests a horizontal line surmounted by a circle, remains
debatable). Though Tanit came to the fore in the fifth century, this
supports but does not prove the view that at this time a major
change took place in religious loyalties in Carthage, whereby Baal
Hammon and Tanit Pene Baal overshadowed the Phoenician Melkart
and Astarte.[20] Nor does the introduction of the cult of Demeter-Kore
into Carthage (in expiation of the sacking of their sanctuary in Syracuse
by the Carthaginians in 396 B.C.) involve the widespread hellenization of
Carthaginian religion;[21] the cult was to be tended by Greeks resident in
Carthage. While not rejecting older beliefs, the Carthaginians may have
become more receptive of new ideas, but on the whole they appear to
have remained conservative. Thus amulets and razors show that Egyptian deities were extremely popular, at least at the level of private
superstition, but these gods seem to have made no inroad into official
beliefs, since their cults are not recorded in the inscriptions.

Sacrifice was a significant part of Punic ritual. That on occasion this
included human sacrifice is not a false accusation by national enemies of
Carthage, but is confirmed by the excavations in the *tophet* at Carthage:
here were found numerous urns containing the burnt bones of children
and two inscriptions which mention infant sacrifice.[22] The children, who
appear to have been generally provided by the leading families, were
mostly under two years old. This sacrifice (*moloch*), which may at periods
have been an annual event, took the form of placing the children in the
hands of a bronze statue of Baal Hammon, whence they were dropped
into a furnace below; Tanit was often associated with Baal. Although

[20] As argued by G. C. Picard 1964[K107], 83ff; G. C. and C. Picard 1961[K113], 62; 1968[K114], 150ff.

[21] As argued by Gaukler 1915[K51], II.521 but rejected by Gsell 1912–20[K54], IV.350.

[22] Dussaud 1946[K34], 371ff. The American excavations of 1976–7 in the eastern part of the *tophet* revealed over 200 urns, mostly of the fourth century, and suggest the possibility of some 20,000 urns deposited between 400–200 B.C. This would suggest that child sacrifice was more a systematic than a sporadic practice: see *CEDAC* 1 (Sept. 1978) 12. See also Stager 1980[K125], 1ff.

child sacrifice was forbidden in the Old Testament (2 *Kings* 23.10; *Jerem.* 7.31; 9.5) and no *tophet* has been found in Phoenicia itself, it was widespread in the West, where *tophets* are known at Hadrumetum (Sousse), Motya, Calaria, Nora and Sulci. In some urns at both Carthage and Hadrumetum only calcined animal bones (sheep and goats) are found. This has suggested a possible increasing substitution for infant sacrifice, but it would seem that at Carthage the percentage of animal victims is higher in urns of the seventh and sixth centuries than in those of the fourth.[23] Further, emergencies demanded desperate measures: thus after their defeat by Agathocles in 310 the Carthaginian nobles, who had previously 'cheated' the god by sacrificing children other than their own, now offered no less than 500 children. The sacrifice of adults was not unknown, but the victims seem to have been confined to defeated enemies and foreigners (though Melkart received one human victim each year). Ordinary animal sacrifices to the gods were of course more common, both large and small, from bulls to birds, and we have a tariff of the priests' shares (*CIS* 165): this inscription, though found at Marseilles, refers to the temple of Baal Saphon at Carthage and gives the 'account of the dues which the controllers of dues have fixed: for each ox, whether the sacrifice be a sin offering or a peace offering or a burnt offering, the priests shall have ten pieces of silver for each, and for sin offering an additional weight of three hundred . . . of the flesh'. The smaller dues for smaller animals and for food and drink follow.

The temples and sanctuaries were served by priests and priestesses (*kohanim*) who tended to come from the same families: thus one inscription mentions seventeen generations, another five.[24] Sometimes a priesthood might be held by a secular official (as by the general Malchus in the sixth century), but probably this was not usual. A hierarchy existed within the priesthood and inscriptions refer to a supervisory body of ten officials. Some priests seem to have been subject to strict taboos. Priests are depicted on three *stelae* at Carthage: one shows a bearded figure, wearing a head-scarf and a linen robe over a short tunic, and holding a patera and flask; another, beardless and wearing a fez-like hat, carries an infant, presumably for sacrifice (Fig. 58). Lesser officials include scribes, musicians and barbers; the last seemingly used the ritual razors that are found in the tombs (some priests were tonsured). The evidence for religious prostitution, whether of women or boys, which was practised in Phoenicia, is doubtful, though what may be 'temple boys' are depicted on some *stelae*. Votive gifts in tombs seem to indicate some beliefs in an after-life. The priests, who held a respected position in Carthaginian society, may well have helped to preserve older Carthaginian traditions,

---

[23] Cintas 1947[K24], 1ff; Stager 1980[K125], 7ff.   [24] Lagrange 1905[K75A], 480.

Fig. 58. Carthaginian stele depicting priest with infant (for sacrifice?).

even after 146 B.C. Indeed, if Tertullian is describing comparatively recent events, as he may well be (*Apol.* 9.2), human sacrifice endured in Africa until the mid-second century A.D. Though in the fourth century B.C. Carthage had become more subjected to Greek influences and had entered the world of Hellenistic economy, she yet stubbornly maintained much of her traditional culture in religion as well as language. But if her cultural development was to some extent moulded by Greece, her political future was to be determined by her relations with Rome.

II. THE ROMANO-CARTHAGINIAN TREATIES

(a) *The early treaties*

Rome and Carthage lived in harmony during the centuries of their earliest contacts, and there was little reason why it should have been otherwise. During most of the sixth century Rome was politically controlled by Etruscan rulers, and Carthage and the Etruscan cities were united by a common rivalry against the Western Greeks. Any trade that early Rome may have developed was stimulated by Etruscan domination; it would therefore be handled through Etruscan channels which were essentially in accord with Carthage.[25] Indeed regal Rome probably had direct treaty relations with Carthage. In referring to the treaties between Carthage and Etruria Aristotle (*Pol.* III.1280 a 36ff) unfortunately mentions only 'Etruscans' (Τυρρηνοί) and does not make it clear whether the Etruscan signatories were the Etruscan League or individual Etruscan cities. In view of the political weakness of the League, separate Etruscan cities are far more likely to have negotiated terms with Carthage, whose commercial ties were stronger with the coastal than the inland cities of Etruria. In either case the first treaty that republican Rome made with Carthage probably represents the renewal of an earlier one contracted by regal Rome. The closeness of the links between Carthage and Etruria has recently been dramatically underlined by the discovery of the gold tablets at Pyrgi (p. 256), the harbour town of Etruscan Caere, with the revelation of the existence of a shrine of the Phoenician goddess Astarte at Pyrgi and the dedication made there by the Etruscan ruler of Caere. This discovery must have seemed less surprising to those scholars who recalled that at Santa Marinella some ten km. further up the coast from Pyrgi lay a settlement called Punicum.

Apart from the indirect evidence offered by archaeology, our knowledge of the early relations of Carthage and Rome derives almost entirely from a series of treaties recorded by some ancient writers. This testimony, which raises numerous problems about their date and number, in

[25] For an alternative interpretation of the presence of Etruscan rulers at Rome see p. 259f.

essence is as follows. Polybius (III.22ff) quotes three treaties before the time of the First Punic War and declares that there were only three: he dates the first to the first year of the Republic (508–507 in his reckoning), the second is undated and the third belongs to the Pyrrhic War in 279–278. Polybius further rejects as false the statement of the pro-Carthaginian Sicilian historian Philinus that there was another treaty which precluded the Romans from entering Sicily and the Carthaginians Italy. Livy records a treaty in 348 (VII.27.2), the presence of a Carthaginian embassy at Rome in 343 (VII.38.2), another treaty in 306 which is 'tertio renovatum' ('renewed for the third time') (IX.43.6), and yet another in 279, 'quarto foedus renovatum ('treaty renewed for the fourth time') (*Ep.* XIII). He also suggests a treaty earlier than that of 348 when in discussing the potential threat of Alexander the Great to the West he refers (IX.19.13) to the Roman and Carthaginian states being united at that time by 'ancient treaties' ('foederibus vetustis iuncta res Punica Romanae esset'). Diodorus (XVI.69.1) gives only one treaty before that of 279/8: this he says was the first. He places it in the consulship of M. Valerius and M. Popillius which according to his chronological system should fall in the Attic year 344/3, but in fact belongs to the Varronian year 348. Of these three authors unfortunately only Polybius provides any details about the content of the treaties. Numerous attempts have been made to try to reconcile the discrepancies in the sources and many scholars have followed the example of Mommsen in questioning the accuracy of Polybius' dating of the first treaty, but before we turn to such problems, the sources of Polybius' information must be examined.

The proximate source presents no problem: Polybius himself provides the answer. He records that at the time of the outbreak of the Second Punic War the existing treaties were referred to in fairly general terms: 'but I think a more particular examination will be useful both to practical statesmen, who require to know the exact truth of the matter, in order to avoid mistakes in any critical deliberations, and to historical students, that they may not be led astray by the ignorance or partisan bias of historians; but that there may be some survey generally recognized as accurate of the treaties between Rome and Carthage from the earliest times to our own day' (III.21.9f). Polybius wished to establish historical truth for its own sake (the reference to ignorance or bias of historians obviously includes Philinus), but there can be little doubt that interest in the topic was heightened in Polybius' own day by the debates which took place in the Senate House and among individual Roman nobles before the outbreak of the Third Punic War. When events were moving towards a resumption of hostilities with Carthage after a lull of half a century, Polybius wanted to place contemporary discussion in an accurate historical setting. This was the more necessary since according to Polybius (III.26.2) even in his day the oldest Romans and Carthaginians and those that had the reputation of taking the greatest interest in public affairs were ignorant of the treaties. This is most surprising since Polybius records that the treaties, engraved on bronze, were preserved in the treasury of the aediles beside the temple of Iuppiter Capitolinus. Thus this general ignorance was presumably occasioned merely by apathy, and no one had bothered to consult the documents until in the late 150s serious interest and concern was felt in Rome about a possible breakdown of peace in North Africa and any potential threat from a flourishing Carthage.

Referring to the first treaty Polybius says that he gives as accurate an interpretation as he can (διερμηνεύσαντες ἡμεῖς ὑπογεγράφαμεν), 'but the ancient Roman language differs so much from that in present use, that some parts of it can be understood only with difficulty, after considerable application by the most knowledgeable Romans' (III.22.3). διερμηνεύσαντες probably means 'interpreting' rather than strictly 'translating' into Greek, since Polybius claims only to reproduce the treaties in general terms: εἰσὶ δ' αἱ συνθῆκαι τοιαίδε τινές. He is often assumed to have found the treaty in some written source, but, if so, the writer must remain quite uncertain. In the fourth book of his *Origines* Cato claimed that before the Second Punic War the Carthaginians broke their treaties for the sixth time (fr. 84 P), but the priority of publication of the relevant books of Cato and of Polybius is not known: although books I–VI of Polybius may have appeared about 150 B.C., and *Origines* IV and V somewhat earlier, the last books, VI and VII, which are likely to have dealt with the antecedents of the Third Punic War at considerable length, appear to have been published after Cato's death in 149. Cato may of course have discussed the treaties in regard to the events of 219–218 B.C., but if they only came to light in the mid-second century, his full treatment probably was to be found in the later books. The possibility that Polybius was allowed to consult Cato's manuscript before its publication is not very strong. Thus if Polybius used published sources, these must remain unidentified.[26]

Stimulated by current interest in earlier Romano-Punic relations, some of the leading Roman statesmen may have consulted the archives in the 150s and a written copy could even have circulated among them. In view of his personal friendship with Scipio Aemilianus, Polybius could then have been given access to this to help him in his historical research. But this is mere hypothesis. Although our chief modern authority feels

---

[26] See Walbank 1972[B185], 20, 80 for a brief summary of his views, which are against the use of Cato, as are those of Nenci 1958[K157], 265ff. See Badian 1966[B6], 7f for dating the *Origines*.

that 'it is highly unlikely that Polybius himself consulted the text of the treaties in the treasury',[27] it is not impossible and it would help to explain Polybius' emphasis on the difficulty of the archaic language (which of course provides one of the strongest arguments for the early date of the treaty). If Polybius saw the treaty in the version of a contemporary writer, he would not be impressed by the language difficulty. His emphasis on this would then amount to little more than an oblique excuse for avoiding autopsy (since Polybius, unlike modern scholars, was not concerned to use the archaic language as an argument to support the early date: he accepted this as an unassailable fact). True, if he had been shown a private copy by (say) Scipio, who had helped him to read it, the linguistic difficulties would have struck him forcibly, since his own incomplete knowledge of Latin makes it improbable that he could attempt fully to understand and translate the treaty himself. But it still remains possible that he consulted the original in the company of some scholarly Roman friend: if he approached the treasury of the aediles with his patron Aemilianus, he would scarcely have found the doors closed to him. However, whatever the intermediate stages, we have little reason to doubt that he has preserved a reasonably accurate record of the substance of the treaties.

In view of the obscurity that surrounds the problem, little need be said about the possible sources of the information given by Diodorus and Livy (pp. 3ff). Fabius Pictor and Cincius Alimentus are among the annalists that have been canvassed as Diodorus' source, while either Valerius Antias or Licinius Macer seems to lie behind much of Livy's first decade.

(b) *The first treaty*

Before giving the terms of the first treaty Polybius stated that it 'was made in the year of L. Iunius Brutus and M. Horatius, the first consuls appointed after the expulsion of the kings and the men who dedicated the temple of Iuppiter Capitolinus. This was twenty-eight years before the crossing of Xerxes into Greece' (III.22.1f). Since Polybius clearly believed the treaty and the Republic to be coeval, it is unnecessary to enter here into the many problems surrounding the names of the first consuls (p. 173f) and the precise dates involved in Polybius' accounts, apart from any light they may throw on the authenticity of the treaty. Recent historians who believe Brutus and Horatius not to have been historical figures use this assumption to argue that the treaty was late. If E. Täubler[28] is right in arguing that Carthaginian practice suggests that the

[27] Walbank 1972[B185], 81 n. 90.   [28] Täubler 1913[J235], 1.270–3.

treaty itself contained neither names nor date, they could easily have been added later by Roman officials in charge of the records: believing the treaty to belong to the first year of the Republic, these men appended the names of the men they considered to have been the consuls of that year. However, at least in the view of the present writer, it is by no means certain that the names in themselves do not represent historical figures, and even if doubts are entertained about Brutus, there is strong reason to believe in Horatius as the dedicator of the temple. In fact the treaty may have contained only Horatius' name, as some believe, since the nearly contemporary treaty of Sp. Cassius of *c.* 493 (p. 274) probably included his name alone, while Cicero (*Balb.* 53) referred to it as struck under the consulship of Cassius and his colleague Postumus Cominius. But whatever the truth, the names should not be used to discredit the date in which Polybius firmly believed.

The clauses of the treaty itself are best set out in analytic form:

INTRODUCTION. There shall be friendship (φιλία) between the Romans and their allies and the Carthaginians and their allies, on these conditions:

I. THE ROMANS

   (a) *Maritime limits*

      The Romans and their allies shall not sail beyond the Fair Promontory, unless forced by storm or by enemies. If any one of them is driven ashore beyond the Promontory, he shall not buy or carry away anything except what is required to repair his ship or for sacrifice [possibly he also had to leave within five days, as in the second treaty].

   (b) *Trade within the permitted limits*

     (i) Libya and Sardinia

        Trade in Libya and Sardinia shall be carried out in the presence of a herald or town-clerk, and the price secured to the seller by the state.

     (ii) Sicily [and Carthage?]

        Any Romans coming to the area of Sicily controlled by Carthage shall enjoy all the commercial rights enjoyed by others. [Since in his comments Polybius adds 'to Carthage itself' and it appears in the second treaty alongside Sicily, it should perhaps be supplied here.]

II. THE CARTHAGINIANS

   (a) The part under Roman control.

     (i) The Carthaginians shall do no injury to the people of Ardea, Antium, the Laurentes (so Ursinus for the ἀρεντίνων of the MSS: see below), Circeii, Tarracina, nor any other Latins that are subject to Rome.

(b) The part not under direct Roman control.
   (i) Regarding those that are not subject, the Carthaginians shall keep their hands off their cities, but if they take any such city they shall hand it over to the Romans undamaged.
   (ii) They shall build no fort in Latin territory.
   (iii) If they enter the district in arms, they shall not pass a night in it.

Since the treaty is drafted in Carthaginian form, the preliminary assertion of friendship, which is the chief positive element, may well be couched in Polybian terms rather than in those of the original. Polybius also records the accompanying oaths, not in the text of the treaty but separately in his later comments on it (III.25.6f). The Carthaginians swore by their ancestral gods (these are specified in more detail in the later treaty between Hannibal and Philip v of Macedon in 215 B.C. (Polyb. VII.9.2)) and the Romans by Iuppiter Lapis in accordance with ancient custom (a ceremony which probably involved invoking Iuppiter and hurling away a stone as a symbol that a perjuror should similarly be cast out by his state).

From the Carthaginian point of view the main emphasis of the treaty is on commerce, from the Roman it is on political conditions in Latium. One major problem is to define the limits set on Roman navigation: this hinges on the identification of the Fair Promontory. Polybius placed the Promontory to the north of Carthage and gives his own opinion on why the Carthaginians forbade the Romans to sail south of it: they wished to exclude them from the Syrtes and the emporia to the south-east. This would mean identifying the Promontory with Cap Bon to the east of Carthage (Map 12); it could not be to the west since in his commentary Polybius says that the Romans were granted access to Carthage itself and this could not have occurred if they had been barred from an area which started to the west of the city and stretched eastwards. However, in the second treaty, as we shall see, the barred zone was extended from the Fair Promontory to Mastia (Cartagena) on the Spanish coast; now if the Fair Promontory was Cap Bon the barrier running from Africa to Spain would have left Carthage itself to the west within the forbidden area, whereas in fact Polybius tells us that it was not. Also elsewhere (1.29.2; 36.11) Polybius calls Cap Bon the Hermaean Promontory (Promunturium Mercuri in Livy). It would seem therefore that the Fair Promontory must be sought west of Cap Bon and of Carthage itself, either at Cap Farina (Ras Sidi Ali el Mekki) which the Romans called Promunturium Pulchri or, less probably, Cap Blanc (Ras Abiad), the Roman Promunturium Candidum (attempts to identify it with Cabo de

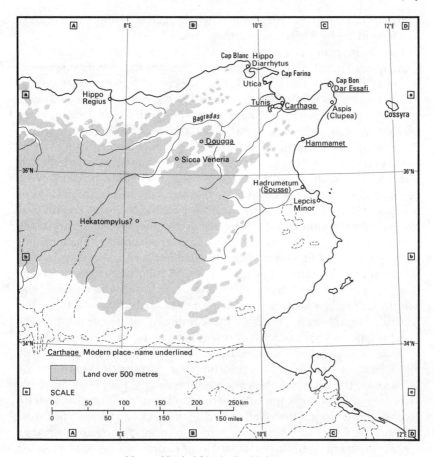

Map 12 North Africa in the third century.

Palos in Spain are less happy). In this case Polybius must have misunderstood the treaty, which will have excluded the Romans not from the Syrtes to the east of Carthage, but from the coast of North Africa along Numidia and Mauretania to the west of Carthage. The permission to trade, under fixed conditions, in Libya, must then refer to the territory east of Cape Farina, that is around the Bay of Tunis and further east, while in Carthage itself, as in western Sicily, conditions were even freer. Thus theoretically the Syrtes coast was open to Rome, but its dangers (from which a Roman fleet suffered in 253 B.C.) were such as to discourage much trade. Thus in general terms the Romans were excluded from much of the southern part of the seas west of Carthage, were given controlled access to the area around Carthage and in Sardinia, and greater freedom in Punic Sicily and Carthage itself.[29]

The main concern of the Romans was to protect Latium from Carthaginian interference; piratical raids rather than large-scale invasion must have been the chief fear. In Latium the cities fell into two categories: those 'subject' to Rome, which included five specifically named towns, and those not thus subject. The former were probably dependent allies (*socii*) who had individual treaties of alliance with Rome, in which Rome's military leadership was recognized, irrespective of Rome's relations with the Latin League as a whole; Rome is known to have had such a treaty with Gabii. The Latin cities which were not 'subject' were probably members of the League which met at Ferentina, of which Rome was a member and perhaps the leading member.[30] Of the five named towns, which lay on or near the coast stretching for some sixty miles south of Rome, that of the Laurentes causes some doubts. These people are possibly to be identified with the inhabitants of a very early settlement supposedly named Laurentum which soon merged with neighbouring Lavinium, or more probably Laurens was the name of the people whose city was called Lavinium (as Ardea was a city of the Rutuli). On the other hand in his comments on the second treaty Polybius mentions the other four towns but not that of the Laurentes; so either he has accidentally omitted it, or the MS reading of ἀρεντίνων in his text of the first treaty might possibly be a corrupted dittography of Ἀρδεατῶν (the people of Ardea) or Ἀντιατῶν (the people of Antium). However, in view of the importance of early Lavinium, demonstrated by recent archaeological discoveries, and its very close religious ties with Rome, it may very well have been named in the first treaty. But whether specifically mentioned or not, it would of course be covered by one or other of the clauses of the treaty. As to Tarracina, which fell to the Volscians before 400 and was then known as Anxur, while it is true that in later times it was called only Tarracina, this name may well be Etruscan and have been the original as well as the later name. Thus in general terms Rome claimed to throw a protective shield over a very wide area in Latium, but there is no suggestion that her interests transcend the boundaries of Latium.

Do these terms accord with what is known about the general historical background of Carthage and Rome and about international conditions

[29] For a recent reaffirmation of the identity of Polybius' Καλὸν ἀκρωτήριον with Cap Farina (Ras Sidi Ali el Mekki) *west* of Carthage see Werner 1975[K167], 21–44. He rejects attempts to identify it with Cap Bon made by Prachner 1969[K161], 157–72 and Petzold 1972[K159], 372ff. Marek 1977[K153], 1–7 tries to have it both ways by identifying it with Cap Bon and then arguing that under this first treaty the barred zone was the Syrtes area, to which the second treaty added Spain south of Mastia and (for trade) the African coast west of Cap Farina.

[30] For a different view see p. 272.

throughout the western Mediterranean near the end of the sixth century, or are they so inappropriate as to throw doubt on the Polybian dating? Throughout much of the sixth century the Carthaginians, often in co-operation with Etruscan cities, had been engaged in a long struggle to check the thrusting expansion of the Greeks in the West. It would thus be reasonable for Carthage to maintain her existing ties and to enter into fresh negotiations with the infant Roman Republic. It may seem surprising that Carthage made no effort to bar the Romans from the Spanish coast, but in all probability she had not yet gained control of the kingdom of Tartessos in Andalusia, which was on good terms with the Greeks. This fits in well with an early date for the first treaty, since by the time of the next treaty in the fourth century the Carthaginians had long conquered Tartessos (whether it be *c.* 500 B.C. as A. Schulten believed, or *c.* 450, as R. Werner maintains)[31] and thus could insist on the exclusion of the Romans from this area – but in 509 they could not do so. The restrictions that Carthage imposed in Sardinia and Sicily pose little difficulty. In Sardinia the Carthaginians had strengthened their hold after the earlier defeat of Malchus: thus the fort on Monte Sirai had been restored in the course of the sixth century, and under Mago and his son Hasdrubal control of the coastal areas was secure. In Sicily in *c.* 510 the Spartan prince Dorieus made an attempt to settle in the western Punic end of the island, but he was soon overwhelmed by a force of Carthaginians, Sicilian Phoenicians and local Elymians. Carthage, once again in control, could offer to treat the Romans on the same footing as any other traders in their Sicilian territory. What is known about Carthaginian influence in Libya, Sardinia and Sicily around 500 B.C. therefore accords with the possibility of a treaty of some such date, but our knowledge of details of Carthaginian policy in these areas at this time is probably too limited to permit further refinement, and to give firm support to a recent suggestion that the treaty must be slightly later than 480.[32]

Before his ill-fated Sicilian venture Dorieus had made an equally unsuccessful attempt to establish a Greek settlement at the mouth of the R. Cinyps in Tripolitania *c.* 513: within three years the Libyan natives, aided by some Carthaginian troops, had driven him and the settlers out. This episode might be brought into direct relation with the first treaty, if the latter did preclude the Romans from the Syrtes area (rather than from the coast westwards of Carthage), but such an argument should be resisted: the incident was only one in a long series of efforts by Carthage to keep others out of this sensitive area, and these continued until the

---

[31] A. Schulten, *Tartessos* (Ed. 2. Hamburg, 1960), 72f.; Werner 1963[A134], 326ff.

[32] Werner 1963[A134], 316–29, in accordance with his view that the Republic was established in *c.* 470 rather than in 509.

second century when they culminated in the aggressions of Massinissa. Tripolitania was probably of little interest to Rome at this time, while the main concern of Carthage with it was to prevent Greek settlement there from threatening her communications with the Phoenicians of the eastern Mediterranean. However that is not to say that an agreement with Rome that regulated, if it did not exclude, trade with this area would not be sought by Carthage.

Thus the interests of Carthage near the end of the sixth century accord quite well with the Polybian date, while K. J. Beloch's attempt to suggest that her international relations in *c.* 384 B.C., when Dionysius of Syracuse sacked Pyrgi, the port of Caere, and when Carthage might be eager to acquire non-Greek allies in the western Mediterranean, would provide a better date, has not met with much favour: though by then Carthage had emerged from a period of comparative isolation into which she had been drawn between her defeat at Himera (480) and her renewed efforts in Sicily in 409, her wide-spread commercial activity had not been revived until about the mid-fourth century, while the Romans can scarcely have been very concerned with overseas affairs immediately after their city had been sacked by the Gauls.[33]

From the Roman point of view also a treaty at the beginning of the Republic presents little difficulty to those who accept that she had become a fairly powerful state under the Etruscans, with widespread interests in Latium, where 'superior Romana res erat' ('the interests of the Roman people predominated': Livy 1.52.4). In a new, or more probably a renewed treaty it would be perfectly natural for the Republic to claim the same position *vis-à-vis* the Latins as the last king had exercised – though the claim was very soon to be challenged and defeated. The very fact that Rome's relations with the Latins deteriorated rapidly and that sixteen years later in the consulship of Sp. Cassius a new alliance was negotiated under which Rome had to abandon any claim to dominance in Latium in exchange for an alliance of equals, strongly supports the Polybian date.

Other considerations, arising from a comparison with the terms of the second Polybian treaty, also support an early date, but these must be postponed until the content of the second treaty has been explored.

(c) *The second treaty*

The formal arrangement of the second treaty, as given by Polybius, differs from the first: whereas the earlier document dealt first with Roman and then with Carthaginian obligations, the second subsumes

[33] See Beloch 1926[A12], 309ff, whose views are rejected by Toynbee 1965[A131], 1.530f.

both contracting parties under various headings. The second section of this later treaty (Polyb. III.24.8–10; see II below) takes the form of a σύμβολον περὶ τοῦ μὴ ἀδικεῖν ('an agreement to refrain from mutual injury') such as occurred in the treaties between Carthage and Etruria according to Aristotle (*Pol.* III.1280 c 35ff) and also in a treaty negotiated by Tyre with its overlord Assurhadon of Assyria in 677.[34] The content of the second treaty also may be set out in analytic form:

There shall be friendship between the Romans and their allies and the Carthaginians, Tyrians (?), and the people of Utica and their allies on these terms:

I. GEOGRAPHICAL LIMITATIONS
  (i) For the Romans
     The Romans shall not plunder, trade or colonize on the further side of the Fair Promontory, Mastia (and?) Tarseum (Μαστίας Ταρσηΐου: see below).
  (ii) For the Carthaginians
     (a) If the Carthaginians capture any city in Latium not subject to Rome, they may keep the goods and men, but must surrender the city.
     (b) If any Carthaginians take captive any member of a people with whom the Romans have a written peace treaty but who are not subject to Rome, they shall not bring them into Roman harbours, but if one is brought in and a Roman lay hold of him, he shall be set free. In like manner the Romans shall be bound to the Carthaginians.

II. CONTRACT REGARDING MUTUAL INJURIES
  (i) For the Romans
     If a Roman takes water or provision from any place within the jurisdiction of Carthage, he shall not injure, while so doing, any member of a people with whom the Carthaginians have peace and friendship.
  (ii) For the Carthaginians
     Neither shall a Carthaginian in like case.
  (iii) Both parties
     If a Roman or Carthaginian break the agreement, the other party shall not take private vengeance, but [if any one does break the agreement] the wrong shall be a matter of state adjustment.

[34] See D. D. Luckenbill, *Ancient Records of Assyria and Babylonia* (Chicago, 1927), II.229.

III. SPECIAL CONDITIONS
   (i) For the Romans
      (a) Sardinia and Libya
         No Roman shall trade or colonize in Sardinia and Libya nor [land in a Sardinian or Libyan port for any other purpose than] to take in provisions or repair his ship. If he be driven there by storm, he shall depart within five days.
      (b) Sicily and Carthage
         In the Carthaginian province of Sicily and at Carthage he may do and sell anything that is permitted to a citizen.
   (ii) For the Carthaginians
      A Carthaginian may do likewise in Rome.

Unlike the first treaty, the second mentions by name one (or two) of the allies of Carthage. The inclusion of Utica, now a privileged ally, indicates greater Carthaginian control in North Africa, but the mention of Tyre raises doubts: it should perhaps be rejected on the ground that Polybius may have misunderstood some Punic phrase such as 'the Tyrians of Carthage', which was their official title. The reference to $Μαστίας$ $Ταρσηίου$ is also difficult; although Polybius seems to believe that Mastia was in Africa, it was almost certainly the site in Spain where New Carthage (Cartagena) was later founded. In his introductory remarks to the treaty (III.24.2) Polybius seems to take Mastia and Tarseum as two settlements, but more probably they are to be linked (he may have misunderstood an archaic Latin genitive, 'Mastiam Tarseiom') and Tarseum is to be connected with the Tartessians whose territory ended just north of Cartagena at the River Tader. The object of this provision was to extend the prohibited area: hitherto it included only the North African coast west of Cape Farina, but now it was to embrace the whole of the western end of the Mediterranean as far north on the Spanish coast as Cartagena, subject no doubt to the exceptions caused by accident mentioned later in the treaty.

   The text of this second treaty, as given by Polybius, does not specify any cities in Latium by name, but in his comments Polybius says that the Romans again stressed that the Carthaginians should not harm the coastal cities of Ardea, Antium, Circeii and Tarracina (either he has carelessly omitted Lavinium or the name should be excluded from the first treaty). This comment however may be merely a gloss by Polybius and, if so, the names will not have appeared in the treaty. The towns which had written peace treaties with Rome and were not subject to her were *foederati*, such as Tibur and Praeneste in Latium, and possibly (depending on the date) other cities as far afield as Tarquinii, Caere, and even Tarentum. The treaty then returns to trading rights and completely excludes the Romans from Sardinia and Libya, which previously had been open to them under controlled conditions, though Punic Sicily and Carthage itself remained accessible.

Polybius unfortunately does not date this treaty, but during much of the fifth century the Romans were subjected to great internal and external pressure and were not perhaps likely to have been much concerned with overseas affairs. Gradually they gained sufficient strength to defeat the Aequi and Volsci and to capture Etruscan Veii, an event which must have impressed the Carthaginians, but then came the Gallic Sack of Rome. After some decades of slow recovery, by 350 B.C. Etruria was neutralized by Rome's long-term non-aggression agreements with Tarquinii and Caere, an alliance had recently been made with the Samnites, and though the Latins after their defeat in 358 were to prove less settled than might appear, Roman power in Italy was obviously increasing (pp. 320ff), as might be noted at Carthage. Thus *c.* 350 seems a reasonable *terminus post quem* for the treaty, while a *terminus ante quem* some ten years later is provided by the absence from the treaty of any reference to Roman control in Campania. Thus the 340s provide a suitable period, while Livy in fact records (VII.27.21) the conclusion of a treaty in 348, when Carthaginian envoys came to Rome 'amicitiam ac societatem petentes' ('seeking friendship and alliance')[35]; this date is also supported obliquely by Diodorus' muddled statement (see above). True, Diodorus says that this was the first treaty; Livy, however, although not mentioning any earlier one, does not say that the pact of 348 was the first. It would therefore seem unnecessary, if not perverse, to seek any other date. (Attempts to place Polybius' first two treaties in 348 and 306 respectively[36] founder on the absence of any reference to the Campanian cities in the second treaty.)

This dating gains support from the form and content of the two treaties, and above all from Polybius' stress upon the difficult Latinity of the earlier one. This in itself suggests a considerable lapse of time between the two. The theory[37] that the second is essentially only a supplement to the first and that therefore the time-gap must have been small, has not met with wide acceptance. Rather, Polybius treats the second as a completely new agreement, and not as a mere string of amendments. The difference in structure (p. 526f) also suggests a longish

[35] Calderone 1980[K141], 365ff dates Livy's treaty to 344 (because of the 'Dictator Years' (p. 348)) and believes that it was a military alliance (*societas*) and so cannot be equated with either of the Polybian treaties, which established only *amicitia* ('friendship').

[36] As argued by Täubler 1913[J235], 1.373–4 and Schachermeyr 1930[K165], 371ff.

[37] Aymard 1957[K138], 277–93, criticized by Toynbee 1965[A131], 1.536f.

interval and Carthage may well have adopted the form of a σύμβολον περὶ
τοῦ μὴ ἀδικεῖν from Greek practice sometime between c. 500 and 348. In
context also there are major differences. Rome's position in Latium is
different (the more so if the four Latin cities named in the second treaty
are merely a gloss by Polybius himself). The importance of the appearance in 349 of a hostile Greek fleet off the coast of Latium and the mouth
of the Tiber, recorded by Livy (VII.25.4; 26.14), has been variously
assessed. If it was merely a passing piratical raid (such as the attack of
Dionysius I on Pyrgi in 384–383), it will at very least have drawn
attention to the need to protect Latium. This much may be said without
accepting the theory that the Greek fleet came from Syracuse (as Livy
suspected, but did not know) to co-operate with the Gauls who were
attacking Latium,[38] or the further suggestion that the Romano-Punic
treaty was designed not to protect a friendly Latium largely under
Roman control but rather to counter a mainly independent and hostile
Latin League which had appealed to the Greeks for help: on this view
Carthage will have made her second agreement with Rome, stimulated
by her perennial enmity with the Greeks and annoyed by the piratical
activities such as those of Antium which disturbed the peace of the coast
of Latium.[39] Further, the outburst of new coinage issued by Carthage in
the 340s (see above, p. 507) suggests that she was reassessing her general
strategic position. Finally, the very considerable extension in the second
treaty of the areas where the Romans were barred or more closely
circumscribed suggests a development of Carthaginian power which will
not have occurred in a very short period. Thus the Livian date of 348 has
strong claims to be the year of this second Polybian treaty.

(d) *Later treaties*

Livy records that after the treaty of 348 Carthaginian envoys again went
to Rome in 343 to congratulate the Romans on their victory over the
Samnites and to offer a gold crown weighing 25 lbs. to Iuppiter
Capitolinus (VII.38.2); no specific mention of a renewal of any treaty is
made. Then in 306, according to Livy (IX.4; 26), Carthaginian envoys
went once again to Rome where the treaty was renewed (*renovatum*) for
the third time (*tertio*); the later treaty of 279/8 was described by the Livian
Epitomator (XIII) as 'quarto . . . renovatum ('renewed for the fourth
time': p. 518). Thus if Livy's 'renovatum' is taken literally, there were
five treaties down to and including that of 279/8 (an original one which
was four times renewed); alternatively the word may be used merely to
indicate that there were three and four agreements. If the latter view is

[38] So Sordi 1960[J230], 104ff; cf. p. 321.   [39] See Ferenczy 1976[A48], 79ff.

taken and the treaty of 306 was for Livy the third, either his account would imply an original one in the earlier Republic (at the beginning?) which he has not mentioned, and a second in 348, or he will have put the first in 348 and perhaps thought that a second was negotiated in 343 when the Carthaginians may have expected more than verbal thanks for their golden crown. If on the other hand *renovatum* is taken to imply five treaties, then four will have been made before 279/8 and this would leave room for the so-called Philinus treaty, if in fact that represented a separate negotiation.

In general the 340s were years when the Carthaginians would wish to ensure Roman friendship and to limit their active interest outside Italy. After the overthrow of Hanno's attempt to establish a tyranny at Carthage, the aristocratic regime was now firmly established, and was planning renewed interference in Sicily where Timoleon intervened in Syracuse after the struggles of Dionysius II and Dion for the city. In 343 the Carthaginians sent a force to Syracuse where it met with little success. They followed this up some two years later by despatching a much more imposing expedition, only to see it soundly defeated by Timoleon in a great battle by the river Crimisus. While the Sicilian Greeks were facing these difficulties, the Greeks of southern Italy, who were struggling to maintain themselves against pressure from the Bruttians and Lucanians in their mountainous hinterland, were forced to seek help from a series of Greek mercenary commanders, of whom the first, Archidamus of Sparta, arrived in Italy in 343. Although this area in the extreme south still lay beyond the political horizon of the Romans, they may nevertheless have been glad to renew their good relations with Carthage, just in case she might (in the event of victories in Sicily) think of interfering with the Greeks in South Italy.

But there was another sensitive area nearer Latium, namely Campania, to which Roman interests were clearly extending, whatever may be thought of the details of the First Samnite War which was alleged to have commenced in 343 (p. 359). Rome might well wish to receive some acknowledgement from Carthage of these extending interests, while Carthage would wish to see such an important market as Campania remaining open to her merchants. Thus general events throughout the central Mediterranean world would lead Rome and Carthage in the 340s to renew their earlier ties: if there was any formal agreement in 343, it could either have been a reiteration of the previous treaty or might even have included some new terms and thus qualify as one of Livy's treaties. It may be objected that two treaties in five years are unlikely, but the horizon had changed somewhat for both parties: in 343 Carthage was face to face with Timoleon, as was Rome both with the Samnites and the threat of the Great Latin War.

The fact of a treaty in 306 (Livy IX.43.26) should be accepted, although its content is unknown except in so far as it can be surmised from Rome's position in Italy and possibly from the essential clause of the 'Philinus' treaty. Rome was much stronger than in 348 or 343: she was encircling Samnium and seemed about to emerge victorious from her long struggle with its people (pp. 372ff). Carthage too seemed poised on the edge of victory over Agathocles whose invasion of Africa had suffered defeat in 307, while a Carthaginian army was besieging Syracuse. Thus both Rome and Carthage, confident of victory yet conscious of the uncertainties of war, might think it wise to negotiate from growing strength – in case that strength should suffer any unexpected set-back. The treaty is therefore likely to have recognized Rome's new position in Italy. This is made more probable by Polybius' statement that in the treaty between Rome and Carthage made in 279/8 during the Pyrrhic War, they agreed to 'maintain all the previous agrements' (III.25.2). Now it is unlikely that the Romans in 279, when they had contacts with the extreme south of Italy, would have been content to see their interests restricted largely to Latium as under Polybius' first two treaties: in consequence a wider definition of their Italian interests might be expected in the treaty of 306 (whether or not any extension occurred in 343, if there was an agreement that year). This thought has led some scholars to suppose that the treaty of 306 contained the far-reaching agreement which according to Philinus defined Italy and Sicily as the respective spheres of interest of Rome and Carthage and forbade either to interfere in the other's territory (cf. pp. 457; 475).

The existence of a formal agreement that Carthage should refrain from interfering in Italy and the Romans in Sicily was asserted by the Sicilian historian Philinus according to the express statement of Polybius (III.26.2–5) who indignantly denied the fact, pointing out that such a treaty, had it existed, would have involved the Romans in treaty-breaking when they crossed over to Sicily at the beginning of the First Punic War in 264: 'there is, as a fact, no such document at all, nor ever was there'. The basis of this vehement denial was that Polybius found no such treaty in the treasury of the aediles.

In other matters Polybius regarded Philinus as a reliable historian and even used his work as one of the two main sources for his own history of the First Punic War, balancing the pro-Carthaginian Philinus with the pro-Roman Fabius. Of these two historians he wrote (1.14.2f): 'judging from their lives and principles, I do not suppose that they intentionally stated what was false, but I think that they are in much the same state of mind as men in love. Partisanship and complete prepossession made Philinus think that all the actions of the Carthaginians were characterized by wisdom, honour and courage: those of the Romans by the reverse.

Fabius thought the exact opposite.' Polybius' outburst against Philinus was therefore based on an honest belief that he was mistaken on an issue in which the honour of Rome was involved. Indeed Polybius goes so far as to admit that the Romans could be blamed for their alliance with the Mamertines which ultimately led to their intervention in Sicily, but he will not have it that they crossed the Straits in contravention of a treaty and of their solemn oaths.

If therefore the essential honesty of neither historian is to be impugned, one or other may have been the victim of national propaganda. So little is known about Philinus that any question of his having consulted the archives in Carthage must remain completely open, as also must the state and completeness of any such records. In view of the commercial activities of the Carthaginians and Aristotle's remarks about their treaty-making, their record office was probably well looked after and there is no reason why Philinus' treaty, if it existed, should not have been preserved in Carthage, and since by implication it branded Rome as the aggressor in 264, there would be no need to conceal it from any enquirer. For the Romans the boot was on the other foot, and national honour would gain by the suppression of any copy in their archives. Indeed some scholars go so far as to suppose that at some point the treaty was deliberately destroyed in the interests of Rome's good name. This presumably could have been done by a clerk at the record office at the instigation of some higher authority (after all, in 52 B.C. Pompey broke into the Aerarium and altered the text of a law on his own responsibility: Suet. *Iul.* 28.3).

Alternatively, if not deliberately 'mislaid', the Roman copy of the treaty could simply have been lost in the course of time. We know little about the filing of state documents in the time of Polybius and nothing about the treasury (ταμιεῖον) of the aediles beyond his reference to it: was it an organized record office or merely a store-room? But we do know that Roman handling of documents was unexpectedly haphazard in the days of Cicero who complained bitterly: 'we have no guardianship of the laws, and therefore they have to be whatever our clerks (*apparitores*) want them to be: we get them from the state copyists (*a librariis*) but have no official records. The Greeks were more careful about this, for they elected guardians of the law, νομοφύλακες' (*Leg.* III.46). About the Philinus treaty we can only speculate. If there was a bronze copy like the three treaties quoted by Polybius, it could have been turned to the wall in order to use the back for another inscription (as was done later to the Lex Acilia to provide for the *lex agraria* now on the reverse[40]). However, all original treaties must have been written documents on skin or papyrus

[40] H. B. Mattingly *JRS* 59 (1969), 138f.

sworn to by the contracting parties, who presumably would file copies in their own archives, and we cannot be certain that all treaties were also set up in bronze. If only the original written document survived, it would be more difficult to trace, more easily lost and more easy to suppress. So Polybius' failure to find such a document (whether by personal search or through the medium of his friends) cannot be regarded as sure proof that it never existed. On the other hand, if the non-existence of such a treaty redounded to Rome's interest in 264, equally its existence could have been invented by their opponents. In that case, granted the essential honesty of Philinus, it must have been the product of the Carthaginian government or an individual which was deliberately foisted upon the unsuspecting historian. This is possible, but if true it is surprising that, so far as we know, no reference to such trickery was made by that great hater of the Carthaginians, Cato, who was so eager to denounce them as *foedifragi* ('treaty-breakers').

If therefore the hypothesis of the propagating of a falsehood has to be balanced against the suppression of a truth, any further evidence which could be added to one of the scales must come from literary allusions, direct or implied, and the possibility of fitting such a treaty into the general series. There is one such allusion: Servius in his commentary on Vergil (*Schol. Dan. Aen.* iv.628): 'in foedere cautum fuit ut neque Romani ad litora Carthaginiensium accederent neque Carthaginienses ad litora Romanorum',[41] where the two *litora* ('shores') must surely represent the 'Italy' and 'Sicily' of the Philinus agreement. However the value to be placed on Servius' testimony remains ambiguous, since it is uncertain whether his statement derives ultimately from Philinus (although this does not seem probable in view of Philinus' later eclipse by Polybius) or from an independent tradition. But more significant perhaps is the episode of 272 B.C. when a Carthaginian fleet appeared off Tarentum: 'quo facto ab his foedus violatum est'[42] (Livy, *Ep.* XIV). This illegal intervention was a cause of the First Punic War according to the words which Livy puts into the mouth of Hanno when he was pleading to the Carthaginians to prevent the Saguntine affair from starting a second war: 'we could not keep our hands off Tarentum, that is from Italy, as by treaty bound' ('sed Tarento, id est Italia, non abstinueramus ex foedere': Livy XXI.10.8). This treaty obligation to keep their hands off Italy corresponds exactly with the ἀπεχέσθαι Ἰταλίας ('to keep away from Italy') of the Philinus agreement. Since the Punic fleet wisely did not press its effort to help the Tarentines against the Romans, the incident was merely a technical breach of obligations and did not immediately

---

[41] 'It was provided by treaty that the Romans should not approach the shores of the Carthaginians nor the Carthaginians those of the Romans.'

[42] 'This action involved a breach of the treaty on their part.'

lead to any undesirable consequences. Finally, another agreement points in the same direction. In the treaty which Rome made with Carthage in 279/8 during the Pyrrhic War (Polybius' third treaty) it was enacted that 'it may be lawful to assist each other in the territory of the party who is the victim of [Pyrrhus'] aggression', namely Sicily or Campania and Latium (below p. 536). This clause implies that in 279/8 a legal barrier precluded the Carthaginians from landing in Italy and the Romans from crossing to Sicily.

If in view of these scraps of evidence some such reciprocal self-denying agreement, defining Italy and Sicily as 'spheres of influence', seems probable, when was it negotiated? The year 306 has much in its favour, but some think it a little too early and that Rome would scarcely claim to speak for all Italy before she had become involved with the Greek cities in the toe and heel, and that the Carthaginians would not be worrying about any possible Roman interference in Sicily. On the other hand in 306 Rome doubtless felt that both Samnites and Etruscans were virtually defeated and that she had no substantial rivals in all Italy. If she thought of the Italiotes, she may well have asserted an inclusive claim to all Italy in order soon to be able to deal with them free from Carthaginian, though not as events turned out from Greek, external interference. Alternatively, if 306 be rejected, some have tried to link the agreement to the Pyrrhus treaty of 279/8, by suggesting that it was a secret clause of this third Polybian pact, diplomatically arranged by Mago on his visit to Rome,[43] but this clashes with another clause which allowed the sending of troops on Carthaginian ships to Italy or Sicily. Others[44] incline to suppose that the treaty of 279/8 contained some vague, but not explicit, recognition of spheres of influence and that after the First Punic War this was built up by Carthaginian propaganda, to which Roman propagandists will have replied by exaggerating the incident of the Punic fleet at Tarentum. Finally, it may be noted that if the interdict is accepted as having some sort of historical basis, its application need not have been absolute: like the later Ebro treaty which forbade the Carthaginians to cross the Ebro only ἐπὶ πολέμῳ ('to wage war') (Pol. 11.13.7), its ban may have been military and political rather than commercial.[45]

Even less certain, both in fact and in dating, is the possible appearance of Corsica in one of these treaties. In the passage of Servius quoted above

[43] So Schachermeyr 1930[K165], 378–80 and Heuss 1949[K180], 459–60. Secret treaties or clauses were virtually unknown in the world of Greek diplomacy (see G.E.M. de Ste Croix, *CQ* 51 (1963), 114ff) and such a clause is highly improbable in Pyrrhus' treaty.

[44] See De Sanctis 1907–64[A37], III.100 and Walbank 1957–79[B182], 1.354.

[45] Historians who have recently argued in favour of the Philinus treaty (306) include Meister 1970[K154], 408–23; 1975[B107], 124ff; Mitchell 1971[K156], 633–55. Cf. also Hampl 1972[K179], 422ff; Musti 1972[B120], 1139f. The attack on the treaty has been renewed by Badian 1980[K139], 161–9.

he adds that by treaties Corsica should become a no man's land: 'in foederibus similiter cautum est ut Corsica esset media inter Romanos et Carthaginienses'. Although Polybius in another context (1.10.5) says that Carthage was mistress of all the islands in the Sardinian and Tyrrhenian seas, there is no direct evidence that these included Corsica, which the Romans captured (from the natives?) in 259. Since the island does not appear as a bone of contention between Rome and Carthage before 264, it might well have figured in a clause omitted (carelessly?) by Polybius or in a treaty which Polybius did not know. The most likely is the Philinus agreement, since Servius apparently links the two, and if Corsica did not appear in any treaty why did Servius or his source mention it? Did they just invent it, and if so why? Or is it merely some busybody's gloss?

The agreement of 279/8, Polybius' third treaty, was probably made just after Pyrrhus had defeated the Romans at Ausculum: the Carthaginians, who were not at war with Pyrrhus, nevertheless feared that he might gain a final victory over the Romans and then be tempted to cross to Sicily to help the Greek cities. Thus in order to keep Pyrrhus in Italy, they negotiated afresh with Rome. As we have seen, they agreed to maintain all earlier agreements: these almost certainly included a fairly extensive recognition of Roman interests in Italy and indeed, if the 'Philinus' treaty be accepted as pre-Pyrrhic, the whole of Italy will have been included. Polybius then adds (III.25.3–6) the new arrangements: 'If they make a written alliance (*symmachia*) against Pyrrhus, let them make it, each or both, with such provision that they may be allowed to assist each other in the territory of the party who is the victim of aggression.'[46] Such potential mutual aid was thus permissive, not obligatory. Then followed two clauses providing help for the Romans: 'no matter which party requires help, the Carthaginians are to provide the ships for transport and return journey (reading ἄφοδον), but each shall provide the pay for its own men. The Carthaginians, if necessary, shall come to the help of the Romans by sea also, but no one shall compel the crews to land against their will.'

The treaty was presumably negotiated by the Carthaginian admiral Mago who appeared off the mouth of the Tiber with an imposing fleet of 120 ships, offering Rome help. The chronology (with the possibility of two visits) and many details of the episode are obscure.[47] A patriotically

---

[46] This is the translation by F. W. Walbank, with the change of 'alliance with' to 'alliance against', a view which he himself now favours, since *symmachia* is a strange word for a potential peace, especially one that might be made sometime by partners who were not even yet in alliance against Pyrrhus. This interpretation was put forward independently by Meister 1970[K154], 408–23 (cf. 1975[B107], 136) and by Mitchell 1971[K156], 648ff: it is attractive.

[47] See Justin. XVIII.2; Val. Max. III.7.10. Passerini 1943[J283], 92–112 dates Mago's visit to late 279 and the treaty to early 278. Cf. Rosenthal-Lefkowitz 1959[J285], 147–77; Petzold 1969[B136], 149ff; Hampl 1972[K179], 412ff. For further discussion of the background and context of the treaty see pp. 475ff.

slanted version depicts the Romans brusquely refusing aid. No doubt no direct military aid was accepted (and the modern theory that Mago handed over a large sum of money is not based on direct ancient testimony, though in view of the golden crown offered in 343 he may not have come empty-handed); nevertheless the result of the visit was the agreement which Polybius records. The great size of the Punic armada merely reinforced the importance that Carthage placed on trying to keep Pyrrhus out of Sicily by negotiating with Rome. If it was designed to impress Rome with the strength of Carthage, it was the strength of an ally of over two hundred years standing.

The history of these early treaties must remain uncertain in many points; all that has been attempted here is to set forth their recorded terms, to indicate the evidence and to suggest a probable pattern of development. A vast number of alternative and often mutually contra-dictory solutions have been advanced since the days of Mommsen. They tend to fall into four categories: those which set Polybius' first treaty either at the beginning of the Republic or in the fourth century, and those which either do or do not accept a maximum of three treaties. Many combinations have been attempted, but no single solution has been found to convince everyone. What does result very clearly is that for a very long period of time both cities found it in their mutual self-interest to maintain friendly agreements which would last as long as Carthage was prepared not to promote her commercial interests in certain areas by aggressive force and Rome was primarily concerned with the peoples of Italy. However, Carthaginian concern with the Greeks in Sicily and Roman concern with the Greeks in southern Italy unfortunately ulti-mately brought the two powers face to face across the narrow Straits of Messana.

III. THE FIRST PUNIC WAR

(a) *The Mamertines and war*

A slight shadow may have been cast on the age-old good relations between Rome and Carthage by the appearance of the Punic fleet off Tarentum in 272 B.C. (p. 534), but no crisis had followed. However, the development of events in Sicily (Map 13) offered some substance to the alleged prophetic remark made by Pyrrhus when he was leaving the island: 'What a cockpit [literally 'wrestling-ground'] we are now leaving for Carthaginian and Roman to fight in' (Plut. *Pyrrh.* 23.8: p. 481). For decades the Carthaginians had kept up persistent pressure on the Sicilian Greeks: though their expansion had been checked first by Agathocles and then by Pyrrhus, they had returned to the attack, defeated the Syracusan fleet and reduced the Greek cities of central Sicily. But this was not the only threat that faced Syracuse. For some time eastern Sicily had

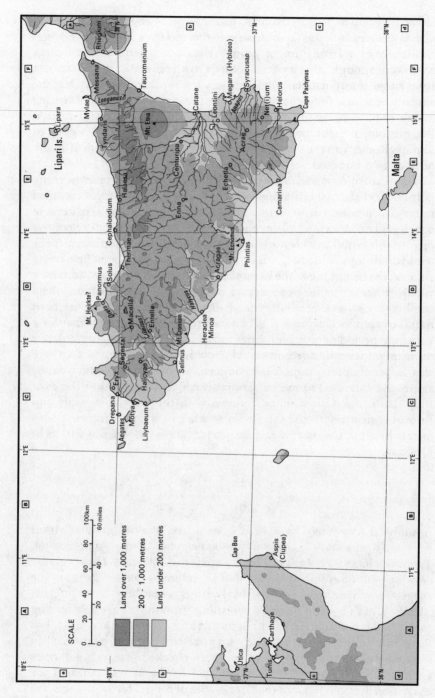

Map 13 Sicily in the First Punic War.

been subjected to attacks from the Mamertines, Agathocles' discharged Italian mercenaries who had seized Messana between 288 and 283 and, though temporarily checked by Pyrrhus, continued to plunder the surrounding countryside, Carthaginian and Greek alike. Syracuse under its *strategos* Hiero made two attempts to deal with them: after an initial defeat (*c.* 275/4), a few years later (either *c.* 269 or *c.* 265) he captured Halaesa and Tyndaris, routed the Mamertines on the river Longanus, and assumed the title of king.[48] He then advanced against Messana, but Carthage was not willing to allow Syracuse to capture a key position which controlled the Straits: a Punic admiral, who was off Lipara keeping an eye on events, intervened and installed a Carthaginian garrison in the citadel of Messana with the approval of the Mamertines. Hiero accepted the situation and withdrew, disappointing the hopes of the poet Theocritus (*Id.* XVI.76ff) that he would continue the struggle like a hero of old, while the Carthaginians added to their success by occupying Tyndaris. But the Mamertines were uncomfortable about their acceptance of the Punic garrison, since they had no desire to become permanently subservient to Carthage and yet lacked the strength to stand on their own feet after their losses at the Longanus battle, especially as they were no longer helped by the rebel garrison in Rhegium. Some therefore proposed to seek a more formal agreement with Carthage by which their independence would be respected, but others, who argued that help should be sought from a less alien people, the Romans, and that the Punic garrison should be asked to withdraw, gained the day.

The three main actors in the developing drama may well have recalled the consequences of another recent appeal for Roman help which had been made by Rhegium, Messana's neighbour across the Straits. The cause of this appeal according to Polybius (1.7.6) was apprehension of attack by Pyrrhus and fear of the Carthaginians who controlled the sea, though Dionysius of Halicarnassus refers (*Ant. Rom.* xx.4) to Rhegium's fear of Bruttians, Lucanians and Tarentines; if the latter be followed, the appeal will have been in 282, if the former in 280. The reference to the threat of Carthaginian domination by sea is interesting, even if it is difficult to suppose that Greek Rhegium had much to fear from Pyrrhus; indeed the Mamertines might seem a greater threat. However that may be, the Romans installed a garrison of Campanian troops of uncertain number (the sources vary between 1200 and 4500), but before long it imitated the conduct of the Mamertines and with their co-operation it revolted and gained control of Rhegium by force. Rome, engaged in her struggle with Pyrrhus, delayed action, and this allowed the rebel troops in Rhegium to seize Croton and destroy Caulonia. But in 270 a consul,

---

[48] For a summary of the chronological problems see Walbank 1957–79[B182], 1.54f.

540II. CARTHAGE AND ROME

helped possibly by some Syracusan troops sent by Hiero (Zonar. VIII.6), took stern vengeance: he captured Rhegium, killed most of the garrison and sent the 300 survivors to Rome to be scourged and executed in the Forum as a public vindication of Roman *fides* to her allies: Rhegium was handed back to its own citizens. These events must surely have been in the minds of the Mamertines, Romans and Carthaginians when Rome was faced by this new appeal from the Mamertines.

Polybius' description of the senate's reaction to this appeal is conditioned to some extent by his use of Fabius Pictor whose account was obviously pro-Roman if not a tendentious justification of Roman conduct, but its essential accuracy need not be questioned. The senate was divided by the equally pressing demands of right and expediency. On the one hand some felt that it would be morally wrong to help the Mamertines who had seized Messana in much the same way as the Campanian mercenaries had seized Rhegium: indeed the Mamertines had even aided the Campanians. Rome had annihilated the latter: how could she be justified in helping the former? But on the other hand possible Carthaginian reaction could not be neglected; although the question at issue was merely aid to the Mamertines, few Roman senators can have failed to see that to countenance or even co-operate in the expulsion of a Punic garrison might have very serious consequences. It may be that Polybius, influenced as he must have been by later events, saw the Carthaginian threat in too sombre a light, when he emphasized their empire in Africa, 'a great part of Spain' (surely exaggerated for 264) and the islands in the Sardinian and Tyrrhenian Seas; further he suggested that if the Mamertines were not helped, the Carthaginians would conquer Syracuse, master the whole of Sicily, thus encircle Italy and 'build a bridge' (γεφυρῶσαι) over to Italy (1.10.5ff). Now it may be that Carthage in fact had no hostile intent towards Italy,[49] but that is not to say that Rome, sensitive to the possibility of foreign invasions of Italy after her war with Pyrrhus which had resulted indirectly from an appeal by Thurii, may not have harboured lurking suspicions about the ultimate Carthaginian intentions. Further, Rome now had allies in southern Italy and responsibilities towards them. If they were not in danger of attack, at least their commercial interests might be threatened: what kind of a trading monopoly would Carthage extend to all Sicilian harbours if she controlled Messana and the rest of the island, and might not the resultant economic pressure lead some of the southern Italians to think of casting in their lot with Carthage and possibly even to seek Punic garrisons as the Mamertines had done? And how would Rome herself view Carthaginian control of the Straits which could compel her own weak little navy to

[49] As argued by Heuss 1949[K180], 457–513.

have to sail all the way around Sicily to reach Tarentum and the Adriatic, exposed at all points to the dominant Punic fleet? By re-asserting their protective interest in their ally Rhegium the Romans six years earlier had secured control over the Straits; were they now to risk the consequences of a Carthaginian occupation of Messana across the narrow waters? Surely some such thought must have weighed heavily on many senators, even if they did not go on to speculate in more detail on the full consequences of a break with Carthage and the dangers of fighting a war in Sicily without adequate sea-power.

Roman interference in Sicily, however, would aggravate not only Carthage but also Syracuse, and Rome had to try to assess Hiero's reaction and power. Syracuse has in fact been regarded as the primary potential enemy by some scholars and this view has been developed into a belief that it was the potential influence of Syracuse, not of Carthage, on southern Italian affairs that the Romans feared. The whole course of the events of the first years of the subsequent war is interpreted in the light of this theory: the conflict started as a war betweeen Rome and Hiero, and only in the winter of 263/2, when it was clear that the Romans were not going to leave Sicily, did Carthage take effective hostile action and a real *Punic* war begin. But while in its discussions in 264 the senate may have given more thought to Syracuse than the Polybian tradition allows, and though the war started as a conflict for Messana, it can scarcely be doubted that Appius Claudius declared war on Carthage, not Syracuse, in 264.[50]

The weight of the ethical argument against helping the Mamertines is not easy to assess. It would be unfair to reject entirely Polybius' belief that it genuinely worried some senators. Yet the Mamertines had now held Messana for a quarter of a century and could be regarded as an independent state with which Rome could legitimately enter into relations, while their earlier opposition to Pyrrhus might commend them to the Romans. Some Romans might even have taken note of the appeal of the Mamertine envoys to their common Italian origin (ὁμόφυλοι: Polyb. 1.10.2).[51] Further, the parallel with Rhegium could not be pressed too far, since Rhegium had been an ally of Rome, whereas the Romans had earlier been under no obligation to protect Messana from the Mamertines. Some senators may of course have used the moralistic argument to mask their conservative dislike of an expansionist policy which might increase

---

[50] Cf. Heuss 1949[K180], 478ff, whose stress on Syracuse rather than Carthage as the primary enemy has been developed by Molthagen 1975[K191], 89–127 as indicated above. The latter's theory has been accepted by Dahlheim 1977[J157], 16 n. 3, but rejected by Welwei 1978[K206], 573–87.

[51] A more favourable tradition about the Mamertine occupation of Messana was preserved in the *Bellum Carthaginiense* of the Oscan writer Alfius (of the Augustan age): they went to help the hard-pressed Messanians who invited them to stay and settle (cf. Cichorius 1922[A26], 58ff). Could this version, even if only Mamertine propaganda, have been in circulation in 264?

the power of the people and of any popular leaders whom an overseas war might bring into prominence. Another possible reason for rejecting the Mamertine appeal was the Philinus treaty which forbade Roman intervention in Sicily. Such an argument naturally does not appear in Polybius since, as we have seen, he rejected the existence of such a treaty, while any pro-Roman writer who accepted its historicity would be ready conveniently to overlook it since, if it was still valid in 264, it would have made the Romans treaty-breakers. Indeed the view could well have been taken that it was (probably) some forty years old and that the Carthaginians themselves had in effect annulled the agreement by their action at Tarentum in 272.

Torn between the two lines of argument the senate after long debate did not sanction the proposal (τὴν γνώμην) for helping the Mamertines but apparently referred the question to the people. Since the immediate issue was not one of war but of alliance, the body consulted will less probably have been the *comitia centuriata* than a tribal assembly, and this will have been the *comitia tributa* rather than the *concilium plebis* because the matter was introduced by the consul Appius Claudius.[52] Though the people were exhausted by recent wars and needed rest, they responded to the arguments put forward by Claudius who, according to Polybius, blatantly talked not merely of help for the Mamertines but of war and stressed the advantages that would result, both to the general good by checking Carthage and to the individual Roman from war-booty. The *comitia* then ratified τὸ δόγμα; this word, used by Polybius (1.11.3), has caused much discussion since it usually means a *senatus consultum* whereas in this debate the senate apparently had not reached a formal decision which it had referred to the *comitia*. However, since δόγμα could also be used for the less formal *senatus auctoritas*, Polybius may here simply be using it for a measure discussed but not decreed by the senate.[53] After the vote of the *comitia* Appius Claudius was ordered to cross over to Messana and help the Mamertines; since the appointment was presumably made by the senate, this body may at the same time have given its approval to the decision of the *comitia*. But what had the *comitia* actually voted? Certainly not war, despite much talk of potential war, and possibly not

---

[52] Polybius 1.11.2 calls the proposers στρατηγοί; here he probably means consuls rather than military commanders. But as one consul was campaigning in Etruria, the matter must have been handled by the other, Appius Claudius, alone. There has been much discussion as to which popular assembly was consulted.

[53] Cf. Walbank 1957–79[B182], 1.60, III.757f; *Res gestae* 20.4. The difficulty has been met on totally different lines by Täubler 1913[J235], 1.100 n. 2 and De Martino 1972–5[A35], II.276ff who assume that οἱ πολλοί ('the many' who ἔκριναν βοηθεῖν 'determined to send assistance') were not the people but a majority of the senate (cf. Polyb. v.49.1 and XXXIII.18.11 for other such possible uses of οἱ πολλοί). On this interpretation after indecision a majority of senators were persuaded by Claudius to accept the appeal, and the *senatus consultum* (δόγμα) was then ratified by the people. This view has recently been revived and supported by Calderone 1977[K171], esp. 25ff; 1981[K172], esp. 34ff.

even a formal *foedus* with the Mamertines; this may have come later, whereas the Mamertine envoys in Rome at this point may only have been making a *deditio* ((formal) surrender) and requesting help.[54]

After the appointment of Appius Claudius Caudex the Mamertines succeeded in ejecting the Punic garrison; this they achieved by their own efforts, so Polybius implies. However, an alternative version, given by Dio (xi fr. 43.7–10 vol. I, p. 146f Boiss.) and Zonaras (viii.8) may well be true; while still engaged in preparing his forces, Appius Claudius sent on an advance guard under his relative C. Claudius who forced the Straits with little opposition, despite a boast by the Carthaginian admiral that he would not let the Romans so much as wash their hands in the sea; in fact, after a slight skirmish, he returned a few ships that he had captured. The Carthaginian commander of the garrison in Messana was no less cautious: faced by the forces of C. Claudius and Mamertine pressure he evacuated the citadel without a fight, but crucifixion was the price he subsequently had to pay for this lack of initiative. The Punic commanders in the field appear to have been left without adequate instructions from home on how to respond to this pressure from the Romans who had in fact not declared war. While Appius Claudius was still busy preparing his forces, both the Carthaginians and Hiero, objecting to this threat of interference in Sicily by a third power, agreed to sink the traditional hostility between Greek and Carthaginian and formed an unnatural alliance. Carthaginian troops were sent to Sicily under the command of Hanno, who proceeded to garrison Acragas and encamped north-west of Messana; a Punic fleet anchored to the north of the town, while Hiero advanced and camped to the south: Messana was efficiently blockaded. Appius Claudius, either before he managed to get his legions across the Straits by night or thereafter, sent envoys to the Carthaginians and Hiero, to negotiate for raising the siege of a town which was under Roman protection.[55] On their refusal to compromise a state of war obviously existed, as was made clear by the declaration of war which Ennius put into the mouth of Claudius: 'Appius indixit

---

[54] So Rich 1976[G694], 120, who also rejects the view proposed by Reuss (1901[K194], 105ff) and revived by Hoffmann (1969[K181], 171ff), Schwarte (1972[K199], 210ff) and Petzold (1969[B136], 168ff), that Polybius has combined into one two appeals by the Mamertines and two votes of the Roman people: first the people voted on an alliance, and later, after Messana was besieged by the Carthaginians and Hiero, they voted to send out help under Appius Claudius. This view gains some support from the most natural interpretation of a somewhat ambiguous passage of Polybius (iii.26.6) which however seems to contradict his account in Book i. In view of this and in the absence of any reference to two appeals in any other source, it may be somewhat bold to prefer his incidental references in Book iii to his narrative account of events in Book i.

[55] According to Diodorus (xxiii.1.4; from Philinus?) Appius was sent out only after the Romans knew that the Carthaginians and Hiero had attacked Messana. This view however may have arisen because of the length of Appius' preparations; when he was ready, the attack may already have started.

Carthaginiensibus bellum' ('Appius declared war on the Carthaginians': Ennius, *Ann.* 216 Skutsch). But the precise legal position is less certain; it is possible that no formal war-vote was passed by the Roman people and that their vote that help be sent to the Mamertines empowered Claudius to implement this order in whatever way he judged fit. If, however, there was a vote for war, the *comitia centuriata* must have met (as the result of a further appeal by the Mamertines?) and an adaptation of the old fetial law presumably followed: senatorial envoys (*legati*) were appointed (or could Claudius himself have been authorized to act as deputy?) and were granted conditional authorization to declare war if the Carthaginians and Hiero rejected a formal demand for reparation (*rerum repetitio*).[56] At any rate, whatever the formalities, Rome was now at war with Carthage and Syracuse.

Rome had taken a momentous step. For the first time in her history she had involved herself in military action outside Italy. True, the Straits were narrow and Sicily was almost part of Italy, but Roman troops had to be carried across and kept supplied in an island when Roman naval power was negligible compared with the great fleets of her enemies. No doubt the Romans who had advocated this policy envisaged only limited action and certainly not a war that was to last nearly a generation, but they do not seem to have realized the difficulty of containing a conflict once started: since the protection they had granted to Thurii and other Greek cities in southern Italy in the late 280s had led to war with Tarentum and in consequence to Pyrrhus' invasion, had they any solid grounds to expect that their protection of Messana might not involve more than a limited clash with Carthage and Hiero? That they anticipated some sort of clash when they offered this protection is shown by the prospect of booty that Claudius dangled before the people. Indeed Claudius' personal ambition and desire for military glory may well have been among the proximate causes of the war. Further, he was a member of a family which had advocated expansion in the south and perhaps had some interest in the Italian world of commerce (pp. 447; 450). But there does not appear to have been any predetermined policy on the part of Rome to challenge Carthage, while Carthage certainly wanted peace in order to maintain and if possible to expand her commerce and her *mare clausum* policy. A series of episodes created some mutual suspicions and the two sides drifted into war. When the minor states between them had been eliminated or assimilated the two great powers of the western Mediterranean suddenly found themselves face to face across the Straits

[56] For recent discussion see Rich 1976[K694], 119ff, who argues against a war-vote. He also suggests that the fragment of Naevius which is concerned with the fetials ('scopas atque verbenas / sagmina sumpserunt' 'they took twigs and shoots as sacred sprigs') applies not to the declaration of the First Punic War but to the subsequent peace treaty (cf. Schwarte 1972[K199], 218ff).

of Messana. Dissimilar in culture and interests, they lacked either the diplomatic skills or perhaps the real desire to try to patch up an age-long friendship which had begun to wear a little thin.

(b) *War by land and sea*[57]

Hostilities opened with successive attacks by Appius Claudius on the separated camps of Hiero and Hanno, but the course of events is obscure since Polybius gives one account and rejects a different version provided by Philinus. According to Polybius (1.11.13–12.4) Claudius' two engagements were successful: Hiero then hastily withdrew to Syracuse, whither he was pursued by the victorious Claudius who proceeded to besiege the city, while in the meantime the defeated Carthaginians had withdrawn from Messana to the protection of neighbouring cities. According to Philinus' version (Polyb. 1.15.1–11), however, the Romans were worsted in both engagements, yet Hiero withdrew. It may be that both engagements were indecisive, with both sides claiming victory, and that Hanno retired to protect and garrison the Punic cities, while Hiero, disappointed that his allies had allowed the Romans to cross over into Sicily virtually unopposed, decided to return home. Two hypotheses, though not without attendant difficulties, are attractive, namely that Claudius' advance against Syracuse should be rejected as a doublet of that of the consul Valerius in the following year, and that Hiero did not retreat until 263 when he was faced by stronger Roman forces.[58] This suggestion, that Claudius was far from successful, would help to explain the senate's displeasure with him, the Roman people's discontent with the conduct of the war and the fact that it was not he, but his successor Valerius, who won the *cognomen* of Messalla, received a triumph and set up in the Senate-House a painting of his victory over the Carthaginians and Hiero.

In the following year (263) the Romans determined on decisive action in Sicily by sending out both consuls, M'. Valerius Maximus (Messalla) and M'. Otacilius Crassus, with a double consular force and a full contingent of allies, some 40,000 men. Since Otacilius was a plebeian *novus homo* and the Valerian *gens* was traditionally opposed to the Claudii,

---

[57] In the period of the First Punic War minor chronological problems arise from the uncertainty as to whether the Roman calendar and the Julian years concided (cf. p. 174 n. 7), and, if not, the extent of the discrepancy. See Morgan 1977[K193], 89–117, who argues that in the early years of the war the Roman calendar was regularly a month or more ahead of the Julian, but that between the spring of 258 and that of 255 they were brought into rough agreement by means of a special intercalation of two months and remained so for the rest of the war.

[58] So Beloch 1912–27[A11], IV.2, 533ff and De Sanctis 1907–64[A37], III.109 respectively. Some consequential adjustments of the tradition are not easy: see Walbank 1957–79[B182], 1.66f. Cf. also Meister 1975[B107], 129ff. On the political, as well as the military, considerations that influenced Hiero see Frézouls 1979[K177], 965–89.

the result of the consular elections must be regarded as a criticism of Appius Claudius and the handling of the war. A line of Naevius ('Manius Valerius / consul partem exerciti in expeditionem / ducit', 'the consul Manius Valerius leads out part of the army on campaign': fr. 32 Mor.) suggests that Valerius may have reached Sicily before his colleague; at any rate his activities are given more prominence in the tradition. The main task was to free Messana if that had not already been achieved, and to force both Carthaginians and Hiero to recognize Rome's Messanian alliance. The consuls advanced into Syracusan territory, and captured the border town of Adranum, south of Etna. Many towns soon surrendered to Rome: Halaesa, Centuripa, Catane, probably Enna, and before long Camarina, while the siege of Echetla (Polyb. 1.15.10) may belong to this campaign (the figure of sixty-seven towns, however, given by Diodorus XXIII.4, may result from the later number of Sicilian towns after the Punic Wars). Alaesa and Centuripa became *sine foedere immunes ac liberae* ('free and exempt from taxation without treaty'), the only such privileged cities in eastern Sicily. But the lack of naval power made the task of supplying the large Roman armies difficult, while they could have little expectation of taking Syracuse itself without control of the sea. Hiero however reckoned that the Romans had brighter prospects than the Carthaginians, and his subjects showed some restlessness at the continuance of an alliance between Greeks and Carthaginians; further, he may have felt that his Punic allies whom he had abandoned at Messana might be somewhat luke-warm in giving further support. He therefore decided to change sides and made overtures, to which the Romans, anxious about their supplies, readily responded. He was granted a treaty under which he surrendered his prisoners of war without ransom and paid a fairly light indemnity of 100 talents (the 25 talents mentioned by Diodorus (XXIII.4.1) are probably a misunderstanding of a first instalment rather than an additional annual tribute). In return he remained king of Syracuse and retained control of some thirty miles of territory around the city, including Acrae, Leontini, Megara, Helorus, Netum and Tauromenium. In fairness to Carthage it should be added that a Punic fleet did in fact arrive to help him, but it was too late; he had already made his peace with Rome. This treaty was ratified by the Roman people and was renewed in 248. Under Roman protection and honoured by the Greeks, Hiero enjoyed a long and prosperous reign, remaining loyal to Rome until his death nearly fifty years later in 215.[59]

In view of the co-operation of Hiero the Romans decided to send only

---

[59] Eckstein 1980[K175], 183ff argues that the agreement of 263 was not a formal military alliance (*foedus sociale*), but a less formal relationship of friendship – *amicitia* (φιλία) – which was merely extended to the indefinite future (φιλία ἀΐδιος) when renewed in 248. If this is accepted, Hiero's frequent aid to Rome rested on good-will rather than on treaty obligation.

two legions to Sicily in 262, but they changed their minds and sent four when they heard that the Carthaginians were recruiting Ligurian, Celtic and Iberian mercenaries for service in the island. Both sides were thus getting further involved. The new consuls won the support of Segesta and Halicyae in the Punic part of the island (these cities also became *civitates liberae* (free communities)) and advanced against the enemy's head-quarters at Acragas. The city lay on a hill sloping down to the south where alone it could be attacked. Here the consuls built two camps at points to the south-west and south-east, and after some preliminary skirmishes they joined the camps up by a double line of trenches in order to besiege the city and to ward off the relieving force that might ultimately be expected. This arrived after the city had endured siege for five months; commanded by Hanno, it was a somewhat unco-ordinated but strong force of 50,000 infantry, 6000 cavalry and 60 elephants according to Philinus (Diod. xxIII.8, but Orosius (IV.7.5) gives only 30,000, 1500 and 30 respectively). This is probably the first time that the Carthaginians made use of elephants; they showed considerable enterprise in the very hazardous task of shipping them across the open sea from Africa, but they seem to have been less skilful in employing them in the subsequent battle. After some preliminary engagements Hanno camped on a neighbouring hill to the west and cut off the Roman supplies, which Hiero loyally tried to maintain. But after two months (Dec. 262 and Jan. 261) the Punic commander in the city, Hannibal, could not face starvation much longer, so Hanno gave battle on the ground between his and the Roman south-west camp in a desperate attempt to relieve the city with its 50,000 inhabitants. After a hard struggle the Romans forced an advanced line of Punic mercenaries back on to the elephants and the other troops, thus throwing them into confusion and gaining the victory; the Romans killed 8 elephants, wounded 33 and rounded up the survivors. Thus the first attested use of the elephant-corps, which had been placed in a curious position between ranks, had not proved very successful. But the Roman losses were so heavy that Hannibal and his garrison of mercenaries managed to break out from the doomed city.[60] The next day the Romans sacked the city and sold the inhabitants into slavery. This savage act merely antagonized Greek sentiment throughout the island, whereas clemency might have swung it the other way. In fact in the campaigning of 261 the Romans made little progress: though some inland towns went over to them, some coastal cities, threatened by the Punic fleet, decided to revert to Carthage. Further, some naval reinforcements which Carthage had sent in the

[60] Hanno's losses in his two battles according to Philinus (Diod. xxIII.8.1) were only 300 infantry and 200 cavalry and 4000 prisoners, with 8 elephants killed and 33 disabled, but the Roman losses for the whole siege are put at 30,000 infantry and perhaps 450 cavalry (Diod. xxIII.9.1).

previous year to Sardinia now began to raid the coast of Italy. Thus events in both Sicily and Italy focused Roman attention on her weakness at sea.

Deadlock had been reached and it was resolved by action which profoundly affected Rome's future. According to Polybius the capture of Acragas led the Romans to determine to expel the Carthaginians completely from Sicily, and their inability to take the coastal towns induced them to build a fleet.[61] They must have realized that only by challenging the enemy's naval power could they hope for overwhelming victory as opposed to a compromise peace, and they deliberately abandoned any idea of a negotiated settlement for a policy of total war. Polybius, however, may have dramatically compressed a gradual realization into a sudden revolutionary change, since there is some evidence to suggest that some Romans, such as Appius Claudius, may have nurtured imperialistic ambitions from the beginning of the war, and that some, such as M'. Valerius Messalla, may have advocated building a navy before 261 (Diod. XXIII.2.1; *Ined. Vat.* 4); further, the capture of Acragas may have been a weaker factor than Polybius suggests, and the raiding of the Italian coast a stronger one. But whether his views were affected by later reflection or do in fact represent contemporary opinion, the year 261 clearly marked a crucial stage in Rome's conduct of the war and in her drive to imperial expansion. Paradoxically, the Roman decision may even have given some encouragement to the Carthaginians who, unable to win the war by land in Sicily, may have welcomed the opportunity to pit their centuries-old naval skill against a people with so little experience of the sea.

The Romans had no tradition of sea-faring; rather, their roots were in the land. Under Etruscan rule a temporary interest in international commerce may have led some to cast a passing glance seaward, but subsequently they made no attempt to create a navy to counter piratical raids on the coast of Latium. However, in 311, when their horizon had extended to Campania, they did set up *duumviri navales* who commanded a squadron of twenty triremes (p. 410), but the vessels may well have been only fitted out when needed and then laid up (thus the army of Appius Claudius crossed to Sicily on ships from allied towns because there was no Roman squadron ready equipped). The crews, if not the ships, were mainly provided by Rome's naval allies (*socii navales*), while after the

---

[61] A milestone from the road from Acragas to Panormus built by a certain Aurelius Cotta has been used as evidence that the Romans intended to stay permanently in Sicily: see di Vita 1955[B269], 10ff = *AÉ* 1957, 158 = *ILLRP* 1277. This view however rests on identifying this Cotta with the consul of 252, whereas he might have been the consul of 200, C. Aurelius Cotta, since an inscription concerning the latter (*CIL* I².610; *ILLRP* 75) is not dissimilar epigraphically: see J. Reynolds 1960[B259], 206f.

Pyrrhic war, during which Rome had been able to count on Carthaginian naval help if needed, her allies may well have supplied ships as well; but these would not number more than some twenty-five triremes and penteconters. With this development may be linked the establishment of four *quaestores classici* in 267.[62] But if Rome was to challenge Carthage by sea she needed far more than this scratch force. She therefore determined to build 100 quinqueremes and 20 triremes, the latter being perhaps a replacement for the outworn duoviral squadron. But her ship-wrights lacked the knowledge to build quinqueremes, since such ships had not been used in Italy, although for some time they had been the standard vessel of the Punic navy. The story goes that the Romans acquired a Punic vessel that had run aground in 264 and, using it as a model, they constructed 100 quinqueremes within sixty days from felling the timber. This account has often been received with an element of scepticism, but it derives strong support from the remains of the Punic ship recently found off western Sicily (see p. 497). The timbers of this vessel, which were numbered by letters, were obviously pre-fabricated and mass-produced. Thus the Romans may have copied not merely details of construction but also methods of production and by a stupendous effort in fact have created this great up-to-date fleet in a remarkably short time. Very large numbers of rowers were required; the majority were supplied by the maritime cities of Italy while the Romans provided the rest. Training, however, was needed not only by the land-lubbers of Rome but by all, since rowing a quinquereme involved a different technique from handling a trireme (a quinquereme was probably rowed by five men to each oar, or less probably by a group of three men to an upper oar and two to a lower). For this purpose wooden stages were said to have been erected on land on which the crews were trained to handle their oars; this story of shore-training is perfectly reasonable and can be paralleled by actions of both the Athenian Chabrias and M. Agrippa in 27 B.C. (Polyaenus, *Strat.* III.11.7 and Dio XLVIII.51.5). It is worth stressing that this new fleet was the result of *Roman* organization, construction and financing. At this time the southern Greeks had only small fleets and no quinqueremes; their main contribution was doubtless to help man the new ships and probably to supply many officers and steersmen, but the ships seem to have been built near Rome and by Roman labour.

The new ships, however, were more heavily built than the Punic quinqueremes, because of the way in which Rome tried to solve another problem: it was easier to build ships than to gain the necessary seaman-ship to meet the manoeuvring and ramming tactics of the enemy. The solution was to turn sea-battles into land-battles by adopting boarding

---

[62] Above, p. 438 (with a different interpretation). A third view: W. V. Harris, *CQ* N.S. 26 (1976), 92–106 (two additional quaestors appointed with general financial functions).

tactics. A new device, which the troops called *corvus*, the 'crow', was invented to prevent the enemy from disengaging after the preliminary prow-to-prow contact and from returning to ram the less manoeuvrable Roman ship. A round pole, 24 feet high and 10 inches in diameter, was erected in the bows, with a pulley at the top. At its base was set a gangway, 36 feet long and 4 wide; this had an oblong slot which allowed the pole to go through about 12 feet from the inboard end. The gangway could swivel round the pole; underneath at the far end it had an iron spike, while on the upper side was a ring from which a rope passed to the pulley at the top of the pole, thus allowing the gangway to be raised up. When the ship went into action, the raised gangway was dropped on to the enemy's prow, the spike held the two ships together, and Roman legionaries boarded the enemy; the gangway could be dropped either directly beyond the prow or, thanks to the swivel, sideways (but perhaps only within an angle of some ninety degrees) if the ships were alongside each other (Fig. 59). Details of the construction have been much debated. The hypothesis of hinges which would have allowed the gangway to be raised to a full vertical position should be rejected, since they are not mentioned by Polybius; rather, the slot in the gangway permitted its outward end to be lifted considerably less than ninety degrees; nevertheless its weight will have driven home the spike on contact with the enemy's deck.

The new naval force under the command of Cn. Cornelius Scipio, one of the consuls of 260, had only a brief period of training at sea. While it was gradually mustering at Messana, Scipio sailed with seventeen ships to Punic-held Lipara which he had reason to believe was ready to go over to Rome. However Hannibal, the general at Panormus, sent twenty ships by night to Lipara which bottled Scipio up in the harbour. At dawn the Romans panicked and sought safety on land: Scipio was captured together with his ships and gained the suitable *cognomen* of Asina ('the She-ass'), though before 254 by an exchange of prisoners he had returned to Rome and was even re-elected to the consulship. This version of events given by Polybius (1.21.4–9: from Philinus?) differs from a more exculpatory annalistic account and indeed from a remark by Polybius himself (VIII.35.9) which made Scipio a victim of Carthaginian treachery. Polybius goes on to record (ib. 35.9–12) that shortly afterwards Hannibal himself on a reconnoitring mission with fifty ships blundered into the Roman fleet and lost the majority of his vessels: attempts to suggest that Polybius is here unwittingly giving Philinus' version of the subsequent battle at Mylae are not very happy, but on the other hand the story of a Roman success at sea at this point does not inspire great confidence.[63]

[63] A version of Mylae: see Beloch 1912–27[A11], IV.1, 654 n. 1; De Sanctis 1907–64[A37], III.129 n. 73. But see Thiel 1954[G736], 122ff, 181f. The historicity of the engagement must remain an open question.

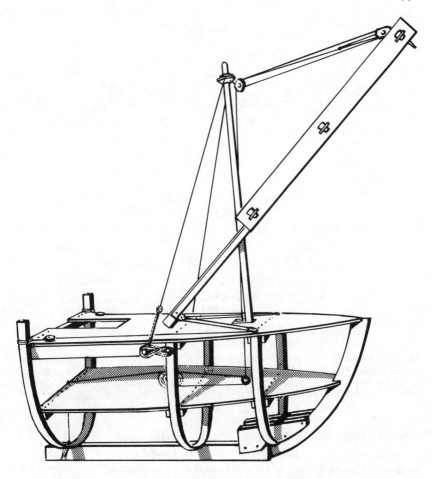

Fig. 59. Illustrative model of the *corvus* (the details of the ship itself and its construction are not intended as an authentic representation). From Wallinga 1956 [K205], pl. 1.

The Roman naval command was taken over by the other consul, C. Duillius, who was in charge of land forces in Sicily. Here the Romans suffered a set-back at Segesta, where a military tribune, C. Caecilius, had been defeated by the Carthaginian Hamilcar (Zonar. VIII.11), but Duillius relieved the siege of Segesta and captured Macella (Macellaro, 24 km. east of Segesta?). Although Polybius (1.24.2) places this success after Duillius' victory at Mylae, the Fasti Triumphales and Duillius' laudatory Inscription (Fig. 60) imply that the land-success preceded the naval one. At any rate Duillius with perhaps 140 ships, including allied auxiliary vessels, encountered the Punic fleet of some 130 ships under Hannibal off Mylae near the north-east corner of Sicily. Trusting to the inexperience of the Romans, Hannibal did not wait to draw up his ships

Fig. 60. Commemorative inscription of C. Duillius (*cos.* 260) recording his relief of Segesta, capture of Macella, victory at Mylae and triumph. The inscription is of the early imperial period but may reproduce the original inscription on the column adorned with ships' prows set up in Duillius' honour.

in strict battle order: they rowed straight into the enemy. But when their 30 front ships were grappled by the novel *corvi* and were boarded by soldiers, the rest turned aside and tried to catch their opponents broadside or on the stern. Polybius says that they were kept off by the *corvi* which swung round in all directions, but since these 'crows' were mounted on the prows, this would in fact have been impossible; so the suggestion that behind the first line of ships the Romans had stationed a second which protected their rear is attractive.[64] At any rate the Carthaginians were forced to withdraw with the loss of fifty ships, including Hannibal's flag-ship, a *hepteres* previously captured from Pyrrhus, and some 10,000 men captured or killed. Thus in her first real naval venture on the sea Rome had won a spectacular victory. Well might Duillius be granted the first naval triumph in Rome's history and be honoured by the erection in the Forum of a column (*columna rostrata*) decorated with the bronze rams of the captured vessels. His skill at sea

[64] Thiel 1954[G736], 185.

was curiously not employed again: he re-emerges into the light of history only once, as dictator to hold the elections in 231. Scipio the Ass was more lucky.

Despite her defeat Carthage still had a considerable navy and a firm grip on Panormus and Lilybaeum. Hamilcar (probably not to be identified with Hamilcar Barca) therefore moved to the attack: after inflicting a serious reverse on the Romans at Thermae (spring 259?), he advanced as far as Enna and Camarina and fortified Drepana in his rear. To check this advance the Romans prolonged the command of C. Aquillius Florus throughout the winter and in 258 sent out another consular army under A. Atilius Caiatinus to join him. Together the Roman commanders advanced towards Panormus, where Hamilcar declined battle, and then recaptured Enna and Camarina, thus confining the Carthaginians once again to the western end of the island. Aquillius received a triumph. Meantime one of the consuls of 259, L. Cornelius Scipio, a brother of Asina, led an expedition against Sardinia and Corsica. This move could scarcely have a crucial effect on the main issues of the war, but it afforded practice in mounting overseas expeditionary forces, and it reduced raids on the Italian coast. Scipio captured Aleria on Corsica (his epitaph with some exaggeration claims: 'hec cepit Corsica Aleriaque urbe, / dedet Tempestatebus aide meretod' ('he took Corsica and the city of Aleria: he gave a shrine to the Tempestates in just requital'): *ILS* 2; *ILLRP* 319; (Fig. 61)), but he failed to take the Punic fortress of Olbia in northern Sardinia. His successor C. Sulpicius Paterculus in 258, however, defeated the enemy's fleet off Sulci: Hannibal paid for his incompetence by being crucified by his own men, while Sulpicius celebrated a triumph over the Carthaginians and Sardinians. In 257 all Roman effort was abandoned in Sardinia, where Carthage retained Sulci and her other colonies. Little was achieved in Sicily, except that the consul C. Atilius Regulus raided

Fig. 61. Funerary inscription of L. Cornelius Scipio (*cos.* 259) recording his qualities, offices, military achievements ('conquest' of Corsica and capture of Aleria) and dedication of a shrine to the Tempestates. From Coarelli 1972 [B307], fig. G.

Melita (Malta), fell in with the Punic fleet off Tyndaris some 24 km. west of Mylae, and sank eighteen vessels. These successes were a happy prelude to a much greater effort for which Rome was now bracing herself.

(c) *The invasion of Africa*

Since neither side was prepared to negotiate, the Romans had either to intensify their efforts in the ding-dong struggle in Sicily or else strike boldly at the heart of the enemy and thus force her to relax her grip on the island. They chose the bolder course of attempting to land an expedition-ary force in Africa, an unprecedented venture for them (Agathocles' previous invasion would not provide much encouragement). It may have been their preparations for this immense effort that had slowed down their activity in 257. They needed to build up their fleet and if possible to outbuild Carthage. Both sides made strenuous efforts and in the subsequent battle at Ecnomus the Romans probably had 230 ships (rather than the Polybian figure of 330), with 80 transports and perhaps 100,000 men needed for the crews, while the Carthaginians put at least 200 and possibly 250 ships to sea.[65] Further, the legionary forces, 500 horses and all the supplies that would be needed on landing in Africa had to be transported. The success of the whole expedition rested primarily upon the fleet: if it could not defeat or evade the Punic navy, the losses in manpower would be terrific. In the summer of 256 the assembled armada, under the command of L. Manlius Vulso and M. Atilius Regulus (probably a brother of the consul of 257), sailed down the eastern coast of Sicily round the south-east promontory and embarked their land forces (probably some 18,400 men) at Cape Ecnomus. They then sailed forth to meet the enemy who advanced eastwards from Heraclea.

The general course of the battle is clear, the precise Roman formation less so. The Carthaginians sailed in one long line abreast, hoping to outflank the enemy; their left wing, on the shoreward end of the line, was formed at an advanced angle to the rest of the line in order to facilitate the outflanking on the Roman right. According to Polybius (1.26.10f) the Romans advanced in four squadrons: the first two formed a wedge-like spearhead (the ships being in echelon), while the third, towing the transports, formed a base to the triangular wedge; behind these was the fourth squadron, nicknamed the *triarii* after the usage of land forces. This wedge-like formation has been rejected by some historians: thus W. W. Tarn wrote, 'no captains, let alone Roman captains, could have

---

[65] The traditions and difficulties about the number of ships have been fully discussed and cannot be treated here; see Tarn 1907[K201], 48–60; De Sanctis 1907–64[A37], 111.135 n. 98; Thiel 1954[G736], 83ff; Walbank 1957–79[B182], 1.82ff.

kept station'.[66] Polybius' misunderstanding, if such it be, could be explained by supposing that they *appeared* to the enemy to be in a wedge-shape (Polybius' account seems ultimately to be based on an eye-witness and to come from Philinus, with some additions from Fabius). This could have occurred either if the first two squadrons sailed in line ahead and then deployed into line abreast or if they sailed in line abreast and then the centre rowed forward more quickly than the wings. In the battle, whatever the formation, the first two Roman squadrons, led by the two flagships of Manlius Vulso and Regulus, broke through the Carthaginian centre which was deliberately falling back with the intention of upsetting the Roman order (and possibly even of exposing the rear of the Roman front line since the third Roman line was slower and could not keep up). However, thanks to the *corvus* the Romans were victorious. Meantime the third Roman squadron, which slipped the transports, was forced inshore by the Punic left wing but was saved from being driven aground because fear of the *corvus* kept the enemy at a respectful distance. The fourth Roman squadron was hard pressed by the Punic right. However, part of the victorious squadron under Regulus returned in time to save the fourth squadron by driving off the Carthaginian right wing; he then joined the other victorious squadron under Vulso and together they converged on the Punic left near the shore, where they sank 30 and captured 50 vessels. The Roman losses were only 24. It was a spectacular victory which smashed open the gateway to Africa.

After a pause to repair and refit, the Romans sailed to Africa and landed at Aspis (Clupea) on the east of the Cap Bon peninsula. Here they had good communications with Sicily, could threaten Carthage from the rear and cut her off from many of her subject cities. They captured Aspis, ravaged the rich countryside and seized over 20,000 slaves. Then on instructions from Rome, one consul was recalled with the fleet, while Regulus was left with 15,000 infantry, 500 cavalry and 40 ships. Realizing that the Romans were digging in for the winter the Carthaginians elected Hasdrubal, son of Hanno, and Bostarus as generals and recalled Hamilcar from Sicily, whence he brought 5000 infantry and 500 cavalry. Since Regulus was acting with extreme caution and making no attempt to join hands with some Numidian chiefs who were restive, these three commanders decided to attack and marched against him while he was besieging Adys, probably some 24 km. south of Carthage, but they were defeated on unfavourable hilly ground which prevented the proper use of their cavalry and elephants. Regulus then seized Tunis where he

---

[66] Tarn 1930[K202], 151. The formation is also rejected by De Sanctis 1907–64[A37], III.141 n. 202 and Thiel 1954[G736], 119, 214, but is accepted by Kromayer 1922–9[K186] Röm. Abt. col. 5.

encamped for the winter, during which negotiations took place. According to Polybius (1.31.4: Fabius?) Regulus took the initiative in order to avoid being superseded, but Diodorus (XXIII.12.1) and others (probably following Philinus) attribute it to Carthage and war-weariness. However Regulus laid down such harsh terms (the details given by Dio Cassius (XI fr. 43.22–3, vol. I, p. 160–1 Boiss.) amount to a complete surrender, but they are scarcely reliable) that they were rejected. But apart from Regulus' folly in making any compromise unnegotiable the attainment of peace was probably impossible since Rome would presumably have insisted on the complete evacuation of Sicily, while Carthage would scarcely have been willing to surrender the western end of the island.

By the spring of 255 Carthaginian spirits had revived since during the winter a group of Spartan mercenaries arrived under their leader Xanthippus who inspired both commanders and soldiers and encouraged them to believe that they could defeat the Roman legions if they used their strength in cavalry and elephants on level ground. So it fell out. Carthaginian citizens for long had not fought in wars abroad: now they had to fight in defence of their lives and they supplied perhaps two-thirds of a force of some 12,000 infantry, 4000 cavalry and 100 elephants (Carthaginian elephant-hunters must have been busy making good the losses suffered at Acragas). After some intensive training this force marched out, and Regulus, instead of waiting for reinforcements from Italy, advanced with slightly greater overall numbers to fight in a plain on ground chosen by the enemy. Xanthippus placed his phalanx behind a line of elephants, and the cavalry on the wings. The Romans made their centre shorter and deeper, but they were only trampled to death the more easily. The battle was decided when the Punic cavalry defeated the Roman horse and then outflanked and surrounded the infantry; a small group on the Roman left managed to rout the Carthaginian mercenaries, but retreated with severe losses as the general resistance crumbled. The Romans paid a heavy price for Regulus' failure to strengthen his cavalry by co-operating with the Numidian chiefs. Regulus and 500 others were taken prisoner and only 2000 Romans escaped to Clupea; the rest were dead. The African expedition thus ended in disaster. Regulus' fate was soon embellished by legend: he was sent to Rome on parole to negotiate, but he refused to advise the senate to make peace and returned voluntarily to suffer torture and death in Carthage. In reality he died in captivity and the legend may have been designed to obscure the fact that his widow tortured two Punic prisoners entrusted to her in Rome.

Rome's intention had been to prepare a fleet to blockade Carthage by sea while Regulus attacked by land. However, before it could set sail news came of the disaster in Africa: nevertheless some 210 vessels under the command of the two consuls set forth with the changed purpose of

rescuing the survivors at Clupea.[67] Their approach was contested by a
fleet of some 200 ships which the Carthaginians had been repairing or
building. *En route* they occupied Cossyra (Pantelleria) and then, probably
in May 255, they engaged the enemy off the Hermaean Promontory (Cap
Bon) and successfully jammed their opponents against the shore, capturing many ships (114, or less probably 24). They rescued the survivors at
Clupea and raided the countryside for provisions, an episode which the
annalistic tradition (Zonar. VIII.14.3; Oros. IV.9.7; Eutrop. II.22.2)
blows up into a Roman victory by land. They then started on the journey
back to Sicily, but fresh disaster awaited them. They encountered a
terrific storm between Camarina and Cape Pachynus which drove most
of the ships, hampered by their *corvi*, on to the rocks: only 80 of the 264
survived. Some 25,000 soldiers and 70,000 rowers (who perhaps included some conscripted Carthaginians) drowned in this unprecedented
calamity. However, since the consuls were granted a triumph for their
victory off Cap Bon, presumably the subsequent tragedy was regarded as
due to natural causes rather than to bad seamanship despite the criticism
which Polybius levels at the consuls (1.37.4ff).

(d) *Stalemate and checkmate*

Since their anticipated short-cut to victory had failed, the Romans now
faced the task of intensifying their efforts in Sicily. Here there was little
prospect of taking the coastal cities unless they could be assaulted by sea
as well as by land, and so the daunting task of building up the navy once
again had to be faced. Helped by the imposition of new taxes a fresh fleet
was prepared and by the spring of 254 Rome again had some 220 ships
and the ability to face Carthage once more by sea. Four legions were sent
to Sicily, where Cn. Cornelius Scipio Asina, who had regained his
freedom and the consulship, captured Cephaloedium (Cefalù) but failed
in an attempt upon Drepana. He then launched attacks by land and sea on
Panormus (Palermo), which comprised two settlements (Map 14): the
Old City which lay between two streams running into the harbour
(modern Cala), and the New City, probably to the south. After the
Romans had stormed the latter with the help of Greek engineers, the Old
City capitulated, where 14,000 inhabitants were ransomed but 13,000
unable to pay two minae were enslaved. Some other cities on the north
coast, including Solus and Tyndaris, now went over to Rome. The
Carthaginians, who were busy checking a revolt of Numidians in Africa,
had not sufficient troops in Sicily to provoke a pitched battle. Their

---

[67] Polyb. 1.36.10 gives the Romans 350 ships, but see above, n. 65. In the subsequent battle they
probably had 250 since the 210 were joined by the forty which had been left behind at Aspis; they
captured 114 ships according to Polyb. 1.26.11, only twenty-four according to Diod. XXIII.18.1.

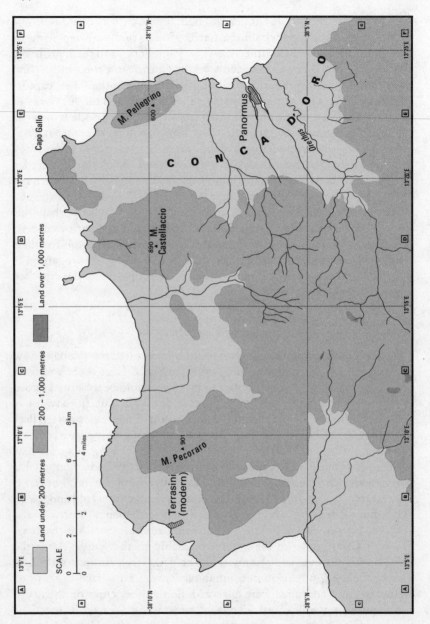

Map 14 Panormus and its hinterland.

general, Carthalo, however, made one counter-attack: he stormed Acragas, which he burnt to the ground since he was too weak to hold it. The Carthaginian grip on the island was now confined largely to the western cities of Drepana, Lilybaeum, Selinus, Heraclea Minoa, and the isolated Thermae, together with the Lipari and Aegates Islands. The consuls of 253 made an unsuccessful assault upon Lilybaeum and then unwisely dispersed their efforts by an ineffectual raid on the east coast of Tunisia, where their ships ran into difficulties on the shoals of the Syrtes. But more serious trouble occurred when at the end of the season the consuls decided to sail back from Panormus to Rome directly across the open sea instead of keeping to the coast: they encountered a heavy storm and lost 150 ships, together with tens of thousands of rowers and soldiers, thus reducing the navy to about only 70 vessels for the next three years. The Carthaginians also were becoming exhausted, though at some time (probably in 253–251 rather than 255–254) they sent some reinforcements to Sicily under Hasdrubal. These included 140 elephants, which in the skirmishing in western Sicily often kept the Roman forces at a respectful distance, since the legionaries were mindful of the havoc wrought by the elephants in the defeat of Regulus. During this some-what uneventful period the Romans did manage to capture Thermae and the Lipari Islands in 252.

Rome finally resolved on a new effort by sea. The consuls elected for 250 had experience in naval warfare (C. Atilius Regulus had fought at Tyndaris, L. Manlius Vulso at Ecnomus) and fifty new ships were built, bringing the fleet up to 120. The Carthaginians also began to build up their naval forces. But before the consuls left Rome a victory had been won in Sicily. Hasdrubal, knowing that one of the consuls of 251 had returned to Rome in the winter and that the other, L. Caecilius Metellus, remained at Panormus with only two legions, decided to strike before he found himself attacked by the two consuls of 250 and by Metellus whose command was prorogued. In June 250[68] he advanced from Lilybaeum against Panormus, ravaging the surrounding countryside, the Conca d'Oro. Metellus lay low and thus enticed Hasdrubal over the Oreto up to some prepared trenches near the city wall. Here the elephants were met by showers of missiles, and maddened by their wounds they stampeded back onto their own forces. The confusion was completed when Metellus launched a sally on Hasdrubal's flank and inflicted a severe defeat on the enemy who (according to Oros. IV.9.15) lost 20,000 out of 30,000 men. Diodorus (XXIII.21) adds that the Celtic mercenaries were drunk, while Zonaras (VIII.14) records that Metellus had uncovered a fifth column plot in Panormus and that a Punic fleet had sailed up but

[68] On the chronology (250 B.C. rather than 251) see De Sanctis 1907–64[A37], III.262; Walbank 1957–79[B182], I.102; Morgan 1972[K192], 121–9.

could do nothing; this may well be true, since Hasdrubal in the event of victory may have hoped to invest the city. The elephants were captured or rounded up (the numbers given vary between 142 and 60). After being transported across the Straits, they were displayed in the Circus in Rome, giving the Roman people their first sight of African elephants. Although the Romans apparently thought them too double-edged a weapon to incorporate in their own army, the *gens Caecilia* adopted the elephant as a kind of family badge and, when mint-masters, they often placed its image on the Roman coinage. Hasdrubal was recalled to Carthage where he was impaled.

When the Roman consuls of 250 arrived they concentrated on the siege of Lilybaeum (Map 15), which was the only remaining Punic base except Drepana. Their forces, excluding the ships' crews, may have numbered some 35,000–40,000 men (perhaps under the full strength of 4 legions of 8000 each, and 100 marines for each of the 120 ships). The city, which lay on a promontory, was defended on the landward side by strong walls and a deep ditch; its harbour on the north (the modern harbour is to the south) was protected by shoals which made navigation difficult. Its garrison comprised some 10,000 men, partly Celts, partly Greeks. The Romans cut it off from the mainland by establishing camps on each side of the city and joined them up by fortifications. A close siege followed, with strenuous attempts to batter down or undermine the towers: the Romans no doubt learnt much of the technique of siege-warfare from the Sicilians. An attempt to betray the city to the Romans was thwarted by the loyalty of a Greek officer. Then Hannibal, son of the Hamilcar who had been defeated at Ecnomus, boldly ran the blockade with 50 ships, disembarked 10,000 soldiers and then sailed out again by night in safety to Drepana where lay the main fleet which the Carthaginians had been building up under the command of Hannibal's friend, Adherbal. The Carthaginian government was kept informed about the course of the siege by the exploits of another Hannibal, 'the Rhodian', who several times managed to run the blockade (vivid details of his exploits, given by Polybius (1.46.4–47.10), probably derive from an eye-witness, possibly Philinus himself). Encouraged by such daring and by a successful attempt to burn the Roman siege-works, the defenders withstood the blockade, especially as Roman supplies were threatened by Punic cavalry from Drepana though Hiero loyally sent help to the Romans. Lilybaeum was still resisting eight years later when the war ended.

The consuls of 249 took to Sicily 10,000 *socii navales* who would provide fresh crews for some forty ships. One, P. Claudius Pulcher, probably a son of the consul of 264, boldly decided to attack the enemy fleet at Drepana before its commander, Adherbal, learnt that the Roman fleet had gained fresh striking power with the arrival of the new crews,

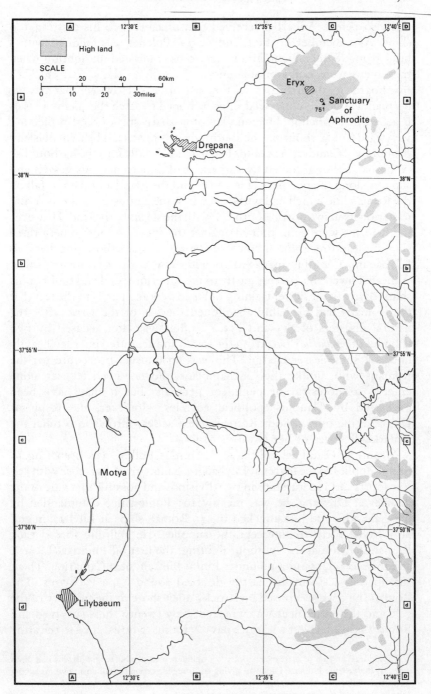

Map 15 Drepana, Eryx and Lilybaeum.

and also before Adherbal received reinforcements to his existing 100 ships. As a member of the Claudian *gens* Pulcher was credited with a headstrong temperament, and is said to have insisted on fighting when the omens were unfavourable and to have flung the sacred chickens overboard: 'let them drink since they will not eat'. However that may be, his plan was not ill-conceived since he hoped to catch the enemy vessels beached or at anchor. Drepana lay on a sharp spit of land projecting westwards; its harbour on the south side was protected by a small island (Columbia). Claudius' 120 ships began to sail boldly into the harbour but Adherbal, although taken by surprise, had time to man his vessels and slip out along the northern side and round the island and then to fall on the Roman line which had withdrawn in some confusion and was trying to station itself in a north–south line with the sterns to the land. However the Romans were soon pinned against the shore and lost ninety-three ships by capture, though some of the crews got ashore and back to Lilybaeum. Claudius managed to withdraw with some thirty ships. Adherbal owed this success partly to the superior speed and build of his ships, partly to the better training of his rowers and partly to the fact that the Romans had probably abandoned the use of the *corvus* after the natural disasters of 255 and 253. Claudius was later accused by two tribunes of *perduellio* ('betraying the state') and acquitted but then heavily fined on some lesser charge. This was an unusual procedure for the Romans who, unlike the Carthaginians, did not even try, let alone crucify, unsuccessful or negligent generals, but it may have been prompted by Claudius' political enemies. However, the result of Drepana, the only serious Roman defeat at sea, throws into relief the remarkable series of her naval victories.

Meantime Claudius' colleague, L. Iunius Pullus, was preparing to bring supplies to the forces at Lilybaeum. Sailing from Syracuse with 800 transports and 120 warships in two divisions and possibly unaware of the disaster at Drepana, he was met by 100 Punic ships commanded by Carthalo who had just attacked the 30 Roman ships at Lilybaeum and now sailed forth to intercept the supplies. He skilfully forced each Roman division ashore without fighting, the first off Phintias (Licata), and the second, coming up under Iunius himself, near Camarina. Then, anticipating a storm, he hastily doubled round Cape Pachynus. The Roman ships were exposed on a rocky open shore to the full fury of the gale and the entire fleet was wrecked: only twenty ships survived and Rome was in effect left without a navy.[69] Iunius, who escaped to the army

---

[69] Diodorus' version of these events (XXIV.1.7–9) differs considerably from Polybius 1.24. Both probably derive from Philinus, Diodorus giving an abridged version of Philinus, Polybius having 'corrected' Philinus partly in the light of Fabius' version. See Walbank 1957–79[B182], I.117f, who defends Polybius' version against Thiel's attempt (1954[G736], 287 n. 734) to defend Diodorus.

at Lilybaeum, then marched northwards and managed to seize both the old city of Eryx and also the adjacent temple of Aphrodite (on modern Mte San Giuliano), the most splendid temple in Sicily.[70] This was a shrewd stroke since Mt Eryx rises up behind Drepana and commanded all the roads leading to the city. Thus stalemate was again reached: Rome had lost control of the sea, but the two towns in Sicily still held by the Carthaginians were isolated from the rest of the island.

The subsequent failure of the Carthaginians actively to exploit their naval superiority is surprising: even more surprising is that they seem even to have laid up most of their fleet at Carthage. Part of the explanation may lie in events in Africa. Here the Numidians, who had attacked Punic territory during the invasion of Regulus, had been pitilessly punished in 254, but around 247 Hanno the 'Great' led an expedition into the interior as far as Hekatompylus (probably Theveste, modern Tebessa) where he showed slightly greater clemency, though taking 3000 hostages. Since in 241 he was στρατηγὸς ἐν τῇ Λιβύῃ ('commander in Libya': Polyb. 1.67.1) he may have been in command of the interior for some years previously. At any rate he appears to have sponsored a policy of expansion in Africa and perhaps represented the interests of the landed aristocracy. He was also an opponent of Hamilcar Barca who was sent as Carthaginian commander to Sicily in 247 and is sometimes regarded as a leader of mercantile imperialism, but it must remain uncertain how far there was any deep cleavage in Carthaginian policy between 'land' and 'trade', between African and overseas interests.[71] Whether it was due to pressure by Hanno and his supporters, or to more serious and prolonged warfare in Africa than our sources record which made it impossible for Carthage to keep both a large army and a large fleet, or simply to lethargy on the part of the Carthaginians who hoped (very mistakenly) that the exhausted Romans would get tired of besieging western Sicily and be prepared to make peace before very long – whatever the causes, the Carthaginians seem to have missed a splendid opportunity in view of Rome's exhaustion. Yet possibly their own finances were strained more than we know, since at some point they asked for a loan of 2000 talents from Ptolemy of Egypt, who politely declined because since 273 he had been a 'friend' of Rome and wished to remain neutral (App. *Sic.* 1). At Rome also the treasury was depleted and the census of 237 B.C. ('Table 1,

[70] Iunius' fate is uncertain. Either he was captured during an attack on Eryx but released under an exchange of prisoners in 247 (Zonar. VIII.15.10; Livy, *Epit.* XIX) or also having disregarded the auspices he was prosecuted in Rome and committed suicide (Cic. *Nat. D.* II.7 et al.). At any rate a *scriba*, M. Claudius Glicia, was appointed dictator (a move by Claudius Pulcher's friends in Rome to improve his prospects?) but he was forced to abdicate and A. Atilius Caiatinus (*cos.* 258 and 254), with L. Caecilius Metellus (*cos.* 251) as *magister equitum*, was appointed dictator and sent to Sicily, being the first dictator to lead an army outside Italy.

[71] Such a clash was suggested by Frank 1926[B56], 311ff; 1928[K176], 698. Cf. above, pp. 492f; 508.

p. 137) revealed a decline in the adult male citizens of 50,000 or some 17
per cent in the previous twenty years, while the losses of the allied states
must have been of a similar order. Thus Rome lacked the money and the
manpower, if not the will, to build yet another fleet in the immediate
future. But she retained her traditional policy of negotiating only after
victories and so fought on. The consuls elected for 248 were the men who
had already held this office in 252 when they had served with caution in
Sicily. One heartening event was that Hiero showed his confidence in
Rome's future by renewing his alliance which was now put on a
permanent basis.

Carthalo in 248 raided the coast of southern Italy, and his successor
Hamilcar Barca followed suit with raids on Locri and Bruttium. Rome
replied by strengthening the coast further north by establishing citizen
colonies at Alsium (247) and Fregenae (245) and in 244 a Latin colony
was sent to Brundisium. A raid by some Roman privateers on Hippo
Diarrhytus (Bizerta) did not amount to much. Hamilcar then landed west
of Panormus and succeeded in fortifying a position on a mountain
named Heirkte behind the city; he anchored his ships at its base.[72] From
this centre with perhaps some 15–20,000 men he held the Romans at bay
for three years, threatening their communications, harassing them by
skirmishes, and again raiding the Italian coast as far north as Cumae. In
244 he pressed westwards and captured the old hill-town of Eryx behind
Drepana, but the Romans held the temple of Aphrodite itself at the top of
the mountain and also a point lower down between the temple and
Drepana, and thus prevented him from seriously interfering with the
siege of this city. The Romans knew that the war could not be won by
land and now that they had enjoyed a few years' breathing-space they
determined to build a new navy. The senate decided that a loan, repay-
able in the event of victory, should be raised and that groups of two or
three men should each provide a quinquereme; how much pressure the
senate put on its richer members for 'voluntary' contributions is uncertain; unlike the trierarchs at Athens, these men were asked only for a loan,
not a gift. The allies, who had had to provide the crews, also faced a very
heavy burden. However, it was a great effort which resulted in 200
warships, built on the lighter model of a ship of Hannibal the Rhodian
which had been captured at Lilybaeum; by not equipping these new
vessels with *corvi*, the Romans showed that they were going to follow
Punic methods of combat at sea.

[72] Heirkte (Map 14) has been identified with Mte Pellegrino (e.g. by De Sanctis 1907–64[A37],
III.181 n. 83; Ziegler 1910[K208], 2645), though Mte Castellaccio seems to have a better claim (cf.
Kromayer-Veith 1903–31[K185], III.1, 4ff; Walbank 1957–79[B182], 1.120f). Recently V. Giustolisi
(1975[K178]) has found traces of a camp on Mte Pecoraro, west of Mte Castellacio, with associated
pottery of the first half of the third century; this he suggests was Heirkte. A ship found off Terrasina,
west of Palermo, appears to be of mid-third-century date, with amphorae and two Roman swords: it
might have been a merchantman with a military guard or a transport.

In the summer of 242 the fleet, commanded by the consul C. Lutatius Catulus, accompanied not by his colleague but by a praetor Q. Valerius Falto, sailed to Sicily, where there was no enemy fleet to challenge its arrival. Thus Lutatius could blockade the harbours of Drepana and Lilybaeum and had more time to train his oarsmen. By the spring of 241 the Carthaginians had raised some 170 ships or so, but they were probably undermanned and the crews were not well trained; possibly some 60 per cent of these crews were Carthaginian citizens who did not usually have to serve in the navy. They planned to land stores in Sicily and then to embark Hamilcar and his best mercenaries to act as marines, but they were forestalled off the Aegates Insulae by Lutatius who boldly decided on action despite a stormy sea. Suffering from inadequate equipment and weighed down with freight through lack of transports, they were speedily defeated. The Romans sank 50 ships and captured another 70 and nearly 10,000 prisoners; according to Orosius (IV.10.7) and Eutropius (II.27) the Romans lost only 12 of their own vessels. Lutatius and his praetor later returned to Rome and were granted naval triumphs; Hanno, the Punic admiral, who thanks to a sudden change in the wind had got away with 50 ships, returned home to face crucifixion. Carthage could do no more: without sea power she could no longer supply her forces in Sicily. The long war was over.

Hamilcar was given full powers to negotiate a peace treaty. He and Lutatius agreed that there should be friendship ($\phi\iota\lambda\iota\alpha$) between Rome and Carthage, that Carthage should evacuate Sicily and not make war on Hiero or his allies, return all prisoners without ransom, and pay 2200 Euboeic talents by instalments over twenty years. In view of Rome's losses in the war and of the wealth of Carthage these terms were quite lenient, and might seem acceptable to the Roman people since they had gained control of Sicily, the chief objective of the war. However they took a harsher view and refused to ratify them. Ten commissioners were sent to Sicily; they stiffened the terms by adding 1000 talents to be paid immediately and cutting the time of payment down to ten years, while all islands between Sicily and Italy (these would be Lipari and the Aegates) must be evacuated by Carthage. This is Polybius' account at 1.62.8–63.3, but in his discussion of all the Romano-Punic treaties (III.27.2–6) he gives the final terms more formally, and these also include the following stipulations: the allies of neither side were to be attacked by the other; neither party was to impose any contribution nor erect any public building nor recruit soldiers in the dominions of the other, nor make any compact of friendship with the allies of the other. The extension of terms to include all allies on both sides seems to represent a gain to Carthage over the first draft, perhaps a concession granted to Hamilcar in return for his acceptance of the heavier financial obligations. But there was serious ambiguity: were any people who became allies later on covered by the relevant clause? The Romans assumed that they were, but the Carthaginians took the opposite view. The issue later became crucial when the status of Saguntum was questioned (Polyb. III.29.4ff). For the moment however peace reigned after twenty-four years.

Polybius attributed Rome's success to the moral and political virtues of her citizens and institutions. At the beginning of the war both sides were uncorrupted in principle, moderate in fortune and equal in strength (1.17.12); at the end they were still equal in enterprise, lofty in spirit and ambitious for supremacy, but the individual soldiers of Rome were far superior, though Hamilcar gained the palm for genius and daring (1.64.5–6). Thus the patriotism of a citizen army, supported by loyal allies in Italy and by Hiero in Sicily (where it is noteworthy that the Greeks failed to rally to the Romans despite their long hostility to Carthage), gave Rome a superiority in manpower and morale that Carthage with her mercenary forces could not match. The senatorial government provided a continuous drive and direction to the war, but no really outstanding Roman generals emerged, partly perhaps because of the system of annual commands, whereas Carthaginian commanders had longer to gain experience in office; many were very competent and one at least, Hamilcar, showed unusual ability and determination. The Roman army formed a very efficient machine, though it did not adapt its tactics to face cavalry and elephants, but Rome's most remarkable achievement was in taking to the sea, in the spectacular series of victories against the age-long maritime skill of her opponent, and in her determination to build fleet after fleet when she found that wind and weather were more devastating than her human enemy. Well might she place the representation of a ship on the bronze coinage that she was soon to issue. She was no longer a purely Italian power. Though she had not entered the war with any intention of conquering all Sicily, she had nevertheless gained the island and acquired the experience, courage and means that would enable her not only to aim at a world empire but to achieve it. So judged Polybius (1.63.9), but he was writing in the light of later events and the implications of his remarks may be premature. Rome's desire for empire was a very slow growth: the seed may have been sown, but it was long before its shoots appeared above ground.

(e) *Revolt in Africa and Sardinia*

The end of the war with Rome brought little respite to Carthage. Arrears of pay had made her mercenaries in Sicily mutinous in 248; Carthalo and then Hamilcar Barca dealt with them severely: some were cut down, others drowned (Zonar. VIII.16). At the end of the war some 20,000 who returned to Carthage were herded into Sicca Veneria (El Kef) while the

Carthaginians, through lack of resources or meanness, temporized. This motley assembly of Iberians, Celts, Ligurians, Balearic islanders, half-breed Greeks and, by far the largest number, Libyans, then marched on Tunis and put themselves under the leadership of Matho, a Libyan, and Spendius, a runaway Roman slave. Revolt spread rapidly among the subject Libyans, and before long to Numidia. Two towns, which remained loyal to Carthage, were besieged, Utica by Spendius and Hippo Diarrhytus (Bizerta) by Matho. The rebels, who may have numbered some 40,000 in all, had thus isolated Carthage from the rest of Libya and forced on her a war that was far more dangerous than that against the Romans in Sicily, since her very existence was at stake. Indeed the Carthaginians might fear that the rebels would try to set up an independent state, as the Mamertines had done: at any rate they became sufficiently co-ordinated to issue an extensive coinage, which betokens a degree of political as well as military organization. The first issues were Carthaginian types, some with the ethnic ΛIBYΩN added; then came a series of native types, all with the ethnic and very often overstruck on ordinary Carthaginian coins, the main types being Head of Herakles/prowling lion, or Zeus/charging bull. The debasement of the silver (and of the few gold pieces) indicates the poor state of Carthaginian finances, while the use of ΛIBYΩN suggests an ethnic basis to the revolt.[73]

Hanno raised a force which included 100 elephants but he failed to relieve Utica (spring 240) and the command was transferred to Hamilcar, perhaps on political as much as on military grounds. With a force of some 10,000 men, including a large cavalry detachment and seventy elephants, Hamilcar inflicted a defeat on the rebels who had further cut off Carthage by occupying the only bridge over the Bagradas, which ran between Carthage and Utica. The tactics of this battle of the Bagradas are not wholly clear, but Hamilcar owed his success partly to a feigned retreat. Thereafter on Matho's advice Spendius kept to higher ground to avoid the Punic cavalry and elephants. He was joined by Numidian and Libyan reinforcements and succeeded in manoeuvring Hamilcar into a dangerous position, but the Carthaginian managed to fight his way out and tried to check the revolt by showing leniency to his prisoners. However Spendius thwarted any hope of compromise by torturing 700 of his prisoners. The revolt had spread not only to Numidia, but to Sardinia where the Punic mercenaries rebelled and killed their Carthaginian commander. When the Carthaginians sent reinforcements to the island, they joined the rebels, crucified their commander and officers and tortured and murdered all the Carthaginians in the island. Like their fellows in Africa, with whom they were in touch, they too issued a coinage: this was only of bronze and was often overstruck on Sardo-Punic issues; it shows the head of Isis / three corn ears or less commonly head of Tanit / single ear of corn or else a plough.[74] In Africa Spendius and Matho gained control of Utica and Hippo and moved against Carthage itself from their base at Tunis, though without sea-power their prospects were slight. The Carthaginians in fact received substantial supplies from Hiero and indeed from Rome. They had recently captured some Italian traders bringing goods to the rebels, but when the Romans complained they returned 500 prisoners. The Romans were pleased and henceforth allowed supplies to be sent to Carthage but not to the rebels, and a general exchange of prisoners took place. These cordial relations were strengthened when Rome declined an invitation from the rebels in Sardinia to occupy the island and also a slightly later appeal from Utica.

The 'Truceless War' in Africa continued with increasing cruelties and atrocities and with no regard for the normal conditions of warfare. Since Hanno and Hamilcar were at logger-heads, the Carthaginians took the unusual step of letting the army choose between them and it chose Hamilcar who soon succeeded in annihilating Spendius' force at Prion (possibly near Sidi Jedid, west of Hammamet, but more probably nearer Tunis). He then closed in on Matho at Tunis and encamped at the south end of the isthmus on which Tunis lay, while Hannibal (the man who took Hanno's place, and possibly the blockade-runner at Lilybaeum) tried to hold the northern end. But Matho, stung to action by the gruesome sight of Spendius and other prisoners being crucified, was too quick for him and captured Hannibal and his camp. He then crucified Hannibal on the cross on which Spendius had just died and massacred thirty leading Carthaginians. Hamilcar, forced to raise the siege of Tunis, withdrew to the mouth of the Bagradas. In the ensuing winter new forces were raised and Hamilcar and Hanno were forced into a reconciliation by the thirty members of the Carthaginian council: Hamilcar's discomfiture at Tunis had given Hanno's faction a chance to re-establish his authority. A final battle was fought at an unknown site, with probably 40,000 Carthaginians against 30,000 rebels who were overwhelmed. The rest of Libya submitted at once, apart from Utica and Hippo which were forced to surrender after short sieges by Hamilcar and Hanno. Matho was led in a triumphal procession through the streets of Carthage and then tortured. Thus ended the war (probably in 237 rather than 238) which Polybius describes at length (1.65–88), a war which 'far surpassed all the wars we know of in cruelty and inhumanity'. Carthage thus survived a ghastly struggle that threatened her very life. Polybius however ended his account of it in his first book by devoting a paragraph to an event of great significance for the future: Rome's seizure of Sardinia.

[74] See Robinson 1943[K120], 1ff.

As soon as the Carthaginians were free from the Libyan war they determined to recover Sardinia, and since their relations with Rome were so good, they can have expected little trouble. But when the rebel mercenaries in Sardinia had been driven out by the natives, had crossed over to Italy and appealed to Rome, the Romans suddenly reversed their policy before the island was occupied by Punic forces. If they acted with decision Carthage could hardly stop them since she virtually lacked a fleet and had few resources left. However, when Carthage understood that Rome was going to intervene, she informed Rome that she had prior claims and intended to occupy the island herself. The Romans promptly alleged that her preparations were directed against themselves and bluntly passed a war-vote against her. The exact course of the subsequent diplomatic negotiations cannot be recovered from Polybius' somewhat vague and brief account. It is likely that a senatorial legation conveyed to Carthage news of this declaration in the form of an ultimatum (*rerum repetitio*) and then refrained from an *indictio belli* when the Carthaginians accepted their terms, so that war was never fully declared. Alternatively, the Romans may only have notified the Carthaginians of their decision and have left it to them to send an embassy to Rome to try to persuade them to change their minds.[75] But whether or not a full declaration of war was ever passed, no hostilities followed because Carthage capitulated and accepted Rome's terms. She agreed to surrender Sardinia and pay 1200 talents – a settlement denounced by Polybius as 'contrary to all justice'. This was unprovoked aggression and treaty-breaking by Rome. There was no excuse. Rome could not justifiably claim that Carthage had forfeited her rights in Sardinia either because she had left it in rebel hands for a year or two or because of the previous capture of Italian merchants who had been helping the rebels, and Sardinia certainly could not be classed among 'the islands between Sicily and Italy' which had been granted to Rome by the treaty of 241, though Roman annalists might try to argue otherwise. But some reason there must have been. Rome was presumably suddenly persuaded (perhaps after sharp differences in the senate) of the potential future danger of allowing Carthage to control an island so near to Italy. It is a tragedy that the Romans had not taken this view in 241 since if they had then insisted on the surrender of Sardinia it is difficult to see how the Carthaginians could have refused: it would have caused anger in place of the brief period of friendship, but it might have been accepted as inevitable. As it was, though in fact an extra clause had as it were been added to the Peace of Lutatius (the terms were embodied in an ἐπισυνθήκή (codicil) to the treaty of 241, and not in a fresh *foedus*), Carthage felt such a deep sense of injustice that relations were permanently embittered and the way was paved for another Punic war.

[75] For the former view see Walbank 1949[G745], 15f and 1957–79[B182], 1.149; for the latter see Rich 1976[K694], 64ff.

POSTSCRIPT. THE EMERGENCE OF THE PROVINCIAL SYSTEM[76]

A. E. ASTIN

The First Punic War set in train a transformation of relationships throughout the Mediterranean world. This was the first phase of a new age of expansion, in which already Roman horizons had been extended beyond Italy, the power structure of the western Mediterranean had been radically changed, and Rome's dealings with extra-Italian powers had led to permanent control of overseas territories. For it is evident that, whatever motives may have been at work in Rome – the desire to exclude Carthage from strategic territories, or the straightforward exploitation of resources, or even the positive enjoyment of dominion – there was no intention of withdrawing either from Sicily or from Sardinia and Corsica.

It is commonly said that the acquisition of these overseas territories presented Rome with new problems, or at least posed new questions; yet it may be doubted whether it was perceived immediately as having done so. In Sicily a pattern of control had been shaped largely by relationships established on an *ad hoc* basis, no doubt with much regard to short-term considerations during the prolonged struggle for the island. When the war ended it is likely at first to have been assumed that these relationships would continue of themselves and would function as before; even the payment of tribute, probably begun during the war and systematized on the model of the methods used in the kingdom of Syracuse, was perhaps expected to operate more or less automatically. It may be guessed that it was this legacy of relationships rather than any conscious abandonment of an earlier policy which accounts for the almost total absence from the Sicilian scene of bilateral treaties such as had been employed to shape Rome's relationships with the peoples of Italy. Nevertheless in the course of time Rome did find a need to take new measures – measures the very modesty and simplicity of which were ultimately to have profound implications for the manner in which a vast empire was administered.

The administrative provision made for Sicily in the years immediately after the war is not known. Perhaps there was virtually none beyond a reliance on messages between the Sicilian communities and the magistrates and senate in Rome, supplemented by occasional visits to the island by senatorial envoys or military officers. At any rate, it is most unlikely that one of the senior magistrates was normally stationed there, for they still numbered only four – the two consuls and two praetors – and there

---

[76] This section was contributed after the death of Professor Scullard. Its subject-matter was discussed by him in his *History of the Roman World, 753 to 146 B.C.* (1980[A119]) 179–86. The most important extended discussion remains Badian 1958[A8], chapter 11.

was much to occupy them elsewhere.[77] But therein lies a major difference from the war-years, when the presence of a senior magistrate to conduct the war had provided also an immediate and clearly located source of overriding authority within the island. Subsequent events suggest that over a period of time the absence of this element from the nexus of relationships began to have discernible consequences. It can be conjectured that such consequences manifested themselves in uncertain and disputed rights of jurisdiction; perhaps in difficulties over the calculation or collection of tribute; and conceivably in disorders. A possible response would have been a wholesale revision of the relationships, such as the general imposition of treaties on the familiar Italian model; but a simpler solution was chosen, namely to restore to the island the focus of authority which had been removed at the end of the war – in other words, to arrange for a magistrate to be sent to Sicily each year. Furthermore this was a choice which, besides having the virtue of simplicity, could well have been influenced also by recent experience in Sardinia, where rather different circumstances had nevertheless created a need for a similar solution. The formal seizure of Sardinia had been followed by prolonged resistance on the part of the native population. The resulting wars of conquest required the presence of a Roman magistrate in command of an army in virtually every year,[78] which in turn must have created a sense of a continuing need for a substantial military presence. In Roman terms that implied a continuing magisterial presence.

Thus in both Sicily and Sardinia the need for new provision emerged over a period of time. Fourteen years after the conclusion of the First Punic War the response to that need was implemented. The number of praetors was doubled, and of the four elected in 227 one was assigned Sicily as his particular sphere of responsibility – his *provincia* – and another Sardinia and Corsica. The latter was a Marcus Valerius, the former none other than Gaius Flaminius.[79] Their appointment initiated a shift in the meaning of the word '*provincia*', which soon came to signify a subject territory placed under the authority of a Roman magistrate (or, later, pro-magistrate). More importantly it established the pattern of the administration of further such territories as they were acquired. Each was placed under one of the annual magistrates, who commanded any military units assigned to his province but otherwise was supported only by his personal staff. Below that level there generally lay a mosaic of territorially defined communities (*civitates*) which furnished their own leaders and officials. Not surprisingly, such a governor concerned

---

[77] *MRR* 1.221–8.
[78] Evidence collected in *MRR* 1.221–8; see esp. Zonar. VIII.18 and the Fasti Triumphales for these years.   [79] Solin. V.1; Livy, *Epit.* XX; cf. *Dig.* 1.2.2.32.

himself especially with jurisdiction and the maintenance of order; and though he could and sometimes did interfere arbitrarily and with overriding authority in almost any matter, he had neither the inclination nor the means to regulate systematically the general life of his province and the affairs of its communities.

With the expansion of empire came new developments: different methods of collecting taxes were tried; in 197 two more praetors were added, almost certainly in direct response to the recent acquisition of two Spanish provinces,[80] and the evolution of the concept of a 'pro-magistrate' (p. 437) made it possible to extend a governor's term of office to a second year, or sometimes even further. Nevertheless the administration which Rome supplied to each of her provinces continued in the mould created by the early experiences in Sicily and Sardinia, consisting essentially of a powerful governor who was also the military commander but who otherwise had no pyramid of Roman administrators below him.

[80] Livy XXXII.27.6; cf. *Dig.* I.2.2.32.

CHAPTER 12

RELIGION IN REPUBLICAN ROME

J. A. NORTH

I. SOURCES AND METHODS

The first question to be asked in this chapter is whether the attempt to discuss Roman religion before about 200 B.C. can be justified at all. There are good reasons for doubting whether it can; but the position that will be argued here is that, despite the necessary limitations on our understanding of the Romans' religious life, it is possible to establish enough about its structure and working to say something, in very general terms at least, about the relation of religion to society (II, III, IV) and to examine the phenomena of religious change and adaptation within the system (V, VI). The purpose of this introduction is, however, more negative: it is to challenge the validity of the established versions of the 'history' of Roman religion and to show why any new attempt at writing such a history would produce no more than another arbitrary synthesis. Any treatment of the subject must begin from a radical re-assessment of the evidence we have and of the possibilities it offers.

The fundamental problem can be stated very simply: the great bulk of the sources we have for early Roman religion derives from historians and antiquarians who lived in the very late Republic or early Principate, two centuries or more after the end of the period with which this chapter is concerned. It must be very doubtful whether these writers had any understanding of the nature of early republican religion, beyond what they could guess or extrapolate from their knowledge of the recent past. Worse than this, the best-informed of these reconstructions, those of Varro and his successors, are themselves lost to us; they only survive either as brief dictionary entries or in the accounts of still later writers who themselves constitute another layer of the problem, for many of them were early Christians, plundering the antiquarians solely in order to show how absurd, valueless and obscene was the religion of the Classical world which they were seeking to destroy and replace.[1] The underlying

---

[1] The richest Christian sources for the religion of the Republic are Augustine, *De Civ. D.* and Arnobius, *Adv. Gent.*, both drawing generously on the work of Varro, especially on his *Antiquitates rerum divinarum* (p. 10). The fragments are collected (with commentary) by B. Cardauns[B26]; see

attitudes of these Christian authorities have often determined modern accounts of the character and development of Roman religion. Even these difficulties might be less serious, if we at least had a secure understanding of the religious situation and atmosphere of the late republican period which produced the writings of Varro, Cicero, Virgil and Ovid on which we are ultimately dependent; but, in fact, no such secure understanding exists and it is debatable whether we should even try to understand the fifth century B.C. before making some sense of the age of Cicero.

Some categories of information, however, offer us at least a possibility of escaping these limitations and thus finding a starting point. First, we have the calendar of festivals of early Rome; a number of copies survive of the late republican calendar (cf. Fig. 62), mostly set up in or soon after the Augustan age and containing many late accretions, including explanatory comments derived from the antiquarians.[2] It was Mommsen who observed that, incorporated in the extant copies, was an earlier list of festivals; the entries in this list were distinguished because they appeared in capital letters.[3] The republican calendar as we know it was basically solar and not determined by the correlation of months to the phases of the moon; we do not know when this form of calendar was introduced, though it may well have been in the course of the republican period; its introduction might or might not have coincided with the fixing of the list of festivals in capitals. The ritual programme of some of

---

Fig. 62. Reconstruction of the only surviving pre-Julian calendar (Fasti Antiates Maiores: between 84 and 46 B.C.) for January to April. The calendar assigns each day one of the first nine letters of the alphabet (in sequence) to aid identification of the *nundinae* (originally market-days); marks the Kalends (K), Nones (Non.) and Ides (Eidus) of each month; records large letter festivals (e.g. CAR(MENTALIA) on 11 January) and other sacrifices, usually on the anniversary of temple dedications (e.g. to Iuturna on 11 January), and assigns each day a letter or combination of letters indicating whether certain types of public activity are forbidden or permitted (e.g. C(omitialis) indicates that public assemblies may be held). For full details see Michels 1967 [G446]. Reconstruction from Degrassi 1963 [G388], Tab. III.

---

also id. 1978[G370], 8off. But it is quite clear that both writers exploit Varro's material without any concern or capacity to be fair to paganism – the last thing on their minds; they therefore tend to emphasize absurd-seeming elements. The dictionary of Festus (ed. Lindsay, 1913) preserves some of the learning of the Augustan antiquarian Verrius Flaccus (on whom A. Dihle 1958[B44], 1636ff; Frier 1979[B57], 35ff), whose work underlies the notes in the Fasti Praenestini (Degrassi 1963[G388], 107ff). For a survey of the literary sources, Latte 1960[G435], 4–8; useful observations on the problems, Dumézil 1970/71[G399], 3ff; a collection of sources in English is provided by F. C. Grant 1957[G416], but with much space given to philosophical texts. For further bibliography, cf. Brelich 1949 etc.[G366]; Schilling 1972[G490], 317ff.

[2] The inscriptions are collected in Degrassi 1963[G388], who also gives (388ff) a selection of other important sources for each festival, with bibliography and notes. The most accessible account in English is Scullard 1981[G494], replacing for purposes of reference Warde Fowler 1899[G508].

[3] Mommsen in Henzen, Hülsen and Mommsen 1893[D16], 283–304.

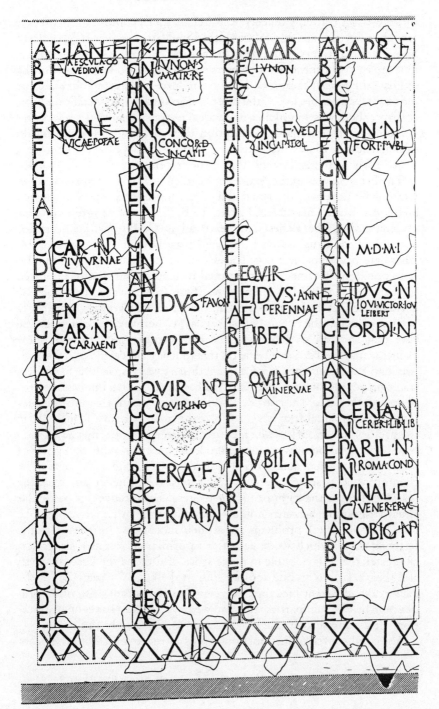

these festivals certainly reflects very archaic social conditions; in no case can it be proved that a festival was introduced later than the regal period.[4] Some were still very prominent in the first century B.C., some totally obscure by that time, even to experts such as Varro. The purpose of the old list (the *feriale*) cannot be known for sure: perhaps it contained the oldest festivals; more likely, the most important at some specific date; or, perhaps, there was an unknown practical purpose behind the selection.[5] It would be an unreliable assumption that anything not appearing in capitals must be a later introduction into the *feriale*. We have, therefore, a list of early festivals; beyond that, little is certain.

The list of names in the *feriale* can be filled out by very mixed sources which offer details of the ritual and of the stories and traditions associated with them. This material gives the best hope of progress towards understanding; the richest source of all is Ovid's *Fasti*, a versified account of the ritual calendar, of which we have the first six months. There are problems here too, because much of what Ovid has to offer does not seem to consist of traditional Roman stories, but of imported Greek ones; it is hard to tell how far these stories were introduced by Ovid himself, in the interests of variety and fun, how far they had already been attached to the rituals before his day; either way, we can hardly be sure that they all date back to the fifth century B.C., though some elements may well do so. The fact is that much of the calendar of festivals was handed down, bereft of any myth or exegesis, in the form of a tradition simply of ritual action. This has very serious implications for the possibility of a history of Roman religion: it means that the interpretation of individual festivals must be problematic for us. Rituals are in themselves notoriously vulnerable to re-interpretation by the participants over a period of time; indeed, to look at it from a different point of view, the strength of such a ritual-system lies exactly in its capacity to be re-interpreted as society evolves new needs over time. In any case, the search either for the right or for the original significance of a particular ritual programme becomes not just difficult, but in principle impossible. Paradoxically, these problems are at their most acute in relation to the festivals about which we have better information; recent research has suggested that it is possible to make sense of some of the lesser festivals and their relations to one another; but in the case, for example, of the Lupercalia, different meanings were evidently read into the ritual programme by different participants and we have, and can have, no justification for assuming that one or another was exclusively right.[6]

A second source of information brings us more directly to the prob-

---

[4] Discussion in Michels 1967[G446], Part II.   [5] Michels 1967[G446], 130ff.
[6] On the value of Ovid as a source, Schilling 1979[G491], 1ff; for the Lupercalia, see below n. 90.

lems of historical development. The annalistic tradition provides a great deal of our information on Roman religion; much of it (say, Livy's account of the procedures for declaring war (1.32.5ff)) must be seen as antiquarian reconstruction incorporated into a historical account, but the historians also claim to know dated facts about religious history. They record vows, special games, the consultation of religious advisers and so on. Brief notices of this kind can provide the framework for elaborate reconstructions; and, even if we cannot test the origin of particular facts of this kind, it is possible to prove that detailed information could survive, at least sometimes. Pliny,[7] for instance, records the actual year in which the procedure of extispicy was amended to take account of the heart as well as other vital organs; this information must have come from an early source, because it is dated in a unique way – by the year of the reign of the *rex sacrorum*, the 'sacred king' who carried on the king's religious duties when kingship was abolished; this can only be a continuing use in priestly records of the dating system abandoned for other purposes when the Republic was founded. This also means that we are dealing with a situation in which at least certain kinds of religious change were accepted, identified as such and in some way recorded. Priests in Rome certainly did keep records to which they could refer to establish points of law; and the *pontifices* in particular kept an annual record of events, including, but not confined to, the sphere of religion. Writing down and recording was very much part of their functions.[8]

So far, the indications are positive; but the limitations of this kind of recording were narrow. Only changes, not continuities, would be recorded; and then only changes of a particular kind, the ones the priestly authorities noticed and chose to record in their collegiate books. Many other changes will have happened over the course of years without record – through mistakes, neglect, forgetfulness, unobserved social evolution, the unconscious re-building of outmoded conceptions; many such things would never even have been noticed, let alone written down. To take these occasional recorded facts and use them to build a straightforward history would result in a most distorted account. It is only if the recorded facts could be fitted into a known scheme of development that they could be raised to the significance of a historical process. But, in fact, unless we already have a conception of how the religion worked, how it related to the social and political realities of the time, how it responded to change, even the few facts we have are robbed of any significance for us.

These short-comings apply even to the best of the literary evidence we have; the way in which scholars have sought to overcome them has been

---

[7] Pliny, *HN* xi.186.

[8] On the books of the *pontifices*, Wissowa 1912[G519], 513; Rohde 1936[G480]. For the pontifical annals, Frier 1979[B57].

to construct the required conceptual scheme from a set of *a priori* assumptions. The elements of such schemes have been: first, some characterization of the original or true nature of Roman religion; secondly, some mechanism for explaining its deterioration or decline.[9] In these theories, which are very similar in structure, however much the details vary, the healthy period of Roman religion is retrojected into the remote past, the late Republic is treated as a period of virtually dead religion; the early Republic then provides a transitional period in which the forces of deterioration gathered strength, while contact with the simplicities of the native religious experience were progressively lost. Amongst the mechanisms of deterioration that have been offered are: (a) the contamination of the native tradition by foreign, especially Greek influences; (b) the sterilization of true religiosity by the growth of priestly ritualism; (c) the alienation of an increasingly sophisticated urban population from an essentially rural religious tradition. In the case of (c), it is hard to believe that any ancient city lost its involvement with and dependence on the seasonal cycle of the agricultural year, let alone the relatively small-town Rome of the third century B.C.[10] The other two are harder to refute, but equally arbitrary; a different approach will be found below, but it will be obvious at once that there is no self-evident connexion between any of these alleged developments and the concepts of deterioration or decline.[11]

Even more fundamental are the issues raised by the first element – the 'true' nature of Roman religion. As we know it in the developed form of the later and middle Republic, some characteristics of the system strike us as peculiar to the Romans and hence as representing a tradition distinct from that of Greeks, Etruscans or even other Italic peoples about whom we know enough to judge at all. The Roman gods, even the greatest of them, lacked personal development and character, while the proliferating lesser gods were little more than a named function in a natural process; the rituals lacked any mythical correlates and seem to have existed essentially as an inherited tradition of repetitious action; the system offered no eschatology, no explanation of creation or man's relation to it; there was no room for prophets or holy men; the antiquarians report the belief that the earliest Romans actually had no representation of their gods, and some deities never had a specifically Roman representation.[12] The temptation, seldom resisted, is to summarize by saying that the Romans were simple, artless, unimaginative and su-

[9] For the most influential versions cf. Warde Fowler 1911[G509]; Latte 1960[G435]; for criticism of Latte's views, Dumézil 1970/71[G399], especially 102ff. A new approach: Scheid 1985[G485], 17ff.   [10] See below (p. 602f).

[11] For discussion of the implications of religious innovation, North 1976[G455], 1ff.

[12] Varro *ap.* Aug. *De civ. D.* iv.31 = fr. 18 (Cardauns); *ap.* Tert. *Apol.* 25.12 = fr. 38 (Cardauns).

Fig. 63. Bronze sheet from Lavinium (sixth-fifth century). The retrograde inscription reads 'Castorei Podlouqueique qurois' 'to the (divine) youths Castor and Pollux' ('qurois' appears to be a direct transliteration of the Greek κούροις but its exact sense here is uncertain: R. Schilling 1960 [G487], 178n. = id. *Rites, cultes, dieux de Rome* (Paris 1979), 339n.).

premely practical, and hence that everything involving art, literary imagination, philosophic awareness or spirituality had to be borrowed from Greeks or Etruscans. Once posited, this conception becomes self-confirming, since if it be agreed that anything truly Roman must also be narrow-minded, anything which fails to conform to the prescribed pattern may be explained as either foreign importation or late retrojection. The technique can also be applied to the detail of Roman ritual or divinatory procedures, to analyse Roman and non-Roman, once again producing circular re-inforcement of the original idea.[13]

Can these methods really detect the genuine Roman tradition? The earliest period about which we can attain any understanding at all is the period of the Etruscan monarchy; but by that time the religion of Rome was already a composite of different traditions, including a native Latin-speaking element, which was already overlaid by other influences. Sixth-century archaeological evidence has made it ever more certain that, whatever the political relations of Rome and Etruria may have been, in cultural and religious terms Rome must be seen as part of a civilization dominated by Etruscans and receptive to the influence of Greeks and possibly of Carthaginians too (cf. Chap. 3). The dedication to the Dioscuri found at Lavinium (Fig. 63)[14] shows unmistakably that we have to reckon with direct Greek contacts, not only with those mediated through the Etruscans; and it is perfectly possible that some of the early republican innovations were also directly influenced from South Italy.[15] Recent research has cut even more deeply into the expected pattern of religious life: Filippo Coarelli's reinterpretation[16] of the material from the Comitium makes it very likely that the area round the Lapis Niger should be identified with the Volcanal; but in the votive deposit from this sanctuary, dating from the second quarter of the sixth century B.C., there was found a black-figure pot with a representation of Hephaestus (Fig. 64); it is thus probable that the identification of Vulcan and Hephaestus had already taken place, and that the Greek image of the god

[13] For instance, in relation to the techniques of extispicy, cf. Schilling 1962[G488], 1371ff = 1979[G491], 183ff.   [14] *ILLRP* 1271a.   [15] See below, p. 620f.
[16] Coarelli 1977[E92], 166ff.

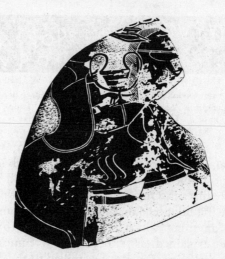

Fig. 64. Fragment of Attic black figure crater depicting the return of Hephaestus to Olympus (c. 570–560 B.C.). From the Lapis Niger votive deposit.

had penetrated to his holy place in Rome. This must raise doubt about the supposed 'aniconic' period, though perhaps a single piece of evidence should not be allowed too much weight, even in the context of falsifying a hypothesis. In a different way, the discovery of a religious phenomenon very widespread throughout Central Italy has similar disturbing implications. Several sites have now produced substantial votive deposits consisting primarily of terracottas of parts of the human body;[17] that is to say, there must have been a number of sanctuaries in the early and middle republican period to which individuals went when seeking cures for their diseases; at these sanctuaries, they dedicated terracottas of the afflicted part. Not only does this imply a major cult which we know nothing about, but also a type of religiosity which the accepted model of early Roman religion seems to exclude: for it implies that individuals turned to the gods directly in search of support with their everyday problems of health and disease. On the accepted model, they would have looked for and expected no such help, practical or spiritual. Another recent study[18] has suggested that inscriptions discovered at Tor Tignosa near to Lavinium come from a cult in which incubation was practised as a means of gaining prophetic insight by direct contact with the deity. Virgil and Ovid[19] both describe the use of such a technique in early – or rather mythical – Italy; but this is exactly the kind of evidence which has always

---

[17] Maule and Smith 1959[G445]; Fenelli 1975[G401], 206ff; Comella 1981[G385], 717ff.
[18] Palmer 1974[G461], 79ff.   [19] Virg. Aen. VII.81–106; Ov. Fast. IV.649–72.

been highly suspect on the grounds that it does not fit our preconceptions.

The most familiar attempt to provide a narrative account of the development of religion in Rome was that of Warde Fowler,[20] who sought to place Rome within the scheme of evolution of religion advocated by contemporary anthropologists; he saw the earliest stage as 'animism' and sought to detect in the historical period the gradual development of 'proper' gods and goddesses. The greater complexity of the picture now emerging seems to preclude at least this particular narrative account; if we were to abandon completely the idea of an original core of Roman-ness always identifiable, then we would have to abandon also any attempt to discover a linear progression and hence the attempt to write a historical account of religion in this period. The only other possibility is to take as the starting-point, not a projection backwards of supposedly 'Roman' characteristics from the first century B.C., but the determination of the earliest features by comparison with related societies. For many years, Georges Dumézil has been elaborating theories which would combine evidence from many Indo-European traditions to discover the internal structure of the systems of mythology that are the common inheritance of these peoples. He regards this structure as derived ultimately from the social division of the original Indo-Europeans themselves, which gave rise to a 'tri-functional ideology' causing deities and all related human activities to fall into three divisions: 1. Religion and Law; 2. War; 3. Production, especially agricultural production. Dumézil has been successful in showing that this structure can be detected both in the most archaic Roman religious institutions and in the mythology of the kings, especially the first four.[21] The problem thus presented to the historian of republican (even perhaps of regal) Roman society is that Dumézil has found, encoded in the mythology, a social organization fundamentally opposed to the social organization of republican Rome itself, where, of course, the warriors *were* the peasants, so that the three functions can have no special application. The theories themselves have proved very fertile when dealing with individual festivals or areas of worship; they will no doubt continue to inspire valuable interpretations. But if the Indo-European elements they postulate were, at any period we can analyse, at variance with the actual socio-economic conditions of the time, then it follows that Dumézil's ideas cannot

---

[20] Warde Fowler 1911[G509].

[21] Dumézil himself has written copiously on Rome since the 1930s and provoked more and more discussion as time has passed – some of it hostile, some supportive. See Dumézil 1941–5[G395], for an early statement; 1974[G398] (1970/71[G399] – Eng. transl. of the first edn.) for his fullest account of Roman religion; 1968–73[G396], latest version of the mythology of the Roman kings. For recent discussion see Momigliano 1983[G449], 329ff; Sheid 1985[G485], 74ff; cf. above p. 54f.

provide the starting point for an account of Roman religion: they may explain survivals, fragments of tradition otherwise inexplicable, or the 'meaning' of rituals; but they cannot help to understand early Roman religion as a whole. If so, it must be admitted that, in the present state of our knowledge, no valid basis exists for analysing its early development. We could construct *a priori* theories, but they would be incapable of verification.

The problems considered take the discussion back to the starting point of this introduction, that is to the character of the literary source material on which our ideas are based. One feature of that source material which must never be forgotten is the fact that the information comes either from priestly writings as such or at least in forms evolved by a priestly tradition of recording. The question is to what extent, whether by conscious means or not, some areas were selected and others rejected from the material which has eventually reached us: the emerging archaeological record strongly suggests that the picture is indeed very partial. To put the point in its most extreme form, what we have might be an artificial historiographic construction, expressing a kind of official religion which never actually represented the religious life of the Roman people. An alternative view would be to say that it does represent a reality, but only a reality of elite religion not of popular religion, which is only preserved by the archaeology. The latter form has the disadvantage of importing a distinction which is extremely hard to prove even for much later periods and is perhaps just an anachronism. On either view, it is necessary to be open-minded in assessing what was or was not within the boundaries of the experience of early Romans. The approach adopted in what follows is not to attempt any kind of developmental picture of the Romans' religion, but to assume as a working hypothesis that the main phenomena were more or less constant throughout the republican period; the actual evidence comes mostly from later periods, but we must either use it, on the grounds that institutional change is fairly slow, or abandon the attempt to say anything at all. The possibility cannot be excluded (and will be discussed as it arises) that the picture here constructed was valid for the third century B.C., perhaps for the second half of the fourth, but that earlier republican religion was somehow profoundly different. If so, its character is irretrievably lost to our understanding.

II. THE PRIESTS AND RELIGIOUS AUTHORITY

In the early republican period there were three major colleges of priests – the *pontifices*, the *augures* and the *duoviri* (later *decemviri*) *sacris faciundis*; the *fetiales* were perhaps of comparable importance. These four colleges each had an area of responsibility and within this the senate would treat them as experts and refer to their authority. Other groups of priests had ritual duties, on particular occasions or in relation to particular cults, but were not, so far as we know, officially consulted on points of religious law. The principle of collegiality suggests that the priests were interchangeable for purposes of ritual, that there was no specific ritual programme for an individual; the *pontifices* at least also had a quorum system for taking decisions. When a member died, the surviving colleagues themselves chose a replacement. This general view of the colleges needs some qualification in particular cases. First, the college of *pontifices* had a far more complex structure than the others. They had a recognized leader (*pontifex maximus*), who by the end of the period was elected publicly from the existing *pontifices*, not just chosen by his colleagues; the college also contained, apparently as full members, the *rex sacrorum* and the *flamines* of the gods Iuppiter, Mars and Quirinus; other priests were associated with the college – the Vestal Virgins, the scribes of the *pontifices*, the twelve lesser *flamines*.[22] The fifteen *flamines*, through the very nature of their priesthood, suggest a different principle of organization; each had his own god to whom he was devoted, he had his ritual programme which he had to fulfil and he was to a greater or lesser degree restricted in his movements and behaviour;[23] it is a reasonable guess that this represents an older system, that the *flamines* had once been independent of the collegiate system.

The second area in which priestly activity diverged from the collegiate pattern concerns the *haruspices*. They were certainly consulted by the senate – in the later period, regularly so; but were not apparently organized as a college, at least before the very end of the Republic.[24] There is no reason to doubt the reports from the early Republic, but it may be important that the *haruspices* are sometimes said to have been summoned to Rome from Etruria;[25] if they were really foreign experts invited to advise the senate, and not Romans at all, that would explain their lack of organization. However, *haruspices* also appear in a humbler and altogether more regular role, as readers of the entrails of sacrificial victims; extispicy is an Etruscan speciality and these men too might be Etruscan or of Etruscan extraction. Alternatively, there might have been two quite separate groups under the same name – upper-class advisers

---

[22] Wissowa 1912[G519], 501ff; De Sanctis 1907–64[A37], IV.2.353ff; Latte 1960[G435], 195ff; 401ff; on priesthood in general: Scheid 1985[G485], 36ff.

[23] All the rules applying to the *flamen Dialis* are lovingly collected by the second-century A.D. antiquarian Aulus Gellius, *NA* x.15.

[24] On the *haruspices* in general: Thulin 1910[G498], 2431–68; Wissowa 1912[G519], 543ff; Bloch 1963[G355], 43ff; Latte 1960[G435], 157–60; MacBain 1982[G440], 43ff. M. Torelli (1975[B266], 119ff) argues for a middle republican date for the creation of the *ordo*, but the issue is not decided; cf. MacBain 1982[G440], 47ff. [25] E.g. Livy xxvII.37.6.

drawn from the elite of Etruscan cities, lower-class religious specialists resident in Rome itself. At any rate, their status as outside advisers, whether really or fictionally outside, gives them an ambivalent but influential position; it is not surprising that they also stood outside the normal organization of the Roman colleges. In the conception of the later Romans, Etruria represented an alien religious tradition; from what is now known about the influence of Etruscan practice in the sixth century B.C. and even later, it could be argued that this later view was wrong; but that does not change the significance of what the Romans themselves believed.

There can be no question of placing these various priestly groups in any kind of hierarchy of religious authority. The more important colleges had their own area of concern and of expertise, within which sphere the others never interfered. The *pontifex maximus* had very limited disciplinary powers, but mostly in relation to the priests and priestesses of his own college – the Vestals, the *rex* and the *flamines*.[26] In general, the position of the priests can only be understood in relation to the rest of the city's constitutional system. The capacity for religious action and the capacity for religious decision-making were widely diffused among different Roman authorities and it is not a simple matter to say where the central power of controlling the relations of the Romans and their gods was located. The first step will be to examine the work of the major colleges.

The augurs (*augures*) were the experts on the taking of the auspices (*auspicia*) by a variety of techniques to establish the will of the gods.[27] That is not to say that they were themselves the takers of the auspices: it was usually the magistrates who carried out the ceremonies in their roles as war-leaders or as political or legal actors. In the normal case, an augur would be present as adviser, perhaps as witness; after the event, the augural college would be the source of judgement on the legality of what had been done or not done. The earliest and best-known modes of taking the auspices were derived from the flight and activity of particular species of birds, but the augurs also dealt with the interpretation of thunder and lightning, the behaviour of certain animals and so on.[28] They seem to have had nothing at all to do with the reading of entrails at sacrifices, which was the business of *haruspices*; and they were not consulted about the interpretation of prodigies. Most characteristically, they were concerned with the interpretation of normal 'natural' events, as indications of the attitude of the gods; sometimes, signs came unasked

[26] Wissowa 1912[G519], 509ff; Guizzi 1968[G423]; cf. Bleicken 1957[G353], 345ff.
[27] On the augurs in general: Warde Fowler 1911[G509], 292ff; Wissowa 1912[G519], 523ff; Dumézil 1970/71[G399], 594ff; Catalano 1960[G377]; 1978[G378]; Linderski 1986[G437], 2146ff.
[28] Wissowa 1912[G519], 231–2; Linderski 1986[G437], 2226ff.

and carried their own meaning (*signa oblativa*); but, in relation to a proposed course of action, a particular question was asked and the answer depended on the direction from which the sign came. The taker of the auspices defined a *templum* in the heavens, a rectangle in which he specified left, right, front and back; the meaning of the sign depended on its spatial relationship to these defined points. The celestial rectangle had an earthly correlate to which the same term was applied; a 'temple' in our sense of the word might or might not be a *templum* in this sense; the 'temple' of Vesta, for instance, was an *aedes* not a *templum*. It was also possible for an earthly *templum* not to be a temple in our sense; such were the senate-house (the senate could not meet elsewhere than in a *templum*), the Comitium and the augurs' own centre for taking auspices, the *auguraculum*.[29] The augurs' science, therefore, concerned not just the interpretation of signs, but the definition of boundaries, or perhaps the purification of bounded spaces. They had, in fact, a system of the categorization of space within and without the city, and also of the outside world in relation to Rome.[30] This categorization corresponded to the different types of auspices: the most famous example was the *pomerium*, the augural boundary of the city, which was the limit of the 'urban auspices' (*auspicia urbana*).[31]

All public action in Rome took place within space and according to rituals falling within the province of the augurs. Major decisions were taken in areas sanctified by the augural ritual; each individual meeting was preceded by the taking of the auspices by those responsible for the meeting. The passing of laws, the holding of elections, discussion in the senate – all took place within spaces and times defined by the application of augural ritual; it followed that their validity was dependent on the correct performances of the rituals and on the application of a network of religious rules, whose maintenance was the augurs' concern. One very important issue was the right to take the auspices, which was held by the senior magistrates, who passed it on, year by year, to their successors; if for any reason there was a gap in the succession, the auspices returned to the *patres*, the patrician members of the senate.[32] It is evident that this whole process was central to the relations between the city and the gods, and to the legitimacy of all public transactions. This is, of course, why the augurs were so important politically: their right to examine whether a *vitium* (religious fault) had occurred in any proceeding of the assemblies gave them a critical role in constitutional controversies, at least in the late republican period.

The *pontifices* had a wider range of functions and responsibilities than

29 Weinstock 1934[G511], 480ff; Linderski 1986[G437], 2256ff.
30 Catalano 1978[G378], 440–53.   31 Varro, *Ling.* v.43.
32 Magdelain 1964[H50], 427ff; cf. above, p. 181.

the augurs, less easily defined in simple terms.[33] The best summary might be to say that their duties covered everything not specifically within the activities of the augurs, the *fetiales* and the *duo-/decemviri*. Like these other colleges, they were treated as experts on problems of sacred law and procedure within their province – such matters as the games, sacrifices and vows, the *sacra* connected with Vesta and the Vestals, tombs and burial law, the inheritance of sacred obligations. Their powers of adjudication do not seem at first sight to lie in areas as politically significant as those dealt with by the augurs. The *pontifices* were, however, and continued to be even in the last days of the Republic, as distinguished as the augurs in membership.[34] As already discussed, they were not like the other colleges in their collegiate structure; they also differed from the others in having functions that took them more distinctly outside what we should define as religious. At its grandest, the role envisaged for them by our sources is as the repository of all law, human or divine; Livy suggests that, down to 304 B.C., the formulae without knowledge of which no legal action could begin, were secrets known only to the *pontifices*.[35] Their role in the law outside religion is a most difficult problem; but it is possible that the *pontifices* were the earliest source of legal advice for the citizen, essentially on matters of religious procedure, such as the rules of burial; but, since religious and non-religious law overlapped, the range of advice they offered might have widened in time.[36] More certainly, the *pontifices* were responsible for the calendar; for the supervision of adoptions and some other matters of family law; and for the keeping of an annual record of events.

Their control of the calendar goes beyond interest merely in the annual festivals, although that would have been part of their task. They were responsible too for intercalation, for inserting the extra months needed to keep the calendar in its correct relation to the solar year; the *rex sacrorum* continued to announce the dates of each month, presumably as a survival from the time when months were really begun by the new moon; the college also fixed dates for some of the important festivals which had no set date. The calendar included a great deal of information in the form of marking of the days; these fixed the character of the day – whether the courts could sit, whether the senate or the *comitia* could meet.[37] The organization of public time was, then, pontifical business. Adoptions, wills and inheritances all involved some elements of strictly religious

[33] For the *pontifices* in general: Wissowa 1912[G519], 501ff; Rohde 1936[G480]; De Sanctis 1907–64[A37], IV.2.353ff; Bleicken 1957[G353], 345ff; Latte 1960[G435], 195ff; Scheid 1985[G485], 36ff. [34] See the lists in Szemler 1972[G497], 101ff. [35] Livy IX.46.5; cf. p. 396f.
[36] Livy I.20.6–7 leaves no doubt that the *pontifex* was expected to be available to advise the individual citizen; see also Pomponius in *Dig.* 1.2.2.6, a text which suggests that one in particular was nominated each year for this purpose, at least in the fourth century B.C.
[37] Degrassi 1963[G388], 314ff; Michels 1967[G446], Part I; Scullard 1981[G494], 41ff.

interest, since they all affected the issue of who would maintain into the next generation the family's religious obligations (*sacra familiaria*).[38] Inevitably, the college's duties in this area would have drawn them into wider issues of the continuity of family traditions and the control of property, issues fertile of conflicts between families or between clans (*gentes*). The most unexpected of their duties was, perhaps, the recording of events. What we know for certain, from a remark of Cato the Elder,[39] is that they were responsible in the second century B.C. for publishing the great events of the day on a whitened board, displayed in public; these public reports, according to other sources, formed the basis of a permanent annual record, known to Cicero, and, at least allegedly, going back to the earliest times.[40] It seems very unlikely that this recording function of the *pontifices* would have been added to their duties, had it not always been part of them. If that is right, we are faced with a range of what we should call 'secular' functions, as well as the 'religious' ones. That might seem to imply that they were not an exclusively religious body in early Rome: it would be better to say that we should not be thinking in terms of our own boundary, or indeed of any boundary, between religious and secular areas of life. It is not impossible on this assumption to find coherence in the college's different responsibilities. One hypothesis might be that there was a connexion between their interest in family continuity and their practice of record-keeping; if so, they should be seen as priestly genealogists, concerned with ensuring that status and rights were preserved within those families and *gentes* whose past achievements had earned them their place in Roman society. Their concern would be with the transmission of past rites into the future, the organization of the year's time into its destined functions, the preservation of past action as a control over present status.

Two other colleges have duties which bring them close to the central workings of the city. The fetials (*fetiales*) controlled and performed the rituals through which alone a war could be started acceptably; it was of the first importance that the war should both be and be seen to be a 'just war' (*bellum iustum*).[41] The full extant accounts of their activities date from a period when much of their ritual must have been modified or discontinued; but, if Livy should be believed at all, they were in early times responsible both for ritual action and for what we should call diplomatic action – conveying messages and demanding reparations.[42]

[38] Cicero discusses at length in *De Legibus* II.47ff the conflict that could arise for a pontifical lawyer between the rules over the inheritance of *sacra* in the pontifical law and the ordinary rules of the civil law.   [39] *Origines* fr. 77 (Peter) = Gell. *NA* II.28.6.

[40] Cic. *De Or.* II.52; *Schol. Dan. Aen.* 1.373. For discussion, Frier 1979[B57]; above, pp. 6f; 87f.

[41] On the *fetiales*, Wissowa 1912[G519], 550ff; Latte 1960[G435], 121ff; Samter 1909[G483], 2259ff; Bayet 1971[G351], 9ff. For the 'just war' cf. above, p. 384.

[42] Livy's account of the earliest fetial law (1.32) is under strong suspicion of being based on later antiquarian reconstructions; see Ogilvie ad loc. (Ogilvie 1965[B129], 127ff).

Later on, they could still be called upon by the senate to give their view on the correct procedures for the declaration.[43] The *duoviri*, later *decemviri, sacris faciundis* (two, later ten, men for ritual action) were the guardians of the Sibylline Books. The Books will be discussed in a later section, but there can be no doubt that the college kept and consulted on the senate's instructions prophetic verses of supposedly great antiquity. When prodigies were reported and the senate felt the need of strong remedial action, the Books would produce recommendations for action. When they suggested the introduction of foreign cults, as they repeatedly did, the priests may have had some continuing responsibility for them; the new cults were normally Greek and celebrated in what the Romans called 'the Greek rite' (*Graeco ritu*); but it would be going well beyond the evidence to say that the *decemviri* had the same duties in relation to the Greek cults as the *pontifices* did in relation to Roman ones.[44] It seems that both *fetiales* and *decemviri* kept within closely defined areas of action.

In fact, all the colleges had limited authority, exercised only within a complicated set of procedures that involved non-priests as well as priests. Thus the priests cannot be treated as an independent or self-sufficient religious structure. For one thing, they do not seem ever to have been a separate caste, or a group of specialized, or professional, priests. Later augurs and *pontifices*, for whom we have lists preserved, were simply the most noble of the senators – that is, they were the same men who dominated politics and the law, fought the battles, celebrated triumphs and made great fortunes on overseas commands.[45] Although they were in principle the guardians of religious, even of secret, lore, they were not specially trained or selected on any criterion other than family or political status. The holders of the less distinguished priesthoods are less well known to us, but there is little, if any, sign that they were chosen as religious specialists. That is not to say that priests, or some of them, did not become experts in the traditions and records of their colleges, but they certainly had other things on their minds as well. Cicero regarded this situation as one of the characteristic and important features of the tradition of Rome and as a source of special strength.[46] There is no doubt that by the end of the period under consideration, the priest-politician was an established figure; whether this situation goes right back to the beginnings of the Republic must be more open to debate, though it is

[43] E.g. Livy XXXI.8.3.

[44] On the *decemviri s.f.*, Wissowa 1912[G519], 524ff; Gagé 1935[G406]; Radke 1963[G472], 1114ff; on the Sibylline Books, below (p. 617).

[45] The most famous examples are such men as Caesar, Pompey and Antony, but see the lists in Szemler 1972[G497] for the evidence as to how widespread the practice was; it should be remembered that we do not have lists for the lesser priesthoods, where it is probable that less important figures would have been found.   [46] Cic. *Dom.* 1.

usually assumed that it does. We know the names of some early priests, but can never positively identify them with known consuls, as we can later on.[47] In some respects, the early republican situation must have been quite different from the later one: the number of priests in the major colleges was far smaller – two or three, as compared to eight or nine after 300 B.C.; again, they were almost certainly all patricians – the first non-patricians seem to enter the *decemviri* in 367 B.C., the *pontifices* and augurs only in 300 B.C. Even in the later period, some priests are prevented by traditional rules from entering other areas of public life. The *rex sacrorum* was prevented from holding any office,[48] but he is a special case on any view. The major *flamines* were in some cases prevented by their duties or the regulations of their priesthoods from holding or exercising all the duties of magistrates.[49] After repeated conflicts, these restrictions were step by step relaxed in the late Republic, until the *flamines* came to play the normal role of an aristocrat in public life. It would be possible to argue that the other priests as well were originally excluded from political life and from warfare; but that they had followed the same route as the *flamines*, though at a much earlier date. In this case, the early colleges would have represented more nearly specialized religious institutions; at a later stage these prestigious offices for life might have become tempting prizes for the aristocratic leaders of the day. It would be difficult to disprove this theory; but on balance the established view seems after all likelier to be right: it seems to be characteristic of the augurs and the *pontifices* that they were full colleagues – one could always act instead of another, so that limitations on their movements would never have been so necessary as on those of the *flamines*. The *flamen Dialis*, in particular, had a ritual programme that only he could perform; so rules to keep him in the city had a particular point.[50]

To define more closely how far the priests had authority, their activities need to be put into their proper context. In general, the initiative in relation to religious action lay with the magistrates: it was they who consulted the gods by taking the auspices before meetings or battles; it was they who performed the dedication of temples to the gods; it was they who conducted censuses and the associated lustral ceremonies; it was they who made public vows and held the games or sacrifices needed to fulfil the vows. The priest's role was to dictate or prescribe the prayers and formulae, to offer advice on the procedures or

---

[47] Szemler 1972[G497], chap. 2.

[48] This emerges quite clearly from Livy XL.42.8ff, reporting a conflict in the second century B.C between a potential *rex sacrorum* and the *pontifex maximus* of the time, who wanted him to abdicate a junior magistracy that he was then holding. The outcome was that he kept his magistracy and did not become *rex*.   [49] See Livy, *Epit.* XIX; Livy XXXVII.51.1ff; Cic. *Phil.* XI.18.

[50] Wissowa 1912[G519], 505ff.

simply to attend. Again, when it came to religious decision-making, it was not with the priests, but with the senate that the effective power of decision lay. To take an example, when a bill had been voted through in the assemblies, but by a questionable procedure, the priests might be asked by the senate to comment on whether a fault (*vitium*) had taken place; but, subject to the ruling the priests offered, it would be the senate not the priests who would declare the law invalid on religious grounds.[51] The procedure for dealing with the annual prodigy-reports suggests much the same relationship; the senate heard the reports and decided to which groups of priests, if any, they should be referred; the priests replied to the senate; the senate ordered the appropriate actions to take place; it was often the magistrates who carried out the ceremonials on the city's behalf.[52]

To the modern observer, this procedure makes the priests look rather like a constitutional sub-committee of the senate, but this may be misleading: if the priests could not act, they were accepted as supreme authorities on the sacred law in their area. Once the senate had consulted them, it seems inconceivable that their advice should not be followed. On other occasions, with smaller issues at stake – such matters as the precise drafting of vows, the right procedure for the consecration of buildings, the control of the calendar – the priests must have had freedom of decision. So, religious authority in the general sense can only be located in the interaction, according to rules and conventions, of magistrates, senate and priests, each college in its own sphere. It follows that the relations of religion and politics were similarly interlocked: every political action took place in a religious context and had a religious aspect, essential to its validity. Thus, even if they were not sole arbiters, the priests must from a very early period have occupied a critical position in Roman political life and often been at the centre of controversy. Conflicts over points of ritual and religious procedures should be seen as an inherent part of the normal working of city life, in no way as a symptom of failure or deterioration in the late Republic. Priests must always have been liable to the charge that they were prejudiced in favour of friends and against enemies; the idea that they had once been quite innocent of politics is no more than a romanticizing fiction.

III. THE PLACE OF GODS AND GODDESSES IN THE LIFE OF ROME

The first characteristic of Roman gods and goddesses to strike the observer must be the wide range of different types, all accepted and

---

[51] Asc. *Corn.* p. 68c.
[52] See, e.g., Livy XXXI.12.8–9, where the final action is clearly the magistrate's responsibility.

worshipped as *di deaeque*. At one extreme, there were the great gods – Mars, Iuppiter, Iuno – each having a variety of major functions, traditions and myths (these, admittedly, sometimes borrowed from the Greeks); at the other extreme, deities who performed one narrowly defined function or who appeared only in one narrowly defined ritual context. Even parts of a natural process could have their presiding deity; and the possibility of still further unnamed or unknown gods and goddesses sometimes had to be admitted and allowed for in ritual formulae.[53] The time-honoured way of dealing with this variety of the Romans' conception of their gods is to claim that the gods have become 'frozen' at different points in their evolution. So far as the republican period is concerned, the fact is that all the types co-existed and that there is no sign of uneasiness, any more than there seems to be any uneasiness about adding to the list whether by means of introduction from outside Rome or of recognition of new divine powers. It may be that the priests made some attempts to list and classify the gods, but this does not seem to have produced any movement towards the convergence of the types or to have imposed family relationships or kinship.

There is very little sign of intermediate categories between gods and men. It may be that the dead should be seen as such a category, since they did receive cult, though not as individuals but as a generalized group, under the title of the *di Manes* or *divi parentes*.[54] However, with the exception of the founders – Aeneas, Romulus and perhaps Latinus – men did not become gods, either when alive or after death; even the three exceptions are equivocal because it is not clear how far they themselves become gods, how far they are identified with pre-existing gods (Indiges, Quirinus, Iuppiter Latiaris).[55] Dramatic interaction between humans and gods was not impossible: Mars had sexual intercourse with the virgin Rhea Silvia and so begot Romulus; Numa conversed banteringly with Iuppiter and slept with the nymph Egeria; Faunus or Inuus seized and raped women in the wild woods; Castor and Pollux appeared in moments of peril. But these mythical or exceptional transactions apart, communication between men and gods took place, so far as literary sources inform us, through the medium of ritualized exchange and the interpretation of signs rather than through intervention or inspiration; it has been mentioned already that our archaeological evidence suggests that this was not the full picture.[56]

Our most direct prospect of understanding the character of communication between gods and human beings comes from the surviving texts, prayers, vows and formulae. There is very little that we can be certain

[53] For the formula, see Appel 1909[G344], 8of.

[54] Wissowa 1912[G519], 232ff; De Sanctis 1907–64[A37], IV.2.243ff; Latte 1960[G435], 98; Weinstock 1971[G517], 291ff.   [55] Liou-Gille 1980[G438].   [56] See above (p. 580).

comes from an early date, but there is a sufficient body of material from the third and second centuries B.C. to give us some grasp of the underlying conceptions. A great deal of emphasis was placed on the spoken word and on the need for the most meticulous repetition of the correct formulae; supposedly, the slightest error in performance had to lead to the repetition of the whole ritual.[57] High value was also placed on the keeping of records and on the preservation of ancient writings and traditions. If the word was important, it was presumably preserved with care. But there are difficulties too: first, the preserved texts were originally part of a ritual complex, which we can only sketchily recreate and which would have modified the meaning of the words in use; secondly, the very value placed on the precise wording as part of the ritual performance is liable to cause the formulae to survive in use after the initial meaning has been forgotten or ceased to be operative. Some prayer formulae are reported to have been quite incomprehensible to those who used them in the later period. This risk is less in the case of the formulae of vows, because they do refer to a specific moment and, even though they necessarily incorporate traditional elements, must be renewed and rethought on each new occasion.

The public vows which survive are very specific and precise undertakings, made to named gods, laying down the conditions under which the vow will be fulfilled and the nature of the gift or ritual action with which the help of the god will be rewarded; these take the form of offerings, sacrifices, special games, the building of temples and so on. They can be made in special circumstances or even in a crisis; there are also regular annual vows for the safety of the *res publica*, taken by the year's consul. The most elaborate example we have dates from the early years of the Hannibalic War, though of course its wording reflects far earlier traditions.[58] It refers to the celebration of the sacred spring (*ver sacrum*), that is the offering to the gods, in this case Iuppiter, of the whole product of a single spring – pigs, sheep, goats and cattle. This extraordinary offer (which we otherwise know only from mythical accounts of early Italy) was made subject to a series of reservations: the people were to lay down the dates which would constitute the 'spring'; if there were to be any error or irregularity in the sacrificial procedure the sacrifice would nevertheless count as properly conducted; if any intended victim were to be stolen, the blame should fall on others than the Roman people or the owner. The circumstances were admittedly unique, because the *ver sacrum* would have involved sacrifices performed all over Roman territory, by large numbers of people outside the supervision of the priests.

---

[57] North 1976[G455], 1ff; cf. Köves-Zulauf 1972[G433], 21ff.

[58] The text is from Livy XXII.10; discussion: Heurgon 1957[J60], 36ff; Eisenhut 1955[J43], 911ff; North 1976[G455], 5–6. Cf. also p. 284.

Even so, the implications are important. The formula specifies for the benefit of the gods what will, and what will not, count as appropriate fulfilment of the vow. It is sometimes said that Roman vows were contractual in the sense that the gods were seen as laid under an obligation by the fact of the taking of the vow. In general, this is simply not true. The Romans offered honour and worship in return for benevolence; the gods were free to be benevolent or not; if they were not, no obligation arose. There was, of course, a reciprocity, as in any other religious transaction. The human side consisted of benefits very much in this world. The gods' side was defined with care in the original formula. They were bound only in one sense, that is that they would accept precisely what they were offered – no more, no less. Just as, Polybius[59] tells us, a Roman expected to be paid his debt on the agreed day, not a day later but not a day earlier either. Roman gods may not have been anthropomorphic in form, but their assumed mentality and behaviour mirror those of their worshippers on a larger scale. There is no sense in which the gods should be seen as all-powerful or irresponsible, nor men as their helpless slaves. They could not be controlled but they could be negotiated with; they were indeed bound to the human community by a network of obligations, traditions, rules, within which the skill of the priests, magistrates and senate could keep them on the side of the city.

Vow forms of one kind or another were used in quite a wide range of transactions. In the case of war the gods of the enemy could be seduced by *evocatio*, a vow offering them continuance of cult or possibly even a temple in Rome, if they withdrew their protection.[60] In the course of the war the general might vow a temple to a god or goddess, not necessarily a warlike one. In face of a disaster in battle, the general (though only if he was *cum imperio*) could dedicate himself and the legions of the enemy to the gods of the dead and to the Earth. In effect, he made himself *sacer*, sacred, almost like the animal victim of a normal sacrifice; he then had to mount a horse and rush precipitately to his death on the enemies' spears. This is first reported as having happened in 340 B.C., the consul being Decius Mus (p. 362); his son and grandson followed his example (pp. 379; 472). This is different from the normal order of events, in that the consul's death was the fulfilment of the vow, and therefore took place before the gods had had the opportunity to do their part. If the consul failed to die, according to Livy, an over life-size image was buried in the earth, evidently in fulfilment of the unsatisfied vow.[61]

[59] XXXI.27, especially 27.10–11.
[60] For the formula see Macrobius III.9.7ff; discussion: Wissowa 1912[G519], 383ff; Dumézil 1970/71[G399], 424ff; Le Gall 1976[G409], 519ff.
[61] Livy VIII.9ff (the fullest account, 340 B.C.); X.28.12ff (295 B.C.); Cic. *Fin.* II.61; *Tusc.* I.89; Dio Cass. *ap.* Zonar. VIII.5 (279 B.C.); full discussion and analysis of the major text by H. S. Versnel 1980[G506], 135ff.

Vows and prayers were recorded in the annals and manageable to the historian, precisely because they were verbal and hence transmittable. It would be a mistake to think that there were not other ways in which important communication took place between men and gods. The story of Decius in 340, which has just been mentioned, contains two direct messages from gods to men. The first is almost unique in Livy, in that it consists of a dream, warning Decius of what is to come; the second is a far more usual element in the tradition:

The Roman generals sacrificed before they went into battle. The *haruspex* revealed to Decius that the liver of his victim had a lobe cut from its 'familiar' part, in other respects it was acceptable to the gods. (His colleague) Manlius had carried his sacrifice through successfully (*egregie litasse*). 'It is enough', said Decius, 'if he has succeeded.'

(Livy VIII.9.1)

The word used here for carrying the sacrifice through is 'litare' (as a noun: 'litatio'); it can be used simply to mean sacrifice, but it involves the successful completion and acceptance of the victim by the gods. In this case, Decius already knew that he was destined to die for the legions and hence that it did not matter that it should be only his colleague who achieved *litatio*; normally the failure to do so would have been a disastrously bad sign.[62]

Animal sacrifice was the central ritual of many religious occasions; we know enough about it from both literary and archaeological evidence to understand the main stages.[63] In structure, as opposed to detail, the ritual was closely related to Greek sacrifice. The victim was tested and checked to make sure it was suitable; precise rules controlled the choice of sex, age, colour and type of victim, in relation to the deity and the occasion. After a procession to the altar and preparatory rites, a prayer was said in which the recipient was named; then the victim was made sacred by the placing of wine and meal on its head and it was at this moment (so it was believed) that the signs (if any) appeared in the entrails that would imply the gods' rejection of the offering.[64] The victim had to be killed by a single blow; its *exta* (entrails) were examined by the *haruspices*; assuming that they were acceptable, the animal was then butchered, cooked and eventually eaten by the worshippers. If the *exta* showed unacceptable signs, further victims could be sacrificed until one was accepted and

---

62 Livy VIII.10.12.

63 For the important, though later, evidence of the sculptured reliefs, cf. Scott Ryberg 1955[G482]; the literary evidence for sacrifice is plentiful but extremely scattered; the only coherent accounts are the attack on sacrifice by the Christian Arnobius, *Adv. Gent.* VII; and the comparison between Greek and Roman practices in Dion. Hal. *Ant. Rom.* VII.72.15–18. Modern discussion: Warde Fowler 1911[G509], 176ff; Wissowa 1912[G519], 409ff; Dumézil 1970/71[G399], 557ff; Scholz 1980[G493], 289ff.   64 Cic. *Div.* II.37.

litatio achieved. The whole process was evidently bound by rules and by traditional lore; any error or misfortune – the victim escaping or struggling, the *exta* slipping when offered up at the altar – would have been very inauspicious.[65] The butchering was a specialized business, because we know about a technical sacred vocabulary for the different cuts offered to the god.[66] This separation of the meat between worshippers and gods implies that the sacrificial ritual involved a symbolic representation of their relationship. To draw on conceptions developed in the study of the parallel Greek situation,[67] it can be said that we have a ritualized redefinition in terms of diet of the boundary between gods and humans. But it is important also that the ritual offered opportunities for the exchange of messages – prayers from men to gods, acceptance or warnings from gods to men.

Warnings also came uninvited, from outside the ritual process; these were prodigies and the lists of them which Livy preserves in his third, fourth and fifth decades provide us with one of our best indications of the style of Roman religious activity.[68] Prodigies included natural disasters, such as floods, famines, even plagues, and a whole range of unusual meteorological events (the raining of 'stones', 'blood', 'milk' etc.); lightning striking significant or holy objects; monsters and deformed births; wild animals penetrating the city's space. There is relatively little which would be called miraculous or supernatural in our terms; rather, these events depart from the Romans' conception of what was normal, which was, of course, not necessarily the same as ours. It would be going outside the evidence to say that the Romans regarded the prodigy as resulting from a direct intervention by the gods, but it did imply that something relating to the gods had gone seriously wrong. The procedure was that prodigies were reported to the senate in Rome; they were taken to indicate some kind of rupture in the proper relationship of Rome to its gods and hence called for religious action by the authorities. Here, then, more than anywhere else, we find a divine irruption into human lives, demanding a response. The response was subject to routine: the senate accepted the prodigy, or could rule that it had no public significance;[69] once accepted, it could be referred to the *decemviri* or the *haruspices* for advice and the appropriate actions (*remedia*) to be taken by priests, magistrates or even people, determined. The effect of this action was

---

[65] Serv. *Aen.* II.104; Festus (ep.) 351 L; Suet. *Iul.* 59 (where Caesar ignores the omen).

[66] We have to rely for information here on the hilarious and hostile account of Arnobius, *Adv. Gent.* VII.24.

[67] See e.g. M. Detienne and J.–P. Vernant (edd.) *La cuisine du sacrifice en pays grec* (Paris 1979).

[68] Bloch 1963[G355].

[69] The senate ruled in 169 B.C. that certain reported prodigies were not acceptable for public purposes, according to Livy XLIII.13; this is the only time that such a decision is mentioned in our sources, but presumably represents the regular procedure. Discussion in MacBain 1982[G440], 25ff.

neutralization of the warning. The signs were not taken to indicate fated or irrelevant processes, nor were they taken as the opportunity for formal divination, since all prodigies were bad signs. It was only in the last two centuries B.C. that the prodigy began to be more elaborately interpreted by the *haruspices*, even sometimes taken to be a potentially good sign. Earlier than this, Livy indicates that some prodigies were regarded as particularly horrifying and that large numbers were reported at times of grave danger to the city. The sources of senatorial and priestly skill and wisdom would be used to avert the dangers, though there was no guarantee of success. So, from a functional point of view, the system provided a means of coping with crises, by focusing fears into an area within which the ruling class could claim special inherited expertise. The *remedia* offered an opportunity for holding elaborate ceremonies, some-times including new festivals or new entertainments, promoting morale and social solidarity.

For all this the overwhelming bulk of the evidence comes from the later republican period, so the problem once again is whether it is a justified assumption that these practices date back to the early period. The first decade of Livy's history mentions occasional prodigies but has no regular lists; Julius Obsequens, who made a collection of Livy's prodigy-lists, began with the year 249 B.C.;[70] that may suggest that Livy provided no regular lists until the nineteenth book of his *History*. But even if something did change in 249 B.C., it might have been the way records were kept, not the way prodigies were regarded or dealt with. The lists must have changed greatly in any case, because the later ones draw on the whole of Roman and even non-Roman Italy, whereas the earlier would have come from the immediate area of Rome. The early evidence suggests that prodigies played the same role as later, though obviously the years of the Republic saw a gradual expansion and routin-ization of the procedure.

It is unavoidable that an account such as this one should rely mostly on those transactions which leave a mark in the historical record; but the gods, or reminders of them, were always present in Roman public and private space. It may not be easy to estimate the impact on a society whose physical environment and experience are known to us at such a remove, but we should at least remember how much we do not know. The early republican city must have been dominated by the great temple of the Capitoline triad, Iuppiter, Iuno and Minerva, which seems to have been built on a far greater scale than any of the subsequent republican sacred buildings.[71] Many of what are later great temples will have been

---

[70] The date comes from the title in the *editio princeps*; text (ed. O. Rossbach) in *T. Livi Periochae omnium librorum, fragmenta Oxyrhynchi reperta, Iulii Obsequentis prodigiorum liber* (Teubner: Leipzig 1910); translation in *Loeb Classical Library, Livy* vol. XIV, 237ff (Cambridge Massachusetts 1959).

[71] Castagnoli 1979[G374], 145ff; above, p. 251f.

simply altars or holy places: others were already temples, but on a small scale compared to Iuppiter's. All the same, the city's public centre, the Forum first laid down under the later kings (p. 75f) and developed in the early Republic, will have been bounded at least on the south by sacred buildings – the temples of Saturn, the Castores, Vesta and also by the Regia – the religious centre of the *rex sacrorum* and the *pontifices*.[72]

We can assume that, at any rate by this time, where there were temples there were also cult images; we have no way of telling how far these images would have been disseminated, whether there would have been terracotta reproductions, whether private houses would then, as they did later, have contained their own images of the household gods. By the end of the Republic the images of the gods were omnipresent and had their own ceremonial: they appeared before the temples on special couches (*pulvinaria*) so that offerings could be given them; they were carried in procession on special litters and their symbols in carriages (*tensae*); at the *ludi* they had their own places from which they watched the racing in the circus.[73] This must all have been happening by the third century B.C.; it is harder to be sure how much of it goes back to the fifth century, or earlier. We have from Dionysius of Halicarnassus[74] what purports to be a description of a fifth-century procession from the Capitoline temple to the Circus Maximus before the games. Dionysius says he found this account in Fabius Pictor, but, even if Fabius himself thought it was a fifth-century document or record which he was using, there are good reasons to doubt the reliability of the date; however, the practice must at the latest have been well established by Fabius' own time in the third century.[75] In Dionysius' words:

The images of the gods came last of all in the procession, borne on the shoulders of men, each having the same appearance as those which the Greeks make, as well as the same clothes, the same symbols and the same gifts, which they had traditionally invented or bestowed on the human race. . .

(Dion. Hal. *Ant. Rom.* VII.72.12)

At the heart of the oldest sets of *ludi*, there was also a ceremony called the *epulum Iovis*, the feast of Iuppiter, which was presumably the offering or sharing of a meal in the presence of the image of Iuppiter from the Capitol. The history of the *ludi* is itself a matter of great controversy, but if any of the ceremonial goes back to the early Republic, it seems likely that the procession of the images is amongst the original elements.[76]

---

[72] Coarelli 1983[E94].

[73] For the ritual of the *ludi*: Wissowa 1912[G519], 449ff; Piganiol 1923[G469]; Piccaluga 1965[G467]; Versnel 1970[G742], 258ff; Weinstock 1971[G517], 282ff.

[74] Dion. Hal. *Ant. Rom.* VII.70ff.   [75] See Piganiol 1923[G469].

[76] For the *epulum Iovis*: Degrassi 1963[G388], 509; 530; Warde Fowler 1899[G508], 216ff; Wissowa 1912[G519], 127; Scullard 1981[G494], 186–7.

Much about the Roman gods is and must remain obscure; but it is possible to discern at least in rough outline their place in the life of Rome. They are very much involved in the political and military activity of the city and their areas of power can be defined very much in terms of the city's social structure, as will be clearer from the next section. They are seen as forces outside the human community with whom the man of learning and skill, knowing the rules, traditions and rituals, can negotiate and communicate in terms of a complex system, so that the historical process is determined by the actions of men and gods together. The activities of the city's leaders on the city's behalf cannot be conceived except in the context of such a procedure of negotiation and joint action. There seems no reason to think that Roman gods act typically either by way of dramatic intervention in human life or as immanent forces realizing themselves through human actors. They are essentially other than men and apart from men, and yet constantly involved in human activities. Their benevolence is essential to success, but it can never be assumed to be available without continuous human effort to maintain the right relationship.

IV. RELIGION AND ACTION

In many ways the categories and vocabulary to be met with in the religion of Rome seem comfortably similar to those familiar from religions current today – prayer, sacrifice, vows, sacred books, even divination; but translating from one religious system into the terms of another is never a simple matter and, in this case, the apparent familiarity is deceptive. It is in considering the relationship between religion and the social organization of republican Rome that the differences become most acutely obvious. The sharpest difference of all is that the Rome of this period had no religious groups whose purpose it was to practise a particular form of devotion or to worship a particular god or set of gods; any individual citizen might belong to a group that had religious duties to perform; but he would belong to it by reason of his birth, as was the case with family or gentile cults, or by reason of where he lived or of his occupation, not by any act of choice. We certainly know from quite an early republican date of *collegia* ('associations') oriented towards a particular god and having a membership from a particular group of people; but we do not know of groups consisting of men who had decided to join together on grounds of religious conviction. Indeed, the very notion of religious conviction is problematic in this situation.

The implications of this difference determine the character of religious life at both the social and the individual level. At the social level, it means that there were no autonomous religious groups, with their own special value-systems, ideas or beliefs to defend or advocate; hence there was little chance that religion would ever represent a force for advocating change or reform. At the individual level, it means that men and women were not faced with the need to make (or opportunity of making) acts of religious commitment; that in turn implies that they had no religious biographies, no moments of profound new experience or revelation such as to determine the course of their future lives. It also means that religious 'experiences', 'feelings' or 'beliefs' must all have had quite different significances and resonances in this society; for us, for instance, the individual's beliefs play a central part in determining his religious life and the loss of belief necessarily implies a crisis, bringing a change of allegiance or the total abandonment of religious life. No doubt, Romans from an early period, or in any period, might have been sceptical about the gods and their supposed activities; but, given that such doubts could not lead anywhere in terms of religious action, they would have constituted no more than a personal eccentricity. It is only in a religious context where beliefs determine choices, that believing as such becomes a central element in the system. In republican Rome, where no such choices existed, the individual's beliefs must have been of marginal importance in his or her life.

In looking at the way in which religion and society interacted, what we find is, therefore, not special institutions and activities, set aside from everyday life and designed to pursue religious objectives or the religious life, but rather a situation in which all institutions and all activities have some religious aspect or associated rituals. As we have already seen, the whole of the political and constitutional system was conducted within an elaborate network of religious ceremonial and regulation which had the effect of bringing the time, space and hence the validity of political action into the divine sphere. The world of decision-taking, of elections and of legislation was the area in which the gods might be expected to be most interested; but, in fact, all important areas of life, public or private, had some religious correlates. It is not difficult to show, by an antiquarian collection of evidence, that there were rituals connected with warfare, with agriculture, or with family life. It is much more difficult to assess how all this information should influence our understanding of Roman life.

Warfare was already sanctified by the rituals of the old calendar of festivals. In March – originally the first month of the year – there was a coherent and interconnected set of festivals, mostly directed to Mars and unmistakably marking the preparations for a new season of war-making. There was a corresponding set in October, somewhat less elaborate, but also evidently marking the end of the season, the putting aside of arms for the winter.[77] On both occasions a central role was played by the Salii,

[77] Degrassi 1963[G388], 417ff; 521ff; Warde Fowler 1911[G509], 96ff; Wissowa 1912[G519], 144ff; Scullard 1981[G494], 85ff; 193ff.

priests of Mars and Quirinus, created to guard the special symbols fallen from the sky – the *ancilia*; the priests were all patricians, who danced through the streets, dressed in the armour of archaic foot-soldiers.[78] There is much argument about what these ceremonies originally meant, but there can be little doubt that at least by republican times they must have represented a celebration of the annual rhythm of war-making. In the Republic the actual conduct of warfare was in the hands of the consuls and they commanded under their own auspices; but at all periods, action was preceded by consultation of the gods and by sacrifices, whose rejection by the gods would imply a warning not to join battle. Meanwhile, the participants in the warfare would seek advantage through the establishment of a better relationship with the gods. At the opening of the campaign the ritual of the fetial priests was intended to ensure that the war was acceptable to the gods as a just war; sacrifices were held in order to obtain confirmation of the divine attitude and vows were taken to induce the gods to look favourably.[79] In the field, too, the commander might take vows to be fulfilled if the battle turned out well; at any rate by the end of the third century, this part of the process had become sufficiently familiar to be parodied by Plautus:

> The generals of both sides, ours and theirs,
> Take vows to Iuppiter and exhort the troops . . .
> (Plautus, *Amphitruon* 231–2)

It was also possible to seek to influence the enemies' gods by the offer of cult in return for their withdrawal of support. There is here, as always, an underlying tension between faith in the gods and the facts of life: if the gods are really benevolent and powerful, why should things ever go wrong? Any system which is able to function at all must offer answers to such questions; only the most obvious is that military disasters are connected with mistakes, noticed too late, in the necessary rituals.

If religion and religious ritual penetrated the area of warfare, warfare and its consequences could to some extent penetrate the religious sphere of the city. The vows taken by generals could lead to spectacular war-memorials in the form of temples in the city; and the spoils of war might either find their way into the temples by way of dedication, or finance the building of monuments commemorating the generals' achievements.[80] Less permanent, though perhaps even more spectacular and desirable, was the triumph in which the victorious returning war-leader paraded through the city's streets at the head of his troops, presenting his spoils

---

[78] Salii: Wissowa 1912[G519], 555ff; Latte 1960[G435], 114ff; Ogilvie 1965[B129], 98f.
[79] See, for instance, Livy XXXVI.1–3 for the various religious proceedings in expectation of war in 191 B.C.   [80] See Harris 1979[A61], 20f; 261f.

RELIGION AND ACTION

601

and his prisoners to the cheering *plebs Romana*. He entered the city by a special gateway, the Porta Triumphalis, splendidly dressed and riding in a chariot drawn by four horses; his procession made its way to the heart of the city by a special route leading eventually to the temple of Iuppiter Capitolinus, where he laid wreaths of laurel in the statue's lap. He himself was dressed and his face painted red, exactly like the statue of Iuppiter.[81] The triumphator's name was then added to the special triumphal *fasti*: the supreme ambition of a Roman noble was achieved. In some sense, the triumphing general had been deified for the day and hence (true or not) we have the story of the slave who stood at his shoulder and whispered: 'Look round and remember that you are a man.'[82] In any case, much of the ceremonial involved the temporary reversal of the usual forms – the general and his army were never otherwise allowed inside the city and the troops were licensed for this one day to shout abuse and obscenities at their general. Dressed as the god, no doubt in the symbolic terms of the ritual he was the god. But at the grand sacrifice of white oxen, with which the procession ended, it was the *triumphator* who sacrificed, Iuppiter who received the victims.

Warfare, like politics, belonged very much to the public area of life in which the gods of Rome had their major interest and concern. When we turn to the rituals of the agricultural year, the city was not responsible for the activity as such, but did undertake to mediate on the farmer's behalf. The ancient calendar of festivals contains rituals connected with grain-crops, with wine-production and with animal husbandry; it is interesting that olive-growing, though it probably arrived from Greece in the course of the sixth century B.C., did not find any place in the calendar. Some of these festivals seem straightforward and unproblematic; thus, for instance, the Robigalia of 25 April was a sacrifice to protect the growing crops from blight.[83] The timing of the two vine festivals of 23 April and 19 August is less easy to understand, since neither date seems to correspond to the time of harvesting.[84] So far as the grain-crops are concerned, there were festivals to mark the sowing of the seed at the end of January – though sowing would have been taking place from autumn onwards; a cluster of festivals in April to Tellus (this is the Fordicidia, the sacrifice of a pregnant cow) and to Ceres, the goddess of corn, as well as the Robigalia already mentioned; all these quite appropriately accom-

---

[81] The triumph: Versnel 1970[G742]; Ehlers 1948[G572], 493ff; Weinstock 1971[G517], 60ff; Scullard 1981[G494], 213ff.

[82] Pliny, *HN* XXVIII.39; Tert. *Apol.* 33.4.

[83] Robigalia (April 25): Degrassi 1963[G388], 448; Latte 1960[G435], 67ff; Scullard 1981[G494], 108.

[84] Vinalia (23 April, 19 August): Degrassi 1963[G388], 446; 498; Wissowa 1912[G519], 115ff; 289ff; Schilling 1954[G486], 98ff; Latte 1960[G435], 75ff; 184; Scullard 1981[G494], 106ff.

panied the period of the growing crops.[85] The festivals of high summer celebrated the harvesting, storing and protecting of the crops against various dangers.[86] The clearest occasion on which the care of animals was the objective was at the Parilia (21 April), the festival of the *pastores* and, incidentally, the birthday of Rome itself.[87] There are, then, festivals which mark at least some of the most important moments of the agricultural year, relating to the different activities of the farm's life.

Much discussion of this cycle of festivals is under-pinned by the assumption that by the end of the period we are considering all these festivals were well on their way to becoming antiquarian survivals having no significance for contemporary, urban-dwelling Romans. It is no doubt true that in Roman religious practice, as in many others, rituals were maintained from year to year out of a general sense of scrupulous-ness, even where no particular significance was being attached to them; it is also true that by the last years of the Republic, antiquarians were no longer able to say what some of the festivals meant. By that time, perhaps, Rome the city had grown so much and its largely immigrant population become so urbanized and so attached to imported religions, that there would have been little meaning left in the old agricultural rituals, though, even for the later date, this would be very hard to prove. For the third century B.C., however, Rome was still very much open to the countryside; many of its residents would have owned farms or at least worked on them intermittently, others would have had relations who did; and they would all have been totally dependent on the produce of the local agricultural economy for their food-supply.[88] It is sometimes suggested that the simple fact that the festivals had fixed dates in a calendar tied to the solar year (or rather a four-year cycle related to the solar year) made those festivals, or at least some of them, meaningless: so a festival intended to coincide, say, with the harvest would sometimes be late, sometimes early, only occasionally coincide; worse, the insertion of the intercalary month was at times neglected by the *pontifices* so that the calendar would be out of phase with the seasons and the celebrations even more grotesquely mistimed. All this rests on multiple misunder-standings. The early Roman calendar was in fact fairly advanced in its workings and we have no evidence that anything went seriously wrong with it before the mysterious aberrations at the end of the third century

[85] Sementivae (late January, but not fixed): Wissowa 1912[G519], 193; Bayet 1971[G351], 177ff; Scullard 1981[G494], 68. Fordicidia (April 15): Degrassi 1963[G388], 440ff; Latte 1960[G435], 68; Dumézil 1970/71[G399], 371ff; Scullard 1981[G494], 102. Cerealia (April 19): Degrassi 1963[G388], 442; Le Bonniec 1958[G360], 108ff; Latte 1960[G435], 68; Dumézil 1970/71[G399], 374ff; Scullard 1981[G494], 102.   [86] Dumézil 1975[G400].

[87] Parilia (April 21): Degrassi 1963[G388], 443; Wissowa 1912[G519], 199; Latte 1960[G435], 87; Dumézil 1975[G400], 188ff; Scullard 1981[G494], 103ff.

[88] Cf. above, p. 408f (with a different view).

B.C., which were presumably caused somehow by the troubles of the Hannibalic War period.[89] Meanwhile, the whole case depends on the assumption that the Romans were very simple-minded or 'primitive' in their conception of the relation between religious act and agricultural process; if one is to believe that the precise date of the religious act is essential to the relationship, one must say also that if the act were not performed at the right moment, the crops would die, the harvest fail, or the stored grain rot. Nothing known to us about the Romans and their gods suggests that this was true; what we should rather expect is that the gods would stay favourable provided the ritual was properly performed at the time prescribed by the priests, following tradition and rule.

There is another underlying assumption to be considered: that each festival had a simple meaning and a simple reference. The Robigalia provides the model here, for our sources connect it with mildew on the corn and with nothing else. In fact, even this case is questionable, if only because the sources are so inadequate, but in many other festivals there were more interpretations than one, or perceived ambiguities in the ritual.[90] It is only a working assumption that in every case there must once have been an unambiguous message in an unambiguous context, which was only later on forgotten, misunderstood or confused. To take even the crudest of categorizations: can we assume that every festival must be either military or agricultural, but not both? A similar problem arises in the categorization of the gods, because the tendency of some of the most important of the Roman gods and goddesses is towards complexity of function. In some cases this has led to extensive debates about the original character of particular gods, based again on the assumption that they must have started as powers in a particular area of action and only acquired more complex roles with the passing of time. In Dumézil's perspective (p. 581), it is fundamental that the earliest gods should have reflected the three original functions of the Indo-Europeans – gods of law and authority, gods of war, gods of production and agriculture; if Roman gods fail to fit, that must be explained as the subsequent accretion of different tasks. The three functions appear most clearly in the gods of the 'old triad' – Iuppiter, Mars, Quirinus, the gods of the three main *flamines*; these three illustrate my point very clearly, because if Dumézil is right, all three eventually developed into the domains of at least one and possibly both of the others. Iuppiter, the god

[89] Michels 1967[G446], 145ff. On the calendar in the period of the First Punic War cf. p. 545 n. 57.
[90] For the most disputed, see above p. 602 n. 87 for the Parilia; below p. 604 n. 95 for the October horse; for the debate on the Lupercalia (15 February), Scholz 1980[G493], 289ff; Ulf 1982[G501] (with survey of earlier views, 83ff). Different sources imply that the festival was (a) a fertility ritual; (b) a purificatory or protective ritual; but it is most significant that it can evidently be re-perceived by Caesar and his supporters as a coronation.

of the highest city authority, also received the war-vows of the departing general and provided the centre of the triumphal procession on his return; but he also presided over the harvest in the vineyards.[91] Mars, the god of war, protected the crops and was hence very prominent in the prayers and rituals of the farmer.[92] Quirinus, who was far less prominent in republican times, appears to have been a war god like Mars, but was also connected with the mass of the population and with production; he was then chosen as the divine aspect of Romulus, the first king of Rome.[93] Another clear instance would be Iuno, who is very much a political goddess in Rome and its area, but also a warrior goddess and the goddess of women and childbirth.[94]

In developing these characteristics, Roman gods and goddesses were doing no more and no less than reflecting the lives of their worshippers. The Roman farmer was a soldier and a voter as well; it is not surprising if the protectors of his endeavours show a similar flexibility. If so, it becomes very unlikely that the festivals and their significance should have remained fixed within categories that applied neither to the gods nor to the worshippers. If, then, we hear from one source that the sacrifice of a horse to Mars on 15 October (the *equus October*) was intended to make the crops prosper, from another that it was a war-ritual, connected with other October ceremonies concerned with the return of the army from its year's campaigning, we cannot assume *a priori* that one of these meanings must be 'right', the other 'wrong'.[95] It is perfectly possible that both meanings had validity at the same time; or that the ritual had different meanings for different groups of people.

This brings up the question of how far the individual citizen was involved at all in the festivals of the old calendar. For the most part they were conducted on the city's behalf by dignitaries – priests, priestesses, magistrates. The only obligation that generally lay on the individual citizen was simply to abstain from work while the ceremonies were going on. There was even some debate, reminiscent of rabbinical debate about the Sabbath, as to what exactly would count as work and what not for this

[91] Iuppiter and the triumph: Versnel 1970[G742], ch. 11; Iuppiter and the vines: cf. above p. 601 n. 84.

[92] It is necessary to Dumézil's whole position to interpret Mars as the war god, the god of the second function; see Dumézil 1970/71[G399], 205ff. But a good deal of the evidence will not fit this view – e.g. Cato, *Agr.* 141, in which Mars is quite clearly protecting the farmers; for different interpretations, cf. Warde Fowler 1911[G509], 131ff; De Sanctis 1907–64[A37], IV.2. 149ff; Latte 1960[G435], 114ff; Scholz 1970[G492].

[93] Latte 1960[G435], 113; Koch 1960[G431], 17ff; 1963[G432], 1306ff; Brelich 1960[G367], 63ff; Gagé 1966[G407], 1591ff; Dumézil 1970/71[G399], 246ff; Liou-Gille 1980[G438], 135ff.

[94] De Sanctis 1907–64[A37], IV.2.137ff; Latte 1960[G435], 104ff; Palmer 1974[G461], 3ff.

[95] On the problem of the October horse (15 October): Degrassi 1963[G388], 521; Warde Fowler 1899[G508], 241ff; Latte 1960[G435], 119f; Bayet 1969[G350], 82f; Scholz 1970[G492]; Dumézil 1975[G400], 145ff; Scullard 1981[G494], 193.

purpose.[96] This seems to have been the extent of the citizen's necessary involvement. If so, it might be that these public performances were something quite apart from the individual's life, offering him no involvement and no satisfaction, only the remote awareness that somebody somewhere was protecting the city's relationship with the gods. If this argument were to be pursued further, the next step would be to say that the religion of individuals did not lie in the state cults at all, but in the cults of his family, his house or his farm. The *paterfamilias* was responsible for maintaining the traditional rites of his household, the worship of the Lares and Penates and the other *sacra* inherited from his ancestors and destined to be passed on to his descendants (the *sacra familiae*):[97] on the estate, as we learn from the handbook of Cato the Elder,[98] the *familia*, including the slaves, would gather together for ceremonies to purify the fields and to pray to the gods for protection and for the fertility of crops and herds. Within the family, there were also, of course, the stages of life to be marked by *rites de passage* – the acceptance of the baby, the admission of the child into the adult world, marriage, death and burial; all these fell within the sphere of family responsibility, even if the *pontifices* were responsible for the law in some respects and were available to give advice.[99]

It might seem a possibility that these private cults would have afforded a separate religious world within which the individual Roman might have found the personal experience of superhuman beings, the sense of community and of his place in it, which the remoteness of the official cult denied him, but which he needed to make sense of the world. As a matter of fact, the terracottas dedicated in the context of health-cult may, as was suggested in an earlier section,[100] give us cause to doubt whether the individual's religious experience was in fact as narrowly bounded as literary sources have been thought to imply. As far as family cults are concerned, however, it is not so easy to believe in this deep but unattested religious life: what has happened is that historians have projected into this area, about which we really know so little, the elements that they postulate as essential to any religion – personal prayer and contact with the divine, deep feelings and beliefs about man's relation to universal forces – and that are missing from the public religious life of the Romans. The theoretical problem is whether the elements of religious life can be postulated *a priori* for any society, or whether they are different and specific in different cultural situations. Almost all the evidence we have suggests that in Rome in particular religious life focused on the public cults, on the relationship between the city and the city's gods and

[96] Scullard 1981[G494], 39–40.   [97] Above, p. 587 n. 38.   [98] Cato, *Agr.* 141.
[99] Above, p. 586 n. 36.   [100] Above, p. 580.

goddesses; the citizen participated through his identification with the
city and its interests, not to be underestimated in a period when the
citizen was voter as well as fighter in the city's cause. If so, we should
accept that the Romans' religious experience was profoundly different
from our own and that it is impossible to postulate what elements it
should or should not have contained.

The separation between city cult and family or farm cult should not in
any case be exaggerated. In some festivals, a central ceremony performed
in the city was accompanied by rites conducted in families or in the
countryside; in others, the only acts reported took place in the family,
though we may assume that there was some corresponding public ritual;
other festivals again took place in groups such as the *curiae*, the ancient
divisions of the Roman people.[101] The festivals for the dead (the
Parentalia in February and the Lemuria in May) were basically family
festivals in relation to the ancestors, though a Vestal performed a public
act of *parentatio* on the first day of the Parentalia;[102] at the Parilia in April,
our descriptions of what took place clearly refer to the farm, with the
shepherd and even the sheep leaping over bonfires;[103] at the Saturnalia in
December, there were sacrifices at the temple of Saturn to open the
festivities, but the feasting, exchanging of roles between masters and
slaves, merrymaking and present-giving evidently all took place in the
households.[104] There were also quite specifically rural festivals – the
Ambarvalia (lustration of the fields), the Sementivae (festival of sowing)
and the Compitalia (celebrated at the crossroads both in Rome and in the
countryside); these do not have fixed dates in the calendars, though they
were a regular part of the ritual year.[105] On still other occasions, although
the festival had a public celebration it provided the context and occasion
for a family event: so at the Liberalia (17 March) boys after the age of
puberty took their *toga virilis*, the mark of their admission to the adult
community.[106] Sometimes the relationship of public and private elements is very obscure: at the Matralia (11 June) the public ceremonial
took place at the temple of Mater Matuta in the Forum Boarium; at this
festival, the matrons prayed for their nephews and nieces first, not their
own children; it seems likely that this means women throughout the city,

[101] *Curiae* at the Fornacalia: Ov. *Fast.* 11.527–32; Dion. Hal. *Ant. Rom.* 11.23; Latte 1960[G435],
143; Scullard 1981[G494], 73.
[102] Parentalia (13–21 February): Degrassi 1963[G388], 408f; Latte 1960[G435], 98f; Scullard
1981[G494], 74f. Lemuria (9, 11, 13 May): Degrassi 1963[G388], 454; Latte 1960[G435], 99; Scullard
1981[G494], 118f.
[103] Parilia (21 April): Ov. *Fast.* IV.735ff; cf. Prop. IV.4.75ff; Tib. 11.5.89ff. See also p. 602 n. 87.
[104] Saturnalia (17–23 December): Degrassi 1963[G388], 539; Latte 1960[G435], 254f; Scullard
1981[G494], 205ff.
[105] Sementivae: above p. 602 n. 85. Compitalia (December/January): Latte 1960[G435], 90f;
Scullard 1981[G494], 58. Ambarvalia (May): Latte 1960[G435], 42; Scullard 1981[G494], 124ff.
[106] Ov. *Fast.* III.771ff.

not just those present at the temple, but it is very hard to be sure.[107] However that may be, it is quite certain that a good deal of private ritual accompanied public events.

The ritual activities of the Vestal Virgins afford another quite different area in which there are connexions between public and private religion, suggesting that these should not be separated in conception but seen as a single system, operating with the same set of religious possibilities. The Vestals are quite set apart from the other priestly groups.[108] They lived in a special house by the *aedes* of Vesta. They wore special dress, containing some of the features of that of a bride. They had a specially privileged legal status, including the right of making a will without the compliance of a guardian (*tutor*). They had (for Rome) unique religious responsibilities and were subject to unique penalties if they failed either by letting the sacred fire go out or by losing their virginity.[109] It is also the case that we know a good deal more about their ritual programme than about that of any other priestly group in Rome; nor does that seem to be a mere accident of transmission, but genuinely reflects the high importance of what they did for Rome.[110] They were involved in ceremonies and symbolic acts, as argued below, which affected many areas of life in Rome; but they and the cults connected with them also seem to have been of the greatest importance to the religious structure of the other Latin cities. We know that there had been Vestals in both the cities from which Rome claimed descent – Alba Longa and Lavinium (pp. 56ff); the Romans took pains in later times to maintain the priesthoods and rites in both these places.[111] It seems certain that we are dealing with a deeply embedded and characteristic area of the religious life of the Latins, one in which many other elements of religious life can be found interacting and interlocking.

The Vestals' activities included a good deal of what might be called household work: there is an obvious parallel between Vesta, the hearth of the city, and the hearths of the houses of individual families; in terms of this parallelism the Vestals would have represented the women of the household.[112] They were responsible for tending the sacred fire which had never to be allowed to go out; they guarded the storehouse (*penus*)

[107] Matralia (11 June): Degrassi 1963[G388], 468f; Warde Fowler 1899[G508], 154ff; Latte 1960[G435], 87; Dumézil 1970/71[G399], 50ff introduces very illuminating parallels from Vedic India; for the sixth-century temples of Mater Matuta and Fortuna in the Forum Boarium, cf. Castagnoli 1979[G374], 145ff.

[108] The Vestals: Wissowa 1912[G519], 507ff; Koch 1958[G430], 1732ff; Latte 1960[G435], 108ff; Koch 1960[G431], 1ff; Guizzi 1962[G422]; Ampolo 1971[E69], 443ff; Radke 1981[G474], 343ff.

[109] Plut. *Numa* 10; *Quaest. Rom.* 96; Dion. Hal. *Ant. Rom.* XII.67.4; see Koch 1960[G431], 1ff; Guizzi 1962[G422], 141ff; Cornell 1981[G386], 27ff.   [110] Rohde 1936[G480], 106ff.

[111] Wissowa 1912[G519], 520–1; Weinstock 1937[G513], 428ff; Alföldi 1965[I3], 250ff; Dury-Moyaers 1981[E24]; Radke 1981[G474], 343ff.

[112] See the discussion in Beard 1980[G352], 12ff.

and they ritually cleaned it out and expelled the dirt; they gathered the first ears of corn from the harvest, ground and baked them to provide the sacred corn-meal (*mola salsa*) that was used to sanctify the victim at sacrifices.[113]

The simplest hypothesis to explain all this activity would be that the life of the Vestals was the life of the ancient regal household and that they themselves represented the women of the king's family. The problem is to know which women of the king's family. They fit neither the role of wives nor that of daughters. Virgins would scarcely have done as wives; daughters of the household could scarcely have reached the status and privileges of the Vestal, whose legal status is precisely not that of a dependent relation.[114] It seems quite certain that the king's household is offering us too simple a picture; in any case, the Vestals' ritual connexions are with the *pontifex* not with the king. A recent study[115] has suggested that the key lies precisely in the ambiguity of their status – they were marginal between matrons and virgins, marginal too between men and women. It is this intermediate sexual status that marked their separateness and their sacredness. But they were marginal in other ways too: they mediated the realms of public and private, by carrying on private duties in the public sphere; and their ritual programme involved them in all major aspects of Roman life, so linking separate parts of life. If anything went wrong in the house of the Vestals, the threat was not to any particular activity but to the whole *salus* of the Roman people; so unchastity was not just an offence, it occasioned prodigies requiring extraordinary measures of expiation.[116] *Salus* was not just the safety of the city; it included the health and fertility of the whole community, its animals and its farms.[117] At the Fordicidia, after the pregnant cow had been sacrificed to Tellus (the Earth), the unborn calf was taken and burned by the senior Vestal: the calf too was an ambiguous being – living but not born, sacrificed but not capable of being a proper victim; its ashes were then preserved by the Vestals and used, mixed with the dried blood of the previous October's 'October horse', to sprinkle on the bonfires of the Parilia, for the purification of the shepherd and the sheep.[118] The precise implications of this set of symbolic acts may not be recoverable; but it does make clear the importance of the Vestals in linking the fertility of the earth, the health and safety of the flocks, and the city's security in the military sense. Human fertility was also involved in the Vestals' sphere; and here, for once, we have the help of myths which fit with and clarify a set of rituals. It is told of various founders or heroes of Latium that they were born of a virgin impregnated either by a spark from the

---

113 Latte 1960[G435], 108ff.   114 On legal aspects in particular see Guizzi 1962[G422].
115 Beard 1980[G352], 12ff.   116 Cornell 1981[G386], 31ff.   117 Koch 1960[G431], 11ff.
118 Above p. 602 n. 85 and n. 87.

hearth or by a phallus which sprang from the hearth.[119] The Roman
Vestals were not only responsible for guarding the hearth, the undying
flame, but also for the keeping of a phallus in the *aedes Vestae*.[120] The
significance of the flame must therefore, in at least one of its aspects, lie in
its connexion with the foundation, generation and continuation of the
race. Vesta herself encapsulated all the elements; she was the flame, she
was the virgin, she was Vesta the Mother.

Once it is clear how the Vestals, themselves withdrawn from all the
ordinary activities of life, linked all the different areas of that life at the
ritual level, it becomes easier to see why there was so powerful an
association between them and the survival of Rome. They provided the
home for the various talismans of that survival.[121] In a real crisis, it was
the *sacra* in their care that had to be saved at any cost, even the cost of
one's own family, as in the case of the plebeian who saved them from the
Gauls.[122] There is ample evidence to show how deeply, even at a quite
late date, the Romans felt the threat to their city, if there was any
suggestion of an irregularity involving the Vestals or their *sacra*.[123]

It is not enough to think of these cults, or the others discussed in this
section, only in terms of the dangers that would arise if they were not
performed; it is essential to assess their positive value as well. To do so,
however, implies an understanding of what it was that a Roman expected
his religion to do for him. It was suggested earlier in this section that to
speak in terms of his 'feelings', 'experiences' or 'beliefs' is to risk
introducing misleading notions about the individual's religious needs or
'spiritual life'. If to do that is excluded, then it would be possible to argue
that religion is the wrong word for what is under discussion; this is a
matter of verbal choice and not one that can profitably be pursued here.
What we can say is that the gods and the rituals addressed to those gods
enter into every institution and every transaction of public life; into the
whole of the Romans' system of orienting themselves in time and space;
it provided them with an essential point of reference in their organization
of society and in particular their organization of power. We tend to think
of the rituals of power as no more than reflections of the reality of power,
established by quite other, more practical means; but in a society which
had no policemen, no secret services, no security firms, the symbolism of
power was far closer to constituting the reality of power as well. In this
sense, religion played an essential part in the functioning of ancient city
life.

---

[119] Servius Tullius: Dion. Hal. *Ant. Rom.* iv.2; Pliny, *HN* xxxvi.204; Ov. *Fast.* vi.627ff; Plut. *De
fort. Rom.* 10. Romulus: Plut. *Rom.* 2.3–5. Caeculus of Praeneste: Serv. *Aen.* vii.678.

[120] Pliny, *HN* xxviii.39.   [121] Dion. Hal. *Ant. Rom.* ii.66.

[122] Livy v.40.7–10, with Ogilvie 1965[B129], 723; above, p. 306.

[123] See, for instance, Cic. *Font.* 46–8.

V. ADJUSTING TO THE NEW REPUBLIC

The last two sections of this chapter attempt, within the severe limits our sources impose, to examine some aspects of historical change, in contrast to the static account of phenomena given so far. This section deals with the only event of which it can certainly be said that it radically changed the nature of the city's religious and political life, that is the overthrow of the monarchy in the late sixth century; the final section will deal with the continuing tradition of change and innovation during the period of the early to middle Republic.

The first problem which the founders of the Republic must have faced was what they should do about the kingship. The step of abolishing kings and replacing them by magistrates with a fixed term of office was a revolutionary one in its religious as well as political implications and should still be seen as such, even if the Romans had precedents amongst their neighbours for what they did. In simple terms, the solution was that the title *rex* should continue to be borne in Rome; its bearer was to be a patrician, a member of the college of *pontifices* chosen for life, called in full the *rex sacrorum*.[124] This 'religious' king and his successors continued to be members of the pontifical college throughout the republican period, though seldom mentioned.[125] It must have been a difficult and delicate task to define the new king's position in relation to the other priests, but especially to the other members of the college to which he would now belong.

Here as so often, the only secure knowledge of the situation comes from the late republican period. By that time, the *rex* had become an obscure member of the college, with a largely forgotten range of ritual duties; meanwhile the *pontifex maximus*, the elected leader of the *pontifices*, had become the most powerful of the great political priests. The implication in Livy's account of the foundation of the Republic in Book II of his Histories[126] is that the subordination of the *rex* to the *pontifex maximus* dates back to a deliberate decision taken by the founders; this, then, would be the solution to the problem: the king's potential threat was neutralized by making him a priest subordinate to the *pontifex*. It has been argued, however, that this is all anachronistic, another retrojection into the fifth century B.C. of reality as it was known to historians writing in the first century B.C.[127] On this view, the king

---

[124] Wissowa 1912[G519], 504ff; De Sanctis 1907–64[A37], IV.2.355ff; Latte 1960[G435], 195ff; Momigliano 1971[F50], 357ff = *Quarto Contributo* 395ff; Dumézil 1970/71[G399], 576ff; cf. Ampolo 1971[E69], 443ff.

[125] The known *reges* are listed by Szemler 1972[G497], 68; 174f. None of them achieved any special distinction. See also p. 611 n. 130 below.   [126] II.2.1.

[127] The argument is most fully developed by Latte 1960[G435], 195ff; *contra* Dumézil 1970/71[G399], 102ff. The most interesting evidence is the priestly order preserved by Festus 299 L – *rex,*

would originally have kept his authority as head of the religion and only slowly in the centuries that followed would the *pontifex maximus* have emerged as the more powerful figure. There can hardly be any certain answer to this question, but some of the issues involved raise important problems, which must be discussed in more detail.

The *rex sacrorum* was subject to two sets of limitations, which must almost certainly go back to the beginning of the Republic and which give the best indication of the intentions of the founders. First, he was absolutely excluded from playing any part in political life – he could not hold political office of any kind and he did not sit in the senate.[128] This puts him in a different category from the major *flamines*, who seem not to have been excluded from political life, but only limited in what they were allowed to do without violation of their sacred duties. The *flamen Dialis* seems even to have had the right to an automatic seat in the senate, or at least his claim to this was reasserted in the third century on the grounds of lapsed precedents.[129] Evidently, the *rex* was quite deliberately excluded from this sphere. The second limitation placed on the *rex* was that of collegiality: whatever his previous relations with the priests had been, he had evidently been set apart from them, perhaps using the different groups of priests as advisers in his active role; now he was to become a member of one college and not of the others, having a share in religious decision-making, but only in the pontifical sphere and only as a member, like the *flamines* and the *pontifices*.[130] He did retain an important ritual programme of his own – he held a sacrifice on the Kalends of each month, announced the dates of the festivals of the month on the Nones, appeared in the Comitium on certain fixed dates (24 March and 24 May) and sacrificed there.[131]

To characterize this whole reform, it can be argued that there was a deliberate separation of religious elements from political ones; possibly, the Romans were aware of foreign precedents for doing this. At the very least, what happened was a step towards the creation of separate religious and political areas; but, if so, the process was very one-sided and incomplete, because, while the *rex* was certainly stripped of his power of action in everyday life, it is very far from true that he kept all his religious

three *flamines, pontifex maximus*. This must indeed reflect some archaic reality quite unlike the known late republican order, but it is impossible to show that it is the reality of the early republican rather than of the regal period. [128] Above, p. 589 n. 48.

[129] Livy XXXI.50.7; the point was established by C. Valerius Flaccus who had become *flamen* against his will (Livy XXVII.8.4); he later rose to be praetor in 183 B.C. (*MRR* 1.379).

[130] Cic. *Har. Resp.* 12 gives a list of the members of the college of *pontifices* present at a particular meeting of the college; the *rex sacrorum* of the time is listed like the others, that is, in the order in which they joined the college.

[131] For his ritual programme: Degrassi 1963[G388], 327ff (Kalends and Nones); 415f (Feb. 24); 430 (March 24); 461 (May 24); 538 (Dec. 15); Weinstock 1937[G512], 861f; Momigliano 1971[F50], 357ff = *Quarto Contributo* 395ff.

authority. It would, therefore, be a misinterpretation to say that the gods were conceived of as willing to accept changes in the secular sphere, but unwilling to accept them in their own sphere. For instance, one essential element of the king's religious position must have been his conduct of the auspices, but these were transferred wholesale to the new magistrates. Moreover, if the king had exercised general authority over religion (and it is difficult to think he had not), this authority must have been divided under the Republic between the senate, the magistrates and the priests; even if this should be thought of as a slow evolution not a sudden decision, it must have been to some extent apparent to contemporaries. In other words, the gods were not seen as frozen in old ways: there could be religious changes decided on by the community, no doubt after proper consultation with the gods themselves. That this was possible shows an important and continuing principle in Roman religious life.

Once it has been accepted that placing the *rex* in one college and excluding him from any other office already implied major changes in his religious as well as his political position, it is perhaps a secondary issue whether the *pontifex maximus* was made the head of the college at once or only slowly became so. It follows from the structure analysed in earlier sections, that the senior *pontifex* would sooner or later have emerged as the more important figure, irrespective of anyone's plans or intentions, simply because he had access to more of the areas into which religious authority was disseminated, especially to the senate. It is inconceivable that the *rex* should have maintained his authority, given his disadvantages in terms of how the republican system eventually worked; it is only if the system worked quite differently in the early Republic (the possibility is discussed above, p. 579f), that sense could be made of the idea of the *rex* as the true religious leader at that time; only given a separate religious area could there have been a religious leader isolated from political life. In the Rome we know from later, the *pontifex maximus* had to become the dominant figure. The record of the early priests does not help here: it is remarkable that, despite the fact that record-keeping was a priestly occupation, neither *reges sacrorum* nor *pontifices maximi* appear to have been major political figures in the early history of the Republic.[132]

The only hope of making further progress with the problem is through consideration of the position eventually occupied by the *pontifex maximus*. It is misleading to call him a high priest: most of his actions seem to have been taken on behalf of, or as agent of, the college; he had no elaborate programme of rituals that he alone could carry out, as for instance did the *flamines*; he had the right to impose fines on priests to recall them to their religious duties, subject to appeal to the people, but

132 See above, p. 610 n. 125.

this is a right he may perfectly well already have possessed under the kings, certainly not one he is likely to have inherited from the *rex*.[133] There is only one area in which he had special authority of his own and that is in relation to the Vestals and their cult. He performed the ceremony of the induction of a new Vestal, using an ancient form of words; he and the Vestals alone had the right of access to their holiest places of cult; he exercised disciplinary powers over them if they failed in their obligations; he acted ritually with them on certain occasions.[134] In doing all this, the *pontifex* was exercising power in the most sensitive of all areas of ritual communication between men and gods. If any sense is to be made of the idea that the *pontifex* had at some stage replaced the *rex*, this seems a likely area in which it could have happened. If the Vestals were indeed originally the daughters of the royal household, their original sacred links would necessarily have been with the king; if so, the *pontifex* must have replaced him at least in this role.[135] In fact, this whole construction is flimsy: the Vestals cannot be regarded as the daughters of a household (see above, p. 608f) and the king's special connexion with them is no more than a guess. But, more importantly for the present argument, the idea of a transfer from *rex* to *pontifex* in this area seems to make nonsense of the whole supposed reform: the theory of the reform is supposed to be that some of the king's ritual performances were so specific to that role and so holy that the gods would only accept them from a king; if the king's association with the Vestals could conceivably be handed over to the *pontifex*, in defiance of the supposed age-old links between the king and his sometime daughters, there seems to be no reason left for the title to have survived at all. The simplest view is that the *pontifex* had his special connexion with the Vestals because he had always had such a connexion, even in the days when the kings were really kings.

The purpose underlying these detailed arrangements was that whoever bore the title *rex* should never again be in a position to threaten the city with a tyranny. There was also a religious penalty invoked against any aspirant to tyranny: he could be declared *sacer*, that is to say dedicated to the gods, meaning that he could be killed without the killer incurring retribution.[136] It might be expected that there would be other signs of a reaction either against monarchy as such, or at least against the Etruscan regime which had just been removed; but in some ways, the continuities

---

[133] For his right to impose a fine (*multa*), see, for instance, Livy xxxvii.51.4ff; xl.42.9ff; Bleicken 1957[G353], 345ff. [134] Guizzi 1962[G422].

[135] The only evidence that gives colour to the idea is the ritual formula quoted by Servius, *Aen.* x.228: 'vigilasne, rex? vigila.' (Are you on the watch, king? Be on the watch.) This shows the Vestals in their role as defenders of the safety of Rome (cf. Koch 1960[G431], 11ff), the guardians of the undying flame; it is hardly necessary to explain it as a survival from primitive household life.

[136] Livy ii.8.2.

between regal and republican Rome seem more striking than the immediate changes. The most striking continuity of all concerns Iuppiter Capitolinus and his grandiose new temple. The tradition is that the temple was built by the last Tarquin, finished by the time of his fall, dedicated by the very first college of magistrates of the Republic.[137] Various criticisms can be made of this as a historical account, but it does at least encapsulate the ambivalent standing of the cult between monarchy and Republic. The position of Iuppiter within the triad, the dominant position and scale of the building, the nature of the cult-practice, all suggest that the king designed the temple as a grandiose expression of his power and that of his regime. It would perhaps have been going too far to expect that the temple would have been razed to the ground when the Tarquins fell; but it is still surprising that what happened was the precise opposite — the cult became central to the new republican era. It was the focus of the religious activity of the annual magistrates; the god was accepted as the fount of the *auspicia* upon which the relationship of the city with the gods rested; the victorious generals of Rome returned to Rome to lay their laurels at the feet of Iuppiter Capitolinus.[138] The ceremonial of the triumph and the related ceremonial of the procession before the games (*pompa circensis*) illustrate the point vividly; the celebrator in each case is actually dressed up — and made up — in the guise of the king and, at the same time, of the statue of Iuppiter himself, as he appeared in the Capitoline temple. This can hardly be understood except as the retention of consciously regal ceremonial under the new regime.[139]

This is not the only example of the survival into the Republic of symbols of power belonging to Etruscan monarchic practice, though it is perhaps the most dramatic one.[140] It seems comprehensible only on the assumption that the Etruscan ceremonial was not perceived by the Romans as in any way alien or arbitrarily imposed on them. The religious world they knew had become saturated with Greek and Etruscan influences that had merged with and transformed the Latin culture of their ancestors. Iuppiter was, after all, an ancient Latin deity with an ancient Latin name. Meanwhile, there was no alternative high culture or vocabulary of ceremonial to which they could turn. They were part of a loosely defined Etruscan cultural empire and it would probably have been as difficult then as it is now to define the boundaries between Etruscan and Roman religion, even had they conceived of doing so.

There is a different sense also in which the tradition about the

---

[137] For the tradition of the dedication in republican times: Livy II.8; Cic. *Dom.* 139; Tac. *Hist.* III.72; Dion. Hal. *Ant. Rom.* v.35.3; above, p. 177f.

[138] *Auspicia*: Cic. *Leg.* II.20; Wissowa 1912[G519], 119. Triumph: Livy XLV.39.11; Versnel 1970[G742], 66ff.   [139] Bonfante Warren 1970[G536], 49ff.

[140] Dion. Hal. *Ant. Rom.* III.61–2; for a vigorous statement of the case, Alföldi 1965[I3], 200ff.

changeover from monarchy to Republic is surprisingly muted: the tradition is that most of the major features of the constitution and the religion of Rome were devised and put into effect by the kings, who are presented in our first-century sources as successive founders of the different areas of public life (pp. 90ff). Little credit is given to the leaders of the republican period. In the form in which we have this, it is of course a literary construction put together in the late republican period.[141] It incorporates far earlier myths, legends and conceptions about the deeds of the founders and the early kings, but it would be very hazardous to assume that the general message of the tradition would have been recognizable to Romans of the fifth century B.C. All the same there does seem to be a shortage of information of this kind referring to the early Republic; and unless all these traditions about the contributions of the monarchs are to be written off as late fictions, they must at least have been transmitted through the early republican period. If the early republicans were themselves deeply hostile to any suggestion of monarchy or of monarchic practice, it is very hard to see how that could possibly have happened. Again, we seem to have to reckon with strong continuities as well as a sharp disruption, if sense is to be made of the tradition which has come down to us.

The overall result of the events that have been considered might be called the republican religious order. We have seen earlier that one of its most remarkable characteristics was that authority over religious matters was so widely diffused. The result is that no individual or family could construct a monopoly of religious, any more than of political, power. It can hardly be altogether an accident that the religious and political aspects of the system should reflect one another in this respect. But the situation is not one of straightforward imitation: priests are not officials elected for one year as were magistrates, but chosen by the surviving members of the college for life; and the differentiation of the priestly groups must already have been a remarkable feature of Roman religious organization in the time of the kings, as the Roman tradition itself implies. The similarity must then have resulted, not from the same decisions being taken, but by similar objectives being aimed at. If it is assumed that the king in the regal period acted as the central religious authority co-ordinating the advice of the different colleges, then his subordinates, whether by planning or not, would have produced a diffusion of authority; if that is the right way to look at it, then the steps considered in this section were indeed the first moves towards a republican type of religion.

---

[141] See especially Cic. *Rep.* ii; Livy i.

VI. INNOVATION AND CHANGE

It was argued in the first section of this chapter that a narrative history of early Roman religion, giving the 'facts' and placing them in an evolutionary or explanatory sequence, was impossible or, rather, attainable only at the price of imposing an arbitrary *a priori* scheme. Later sections have tried to show that religion in Rome in the republican period was not a separate area of life but integrated into the political and social structure, in such a way that every group or activity had its religious aspect. For this reason, too, it is arguable that there cannot be a separate history of Roman religion in the way there can be a separate history of Christianity.

In the period under consideration, there were many changes and innovations – new temples and cults, new or revised ceremonies, changes of procedure or of the rules of membership in the priestly colleges; there was another category of change too that we might infer or guess at, for one of the implications of the system was that social, political or economic changes, or changes in Rome's relations with other states, would all have had religious repercussions. This second category is likely to have had profounder effects in the long run, but it is the first category that our sources tell us about, the ones noticed by contemporary recorders. The most serious distinction (which may but does not necessarily correspond to the two categories) is between changes that could be assimilated to the overall structure and those which threatened to transform it. Innovation in one form or another is certainly a central feature of the situation; and scholars have in the past been misled into thinking that each new cult meant a confession of failure, an effort by despairing priests to shore up a collapsing edifice. In fact, the new gods, goddesses and rituals were for the most part assimilated without difficulty to the existing complex of old cults. Sometimes, they were definitely recognized as non-Roman, but accepted through *evocatio*, through the vows of generals or through the recommendations found in the Sibylline Books. More and more as time passed, and especially in the third century B.C., they were abstractions or personifications – Concord, Victory, Hope, Faith, Honour and Virtue.[142] In some cases, it may be that an abstraction came to take on a more specific personality, as was perhaps the case with Venus.[143] The third century saw an intensification of the process, as Rome's frontiers and contacts widened and as her military successes brought in new resources to be invested in building projects. Thus, Aesculapius (Asclepius, the Greek god of healing) was introduced in the 290s; underworld gods, Dis Pater and Proserpina, were

---

[142] De Sanctis 1907–64[A37], IV.2.295ff; Latte 1960[G435], 233–42; Weinstock 1971[G517], 168f (Fides); 260 (Concordia); 230ff (Honos/Virtus); for Victoria, below, p. 617 n. 146.

[143] Schilling 1954[G486].

a central part of the Secular Games, probably first celebrated in 249 B.C.; and the later years of the century saw a still further quickening of the process.[144] Sometimes, again, ancient gods or goddesses were offered a completely new type of cult: in the case of Ceres, whose cult is already quite well established in the rituals of the old calendar, a quite distinct set of observances, known to the Romans as the 'Greek rites' (*Graeca sacra*), was introduced at some point before the Hannibalic Wars.[145] In at least one case we can trace the impact on their decisions of events outside the Roman area, because the cult of Victoria, not an old Roman cult, was evidently derived from their awareness of Greek Victory cults in the late fourth century and especially of the conquests and the far-famed invincibility of Alexander the Great. Victoria received a temple in 294 B.C.; at the same period other Roman war gods began to attract the title Victor or Invictus. Before long, as the early Roman issues of coinage show, the new goddess was playing a prominent role in the Roman imagery of war.[146]

Many innovations were inspired by the Sibylline Books, the collections of oracles, kept and consulted by the *decemviri sacris faciundis*, which served to provide legitimation for what might otherwise have been seen as deviations from the ancestral tradition. The story of the purchase of these Books dates their arrival to the later regal period, when King Tarquin the Proud bought them from an old woman who offered him nine for a certain price; when he refused to buy, she destroyed three of them and offered him the remaining three for the same price; he refused again, so she destroyed three more and offered him the last three, still for the same price. Impressed at last, he paid the price and these three were the books kept by the college.[147] In other accounts, and regularly in the later tradition, the books are called Sibylline and connected with the Sibyl of Cumae; they were believed to contain the destiny of the Romans.[148] The anecdote, the connexion with the Sibyl of Cumae and the broad prophetic content may all be late accretions to the tradition; but it is clear enough that the Romans did have a set of oracles in Greek verse, regarded as of early origin though not so early as the foundation of the main institutions in the time of King Numa. The many consultations of the books recorded in the historians do not suggest that the books contained very much that we should call prophetic, but rather sets of *remedia*, rituals through which the threatened harm implied by the

[144] Aesculapius: Livy x.47.7; Latte 1960[G435], 225ff. Secular Games: Latte 1960[G435], 246ff; Nilsson 1920[G453], 1696ff; Weinstock 1971[G517], 191ff.
[145] Le Bonniec 1958[G360], 379ff; for the date of the arrival of the new cult see Arnobius, *Adv. Gent.* II.73. [146] Weinstock 1958[G516], 2504ff; 1971[G517], 91ff; above, pp. 416; 418.
[147] The story of King Tarquin, the old woman and the books: Dion. Hal. *Ant. Rom.* IV.62. The books: Diels 1890[G393]; Hoffman 1933[G426]; Gagé 1935[G406]; Latte 1960[G435], 160f; Radke 1963[G472], 1115ff. [148] On the origins of the connexion cf. Radke 1963[G472], 1146.

prodigies might be averted. It was in this context that the Books
suggested new cults and rituals, providing legitimation by their antiquity
and their foreignness. Another source of foreign wisdom, also available
to the senate, was provided by the *haruspices* summoned from Etruscan
cities; so far as Roman evidence goes, these too were in the early period
offering little or nothing that could be called prophecy.[149] The lack of
evidence is not necessarily to be trusted; this may very well be a case
where the nature of the tradition is censoring our information and
obscuring the variety of religious life in the period. It is certain that a
tradition of prophetic skill survived amongst the Etruscans and that they
still possessed it in the late republican period. Whatever the role of the
senate's various advisers, there is no doubt that the introduction of new
deities and forms continued throughout the period. At the same time, the
Romans were establishing their practice of admitting new citizens from
the surrounding area into their community as full citizens (pp. 281; 318f);
these open boundaries at the human level are surely inseparable from
open boundaries to foreign gods.[150]

To say that innovation was a normal mode of the functioning of this
religious system, and hence supportive of it not threatening to it, is not to
say that successive introductions did not bring with them new attitudes
or ideas, enshrined in the new cults. The problem is to assess which were
the new attitudes or ideas, given that we have such an inadequate grasp of
the religious possibilities in earlier times. Thus, the *lectisternium* ritual of
399 B.C. has often been seen as a great turning-point, partly because of the
choice of deities involved – clearly under Greek influence; partly because
the statues of the deities were brought out and offered a meal, an apparent
step on the road to complete anthropomorphism. But Greek influence,
we now know, goes back more than a century; and even the meal seems
likely to have been following the model of the *epulum Iovis*, celebrated at
the games in September and November.[151] Another great turning-point
in modern accounts has been the arrival of healing cults, beginning with
Aesculapius, whose temple was dedicated in the early third century: but
here again the discovery of healing-cults, with a female presiding deity,
widely spread in Central Italy forces us to reassess what if anything was
new to Rome in the Aesculapius cult, apart from the gender of the
deity.[152]

[149] For the *haruspices* in general cf. above, p. 583 n. 24; for their *responsa* in this period: MacBain
1982[G440], 43ff (lists at 82ff); their reticence should be contrasted with the unmistakably prophetic
elements in the *responsum* discussed in Cicero's *Har. Resp.*

[150] North 1976[G455], 11.

[151] The *lectisternium* of 399 B.C.: Livy v.13; see Warde Fowler 1911[G509], 262ff; Bayet
1926[G348], 260ff; Gagé 1935[G406], 168ff; Latte 1960[G435], 242ff; Ogilvie 1965[B129], 655ff.
Epulum Iovis: above, p. 597, n. 76.

[152] See above, p. 580. Aesculapius: Livy x.47.7; cf. Ov. *Met.* xv.626. For the myth of his arrival:
Latte 1960[G435], 225ff.

There are all the same some instances where it is possible to be certain that changes did occur: in the Greek rites of Ceres, introduced in the third century B.C., as opposed to the original Italian cults, the festival centres on the women of the community, especially on mothers and daughters, reflecting the relationship of the two goddesses Ceres and Proserpina.[153] There had naturally always been a place for women in cult-practice and certain festivals in which they had specific roles; there were also various goddesses devoted to the special concern of women with fertility and child-birth. Little or nothing was under women's control: the priests were all male, except for the Vestals who had to be conceded a quasi-male status to mark them off from their sisters. Women could certainly make vows and dedications in private contexts; and there are even hints that private cults were specially women's responsibility. The new Greek rites, however, brought with them Greek priestesses, who had to be given Roman citizenship, and a distinct place in public ceremonial and procession for the women of Rome.[154] There was, of course, nothing threatening about this: male priests were in ultimate control; and the Ceres cult gave ritual reinforcement to the family and reproductive roles of women. All the same, it represents the giving of more prominence to women in religious life and may well foreshadow later developments in the progress of women towards a degree of independence.

The obvious direction to look for religious change of deep significance would be the area of social conflict, more particularly to the conflicts that produced the oligarchy of the third century B.C., composed of the dominant plebeian as well as the traditional patrician families. It is implicit in the conception of religious life proposed in this chapter, that any long-standing division in society would eventually find some religious expression, since any kind of continuing, coherent action would have had to be put into relation with the gods and their involvement in Roman life. To a limited extent, it may be possible to detect the lines along which this might have happened, both in the great struggle between the plebeians and the patricians and in the even more obscure struggle between the great *gentes* and the interest of the city institutions. The recorded information about either plebeian or gentile religion is, however, very flimsy; and since, at least in the early stages, it is still very controversial what was happening at the level of social conflict, any reconstruction of the religious effects must be even more tentative. It seems to be beyond dispute that the patrician families claimed special authority in relation to the community's religious life. The strong form of that claim – that only patricians could communicate with the gods through the auspices[155] – can never have been established, since there were

---

[153] Le Bonniec 1958[G360], 379ff.   [154] Cic. *Balb.* 55.   [155] Livy IV.2.

apparently non-patrician senior magistrates at least intermittently in every period; but the patricians did control the priesthoods, or at least the most important ones, as they easily could through the system of collegiate co-option. There is no reason to doubt the tradition that plebeians attained priesthoods when specially reserved places were created for them in the colleges: this happened in 367 B.C. for the *duoviri* – then increased to ten, and in 300 B.C. for the augurs and *pontifices*, increased to eight or nine.[156] Other priestly places, including reserved places in the major colleges, continued to be a patrician preserve. In this sense, the religion of the city in the fifth century B.C. was controlled by the patricians.

It is an important question how far the plebeians developed their own religion in the fifth century B.C. They certainly adopted the temple of Ceres, Liber and Libera as their centre and as the storehouse of their records, guarded by the *aediles*, who probably took their title from the temple;[157] it is tempting to see the *aediles* as the priests of the movement, while the tribunes are the magistrates, but there is no clear evidence that they so acted.[158] In the case of Ceres, Liber and Libera and possibly of other temples built in the early years of the fifth century, it has been suggested that they not only show the influence of the plebeians, but also that of the South Italian Greeks.[159] Mercury, corresponding to Hermes, was said to have had his temple dedicated by a plebeian and had strong associations with trade and traders.[160] The temple of the Castores is more problematic; we know that the cult of the Dioscuri in thoroughly Greek form existed at Lavinium (p. 579), which had such close links with Rome. The Roman cult, however, shows its own very characteristic forms, especially its emphasis on Castor to the exclusion of Pollux – irresistibly reminiscent of the emphasis on Romulus to the exclusion of Remus.[161] Also, the Dioscuri ought to be the patrons of the cavalry, who may not be specially patrician, but are not specially plebeian either.[162] It remains a possibility that all these cults reflect South Italian contacts and hence a

---

[156] 367 B.C.: Livy VI.37.12; 42.2; Wissowa 1912[G519], 534f. Lex Ogulnia of 300 B.C.: Livy x.6–9; Wissowa 1912[G519], 492.

[157] De Sanctis 1907–64[A37], IV.2.194f; Le Bonniec 1958[G360], 348; above, p. 225f.

[158] Sabbatucci 1954[G705]; Richard 1978[H76], 580ff.

[159] Ceres, Liber, Libera: Dion. Hal. *Ant. Rom.* VI.17 (who gives the tradition that the recommendation came from the Sibylline Books); for discussion: Le Bonniec 1958[G360], 236ff; Latte 1960[G435], 161f. The suggestion of South Italian connexions: Momigliano 1967[H61], 310f; discussion: Richard 1978[H76], 509ff.

[160] Mercury: Livy II.27.5–6; cf. Ogilvie 1965[B129], 303f; Richard 1978[H76], 513ff; Combet-Farnoux 1980[G384], 18ff.

[161] Foundation of the temple: Livy II.42.5; the problem of its origins: Latte 1960[G435], 173ff; Ogilvie 1965[B129], 288; 347; Richard 1978[H76], 510f; character of the Roman cult: Schilling 1960[G487], 177ff.   [162] Richard 1978[H76], 484ff; cf. above, p. 167f.

specifically plebeian religious life; but it should be remembered, first, that the dedication of temples accepted by the state must have been under patrician control if anything was and, secondly, that we depend on dates preserved in the priestly, that is, patrician tradition for whatever knowledge we have. If plebeian temples began their lives as part of a revolutionary enterprise, it seems unlikely that we should hear about their existence earlier than the date of the officially accepted dedication ceremony.

There are other areas where the plebeians may have made a distinctive contribution: one of the oldest sets of *ludi* (games) were called plebeian and here there is no doubt of the connexion. In fact, Cicero calls these games the oldest of all and they have at their heart one of the two 'feasts of Iuppiter'.[163] It is a controversial but not indefensible idea that games as such (as opposed to the ludic elements in archaic festivals) were a plebeian contribution to Roman life. In this case they may have been originally unrecognized and subsequently accepted by the religious authorities. Finally, on the view argued in this chapter, it is inevitable that the political activities of the plebeians must have had religious aspects: the electing of magistrates and the passing of laws (*plebiscita*) could not have taken place without the gods' involvement. No doubt, whatever religious forms the plebeians employed were rejected as invalid by the patrician priests, but eventually accepted as were plebeian assemblies and magistrates. Little reflection of this survives: the plebeians certainly took oaths to guarantee their tribunes;[164] and late-republican tribunes claimed powers to report omens and to perform consecration and cursing;[165] all these must once have been resisted and subsequently accepted by the priestly authorities.

The cults of the *gentes* present a rather similar problem; we have enough evidence to show that they were once an important factor, but scarcely enough to assess their significance. Certain *gentes* did maintain ancient cults in the late Republic, not always located in Rome itself; thus the cult of the Iulii was celebrated at Bovillae in Latium.[166] The dedication to Mars by the *sodales* of Poplios Valesios discovered at Satricum (it is not clear whether he himself came from Rome, Satricum or elsewhere) seems to give a glimpse of a quite different social organization in which the clients or the war-band of a leader might act as a unity for religious purposes.[167] It is at least a possible view of the situation in the early decades of the Republic, that the city's control had broken down to the point where control of religion as of other areas had passed into the hands

---

[163] Cic. II *Verr.* 5.36; cf. Le Bonniec 1958[G360], 350ff; Richard 1978[H76], 118ff.
[164] Festus 422 L.   [165] Bayet 1960[G349], 46ff.
[166] *ILLRP* 270; cf. Weinstock 1971[G517], 8ff.
[167] Versnel in Stibbe et al. 1980[B263]; 1982[B268], 193ff; above, p. 97.

of the great leaders of the *gentes*.[168] If such a situation ever existed, little
trace of it has survived into the later tradition. The lack of information
about gentile religion is even more surprising than that about plebeian
religion. After all, on some views the plebeians were a powerful active
group for a relatively short period in the early Republic, after which their
activity was absorbed into those of the city as a whole; the *gentes* must
have had cult activities of the greatest importance for centuries. The
almost total disappearance of this may suggest a deliberate policy on the
part of the priests.

It has to be a matter for speculation whether there was a time of
conflict at the end of the early republican period, when some of these
issues might have been raised and resolved. The last few years of the
fourth century (pp. 394ff) offer at least hints of such conflict. The
censorship of Appius Claudius Caecus in 312 B.C. saw the control of a
major cult – that of Hercules at the Ara Maxima – transferred from the
gens Potitia to the state; this is the only trace of the removal of gentile
control of a cult, but it may not have been so isolated as it now seems.[169]
The same period is said to have seen two separate conflicts between
Appius' freedman Cn. Flavius and the college of *pontifices* over the
publication of some of their secrets and also over the correct procedure
for the dedication of temples.[170] In 300 B.C., the plebeians gained access
to the two major colleges under the Lex Ogulnia; finally it was probably
in the early decades of the third century that the very important but
unreported reform was carried which transferred the choice of the
pontifex maximus from the members of the college to a specially devised
form of popular election.[171] There seems to be enough here to make it
quite certain that major religious issues were under debate. It is not so
easy to see the trend of events or their significance. One element is the
attack on the patrician monopoly; another is the limitation of the power
and independence of the priestly colleges; a third is the centralization of
religious control in the state institutions. This may all help to explain the
succession of authoritative priestly figures, several of them plebeians,
which characterizes the third and second centuries. If there is any
substance in the speculation that early priests might have been more
isolated from public life, this will be the point where the priest-politician
emerged as a characteristic figure.[172]

168 Momigliano 1967[H61], 305ff; Versnel in Stibbe et al. 1980[B263], 117ff.
169 Livy IX.29.9. For the cult: Bayet 1926[G348]; Latte 1960[G435], 213ff. For a different view of
the events of 312: Palmer 1965[G460], 294ff.   170 Livy IX.46.
171 Livy XXV.5.2–3 (212 B.C.) gives us the first explicit mention of *comitia* for the election of the
pontifex maximus; but there is no reason to regard this as the first such election.
172 Cf. above, p. 588f. The first influential *pontifex maximus* known to us is Ti. Coruncanius
(Münzer and Jörs 1901[G452], 1663ff), the first plebeian to hold the office (Livy, *Epit.* XVIII),
probably by the 250s. It seems likely, but not certain, that election had been introduced earlier than
this.

If this approach is right, then in or around the late fourth century, the religious consequences of social conflict, like those of religious innovation or of simple neglect, were absorbed within the flexible, always changing boundaries of the system. None of these processes needs to be perceived as anything other than the normal processes of a living set of human institutions. Nothing seems to be illuminated at this date by talking in terms of decline, decay, deterioration or dissolution. One isolated story is sometimes quoted to illustrate the rise of scepticism in the elite as the result of contact with the Greeks: that is the famous incident of 249 B.C. when the naval commander – another Claudius – found that his wish to join battle was impeded by the bad omen of the sacred chickens refusing to eat; he threw them in the sea, remarking: 'If they will not eat, let them drink'.[173] The point of the story, it need hardly be said, is that he lost the battle; this is a category of anecdote confirmatory of the system, if not essential to it. We do know, from the occasional Plautine reference, that at least a superficial awareness of the views of Stoics and Epicureans had reached Rome by the end of the third century;[174] but there is no reason to think that any serious opposition was felt between Greek academic theories and traditional Roman forms of action before Cicero's time at the earliest. It takes time for the implications of new and unfamiliar modes of thought to disturb assumptions built into a whole social and symbolic system.

It is not quite enough, however, to say that we have plenty of evidence of change within the system, but none of deep change which might threaten the system. The religious life of the Republic as described in earlier sections of this chapter did undergo a process of transformation, so that Cicero and Augustus lived in a very different religious environment from Appius Claudius Caecus. One side of the transformation was the retreat of the sacred from areas in which it had once had its part to play. The other and more positive side was the emergence of new religious forces and forms of organization, most importantly, the emergence of specifically religious groups and hence specifically religious choices for the individual of the kind which, we have seen,[175] had not existed at all in early Rome. It is important not to confuse the transformation of the religious system of the middle Republic with the deterioration of Roman religion as such. The age in which Cicero lived was in many ways an innovative and vigorous period in religious history; it was witnessing changes in progress which were to produce an entirely new relationship between religion and society; the effects of this were eventu-

[173] Cic. *Nat. D.* II.7; above, p. 562.
[174] There are, for instance, quite frequent references in Plautus to Stoic or Epicurean attitudes to the gods: e.g. *Merc.* 4–7; *Epid.* 610–11; *Capt.* 313–15; *Rud.* 9–30; *Cas.* 346–9; *Aul.* 88.
[175] Above, p. 598f.

ally to be subsumed into the triumph of Christianity, but it is clear enough that developments within pagan life to some extent anticipated and facilitated the process. The first unmistakable sign of the beginning of a new age in religious history, comes to us almost by accident when the senate decided to destroy the worship of Bacchus through the whole of Italy in the 180s B.C.[176] A movement so alien in its organization to the native tradition cannot have established itself through so many areas of Italy suddenly; there must have been many years of earlier development. That this is so is confirmed both by the occasional reference to the cult in Plautus' plays from the end of the third century onwards and also by archaeological evidence of its presence.[177] The second half of the third century emerges as the period when, though there is scarcely a hint from our historical sources, profound changes of religious attitude must have been under way in much of Italy.

[176] Livy xxxix.8ff; *ILLRP* 511.   [177] North 1979[G456], 87ff.

APPENDIX

A. DRUMMOND

I. EARLY ROMAN CHRONOLOGY

The so-called Varronian system of chronology used in this volume
effectively placed the foundation of Rome in 753 B.C., the first consuls in
509 and the Gallic Sack of Rome in 390, and was largely followed by the
Capitoline Fasti (p. 347). It was, however, a creation of the mid-first
century B.C. (perhaps of Atticus rather than Varro) and incorporated the
dictator–years, which appear to be a late invention (p. 348);[1] it is not,
therefore, representative of the chronologies employed by the Roman
historians, to whom the dictator–years were foreign. Those chronologies,
however, are imperfectly known since few relevant data are preserved
from the lost early chroniclers of Rome and not all the surviving
authorities are systematic, accurate or even internally consistent in their
chronologies. Thus Livy (probably following the pattern of his Latin
predecessors) is generally content to chart the passage of the years merely
by recording the successive consular colleges and only occasionally
employs dates 'from the foundation of the city' (*ab urbe condita*). As a
result, it is very doubtful whether he worked with a clearly defined
overall chronological system, particularly since his own narrative omits
certain consular years (490–489 and 376 on the Varronian scheme)[2]
which his dates 'from the foundation of the city' seem to include and
some of these latter dates themselves appear to be mutually incompatible.
The most satisfactory explanation of these last inconsistencies is that
Livy's dates 'from the foundation of the city' derive from two different
schemes (presumably to be found ultimately in different sources), which
placed the foundation of Rome in 751 or 750 respectively, the establishment of the Republic in 507 or 506 and the Gallic Sack in 386; but even
this remains hypothetical. In Diodorus the confusion is still more acute,
despite his correlation of consular colleges with Greek olympiads and

---

[1] In partial compensation the 'Varronian' chronology probably allowed only two years for the
Decemvirates (451–450) in contrast to the three years of other chronologies.

[2] The single college which he gives in place of those of 507–6 (II.15.1) may be presupposed in the
dates 'from the foundation of the city' in III.33.1 and IV.7.1.

Athenian archons. For although he appears to accept the Greek synchronism which located the Gallic Sack in ol. 98.2 (387/6 B.C.),[3] his list of
consuls has been so blatantly manipulated to fit it[4] and is otherwise so
replete with manifest error[5] that his synchronization of Greek and
Roman dates (and therefore the modern translation of the latter into B.C.
terms) remains worthless. Of the extant historians only Dionysius has
serious claims to have attempted a coherent chronology of the Republic
and to have correlated it fully with Greek dates (a topic on which he
wrote in a separate work now lost (*Ant. Rom.* 1.74.2)). He places the
foundation of the city in ol. 7.1 (752/1 B.C.), the first consuls in ol. 68.2
(508/7 B.C.) and the Gallic Sack in ol. 98.1 (388/7 B.C.).[6] A century earlier
Polybius gave the same date for the Republic and dates only one year later
for the foundation and the Gallic Sack.[7] This broad consistency with the
chronological schemes known for Dionysius and conjectured in Livy,
together with the general agreement between the surviving consular lists
(p. 18f),[8] may indicate that a comparatively uniform republican chronology was employed by, or implicit in, the Roman historical tradition
from the mid-second century; the few foundation dates which we have
from other works of this period[9] support that hypothesis. The earliest
historians, however, gave discrepant and diverse foundation dates:
Timaeus 814/13 B.C., Fabius Pictor ol. 8.1 (748/7), Cincius Alimentus ol.
12.4 (729/8).[10] This has prompted suggestions that one or more of these
authors had radically different consular lists from those found later and

[3] Such olympiad dates are usually correlated with the Roman consuls who enter office in the
course of the olympiad year concerned. The variation in the dates of entry into office in the early
Republic (p. 174 n. 7) makes such a uniform correlation still more artificial.

[4] Through the wholesale repetition of the colleges of 394–390 (Perl 1957[D25], 113f).

[5] Notably his complete omission of the colleges of 423–419. The only major distinctive variants
in Diodorus worth consideration are the additional colleges apparently or certainly included after
those of 458, 457 and 428 and the alternative college under 349; but even these are of dubious merit.
See Perl 1957[D25].

[6] Dion. Hal. *Ant. Rom.* 1.74.4–75.3; v.1.1. There are, however, some difficulties in explaining
Dionysius' distinctive date for the Gallic Sack (*Ant. Rom.* 1.74.4) and the chronological data in *Ant.
Rom.* 1.3.4 and (especially) 1.8.1. For discussion and bibliography see Werner 1963[A134], 134ff.

[7] Cf. Polyb. III.22.2; VI.11a.2; 1.6.1f with Walbank 1957–79[B182] ad loc.

[8] Including that of Diodorus when purged of its grosser errors (Perl 1957[D25], esp. 106–22).

[9] According to Dion. Hal. *Ant. Rom.* 1.74.2f Cato's location of the foundation of Rome 432 years
later than the fall of Troy implied a date of ol. 7.1 (752/1 B.C.) on Eratosthenes' chronology (some
believe that Dionysius has misrepresented Cato, whose figure in fact implied ol. 7.2: see Werner
1963[A134], 113–19). ol. 7.2 recurs in Cic. *Rep.* 11.18 (from Polybius?), in Diod. fr. VII.5.1 and
reputedly in Lutatius Catulus and Cornelius Nepos (Solinus 1.27). Dion. Hal. *Ant. Rom.* 1.74.3 may
imply that the data of 'τοῦ παρὰ τοῖς ἀρχιερεῦσι κειμένου πίνακος' (presumably the pontifical
whiteboard itself or a transcription) could be, or had been, used to achieve a similar date.

It is possible that other second-century historians had slightly different chronologies (cf. esp.
Cassius Hemina fr. 20P; Piso fr. 36P (cf. also 26P); Gellius fr. 25 and 27P) but the accuracy and/or
implications of the relevant fragments are controversial.

[10] Naevius and Ennius apparently dated the foundation of Rome soon after the Trojan war (p. 82)
but the details of their overall chronology (if they had one) elude us.

hence gave an earlier or later date for the establishment of the city,[11] but more probably the variation is to be explained by differences in the length assigned to the monarchy: Fabius Pictor's chronology for the early fourth century, for example, may already have conformed broadly to that current later[12] and have included, *inter alia*, the spurious anarchy (375–371 B.C.). As that fiction demonstrates, however, the consular lists available to Roman historians proved an inadequate basis for synchronization with external data, which thereby showed them to be chronologically defective (p. 349). Whilst, therefore, it remains regrettable that modern convention employs the still less satisfactory Varronian chronological system (and its corresponding B.C. correlation), the adoption of another scheme (e.g. that of Dionysius) would bring only a limited improvement: for all ancient reconstructions of early republican chronology suffered from inherent weaknesses now beyond total remedy.[13]

II. THE CONSULAR *FASTI*: 509–220 B.C.

The following list derives from a variety of literary and epigraphic texts, most of which do not usually give the magistrate's full name; as a result, many entries are an amalgam of material from different sources.[14] Whilst some attempt has been made to signal individual uncertainties,[15] only the most significant or credible variants have been included, without discus-

---

[11] Cf. Pinsent 1975[D26], 2–3 etc. Timaeus' date may depend primarily on his desire to achieve a symbolic synchronization of the foundation of Rome and Carthage (p. 82).

[12] If Aulus Gellius, *NA* v.4.3 derives from a Latin version of his work and 'duovicesimo' means 'twenty-second'. For the passage and its implications cf. Werner 1963[A134], 119–29; above, p. 348.

[13] Pliny, *HN* XXXIII.19 reports that in the inscription on his temple of Concord Cn. Flavius dated the shrine's dedication 204(?) years after the dedication of the Capitoline temple. Since Flavius performed the dedication as curule aedile in 303 B.C. on pre-Varronian chronologies (304 B.C. on Varro's), this would imply that already at the end of the fourth century the consecration of the Capitoline temple was assigned its Polybian date of 507 B.C. and, as a result, it would be of great significance (not least for the history of the consular *fasti*) if we could determine the basis of Flavius' calculation. Since it was later believed that the Capitoline temple was dedicated in the first year of the Republic, it might be suggested that Flavius had access to, and employed, a consular list, which will then already have resembled closely those current later. Otherwise it is supposed that he was able to compute the dedication date of the Capitoline temple independently of the *fasti* (perhaps by counting the annual nails (p. 187)); in that case his calculation itself or the chronological evidence on which it was based may have been used as a check on, or even the basis of, the later consular lists and their implied date for the start of the Republic. However, given our ignorance of the means by which Flavius reached his alleged figure all such theories are necessarily speculative (and are open to challenge on other counts); indeed, the import of Flavius' own alleged figure is controversial. Rather than acting as a chronological lynch-pin it may itself have been used to date Flavius' aedileship (or even the dedication of the Capitoline temple) in conformity with later pre-Varronian chronologies or Pliny may have misunderstood his source and have attributed to Flavius a calculation which was in fact the work of that source.　　[14] Degrassi 1947[D7], 346ff; *MRR* I.

[15] The use of the question mark does not, however, necessarily imply serious doubt and even where variants are cited there are usually sound reasons for preferring one of the alternatives given.

sion. Beyond the issue of the overall reliability of the list (pp. 173ff),
especial doubt attaches to the *cognomina* attributed to fifth- and fourth-
century consuls: *cognomina* themselves may have been included in records
of consulships relatively late and multiple *cognomina* before the later
fourth century may reflect a combination of two different
reconstructions.[16]

Roman numerals after a name denote repeated tenure of the consulship or consular tribunate (in keeping with the practice of ancient
sources, repeated consulships and repeated consular tribunates of the
same individual are numbered separately). Material in brackets represents modern additions. So far as possible the order of names within each
year is that of Livy (or, where his text fails, of authors generally
dependent on Livy), but this has no special authority.[17]

509	L. Iunius Brutus		L. Tarquinius Collatinus
suf.:	Sp. Lucretius Tricipitinus (omitted by some early authorities: Livy II.8.5) M. Horatius Pulvillus (Polybius III.22.1 gives Brutus and Horatius as the first consuls)	*suf.*:	P. Valerius Poplicola
508	P. Valerius Poplicola II		T. Lucretius Tricipitinus
507	P. Valerius Poplicola III		M. Horatius Pulvillus II
506	Sp. Larcius Rufus (Flavus?) (In place of the colleges of 507/6 Livy II.15.1 gives one pair of consuls: P.(?) Lucretius and P. Valerius Poplicola (III))		T. Herminius Aquilinus
505	M. Valerius Volusus(?)		P. Postumius Tubertus
504	P. Valerius Poplicola IV		T. Lucretius Tricipitinus II
503	Agrippa Menenius Lanatus		P. Postumius Tubertus II
502	Opiter Verginius Tricostus		Sp. Cassius Vicellinus
501	Postumus Cominius Auruncus		T. Larcius Flavus Rufus
500	Ser. Sulpicius Camerinus Cornutus		M'. Tullius Longus
499	T. Aebutius Helva Flavus(?)		C. or P. Veturius Geminus Cicurinus
498	Q. Cloelius Siculus		T. Larcius Flavus Rufus II
497	A. Sempronius Atratinus		M. Minucius Augurinus
496	A. Postumius Albus Regillensis		T. Verginius Tricostus Caeliomontanus

---

[16] Cichorius 1886[D4], 177ff; 219ff.

[17] Whilst the spelling of family names has been standardized, the diversity of form and/or spelling
of certain *cognomina* in different sources has been deliberately allowed to stand. Only where the same
individual appears more than once has uniformity been consciously pursued.

495	Ap. Claudius Sabinus Inregillensis	P. Servilius Priscus Structus
494	A. Verginius Tricostus Caeliomontanus	T. Veturius Geminus Cicurinus
493	Sp. Cassius Vicellinus II	Postumus Cominius Auruncus II
492	T. Geganius Macerinus	P. Minucius Augurinus
491	M. Minucius Augurinus II	A. Sempronius Atratinus II
490	Q. Sulpicius Camerinus Cornutus	Sp. Larcius Flavus (*or* Rufus?) II
489	C. Iulius Iullus	P. Pinarius Rufus Mamertinus
488	Sp. Nautius Rutilus	Sex. Furius
487	T. Sicinius (Dion. Hal. and Cassiodorus) *or* T. Siccius Sabinus(?)	C. Aquillius Tuscus(?)
486	Sp. Cassius Vicellinus III	Proculus Verginius Tricostus Rutilus
485	Ser. Cornelius Maluginensis	Q. Fabius Vibulanus
484	L. Aemilius Mamercus	K. Fabius Vibulanus
483	M. Fabius Vibulanus	L. Valerius Potitus Volusus Poplicola
482	Q. Fabius Vibulanus II	C. Iulius Iullus
481	K. Fabius Vibulanus II	Sp. Furius (Medullinus?) Fusus
480	M. Fabius Vibulanus II	Cn. Manlius Cincinnatus(?)
479	K. Fabius Vibulanus III	T. Verginius Tricostus Rutilus
478	L. Aemilius Mamercus II	C. Servilius Structus *or* (Diod.) C. Cornelius Lentulus
		suf.: [Opet. Verginius? E]squilinus
477	C.(?) Horatius Pulvillus	T. Menenius Lanatus
476	A. Verginius Tricostus Rutilus	Sp.(?) Servilius Structus
475	C. Nautius Rutilus	P. Valerius Poplicola
474	L. Furius Medullinus	A.(?) Manlius Vulso
473	L. Aemilius Mamercus III	Vopiscus(?) Iulius Iullus *or* Opet. Verginius
472	L. Pinarius Mamercinus Rufus	P. Furius (Medullinus?) Fusus
471	Ap. Claudius (Crassus?) Inregillensis Sabinus	T. Quinctius Capitolinus Barbatus
470	L. Valerius Potitus Volusus Poplicola II	Ti.(?) Aemilius Mamercus

469	T. Numicius Priscus	A. Verginius Caeliomontanus
468	T. Quinctius Capitolinus Barbatus II	Q. Servilius Structus Priscus
467	Ti.(?) Aemilius Mamercus II	Q. Fabius Vibulanus
466	Q. Servilius (Structus) Priscus II	Sp. Postumius Albus Regillensis
465	Q. Fabius Vibulanus II	T. Quinctius Capitolinus (Barbatus) III
464	A. Postumius Albus Regillensis	Sp. Furius Medullinus Fusus
463	L. Aebutius Flavus Helva	P. Servilius Structus Priscus
462	L. Lucretius Tricipitinus	T. Veturius Geminus Cicurinus
461	P. Volumnius Amintinus Gallus	Ser. Sulpicius Camerinus Cornutus
460	C. Claudius Inregillensis Sabinus	P. Valerius Poplicola II
		suf.: L. Quinctius Cincinnatus
459	Q. Fabius Vibulanus III	L. Cornelius Maluginensis Uritinus
458	[..........] Carve[......] (Capitoline Fasti)	C.(?) Nautius Rutilus II

(*suf.*:) L. Minucius Esquilinus
    Augurinus

(After these consuls Diodorus may have included an additional college.)

457	Q. Minucius Esquilinus Augurinus(?) *or* (Diodorus) L. Postumius	C.(?) Horatius Pulvillus II(?)

(After these consuls Diodorus inserts an additional college: L. Quinctius Cincinnatus and M. Fabius Vibulanus)

456	M. Valerius Maximus Lactuca	Sp. Verginius Tricostus Caeliomontanus
455	T. Romilius Rocus Vaticanus	C. Veturius Cicurinus
454	Sp. Tarpeius Montanus Capitolinus	A. Aternius Varus Fontinalis
453	P. Curiatius Fistus Trigeminus *or* (Dion. Hal.) P. Horatius	Sex. Quinctilius (Varus?)
		suf.: Sp. Furius (Medullinus Fusus II?) (only in Dion. Hal.)
452	T.(?) Menenius Lanatus	P. Sestius Capito Vaticanus *or* (Dion. Hal.) P. Siccius

451 First Decemvirate:
Ap. Claudius Crassus Inrigillensis Sabinus II   consuls *or*
T. Genucius Augurinus *or* (Diod.)   consuls
T. Minucius   elect

P. Sestius (Capito Vaticanus)
Sp.(?) Veturius Crassus Cicurinus
C. Iulius Iullus
A. Manlius Vulso
Ser.(?) Sulpicius Camerinus (Cornutus?)
P. Curiatius (Fistus Trigeminus) *or* (Dion. Hal.) P. Horatius
T. Romilius (Rocus Vaticanus)
Sp. Postumius Albus (Regillensis)

450 Second Decemvirate:
Ap. Claudius Crassus Inrigillensis Sabinus
M. Cornelius Maluginensis
M.(?) Sergius Esquilinus
L. Minucius Esquilinus Augurinus
Q. Fabius Vibulanus
Q. Poetelius
T. Antonius Merenda
K. Duillius
Sp. Oppius Cornicen
M'. Rabuleius

449	L. Valerius Poplicola Potitus	M. Horatius [....]rrin. Barbatus
448	Lars(?) Herminius Coritinesanus	T. Verginius Tricostus Caeliomontanus
447	M. Geganius Macerinus	C.(?) Iulius
446	T. Quinctius Capitolinus Barbatus IV	Agrippa Furius Fusus
445	M. Genucius Augurinus	C.(?) Curtius Chilo *or* (Livy) P. Cur⟨i⟩atius
444	A. Sempronius Atratinus L. Atilius Luscus T. Cloelius Siculus	

Suffect consuls (in the Linen Books and Ardeate treaty):
	L. Papirius Mugillanus	L. Sempronius Atratinus
443	M. Geganius Macerinus II	T. Quinctius Capitolinus Barbatus V
442	M. Fabius Vibulanus	Post. Aebutius Helva Cornicen

441   C.(?) Furius Pacilus Fusus   M'.(?) Papirius Crassus
440   Proculus Geganius Macerinus   T. Menenius Lanatus II *or*
                                          (Livy) L. Menenius Lanatus
439   T. Quinctius Capitolinus   Agrippa Menenius Lanatus
      (Barbatus) VI
438   L. Quinctius Cincinnatus (*cos.* 428/7?)
      Mam. Aemilius Mamercus
      L. *or* C. Iulius Iullus (*cos.* 430?)
437   M. Geganius Macerinus III   L. Sergius Fidenas
suf.(?):[M. Valerius Lactuca
         Maxi]mus (Degrassi 1947
         [D7], 538)
436   M.(?) Cornelius   L. Papirius Crassus
      Maluginensis
435   C. Iulius II(?)   L.(?) Verginius Tricostus
434   *Either* (a) M. Manlius Capitolinus
                Q. Sulpicius Camerinus Praetextatus
                Ser. Cornelius Cossus
                   (So the early writers: Livy iv.23.2)
          or   (b) C. Iulius III(?)   L(?) Verginius (Tricostus) II
                   (So the Linen Books according to Licinius Macer)
          or   (c) M. Manlius (Capitolinus?)   Q. Sulpicius (Camerinus
                                                      Praetextatus?)
                   (So Valerius Antias and the Linen Books
                   according to Q. Aelius Tubero)
433   M. Fabius Vibulanus (*cos.* 442)
      M. Folius Flaccinator
      L. Sergius Fidenas (*cos.* 437, 429)
432   L. Pinarius Mamercinus
      L. Furius Medullinus
      Sp. Postumius Albus
431   T. Quinctius Poenus   C.(?) Iulius Mento
      Cincinnatus
430   L.(?) Papirius Crassus (II?)   L.(?) Iulius Iullus
429   L. Sergius Fidenas II   Hostus(?) Lucretius
                                          Tricipitinus
428   A. Cornelius Cossus   T. Quinctius Poenus
                                          Cincinnatus II
      (After these consuls Diodorus inserts an additional college:
      L. Quinctius (Cincinnatus II?) and A. Sempronius (Atratinus?).)
427   C. Servilius Structus *or* (?)   L. Papirius Mugillanus
      Ahala

426 T. Quinctius Poenus (Cincinnatus) (*cos.* 431, 428)
C. Furius (Pacilus) Fusus (*cos.* 441?)
M. Postumius
A. Cornelius Cossus (*cos.* 428)

425 A. Sempronius Atratinus (*cos.* 428/7?)
L. Quinctius Cincinnatus (II) (*cos.* 428/7?)
L. Furius Medullinus (II)
L. Horatius Barbatus

424 Ap.(?) Claudius Crassus
Sp. Nautius Rutilus
L. Sergius Fidenas (II) (*cos.* 437, 429)
Sex. Iulius Iullus

423 C. Sempronius Atratinus   Q. Fabius Vibulanus

422 L. Manlius Capitolinus
Q. Antonius Merenda
L. Papirius Mugillanus (*cos.* 427)

421 N.(?) Fabius Vibulanus   T. Quinctius Capitolinus
Barbatus

420 L. Quinctius Cincinnatus III (*cos.* 428/7?) *or* (T. Quinctius
Poenus) Cincinnatus II (*cos.* 431, 428)
L. Furius Medullinus III
M. Manlius Vulso
A. Sempronius Atratinus (II) (*cos.* 428/7?)

419 Agrippa Menenius Lanatus (*cos.* 439)
P. Lucretius Tricipitinus
Sp. Nautius Rutilus
C. Servilius (Structus *or* (?) Axilla) (*cos.* 427) (Capitoline Fasti
only)

418 L. Sergius Fidenas III (*cos.* 437, 429)
M. Papirius Mugillanus (*cos.* 411)
C. Servilius Structus *or* (?) Axilla II (*cos.* 427?) *or*
(Livy) C. Servilius

417 Agrippa Menenius Lanatus II (*cos.* 439)
C. Servilius Structus *or* (?) Axilla III (*cos.* 427?) *or* L.(?)
Servilius Structus II (Livy)
P. Lucretius Tricipitinus II
Sp. Veturius (Crassus) *or* (Livy) Sp. Rutilius Crassus

416 A. Sempronius Atratinus III (*cos.* 428/7?)
M. Papirius Mugillanus II
Sp. Nautius Rutilus II
Q. Fabius (Vibulanus) (*cos.* 423)

415 P. Cornelius Cossus
C. Valerius Potitus (Volusus)

Q. Quinctius Cincinnatus
(N.?) Fabius Vibulanus (*cos.* 421?)
414　Cn.(?) Cornelius Cossus (*cos.* 409)
L.(?) Valerius Potitus (*cos.* 393(?), 392)
Q.(?) Fabius Vibulanus II(?) (*cos.* 423?)
P.(?) Postumius (Albinus) Regillensis
413　A.(?) Cornelius Cossus　　　L. Furius Medullinus
412　Q. Fabius Ambustus　　　　C. Furius Pacilus
　　　Vibulanus
411　M. Papirius Mugillanus　　　Sp.(?) Nautius Rutilus
410　M'. (?) Aemilius Mamercinus　C. Valerius Potitus Volusus
409　Cn. Cornelius Cossus　　　　L. Furius Medullinus II
408　C. Iulius Iullus
P. Cornelius Cossus
C. Servilius Ahala
407　L. Furius Medullinus (*cos.* 413, 409)
C. Valerius Potitus Volusus II (*cos.* 410)
N.(?) Fabius Vibulanus II (*cos.* 421?)
C. Servilius Ahala II
406　P. Cornelius Rutilus Cossus
Cn. Cornelius Cossus
N.(?) Fabius Ambustus
L. Valerius Potitus II(?) (*cos.* 393(?), 392)
405　T. Quinctius Capitolinus Barbatus (*cos.* 421)
Q. Quinctius Cincinnatus II
C. Iulius Iullus II
A. Manlius Vulso Capitolinus
L. Furius Medullinus II (*cos.* 413, 409)
M'. (?) Aemilius Mamercinus (*cos.* 410)
404　C. Valerius Potitus Volusus
M'. Sergius Fidenas
P. Cornelius Maluginensis
Cn. Cornelius Cossus II
K.(?) Fabius Ambustus
Sp. Nautius Rutilus III (*cos.* 411?)
403　M'.(?) Aemilius Mamercinus II (*cos.* 410)
L. Valerius Potitus III(?) (*cos.* 393(?), 392)
Ap. Claudius Crassus (*cos.* 349?)
M. Quinctilius Varus
L. Iulius Iullus
M. Furius Fusus *or* (Livy) M. Postumius
(Livy erroneously adds the censors of 403: M. Furius Camillus
and M. Postumius Albinus)

402 C. Servilius Ahala III
     Q. Servilius Fidenas
     L. Verginius Tricostus Esquilinus
     Q. Sulpicius Camerinus Cornutus
     A. Manlius Vulso Capitolinus II
     M'. Sergius Fidenas II

401 L. Valerius Potitus IV (*cos.* 393(?), 392)
     M. Furius Camillus
     M'.(?) Aemilius Mamercinus III (*cos.* 410)
     Cn. Cornelius Cossus III
     K.(?) Fabius Ambustus II(?)
     L. Iulius Iullus

400 P. Licinius Calvus Esquilinus
     P. Manlius Vulso
     (L.?) Titinius Pansa Saccus
     P. Maelius Capitolinus
     Sp.(?) Furius Medullinus
     L. Publilius Philo Vulscus

399 M. Veturius Crassus Cicurinus
     M. Pomponius Rufus
     C.(?) Duillius Longus
     Voler. Publilius Philo
     Cn. Genucius Augurinus
     L. Atilius Priscus

398 L. Valerius Potitus V (*cos.* 393(?), 392)
     (M.) Valerius Lactucinus Maximus
     M. Furius Camillus II
     L. Furius Medullinus III (*cos.* 413, 409)
     Q. Servilius Fidenas II
     Q. Sulpicius Camerinus (Cornutus) II

397 L. Iulius Iullus II
     (L.) Furius Medullinus IV (*cos.* 413, 409)
     L. Sergius Fidenas
     A. Postumius (Albinus) Regillensis
     P. Cornelius Maluginensis (*cos.* 393?)
     A.(?) Manlius (Vulso Capitolinus III(?))

396 L. Titinius Pansa Saccus II
     P. Maelius Capitolinus II
     Cn. Genucius (Augurinus) II
     L. Atilius (Priscus) II
     P. Licinius Calvus Esquilinus II(?)
     Q. Manlius Vulso

395 P. Cornelius Cossus
P. Cornelius Scipio
M. Valerius (Lactucinus) Maximus II
K. Fabius Ambustus III(?)
L. Furius Medullinus V (*cos.* 413, 409)
Q. Servilius (Fidenas) III

394 M. Furius Camillus III
L. Furius Medullinus VI (*cos.* 413, 409)
C. Aemilius (Mamercinus)
L. Valerius Publicola
Sp. Postumius
P. Cornelius (Maluginensis *or* Cossus *or* Scipio) II

393 [L. Valerius] Potitus   [P. *or* Ser.? Cornel]ius
                                   Maluginensis
(Both in the Capitoline Fasti only; they may not have entered office)
suf.: L. Lucretius Flavus (Tricipitinus) Ser. Sulpicius Camerinus

392 L. Valerius Potitus II   M.(?) Manlius Capitolinus

391 L. Lucretius (Flavus) Tricipitinus (*cos.* 393)
Ser. Sulpicius (Camerinus) (*cos.* 393)
L. *or* M. Aemilius Mamercinus
L. Furius Medullinus VI (*cos.* 413, 409)
Agrippa Furius
C. Aemilius (Mamercinus) II

390 Q. Fabius Ambustus (II?)
K.(?) Fabius (Ambustus) (IV?)
N.(?) Fabius (Ambustus) (II)
Q. Sulpicius Longus
Q. Servilius (Fidenas) IV
P. Cornelius Maluginensis (II) (*cos.* 393(?))

389 (L.) Valerius Publicola II
L. Verginius Tricostus (Esquilinus II?)
P. Cornelius
A. Manlius (Capitolinus)
L. Aemilius (Mamercinus) (II?)
L. Postumius Albinus (Regillensis)
L. Papirius (Diod. only)
M. Furius (Diod. only)

388 T. Quinctius Cincinnatus Capitolinus
Q. Servilius Fidenas V
L. Iulius Iullus
L. Aquillius Corvus
L. Lucretius (Flavus) Tricipitinus (II) (*cos.* 393)
(Ser.) Sulpicius Rufus

387   L. Papirius Cursor
      Cn. Sergius (Fidenas Coxo)
      L. Aemilius (Mamercinus III)
      Licinus Menenius Lanatus
      L. Valerius Publicola III
      L. Quinctius (Diod. only)
      L. Cornelius (Diod. only)
      A. Manlius (Capitolinus II?) (Diodorus only)

386   M. Furius Camillus (IV)
      Ser.(?) Cornelius Maluginensis
      Q. Servilius Fidenas VI
      L. Quinctius Cincinnatus (Capitolinus) (II?)
      L. Horatius Pulvillus
      P. Valerius (Potitus Poplicola)

385   A. Manlius Capitolinus II (*or* III)
      P. Cornelius II
      T. Quinctius (Cincinnatus) Capitolinus II
      L. Quinctius Cincinnatus(?) Capitolinus II (*or* III?)
      L. Papirius Cursor II
      (Cn. Sergius Fidenas Coxo II?)

384   Ser. Cornelius Maluginensis II(?)
      P. Valerius Potitus (Poplicola) II
      M. Furius Camillus V
      Ser. Sulpicius Rufus II
      C.(?) Papirius Crassus
      T. Quinctius Cincinnatus (Capitolinus) II

383   L. Valerius Publicola IV
      A. Manlius (Capitolinus) III (*or* IV)
      Ser. Sulpicius (Rufus) III
      L. Lucretius Flavus (Tricipitinus) III (*cos.* 393)
      L. Aemilius (Mamercinus IV?)
      M. Trebonius

382   Sp. Papirius Crassus
      L. Papirius (Mugillanus?)
      Ser. Cornelius Maluginensis III(?)
      Q. Servilius Fidenas
      C. Sulpicius
      L. Aemilius (Mamercinus V(?))

381   M. Furius Camillus VI
      A. Postumius Regillensis
      L. Postumius (Albinus) Regillensis (II)
      L. Furius (Medullinus)
      L. Lucretius (Flavus) Tricipitinus (IV) (*cos.* 393)
      M. Fabius Ambustus

380   L. Valerius Publicola V
      P. Valerius Potitus Poplicola III
      Cn. Sergius Fidenas Coxo III
      Licinus Menenius Lanatus II
      Ti. Papirius Crassus
      Ser. Cornelius Maluginensis IV(?)
      L. Papirius Mugillanus II
      C. Sulpicius Peticus (*cos.* 364, 361, 355, 353, 351)
      L. Aemilius Mamercinus VI(?)
379   P. Manlius Capitolinus
      C., P. *or* Cn. Manlius
      L. Iulius (Iullus II)
      C. Sextilius
      M.(?) Albinius
      L. Antistius
      C. Erenucius (=Genucius?) (Diod. only)
      P. Trebonius (Diod. only)
378   Sp.(?) Furius
      Q. Servilius Fidenas II
      Licinus Menenius (Lanatus) III *or* (Diod.) C. Licinius
      P. Cloelius Siculus
      M. Horatius
      L. Geganius
377   L. Aemilius Mamercinus (*cos.* 366, 363?)
      P.(?) Valerius (Potitus Poplicola) IV
      C. Veturius (Crassus Cicurinus?)
      Ser. Sulpicius Rufus (IV) *or* Ser. Sulpicius (Praetextatus)
      L. Quinctius Cincinnatus III (*or* IV?)
      C. Quinctius Cincinnatus
376   L. Papirius (Mugillanus (III?))
      (Licinus) Menenius Lanatus IV(?)
      Ser. Cornelius (Maluginensis V(?))
      Ser. Sulpicius Praetextatus (II(?))
375-371 'Anarchy' (assigned a duration of one year in Diodorus)
370   L. Furius Medullinus (II)
      A. Manlius (Capitolinus IV (*or* V))
      Ser. Sulpicius Praetextatus III(?)
      Ser. Cornelius Maluginensis VI(?)
      (P.) Valerius Potitus Poplicola V(?)
      C. Valerius
369   Q. Servilius Fidenas III
      C. Veturius (Crassus Cicur)inus II
      A. Cornelius Cossus
      M. Cornelius Maluginensis

Q. Quinctius
M. Fabius Ambustus II
368 T. Quinctius (Cincinnatus?) Capitolinus
Ser. Cornelius Maluginensis VII(?)
Ser. Sulpicius Praetextatus IV(?)
Sp. Servilius Structus
L. Papirius Crassus
L. Veturius Crassus Cicurinus
367 A. Cornelius Cossus II
M. Cornelius Maluginensis II
M. Geganius Macerinus
P. Manlius Capitolinus II
L. Veturius Crassus Cicurinus II
P. Valerius Potitus Poplicola VI(?)

366	L. Sextius Sextinus Lateranus	L. Aemilius Mamercinus
365	L. Genucius Aventinensis	Q. Servilius Ahala
364	C. Sulpicius Peticus	C. Licinius Stolo *or* C. Licinius Calvus
363	Cn.(?) Genucius Aventinensis	L. Aemilius Mamercinus II
362	Q. Servilius Ahala II	L. Genucius Aventinensis II
361	C. Sulpicius Peticus II	(C. Licinius) Stolo *or* C. Licinius Calvus
360	C. Poetelius Libo Visolus	M. Fabius Ambustus
359	M. Popillius Laenas	Cn. Manlius Capitolinus Imperiosus
358	C.(?) Fabius Ambustus	C. Plautius Proculus
357	C. Marcius Rutilus	Cn. Manlius Capitolinus (Imperiosus II?)
356	M. Fabius Ambustus II	M. Popillius Laenas II
355	C. Sulpicius Peticus III	M. Valerius Publicola
354	M. Fabius Ambustus III	T. Quinctius (Poenus) Capitolinus *or* M. Popillius (Laenas III)
353	C. Sulpicius Peticus IV	M. Valerius Publicola II
352	P. Valerius Publicola	C. Marcius Rutilus II
351	C. Sulpicius Peticus V	T. Quinctius Poenus (Capitolinus) II(?)
350	M. Popillius Laenas III (*or* IV)	L. Cornelius Scipio
349	L. Furius Camillus	Ap. Claudius Crassus Inrigillensis

(In place of these consuls Diodorus gives: M. Aemilius and
T. Quinctius (Poenus Capitolinus III?).)

348	M. Valerius Corvus	M. Popillius Laenas IV (or V)
347	T. Manlius Imperiosus Torquatus	C. Plautius Venox
346	M. Valerius Corvus II	C. Poetelius Libo Visolus II
345	M. Fabius Dorsuo	Ser. Sulpicius Camerinus Rufus

(Diodorus puts this college before that of 348)

344	C. Marcius Rutilus III	T. Manlius (Imperiosus) Torquatus II
343	M. Valerius Corvus III	A. Cornelius Cossus Arvina
342	C. Marcius Rutilus IV	Q. Servilius Ahala III
341	C. Plautius Venox II	L. Aemilius Mamercinus
340	T. Manlius (Imperiosus) Torquatus III	P. Decius Mus
339	Ti.(?) Aemilius Mamercinus	Q. Publilius Philo
338	L. Furius Camillus	C. Maenius
337	C. Sulpicius Longus	P. Aelius Paetus
336	L. Papirius Crassus	K. Duillius
335	M. Valerius Corvus IV	M. Atilius Regulus Calenus
334	T. Veturius Calvinus	Sp. Postumius Albinus
(333	Dictator year)	
332	A. Cornelius Cossus Arvina II	Cn. Domitius Calvinus
331	M. Claudius Marcellus	C.(?) Valerius Potitus or Flaccus
330	L. Papirius Crassus II(?)	L. Plautius Venox
329	L. Aemilius Mamercinus Privernas II	C. Plautius Decianus
328	P.(?) Plautius Proculus or Decianus (or?) Venox	P. Cornelius Scapula or Scipio Barbatus
327	L. Cornelius Lentulus	Q. Publilius Philo II
326	C. Poetelius Libo (Visolus) III	L. Papirius Cursor or Mugillanus
325	L. Furius Camillus II	D. Iunius Brutus Scaeva
(324	Dictator year)	
323	C. Sulpicius Longus II	(Q. Aulius) Cerretanus or (Diod.) C. Aelius or (Livy) Q. Aemilius Cerretanus
322	Q. Fabius Maximus Rullianus	L. Fulvius Curvus
321	T. Veturius Calvinus II	Sp. Postumius Albinus II
320	Q. Publilius Philo III	L. Papirius Cursor II(?)
319	L. Papirius Cursor III or L. Papirius Mugillanus (II)	Q. Aulius Cerretanus II or (Diod.) Q. Aelius
318	M. Folius Flaccinator	L. Plautius Venox

317	C. Iunius Bubulcus Brutus	Q. Aemilius Barbula
316	Sp. Nautius Rutilus	M. Popillius Laenas
315	L. Papirius Cursor IV(?)	Q. Publilius Philo IV
314	M. Poetelius Libo	C. Sulpicius Longus III
313	L. Papirius Cursor V	C. Iunius Bubulcus Brutus II
312	M. Valerius Maximus (Corvinus?)	P. Decius Mus
311	C. Iunius Bubulcus Brutus III	Q. Aemilius Barbula II
310	Q. Fabius Maximus Rullianus II	C. Marcius Rutilus
(309	Dictator year)	
308	Q. Fabius Maximus Rullianus III	P. Decius Mus II
307	Ap. Claudius Caecus	L. Volumnius Flamma Violens
306	P. Cornelius Arvina	Q. Marcius Tremulus

(The consular colleges of 307 and 306 were both omitted in Calpurnius Piso's history; the reason is not known.)

305	L. Postumius Megellus	Ti.(?) Minucius Augurinus
		suf.: M. Fulvius Curvus Paetinus ('some sources': Livy IX.44.15)
304	P. Sulpicius Saverrio	P. Sempronius Sophus
303	L. Genucius Aventinensis	Ser. Cornelius Lentulus
302	M. Livius Denter	M. Aemilius Paullus
(301	Dictator year)	
300	M. Valerius Corvus V(?)	Q. Appuleius Pansa
299	M. Fulvius Paetinus	T. Manlius Torquatus
		suf.: M. Valerius (Corvus) VI(?)
298	L. Cornelius Scipio Barbatus	Cn. Fulvius Maximus Centumalus
297	Q. Fabius Maximus Rullianus IV	P. Decius Mus III
296	L. Volumnius (Flamma) Violens II	Ap. Claudius Caecus II
295	Q. Fabius Maximus Rullianus V	P. Decius Mus IV
294	L. Postumius Megellus II	M. Atilius Regulus
293	L. Papirius Cursor	Sp. Carvilius Maximus
292	Q. Fabius Maximus Gurges	D. Iunius Brutus Scaeva

291	L. Postumius Megellus III	C. Iunius Bubulcus Brutus
290	P. Cornelius Rufinus	(M'.) Curius Dentatus
289	M. Valerius Maximus Corvinus II	Q. Caedicius Noctua
288	Q. Marcius Tremulus II	P. Cornelius Arvina (II)
287	M. (Claudius) Marcellus	C. Nautius Rutilus
286	M. Valerius Maximus Potitus	C. Aelius Paetus
285	C. Claudius Canina	M. Aemilius Lepidus
284	C. Servilius Tucca	L. Caecilius Metellus Denter
	suf.:	M'.Curius (Dentatus II) (Polybius only)
283	P. Cornelius Dolabella	Cn. Domitius Calvinus Maximus
282	C. Fabricius Luscinus	Q. Aemilius Papus
281	L. Aemilius Barbula	Q. Marcius Philippus
280	P. Valerius Laevinus	Ti. Coruncanius
279	P. Sulpicius Saverrio	P. Decius Mus
278	C. Fabricius Luscinus II	Q. Aemilius Papus II
277	P. Cornelius Rufinus II	C. Iunius Bubulcus Brutus II
276	Q. Fabius Maximus Gurges II	C. Genucius Clepsina
275	M'. Curius Dentatus II (or III)	L. Cornelius Lentulus Caudinus
274	Ser. Cornelius Merenda	M'. Curius Dentatus III (*or* IV)
273	C. Fabius Licinus Dorso	C. Claudius Canina II
272	L. Papirius Cursor II	Sp. Carvilius Maximus II
271	K. Quinctius Claudus	L. Genucius Clepsina
270	C. Genucius Clepsina II	Cn. Cornelius Blasio
269	Q. Ogulnius Gallus	C. Fabius Pictor
268	P. Sempronius Sophus	Ap. Claudius Russus
267	M. Atilius Regulus	L. Iulius Libo
266	D. Iunius Pera	N. Fabius Pictor
265	Q. Fabius Maximus (Gurges)	L. Mamilius Vitulus
264	Ap. Claudius Caudex	M. *or* Q. Fulvius Flaccus
263	M'.Valerius Maximus Messalla	M'. Otacilius Crassus
262	L. Postumius Albinus Megellus	Q. Mamilius Vitulus
261	L. Valerius Flaccus	T. Otacilius Crassus
260	Cn. Cornelius Scipio Asina	C. Duillius
259	C. Aquillius Florus	L. Cornelius Scipio
258	A. Atilius Caiatinus *or* Calatinus	C. Sulpicius Paterculus

257	Cn. Cornelius Blasio II	C. Atilius Regulus
256	Q. Caedicius	L. Manlius Vulso Longus
suf.:	M. Atilius Regulus II	
255	M. Aemilius Paullus	Ser. Fulvius Paetinus Nobilior
254	Cn. Cornelius Scipio Asina II	A. Atilius Caiatinus *or* Calatinus II
253	Cn. Servilius Caepio	C. Sempronius Blaesus
252	C. Aurelius Cotta	P. Servilius Geminus
251	L. Caecilius Metellus	C. Furius Pacilus
250	C. Atilius Regulus II	L. Manlius Vulso (Longus) II
249	P. Claudius Pulcher	L. Iunius Pullus
248	P. Servilius Geminus II	C. Aurelius Cotta II
247	L. Caecilius Metellus II	N. Fabius Buteo
246	M. Fabius Licinus	M'. Otacilius Crassus II
245	M. Fabius Buteo	C. Atilius Bulbus
244	A. Manlius Torquatus Atticus	C. Sempronius Blaesus II
243	C. Fundanius Fundulus	C. Sulpicius Galus
242	C. Lutatius Catulus *or* (Cassiodorus) Cerconius	A. Postumius Albinus
241	Q. Lutatius Cerco *or* Catulus	A. Manlius Torquatus Atticus II
240	C. Claudius Centho	M. Sempronius Tuditanus
239	C. Mamilius Turrinus	Q. Valerius Falto
238	Ti. Sempronius Gracchus	P. Valerius Falto
237	L. Cornelius Lentulus Caudinus	Q. Fulvius Flaccus
236	C. Licinius Varus	P. Cornelius Lentulus Caudinus
235	T. Manlius Torquatus	C. Atilius Bulbus II
234	L. Postumius Albinus	Sp. Carvilius Maximus Ruga
233	Q. Fabius Maximus Verrucosus	M'. Pomponius Matho
232	M. Aemilius Lepidus	M. Publicius Malleolus
231	C. Papirius Maso	M. Pomponius Matho
230	M. Aemilius Barbula	M. Iunius Pera
229	L. Postumius Albinus II	Cn. Fulvius Centumalus
228	Q. Fabius Maximus Verrucosus II	Sp. Carvilius Maximus Ruga II
227	P. Valerius Flaccus	M. Atilius Regulus
226	L. Apustius Fullo	M. Valerius Maximus Messalla
225	C. Atilius Regulus	L. Aemilius Papus
224	T. Manlius Torquatus II	Q. Fulvius Flaccus II
223	C. Flaminius	P. Furius Philus

222	M. Claudius Marcellus	Cn. Cornelius Scipio Calvus
221	P. Cornelius Scipio Asina	M. Minucius Rufus
(?suf.:	M. Aemilius Lepidus II)	
220	M. Valerius Laevinus	(Q. Mucius) Scaevola
suf.(?):	L. Veturius Philo	C. Lutatius Catulus

CHRONOLOGICAL TABLE

Notes: (i) The dates here given for Roman republican history are based on the conventional translation of the relevant Roman consular year into B.C. terms. This may, however, be misleading since there was no fixed date for the start of the consular year until 222 B.C., when the Ides of March seems to have become the norm (altered to 1 January in 153 B.C.). As a result, for the period covered by this Table the consular year may seldom (if ever) have coincided with the calendar year of modern reckoning.

(ii) The Varronian chronological scheme employed here for those events of Roman history (columns 1 and 2) which are recorded by literary sources is defective for the period before 300 B.C. (p. 625). Such dates cannot, therefore, be synchronized with items in column 3, whose date usually derives from Greek sources.

(iii) The Table for the most part reproduces the data of the literary tradition for non-archaeological items. In consequence, the authenticity and/or date of many such items are controversial.

	ROME: INTERNAL HISTORY	ROME: EXTERNAL RELATIONS	GREECE, CARTHAGE AND THE WESTERN MEDITERRANEAN
	c. 1600–1000? Middle and late Bronze Age. Appennine and Sub-Appennine material from Sant' Omobono fill. c. 1100? Foundation of Rome according to Ennius.		
1000	c. 1000–900 Latial Culture I (Final Bronze Age). Forum tombs. Palatine tomb(?). Cremation (with hut urns) predominant. ?Earliest material from Capitol.		c. 1000–900? Final Bronze Age (Proto-Villanovan) in Etruria (and at Capua).
900	c. 900–830 Latial Culture IIA (Iron Age). Forum and Forum Augustum tombs. Progressive introduction of inhumation (fossa tombs). c. 830–770 Latial Culture IIB. Forum tombs cease: Esquiline necropolis begins. Inhumation predominant. 814/13 Foundation of Rome according to Timaeus.		c. 900–730/20 Iron Age Villanovan in Etruria (and at Capua and Pontecagnano).
800	c. 770–730 Latial Culture III. Esquiline and Quirinal tombs. Hut remains on Palatine, in Forum and Forum Boarium. Votive material at S. Maria della Vittoria (Quirinal). Euboean-Cycladic pottery, especially at Sant' Omobono. Introduction of wheel-made pottery.		814/13 Foundation of Carthage according to Timaeus. c. 775–750 Euboean colony at Pithecusae (Ischia).

	Reign of Rome / Latial Culture	Reign events	Colonies and settlements
750	753 Foundation of Rome according to Atticus and Varro. 753–715 Reign of Romulus. Creation of basic political and religious institutions. Incorporation of Sabines and joint rule with Titus Tatius.	753–715 Reign of Romulus: Conquest of Caenina, Antemnae, Crustumerium. Acquisition of Septem Pagi. Campaign against Fidenae. Colony at Fidenae.	c. 750–725 Euboean colony at Cumae. c. 750–700 Start of Phoenician settlements at Carthage, Utica, Motya, Panormus(?), in south Spain and Sardinia. 734 Chalcidian colony at Naxus. 733 Corinthian colony at Syracuse. c. 730 Cumaean–Euboean colony at Zancle. Rhegium founded from Zancle. c. 730/720–580 Orientalizing phase in Etruria (south of Appennines) and Campania.
	c. 730–630 Latial Culture IVA (early and middle orientalizing). Esquiline tombs. Child burials in Forum. Huts in Forum and Forum Boarium.		
	715–672 Reign of Numa. Creation of major public religious institutions.		c. 720 Achaean colony at Sybaris. c. 709 Achaean colony at Croton. c. 706–705 Spartan colony at Tarentum.
700			c. 700 Alphabet introduced in Central Italy. 688 Rhodian–Cretan colony at Gela. c. 680–650? Ionian colony at Siris. 679 or 673 'Locrian' colony at Epizephyrian Locri. c. 675? Cumaean(?) colony at Parthenope (Naples).
	672–640 Reign of Tullus Hostilius.	672–640 Reign of Tullus Hostilius: Absorption of Alba Longa. Establishment of Roman hegemony in Latium. Wars against Fidenae, Veii and Sabines.	

	ROME: INTERNAL HISTORY	ROME: EXTERNAL RELATIONS	GREECE, CARTHAGE AND THE WESTERN MEDITERRANEAN
650			c. 656? Fall of Bacchiads at Corinth; emigration of Demaratus.
			c. 650? Achaean colonies at Caulonia and Metapontum.
			Hoplite armour introduced in Central Italy.
			c. 650 Acquarossa houses; first phase of 'palace'.
			'Palace' building at Murlo (Poggio Civitate).
			Upsurge in Etruscan influence in Campania.
			Upsurge in population and prosperity at Carthage.
			648 Zancle establishes colony at Himera.
640	640–616 Reign of Ancus Marcius.	640–616 Reign of Ancus Marcius: Conquest of Ficana, Politorium, Tellenae, Medullia.	632 Theran colony at Cyrene.
630	c. 630–570 Latial Culture IVB (late orientalizing). Progressive reduction in grave goods. Esquiline tomb 125 (chamber tomb). Sun-dried brick and tile construction begins.	Roman colony at Ostia. Defeats of Veientes, Sabines and Volsci and capture of Fidenae and Velitrae (Dion. Hal.).	628 Colony founded at Selinus from Megara (Hyblaea).
625	c. 625 Paving of Forum (with Comitium). First structure at Regia.		c. 625–600? Sybarite colony at Posidonia. Late seventh-century Phoenician fort on Mt Sirai (Sardinia).
	c. 625–600 Open-air shrine at Sant' Omobono. Earliest pottery from pozzo near temple of Vesta. First phase of Curia Hostilia. Votive deposit on Capitol.		

Date	Rome		Wider world
600	616–578 Reign of Tarquinius Priscus. Expansion of senate and cavalry. c. 600 Earliest preserved inscription from Rome.	616–578 Reign of Tarquinius Priscus: (Re)-establishment of Roman hegemony in Latium (and Etruria (Dion. Hal.)).	c. 600 Phocaean defeat of Etrusco-Carthaginian fleet; foundation of Massalia. c. 600? Celtic infiltration into North Italy begins. c. 600–575 Second phase of Murlo 'palace'. c. 600–550 Achaean colonies overwhelm Siris.
590			598 Syracusan colony at Camarina. 590–580 Shrine to Aphrodite-Turan founded at Gravisca.
580	c. 580 Rebuilding of Regia and(?) Curia Hostilia after destruction by fire.		580 Geloan–Rhodian colony at Acragas. 580–570 (Phoenicians and) Elymians repulse Pentathlus' attempt to colonize Lilybaeum. Survivors settle on Lipara and attack Etruscan shipping. c. 580–570 (or 535) Phocaean settlement at Elea.
570	578–534 Reign of Servius Tullius. Introduction of centuriate organization and urban (and rural?) tribes. City wall. c. 575? First temple building at Sant' Omobono. First phase of Lapis Niger sanctuary.	578–534 Reign of Servius Tullius: Common Latin shrine of Diana on Aventine.	c. 570? Earliest phase of shrine of thirteen altars at Lavinium.
560			c. 565–560 Phocaean occupation of Alalia (Corsica).
550	c. 550–525 Regia destroyed by fire and rebuilt. c. 550–525? Reconstruction of Sant'Omobono sanctuary.		c. 550 Carthaginian 'Malchus', after victories in Sicily, defeated by natives of Sardinia.

650

	ROME: INTERNAL HISTORY	ROME: EXTERNAL RELATIONS	GREECE, CARTHAGE AND THE WESTERN MEDITERRANEAN
540	534–509 Reign of Tarquinius Superbus.	534–509 Reign of Tarquinius Superbus: Control of Gabii secured. Campaign against Volsci; Suessa Pometia taken. Colonies at Signia, Circeii (and Cora and Pometia?). Sabine war (Dion. Hal.). Roman 'friendship' with Massalia.	c. 540 Caeretan and Carthaginian fleets defeated by Phocaeans at Alalia. Increased Etruscan presence on Corsica.
530			531 Samian colony at Dicaearchia (Puteoli).
c. 530 Pythagoras arrives at Croton.
524 Cumaean land victory over Etrusco-Italic force.
520			c. 525–500 onwards? Etruscan expansion in Po valley.
520–510 Origin of Spina.
510	c. 510–500 Reconstruction of Regia. ?Destruction of Sant' Omobono sanctuary.
509 First year of Republic. Introduction of consulship; creation of *rex sacrorum*. Valerian laws of appeal and against attempts at kingship.
509 or 507 Dedication of Capitoline temple.
c. 504 Migration of Attus Clausus to Rome.
501 or 498 First dictator appointed.	509 Polybius' first Romano-Punic treaty.	c. 514–512 Abortive settlement of Spartan Dorieus in Tripolitania. Dorieus expelled by Carthaginians and Libyans.
511/10 Crotoniate defeat of Sybarites at R. Crathis. Sybaris destroyed.
c. 510 Abortive attempt of Dorieus to settle in Phoenician Sicily.
c. 510–500? Miltiades' conquest of Lemnos.

505

500

495

508/7 Lars Porsenna besieges (and takes?) Rome.
505 onwards Occasional conflicts with Sabines.
504 Fidenae captured.
503–2 Pometia and Cora 'desert' to Aurunci. War against Aurunci.
501 (Continuing?) Latin disaffection from Rome.

499 Praeneste 'defects' to Rome.
499 or 496 Latins defeated at Lake Regillus.
498 Colony at Fidenae.

495 Colony at Signia.
494 Colony at Velitrae.
494 onwards Successive 'wars' against Volsci and/or Aequi.

493 Cassian treaty between Rome and Latins. Corioli taken from Volsci.
492 Colony at Norba.

497? Temple of Saturn dedicated.

495 Temple of Mercury dedicated. Number of tribes now twenty-one.

494/3 First Secession; plebeian tribunate created.
493 Temple of Ceres, Liber and Libera dedicated.

504 Porsenna's army defeated at Aricia by Latins and Aristodemus of Cumae.

c. 500? (Re?)dedication of grove of Diana at Aricia by Latin League.
c. 500 or 450? Carthaginian expansion in south Spain.
c. 500–480? Thefarie Velianas dedicates shrine of Uni-Astarte at Pyrgi.
c. 500–475 Tarentine victories over Messapians, Peucetians and Iapygians.

c. 498–491 Hippocrates of Gela secures Naxos, Zancle, Leontini and Camarina and attacks Syracuse.
c. 497 Aristagoras proposes Ionian occupation of Sardinia or Myrcinus in Thrace.
495 Volsci control Cora and Pometia.
c. 494 Dionysius of Phocaea attacks Etruscan and Carthaginian shipping from north Sicily.
494/3 Anaxilas tyrant of Rhegium.
493 Volsci control Ardea. Samian fugitives seize Zancle.

Date	ROME: INTERNAL HISTORY	ROME: EXTERNAL RELATIONS	GREECE, CARTHAGE AND THE WESTERN MEDITERRANEAN
490	491 Exile of Coriolanus.		c. 490 Massalia defeats Carthaginians off Cape Nao.
			c. 490–486? Gelon of Gela campaigns against Punic Sicily; forms alliance with Theron of Acragas.
			c. 489? Anaxilas secures Zancle (renamed Messana).
		489–8 Advance of Volscians under Coriolanus on Rome.	c. 489–485? Alliance of Anaxilas with Terillus of Himera.
		487 Major engagement against Volsci? Campaign against Hernici.	
		486 Hernici defeated. Alliance with Hernici.	
485	486 Agrarian proposals of Sp. Cassius.		485 Gelon tyrant of Syracuse.
	485 Sp. Cassius executed for aiming at tyranny.		c. 484 Syracuse destroys Megara (Hyblaea) and Camarina.
	484 Temple of Castor dedicated.	484 Treaty with Tusculum.	483 Theron secures Himera. Terillus appeals to Carthage.
		483–474 First Veientan War.	
480			480 Syracusan victory over Carthaginians at Himera.
		477 Defeat of Fabii at Cremera.	c. 476 Anaxilas attacks Locri but is restrained by Hiero of Syracuse.
475		474 Forty-year truce with Veii.	474 Hiero and Cumaeans defeat 'Etruscan' fleet off Cumae. Syracusan fort on Pithecusae.
			c. 473 Iapygians defeat Tarentum (and Rhegium).

470	471 Publilian plebiscite introduces tribal basis to plebeian assembly (and an increase in the tribunate to four or five?).		*c.* 470–400? Expansion of Carthaginian power in North Africa.
465	466 Temple to Dius Fidius dedicated.	467 Colony at Antium.	
460	462 C. Terentilius Harsa proposes legislative commission.	460 Ap. Herdonius seizes Capitol. 459 Antium defects to the Volsci. 458 Cincinnatus defeats Aequi at Mt. Algidus.	458/7 Athenian alliances with Segesta and Halicyae.
455	457? Increase in plebeian tribunate to ten. 456 Icilian plebiscite *de Aventino publicando.* 454 Despatch of embassy to study Greek law codes. Lex Aternia Tarpeia on fines.		453 In response to Etruscan piracy Syracuse takes Elba and ravages coastal Etruria and Corsica.
450	452 Lex Menenia Sestia on fines. 451 First Decemvirate. 450 Second Decemvirate. Completion of Twelve Tables. Second Secession: 449 Valerio-Horatian laws on (a) appeal; (b) validity of plebiscites; (c) tribunician sacrosanctity. Duillian plebiscites on (a) appeal; (b) maintenance of tribunate. 448 Trebonian plebiscite bars co-option to tribunate. 446 Election of quaestors introduced (Tacitus).		448–446? Athenian alliances with Rhegium and Leontini.
445	445 Canuleian plebiscite to permit patrician– plebeian intermarriage.		

	ROME: INTERNAL HISTORY	ROME: EXTERNAL RELATIONS	GREECE, CARTHAGE AND THE WESTERN MEDITERRANEAN
	444 First consular tribunes appointed. 443 First censors appointed.	444 Treaty with Ardea. 442 Colony at Ardea.	444 Panhellenic colony at Thurii. c. 443 Thurii and Tarentum at war. c. 440? Athenian *strategos* Diotimus visits Naples.
440	439 Sp. Maelius killed for aiming at tyranny.	437–426 Second Veientan War. 437 (or 428 or 426) Cossus wins *spolia opima* against Veientes.	
435	435 First census held at Villa Publica. Censors limited to eighteen months in office.		433 Athens renews alliances with Leontini, Rhegium, Segesta and Halicyae. 433/2 Tarentum founds Heraclea.
430	431 Temple of Apollo dedicated. 430 Lex Papiria Iulia on fines.	431 Aequi and Volsci defeated at Algidus.	c. 430–420 'Samnites' secure domination in Campania. c. 430–400 Expansion of Lucanians in south-west Italy, including absorption of Posidonia. 427–424 Leontini secures Athenian intervention against Syracuse. Conference of Gela forces Athenian withdrawal.
425	421 Quaestors increased to four.	426 Fidenae taken. 425 Twenty-year truce with Veii.	423 'Samnites' seize control of Capua. 421/0 'Samnite' capture of Cumae.

415	414/13 Small Etruscan (and Campanian?) participation in Sicilian expedition.	418 Capture of Labici from Aequi. Colony at Labici.	
	410/9 Carthaginian expedition against Sicily in support of Segesta. Selinus and Himera sacked.	415–14 Bolae captured from Aequi.	
410	408 Hermocrates of Syracuse ravages Motya and Panormus.	413 Ferentinum captured from Volsci.	409 First plebeian quaestors.
		410 Carventum captured from Aequi and Volsci.	
		409 Carventum lost to Aequi and Volsci. Verrugo taken.	
	406 New Carthaginian expedition against Sicily; Acragas captured.	407 Verrugo lost to Volsci.	406 First six-member college of consular tribunes. Introduction of *stipendium*.
405	405 Carthage takes Gela and Camarina. Peace between Syracuse and Carthage: Acragas, Selinus and Thermae ceded to Carthage; Gela and Camarina to be tributary.	406–396 Third Veientan War.	
		406 Tarracina captured from Volsci.	
	403 Dionysius I of Syracuse takes Catane and Naxus. Submission of Leontini.	404 Artena captured from Volsci.	
400	398–392 First war of Dionysius with Carthage.	401 Colony at Velitrae.	400 First plebeian consular tribunes.
	398 Dionysius secures allegiance of Gela, Camarina, Acragas, Thermae and Eryx and takes Motya.		399 *Lectisternium* introduced.
	397 Carthaginian force restores Punic position. Lilybaeum founded. Messana destroyed. Major Punic naval victory and advance on Syracuse.		
	396 Carthage defeated and forced to withdraw from Syracuse. Dionysius restores Messana. Carthage quells North African revolt.	396 Defeat by, and victory over, Falerii and Capena. Veii captured.	396 Temple of Mater Matuta dedicated.

	ROME: INTERNAL HISTORY	ROME: EXTERNAL RELATIONS	GREECE, CARTHAGE AND THE WESTERN MEDITERRANEAN
395		395 Capena conquered. Colony at Vitellia. 394 Falerii subdued. Roman offering sent to Massaliote treasury at Delphi. 393 Colony at Circeii. Labici taken. Revolt of Satricum and Velitrae.	395–392 Dionysius secures control of Sicels.
	392 Temple of Iuno Regina dedicated.		392 Carthage forced to terms: Dionysius' control of Sicels and Tauromenium recognized.
	391 Exile of Camillus.	391 Volsinii compelled to make twenty-year truce.	
390		390 Gallic victory at Allia. Gauls capture Rome. Camillus defeats Gauls. *Hospitium publicum* established between Caere and Rome. 390/389 Latin and Hernican partnership with Rome lapses. Some Latins ally with Volsci.	390 Dionysius besieges Rhegium with Locrian aid.
		389 'Etruscans' capture Sutrium. Camillus defeats Volscian Antiates, Aequi and Etruscans; retakes Sutrium. Roman alliance with Massalia. Surviving inhabitants of Veii, Falerii and Capena given Roman citizenship.	389 Dionysius with Lucanian support defeats Thurii at Laus. Dionysius defeats Italiots at Elleporus; Caulonia and Hipponium taken.
	388 Temple of Mars dedicated.	388 Tarquinian territory invaded; Cortuosa and Contenebra taken. Campaign against Aequi.	
	387 Stellatina, Tromentina, Sabatina and Arniensis tribes created.		

385	384 (or 385) M. Manlius Capitolinus executed for aiming at tyranny. 383 Five-man commission for distribution of *ager Pomptinus* appointed.	386 Camillus defeats Volsci, Latins and Hernicans; secures Sutrium and Nepet. Five hundred Roman colonists sent to Sardinia. 385 Colony at Satricum. 383? Latin colonies at Sutrium and Nepet. 383 Lanuvium joins Volsci. 382 Latin colony at Setia. Praeneste allies with Volsci. 381 Tusculum annexed. 380 Latins defeated; surrender of Praeneste. Velitrae captured. c. 380–350? Fortified settlement at Ostia.	386 Dionysius takes Rhegium. 'Alliance' with Gauls. Peace of Antalcidas. c. 385 Dionysius establishes colony at Atria. 384 Dionysius sacks Pyrgi; establishes base on Corsica. 382?–374? Second war of Dionysius with Carthage.
380	380 Tribunician agitation over debt.		379 Dionysius takes Croton.
375	378 Renewed debt agitation. Tax levied for construction of city wall. 375 Temple of Iuno Lucina dedicated. 368 First plebeian *magister equitum*. 376–367 Agitation culminating in passage of Licinio-Sextian rogations on (i) debt; (ii) occupation of public land; (iii) admission of plebeians to consulship.	377 Tusculum recovered from Latins.	375? Syracusan victory at Cabala; Carthaginians defeat Dionysius at Cronium. 374? R. Halycus becomes boundary of Punic Sicily.
370	367 *Duoviri sacris faciundis* increased to ten and plebeians admitted to priesthood. Temple of Concord vowed. 366 Consulship re-established. First plebeian consul. Praetorship and curule aedileship instituted.	370–367 Siege and recapture of Velitrae. 367 Gallic raid: victory of Camillus.	c. 368–367 Third war of Dionysius with Carthaginians leaves Punic *epikrateia* intact.

	ROME: INTERNAL HISTORY	ROME: EXTERNAL RELATIONS	GREECE, CARTHAGE AND THE WESTERN MEDITERRANEAN
365	364 *Ludi scaenici* introduced.	362 Major engagements between Rome and Hernici. 361 Ferentinum captured from Hernici. Gallic raid and defeat at Anio. 361–354 War with Tibur. ?–354 War with Praeneste. 360 Hernici defeated. Gallic raid and defeat (Livy).	
360	358 Poetelian law against electoral malpractice. Plebiscite restricts assemblies to Rome and vicinity. Pomptina and Publilia tribes created. 357 Five per cent tax on manumissions introduced. Plebiscite limits interest rates to 8⅓ per cent. 356 First plebeian dictator.	358 Hernici defeated. Hernican alliance renewed. Latin alliance renewed. Gallic raid and defeat (Livy). 358–351 War with Tarquinii and (from 357) Falerii. 357 Gallic raid (Livy). Attack on Privernum.	c. 358/5 Dionysius II restores Rhegium and campaigns against Lucanians. 356 Bruttii secure independence from Lucanians.
355	355–3, 351, 349, 345, 343 Both consuls patrician. 352 *Quinqueviri mensarii* appointed to meet debt crisis.	354 Romano-Samnite treaty. Truce with Praeneste. Surrender of and alliance with Tibur. 353 100-year truce with Caere.	c. 355–345 Internal Syracusan weakness permits consolidation of Punic position in Sicily.

350	351 First plebeian censor.	351 Forty-year truces with Tarquinii and Falerii. 350 Gallic raid and defeat. 349 Gallic raid and defeat. 348 Second(?) Romano-Punic treaty. Satricum restored by Volsci. 346 Volsci defeated at Antium and Satricum; Satricum destroyed.	c. 345 (= Varronian 349) Greek (Syracusan?) fleet raids coast of Latium. 345/4 Syracusan Hicetas (tyrant of Leontini) employs Carthaginian aid against Dionysius II. 345 Punic capture of Entella. 344 Dionysius II surrenders to Timoleon. c. 344? Hanno's bid for tyranny at Carthage fails. 344/3 Unsuccessful blockade of Timoleon by Hicetas and Carthaginians. 343 Timoleon raids Punic *epikrateia* and 'frees' Entella. Archidamus of Sparta assists Tarentum against Lucanians and Messapians.
345	347 Measures to ease debt repayment. 344 Usurers tried and convicted. Temple of Iuno Moneta dedicated. 342 Genucian bills on (a) plebeian tenure of consulship; (b) prohibition of lending at interest; (c) prohibition of concurrent tenure of offices and of repeated tenure of an office within ten years. Army reforms after mutiny.	345 Attack on Aurunci. Sora taken from Volsci. 343 Samnites attack Sidicini and Campanians. Capua appeals to Rome. Rome expels Samnites and occupies Capua (First Samnite War). Carthaginian embassy to Rome. Roman victories at Mt. Gaurus, Saticula and Suessula.	

	ROME: INTERNAL HISTORY	ROME: EXTERNAL RELATIONS	GREECE, CARTHAGE AND THE WESTERN MEDITERRANEAN
		341 Romano-Samnite treaty renewed. Sidicini and Campanians ally with Latins and Volsci. Volscians of Privernum defeated.	341 Syracusan defeat of Punic force at Crimisus.
340		340 Latins and Campanians defeated at Veseris and Trifanum. Latin and Privernate land and *ager Falernus* confiscated. *Equites Campani* given *civitas* (*sine suffragio?*).	
	339 Publilian bills on (a) plebeian tenure of consulship; (b) *patrum auctoritas* in advance of legislative assemblies; (c) universal validity of plebiscites.	339 Further Latin defeat.	339 Peace between Timoleon and Carthage: R. Halycus remains boundary of Punic Sicily.
		338 Reduction of rebel Latin towns. Roman settlement of Latium: dissolution of Latin League and incorporation in Roman state of Lanuvium, Aricia, Nomentum and Pedum. Roman settlers sent to Velitrae. Fundi, Formiae, Capua, Suessula and Cumae given *civitas sine suffragio*. Roman colony at Antium.	338 Archidamus killed at Mandonium. 338/7 Timoleon resettles Gela and Acragas.
		337 Campaigns against Sidicini, Aurunci and Volsci.	
	336 First plebeian praetor.	336–335 Further campaigns against Sidicini. Teanum Sidicinum and Cales taken.	
335		334 Latin colony at Cales.	c. 334–331 Alexander I of Molossia responds to Tarentum's appeal, campaigns successfully against Iapygians, Lucanians, Samnites and Bruttii but loses Tarentine allegiance.

332 Maccia and Scaptia tribes created.	332 Acerrae given *civitas sine suffragio*.	331/0 Alexander killed at Pandosia, fighting Lucanians and Bruttii.
	331 Peace with Gauls.	330 Carthage aids Syracusan aristocracy.
	330 War with Privernum.	*c.* 330 Syracusan aid to Croton against Bruttii.
326 (or 313) Lex Poetelia prohibits *nexum*. Q. Publilius Philo first proconsul.	329 Roman colony at Tarracina. Surrender of Privernum. Privernum given *civitas sine suffragio*.	
c. 326? Earliest Romano-Campanian bronze coins.	328 Latin colony at Fregellae.	
	327 Rome lays siege to Naples and its Samnite garrison.	
	326 Start of Second Samnite War. Roman operations in west Samnium. Samnite garrison expelled from Naples. Alliance of Naples with Rome.	
	325 Rome attacks Vestini; Cutina and Cingilia taken. Samnites defeated at Imbrinium.	325/2 Epirote League established.
	323 Roman operations in Apulia and Samnium.	
	322 Samnites defeated.	
	321 Roman surrender at Caudine Forks.	
	320 Roman victory at Luceria. Samnites control Fregellae.	
	319 Samnite defeat. Ferentinum and Satricum captured.	
318 Oufentina and Falerna tribes created. Censors select senate.	318 Two-year truce with Samnites. Roman campaigns in Apulia and Lucania secure adhesion of Teanum Apulum and Canusium.	
	317 Forentum (Apulia) and Nerulum (Lucania) secured.	317 Molossian king Aiacides deposed.
	316 Hostilities with Samnites renewed. Rome attacks Saticula.	316/15 Agathocles becomes ruler of Syracuse.

330

325

320

315

662

ROME: INTERNAL HISTORY	ROME: EXTERNAL RELATIONS	GREECE, CARTHAGE AND THE WESTERN MEDITERRANEAN
315 c. 315? Production of Ficoroni cista.	315 Rome captures Saticula. Samnites seize Plistica, defeat Romans at Lautulae and raid south Latium. Sora defects to Samnites. 315 or 314 Latin colony at Luceria.	c. 315 Timaeus of Tauromenium, exiled by Agathocles, withdraws to Athens. 315/14? Agathocles attacks Messana; Carthaginian diplomatic intervention. Alliance of Acragas with Messana and Gela. Abortive intervention of Akrotatos of Sparta. Peace between Acragan alliance and Agathocles; Punic hegemony in W. Sicily recognized.
314 Enquiry into Campanian disaffection and electoral malpractice at Rome. Late fourth century. Redevelopment of Portus area at Rome. Temples of Portunus and Hercules Invictus founded.	314 Samnite defeat (at Tarracina?). Rome recaptures Sora and subdues Aurunci.	
312 Censorship of Ap. Claudius Caecus: initiation of Via Appia and Appian aqueduct; contentious revision of senatorial roll and reorganization of tribal registration; cult of Hercules at Ara Maxima transferred to public supervision.	313 Rome recovers Fregellae, captures Nola, Calatia and Atina, and attacks Bovianum. Latin colonies at Suessa Aurunca, Saticula and Pontiae. 312 Latin colony at Interamna on Liris. Defeat of Samnites (and Sorani?). Attack on Marrucine Pollitia.	312/11? Agathocles secures Messana and attacks Acragas. Carthaginians relieve Acragas. Agathocles invades Punic epikrateia.
311 Institution of duumviri navales. Election introduced for military tribunate.	311 'Etruscan' attack on Sutrium repulsed. Cluviae retaken; Bovianum of Pentri captured.	311/10 Carthaginians defeat Agathocles on southern Hemeras; advance on Syracuse.

310	310–307 Agathocles campaigns in North Africa. 310/309 Syracuse defeats Punic force in Anapus valley; lifts land blockade. 309/8 Acragas mobilizes south Sicily against Syracuse. 308 Attempted coup by Bomilcar at Carthage foiled. 308/7 Defeats of Acragas reestablish Syracusan control of south Sicily. 307 Agathocles makes substantial gains in Punic *epikrateia* and, with Etruscan aid, raises naval blockade of Syracuse. Agathocles defeated in North Africa. 306 Pyrrhus installed as king of the Molossians. Peace between Agathocles and Carthage: Halycus restored as frontier of Punic Sicily.	310 Roman victories in south (and central?) Etruria. Thirty-year truces with Perusia, Cortona and Arretium. Alliance with Camerinum. Rome captures Allifae. Samnites defeated at Longulae. 308 Roman victory in Umbria; surrender of Mevania; alliance with Ocriculum. Forty-year truce with Tarquinii renewed. 307 Samnites take Sora and Caiatia. Samnite defeat near Allifae. Roman campaign against Sallentini. 306 Samnites invade north Campania. Samnites defeated. Defeat of Hernici; 'rebel' Hernicans given *civitas sine suffragio*. Third(?) Romano-Punic treaty (= 'Philinus treaty'?). *c.* 306–5 Official contacts between Rome and Rhodes?	*c.* 310? First Roman silver coins. 307? Via Valeria begun.
305	305 Agathocles defeats Syracusan exiles at Torgium.	305 Rome captures Bovianum and defeats Samnites. Sora recovered. Arpinum and Cesennia taken. Subjugation of Paeligni. 304 Conclusion of Second Samnite War; Romano-Samnite treaty renewed. Aequi subjugated. Roman alliances with Marsi, Paeligni, Marrucini and Frentani.	304 Cn. Flavius, a freedman's son, becomes curule aedile, publishes *legis actiones* and calendar, and dedicates shrine of Concord. Censors reverse Ap. Claudius' tribal reorganization. Institution (or reorganization) of *transvectio equitum*.

ROME: INTERNAL HISTORY	ROME: EXTERNAL RELATIONS	GREECE, CARTHAGE AND THE WESTERN MEDITERRANEAN
	303 Latin colonies at Sora and Alba Fucens. Trebula Suffenas and Arpinum given *civitas sine suffragio*: also Frusino (or in 306).	303/2 Cleonymus of Sparta assists Tarentum against the Lucanians (and Rome). Tarentum appeals to Agathocles.
	?303/2 Roman treaty with Tarentum.	
302 Temple of Salus dedicated.	302 Popular rising at Arretium suppressed. Roman alliance with Vestini. Cleonymus of Sparta defeated; recovery of *ager Sallentinus*.	302 Cassander of Macedon deposes Pyrrhus.
300 Ogulnian plebiscite admits plebeians to enlarged pontificate and augurate. Valerian law of appeal.	300 Roman attack on Nequinum.	c. 300–296 Agathocles intervenes in South Italy, takes Corcyra, forces Bruttii into alliance but is then defeated by them.
299 Creation of Aniensis and Teretina tribes.	299 Nequinum taken. Latin colony at Narnia.	299 Gallic raid on Etruria.
	298 Latin colony at Carseoli. Roman alliance with Lucanians initiates Third Samnite War. Roman victories in Etruria and Samnium.	
	297 Apuli defeated at Malventum (Beneventum). Samnite territory ravaged; Cimetra taken.	297 Pyrrhus recovers Molossian throne.
296 Temple of Bellona vowed. Bronze statue group of Romulus and Remus set up.	296 Samnite defeat at R. Volturnus. Rome takes Murgantea, Romulea and Ferentinum. Etrusco-Samnite force defeated. Coalition of Samnites, Etruscans, Umbrians and Gauls.	

	Temples	Rome and the West	The Greek world
295	**295** Temple of Iuppiter Victor vowed.	Rome suppresses popular rising in Lucania. Roman colonies at Minturnae and Sinuessa. **295** Samnites and Gauls defeated at Sentinum.	**295** Pyrrhus marries Agathocles' daughter Lanassa and receives Corcyra. Agathocles secures Croton; alliance with Iapygians and Peucetians.
	294 Temple of Victoria dedicated. Temple of Iuppiter Stator vowed.	**294** Rusellae taken. Forty-year truce with Arretium, Cortona, Perusia. Roman successes in Samnium.	**294** Pyrrhus receives Ambracia, Acarnania, Amphilochia from Alexander V of Macedon.
	293 Temple of Fors Fortuna vowed. Temple of Quirinus dedicated.	**293** Major Samnite defeat at Aquilonia. Rome captures Duronia, Cominium, Aquilonia, Saepinum, Velia, Palumbinum and Herculaneum. Fifty-year truce with Falerii. **292** Roman defeat in Samnium. Roman campaigns in Etruria.	**293** Campaigns of Agathocles against Bruttii. Agathocles secures Hipponium.
	291 Temple of Aesculapius dedicated.	**291** (Re-)capture of Cominium and Venusia. Latin colony at Venusia. Major victory over Samnites.	*c.* 291/0 Demetrius Poliorcetes wins Corcyra from Pyrrhus, makes alliance with Agathocles and marries Lanassa.
290		**290** Defeat and submission of Samnites concludes Third Samnite War. Sabines and Praetuttii defeated and become *cives sine suffragio*; *viritim* settlements of M'. Curius Dentatus. 290–286? Latin colony at Hadria.	**289** Death of Agathocles. Pyrrhus defeats forces of Demetrius Poliorcetes in Aetolia. *c.* 288? 'Mamertines' settle in Messana. 288/7 Partition of Macedonia by Lysimachus and Pyrrhus.

666

ROME: INTERNAL HISTORY	ROME: EXTERNAL RELATIONS	GREECE, CARTHAGE AND THE WESTERN MEDITERRANEAN
c. 287 Third Secession. Hortensian law makes plebiscites binding on community. 287 or 285? Via Clodia begun.		284? Pyrrhus forced to withdraw from Macedon.
283? Via Caecilia begun.	284 (or 283) Romans defeated by Senones at Arretium. Senones subdued and territory confiscated(?). 284? Roman colony at Sena Gallica. 283 (or 282) Boii (or Senones?) and Etruscans defeated at L. Vadimon. 282 (or 281) Renewed conflict with Etruscans and Boii. Treaty with Boii. 282 or 280 Rhegium appeals to Rome; Rome installs garrison of Campanians which subsequently seizes town. 282 Rome relieves Thurii from Lucanian pressure. Tarentum attacks Roman naval squadron and forces Roman withdrawal from Thurii.	282/1 Tarentum provides Pyrrhus with naval aid for recovery of Corcyra.
c. 281 Second issue of Roman silver didrachms.	281 Rome attacks Tarentum, which appeals to Pyrrhus. 280 Pyrrhus crosses to Italy, defeats Rome at Heraclea, advances to Anagnia but withdraws to Tarentum. Roman defeat of Volsinii and Vulci. 280–279 Abortive negotiations between Pyrrhus and Rome.	281 Tarentum appeals to Pyrrhus for aid. Pyrrhus concludes treaty with Ptolemy Ceraunus of Macedon. 280/79 Hicetas of Syracuse suffers heavy defeat in attack on Carthaginian *epikrateia*. 280 or 279 Gauls invade Thrace and Macedon. Defeat and death of Ceraunus.

285

280

278 Temple of Summanus vowed.	279 Pyrrhus defeats Romans at Ausculum. Syracuse invites Pyrrhus to lead war against Carthage.	279 Thoenon replaces Hicetas as tyrant of Syracuse but is expelled. Syracuse seeks Pyrrhus' aid against Carthage.
	279/8 Fourth(?) Romano-Punic treaty.	278 Carthage blockades Syracuse. Pyrrhus crosses to Sicily. Carthaginian blockade lifted.
	278 Pyrrhus crosses to Sicily. Roman victories over Tarentines, Lucanians, Samnites and Bruttii. Roman treaty with Heraclea.	278–276 Initial successes of Pyrrhus in Sicily undermined by failure to take Lilybaeum and Greek disaffection.
	277 Roman defeat at Mt Cranita. Rome captures Croton.	
	277–276 Roman successes against Samnites, Lucanians and Bruttii.	276 Pyrrhus returns to Italy but is defeated at sea by Carthaginians.
	276 Pyrrhus returns to Italy.	275 Pyrrhus withdraws to Epirus.
275	275 Pyrrhus defeated at Malventum (Beneventum); returns to Epirus. Roman campaign against Samnites and Lucanians.	275/4 Hiero of Syracuse defeated by Mamertines of Messana.
		274 Pyrrhus recovers Macedonian throne.
	274/3? Caeretan 'revolt' suppressed; Caere given *civitas sine suffragio*.	
	273 Latin colonies at Cosa and Paestum. Embassy to Ptolemy Philadelphus.	
272 Anio Vetus aqueduct begun. Temple of Consus vowed.	272 Campaign against Samnites, Lucanians and Bruttii. Tarentum taken. Carthaginian fleet appears off Tarentum.	272 Pyrrhus killed at Argos in campaign against Antigonus Gonatas.
272? Arrival of Livius Andronicus in Rome.		
270	270 Rhegium captured; Campanians executed.	
269? First silver coins minted at Rome.	269 Campaign in Bruttium.	
	269–268 Conquest of Picentes (incorporated as *cives sine suffragio*).	
268 Temple of Tellus vowed.	268 Latin colonies at Beneventum and Ariminum. Lowland Sabines incorporated as full citizens.	

ROME: INTERNAL HISTORY	ROME: EXTERNAL RELATIONS	GREECE, CARTHAGE AND THE WESTERN MEDITERRANEAN
267 Quaestors increased to six or eight. Temple of Pales vowed.	267 Campaign against Sallentini; Brundisium taken.	
	266 Campaign against Sarsinates. Defeat of Sallentini and Messapii.	
	265–264 Rome destroys Volsinii Veteres (replaced by Volsinii Novi).	c. 265? Hiero of Syracuse defeats Mamertines of Messana at the Longanus. Carthage installs garrison at Mamertine request.
264 Temple of Vortumnus vowed.	264 Mamertines of Messana appeal to Rome for aid against Carthage. Ap. Claudius Caudex sent to assist Mamertines. Mamertines eject Punic garrison. Alliance between Carthage and Hiero of Syracuse; blockade of Messana. After two engagements Hiero and Hanno withdraw from Messana. Ap. Claudius advances on Syracuse. Latin colony at Firmum. Roman colony at Castrum Novum (and Pyrgi?).	
	263 Rome gains control of Adranum, Halaesa, Centuripa, Catane, Camarina (and Enna?). Alliance of Hiero with Rome. Latin colony at Aesernia.	
	262 Rome secures adhesion of Segesta and Halicyae. Carthage sends naval reinforcements to Sardinia.	
	262/1 Roman siege and sack of Acragas.	

265

c. 260 Death of Timaeus.

261 Carthage raids Italian coast from Sardinia.
Creation of Roman fleet.
260 Defeat and capture of Cn. Cornelius Scipio at Lipara.
Roman naval victory over Hannibal?
Roman defeat at Segesta. Naval victory of C. Duillius at Mylae. Duillius relieves Punic siege of Segesta.
259 Hamilcar Barca defeats Rome at Thermae; advances to Enna and Camarina.
L. Cornelius Scipio captures Aleria in Corsica.
258 Rome attacks Panormus; retakes Enna and Camarina.
C. Sulpicius Paterculus defeats Carthaginians off Sulci (Sardinia).
257 Roman raid on Malta and minor naval victory off Tyndaris.
256 Roman expeditionary force under Regulus defeats Carthaginian fleet at Ecnomus, lands in North Africa, defeats Carthaginians and seizes Tunis.
256/5 Abortive negotiations between Regulus and Carthage.
255 Spartan Xanthippus arrives at Carthage. Regulus defeated.
Roman fleet victorious off Cap Bon; survivors of Regulus' force rescued at Clupea.
Major Roman storm losses off Camarina.
255/4 Reconstruction of Roman fleet.

259 Temple of Tempestates vowed.

258 Temple of Spes vowed.

255–2 First plebeian *pontifex maximus* appointed.

260

255

	ROME: INTERNAL HISTORY	ROME: EXTERNAL RELATIONS	GREECE, CARTHAGE AND THE WESTERN MEDITERRANEAN
	254 Temple of Fides dedicated.	254 Romans capture Cephaloedium and Panormus. Carthage holds Drepana and sacks Acragas.	
		c. 254 Carthage punishes Numidian disaffection.	
		253 Unsuccessful Roman attack on Lilybaeum; ineffective raid on E. Tunisia; further serious storm losses.	
		252 Rome captures Thermae Himeraeae and Lipara Islands.	
		251/0 Hasdrubal defeated near Panormus.	
250		250–241 Roman siege of Lilybaeum.	
	249 *Ludi saeculares* instituted.	249 Roman naval defeat at Drepana. Naval battle off C. Pachynus followed by major Roman storm losses. Rome seizes Eryx.	
		248 Mutiny of Carthaginian mercenaries in Sicily suppressed. Alliance between Hiero and Rome renewed.	
		248–244 Carthaginian raids on Italian coast.	
		247? Hanno defeats Numidians at Hekatompylus.	
		247 Hamilcar Barca sent to Sicily and secures Mt. Heirkte.	
245		Roman colony at Alsium.	
		245 Roman colony at Fregenae.	
		244 Hamilcar captures Eryx. Latin colony at Brundisium.	

242 Institution of *praetor peregrinus*.	242 New Roman fleet blockades Drepana and Lilybaeum.	
	242/1 Punic defeat off Aegates Islands.	241 Carthaginian mercenaries at Sicca Veneria revolt and march on Tunis.
241? Via Aurelia begun.	241 End of First Punic War. Peace treaty gives Rome control of Sicily. Latin colony at Spoletium. Defeat of Falerii; destruction of Falerii Veteres.	
241 Clivus Publicius and temple of Flora built. Establishment of Floralia. Temple of Iuturna and Nymphs dedicated.		
240 Quirina and Velina tribes created.		240? Hamilcar defeats mercenaries at the Bagradas. Carthaginian mercenaries in Sardinia revolt. Mercenaries secure Utica and Hippo.
240? Livius Andronicus produces first play at Rome.		239? Mercenary force crushed at Prion. Carthaginian force captured at Tunis.
	c. 239 Acarnanian appeal to Rome: Roman embassy to Aetolia rebuffed?	239 Ennius born at Rudiae.
	239? Rome assists Carthage in Mercenary War. Rome declines mercenary invitation to occupy Sardinia.	238? Final defeat of mercenaries.
238 Temple of Flora dedicated.	238–230 Roman campaigns in Liguria.	
	238–236 Roman campaigns against Boii in north-east Italy.	
	238? Renewed mercenary appeal leads to Roman occupation of Sardinia.	237–229 Campaigns of Hamilcar Barca in Spain.
235	236–231 Roman campaigns in Corsica and Sardinia.	
235? Cn. Naevius presents first play.		
233 Temple of Honos vowed.		
232 Flaminian plebiscite for viritane distribution of *ager Gallicus and Picenus*.	231 Roman embassy to Hamilcar in Spain.	
231 Shrine of Fons dedicated.	231? Roman alliance with Saguntum.	

	ROME: INTERNAL HISTORY	ROME: EXTERNAL RELATIONS	GREECE, CARTHAGE AND THE WESTERN MEDITERRANEAN
230	c. 230 Reform of *comitia centuriata*.	230 Protest to Illyrian queen Teuta over attacks on Italian shipping. Murder of Roman envoy provokes First Illyrian War.	230 Illyrian raids on Epirus. Achaeans and Aetolians send aid to Epirus against Illyria. Epirote alliance with Teuta of Illyria.
		229–228 Roman operations in Illyria; peace concluded.	229 Achaeans and Aetolians defeated off Paxos by Illyrians.
		228 Rome admitted to Isthmian Games.	c. 228 Foundation of New Carthage.
	227 Praetors increased to four.	227 Praetors sent to govern Sicily and Sardinia (with Corsica).	
		226 'Ebro treaty' between Rome and Carthage.	
225	c. 225? Via Minucia begun.	225 Gallic invasion of Italy; Roman force defeated in Etruria; Roman victory at Telamon.	
		Roman campaign in Sardinia.	
		224 Subjugation of Boii.	
		223 Insubres defeated at R. Clusius.	
		222 Insubres defeated at Acerrae and Clastidium. Mediolanum taken.	
		221 Roman successes in Istria.	
		c. 221 Roman intervention at Saguntum.	
220	220 Construction of Via Flaminia and Circus Flaminius. Freedmen restricted to four urban tribes?	220 Roman campaign in North Italy.	

BIBLIOGRAPHY

ABBREVIATIONS

A & A *Antike und Abendland*

AAN *Atti della Accademia di Scienze morali e politiche della Società nazionale di Scienze, Lettere ed Arti di Napoli*

AAnt. Hung. *Acta Antiqua Academiae Scientiarum Hungaricae*

AArch. Hung. *Acta Archaeologica Academiae Scientiarum Hungaricae*

AATC *Atti e Memorie dell' Accademia Toscana 'La Columbaria'*

AAWW *Anzeiger der Österreichischen Akademie der Wissenschaften in Wien*, Phil.-hist. Klasse

AClass. *Acta Classica*

AÉ *L'Année Épigraphique*

AIIN *Annali dell'Istituto Italiano di Numismatica*

AION (Archeol) *Annali dell'Istituto Universitario Orientale di Napoli.* Seminario di studi del mondo classico. Sezione di archeologia e storia antica

AJA *American Journal of Archaeology*

AJAH *American Journal of Ancient History*

AJPhil. *American Journal of Philology*

ALL *Archiv für Lateinische Lexikographie und Grammatik*

Anc. Soc. *Ancient Society*

Annales (ESC) *Annales (Économie, Sociétés, Civilisations)*

ANRW *Aufstieg und Niedergang der römischen Welt*, ed. H. Temporini and W. Haase. Berlin–New York, 1972–

ANSMN *American Numismatic Society, Museum Notes*

Ant. Class. *L'Antiquité Classique*

Ant. Journ. *Antiquaries Journal*

A & R *Atene e Roma*

Arch. Class. *Archeologia Classica*

Arch. Laz. *Archeologia Laziale*

ARID *Analecta Romana Instituti Danici*

ASGP *Annali del Seminario Giuridico di Palermo*

ASNP *Annali della Scuola Normale Superiore di Pisa*, Classe di lettere e filosofia

AUB *Annales Universitatis Budapestinensis de Rolando Eötvös nominatae*

BAR *British Archaeological Reports*

BCAR *Bullettino della Commissione Archeologica Comunale in Roma*

BICS   *Bulletin of the Institute of Classical Studies* (London)

BIDR   *Bollettino dell'Istituto di Diritto romano* (Milan)

BPI   *Bullettino di Paletnologia Italiana*

Bruns   C. G. Bruns (ed.), *Fontes Iuris Romani Antiqui*. Ed. 7. Tübingen, 1909

CAH   *Cambridge Ancient History*

CEDAC   Centre d'études et de documentation archéologique de la conservation de Carthage, *Bulletin*

CIL   *Corpus Inscriptionum Latinarum*

CISA   *Contributi dell'Istituto di Storia Antica dell'Università del Sacro Cuore Milano*

C & M   *Classica et Mediaevalia*

CPhil.   *Classical Philology*

CQ   *Classical Quarterly*

CR   *Classical Review*

CRAcad. Inscr.   *Comptes Rendus de l'Académie des Inscriptions et Belles-Lettres*

CSCA   *California Studies in Classical Antiquity*

CSSH   *Comparative Studies in Society and History*

DArch.   *Dialoghi di Archeologia*

De Martino, *Diritto e società nell'antica Roma*   F. De Martino, *Diritto e società nell'antica Roma*. Rome, 1979

EHR   *English Historical Review*

Entretiens Hardt   *Entretiens sur l'antiquité classique*, Fondation Hardt. Vandoeuvres-Geneva

Gli Etruschi e Roma   *Gli Etruschi e Roma (Incontro di studio in onore di Massimo Pallottino)*. Rome, 1981

FIRA   S. Riccobono et al., *Fontes Iuris Romani Anteiustiniani*. 3 vols. Florence, 1940–3

Fraccaro, *Opuscula*   P. Fraccaro, *Opuscula*. 4 vols. Pavia, 1965–7 (I–III) and 1975 (IV)

Gelzer, *Kl. Schr.*   M. Gelzer, *Kleine Schriften*. 3 vols. Wiesbaden, 1962–4

GL   H. Keil (ed.), *Grammatici Latini*. 8 vols. 1855–1923

G & R   *Greece and Rome*

Guarino, *Le origini quiritarie*   A. Guarino, *Le origini quiritarie*. Naples, 1973

Harv. Theol. Rev.   *Harvard Theological Review*

Hommages J. Bayet   *Hommages à J. Bayet* (Collection Latomus 70). Brussels, 1964

Hommages A. Grenier   *Hommages à A. Grenier* (Collection Latomus 58). 3 vols. Brussels, 1962

Hommages M. Renard   *Hommages à M. Renard* (Collection Latomus 101–3). 3 vols. Brussels, 1969

HSCP   *Harvard Studies in Classical Philology*

HZ   *Historische Zeitschrift*

IG   *Inscriptiones Graecae*

IH   *L'Information Historique*

IJ   *The Irish Jurist*

ILLRP   A. Degrassi, *Inscriptiones Latinae Liberae Rei Publicae*. 2 vols. Ed. 2. Florence, 1965

ILS   H. Dessau, *Inscriptiones Latinae Selectae*. 3 vols. Berlin, 1892–1916

Inscr. Ital.   Inscriptiones Italiae
JA   Journal Asiatique
Jac. *FGrH*   F. Jacoby, *Die Fragmente der griechischen Historiker.* 3 parts, 11 vols.
    Berlin–Leiden, 1923–58
JDAI   Jahrbuch des Deutschen Archäologischen Instituts
JHS   Journal of Hellenic Studies
JNG   Jahrbuch für Numismatik und Geldgeschichte
JRS   Journal of Roman Studies
Latte, *Kleine Schriften*   K. Latte, *Kleine Schriften zu Religion, Recht, Literatur und
    Sprache der Griechen und Römer.* Munich, 1968
LCM   Liverpool Classical Monthly
LÉC   Les Études Classiques
LQR   Law Quarterly Review
MAAR   Memoirs of the American Academy in Rome
MAL   Memorie della Classe di Scienze morali e storiche dell' Accademia dei Lincei
*MDAI(R)   Mitteilungen des Deutschen Archäologischen Instituts (Römische
    Abteilung)*
*MÉFR(A)   Mélanges d'Archéologie et d'Histoire de l'École Française de Rome
    (Antiquité)*
*Mélanges J. Carcopino   Mélanges d'archéologie, d'épigraphie et d'histoire offerts à J.
    Carcopino.* Paris, 1966
*Mélanges J. Heurgon   Italie préromaine et la Rome républicaine: Mélanges offerts à J.
    Heurgon* (Collection de l'École Française de Rome 27). 2 vols. Rome, 1976
Mélanges A. Piganiol   Mélanges d'archéologie et d'histoire offerts à A. Piganiol. 3 vols.
    Paris, 1966
*Mélanges P. Wuilleumier   Mélanges de littérature et d'épigraphie latines, d'histoire
    ancienne et d'archéologie. Hommage à la mémoire de P. Wuilleumier* (Collection
    d'études latines, Série scientifique 35). Paris, 1980
MH   Museum Helveticum
MIL   Memorie dell'Istituto Lombardo, Accademia di Scienze e Lettere, Classe di
    Lettere, Scienze morali e storiche
Miscellanea E. Manni   Φιλίας χάριν. Miscellanea di studi classici in onore di E. Manni.
    6 vols. Rome, 1980
Momigliano, *Secondo Contributo*   A. Momigliano, *Secondo Contributo alla storia
    degli studi classici.* Rome, 1960
Momigliano, *Terzo Contributo*   A. Momigliano, *Terzo Contributo alla storia degli
    studi classici e del mondo antico.* 2 vols. Rome, 1966
Momigliano, *Quarto Contributo*   A. Momigliano, *Quarto Contributo alla storia
    degli studi classici e del mondo antico.* Rome, 1969
Momigliano, *Quinto Contributo*   A. Momigliano, *Quinto Contributo alla storia
    degli studi classici e del mondo antico.* 2 vols. Rome, 1975
Momigliano, *Sesto Contributo*   A. Momigliano, *Sesto Contributo alla storia degli
    studi classici e del mondo antico.* 2 vols. Rome, 1980
Momigliano, *Settimo Contributo*   A. Momigliano, *Settimo Contributo alla storia
    degli studi classici e del mondo antico.* Rome, 1984
MRR   T. R. S. Broughton and M. L. Patterson, *The Magistrates of the Roman
    Republic.* 3 vols. New York, 1951–2 (I–II); Atlanta, 1986 (III)

Münch. Beitr. Papyr. *Münchener Beiträge zur Papyrusforschung und antiken Rechtsgeschichte*

NAC *Numismatica e Antichità Classiche*

NRS *Nuova Rivista Storica*

NSc. *Notizie degli Scavi di Antichità*

Num. Chron. *Numismatic Chronicle*

Op. Rom. **Opuscula Romana**

PBSR *Papers of the British School at Rome*

PCPhS *Proceedings of the Cambridge Philological Society*

PP *Parola del Passato*

PPS *Proceedings of the Prehistoric Society* (London)

RAL *Rendiconti della Classe di Scienze morali, storiche e filologiche dell' Accademia dei Lincei*

RBPhil. *Revue Belge de Philologie et d'Histoire*

RE *Paulys Real-Encyclopädie der classischen Altertumswissenschaft*

RÉL *Revue des Études Latines*

Rev. Arch. *Revue Archéologique*

Rev. Ét. Anc. *Revue des Études Anciennes*

Rev. Hist. Rel. *Revue de l'Histoire des Religions*

Rev. Phil. *Revue de Philologie*

RHD *Revue d'Histoire du Droit. Tijdschrift voor Rechtsgeschiedenis*

RHDFÉ *Revue Historique de Droit Français et Étranger*

Rh. Mus. *Rheinisches Museum*

RIDA *Revue Internationale des Droits de l'Antiquité*

RIL *Rendiconti dell'Istituto Lombardo*, Classe di Lettere, Scienze morali e storiche

Riv. Fil. *Rivista di Filologia e di Istruzione Classica*

RPAA *Rendiconti della Pontificia Accademia di Archeologia*

RRC M. H. Crawford, *Roman Republican Coinage.* 2 vols. Cambridge, 1974

RSA *Rivista Storica dell' Antichità*

RSI *Rivista Storica Italiana*

RSL *Rivista di Studi Liguri*

RSO *Rivista degli Studi Orientali*

RStud. Fen. *Rivista di Studi Fenici*

S & C *Scrittura e Civiltà*

SCO *Studi Classici e Orientali*

SDHI *Studia et Documenta Historiae et Iuris*

SGDI H. Collitz and F. Bechtel, *Sammlung der griechischen Dialekt-Inschriften.* Göttingen, 1884–1915

SHAW *Sitzungsberichte der Heidelberger Akademie der Wissenschaften*, Phil.–hist. Klasse

SIG W. Dittenberger, *Sylloge Inscriptionum Graecarum.* 4 vols. Ed. 3. Leipzig, 1915–24

SMSR *Studi e Materiali di Storia delle Religioni*

SNR *Schweizerische Numismatische Rundschau*

SO *Symbolae Osloenses*

Stud. Clas. *Studii Clasice*

Stud. Etr.   *Studi Etruschi*

Stud. Rom.   *Studi Romani*

Stud. Stor.   *Studi Storici*

Studi V.Arangio-Ruiz   *Studi in onore di V. Arangio-Ruiz*. 4 vols. Naples, 1953

TAPA   *Transactions and Proceedings of the American Philological Association*

TLE   M. Pallottino, *Testimonia Linguae Etruscae*

Walbank, *Selected Papers*   F. W. Walbank, *Selected Papers. Studies in Greek and Roman History and Historiography.* Cambridge, 1985

WS   *Wiener Studien*

ZSS   *Zeitschrift der Savigny-Stiftung für Rechtsgeschichte* (Romanistische Abteilung)

BIBLIOGRAPHY

A. GENERAL AND REFERENCE WORKS

1. Alföldi, A. *Die Struktur des voretruskischen Römerstaates* (Bibliothek der klassischen Altertumswissenschaften N. F. I. Reihe, 5). Heidelberg, 1974. (Reviews by J. Poucet, *Ant. Class.* 44 (1975) 646–51; H. S. Versnel, *Bibliotheca Orientalis* 23 (1976) 391–401; R. Werner, *Gymnasium* 83 (1976) 228–38 and *HZ* 222 (1976) 146–51)
2. Alföldi, A. *Römische Frühgeschichte. Kritik und Forschung seit 1964*. Heidelberg, 1976
3. Altheim, F. *Epochen der römischen Geschichte*. 2 vols. Frankfurt, 1934–5
4. Altheim, F. *Römische Geschichte*. 2 vols. Ed. 2. Berlin, 1956
5. Altheim, F. *Untersuchungen zur römischen Geschichte*. Frankfurt, 1961
6. *Atti del convegno internazionale sulla città antica in Italia 1970* (Centro Studi e Documentazione sull'Italia Romana, Atti 3). Varese–Milan, 1971
7. *Atti del convegno internazionale sul tema: Dalla tribù allo stato; Roma 13–16 aprile 1961* (Accademia Nazionale dei Lincei: Problemi attuali di scienza e di cultura. Quad. 54). Rome, 1962
8. Badian, E. *Foreign Clientelae (264–70 B.C.)*. Oxford, 1958
9. Badian, E. 'Figuring out Roman slavery' (review-discussion of K. Hopkins, *Conquerors and Slaves* (Cambridge, 1978)), in *JRS* 72 (1982) 164–9
10. Barbagallo, C. *Il problema delle origini di Roma. Da Vico a noi*. Milan, 1926
11. Beloch, K. J. *Griechische Geschichte*. 4 vols. Ed. 2. Strasbourg, 1912–1927
12. Beloch, K. J. *Römische Geschichte bis zum Beginn der punischen Kriege*. Berlin, 1926
13. Benveniste, E. *Le vocabulaire des institutions indo-européennes*. 2 vols. Paris, 1969. Translated as:
14. Benveniste, E. *Indo-European Language and Society*. London, 1973
15. Bernardi, A. 'L'Italia antichissima e le origini di Roma', in *Nuove questioni di storia antica* 241–81. Milan, 1968
16. Bickerman, E. J. 'Some reflections on early Roman history', *Riv. Fil.* 97 (1969) 393–408
17. Bickerman, E. J. and Smith, M. *The Ancient History of Western Civilization*. New York, 1976
18. Bleicken, J. *Die Verfassung der römischen Republik*. Ed. 3. Paderborn, 1982
19. Bloch, R. *Les origines de Rome*. Ed. 5. Paris, 1967. First edition (Paris, 1959) translated in a revised and expanded version as *The Origins of Rome* (London, 1960)

20. Broughton, T. R. S. and Patterson, M. L. *The Magistrates of the Roman Republic* (Philological Monographs of the American Philological Association 15.1 and 2). 3 vols. New York, 1951–2 (I–II); Atlanta, 1986 (III)
21. Brunt, P. A. *Italian Manpower 225 B.C.–A.D. 14.* Oxford, 1971
22. Capogrossi Colognesi, L. *Storia delle istituzioni romane arcaiche.* Rome, 1978
23. Carcopino, J. *Virgile et les origines d'Ostie.* Paris, 1919
24. Catalano, P. *Populus Romanus Quirites.* Turin, 1974
25. Ciaceri, E. *Le origini di Roma.* Milan, 1937
26. Cichorius, C. *Römische Studien.* Berlin–Leipzig, 1922
27. Cornelius, F. *Untersuchungen zur frühen römischen Geschichte.* Munich, 1940
28. Cornewall Lewis, G. *An Inquiry into the Credibility of the Early Roman History.* 2 vols. London, 1855
29. *La cultura italica. Atti del convegno della Società Italiana di Glottologia Pisa 19 e 20 dicembre 1977.* Pisa, 1978
30. Dahlheim, W. *Gewalt und Herrschaft. Das provinziale Herrschaftssystem der römischen Republik.* Berlin, 1977
31. De Coulanges, N. D. F. *La cité antique.* Ed. 1. Paris, 1864. Translated as *The Ancient City* (with new foreword by A. Momigliano and S. C. Humphreys). Baltimore–London, 1980
32. De Francisci, P. 'La comunità sociale e politica romana primitiva', *SDHI* 22 (1956) 1–86
33. De Francisci, P. *Primordia Civitatis* (Pontificio Instituto Utriusque Iuris: Studia et Documenta 2). Rome, 1959
34. De Francisci, P. *Variazioni su temi di preistoria romana.* Rome, 1974
35. De Martino, F. *Storia della constituzione romana.* 5 vols. Ed. 2. Naples, 1972–5
36. De Martino, F. *Diritto e società nell'antica Roma* (Biblioteca di storia antica 6), edd. A. Dell'Agli and T. S. Vigorita. Rome, 1979
37. De Sanctis, G. *Storia dei Romani.* 4 vols. Turin, 1907–64
38. De Sanctis, G. 'La légende historique des premiers siècles de Rome', *Journal des Savants* 7 (1909) 126–32, 205–14
39. De Sanctis, G. *Roma dalle origini alla monarchia* (*Storia dei Romani* 1 in a different, posthumous version). Florence, 1980
40. Dondera, I. and Pensabene, P. (edd.). *Roma repubblicana fra il 509 e il 270 a.C.* Rome, 1982
41. Dumézil, G. *Naissance de Rome.* Ed. 6. Paris, 1944
42. Dumézil, G. *L'héritage indo-européen à Rome.* Paris, 1949
43. Dumézil, G. *L'idéologie tripartie des Indo-Européens.* Brussels, 1958
44. Erasmus, H. J. *The Origins of Rome in Historiography from Petrarch to Perizonius* (diss. Assen). Leiden, 1962
45. Errington, R. M. *The Dawn of Empire. Rome's Rise to World Power.* London, 1971
46. *Gli Etruschi e Roma (Incontro di studio in onore di Massimo Pallottino).* Rome, 1981
47. Fell, R. A. L. *Etruria and Rome.* Cambridge, 1924
48. Ferenczy, E. *From the Patrician State to the Patricio-Plebeian State.* Budapest, 1976

49. Fraccaro, P. 'La storia romana arcaica', *RIL* 85 (1952) 85–118 = id. *Opuscula* I. 1–23

50. Fraccaro, P. *Opuscula* I–III. Pavia, 1956–7

51. Fraccaro, P. 'The history of Rome in the regal period', *JRS* 47 (1957) 59–65

52. Fraser, P. M. *Ptolemaic Alexandria*. 3 vols. Oxford, 1972

53. Gagé, J. *Huit recherches sur les origines italiques et romaines*. Paris, 1950

54. Gagé, J. *Enquêtes sur les structures sociales et réligieuses de la Rome primitive*. Brussels, 1977

55. Gelzer, M. *Vom römischen Staat*. Leipzig, 1943

56. Gjerstad, E. *Early Rome*. 6 vols. Lund, 1953–73

57. Gjerstad, E. *Legends and Facts of Early Roman History* (Scripta Minora Regiae Societatis Humanarum Litterarum Lundensis 1960/61 n. 2). Lund, 1962

58. Gjerstad, E. 'Discussions concerning early Rome', *Op. Rom.* 3 (1960) 69–102

59. Gjerstad, E. 'Discussions concerning early Rome 3', *Historia* 16 (1967) 257–78

60. Guarino, A. *Le origini quiritarie*. Naples, 1973

61. Harris, W. V. *War and Imperialism in Republican Rome 327–70 B.C.* Oxford, 1979

62. Heinze, R. *Von den Ursachen der Grösse Roms*. Ed. 5. Leipzig, 1938 = id. *Vom Geist des Römertums* 9–27. Ed. 3. Darmstadt, 1960

63. Heurgon, J. *Rome et la Méditerranée occidentale jusqu'aux guerres puniques*. Paris, 1969. Translated as:

64. Heurgon, J. *The Rise of Rome to 264 B.C.* London, 1973

65. Holland, L. A. *Janus and the Bridge* (Papers and Monographs of the American Academy in Rome 21). Rome, 1961

66. Homo, L. *Primitive Italy and the Beginnings of Roman Imperialism*. London, 1927

67. Hopkins, K. *Conquerors and Slaves*. Cambridge, 1978

68. Hopkins, K. *Death and Renewal*. Cambridge, 1983

69. *The Imperialism of Mid-Republican Rome: Proceedings of a Conference held at the American Academy in Rome, Nov. 5–6, 1982* (Papers and Monographs of the American Academy in Rome 29), ed. W. V. Harris. Rome, 1984

70. Lange, L. *Römische Alterthümer*. 3 vols. Ed. 2. Berlin, 1863–76

71. *Lingue a contatto nel mondo antico. Atti del convegno della Società Italiana di Glottologia. Napoli, 12 e 13 maggio 1976*. Pisa, 1978

72. Lintott, A. W. *Violence, Civil Strife and Revolution in the Classical City, 750–330 B.C.* London, 1982

73. von Lübtow, U. *Das römische Volk, sein Staat und sein Recht*. Frankfurt, 1955

74. Madvig, J. *Die Verfassung und Verwaltung des römischen Staates*. 2 vols. Leipzig, 1881–2

75. Majak, I. L. 'Die Königszeit und die frühe römische Republik', in *Die Geschichte des Altertums im Spiegel der sowjetischen Forschung* (Erträge der Forschung 146), ed. H. Heinen, 165–98. Darmstadt, 1980

76. Mansuelli, G. A. *Les Étrusques et les commencements de Rome*. Paris, 1955

77. Marquardt, J. and Wissowa, G. *Römische Staatsverwaltung* (Handbuch der römischen Alterthümer 4–6). 3 vols. Ed. 2. Leipzig, 1881–5

78. Meier, Chr. *Res publica amissa. Eine Studie zu Verfassung und Geschichte der späten römischen Republik.* Wiesbaden, 1966
79. Meyer, Ed. *Geschichte des Altertums.* 3 vols. Ed. 2. Stuttgart, 1907–37 (vol. 1, Ed. 3. Stuttgart, 1913)
80. Meyer, Ernst. *Römischer Staat und Staatsgedanke.* Ed. 3. Zurich, 1964
81. Meyer, J. C. *Pre-Republican Rome. An Analysis of the Cultural and Chronological Relations 1000–500 B.C.* (*ARID* Suppl. 11). Odense, 1983
82. *Modes de contacts et processus de transformation dans les sociétés antiques. Actes du colloque de Cortone (24–30 mai 1981) organisé par la Scuola Normale Superiore et l'École Française de Rome, avec la collaboration du Centre de Recherches d'Histoire Ancienne de l'Université de Besançon* (Collection de l'École Française de Rome 67). Pisa–Rome, 1983
83. Momigliano, A. 'An interim report on the origins of Rome', *JRS* 53 (1963) 95–121 = id. *Terzo Contributo* 545–98
84. Momigliano, A. *Terzo contributo alla storia degli studi classici e del mondo antico* 545–698. Rome, 1966
85. Momigliano, A. *Quarto contributo alla storia degli studi classici e del mondo antico* 273–499. Rome, 1969
86. Momigliano, A. 'Le origini della repubblica romana', *RSI* 81 (1969) 5–43
87. Momigliano, A. 'The origins of the Roman republic', in *Interpretation: Theory and Practice*, ed. C. S. Singleton, 1–34. Baltimore, 1969. = id. *Quinto Contributo* 293–332
88. Momigliano, A. *Alien Wisdom.* Cambridge, 1975
89. Momigliano, A. 'New paths of classicism in the nineteenth century', *History and Theory* 21.4, Beiheft 21 (1982) 1–63
90. Mommsen, Th. *Römische Forschungen.* 2 vols. Berlin, 1864–79
91. Mommsen, Th. *Römische Staatsrecht.* 3 vols. Ed. 3. Leipzig, 1887–8
92. Mommsen, Th. *Römische Geschichte.* 4 vols. Ed. 8. Berlin, 1888–94. Translated as *The History of Rome.* 5 vols. London, 1894
93. Niebuhr, B. G. *Römische Geschichte.* 3 vols. Ed. 2. Berlin, 1828–32. Translated as:
94. Niebuhr, B. G. *History of Rome.* London, 1838
95. Ogilvie, R. M. Review of E. Gjerstad, *Legends and Facts of Early Roman History* (Lund, 1962) in *CR* N.S. 14 (1964) 85–7
96. Ogilvie, R. M. *Early Rome and the Etruscans.* Glasgow, 1976
97. *L'onomastique latine. Paris, 13–15 octobre 1975* (Colloques Internationales du C.N.R.S. n. 564). Paris, 1977
98. *Les origines de la république romaine* (*Entretiens Hardt* 13). Geneva, 1967
99. Pais, E. *Storia di Roma.* 2 vols. Turin, 1898–9 (Ed. 2 as *Storia critica di Roma durante i primi cinque secoli.* 4 vols. Rome, 1913–20)
100. Pais, E. *Ancient Legends of Roman History.* London, 1906
101. Pais, E. *Ricerche sulla storia e sul diritto pubblico di Roma.* Serie i–iv. Rome, 1915–21
102. Palmer, R. E. A. *The Archaic Community of the Romans.* Cambridge, 1970
103. Peruzzi, E. *Origini di Roma.* 2 vols. Florence–Bologna, 1970–3
104. Piganiol, A. *Essai sur les origines de Rome.* Paris, 1916
105. Piganiol, A. *Histoire de Rome.* Ed. 5. Paris, 1962
106. Piganiol, A. *Scripta varia II: Les origines et la république.* Brussels, 1973

107. von Pöhlmann, R. *Geschichte der sozialen Frage und des Sozialismus in der antiken Welt* 327–41. Ed. 3. Munich, 1925

108. Poucet, J. *Les origines de Rome: tradition et histoire* (Publications des Facultés Universitaires Saint-Louis 38). Brussels, 1985

109. *Dalla preistoria alla espansione di Roma* (especially the chapter on 'Roma arcaica' by C. Ampolo, 299–311). Milan, 1981

110. Raaflaub, K. A. (ed.). *Social Struggles in Archaic Rome*. California, 1986

111. Ridgway, D. and F. R. (edd.). *Italy before the Romans. The Iron Age, Orientalizing and Etruscan Periods*. London–New York, 1979

112. Rizzo, F. P. *Studi ellenistico-romani*. Palermo, 1974

113. *Roma arcaica e le recenti scoperte archeologiche; giornate di studio in onore di U. Coli* (Circolo Toscano di Diritto Romano e Storia del Diritto 6). Milan, 1980

114. Rotondi, G. *Leges publicae populi Romani*. Milan, 1912

115. Rubino, J. *Untersuchungen über römische Verfassung und Geschichte*. Cassel, 1839

116. Sabbatucci, D. *Il mito, il rito e la storia*. Rome, 1978

117. Schwegler, A. *Römische Geschichte*. 3 vols. Tübingen, 1853–8

118. Scullard, H. H. *The Etruscan Cities and Rome*. London, 1967

119. Scullard, H. H. *A History of the Roman World (753–146 B.C.)*. Ed. 4. London, 1980

120. Sereni, E. *Comunità rurali nell'Italia antica*. Rome, 1955

121. Serrao, F. (ed.). *Legge e società nella repubblica romana* 1. Naples, 1981

122. Serrao, F. *Diritto privato, economia e società nella storia di Roma* 1.i. Naples, 1984

123. Sherwin-White, A. N. *The Roman Citizenship*. Ed. 2. Oxford, 1973

124. Siber, H. *Römisches Verfassungsrecht in geschichtlicher Entwicklung*. Lahr, 1952

125. Starr, C. G. *The Beginnings of Imperial Rome*. Ann Arbor, 1981

126. Stier, H. E. *Roms Aufstieg zur Weltmacht und die griechische Welt*. Cologne–Opladen, 1957

127. Stuart Jones, H. 'The primitive institutions of Rome', *CAH* VII.407–35. Ed. 1. Cambridge, 1928

128. Stuart Jones, H. and Last, H. 'The early republic', *CAH* VII.436–84. Ed. 1. Cambridge, 1928

129. Tondo, S. *Profilo di storia costituzionale romana* 1. Milan, 1981

130. Toubert, P. *Les structures du Latium médiéval: le Latium méridional et la Sabine du IXe siècle à la fin du XII siècle* (Bibliothèque des Écoles Françaises d'Athènes et de Rome 221). Rome, 1973

131. Toynbee, A. J. *Hannibal's Legacy*. 2 vols. London, 1965

132. Vogt, J. (ed.). *Rom und Karthago*. Leipzig, 1942

133. Weber, M. *Wirtschaft und Gesellschaft*. Ed. 4. Tübingen, 1956. Translated as *Economy and Society: An Outline of Interpretive Sociology*. 3 vols. New York, 1968

134. Werner, R. *Der Beginn der römischen Republik*. Munich–Vienna, 1963

B. SOURCES AND EVIDENCE

a. LITERARY AND DOCUMENTARY SOURCES

See also A51, 108; D11–12, 28, 51; E101; F65–6; G122, 421, 588, 663; H20, 25, 54–5, 71, 88, 93, 119; I23; J47–8, 180, 185, 201, 270; K187, 197, 199.

1. Aalders, G. J. D. *Die Theorie der gemischten Verfassung im Altertum.* Amsterdam, 1968
2. Altheim, F. 'Diodors römische Annalen', *Rh. Mus.* N.F. 93 (1950) 267–86
3. Ampolo, C. 'La storiografia su Roma arcaica e i documenti', in *Tria corda: scritti in onore di Arnaldo Momigliano* 9–26. Como, 1983
4. Andrén, A. 'Dionysius of Halicarnassus on Roman monuments', in *Hommages à L. Herrmann* 84–104. Brussels, 1960
5. Avenarius, G. *Lukians Schrift zur Geschichtsschreibung.* Meisenheim, 1956
6. Badian, E. 'The early historians', in *Latin Historians*, ed. T. A. Dorey, 1–38. London, 1966
7. Badian, E. 'An un-serious Fabius', *LCM* 1 (1976) 97–8
8. Balsdon, J. P. V. D. 'Dionysius on Romulus, a political pamphlet?', *JRS* 61 (1971) 18–27
9. Bayet, J. *Tite-Live Histoire Romaine, Livres I–VII* (Collection Budé). 7 vols. Paris, 1954–68
10. Bloch, R. *Tite Live et les premiers siècles de Rome.* Paris, 1965
11. Bömer, F. 'Naevius und Fabius Pictor', *SO* 29 (1952) 34–53
12. Bottin, C. 'Les sources de Diodore de Sicile pour l'histoire de Pyrrhus, des successeurs d'Alexandre le Grand et d'Agathocle', *RBPhil.* 7 (1929) 1307–27
13. Bowersock, G. W. *Augustus and the Greek World* 122–39. Oxford, 1965
14. Brink, C. O. 'Tragic history and Aristotle's school', *PCPhS* N.S. 6 (1960) 14–19
15. Brink, C. O. and Walbank, F. W. 'The construction of the sixth book of Polybius', *CQ* N.S. 4 (1954) 97–122
16. Briscoe, J. 'The first decade', in *Livy*, ed. T. A. Dorey, 1–20. London, 1971
17. Briscoe, J. *A Commentary on Livy Books XXXI–XXXIII.* Oxford, 1973
18. Briscoe, J. *A Commentary on Livy Books XXXIV–XXXVII.* Oxford, 1981
19. Brunt, P. A. 'Cicero and historiography', in *Miscellanea E. Manni* (1980) I.309–40
20. Bung, P. *Q. Fabius Pictor der erste römische Annalist.* Cologne, 1950
21. Burck, E. 'Zum Rombild des Livius. Interpretationen zur zweiten Pentade', *Der altsprachlich Unterricht* 3. Reihe, 2 (1957) 34–75 = id. *Vom Menschenbild in der römischen Literatur* I.321–53. Heidelberg, 1966
22. Burck, E. *Die Erzählungskunst des T. Livius.* Ed. 2. Berlin, 1964
23. Burck, E. 'Die römische Expansion im Urteil des Livius', *ANRW* II.30.2 (1982) 1148–89
24. *The Cambridge History of Classical Literature II: Latin Literature*, edd. E. J. Kenney and W. V. Clausen. Cambridge, 1982
25. Cantarelli, L. 'Origine degli Annales Maximi', *Riv. Fil.* 26 (1898) 209–29

26. Cardauns, B. *M. Terentii Varronis Antiquitates Rerum Divinarum* (*Der Akademie der Wissenschaften und der Literatur in Mainz, Abhandlungen der Geistes- und sozialwissenschaftliche Klasse*. Einzelveröffentlichung). 2 vols. Wiesbaden, 1976

27. Cardauns, B. 'Stand und Aufgabe der Varroforschung (mit einer Bibliographie der Jahre 1935–1980)', *Der Akademie der Wissenschaften und der Literatur in Mainz. Abhandlungen der Geistes- und sozialwissenschaftliche Klasse* 1982 n. 4

28. Càssola, F. 'Diodoro e la storia romana', *ANRW* ii.30.1 (1982) 724–73

29. Castagnoli, F. 'Topografia romana e tradizione storiografica su Roma arcaica', *Arch. Class.* 25–6 (1973–4) 123–31

30. Cloud, J. D. 'Livy's source for the trial of Horatius', *LCM* 2 (1977) 205–13

31. Cloud, J. D. 'The date of Valerius Antias', *LCM* 2 (1977) 225–7

32. Cornell, T. J. 'Notes on the sources for Campanian history in the fifth century B.C.', *MH* 31 (1974) 193–208

33. Cornell, T. J. 'Etruscan historiography', *Annali della Scuola Normale Superiore di Pisa* 3 (1976) 411–40

34. Cornell, T. J. 'Alcune riflessioni sulla formazione della tradizione storiographica su Roma arcaica', in *Roma arcaica e le recenti scoperte archeologiche: giornate di studio in onore di U. Coli* (Circolo Toscano di Diritto Romano e Storia del Diritto 6) 19–34. Milan, 1980

35. Cornell, T. J. 'The formation of the historical tradition of early Rome', in *Past Perspectives: Studies in Greek and Roman Historical Writing*, edd. I. S. Moxon, J. D. Smart and A. J. Woodman, 67–86. Cambridge, 1986

36. Cornell, T. J. 'The value of the literary tradition concerning archaic Rome', in *Social Struggles in Archaic Rome*, ed. K. A. Raaflaub, 52–76. California, 1986

37. Costanzi, V. 'Diocle di Pepareto', *Studi Storici per l'Antichità Classica* 3 (1910) 74–87

38. Crake, J. E. A. 'The Annals of the Pontifex Maximus', *CPhil.* 35 (1940) 375–86

39. Dahlmann, H. *Varro und die hellenistische Sprachtheorie* (Problemata 5). Berlin, 1932

40. Dahlmann, H. 'M. Terentius Varro (Terentius 84)', *RE* Suppl. 6 (1935) 1172–277

41. Dahlmann, H. *Varro De Lingua Latina Buch VIII* (*Hermes* Einzelschriften 7). Berlin, 1940

42. Daly, L. J. 'Livy's *veritas* and the *spolia opima*. Politics and the heroics of A. Cornelius Cossus (4.19–20)', *Ancient World* 4 (1981) 49–63

43. Dessau, H. 'Livius und Augustus', *Hermes* 41 (1906) 142–51

44. Dihle, A. 'M. Verrius Flaccus (Verrius 2)', *RE* 2.Reihe, 8 (1958) 1636–45

45. Dorey, T. A. (ed.). *Livy* (Greek and Latin Studies, Classical Literature and its Influence). London, 1971

46. Dumézil, G. 'Grandeur et décadence des Étrusques chez les poètes augustéens', *Latomus* 10 (1951) 293–6

47. Eckstein, A. M. 'The perils of poetry. The Roman 'poetic tradition' on the outbreak of the First Punic War', *AJAH* 5 (1980) 174–92

48. Erb, N. *Kriegsursachen und Kriegsschuld in der ersten Pentade des T. Livius* (diss. Zurich, 1963)

49. Errington, R. M. 'The chronology of Polybius' *Histories*, Books I and II', *JRS* 57 (1967) 96–108

50. Fasce, S. 'Le guerre galliche di Livio e l'epopea mitologica celtica', *Maia* 37 (1985) 27–44

51. Ferenczy, E. 'Critique des sources de la politique extérieure romaine de 390 à 340 avant notre ère', *AAnt. Hung.* 1 (1951) 127–59

52. Ferrary, J.-L. 'L'archéologie du *De Re Publica* (2,2,4–37,63): Cicéron entre Polybe et Platon', *JRS* 74 (1984) 87–98

53. Flacelière, R. (ed.). *Plutarque Vies VI.1: Pyrrhos* (Collection Budé). Paris, 1971

54. Fraccaro, P. *Studi Varroniani. De gente populi Romani libri IV.* Padua, 1907

55. Fraenkel, E. 'Naevius (2)', *RE* Suppl. 6 (1935) 622–40

56. Frank, T. 'Two historical themes in Roman literature', *CPhil.* 21 (1926) 311–16

57. Frier, B. W. *Libri annales pontificum maximorum. The Origins of the Annalistic Tradition* (Papers and Monographs of the American Academy in Rome 27). Rome, 1979

58. von Fritz, K. *The Theory of the Mixed Constitution in Antiquity.* New York, 1954

59. Gabba, E. (ed.). *Appiani Bellorum Civilium Liber Primus* (Introduction, text and commentary). Florence, 1958

60. Gabba, E. 'Studi su Dionigi di Alicarnasso, I: La costituzione di Romolo', *Athenaeum* N.S. 38 (1960) 175–252

61. Gabba, E. 'Studi su Dionigi da Halicarnasso, II. Il regno di Servio Tullio', *Athenaeum* N.S. 39 (1961) 98–121

62. Gabba, E. 'Studi su Dionigi d'Alicarnasso, III: La proposta di legge agraria di Spurio Cassio', *Athenaeum* N.S. 42 (1964) 29–41

63. Gabba, E. 'Considerazioni sulla tradizione letteraria sulle origini della repubblica', in *Les origines de la république romaine* (*Entretiens Hardt* 13) 133–74. Geneva, 1967

64. Gabba, E. 'Dionigi e la "Storia di Roma arcaica"', in *Association G. Budé. Actes du IXe Congrès (Rome, 13–18 avril 1973)* I.218–29. Paris, 1975. =

65. Gabba, E. 'La "storia romana arcaica" di Dionigi di Alicarnasso', *ANRW* II.30.1 (1982) 799–816

66. Gelzer, M. 'Römische Politik bei Fabius Pictor', *Hermes* 68 (1933) 129–66 = id. *Kleine Schriften* III.51–92

67. Gelzer, M. 'Der Anfang römischer Geschichtsschreibung', *Hermes* 69 (1934) 46–55 = id. *Kleine Schriften* III.93–103

68. Gelzer, M. 'Nochmals über den Anfang der römischen Geschichtsschreibung', *Hermes* 82 (1954) 342–48 = id. *Kleine Schriften* III.104–10

69. Gentili, B. 'Storiografia greca e storiografia romana arcaica', *Studi Urbinati di Storia, Filosofia e Letteratura* 49 (1975) 13–38

70. Gentili, B. and Cerni, G. *Le teorie del discorso storico nel pensiero greco e la*

storiografia romana arcaica (Università di Urbino. Istituto di Filologia Classica. Filologia e Critica 15). Rome, 1975

71. Gutberlet, D. *Die erste Dekade des Livius als Quelle zur gracchischen und sullanischen Zeit* (Beiträge zur Altertumswissenschaft 4). Hildesheim, 1985

72. Hanell, K. 'Zu Problematik der älteren römischen Geschichtsschreibung', in *Histoire et historiens dans l'antiquité (Entretiens Hardt 4)* 147–70. Geneva, 1956

73. Henderson, M. I. Review of H. H. Scullard, *Roman Politics 200–150 B.C.* (Oxford, 1951) in *JRS* 42 (1952) 114–6

74. Henderson, M. I. Review of P. G. Walsh, *Livy: His Historical Aims and Methods* (Cambridge, 1961) in *JRS* 52 (1962) 277–8

75. Heurgon, J. 'L. Cincius e la loi du *clavus annalis*', *Athenaeum* N.S. 42 (1964) 432–7

76. Hill, H. 'Dionysius of Halicarnassus and the origins of Rome', *JRS* 51 (1961) 88–93

77. Hoch, H. *Die Darstellung der politischen Sendung Roms bei Livius.* Frankfurt, 1951

78. Hornblower, J. *Hieronymus of Cardia.* Oxford, 1981

79. Horsfall, N. 'Q. Fabius C. filius Pictor; some new evidence', *LCM* 1 (1976) 18

80. Jacoby, F. *Die Fragmente der griechischen Historiker.* 3 parts, 11 vols. Berlin–Leiden, 1923–58

81. Jocelyn, H. D. 'The poems of Quintus Ennius', *ANRW* 1.2 (1972) 987–1026

82. Jocelyn, H. D. 'Varro's *Antiquitates rerum divinarum* and religious affairs in the late Roman republic', *Bulletin of the John Rylands Library* 85 (1982) 148–205

83. Jones, C. P. *Plutarch and Rome.* Oxford, 1971

84. Keil, H. *Commentarius in Varronis rerum rusticarum libros tres.* Leipzig, 1891

85. Kierdorf, W. 'Catos Origines und die Anfänge der römischen Geschichtsschreibung', *Chiron* 10 (1980) 204–24

86. Klein, R. *Königtum und Königszeit bei Cicero* (diss. Erlangen, 1962)

87. Klotz, A. 'Diodors römische Annalen', *Rh. Mus.* N.F. 86 (1937) 206–24

88. Klotz, A. 'Zu den Quellen der Archaiologia des Dionysios von Halicarnassos', *Rh. Mus.* N.F. 87 (1938) 32–50

89. Klotz, A. 'Der Annalist Q. Claudius Quadrigarius', *Rh. Mus.* N.F. 91 (1942) 268–85

90. Klotz, A. *Livius und seine Vorgänger* (Neue Wege zur Antike. 2. Reihe, Interpretationen. Heft 9–11). 3 vols. Amsterdam, 1964

91. Kornemann, E. *Der Priesterkodex in der Regia und die Entstehung der altrömischen Pseudogeschichte.* Tübingen, 1912

92. La Bua, V. *Filino, Polibio, Sileno, Diodoro, il problema delle fonti dalla morte di Agatocle alla guerra mercenaria in Africa.* Palermo, 1966

93. Laqueur, R. 'Timagenes (2)', *RE* 2. Reihe, 6 (1937) 1063–71

94. Laqueur, R. 'Timaios (3)', *RE* 2. Reihe, 6 (1937) 1076–1203

95. Latte, K. 'Der Historiker L. Calpurnius Frugi', *Sitzungsberichte der*

Deutschen Akademie der Wissenschaften zu Berlin. Klasse für Sprache, Literatur und Kunst 1960 n. 7 = id. *Kleine Schriften* 837–47

96. Lefèvre, E. 'Argumentation und Struktur der moralischen Geschichtsschreibung der Römer am Beispiel von Livius' Darstellung des Beginns des römischen Freistaats (2,1–2,15)', in *Livius, Werk und Rezeption. Festschrift für E. Burck zum 80.Geburtstag*, edd. E. Lefèvre and E. Olshausen, 31–57. Munich, 1983

97. Lipovsky, J. *A Historiographical Study of Livy: Books VI–X*. New York, 1981

98. Luce, T. J. 'Design and structure in Livy: 5.32–55', *TAPA* 102 (1971) 265–302

99. Luce, T. J. *Livy. The Composition of his History*. Princeton, 1977

100. McDonald, A. H. 'Theme and style in Roman historiography', *JRS* 65 (1975) 1–10

101. Manganaro, G. 'Una biblioteca storica nel ginnasio di Tauromenion e il P. Oxy. 1241', *PP* 29 (1974) 389–409

102. Manganaro, G. 'Una biblioteca storica nel ginnasio a Tauromenion nel II sec. a.C.', in A. Alföldi, *Römische Frühgeschichte: Kritik und Forschung seit 1964*, 83–96. Heidelberg, 1976

103. Martin, P. M. 'Mutation idéologique dans les figures de héros républicains entre 362 et 279 av. J.C.', *RÉL* 60 (1982) 139–52

104. Mattingly, H. B. 'Q. Fabius Pictor, father of Roman history', *LCM* 1 (1976) 3–7

105. Mattingly, H. B. 'Polybius' use of Fabius Pictor', *LCM* 7.2 (1982) 20

106. Mazzarino, S. *Il pensiero storico classico*. 2 vols. Bari, 1966

107. Meister, K. *Historische Kritik bei Polybios* (Palingenesia 9). Berlin, 1975

108. Mensching, E. 'Livius, Cossus und Augustus', *MH* 24 (1967) 12–32

109. Meyer, Ed. 'Untersuchungen über Diodors römische Geschichte', *Rh. Mus.* N.F. 37 (1882) 610–27

110. Mitchell, R. E. 'The historical and historiographical prominence of the Pyrrhic War', in *The Craft of the Ancient Historian: Essays in Honor of Chester G. Starr*, edd. J. W. Eadie and J. Ober, 303–30. Lanham, 1985

111. Momigliano, A. 'Perizonius, Niebuhr and the character of early Roman tradition', *JRS* 47 (1957) 104–14 = id. *Secondo Contributo* 69–88 = id. *Essays in Ancient and Modern Historiography* 231–51. Oxford, 1977

112. Momigliano, A. 'Some observations on the *Origo gentis Romanae*', *JRS* 48 (1958) 56–73 = id. *Secondo Contributo* 145–76

113. Momigliano, A. 'Atene nel III secolo a.C. e la scoperta di Roma nelle storie di Timeo di Tauromenio', *RSI* 71 (1959) 529–56 = id. *Terzo Contributo* 23–53

114. Momigliano, A. 'Linee per una valutazione di Fabio Pittore', *RAL* ser. 8.15 (1960) 310–20 = id. *Terzo Contributo* 55–68

115. Momigliano, A. 'Timeo, Fabio Pittore e il primo censimento di Servio Tullio', in *Miscellanea di studi alessandrini in memoria di Augusto Rostagni* 180–87. Turin, 1963 = id. *Terzo Contributo* 649–56

116. Momigliano, A. 'Did Fabius Pictor lie?', *New York Review of Books* 16 Sept.

1965, 19–22 = id. *Essays in Ancient and Modern Historiography* 99–105. Oxford, 1977

117. Momigliano, A. *Essays in Ancient and Modern Historiography*. Oxford, 1977
118. Münzer, F. 'Q. Fabius Pictor (Fabius (126))', *RE* 6 (1909) 1836–41
119. Musti, D. *Tendenze nella storiografia romana e greca su Roma arcaica. Studi su Livio e Dionigi di Alicarnasso* (Quaderni Urbinati di Cultura Classica 10). Urbino, 1970
120. Musti, D. 'Polibio negli studi dell'ultimo ventennio (1950–1970)', *ANRW* 1.2 (1972) 1114–81
121. Musti, D. 'Etruschi e Greci nella rappresentazione dionisiana delle origini di Roma', in *Gli Etruschi e Roma* 23–44
122. Nederlof, A. B. *Plutarchus' Leven van Pyrrhus. Historische Commentaar* (diss. Leiden, 1940)
123. Nicolet, C. 'Polybe et les institutions romaines', in *Polybe* (*Entretiens Hardt* 20) 209–58. Geneva, 1974
124. Nitzsch, K. W. *Die römische Annalistik von ihren ersten Anfängen bis auf Valerius Antias*. Berlin, 1873
125. Noè, E. 'Il tentativo di Appio Erdonio nella narrazione di Dionigi', *RAL* ser. 8.32 (1978) 641–65
126. Noè, E. 'Ricerche su Dionigi d'Alicarnasso; La prima stasis a Roma e l'episodio di Coriolano', in *Ricerche di storiografia antica I: Ricerche di storiografia greca di età romana* (Biblioteca di Studi Antichi 22) 21–116. Pisa, 1979
127. Oakley, S. P. *A Commentary on Livy Book IX, 1–28* (Ph.D. thesis. Cambridge, 1984)
128. Ogilvie, R. M. 'Livy, Licinius Macer and the *libri lintei*', *JRS* 48 (1958) 40–6
129. Ogilvie, R. M. *A Commentary on Livy Books 1–5*. Oxford, 1965
130. Pabst, W. *Quellenkritische Studien zur inneren Geschichte der älteren Zeit bei T. Livius und Dionys von Halikarnass* (diss. Innsbruck, 1969)
131. Pédech, P. *La méthode historique de Polybe* (Collection d'Études Anciennes). Paris, 1964
132. Pelling, C. B. R. 'Plutarch's method of work in the Roman lives', *JHS* 99 (1979) 74–96
133. Pelling, C. B. R. 'Plutarch's adaptation of his source material', *JHS* 100 (1980) 127–39
134. Perl, G. 'Der Anfang der römischen Geschichtsschreibung', *Forschungen und Fortschritte* 38 (1964) 185–9, 213–18
135. Peter, H. *Historicorum Romanorum Reliquiae* 1. Ed. 2. Leipzig, 1914
136. Petzold, K.-E. *Studien zur Methode des Polybios und zu ihrer historischen Auswertung*. Munich, 1969
137. Petzold, K.-E. 'Die Entstehung des römischen Weltreiches im Spiegel der Historiographie', in *Livius: Werk und Rezeption. Festschrift für E. Burck* 241–63. Munich, 1983
138. Phillips, J. E. 'Current research in Livy's first decade, 1975–9', *ANRW* II.30.2 (1982) 998–1057

139. Pinsent, J. 'Antiquarianism, fiction and history in the first decade of Livy', *The Classical Journal* 55 (1959) 81–5

140. Pinsent, J. 'Cincius, Fabius and the Otacilii', *Phoenix* 18 (1964) 18–29

141. Plathner, H.-G. *Die Schlachtschilderungen bei Livius.* Breslau, 1934

142. Poma, G. 'La valutazione del Decemvirato nel *De republica* di Cicerone', *RSA* 6–7 (1976–7) 129–46

143. Pöschl, V. *Römischer Staat und griechischer Staatsdenken bei Cicero: Untersuchungen zu Ciceros Schrift De republica.* Berlin, 1936

144. Poucet, J. 'Le premier livre de Tite-Live et l'histoire', *LÉC* 43 (1975) 327–49

145. Puccioni, G. (ed.). *Aureli Victoris Origo gentis Romanae.* Florence, 1958

146. Radke, G. 'Die Überlieferung archaischer lateinischer Texte in der Antike', *Romanitas* 11 (1972) 189–264

147. Rambaud, M. *Cicéron et l'histoire romaine* (Collection d'Études Latines: Série Scientifique 28). Paris, 1953

148. Rawson, E. 'Prodigy lists and the use of the Annales Maximi', *CQ* N.S. 21 (1971) 158–69

149. Rawson, E. 'Cicero the historian and Cicero the antiquarian', *JRS* 62 (1972) 33–45

150. Rawson, E. 'The first Latin annalists', *Latomus* 35 (1976) 689–717

151. Reitzenstein, R. *Verrianische Forschungen.* Breslau, 1887

152. Richard, J.-C. (ed.). *Ps. Aurelius Victor, Les origines du peuple romain* (Collection Budé). Paris, 1983

153. Roberts, L. G. 'The Gallic fire and Roman archives', *MAAR* 2 (1918) 55–65

154. Russell, D. A. F. M. 'Plutarch's life of Coriolanus', *JRS* 53 (1963) 21–8

155. Russell, D. A. F. M. *Plutarch.* London, 1973

156. Saulnier, C. 'L'histoire militaire de la Rome archaïque chez Denys d'Halicarnasse', *Bulletin de l'Association G. Budé* 1972, 283–95

157. Schaeublin, C. 'Sempronius Asellio fr. 2', *Würzburger Jahrbücher für die Altertumswissenschaft* N.F. 9 (1983) 147–55

158. Scheller, P. *De hellenistica historiae conscribendae arte* (diss. Leipzig, 1911)

159. Schroder, W. A. *M. Porcius Cato: Das erste Buch des Origines* (Beiträge zur klassischen Philologie 41). Meisenheim, 1971

160. Schultze, C. *Dionysius of Halicarnassus as an Historian: An Investigation of his Aims and Methods in the Antiquitates Romanae* (D.Phil. thesis. Oxford, 1980)

161. Schultze, C. 'Dionysius of Halicarnassus and his audience', in *Past Perspectives: Studies in Greek and Roman Historical Writing*, edd. I. S. Moxon, J. D. Smart and A. J. Woodman, 121–42. Cambridge, 1986

162. Schwartz, E. 'Diodorus', *RE* 5 (1905) 663–704

163. Schwartz, E. 'Dionysius von Halikarnassos', *RE* 5 (1905) 934–61

164. Seemüller, J. *Die Doubletten in der ersten Dekade des Livius* (diss. Neuberg, 1904)

165. Sigwart, G. 'Römische Fasten und Annalen bei Diodor', *Klio* 6 (1906) 269–86, 341–79

166. Skutsch, O. 'Readings and interpretations in the *Annals*', in *Ennius* (*Entretiens Hardt* 17) 3–29. Geneva, 1971

167. Skutsch, O. 'Notes on Ennius', *BICS* 21 (1974) 75–80

168. Skutsch, O. 'Notes on Ennius III', *BICS* 24 (1977) 1–6

169. Skutsch, O. *The Annals of Q. Ennius*. Oxford, 1985

170. Solodov, J. B. 'Livy and the story of Horatius, 1, 24–26', *TAPA* 109 (1979) 251–68

171. Soltau, W. *Die Anfänge der römischen Geschichtsschreibung*. Leipzig, 1909

172. Strzelecki, W. *Quaestiones Verrianae*. Warsaw, 1932

173. Syme, R. 'Livy and Augustus', *HSCP* 64 (1959) 27–87 = id. *Roman Papers* 1.400–54. Oxford, 1979

174. Timpe, D. 'Fabius Pictor und die Anfänge der römischen Historiographie', *ANRW* 1.2 (1972) 928–69

175. Timpe, D. 'Erwägungen zur jüngeren Annalistik', *A & A* 25 (1979) 97–119

176. Tomasini, O. 'Per l'individuazione di fonti storiografiche anonime latine in Dionigi d'Alicarnasso', *Annali della Facoltà di Lettere e Filosofia, Trieste* 1 (1964–5) 153–74

177. Torelli, Marina R. *Rerum Romanarum fontes ab anno ccxcii ad annum cclxv a.Ch.n.* Pisa, 1978

178. von Ungern-Sternberg, J. 'The formation of the "annalistic tradition": the example of the Decemvirate', in *Social Struggles in Archaic Rome*, ed. K. A. Raaflaub. California, 1986

179. *Varron* (*Entretiens Hardt* 9). Geneva, 1963

180. Verdin, H. 'La fonction de l'histoire selon Denys d'Halicarnasse', *Anc. Soc.* 5 (1974) 289–307

181. Walbank, F. W. 'Polybius, Philinus and the First Punic War', *CQ* 39 (1945) 1–18 = id. *Selected Papers* 77–98

182. Walbank, F. W. *A Historical Commentary on Polybius*. 3 vols. Oxford, 1957–79

183. Walbank, F. W. 'History and tragedy', *Historia* 9 (1960) 216–34 = id. *Selected Papers* 224–41

184. Walbank, F. W. 'The historians of Greek Sicily', *Kokalos* 14–15 (1968–9) 476–98

185. Walbank, F. W. *Polybius* (Sather Classical Lectures 42). Berkeley–Los Angeles, 1972

186. Walbank, F. W. *Selected Papers. Studies in Greek and Roman History and Historiography*. Cambridge, 1985

187. Walsh, P. G. *Livy; His Historical Aims and Methods*. Cambridge, 1961

188. Walsh, P. G. *Livy* (*G & R* New Surveys in the Classics 8). Oxford, 1974

189. Wikén, E. *Die Kunde der Hellenen von dem Land und den Völkern der Apenninenhalbinsel bis 300 v.Chr.* Lund, 1937

190. Wiseman, T. P. *Clio's Cosmetics. Three Studies in Greco-Roman Literature*. Leicester, 1979

191. Wiseman, T. P. 'The credibility of the Roman annalists', *LCM* 8 (1983) 20–2

192. Wiseman, T. P. 'Monuments and the Roman annalists', in *Past Perspectives:*

Studies in Greek and Roman Historical Writing, edd. I. S. Moxon, J. D. Smart and A. J. Woodman, 87–100. Cambridge, 1986

193. Wolski, J. 'La prise de Rome par les Celtes et la formation de l'annalistique romaine', *Historia* 5 (1956) 24–52

194. Zimmerer, M. *Der Annalist Qu. Claudius Quadrigarius*. Munich, 1937

b. EPIGRAPHIC AND NUMISMATIC EVIDENCE. THE DEVELOPMENT
OF ROMAN COINAGE

See also (J)c on Pyrrhus and K(a) on Carthage and the items listed in the Abbreviations as *AÉ, CIL, IG, ILLRP, ILS, Inscr.Ital., SGDI, SIG, TLE*. See further B115, 351, 373; D7; G35, 43, 45, 80, 114, 120, 151, 388, 419; H23; J129.

195. Alföldi, A. 'Timaios' Bericht über die Anfänge der Geldprägung in Rom', *MDAI(R)* 68 (1961) 64–79

196. Ampolo, C. '*Servius rex primus signavit aes*', *PP* 29 (1974) 382–8

197. Bloch, R. 'À propos des inscriptions latines les plus anciennes', in *Acta of the Fifth International Congress of Greek and Latin Epigraphy 1967* 175–81. Cambridge, 1971

198. Bloch, R. 'À propos de l'inscription latine archaïque trouvée à Satricum', *Latomus* 42 (1983) 362–71

199. Breglia, L. 'A proposito dell' 'aes signatum'', *AIIN* 12–14 (1965–7) 269–75

200. Breglia, L. *Numismatica antica: storia e metodologia*. Ed. 2. Milan, 1967

201. Bremmer, J. 'The *suodales* of Poplios Valesios', *Zeitschrift für Papyrologie und Epigraphik* 47 (1982) 133–47

202. Burnett, A. 'The coinages of Rome and Magna Graecia in the late fourth and early third centuries B.C.', *SNR* 56 (1977) 92–121

203. Burnett, A. 'The first Roman silver coins', *NAC* 7 (1978) 121–42

204. Burnett, A. 'The second issue of Roman didrachms', *NAC* 9 (1980) 169–74

205. Colonna, G. 'Una nuova iscrizione etrusca del VII secolo', *MÉFR* 82 (1970) 637–72

206. Colonna, G. 'Ancora sulla fibula prenestina', *Epigraphica* 41 (1979) 119–30

207. Colonna, G. 'Duenos', *Stud. Etr.* 47 (1979) 163–72

208. Colonna, G. '"Graeco more bibere"; l'iscrizione della tomba 115 dell'Osteria dell'Osa', *Arch. Laz.* 3 (1980) 51–5

209. Cornell, T. J. Review-discussion of M. Torelli, *Elogia Tarquiniensia* (Florence, 1975), in *JRS* 68 (1978) 167–73

210. Crawford, M. H. *Roman Republican Coinage*. 2 vols. Cambridge, 1974

211. Crawford, M. H. *La moneta in Grecia e Roma*. Rome–Bari, 1982

212. Crawford, M. H. *Coinage and Money under the Roman Republic: Italy and the Mediterranean Economy*. London, 1985

213. Degrassi, A. *Inscriptiones Latinae Liberae Rei Publicae* (Biblioteca di studi superiori 23 & 40). 2 vols. Ed. 2. Florence, 1965

214. De Simone, C. 'L'iscrizione latina arcaica di Satricum. Problemi

metodologici ed ermeneutici', *Giornale Italiano di Filologia* 33 (1981) 25–56

215. Dumézil, G. 'Remarques sur la stèle archaïque du Forum', in *Hommages J. Bayet* (1964) 172–9

216. Dumézil, G. 'La deuxième ligne de l'inscription de Duenos', in *Hommages M. Renard* (1969) II.244–55

217. Dümmler, F. 'Iscrizione della fibula prenestina', *MDAI(R)* 2 (1887) 40–3

218. Durante, M. 'L'iscrizione di Dueno', *Incontri Linguistici* 7 (1982) 31–5

219. Ernout, A. *Recueil de textes latins archaïques.* Ed. 2. Paris, 1957

220. Franke, P. R. *Die antiken Münzen von Epirus I.* Wiesbaden, 1961

221. Gabrici, E. *La monetazione del bronzo nella Sicilia antica.* Palermo, 1927

222. Gjerstad, E. 'The Duenos vase', in *Septentrionalia et Orientalia. Studia B. Karlgren dedicata* 133–43. Stockholm, 1959

223. Gordon, A. E. 'Notes on the Duenos-vase inscription in Berlin', *CSCA* 8 (1975) 53–72

224. Gordon, A. E. *The Inscribed Fibula Praenestina: Problems of Authenticity* (University of California Publications: Classical Studies 16). Berkeley– Los Angeles–London, 1975

225. Guarducci, M. 'L'epigrafe *REX* nella regia del Foro Romano', in *Akten des VI. Internationalen Kongresses für griechische und lateinische Epigraphik. München, 1972* (Vestigia 17) 381–4. Munich, 1973

226. Guarducci, M. 'La cosidetta Fibula Praenestina', *MAL* ser. 8.24 (1980) 413–574

227. Guarducci, M. 'L'epigrafe arcaica di Satricum e Publio Valerio', *RAL* ser. 8.35 (1981) 479–89

228. Guarducci, M. 'La cosidetta Fibula Praenestina: elementi nuovi', *MAL* ser. 8.28 (1984) 127–77

229. Hamp, E. P. 'Is the fibula a fake?', *AJPhil.* 102 (1981) 151–4

230. Happ, H. 'Zwei lateinische Graffiti archaischer Zeit aus Rom', *Glotta* 46 (1968) 121–36

231. Happ, H. 'Nochmals zum *rex*-graffito aus Rom', *Glotta* 48 (1970) 248–53

232. Helbig, W. 'Sopra una fibula d'oro trovata presso Palestrina', *MDAI(R)* 2 (1887) 37–9

233. Heurgon, J. 'L'*elogium* d'un magistrat étrusque découvert à Tarquinia', *MÉFR* 63 (1951) 119–37

234. Heurgon, J. 'The inscriptions of Pyrgi', *JRS* 56 (1966) 1–15

235. Heurgon, J. 'Recherches sur la fibule d'or inscrite de Chiusi: la plus ancienne mention épigraphique du nom des Étrusques', *MÉFR* 83 (1971) 9–28

236. *Le iscrizioni prelatine in Italia. Colloquio Roma, 14–15 marzo 1977* (Atti dei Convegni Lincei 39). Rome, 1979

237. Karo, G. Review of D. Randall-MacIver, *Villanovans and Early Etruscans* (Oxford, 1924) in *Wiener Prähistorische Zeitschrift* 12 (1925) 143–7

238. Krummery, H. 'Die Fibula Praenestina als Fälschung erwiesen?', *Klio* 64 (1982) 583–9

239. Lazzeroni, R. 'Note sulla fibula prenestina', *SCO* 31 (1981) 227–32

240. Lo Schiavo, F. 'La "fibula prenestina": considerazioni tipologiche', *BPI* N.S. 24 (1975–80) 287–306

241. Mattingly, H. 'Coinage and the Roman state' (review-discussion of M. H. Crawford, *Roman Republican Coinage* (Cambridge, 1974)), in *Num. Chron.* 17 (1977) 199–215

242. Mitchell, R. E. 'The fourth-century origin of Roman didrachms', *ANSMN* 15 (1969) 41–71

243. Moretti, L. 'Chio e la lupa capitolina', *Riv. Fil.* 108 (1980) 33–54

244. Nenci, G. 'Considerazioni sulla storia della monetazione in Plinio (*N.H.* 33.42–7)', *Athenaeum* N.S. 46 (1968) 3–36

245. Pallottino, M. 'Rivista di epigrafia etrusca. 1.Veio, n. 1', *Stud. Etr.* 13 (1939) 455–7

246. Pallottino, M. 'L'ermeneutica etrusca fra due documenti-chiave', *Stud. Etr.* 37 (1969) 79–91 = id. *Saggi di Antichità* 11.533–44. Rome, 1979

247. Palmer, R. E. A. *The King and the Comitium. A Study of Rome's Oldest Public Document* (*Historia* Einzelschriften 11). Wiesbaden, 1969

248. Pfister, R. 'Zur gefälschten Maniosinschrift', *Glotta* 61 (1983) 105–18

249. Piccozzi, V. 'Q. Ogulnio C. Fabio coss.', *NAC* 8 (1979) 159–71

250. Pisani, V. *Testi latini arcaici e volgari.* Turin, 1950

251. Pisani, V. 'L'iscrizione paleolatina di Satricum', *Glotta* 51 (1981) 136–40

252. Prosdocimi, A. L. 'Studi sul latino arcaico II. Sull'iscrizione "Popliosio Valesiosio" di Satricum', *Stud. Etr.* 47 (1979) 183–97

253. Prosdocimi, A. L. 'Studi sull'italico', *Stud. Etr.* 48 (1980) 187–249

254. Prosdocimi, A. L. 'Sull'iscrizione di Satricum', *Giornale Italiano di Filologia* N.S. 15 (1984) 183–230

255. Pugliese Carratelli, G. 'Intorno alle lamine di Pyrgi', *Stud. Etr.* 33 (1965) 221–35

256. Radke, G. 'Zu der archaischen Inschrift von Madonnetta', *Glotta* 42 (1964) 214–19

257. Radke, G. 'Zur Echtheit der Inschrift auf der Fibula Praenestina', *Archäologisches Korrespondenzblatt* 14 (1984) 59–66

258. Ravel, O. E. *Descriptive Catalogue of the Collection of Tarentine Coins formed by M. P. Vlasto.* London, 1947

259. Reynolds, J. 'Inscriptions and Roman studies 1910–1960', *JRS* 50 (1960) 204–9

260. Ridgway, D. 'Manios faked?', *BICS* 24 (1977) 17–30

261. Sarstrom, M. *A Study in the Coinage of the Mamertines.* Lund, 1940

262. Solin, H. 'Zur Datierung ältester lateinischer Inschriften', *Glotta* 47 (1969) 248–53

263. Stibbe, C. M., Colonna, G., De Simone, C. and Versnel, H. S. *Lapis Satricanus* (Nederlands Instituut te Rome, Scripta Minora 5). The Hague, 1980

264. Thomsen, R. *Early Roman Coinage, A Study of the Chronology* (Nationalmuseetsskrifter, Arkaeologisk-historisk Raekke 5, 9 and 10). 3 vols. Copenhagen, 1957 and 1961

265. Torelli, M. 'L'iscrizione "latina" nella coppa argentea della tomba Bernardini', *DArch.* 1 (1967) 38–45

266. Torelli, M. *Elogia Tarquiniensia.* Florence, 1975

267. Truempy, C. 'La fibule de Préneste. Document inestimable ou falsification?', *MH* 40 (1983) 65–74

268. Versnel, H. S. 'Die neue Inschrift von Satricum in historischer Sicht',
     Gymnasium 89 (1982) 193–235
269. di Vita, A. 'Un *milliarium* del 252 a.C. e l'antica via Agrigento-Panormo',
     Kokalos 1 (1955) 10–21
270. Vitucci, G. 'Intorno a un nuovo frammento di elogium', *Riv. Fil.* 31 (1953)
     43–61
271. Weinstock, S. 'Two archaic inscriptions from Latium', *JRS* 50 (1960)
     114–8
272. Wieacker, F. 'Die Manios-Inschrift von Präneste. Zu einer exemplarischen
     Kontroverse', *Nachrichten der Akademie der Wissenschaften in Göttingen* 1.
     Phil.-hist. Klasse, Jahrgang 1984 n. 9
273. Zehnacker, H. *Moneta. Recherches sur l'organisation et l'art des émissions
     monétaires de la république romaine (289–31 av. J.C.)* (Bibliothèque des
     Écoles Françaises d'Athènes et de Rome 222). 2 vols. Paris, 1973
274. Zevi, F. 'Un documento inedito sulla fibula di Manios', *Prospettiva* 5 (1976)
     50–2

C. ARCHAEOLOGICAL EVIDENCE

See also E(a) on foundation cults etc.; E(b) on Rome; J(a) on pre-Roman Italy;
K(a) on Carthage; A56–9, 81, 108, 113; G59, 93, 110, 346–7, 382, 401, 445, 449,
477, 499–500, 534, 715, 718–19; I13–14, 16, 27, 32–3, 35, 49.

275. Åberg, N. *Bronzezeitliche und früheisenzeitliche Chronologie 1: Italien.* Stock-
     holm, 1930
276. Acanfora, M. O., Segre, A. G., Tortorici, E. et al. 'Gli scavi della necropoli
     dell'Osa (Roma)', *BPI* N.S. 23 (1972–4) 253–374
277. *Affreschi romani dalle raccolte dell'Antiquarium Comunale* (Exhibition cata-
     logue). Rome, 1976
278. Algreen-Ussing, G. and Fischer-Hansen, T. 'Ficana, le saline e le vie della
     regione bassa del Tevere', *Arch. Laz.* 7.1 (1985) 65–71
279. Andrén, A. *Architectural Terracottas from Etrusco-Italic Temples* (Skrifter
     utgivna av Svenska Institutet i Rom 4). Lund, 1940
280. Andrén, A. 'Osservazioni sulle terrecotte architettoniche etrusco-italiche',
     Op. Rom. 8 (1974) 1–16
281. *Archeologia Laziale* 1– . Rome, 1978– .
282. Ashby, T. 'La rete stradale romana nell'Etruria meridionale in relazione a
     quella del periodo etrusco', *Stud. Etr.* 3 (1929) 171–85
283. Aubet, E. *Los marfiles orientalizantes de Praeneste.* Barcelona, 1971
284. Beazley, J. D. *Etruscan Vase Painting.* Oxford, 1947
285. Bedini, A. 'Abitato protostorico in località Acqua Acetosa Laurentina',
     Arch. Laz. 1 (1978) 30–4
286. Bedini, A. 'Abitato protostorico in località Acqua Acetosa-Laurentina',
     Arch. Laz. 2 (1979) 21–8
287. Bedini, A. 'Abitato protostorico in località Acqua Acetosa-Laurentina',
     Arch. Laz. 3 (1980) 58–64
288. Bedini, A. 'Contributo alla conoscenza del territorio a sud di Roma in
     epoca protostorica', *Arch. Laz.* 4 (1981) 57–68

289. Bedini, A. 'Edifici di abitazione di epoca arcaica in località Acqua Acetosa Laurentina', *Arch. Laz.* 4 (1981) 253-7

290. Bedini, A. 'Due nuove tombe a camera presso l'abitato della Laurentina: nota su alcuni tipi di sepolture nel VI e V secolo a.C.', *Arch. Laz.* 5 (1983) 28-37

291. Bedini, A. 'Tre corredi protostorici dal Torrino: osservazioni sull'affermarsi e la funzione delle aristocrazie terriere nell' VIII secolo a.C. nel Lazio', *Arch. Laz.* 7.1 (1985) 44-64

292. Bedini, A. and Cordano, F. 'L'ottavo secolo nel Lazio e l'inizio dell'orientalizzante antico alla luce di recenti scoperte nella necropoli di Castel di Decima', *PP* 32 (1977) 274-311

293. Belardelli, C., Bietti Sestieri, A. M., et al. 'Preistoria e protostoria nel territorio di Roma. Modelli di insediamento e vie di comunicazione', in *Il Tevere e le altre vie d'acqua del Lazio antico (Arch. Laz.* 7.2 (1986)) 30-70

294. Bietti Sestieri, A. M. 'Gabii – Dati e ipotesi preliminari sulla necropoli dell'Osteria dell'Osa', *Arch. Laz.* 1 (1978) 47-50

295. Bietti Sestieri, A. M. *Ricerca su una comunità del Lazio protostorico. Il sepolcreto dell'Osteria dell'Osa sulla via Prenestina.* Rome, 1979

296. Bietti Sestieri, A. M. 'La necropoli dell Osteria dell'Osa', *Arch. Laz.* 2 (1979) 15-20

297. Blake, M. E. *Ancient Roman Construction in Italy from the Prehistoric Period to Augustus.* Washington, 1947

298. Bocci Pacini, P. 'Il pittore di Sommavilla Sabina ed il problema della nascità delle figure rosse in Etruria', *Stud. Etr.* 50(1982[1984]) 23-39

299. Boitani, F. 'Veio: nuovi rinvenimenti nella necropoli di Monte Michele', in *Archeologia della Tuscia* 95-103. Rome, 1982

300. Brandt, J. R., Pavolini, C. and Cataldi Dini, M. 'Ficana', *Arch. Laz.* 2 (1979) 29-36

301. Castagnoli, F. 'Roma arcaica e i recenti scavi di Lavinio', *PP* 32 (1977) 340-55

302. Castaldi, E. 'La civiltà appenninica 1959-1976. Per un bilancio critico', in *Studi in onore di F. Rittatore Vonwiller 1: Preistoria e protostoria* 1.57-79. Como, 1982

303. Cataldi, M. 'Ficana: saggio di scavo sulle pendici sud-occidentali di Monte Cugno, nelle vicinanze del moderno casale', *Arch. Laz.* 4 (1981) 274-86

304. Chiarucci, G. 'Albano: nuove scoperte relative ai primi periodi della civiltà laziale', *Arch. Laz.* 6 (1984) 29-34

305. *Civiltà arcaica dei Sabini nella valle del Tevere.* 2 vols. Rome, 1973-4

306. *Civiltà del Lazio primitivo. Palazzo delle Esposizioni. Roma 1976* (Exhibition catalogue). Rome, 1976

307. Coarelli, F. 'Il sepolcro degli Scipioni', *DArch.* 6 (1972) 36-105

308. Coarelli, F. *Guida archeologica di Roma.* Ed. 2. Milan, 1975

309. Coarelli, F. *Guida archeologica del Lazio.* Rome-Bari, 1982

310. Coarelli, F. and La Regina, A. *Guida archeologica dell'Abruzzo e Molise.* Rome-Bari, 1984

311. Colonna, G. 'Preistoria e protostoria di Roma e del Lazio', in *Popoli e civiltà dell'Italia antica* 11.283-346. Rome, 1974

312. Colonna, G. 'Un aspetto oscuro del Lazio antico: le tombe del VI–V secolo a.C.', *PP* 32 (1977) 131–65

313. Colonna, G. 'Vulci nella valle del Fiora e dell'Albegna', in *La civiltà arcaica di Vulci e la sua espansione (Atti del X convegno di studi etruschi e italici)* 189–96. Florence, 1977

314. Conta Haller, G. *Ricerche su alcuni centri fortificati in opera poligonale nell'area campano-sannitica* (Accademia di Archeologia, Lettere e Belle Arti di Napoli, Monumenti 3). Naples, 1978

315. Cornell, T. J. 'Rome and Latium Vetus, 1974–79', in *Archaeological Reports for 1979–80* (Society for the Promotion of Hellenic Studies & British School at Athens, Archaeological Reports 28) 71–89. London, 1980

316. *Un decennio di ricerche archeologiche* II.395–526. Rome, 1978

317. Del Chiaro, M. A. *The Genucilia Group: a Class of Etruscan Red-Figured Plates.* Berkeley, 1957

318. De Rossi, G. M. *Tellenae* (Forma Italiae Regio I, 4). Rome, 1967

319. De Rossi, G. M. *Bovillae* (Forma Italiae Regio I, 15). Florence, 1979

320. Dohrn, T. 'Vulci, Tomba 47 "del Guerriero"', in W. Helbig, *Führer durch die öffentlichen Sammlungen klassischer Altertümer in Rom* III.491–2. Ed. 4. Tübingen, 1969

321. Dohrn, T. *Die Ficoronische Cista.* Berlin, 1972

322. Dragt, G. I. W. 'Le case su fondamenta in pietra', in *Satricum – una città latina* 41–2. Florence, 1982

323. von Duhn, F. *Italische Gräberkunde.* 2 vols. Heidelberg, 1924–39

324. *Ficana – en milesten på veien til Roma.* Ed. 2. Copenhagen, 1981

325. *Ficana. Catalogo della Mostra.* Rome, 1981

326. *Ficana. Rassegna preliminare delle campagne archeologiche 1975–7* (Itinerari Ostiensi 2). Rome, 1977. *Aggiornamento.* Rome, 1978

327. Fischer-Hansen, T. et al. 'Ficana', *Arch. Laz.* 1 (1978) 35–41

328. Frederiksen, M. W. 'Archaeology in South Italy and Sicily, 1973–6', in *Archaeological Reports for 1976–7* (Society for the Promotion of Hellenic Studies and British School at Athens, Archaeological Reports 23) 43–76. London, 1977

329. Frederiksen, M. W. and Ward Perkins, J. B. 'The ancient road systems of the central and northern Ager Faliscus: notes on South Etruria II', *PBSR* 25 (1957) 67–208

330. Fugazzola Delpino, M. A. *Testimonianze di cultura appenninica nel Lazio* (Origines, Studi e Materiali pubbl. a cura dell'Istituto Italiano di Preistoria e Protostoria). Florence, 1976

331. Gabba, E. Review of G. Conta Haller, *Ricerche su alcuni centri fortificati in opera poligonale in area campano-sannitica* (Naples, 1978), in *Athenaeum* N.S. 57 (1979) 171–2

332. Galieti, A. 'Contributo alla conoscenza dell'armatura dei prisci Latini', in *Atti del IV congresso nazionale di studi romani* II.282–9. Rome, 1938 = *Archeologia e Società* 2.2 (1976) 45–50 (with new photographs)

333. Gierow, P. G. *The Iron Age Culture of Latium.* 2 vols. Lund, 1964–6

334. Gierow, P. G. *Relative and Absolute Chronology of the Iron Age Culture of Latium in the Light of Recent Discoveries.* Separately paginated fascicle of *Scripta Minora 1977–8 in honorem E. Gjerstad.* Lund, 1977

335. Gierow, P. G. 'I Colli Albani nel quadro archeologico della civiltà laziale', *Op. Rom.* 14 (1983) 7–18

336. Gjerstad, E. 'Cultural history of early Rome. Summary of archaeological evidence', *Acta Archaeologica* 36 (1965) 1–41

337. Guaitoli, M. 'L'abitato di Castel di Decima', *Arch. Laz.* 2 (1979) 37–40

338. Guaitoli, M. 'Gabii: osservazioni sulle fasi di sviluppo dell'abitato', *Quaderni dell'Istituto di Topografia Antica dell'Università di Roma* 9 (1981) 23–58

339. Guaitoli, M. 'Castel di Decima. Nuove osservazioni sulla topografia dell'abitato alla luce dei primi saggi di scavo', *Quaderni dell'Istituto di Topografia Antica dell'Università di Roma* 9 (1981) 117–50

340. Guaitoli, M., Piccareta, F. and Sommella, P. 'Contributi per una carta archeologica del territorio di Castel di Decima', *Quaderni dell'Istituto di Topografia Antica dell' Università di Roma* 6 (1974) 43–130

341. Guidi, A. et al. 'Cures Sabini', *Arch. Laz.* 7.1 (1985) 77–92

342. Helbig, W. *Führer durch die öffentlichen Sammlungen klassischer Altertümer in Rom.* 4 vols. Ed. 4 (revised by H. Speier). Tübingen, 1963–72

344. Hencken, H. *Tarquinia and Etruscan Origins.* London, 1968

345. Hencken, H. *Tarquinia, Villanovans and Early Etruscans.* 2 vols. Cambridge, 1968

345. Holloway, R. R. *Italy and the Aegean 3000–700 B.C.* (Publications d'Histoire de l'Art et d'Archéologie de l'Université Catholique de Louvain 28. Archeologia Transatlantica 1). Louvain, 1981

346. Jarva, E. 'Area di tombe infantili a Ficana', *Arch. Laz.* 4 (1981) 269–73

347. Jehasse, J. and L. *La nécropole préromaine d'Aléria (1960–1968)* (*Gallia* Suppl. 25). Paris, 1973

348. Johnston, A. W. *Trade-marks on Greek Vases.* Warminster, 1979

349. Judson, S. and Hemphill, P. 'Sizes of settlements in southern Etruria 6th–5th centuries B.C.', *Stud. Etr.* 49 (1981) 193–202

350. Kahane, A., Threipland, L. M. and Ward-Perkins, J. B. 'The Ager Veientanus North and East of Rome', *PBSR* 36 (1968) 1–218

351. Karo, G. 'Tombe arcaiche di Cuma', *BPI* 30 (1904) 1–29

352. La Regina, A. 'Centri fortificati preromani nei territori sabellici dell'Italia centrale', *Poszbna Isdanja* 24 (1975) 271–82

353. La Rocca, E. 'Due tombe dell'Esquilino. Alcune novità sul commercio euboico in Italia centrale nell'VIII secolo a.C.', *DArch.* 8 (1974–5) 86–103

354. Lévêque, P. and Morel, J.-P. *Céramiques hellénistiques et romaines.* Paris, 1980

355. Liverani, P. 'L'Ager Veientanus in età repubblicana', *PBSR* 52 (1984) 36–48

356. Lugli, G. *La tecnica edilizia romana.* 2 vols. Rome, 1957

357. Martelli, M. and Cristofani, M. (edd.). *Caratteri dell'ellenismo nelle urne etrusche.* Florence, 1977

358. Melis, F. and Rathje, A. 'Considerazioni sullo studio dell'architettura domestica arcaica', *Arch. Laz.* 6 (1984) 382–95

359. Montelius, C. *La civilisation primitive en Italie depuis l'introduction des métaux.* 2 vols. Stockholm, 1895–1905

360. Morel, J.-P. *Céramique au vernis noir du Forum romain et du Palatin.* Paris, 1965

361. Morel, J.-P. 'L'atelier des petites estampilles', *MÉFR* 81 (1969) 1–59
362. Morel, J.-P. 'Céramiques de l'Italie et céramiques hellénistiques', in *Hellenismus in Mittelitalien. Kolloquium in Göttingen von 5. bis. 9. Juni 1974 (Abhandlungen der Akademie der Wissenschaften in Göttingen*. Phil.-hist. Klasse III, 97, 1/II), ed. P. Zanker, II.471–501. Göttingen, 1976
363. Morel, J.-P. *La céramique campanienne*. Paris, 1981
364. Morpurgo, L. 'Nemus Aricinum', *Monumenti Antichi* 13 (1903) 297–368
365. Morpurgo, L. 'Nemi. Teatro ed altri edifici romani in contrada La Valle', *NSc* (1931) 237–305, 408
366. Muzzioli, M. P. *Cures Sabini* (Forma Italiae Regio IV,2). Florence, 1980
367. Nielsen, E. and Phillips, K. M. 'Poggio Civitate (Siena). Gli scavi del Bryn Mawr College dal 1966 al 1974', *NSc.* 30 (1976) 113–47
368. Östenberg, C. E. *Case etrusche di Acquarossa*. Rome, 1975
369. Östenberg, C. E. and others. *Luni sul Mignone*. 2 vols. Lund, 1967–75
370. Ogilvie, R. M. 'Eretum', *PBSR* 33 (1965) 70–112
371. Pallottino, M. 'Scavi nel santuario di Pyrgi', *Arch. Class.* 17 (1964) 39–117
372. Pallottino, M. and others (edd.). *Popoli e civiltà dell'Italia antica* (Biblioteca di Storia Patria). Rome, 1972–
373. Palm, J. 'Two groups of Etruscan tombs from Veii', *Opuscula Archaeologica* 7 (1952) 50–86
374. Pareti, L. *La tomba Regolini-Galassi del Museo Gregoriano Etrusco e la civiltà dell'Italia centrale nel VII sec. a.C.* Vatican, 1947
375. Pavolini, C. 'Ficana: edificio sulle pendici sud-occidentali di Monte Cugno', *Arch. Laz.* 4 (1981) 258–68
376. Pavolini, C. and Rathje, A. 'L'inizio dell'architettura domestica con fondamenta in pietra nel Lazio e a Ficana', in *Ficana. Catalogo della Mostra* 75–87. Rome, 1981
377. Peroni, R. 'Per uno studio dell'economia di scambio in Italia nel quadro dell'ambiente culturale dei secoli intorno al 1000', *PP* 24 (1969) 134–60
378. Peroni, R. 'Zur jungbronzezeitlichen Besiedlung und Kultur im westlichen Mittelitalien', in *Jahresbericht des Instituts für Vorgeschichte der Universität Frankfurt* (1975) 33–45
379. Pfister-Roesgen, G. *Die etruskischen Spiegel des fünften Jahrhunderts vor Christus* (Archäologische Studien 2). Frankfurt, 1975
380. Phillips, K. M. 'Italic house models and Etruscan architectural terracottas of the seventh century B.C. from Acquarossa and Poggio Civitate, Murlo', *ARID* 14 (1985) 7–16
381. Pinza, G. *Monumenti primitivi di Roma e del Lazio antico (Monumenti Antichi* 15). Rome, 1905
382. Pinza, G. *Materiali per la etnologia antica toscano-laziale* I. Milan, 1915
383. Pinza, G. *Storia della civiltà latina*. Rome, 1924
384. Potter, T. W. *A Faliscan Town in South Etruria. Excavations at Narce, 1966–71.* London, 1976
385. Potter, T. W. *The Changing Landscape of South Etruria*. London, 1979
386. Poucet, J. 'Le Latium protohistorique et archaïque à la lumière des découvertes archéologiques récentes', *Ant. Class.* 47 (1978) 566–601; 48 (1979) 177–220

387. Puglisi, S. M. *La civiltà appenninica. Origine delle comunità pastorali in Italia.* Florence, 1959

388. Quilici, L. *Collatia* (Forma Italiae Regio I, 10). Rome, 1974

389. Quilici, L. *Roma primitiva e le origini della civiltà laziale.* Rome, 1979

390. Quilici, L. and Quilici Gigli, St. *Antemnae.* Rome, 1978

391. Quilici, L. and Quilici Gigli, St. *Crustumerium.* Rome, 1980

392. Quilici Gigli, St. 'Nota topografica su Ficana', *Arch. Class.* 23 (1971) 26–36

393. Radmilli, A. M. *Piccola guida della preistoria italiana.* Florence, 1962

394. Randall-MacIver, D. *Villanovans and Early Etruscans.* Oxford, 1924

395. Rasmussen, T. B. *Bucchero Pottery from South Etruria.* Cambridge, 1979

396. Rathje, A. 'A banquet service from the Latin city of Ficana', *ARID* 12 (1983) 7–29

397. Ridgway, D. 'The first western Greeks: Campanian coasts and southern Etruria', in *Greeks, Celts and Romans. Studies in Venture and Resistance* (Archaeology into History 1), edd. C. and S. Hawkes, 5–38. London, 1973

398. Riemann, H. 'Beiträge zur römischen Topographie', *MDAI(R)* 76 (1969) 103–21

399. Riis, P. J. *Tyrrhenika. An Archaeological Study of the Etruscan Sculpture in the Archaic and Classical Periods.* Copenhagen, 1941

400. Riis, P. J. *Etruscan Types of Heads: A Revised Chronology of the Archaic and Classical Terracottas of Etruscan Campania and Central Italy* (*Det Kongelige Danske Videnskabernes Selskab* Historisk-filosofiskeskrifter 9.5). Copenhagen, 1981

401. *Roma medio repubblicana. Aspetti culturali di Roma e del Lazio nei secoli IV e III a.C.* (Exhibition catalogue). Rome, 1973

402. Ryberg, I. S. *An Archaeological Record of Rome from the Seventh to the Second Century B.C.* London, 1940

403. Santoro, P. 'Colle del Forno. Loc. Montelibretti (Roma). Relazione di scavo sulle campagne 1971–1974 nella necropoli', *NSc.* 31 (1977) 211–98

404. Santoro, P. 'La necropoli di Colle del Forno', *Arch. Laz.* 3 (1980) 56–7

405. *Satricum—una città latina.* Florence, 1982

406. Shefton, B. B. 'Attisches Meisterwerk und etruskische Kopie', *Wissenschaftliche Zeitschrift der Universität Rostock, Gesellschafts- und Sprachwissenschaftliche Reihe* 16 (1967) 529–37

407. Sommella, P. 'Lavinium. Rinvenimenti preistorici e protostorici', *Arch. Class.* 21 (1969) 18–33

408. Sommella, P. 'La necropoli protostorica rinvenuta a Pratica di Mare', *RPAA* 46 (1973–4) 33–48

409. Strøm, J. *Problems concerning the Origin and Early Development of the Etruscan Orientalizing Style.* Odense, 1971

410. Sundwall, J. *Die älteren italischen Fibeln.* Berlin, 1943

411. Threipland, L. M. 'Veii: a deposit of votive pottery', *PBSR* 37 (1969) 1–13

412. Threipland, L. M. and Torelli, M. 'A semi-subterranean Etruscan building in the Casale Pian Roseto (Veii) area', *PBSR* 38 (1970) 62–121

413. Torelli, M. 'Veio, la città, l'arx e il culto di Giunone Regina', in *Miscellanea T. Dohrn dedicata* 117–28. Rome, 1982
414. Toti, O. *I Monti Ceriti nell'età del ferro*. Civitavecchia, 1959
415. Toti, O. *Allumiere e il suo territorio*. Rome, 1967
416. Vagnetti, L. *Il deposito votivo di lampetti a Veio*. Florence, 1971
417. Vagnetti, L. 'Quindici anni di studi e ricerche sulle relazioni tra il mondo egeo e l'Italia protostorica', in *Magna Grecia e mondo miceneo. Nuovi documenti (22 convegno di studi sulla Magna Grecia, Taranto, 7–11 ottobre 1982)* 9–40. Taranto, 1982
418. Vianello Cordova, A. P. 'Una tomba "protovillanoviana" a Veio', *Stud. Etr.* 25 (1967) 295–306
419. Ward-Perkins, J. B. 'Notes on South Etruria and the Ager Veientanus', *PBSR* 23 (1955) 44–72
420. Ward-Perkins, J. B. 'Etruscan and Roman roads in Southern Etruria', *JRS* 47 (1957) 139–43
421. Ward-Perkins, J. B. 'Veii: the historical topography of the ancient city', *PBSR* 29 (1961) 1–123
422. Ward-Perkins, J. B. and Kahane, A. M. 'The Via Gabina', *PBSR* 40 (1972) 91–126
423. Zaccagni, P. 'Gabii – La città antica ed il territorio', *Arch. Laz.* 1 (1978) 42–6
424. Zevi, F. 'Alcuni aspetti della necropoli di Castel di Decima', *PP* 32 (1977) 241–73
425. Zevi, F., Bartoloni, G., Cataldi Dini, M., Bedini, A. and Cordano, F. 'Castel di Decima: La necropoli arcaica', *NSc.* 29 (1975) 233–408

C. GEOGRAPHY

See also B278, 293.

1. Almagià, R. *Lazio* (Le Regioni d'Italia 11). Turin, 1966
2. Ampolo, C. 'Le condizioni materiali della produzione. Agricoltura e paesaggio agrario', *DArch.* N.S. 2 (1980) 15–46
3. Ashby, T. *The Roman Campagna in Classical Times*. London, 1927
4. Bietti Sestieri, A. M. 'Cenni sull'ambiente naturale', *DArch.* N.S. 2 (1980) 5–13
5. Fornaseri, M., Scherillo, A. and Ventriglia, U. *La regione vulcanica dei Colli Albani*. Rome, 1963
6. Giordano, F. *Cenni sulle condizioni fisico-economiche di Roma e suo territorio*. Florence, 1871
7. Heuberger, H. 'Die Alpengletscher im Spät– und Postglazial: eine chronologische Übersicht', *Eiszeitalter und Gegenwart* 19 (1968) 270–5
8. Le Gall, J. *Le Tibre, fleuve de Rome dans l'antiquité*. Paris, 1952
9. Marimpieri, L. *I terreni dell' Agro Romano*. Rome, n.d.
10. Nissen, H. *Italische Landeskunde*. 2 vols. Berlin, 1883–1902
11. Potter, T. W. 'Valleys and settlement: some new evidence', *World Archaeology* 8 (1976) 207–19

12. Principi, P. 'I terreni agrari del Lazio', *L'Italia Agricola* 88 (1951) 86–101
13. Quilici, L. and Quilici Gigli, St. 'Il Lazio antichissimo e le origini di Roma', *Capitolium* 50 n. 11 (1975) 8–23
14. Smith, C. Delano. *Western Mediterranean Europe. A Historical Geography of Italy, Spain and Southern France since the Neolithic.* London, 1979
15. Strafforrello, G. *Geografia dell'Italia: Provincia di Roma.* Turin, 1894
16. *Il Tevere e le altre vie d'acqua del Lazio antico (Arch. Laz.* 7.2 (1986))
17. Tomasetti, G. *La Campagna Romana, antica, medioevale e moderna.* 4 vols. 1910–26. New revised edition by L. Chiumenti and F. Bilancia. 6 vols. Florence, 1979–80
18. Ventriglia, U. *La geologia della città di Roma.* Rome, 1971
19. Vita-Finzi, C. *The Mediterranean Valleys: Geological Changes in Historical Times.* Cambridge, 1969
20. Ward-Perkins, J. B. 'Etruscan towns, Roman roads and medieval villages: the historical geography of South Etruria', *Geographical Journal* 128 (1962) 389–405
21. Ward-Perkins, J. B. *Landscape and History in Central Italy* (Second J. L. Myres Memorial Lecture). Oxford, 1964

D. THE CHRONOLOGY OF EARLY ROME. THE *FASTI·CONSULARES*

See also A27, 134; B2, 49, 75, 165; F9; G403, 611; H74; K193.

1. Alföldi, A. 'Les *cognomina* des magistrats de la république romaine', in *Mélanges A. Piganiol* (1966) 11.709–22
2. Ampolo, C. 'Gli Aquilii del V secolo a.C. e il problema dei Fasti consolari più antichi', *PP* 30 (1975) 410–16
3. Beloch, K. J. 'Die Sonnenfinsternis des Ennius und der voriulianische Kalender', *Hermes* 57 (1922) 119–33
4. Cichorius, C. *De fastis consularibus antiquissimis* (diss. Leipzig, 1886)
5. Costa, G. *I fasti consolari romani* 1.1–2. Milan, 1910
6. Degrassi, A. 'L'edificio dei Fasti Capitolini', *RPAA* 21 (1945–6) 57–104
7. Degrassi, A. *Inscriptiones Italiae, vol. XIII – Fasti et elogia, fasc. 1 – Fasti consulares et triumphales.* Rome, 1947
8. Drummond, A. 'The dictator years', *Historia* 27 (1978) 550–72
9. Drummond, A. 'Consular tribunes in Livy and Diodorus', *Athenaeum* N.S. 58 (1980) 57–72
10. Fraccaro, P. Review of A. Degrassi, *Inscriptiones Italiae vol. XIII – Fasti et elogia, fasc. 1 – Fasti consulares et triumphales* (Rome, 1947) in *Athenaeum* N.S. 25 (1947) 240–50
11. Frier, B. W. 'Licinius Macer and the *consules suffecti* of 444 B.C.', *TAPA* 105 (1975) 79–97
12. Gabba, E. 'Un documento censorio in Dionigi d'Alicarnasso 1,74,5', in *Synteleia V. Arangio-Ruiz* 1.486–93. Naples, 1964
13. Grafton, A. T. and Swerdlow, N. M. 'The horoscope of the foundation of Rome', *CPhil.* 81 (1986) 148–53

14. Hanell, K. 'Sulla questione del *clavus annalis*', *BCAR* 58 (1930) 163–70
15. Hanell, K. 'Probleme der römischen Fasti', in *Les origines de la république romaine* (*Entretiens Hardt* 13) 175–96. Geneva, 1967
16. Henzen, W., Hülsen, Chr. and Mommsen, Th. *Corpus Inscriptionum Latinarum* 1.1. Ed. 2. Berlin, 1893
17. Holzapfel, L. *Römische Chronologie*. Berlin, 1883–4
18. Janssen, L. F. 'The chronology of early Rome', *Mnemosyne* 23 (1970) 68–81
19. Laroche, R. A. 'The Alban king-list in Dionysius 1.70–71', *Historia* 31 (1982) 112–20
20. Laroche, R. A. 'Early Roman chronology: its schematic nature', in *Studies in Latin Literature and Roman History* III (Collection Latomus 180), ed. C. Deroux, 5–25. Brussels, 1983
21. Leuze, O. *Die römische Jahrzählung*. Tübingen, 1909
22. Mommsen, Th. *Die römische Chronologie bis auf Cäsar*. Ed. 2. Berlin, 1859
23. Pais, E. 'A proposito dell'attendibilità dei fasti dell'antica repubblica romana', *RAL* ser. 5.17 (1908) 33–68
24. Pekáry, T. 'Das Weihedatum des kapitolinischen Iuppitertempels und Plinius *N.H.* 33.19', *MDAI(R)* 76 (1969) 307–12
25. Perl, G. *Kritische Untersuchungen zu Diodors römischer Jahrzählung* (Deutsche Akademie der Wissenschaften zu Berlin. Schriften der Sektion für Altertumswissenschaft 9). Berlin, 1957
26. Pinsent, J. *Military Tribunes and Plebeian Consuls. The Fasti from 444V to 342V* (*Historia* Einzelschriften 24). Wiesbaden, 1975
27. Ridley, R. T. 'Fastenkritik, a stocktaking', *Athenaeum* N.S. 58 (1980) 264–98
28. Ridley, R. T. '*Falsi triumphi, plures consulatus*', *Latomus* 42 (1983) 372–82
29. Sordi, M. 'Sulla cronologia liviana nel IV secolo', *Helikon* 5 (1965) 3–44
30. Stiehl, R. *Die Datierung der Kapitolinischen Fasten* (Untersuchungen zur klassischen Philologie und Geschichte des Altertums 1). Tübingen, 1957
31. Taylor, L. R. 'The date of the Capitoline Fasti', *CPhil.* 41 (1946) 1–11
32. Taylor, L. R. 'Annals of the Roman consulship on the Arch of Augustus', *Proceedings of the American Philosophical Society* 94 (1950) 511–16
33. Taylor, L. R. 'The consular and triumphal Fasti', *CPhil.* 45 (1950) 84–95
34. Taylor, L. R. 'New indications of Augustan editing in the Capitoline Fasti', *CPhil.* 46 (1951) 73–80

E. THE 'FOUNDATION' OF ROME

a. THE FOUNDATION LEGENDS

See also A23; B76, 271, 301, 407; G438, 461; I3, 16, 70.

1. Alföldi, A. *Die troianischen Urahnen der Römer*. Basle, 1956
2. Alföldi, A. 'Die Penaten, Aeneas und Latinus', *MDAI(R)* 78 (1971) 16–22
3. Alföldi, A. 'La louve du Capitole. Quelques remarques sur son mythe à

Rome et chez les Étrusques', in *Hommages à la mémoire de J. Carcopino* 1–11. Paris, 1977

4. Bendinelli, G. 'Gruppo fittile di Enea e Anchise proveniente da Veio', *Riv. Fil.* 76 (1948) 88–97
5. Boas, H. *Aeneas' Arrival in Latium*. Amsterdam, 1938
6. Bömer, R. *Rom und Troia*. Baden-Baden, 1951
7. Briquel, D. 'L'oiseau ominal, la louve de Mars, la truie féconde', *MÉFR(A)* 88 (1976) 31–50
8. Briquel, D. 'La triple fondation de Rome', *Rev.Hist.Rel.* 189 (1976) 145–76
9. Briquel, D. 'Trois études sur Romulus', in *Recherches sur les religions de l'antiquité classique*, ed. R. Bloch, 267–346. Geneva–Paris, 1980
10. Briquel, D. 'En decà de l'épopée, un thème légendaire indo-européen: caractère trifonctionnel et liaison avec le feu dans la geste des rois iraniens et latins', in *L'épopée gréco-latin et ses prolongements européens*, ed. R. Chevallier, 7–31. Paris, 1981
11. Cairns, F. 'Geography and nationalism in the Aeneid', *LCM* 2 (1977) 109–16 (and discussion ib. 129–43)
12. Carcopino, J. *La louve du Capitol*. Paris, 1925
13. Castagnoli, F. '*Roma quadrata*', in *Studies presented to D. M. Robinson* 1.389–99. St Louis, 1951
14. Castagnoli, F. 'I luoghi connessi con l'arrivo di Enea nel Lazio (Troia, Sol Indiges, Numicus)', *Arch. Class.* 19 (1967) 236–47
15. Castagnoli, F. 'La leggenda di Enea nel Lazio', *Stud. Rom.* 30 (1982) 1–15
16. Cazzaniga, I. 'Il frammento 61 degli Annali di Ennio: Quirinus Indiges', *PP* 29 (1974) 363–81
17. Classen, C. J. 'Zur Herkunft der Sage von Romulus und Remus', *Historia* 12 (1963) 447–57
18. Cogrossi, C. 'Atene Iliaca e il culto degli eroi. L'*heroon* di Enea a Lavinio e Latino figlio di Odisseo', in *Politica e religione nel primo scontro tra Roma e l'Oriente* (*CISA* 8), ed. M. Sordi, 79–98. Milan, 1982
19. Cornell, T. J. 'Aeneas and the twins: the development of the Roman foundation legends', *PCPhS* 21 (1975) 1–32
20. Cornell, T. J. 'Aeneas' arrival in Italy', *LCM* 2 (1977) 77–83
21. Cornell, T. J. 'The foundation of Rome in the ancient literary tradition', in *Papers in Italian Archaeology I: The Lancaster Seminar* (*BAR* Suppl. Series 41), edd. H. McK. Blake, T. W. Potter and D. B. Whitehouse, 1.131–40. Oxford, 1978
22. Crawford, M. H. 'A Roman representation of the Keramos Troikos', *JRS* 61 (1971) 153–4
23. Dohrn, T. 'Des Romulus Gründung Roms', *MDAI(R)* 71 (1964) 1–18
24. Dury-Moyaers, G. *Énée et Lavinium* (Collection Latomus 172). Brussels, 1981. (Review-discussion by R. Turcan, *Rev. Hist. Rel.* 200 (1983) 41–66)
25. *Enea nel Lazio: archeologia e mito* (Exhibition catalogue). Rome, 1981
26. Fuchs, W. 'Die Bildgeschichte der Flucht des Aeneas', *ANRW* 1.4 (1973) 615–32
27. Gabba, E. 'Sulla valorizzazione politica della leggenda delle origini troiane

di Roma fra III e II sec.', in *I canali della propaganda nel mondo antico* (*CISA* 4), ed M. Sordi, 84–101. Milan, 1976

28. Gagé, J. 'Comment Énée est devenu l'ancêtre des Silvii Albains', *MÉFR(A)* 88 (1976) 7–30

29. Galinsky, G. K. *Aeneas, Sicily and Rome.* Princeton, 1969

30. Gantz, T. N. 'Lapis Niger. The tomb of Romulus', *PP* 29 (1974) 350–61

31. Giglioli, G. Q. 'Osservazioni e monumenti relativi alla leggenda delle origini di Roma', *Bullettino del Museo della Civiltà Romana* 12 (Supplement to *BCAR* 69 (1941)) 3–7

32. Grant, M. *Roman Myths.* London, 1971

33. Guarducci, M. 'Cippo latino arcaico con dedica a Enea', *Bullettino del Museo della Civiltà Romana* 19 (Supplement to *BCAR* 76 (1956–8)) 1–13

34. Guarducci, M. 'Enea e Vesta', *MDAI(R)* 78 (1971) 73–118

35. Hafner, G. 'Aeneas und Anchises', *Archäologischer Anzeiger* 1979, 24–7

36. Heurgon, J. 'Lars, Largus et Lare Aineia', in *Mélanges A. Piganiol* (1966) ii.655–64

37. Kolbe, H. G. 'Lare Aineia?', *MDAI(R)* 77 (1970) 1–9

38. Lincoln, B. 'The Indo-European myth of creation', *History of Religions* 15 (1975) 121–45

39. Manni, E. 'La fondazione di Roma secondo Antioco, Alcimo e Callia', *Kokalos* 9 (1963) 253–68

40. Manson, M. 'Un personnage d'enfant dans l'épopée antique: Ascagne', *Rev. Phil.* 12 (1938) 53–70

41. Mitchell, R. E. 'Roman coins as historical evidence. The Trojan legends of Rome', *Illinois Classical Studies* 1 (1976) 65–85

42. Momigliano, A. 'How to reconcile Greeks and Trojans', *Mededelingen der Koninklijke Nederlandse Akademie van Wetenschappen. Afdeling Letterkunde* N.S. 45.9 (1982) 231–54 = id. *Settimo Contributo* 437–62

43. Mommsen, Th. 'Die Remuslegende', *Hermes* 16 (1881) 1–23 = id. *Gesammelte Schriften* iv.1–21. Berlin, 1906

44. Mommsen, Th. 'Die Tatiuslegende', *Hermes* 21 (1886) 570–84 = id. *Gesammelte Schriften* iv. 22–35. Berlin, 1906

45. Moyaers, G. 'Énée et Lavinium à la lumière des découvertes archéologiques récentes', *RBPhil.* 55 (1977) 21–50

46. Musti, D. 'Varrone nell'insieme delle tradizioni su Roma quadrata', *Studi Urbinati di Storia, Filosofia e Letteratura* 49 (1975) 297–318

47. Perret, J. *Les origines de la légende troyenne de Rome (281–31).* Paris, 1942. (Review-discussion by P. Boyancé, *Rev. Ét. Anc.* 45 (1943) 275–90 = id. *Études sur la religion romaine* 153–70. Rome, 1972)

48. Perret, J. 'Rome et les Troyens', *RÉL* 49 (1971) 41–3

49. Perret, J. 'Athènes et les légendes troyennes d'Occident', in *Mélanges J. Heurgon* (1976) ii.791–803

50. Porte, D. 'Romulus-Quirinus', *ANRW* ii.17.1 (1981) 300–42

51. Poucet, J. *Recherches sur la légende sabine des origines de Rome.* Kinshasa (Lovanium), 1967

52. Poucet, J. 'Les Sabins aux origines de Rome. Orientations et problèmes', *ANRW* i.1 (1972) 48–135

53. Poucet, J. 'Préoccupations érudits dans la tradition du règne de Romulus', *Ant. Class.* 50 (1981) 664–76

54. Poucet, J. 'Un culte d'Énée dans la région lavinate au quatrième siècle avant Jésus Christ?', in *Hommages à R. Schilling* (Collection d'Études Latines. Série Scientifique 37), edd. H. Zehnacker and G. Hertz, 187–201. Paris, 1983

55. Poucet, J. 'Enée et Lavinium', *RBPhil.* 61 (1983) 144–59

56. Préaux, J. 'Les sept premiers vers de l'Eneide et les découvertes de Lavinium', in *D'Eschyle à nos jours*, ed. G. Cambier, 73–96. Brussels, 1978

57. Puhvel, J. '*Remus et frater*', *History of Religions* 15 (1975) 146–57

58. Schauenburg, K. 'Aeneas und Rom', *Gymnasium* 67 (1960) 176–90

59. Schauenburg, K. '*Αἰνέας καλός*', *Gymnasium* 76 (1969) 42–53

60. Schefold, K. 'Die römische Wölfin und der Ursprung der Romsagen', in *Provincialia. Festschrift für R. Laur-Belart* 428–39. Basle, 1968

61. Schilling, R. 'Romulus l'élu et Rémus le réprouvé', *RÉL* 38 (1960) 182–99 = id. *Rites, cultes, dieux de Rome* (Études et Commentaires 92) 103–20. Paris, 1979

62. Scuderi, R. 'Il mito eneico in età augustea: aspetti filo-etruschi e filo-ellenici', *Aevum* 52 (1978) 88–99

63. Sommella, P. '*Heroon* di Enea a Lavinium. Recenti scavi a Pratica di Mare', *RAL* ser. 8.44 (1971–2) 47–74

64. Sommella, P. 'Das Heroon des Aeneas and die Topographie des antiken Laviniums', *Gymnasium* 81 (1974) 273–97

65. Sordi, M. 'Lavinio, Roma e il Palladio', in *Politica e religione nel primo scontro tra Roma e l'Oriente* (*CISA* 8), ed. M. Sordi, 65–78. Milan, 1982

66. Strasburger, H. 'Zur Sage von der Gründung Roms', *Sitzungsberichte der Heidelberger Akademie der Wissenschaften*, Phil.-hist. Klasse 1968 n. 5. (Review by C. J. Classen, *Gnomon* 43 (1971) 479–84)

67. Torelli, M. Reviews of L. Vagnetti, *Il deposito votivo di lampetti a Veio* (Florence, 1971) and M. B. Jovino, *Capua preromana – Terrecotte votive* II (Florence, 1971) in *DArch.* 7 (1973–4) 396–407

b. THE ORIGINS AND DEVELOPMENT OF THE CITY

See also B(c) for archaeological evidence; A1, 15, 33, 56–9, 65, 81, 93, 95, 108; B29; C13; E13, 30; F53.

68. Alföldi, A. '*Ager Romanus antiquus*', *Hermes* 90 (1962) 187–213

69. Ampolo, C. 'Analogie e rapporti tra Atene e Roma arcaica. Osservazioni sulla Regia, sul *rex sacrorum* e sul culto di Vesta', *PP* 26 (1971) 443–57

70. Ampolo, C. 'Le origini di Roma e la "cité antique"', *MÉFR(A)* 92 (1980) 567–76

71. Ampolo, C. 'La città arcaica e le sue feste: due ricerche sul Septimontium e sull' *equus October*', *Arch. Laz.* 4 (1981) 233–40

72. Ampolo, C. 'Die endgültige Stadtwerdung Roms im VII. und VI. Jh. v. Chr.', in *Palast und Hütte. Beiträge zum Bauen und Wohnen im Altertum von Archäologen, Vor- und Frühgeschichtlichern: Symposium der Alexander-von-*

Humboldt Stiftung Bonn-Bad Godesberg 25–30 November 1979 in Berlin, edd.
D. Papenfuss and V. M Strocka, 319–324. Mainz, 1982

73. Ampolo, C. 'Sulla formazione della città di Roma', Opus 2 (1983) 425–30
74. Ashby, T. and Richmond, I. The Aqueducts of Ancient Rome. London, 1935
75. Aurigemma, S. 'Le mura "Serviane", l'aggere e il fossato all'esterno delle
    mura, presso la nuova stazione ferroviaria di Termini in Roma', BCAR
    78 (1961–2 [1964]) 19–36
76. Barocelli, P. 'Terremare, Palatino, orientazione dei castra e delle città
    romane', BCAR 70 (1942) 131–44
77. von Blackenhagen, P. H. 'Vom Ursprung Roms', Prähistorische Zeitschrift
    34–5 (1949–50) 245–49
78. Brown, F. E. 'New soundings in the Regia: the evidence for the early
    republic', in Les origines de la république romaine (Entretiens Hardt 13)
    45–60. Geneva, 1967
79. Brown, F. E. 'La protostoria della Regia', RPAA 47 (1974–5) 15–36
80. Castagnoli, F. 'Note di topografia romana', BCAR 74 (1951–2) 49–56
81. Castagnoli, F. Ippodamo da Mileto e l'urbanistica a pianta ortogonale 91–9.
    Gubbio, 1963
82. Castagnoli, F. 'Note sulla topografia del Palatino e del Foro Romano',
    Arch. Class. 16 (1964) 173–99
83. Castagnoli, F. 'Note di architettura e di urbanistica', Arch. Class. 20 (1968)
    117–25
84. Castagnoli, F. Topografia e urbanistica di Roma antica. Bologna, 1969
85. Castagnoli, F. 'Topografia e urbanistica di Roma nel IV secolo a.C.', Stud.
    Rom. 22 (1974) 425–43
86. Castagnoli, F. 'Per la cronologia dei monumenti del Comizio', Stud. Rom.
    23 (1975) 187–9
87. Castagnoli, F. 'Cermalo', Riv. Fil. 105 (1977) 15–19
88. Castagnoli, F. 'Aspetti urbanistici di Roma e del Lazio in età arcaica', in
    Deutsches Archäologisches Institut: 150 Jahre Deutsches Archäologisches
    Institut: 1829–1979: Festveranstaltung und Internationales Kolloquium, 17.–22.
    April 1969 in Berlin 133–42. Mainz, 1981
89. Castagnoli, F. 'Il Niger Lapis nel Foro romano e gli scavi del 1955', PP 39
    (1984) 56–61
90. Citarella, A. O. 'Cursus triumphalis and sulcus primigenius', PP 35 (1980)
    401–14
91. Coarelli, F. 'Ara Saturni, Mundus, Senaculum. La parte occidentale del
    Foro in età arcaica', DArch. 9–10 (1976–7) 346–77
92. Coarelli, F. 'Il comizio dalle origini alla fine della repubblica: cronologia e
    topografia', PP 32 (1977) 166–238
93. Coarelli, F. 'Il foro in età arcaica: Regia, via Sacra, Comizio', Arch. Laz. 4
    (1981) 241–8
94. Coarelli, F. Il Foro Romano. 1. Periodo arcaico. Rome, 1983. 2. Periodo
    repubblicano e augusteo. Rome, 1985.
95. Colini, A. M. 'Ambiente e storia dei tempi più antichi [dell'area sacra di
    Sant'Omobono]', PP 32 (1977) 16–19
96. Colini, A. M. et al. 'Area sacra di S. Omobono in Roma. Ricerca

stratigrafica 1974–1976', in *Un decennio di ricerche archeologiche* 11.417–42. Rome, 1978

97. Colonna, G. 'Aspetti culturali della Roma primitiva. Il periodo orientalizzante recente', *Arch. Class.* 16 (1964) 1–12 = id. 'The later orientalising period in Rome' (with additional material) in *Italy before the Romans*, edd. D. and F. R. Ridgway, 223–35. London, 1979

98. Cosentini, C. 'Origini di Roma. Indagini archeologiche e dati storico-tradizionali', in *Studi in memoria di Orazio Condorelli* (Università di Catania, Pubblicazioni della Facoltà di Giurisprudenza 75) 1.349–66. Milan, 1974

99. De Simone, C. 'Il nome del Tevere', *Stud. Etr.* 43 (1975) 145–9

100. Drews, R. 'The coming of the city to central Italy', *AJAH* 6 (1981) 133–65

101. Gelsomino, R. *Varrone e i sette colli di Roma.* Rome, 1975

102. von Gerkan, A. 'Zur Frühgeschichte Roms', *Rh. Mus.* N.F. 100 (1957) 82–97

103. von Gerkan, A. 'Das frühe Rom nach E. Gjerstad', *Rh. Mus.* N.F. 104 (1961) 132–48

104. Gjerstad, E. 'The agger of Servius Tullius', in *Studies presented to D. M. Robinson* 1.413–22. St Louis, 1951

105. Gjerstad, E. 'The fortifications of early Rome', *Op. Rom.* 1 (1954) 50–65

106. Grimal, P. 'Le dieu Janus et les origines de Rome', *Lettres d'Humanité* 4 (1945) 15–121

107. Grimal, P. 'L'enceinte servienne dans l'histoire urbaine de Rome', *MÉFR* 71 (1959) 43–64

108. Holland, L. A. 'Septimontium or Saeptimontium?', *TAPA* 84 (1953) 16–34

109. Loicq, J. 'Les origines de Rome', *Cahiers de Clio* 57 (1979) 35–48

110. Lugli, G. 'I confini del pomerio suburbano di Roma primitiva', in *Mélanges J. Carcopino* (1966) 641–50

111. Magdelain, A. 'Le *pomerium* archaïque et le *mundus*', *RÉL* 54 (1976) 71–109

112. Merlin, A. *L'Aventin dans l'antiquité.* Paris, 1906

113. Meyer, Ernst. 'Zur Frühgeschichte Roms', *MH* 9 (1952) 176–81

114. Müller-Karpe, H. *Vom Anfang Roms. Studien zu den prähistorischen Forums- und Palatingräbern (MDAI(R)* Ergänzung-Heft 5). Heidelberg, 1959

115. Müller-Karpe, H. *Zur Stadtwerdung Roms (MDAI(R)* Ergänzung-Heft 8). Heidelberg, 1962

116. Pallottino, M. 'Le origini di Roma', *Arch. Class.* 12 (1960) 1–36

117. Pallottino, M. 'Fatti e leggende (moderne) sulla più antica storia di Roma', *Stud. Etr.* 31 (1963) 3–37

118. Pallottino, M. 'Le origini di Roma', *ANRW* I.1 (1972) 22–47 = id. 'The origins of Rome', in *Italy before the Romans*, edd. D. and F. R. Ridgway, 197–222. London, 1979

119. Peroni, R. 'Sant' Omobono. Materiali dell'età del ferro', *BCAR* 77 (1959–60 [1962]) 7–32

120. Peroni, R. 'Per una diversa cronologia del sepolcreto arcaico del Foro', in *Civiltà del Ferro. Studi pubblicati nella ricorrenza centenaria della scoperta di Villanova* 461–99. Bologna, 1960

121. Peroni, R. 'L'insediamento subappenninico della valle del Foro e il problema della continuità di insediamento tra l'età di bronzo recente e quella finale nel Lazio', *Arch. Laz.* 1 (1978) 171–6

122. Platner, S. B. and Ashby, T. *A Topographical Dictionary of Ancient Rome.* Oxford, 1929

123. Poucet, J. 'Le Septimontium et la Succusa chez Festus et chez Varron. Un problème d'histoire et de topographie romaines', *Bulletin de l'Institut Historique Belge de Rome* 32 (1960) 25–73

124. Poucet, J. 'L'importance du term "collis" pour l'étude du développement urbain de la Rome archaïque', *Ant. Class.* 36 (1967) 99–115

125. Puglisi, S. M. *Gli abitatori primitivi del Palatino attraverso le testimonianze archeologiche e le nuove indagini stratigrafiche sul Germalo (Monumenti Antichi 41).* Rome, 1951

126. Puglisi, S. M. 'Nuovi resti sepolcrali nella valle del Foro Romano', *BPI* N.S. 8.4 (1952) 5–17

127. Quilici Gigli, St. 'Considerazioni sui confini del territorio di Roma primitiva', *MÉFR(A)* 90 (1978) 567–75

128. Quoniam, P. 'À propos du mur dit de Servius Tullius', *MÉFR* 59 (1947) 41–64

129. Riemann, H. Review of E. Gjerstad, *Early Rome* III (Lund, 1960) in *Göttingische Gelehrte Anzeigen* 222 (1970) 25–66; 223 (1971) 33–86

130. Säflund, G. *Le mura di Roma repubblicana. Saggio di archeologia romana.* Rome, 1932

131. Sartorio, G. P., Colini, A. M. and Buzzetti, C. 'Portus Tiberinus', in *Il Tevere e le altre vie d'acqua del Lazio antico (Arch. Laz.* 7.2 (1986)) 157–97

132. Sartorio, G. P. and Virgili, P. 'Area sacra di S. Omobono', *Arch. Laz.* 2 (1979) 41–7 (with comments by F. Coarelli ib. 123–4)

133. Scrinari, V. S. M. 'Brevi note sugli scavi sotto la chiesa di S. Vito', *Arch. Laz.* 2 (1979) 58–62

134. Sommella, P. 'Appunti tecnici sull'urbanistica di piano romano in Italia', *Arch. Class.* 28 (1976) 10–29

135. Sommella Mura, A. 'L'area sacra di S. Omobono. La decorazione architettonica del tempio arcaico', *PP* 32 (1977) 62–128

136. Sommella Mura, A. 'Roma – Campidoglio ed Esquilino', *Arch. Laz.* 1 (1978) 28–9

137. Stacciolo, R. A. 'A proposito della decorazione frontonale del tempio arcaico di Sant' Omobono', *Arch. Class.* 31 (1979) 286–93

138. Virgili, P. 'L'area sacra di S. Omobono. Scavo stratigrafico (1974–5)', *PP* 32 (1977) 20–34

139. Welin, E. *Studien zur Topographie des Forum Romanum* (Acta Instituti Romani Regni Sueciae ser. 2 (8⁰).6). Lund, 1953

F. THE MONARCHY, THE ESTABLISHMENT OF THE REPUBLIC AND THE LATER ASPIRANTS TO KINGSHIP

See also A33, 38–9, 51, 86–9, 95, 98; B62–3, 86, 125, 225, 230–1, 247; E117; G112, 611, 638; I2–3, 14, 44.

1. Alföldi, A. 'Etruria e Roma intorno al 500 a.C.', in *Atti del I congresso internazionale di archeologia dell'Italia settentrionale, Torino, 21–24 giugno 1961* (Università di Torino, Pubblicazioni della Facoltà di Lettere e Filosofia 14) 3–17. Turin, 1963

2. Basile, M. 'Analisi e valore della tradizione sulla *rogatio Cassia agraria* del 486 a.C.', in *Sesta miscellanea greca e romana* 277–98. Rome, 1978

3. Bauman, R. A. 'The abdication of "Collatinus"', *AClass.* 9 (1966) 129–41

4. Bernardi, A. 'Dagli ausiliari del *rex* ai magistrati della *respublica*', *Athenaeum* N.S. 30 (1952) 3–58

5. Bernardi, A. 'Periodo sabino e periodo etrusco nella monarchia romana', *RSI* 66 (1954) 5–20

6. Bernhöff, F. *Staat und Recht der römischen Königszeit.* Stuttgart, 1882

7. Bessone, E. 'La gente Tarquinia', *Riv. Fil.* 110 (1982) 394–415

8. Bianchi, L. 'Il *magister* Servio Tullio', *Aevum* 59 (1985) 57–68

9. Bloch, R. 'Rome de 509 à 475 environ avant J.C.', *RÉL* 37 (1959) 118–31

10. Bloch, R. 'Le départ des Étrusques de Rome selon l'annalistique et la dédicace du temple de Jupiter Capitolin', *Rev. Hist. Rel.* 159 (1961) 141–56

11. Bottiglieri, S. 'Il caso di Appio Erdonio', *AAN* 88 (1977) 7–20

12. Coarelli, F. 'La doppia tradizione sulla morte di Romolo e gli *auguracula* dell'Arx e del Quirinale', in *Gli Etruschi e Roma* 173–88

13. Coarelli, F. 'Le pitture della tomba François a Vulci. Una proposta di lettura', *DArch.* ser. 3.1.2 (1983) 43–69

14. Coli, U. '*Regnum*', *SDHI* 17 (1951) 1–168 = id. *Regnum*. Florence, 1951 = id. *Scritti di diritto romano* 1.321–483. Milan, 1973

15. Colonna, G. 'Quali etruschi a Roma', in *Gli Etruschi e Roma* 159–68

16. Combet-Farnoux, B. 'Cumes, l'Étrurie et Rome à la fin du VIe siècle et au début du Ve siècle', *MÉFR* 69 (1959) 7–44

17. De Francisci, P. 'Dal "regnum" alla "respublica"', *SDHI* 10 (1944) 150–66

18. De Martino, F. 'Intorno all'origine della repubblica romana e delle magistrature', *ANRW* 1.1 (1972) 217–49 = id. *Diritto e società nell'antica Roma* 88–129

19. De Sanctis, G. 'Mastarna', *Klio* 2 (1902) 96–104

20. Dovere, E. 'Contributo alla lettura delle fonti su Porsenna', *AAN* 95 (1984) 69–126

21. Dubourdieu, A. 'L'exil de Tarquin Collatin à Lavinium', *Latomus* 43 (1984) 733–50

22. Ferenczy, E. 'Lo stato romano fra la monarchia e la repubblica', in *Studi in onore di A. Biscardi* III.101–10. Milan, 1982

23. Gagé, J. 'Les femmes de Numa Pompilius', in *Mélanges de philosophie, de littérature et d'histoire ancienne offerts à P. Boyancé* (Collection de l'École Française de Rome 22), 281–98. Rome, 1974

24. Gagé, J. *La chute des Tarquins et les débuts de la république romaine.* Paris, 1976

25. Gantz, T. N. 'The Tarquin dynasty', *Historia* 24 (1975) 539–54

26. Giannelli, G. 'Il tempio di Giunone Moneta e la casa di Marco Manlio Capitolino', *BCAR* 87 (1980–1 [1982]) 7–36

27. Gioffredi, C. 'Rex, praetores e pontifices nella evoluzione dal regno al regime consolare', BCAR 71 (1943–5) 129–35
28. Gjerstad, E. 'The origins of the Roman republic', in Les origines de la république romaine (Entretiens Hardt 13) 3–43. Geneva, 1967
29. Gjerstad, E. 'Porsenna and Rome', Op. Rom. 7 (1969) 149–61
30. Grise, Y. 'Pourquoi "retuer" un mort? Un cas de suicide dans la Rome royale', in Mélanges d'études anciennes offerts à M. Lebel 261–81. Quebec, 1980
31. Guarino, A. 'La formazione della respublica romana', RIDA ser. 1.1 (1948) 95–112 = id. Le origini quiritarie 48–62
32. Guarino, A. 'Dal regnum alla respublica', Labeo 9 (1963) 346–55 = id. Le origini quiritarie 63–74
33. Guarino, A. 'Post reges exactos', Labeo 17 (1971) 320–9
34. Henderson, M. I. 'Potestas regia', JRS 47 (1957) 82–7
35. Hulsen, C. 'I veri fondatori di Roma', RPAA 2 (1924) 83–6
36. d'Ippolito, F. 'La legge agraria di Spurio Cassio', Labeo 21 (1975) 197–210
37. Jordan, H. Die Könige im alten Italien: ein Fragment. Berlin, 1887
38. Kunkel, W. 'Zum römischen Königtum', in Ius et Lex. Festgabe zum 70. Geburtstag von M. Gutzwiller 3–22. Basle, 1959
39. Lintott, A. W. 'The traditions of violence in the annals of the early Roman republic', Historia 19 (1970) 12–29
40. Lyngby, H. 'Columna Minucia', Eranos 61 (1963) 55–62
41. Magdelain, A. 'Quando rex comitiavit fas', RHDFÉ ser. 4.58 (1980) 5–11
42. Martínez-Pinna, J. 'Tarquinio Prisco y Servio Tulio', Archivo Español de Arqueologia 55 (1982) 35–63
43. Martin, P. M. L'idée de la royauté à Rome, I: De la Rome royale au consensus républicain (Miroir des civilisations antiques 1). Clermont-Ferrand, 1982
44. Martin, P. M. 'Tanaquil, la "faiseuse de rois"', Latomus 44 (1985) 5–15
45. Mastrocinque, A. 'La cacciata di Tarquinio il Superbo. Tradizione romana e letteratura greca', Athenaeum N.S. 61 (1983) 457–80; 62 (1984) 210–29
46. Mastrocinque, A. 'Il cognomen "Publicola"', PP 39 (1984) 211–20
47. Mazzarino, S. Dalla monarchia allo stato repubblicano. Catania, 1945
48. Momigliano, A. 'Due punti di storia romana arcaica', SDHI 2 (1936) 373–98 = id. Quarto Contributo 329–61
49. Momigliano, A. 'Sulla data dell'inizio della repubblica', RSI 75 (1963) 882–8 = id. Terzo Contributo 661–8
50. Momigliano, A. 'Il rex sacrorum e l'origine della repubblica', in Studi in onore di E. Volterra 1.357–64. Milan, 1971 = id. Quarto Contributo 395–402
51. Mommsen, Th. 'Sp. Cassius, M. Manlius, Sp. Maelius, die drei Demagogen der älteren republikanischen Zeit', Hermes 5 (1871) 228–71 = id. Römische Forschungen II.153–220. Berlin, 1879
52. Pallottino, M. 'Servius Tullius à la lumière des nouvelles découvertes archéologiques et épigraphiques', CR Acad. Inscr. 1977, 216–35
53. Pasquali, G. 'La grande Roma dei Tarquinii', Nuova Antologia 1936, 405–16 = id. Terze pagine stravaganti 1–24. Florence, 1942 = id. Pagine stravaganti II 5–21. Florence, 1968
54. Pollera, A. 'La carestia del 439 a.C. e l'uccisione di Spurio Melio', BIDR 82 (1979) 143–68

55. Poma, G. *Gli studi recenti sull'origine della repubblica romana.* Bologna, 1974
56. Préaux, J.-G. 'La sacralité du pouvoir royal à Rome', in *Le pouvoir et le sacré* (Annales du Centre d'Étude des Religions 1) 103–22. Brussels, 1962
57. Richard, J.-C. 'L'oeuvre de Servius Tullius. Essai de mise au point', *RHDFÉ* ser. 4. 61 (1983) 181–93
58. Ridley, R. T. 'The enigma of Servius Tullius', *Klio* 57 (1975) 147–77
59. Rosenberg, A. '*Rex*', *RE* 2. Reihe, 1 (1914) 703–21
60. Scevola, M. L. 'Conseguenze della *deditio* di Roma a Porsenna', *RIL* 109 (1975) 3–27
61. Schachermeyr, F. 'Tarquinius', *RE* 2. Reihe, 4 (1931) 2348–90
62. Thomsen, R. *King Servius Tullius: a Historical Synthesis.* Copenhagen, 1980
63. Tränkle, H. 'Der Anfänge des römischen Freistaats in der Darstellung des Livius', *Hermes* 93 (1965) 312–37
64. Valeri, V. 'Regalità', in *Enciclopedia*, ed. G. Enaudi, 11.742–71. Turin, 1980
65. Valvo, A. 'Le vicende del 44–43 a.C. nella tradizione di Livio e di Dionigi su Spurio Melio', in *Storiografia e Propaganda (CISA* 3), ed. M. Sordi, 157–83. Milan, 1975
66. Valvo, A. 'La sedizione di Manlio Capitolino in Tito Livio', *MIL* 38.1 (1983) 5–64
67. Valvo, A. 'Il cognomen "Capitolinus" in età repubblicana e il sorgere dell'area sacra sull'arce e il Campidoglio', in *I santuari e la guerra nel mondo classico (CISA* 10), ed. M. Sordi, 92–106. Milan, 1984
68. Wesenberg, G. 'Zu Frage der Kontinuität zwischen königlicher Gewalt und Beamtengewalt in Rom', *ZSS* 70 (1953) 58–92
69. Wiseman, T. P. 'Topography and rhetoric: the trial of Manlius', *Historia* 28 (1979) 32–50

G. EARLY ROME

a. SOCIAL, ECONOMIC AND CULTURAL DEVELOPMENT

See also B(b) for coinage; B(c) for archaeological evidence; A7, 9, 13–14, 21–2, 31–3, 41–3, 47, 54, 56–7, 60, 67, 83, 107, 121–2, 125–6, 133; B198, 201, 208, 214, 227, 251–2, 254, 263, 265, 268; C2; E131; F48; G172–3, 183, 187, 189, 198; 211, 230, 234, 314, 387, 395–7, 449, 454, 522, 560, 741; H31, 56, 98; I14: J32, 142, 162, 167; K162.

1. Altheim, F. *Rom und der Hellenismus.* Amsterdam–Leipzig, 1942
2. Ampolo, C. 'Su alcuni mutamenti sociali nel Lazio tra l'VIII e il V secolo', *DArch.* 4–5 (1970–1) 37–68
3. Ampolo, C. 'Demarato. Osservazioni sulla mobilità sociale arcaica', *DArch.* 9–10 (1976–7) 333–45
4. Ampolo, C. 'I gruppi etnici in Roma arcaica: posizione del problema e fonti', in *Gli Etruschi e Roma* 45–70
5. Ampolo, C. 'Il lusso funerario e la città antica', *AION (Archeol)* 6 (1984) 71–102
6. Andrén, A. 'In quest of Vulca', *RPAA* 49 (1976–7 [1978]) 63–83

7. Appleton, C. 'Contribution à l'histoire du prêt à intérêt à Rome', *RHDFÉ* 43 (1919) 467–543

8. Arangio-Ruiz, V. *Le genti e la città*. Messina, 1914 = id. *Scritti di diritto romano* (Pubblicazioni della Facoltà di Giurisprudenza dell'Università di Camerino) 1.519–87. Naples, 1974

9. Bayer, E. 'Rom und die Westgriechen bis 280 v.Chr.', *ANRW* 1.1 (1972) 305–40

10. Beloch, K. J. *Die Bevölkerung der griechisch-römischen Welt*. Leipzig, 1886

11. Benveniste, E. 'Deux modèles linguistiques de la cité', in *Échanges et communications. Mélanges offerts à Cl. Lévi-Strauss à l'occasion de son 60ème anniversaire* 1.589–96. The Hague–Paris, 1970

12. Besnier, R. 'L'état économique de Rome de 509 à 264 a.C.', *RHDFÉ* ser. 4. 33 (1955) 195–226

13. Bettini, M. '*Pater, avunculus, avus* nella cultura romana più arcaica', *Athenaeum* N.S. 62 (1984) 468–91

14. Bianchi Bandinelli, R. *Rome the Centre of Power*. London, 1972

15. Bietti Sestieri, A. M. 'Economy and society in Italy between the late Bronze Age and early Iron Age', in *Archaeology and Italian Society* (*BAR* International Series 102), edd. G. Barker and R. Hodges, 133–55. Oxford, 1981

16. Boëthius, A. and Ward-Perkins, J. B. *Etruscan and Roman Architecture*. London, 1970

17. Bonfante, G. 'The origin of the Latin name-system', in *Mélanges de philologie, de littérature et d'histoire ancienne offerts à J. Marouzeau* 43–59. Paris, 1948

18. Bonfante, G. 'Il nome delle donne nella Roma arcaica', *RAL* ser. 8.25 (1980) 3–10

19. Bonfante, L. 'Historical art: Etruscan and early Roman', *AJAH* 3 (1978) 136–62

20. Botsford, G. W. 'Some problems connected with the Roman *gens*', *Political Science Quarterly* 22 (1907) 663–92

21. Bozza, F. *La possessio dell'ager publicus*. Naples, 1938

22. Brunt, P. A. Review-discussion of W. L. Westermann, *The Slave Systems of Greek and Roman Antiquity* (Philadelphia, 1955) etc. in *JRS* 48 (1958) 164–70

23. Burdese, A. *Studi sull'ager publicus*. Turin, 1952

24. Capogrossi Colognesi, L. 'Le régime de la terre à l'époque républicaine', in *Terre et paysans dépendants dans les sociétés antiques. Colloque international, Besançon, 2–3 mai 1974*, 313–88. Paris, 1979

25. Capogrossi Colognesi, L. 'Alcuni problemi di storia romana arcaica: *ager publicus, gentes* e clienti', *BIDR* 83 (1980) 29–65

26. Capogrossi Colognesi, L. *La terra in Roma antica. Forme di proprietà e rapporti produttivi, I: L'età arcaica*. Rome, 1981

27. Capogrossi Colognesi, L. '*Ager publicus* e *ager gentilicius* nella riflessione storiografica moderna', in *Studi in onore di Cesare Sanfilippo* (Pubblicazioni della Facoltà di Giurisprudenza dell'Università di Catania 96) III.73–106. Milan, 1982

28. Capozza, M. *Movimenti servili nel mondo romano in età repubblicana* I. Rome, 1966
29. Castello, C. *Studi sul diritto familiare e gentilizio romano* I. Turin, 1960
30. Castello, C. 'Lo schiavo tra persone e cose nell'arcaico diritto romano', in *Studi in onore di A. Biscardi* 1.93–116. Milan, 1983
31. Cels-Saint-Hilaire, J. and Feuvrier-Prévotat, C. 'Guerres, échanges, pouvoir à Rome à l'époque archaïque', *Dialogues d'histoire ancienne* 5 (1979) 103–44
32. Clerici, L. *Economica e finanza dei Romani* I. Bologna, 1943
33. Coarelli, F. 'Classe dirigente romana e arti figurative', *DArch.* 4–5 (1970–1) 241–65
34. Coli, U. 'Le origini de la *civitas* romana secondo De Francisci', *Studi Senesi* 71 (1959) 375–423 = id. *Scritti di diritto romano* II.677–717. Milan, 1973
35. Colonna, G. 'Firme arcaiche di artefici nell'Italia centrale', *MDAI(R)* 82 (1975) 181–92
36. Colonna, G. '*Scriba cum rege sedens*', in *Mélanges J. Heurgon* (1976) 1.187–95
37. Colonna, G. 'Nome gentilizio e società', *Stud. Etr.* 45 (1977) 175–92
38. Colonna, G. 'Un tripode fittile geometrico dal Foro Romano', *MÉFR(A)* 89.2 (1977) 471–91
39. Cook, R. M. 'Die Bedeutung der bemalten Keramik für den griechischen Handel', *JDAI* 74 (1959) 114–23
40. Coughanowr, E. 'The plague in Livy and Thucydides', *Ant. Class.* 54 (1985) 152–8
41. Cracco Rugini, L. 'Esperienze economiche e sociali nel mondo romano', in *Nuove questioni di storia antica* 685–813. Milan, 1969
42. Crawford, M. H. 'The early Roman economy', in *Mélanges J. Heurgon* (1976) 1.197–207
43. Cristofani, M. 'Sull' origine e la diffusione dell' alfabeto etrusco', *ANRW* I.2 (1972) 466–89
44. Cristofani, M. 'Artisti etruschi a Roma nell'ultimo trentennio del VI secolo a.C.', *Prospettiva* 9 (1977) 2–7
45. Cristofani, M. 'Rapporto sulla diffusione della scrittura nell'Italia antica', *S&C* 2 (1978) 5–33
46. Cristofani Martelli, M. 'Prime considerazioni sulla statistica delle importazioni greche in Etruria nel periodo arcaico', *Stud. Etr.* 47 (1979) 37–52
47. Crook, J. A. '*Patria potestas*', *CQ* N.S. 17 (1967) 113–22
48. De Martino, F. 'La *gens*, lo stato e le classi in Roma antica', in *Studi V. Arangio-Ruiz* IV.25–49. Naples, 1953. = id. *Diritto e società nell'antica Roma* 51–74
49. De Martino, F. 'Intorno alle origini della schiavitù in Roma', *Labeo* 20 (1974) 163–93 = id. *Diritto e società nell'antica Roma* 130–61
50. De Martino, F. 'Produzione di cereali in Roma nell'età arcaica', *PP* 34 (1979) 241–55
51. De Martino, F. *Storia economica di Roma antica.* 2 vols. Florence, 1980
52. De Martino, F. 'Clienti e condizioni materiali in Roma arcaica', in *Miscellanea E. Manni* (1980) II.681–705

53. De Martino, F. 'Ancora sulla produzione di cereali in Roma arcaica', *PP* 39 (1984) 241–63

54. Denoyez, L. 'Le *paterfamilias* et l'évolution de sa position', in *Synteleia V. Arangio-Ruiz* 1.441–9. Naples, 1964

55. De Robertis, F. M. *Storia delle corporazioni e del regime associativo nel mondo romano* 1. Bari, 1971

56. Dieter, H. 'Zur Rolle der Sklaverei in der frühen römischen Republik', in *Produktivkräfte und Gesellschaftsformationen in vorkapitalistischer Zeit* (Veröffentlichungen des Zentralinstituts für Alte Geschichte und Archäologie der Akademie der Wissenschaften der DDR 12), edd. J. Herrmann and I. Sellnow, 331–8. Berlin, 1982

57. Dumézil, G. *Mariages indo-européens*. Paris, 1979

58. Dumont, J. C. 'Le gentilice: nom de citoyen ou d'esclave?', *Ktema* 6 (1981) 105–14

59. Fayer, C. *Aspetti di vita quotidiana nella Roma arcaica dalle origini all'età monarchica* (Studia Archaeologica 22). Rome, 1982

60. Ferenczy, E. 'Die Bevölkerung vom mindesten Recht Roms zur Zeit der Frührepublik', *A Ant. Hung.* 21 (1973) 153–60

61. Ferenczy, E. 'Eherecht und Gesellschaft in der Zeit der Zwölftafeln', *Oikumene* 2 (1978) 153–61

62. Ferenczy, E. 'Clientela e schiavitù nella repubblica romana primitiva', *Index* 8 (1978–9) 167–72

63. Ferenczy, E. 'Über die alte Klientel', *Oikumene* 3 (1982) 193–201

64. Finley, M. I. 'Between slavery and freedom', *CSSH* 6 (1963–4) 233–49

65. Finley, M. I. 'La servitude pour dettes', *RHDFÉ* ser. 4.43 (1965) 159–84. Revised and translated as 'Debt bondage and the problem of slavery', in M. I. Finley, *Economy and Society in Ancient Greece* (edd. R. Saller and B. D. Shaw) 150–66. London, 1981

66. Finley, M. I. *Ancient Slavery and Modern Ideology*. London, 1980

67. Franciosi, G. *Clan gentilizio e strutture monogamiche* 1. Naples, 1978

68. Franciosi, G. (ed.). *Ricerche sulla organizzazione gentilizia romana* 1. Naples, 1984

69. Frank, T. *An Economic History of Rome*. Ed. 2. London, 1927

70. Frank, T. 'Roman census statistics from 508 to 225 B.C.', *AJPhil.* 51 (1930) 313–24

71. Frank, T. *An Economic Survey of Ancient Rome*. 6 vols. Baltimore, 1933–40

72. Frayn, J. M. 'Subsistence farming in Italy during the Roman period. A preliminary discussion of the evidence', *G&R* 21 (1974) 11–18

73. Frayn, J. M. *Subsistence Farming in Roman Italy*. London, 1979

74. Gabba, E. 'Per la tradizione dell'*heredium* romuleo', *RIL* 112 (1978) 250–8

75. Gabba, E. 'The *collegia* of Numa: Problems of method and political ideas', *JRS* 74 (1984) 81–6

76. Gabba, E. and Pasquinucci, M. *Strutture agrarie e allevamento transumante nell'Italia romana*. Pisa, 1980

77. Garnsey, P., Hopkins, K. and Whittaker, C. R. (edd.). *Trade in the Ancient Economy*. London, 1983

78. Giovannini, A. 'Le sel et la fortune de Rome', *Athenaeum* N.S. 63 (1985) 373–88

79. Gnoli, F. 'Di una recente ipotesi sui rapporti tra *pecus, pecunia, peculium*', *SDHI* 44 (1978) 204–18

80. Gordon, A. E. 'On the origins of the Latin alphabet: modern views', *CSCA* 2 (1969) 157–70

81. Gras, M. 'Vin et société à Rome et dans le Latium à l'époque archaïque', in *Modes de contacts et processus de transformation dans les sociétés antiques* 1067–75. Pisa–Rome, 1983

82. Grenier, A. 'La transhumance des troupeaux en Italie et son rôle dans l'histoire romaine', *MÉFR* 25 (1905) 293–328

83. Guarino, A. '*Lex Manlia de vicesima*', in Μνήμη Γεωργίου Ἀ. Πετροπούλου, edd. A. Biscardi et al., 1.415–20. Athens, 1984

84. Günther, R. 'Die Entstehung der Schuldsklaverei im alten Rom', *AAnt. Hung.* 7 (1959) 231–49

85. Hafner, G. 'Bildnisse des 5. Jhs. v. Chr. aus Rom und Umgebung', *MDAI(R)* 76 (1969) 14–50

86. Hanard, G. 'Aux origines de la famille romaine. Critique de la méthode de P. Bonfante', *Revue Interdisciplinaire d'Études Juridiques* 5 (1980) 63–115; 6 (1981) 127–74

87. Heinze, R. '*Fides*', *Hermes* 64 (1929) 140–66

88. Heitland, W. E. *Agricola: A Study of Agriculture and Rustic Life in the Greco-Roman World from the Point of View of Labour.* Cambridge, 1921

89. Hermon, E. 'Réflexions sur la propriété à l'époque royale', *MÉFR(A)* 90 (1978) 7–31

90. Hoffmann, W. *Rom und die griechische Welt im 4. Jahrhundert (Philologus* Suppl. 27.1). Leipzig, 1934

91. Jasny, N. *The Wheats of Classical Antiquity* (John Hopkins University Studies in Historical and Political Science 62). Baltimore, 1944

92. Jel'Nickij, L. A. *The Origin and Development of Slavery in Rome from the Eighth to the Third Century B.C.* (in Russian). Moscow, 1964

93. Judson, S. and Kahane, A. 'Underground drainageways in southern Etruria and northern Latium', *PBSR* 31 (1963) 74–99

94. Kajanto, I. *The Latin Cognomina* (Societas Scientiarum Fennica, Commentationes Humanarum Litterarum 36.ii). Helsinki, 1965

95. Kaser, M. 'Der Inhalt der *patria potestas*', *ZSS* 58 (1938) 62–87

96. Kaser, M. 'Zur altrömischen Hausgewalt', *ZSS* 67 (1949) 474–97

97. Kaser, M. 'La famiglia romana arcaica', *Annali Triestini* 4 (1950) 43–64

98. Kaufmann, H. *Die altrömische Miete: ihre Zusammenhänge mit Gesellschaft, Wirtschaft und staatlicher Vermögensverwaltung* (Forschungen zum römischen Recht Abh. 18). Cologne, 1964

99. La Rocca, E. 'Note sulle importazioni greche in territorio laziale nell' VIII secolo a.C.', *PP* 32 (1977) 375–97

100. La Rocca, E. 'Ceramica d'importazione greca dell'VIII secolo a.C. a Sant'Omobono. Un aspetto delle origini di Roma', in *La céramique grecque ou de tradition grecque en Italie centrale et méridionale* (Cahiers du Centre Jean-Bérard 3) 45–54. Naples, 1982

101. La Rocca, E. 'Fabio o Fannio. L'affresco medio-repubblicano dell'Esquilino come riflesso dell'arte "rappresentiva" e come espressione di mobilità sociale', *DArch.* ser. 3.2 (1984) 31–54

102. Lemosse, M. 'Affranchissement, clientèle, droit de cité', *RIDA* ser. 1.3 (*Mélanges F. De Visscher* II) (1949) 37–68

103. Lemosse, M. 'L'affranchissement par le cens', *RHDFÉ* ser. 4.27 (1949) 161–203

104. Levi, M. A. *Ne liberi ne schiavi*. Milan, 1976

105. Lévy-Bruhl, H. 'Esquisse d'une théorie sociologique de l'esclavage à Rome', *Revue Général de Droit* 55 (1931) 1–17

106. Lintott, A. W. *Violence in Republican Rome*. Oxford, 1968

107. Luzzatto, G. I. *Le organizzazioni preciviche e lo stato*. Modena, 1948

108. Luzzatto, G. I. 'Il passaggio dall'ordinamento gentilizio alla monarchia in Roma e l'influenza dell'ordinamento delle *gentes*', in *Atti del convegno internazionale sul tema: Dalla tribù allo stato* 193–234. Rome, 1962

109. Magdelain, A. 'Remarques sur la société romaine archaïque', *RÉL* 49 (1971) 103–27

110. *La Magna Grecia e Roma nell'età arcaica (Atti VIII convegno di studi sulla Magna Grecia)*. Naples, 1969

111. Majak, I. L. 'Les rapports agraires dans la Rome archaïque' (in Russian), *Klio* 65 (1983) 169–84

112. Meyer, J. C. 'Roman history in the light of the import of Attic vases to Rome and Etruria in the 6th and 5th centuries B.C.', *ARID* 9 (1980) 47–69

113. Millan Mendez, A. 'Organización primitiva de los pueblos indo-europeos y la politica socio-religiosa de Roma', *Annales de Historia Antigua y Medieval* 17 (1972) 148–209

114. Modestov, B. *Der Gebrauch der Schrift unter den römischen Königen*. Berlin, 1871

115. Mommsen, Th. 'Die römische Clientel', *HZ* 1859, 1.322–79 = id. *Römische Forschungen* 1.355–85. Berlin, 1864

116. Moreau, Ph. 'Plutarque, Augustin, Lévi-Strauss. Prohibition de l'inceste et mariage préférentiel dans la Rome primitive', *RBPhil*. 56 (1978) 41–54

117. Morel, J.-P. 'Sur quelques aspects de la jeunesse à Rome', in *Mélanges J. Heurgon* (1976) II.663–83

118. Moritz, L. A. *Grain-Mills and Flour in Classical Antiquity*. Oxford, 1958

119. Oxé, R. 'Zur älteren Nomenklatur der römischen Sklaven', *Rh. Mus.* N.F. 59 (1904) 108–40

120. Pallottino, M. 'Lo sviluppo socio-istituzionale di Roma arcaica alla luce di nuovi documenti epigrafici', *Stud. Rom.* 27 (1979) 1–14

121. Paribeni, E. 'Considerazioni sulle sculture originali greche di Roma', in *La Magna Grecia e Roma nell'età arcaica (Atti VIII Convegno Magna Grecia, Taranto 1968*) 83–9. Naples, 1969

122. Poma, G. 'Schiavi e schiavitù in Dionigi di Alicarnasso', *RSA* 11 (1981) 69–101

123. Porisini, G. *Produttività e agricoltura: i rendimenti del frumento in Italia dal 1815 al 1922*. Turin, 1971

124. Pulgram, E. 'The origin of the Latin *nomen gentilicium*', *HSCP* 58–9 (1948) 163–87

125. Ramírez, J. L. 'Importaciones de trigo en Roma en el siglo V a.c.', *Faventia* 5 (1983) 97–109

126. Rawson, E. 'Chariot-racing in the Roman republic', *PBSR* 49 (1981) 1–16
127. Reichmuth, J. *Die lateinische Gentilicia und ihre Beziehungen zu den römischen Individualnamen* (diss. Zurich, 1956)
128. Richard, J.-C. 'Sur les prétendues corporations numaïques: à propos de Plutarque, *Num.* 17, 3', *Klio* 60 (1978) 423–8
129. Richardson, E. H. 'The Etruscan origins of early Roman sculpture', *MAAR* 21 (1953) 77–124
130. Rickman, G. *The Corn Supply of Ancient Rome.* Oxford, 1980
131. Riis, P. J. 'Art in Etruria and Latium during the first half of the fifth century B.C.', in *Les origines de la république romaine* (*Entretiens Hardt* 13) 65–91. Geneva, 1967
132. Rix, H. 'Zum Ursprung des römisch-mittelitalischen Gentilnamensystems', *ANRW* 1.2 (1972) 700–58
133. Rodriguez Adrados, F. *El systema gentilicio decimal y los orígenes de Roma.* Madrid, 1948
134. Rouland, N. *Pouvoir politique et dépendance personnelle dans l'antiquité romaine. Genèse et rôle des rapports de clientèle* (Collection Latomus 166). Brussels, 1979
135. Roussel, D. *Tribu et cité.* Paris, 1976
136. Sartori, F. 'La Magna Grecia e Roma', *Archivio Storico per la Campania e la Lucania* 28 (1959) 137–91
137. Scalais, R. 'La production agricole dans l'état romain et les importations de blés provinciaux jusqu'à la seconde guerre punique', *Le Musée Belge* 29 (1925) 143–63
138. Schulze, W. *Zur Geschichte lateinischer Eigennamen.* Berlin, 1904
139. Schulze, W. 'Beiträge zur Wort- und Sittengeschichte II', *Sitzungsberichte der Preussischen Akademie der Wissenschaften* 1918, 481–511 = id. *Kleine Schriften* 160–89. Berlin, 1934
140. Skydsgaard, J. E. 'Transhumance in ancient Italy', *ARID* 7 (1974) 7–36
141. Sombart, W. *Die römische Campagna. Eine sozialökonomische Studie.* Leipzig, 1888
142. Storchi Marino, A. 'La tradizione plutarchea sui *collegia opificum* di Numa', *Annali dell'Istituto Italiano per gli Studi Storici* 3 (1971–2) 1–53
143. Strasburger, H. 'Zum antiken Gesellschaftsideal', *Abhandlungen der Heidelberger Akademie der Wissenschaften*, Phil.-hist. Klasse 1976 n. 4
144. Tamborini, F. 'La vita economica nella Roma degli ultimi re', *Athenaeum* N.S. 8 (1930) 299–328, 452–87
145. Thomas, Y. 'Mariages endogamiques à Rome. Patrimoine, pouvoir et parenté depuis l'époque archaïque', *RHDFÉ* ser. 4.58 (1980) 345–82
146. Thomas, Y. '*Vitae necisque potestas*. Le père, la cité, la mort', in *Du châtiment dans la cité* (Collection de l'École Française de Rome 79) 499–548. Paris, 1984
147. Tibiletti, G. 'Il possesso dell'*ager publicus* e le norme *de modo agrorum* sino ai Gracchi', *Athenaeum* N.S. 26 (1948) 173–236; 27 (1949) 3–42
147A. Tibiletti, G. 'Ricerche di storia agraria romana I: La politica agraria dalla guerra annibalica ai Gracchi', *Athenaeum* N.S. 28 (1950) 183–266
148. Torelli, M. 'Tre studi di storia etrusca', *DArch.* 8 (1974–5) 3–78

149. Torelli, M. 'Rome et l'Étrurie à l'époque archaïque', in *Terre et paysans dépendants dans les sociétés antiques. Colloque international, Besançon, 2–3 mai 1974*, 251–313. Paris, 1979

150. Treggiari, S. *Roman Freedmen during the Late Republic.* Oxford, 1969

151. Ullmann, B. S. 'The Etruscan origin of the Roman alphabet and the name of the letters', *CPhil.* 22 (1927) 372–7

152. Usener, H. 'Italische Volksjustiz', *Rh. Mus.* N.F. 56 (1901) 1–28 = id. *Kleine Schriften* IV.356–82. Leipzig, 1913

153. von Vacano, O.-W. 'Vulca, Rom und die Wölfin. Untersuchungen zur Kunst des frühen Rom', *ANRW* 1.4 (1973) 523–83

154. Vallet, G. 'L'introduction de l'olivier en Italie centrale d'après les données de la céramique', in *Hommages A. Grenier* (1962) III.1554–63

155. Virlouvet, C. *Famines et émeutes à Rome des origines de la république à la mort de Néron.* Rome, 1985

156. Volkmann, H. 'Die Massenversklavungen der Einwohner eroberten Städte in hellenistisch-römischen Zeit', *Abhandlungen der Akademie der Wissenschaften zu Mainz*, Geistes- und sozialwissenschaftliche Klasse 1961 n. 3

157. Watson, A. '*Enuptio gentis*', in *Daube Noster. Essays in Legal History for D. Daube* 331–41. Edinburgh–London, 1974

158. Weber, M. *Die römische Agrargeschichte in ihrer Bedeutung für das Staats- und Privatrecht.* Stuttgart, 1891

159. Weber, M. 'Agrarverhältnisse im Altertum', in *Handwörterbuch der Staatswissenschaften* 1.52–188. Ed. 3. Jena, 1890 = id. *Gesammelte Aufsätze zur Sozial- und Wirtschaftsgeschichte* 1–288. Tübingen, 1924

160. Weber, V. 'Zur Geschichte des römischen Vereinswesens', *Klio* 59 (1977) 247–56

161. Westrup, C. W. *Some Notes on the Roman Slave in Early Times, a Comparative Sociological Study (Hist.-filol. Meddel. udg. af dar Danske Vidensk. Selskab 36.3).* Copenhagen, 1956

162. White, K. D. *Roman Farming.* London, 1970

163. Wieacker, F. '*Endoplorare.* Diebstahlsverfolgung und Gerüft im altrömischen Recht', in *Festschrift für L. Wenger (Münch. Beitr. Papyr. 34–5)* I.129–79. Munich, 1944–5

164. Williams, G. 'Some aspects of Roman marriage ceremonies and ideals', *JRS* 48 (1958) 16–29

165. Yaron, R. '*Vitae necisque potestas*', *RHD* 30 (1962) 243–51

166. Yeo, C. A. 'The overgrazing of ranch-lands in ancient Italy', *TAPA* 79 (1948) 275–309

167. Zancan, L. *Ager publicus. Ricerche di storia e di diritto romano.* Padua, 1935

168. Zehnacker, H. '*Unciarium fenus* (Tacite, *Annales* VI.16)', in *Mélanges P. Wuilleumier* (1980) 353–62

b. LAW

See also the items listed in the *Abbreviations* as Bruns, *FIRA*. See further A114, 121–2, 142, 178; F6; G26, 29–30, 47, 54–5, 89, 95–8, 146, 157, 163, 165, 168, 531, 649, 656, 659; H71.

169. Badian, E. 'Three non-trials in Cicero. Notes on the text, prosopography and chronology of *Divinatio in Caecilium* 63', *Klio* 66 (1984) 291–309

170. Bauman, R. A. *The Duumviri in the Roman Criminal Law and in the Horatius Legend* (*Historia* Einzelschriften 12). Wiesbaden, 1969

171. Behrends, O. Review of A. H. M. Jones, *The Criminal Courts of the Roman Republic and Principate* (Oxford, 1972) in *ZSS* 90 (1973) 462–75

172. Behrends, O. *Der Zwölftafelprozess. Zur Geschichte des römischen Obligationenrechts* (Göttinger rechtswiss. Stud. 92). Göttingen, 1974

173. Behrends, O. 'Das *nexum* im Manzipationsrecht oder die Ungeschichtlichkeit des Libraldarlehens', *RIDA* ser. 3.21 (1974) 137–84

174. Birks, P. 'English beginnings and Roman parallels', *IJ* N.S. 6 (1971) 147–62

175. Birks, P. 'A note on the development of *furtum*', *IJ* N.S. 8 (1973) 349–55

176. Bonfante, P. *Res mancipi e nec mancipi*. Rome, 1888

177. Bonfante, P. *Corso di diritto romano* i–iii and vi. Rome, 1925–33

178. Bonfante, P. *Scritti giuridici* i. Turin, 1926

179. Bonfante, P. *Storia del diritto romano* i. Ed. 4. Milan, 1958 (reprint)

180. Brunt, P. A. Review of W. Kunkel, *Untersuchungen zur Entwicklung des römischen Kriminalverfahrens in vorsullanischer Zeit* (Munich, 1962) in *RHD* 32 (1964) 440–9

181. Burdese, A. 'Riflessioni sulla repressione penale romana in età arcaica', *BIDR* 69 (1966) 342–54

182. Carcopino, J. 'Les prétendues lois royales', *MÉFR* 54 (1937) 344–76

183. Chantraine, H. 'Zur Entstehung der Freilassung mit Bürgerrechtserwerb in Rom', *ANRW* i.2 (1972) 59–67

184. *Du châtiment dans la cité. Supplices corporels et peine de mort dans le monde antique. Table ronde organisée par l'École Française de Rome avec le concours du Centre National de la Recherche Scientifique (Rome 9–11 novembre 1982).* (Collection de l'École Française de Rome 79). Paris, 1984

185. Ciulei, G. 'Gab es einen Einfluss des griechischen Rechts in den Zwölftafeln?', in *Gesellschaft und Recht in griech.-röm. Altertum* (Deutsche Akademie der Wissenschaften zu Berlin. Schriften der Sektion für Altertumswissenschaft 52), ed. M. N. Andreev, ii.21–46. Berlin, 1969

186. Cloud, J. D. '*Parricidium* from the *lex Numae* to the *lex Pompeia de parricidiis*', *ZSS* 88 (1971) 1–66

187. Cosentini, C. *Studi sui liberti: contributo allo studio della condizione giuridica dei liberti cittadini* (Università di Catania. Pubblicazioni della Facoltà di Giurisprudenza 11 & 14). 2 vols. Catania, 1948 and 1950

188. Crifò, G. 'La legge delle XII tavole: osservazioni e problemi', *ANRW* i.2 (1972) 115–33

189. Daube, D. 'Two early patterns of manumission', *JRS* 36 (1946) 57–75

190. Daube, D. *Forms of Roman Legislation*. Oxford, 1956

191. Daube, D. 'Texts and interpretation in Roman and Jewish law', *Jewish Journal of Sociology* 3 (1961) 3–28

192. Daube, D. 'The preponderance of intestacy at Rome', *Tulane Law Review* 39 (1964–5) 253–62

193. Daube, D. *Roman Law: Linguistic, Social and Philosophical Aspects*. Edinburgh, 1969

194. Daube, D. 'The self-understood in legal history', *Juridical Review* N.S. 18 (1973) 126–34

195. Daube, D. 'Money and justiciability', *ZSS* 96 (1979) 1–16

196. Delz, J. 'Die griechische Einfluss auf die Zwölftafelgesetzgebung', *MH* 23 (1966) 69–83

197. De Martino, F. 'Storia arcaica e diritto romano privato', *RIDA* ser. 1.4 (1950) 387–407 = id. *Diritto e società nell'antica Roma* 34–50

198. De Visscher, F. *Le régime romain de la noxalité: de la vengeance collective à la responsabilité individuelle*. Brussels, 1947

199. De Zulueta, F. 'The recent controversy about *nexum*', *LQR* 29 (1913) 137–53

200. De Zulueta, F. *The Institutes of Gaius*. 2 vols. Oxford, 1953

201. Diamond, A. S. *Primitive Law: Past and Present*. Ed. 2. London, 1971

202. Diósdi, G. '*Familia pecuniaque*. Ein Beitrag zum altrömischen Eigentum', *AAnt. Hung.* 12 (1964) 87–105

203. Diósdi, G. *Ownership in Ancient and Preclassical Roman Law*. Budapest, 1970

204. Diósdi, G. *Contract in Roman Law from the Twelve Tables to the Glossators*. Budapest, 1981

205. Ducos, M. *L'influence grecque sur la loi des douzes tables*. Paris, 1978

206. Eder, W. 'The political significance of the codification of law in archaic societies: an unconventional hypothesis', in *Social Struggles in Archaic Rome*, ed. K. A. Raaflaub, 262–300. California, 1986

207. Ferenczy, E. 'Vom Ursprung der *decemviri stlitibus iudicandis*', *ZSS* 89 (1972) 338–44

208. Ferenczy, E. 'Uti legassit . . . ita ius esto', *Oikumene* 1 (1976) 173–83

209. Ferenczy, E. 'Das römisches Strafrecht zur Zeit der Zwölftafeln', *AUB* 7 (1979) 45–51

210. Ferenczy, E. 'Römische Gesandtschaft im Perikleischen Athen', *Oikumene* 4 (1983) 37–42

211. Fraenkel, E. Review of F. Beckmann, *Zauberei und Recht in Roms Fruhzeit* (Münster, 1923) in *Gnomon* 1 (1925) 185–200 = id. *Kleine Beiträge zur klassischen Philologie* 11.400–15. Rome, 1964

212. Franciosi, G. '"Partes secanto", tra magia e diritto', *Labeo* 24 (1978) 263–75

213. Frezza, P. 'La costituzione cittadina di Roma ed il problema degli ordinamenti giuridici preesistenti', in *Scritti in onore di C. Ferrini pubblicati in occasione della sua beatificazione*, ed. A. Gemelli, 1.275–98. Milan, 1947–9

214. Gagé, J. 'Les primitives ordalies tiberines et les recherches ostiennes', in *Hommage à la mémoire de Jerome Carcopino* 119–38. Paris, 1977

215. Gallo, F. *Studi sulla distinzione fra res mancipi e res nec mancipi* (Memorie dell'Istituto Giuridico dell'Università di Torino ser. 2a.102). Turin, 1958

216. Gallo, F. '*Potestas* e *dominium* nell'esperienza giuridica romana', *Labeo* 16 (1970) 17–58

217. Gaudemet, J. '"Uti legassit . . ." (XII Tables V.3)', in *Hommages à R.*

G. EARLY ROME 721

Schilling (Collection d'Études Latines, Série Scientifique 37), edd. H. Zehnacker and G. Hentz, 109–15. Paris, 1983

218. Gioffredi, C. 'Su XII Tab. VI, 1', *SDHI* 27 (1961) 343–50
219. Girard, P. F. 'L'histoire des XII Tables', *Nouvelle Revue Historique de Droit Français et Étranger* 26 (1902) 381–436
220. Greenidge, A. H. J. 'The authenticity of the Twelve Tables', *EHR* 20 (1905) 1–21
221. Heinze, R. '*Supplicium*', *ALL* 15 (1908) 89–105
222. Horak, F. 'Kreditvertrag und Kreditprozess in den Zwölftafeln' (review of O. Behrends, *Der Zwölftafelprozess* (Göttingen, 1974)), *ZSS* 93 (1976) 261–86
223. Imbert, J. '*Fides* et *nexum*', in *Studi V. Arangio-Ruiz* 1.339–63. Naples, 1953
224. d'Ippolito, F. 'Das *ius Flavianum* und die *lex Ogulnia*', *ZSS* 102 (1985) 91–128
225. d'Ippolito, F. *Giuristi e sapienti in Roma arcaica*. Rome–Bari, 1986
226. von Jhering, R. 'Reich und Arm im altrömischen Civilprozess', in id. *Scherz und Ernst in der Jurisprudenz* 175–232. Ed. 10. Leipzig, 1909
227. Jolowicz, H. F. and Nicholas, B. *Historical Introduction to the Study of Roman Law*. Ed. 3. London, 1972
228. Jones, A. H. M. *The Criminal Courts of the Roman Republic and Principate.* Oxford, 1972
229. Karlowa, O. *Römische Rechtsgeschichte.* 2 vols. Leipzig, 1885–1901
230. Kaser, M. 'Die Anfänge der Manumissio und das fiduziarisch gebundene Eigentum', *ZSS* 61 (1941) 153–86
231. Kaser, M. 'Zum Ursprung des geteilten römischen Zivilprozessverfahrens', in *Festschrift für L. Wenger (Münch. Beitr. Papyr.* 34–5) 1.106–28. Munich, 1944–5
232. Kaser, M. *Das altrömische Ius. Studien zur Rechtsvorstellung und Rechtsgeschichte der Römer.* Göttingen, 1949
233. Kaser, M. 'Religione e diritto in Roma antica', *Annali del Seminario Giuridico di Catania* 3 (1949) 77–98
234. Kaser, M. Review of C. Cosentini, *Studi sui liberti* (Catania, 1948–50) in *ZSS* 68 (1951) 576–86
235. Kaser, M. *Eigentum und Besitz im älteren römischen Recht* (Forschungen zum römischen Recht Abh. 1). Ed. 2. Cologne, 1956
236. Kaser, M. 'Typisierter *dolus* im altrömischen Recht', *BIDR* 65 (1962) 79–104
237. Kaser, M. 'The concept of Roman ownership', *Tydskrif vir Hedendaagse Romeins-Hollandse Reg* 27 (1964) 5–19
238. Kaser, M. *Das römische Zivilprozessrecht* (Handbuch der Altertumswissenschaft X. 3.4). Munich, 1966
239. Kaser, M. *Römische Rechtsgeschichte.* Ed. 2. Göttingen, 1967
240. Kaser, M. *Das römische Privatrecht I. Das altrömische, das vorklassische und klassische Recht* (Handbuch der Altertumswissenschaft X. 3.3). Ed. 2. Munich, 1971
241. Kaser, M. 'Die Beziehung von Lex und Ius und die XII Tafeln', in *Studi in memoria di Guido Donatuti* II.523–46. Milan, 1973
242. Kelly, J. M. *Roman Litigation.* Oxford, 1966

243. Kelly, J. M. 'A note on threefold mancipation', in *Daube Noster, Essays in Legal History for David Daube* 183–86. Edinburgh, 1974

244. Kelly, J. M. *Studies in the Civil Judicature of the Roman Republic.* Oxford, 1976

245. Kunkel, W. *Untersuchungen zur Entwicklung des römischen Kriminalverfahrens in vorsullanischer Zeit* (*Abhandlungen der Bayerischen Akademie der Wissenschaften* Phil.-hist. Klasse, N.F. 56). Munich, 1962

246. Kunkel, W. 'Das Konsilium im Hausgericht', *ZSS* 83 (1966) 219–51

247. Kunkel, W. 'Die Funktion des Konsiliums in der magistratischen Strafjustiz und im Kaisergericht', *ZSS* 84 (1967) 218–44

248. Kunkel, W. 'Ein direktes Zeugnis für den privaten Mordprozess im altrömischen Recht', *ZSS* 84 (1967) 382–85

249. Lambert, E. 'La question de l'authenticité des XII Tables et les Annales Maximi', *Nouvelle Revue Historique de Droit Français et Étranger* 26 (1902) 149–200

250. Lambert, E. *La fonction du droit civil comparé.* Paris, 1903

251. Lambert, E. 'L'histoire traditionelle des XII Tables et les critères d'inauthenticité des traditions en usage dans l'école de Mommsen', in *Mélanges Ch. Appleton. Études d'histoire du droit dédiées à M. Ch. Appleton à l'occasion de son XXVe anniversaire de professorat* 501–626. Lyon, 1903

252. Latte, K. 'Religiöse Begriffe in frührömischen Recht', *ZSS* 67 (1949) 47–61 = id. *Kleine Schriften* 329–40

253. Lauria, M. *Ius Romanum* 1.1. Naples, 1963

254. Lauria, M. '. . . usus auctoritas fundi biennium est', in *De iustitia et iure. Festgabe für U. von Lübtow zum 80. Geburtstag,* edd. M. Harder and G. Thielmann, 163–86. Berlin, 1980

255. Lévy-Bruhl, H. *Nouvelles études sur le très ancien droit romain* (Publications de l'Institut de Droit Romain de l'Université de Paris 1). Paris, 1947

256. Lévy-Bruhl, H. *Quelques problèmes du très ancien droit romain.* Paris, 1934

257. Lévy-Bruhl, H. 'La vente de la fille de famille à Rome', in *Festschrift für H. Lewald* 93–100. Basle, 1953

258. Lévy-Bruhl, H. *Recherches sur les actions de la loi.* Paris, 1960

259. von Lübtow, U. 'Zum Nexumproblem', *ZSS* 67 (1949) 112–61

260. MacCormack, G. '*Nexi, iudicati* and *addicti* in Livy', *ZSS* 84 (1967) 350–5

261. MacCormack, G. '*Partes secanto*', *RHD* 36 (1968) 509–18

262. MacCormack, G. 'Formalism, symbolism and magic in early Roman law', *RHD* 37 (1969) 439–68

263. MacCormack, G. 'Roman and African litigation', *RHD* 39 (1971) 221–55

264. MacCormack, G. 'Criminal liability for fire in early and classical Roman law', *Index* 3 (1972) 382–96

265. MacCormack, G. 'The *lex Poetelia*', *Labeo* 19 (1973) 306–17

266. MacCormack, G. 'Anthropology and early Roman law', *IJ* N.S. 14 (1979) 173–87

267. MacCormack, G. 'Fault and causation in early Roman law. An anthropological perspective', *RIDA* ser. 3.28 (1981) 97–126

268. MacCormack, G. 'A note on a recent interpretation of "paricidas esto"', *Labeo* 28 (1982) 43–50

269. Magdelain, A. 'Remarques sur la *perduellio*', *Historia* 22 (1973) 405–22

270. Magdelain, A. 'Aspects arbitraux de la justice civile archaïque à Rome', *RIDA* ser. 3.27 (1980) 205–81

271. Magdelain, A. 'L'acte *per aes et libram* et l'*auctoritas*', *RIDA* ser.3.28 (1981) 127–61

272. Magdelain, A. 'Les mots *legare* et *heres* dans la loi des XII Tables', in *Hommages à R. Schilling* (Collection d'Études Latines, Série Scientifique 37), edd. H. Zehnacker and G. Hentz, 159–73. Paris, 1983

273. Magdelain, A. '*Paricidas*', in *Du châtiment dans la cité. Supplices corporels et peine de mort dans le monde antique* (Collection de l'École Française de Rome 79) 549–71. Rome, 1984

274. Michel, J. H. *Gratuité en droit romain.* Brussels, 1963

275. Michon, L. 'La succession "ab intestato" d'après les XII Tables', *RHDFÉ* 45 (1921) 119–64

276. Mitteis, L. 'Über das Nexum', *ZSS* 22 (1901) 96–125

277. Mommsen, Th. *Römisches Strafrecht.* Leipzig, 1899

278. Münzer, F. 'Hermodorus', *RE* 8 (1913) 859–61

279. Noailles, P. *Fas et ius.* Paris, 1948

280. Ogilvie, R. M. 'The maid of Ardea', *Latomus* 21 (1962) 477–83

281. Pagliaro, A. 'La formula "paricidas esto"', in *Studi in onore di L. Castiglioni* II.669–731. Florence, 1961

282. Paoli, J. 'Le Ius Papirianum et la loi Papiria', *RHDFÉ* ser. 4. 24 (1946–7) 157–200

283. Peppe, L. *Studi sull'esecuzione personale 1: Debiti e debitori nei primi due secoli della repubblica romana* (Università di Roma: Pubblicazioni dell'Istituto di Diritto Romano e dei Diritti dell'Oriente Mediterraneo 60). Milan, 1981

284. Pólay, E. 'Das Jurisprudenzmonopol des Pontifikalkollegiums in Rom und seine Abschaffung', *Acta Classica Universitatis Scientiarum Debreceniensis* 19 (1983) 49–56

285. Pólay, E. '*Iniuria*-Tatbestände im archaische Zeitalter des antiken Rom', *ZSS* 101 (1984) 142–89

286. Prichard, A. M. 'Early *usucapio*', *LQR* 90 (1974) 234–45

287. Prichard, A. M. '*Auctoritas* in early Roman law', *LQR* 90 (1974) 378–95

288. Pugliese, G. '*Res corporales, res incorporales* e il problema del diritto soggettivo', in *Studi V. Arangio-Ruiz* (1953) III.223–60

289. Rabello, A. M. *Effetti personali della 'patria potestas' 1: Dalle origini al periodo degli Antonini* (Pubblicazioni della Università degli Studi di Milano, Istituto di Diritto Romano 12). Milan, 1979

290. Radke, G. 'Sprachliche und historische Beobachtungen zu den *Leges XII tabularum*', in *Sein und Werden im Recht. Festgabe für Ulrich von Lübtow* 223–46. Berlin, 1970

291. Radke, G. 'Versuch einer Sprach- und Sachbedeutung alter römischer Rechtsbegriffe', in *De iustitia et iure. Festgabe für U. von Lübtow zum 80. Geburtstag*, edd. M. Harder and G. Thielmann, 9–44. Berlin, 1980

292. Ruoff-Väänänen, E. 'The Roman senate and criminal jurisdiction during the Roman republic', *Arctos* 12 (1978) 125–33

293. Ruschenbusch, E. 'Die Zwölftafeln und die römische Gesandtschaft nach Athen', *Historia* 12 (1963) 250–3

294. Santalucia, B. 'Osservazioni sui *duumviri perduellionis* e sul procedimento duumvirale', in *Du châtiment dans la cité. Supplices corporels et peine de mort dans le monde antique* (Collection de l'École Française de Rome 79) 439–52. Rome, 1984

295. Scherillo, G. '*Res mancipi et nec mancipi*, cose immobili e mobili', in *Synteleia V. Arangio-Ruiz* 83–96. Naples, 1964

296. Schmidlin, B. 'Zur Bedeutung des *legis actio*: Gesetzesklage oder Spruchklage?', *RHD* 38 (1970) 367–87

297. Schönbauer, E. '*Mancipium* und *nexus*', *Iura* 1 (1950) 300–5

298. Schönbauer, E. 'Studien zum römischen Strafrecht und Strafverfahren', *AAWW* 102 (1965) 251–83

299. Selb, W. 'Vom geschichtlichen Wandel der Aufgabe des *iudex* in der *legis actio*', in *Gedächtnisschrift für Wolfgang Kunkel*, edd. D. Nörr and D. Simon, 391–448. Frankfurt am Main, 1984

300. Siewert, P. 'Die angebliche Übernahme solonischer Gesetze in die Zwölftafeln. Ursprung und Ausgestaltung einer Legende', *Chiron* 8 (1978) 331–44

301. Täubler, E. *Untersuchungen zur Geschichte des Dezemvirats*. Berlin, 1921

302. Thomas, Y. '*Parricidium*, 1: Le père, la famille et la cité (la Lex Pompeia et le système des poursuites publiques)', *MÉFR(A)* 93 (1981) 643–715

303. Thormann, K. F. *Der doppelte Ursprung der Mancipatio* (*Münch. Beitr. Papyr.* 33). Ed. 2. Munich, 1969

304. Tomulescu, C. St. 'Infractions de droit pénal public dans la loi des XII Tables', *RIDA* ser. 3.26 (1979) 437–52

305. Tomulescu, C. St. 'Quelques petites études de droit romain', *BIDR* 82 (1979) 95–117

306. Tondo, S. 'Introduzione alle *leges regiae*', *SDHI* 37 (1971) 1–73

307. Tondo, S. *Leges regiae e paricidas* (*AATC* Studi 26). Florence, 1973

308. Tyrrell, W. B. 'The *duumviri* in the trials of Horatius, Manlius and Rabirius', *ZSS* 91 (1974) 106–25

309. van den Brink, H. '*Ius fasque*', *Labeo* 16 (1970) 140–76

310. Voci, P. 'Diritto sacro romano in età arcaica', *SDHI* 19 (1953) 38–103

311. Voci, P. *Diritto ereditario romano*. 2 vols. Ed. 2. Milan, 1963 and 1967

312. Volterra, E. 'Tite-Live 4,9 et le droit d'Ardée au Ve siècle avant J.-C.', *RIDA* ser. 3.13 (1966) 390–1

313. Watson, A. 'The divorce of Carvilius Ruga', *RHD* 33 (1965) 38–50

314. Watson, A. 'Roman private law and the *leges regiae*', *JRS* 62 (1972) 100–5

315. Watson, A. 'The law of actions and the development of substantive law in the early Roman republic', *LQR* 89 (1973) 387–92

316. Watson, A. *Legal Transplants: An Approach to Comparative Law*. Edinburgh, 1974

317. Watson, A. *Rome of the Twelve Tables: Persons and Property*. Princeton, 1975

318. Watson, A. 'Personal injuries in the Twelve Tables (VIII.1ff.)', *RHD* 43 (1975) 213–22

319. Watson, A. 'The origin of *usus*', *RIDA* ser.3.23 (1976) 265–70

320. Watson, A. 'The death of Horatia', *CQ* N.S. 29 (1979) 436–47

321. Watson, A. 'La mort d'Horatia et le droit pénal archaïque à Rome', *RHDFÉ* ser. 4.57 (1979) 5–20

322. Wenger, L. *Die Quellen des römischen Rechts.* Vienna, 1953

323. Westrup, C. W. *Introduction to Early Roman Law.* 5 vols. London–Copenhagen, 1934–54

324. Wieacker, F. *Hausgenossenschaft und Erbeinsetzung. Über die Anfänge des römischen Testaments.* Leipzig, 1940

325. Wieacker, F. *Vom römischen Recht. Wirklichkeit und Überlieferung.* Leipzig, 1944

326. Wieacker, F. 'Zwölftafelprobleme', *RIDA* ser. 3.3 (1956) 459–91

327. Wieacker, F. 'Die XII Tafeln in ihrem Jahrhundert', in *Les origines de la république romaine (Entretiens Hardt* 13) 291–359. Geneva, 1967

328. Wieacker, F. 'Solon und die XII Tafeln', in *Studi in onore di E. Volterra* III.757–84. Milan, 1971

329. Wieacker, F. 'Ius. Die Entstehung einer archaischen Rechtsordnung im archaischen Rom', in *Rechtswissenschaft und Rechtsentwicklung* (Göttinger Rechtswissenschaftliche Studien 111), ed. H. Immenga, 33–52. Göttingen, 1980

330. Wieacker, F. 'Rechtsaustrag und Rechtsvorstellung im archaischen Rom', in *Entstehung und Wandel rechtlicher Traditionen* (Veröffentlichungen des Instituts für historische Anthropologie 2), ed. W. Fikentscher, 581–609. Freiberg, 1980

331. Wolf, J. G. '*Lanx* und *licium.* Das Ritual der Haussuchung im altrömischen Recht', in *Sympotica Franz Wieacker sexagenario Sasbachwaldeni a suis libata* 59–79. Göttingen, 1970

332. Wolff, H. J. 'Ein Vorschlag zum Verständnis des Manzipationsrituals', in *Beiträge zur europäischen Rechtsgeschichte und zum geltenden Zivilrecht. Festgabe für J. Sontis,* edd. F. Bauer, K. Larenz and F. Wieacker, 53–89. Munich, 1977

333. Yaron, R. 'Two notes on intestate succession', *RHD* 25 (1957) 385–97

334. Yaron, R. 'Minutiae on Roman divorce', *RHD* 28 (1960) 1–12

335. Yaron, R. 'Reflections on *usucapio*', *RHD* 35 (1967) 191–229

336. Yaron, R. '*Si pater filium ter venum duit*', *RHD* 36 (1968) 57–72

337. Yaron, R. 'Semitic elements in early Rome', in *Daube Noster. Essays in Legal History for D. Daube* 343–57. Edinburgh, 1974

c. RELIGION

See also B(c) for archaeological evidence; E(a) for 'foundation' cults; E(b) for Roman shrines; A31, 41–3, 54, 65, 116; B26, 271; D24; F12, 26–7, 41, 50, 56, 67, 224–7, 233, 252, 310, 532–4, 557, 590, 597, 613–14, 618, 627, 652–3, 655, 659, 668–9, 705, 714, 741–2, 747; H50, 83, 89; J43, 60.

338. *Akten des Kolloquiums zum Thema Die Göttin von Pyrgi. Archäologische, linguistische und religionsgeschichtliche Aspekte (Tübingen, 16–17 Januar 1979)* (Biblioteca di Studi Etruschi 12). Florence, 1981

339. Alföldi, A. 'Diana Nemorensis', *AJA* 64 (1960) 137–44

340. Alföldi, A. 'Il santuario federale latino di Diana sull'Aventino e il tempio di Ceres', *SMSR* 32 (1961) 21–39

341. Altheim, F. *Griechische Götter im alten Rom.* Giessen, 1930

342. Altheim, F. *Römische Religionsgeschichte.* Berlin–Leipzig, 1931. Translated as *A History of Roman Religion.* London, 1938

343. Ampolo, C. 'L'Artemide di Marsiglia e la Diana dell'Aventino', *PP* 25 (1970) 200–10

344. Appel, G. *De Romanorum precationibus* (Religionsgeschichtliche Versuche und Vorarbeiten 7.2). Giessen, 1909

345. Banti, L. 'Il culto del cosidetto tempio dell'Apollo a Veii e il problema delle triadi etrusco-italiche', *Stud. Etr.* 17 (1943) 187–224

346. Bartoloni, G., Cataldi Dini, M., and Zevi, F. 'Aspetti dell'ideologia funeraria nella necropoli di Castel di Decima', in *La mort, les morts dans les sociétés anciennes*, edd. G. Gnoli and J.-P. Vernant, 257–73. Cambridge, 1982

347. Bartoloni, G. 'Riti funerari dell'aristocrazia in Etruria e nel Lazio. L'esempio di Veio', *Opus* 3 (1984) 13–29

348. Bayet, J. *Les origines de l'Hercule romain* (Bibliothèque des Écoles Françaises d'Athènes et de Rome 132). Paris, 1926

349. Bayet, J. 'Les malédictions du tribune C. Ateius Capito', in *Hommages à G. Dumézil* (Collection Latomus 45) 46–53. Brussels, 1960 = id. *Croyances et rites dans la Rome antique* 353–65. Paris, 1971

350. Bayet, J. *Histoire politique et psychologique de la religion romaine.* Ed. 2. Paris, 1969

351. Bayet, J. *Croyances et rites dans la Rome antique.* Paris, 1971

352. Beard, M. 'The sexual status of Vestal Virgins', *JRS* 70 (1980) 12–27

353. Bleicken, J. 'Oberpontifex und Pontifikalkollegium. Eine Studie zur römischen Sakralverfassung', *Hermes* 85 (1957) 345–66

354. Bloch, R. 'L'origine du culte des Dioscures à Rome', *Rev. Phil.* 34 (1960) 182–93

355. Bloch, R. *Les prodiges dans l'antiquité classique.* Paris, 1963

356. Bloch, R. 'Recherches sur la religion romaine du VIe siècle avant J.-C.', *CRAcad. Inscr.* 1978, 669–87

357. Bloch, R. (ed.). *Recherches sur les religions de l'antiquité classique.* Geneva–Paris, 1980

358. Bloch, R. 'Recherches sur la religion romaine du VIe siècle et du début du Ve siècle av. J.-Chr.', in id. (ed.) *Recherches sur les religions de l'antiquité classique* 347–82. Geneva–Paris, 1980

359. Bömer, F. *Ahnenkult und Ahnenglaube im alten Rom* (Archiv für Religionswissenschaft Beiheft 1). Leipzig, 1943

360. Le Bonniec, H. *Le culte de Cérès à Rome des origines à la fin de la république.* Paris, 1958

361. Le Bonniec, H. 'Au dossier de la "lex sacra" trouvée à Lavinium', in *Mélanges J. Heurgon* (1976) I.509–17

362. Le Bourdellès, H. 'Nature profonde du pontificat romain. Tentative d'une étymologie', *Rev. Hist. Rel.* 189 (1976) 53–66

363. Le Bourdellès, H. 'Le Flamen et le Brahmane', *RÉL* 57 (1979) 69–84; 58 (1980) 124–5
364. Boyancé, P. *Études sur la religion romaine.* Rome, 1972
365. Brelich, A. *Die geheime Schutzgottheit von Rom.* Zurich, 1949
366. Brelich, A. Bibliographies of Roman religion from 1939 in *Doxa* 2 (1949) 136–66; *Studi Romani* 2 (1954) 570–7; 4 (1956) 590–4; 6 (1958) 591–4; 9 (1961) 301–7; 11 (1963) 581–9; 15 (1967) 70–8; 19 (1971) 315–22; 23 (1975) 195–205; 25 (1977) 401–12; 26 (1978) 78–86; 31 (1983) 307–13
367. Brelich, A. 'Quirinus. Una divinità romana alla luce della comparazione storica', *SMSR* 31 (1960) 63–119
368. Brind'Amour, P. *Le calendrier romain; recherches chronologiques* (Collection d'études anciennes de l'Université d'Ottawa 2). Ottawa, 1983
369. Briquel, D. 'Sur les aspects militaires du dieu ombrien Fisus Sancius', *MÉFR(A)* 90 (1978) 133–52
370. Cardauns, B. 'Varro und die römische Religion', *ANRW* II.16.1 (1978) 80–103
371. Carettoni, G. 'La *domus virginum Vestalium* e la *domus publica* del periodo repubblicano', *RPAA* 51–2 (1978–80) 325–55
372. Castagnoli, F. 'Sul tempio "Italico"', *MDAI (R)* 83–4 (1966–7) 10–14
373. Castagnoli, F. 'Les sanctuaires du Latium archaïque', *CRAcad. Inscr.* 1977, 460–76
374. Castagnoli, F. 'Il culto della Mater Matuta e della Fortuna nel Foro Boario', *Stud. Rom.* 27 (1979) 145–52
375. Castagnoli, F. 'L'introduzione del culto dei Dioscuri nel Lazio', *Stud. Rom.* 31 (1983) 3–12
376. Castagnoli, F. 'Il tempio romano: questioni di terminologia e di tipologia', *PBSR* 52 (1984) 3–20
377. Catalano, P. *Contributo allo studio del diritto augurale* I (Università di Torino. Memorie dell'Istituto Giuridico ser. 2, Mem. 107). Turin, 1960
378. Catalano, P. 'Aspetti spaziali del sistema giuridico-religioso romano. *Mundus, templum, urbs, ager*, Latium, Italia', *ANRW* II.16.1 (1978) 440–53
379. Champeaux, J. *Fortuna. Recherches sur le culte de la Fortuna à Rome et dans le monde romain. Des origines à la mort de César, I: Fortuna dans la religion archaïque* (Collection de l'École Française de Rome 64). Paris, 1982
380. Cloud, J. D. 'Numa's calendar in Livy and Plutarch', *LCM* 4 (1979) 65–71
381. Colonna, G. 'Sull'origine del culto di Diana Aventinensis', *PP* 17 (1962) 57–60
382. Colonna, G. 'L'ideologia funeraria e il conflitto delle culture', *Arch. Laz.* 4 (1981) 229–32
383. Colonna, G. 'Tarquinio Prisco e il tempio di Giove Capitolino', *PP* 31 (1981) 41–59
384. Combet-Farnoux, B. *Mercure romain: le culte public de Mercure et la fonction mercantile à Rome de la république archaïque à l'époque augustéenne* (Bibliothèque des Écoles Françaises d'Athènes et de Rome 238). Rome, 1980

385. Comella, A. 'Tipologia e diffusione dei complessi votivi in Italia in epoca medio e tardo repubblicana', *MÉFR(A)* 93 (1981) 717–803

386. Cornell, T. J. 'Some observations on the "crimen incesti"', in *Le délit religieux dans la cité antique* (Collection de l'École Française de Rome 48) 27–37. Paris, 1981

387. Corsano, M. '*Sodalitas* et gentilité dans l'ensemble lupercal', *Rev. Hist. Rel.* 191 (1977) 137–58

388. Degrassi, A. *Inscriptiones Italiae, vol. XIII – Fasti et elogia, fasc. II – Fasti anni Numani et Iuliani.* Rome, 1963

389. Delatte, A. 'Les doctrines pythagoriciennes des livres de Numa', *Bulletin de l'Académie Royale Belgique* (Classe des Lettres et des Sciences Politiques) ser. 5.22 (1936) 19–40

390. Del Basso, E. 'Virgines Vestales', *AAN* 85 (1974) 161–249

391. *Le délit religieux dans la cité antique* (Collection de l'École Française de Rome 48). Rome, 1981

392. De Marchi, A. *Il culto privato di Roma antica.* 2 vols. Milan, 1896/1903

393. Diels, H. *Sibyllinische Blätter.* Berlin, 1890

394. Drerup, H. 'Zur Zeitstellung des Kapitolstempels in Rom', *Marburger Winckelmann-Programm 1973* [1974] 1–12

395. Dumézil, G. *Jupiter Mars Quirinus.* 3 vols. Paris, 1941–5

396. Dumézil, G. *Mythe et épopée.* 3 vols. Paris, 1968–73

397. Dumézil, G. *Idées romaines.* Paris, 1969

398. Dumézil, G. *La religion romaine archaïque.* Ed. 2. Paris, 1974. First edition translated as:

399. Dumézil, G. *Archaic Roman Religion.* London–Chicago, 1970–1

400. Dumézil, G. *Fêtes romaines d'été et d'automne.* Paris, 1975

401. Fenelli, M. 'Contributi per lo studio del votivo anatomico. I votivi anatomici di Lavinio', *Arch. Class.* 27 (1975) 206–52

402. Flamant, J. 'L'année lunaire aux origines du calendrier pré-julien', *MÉFR(A)* 96.2 (1984) 175–93

403. Foresti, L. A. 'Zur Zeremonie der Nagelschlagung in Rom und Etrurien', *AJAH* 4 (1979) 144–56

404. Fraschetti, A. 'Le sepolture rituali del Foro Boario', in *Le délit religieux dans la cité antiquè* (Collection de l'École Française de Rome 48), ed. J. Scheid, 51–115. Rome, 1981

405. Fugier, H. *Recherches sur l'expression du sacré dans la langue latine.* Paris, 1963

406. Gagé, J. *Apollon romain: essai sur le culte d'Apollon et le développement du 'ritus Graecus' à Rome des origines à Auguste.* Paris, 1935

407. Gagé, J. 'Quirinus fut-il le dieu des Fabii?', in *Mélanges A. Piganiol* (1966) III.1591–1605

408. Gagé, J. 'Les superstitions de l'écorce et le rôle rituel des fûts de troncs d'arbres dans l'Italie primitive', *MÉFR(A)* 91 (1979) 545–70

409. Le Gall, J. '*Evocatio*', in *Mélanges J. Heurgon* (1976) 1.519–24

410. Gerschel, L. 'Saliens de Mars et Saliens de Quirinus', *Rev. Hist. Rel.* 138 (1950) 145–51

411. Gjerstad, E. 'The temple of Saturn in Rome. Its date of dedication and the early history of the sanctuary', in *Hommages A. Grenier* (1962) II.757–62

412. Gjerstad, E. 'The Aventine sanctuary of Diana', *Acta Archaeologica* 41 (1970) 99–107

413. Gjerstad, E. 'Pales, Palilia, Parilia', in *Studia Romana in honorem P. Krarup*, 1–5. Odense, 1976

414. Gordon, A. E. 'On the origin of Diana', *TAPA* 63 (1932) 177–92

415. Gordon, A. E. *The Cults of Aricia*. Berkeley, 1934

416. Grant, F. C. *Ancient Roman Religion* (Library of Liberal Arts 138). New York, 1957

417. Grenier, A. *Les religions étrusque et romaine*. Paris, 1948

418. Guarducci, M. 'Janus Geminus', in *Mélanges A. Piganiol* (1966) III.1607–21

419. Guarducci, M. 'Nuove osservazioni sulla lamina bronzea di Cerere a Lavinio', in *Mélanges J. Heurgon* (1976) 1.411–25

420. Guittard, C. 'Recherches sur la nature de Saturne, des origines à la réforme de 217 av. J.-C.', in *Recherches sur les religions de l'Italie antique*, ed. R. Bloch, 43–71. Geneva, 1976

421. Guittard, C. 'Aspects épiques de la première décade de Tite-Live; le rituel de la *devotio*', in *L'épopée greco-latine*, ed. R. Chevallier, 33–44. Paris, 1981

422. Guizzi, F. *Il sacerdozio di Vesta. Aspetti giuridici dei culti romani*. Naples, 1962

423. Guizzi, F. *Aspetti giuridici del sacerdozio romano. Il sacerdozio di Vesta*. Naples, 1968

424. Hackens, T. 'Capitolium Vetus', *Bulletin de l'Institut Historique Belge de Rome* 33 (1961) 69–88

425. Hauben, H. 'Some observations on the early Roman calendar', *Anc. Soc.* 11–2 (1980–1) 241–55

426. Hoffmann, W. *Wandel und Herkunft der Sibyllinischen Bücher in Rom* (diss. Leipzig, 1933)

427. Hölscher, T. *Victoria Romana*. Mainz, 1967

428. Hookes, E. M. 'The significance of Numa's religious reforms', *Numen* 10 (1963) 87–132

429. Koch, C. *Der römische Iuppiter* (Frankfurter Studien zur Religion und Kultur der Antike 14). Frankfurt, 1937

430. Koch, C. 'Vesta', *RE* 2. Reihe, 8 (1958) 1717–76

431. Koch, C. *Religio. Studien zu Kult und Glauben der Römer*. Nuremberg, 1960

432. Koch, C. 'Quirinus', *RE* 24 (1963) 1306–21

433. Köves-Zulauf, T. *Reden und Schweigen*. Munich, 1972

434. Lambrechts, P. 'Mars et les Saliens', *Latomus* 5 (1946) 111–19

435. Latte, K. *Römische Religionsgeschichte* (Handbuch der Altertumswissenschaft v.4). Munich, 1960

436. Liénard, E. 'Calendrier de Romulus. Les débuts du calendrier romain', *Ant. Class.* 50 (1981) 469–82

437. Linderski, J. 'The augural law', *ANRW* II.16.3 (1986) 2146–312

438. Liou-Gille, B. *Cultes 'heroiques' romains. Les fondateurs*. Paris, 1980

439. Loicq, J. 'Mamurius Veturius et l'ancienne représentation italique de l'année', in *Hommages J. Bayet* (1964) 401–26

440. MacBain, B. *Prodigy and Expiation: a Study in Religion and Politics in Republican Rome* (Collection Latomus 177). Brussels, 1982

441. Maddoli, G. 'Il rito degli Argei e le origini del culto di Hera a Roma', *PP* 26 (1971) 153–66

442. Martinez-Pinna, J. 'Evidenza di un tempio di Giove Capitolino a Roma all'inizio del VI sec. a.C.', *Arch. Laz.* 4 (1981) 249–52

443. Martin, P. M. 'Architecture et politique: le temple de Jupiter Capitolin', *Caesarodunum* 18 bis (1983) 9–29

444. Martorana, G. 'Un' ipotesi sui Lupercalia', in *Studi di storia antica offerti dagli allievi a E. Manni* 1.241–58. Rome, 1976

445. Maule, Q. F. and Smith, H. R. W. *Votive Religion at Caere: Prolegomena.* Berkeley–Los Angeles, 1959

446. Michels, A. K. *The Calendar of the Roman Republic.* Princeton, 1967

447. Momigliano, A. 'Camillus and Concord', *CQ* 36 (1942) 111–20 = id. *Secondo Contributo* 89–104

448. Momigliano, A. 'Sul *dies natalis* del santuario federale di Diana sull'Aventino', *RAL* ser. 8.17 (1962) 387–92 = id. *Terzo Contributo* 641–8

449. Momigliano, A. 'Premesse per una discussione su Georges Dumézil', *Opus* 2 (1983) 329–42

450. Moskovszky, E. 'Larentia and the god. Archaeological aspects of an ancient Roman legend', *A Arch. Hung.* 25 (1973) 241–64

451. Münzer, F. 'Die römischen Vestalinnen bis zur Kaiserzeit', *Philologus* N.F. 46 (1937–8) 47–67, 199–222

452. Münzer, F. and Jörs, P. 'Ti. Coruncanius (Coruncanius 3)', *RE* 4 (1901) 1663–5

453. Nilsson, M. P. 'Saeculares ludi', *RE* 2. Reihe, 1 (1920) 1696–1720

454. Norden, E. *Aus altrömischen Priesterbüchern* (Skrifter utgivna av. Kungl. Humanistika Vetenskapssamfundet i Lund 29). Lund, 1939

455. North, J. A. 'Conservatism and change in Roman religion', *PBSR* 44 (1976) 1–12

456. North, J. A. 'Religious toleration in republican Rome', *PCPhS* 25 (1979) 85–103

457. Ogilvie, R. M. 'Some cults of early Rome', in *Hommages M. Renard* (1969) II.566–72

458. Olshausen, E. 'Über die römischen Ackerbrüder. Geschichte eines Kultes', *ANRW* II.16.1 (1978) 820–32

459. Pairault, F. H. 'Diana Nemorensis, déesse latine, déesse hellenisée', *MÉFR* 81 (1969) 425–71

460. Palmer, R. E. A. 'The censors of 312 B.C. and the state religion', *Historia* 14 (1965) 294–324

461. Palmer, R. E. A. *Roman Religion and Roman Empire. Five Essays* (The Harvey Foundation Series 154). Philadelphia, 1974

462. Palmer, R. E. A. 'Roman shrines of female chastity from the Caste Struggle to the Papacy of Innocent I', *RSA* 4 (1974) 113–59

463. Pena, M. J. 'La dedicación y el dedicante del templo de Júpiter Capitolino', *Faventia* 3 (1981) 149–70

464. Pena Gimeno, M. J. 'Artemis-Diana y algunas cuestiones en relacion con sua iconografia y suo culto en Occidente', *Ampurias* 35 (1973) 109–34

465. Peruzzi, E. 'Haruspices Sabinorum', PP 24 (1969) 5–33

466. Peyre, C. 'Castor et Pollux et les Pénates pendant la période républicaine', MÉFR 74 (1962) 433–62

467. Piccaluga, G. Elementi spettacolari nei rituali festivi romani. Rome, 1965

468. Piccaluga, G. Terminus. I segni di confine nella religione romana. Rome, 1974

469. Piganiol, A. Recherches sur les jeux romains (Publications de la Faculté des Lettres de l'Université de Strasbourg 13). Strasbourg, 1923

470. Pötscher, W. 'Die Lupercalia: eine Strukturanalyse', Grazer Beiträge 11 (1984) 221–49

471. Prowse, K. R. 'Numa and the Pythagoreans: a curious incident', G&R N.S. 11 (1964) 36–42

472. Radke, G. 'Quindecimviri', RE 24 (1963) 1114–48

473. Radke, G. Die Götter Altitaliens (Fontes et Commentationes 3). Ed. 2. Münster, 1979

474. Radke, G. 'Die "Dei Penates" und Vesta in Rom', ANRW II.17.1 (1981) 343–73

475. Radke, G. 'Quirinus', ANRW II.17.1 (1981) 276–99

476. Richard, J.-C. '"M. Laetorius primi pili centurio"; à propos de la dédicace du temple de Mercure', in Scritti in memoria di A. Brelich, edd. V. Lanternari, M. Massenzio and D. Sabbatucci, 501–9. Bari, 1982

477. Richardson, E. H. 'The gods arrive', Archaeological News 6 (1976) 125–33

478. Ries, J. 'Héritage indo-européen et religion romaine. À propos de La religion romaine archaïque de Georges Dumézil', Revue Théologique de Louvain 7 (1976) 476–89

479. Riis, P. J. 'The cult image of Diana Nemorensis', Acta Archaeologica 37 (1966) 67–75

480. Rohde, G. Die Kultsatzungen der römischen Pontifices. Berlin, 1936

481. Rose, H. J. Ancient Roman Religion. London, 1949

482. Ryberg, I. S. Rites of the State Religion in Roman Art (Memoirs of the American Academy in Rome 23). New Haven, 1955

483. Samter, E. 'Fetiales', RE 6 (1909) 2259–65

484. Scheid, J. La religione a Roma. Rome, 1983

485. Scheid, J. Religion et piété à Rome. Paris, 1985

486. Schilling, R. La religion romaine de Vénus. Paris, 1954

487. Schilling, R. 'Les castors romains à la lumière des traditions indo-européennes', in Hommages à G. Dumézil (Collection Latomus 45) 177–92. Brussels, 1960 = R. Schilling, Rites, cultes, dieux de Rome (Études et Commentaires 92) 338–52. Paris, 1979

488. Schilling, R. 'À propos des "exta": l'extispicine étrusque et la "litatio" romaine', in Hommages A. Grenier (1962) III.1371–8 = R. Schilling, Rites, cultes, dieux de Rome (Études et Commentaires 92) 183–90. Paris, 1979

489. Schilling, R. 'L'originalité du vocabulaire religieux latin', RBPhil. 49 (1971) 31–54 = id. Rites, cultes, dieux de Rome (Études et Commentaires 92) 30–53. Paris, 1979

490. Schilling, R. 'Les études relatives à la religion romaine (1950–70)', ANRW I.2 (1972) 317–47

491. Schilling, R. *Rites, cultes, dieux de Rome* (Études et Commentaires 92). Paris, 1979

492. Scholz, U. W. *Studien zum altitalischen und altrömischen Marskult und Marsmythos* (Bibliothek der klassischen Altertumswissenschaften N.F. 2.Reihe, 35). Heidelberg, 1970

493. Scholz, U. W. 'Zur Erforschung der römischen Opfer (Beispiel: die Lupercalia)', in *Le sacrifice dans l'antiquité* (*Entretiens Hardt* 27) 289–340. Geneva, 1980

494. Scullard, H. H. *Festivals and Ceremonies of the Roman Republic*. London, 1981

495. Simon, E. 'Apollo in Rom', *JDAI* 93 (1978) 202–27

496. Syme, R. *Some Arval Brethren*. Oxford, 1980

497. Szemler, G. J. *The Priests of the Roman Republic* (Collection Latomus 127). Brussels, 1972

498. Thulin, C. 'Haruspices', *RE* 7 (1910) 2431–68

499. Torelli, M. 'Il santuario di Hera a Gravisca', *PP* 26 (1971) 44–67

500. Torelli, M. 'Il santuario greco di Gravisca', *PP* 32 (1977) 398–458

501. Ulf, C. *Das römische Lupercalienfest*. Darmstadt, 1982

502. van Berchem, D. 'Hercule-Melqart à l'Ara Maxima', *RPAA* 32 (1959–60) 61–8

503. van Berchem, D. 'Trois cas d'asylie archaïque', *MH* 17 (1960) 21–33

504. van Berchem, D. 'Sanctuaires d'Hercule-Melqart: contribution à l'étude de l'expansion phénicienne en Méditerranée', *Syria* 44 (1967) 73–109, 307–38

505. Versnel, H. S. 'Two types of Roman *devotio*', *Mnemosyne* 29 (1976) 365–410

506. Versnel, H. S. 'Self-sacrifice, compensation and the anonymous gods', in *Le sacrifice dans l'antiquité* (*Entretiens Hardt* 27) 135–94. Geneva, 1980

507. Verzar, M. 'Pyrgi e l'Afrodite di Cipro. Considerazioni sul programma decorativo del tempio B', *MÉFR(A)* 92 (1980) 35–86

508. Warde Fowler, W. *The Roman Festivals*. London, 1899

509. Warde Fowler, W. *The Religious Experience of the Roman People*. London, 1911

510. Weinrib, E. J. '*Obnuntiatio*. Two problems', *ZSS* 87 (1970) 395–425

511. Weinstock, S. '*Templum*', *RE* 2. Reihe, 5 (1934) 480–5

512. Weinstock, S. '*Nonalia sacra*', *RE* 17 (1937) 861–2

513. Weinstock, S. 'Penates', *RE* 19 (1937) 417–57

514. Weinstock, S. '*Libri fulgurales*', *PBSR* 19 (1951) 122–53

515. Weinstock, S. 'Victor and Invictus', *Harv. Theol. Rev.* 50 (1957) 211–47

516. Weinstock, S. 'Victoria', *RE* 2. Reihe, 8 (1958) 2501–42

517. Weinstock, S. *Divus Iulius*. Oxford, 1971

518. Wissowa, G. *Gesammelte Abhandlungen zur römischen Religions- und Stadtgeschichte*. Munich, 1904

519. Wissowa, G. *Religion und Kultus der Römer* (Handbuch der Altertumswissenschaft V.4). Ed. 2. Munich, 1912

d. POLITICAL AND MILITARY INSTITUTIONS

See also F for the monarchy; H(a) for plebeian institutions; A18, 22, 24, 35, 60, 70, 73–4, 77, 80, 91, 102, 114–15, 124, 127, 129, 270; B115, 270, 332; G292; H1–4, 10, 32, 45, 51, 57, 59, 62, 114, 126; J105, 135, 144, 168.

520. Adcock, F. E. 'Consular tribunes and their successors', *JRS* 47 (1957) 9–14
521. Alföldi, A. '*Hasta summa imperii*. The spear as embodiment of sovereignty in Rome', *AJA* 63 (1959) 1–27
522. Alföldi, A. 'Zur Struktur des Römerstaates im 5. Jahrhundert v.Chr.', in *Les origines de la république romaine* (*Entretiens Hardt* 13) 223–78. Geneva, 1967
523. Anderson, J. K. 'Homeric, British and Cyrenaic chariots', *AJA* 69 (1965) 349–52
524. Astin, A. E. 'The censorship of the Roman republic: frequency and regularity', *Historia* 31 (1982) 174–87
525. Badian, E. Review-discussion of L. R. Taylor, *The Voting Districts of the Roman Republic* (Rome, 1960) in *JRS* 52 (1962) 200–10
526. Béranger, J. '*Imperium*, expression et conception du pouvoir impérial', *RÉL* 55 (1977) 325–44
527. Beseler, G. 'Triumph und Votum', *Hermes* 44 (1909) 352–61
528. Biscardi, A. '*Auctoritas patrum*', *BIDR* 48 (1941) 403–521
529. Bleicken, J. '*Coniuratio*. Die Schwurszene auf den Münzen und Gemmen der römischen Republik', *JNG* 13 (1963) 51–70
530. Bleicken, J. *Staatliche Ordnung und Freiheit in der römischen Republik* (Frankfurter Althistorische Studien 6). Kallmünz, 1971
531. Bleicken, J. *Lex Publica. Gesetz und Recht in der römischen Republik*. Berlin, 1975
532. Bleicken, J. 'Zum Begriff der römischen Amtsgewalt: *auspicium-potestas-imperium*', *Nachrichten der Akademie der Wissenschaften in Göttingen 1.* Phil.-hist. Klasse 1981 n. 9
533. Bloch, R. 'Sur les danses armées des Saliens', *Annales (E.S.C.)* 13 (1958) 706–15
534. Bloch, R. 'Une tombe villanovienne près de Bolsena et la danse guerrière dans l'Italie primitive', *MÉFR* 70 (1958) 7–37
535. Boddington, A. 'The original nature of the consular tribunate', *Historia* 8 (1959) 356–64
536. Bonfante Warren, L. 'Roman triumphs and Etruscan kings: the changing face of the triumph', *JRS* 60 (1970) 49–66
537. Botsford, G. W. *The Roman Assemblies from their Origin to the End of the Republic*. New York, 1909
538. Branca, G. 'Cic. *de domo* 14.38 e *auctoritas patrum*', *Iura* 20 (1969) 49–51
539. Brisson, J.-P. (ed.). *Problèmes de la guerre à Rome*. Paris, 1969
540. Brunt, P. A. Review of G. Pieri, *L'histoire du cens jusqu'à la fin de la république romaine* (Paris, 1968) in *RHD* 37 (1969) 263–7
541. Cadoux, T. J. Review-discussion of G. Vitucci, *Ricerche sulla praefectura urbi in età imperiale (sec. I–III)* (Rome, 1956) in *JRS* 49 (1959) 152–60

542. Campanile, E. 'Una struttura indoeuropea a Roma', *Studi e saggi linguistici* 15 (1975) 36–44

543. Cancelli, F. *Studi sui censores e sull' arbitratus della lex contractus* (Università di Roma. Pubblicazioni dell'Istituto di Diritto Romano e dei Diritti dell'Oriente Mediterraneo 34). Milan, 1957

544. Cancelli, F. 'Postilla sul potere dei *censores*', *Labeo* 6 (1960) 225–7

545. Carcopino, J. 'Correction à un texte de Festus sur le plébiscite ovinien', *Bulletin de la Société Nationale des Antiquaires de France* 1929, 75–92

546. Castello, C. 'Intorno alla legittimità della *lex Valeria de Sulla dictatore*', in *Studi in onore di P. De Francisci* III.37–60. Milan, 1956

547. Cohen, D. 'The origin of Roman dictatorship', *Mnemosyne* ser. 4.10 (1957) 300–18

548. Coli, U. 'Sui limiti di durata delle magistrature romane', in *Studi V.Arangio-Ruiz* IV.395–418. Naples, 1953 = id. *Scritti di diritto romano* 1.485–508. Milan, 1973

549. Coli, U. 'Tribù e centurie dell'antica repubblica romana', *SDHI* 21 (1955) 181–222 = id. *Scritti di diritto romano* II.571–611. Milan, 1973

550. Coli, U. 'Sur la notion d'*imperium* en droit public romain', *RIDA* ser. 3.7 (1960) 361–87 = id. *Scritti di diritto romano* II.719–42. Milan, 1973

551. Combès, G. *Imperator*. Paris, 1966

552. Couissin, P. *Les armes romaines: essai sur les origines et l'évolution des armes individuelles du légionnaire romain*. Paris, 1926

553. Cram, R. V. 'The Roman censors', *HSCP* 51 (1940) 70–110

554. Crifò, G. *Ricerche sull' 'exilium' nel periodo repubblicano*. Milan, 1961

555. Crifò, G. 'Attività normativa del senato in età repubblicana', *BIDR* 71 (1968) 31–115

556. D'Amati, N. 'Natura e fondamento del *tributum* romano', *Annali della Facoltà di Giurisprudenza di Bari* 16 (1962) 143–69

557. De Francisci, P. 'Intorno alla natura e alla storia dell'*auspicium imperiumque*', in *Studi in memoria di E. Albertario* 1.397–432. Milan, 1953

558. De Francisci, P. 'Per la storia dei "comitia centuriata"', in *Studi V. Arangio-Ruiz* IV.1–32. Naples, 1953

559. De Francisci, P. 'Intorno all'origine etrusca del concetto d'*imperium*', *Stud. Etr.* 24 (1955–6) 19–43

560. De Martino, F. 'Territorio, popolazione ed ordinamento centuriato', *BIDR* 80 (1977) 1–22 = id. *Diritto e società nell'antica Roma* 162–82

561. De Martino, F. 'Sulla storia dell'*equitatus* romano', *PP* 35 (1980) 143–60

562. De Sanctis, G. 'Le origini dell'ordinamento centuriato', *Riv. Fil.* 61 (1933) 289–98

563. Deubner, L. 'Die Tracht des römischen Triumphators', *Hermes* 69 (1934) 316–23

564. Develin, R. '*Comitia tributa plebis*', *Athenaeum* N.S. 53 (1975) 302–37

565. Develin, R. '*Comitia tributa* again', *Athenaeum* N.S. 55 (1977) 425–6

566. Develin, R. '*Lex curiata* and the competence of magistrates', *Mnemosyne* ser. 4.30 (1977) 49–65

567. Develin, R. 'The Atinian plebiscite, tribunes and the senate', *CQ* N.S. 28 (1978) 141–4

568. Develin, R. 'The third-century reform of the *comitia centuriata*', *Athenaeum* N.S. 56 (1978) 346–77

569. De Visscher, F. '*Conubium* et *civitas*', *RIDA* ser. 2.1 (1952) 401–22 = id. *Études de droit romain public et privé* III.147–67. Milan, 1966

570. De Visscher, F. '*Ius Quiritium, civitas Romana* et nationalité moderne', in *Studi in onore di U. E. Paoli* 239–51. Florence, 1955

571. Devoto, G. 'Tre aspetti della romanità arcaica', *RSI* 80 (1968) 658–68

572. Ehlers, W. '*Triumphus*', *RE* 2.Reihe, 7 (1948) 493–511

573. Ferenczy, E. 'Zu Verfassungsgeschichte der Frührepublik', in *Beiträge zur alten Geschichte und deren Nachleben. Festschrift für F. Altheim* 1.136–50. Berlin, 1969

574. Ferenczy, E. 'Die Grundgesetze der römischen Republik', in *Sein und Werden im Recht. Festgabe für Ulrich von Lübtow* 267–80. Berlin, 1970

575. Ferenczy, E. 'Die erste Entwicklungsphase der Verfassung der römischen Republik. Vom Verfall der Monarchie bis zum Dezemvirat', *AUB* 3 (1975) 65–80

576. Ferenczy, E. 'L'immigrazione della *gens Claudia* e l'origine delle tribù territoriali', *Labeo* 22 (1976) 362–4

577. Ferenczy, E. 'Über das Interregnum', in *De iustitia et iure. Festgabe für U. von Lübtow zum 80. Geburtstag*, edd. M. Harder and G. Thielmann, 45–52. Berlin, 1980

578. Fraccaro, P. 'La riforma dell'ordinamento centuriato', in *Studi in onore di P. Bonfante* (Pavia, 1929) 1.105–22 = id. *Opuscula* II.171–90

579. Fraccaro, P. 'La storia dell'antichissimo esercito Romano e l'età dell'ordinamento centuriato', in *Atti del II congresso nazionale di studi romani* III.91–7. Rome, 1931 = id. *Opuscula* II.287–92

580. Fraccaro, P. '*Tribules* ed *aerarii*. Una ricerca di diritto pubblico romano', *Athenaeum* N.S. 11 (1933) 150–72 = id. *Opuscula* II.149–70

581. Fraccaro, P. 'Ancora sull'età dell'ordinamento centuriato', *Athenaeum* N.S. 12 (1934) 57–71 = id. *Opuscula* II.293–306

582. Fraccaro, P. *Opuscula* IV (*Della guerra presso i Romani*). Pavia, 1975

583. Frederiksen, M. W. 'Changes in the patterns of settlement', in *Hellenismus in Mittelitalien. Kolloquium in Göttingen von 5. bis 9. Juni 1974 (Abhandlungen der Akademie der Wissenschaften in Göttingen*, Phil.-hist. Klasse III.97.1/II), ed. P. Zanker, II.341–55. Göttingen, 1976

584. Frezza, P. 'L'istituzione della collegialità in diritto romano', in *Studi in onore di Siro Solazzi nel cinquantesimo anniversario del suo insegnamento universitario* 507–42. Naples, 1948

585. Friezer, E. *De ordering van Servius Tullius* (diss. Amsterdam, 1957)

586. Friezer, E. '*Interregnum* und *patrum auctoritas*', *Mnemosyne* ser. 4.12 (1959) 301–29

587. Gabba, E. 'Esercito e fiscalità a Roma in età repubblicana', in *Armées et fiscalité dans le monde antique: Paris 14–16 octobre 1976* (Colloques Nationaux du Centre National de la Recherche Scientifique n.936) 13–33. Paris, 1977

588. Gabba, E. 'Dionigi e la dittatura a Roma', in *Tria corda: scritti in onore di Arnaldo Momigliano* 215–28. Como, 1983

589. Gagé, J. 'Les traditions des Papirii et quelques-unes des origines de l'*equitatus* romain et latin', *RHDFÉ* ser. 4.33 (1955) 20–50, 165–94

590. Gagé, J. 'Les autels de Titus Tatius. Une variante sabine des rites d'intégration dans les curies', in *Mélanges J. Heurgon* (1976) 1.309–22

591. Garlan, Y. *La guerre dans l'antiquité*. Paris, 1972. Translated as: *War in the Ancient World*. London, 1975

592. Gatti, C. 'Riflessioni sull'istituzione dello *stipendium*', *Acme* 23 (1970) 131–5

593. Gatti, C. 'A proposito degli *accensi* nell'ordinamento centuriato', *Athenaeum* N.S. 51 (1973) 377–82

594. Gauthier, Ph. '"Generosité" romaine et "avarice" grecque. Sur l'octroi du droit de cité', in *Mélanges d'histoire ancienne offerts à William Seston* 207–15. Paris, 1974

595. Gauthier, Ph. 'La citoyenneté en Grèce et à Rome: participation et intégration', *Ktema* 6 (1981) 167–79

596. Gintowt, E. '*Dictator Romanus*', *RIDA* ser. 1.2 (1949) 385–94

597. Gioffredi, C. 'Sulle attribuzioni sacrali dei magistrati romani', *Iura* 9 (1958) 22–49

598. Gioffredi, C. 'Libertà e cittadinanza', in *Studi in onore di E. Betti* II.509–29. Milan, 1962

599. Giovannini, A. *Consulare Imperium* (Schweizerische Beiträge zur Altertumswissenschaft Heft 16). Basle, 1983

600. Giovannini, A. 'Les origines des magistratures romaines', *MH* 41 (1984) 15–30

601. Giovannini, A. '*Auctoritas patrum*', *MH* 42 (1985) 28–36

602. Gjerstad, E. 'Innenpolitische und militarische Organisation in frührömischer Zeit', *ANRW* I.1 (1972) 136–88

603. Gluck, J. J. 'Reviling and monomachy as battle-preludes in ancient warfare', *AClass.* 7 (1964) 25–31

604. Greenhalgh, P. A. *Early Greek Warfare*. Cambridge, 1973

605. Grelle, F. *Stipendium vel tributum*. Naples, 1963

606. Grieve, L. J. 'The reform of the *comitia centuriata*', *Historia* 34 (1985) 278–309

607. Gschnitzer, F. '*Exercitus*. Zur Bezeichnung und Geschichte des Heeres im frühen Rom', in *Studien zur Sprachwissenschaft und Kulturkunde. Gedenkschrift für W. Brandenstein* (Innsbrucker Beiträge zur Kulturwissenschaft 14) 181–90. Innsbruck, 1968

608. Guarino, A. 'Notazioni romanistiche: la genesi storica dell'*auctoritas patrum*', in *Studi in onore di Siro Solazzi nel cinquantesimo anniversario del suo insegnamento universitario* 21–31. Naples, 1948

609. Guarino, A. '*Praetor maximus*', *Labeo* 15 (1969) 199–201 = id. *Le origini quiritarie* 77–9

610. Hackl, O. *Die sogennante servianische Heeresreform* (diss. Munich, 1959)

611. Hanell, K. *Das altrömische eponyme Amt*. Lund, 1946

612. Hausmaninger, H. '*Bellum iustum* und *iusta causa belli* im älteren römischen

Recht', *Österreichische Zeitschrift für öffentliches Recht* N.F. 11 (1961) 335–45

613. Helbig, W. 'Die Castores als Schutzgötter des römischen Equitatus', *Hermes* 40 (1905) 101–15

614. Helbig, W. 'Sur les attributs des Saliens', *Memoires de l'Académie des Inscriptions et Belles Lettres* 37 (1906) 205–76

615. Helbig, W. 'Zur Geschichte des römischen Equitatus', *Abhandlungen der Königlichen Bayerischen Akademie der Wissenschaften zu München*, Phil.-hist. Klasse 23 (1909) 267–317

616. Heurgon, J. 'Magistratures romaines et magistratures étrusques', in *Les origines de la république romaine* (*Entretiens Hardt* 13) 97–127. Geneva, 1967

617. Heuss, A. 'Zur Entwicklung des Imperiums der römischen Oberbeamten', *ZSS* 64 (1949) 57–133

618. Heuss, A. 'Gedanken und Vermutungen zur frühen römischen Regierungsgewalt', *Nachrichten der Akademie der Wissenschaften in Göttingen*, Phil.-hist. Klasse 1982 n. 10

619. Hill, H. 'Equites and Celeres', *CPhil.* 33 (1938) 283–90

620. Holzapfel, L. 'Die drei ältesten römischen Tribus', *Klio* 1 (1901) 228–55

621. Ilari, V. 'I *celeres* e il problema dell' *equitatus* nell'età arcaica', *Rivista Italiana per le Scienze Giuridiche* 78 (1971) 117–65

622. Ilari, V. *Gli Italici nelle strutture militari romane.* Milan, 1974

623. Jahn, J. *Interregnum und Wahldiktatur* (Frankfurter Althistorische Studien 3). Kallmünz, 1970

624. Janssen, L. F. *Abdicatio: Nieuwe onderzoekingen over de dictatur* (diss. Amsterdam, 1960)

625. Janssen, L. F. 'Einige kritische Bemerkungen zum Problem der *creatio*', in *Studi in onore di E. Volterra* IV.391–400. Milan, 1971

626. Jashemski, W. *The Origins and History of Proconsular and Propraetorian Imperium* (diss. Chicago, 1950)

627. Jones, A. H. M. Review of A. Magdelain, *Recherches sur l'imperium. La loi curiate et les auspices d'investiture* (Paris, 1968) in *RHD* 37 (1969) 600–3

628. Kloft, H. *Prorogation und ausserordentliche Imperium, 326–81 v.Chr.* Meisenheim am Glan, 1977

629. Klotz, A. 'Zur Geschichte der römischen Zensur', *Rh. Mus.* N.F. 88 (1939) 27–36

630. Köves-Zulauf, T. 'Der Zweikampf des Valerius Corvus und die Alternativen römischen Heldentums', *Antike und Abendland* 31 (1985) 66–75

631. Kubitschek, W. *De Romanorum tribuum origine ac propagatione.* Vienna, 1882

632. Kunkel, W. 'Bericht über neuere Arbeiten zur römischen Verfassungsgeschichte I', *ZSS* 72 (1955) 288–325

633. Kunkel, W. 'Bericht über neuere Arbeiten zur römischen Verfassungsgeschichte II', *ZSS* 73 (1956) 307–25

634. Kunkel, W. Review of L. F. Janssen, *Abdicatio. Nieuwe onderzoekingen over de dictatur* (Amsterdam, 1960) in *ZSS* 78 (1961) 537–9

635. Kunkel, W. 'Magistratische Gewalt und Senatsherrschaft', *ANRW* I.2 (1972) 3–22

636. Labruna, L. '*Quirites*', *Labeo* 8 (1962) 340–8

637. Laqueur, R. 'Ueber das Wesen des römischen Triumphs', *Hermes* 44 (1909) 215–36

638. Last, H. M. 'The Servian reforms', *JRS* 35 (1945) 30–48

639. Latte, K. 'Zwei Exkurse zum römischen Staatsrecht', *Nachrichten von der Königlicher Gesellschaft der Wissenschaften zu Göttingen*, Phil.-hist. Klasse N. F. Fachgruppe 1: Altertumswissenschaft 1 (1934–6 (1936)) 59–77 = id. *Kleine Schriften* 341–58

640. Latte, K. 'The origin of the Roman quaestorship', *TAPA* 67 (1936) 24–33 = id. *Kleine Schriften* 359–66

641. Leifer, F. *Die Einheit des Gewaltsgedankens im römischen Staatsrecht*. Munich–Leipzig, 1914

642. Leifer, F. *Studien zum antiken Ämterwesen* (*Klio* Beiheft 23). Leipzig, 1931

643. Lemosse, M. 'Les éléments techniques de l'ancien triomphe romain et le problème de son origine', *ANRW* 1.2 (1972) 441–53

644. Letta, C. 'Cic., *De Rep.* 11, 22 e l'ordinamento centuriato', *SCO* 27 (1977) 193–282

645. Leuze, O. *Zur Geschichte der römischen Censur*. Halle, 1912

646. Levy, E. '*Civitas* und *libertas*', *ZSS* 78 (1961) 142–72

647. von Lübtow, U. 'Die *lex curiata de imperio*', *ZSS* 69 (1952) 154–71

648. Luzzatto, G. I. 'Appunti sulle dittature *imminuto iure*. Spunti critici e ricostruttivi', in *Studi in onore di Pietro De Francisci* 111.405–59. Milan, 1956

649. Luzzatto, G. I. 'Il verbo *praeire* delle più antiche magistrature romano-italiche', *Eos* 48.1 (*Symbolae R. Taubenschlag dedicatae* 1) (1956) 439–71

650. McCartney, E. 'The military indebtedness of early Rome to Etruria', *MAAR* 1 (1917) 121–67

651. McFayden, D. 'A constitutional doctrine re-examined', in *Studies in Honor of F. W. Shipley* 1–15. St Louis, 1942

652. Magdelain, A. 'Note sur la loi curiate et les auspices des magistrats', *RHDFÉ* ser. 4.42 (1964) 198–203

653. Magdelain, A. *Recherches sur l'imperium. La loi curiate et les auspices d'investiture*. Paris, 1968

654. Magdelain, A. 'Praetor *maximus* et *comitiatus maximus*', *Iura* 20 (1969) 257–86

655. Magdelain, A. 'L'inauguration de l'*urbs* et l'*imperium*', *MÉFR(A)* 89.1 (1977) 11–29

656. Magdelain, A. *La loi à Rome. Histoire d'un concept* (Collection d'Études Latines. Série Scientifique 34). Paris, 1978

657. Magdelain, A. 'Les *accensi* et le total des centuries', *Historia* 27 (1978) 492–5

658. Magdelain, A. 'Le suffrage universel à Rome au Ve siècle av. Jésus-Christ', *CRAcad. Inscr.* 1979, 698–713

659. Magdelain, A. 'Quirinus et le droit (*spolia opima, ius fetiale, ius Quiritium*)', *MÉFR(A)* 96.2 (1984) 195–237

660. Mancuso, G. 'Alle radici della storia del *senatus*', *ASGP* 33 (1972) 169–335

661. Mancuso, G. '*Patres conscripti*. Un'ipotesi sulla composizione dell'antico senato romano', *ASGP* 36 (1976) 253–88

662. Mannino, V. *L'auctoritas patrum* (Pubblicazioni dell'Istituto di Diritto Romano e dei Diritti dell'Oriente Mediterraneo 54). Milan, 1979
663. Marino, R. 'Tradizione storiografica sull'introduzione del trionfo a Roma', *Stud. Rom.* 28 (1980) 161–71
664. Martinez-Pinna Nieto, J. *Los origenes del ejército romano. Estudio de las formas pre-militares en su relación con las estructuras sociales de la más primitiva.* Madrid, 1981
665. Martorana, G. *Intra pomerium, extra pomerium.* Palermo (Università), 1978
666. Mazzarino, S. *'Dicator e dictator'*, *Helikon* 7 (1967) 426–7
667. Meier, Chr. *'Praerogativa centuria'*, *RE* Suppl. 8 (1956) 567–98
668. Meier, Chr. Review of A. Magdelain, *Recherches sur l'imperium. La loi curiate et les auspices d'investiture* (Paris, 1968) in *ZSS* 86 (1969) 487–93
669. Ménager, L. R. 'Les collèges sacerdotaux, les *tribus* et la formation primordiale de Rome', *MÉFR(A)* 88 (1976) 455–543
670. Metzger, H. and van Berchem, D. 'Hippeis', in *Gestalt und Geschichte. Festschrift für K. Schefold* 155–8. Bern, 1967
671. Meyer, Ed. 'Das römische Manipularheer, seine Entwicklung und seine Vorstufen', *Abhandlungen der Preussischen Akademie der Wissenschaften*, Phil.-hist. Klasse 1923 n. 3 = id. *Kleine Schriften* ii.193–329 (with a new Appendix: 'Zur älteren römischen Geschichte'). Ed. 2. Halle, 1924
672. Meyer, Ernst. 'Vom griechischen und römischen Staatsgedanken', in *Eumusia, Festgabe für E. Howald*, 30–53. Zurich, 1947 = *Das Staatsdenken. der Römer* (Wege der Forschung 46), ed. R. Klein, 65–86. Darmstadt, 1966
673. Millan Mendez, A. *'Sacramentum militiae'*, *Hispania Antiqua* 6 (1976) 27–42
674. Momigliano, A. 'Ricerche sulle magistrature romane: i. Il *dictator clavi figendi causa.* ii. *Imperator.* iii. L'origine del tribunato della plebe. iv. L'origine della edilità plebea. v. Tribù umbro-sabelle e tribù romane', *BCAR* 58 (1930) 29–42, 42–55; 59 (1931) 157–77; 60 (1932) 217–28, 228–32 = id. *Quarto Contributo* 273–327
675. Momigliano, A. 'Studi sugli ordinamenti centuriati', *SDHI* 4 (1938) 509–20 = id. *Quarto Contributo* 363–75
676. Momigliano, A. *'Praetor maximus* e questioni affini', in *Studi in onore di G. Grosso* i. 159–75. Turin, 1968 = id. *Quarto Contributo* 403–17
677. Moore, O'Brien, 'Senatus', *RE* Suppl. 6 (1935) 660–800
678. Morel, J.-P. '"Pube praesenti in contione, omni poplo" (Plaut., *Pseud.* 126)', *RÉL* 42 (1964) 375–88
679. Nicholls, J. J. 'Cicero, *De republica* 2.39–40 and the centuriate assembly', *CPhil.* 59 (1964) 102–5
680. Nicholls, J. J. 'The content of the *lex curiata*', *AJPhil.* 88 (1967) 257–78
681. Nicolet, C. *L'ordre équestre à l'époque républicaine* i. Paris, 1966
682. Nicolet, C. *Tributum. Recherches sur la fiscalité directe à l'époque républicaine* (Antiquitas 1.Reihe, 24). Bonn, 1976
683. Nicolet, C. 'L'idéologie du système centuriate et l'influence de la philosophie politique grecque', in *La filosofia greca e il diritto romano. Colloquio italo-francese (Roma, 14–17 aprile 1973)* (Accademia Nazionale dei Lincei. Quaderni n. 221.1) 111–37. Rome, 1976

684. Nicolet, C. *Le métier de citoyen dans la Rome républicaine*. Paris, 1976. Translated as:

685. Nicolet, C. *The World of the Citizen in Republican Rome*. London, 1980

686. Oakley, S. P. 'Single combat in the Roman republic', *CQ* N.S. 35 (1985) 392–410

687. Pagliaro, A. '*Proletarius*', *Helikon* 7 (1967) 395–401

688. Perret, J. '*Cives* ou *Quirites*', in *Mélanges P. Wuilleumier* (1980) 269–75

689. Pieri, G. *L'histoire du cens jusqu'à la fin de la république romaine* (Publications de l'Institut de Droit Romain de l'Université de Paris 25). Paris, 1968

690. Pieri, G. 'Statut de personnes et organisation politique aux origines de Rome', *RHDFÉ* ser. 4.59 (1981) 583–92

691. Porzig, W. '*Senatus populusque Romanus*', *Gymnasium* 63 (1956) 318–26

692. Radke, G. '"Res Italae Romanorumque triumphi" (Verg. *Aen.* 8, 626)', *Fortwirkende Antike* 6 (1974) 78–104

693. Rawson, E. 'The literary sources for the pre-Marian army', *PBSR* 39 (1971) 13–31

694. Rich, J. W. *Declaring War in the Roman Republic in the Period of Transmarine Expansion* (Collection Latomus 149). Brussels, 1976

695. Richard, J.-C. '*Classis- infra classem*', *Rev. Phil.* 51 (1977) 229–36

696. Richard, J.-C. '*Proletarius.* Quelques remarques sur l'organisation servienne', *Ant. Class.* 47 (1978) 438–47

697. Richard, J.-C. 'Sur le vote des centuries équestres: Cic. *Phil.* 2.82', in *Mélanges P. Wuilleumier* (1980) 317–23

698. Richard, J.-C. 'Variations sur le thème de la citoyenneté à l'époque royale', *Ktema* 6 (1981) 89–103

699. Richard, J.-C. '"Praetor collega consulis est": contribution à l'histoire de la préture', *Rev. Phil.* 56 (1982) 19–31

700. Ridley, R. T. 'The origin of the Roman dictatorship. An overlooked opinion', *Rh. Mus.* N.F. 122 (1979) 303–9

701. Ridley, R. T. 'Livy and the *concilium plebis*', *Klio* 62 (1980) 337–54

702. Rilinger, R. 'Die Ausbildung von Amtswechsel und Amtsfristen als Problem zwischen Machtbesitz und Machtgebrauch in der mittleren Republik (342–217 v.Chr.)', *Chiron* 8 (1978) 247–312

703. Rosenberg, A. *Untersuchungen zur römischen Zenturienverfassung*. Berlin, 1911

704. Rudolph, H. 'Das Imperium der römischen Magistrate', *Neue Jahrbücher für Antike* 104 (1939–40) 145–64

705. Sabbatucci, D. 'L'edilità romana: magistratura e sacerdozio', *MAL* ser. 8.6 (1954) 255–333

706. Saulnier, C. *L'armée et la guerre dans le monde étrusco-romain*. Paris, 1980

707. Scarlata Fazio, M. 'Sul passaggio della magistratura unica a quella collegiale', in *Studi in onore di Cesare Sanfilippo* (Pubblicazioni della Facoltà di Giurisprudenza dell'Università di Catania 96) II.541–5. Milan, 1982

708. Schönbauer, E. 'Die römische Centurienverfassung in neuer Quellenschau', *Historia* 2 (1953–4) 21–49

709. Sealey, R. 'Consular tribunes once more', *Latomus* 18 (1959) 521–30

710. Seston, W. 'La citoyenneté romaine', in *XIIIe Congr. internat. des Sciences*

historiques (Moscow, 16–23 octobre 1970) 31–52. Moscow, 1973 = W. Seston, *Scripta Varia. Mélanges d'histoire romaine, de droit, d'épigraphie et d'histoire du christianisme* (Collection de l'École Française de Rome 43) 3–18. Paris, 1980

711. Shatzman, I. 'The Roman general's authority over booty', *Historia* 21 (1972) 177–205

712. Siber, H. 'Die ältesten römischen Volksversammlungen', *ZSS* 57 (1937) 233–71

713. Siber, H. 'Zur Kollegialität der römischen Zensoren', in *Festschrift für F. Schulz* I. 466–474. Weimar, 1951

714. Sini, F. 'A proposito del carattere religioso del *dictator*. Note metodologiche sui documenti sacerdotali', *SDHI* 42 (1976) 401–24

715. Snodgrass, A. M. 'The hoplite reform and history', *JHS* 85 (1965) 110–22

716. Soltau, W. 'Der Ursprung der Diktatur', *Hermes* 49 (1914) 352–68

717. Stark, R. 'Ursprung und Wesen der altrömischen Diktatur', *Hermes* 75 (1940) 206–14

718. Stary, P. F. 'Foreign elements in Etruscan arms and armour: 8th to 3rd centuries B.C.', *PPS* N.S. 45 (1979) 179–206

719. Stary, P. F. *Zur eisenzeitlichen Bewaffnung und Kampfesweise in Mittelitalien.* Mainz, 1981

720. Staveley, E. S. 'The reform of the *comitia centuriata*', *AJPhil.* 74 (1953) 10–33

721. Staveley, E. S. 'The significance of the consular tribunate', *JRS* 43 (1953) 30–6

722. Staveley, E. S. 'The conduct of elections during an *interregnum*', *Historia* 3 (1954–5) 193–211

723. Staveley, E. S. 'Tribal legislation before the *lex Hortensia*', *Athenaeum* N.S. 33 (1955) 3–31

724. Staveley, E. S. 'Forschungsbericht. The constitution of the Roman republic 1940–1954', *Historia* 5 (1956) 74–122

725. Staveley, E. S. 'Cicero and the *comitia centuriata*', *Historia* 11 (1962) 299–314

726. Staveley, E. S. *Greek and Roman Voting and Elections.* London, 1972

727. Sumner, G. V. 'Cicero on the *comitia centuriata*: De re publica II, 22, 39–40', *AJPhil.* 81 (1960) 136–56

728. Sumner, G. V. 'The legion and the centuriate organisation', *JRS* 60 (1970) 61–79

729. Suolahti, J. *The Roman Censors. A Study on Social Structure.* Helsinki, 1955

730. Täubler, E. 'Die umbrisch-sabellischen und die römischen Tribus', *SHAW* 1929–30 n. 4

731. Taylor, L. R. 'The four urban tribes and the four regions of ancient Rome', *RPAA* 27 (1952–4) 225–38

732. Taylor, L. R. 'The centuriate assembly before and after the reform', *AJPhil.* 78 (1957) 337–54

733. Taylor, L. R. *The Voting Districts of the Roman Republic* (Papers and Monographs of the American Academy in Rome 20). Rome, 1960

734. Taylor, L. R. 'The corrector of the codex of Cicero's De Republica', *AJPhil.* 82 (1961) 337–45

735. Taylor, L. R. *Roman Voting Assemblies*. Ann Arbor, 1966
736. Thiel, J. H. *A History of Roman Sea Power before the Second Punic War*. Amsterdam, 1954
737. Thomsen, R. 'The pay of the Roman army and the property qualifications of the Servian census', *C & M* 9 (*Festschrift für F. Blatt*) (1973) 194–208
738. Tibiletti, G. 'Evoluzione di magistrato e popolo nello stato Romano', *Studia Ghisleriana* 2.1 (1950) 3–21
739. Tondo, S. 'Il *sacramentum militiae* nell'ambiente culturale romano', *SDHI* 29 (1963) 1–123
740. Tondo, S. 'Sul *sacramentum militiae*', *SDHI* 34 (1968) 376–96
741. van Berchem, D. 'Rome et le monde grec au VIe siècle av. notre ère', in *Mélanges A. Piganiol* (1966) II.739–48
742. Versnel, H. S. *Triumphus. An Enquiry into the Origin, Development and Meaning of the Roman Triumph*. Leiden, 1970
743. Vigneron, P. *Le cheval dans l'antiquité gréco-romaine*. Nancy, 1968
744. Voci, P. 'Per la definizione dell'*imperium*', in *Studi in memoria di E. Albertario* II.65–102. Milan, 1953
745. Walbank, F. W. 'Roman declaration of war in the third and second centuries', *CPhil.* 44 (1949) 15–19 = id. *Selected Papers* 101–6
746. Wallisch, E. 'Name und Herkunft des römischen Triumphs', *Philologus* 99 (1955) 245–58
747. Warde Fowler, W. 'Juppiter and the triumphator', *CR* 30 (1916) 153–7
748. Weeber, K.-W. '*Troiae lusus*. Alter und Entstehung eines Reiterspiels', *Anc. Soc.* 5 (1974) 171–96
749. Weigel, R. D. 'Roman colonisation and the tribal assembly', *PP* 38 (1983) 191–6
750. Wesenberg, G. '*Praetor maximus*', *ZSS* 65 (1947) 319–26
751. Westrup, C. W. 'Sur les *gentes* et les *curiae* de la royauté primitive', *RIDA* ser. 3.1 (1954) 43–73
752. Wiesner, J. 'Reiter und Ritter im ältesten Rom', *Klio* 13 (1944) 43–100
753. Wilcken, U. 'Zur Entwicklung des römischen Diktatur', *Abhandlungen der Preussischen Akademie der Wissenschaften*, Phil.-hist. Klasse 1940 n. 1
754. Willems, P. *Le sénat de la république romaine*. 2 vols. Ed. 2. Louvain, 1883–5 (reprinted Darmstadt, 1968)
755. Willems, P. *Le droit public romain*. Ed. 7. Louvain, 1910
756. Wolff, H. J. 'Interregnum und Auctoritas Patrum', *BIDR* 64 (1961) 1–14
757. Ziegler, K.-H. 'Kriegsverträge im antiken römischen Recht', *ZSS* 102 (1985) 40–90

H. EARLY REPUBLICAN ROME: INTERNAL POLITICS

a. PATRICIATE AND PLEBS. THE 'STRUGGLE OF THE ORDERS' TO THE LEX HORTENSIA

See also A16, 48, 60, 72, 86–7, 102; B126, 130; F35, 37, 147, 147a; G269, 447, 564–5, 567, 569, 638, 721, 723.

1. Alföldi, A. *Der frührömische Reiteradel und seine Ehrenabzeichen*. Baden-Baden, 1952
2. Alföldi, A. 'Il dominio della cavalleria dopo la caduta dei re in Grecia ed a Roma', *Rendiconti dell'Accademia di Archeologia, Lettere e Belle Arti di Napoli* 40 (1965) 21–34
3. Alföldi, A. 'Die Herrschaft der Reiterei in Griechenland und Rom nach dem Sturz der Könige', in *Gestalt und Geschichte. Festschrift für K. Schefold* 13–45. Bern, 1967
4. Alföldi, A. '*(Centuria) procum patricium*', *Historia* 17 (1968) 444–60
5. Altheim, F. *Lex sacrata: die Anfänge der plebeischen Organisation* (Albae Vigiliae 1). Amsterdam, 1940
6. Altheim, F. 'Patriziat und Plebs', *Die Welt als Geschichte* 7 (1941) 217–33
7. Angelini, P. *Ricerche sul patriziato*. Milan, 1979
8. Bauman, R. A. 'The *lex Valeria de provocatione* of 300 B.C.', *Historia* 22 (1973) 37–47
9. Bernardi, A. 'Patrizi e plebei nella costituzione della primitiva repubblica romana', *RIL* 79 (1945–6) 3–14
10. Bernardi, A. 'Ancora sulla costituzione della primitiva repubblica romana', *RIL* 79 (1945–6) 15–26
11. Bertelli, L. 'L'apologo di Menenio Agrippa. Incunabulo della "Homonoia" a Roma?', *Index* 3 (1972) 224–34
12. Binder, J. *Die Plebs: Studien zur römischen Rechtsgeschichte*. Leipzig, 1909 (reprinted Rome, 1965)
13. Bleicken, J. 'Ursprung und Bedeutung der Provokation', *ZSS* 76 (1959) 324–77
14. Bleicken, J. *Das Volkstribunat der klassischen Republik* (Zetemata Heft 13). Ed. 2. Munich, 1968
15. Bleicken, J. 'Das römische Volkstribunat. Versuch einer Analyse seiner politischen Funktion in republikanischer Zeit', *Chiron* 11 (1981) 87–108
16. Botsford, G. W. 'The social composition of the primitive Roman *populus*', *Political Science Quarterly* 21 (1906) 498–526
17. Brunt, P. A. *Social Conflicts in the Roman Republic*. London, 1971
18. Cornell, T. J. 'The failure of the plebs', in *Tria corda: scritti in onore di Arnaldo Momigliano* 101–20. Como, 1983
19. Crifò, G. 'Alcune osservazioni in tema di *provocatio ad populum*', *SDHI* 29 (1963) 288–95
20. Dal Cason, F. 'La tradizione annalistica sulle più antiche legge agrarie: riflessioni e proposte', *Athenaeum* N.S. 63 (1985) 174–83
21. Dell'Oro, A. *La formazione dello stato patrizio-plebeo*. Milan, 1950
22. De Martino, F. 'Riforme del IV sec. a.C.', *BIDR* 78 (1975) 29–70 = id. *Diritto e società nell'antica Roma* 183–224
23. De Martino, F. 'Postilla a riforme del IV secolo a.C.', *BIDR* 80 (1977) 51–3
24. De Sanctis, G. 'La *lex tribunicia prima*', in *Miscellanea in onore di G. Mercati* (Studi e Testi 125) 539–44. Rome, 1946
25. Develin, R. '*Provocatio* and plebiscites: early Roman legislation and the historical tradition', *Mnemosyne* ser. 4.31 (1978) 45–60
26. Develin, R. 'A peculiar restriction on candidacy for plebeian office', *Antichthon* 15 (1981) 111–17

27. Develin, R. 'The integration of the plebeians into the political order after 366 B.C.', in *Social Struggles in Archaic Rome*, ed. K. A. Raaflaub, 327–52. California, 1986

28. Ellul, J. 'Réflexions sur la révolution, la plèbe et le tribunat de la plèbe', *Index* 3 (1972) 155–67

29. Ferenczy, E. 'The rise of the patrician–plebeian state', *A Ant. Hung.* 14 (1966) 113–39

30. Forni, G. 'Manio Curio Dentato, uomo democratico', *Athenaeum* N.S. 31 (1953) 170–240

31. Frezza, P. 'Secessioni plebee e rivolte servili nella Roma antica', *SDHI* 45 (1979) 310–27

32. von Fritz, K. 'The reorganisation of the Roman government in 366 B.C. and the so-called Licinio-Sextian laws', *Historia* 1 (1950) 3–44 = id. *Antike Verfassungsgeschichte und Verfassungstheorie* 329–73. Berlin, 1976

33. von Fritz, K. '*Leges sacratae* and *plebei scita*', in *Studies presented to D. M. Robinson* 11.893–905. St Louis, 1953 = id. *Antike Verfassungsgeschichte und Verfassungstheorie* 374–87. Berlin, 1976

34. Gabba, E. *Le rivolte militari romane dal IV secolo a.C. ad Augusto.* Florence, 1975

35. Gagé, J. 'La *plebs* et le *populus* et leurs encadrements respectifs dans la Rome de la première moitié du Ve siècle av. J.C.', *Revue Historique* 243 (1970) 5–30

36. Gioffredi, C. 'Il fondamento della *tribunicia potestas* e i procedimenti normativi dell'ordine plebeo (*sacrosanctum-lex sacrata-sacramentum*)', *SDHI* 11 (1945) 37–64

37. Giovannini, A. 'Volkstribunat und Volksgericht', *Chiron* 13 (1983) 545–66

38. Giuffré, V. '*Plebei gentes non habent*', *Labeo* 16 (1970) 329–34

39. Guarino, A. 'L'*exaequatio* dei *plebiscita* ai *leges*', in *Festschrift für F. Schulz* 1.458–65. Weimar, 1951

40. Guarino, A. *La rivoluzione della plebe.* Naples, 1975

41. Guarino, A. 'Genesi e ragion d'essere del patriziato', *Labeo* 21 (1975) 343–53

42. Guarino, A. 'La *perduellio* e la plebe', *Labeo* 21 (1975) 73–7

43. Hahn, I. 'The plebeians and clan society', *Oikumene* 1 (1976) 47–75

44. Halpérin, J.-L. 'Tribunat de la plèbe et haute plèbe (493–218 av. J.-C.)', *RHDFÉ* ser.4.62 (1984) 161–82

45. Kienast, D. 'Die politische Emanzipation der Plebs und die Entwicklung des Heerwesens im frühen Rom', *Bonner Jahrbücher* 175 (1975) 83–112

46. Levi, M. A. 'Roma arcaica e il connubio fra plebei e patrizi', *PP* 38 (1983) 241–59

47. Linderski, J. 'Religious aspects of the Conflict of the Orders: the case of *confarreatio*', in *Social Struggles in Archaic Rome*, ed. K. A. Raaflaub, 244–61. California, 1986

48. Lintott, A. W. '*Provocatio*. From the Struggle of the Orders to the Principate', *ANRW* 1.2 (1972) 226–67

49. Maddox, G. 'The economic causes of the *lex Hortensia*', *Latomus* 42 (1983) 277–86

50. Magdelain, A. '*Auspicia ad patres redeunt*', in *Hommages J. Bayet* (1964) 427–73
51. Magdelain, A. '*Procum patricium*', in *Studi in onore di E. Volterra* II.247–66. Milan, 1971
52. Mancuso, G. '*Patres minorum gentium*', *ASGP* 34 (1973) 397–419
53. Martin, J. 'Die Provocation in der klassischen und späten Republik', *Hermes* 98 (1970) 72–96
54. Mazzarino, S. 'Sul tribunato della plebe nella storiografia romana', *Helikon* 11–12 (1971–2) 99–119
55. Mazzarino, S. 'Note sul tribunato della plebe nella storiografia romana', *Index* 3 (1972) 175–91
56. Ménager, L. R. 'Nature et mobiles de l'opposition entre la plèbe et le patriciat', *RIDA* ser. 3.19 (1972) 367–97
57. Meyer, Ed. 'Der Ursprung des Tribunats und die Gemeinde der vier Tribus', *Hermes* 30 (1895) 1–24 = id. *Kleine Schriften* 1.333–61. Ed. 2. Halle, 1924
58. Mitchell, R. E. 'The definition of *patres* and *plebs*: an end to the Struggle of the Orders', in *Social Struggles in Archaic Rome*, ed. K. A. Raaflaub, 130–74. California, 1986
59. Momigliano, A. '*Procum patricium*', *JRS* 56 (1966) 16–24 = id. *Quarto Contributo* 377–94
60. Momigliano, A. 'Osservazioni sulla distinzione fra patrizi e plebei', in *Les origines de la république romaine* (*Entretiens Hardt* 13) 199–221. Geneva, 1967 = id. *Quarto Contributo* 419–36
61. Momigliano, A. 'L'ascesa della plebe nella storia arcaica di Roma', *RSI* 79 (1967) 297–312 = id. *Quarto Contributo* 437–54 = n. 64 (below)
62. Momigliano, A. 'Cavalry and patriciate. An answer to Professor A. Alföldi', *Historia* 18 (1969) 385–8 = id. *Quinto Contributo* 635–9
63. Momigliano, A. 'Prolegomena a ogni futura metafisica sulla plebe romana', *Labeo* 23 (1977) 7–15 = id. *Sesto Contributo* 477–86
64. Momigliano, A. 'The rise of the plebs in the archaic age of Rome', in *Social Struggles in Archaic Rome*, ed. K. A. Raaflaub, 175–97. California, 1986
65. Néraudau, J.-P. 'Jeunesse et politique à Rome au Ve siècle av. J.C., d'après Tite-Live III', in *Mélanges P. Wuilleumier* (1980) 251–60
66. Nestle, W. 'Die Fabel des Menenius Agrippa', *Klio* 21 (1927) 350–60
67. Niccolini, G. *Il tribunato della plebe*. Milan, 1932
68. Niese, B. 'Das sogennante Licinisch-Sextisch Ackergesetz', *Hermes* 23 (1888) 410–23
69. Olivesi, A. 'Manius Curius Dentatus et le mouvement démocratique à Rome au début du IIIe siècle av.J.-C.', *IH* 18 (1956) 85–90
70. Poma, G. 'Le secessioni e il rito dell'infissione del *clavus*', *RSA* 8 (1978) 39–50
71. Poma, G. *Tra legislatori e tiranni: problemi storici e storiografici sull'età delle XII Tavole* (Studi di storia 2). Bologna, 1984
72. Raaflaub, K. A. 'The Conflict of the Orders in archaic Rome: a comprehensive and comparative approach', in *Social Struggles in Archaic Rome*, ed. K. A. Raaflaub, 1–51. California, 1986

73. Raaflaub, K. A. 'From protection and defense to offense and participation: stages in the Conflict of the Orders', in *Social Struggles in Archaic Rome*, ed. K. A. Raaflaub, 198–243. California, 1986

74. Ranouil, P. C. *Recherches sur le patriciat*. Paris, 1975

75. Richard, J.-C. 'Édilité plébéienne et édilité curule; à propos de Denys d'Halicarnasse, *AR* VI.95.4', *Athenaeum* N.S. 55 (1977) 428–34

76. Richard, J.-C. *Les origines de la plèbe romain. Essai sur la formation du dualisme patricio-plébéien* (Bibliothèque des Écoles Françaises d'Athènes et de Rome 232). Paris, 1978

77. Richard, J.-C. 'Sur le plébiscite *ut liceret consules ambos plebeios creari*', *Historia* 28 (1979) 65–75

78. Richard, J.-C. 'Sur le droit de la plèbe à exercer la censure: à propos de Liv. 8.12.16', *Mnemosyne* ser. 4.34 (1981) 127–35

79. Richard, J.-C. 'Patricians and plebeians: the origin of a social dichotomy', in *Social Struggles in Archaic Rome*, ed. K. A. Raaflaub, 105–29. California, 1986

80. Ridley, R. T. 'Notes on the establishment of the tribunate of the plebs', *Latomus* 27 (1968) 535–54

81. Rodríguez-Ennes, L. 'La *provocatio ad populum* como garantia fundamental del ciudadano romano frente al poder coercitivo del magistrado en la época republicana', in *Studi in onore di A. Biscardi* IV.73–114. Milan, 1983

82. Rosenberg, A. 'Studien zur Entstehung der Plebs', *Hermes* 48 (1913) 359–77

83. Sabbatucci, D. 'Patrizi e plebei nello sviluppo della religione romana', *SMSR* 24–5 (1953–4) 76–92

84. Schaefer, A. 'Zur Geschichte des römischen Consulats', *Jahrbücher für classische Philologie* 113 (1876) 569–83

85. Shatzman, I. 'Patricians and plebeians: the case of the Veturii', *CQ* N.S. 23 (1973) 65–77

86. Siber, H. *Die plebejischen Magistraturen bis zur Lex Hortensia*. Leipzig, 1936

87. Siena, E. 'La politica democratica di Quinto Publilio Filone', *Stud. Rom.* 4 (1956) 509–22

88. Sordi, M. 'La *lex Maria de suffragiis ferendis* e il tribunato di C. Letorio nel 471 vulg. (storia e pseudostoria nell'annalistica romana)', *Athenaeum* N.S. 50 (1972) 132–41

89. Sordi, M. 'Il santuario di Cerere, Libero e Libera e il tribunato della plebe', in *Santuari e politica nel mondo antico* (*CISA* 9), ed. M. Sordi, 127–39. Milan, 1983

90. Staveley, E. S. '*Provocatio* during the fifth and fourth centuries B.C.', *Historia* 3 (1954–5) 412–28

91. Staveley, E. S. 'The nature and aims of the patriciate', *Historia* 32 (1983) 24–57

92. Stuart Jones, H. and Last, H. 'The making of a united state', *CAH* VII.519–53. Ed. 1. Cambridge, 1928

93. Stuveras, R. 'La vie politique au premier siècle de la république romaine à travers la tradition littéraire', *MÉFR* 76 (1964) 295–342; 77 (1965) 35–67

94. Toher, M. 'The Tenth Table and the Conflict of the Orders', in *Social Struggles in Archaic Rome*, ed. K. A. Raaflaub, 301–26. California, 1986
95. Triebel, C. A. M. *Ackergesetze und politische Reformen* (diss. Bonn, 1980)
96. von Ungern-Sternberg, J. 'The end of the Conflict of the Orders', in *Social Struggles in Archaic Rome*, ed. K. A. Raaflaub, 353–77. California, 1986
97. Urban, R. 'Zur Entstehung des Volkstribunats', *Historia* 22 (1973) 761–4
98. Werner, R. 'Vom Stadtstaat zum Weltreich. Grundzüge der innenpolitischen und sozialen Entwicklung Roms', *Gymnasium* 80 (1973) 209–35, 437–57
99. Zusi, L. 'Patriziato e plebe', *Critica Storica* 6 (1975) 177–230

b. ARISTOCRATIC POLITICS IN THE FOURTH AND THIRD CENTURIES

See also A68; B73, 190, 307; G101, 224–5, 460, 702; H30, 69, 87.

100. Afzelius, A. 'Zur Definition der römischen Nobilität vor der Zeit Ciceros', *C&M* 7 (1945) 150–200
101. Amatucci, A. G. 'Appio Claudio Cieco', *Riv. Fil.* 22 (1894) 227–58
102. Brunt, P. A. '*Nobilitas* and *novitas*', *JRS* 72 (1982) 1–22
103. Càssola, F. *I gruppi politici romani nel III secolo a.C.* Trieste, 1962
104. Corbett, J. H. C. *Flaminius and Roman Policy in North Italy* (diss. Toronto, 1968)
105. Develin, R. 'Flaminius in 232 B.C.', *Ant. Class.* 45 (1976) 638–43
106. Develin, R. *Patterns in Office-holding, 366–49 B.C.* (Collection Latomus 161). Brussels, 1979
107. Develin, R. *The Practice of Politics at Rome 366–167 B.C.* (Collection Latomus 188). Brussels, 1985
108. Dorey, T. A. 'The dictatorship of Minucius', *JRS* 45 (1955) 92–6
109. Ferenczy, E. 'The censorship of Appius Claudius Caecus', *A Ant. Hung.* 15 (1967) 27–61
110. Fraccaro, P. '*Lex Flaminia de Agro Gallico et Piceno viritim dividundo*', *Athenaeum* 7 (1919) 73–93 = id. *Opuscula* II.191–205
111. Frank, T. 'Rome after the conquest of Sicily', *CAH* VII.793–820. Ed. 1. Cambridge, 1928
112. Garzetti, A. 'Appio Claudio Cieco nella storia politica del suo tempo', *Athenaeum* N.S. 25 (1947) 175–224
113. Gelzer, M. *Die Nobilität der römischen Republik*. Leipzig, 1912. Translated as *The Roman Nobility*. Oxford, 1969
114. Gintowt, E. 'Le changement du caractère de la tribus romaine attribué à Appius Claudius Caecus', *Eos* 43 (1948–9) 198–210
115. Jacobs, K. *Gaius Flaminius* (diss. Hoorn, 1937)
116. Lejay, P. 'Appius Claudius Caecus', *Rev. Phil.* 44 (1920) 92–141
117. Lippold, A. *Consules: Untersuchungen zur Geschichte des römischen Konsulates von 264 bis 201 v.Chr.* Bonn, 1963
118. MacBain, B. 'Appius Claudius Caecus and the Via Appia', *CQ* N.S. 30 (1980) 356–72

119. Mommsen, Th. 'Die patricischen Claudier', *Monatsbericht der Königlicher Preussischen Akademie der Wissenschaften* 1861, 317–38 = id. *Römische Forschungen* 1.285–318. Berlin, 1864

120. Münzer, F. *Römische Adelsparteien und Adelsfamilien.* Stuttgart, 1920

121. Münzer, F. 'L.Papirius Crassus (Papirius 46)', *RE* 18 (1949) 1035–6

122. Münzer, F. 'L.Papirius Crassus (Papirius 47)', *RE* 18 (1949) 1036

123. Nicolet, C. 'Appius Claudius Caecus et le double forum de Capoue', *Latomus* 20 (1961) 683–720

124. Phillips, E. J. 'Roman politics during the Second Samnite War', *Athenaeum* N.S. 50 (1972) 337–56

125. Radke, G. 'Die territoriale Politik des C.Flaminius', in *Beiträge zur Alten Geschichte und deren Nachleben. Festschrift für F. Altheim*, edd. R. Stiehl and H. E. Stier, 366–86. Berlin, 1969

126. Rilinger, R. *Der Einfluss des Wahlleiters bei den römischen Konsulwahlen von 366 bis 50 v.Chr.* (Vestigia 24). Munich, 1976

127. Scullard, H. H. *Roman Politics 220–150 B.C.* Ed. 2. Oxford, 1973

128. Staveley, E. S. 'The political aims of Appius Claudius Caecus', *Historia* 8 (1959) 410–33

129. Yavetz, Z. 'The policy of Flaminius and the *plebiscitum Claudianum*', *Athenaeum* N.S. 40 (1962) 325–44

I. LATIUM, THE LATINS AND ROME

See also B(c) for archaeological evidence; E(a) for 'foundation' cults; G(c) for other cults; K(b) for the first Carthaginian treaty; A2, 123, 134; C13; E88, 100; F16, 53.

1. Alföldi, A. 'Rom und der Latinerbund um 500 v.Chr.', *Gymnasium* 67 (1960) 193–6

2. Alföldi, A. 'Die Etrusker in Latium und Rom', *Gymnasium* 70 (1963) 385–93

3. Alföldi, A. *Early Rome and the Latins.* Ann Arbor, 1965

4. *Alle origini del latino. Atti del convegno della Società Italiana di Glottologia, Pisa 7–8 dicembre 1980*, ed. E. Vineis. Pisa, 1982

5. Ampolo, C. 'Ricerche sulla lega latina I: Caput aquae Ferentinae e lacus Turni', *PP* 36 (1981) 219–33

6. Ampolo, C. 'Ricerche sulla lega latina, II: La dedica di Egerius Baebius (Cato fr. 58 Peter)', *PP* 38 (1983) 321–6

7. Ashby, T. 'Alba Longa', *Journal of Philology* 27 (1901) 37–50

8. Bellini, V. 'Sulla genesi e la struttura delle leghe dell'Italia antica III: Le leghe laziali', *RIDA* ser. 3.8 (1961) 167–227

9. Beloch, K. J. 'Die Weihinschrift des Dianahaines im Aricia', *Neue Jahrbücher für Philologie* 127 (1883) 169–75

10. Bernardi, A. 'L'interesse di Caligola per la successione del *rex nemorensis* e l'arcaica regalità nel Lazio', *Athenaeum* N.S. 31 (1953) 273–87

11. Bernardi, A. 'Dai *populi Albenses* ai *Prisci Latini* nel Lazio arcaico', *Athenaeum* N.S. 42 (1964) 223–60

12. Bernardi, A. *Nomen Latinum*. Pavia, 1973

13. Bietti Sestieri, A. M. and De Santis, A. 'Indicatori archeologici di cambiamento nella struttura delle comunità laziali nell'8 sec. a.C.', *DArch.* ser. 3.3 (1985) 35–46

14. Blakeway, A. 'Demaratus: a study of some aspects of the earliest hellenisation of Latium and Etruria', *JRS* 25 (1935) 129–49

15. Bruun, P. 'The *foedus Gabinum*', *Arctos* 5 (1967) 51–66

16. Castagnoli, F. and others. *Lavinium I: Topografia generale, fonti e storia delle ricerche*. Rome, 1972. *Lavinium II: Le tredici are*. Rome, 1975

17. Cicala, V. 'A proposito di una dedica a Diana Nemorensis', *RSA* 6–7 (1976) 301–5

18. *Le città latine fino al 338 a.C.* (*Arch. Laz.* 6 (1984) 325–418)

19. Colonna, G. 'Il *lucus Ferentinae* ritrovato?', *Arch. Laz.* 7.1 (1985) 40–3

20. Cozzoli, U. 'Aristodemo Malaco', in *Miscellanea greca e romana* (Studi pubblicati dall'Istituto Italiano per la Storia Antica 16) 5–29. Rome, 1965

21. Deroy, L. 'Le combat légendaire des Horaces et des Curiaces', *LÉC* 41 (1973) 197–206

22. De Sanctis, G. 'Sul Foedus Cassianum', in *Atti del I congresso nazionale di studi romani* 1.231–9. Rome, 1929

23. Dispersia, G. 'Le polemiche sulla guerra sociale nell'ambasceria latina di Livio VIII, 4–6', in *Storiografia e propaganda* (*CISA* 3), ed. M. Sordi, 111–20. Milan, 1975

24. Ernout, A. 'Les éléments étrusques du vocabulaire latin', *Bulletin de la Société de Linguistique de Paris* 89 (1929) 82–124

25. Ferenczy, E. 'Zum Problem des Foedus Cassianum', *RIDA* ser. 3.22 (1975) 223–32

26. Ferenczy, E. 'Κοινὸν τῶν Λατίνων', in Μνήμη Γεωργίου 'Α. Πετροπούλου, edd. A. Biscardi et al., 1.365–78. Athens, 1984

27. *La formazione della città nel Lazio* (*DArch.* N.S. 2 (1980) fasc. 1–2)

28. Friedmann, B. *Die ionischen und attischen Wörter im Altlatein*. Helsingfors, 1937

29. Gagé, J 'Mettius Fufetius: un nom ou un double titre? Remarques sur les structures de l'ancienne société albaine', *RHDFÉ* ser. 4. 53 (1975) 201–24

30. Gelzer, M. 'Latium', *RE* 12 (1924) 940–63

31. Gierow, P. G. 'Da Alba Longa a Lavinio', *Opuscula Romana* 7 (1969) 139–48

32. *Greci e Latini nel Lazio antico. Atti del convegno della Società Italiana per lo Studio dell' Antichità Classica* (*Roma 26 marzo 1981*). Rome, 1982

33. Guaitoli, M. 'Considerazioni su alcune città ed insediamenti del Lazio in età protostorica ed arcaica', *MDAI(R)* 84 (1977) 5–25

34. Guarino, A. '*Commercium* e *ius commercii*', in id. *Le origini quiritarie* 266–82

35. Guidi, A. 'Sulle prime fasi dell'urbanizzazione nel Lazio protostorico', *Opus* 1 (1982) 279–89

36. Instinsky, H. U. 'Die Weihung des Heiligtums der Latiner im Hain von Aricia', *Klio* 30 (1937) 118–22

37. Kaser, M. 'Zum Begriff des Commercium', in *Studi V. Arangio-Ruiz* (1953) II.131–67

38. *Lazio arcaico e mondo greco* (*PP* 32 (1977) fasc. 172–7)

39. *Il Lazio nell'antichità romana*, ed. R. Lefèvre. Rome, 1982

40. Maddoli, G. 'Contatti antichi del mondo latino col mondo greco', in *Alle origini del latino. Atti del convegno della Società Italiana di Glottologia, Pisa 7–8 dicembre 1980*, ed. E. Vineis, 43–64. Pisa, 1982

41. Majak, I. L. Review of E. Peruzzi, *Aspetti culturali del Lazio primitivo* (Florence 1977) in *Vestnik Drevnej Istorii* 153 (1980) 200–15

42. Manni, E. 'Le tracce della conquista volsca del Lazio', *Athenaeum* N.S. 27 (1939) 233–79

43. Manni, E. 'Aristodemo di Cuma detto il malaco', *Klearchos* 7 (1965) 63–78

44. Momigliano, A. Review-discussion of A. Alföldi, *Early Rome and the Latins* (Ann Arbor, 1965) in *JRS* 57 (1967) 211–16 = id. *Quarto Contributo* 487–99

45. Mommsen, Th. 'Die Erzählung von Cn. Marcius Coriolanus', *Hermes* 4 (1870) 1–26 = id. *Römische Forschungen* II.113–42. Berlin, 1879

46. Palmer, L. R. *The Latin Language*. London, 1954

47. Pareti, L. 'Sulla battaglia del lago Regillo', *Stud. Rom.* 7 (1959) 18–30

48. Pascal, C. B. '*Rex nemorensis*', *Numen* 23 (1976) 23–39

49. Peruzzi, E. *Aspetti culturali del Lazio primitivo*. Florence, 1978

50. Peruzzi, E. *Mycenaeans in Early Latium*. Rome, 1980

51. Piganiol, A. 'Romains et Latins: la légende des Quinctii', *MÉFR* 38 (1920) 285–316

52. Pisani, V. *Storia della lingua latina* I (Manuale storico della lingua latina I). Turin, 1962

53. Pugliese Carratelli, G. 'Greci d'Asia in Occidente tra il sec. VII e il VI', *PP* 21 (1966) 155–65

54. Pugliese Carratelli, G. 'Lazio, Roma e Magna Grecia prima del secolo IV a.C.', *PP* 23 (1968) 321–47

55. Quilici Gigli, St. 'A proposito delle ricerche sull'ubicazione di Alba Longa', *PP* 38 (1983) 140–9

56. Radke, G. *Archaisches Latein*. Darmstadt, 1981

57. Reichenberger, A. 'Die Coriolan-Erzählung', in *Wege zu Livius*, ed. E. Burck, 382–91. Darmstadt, 1967

58. Ribezzo, R. 'Fatti, fonti e metodi di studio per la toponomastica di Roma e del Lazio delle origini', *Onomastica* 2 (1948) 29–48

59. Rosenberg, A. 'Zur Geschichte des Latinerbundes', *Hermes* 54 (1919) 113–73

60. Rosenberg, A. 'Die Entstehung des sogenannten Foedus Cassianum und des latinischen Rechts', *Hermes* 55 (1920) 337–63

61. Salmon, E. T. 'Historical elements in the story of Coriolanus', *CQ* 24 (1930) 96–101

62. Salmon, E. T. 'Rome and the Latins', *Phoenix* 7 (1953) 93–104, 123–35

63. Sautel, G. 'Essai sur la notion romaine de *commercium* à l'époque ancienne', in *Varia: Études de droit romain* (Publications de l'Institut de Droit Romain de l'Université de Paris 9) 1–98. Paris, 1952

64. Scevola, M. L. 'Civiltà preistorica e protostorica della zona anziate', *RIL* 93–4 (1959–60) 417–36
65. Scevola, M. L. 'Anzio Volsca', *RIL* 100 (1966) 205–43
66. Schilling, R. 'Une victime des vicissitudes politiques: la Diane latine', in *Hommages J. Bayet* (1964) 650–67
67. Soltau, W. 'Das sogenannte Latinerbundniss des Spurius Cassius', *WS* 35 (1913–14) 257–66
68. Tilly, B. 'The identification of Laurentum', *Arch. Class.* 28 (1976) 283–93
69. Torelli, M. 'Colonizzazioni etrusche e latine di epoca arcaica: un esempio', in *Gli Etruschi e Roma* 71–82
70. Torelli, M. *Lavinio e Roma – uno studio di storia religiosa e sociale.* Rome, 1984
71. Torelli, Marina R. 'Il problema storico della più antica colonizzazione latina', *Arch. Laz.* 2 (1979) 193–6
72. Zoeller, M. *Latium und Rom.* Leipzig, 1878

J. ROME: EXTERNAL RELATIONS TO 264 B.C.

a. THE PEOPLES AND CULTURES OF PRE-ROMAN ITALY

See also G(c) for cults; A7, 29; B209, 236, 266, 314, 331, 352, 372; G616, 650, 715, 718–19.

1. Ampolo, C. 'Fertor Resius *rex Aequicolus*', *PP* 27 (1972) 409–12
2. Arias, P. E. 'I Galli nella regione emiliana', *Emilia Preromana* 1 (1948) 33–41
3. *Atti del colloquio sul tema: L'Etrusco arcaico (Firenze, 4–5 ottobre 1974)* (Bibl. di Studi Etruschi 10). Florence, 1976
4. *Die Aufnahme fremder Kultureinfluss in Etrurien und das Problem des Retardierens in der etruskischen Kunst (Mannheim 8.–10.2.1980)* (Schriften des Deutschen Archäologen Verbands 5). Mainz, 1981
5. Baldacci, P. 'La celtizzazione dell'Italia settentrionale nel quadro della politica mediterranea', in *Popoli e facies culturali celtiche a nord e a sud delle Alpi dal V al I secolo a.C.*, 147–55. Milan, 1983
6. Banti, L. 'Rapporti tra Etruria ed Umbria avanti il V sec. a.C.', in *I problemi di storia e archeologia dell'Umbria. Atti del 1 convegno di studi umbri, Gubbio, 26–31 maggio 1963*, 161–74. Perugia, 1964
7. Barfield, L. *Northern Italy before Rome.* London, 1971
8. Barker, G. W. W. 'The conditions of cultural and economic growth in the Bronze Age of Central Italy', *PPS* 38 (1972) 170–208
9. Barker, G. W. W. 'The archaeology of Samnite settlement', *Antiquity* 51 (1977) 20–4
10. Barker, G. W. W. *Landscape and Society: Prehistoric Central Italy.* London, 1981
11. Barker, G. W. W., Lloyd, J. A. and Webley, D. 'A classical landscape in Molise', *PBSR* 46 (1978) 135–51
12. Beloch, K. J. *Campanien.* Ed. 2. Breslau, 1890

13. Bianchi-Bandinelli, R. and Giuliano, A. *Les étrusques et l'Italie avant Rome*. Paris, 1973

14. Bonfante, L. *Out of Etruria. Etruscan Influence North and South* (*B.A.R*. Int. Ser. 103). Oxford, 1981

15. Bosch-Gimpera, P. 'Les mouvements celtiques, essai de réconstruction', *Études Celtiques* 5.2 (1950–1) 352–400; 6.1 (1952) 71–126; 6.2 (1953–4) 328–55; 7.1 (1955) 147–69

16. Campanile, E. and Letta, C. *Studi sulle magistrature indigene e municipali in area italica*. Pisa, 1979

17. Camporeale, G. 'La terminologia magistratuale nelle lingue osco-umbre', *AATC* 21 (1956) 31–108

18. Camporeale, G. 'Sull'organizzazione statuale degli Etruschi', *PP* 13 (1958) 5–25

19. Camporeale, G. 'Saghe greche nell'arte etrusca arcaica', *PP* 19 (1964) 428–50

20. Camporeale, G. 'Banalizzazioni etrusche di miti greci', in *Studi in onore di L. Banti* 111–123. Rome, 1965

21. Camporeale, G. 'Banalizzazioni etrusche di miti greci II', *Stud. Etr.* 36 (1968) 21–35

22. Camporeale, G. 'Banalizzazioni etrusche di miti greci III', *Stud. Etr.* 37 (1969) 59–76

23. *I Celti d'Italia*, ed. E. Campanile. Pisa, 1981

24. Chevallier, R. 'La Celtique du Pô, position des problèmes', *Latomus* 21 (1962) 366–70

25. Coli, U. 'Stati-città e unioni etniche nella preistoria greca e italica', in *Studi in onore di P. De Francisci* IV.505–33. Milan, 1956 = U. Coli, *Scritti di diritto romano* II.543–67. Milan, 1973

26. Coli, U. 'L'organizzazione politica dell'Umbria preromana', in *I problemi di storia e archeologia dell'Umbria. Atti del I convegno di studi umbri, Gubbio, 26–31 maggio 1963*, 133–60. Perugia, 1964 = id. *Scritti di diritto romano* II.835–60. Milan, 1973

27. Colonna, G. 'La Sicilia e il Tirreno nel V e IV secolo', *Kokalos* 26–7 (1980–81) 157–83

28. Colonna, G. 'Apollon, les Étrusques et Lipara', *MÉFR(A)* 96.2 (1984) 557–78

29. *Il commercio etrusco arcaico. Atti dell'incontro di studio 5–7 dicembre 1983* (Quaderni del Centro di Studio per l'Archeologia Etrusco-Italica 9), edd. M. Cristofani et al. Rome, 1985

30. *Il commercio greco nel Tirreno in età arcaica. Atti del seminario in memoria di Mario Napoli*. Salerno, 1981

31. Crawford, M.H. Review of E. Campanile and C. Letta, *Studi sulle magistrature indigene e municipali in area italica* (Pisa, 1979) in *Athenaeum* N.S. 59 (1981) 542–3

32. Cristofani, M. 'Il "dono" nell'Etruria arcaica', *PP* 30 (1975) 132–52

33. Cristofani, M. *Città e campagna nell'Etruria settentrionale*. Arezzo–Novara, 1976

34. De Marinis, R. 'The La Tène culture of the Cisalpine Gauls', *Keltske Studije* 1977

35. De Niro, A. *Il culto d'Ercole tra i Sanniti Pentri e Frentani*. Rome, 1977

36. De Simone, C. *Die griechischen Entlehnungen im Etruskischen*. 2 vols. Wiesbaden, 1968–70

37. De Simone, C. 'Etrusco Tursikina: sulla formazione ed origine dei gentilizi etruschi in -kina (-cina)', *Stud. Etr.* 40 (1972) 153–81

38. De Simone, C. 'Un nuovo gentilizio etrusco di Orvieto ("Katacina") e la cronologia della penetrazione celtica (gallica) in Italia', *PP* 33 (1978) 370–95

39. Devoto, G. *Gli antichi Italici*. Ed. 3. Florence, 1968

40. Devoto, G. 'Protosabini, Sabini e Postsabini', *Stud. Etr.* 39 (1971) 107–14

41. Dohrn, T. 'Die Etrusker und die griechische Sage', *MDAI(R)* 73–4 (1966–7) 15–28

42. Dohrn, T. *Die etruskische Kunst im Zeitalter der griechischen Klassik: die Interimsperiode*. Mainz, 1982

43. Eisenhut, W. '*Ver sacrum*', RE 2.Reihe, 8 (1955) 911–23

44. De Franciscis, A. *Stato e società in Locri Epizefiri*. Naples, 1972

45. Frankfort, T. 'Les classes serviles en Étrurie', *Latomus* 18 (1959) 3–22

46. Frederiksen, M. W. 'Campanian cavalry. A question of origins', *DArch.* 2 (1968) 3–31

47. Frederiksen, M. W. Review-discussion of E. T. Salmon, *Samnium and the Samnites* (Cambridge, 1967) in *JRS* 58 (1968) 224–9

48. Frederiksen, M. W. *Campania*. London, 1984

49. *I Galli et l'Italia* (Exhibition catalogue). Rome, 1978

50. Gras, M. 'La Sicilie et l'Italie centrale au VIIe siècle et dans la première moitié du VI siècle avant J.C.', *Kokalos* 26–7 (1980–81) 99–138

51. Grenier, A. *Les Gaulois*. Paris, 1945

52. Grilli, A. 'I capitoli sui Galli in Livio', in *Studi in onore di F. Rittatore Vonwiller*, 183–92. Como, 1980

53. Hampe, R. and Simon, E. *Griechische Sagen in der frühen etruskischen Kunst*. Mainz, 1964

54. Harmand, J. *Les Celtes au second âge du fer*. Paris, 1970

55. Hatt, J.-J. 'Les invasions celtiques en Italie du Nord', *Bulletin de la Société Préhistorique Française* 57 (1960) 362–72

56. Hatt, J.-J. 'Sur les traces des invasions celtiques en Italie du Nord', *RÉL* 38 (1960) 69–70

57. Hatt, J.-J. *Celtes et Gallo-romains*. Paris, 1970

58. Hencken, H. 'Syracuse, Etruria and the north', *AJA* 62 (1958) 259–72

59. Heurgon, J. *Recherches sur l'histoire, la religion, et la civilisation de Capoue préromaine des origines à la deuxième guerre punique*. Paris, 1942

60. Heurgon, J. *Trois études sur le 'ver sacrum'* (Collection Latomus 26). Brussels, 1957

61. Heurgon, J. 'L'état étrusque', *Historia* 6 (1957) 63–97

62. Heurgon, J. 'Les pénestes étrusques chez Denys d'Halicarnasse (IX, 5, 4)', *Latomus* 18 (1959) 713–23

63. Heurgon, J. 'Classes et ordres chez les Étrusques', in *Recherches sur les structures sociales dans l'antiquité classique. Caen 25–26 avril 1969*, 29–41. Paris, 1970

64. Heurgon, J. 'Onomastique étrusque: la dénomination gentilice', in *L'onomastique latine*, 25–34. Paris, 1977

65. Heurgon, J. 'À propos de l'inscription "Tyrrhénienne" de Lemnos', *CRAcad. Inscr.* 1980, 578–600

66. Homeyer, H. 'Zum Keltenexkurs in Livius' 5. Buch (33.4–35.3)', *Historia* 9 (1960) 345–61

67. Hubert, H. *Les Celtes depuis l'époque de La Tène et la civilisation celtique*. Ed. 2. Paris, 1950

68. Hus, A. *Les siècles d'or de l'histoire étrusque (675–465 avant J.C.)*. Brussels, 1976

69. Hus, A. *Les Étrusques et leur destin*. Paris, 1980

70. Judson, S. and Hemphill, P. 'Sizes of settlements in Southern Etruria 6th–5th centuries B.C.', *Stud. Etr.* 49 (1981) 193–202

71. Jullian, C. *Histoire de la Gaule*. 8 vols. Paris, 1908–26

72. Kornemann, E. 'Zur altitalischen Verfassungsgeschichte', *Klio* 14 (1915) 190–206

73. Kruta, V. *Les Celtes*. Paris, 1976

74. Kruta, V. 'Celtes de Cispadane et transalpines aux IV et III siècles av. notre ère: données archéologiques', *Stud. Etr.* 46 (1978) 149–74

75. Kruta-Poppi, L. 'Les Celtes à Marzabotto', *Études Celtiques* 14.2 (1975) 345–76

76. Lambrechts, R. *Essai sur les magistratures des républiques étrusques*. Brussels, 1959

77. La Regina, A. 'Cluviae e il territorio Carecino', *RAL* ser. 8.22 (1967) 88–99

78. La Regina, A. 'Contributi dell'archeologia alla storia sociale: territori sabellici e sannitici', *DArch.* 4–5 (1970–71) 443–73

79. La Regina, A. 'Appunti su entità etniche e strutture istituzionali nel Sannio antico', *AION (Archeol)* 3 (1981) 129–37

80. Laviosa-Zambotti, P. 'L'invasione gallica in Val Padana', in *Storia di Milano*, 1.67–110. Milan, 1953

81. Letta, C. *I Marsi e il Fucino nell'antichità*. Milan, 1972

82. Mansuelli, G. A. *I Cisalpini*. Florence, 1962

83. Mansuelli, G. A. 'Problemi storici della civiltà gallica in Italia', in *Hommages A. Grenier* (1962) III.1067–93

84. Mansuelli, G. A. 'La formazione delle civiltà storiche nella valle padana orientale', *Stud. Etr.* 33 (1965) 3–47

85. Mansuelli, G. A. 'Etruschi e Celti nella valle del Po', in *Hommages M. Renard* (1969) II.485–504

86. Martini, W. 'Überlegungen zur Genese der etruskischen Kultur', *JDAI* 96 (1981) 1–27

87. Nava, M. L. *Stele Daunie*. 2 vols. Florence, 1980

88. Negroni-Catacchio, M. 'Le fasi finali della civiltà di Golasecca nel ambito

degli aspetti culturali della Val Padana fino alla romanizzazione', in *Popoli e civiltà dell'Italia antica* IV.329–56. Rome, 1975

89. Nicolet, C. 'Les "Equites Campani" et leurs représentations figurées', *MÉFR* 74 (1962) 463–517

90. Pallottino, M. 'Nuovi spunti di ricerca sul tema delle magistrature etrusche', *Stud. Etr.* 24 (1955–6) 45–72

91. Pallottino, M. 'Il filoetruschismo di Aristodemo di Cuma e la data della fondazione di Capua', *PP* 11 (1956) 81–8

92. Pallottino, M. *Saggi di antichità I: alle origini dell'Italia antica.* Rome, 1979

93. Pallottino, M. *Saggi di antichità II: Documenti per la storia della civiltà etrusca.* Rome, 1979

94. Pallottino, M. *Genti e culture dell'Italia preromana.* Rome, 1981

95. Pallottino, M. *Storia della prima Italia.* Milan, 1984

96. Pallottino, M. *Etruscologia.* Ed. 7. Milan, 1984. Sixth edition translated (with additions) as *The Etruscans.* London, 1975

97. Pallottino, M. 'Oriundi forestieri nella onomastica e nella società etrusca', in *Studi di antichità in onore di G. Maetzke* II.401–5. Rome, 1984

98. Panuccio, R. 'Per una nuova collocazione cronologica di alcune delle tavolette bronzee di Locri Epizefiri', *RIL* 108 (1974) 105–20

99. Pareti, L. 'La disunione politica degli Etruschi e i suoi riflessi storici e archeologici', *RPAA* 7 (1931) 89–100

100. *Popoli e facies culturali celtiche a nord e a sud delle Alpi dal V a I secolo a.C. Atti del colloquio internazionale, Milano, 14–16 novembre 1980.* Milan, 1983

101. Radke, G. 'Volsci', *RE* 2.Reihe, 9 (1961) 773–827

102. Restelli, A. 'Etruschi ed Umbri nel III secolo a.C.', in *Conoscenze etniche et rapporti di convivenza nell'antichità (CISA* 6), ed. M. Sordi, 150–7. Milan, 1979

103. Ridgway, D. *The Etruscans* (University of Edinburgh, Department of Archaeology Occasional Paper 6). Edinburgh, 1981 = *CAH* IV. Ed. 2, Chap. 13. Cambridge, 1988

104. Rix, H. *Das etruskische Cognomen.* Wiesbaden, 1963

105. Rosenberg, A. *Der Staat der alten Italiker. Untersuchungen über die ursprüngliche Verfassung der Latiner, Osker und Etrusker.* Berlin, 1913

106. Salmon, E. T. *Samnium and the Samnites.* Cambridge, 1967

107. Sartori, F. *Problemi di storia costituzionale italiota* (Università degli Studi di Padova. Pubblicazioni dell'Istituto di Storia Antica 1). Rome, 1953

108. Sartori, F. 'Costituzioni italiote, italiche, etrusche', *Stud. Clas.* 10 (1968) 1–22

109. Saulnier, C. *L'armée et la guerre chez les peuples samnites.* Paris, 1983

110. Scevola, M. L. 'Pirateria anziate', in *Studi di storia antica in memoria di L. De Regibus* (Pubblicazioni dell'Istituto di Storia Antica, Università di Genova 6) 135–44. Genoa, 1969

111. Schauenburg, K. 'Zu griechischen Mythen in der etruskischen Kunst', *JDAI* 85 (1970) 28–81

112. Sereni, E. 'Città e campagna nell'Italia preromana', *Critica Marxista* 9 (1966) 13–100

113. Sordi, M. 'La leggenda di Arunte chiusino e la prima invasione gallica in Italia', *RSA* 6–7 (1976–7) 111–17

114. Sordi, M. 'Il giuramento della *legio linteata* e la guerra sociale', in *I canali della propaganda nel mondo antico (CISA* 4), ed. M. Sordi, 160–8. Milan, 1976

115. Sprenger, M. *Die etruskische Plastik des 5. Jahrhunderts v.Chr. und ihr Verhältnis zur griechischen Kunst* (Studia Archaeologica 14). Rome, 1972

116. *Storia della società italiana I: Dalla preistoria all'espansione romana.* Milan, 1981

117. *Studi sulla città antica. Atti del convegno di studi sulla città etrusca e italica preromana.* Bologna, 1970

118. *Le tavole di Locri. Atti del colloquio sugli aspetti politici, economici, cultuali e linguistici dei testi dell'archivio locrese, Napoli 26–27 aprile 1977*, ed. D. Musti. Rome, 1979

119. Tibiletti, G. 'Considerazioni sulle popolazioni dell'Italia preromana', in *Popoli e civiltà dell'Italia antica* VII.15–49. Rome, 1978

120. Torelli, M. 'Beziehungen zwischen Griechischen und Etruskischen im 5. und 4. Jhdt. v.u.Z.', in *Hellenische Poleis*, ed. E. Ch. Welskopf, II.823–40. Berlin, 1974

121. Torelli, M. 'Greek artisans and Etruria: a problem concerning the relationship between the two cultures', *Archaeological News* 5 (1976) 134–8

122. Torelli, M. *Storia degli Etruschi.* Bari, 1981

123. Torelli, M. 'Il commercio greco in Etruria tra l'VIII ed il VI secolo a.C.', in *Il commercio greco nel Tirreno in età arcaica. Atti del seminario in memoria di Mario Napoli* 67–82. Salerno, 1981

124. Torelli, M. 'Delitto religioso. Qualche indizio sulla situazione in Etruria', in *Le délit religieux dans la cité antique* (Collection de l'École Française de Rome 48) 1–7. Rome, 1981

125. Torelli, M. 'Polis e palazzo – architettura, ideologia e artigianato greco in Etruria tra VII e VI sec. a.C.', in *Architecture et société de l'archaïsme grec à la fin de la république romaine. Actes du colloque international organisé par le Centre National de la Recherche Scientifique et l'École Française de Rome (Rome 2–4 décembre 1980)* (Collection de l'École Française de Rome 66) 471–99. Paris–Rome, 1983

126. Trump, D. H. *Central and Southern Italy before Rome.* London, 1966

127. Vallet, G. *Rhégion et Zancle. Histoire, commerce et civilisation des cités chalcidiennes du détroit de Messine* (Bibliothèque des Écoles Françaises d'Athènes et de Rome 189). Paris, 1958

128. van Wonterghem, F. 'Le culte d'Hercule chez les Paeligni', *Ant. Class.* 42 (1973) 36–48

129. Vetter, E. *Handbuch der italischen Dialekte* I. Heidelberg, 1953

130. Weeber, K.-W. *Geschichte der Etrusker.* Stuttgart–Berlin, 1979

131. Wuilleumier, P. *Tarente, des origines à la conquête romaine.* Paris, 1939

132. Zuffa, M. 'Celti nell'Italia adriatica', in *Atti del I Convegno di studi ant. adriatiche* (1971) 97–159

b. ROMAN EXPANSION IN ITALY

See also A30, 48, 61, 69, 123; B50–1, 119, 127, 193, 282, 420; C20–1; G101, 622, 749; H98, 104–5, 110, 125; J47–8, 59, 106.

133. Adcock, F. E. 'The conquest of central Italy', *CAH* VII.581–616. Ed. 1. Cambridge, 1928
134. Afzelius, A. *Die römische Eroberung Italiens (340–264 v. Chr.)*. Copenhagen, 1942
135. Anziani, D. *'Caeritum tabulae'*, *MÉFR* 31 (1911) 435–56
136. Bayet, J. 'Tite Live et la précolonisation romaine', *Rev. Phil.* 12 (1938) 97–119
137. Beloch, K. J. *Der italische Bund unter Roms Hegemonie*. Leipzig, 1880
138. Beloch, K. J. 'La conquista romana della regione sabina', *Rivista di Storia Antica e Scienze Affini* 9 (1904) 269–77
139. Bengtson, H. *Die Staatsverträge des Altertums* II: *Die Verträge der griechisch-römischen Welt von 700 bis 338 v.Chr.* Munich–Berlin, 1962
140. Bernardi, A. *'I cives sine suffragio'*, *Athenaeum* N.S. 16 (1938) 239–77
141. Bernardi, A. 'Roma e Capua nella seconda metà del quarto secolo a.C.', *Athenaeum* N.S. 20 (1942) 86–103; 21 (1943) 21–31
142. Bernardi, A. 'Incremento demografico di Roma e colonizzazione latina dal 338 a.C. all'età dei Gracchi', *Nuova Rivista Storica* 30 (1946) 272–89
143. Binneboessel, P. *Untersuchungen über Quellen und Geschichte des zweiten Samniterkrieges* (diss. Halle, 1893)
144. Bitto, I. *'Tribus e propagatio civitatis* nei secoli IV e III a.C.', *Epigraphica* 30 (1968) 20–58
145. Bleicken, J. 'Rom und Italien', in *Propylaeen Weltgeschichte: ein Universalgeschichte*, edd. G. Mann and A. Heuss, 27–96. Berlin, 1963
146. Brandt, J. Rasmus. 'Ostia, Minturno, Pyrgi. The planning of three Roman colonies', *Acta ad archaeologiam et artium historiam pertinentia Instituti Romani Norvegiae* ser. 2.5 (1985) 25–88
147. Brown, F. E. *Cosa: the Making of a Roman Town*. Ann Arbor, 1980
148. Bruno, B. *La terza guerra sannitica* (Studi di Storia Antica 6). Rome, 1906
149. Brunt, P. A. 'The enfranchisement of the Sabines', in *Hommages M. Renard* (1969) II.121–9
150. Burger, C. P. *Der Kampf zwischen Rom und Samnium bis zum vollständigen Siege Roms um 312 v. Chr.* Amsterdam, 1898
151. Catalano, P. *Linee del sistema sovranazionale romano* I. Turin, 1965
152. Coarelli, F. 'Fregellae e la colonizzazione latina nella valle del Liri', *Arch. Laz.* 2 (1979) 197–204
153. Colonna, G. 'Un "trofeo" di Novio Fannio, comandante sannita', in *Studi di antichità in onore di G. Maetzke*, II.229–41. Rome, 1984
154. Corbett, J. H. 'Rome and the Gauls, 285–80 B.C.', *Historia* 20 (1971) 656–64
155. Costanzi, V. 'Osservazioni sulla terza guerra sannitica', *Riv. Fil.* 47 (1919) 161–215
156. Crawford, M. H. *'Foedus* and *sponsio'*, *PBSR* 41 (1973) 1–7

157. Dahlheim, W. *Struktur und Entwicklung des römischen Volkerrechts*. Munich, 1968

158. Delplace, C. 'L'intervention étrusque dans les dernières années de la deuxième guerre samnite (312–308)', *Latomus* 26 (1967) 454–66

159. De Visscher, F. 'La *deditio* internationale et l'affaire des Fourches Caudines', *CR Acad. Inscr.* 1946, 82–95

160. Didu, I. 'Il supposto invio di coloni romani in Sardegna nell'anno 378–7 a.C.', *Athenaeum* N.S. 50 (1972) 310–29

161. Fraccaro, P. 'L'organizzazione politica dell'Italia romana', in *Atti del congresso internazionale di diritto romano, Roma, 22–29 aprile 1933*, I.195–208. Pavia, 1934 = P. Fraccaro, *Opuscula* I.103–14

162. Fraccaro, P. 'Assegnazioni agrarie e censimenti romani', in *Scritti in onore di C. Ferrini pubblicati in occasione della sua beatificazione* (Pubblicazioni dell'Università Cattolica di Milano N.S. 17) I.262–74. Milan, 1947–9 = P. Fraccaro, *Opuscula* II.87–102

163. Frank, T. 'On Rome's conquest of Sabinum, Picenum, and Etruria', *Klio* 11 (1911) 367–81

164. Frank, T. *Roman Imperialism*. New York, 1914

165. Freeman, E. A. *History of Federal Government in Greece and Italy*. London, 1863

166. Frezza, P. 'Le forme federative e la struttura dei rapporti internazionali nell'antico diritto romano', *SDHI* 4 (1938) 363–428

167. Frezza, P. 'Intorno alla leggenda dei Fabi al Cremera', in *Scritti in onore di C. Ferrini pubblicati in occasione della sua beatificazione* (Pubblicazioni dell'Università Cattolica di Milano N.S. 17) I.295–306. Milan, 1947–9

168. Gabba, E. 'Istituzioni militari e colonizzazione in Roma mediorepubblicana', *Riv. Fil.* 103 (1975) 144–54

169. Gabba, E. 'Per un'interpretazione storica della centuriazione romana', *Athenaeum* N.S. 63 (1985) 265–84

170. Galsterer, H. *Herrschaft und Verwaltung im republikanischen Italien. Die Beziehungen Roms zu den italischen Gemeinden von Latinerfrieden 338 v.Chr. bis zum Bundesgenossenkrieg 91 v.Chr.* (Münch. Beitr. Papyr. 68). Munich, 1976

171. Göhler, J. *Rom und Italien*. Breslau, 1939

172. Grieve, L. J. 'The etymology of *municeps*', *Latomus* 41 (1982) 771–2

173. Hantos, T. *Das römische Bundesgenossensystem in Italia* (Vestigia 34). Munich, 1983

174. Harris, W. V. 'Roman *foedera* in Etruria', *Historia* 14 (1965) 282–92

175. Harris, W. V. *Rome in Etruria and Umbria*. Oxford, 1971

176. Hirschfeld, O. 'Zur Camillus-Legende', in *Festschrift für L. Friedländer* 125–38. Leipzig, 1895

177. Holleman, A. W. 'Myth and historiography. The tale of the 306 Fabii', *Numen* 23 (1976) 210–18

178. Homo, L. 'The Gallic wars of Rome', *CAH* VII.554–80. Ed. 1. Cambridge, 1928

179. Horn, H. *Foederati*. Frankfurt, 1930

180. Horsfall, N. 'From history to legend. M. Manlius and the geese', *Classical Journal* 76 (1981) 298–311

181. Horsfall, N. 'The Caudine Forks: topography and illusion', *PBSR* 50 (1982) 45–52
182. Hubaux, J. *Rome et Véies: recherches sur la chronologie légendaire du moyen âge romain.* Liège, 1958
183. Humbert, M. 'L'incorporation de Caere dans la *civitas Romana*', *MÉFR* 84 (1972) 231–68
184. Humbert, M. *Municipium et civitas sine suffragio. L'organisation de la conquête jusqu'à la guerre sociale* (Collection de l'École Française de Rome 36). Rome, 1978
185. Klotz, A. 'Livius' Darstellung des zweiten Samniterkrieges', *Mnemosyne* ser. 3.6 (1938) 83–102
186. Kornemann, E. '*Coloniae*', *RE* 4 (1900) 511–88
187. Kornemann, E. '*Municipium*', *RE* 16 (1933) 570–638
188. Kramer, F. R. 'Massilian diplomacy before the Second Punic War', *AJPhil.* 69 (1948) 1–26
189. McKendrick, P. 'Roman colonization', *Phoenix* 6 (1952) 139–46
190. Manni, E. *Per la storia dei municipii fino alla guerra sociale.* Rome, 1947
191. Manni, E. 'Sur l'origine des *municipia* romains', *RHDFÉ* ser. 4.47 (1969) 66–77
192. Martinez-Pinna, J. 'Camilo y los galos. Nota sobre la invasione celta en Italia en el siglo IV', *Hispania Antiqua* 8 (1978) 7–16
193. Meiggs, R. *Roman Ostia.* Ed. 2. Oxford, 1973
194. Morgan, M. G. 'The defeat of L. Metellus Denter at Arretium', *CQ* N.S. 22 (1972) 309–25
195. Napoli, M. *Napoli greco-romana.* Naples, 1959
196. Nenci, G. 'Le relazioni con Marsiglia nella politica estera romana', *RSL* 24 (1958) 24–97
197. Nicolet, C. *Rome et la conquête du monde méditerranéen (264–27 av. J.C.) 1. Les structures de l'Italie romaine.* Paris, 1977
198. Nissen, H. 'Die Caudinische Friede', *Rh.Mus.* N.F. 25 (1870) 1–65
199. Pais, E. 'La flotta greca che nel 349 a.C. comparve davanti alle coste del Lazio', *Stud. Stor.* 2 (1893) 429–443
200. Pais, E. 'Serie cronologica delle colonie romane e latine dall'età regia fino all'impero', *MAL* ser. 5.17 (1924) 311–55
201. Pareti, L. 'Le lotte dei Romani contro gli Etruschi nell'opera liviana', *A & R* N.S. 12 (1931) 211–30
202. Pfiffig, A. J. *Die Ausbreitung des römischen Städtewesens in Etrurien und die Frage der Unterwerfung der Etrusker.* Florence, 1966
203. Pfiffig, A. J. 'Das Verhalten Etruriens im Samniterkrieg und nachher bis zum 1. punischen Krieg', *Historia* 17 (1968) 307–50
204. Piccirilli, C. 'Camillo fra Roma e Cere', *PP* 35 (1980) 415–31
205. Piganiol, A. *La conquête romaine.* Ed. 5. Paris, 1967
206. Pinsent, J. 'The original meaning of *municeps*', *CQ* N.S. 4 (1954) 158–64
207. Pinsent, J. '*Municeps* II', *CQ* N.S. 7 (1957) 89–97
208. Pohl, I. 'Was early Ostia a colony or a fort?', *PP* 38 (1983) 123–30
209. Poucet, J. '*Acta triumphalia et falsi triumphi.* Le triomphe remporté sur les Samnites et les Nequinates par le consul Fulvius en 299 av. J.C. et les

falsi triumphi de la *gens Fulvia* à l'époque des guerres samnites', in *Recueil commémoratif du Xe anniversaire de la Faculté de Philosophie et Lettres* (Publ. de l'Univ. Lovanium de Kinshasa 22) 205–19. Louvain, 1968

210. Rowland, R. J. 'Rome's earliest imperialism', *Latomus* 42 (1983) 749–62
211. Rudolph, H. *Stadt und Staat im römischen Italien.* Leipzig, 1935
212. Salmon, E. T. 'The *pax Caudina*', *JRS* 19 (1929) 12–18
213. Salmon, E. T. 'Rome's battles with Etruscans and Gauls in 284–282 B.C.', *CPhil.* 30 (1935) 25–31
214. Salmon, E. T. 'Roman expansion and Roman colonisation in Italy', *Phoenix* 9 (1955) 63–75
215. Salmon, E. T. 'The resumption of hostilities after the Caudine peace', *TAPA* 87 (1956) 98–108
216. Salmon, E. T. 'Colonial foundations during the Second Samnite War', *CPhil.* 58 (1963) 235–8
217. Salmon, E. T. 'The *coloniae maritimae*', *Athenaeum* N.S. 41 (1963) 3–38
218. Salmon, E. T. *Roman Colonisation under the Republic.* London, 1969
219. Salmon, E. T. *The Making of Roman Italy.* London, 1982
220. Scevola, M. L. 'Sulla prima guerra sannitica', *Aevum* 42 (1968) 291–7
221. Scevola, M. L. 'Sulla più antica espansione territoriale romana in Campania', *RIL* 107 (1973) 1002–40
222. Schachermeyr, R. 'Die gallische Katastrophe', *Klio* 23 (1929) 277–305
223. Schmitt, H. H. *Rom und Rhodos. Geschichte ihrer politischen Beziehungen seit der ersten Berührung bis zum Aufgehen des Inselstaates im römischen Weltreich* (*Münch. Beitr. Papyr.* 40). Munich, 1957
224. Schmitt, H. H. *Die Staatsverträge des Altertums III: Die Verträge der griechisch-römischen Welt von 338 bis 200 v.Chr.* Munich, 1969
225. Schwarte, H.-H. 'Zum Ausbruch des zweiten Samnitenkrieges (326–304 v.Chr.)', *Historia* 20 (1971) 368–75
226. Skutsch, O. 'The fall of the Capitol', *JRS* 43 (1953) 77–8
227. Skutsch, O. 'The fall of the Capitol again: Tacitus, *Ann.* 11.23', *JRS* 68 (1978) 93–4
228. Solari, A. 'Cincinnato e le lotte contro gli Equi e i Volsci secondo Livio', in G. N. Columba et al., *Studi Liviani*, 67–80. Rome, 1934
229. Sommella, P. *Antichi campi di battaglia in Italia.* Rome, 1967
230. Sordi, M. *I rapporti romano-ceriti e le origini della civitas sine suffragio.* Rome, 1960
231. Sordi, M. 'L'excursus sulla colonizzazione romana in Velleio e le guerre sannitiche', *Helikon* 6 (1966) 627–38
232. Sordi, M. *Roma e i Sanniti nel IV secolo.* Bologna, 1969
233. Sordi, M. 'Il Campidoglio e l'invasione gallica del 386 a.C.', in *I santuari e la guerra nel mondo classico* (*CISA* 10), ed. M. Sordi, 82–91. Milan, 1984
234. Spaeth, J. W. *The Causes of Rome's Wars 343–269 B.C.* (diss. Princeton, 1926)
235. Täubler, E. *Imperium Romanum. Studien zur Entwicklungsgeschichte des römischen Reiches* I. Leipzig, 1913
236. Tibiletti, G. 'Latini e Ceriti', in *Studi giuridici e sociali in memoria di E. Vanoni* (*Studia Ghisleriana* ser. 1.3) 239–49. Pavia, 1961
237. Torelli, M. and Coarelli, F. 'I Galli a Roma', in *I Galli e l'Italia*, 226–30. Rome, 1978

238. Veyne, P. '*Foederati*: Tarquinies, Camérinum, Capène', *Latomus* 19 (1960) 429–36
239. Veyne, P. 'Y a-t-il eu un impérialisme romain?', *MÉFR(A)* 87 (1975) 793–855
240. Vitucci, G. 'A proposito dei primi contatti fra Umbri e Romani', in *I problemi di storia e archeologia dell'Umbria. Atti del I convegno di studi umbri, Gubbio, 26–31 maggio 1963*, 291–301. Perugia, 1964
241. Waley, D. *Die italienischen Stadtstaaten*. Munich, 1969
242. Westington, M. M. *Atrocities in Roman Warfare to 133 B.C.* (diss. Chicago, 1938)
243. Whatmough, J. *The Foundations of Roman Italy*. London, 1937
244. Wiseman, T. P. 'Roman republican road-building', *PBSR* 38 (1970) 122–52

C. PYRRHUS

See also B12, 53, 92, 110, 122, 220–1, 258; J44, 98, 118, 131.

245. Accame, S. 'La diarchia dei Molossi', *Riv. Fil.* 62 (1934) 522–34
246. Adcock, F. E. *The Greek and Macedonian Art of War*. Berkeley–Los Angeles, 1967
247. Aymard, A. 'L'usage du titre royal dans la Grèce classique et hellénistique', *RHDFÉ* ser. 4.27 (1949) 579–90
248. Babelon, J. 'Le roi Pyrrhos', in *Centennial Publication of the American Numismatic Society*, ed. H. Ingholt, 53–71. New York, 1958
249. Bengtson, H. 'Pyrrhus', in id. *Herrschergestalten des Hellenismus*, 91–110. Munich, 1975
250. Berve, H. 'Das Königtum des Pyrrhos in Sizilien', in *Neue Beiträge zur klass. Altertumswissenschaft. Festschrift für B. Schweitzer*, ed. R. Lullies, 272–7. Stuttgart, 1954
251. Bickerman, E. 'Apocryphal correspondence of Pyrrhos', *CPhil.* 42 (1947) 137–46
252. Breglia, L. 'Nuovi elementi di conoscenza per la circolazione monetale e la storia dell'Epiro', *Rendiconti dell'Accademia di Archeologia, Lettere e Belle Arti di Napoli* 21 (1941) 193–260
253. Carcopino, J. 'Pyrrhus', in id. *Profils de Conquérants* 11–108. Paris, 1961
254. Ciaceri, E. *Sulla spedizione del re Pirro in Sicilia*. Catania, 1902
255. Cross, G. N. *Epirus. A Study in Greek Constitutional Development*. Cambridge, 1932
256. Frank, T. 'Pyrrhus', *CAH* VII.638–64. Ed. 1. Cambridge, 1928
257. Franke, P. R. *Alt-Epirus und das Königtum der Molosser* (diss. Erlangen, 1954). Kallmünz, 1955
258. Gagé, J. 'Pyrrhus et l'influence religieuse de Dodone dans l'Italie primitive', *Rev. Hist. Rel.* 145 (1954) 137–65; 146 (1954) 18–50, 129–39; 147 (1955) 1–31
259. Garoufalias, P. *Pyrrhus, King of Epirus*. Ed. 2. London, 1979
260. Griffith, G. T. *The Mercenaries of the Hellenistic World*. Ed. 2. Cambridge, 1968

762   BIBLIOGRAPHY

261. Hamburger, O. *Untersuchungen über den pyrrhischen Krieg* (diss. Würzburg, 1927)
262. Hammond, N. G. L. *Epirus*. Oxford, 1967
263. Hoffmann, W. 'Der Kampf zwischen Rom und Tarent im Urteil der antiken Überlieferung', *Hermes* 71 (1936) 11–24
264. Holleaux, M. *Rome, la Grèce et les monarchies hellénistiques au IIIe siècle av. J.-C.* Paris, 1921
265. Jacquemod, M. 'Sulle direttive politiche di Pirro in Italia', *Aevum* 6 (1932) 445–72
266. Judeich, W. 'König Pyrrhos' römische Politik', *Klio* 20 (1926) 1–18
267. Kienast, D. 'Pyrrhos', *RE* 13 (1963) 108–65
268. Klotzsch, C. *Epeirotische Geschichte*. Berlin, 1911
269. La Bua, V. 'Prosseno e gli ὑπομνήματα Πύρρου', in *Terza miscellanea greca e romana* (Studi pubblicati dall'Istituto Italiano per la Storia Antica 21) 1–61. Rome, 1971
270. La Bua, V. 'Pirro in Pompeo Trogo-Giustino', in *Scritti storico-epigrafici in memoria di M. Zambelli*, ed. L. Gasperini, 181–205. Rome, 1978
271. Larsen, J. A. O. *Representative Government in Greek and Roman History*. Oxford, 1966
272. Launey, M. *Recherches sur les armées hellénistiques*. 2 vols. Paris, 1949–50
273. Lepore, E. 'Il problema storico dei rapporti fra l'Epiro e la Sicilia', *Kokalos* 10/11 (1964/5) 489–502
274. Lévêque, P. *Pyrrhos*. Paris, 1957
275. Lévêque, P. 'Monnaies et finances des cités italiotes engagées dans la guerre pyrrhique', in *Armées et fiscalité dans le monde antique: Paris 14–16 octobre 1976* (Colloques Nationaux du Centre National de la Recherche Scientifique 936) 455–73. Paris, 1977
276. Manni, E. 'Pirro e gli stati greci nel 281/0 a.C.', *Athenaeum* N.S. 26 (1948) 102–21
277. Nederlof, A. B. *Pyrrhus van Epirus*. Amsterdam, 1978
278. Nenci, G. *Pirro. Aspirazioni egemoniche ed equilibrio mediterraneo*. Turin, 1953
279. Nenci, G. 'Il segno regale et la taumaturgia di Pirro', in *Miscellanea di studi alessandrini in memoria di A. Rostagni*, 152–61. Turin, 1963
280. Niese, B. 'Zur Geschichte des pyrrhischen Krieges', *Hermes* 31 (1896) 481–507
281. Nilsson, M. P. *Studien zur Geschichte des alten Epeiros*. Lund, 1909
282. Nilsson, M. P. *Cults, Myths, Oracles and Politics in Ancient Greece*. Lund, 1951 (reprinted New York, 1972)
283. Passerini, A. 'Sulle trattative dei Romani con Pirro', *Athenaeum* N.S. 21 (1943) 92–112
284. Poulsen, F. 'Bildnisse der Gegner Roms', *Die Antike* 14 (1938) 137–42
285. Rosenthal-Lefkowitz, M. 'Pyrrhus' negotiations with the Romans, 280–278 B.C.', *HSCP* 64 (1959) 147–77
286. Sandberger, F. *Prosopographie zur Geschichte des Pyrrhos* (diss. Munich, 1971)
287. von Scala, R. *Der pyrrhische Krieg* (diss. Berlin–Leipzig, 1884)
288. Schubert, R. *Geschichte des Pyrrhos*. Königsberg, 1894
289. Scullard, H. H. *The Elephant in the Greek and Roman World*. London, 1974

290. Vartsos, J. A. *AKMH TOY ΠΥΡΡΟΥ ΚΑΙ ΕΠΕΜΒΑΣΙΣ ΑΥΤΟΥ ΕΙΣ ΤΗΝ ΜΑΚΕΔΟΝΙΑΝ*. Athens, 1964
291. Vartsos, J. A. *Ο ΠΥΡΡΟΣ ΕΝ ΙΤΑΛΙΑ*. Athens, 1967
292. Vartsos, J. A. 'Osservazioni sulla campagna di Pirro in Sicilia', *Kokalos* 16 (1970) 89–97
293. Weizkiwski, I. I. 'Zur Geschichte des Pyrrhos-Krieges', *Naukovi zapiski L'vivskovo derzavnovo universiteta imeni Ivana Franka, serija istoricua* 37 (1955) 173–90. German résumé in *Bibliotheca Classica Orientalis* 4 (1959) 18–23
294. Will, E. 'The formation of the Hellenistic kingdoms', *CAH* VII.1.101–17. Ed. 2. Cambridge, 1984

K. ROME AND CARTHAGE

a. CARTHAGE: HISTORY, INSTITUTIONS AND CULTURE

1. Amadasi, M. G. Guzzo. *Le iscrizioni fenicie e puniche delle colonie in Occidente*. Rome, 1967
2. Amadasi, M. G. Guzzo et al. *Monte Sirai* II–IV. Rome, 1965–7
3. Astruc, M. 'Traditions funéraires de Carthage', *Cahiers de Byrsa* 6 (1956) 29–58
4. *Atti del I convegno internazionale di studi fenici e punici (Roma, 5–10 novembre 1979)* (Collezione di studi fenici 16). Rome, 1983
5. Baradez, J. 'Nouvelles recherches sur les ports antiques de Carthage', *Karthago* 9 (1958) 45–78
6. Barreca, F. *La civiltà di Cartagine*. Cagliari, 1964
7. Barreca, F. et al. *Monte Sirai* I. Rome, 1964
8. Beloch, K. J. 'Die Könige von Karthago', *Klio* 7 (1907) 19–28 = id. *Griechische Geschichte* III.2.107–20. Strasbourg, 1923
9. Bengtson, H. 'Zur karthagischen "strategie"', *Aegyptus* 32 (1952) 158–62
10. Benichou-Safar, H. *Les tombes puniques de Carthage. Topographie, structures, inscriptions et rites funéraires*. Paris, 1981
11. Benichou-Safar, H. 'À propos des ossements humains du tophet de Carthage', *RStud. Fen.* 9 (1981) 5–9
12. Berthier, A. and Charlier, R. *La sanctuaire punique d'El Hofra à Constantine*. Paris, 1955
13. Bisi, A. M. *Le stele puniche* (Studi Semitici 2). Rome, 1967
14. Bondi, S. F. 'I Libifenici nell'ordinamento cartaginese', *RAL* ser. 8.26 (1971) 653–61
15. Bondi, S. F. 'Monte Sirai, un insediamento punico nell'entroterra sardo', *RPAA* 51–2 (1978–80) 171–94
16. Bunnens, G. *L'expansion phénicienne en Méditerranée. Essai d'interprétation fondé sur une analyse des traditions littéraires* (Études de philologie, d'archéologie et d'histoire anciennes 17). Brussels–Rome, 1979
17. Capuzzi, A. 'I sacrifici animali a Cartagine', *Studi Magrebini* 2 (1968) 45–76

18. Carrié, J. M. and Sanviti, N. 'Fouilles françaises à Carthage, 1974–1975. Le secteur B', *Antiquités Africaines* 11 (1977) 51–66

19. *I Cartaginesi in Sicilia all'epoca dei due Dionisi (Colloquio Palermo 4–6.6.1981)* (*Kokalos* 28–9 (1982–3) 127–277)

20. Carton, L. *Un sanctuaire punique découvert à Carthage.* Paris, 1929

21. CEDAC (Centre d'études et de documentation archéologique de la conservation de Carthage), Institut national d'archéologie et d'art de Tunisie. *Bulletin* 1– (1978–), with bibliographies

22. Charlier, R. 'La nouvelle série de stèles puniques de Constantine', *Karthago* 4 (1953) 1–49

23. Cintas, P. *Amulettes puniques.* Tunis, 1946

24. Cintas, P. 'Sanctuaire punique de Sousse', *Revue Africaine* 91 (1947) 1–80

25. Cintas, P. *Céramique punique.* Paris, 1950

26. Cintas, P. 'Dar Essafi', *CRAcad. Inscr.* 1953, 256–60

27. Cintas, P. *Manuel d'archéologie punique.* 2 vols. Paris, 1970–6

28. Coacci Polselli, G. 'L'epigrafia punica in Sicilia', *Kokalos* 26–7 (1980–1) 19–26

29. Cooke, G. A. *A Textbook of North Semitic Inscriptions.* Oxford, 1903

30. *Corpus Inscriptionum Semiticarum.* 3 vols. 1881–

31. Decret, F. *Carthage ou l'empire de la mer.* Paris, 1977

32. Donner, H. and Rollig, W. *Kanaanaische und aramaische Inschriften.* Wiesbaden, 1962–5

33. Dupont-Sommer, A. 'Une nouvelle inscription punique de Carthage', *CRAcad. Inscr.* 1968, 116–33

34. Dussaud, R. 'Précisions épigraphiques touchant les sacrifices puniques d'enfants', *CRAcad. Inscr.* 1946, 371–87

35. Duval, R. 'Mise au jour de l'enceinte extérieure de la Carthage punique', *CRAcad. Inscr.* 1950, 53–9

36. Ehrenberg, V. *Karthago.* Leipzig, 1927 = id. *Polis und Imperium* 549–86. Zurich–Stuttgart, 1965

37. *Excavations at Carthage: the British Mission 1. The Avenue du Président Habib Bourguiba Salammbo* i. H. H. Hurst and S. P. Roskams, *The Site and Finds other than Pottery.* ii. M. G. Fulford and D. P. S. Peacock, *The Pottery and other Ceramic Objects from the Site.* Sheffield, 1984

38. Fantar, M. H. '*Pavimenta Punica* et signe dit de Tanit dans les habitations de Kerkouane', *Studi Magrebini* 1 (1965) 57–65

39. Fantar, M. H. 'Présence punique au Cap Bon', *Kokalos* 18–19 (1972–3) 264–77

40. Ferron, J. and Pinard, M. 'Les fouilles de Byrsa 1952–54', *Cahiers de Byrsa* 5 (1955) 31–81; 9 (1960–1) 77–170

41. Fevrier, J. G. 'Molchomor', *Rev. Hist. Rel.* 143 (1953) 8–18

42. Fevrier, J. G. 'Remarques sur le grand tarif dit de Marseille', *Cahiers de Byrsa* 8 (1958–9) 35–43

43. Fevrier, J. G. 'Essai de reconstitution de sacrifice molek', *JA* 248 (1960) 167–87

44. Foucher, L. *Hadrumetum.* Paris, 1964

45. Fouchet, M. P. *L'art à Carthage*. Paris, 1962
46. Frost, H. 'The discovery of a Punic ship', *International Journal of Nautical Archaeology* 1 (1972) 113–17
47. Frost, H. 'The Punic wreck off Sicily', *Mariner's Mirror* 59 (1973) 229–30
48. Frost, H., Werner, A. E. and Oddy, W. A. 'Marsala (Trapani). Relitto di una nave punica del III secolo a.C. al largo dell'Isola Lunga. La prima campagna di scavi 1971', *NSc.* 26 (1972) 651–74
49. Garbini, G. 'Note di epigraphia punica', *RSO* 43 (1968) 5–17
50. Garbini, G. 'Dieci anni di epigrafia punica nel Magreb, 1965–1974', *Studi Magrebini* 6 (1974) 1–36
51. Gaukler, P. *Nécropoles puniques de Carthage.* 2 vols. Paris, 1915
52. de la Genière, J. 'Réflexions sur Sélinonte e l'Ouest Sicilien', *CRAcad. Inscr.* 1977, 251–64
53. Groag, E. *Hannibal als Politiker.* Vienna, 1929
54. Gsell, S. *Histoire ancienne de l'Afrique du Nord.* 4 vols. Paris, 1912–20
55. Halff, G. 'L'onomastique punique de Carthage', *Karthago* 12 (1963–4) 63–145
56. Hans, L. M. *Karthago und Sizilien. Die Entstehung und Gestaltung der Epikratie auf dem Hintergrund der Beziehungen der Karthager zu den Griechen und den nicht-griechischen Völkern Siziliens* (Historische Texte und Studien 7). Hildesheim, 1983
57. Harden, D. B. 'The topography of Punic Carthage', *G & R* 9 (1938) 1–12
58. Harden, D. B. *The Phoenicians.* London, 1962
59. Henderson, B. W. 'The Carthaginian councils', *Journal of Philology* 24 (1895) 119–30
60. Hours-Meidan, M. *Carthage.* Paris, 1947
61. Hours-Meidan, M. 'Les représentations figurées sur les stèles de Carthage', *Cahiers de Byrsa* 1 (1951) 15–160
62. Hurst, H. 'Excavations at Carthage, 1974', *Ant. Journ.* 55 (1975) 11–40; for 1975 ib. 56 (1976) 177–97; for 1976 ib. 57 (1977) 232–61; for 1977 ib. 59 (1979) 19–49
63. Huss, W. 'Die Religion der Karthager', in *Beiträge zur Geschichte*, edd. W. Huss and K. Strobel, 7–17. Bamberg, 1983
64. Huss, W. 'Der karthagische Sufetat', in *Althistorische Studien. Hermann Bengtson zum 70. Geburtstag* (*Historia* Einzelschriften 40), ed. H. Heinen, 24–43. Wiesbaden, 1983
65. Huss, W. *Geschichte der Karthager* (Handbuch der Altertumswissenschaft III.8). Munich, 1985
66. Isserlin, B. J. S. et al. 'Motya, 1955', *PBSR* 26 (1958) 1–29
67. Isserlin, B. J. S. et al. 'Motya, a Phoenician Punic site near Marsala', *Annual of the Leeds Oriental Society* 4 (1962–3) 84–131
68. Isserlin, B. J. S. and du Plat Taylor, J. *Motya. A Phoenician and Carthaginian City in Sicily* I. Leiden, 1974
69. Jahn, J. 'Literaturüberblicke der griechischen Numismatik: Karthago und Nordafrika', *Chiron* 7 (1977) 411–85
70. Jenkins, G. K. and Lewis, R. B. *Carthaginian Gold and Electrum Coins.* London, 1963

71. Jenkins, G. K. 'Coins of Punic Sicily', *SNR* 50 (1971) 25–78
72. Jenkins, G. K. 'Coins of Punic Sicily, II: Carthage series I', *SNR* 53 (1974) 23–41
73. Jenkins, G. K. 'Coins of Punic Sicily, III', *SNR* 56 (1977) 5–65
74. Julien, C. A. *Histoire de l'Afrique du Nord. Des origines à la conquête arabe.* Ed. 2 (revised by C. Courtois). Paris, 1951
75. Krahmalkov, C. 'Notes on the rule of the Sōphtim in Carthage', *RStud. Fen.* 2 (1974) 171–7
75A. Lagrange, M. J. *Études sur les religions sémitiques.* Ed. 2. Paris, 1905
76. Lancel, S. et al. 'Fouilles françaises à Carthage, 1974–75', *Antiquités Africaines* 11 (1977) 13–130
77. Lapeyre, G. and Pellegrin, A. *Carthage punique.* Paris, 1942
78. Lézine, A. *Architecture punique. Recueil de documents.* Paris, 1962
79. Mahjoubi, H. and Fantar, M. H. 'Une nouvelle inscription carthaginoise', *RAL* ser. 8.21 (1966) 201–10
80. Martin, R. 'Histoire de Sélinonte d'après les fouilles récentes', *CRAcad. Inscr.* 1977, 46–63
81. Masson, O. 'Inscription d'Inibalos en Sicile', *Semitica* 26 (1976) 93–6
82. Maurin, L. 'Himilcon le Magonide', *Semitica* 12 (1962) 5–43
83. Meltzer, O. and Kahrstedt, U. *Geschichte der Karthager.* 3 vols. Berlin, 1879, 1896, and (Kahrstedt) 1913
84. Morel, J.-P. 'Kerkouane, ville punique du Cap Bon', *MÉFR* 81 (1969) 473–518
85. Moscati, S. 'Il sacrificio dei fanciulli', *RPAA* 38 (1965–6) 61–8
86. Moscati, S. 'La penetrazione fenica e punica in Sardegna', *MAL* ser. 8.12 (1966) 215–50
87. Moscati, S. 'Scoperte puniche in Sardegna', *RPAA* 39 (1966–7) 15–32
88. Moscati, S. 'Considerazioni sulla cultura fenicio-punica in Sardegna', *RAL* ser. 8.22 (1967) 129–52
89. Moscati, S. *The World of the Phoenicians.* London, 1968
90. Moscati, S. 'L'expansion phénico-punique dans la Méditerranée occidentale', in *Actes du 2e congrès internationale d'étude des cultures de la Méditerranée occidentale,* ed. M. Galley, I.9–33. Algiers, 1978
91. Moscati, S. 'La Sicilia tra l'Africa fenicio-punica e il Tirreno', *Kokalos* 26–7 (1980–1) 80–94
92. Moscati, S. *Cartaginesi.* Milan, 1982
93. *New Light on Ancient Carthage. Papers of a Symposium sponsored by the Kelsey Museum of Archaeology, the University of Michigan, marking the Fiftieth Anniversary of the Museum,* ed. J. G. Pedley. Ann Arbor, 1980
94. Niemeyer, H. G. 'Die Phönizier und die Mittelmeerwelt im Zeitalter Homers', *Jahrbuch des römisch-germanischen Zentralmuseums* 31 (1984) 3–94
95. Pareo, E. B. 'I supremi magistrati a Cartagine', in *Contributi in onore di A. Garzetti* 61–87. Genoa, 1978
96. Pesce, G. *Sardegna punica.* Cagliari, 1961
97. *Phönizier im Westen. Die Beiträge des internationalen Symposions über die phönizische Expansion im westlichen Mittelmeerraum in Köln vom 24.–27. April 1979* (Madrider Beiträge 8), ed. H. G. Niemeyer. Mainz, 1982

98. Picard, C. *Carthage*. Paris, 1951
99. Picard, C. 'Vestiges d'un édifice punique à Carthage', *Karthago* 3 (1951–52) 117–26
100. Picard, C. *Catalogue du Musée Alaoui*. Tunis, 1954
101. Picard, C. '*Sacra punica*; étude sur les masques et les rasoirs de Carthage', *Karthago* 13 (1967) 1–115
102. Picard, C. 'Thèmes hellénistiques sur les stèles de Carthage', *Antiquités Africaines* 1 (1967) 9–30
103. Picard, C. 'Les représentations de la sacrifice molk sur les ex-voto de Carthage', *Karthago* 17 (1973–4) 67–138
104. Picard, G. C. 'Un quartier de maisons puniques à Carthage', *Rev. Arch.* 1958, 1. 21–32
105. Picard, G. C. *Les religions de l'Afrique antique*. Paris, 1954
106. Picard, G. C. *Le monde de Carthage*. Paris, 1956. Translated as:
107. Picard, G. C. *Carthage*. London, 1964
108. Picard, G. C. 'Les sufètes de Carthage chez Tite-Live et Cornelius Nepos', *RÉL* 41 (1963) 269–81
109. Picard, G. C. 'L'administration territoriale de Carthage', in *Mélanges A. Piganiol* (1966) III.1257–65
110. Picard, G. C. 'Les rapports entre gouvernants et gouvernés à Carthage', *Recueils de la Société Jean Bodin* 23 (1968) 129–38
111. Picard, G. C. 'La révolution démocratique de Carthage', in *Conférence de la Société d'Études Latines de Bruxelles* (Collection Latomus 62) 113–30. Brussels, 1968
112. Picard, G. C. and C. *La vie quotidienne à Carthage au temps de Hannibal*. Ed. 2. Paris, 1964. First edition translated as:
113. Picard, G. C. and C. *Daily Life in Carthage in the Time of Hannibal*. London, 1961
114. Picard, G. C. and C. *The Life and Death of Carthage*. London, 1968
115. Poinssot, L. and Lantier, R. 'Un sanctuaire de Tanit à Carthage', *Rev. Hist. Rel.* 76 (1923) 32–68
116. Rakob, F. 'Deutsche Ausgrabungen in Karthago. Die punischen Befunde', *MDAI(R)* 91 (1984) 1–22
117. *La religione fenicia. Matrici orientali e sviluppi occidentali. Atti del colloquio in Roma, 6 marzo, 1979*. Rome, 1981
118. *Répertoire d'épigraphie sémitique* 1. Paris, 1900–5
119. Reyniers, F. 'Remarques sur la topographie de Carthage à l'époque de la troisième guerre punique', in *Mélanges A. Piganiol* (1966) III.1281–90
120. Robinson, E. S. G. 'The coinage of the Libyans and kindred Sardinian issues', *Num. Chron.* ser. 6.3 (1943) 1–13
121. Robinson, E. S. G. 'A hoard of coins of the Libyans', *Num. Chron.* ser 6.13 (1953) 27–32
122. Robinson, E. S. G. 'The Libyan hoard. Addenda, and the Libyan coinage in general', *Num. Chron.* ser. 6.16 (1956) 9–14
123. Senay, P. (ed.). *Carthage* 5 (Cahiers des études anciennes). Quebec, 1981
124. Simonetti, A. 'Sacrifici umani e uccisioni rituali nel mondo fenicio-

punico. Il contributo delle fonti letterarie classiche', *RStud. Fen.* 11
(1983) 91–111

125. Stager, L. E. 'The rite of child sacrifice at Carthage', in *New Light on
Ancient Carthage*, ed. J. G. Pedley, 1–11. Ann Arbor, 1980

126. Susemihl, F. and Hicks, R. D. *The Politics of Aristotle, Books I–IV*, 340–50.
London, 1894

127. Sznycer, M. 'Carthage et la civilisation punique', in C. Nicolet, *Rome et la
conquête du monde méditerranéen II. Genèse d'un empire* 545–93. Paris, 1978

128. Sznycer, M. 'L'expansion phénico-punique dans la Méditerranée
occidentale. Problèmes et méthodes', in *Actes du 2e congrès internationale
d'étude des cultures de la Méditerranée occidentale*, ed. M. Galley, 1.35–48.
Algiers, 1978

129. Teixidor, J. 'Bulletin d'épigraphie sémitique', *Syria* 46 (1969) 340–4

130. Tusa, V. 'La civiltà punica', in *Popoli e civiltà dell'Italia antica*, III.9–142.
Rome, 1974

131. Tusa, V. 'La Sicilia fenicio-punica', *Dialogues d'Histoire Ancienne* 9 (1983)
237–85

132. Tusa, V. et al. *Mozia*. 4 vols. Rome, 1964–7

133. Vattioni, F. 'Per una ricerca sull'antroponomia fenicio-punica', *Studi
Magrebini* 11 (1979) 43–123; 12 (1980) 1–82

134. Vercoutter, J. *Les objets égyptiens et égyptisants du mobilier funéraire
carthaginois*. Paris, 1945

135. Warmington, B. H. *Carthage*. Ed. 2. London, 1969

136. Weber, O. R. J. *Etruskisch-karthagische Beziehungen. Historisch-archäologische
Untersuchung* (diss. Vienna, 1983)

137. Whittaker, C. R. 'Carthaginian imperialism in the fifth and fourth centuries', in *Imperialism in the Ancient World*, edd. P. D. A. Garnsey and
C. R. Whittaker, 59–90. Cambridge, 1978

b. THE EARLY ROMANO–CARTHAGINIAN TREATIES

See also A134; B182, 234, 255, 371; G338; J235.

138. Aymard, A. 'Les deux premiers traités entre Rome et Carthage', *Rev. Ét.
Anc.* 59 (1957) 277–93

139. Badian, E. 'Two Polybian treaties', in *Miscellanea E. Manni* (1980) 1.161–9

140. Beaumont, B. L. 'The date of the first treaty between Rome and Carthage',
JRS 29 (1939) 74–86

141. Calderone, S. 'Livio e il secondo trattato romano-punico in Polibio', in
Miscellanea E. Manni (1980) II.363–75

142. Cary, M. 'A forgotten treaty between Rome and Carthage', *JRS* 9 (1919)
67–77

143. Costanzi, V. 'Sulla cronologia del primo trattato fra Roma e Cartagine',
Riv. Fil. 53 (1925) 381–94

144. David, M. 'The treaties between Rome and Carthage', in *Symbolae ad ius et
historiam antiquitatis pertinentes I. Chr. van Oven dedicatae*, 231–50. Leiden,
1946

145. Ferenczy, E. 'Zur Vorgeschichte des zweiten römisch-punischen Vertrags', *A Ant. Hung.* 16 (1968) 209–13

146. Ferenczy, E. 'Die römisch-punischen Verträge und die Protohistorie des Commercium', *RIDA* ser. 3.16 (1969) 259–92

147. Ferron, J. 'Les relations de Carthage avec l'Étrurie', *Latomus* 25 (1966) 689–709

148. Ferron, J. 'Un traité d'alliance entre Caere et Carthage contemporain des derniers temps de la royauté étrusque à Rome', *ANRW* i.1 (1972) 189–216

149. Hampl, F. 'Das Problem der Datierung der ersten Verträge zwischen Rom und Karthago', *Rh. Mus.* N.F. 101 (1958) 58–75

150. Hoyos, B. D. 'The Roman-Punic pact of 279 B.C.: its problems and its purpose', *Historia* 33 (1984) 402–39

151. Hoyos, B. D. 'Treaties true and false: the error of Philinus of Agrigentum', *CQ* N.S. 35 (1985) 92–109

152. Last, H. 'The date of the first treaty between Rome and Carthage', *CAH* vii.859–62. Ed. 1. Cambridge, 1928

153. Marek, C. 'Die Bestimmungen des zweiten römisch-punischen Vertrags über die Grenzen der karthagischen Hoheitsgewässer', *Chiron* 7 (1977) 1–7

154. Meister, K. 'Der sogenannte Philinosvertrag', *Riv. Fil.* 98 (1970) 408–23

155. Meister, K. 'Das Datum des römisch-karthagischen Vertrages κατὰ τὴν Πύρρου διάβασιν', *PP* 26 (1971) 196–201

156. Mitchell, R. E. 'Roman-Carthaginian treaties: 306 and 279/8 B.C.', *Historia* 20 (1971) 633–65

157. Nenci, G. 'Il trattato romano-carthaginese κατὰ τὴν Πύρρου διάβασιν', *Historia* 7 (1958) 263–99

158. Nissen, H. 'Die römisch-karthagischen Bündnisse', *Neue Jahrbücher für Philologie* 95 (1867) 321–32

159. Petzold, K.-E. 'Die beiden ersten römisch-karthagischen Verträge und das Foedus Cassianum', *ANRW* i.1 (1972) 364–411

160. Piganiol, A. 'Observations sur la date des traités conclus entre Rome et Carthage', *Le Musée Belge* 27 (1923) 177–88

161. Prachner, G. 'Zum Καλὸν ἀκρωτήριον (Polybius 3, 22, 5)', in *Beiträge zur Alten Geschichte und deren Nachleben. Festschrift für Franz Altheim*, edd. R. Stiehl and H. E. Stier, i.157–72. Berlin, 1969

162. Rebuffat, R. 'Les Phéniciens à Rome', *MÉFR* 78 (1966) 7–48

163. Rupprecht, E. 'Zu den Karthagerverträgen', *Klio* 32 (1939) 106–8

164. Scevola, M. L. 'Una testimonianza trascurata di Livio sul più antico trattato romano-cartaginese', *Athenaeum* N.S. 21 (1943) 122–4

165. Schachermeyr, F. 'Die römisch-punischen Verträge', *Rh. Mus.* N.F. 79 (1930) 350–80

166. Strachan-Davidson, J. L. *Selections from Polybius*, 50–72. Oxford, 1888

167. Werner, R. 'Das Καλὸν ἀκρωτήριον des Polybios', *Chiron* 5 (1975) 21–44

168. Wickert, L. 'Zu den Karthagerverträgen', *Klio* 31 (1938) 349–64

C. THE FIRST PUNIC WAR

See also A45, 61, 132; B47, 92, 181–2, 261, 269; G694, 736, 745.

169. Berve, H. *König Hieron II*. Munich, 1959
170. Bisi, A. M. 'Ricerche sulle fortificazioni puniche di Lilibeo (Marsala)', *Arch. Class.* 20 (1968) 259–65
171. Calderone, S. 'Di un antico problema di esegesi polibiana. I, 11, 1–3', *AAnt. Hung.* 25 (1977) 383–7
172. Calderone, S., Bitto, I., De Salvo, L. and Pinzone, A. 'Polibio I, 11, 1sq.', *Quaderni Urbinati di Cultura Classica* N.S. 7 (1981) 7–78
173. Caven, B. *The Punic Wars*. London, 1980
174. Eckstein, A. M. 'Polybius on the rôle of the senate in the crisis of 264 B.C.', *Greek, Roman and Byzantine Studies* 21 (1980) 175–90
175. Eckstein, A. M. '*Unicum subsidium populi Romani*: Hiero II and Rome, 263–215 B.C.', *Chiron* 10 (1980) 183–203
176. Frank, T. 'Rome and Carthage: the First Punic War', *CAH* VII.665–98. Ed. 1. Cambridge, 1928
177. Frézouls, E. 'Hiéron, Carthage et Rome', in *Miscellanea E. Manni* (1980) III.965–89
178. Giustolisi, V. *Le nave romane di Terrasina e l'avventura di Amilcare sul Monte Heirkte*. Palermo, 1975
179. Hampl, F. 'Zur Vorgeschichte des ersten und zweiten punischen Krieges', *ANRW* I.1 (1972) 412–41
180. Heuss, A. 'Der erste punische Krieg und das Problem des römischen Imperialismus', *HZ* 169 (1949) 457–513
181. Hoffmann, W. 'Das Hilfsgesuch der Mamertiner am Vorabend des ersten punischen Krieges', *Historia* 18 (1969) 153–80
182. Hoyos, B. D. 'The Carthaginian and Roman commanders in 264. Who was who', *LCM* 8 (1983) 120–2
183. Hoyos, B. D. 'Polybius' Roman οἱ πολλοί in 264 B.C.', *LCM* 9 (1984) 88–93
184. Hoyos, B. D. 'The rise of Hiero II: Chronology and campaigns 275–264 B.C.', *Antichthon* 19 (1985) 32–56
185. Kromayer, J. and Veith, G. *Antike Schlachtfelder. Bausteine einer antiken Kriegsgeschichte*. 5 vols. Berlin, 1903–31
186. Kromayer, J. and Veith, G. *Schlachten-Atlas zur antiken Kriegsgeschichte*. 4 vols. Leipzig, 1922–9
187. La Bua, V. 'Cassio Dione–Zonara ed altre tradizioni sugli inizi della prima guerra punica', in *Scritti sul mondo antico in memoria di F. Grosso* (Università di Macerata, Pubblicazioni della Facoltà di Lettere e Filosofia 9) 241–71. Rome, 1981
188. Leuze, O. 'Die Kämpfe um Sardinien und Korsika im ersten punischen Kriege', *Klio* 10 (1910) 406–44
189. Lippold, A. 'Der Consul Appius Claudius und der Beginn des ersten punischen Krieges', *Orpheus* 1 (1954) 154–69
190. Meyer, P. *Der Ausbruch des ersten punischen Krieges*. Berlin, 1908

191. Molthagen, J. 'Der Weg in den ersten punischen Krieg', *Chiron* 5 (1975) 89–127

192. Morgan, M. G. 'Polybius and the date of the battle of Panormus', *CQ* N.S. 22 (1972) 121–9

193. Morgan, M. G. 'Calendars and chronology in the First Punic War', *Chiron* 7 (1977) 89–117

194. Reuss, F. 'Zur Geschichte des ersten punischen Krieges', *Philologus* 60 (1901) 105–48

195. Roussell, D. *Les Siciliens entre les romains et les carthaginois*. Paris, 1970

196. Ruschenbusch, E. 'Der Ausbruch des 1. punischen Krieges', *Talanta* 12–13 (1980–1) 55–76

197. Ruschenbusch, E. 'Ein literarisches Vorbild für die Senatsdebatte über das Hilfgesuch der Mamertiner', *Rh. Mus.* 127 (1984) 263–5

198. Schenk von Stauffenberg, A. *König Hieron der Zweite von Syrakus*. Stuttgart, 1933

199. Schwarte, K. H. 'Naevius und der Beginn des ersten punischen Krieges', *Historia* 21 (1972) 206–23

200. Sordi, M. 'I *corvi* di Duilio', *Riv. Fil.* 95 (1967) 260–8

201. Tarn, W. W. 'The fleets of the First Punic War', *JHS* 27 (1907) 48–60

202. Tarn, W. W. *Hellenistic Military and Naval Developments*. Cambridge, 1930

203. Uggeri, G. 'Gela, Finzia e l'Alico nella battaglia del 249 a.C.', *PP* 23 (1968) 120–31

204. Vallone, A. 'I Mamertini in Sicilia', *Kokalos* 1 (1955) 22–61

205. Wallinga, H. T. *The Boarding-Bridge of the Romans*. Groningen, 1956. (Review by J. S. Morrison, *JRS* 47 (1957) 270–1)

206. Welwei, K.-W. 'Hieron II von Syrakus und der Ausbruch des ersten punischen Krieges', *Historia* 27 (1978) 573–87

207. Winter, F. E. *Greek Fortifications*. London, 1971

208. Ziegler, K. 'Heirkte', *RE* 7 (1910) 2645

INDEX

NOTES

(1) References in italics are to maps (by map number) and illustrations (by page number).
(2) Romans are indexed under their gentile names.
(3) Arrangement of material within entries is predominantly chronological, though some material of a topical nature is alphabetically ordered.
(4) Footnotes are referred to only where the subject is not mentioned in the corresponding page of text.

anthropology, comparative, 29, 113; on
socio-economic problems, 325, 329; on
religion, 581
Antiates, 363
Antigone, queen of Molossians, 459
Antigonus Gonatas, king of Macedon, 463,
469, 482, 483, 484, 667
Antiochus I, king of Syria, 463, 482
Antiochus of Syracuse (historian), 3
antiquarian writers, 9–11; *see also individual
writers*
Antium, *1 Dd, 2 Bb, 3 Bd, 7 Aa, 10 Bb, 11 Fb*;
regal period, 63, 85, 255, 521; Latin
colony (467), 278–9, 280, 653; defects to
Volsci, 279, 282, 653; Rome defeats
Volsci at, 290, 301, 656, 659; Roman
colony (338), 365, *390*, 420, 660; navy,
365; temple of Fortunae, 50
Antonii (*gens*), 193–4, 207, 208
Antonius Merenda, Q. (cons. trib. ?422), 193,
633
Antonius Merenda, T. (*decemvir* 450), 194,
631
Anxur, *see* Tarracina
Aous, gorges of; battle, 483
Aphrodite, cult of; in emporia, 48, 49–50; at
Eryx, *15 Ca*
Apollo, cult of, 138, 513
Apollonia, *11 Gb*, 462
appeal, legal, 400; to citizen community
(*provocatio ad populum*), 157, 211, 219–21,
225, 241, 400; *comitia centuriata* and, 92;
laws: Valerian (509), 219–20; Valerio-
Horatian (449), 219–20, 228–9, 653;
Valerian (300), 664; *see also* assistance
Appennine period (Bronze Age), 64, 646
Apulia, *5 Db, 10 Db, 11 Gb*; Latin colonies in,
421; Pyrrhic war, 472, 477; Second
Samnite War, 363, 371, 661; Third
Samnite War, 664; Roman conquest of
southern, 422; coinage, 415; culture, 357
aqueducts: Anio Vetus, *406–7*, 408, 450, 667;
Aqua Appia, 395, *406–7*, 408, 662
Aquillius Corvus, L. (cons. trib. 388), 239,
636
Aquillius Florus, C. (*cos.* 259), 553, 642
Aquillius Tuscus, C. (*cos.* 487), 175, 290, 629
Aquilonia, 380, 389, 665
Aquinum, *7 Ba*, 421, 431
archaeology, 15–16, 29; archaic period,
30–51, *62*; literary tradition confirmed
by, 31, 38, 51, 56, 81, 82–7, 250–1, (on
date of fall of monarchy), 177, 179;
Carthage, 499–502; Etruria (C6th
unrest), 258; Latial Periods, First and
Second, 34–5, 38–9; Rome, (archaic), *62*,
63, *75*, (C5th economy), 113, 286–7,

(C3rd economy), 411–12; South Etruria
Survey, 138–9, *140–3*
Archidamus of Sparta (mercenary
commander), 457, 531, 659, 660
architecture: C7–6th sanctuaries and palaces,
37, 39–48; Carthage, 499, 501–2; Rome,
(C5th), 129, 130, (C3rd), 405, *406–7*, 408;
see also under Rome, *and*: dwellings;
temples
Ardea, *1 Dd, 2Bb, 3 Bd, 7 Aa*; early
occupation, 31, 64; Etruscans at, 16;
Latial Culture Phase III bronze deposit,
66; and regal Rome, 85, 253, 521; and
early republican Rome, 273, treaty
(444), 8, 14, 174–5n, 631, 654; Latin
colony, 279, 280, *390*, 420, 654; probably
loyal to Rome after Gallic Sack, 317;
religious ceremonies, Latin, 266; size,
246, 247; temples; Aphrodisium, 50
Argei, festival of the, 84
Argos, 484, 667
Aricia, *1 Dc–d, 2 Bb, 3 Bd, 246*; battle between
Porsenna and Latins, 1–2, 257, 258, 259,
651; and Latin League, 317; Grove of
Diana, 14, 85, 86, 266, 272–4, 651;
incorporation in Roman state, 365, 420,
660; *see also* Ferentina, Grove of
Ariminum (Rimini), *4 Fc, 11 Fb*; Latin colony
founded, 381, *390*, 405, 425, 667; Gallic
raids, 432, 453
Aristagoras of Miletus, 651
aristocracies, archaic: emergence, 34–9;
development, 80–1; effect of hoplite
warfare on, 35–6; display of wealth,
68–9; Etruscan, 35–9, 89; fraternities,
158; Latin, 35–9, 270; patricians, 167–8,
171; patronage, 35–6, 39, 98–9, 101–6,
145, 162; personal honour, 157, 178;
Phoenician, 492; Roman, regal period,
100–1, 102, 145, (and fall of monarchy),
178, 205; and temple construction, 132;
trade stimulated by lifestyle of, 48, 124;
see also: nobility; patriciate
Aristodemus, tyrant of Cumae, 1–2, 93–4,
177, 257, 258, 263, 651
Aristotle, 2, 23, 419
armour: Roman, C5th, 124, 163, 164; Samnite
influence on Roman army, 373
army, Carthaginian, *see under* Carthage
army, Roman, 383–91; allies' contributions,
379, 385, 386–9, (in First Punic War),
545, 566; efficiency, 566; C5th growth,
124, 194; Campanian *legio*, 428; census as
military review, 197; centuriate
organization, 36, 104, 199–201, 207–9;
comitia curiata and, 199; commanders,
172, 189, 190, 191, 193, 600; efficiency,

790   INDEX

Iuppiter (*cont.*)
    603–4; Stator, 408, 665; Victor, 408, 418,
    615; *see also*: Rome (temples: Capitoline)
ius, *see*: justice; law
ius suffragii ferendi (Latin right), 427
ivory: lion, Sant' Omobono, 78, *79*; Punic,
    510; Tibur, 74

Janus, cult of, 109, 383, 453
jewellery: Latial Phase III, 69; Punic, 510,
    512
Juba, king of Mauretania, 513
judicial wager (*sacramentum*), 233–4
jurisprudence, Ap. Claudius Caecus' work on,
    399
justice, 144–5; C5th, 144–5; civil, (plebeian
    movement and), 218, 224, 237, 242,
    (individual initiative in), 144–5, 155–7,
    162, 215–16, 218; *comitia centuriata* and,
    105, 201–2, 226; consuls' role, 172, 189;
    criminal, 105, 201–2; deterrent wager,
    233–4; judges (*iudices decemviri*), 226–7,
    229; patronage and, 160, 162, 233, 234;
    plebeian magistrates and, 224, 226, 237;
    praetor urbanus and, 438; *see also*: appeal;
    assistance; formulae; law; reparation;
    revenge; Twelve Tables

Kalaturus Phapenas of Caere, 81, 100
Kalends; religious rites, 611
kings, Roman, 87–96, 647–50; and
    aristocracy, 102, 145, 178, 179–82, 205;
    as band chiefs, 97–9, 106, 205;
    chronology, 176–8; consuls as
    successors, 189–90; divinization, 57, 109;
    dual kingship, 57, 59; fall, 23, 93–4, 172,
    173, 257–64, 650, (aristocracy and), 178,
    182, 205; Mastarna as possible, 94, *95*,
    96, 97; mythology, 581; recognition of,
    105, 106; *rex sacrorum* as successor, 97,
    107, 190, 610–13; role and powers,
    106–8; sacerdotal functions, 96–7, 106–7,
    190, 610–15; sources, 87–90; *see also under*
    individual kings, and: monarchy; regal
    period
kinship structures, 144, 154–7, 182; First/
    Second Latial Period, 34, 38; *see also*:
    family; *gentes*
La Ferriera, *141*
La Rustica, *2 Bb*, 68
La Tène culture, 303
La Tolfa, *1 Cb–Db*, 64
La Torre, *140*
Labici, *2 Bb*, *246*; Coriolanus takes, 288;
    colonized by Rome, 278, 280, 281, 420,
    655; Rome conquers (393), 656
labour, 125–6; agricultural, 119–20, 123, 141;

C5th Roman, 125–6; clients used as, 331;
    debt-bondage as form of, 330–1, 333;
    division of, archaic, 38, 39; for Roman
    city wall, C4th, 332–3; semi-seasonal,
    236; wage-, 121, 331; work-exchange,
    154; *see also* slavery
Laevinus, P. Valerius, *see under* Valerius
Lanassa, wife of Pyrrhus, 461, 474, 665
land: archaic ownership structures, 56;
    (338–264), 403, 405; C4th problems
    over, 324, 325–9; C5th: (ownership),
    139, 144, (shortage), 136, 141–2, 147,
    165, 242, (alleviated), 327, 332, 334,
    433
    inheritance, 147, 150; as motive for war,
    384; ownership: (citizenship and), 211,
    (family), 38, 165–6, (Latin rights of),
    269, 270, (by nobility), 165–6, 444,
    (qualification for military service),
    118–19, (property boundaries), 119, 139,
    (plebeian movement and), 238, 242, 327,
    (regal period), 99–100, (rural, by
    patricians), 65–6, 140, 165–6, 179; size of
    holdings, 100, 121, 150, 325–6; Veii:
    distribution, 312–13; viritane allotments,
    121, 327–8, 421, 450, 452, 665,
    (Flaminian plebiscite), 432–3, 454, 671;
    see also: *ager publicus*; *heredium*
languages, 81; *see also individual languages*
Lanuvium, *2 Bb*, *246*; archaic tombs, 37, 50,
    65; and Latin revolt, 273; loyal to Rome
    after Sack, 317; ally of Volsci against
    Rome, 318, 657; incorporated into
    Rome, 363, 365, 366, 420, 660
Laos, *7 Dc*, 656
Lapis Satricanus, *see* Valerius, Publius
Larcius, T. (*cos.* 501, 498), 192
Lares (household gods), 605
Laris Velchaina of Satricum, 74, 81
Larissa: palace, 40, 44
Latial Culture, 63–4, 646–8; cultural unity,
    269; Phase I, 31, 34–5, 38–9, 64–5, 265,
    646; Phase II, 34–5, 38–9, 65–6, 646,
    (IIA), 265, 646, (IIB), 65–6, 646; Phase
    III, 66–8, 646; Phase IV (Orientalizing),
    34, 36, 40, 48, 68–75, 80, 81, 269, 270,
    647, 648
Latiar (Latin festival), 265–6
latifundia, 334, 413–14
Latin language, 86–7; *see also*: alphabet;
    literature
Latin League, 84–6, 264–74; army, 275–6,
    277; booty, sharing of, 277, 278;
    dictatorship, 192, 273, 274; dissolution,
    366, 660; political/military league, 271–4;
    levy, 321; religious rites, 70, 80–1, 85,
    265–9, 270, 651; sanctuaries, *see under*

Aricia; Lavinium; *and see*: Alban Mount;
Ferentina, Grove of
Latin rights, 151, 269–71, 275, 366–7, 427; in
colonies, 278, 368
Latini, *5 Ab*; *see also* Latium
Latinus (legendary son of Odysseus), 57, 253,
265–6, 591
Latium, *1 Dc–d, 3 Bd, 5 Ab, 11 Fb*, 243–308;
archaeology, 15, 30; Latial Culture, *see
separate entry*
archaic period, *1 Dc–d*, (aristocracy), 34–9,
68–9, 270, (burials), 34–5, 73,
(colonization), 38, (communications),
63–4, (foreign influence), 34, 81, (and
Etruria), 31, 51, 81, (metallurgy), 34, 66,
(orientalizing style), 68–9, 269, (political
structures), 262, 264–5, (pottery), 34,
(public building), 37, (size of city-states),
246–7, (social structure), 80–1, 270,
(trade), 48, 50, (urbanization), 36, 269
and regal Rome, 84–6, 91, 92, 243–57, 262,
263, 647, 649; war against Porsenna,
257, 263; republics established, 262; and
Tarquinius Superbus, 93–4, 253, 258,
268; relations with Rome by beginning
of Republic, 85–6, 521, 524, 526, 529,
530; 'revolt', 191, 262–3, 272–4, 281,
290, 317–18, 651; Cassian treaty, 14, 86,
128, 136, 153, 263–4, 274–5, 526, 651,
(and Latin rights), 271, (on division of
spoils), 277, (ends Roman incursions in
Latium), 136, 281–2; and Rome (C5th),
274–81
incursions of Sabines, Aequi and Volsci,
281–94; helps Rome against Appius
Herdonius, 98; Roman advance (end
C5th), 300–1, 316; disaffection from
Rome (380s), 310, 317, 656, 657; C4th
Roman expansion, 309,
311–12, 317–21, 322–3, *382*, 656–60;
alliance renewed (358), 320, 658; Greek
naval raids (349), 321, 530, 659; extent
of Roman domination, 323, 527, 528–9;
Latin war (341–338), 360–3, 660;
settlement, 364–8, 660; Samnite
incursion, 372, 662; position (by 281),
420
L. Adiectum, 367–8; citizenship, 361, 365,
366; city chronicles, 89; coastal
garrisons, 365; colonization, 38,
(participation in Roman), 388;
constitutions, 269, 270; cultural unity,
15–16, 269, 427; in Roman
'commonwealth', 210, 362, 364–8,
420–1; legends, 58, 59, 61; malarial
areas, 138; metallurgy, 34; mobility,
social, 270; nobility, Latin members of

Roman, 444, 450; piracy, 206, 548;
political federal association, 65, 266;
alleged political role of Alba Longa,
264–5
religion, 80–1, 265–9, 607; settlement
patterns, 138–9, *140–3*; social structure,
80–1, 270; temple building, 132;
territory (C4th–3rd), *382*; thirty peoples
of, 65, 85, 266; trade, 128; urbanization,
269; Vestals, 607; *see also individual towns,
and*: allies (Latin); colonies, (Latin);
Latin League; Latin rights
Laurentes, 521, 524
Laurentina, 38, 70–1, 73
Laurentum, *see* Lavinium
Laus, *7 Dc*; battle of, 656
Lautulae, *7 Ba*, 372
Lavinium, *1 Dd, 2 Ab, 71*; Aeneas cult, 55,
60–1, 69, 70; archaeology, 15, 64;
acropolis, *71*; archaic period, 35, 36, 38,
69–70, *246*; Dioscuri, cult of, *579*, 620;
and Latin League, 50, 70, 85, 266–7;
relations with Rome: (beginning of
Republic), 85, 255, 524, (380s), 273, 317,
(340s–30s), 362, (status in
commonwealth), 420; legends, 55, 58,
59, *60–1*; Penates Populi Romani at, 61,
85; sanctuaries, 69–70, 649,
(Aphrodisium, pan-Latin), 50, (heroon),
60–1, 69, *71*, (Minerva, eastern sanctuary
of), 70, *71, 72*, (of thirteen altars), 70, *71*,
266–7, 649; tombs, 55, *170, 171*; Vestals,
607; votive sculpture, 132
law, Roman: action, initiation of, 155 (*see also*
formulae); of annual nail, 14, 22, 138,
187–8; *comitia centuriata* and, 92, 185,
190, 203–4; *comitia curiata* and, 105;
concept of citizen community and, 211;
on debt-bondage, 333–4; declaration as
invalid, 590; enforcement, C5th, 144–5;
family, 105, 198, 586–7; fetial, 544; fines,
123, 211, 653, 654; Greek models, 106,
111–12, 227, 231, 653; guardianship of
records, 533; Ius (Flavianum), 397,
(Papirianum), 107–8; kings and, 107–8;
magistrates and, 172, 189, 224, 226, 232,
237; Numa and, 107–8; and order, 393;
patrician expertise, 179, 182, 204, 232,
233; plebiscites, 213, 222, 223, 225, 337,
341–2, 621, 658, 666, (*see also under* leges
below); priests and, 110, 232, 583, 586,
589, 622; religion and, 585, 599, 621;
reparation, 153, 544; sacred, 86, 108,
583, 586; senate and, 102, 103; as source
for early Roman history, 29; sumptuary,
450, (Twelve Tables on), 116, 130, 145n,
166, 168, 171, 237; and trade,

620; and Quirinus, 604; reign, 294, 647; and social structure, 55, 57, 83, 101, 104–5, 159; statue, C3rd bronze, 412, 664
Roviano (Aequian hill-fort), *3 Bc*
Rudiae, 671
Rullianus, Q. Fabius Maximus, *see under* Fabius
Rusaddir, *11 Cc*, 503
Rusellae, *1 Cb, 6 Cb*, 36, 37, 380, 389, 665
Rusuccuru, *11 Dc*, 503
Rutile Hipukrates of Tarquinii, 81, 91, 100

Sabatina (tribe), 313, *404*, 656
Sabellian peoples, 284, 285, 376
Sabines, *1 Db, 5 Aa–Ba*; early contacts with Rome, 30, 57, 59, 98, 251, 286, 647, 648, (and Quirinal), 75, 86–7; Tarquinius Superbus' campaigns, 650; wars against early Roman republic, 281, 290, 651; C5th incursions, 284, 293, (Ap. Herdonius), 59, 98, 286, 292, 653; Roman annexation, 380, 403, 421, 431, 665; settlement of *ager Sabinus*, 447, 450; full franchise for lowland, 425, 429, 430, 431, 667
Sabrata, *11 Fd*, 503
sacer, individual as, 109, 213, 593, 613; *see also devotio*
sacramentum (judicial wager), 233–4
'Sacred Band', Carthaginian, 494
Sacred Mount, 212
sacrifices, 589–90, 594–5; Carthage, 514–15, *516*, 517; human, 322, 517; by *rex sacrorum*, 611; October horse, 603n, 604, 608; Vestals and, 608; and war, 322, 600, 601
Saepinum, *7 Ca*, 356, *358*, 380, 389, 665
Saguntum, *11 Cc*; and settlement after First Punic War, 566; alliance with Rome, 454, 671; Roman intervention, 451, 452, 453, 672
sailing, *see*: navy; seafaring
sale: 'by bronze and balance', 119, 124–5, 127, 235; of children, 126, 143, 165, 330
Salii (priests), 86, 90; *carmen*, 111; patrician monopoly, 102, 179, 343; rites, 109, 111, 599–600
Sallentini, 357, 364, 663, 664, 668
salt: Tiberine deposits, 64, 124, 294, 297; trade, 126, 130, 211
Salui, *4 Ac*, 303
Samnite League, 356, 357
Samnium and Samnites, *1 Fd-Ge, 5 Cb–Db, 10 Cb, 358*; C5th migration, 259, 284–5, 357; alliance with Rome, 323, 360, 529, 658; First Samnite War, 359–60, 363;

war against Tarentum and Alexander I of Molossia, 660; garrison in Naples, 661; Second Samnite War, 363, 368–72, 373, 375, 532, 661–2, 663; Third Samnite War, 17n, 363, 377–80, 389, 664; in Pyrrhic War, 364, 381, 463, 467, 469, 470, 475, 478, 480, 481, 482, 667; settlement by Rome, 422–3, 429
agriculture, 353; archaeology, 16; army oath of loyalty, 219n; enslavement of prisoners by Rome, 389; and Etruscans, 378–9, 421; hill-forts, 356–7, *358–9*; Latin colonies as defence against, 421, 423; 'linen legion', 380; Oscan culture, 357; political organization, 353, 356–7; population, 353; region, 351, *352*, 353; religion, 356; Roman aggression towards, 371–2
Samos, 651
S. Angelo, Mt, *140–3*
S. Martino in Gattara; cemetery, 305
Sanates, 86, 116
sarcophagi, 287, 412, 501, 507
Sardinia, *11 Eb–c*; Phoenician occupation, 68, 647, 648; Carthaginian control, 487, 503, 505, 525, 528, 529, 649; Aristagoras and, 651; Roman colonization, 315, 657; in First Punic War, 547–8, 553, 668, 669; in Mercenary War, 567–8, 569, 671; Roman annexation, 451, 453, 569, 671; provincial administration, 438, 571, 672; Roman campaign (225), 672; mercenaries, 494, 495; Punic razors and jewellery, 512; trade, 128, 521, 524
Sarsinates, 364, 425, 668
Saticula, *5 Cb, 7 Ca, 10 Cb*; Samnite Wars, 356, 372, 659, 661, 662; Latin colony, *390*, 405, 421, 662
Satricum, *2 Bb*; Etruscans at, 16; orientalizing period, 74; palace, 37, 45, 48; Coriolanus takes, 288; revolt (393), 656; colony, 280, 316, 428, 657; Volscian wars, 318, 363, 659; Second Samnite war, 661
inscriptions, (Publius Valerius), 12, 15, 81, 97, 98, 158, 292, 621, (Laris Velchaina), 74, 81; temple of Mater Matuta, 12, 50, 74; urban area, *247*
Saturn; Baal Hammon equated with, 514
Saturnalia (festival), 606
Scaevola, P. Mucius, *see under* Mucius
Scaptia (tribe), 362, 366, 403, *404*, 661
scarabs, 59, 512
scepticism, religious, 623
'Sciarra youth' bronze, 129
Scipiones (family), 454, 455; *see also* Cornelius
sculpture: C5th, 129, 131, 132; C3rd Roman,

War, Punic (Second), 345, 451, 453, 455, 502–3

War, Pyrrhic, 381, 462–83, 666–7; causes of, 544; and coinage, 416, *417*; lasting effect on Rome, 419, 484; Roman levy, 467, 482; senate decision against peace (279), 399, 448, 471; *see also* Pyrrhus

War, Truceless, *see* War, Mercenary

war-bands, *see* bands, warrior

warfare, techniques of: brigandage, 292–3; Carthaginian, 495; chariot, 495; elephants, 495–6; Gallic wars, 321–2; hoplite, *36*, *45*, 146, (C7th introduction), 35–7, 81, 648, (Greek influence), 111, (Servian organization and), 92, 163, (social effects), 35–7, 39, 199–200, 207–9, 240; raiding and skirmishing, 291–4, 321–2; siege techniques, 37, 560; Veientine wars, 294, 295

water supply: Carthage, 501, 502; Rome, *see* aqueducts

wealth: archaic, 68, 73, 74–5, 80, 92–3; C5th distribution, 144, 171; C4th-3rd increase in Roman, 403; Carthage, 486–7, 492–3, 506; livestock as, 122–4; Rome, (determinant of status), 92–3, 103–4, 146, 163, 197–8, 199–200; idealistic scorn for, 449; patrician, 168, 182, 412–13; plebeian, 166, 171, 412–13; *see*

also economy

welfare, public, 211

wheat: Carthage, 508; Rome, (C8th), 63, (C5th imports in crisis), 118, 126–7, 128, 130, 133–4, 183, 211, 237, 409, (rituals connected with), 245, 601, 602n, 603

wills, 144, 210; 'by bronze and balance', 116, 148, 149, 232; *comitia curiata* and, 198; *pontifices* and, 586–7; Vestals', 607

wine production, 50, 63, 119, 508, 601

women: and cult-practice, 619; inheritance, 149; at symposia, 100; *see also*: marriage; Vestal Virgins

wood-working, Punic, 509

woodland, 134, 135, 140

workforce, *see*: labour; slavery

wrecks, 497, 549

writing, 11, 81, 232

Xanthippus of Sparta (mercenary leader), 495, 556, 669

xenia, *see* guest-friendship

youth groups, archaic, 55, 57, 58; *see also* bands, warrior

Zancle, 647, 648, 651, 652; *see also* Messana

Zonaras (historian), 4n